Price $27.95

TENNESSEE STATISTICAL ABSTRACT 1990

Betty B. Vickers, Editor
Melissa A. Kirby, Assistant Editor

Center for Business and Economic Research
College of Business Administration
The University of Tennessee, Knoxville

July 1990

The move to annual editions of the *Tennessee Statistical Abstract* was partly a result of constraints undertaken in the face of severe budgetary limitations in national and state government and higher education. Current statistical data at the national and local area levels which have been readily available to researchers in the past are often not available now in reference libraries, and a number of federal and state statistical programs have been eliminated or reduced. More important to data users is the fact that some federal and state agencies still collect the data but can no longer make them publicly available. Also, many government publications which formerly were free are now available only by subscription or specific inquiry. These conditions are of continuing concern to the statistical community and indeed, to everyone who supports informed decision making. Therefore, each of these kinds of data has been collected and is reported in the *1990 Tennessee Statistical Abstract.* This *Abstract* is the only published and readily available source of many of these data.

Twelfth Edition, July 1990
Library of Congress Catalogue No. 68-66499

SUGGESTED CITATION
The University of Tennessee, Knoxville
Center for Business and Economic Research
Tennessee Statistical Abstract 1990
Knoxville, Tennessee, 1990

Cover Photo: The Giles County Courthouse, Pulaski, Tennessee. Photo courtesy of the Image Taker.

UT Authorization No. E01-1490-001-91

ISBN 0–940191–13–X

1990 TENNESSEE STATISTICAL ABSTRACT PROJECT STAFF

Betty B. Vickers, *Research Associate and Editor, TSA*

Melissa A. Kirby, *Research Assistant and Assistant Editor, TSA*

Vickie C. Cunningham
Research Assistant

Lucie C. Polk
Research Assistant

Krisztina Martin-Hajdu
AIESEC Intern

Jeanne P. McDonald
Managing Editor of Publications

Joan M. Snoderly
Associate Editor of Publications

Lynn J. Landry
Publications Coordinator

Patricia A. Hunley
Word Processing Group Supervisor

Scott A. Calbaugh
Student Assistant

INTRODUCTION: NOTE FOR DATA USERS

The *Tennessee Statistical Abstract* attempts to provide, in a single convenient reference, the most useful of the available current data as well as some historical time-series data. Every effort is made to insure the accuracy of the data reproduction and computations. Responsibility for errors in reproduction of data or in calculations, however, is assumed by the Center for Business and Economic Research.

For proper understanding of the data, the user is urged to read carefully the chapter prefaces and any footnotes accompanying the tables. Those who intend to employ these data for research or for other purposes where the choice of statistics must be defended will need to become familiar with the methodology guiding the collection and computation of the relevant data. Data may have been collected either by a census–a "complete" count of the population of interest–or by a sample survey, and methods of sampling will vary, affecting the validity of the information for various uses. Specialized information on the methodology behind the data cannot be included in the *Abstract*, but the source notes at the end of each table will lead the reader to that information.

Much of the value of the *Abstract* lies in its many references to other sources of information. There are 26 libraries in Tennessee designated as federal depository libraries, which house a variety of federal publications and have reference staffs to assist in locating information. In addition, the Bureau of the Census has designated a Tennessee State Data Center, a joint project of the Tennessee State Planning Office, Nashville, and the Center for Business and Economic Research, The University of Tennessee, Knoxville. The State Data Center, 16 affiliate data centers, and a census depository library (in addition to the federal depository libraries) a list of which follows, maintain for public use a collection of all census publications relating to Tennessee.

The cost of collecting and processing data for specialized concerns and small geographic areas is often prohibitive. Also, data are not provided for a subject until expressed interest demands it, or, where concepts and interest exist, there may be no appropriate agency to represent the interests and establish data collection. New data are incorporated into the *Abstract* as collected and substitutions are made when appropriate. For example, interest and need for foreign trade data prompted the Foreign Trade Division, Bureau of the Census, to enhance data collection and distribution efforts in order to provide states with information on exports and imports. These data are included in Rankings Table 20.14. We solicit your suggestions about other sources of data as well as areas about which you wish to have more detailed information.

PREFACE

The *1990 Tennessee Statistical Abstract* is the seventh annual edition and the twelfth published by the Center for Business and Economic Research (CBER) since publication began in 1969. The annual publication of the *Abstract* is facilitated both by your purchase and by CBER's continued commitment to support informed decison-making in Tennessee.

The 1990 edition was produced using Ventura Publisher® desktop design package and LOTUS® data files. This process results in a more professional presentation at a reduced production cost and permits continuous access to machine readable data files. Although technological advancement and private and public sector data initiatives provide access to an ever-increasing supply of data, barriers to informed decision-making remain.

First, the availability of data in electronic media excludes many data users either because they do not have the technical equipment or user knowledge to access these data or because the existence of the data is veiled by the medium. Published indexes to electronically disseminated information should be readily available to data users. A statistical abstract serves as an index to both published and unpublished data and data sources. Secondly, the imposition of user fees either by the public or the private sector excludes both the casual data user and those who cannot afford the purchase price. Although arguments for recovering the costs of value added services have merit, these charges should not prohibit access to public data. Finally, the abundance of data engenders an "information-poor" class, because a data user must deal with a multitude of different measurements for each data item and is often hindered in the selection of the best measure by the absence of collection dates, methodology or source.

The necessity for maintaining standards in data presentation, whether electronic or print, underscores the importance of compendia such as the *Statistical Abstract of the United States* and state counterparts like the *Tennessee Statistical Abstract.* Unless agencies such as ours assume lead responsibility for accessing, compiling, and publishing statistical information, standards may fall victim to indiscriminate accessibility.

Numerous federal, state, and private publications were used in compiling this volume, and source documentation has been made as complete as possible. The chapter prefaces and the source notes following each table provide valuable direction to the user who wishes to obtain additional information. All data users should be aware of the inherent limitations of data of all kinds and are urged to read the "Notes for Data Users" on page iv.

In this *1990 Tennessee Statistical Abstract*, data are given primarily for 1987 and 1988 for the state of Tennessee, its Metropolitan Statistical Areas, counties, and, where data are available and space permits, for towns. Also presented are comparisons between Tennessee and other southeastern states. The reporting lag is the time required by the collecting agencies to accumulate and process the data.

To encourage circulation, the price of the *Tennessee Statistical Abstract* is set to barely cover the marginal cost of printing. We want and need your feedback on content, your repeat purchase of annual editions of the *Abstract,* and your recommendation to other potential purchasers. We encourage the placement of a standing order for annual editions of the *Abstract.* Use either the card enclosed for this purpose or contact the Editor, *Tennessee Statistical Abstract*, Center for Business and Economic Research, College of Business Administration, The University of Tennessee, Knoxville, Tennessee, 37996-4170, (615) 974-5441.

Compiling the *Tennessee Statistical Abstract* is a task that requires a variety of talents ranging from graphic arts to statistical detective work, sophisticated desktop publishing skills, and editorial judgment. Each CBER staff member and student assistant gave countless hours in the attempt to insure that the *Abstract* is as useful and accurate as possible. The list of those contributing to the *1990 Tennessee Statistical Abstract* may be found on page iii. We are grateful for their dedication, patience, and cooperation. We also appreciate the work of Dick Lefevre of the Department of Art at The University of Tennessee for cover design and of Will Fontanez, cartographer, The University of Tennessee, Department of Geography, for creation of the county maps. Tennessee state government personnel, too numerous to list individually, have been generous in providing data and answering questions; and finally, the reference staff of UTK Library has provided assistance in locating materials throughout this research effort.

David A. Hake, *Director*
Betty B. Vickers, *Research Associate*

Center for Business and Economic Research
College of Business Administration
The University of Tennessee, Knoxville
Knoxville, Tennessee

TABLE OF CONTENTS

LIST OF FIGURES

TENNESSEE STATE DATA CENTER

Tennessee State Planning Office, 309 John Sevier Building, 500 Charlotte Avenue, Nashville, TN 37219, (615) 741-1676

Center for Business and Economic Research, Suite 100, Glocker Business Administration Building, The University of Tennessee, Knoxville, TN 37996-4170, (615) 974-5441

EAST TENNESSEE DATA RESOURCES

Federal Depository Libraries

E. W. King Library, King College, Bristol, TN 37620, (615) 968-1187

Sherrod Library, East Tennessee State University, P. O. Box 22450A, Johnson City, TN 37614-0002, (615) 929-4337

Carson-Newman College Library, Russell Avenue, Jefferson City, TN 37760, (615) 475-9061

Lawson-McGhee Public Library, 500 Church Street, SW, Knoxville, TN 37902-2505 (615) 544-5750

The University of Tennessee Law Library, College of Law, 1505 W. Cumberland, Knoxville, TN 37996-1800, (615) 974-4381

John C. Hodges Library, The University of Tennessee at Knoxville, Knoxville, TN 37996-1000, (615) 974-4127

U.S. TVA Technical Library, 1101 Market Street, Chattanooga, TN 37402, (615) 751-4913

Cleveland State Community College Library, P. O. Box 3570, Cleveland, TN 37320-3570, (615) 472-7141

Chattanooga Hamilton County Bicentennial Library, 1001 Broad Street, Chattanooga, TN 37402-2652, (615) 757-5310

Jesse Ball DuPont Library, University of the South, Sewanee, TN 37375-4005, (615) 598-5931

Census Depository Library

J. Fred Johnson Memorial Library, Broad and New Streets, Kingsport, TN 37660-4292, (615) 229-9465

State Data Center Affiliates

First Tennessee-Virginia Development District, 207 North Boone Street, Johnson City, TN 37601, (615) 928-0224

East Tennessee Development District, Westwood Building, 5615 Kingston Pike, P. O. Box 19806, Knoxville, TN 37939-2806, (615) 584-8553

Southeast Tennessee Development District, 216 West 8th Street, Suite 300, Chattanooga, TN 37402, (615) 266-5781

Oak Ridge Public Library, Civic Center, Oak Ridge, TN 37830, (615) 483-6386

Knoxville/Knox County Metropolitan Planning Commission, Suite 403, 400 Main Avenue, Knoxville, TN 37902-2476, (615) 521-2500

MIDDLE TENNESSEE DATA RESOURCES

Federal Depository Libraries

University Library, Tennessee Technological University, P. O. Box 5066, Cookeville, TN 38505, (615) 372-3408

Andrew L. Todd Library, Middle Tennessee State University, P. O. Box 13, Murfreesboro, TN 37132, (615) 898-2772

Public Library of Nashville and Davidson County, 8th Avenue N. and Union, Nashville, TN 37203-3585, (615) 259-6004

Fisk University Library, 17th Avenue N., Nashville, TN 37208-3051, (615) 329-8641

Brown-Daniel Library, Tennessee State University, 3500 J. Merritt Blvd., Nashville, TN 37209-1561, (615) 320-3682

Vanderbilt Law Library, College of Law, Nashville, TN 37240, (615) 322-2568

Vanderbilt University Library, 419 21st Avenue S., Nashville, TN 37240-0007, (615) 322-7100

Felix G. Woodward Library, Austin Peay State University, Clarksville, TN 37044, (615) 648-7618

Tennessee State Law Library, Supreme Court Building, 401 7th Avenue N., Nashville, TN 37219, (615) 741-2016

Tennessee State Library and Archives, State Library Division, 403 7th Avenue N., Nashville, TN 37219, (615) 741-2451

John W. Finney Memorial Library, Columbia State Community College, P. O. Box 1315, Columbia, TN 38401, (615) 388-0120

State Data Center Affiliates

Upper Cumberland Development District, 1225 Burgess Falls Road, Cookeville, TN 38501, (615) 432-4111

Greater Nashville Regional Council, 7th Floor Stahlman Building, Box 233, 211 Union Street, Nashville, TN 37201, (615) 259-5491

South Central Tennessee Development District, P. O. Box 1346, Columbia, TN 38402-1346, (615) 381-2040

Department of Economic and Community Development, 8th Floor, Rachel Jackson Building, Nashville, TN 37219, (615) 741-1995

WEST TENNESSEE DATA RESOURCES

Federal Depository Libraries

Paul Meek Library, The University of Tennessee at Martin, Martin, TN 38238-5047, (901) 587-7060

Luther L. Gobbel Library, Lambuth College, Lambuth Blvd., Jackson, TN 38301-5296, (901) 425-2500

Memphis and Shelby County Public Library and Information Center, 1850 Peabody Avenue, Memphis, TN 38104-4025, (901) 725-8855

Cecil C. Humphreys School of Law Library, Memphis State University, Memphis, TN 38152, (901) 678-2426

Regional Depository and State Data Center Affiliate

John W. Brister Library, Memphis State University, Memphis, TN 38152, (901) 678-2206

State Data Center Affiliates

Northwest Tennessee Development District, 124 Weldon Street, P. O. Box 63, Martin, TN 38237 (901) 587-4215

Southwest Tennessee Development District, 416 East Lafayette Street, P. O. Box 2385, Jackson, TN 38301, (901) 422-4041

Library, The University of Tennessee at Martin, Martin, TN 38238, (901) 587-7065

Memphis Delta Development District, 157 Poplar Avenue, B150, Memphis, TN 38103, (901) 576-4610

Bureau for Business and Economic Research, Memphis State University, Memphis, TN 38152, (901) 454-2281

Memphis and Shelby County Office of Planning and Development, City Hall, 125 N. Mid-America Mall, Room 419, Memphis, TN 38103, (901) 576-6763

FIGURE 0.1
Counties, Metropolitan Areas, and Selected Places

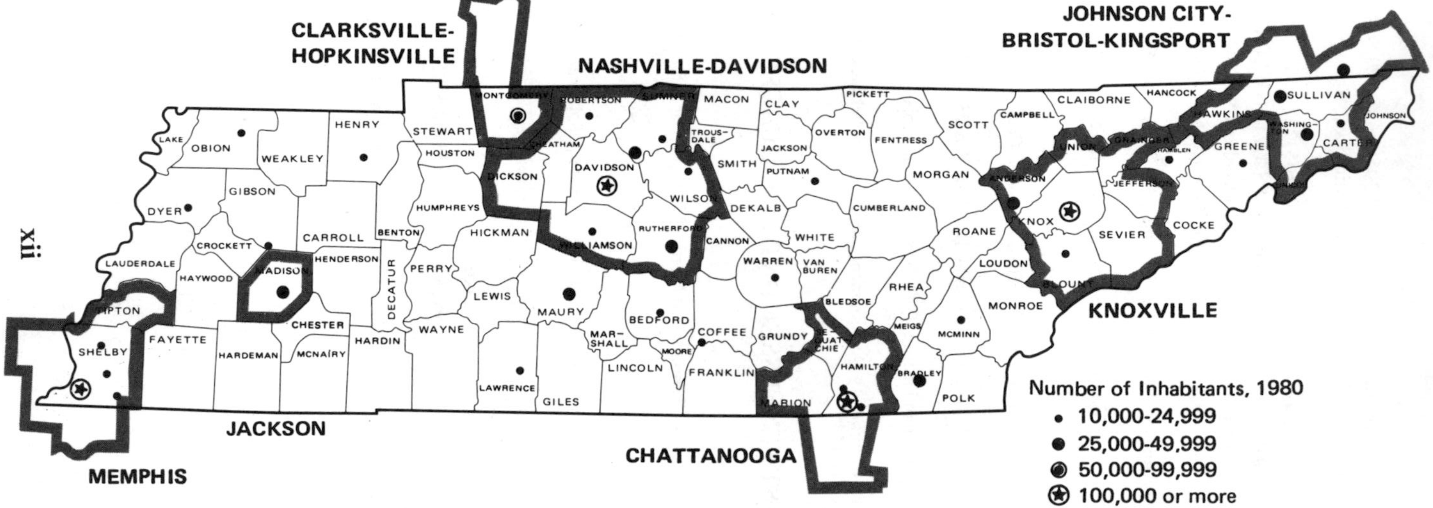

Note: Grainger, Jefferson and Sevier Counties were added to the Knoxville Metropolitan Statistical Area effective June 30, 1983 and Jackson was recognized as an MSA June 30, 1985.
Source: U.S. Department of Commerce, Bureau of the Census, *Census of Population: 1980*; and U.S.. Office of Management and Budget, June 30, 1985.

As the *1990 Tennessee Statistical Abstract* goes to press, data users anxiously await results from the *1990 Bicentennial Census of Population and Housing*. Since its beginning in 1790, the decennial census has provided the only data which count and describe all individuals and households in the United States. Until these rich details of age, race, income, family characteristics and employment are reported in 1991-1993, data users must be satisfied with data provided in the *1980 Census* reports and estimates based on those data.

Population estimates for Tennessee, its counties and municipalities are currently reported for July 1, 1988. State and county estimates are reported annually, while municipal populations are estimated biennially. These estimates are produced by the Bureau of the Census in cooperation with the Tennessee State Planning Office and published in *Current Population Reports*.

Mid-decade county estimates of households in Table 1.10 and 1985 population estimates detailed by age and sex in Table 1.8 are new to this edition of the *Abstract*. Both data items are unpublished and should provide valuable information to decision makers who rely on county-level data.

One statistical unit the user of the *Abstract* will find frequently is the Metropolitan Statistical Area (MSA). Such areas are aggregates of whole counties, including their rural areas, which meet established criteria of population density and economic integration with a large central city. Tennessee's seven metropolitan areas, with their component counties, are shown in Figure 0.1. The most recent change in Tennessee MSAs was effective June 30, 1985, when the U.S. Office of Management and Budget announced the designation of MSA status to Jackson, Tennessee. Jackson qualified for recognition as an MSA when its population was estimated at greater than 50,000 persons. Detail for the Jackson MSA are reported only for data collected or estimated after June 30, 1985. However, MSA data for Jackson will be the same as that reported in county tables for Madison County.

Data users should be aware that as cities and their environs grow, new counties may be added to the Metropolitan Statistical Areas. Such changes have occurred in every Tennessee MSA since their designation in the 1950s. Current and historical data in Table 1.5 have been revised so that geographic areas are consistent throughout. Readers using time-series MSA data should determine what geographic areas are covered. This information is detailed in chapter prefaces and table footnotes in the *Abstract*, but greater care must be taken when using time series data from other sources.

TABLE OF CONTENTS

TABLE 1.1-- URBAN AND RURAL POPULATION, TENNESSEE, 1790–1980, DECENNIAL CENSUS YEARS

Year	Total	Urban	Rural	Urban as percentage of total	Rural as percentage of total
1980	4,591,120	2,773,573	1,817,547	60.4	39.6
1970	3,926,018	2,318,458	1,605,229	59.1	40.9
1960	3,567,089	1,864,828	1,702,261	52.3	47.7
1950	3,291,718	1,452,602	1,839,116	44.1	55.9
1940	2,915,841	1,027,206	1,888,635	35.2	64.8
1930	2,616,556	896,538	1,720,018	34.3	65.7
1920	2,337,885	611,226	1,726,659	26.1	73.9
1910	2,184,789	441,045	1,743,744	20.2	79.8
1900	2,020,616	326,639	1,693,977	16.2	83.8
1890	1,767,518	238,394	1,529,124	13.5	86.5
1880	1,542,359	115,984	1,426,375	7.5	92.5
1870	1,258,520	94,237	1,164,283	7.5	92.5
1860	1,109,801	46,541	1,063,260	4.2	95.8
1850	1,002,717	21,983	980,734	2.2	97.8
1840	829,210	6,929	822,281	0.8	99.2
1830	681,904	5,566	676,338	0.8	99.2
1820	422,823	0	422,823	0.0	100.0
1810	261,727	0	261,727	0.0	100.0
1800	105,602	0	105,602	0.0	100.0
1790	35,691	0	35,691	0.0	100.0

Note: 1790 population is that of territory south of the Ohio River, including area now constituting parts of Mississippi, Alabama, and Georgia. Definition of urban population before 1950: All persons living in incorporated places of 2,500 or more inhabitants and in areas (usually minor civil divisions) classified as urban under special rules relating to population size and density.

Current definition of urban population:

1) All persons living in places of 2,500 or more inhabitants but excluding those in rural portions of extended cities.

2) All persons living in any territory within urbanized areas.

Source: U.S. Department of Commerce, Bureau of the Census, *1980 Census of Population, Number of Inhabitants, Tennessee*, and earlier editions.

FIGURE 1.1
Percentage Change in Population Between Census Years, United States and Tennessee, 1840–1980

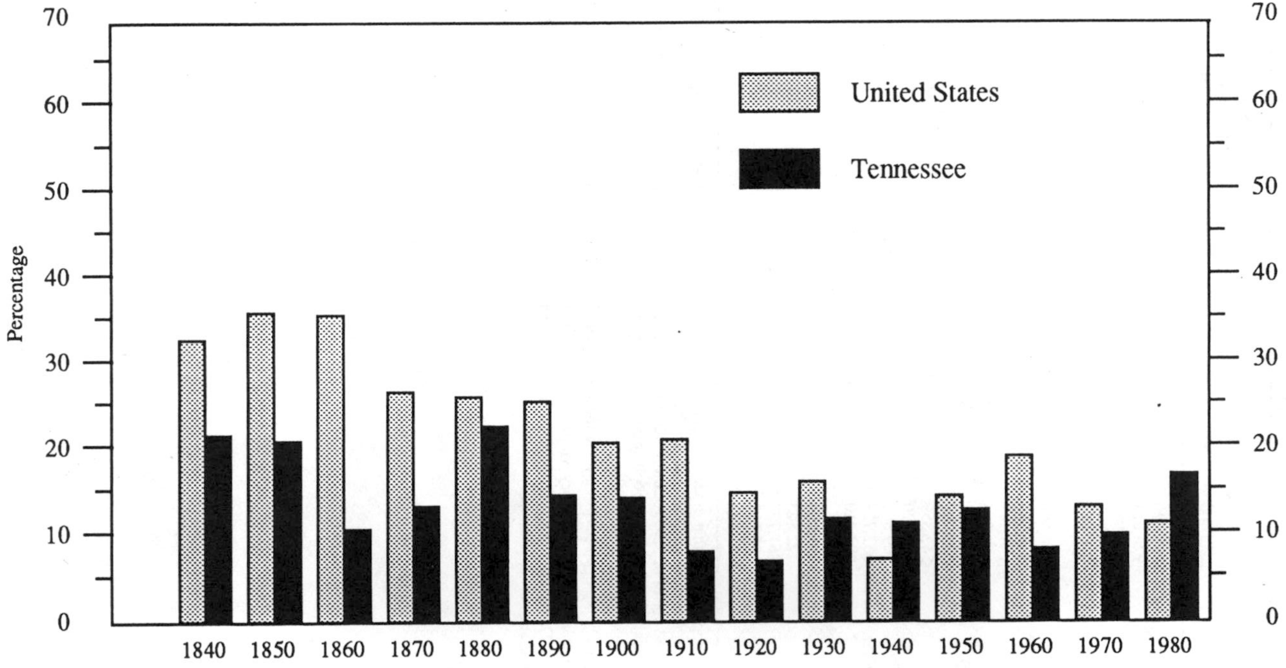

Note: Percentage change for the U.S. 1970 to 1980 was computed by the Center for Business and Economic Research from PHC80-51-1. Earlier years are from *Census of Population: 1970, Number of Inhabitants*, U.S. Summary.
Source: U.S. Department of Commerce, Bureau of the Census. *Census of Population: 1980, Number of Inhabitants, Tennessee.*

TABLE 1.2-- POPULATION AND PERCENTAGE CHANGE, TENNESSEE AND UNITED STATES, 1790–1980, DECENNIAL CENSUS YEARS, AND POPULATION ESTIMATES, 1981–1988

Year	Population: Tennessee	Population: United States	Percent increase in each decade: Tennessee	Percent increase in each decade: United States	Tennessee as a percentage of United States
1988	4,895,000	245,807,000	(X)	(X)	2.0
1987[r]	4,855,000	243,419,000	(X)	(X)	2.0
1986[r]	4,800,000	241,107,000	(X)	(X)	2.0
1985[r]	4,766,000	238,736,000	(X)	(X)	2.0
1984[r]	4,728,000	236,477,000	(X)	(X)	2.0
1983[r]	4,690,000	234,284,000	(X)	(X)	2.0
1982[r]	4,667,000	231,996,000	(X)	(X)	2.0
1981	4,639,000	229,637,000	(X)	(X)	2.0
1980	4,591,120	226,545,805	16.9	11.4	2.0
1970	3,926,018	203,302,031	10.0	13.3	1.9
1960	3,567,089	179,323,175	8.4	19.0	2.0
1950	3,291,718	150,697,361	12.9	14.5	2.2
1940	2,915,841	131,669,275	11.4	7.2	2.2
1930	2,616,556	122,775,046	11.9	16.1	2.1
1920	2,337,885	105,710,620	7.0	14.9	2.2
1910	2,184,789	91,972,266	8.1	21.0	2.4
1900	2,020,616	75,995,575	14.3	20.7	2.7
1890	1,767,518	62,947,714	14.6	25.5	2.8
1880	1,542,359	50,155,783	22.6	26.0	3.1
1870	1,258,520	39,818,449	13.4	26.6	3.2
1860	1,109,801	31,443,321	10.7	35.6	3.5
1850	1,002,717	23,191,876	20.9	35.9	4.3
1840	829,210	17,069,453	21.6	32.7	4.9
1830	681,904	12,866,020	61.3	33.5	5.3
1820	422,823	9,638,453	61.6	33.1	4.4
1810	261,727	7,239,881	147.8	36.4	3.6
1800	105,602	5,308,483	195.9	35.1	2.0
1790	35,691	3,929,214	(X)	(X)	0.9

Note: United States includes Alaska and Hawaii beginning in 1960. Data are as of April 1, for decennial census years, and as of July 1, for years 1981–1988.

r revised.

(X) not applicable.

Source: U.S. Department of Commerce, Bureau of the Census, *Current Population Reports*, Series P-25, No. 1044; *1980 Census of Population*, and earlier editions.

TABLE 1.3-- POPULATION BY AGE, BY RACE, AND BY SEX, TENNESSEE, 1980

Age group	Total		White		Black		Other races[1]	
	Male	Female	Male	Female	Male	Female	Male	Female
Total (all ages)	2,216,600	2,374,520	1,862,465	1,972,987	339,168	386,774	14,967	14,759
Under 5 years	167,368	158,720	131,846	124,236	33,962	33,005	1,560	1,479
5–9	179,209	170,719	142,948	135,469	34,955	33,897	1,306	1,353
10–14	189,403	180,537	152,427	143,781	35,867	35,703	1,109	1,053
15–19	219,497	210,756	176,592	167,597	41,288	41,988	1,617	1,171
20–24	209,291	214,122	171,073	171,620	35,843	40,862	2,375	1,640
25–34	365,548	379,075	309,881	314,717	52,303	60,759	3,364	3,599
35–44	259,838	274,003	229,941	235,925	27,977	36,152	1,920	1,926
45–54	221,088	244,278	195,437	210,279	24,729	32,844	922	1,155
55–64	197,720	232,360	174,301	202,220	22,991	29,540	428	600
65–74	138,519	184,508	119,367	158,408	18,905	25,621	247	479
75 and over	69,119	125,442	58,652	108,735	10,348	16,403	119	304
Median age	28.7	31.4	29.1	32.6	23.2	26.0	n.a.	n.a.

Note: Table 20.1 gives 1988 population estimates, by age, for the Southeastern States and United States.

n.a. not available.

1. Data for other races were computed by the Center for Business and Economic Research.

Source: U.S. Department of Commerce, Bureau of the Census, *1980 Census of Population, General Population Characteristics, Tennessee.*

TABLE 1.4-- PERSONS 100 YEARS AND OVER, BY AGE, BY SEX, AND BY EDUCATIONAL ATTAINMENT, TENNESSEE, 1980

Age	Total	Elementary, 0 to 8 years	High school 1 to 3 years	High school 4 years	College 1 to 3 years	College 4 or more years
Total	579	403	67	72	15	22
100–104 years	468	333	44	64	15	12
105–109 years	91	58	23	0	0	10
110 years and over	20	12	0	8	0	0
Male	178	155	13	8	2	0
100–104 years	146	130	6	8	2	0
105–109 years	30	23	7	0	0	0
110 years and over	2	2	0	0	0	0
Female	401	248	54	64	13	22
100–104 years	322	203	38	56	13	12
105–109 years	61	35	16	0	0	10
110 years and over	18	10	0	8	0	0

Note: The centenarian data shown are from the "not allocated" distribution. This is the best estimate of the centenarian population that can be provided for each state, but it still represents an inflation of the true count of centenarians. For a complete explanation of this overcount and the statistical procedures involved, see the original source.

Source: U.S. Department of Commerce, Bureau of the Census, *Current Population Reports*, Special Studies, Series P-23, No. 153.

TABLE 1.5-- POPULATION AND SELECTED STATISTICS, METROPOLITAN STATISTICAL AREAS, 1950–1980, DECENNIAL CENSUS YEARS

MSA and counties	Population 1980	Population 1970	Population 1960	Population 1950	Land area (sq. mi.)	Percentage of 1980 population White	Percentage of 1980 population Rural
Chattanooga	426,540	370,857	339,887	295,168	2,102	85.4	25.5
Tennessee: Hamilton, Marion, Sequatchie							
Georgia: Catoosa, Dade, Walker							
Clarksville-Hopkinsville	150,220	118,945	112,549	86,545	1,261	75.9	30.2
Tennessee: Montgomery							
Kentucky: Christian							
Johnson City-Kingsport-Bristol	433,638	373,591	347,132	324,976	2,865	97.6	44.4
Tennessee: Carter, Hawkins, Sullivan, Unicoi, Washington							
Virginia: Scott, Washington, Bristol City[1]							
Knoxville	565,970	476,538	434,828	401,903	2,750	93.2	41.5
Anderson, Blount, Grainger, Knox, Jefferson, Sevier, Union							
Memphis	913,472	834,103	727,038	583,958	2,308	59.3	10.8
Tennessee: Shelby, Tipton							
Arkansas: Crittenden							
Mississippi: DeSoto							
Nashville-Davidson	850,505	699,271	596,865	501,608	4,060	83.0	24.9
Cheatham, Davidson, Dickson, Robertson, Rutherford, Sumner, Williamson, Wilson							

Note: Data revised to provide population for comparable land areas. MSA boundaries are as defined by the Office of Management and Budget June 30, 1983. Land area and percentages were computed by the Center for Business and Economic Research. Table 20.2 gives 1988 population estimates for all MSA's in the Southeastern States.

1. In Virginia the cities are independent of counties.

Source: U.S. Department of Commerce, Bureau of the Census, *1980 Census of Population, Number of Inhabitants*; and *General Population Characteristics*; and earlier editions.

TABLE 1.6-- POPULATION LIVING IN GROUP QUARTERS, BY AGE AND BY TYPE OF QUARTERS, TENNESSEE, 1980

		Noninstitutional residents				Inmates of institutions			
Age	Total	Boarding house	Military	College dormitory	Other	Mental hospital	Home for aged	Corrections institution	Other
Total (all ages)	111,441	3,307	12,490	47,525	2,777	6,215	22,014	10,493	6,620
Under 5	511	315	20	18	67	46	15	0	30
5–9	561	178	0	0	67	102	0	0	214
10–14	1,371	51	5	70	136	125	8	36	940
15–19	32,805	219	6,244	22,549	549	283	18	996	1,947
20–24	33,305	252	4,820	23,534	573	535	41	3,227	323
25–29	5,864	399	854	924	103	583	58	2,713	230
30–34	3,216	298	285	109	114	491	53	1,683	183
35–39	1,935	260	165	73	71	467	87	695	117
40–44	1,319	76	37	41	67	421	88	454	135
45–49	1,246	130	31	27	111	429	104	237	177
50–54	1,571	116	7	6	138	569	266	218	251
55–59	1,645	176	0	36	107	425	399	150	352
60–64	2,058	291	7	29	90	484	794	44	319
65–69	2,756	277	7	35	89	396	1,602	33	317
70–74	2,988	42	0	26	139	297	2,279	7	198
75–79	4,794	139	8	27	122	187	4,096	0	215
80–84	5,301	60	0	8	84	217	4,598	0	334
85 and over	8,195	28	0	13	150	158	7,508	0	338

Source: U.S. Department of Commerce, Bureau of the Census, *1980 Census of Population, Detailed Population Characteristics, Tennessee.*

TABLE 1.7-- TOTAL POPULATION, TENNESSEE AND COUNTIES, 1950–1980, DECENNIAL CENSUS YEARS, AND ESTIMATES FOR 1986, 1987, AND 1988

County	Population estimates							Change, 1980–1988		
								Total		
	1988 P	1987 r	1986 r	1980	1970	1960	1950	Number	%	Net migration
TENNESSEE	4,895,000	4,855,000	4,800,000	4,591,023	3,926,018	3,567,089	3,291,718	304,000	6.6	118,000
Anderson	70,700	70,100	69,200	67,346	60,300	60,032	59,407	3,400	5.0	1,600
Bedford	29,500	29,300	29,200	27,916	25,039	23,150	23,627	1,500	5.5	1,000
Benton	14,900	14,900	15,000	14,901	12,126	10,662	11,495	0	0.2	100
Bledsoe	9,900	10,000	9,800	9,478	7,643	7,811	8,561	400	4.5	200
Blount	84,600	83,600	82,400	77,770	63,744	57,525	54,691	6,800	8.8	4,500
Bradley	74,300	73,000	72,300	67,547	50,686	38,324	32,338	6,800	10.0	3,300
Campbell	35,000	35,000	35,600	34,923	26,045	27,936	34,369	100	0.3	-900
Cannon	10,900	10,900	10,800	10,234	8,467	8,537	9,174	700	6.7	500
Carroll	28,100	28,100	28,000	28,285	25,741	23,476	26,553	-200	-0.8	-200
Carter	51,300	51,600	51,400	50,205	43,259	41,578	42,432	1,100	2.1	200
Cheatham	26,700	25,900	24,800	21,616	13,199	9,428	9,167	5,100	23.6	3,800
Chester	12,900	13,000	12,800	12,727	9,927	9,569	11,149	200	1.3	-100
Claiborne	26,800	26,400	26,400	24,595	19,420	19,067	24,788	2,200	9.0	1,400
Clay	7,900	7,900	7,900	7,676	6,624	7,289	8,701	300	3.6	200
Cocke	29,400	29,300	29,300	28,792	25,283	23,390	22,991	600	2.2	200
Coffee	42,200	41,800	41,300	38,311	32,572	28,603	23,049	3,900	10.1	2,200
Crockett	14,000	14,100	14,300	14,941	14,402	14,594	16,624	-1,000	-6.5	-1,100
Cumberland	33,400	32,700	31,700	28,676	20,733	19,135	18,877	4,800	16.6	3,800
Davidson	507,300	507,000	498,800	477,811	447,877	399,743	321,758	29,500	6.2	4,700
Decatur	10,900	11,100	11,100	10,857	9,457	8,324	9,442	0	0.2	0
DeKalb	14,400	14,400	14,400	13,589	11,151	10,774	11,680	900	6.3	600
Dickson	34,700	33,800	32,900	30,037	21,977	18,839	18,805	4,600	15.4	3,400
Dyer	35,000	34,500	34,300	34,663	30,427	29,537	33,473	300	0.9	-500
Fayette	26,400	26,300	25,800	25,305	22,692	24,577	27,535	1,100	4.3	-200
Fentress	15,700	15,700	15,700	14,826	12,593	13,288	14,917	900	6.0	500
Franklin	34,400	34,100	33,900	31,983	27,289	25,528	25,431	2,400	7.4	1,600
Gibson	48,300	48,600	48,800	49,467	47,871	44,699	48,132	-1,200	-2.4	-1,100
Giles	25,100	25,000	24,800	24,625	22,138	22,410	26,961	500	2.1	0

TABLE 1.7-- TOTAL POPULATION, TENNESSEE AND COUNTIES, 1950–1980, DECENNIAL CENSUS YEARS, AND ESTIMATES FOR 1986, 1987, AND 1988 (Continued)

County	Population estimates							Change, 1980–1988		
								Total		
	1988 P	1987 r	1986 r	1980	1970	1960	1950	Number	%	Net migration
Grainger	17,400	17,300	17,400	16,751	13,948	12,506	13,086	700	4.1	300
Greene	56,300	56,500	56,600	54,422	47,630	42,163	41,048	1,900	3.5	900
Grundy	14,400	14,600	14,400	13,787	10,631	11,512	12,558	600	4.5	100
Hamblen	51,700	51,300	51,700	49,300	38,696	33,092	23,976	2,400	4.8	800
Hamilton	291,800	289,500	285,500	287,643	255,077	237,905	208,255	4,100	1.4	-6,700
Hancock	6,800	6,900	6,800	6,887	6,719	7,757	9,116	-100	-1.5	-300
Hardeman	24,400	24,300	24,100	23,873	22,435	21,517	23,311	500	2.1	-300
Hardin	22,400	22,400	22,300	22,280	18,212	17,397	16,908	100	0.6	-100
Hawkins	45,400	45,100	45,000	43,751	33,757	30,468	30,494	1,600	3.8	400
Haywood	21,100	21,100	21,000	20,318	19,596	23,393	26,212	800	3.7	200
Henderson	22,800	22,700	22,600	21,390	17,360	16,115	17,173	1,400	6.7	1,100
Henry	29,400	29,400	29,400	28,656	23,749	22,275	23,828	700	2.5	800
Hickman	16,700	16,400	16,300	15,151	12,096	11,862	13,353	1,500	10.0	1,300
Houston	7,200	7,100	7,000	6,871	5,853	4,794	5,318	300	4.7	300
Humphreys	16,100	16,000	16,100	15,957	13,560	11,511	11,030	200	1.2	-100
Jackson	9,400	9,400	9,300	9,398	8,141	9,233	12,348	0	0.3	100
Jefferson	33,400	33,200	33,200	31,284	24,940	21,493	19,667	2,100	6.9	1,500
Johnson	14,000	14,100	14,200	13,745	11,569	10,765	12,278	200	1.5	0
Knox	331,000	328,900	326,700	319,694	276,293	250,523	223,007	11,300	3.5	600
Lake	7,500	7,700	7,700	7,455	8,074	9,572	11,655	100	0.8	100
Lauderdale	25,100	25,100	25,100	24,555	20,271	21,844	25,047	500	2.2	-100
Lawrence	35,200	35,000	35,000	34,110	29,097	28,049	28,818	1,100	3.2	-100
Lewis	10,600	10,500	10,400	9,700	6,761	6,269	6,078	900	9.3	500
Lincoln	27,600	27,200	27,100	26,483	24,318	23,829	25,624	1,100	4.1	600
Loudon	31,200	30,900	30,500	28,553	24,266	23,757	23,182	2,600	9.2	2,100
McMinn	43,600	43,700	43,300	41,878	35,462	33,662	32,024	1,700	4.1	800
McNairy	24,000	23,900	23,600	22,525	18,369	18,085	20,390	1,500	6.4	1,200

TABLE 1.7-- TOTAL POPULATION, TENNESSEE AND COUNTIES, 1950–1980, DECENNIAL CENSUS YEARS, AND ESTIMATES FOR 1986, 1987, AND 1988 (Continued)

	Population estimates							Change, 1980–1988		
								Total		
County	1988 P	1987 r	1986 r	1980	1970	1960	1950	Number	%	Net migration
Macon	16,200	16,100	16,100	15,700	12,315	12,197	13,599	500	2.9	200
Madison	78,200	78,000	78,000	74,546	65,774	60,655	60,128	3,700	5.0	900
Marion	25,600	25,400	25,300	24,416	20,577	21,036	20,520	1,200	4.7	500
Marshall	21,300	21,200	20,800	19,698	17,319	16,859	17,768	1,600	8.1	1,400
Maury	55,300	55,000	54,100	51,095	44,028	41,699	40,368	4,200	8.2	2,700
Meigs	8,400	8,200	8,000	7,431	5,219	5,160	6,080	1,000	13.2	700
Monroe	31,100	31,000	30,700	28,700	23,475	23,316	24,513	2,400	8.4	1,400
Montgomery	97,000	94,200	92,700	83,342	62,721	55,645	44,186	13,700	16.4	4,800
Moore	4,900	4,800	4,800	4,510	3,568	3,454	3,948	400	9.7	300
Morgan	17,700	17,700	17,300	16,604	13,619	14,304	15,727	1,100	6.7	700
Obion	32,700	33,100	33,000	32,781	30,247	26,957	29,056	0	-0.1	-300
Overton	17,900	17,900	17,700	17,575	14,866	14,661	17,566	300	1.9	100
Perry	6,500	6,400	6,400	6,111	5,238	5,273	6,462	400	7.1	500
Pickett	4,500	4,600	4,600	4,358	3,774	4,431	5,093	200	4.2	100
Polk	13,900	13,900	13,800	13,602	11,669	12,160	14,074	300	2.2	100
Putnam	52,300	51,600	51,000	47,690	35,487	29,236	29,869	4,600	9.6	3,200
Rhea	25,300	25,000	25,000	24,235	17,202	15,863	16,041	1,000	4.2	200
Roane	49,600	49,500	49,600	48,425	38,881	39,133	31,665	1,200	2.4	100
Robertson	42,800	41,900	40,500	37,021	29,102	27,335	27,024	5,700	15.5	4,100
Rutherford	111,700	107,300	102,600	84,058	59,428	52,368	40,696	27,600	32.8	21,000
Scott	20,600	20,800	20,800	19,259	14,762	15,413	17,362	1,300	6.9	400
Sequatchie	9,000	8,900	8,900	8,605	6,331	5,915	5,685	400	4.5	100
Sevier	49,800	48,700	47,400	41,418	28,241	24,251	23,375	8,400	20.2	6,600
Shelby	819,800	812,400	804,300	777,113	722,111	627,019	482,393	42,600	5.5	-8,900
Smith	14,800	14,800	14,700	14,935	12,509	12,059	14,098	-200	-1.0	-500
Stewart	9,400	9,400	9,300	8,665	7,319	7,851	9,175	800	8.8	800
Sullivan	147,400	147,300	146,400	143,968	127,329	114,139	95,063	3,500	2.4	-200
Sumner	102,400	100,100	96,800	85,790	56,266	36,217	33,533	16,600	19.4	11,300

TABLE 1.7-- TOTAL POPULATION, TENNESSEE AND COUNTIES, 1950–1980, DECENNIAL CENSUS YEARS, AND ESTIMATES FOR 1986, 1987, AND 1988 (Continued)

County	Population estimates			1980	1970	1960	1950	Change, 1980–1988		
								Total		Net migration
	1988 p	1987 r	1986 r					Number	%	
Tipton	38,100	37,200	36,100	32,930	28,001	28,564	29,782	5,200	15.8	3,100
Trousdale	6,200	6,100	6,000	6,137	5,155	4,914	5,520	0	0.4	-100
Unicoi	16,700	16,700	16,800	16,362	15,254	15,082	15,886	400	2.2	200
Union	12,700	12,400	12,300	11,707	9,072	8,498	8,670	900	8.1	300
Van Buren	4,700	4,800	4,800	4,728	3,758	3,671	3,985	0	0.1	-200
Warren	34,200	34,100	33,600	32,653	26,972	23,102	22,271	1,500	4.6	400
Washington	91,700	91,400	91,300	88,755	73,924	64,832	59,971	3,000	3.4	600
Wayne	14,200	14,200	14,200	13,946	12,365	11,908	13,864	200	1.5	-100
Weakley	32,600	32,600	32,800	32,896	28,827	24,227	27,962	-300	-0.8	-300
White	20,500	20,300	20,300	19,567	16,329	15,577	16,204	900	4.7	500
Williamson	77,800	75,100	72,100	58,108	34,423	25,267	24,307	19,700	33.8	15,800
Wilson	68,600	66,600	63,800	56,064	36,999	27,668	26,318	12,500	22.3	9,400

p provisional.
r revised.
Source: U.S. Department of Commerce, Bureau of the Census, *1980 Census of Population, Number of Inhabitants, Tennessee*, and earlier editions; and direct correspondence.

FIGURE 1.2
Percentage Population Increase in Tennessee Counties, 1980–1988
(Tennessee percentage increase = 6.6)

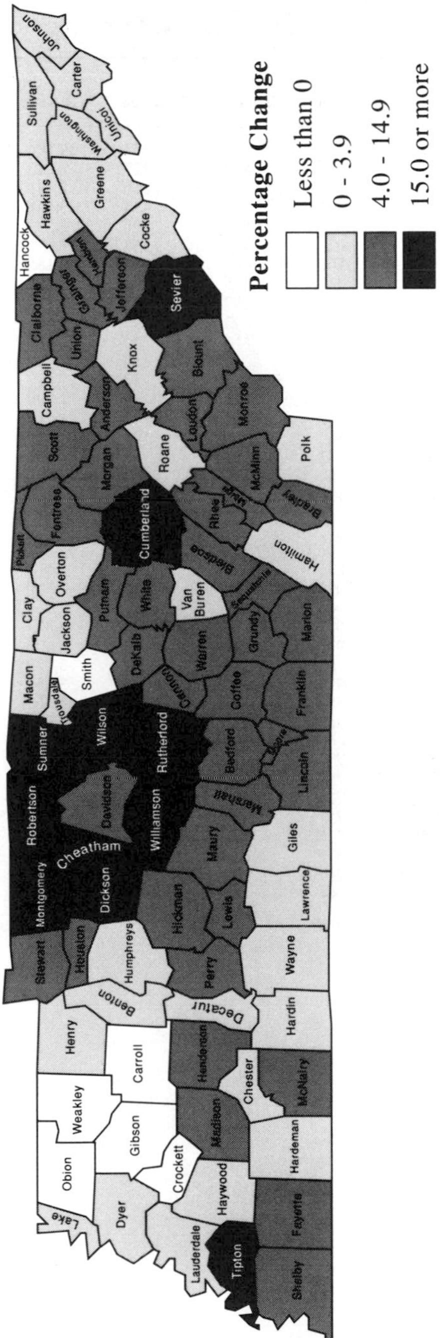

Source: U.S. Department of Commerce, Bureau of the Census, direct correspondence.

TABLE 1.8-- POPULATION ESTIMATES, BY AGE AND BY SEX, COUNTIES, 1985

Age group	Anderson	Bedford	Benton	Bledsoe	Blount	Bradley	Campbell	Cannon
MALE	33,207	14,307	7,312	5,048	39,104	35,010	17,111	5,203
0-4	2,323	927	469	377	2,843	2,539	1,061	432
5-9	2,159	1,100	470	316	2,451	3,199	1,320	470
10-14	2,623	1,396	663	454	3,148	2,720	1,595	449
15-19	2,230	1,097	587	390	3,202	3,152	1,563	407
20-24	2,230	1,026	501	568	2,958	3,330	1,259	312
25-29	2,963	908	495	480	3,185	3,299	1,205	234
30-34	2,986	1,332	715	379	3,525	3,034	1,301	455
35-39	2,514	917	357	374	3,170	2,608	1,411	366
40-44	2,404	900	443	297	2,732	2,404	1,189	310
45-49	1,938	773	416	336	2,028	1,846	854	358
50-54	1,659	685	376	169	1,813	1,422	818	266
55-59	1,742	749	291	217	1,677	1,372	865	267
60-64	1,748	717	411	189	1,799	1,226	781	247
65-69	1,462	630	363	177	1,711	1,025	642	221
70-74	1,156	503	348	149	1,399	845	524	178
75-79	612	373	221	99	786	540	372	128
80-84	296	169	112	52	449	266	221	68
85+	162	105	74	25	228	183	130	35
FEMALE	35,628	14,606	7,790	4,588	42,620	36,801	18,554	5,597
0-4	2,026	875	455	297	2,410	2,329	1,111	361
5-9	2,235	1,095	633	325	2,510	2,622	1,323	435
10-14	2,403	1,066	487	297	2,965	2,535	1,484	418
15-19	2,196	1,074	571	322	3,304	3,037	1,629	402
20-24	2,224	977	336	457	3,402	3,539	1,147	273
25-29	3,053	1,162	646	327	3,229	3,036	1,326	435
30-34	2,909	978	486	373	3,582	3,008	1,366	503
35-39	3,070	883	589	352	3,205	3,042	1,345	378
40-44	2,270	965	362	355	3,006	2,520	1,141	369
45-49	1,960	660	507	268	2,192	1,950	930	309
50-54	1,716	779	257	165	1,994	1,564	894	260
55-59	1,989	750	418	222	2,131	1,688	974	271
60-64	2,176	714	465	200	2,252	1,648	997	266
65-69	1,811	751	460	187	2,063	1,383	964	296
70-74	1,456	656	422	151	1,770	1,095	770	228
75-79	1,041	570	303	139	1,243	888	547	185
80-84	601	347	203	63	734	529	373	112
85+	492	304	190	88	628	388	233	96

TABLE 1.8-- POPULATION ESTIMATES, BY AGE AND BY SEX, COUNTIES, 1985 (Continued)

Age group	Carroll	Carter	Cheatham	Chester	Claibome	Clay	Cocke	Coffee
MALE	13,544	25,320	11,875	6,166	13,289	3,997	14,037	19,811
0-4	973	1,659	950	410	980	279	816	1,667
5-9	1,098	1,965	1,162	480	1,094	307	1,048	1,386
10-14	1,089	1,838	859	377	1,053	331	1,127	1,544
15-19	1,113	2,032	1,071	653	1,006	348	1,117	1,602
20-24	759	2,217	643	567	1,050	216	1,165	1,439
25-29	1,036	2,071	963	565	955	297	1,149	1,354
30-34	827	2,100	1,149	522	1,272	315	1,209	1,371
35-39	929	1,927	1,192	408	1,193	384	1,023	1,515
40-44	866	1,710	896	335	919	205	1,007	1,543
45-49	719	1,411	662	383	726	234	765	1,023
50-54	566	1,261	456	229	628	159	813	1,252
55-59	823	1,196	497	254	477	197	749	1,106
60-64	777	1,131	419	263	668	218	614	940
65-69	651	1,009	322	226	439	174	483	727
70-74	561	821	287	196	358	144	435	610
75-79	412	515	189	155	251	83	275	376
80-84	228	293	113	84	140	66	148	231
85+	117	164	45	59	80	40	94	125
FEMALE	14,693	26,105	12,098	6,667	13,600	3,925	15,320	21,019
0-4	855	1,587	858	483	799	270	846	1,311
5-9	786	1,793	1,020	473	1,014	220	1,001	1,539
10-14	1,225	1,648	1,204	383	960	291	1,277	1,623
15-19	1,100	1,897	782	699	1,202	268	1,198	1,551
20-24	757	2,091	804	578	1,006	354	1,184	1,212
25-29	1,007	2,185	1,035	376	1,053	212	1,167	1,480
30-34	870	2,048	1,285	476	1,330	333	1,085	1,559
35-39	1,153	1,765	966	331	956	279	1,185	1,437
40-44	940	1,664	917	397	965	226	1,082	1,521
45-49	715	1,313	678	318	686	245	988	1,248
50-54	711	1,269	461	322	537	193	878	1,129
55-59	881	1,296	508	355	543	183	781	1,147
60-64	819	1,370	366	418	748	175	644	1,194
65-69	801	1,327	381	324	577	224	664	969
70-74	781	1,170	361	291	492	169	577	778
75-79	598	862	228	207	353	129	397	625
80-84	382	453	139	137	226	88	218	421
85+	312	367	105	99	153	66	148	275

TABLE 1.8-- POPULATION ESTIMATES, BY AGE AND BY SEX, COUNTIES, 1985 (Continued)

Age group	Crockett	Cum-berland	Davidson	Decatur	DeKalb	Dickson	Dyer	Fayette
MALE	6,680	15,090	233,855	5,471	6,861	15,601	16,637	12,617
0-4	492	1,000	16,050	327	528	1,182	1,242	1,243
5-9	406	1,246	13,994	407	503	1,164	1,139	1,128
10-14	517	1,193	15,211	449	492	1,170	1,479	1,245
15-19	559	1,365	18,855	490	621	1,368	1,670	1,277
20-24	331	903	27,018	270	510	1,176	1,330	982
25-29	500	1,104	27,423	320	566	1,289	1,365	774
30-34	452	1,165	22,000	449	388	1,321	1,246	874
35-39	636	1,189	16,862	446	432	1,065	1,089	720
40-44	563	1,004	12,785	359	430	1,045	1,060	601
45-49	264	703	11,659	235	382	998	759	587
50-54	336	750	10,646	302	340	801	808	618
55-59	301	688	10,965	317	282	677	718	520
60-64	298	705	9,325	310	481	645	726	565
65-69	369	810	7,837	257	292	583	698	482
70-74	263	611	5,736	205	271	476	580	413
75-79	216	373	3,967	161	180	358	419	303
80-84	106	176	2,142	106	93	195	198	143
85+	71	105	1,380	61	70	88	111	142
FEMALE	7,619	16,082	257,665	5,698	7,350	16,331	17,848	12,798
0-4	568	926	15,774	372	480	996	1,167	989
5-9	573	1,152	13,623	285	591	1,013	1,267	1,014
10-14	523	1,115	14,308	519	426	1,315	1,114	1,007
15-19	566	1,452	17,183	446	599	1,344	1,338	1,074
20-24	454	868	28,745	355	354	1,191	1,390	936
25-29	502	1,108	26,968	369	679	1,402	1,211	844
30-34	483	1,244	21,602	331	276	1,182	1,250	994
35-39	552	1,165	17,696	371	484	1,213	1,462	734
40-44	396	983	14,666	271	546	1,052	921	709
45-49	341	816	12,805	260	388	829	836	754
50-54	337	776	12,330	340	391	778	916	511
55-59	336	940	13,148	310	404	731	836	677
60-64	470	926	12,530	357	433	776	982	702
65-69	421	858	10,851	341	386	780	912	585
70-74	423	672	9,171	287	359	684	870	476
75-79	347	497	7,475	249	261	470	659	391
80-84	170	314	4,789	141	164	307	391	195
85+	157	270	4,001	94	129	268	326	206

TABLE 1.8-- POPULATION ESTIMATES, BY AGE AND BY SEX, COUNTIES, 1985 (Continued)

Age group	Fentress	Franklin	Gibson	Giles	Grainger	Greene	Grundy	Hamblen
MALE	7,478	16,833	23,152	11,835	8,586	27,307	7,148	26,172
0-4	479	1,140	1,676	886	622	1,663	638	1,820
5-9	561	1,577	1,579	876	791	2,172	687	1,849
10-14	750	1,547	2,158	946	809	2,441	673	2,131
15-19	549	1,727	2,020	985	801	2,271	570	2,544
20-24	512	1,183	1,566	931	626	1,710	555	2,183
25-29	508	1,206	1,630	889	509	1,741	433	1,996
30-34	637	1,052	1,516	783	701	2,447	468	1,875
35-39	668	1,230	1,558	825	720	2,140	587	2,226
40-44	502	1,160	1,429	703	635	1,913	484	1,838
45-49	359	1,005	1,164	750	364	1,786	362	1,702
50-54	372	756	1,189	461	379	1,636	332	1,543
55-59	360	778	1,155	569	396	1,403	285	1,109
60-64	345	696	1,199	690	318	1,117	375	1,261
65-69	298	683	1,072	547	324	1,044	230	817
70-74	226	494	996	407	258	879	211	643
75-79	180	338	668	335	196	532	142	351
80-84	108	163	360	154	66	264	65	188
85+	64	98	217	98	71	148	51	96
FEMALE	8,121	16,610	25,725	13,235	8,798	29,228	7,407	26,803
0-4	521	995	1,532	737	535	1,770	558	1,642
5-9	692	1,136	1,549	827	590	1,931	588	1,896
10-14	684	1,285	1,691	948	685	2,126	749	1,723
15-19	714	1,302	1,502	1,140	753	2,249	674	2,020
20-24	444	1,243	1,463	1,073	517	1,786	457	1,917
25-29	574	1,329	1,560	799	684	2,151	497	2,406
30-34	702	1,339	2,030	867	525	2,509	478	2,130
35-39	570	1,149	1,808	775	787	2,120	474	1,968
40-44	561	1,027	1,359	1,029	662	2,077	489	2,160
45-49	412	891	1,433	680	542	1,677	426	1,646
50-54	326	877	1,574	573	419	1,615	263	1,414
55-59	438	666	1,474	778	437	1,414	313	1,344
60-64	365	870	1,475	741	454	1,444	440	1,356
65-69	366	738	1,527	668	375	1,377	313	1,083
70-74	304	701	1,392	609	316	1,110	266	808
75-79	224	531	1,095	466	254	883	182	639
80-84	128	319	675	291	161	541	134	363
85+	96	212	586	234	102	448	106	288

TABLE 1.8-- POPULATION ESTIMATES, BY AGE AND BY SEX, COUNTIES, 1985 (Continued)

Age group	Hamilton	Hancock	Hardeman	Hardin	Hawkins	Haywood	Hender-son	Henry
MALE	135,036	3,336	11,747	11,038	22,511	9,950	10,798	14,290
0-4	9,614	299	983	778	1,476	807	946	1,181
5-9	10,053	204	997	830	1,824	931	817	1,323
10-14	10,244	285	1,198	899	2,057	925	736	972
15-19	10,967	299	885	923	1,841	816	898	937
20-24	12,198	193	866	561	1,454	884	1,078	717
25-29	12,329	296	866	705	1,825	838	796	941
30-34	11,268	222	1,141	889	1,877	672	783	1,023
35-39	11,121	157	738	920	2,017	600	720	968
40-44	7,801	229	681	699	1,652	545	655	774
45-49	6,982	205	481	704	1,182	500	490	750
50-54	6,585	214	521	589	992	342	413	790
55-59	6,744	183	556	585	1,206	386	545	803
60-64	5,869	147	523	563	963	378	615	893
65-69	4,971	137	434	458	766	427	461	777
70-74	3,462	136	337	381	651	367	398	627
75-79	2,609	84	279	311	391	257	227	449
80-84	1,327	29	144	152	205	171	114	210
85+	892	17	117	91	132	104	106	155
FEMALE	149,216	3,559	12,199	11,349	22,696	10,792	11,701	14,991
0-4	8,548	269	816	709	1,380	856	927	1,014
5-9	9,238	293	898	845	1,776	731	960	852
10-14	9,615	233	1,016	959	1,853	976	678	946
15-19	10,713	344	1,019	900	1,348	885	915	988
20-24	13,186	278	834	559	1,506	617	867	951
25-29	13,006	202	884	669	2,196	1,094	981	862
30-34	12,714	215	945	693	1,785	820	1,009	1,085
35-39	11,094	243	985	869	1,905	602	674	1,048
40-44	8,820	177	585	883	1,445	504	596	829
45-49	7,795	208	496	604	1,216	465	568	726
50-54	7,581	213	623	583	1,167	465	517	787
55-59	7,956	140	554	537	1,006	456	512	850
60-64	7,068	216	611	622	1,114	509	652	990
65-69	6,418	186	527	566	967	498	524	888
70-74	5,631	138	493	500	820	516	508	853
75-79	4,514	114	402	401	638	373	380	603
80-84	2,836	58	260	246	326	226	247	402
85+	2,483	32	251	204	248	199	186	317

TABLE 1.8-- POPULATION ESTIMATES, BY AGE AND BY SEX, COUNTIES, 1985 (Continued)

Age group	Hickman	Houston	Hum-phreys	Jackson	Jefferson	Johnson	Knox	Lake
MALE	8,222	3,401	7,664	4,676	16,308	7,114	158,571	3,829
0-4	533	194	529	366	1,026	410	10,466	267
5-9	460	233	579	361	1,172	651	11,059	399
10-14	622	294	767	349	1,248	599	11,115	386
15-19	680	281	562	416	1,321	627	13,588	323
20-24	909	301	396	349	1,677	567	15,957	227
25-29	588	164	402	275	1,319	419	15,653	305
30-34	678	302	696	244	1,285	407	14,910	285
35-39	631	286	629	333	1,324	614	12,611	201
40-44	546	216	501	280	1,031	409	9,510	208
45-49	553	182	456	257	855	431	8,270	190
50-54	322	155	378	252	854	368	7,017	187
55-59	340	146	455	191	748	336	6,952	163
60-64	491	168	387	335	801	384	6,696	250
65-69	306	175	326	218	593	318	5,443	150
70-74	290	126	252	203	465	259	4,024	107
75-79	159	91	202	131	319	152	2,816	94
80-84	70	53	94	71	172	84	1,469	39
85+	44	34	53	45	98	79	1,015	48
FEMALE	7,729	3,647	8,288	4,644	16,752	6,987	170,702	4,041
0-4	493	196	484	266	854	343	10,022	178
5-9	550	281	534	257	1,079	441	10,749	360
10-14	596	321	822	323	1,264	603	10,665	304
15-19	545	343	563	343	1,396	373	12,285	310
20-24	536	182	677	231	1,465	484	16,751	314
25-29	415	191	411	307	1,394	436	14,813	279
30-34	554	343	709	279	1,215	560	15,165	341
35-39	654	259	609	396	1,209	501	12,747	244
40-44	397	214	523	363	994	498	9,468	158
45-49	426	222	377	260	870	351	8,642	278
50-54	447	177	472	252	861	423	7,964	189
55-59	385	186	476	217	840	442	8,518	215
60-64	453	108	366	281	901	348	8,216	221
65-69	405	182	414	255	788	352	7,305	172
70-74	311	170	321	242	646	296	6,316	161
75-79	279	122	244	198	442	246	5,012	137
80-84	152	80	170	94	285	168	3,380	102
85+	131	70	116	80	249	122	2,684	78

TABLE 1.8-- POPULATION ESTIMATES, BY AGE AND BY SEX, COUNTIES, 1985 (Continued)

Age group	Lauderdale	Lawrence	Lewis	Lincoln	Loudon	McMinn	McNairy	Macon
MALE	12,073	17,116	5,008	12,965	14,493	20,772	11,537	7,918
0-4	1,005	1,363	299	997	1,026	1,452	935	581
5-9	995	1,467	608	959	1,046	1,616	817	615
10-14	1,004	1,382	468	1,046	1,117	1,980	909	606
15-19	990	1,715	380	1,199	1,184	1,589	889	792
20-24	864	1,068	274	924	1,014	1,383	1,036	713
25-29	948	1,476	426	1,000	1,115	1,698	690	533
30-34	1,009	1,273	511	922	1,223	1,631	766	511
35-39	1,044	1,010	432	943	1,190	1,430	741	618
40-44	773	1,113	208	773	821	1,395	586	577
45-49	478	1,016	261	656	869	1,169	820	373
50-54	547	690	247	645	821	996	654	416
55-59	443	924	202	618	740	1,052	734	320
60-64	490	699	160	689	713	1,193	533	344
65-69	469	722	192	580	610	760	443	298
70-74	433	514	150	453	466	646	439	262
75-79	328	340	113	300	286	389	297	191
80-84	159	212	40	169	143	272	149	104
85+	94	132	37	92	109	121	99	64
FEMALE	12,850	17,740	5,411	13,993	15,922	22,416	11,946	8,058
0-4	950	1,237	290	1,032	906	1,450	798	603
5-9	1,090	1,257	488	862	1,090	1,763	844	557
10-14	950	1,166	547	1,089	1,227	15,555	793	536
15-19	1,014	1,362	445	940	1,088	1,649	789	591
20-24	805	1,274	323	817	975	1,314	636	628
25-29	921	1,236	427	946	926	1,907	760	602
30-34	944	1,263	433	1,132	1,406	1,799	805	550
35-39	871	1,139	443	962	1,114	1,686	801	558
40-44	710	1,105	446	899	1,188	1,324	811	535
45-49	657	1,018	210	784	815	1,252	786	362
50-54	473	1,012	189	684	934	1,060	641	398
55-59	614	850	265	610	862	1,124	681	358
60-64	678	893	180	920	951	1,194	675	433
65-69	688	921	231	688	784	1,010	611	379
70-74	571	699	200	612	667	826	551	332
75-79	384	622	150	469	433	748	454	303
80-84	312	388	84	326	271	433	299	195
85+	218	298	60	221	285	322	211	138

TABLE 1.8-- POPULATION ESTIMATES, BY AGE AND BY SEX, COUNTIES, 1985 (Continued)

Age group	Madison	Marion	Marshall	Maury	Meigs	Monroe	Mont-gomery	Moore
MALE	36,713	12,282	10,243	25,700	3,909	14,494	45,859	2,571
0-4	3,060	955	727	2,115	234	996	2,681	223
5-9	3,069	1,144	870	1,912	297	971	2,829	258
10-14	2,988	796	950	1,857	476	1,318	3,302	213
15-19	2,954	1,044	811	1,950	362	1,393	4,077	167
20-24	2,900	1,031	680	2,089	266	1,165	7,295	136
25-29	3,243	852	664	2,126	219	1,033	5,665	195
30-34	3,467	1,054	792	2,391	349	1,158	4,169	238
35-39	2,485	1,057	843	1,814	276	1,135	3,336	169
40-44	1,824	780	681	1,640	335	1,014	2,322	148
45-49	1,762	628	505	1,342	138	649	2,266	144
50-54	1,600	691	472	1,181	226	596	1,907	168
55-59	1,771	592	510	1,208	164	749	1,652	105
60-64	1,619	444	481	1,251	195	695	1,407	140
65-69	1,371	424	439	1,005	157	618	1,068	102
70-74	1,082	356	375	803	97	460	840	77
75-79	800	252	245	539	58	289	555	53
80-84	439	122	123	258	43	143	282	21
85+	279	60	75	219	17	112	206	14
FEMALE	40,980	12,541	10,418	27,578	3,911	15,817	44,066	2,420
0-4	2,977	794	644	1,885	216	1,062	2,592	133
5-9	2,875	963	638	2,098	232	1,299	2,973	109
10-14	2,573	1,021	809	1,523	419	1,421	2,903	185
15-19	3,195	980	748	2,067	328	1,419	4,079	193
20-24	3,755	874	582	1,885	299	926	5,309	192
25-29	3,673	890	696	2,428	219	1,083	4,212	137
30-34	3,092	953	701	2,165	381	1,173	3,737	222
35-39	2,829	916	781	1,973	430	1,234	3,345	153
40-44	2,078	892	784	1,666	252	877	2,665	141
45-49	1,814	581	470	1,253	178	816	2,511	161
50-54	1,899	653	503	1,403	214	777	2,011	108
55-59	1,925	657	562	1,401	152	691	1,770	190
60-64	1,876	576	536	1,493	169	762	1,672	172
65-69	1,791	524	603	1,303	170	728	1,382	119
70-74	1,547	530	472	1,185	117	582	1,061	84
75-79	1,387	371	383	830	68	474	885	61
80-84	928	218	271	567	48	256	507	41
85+	766	148	235	453	19	237	452	19

TABLE 1.8-- POPULATION ESTIMATES, BY AGE AND BY SEX, COUNTIES, 1985 (Continued)

Age group	Morgan	Obion	Overton	Perry	Pickett	Polk	Putnam	Rhea
MALE	8,796	15,849	8,906	3,450	2,127	6,777	25,117	12,253
0-4	664	1,151	614	212	138	344	1,905	858
5-9	796	1,362	736	260	196	651	1,523	1,125
10-14	843	1,233	674	299	192	709	1,628	1,124
15-19	728	1,252	798	297	138	664	2,519	1,019
20-24	525	1,020	616	376	62	448	3,593	879
25-29	686	1,151	451	303	196	462	2,164	1,041
30-34	860	1,357	654	232	95	569	1,575	1,057
35-39	624	1,317	741	238	169	528	1,848	863
40-44	538	997	714	250	163	473	1,602	823
45-49	544	811	487	183	104	404	1,087	604
50-54	424	752	391	101	121	296	1,109	561
55-59	337	684	527	156	106	254	1,145	516
60-64	371	698	399	154	125	315	983	533
65-69	294	712	407	138	104	240	841	437
70-74	265	577	276	106	105	206	694	373
75-79	158	388	218	92	56	117	481	252
80-84	82	255	111	33	36	66	233	126
85+	57	132	92	20	21	31	187	62
FEMALE	8,164	17,383	8,965	3,090	2,385	6,906	25,602	12,443
0-4	513	1,084	526	224	156	272	1,463	677
5-9	540	1,095	659	227	149	455	1,241	953
10-14	695	1,157	804	102	186	812	1,280	1,090
15-19	761	1,223	703	124	196	503	2,576	998
20-24	404	1,139	402	226	174	532	3,106	940
25-29	601	1,264	566	233	174	412	2,075	1,043
30-34	617	1,303	720	208	163	684	1,896	982
35-39	618	1,332	624	148	157	544	1,768	975
40-44	558	1,120	580	325	137	457	1,628	756
45-49	535	842	531	187	127	384	1,116	605
50-54	448	854	498	157	129	316	1,191	573
55-59	342	939	424	180	112	291	1,268	488
60-64	433	905	457	189	123	280	1,262	565
65-69	352	909	457	148	105	313	1,146	554
70-74	308	834	390	170	113	270	911	505
75-79	212	599	280	115	96	190	814	355
80-84	121	453	200	74	54	114	463	207
85+	106	331	144	53	34	77	398	177

TABLE 1.8-- POPULATION ESTIMATES, BY AGE AND BY SEX, COUNTIES, 1985 (Continued)

Age group	Roane	Robert-son	Ruther-ford	Scott	Sequat-chie	Sevier	Shelby	Smith
MALE	24,515	19,230	48,503	10,149	4,392	22,655	383,192	7,023
0-4	1,702	1,588	3,825	724	249	1,434	32,251	533
5-9	2,300	1,595	3,994	1,109	359	1,749	29,090	584
10-14	1,973	1,446	3,632	969	473	2,014	30,851	524
15-19	2,015	1,574	4,341	1,114	456	1,681	35,869	478
20-24	1,359	1,561	5,209	724	399	1,674	39,980	437
25-29	1,676	1,507	4,766	798	351	1,970	37,979	476
30-34	2,219	1,524	3,873	826	380	2,041	34,169	689
35-39	2,005	1,405	4,136	775	276	1,875	29,451	437
40-44	1,602	1,199	3,213	507	293	1,585	20,975	430
45-49	1,343	1,032	2,110	496	291	1,132	16,478	349
50-54	1,240	909	2,151	415	155	990	15,456	373
55-59	1,345	903	1,854	373	151	1,148	16,183	332
60-64	1,356	886	1,827	406	148	1,083	14,546	393
65-69	909	697	1,380	296	136	837	11,366	317
70-74	648	591	968	255	130	646	8,195	263
75-79	441	440	660	202	75	436	5,623	206
80-84	240	197	323	94	44	219	2,771	115
85+	142	176	241	66	26	141	1,959	87
FEMALE	25,199	20,264	50,158	10,604	4,514	23,974	420,591	7,533
0-4	1,507	1,432	3,437	827	307	1,513	30,969	533
5-9	1,647	1,583	3,834	938	355	1,779	29,542	544
10-14	1,807	1,619	3,528	911	419	1,774	30,835	598
15-19	1,733	1,757	4,564	918	394	1,809	32,480	562
20-24	1,291	1,237	5,869	696	308	1,696	40,158	503
25-29	2,187	1,648	4,809	966	309	2,040	39,561	526
30-34	2,168	1,660	4,106	997	361	2,301	36,965	483
35-39	1,844	1,534	3,999	755	346	1,783	31,687	579
40-44	1,656	1,202	2,780	582	317	1,454	22,927	429
45-49	1,505	962	2,436	480	245	1,241	19,924	356
50-54	1,378	929	2,244	423	203	1,377	19,257	393
55-59	1,443	903	1,795	408	193	1,134	19,409	357
60-64	1,385	947	1,846	438	158	1,017	18,102	315
65-69	1,187	850	1,472	410	181	951	14,873	388
70-74	877	726	1,252	309	150	858	12,403	383
75-79	694	590	982	259	113	597	9,918	272
80-84	509	387	652	178	95	351	6,213	179
85+	381	298	553	109	60	299	5,368	133

TABLE 1.8-- POPULATION ESTIMATES, BY AGE AND BY SEX, COUNTIES, 1985 (Continued)

Age group	Stewart	Sullivan	Sumner	Tipton	Trousdale	Unicoi	Union	Van Buren
MALE	4,732	69,770	47,258	17,657	3,061	8,335	6,185	2,339
0-4	264	4,263	3,556	1,711	259	588	501	242
5-9	323	5,519	4,064	1,549	299	497	353	195
10-14	366	5,659	4,316	1,664	184	774	535	191
15-19	428	5,577	3,613	1,830	199	766	631	165
20-24	253	4,468	3,120	1,434	195	558	457	108
25-29	374	5,060	4,133	1,201	351	631	471	119
30-34	310	5,567	4,432	1,169	224	587	489	256
35-39	391	6,083	4,441	1,255	206	543	593	179
40-44	309	5,106	3,271	1,002	165	568	447	157
45-49	224	4,572	2,615	969	197	490	346	140
50-54	295	3,720	2,287	941	102	442	329	126
55-59	283	3,774	1,947	764	163	405	225	130
60-64	252	3,404	1,745	582	158	494	212	89
65-69	222	2,649	1,436	522	111	348	215	100
70-74	191	2,104	1,009	509	108	267	174	56
75-79	122	1,280	671	306	73	181	97	47
80-84	73	574	382	155	40	115	64	19
85+	52	391	220	94	27	81	46	20
FEMALE	4,542	75,900	46,585	17,603	2,785	8,537	6,055	2,549
0-4	315	4,214	3,292	1,612	228	478	456	183
5-9	244	4,934	3,509	1,245	91	501	488	246
10-14	257	5,550	3,437	1,396	202	743	432	183
15-19	353	5,157	3,221	1,391	229	468	484	180
20-24	121	4,873	3,028	1,170	201	443	459	143
25-29	406	5,409	4,099	1,350	198	656	403	255
30-34	261	6,010	4,386	1,477	249	583	564	194
35-39	293	6,420	4,010	1,224	151	752	512	258
40-44	430	5,433	3,390	1,127	115	444	430	105
45-49	362	4,431	2,514	877	148	454	331	190
50-54	182	4,116	2,303	946	171	401	219	112
55-59	256	4,455	1,884	747	150	559	254	110
60-64	215	4,130	2,148	707	147	538	312	95
65-69	257	3,534	1,693	686	155	450	237	96
70-74	227	2,873	1,431	642	139	394	191	81
75-79	192	2,071	1,020	490	100	303	144	56
80-84	81	1,308	691	286	62	202	90	31
85+	90	982	529	230	49	168	49	31

TABLE 1.8-- POPULATION ESTIMATES, BY AGE AND BY SEX, COUNTIES, 1985 (Continued)

Age group	Warren	Wash-ington	Wayne	Weakley	White	William-son	Wilson
MALE	16,748	45,658	6,908	16,181	9,747	34,568	31,297
0-4	1,211	2,927	571	1,154	504	2,756	2,302
5-9	1,309	2,948	544	1,135	695	3,232	2,666
10-14	1,594	3,495	586	1,185	701	3,280	2,722
15-19	1,372	3,579	551	1,538	776	2,750	2,666
20-24	1,201	4,687	516	1,882	644	1,410	2,065
25-29	1,394	3,795	530	1,300	543	2,550	2,599
30-34	1,425	3,902	534	1,158	762	3,101	2,790
35-39	1,146	3,990	511	891	925	3,408	3,092
40-44	1,037	3,156	334	970	735	3,003	2,325
45-49	778	2,333	387	872	605	2,411	1,823
50-54	779	2,059	354	630	566	1,618	1,253
55-59	805	2,194	315	625	531	1,491	1,269
60-64	849	2,207	392	747	468	1,221	1,096
65-69	657	1,592	278	678	451	883	1,011
70-74	506	1,271	221	613	375	620	718
75-79	368	802	147	408	245	436	495
80-84	175	401	88	236	142	222	245
85+	142	320	49	159	79	176	160
FEMALE	16,767	46,985	7,279	17,064	10,194	34,077	31,161
0-4	1,188	2,805	550	913	629	2,438	2,039
5-9	1,210	2,892	427	1,112	580	2,861	2,401
10-14	1,096	3,242	635	1,080	802	2,710	2,349
15-19	1,010	3,714	599	1,928	781	2,328	2,297
20-24	1,188	4,568	471	1,757	488	1,564	1,418
25-29	1,297	3,636	553	1,103	691	2,592	2,801
30-34	1,326	3,982	634	1,235	765	3,451	2,975
35-39	1,265	3,473	501	990	782	3,603	3,248
40-44	903	2,826	416	847	733	2,934	2,130
45-49	911	2,579	440	895	539	2,109	1,911
50-54	895	2,067	350	649	469	1,695	1,268
55-59	956	2,227	293	756	518	1,337	1,335
60-64	854	2,239	329	743	589	1,026	1,269
65-69	794	1,944	330	886	538	1,044	1,155
70-74	650	1,713	305	811	504	883	973
75-79	557	1,360	224	573	386	646	732
80-84	396	889	148	449	225	433	476
85+	271	829	74	337	175	423	384

Source: U.S. Department of Commerce, Bureau of the Census, Population Estimates Branch, *Experimental County Estimates by Age, Sex, and Race*, prepared for the National Cancer Institute, September 1988.

TABLE 1.9-- POPULATION, BY RACE, TENNESSEE AND COUNTIES, 1980

County	Total	White	Black	American Indian	Other
TENNESSEE	4,591,120	3,835,452	725,942	5,013	24,713
Anderson	67,346	64,043	2,594	164	545
Bedford	27,916	24,860	3,008	14	34
Benton	14,901	14,490	368	9	34
Bledsoe	9,478	9,125	320	8	25
Blount	77,770	74,859	2,582	99	230
Bradley	67,547	64,392	2,668	168	319
Campbell	34,923	34,643	170	57	53
Cannon	10,234	10,022	187	6	19
Carroll	28,285	24,956	3,243	23	63
Carter	50,205	49,647	426	42	90
Cheatham	21,616	20,971	595	23	27
Chester	12,727	11,330	1,367	5	25
Claiborne	24,595	24,202	314	46	33
Clay	7,676	7,545	112	8	11
Cocke	28,792	28,020	668	25	79
Coffee	38,311	36,725	1,340	29	217
Crockett	14,941	12,084	2,828	10	19
Cumberland	28,676	28,600	6	22	48
Davidson	477,811	366,448	106,369	533	4,461
Decatur	10,857	10,350	481	12	14
DeKalb	13,589	13,282	268	9	30
Dickson	30,037	28,307	1,672	17	41
Dyer	34,663	30,482	4,101	38	42
Fayette	25,305	12,465	12,804	14	22
Fentress	14,826	14,795	2	11	18
Franklin	31,983	29,587	2,279	21	96
Gibson	49,467	39,908	9,450	26	83
Giles	24,625	21,106	3,452	6	61
Grainger	16,751	16,595	136	8	12
Greene	54,422	53,010	1,233	53	126
Grundy	13,787	13,772	2	5	8
Hamblen	49,300	46,747	2,341	67	145
Hamilton	287,740	229,976	55,840	308	1,616
Hancock	6,887	6,833	38	3	13
Hardeman	23,873	15,069	8,725	17	62
Hardin	22,280	21,246	986	6	42
Hawkins	43,751	42,778	826	61	86
Haywood	20,318	9,876	10,420	3	19
Henderson	21,390	19,450	1,901	10	29
Henry	28,656	25,425	3,148	31	52
Hickman	15,151	14,311	817	16	7
Houston	6,871	6,524	331	5	11
Humphreys	15,957	15,284	629	11	33
Jackson	9,398	9,367	21	1	9
Jefferson	31,284	30,259	922	46	57
Johnson	13,745	13,623	86	8	28
Knox	319,694	288,675	28,006	426	2,587
Lake	7,455	6,013	1,437	2	3
Lauderdale	24,555	16,769	7,597	133	56
Lawrence	34,110	33,518	508	21	63

TABLE 1.9-- POPULATION, BY RACE, TENNESSEE AND COUNTIES, 1980 (Continued)

County	Total	White	Black	American Indian	Other
Lewis	9,700	9,473	156	16	55
Lincoln	26,483	23,765	2,637	21	60
Loudon	28,553	28,055	421	32	45
McMinn	41,878	39,629	2,043	68	138
McNairy	22,525	21,036	1,434	15	40
Macon	15,700	15,608	70	9	13
Madison	74,546	51,955	22,322	28	241
Marion	24,416	23,262	1,102	25	27
Marshall	19,698	17,704	1,960	13	21
Maury	51,095	42,500	8,464	43	88
Meigs	7,431	7,279	138	8	6
Monroe	28,700	27,745	888	11	56
Montgomery	83,342	66,415	14,684	191	2,052
Moore	4,510	4,293	209	5	3
Morgan	16,604	16,430	118	17	39
Obion	32,781	29,583	3,107	33	58
Overton	17,575	17,493	44	28	10
Perry	6,111	5,954	143	7	7
Pickett	4,358	4,340	1	16	1
Polk	13,602	13,566	5	13	18
Putnam	47,690	46,359	768	42	521
Rhea	24,235	23,485	611	45	94
Roane	48,425	46,731	1,526	34	134
Robertson	37,021	31,970	4,960	29	62
Rutherford	84,058	74,671	8,593	90	704
Scott	19,259	19,161	6	69	23
Sequatchie	8,605	8,548	18	17	22
Sevier	41,418	41,112	162	46	98
Shelby	777,113	445,458	324,664	747	6,244
Smith	14,935	14,308	600	12	15
Stewart	8,665	8,501	133	14	17
Sullivan	143,968	140,855	2,607	145	361
Sumner	85,790	80,348	5,084	99	259
Tipton	32,930	24,021	8,786	30	93
Trousdale	6,137	5,227	898	7	5
Unicoi	16,362	16,300	4	18	40
Union	11,707	11,681	1	17	8
Van Buren	4,728	4,714	4	4	6
Warren	32,653	31,351	1,199	30	73
Washington	88,755	85,269	3,004	89	393
Wayne	13,946	13,760	168	5	13
Weakley	32,896	30,485	2,070	29	312
White	19,567	19,097	431	9	30
Williamson	58,108	52,657	5,202	40	209
Wilson	56,064	50,934	4,873	61	196

Source: U.S. Department of Commerce, Bureau of the Census, *1980 Census of Population, General Population Characteristics, Tennessee.*

TABLE 1.10--NUMBER OF HOUSEHOLDS AND AVERAGE POPULATION PER HOUSEHOLD, TENNESSEE AND COUNTIES, 1980 AND 1985

County	Number of households		Change, 1980 to 1985		Average population per household	
	1985	1980	Number	%	1985	1980
TENNESSEE	1,757,000	1,618,505	138,000	8.5	2.65	2.77
Anderson	26,900	24,616	2,300	9.2	2.53	2.70
Bedford	10,600	9,943	600	6.2	2.70	2.77
Benton	5,800	5,577	200	3.2	2.59	2.64
Bledsoe	3,100	2,979	200	5.3	2.77	2.88
Blount	30,800	28,177	2,700	9.4	2.61	2.72
Bradley	25,900	23,026	2,900	12.5	2.71	2.87
Campbell	12,900	12,087	800	6.9	2.74	2.88
Cannon	3,800	3,625	200	6.0	2.78	2.80
Carroll	10,500	10,321	200	1.9	2.63	2.70
Carter	19,000	17,868	1,200	6.6	2.66	2.76
Cheatham	8,200	7,063	1,100	16.1	2.91	3.04
Chester	4,600	4,210	400	8.3	2.62	2.75
Claiborne	9,500	8,295	1,200	14.7	2.75	2.91
Clay	2,900	2,731	200	6.5	2.69	2.79
Cocke	11,000	10,154	900	8.5	2.65	2.83
Coffee	15,100	13,649	1,500	10.7	2.67	2.77
Crockett	5,400	5,380	(a)	(a)	2.64	2.76
Cumberland	11,200	9,887	1,300	13.6	2.75	2.88
Davidson	194,100	177,737	16,400	9.2	2.44	2.58
Decatur	4,200	4,081	200	3.9	2.61	2.64
DeKalb	5,300	4,956	300	6.1	2.68	2.72
Dickson	11,800	10,468	1,300	12.3	2.70	2.85
Dyer	13,100	12,696	400	3.2	2.61	2.71
Fayette	8,100	7,431	700	9.0	3.11	3.35
Fentress	5,600	5,027	500	10.4	2.80	2.94
Franklin	11,600	10,792	800	7.8	2.79	2.87
Gibson	18,900	18,202	700	4.0	2.55	2.69
Giles	9,400	8,825	600	6.4	2.62	2.75
Grainger	6,100	5,694	400	6.4	2.83	2.92
Greene	20,700	19,157	1,500	7.9	2.65	2.76
Grundy	4,900	4,510	400	8.2	2.96	3.05
Hamblen	19,600	17,257	2,300	13.4	2.68	2.84
Hamilton	107,500	103,319	4,200	4.1	2.58	2.71
Hancock	2,400	2,351	(a)	0.7	2.91	2.93
Hardeman	8,200	7,623	600	7.6	2.83	3.00
Hardin	8,100	7,970	100	1.9	2.73	2.77
Hawkins	16,500	15,288	1,200	7.9	2.74	2.86
Haywood	7,100	6,513	600	8.7	2.92	3.10
Henderson	8,300	7,686	600	7.5	2.69	2.76
Henry	11,400	10,914	500	4.6	2.54	2.60
Hickman	5,500	5,094	400	7.3	2.74	2.84
Houston	2,500	2,410	100	3.4	2.79	2.83
Humphreys	5,900	5,634	200	4.0	2.70	2.82
Jackson	3,400	3,363	100	2.1	2.70	2.78
Jefferson	11,800	10,623	1,200	11.2	2.66	2.81
Johnson	5,200	4,840	400	8.5	2.67	2.83
Knox	126,700	117,951	8,800	7.4	2.51	2.61
Lake	2,800	2,575	300	10.3	2.71	2.84
Lauderdale	8,700	8,281	400	5.0	2.77	2.86
Lawrence	12,600	11,867	700	6.1	2.74	2.85

TABLE 1.10--NUMBER OF HOUSEHOLDS AND AVERAGE POPULATION PER HOUSEHOLD, TENNESSEE AND COUNTIES, 1980 AND 1985 (Continued)

County	Number of households				Average population per household	
			Change, 1980 to 1985			
	1985	1980	Number	%	1985	1980
Lewis	3,400	3,055	400	11.9	2.72	2.84
Lincoln	10,000	9,533	500	4.7	2.67	2.75
Loudon	11,300	10,289	1,000	10.2	2.65	2.75
McMinn	15,800	14,727	1,100	7.2	2.71	2.81
McNairy	8,800	8,179	700	8.1	2.63	2.73
Macon	5,800	5,645	200	3.1	2.71	2.75
Madison	28,900	26,713	2,200	8.2	2.61	2.71
Marion	8,800	8,270	500	6.3	2.79	2.93
Marshall	7,600	7,144	500	6.3	2.68	2.72
Maury	19,900	18,180	1,700	9.6	2.64	2.78
Meigs	2,700	2,520	200	8.0	2.86	2.95
Monroe	10,500	9,637	900	9.2	2.81	2.93
Montgomery	31,600	27,198	4,400	16.1	2.67	2.87
Moore	1,800	1,534	300	17.5	2.76	2.94
Morgan	5,800	5,389	400	7.0	2.87	3.00
Obion	12,800	12,079	800	6.4	2.57	2.70
Overton	6,300	6,122	200	3.3	2.79	2.85
Perry	2,600	2,240	300	14.2	2.53	2.71
Pickett	1,600	1,542	100	5.2	2.78	2.82
Polk	4,800	4,607	100	3.2	2.86	2.95
Putnam	18,600	16,706	1,900	11.5	2.50	2.65
Rhea	8,800	8,285	500	6.2	2.74	2.85
Roane	18,300	17,078	1,200	7.3	2.70	2.82
Robertson	13,700	12,532	1,200	9.4	2.85	2.93
Rutherford	34,100	28,002	6,100	21.9	2.74	2.84
Scott	6,900	6,200	700	10.8	3.00	3.09
Sequatchie	3,000	2,891	200	5.3	2.87	2.93
Sevier	17,000	14,741	2,300	15.6	2.72	2.79
Shelby	291,500	269,186	22,300	8.3	2.68	2.81
Smith	5,300	5,392	-100	-1.5	2.72	2.76
Stewart	3,500	3,104	400	11.3	2.68	2.79
Sullivan	54,600	52,022	2,600	5.0	2.64	2.75
Sumner	33,400	28,557	4,900	17.1	2.79	2.99
Tipton	12,000	10,778	1,200	11.6	2.91	3.04
Trousdale	2,100	2,227	-100	-4.5	2.73	2.73
Unicoi	6,300	5,948	300	5.1	2.68	2.74
Union	4,300	3,947	400	9.4	2.82	2.96
Van Buren	1,700	1,590	100	6.6	2.88	2.97
Warren	12,700	11,869	800	7.0	2.62	2.74
Washington	33,400	31,191	2,300	7.2	2.59	2.71
Wayne	5,100	4,792	300	5.9	2.76	2.88
Weakley	11,600	11,567	(a)	0.1	2.57	2.60
White	7,500	6,988	500	7.3	2.64	2.78
Williamson	22,900	18,723	4,200	22.6	2.97	3.08
Wilson	21,900	18,863	3,000	16.1	2.81	2.94

Note: The numeric change given above is based upon rounded household numbers. The percentage change shown is based on unrounded numbers which were not published. This percentage is more accurate than that which would be calculated from using the published, rounded numbers.

a. Zero or rounds to zero.

Source: U.S. Department of Commerce, Bureau of the Census, direct correspondence.

TABLE 1.11--NET MIGRATION, BY SEX, BY RACE, AND BY AGE, TENNESSEE AND COUNTIES, 1975–1980

County	Total net migration	Sex		Race[1]		Age[2]			
		Male	Female	White	Black	5–19	20–44	45–64	65 and over
TENNESSEE	132,380	69,216	63,164	117,338	7,354	44,432	59,953	21,905	6,090
Anderson	219	57	162	296	-298	-579	645	-8	161
Bedford	647	495	152	989	-349	380	282	187	-202
Benton	703	379	324	644	73	314	141	125	123
Bledsoe	75	108	-33	70	-34	-15	44	56	-10
Blount	4,515	1,838	2,677	4,225	138	1,191	2,139	672	513
Bradley	3,657	1,750	1,907	3,205	215	940	2,092	251	374
Campbell	1,400	668	732	1,362	20	492	468	383	57
Cannon	1,016	491	525	1,015	-8	429	276	201	110
Carroll	908	401	507	939	-109	428	74	392	14
Carter	2,016	1,170	846	1,973	48	688	1,039	278	11
Cheatham	1,808	808	1,000	1,913	-84	584	986	157	81
Chester	803	312	491	666	110	570	-86	209	110
Claiborne	1,573	786	787	1,609	-40	383	688	354	148
Clay	300	180	120	296	4	95	94	89	22
Cocke	-488	-331	-157	-420	-41	-260	-340	104	8
Coffee	2286	980	1306	2012	183	717	679	681	209
Crockett	-302	-273	-29	-189	-119	-86	-152	65	-129
Cumberland	2,880	1,300	1,580	2,863	0	959	771	772	378
Davidson	-5,785	-2,369	-3,416	-9,723	3,111	-3,869	847	-2,214	-549
Decatur	1,017	526	491	961	74	398	259	264	96
DeKalb	470	255	215	443	15	241	-13	281	-39
Dickson	1,986	896	1,090	1,846	99	471	1,008	461	46
Dyer	-29	136	-165	231	-274	58	-147	132	-72
Fayette	575	417	158	1,206	-623	17	-73	492	139
Fentress	112	-1	113	107	0	22	-23	102	11
Franklin	2,051	1,271	780	1,920	77	1,183	485	285	98
Gibson	-311	-139	-172	289	-559	-352	-573	430	184
Giles	806	193	613	578	92	227	127	220	232

TABLE 1.11--NET MIGRATION, BY SEX, BY RACE, AND BY AGE, TENNESSEE AND COUNTIES, 1975–1980 (Continued)

County	Total net migration	Sex		Race[1]		Age[2]			
		Male	Female	White	Black	5–19	20–44	45–64	65 and over
Grainger	1,052	557	495	986	50	477	307	141	127
Greene	1,725	889	836	1,675	8	877	318	416	114
Grundy	-400	-268	-132	-335	-24	-84	-382	48	18
Hamblen	388	374	14	409	-70	-100	-3	513	-22
Hamilton	2,554	719	1,835	2,937	-653	128	2,667	39	-280
Hancock	-56	-63	7	-56	0	36	-71	46	-67
Hardeman	-411	-71	-340	236	-645	-194	-134	-68	-15
Hardin	422	344	78	480	-52	365	-102	257	-98
Hawkins	3,287	1,709	1,578	3,248	-11	954	1,697	513	123
Haywood	352	235	117	640	-288	34	209	127	-18
Henderson	-206	-160	-46	-35	-159	-66	-36	11	-115
Henry	440	248	192	494	-86	87	-188	447	94
Hickman	1,229	908	321	902	225	238	665	305	21
Houston	534	204	330	437	81	271	275	87	-99
Humphreys	267	37	230	297	-34	103	-38	181	21
Jackson	502	283	219	520	-18	197	81	159	65
Jefferson	2,503	1,181	1,322	2,546	-44	803	986	304	410
Johnson	-28	61	-89	-69	-13	-40	-191	189	14
Knox	11,742	5,597	6,145	9,985	1,057	5,151	5,938	572	81
Lake	-98	-16	-82	-56	-42	29	-244	40	77
Lauderdale	-29	41	-70	-246	209	-127	-10	-17	125
Lawrence	437	321	116	471	-19	109	-9	229	108
Lewis	929	450	479	883	-4	412	358	84	75
Lincoln	-898	-506	-392	-858	-146	-123	-496	-349	70
Loudon	1,103	419	684	1,174	-61	316	169	312	306
McMinn	1,163	478	685	1,101	84	408	185	405	165
McNairy	-414	-163	-251	-449	3	-199	-523	360	-52
Macon	1,208	690	518	1,196	0	451	556	123	78
Madison	742	335	407	708	24	434	-156	332	132
Marion	132	43	89	278	-155	-1	38	80	15

TABLE 1.11--NET MIGRATION, BY SEX, BY RACE, AND BY AGE, TENNESSEE AND COUNTIES, 1975–1980 (Continued)

County	Total net migration	Sex		Race[1]		Age[2]			
		Male	Female	White	Black	5–19	20–44	45–64	65 and over
Marshall	1,061	669	392	1,198	-166	453	367	154	87
Maury	693	299	394	585	82	-42	557	94	84
Meigs	972	460	512	949	23	372	408	145	47
Monroe	511	94	417	558	-33	556	-287	210	32
Montgomery	12,891	7,895	4,996	8,970	2,887	3,270	8,492	836	293
Moore	213	144	69	136	77	-9	33	158	31
Morgan	1,178	697	481	1,106	44	464	294	353	67
Obion	-257	-225	-32	-79	-184	-267	-70	67	13
Overton	323	199	124	336	-13	264	-42	158	-57
Perry	105	256	-151	99	19	-107	158	19	35
Pickett	144	10	134	142	0	74	16	65	-11
Polk	801	384	417	802	0	460	398	70	-127
Putnam	3,846	2,009	1,837	3,498	68	1,433	1,594	417	402
Rhea	1,865	960	905	1,789	66	829	744	308	-16
Roane	2,356	1,365	991	2,306	68	760	899	507	190
Robertson	2,309	1,079	1,230	2,351	-61	909	990	392	18
Rutherford	10,744	4,916	5,828	9,717	583	4,128	5,009	1,320	287
Scott	813	437	376	813	0	431	232	109	41
Sequatchie	1,008	498	510	979	0	429	423	105	51
Sevier	4,735	2,292	2,443	4,661	16	1,600	2,246	803	86
Shelby	-6,468	-2,820	-3,648	-11,257	3,236	-844	-2,646	-2,735	-243
Smith	830	344	486	851	-15	369	344	145	-28
Stewart	-119	71	-190	-124	-11	-12	-151	36	8
Sullivan	748	149	599	578	51	752	-378	522	-148
Sumner	7,477	4,290	3,187	7,525	-61	1,544	3,999	1,458	476
Tipton	38	292	-254	929	-964	0	-277	272	43
Trousdale	-25	52	-77	-3	-22	-8	36	44	-97
Unicoi	-290	-75	-215	-339	0	21	-303	28	-36
Union	501	265	236	494	0	110	240	94	57
Van Buren	152	-3	155	146	0	59	12	113	-32

TABLE 1.11--NET MIGRATION, BY SEX, BY RACE, AND BY AGE, TENNESSEE AND COUNTIES, 1975–1980 (Continued)

County	Total net migration	Sex		Race[1]		Age[2]			
		Male	Female	White	Black	5–19	20–44	45–64	65 and over
Warren	1,499	1,033	466	1,493	-26	322	568	377	232
Washington	4,951	2,616	2,335	4,627	92	1,645	2,530	587	189
Wayne	-176	-137	-39	-133	-43	-65	-190	81	-2
Weakley	3,045	1,390	1,655	2,457	385	1,792	1,083	259	-89
White	941	567	374	1,007	-67	238	276	302	125
Williamson	10,806	5,827	4,979	10,801	7	3,802	5,035	1,743	226
Wilson	7,080	3,737	3,343	6,545	378	2,128	3,711	982	259

Note: Net migration is total in-migration less out-migration.

1. Total net migration includes races not shown separately.

2. Age in 1980. Persons under age 5 in 1980 are excluded.

Source: U.S. Department of Commerce, Bureau of the Census, *1980 Census of Population, Gross Migration for Counties: 1975 to 1980*, supplementary report.

TABLE 1.12--LAND AREA, POPULATION DENSITY, AND POPULATION LIVING IN URBAN AND RURAL AREAS, TENNESSEE AND COUNTIES, 1980

County	Land area (square miles)	Population per square mile	Population		Percentage of total population	
			Urban	Rural	Urban	Rural
TENNESSEE	41,155	111.6	2,773,573	1,817,547	60.4	39.6
Anderson	339	198.7	33,138	34,208	49.2	50.8
Bedford	475	58.8	13,530	14,386	48.5	51.5
Benton	392	38.0	3,279	11,622	22.0	78.0
Bledsoe	407	23.3	0	9,478	0.0	100.0
Blount	558	139.4	39,106	38,664	50.3	49.7
Bradley	327	206.6	30,775	36,772	45.6	54.4
Campbell	479	72.9	10,996	23,927	31.5	68.5
Cannon	266	38.5	0	10,234	0.0	100.0
Carroll	600	47.1	9,051	19,234	32.0	68.0
Carter	341	147.2	25,911	24,294	51.6	48.4
Cheatham	303	71.3	0	21,616	0.0	100.0
Chester	289	44.0	4,449	8,278	35.0	65.0
Claiborne	432	56.9	2,530	22,065	10.3	89.7
Clay	227	33.8	0	7,676	0.0	100.0
Cocke	432	66.6	7,580	21,212	26.3	73.7
Coffee	429	89.3	22,744	15,567	59.4	40.6
Crockett	266	56.2	2,615	12,326	17.5	82.5
Cumberland	682	42.0	6,394	22,282	22.3	77.7
Davidson	501	953.7	468,157	9,654	98.0	2.0
Decatur	330	32.9	0	10,857	0.0	100.0
DeKalb	291	46.7	3,839	9,750	28.3	71.7
Dickson	491	61.2	7,040	22,997	23.4	76.6
Dyer	520	66.7	18,650	16,013	53.8	46.2
Fayette	705	35.9	0	25,305	0.0	100.0
Fentress	498	29.8	0	14,826	0.0	100.0
Franklin	543	58.9	6,127	25,856	19.2	80.8
Gibson	602	82.2	22,893	26,574	46.3	53.7
Giles	610	40.4	7,184	17,441	29.2	70.8
Grainger	273	61.4	0	16,751	0.0	100.0
Greene	619	87.9	14,097	40,325	25.9	74.1
Grundy	361	38.2	0	13,787	0.0	100.0
Hamblen	156	316.0	19,683	29,617	39.9	60.1
Hamilton	539	533.8	259,049	28,691	90.0	10.0
Hancock	224	30.7	0	6,887	0.0	100.0
Hardeman	670	35.6	6,597	17,276	27.6	72.4
Hardin	578	38.5	6,992	15,288	31.4	68.6
Hawkins	486	90.0	14,900	28,851	34.1	65.9
Haywood	534	38.0	9,307	11,011	45.8	54.2
Henderson	520	41.1	5,934	15,456	27.7	72.3
Henry	560	51.2	10,812	17,844	37.7	62.3
Hickman	610	24.8	2,824	12,327	18.6	81.4
Houston	200	34.4	0	6,871	0.0	100.0
Humphreys	527	30.3	4,405	11,552	27.6	72.4
Jackson	308	30.5	0	9,398	0.0	100.0
Jefferson	266	117.6	5,612	25,672	17.9	82.1
Johnson	297	46.3	0	13,745	0.0	100.0
Knox	506	631.8	245,534	74,160	76.8	23.2
Lake	168	44.4	0	7,455	0.0	100.0
Lauderdale	475	51.7	6,366	18,189	25.9	74.1
Lawrence	617	55.3	10,184	23,926	29.9	70.1

TABLE 1.12--LAND AREA, POPULATION DENSITY, AND POPULATION LIVING IN URBAN AND RURAL AREAS, TENNESSEE AND COUNTIES, 1980 (Continued)

County	Land area (square miles)	Population per square mile	Population		Percentage of total population	
			Urban	Rural	Urban	Rural
Lewis	282	34.4	3,922	5,778	40.4	59.6
Lincoln	571	46.4	7,559	18,924	28.5	71.5
Loudon	235	121.5	9,389	19,164	32.9	67.1
McMinn	429	97.6	15,838	26,040	37.8	62.2
McNairy	562	40.1	3,979	18,546	17.7	82.3
Macon	307	51.1	3,808	11,892	24.3	75.7
Madison	558	133.6	50,338	24,208	67.5	32.5
Marion	512	47.7	6,269	18,147	25.7	74.3
Marshall	376	52.4	8,760	10,938	44.5	55.5
Maury	616	82.9	29,747	21,348	58.2	41.8
Meigs	189	39.3	0	7,431	0.0	100.0
Monroe	648	44.3	7,609	21,091	26.5	73.5
Montgomery	539	154.6	58,236	25,106	69.9	30.1
Moore	129	35.0	0	4,510	0.0	100.0
Morgan	523	31.7	59	16,545	0.4	99.6
Obion	550	59.6	13,171	19,610	40.2	59.8
Overton	433	40.6	3,372	14,203	19.2	80.8
Perry	412	14.8	0	6,111	0.0	100.0
Pickett	159	27.4	0	4,358	0.0	100.0
Polk	437	31.1	0	13,602	0.0	100.0
Putnam	399	119.5	23,145	24,545	48.5	51.5
Rhea	309	78.4	5,913	18,322	24.4	75.6
Roane	357	135.6	21,948	26,477	45.3	54.7
Robertson	476	77.8	13,994	23,027	37.8	62.2
Rutherford	605	138.9	47,179	36,879	56.1	43.9
Scott	528	36.5	3,275	15,984	17.0	83.0
Sequatchie	266	32.3	3,681	4,924	42.8	57.2
Sevier	590	70.2	7,766	33,652	18.8	81.2
Shelby	772	1,006.6	747,016	30,097	96.1	3.9
Smith	313	47.7	2,672	12,263	17.9	82.1
Stewart	454	19.1	0	8,665	0.0	100.0
Sullivan	415	346.9	106,315	37,653	73.8	26.2
Sumner	529	162.2	50,325	35,465	58.7	41.3
Tipton	454	72.5	6,065	26,865	18.4	81.6
Trousdale	114	53.8	2,674	3,463	43.6	56.4
Unicoi	186	88.0	7,652	8,710	46.8	53.2
Union	218	53.7	0	11,707	0.0	100.0
Van Buren	273	17.3	0	4,728	0.0	100.0
Warren	431	75.8	10,683	21,970	32.7	67.3
Washington	326	272.3	57,242	31,513	64.5	35.5
Wayne	734	19.0	0	13,946	0.0	100.0
Weakley	581	56.6	9,130	23,766	27.8	72.2
White	373	52.5	4,864	14,703	24.9	75.1
Williamson	584	99.5	28,976	29,132	49.9	50.1
Wilson	571	98.2	22,718	33,346	40.5	59.5

Note: Urban population includes all persons living in urbanized areas and in places of 2,500 or more inhabitants outside urbanized areas. Rural population is all population not classified as urban.

Source: U.S. Department of Commerce, Bureau of the Census, *1980 Census of Population, Number of Inhabitants, Tennessee*.

TABLE 1.13--LOCATION AND POPULATION, INCORPORATED URBAN PLACES, 1960–1980, DECENNIAL CENSUS YEARS, AND 1986 AND 1988

Incorporated urban place	County	1988	1986	1980	1970	1960	Percent change 1980–1988
Adams	Robertson	660	640	600	458	(X)	10.0
Adamsville	McNairy	1,670	1,560	1,453	1,344	1,046	14.9
Alamo	Crockett	2,490	2,580	2,615	2,499	1,665	-4.8
Alcoa	Blount	6,790	6,660	6,870	7,739	6,395	-1.2
Alexandria	DeKalb	630	680	689	680	599	-8.6
Algood	Putnam	2,370	2,390	2,406	1,808	886	-1.5
Allardt	Fentress	880	860	654	610	(X)	34.6
Altamont	Grundy	710	730	679	546	552	4.6
Ardmore	Giles	730	710	835	601	195	-12.6
Arlington	Shelby	2,160	1,960	1,778	1,349	620	21.5
Ashland City	Cheatham	2,790	2,680	2,329	2,027	1,400	19.8
Athens	McMinn	12,080	12,140	12,080	11,790	12,103	0.0
Atoka	Tipton	980	820	691	446	357	41.8
Atwood	Carroll	1,220	1,190	1,143	937	461	6.7
Auburntown	Cannon	240	230	204	213	256	17.6
Baileyton	Greene	380	380	333	258	206	14.1
Baneberry	Jefferson	10	10	12	(X)	(X)	-16.7
Bartlett	Shelby	26,370	22,910	18,691[a]	1,150	508	41.1
Baxter	Putnam	1,300	1,280	1,411	1,229	853	-7.9
Beersheba Springs	Grundy	600	590	643	560	577	-6.7
Bell Buckle	Bedford	420	460	450	393	318	-6.7
Belle Meade	Davidson	3,570	3,410	3,182	2,933	3,082	12.2
Bells	Crockett	1,390	1,430	1,571	1,474	1,232	-11.5
Benton	Polk	1,250	1,240	1,115	749	638	12.1
Berry Hill	Davidson	1,380	1,280	1,113	1,517	1,551	24.0
Bethel Springs	McNairy	950	920	873	781	533	8.8
Big Sandy	Benton	640	640	650	539	492	-1.5
Blaine	Grainger	1,350	1,230	1,147	(X)	(X)	17.7
Bluff City	Sullivan	1,240	1,190	1,121	985	948	10.6
Bolivar	Hardeman	6,460	6,360	6,597	6,674	3,338	-2.1
Braden	Fayette	240	260	293	(X)	(X)	-18.1
Bradford	Gibson	990	1,040	1,146	968	763	-13.6
Brentwood	Williamson	16,820	14,300	10,701	4,099	(X)	57.2
Brighton	Tipton	1,150	1,050	976	952	652	17.8
Bristol	Sullivan	23,400	23,460	23,986	20,064	17,582	-2.4
Brownsville	Haywood	10,330	10,230	9,307	7,011	5,424	11.0
Bruceton	Carroll	1,490	1,550	1,579	1,450	1,158	-5.6
Bulls Gap	Hawkins	950	910	821	774	682	15.7
Burlison	Tipton	440	410	386	397	(X)	14.0
Burns	Dickson	1,080	960	777	456	386	39.0
Byrdstown	Pickett	820	870	884	582	613	-7.2
Calhoun	McMinn	640	660	590	624	(X)	8.5
Camden	Benton	3,300	3,460	3,586	3,052	2,774	-8.0
Carthage	Smith	2,390	2,400	2,672	2,491	2,021	-10.6
Caryville	Campbell	2,100	2,140	2,039	648	(X)	3.0
Cedar Hill	Robertson	480	440	420	355	(X)	14.3
Celina	Clay	1,650	1,640	1,580	1,370	1,228	4.4
Centertown	Warren	340	320	300	181	169	13.3
Centerville	Hickman	3,020	2,910	2,824	2,592	1,678	6.9
Chapel Hill	Marshall	860	850	861	752	630	-0.1
Charleston	Bradley	970	940	756	792	764	28.3
Charlotte	Dickson	860	840	788	610	551	9.1
Chattanooga	Hamilton	162,670	162,170	169,514[a]	119,923	130,009	-4.0

TABLE 1.13--LOCATION AND POPULATION, INCORPORATED URBAN PLACES, 1960–1980, DECENNIAL CENSUS YEARS, AND 1986 AND 1988 (Continued)

Incorporated urban place	County	1988	1986	1980	1970	1960	Percent change 1980–1988
Church Hill	Hawkins	4,290	4,320	4,110	2,822	769	4.4
Clarksburg	Carroll	370	400	400	349	(X)	-7.5
Clarksville	Montgomery	72,620	67,180	60,591	31,719	22,021	19.9
Cleveland	Bradley	26,540	26,140	26,415	21,446	16,196	0.5
Clifton	Wayne	870	860	773	737	708	12.5
Clinton	Anderson	8,860	8,420	7,790[a]	4,794	4,943	13.7
Coalmont	Grundy	640	670	625	518	458	2.4
Collegedale	Hamilton	4,270	4,240	4,607	3,031	(X)	-7.3
Collierville	Shelby	12,190	9,940	7,839	3,651	2,020	55.5
Collinwood	Wayne	1,060	1,070	1,064	922	596	-0.4
Columbia	Maury	28,910	28,170	26,570[a]	21,471	17,624	8.8
Cookeville	Putnam	24,570	23,920	21,604[a]	14,403	7,805	13.7
Copperhill	Polk	370	350	418	563	631	-11.5
Cornersville	Marshall	760	740	722	655	314	5.3
Cottage Grove	Henry	90	100	117	119	130	-23.1
Covington	Tipton	6,900	6,660	6,065	5,801	5,298	13.8
Cowan	Franklin	1,870	1,860	1,790	1,772	1,979	4.5
Crab Orchard	Cumberland	1,090	1,040	1,065	(X)	(X)	2.3
Cross Plains	Robertson	910	830	655	(X)	(X)	38.9
Crossville	Cumberland	7,670	7,200	6,394	5,381	4,668	20.0
Cumberland City	Stewart	270	280	276	416	314	-2.2
Cumberland Gap	Claiborne	320	290	263	231	291	21.7
Dandridge	Jefferson	1,400	1,460	1,383	1,270	829	1.2
Dayton	Rhea	5,430	5,420	5,582[a]	4,361	3,500	-2.7
Decatur	Meigs	1,200	1,130	1,069	698	681	12.3
Decaturville	Decatur	1,010	1,080	1,004	958	571	0.6
Decherd	Franklin	2,350	2,400	2,233	2,148	1,704	5.2
Dickson	Dickson	7,820	7,370	7,040	5,665	5,028	11.1
Dover	Stewart	1,270	1,240	1,197	1,179	736	6.1
Dowelltown	DeKalb	300	280	341	329	279	-12.0
Doyle	White	290	320	344	446	(X)	-15.7
Dresden	Weakley	2,160	2,200	2,256	1,939	1,510	-4.3
Ducktown	Polk	560	530	583	562	741	-3.9
Dunlap	Sequatchie	3,920	3,900	3,681	1,672	1,488	6.5
Dyer	Gibson	2,440	2,430	2,442	2,501	1,909	-0.1
Dyersburg	Dyer	15,800	15,670	15,856	14,523	12,499	-0.4
Eagleville	Rutherford	480	460	444	437	363	8.1
East Ridge	Hamilton	21,430	20,810	21,236	21,799	19,570	0.9
Eastview	McNairy	570	550	552	423	(X)	3.3
Elizabethton	Carter	12,030	12,300	12,431	12,269	10,896	-3.2
Elkton	Giles	500	480	540	341	199	-7.4
Englewood	McMinn	2,030	1,970	1,840	1,878	1,574	10.3
Enville	McNairy-Chester	270	250	287	228	250	-5.9
Erin	Houston	1,630	1,620	1,614	1,165	1,097	1.0
Erwin	Unicoi	5,150	5,190	5,283	4,715	3,210	-2.5
Estill Springs	Franklin	1,690	1,630	1,324	919	734	27.6
Ethridge	Lawrence	690	620	548	(X)	(X)	25.9
Etowah	McMinn	3,660	3,670	3,898	3,736	3,223	-6.1
Fairview	Williamson	4,910	4,620	3,648	1,630	1,017	34.6
Farragut	Knox	8,950	7,820	6,279	(X)	(X)	42.5
Fayetteville	Lincoln	7,670	7,700	7,651[a]	7,691	6,804	0.2
Finger	McNairy	290	290	245	(X)	(X)	18.4

TABLE 1.13--LOCATION AND POPULATION, INCORPORATED URBAN PLACES, 1960–1980, DECENNIAL CENSUS YEARS, AND 1986 AND 1988 (Continued)

Incorporated urban place	County	1988	1986	1980	1970	1960	Percent change 1980–1988
Forest Hills	Davidson	5,040	4,800	4,516	4,255	2,101	11.6
Franklin	Williamson	20,060	18,500	13,424[a]	9,497	6,977	49.4
Friendship	Crockett	620	720	763	441	399	-18.7
Friendsville	Blount	940	880	694	575	606	35.4
Gadsden	Crockett	570	570	683	523	222	-16.5
Gainesboro	Jackson	1,150	1,140	1,119	1,101	1,021	2.8
Gallatin	Sumner	20,670	19,350	17,191	13,253	7,901	20.2
Gallaway	Fayette	830	900	804	304	(X)	3.2
Garland	Tipton	360	340	301	292	168	19.6
Gates	Lauderdale	770	780	729	523	291	5.6
Gatlinburg	Sevier	3,900	3,780	3,500	2,329	1,764	11.4
Germantown	Shelby	31,720	29,360	22,722[a]	3,474	1,104	39.6
Gibson	Gibson	520	540	458	302	297	13.5
Gilt Edge	Tipton	410	390	404	406	(X)	1.5
Gleason	Weakley	1,160	1,200	1,335	1,314	900	-13.1
Goodlettsville	Davidson-Sumner	10,440	9,540	8,327	6,168	3,163	25.4
Gordonsville	Smith	960	920	893	601	249	7.5
Grand Junction	Hardeman	390	380	366	427	446	6.6
Graysville	Rhea	1,410	1,440	1,380	951	838	2.2
Greenback	Loudon	630	590	546	318	285	15.4
Greenbrier	Robertson	3,450	3,270	3,180	2,279	1,238	8.5
Greeneville	Greene	14,890	14,860	14,097	13,722	11,759	5.6
Greenfield	Weakley	1,990	2,050	2,109	2,050	1,779	-5.6
Gruetli-Laager	Grundy	1,980	2,010	2,021	(X)	(X)	-2.0
Guys	McNairy	520	510	486	(X)	(X)	7.0
Halls	Lauderdale	2,260	2,320	2,444	2,323	1,890	-7.5
Harriman	Roane	8,300	8,360	8,303	8,734	5,931	0.0
Hartsville	Trousdale	2,360	2,350	2,674	2,243	1,712	-11.7
Henderson	Chester	4,360	4,410	4,449	3,581	2,691	-2.0
Hendersonville	Sumner	31,610	30,170	26,561	412	(X)	19.0
Henning	Lauderdale	690	700	638	605	466	8.2
Hickory Valley	Hardeman	240	250	252	180	179	-4.8
Hohenwald	Lewis	3,920	3,930	3,922	3,385	2,194	-0.1
Hollow Rock	Carroll	1,190	1,110	955	722	568	24.6
Hornbeak	Obion	440	450	452	418	307	-2.7
Hornsby	Hardeman	430	410	401	212	228	7.2
Humboldt	Gibson	9,710	9,870	10,209	10,066	8,482	-4.9
Huntingdon	Carroll	3,990	4,040	4,345	3,661	2,119	-8.2
Huntland	Franklin	1,010	1,050	983	849	500	2.7
Huntsville	Scott	520	520	519	337	(X)	0.2
Iron City	Lawrence-Wayne	480	480	482	504	(X)	-0.4
Jacksboro	Campbell	1,920	1,810	1,722	689	(X)	11.5
Jackson	Madison	53,320	52,810	49,258[a]	39,996	34,376	8.2
Jamestown	Fentress	2,260	2,370	2,364	1,899	1,727	-4.4
Jasper	Marion	2,740	2,560	2,633	2,009	1,450	4.1
Jefferson City	Jefferson	5,480	5,770	5,639[a]	5,124	4,550	-2.8
Jellico	Campbell	2,520	2,690	2,798	2,235	2,210	-9.9
Johnson City[1]	Carter-Washington	43,350	44,700	43,706[a]	33,770	31,187	-0.8
Jonesborough	Washington	2,860	2,810	2,829	1,510	1,148	1.1
Kingsport	Hawkins-Sullivan	31,440	31,470	32,027	31,938	26,314	-1.8

TABLE 1.13--LOCATION AND POPULATION, INCORPORATED URBAN PLACES, 1960–1980, DECENNIAL CENSUS YEARS, AND 1986 AND 1988 (Continued)

Incorporated urban place	County	1988	1986	1980	1970	1960	Percent change 1980–1988
Kingston	Roane	4,830	4,780	4,561	4,142	2,010	5.9
Kingston Springs	Cheatham	1,420	1,230	1,017	312	(X)	39.6
Knoxville	Knox	172,080	173,210	175,045	174,587	111,827	-1.7
Lafayette	Macon	3,920	3,800	3,808	2,583	1,590	2.9
LaFollette	Campbell	7,950	8,140	8,198	6,902	6,204	-3.0
LaGrange	Fayette	160	160	185	213	217	-13.5
Lake City	Anderson	2,580	2,440	2,335	1,923	1,914	10.5
Lakeland	Shelby	1,030	690	612	(X)	(X)	68.3
Lakesite	Hamilton	1,080	870	651	(X)	(X)	65.9
Lakewood	Davidson	2,690	2,520	2,325	2,282	1,896	15.7
LaVergne	Rutherford	7,020	6,850	5,793[a]	(X)	(X)	21.2
Lawrenceburg	Lawrence	11,230	10,950	10,184	8,889	8,042	10.3
Lebanon	Wilson	14,410	13,950	13,004[a]	12,492	10,512	10.8
Lenoir City	Loudon	6,040	5,830	5,505[a]	5,324	4,979	9.7
Lewisburg	Marshall	9,510	9,290	8,760	7,207	6,338	8.6
Lexington	Henderson	6,260	6,270	5,934	5,024	3,943	5.5
Liberty	DeKalb	350	340	365	332	293	-4.1
Linden	Perry	1,240	1,170	1,087	1,062	1,086	14.1
Livingston	Overton	3,170	3,090	3,372	3,050	2,817	-6.0
Lobelville	Perry	1,090	1,050	993	773	449	9.8
Lookout Mountain	Hamilton	1,760	1,820	1,886	1,741	1,817	-6.7
Loretto	Lawrence	1,730	1,630	1,612	1,375	929	7.3
Loudon	Loudon	4,430	4,260	4,199	3,728	3,812	5.5
Luttrell	Union	940	940	962	819	(X)	-2.3
Lynchburg	Moore	4,950	4,940	4,510	538	396	9.8
Lynnville	Giles	400	420	383	327	362	4.4
McEwen	Humphreys	1,590	1,540	1,352	1,237	979	17.6
McKenzie[2]	Carroll-Henry-Weakley	5,400	5,330	5,405	4,873	3,780	-0.1
McLemoresville	Carroll	320	320	311	328	285	2.9
McMinnville	Warren	11,060	10,790	11,227[a]	10,662	9,013	-1.5
Madisonville	Monroe	3,410	3,240	2,884	2,614	1,812	18.2
Manchester	Coffee	7,730	7,630	7,250	6,208	3,930	6.6
Martin	Weakley	9,120	9,390	8,898	7,781	4,750	2.5
Maryville	Blount	18,170	18,060	17,480	13,808	10,348	3.9
Mason	Tipton	470	490	471	443	407	-0.2
Maury City	Crockett	950	950	989	813	624	-3.9
Maynardville	Union	1,010	950	924	702	620	9.3
Medina	Gibson	720	690	687	755	722	4.8
Medon	Madison	150	150	169	136	97	-11.2
Memphis	Shelby	645,190	652,640	646,170[a]	623,988	497,524	-0.2
Michie	McNairy	570	540	530	377	(X)	7.5
Middleton	Hardeman	730	700	596	654	461	22.5
Milan	Gibson	7,850	7,950	8,083	7,313	5,208	-2.9
Milledgeville	Hardin-Chester-McNairy	400	380	392	349	(X)	2.0
Millersville	Sumner	1,730	1,620	1,415	(X)	(X)	22.3
Millington	Shelby	17,840	18,200	20,236	21,177	6,059	-11.8
Minor Hill	Giles	540	540	564	315	(X)	-4.3
Mitchellville	Sumner	190	200	209	177	184	-9.1
Monteagle	Marion-Grundy	1,250	1,240	1,126	934	(X)	11.0

TABLE 1.13--LOCATION AND POPULATION, INCORPORATED URBAN PLACES, 1960–1980, DECENNIAL CENSUS YEARS, AND 1986 AND 1988 (Continued)

Incorporated urban place	County	1988	1986	1980	1970	1960	Percent change 1980–1988
Monterey	Putnam	2,730	2,710	2,610	2,351	2,069	4.6
Morrison	Warren	590	610	587	379	294	0.5
Morristown	Hamblen	20,800	19,650	21,422[a]	20,318	21,267	-2.9
Moscow	Fayette	490	500	499	448	368	-1.8
Mosheim	Greene	2,050	1,950	1,539	(X)	(X)	33.2
Mount Carmel	Hawkins	5,630	5,470	3,764	2,821	(X)	49.6
Mount Juliet	Wilson	3,870	3,580	2,879	(X)	(X)	34.4
Mount Pleasant	Maury	3,660	3,670	3,891	3,530	2,921	-5.9
Mountain City	Johnson	2,330	2,310	2,125	1,883	1,379	9.6
Munford	Tipton	2,900	2,690	2,336	1,281	1,014	24.1
Murfreesboro	Rutherford	45,820	40,960	32,845	26,360	18,991	39.5
Nashville[3]	Davidson	481,380	473,670	455,651	426,029	154,563	5.6
New Hope	Marion	760	680	681	(X)	(X)	11.6
New Johnsonville	Humphreys	1,800	1,770	1,824	970	559	-1.3
New Market	Jefferson	1,230	1,250	1,216	(X)	(X)	1.2
New Tazewell	Claiborne	1,850	1,700	1,677	1,192	768	10.3
Newbern	Dyer	2,710	2,750	2,794	2,124	1,695	-3.0
Newport	Cocke	7,360	7,480	7,580	7,328	6,448	-2.9
Niota	McMinn	960	890	765	629	679	25.5
Normandy	Bedford	130	120	118	122	119	10.2
Norris	Anderson	1,500	1,460	1,374	1,359	1,389	9.2
Oak Hill	Davidson	5,030	4,790	4,609	4,645	4,490	9.1
Oak Ridge	Anderson-Roane	27,710	26,920	27,662	28,319	27,169	0.2
Oakdale	Morgan	280	290	323	376	470	-13.3
Oakland	Fayette	670	580	472	353	306	41.9
Obion	Obion	1,230	1,220	1,282	1,010	1,097	-4.1
Oliver Springs	Anderson-Morgan-Roane	3,750	3,910	3,659	3,405	1,163	2.5
Oneida	Scott	4,440	4,470	4,271[a]	2,602	2,480	4.0
Orlinda	Robertson	390	390	382	347	(X)	2.1
Orme	Marion	190	190	181	122	171	5.0
Palmer	Grundy	900	900	1,027	898	1,069	-12.4
Paris	Henry	10,390	10,470	10,728	9,892	9,325	-3.2
Parker's Crossroads	Henderson	190	190	186	(X)	(X)	2.2
Parrottsville	Cocke	110	110	118	115	91	-6.8
Parsons	Decatur	2,370	2,330	2,422	2,167	1,859	-2.1
Pegram	Cheatham	1,390	1,270	1,081	(X)	(X)	28.6
Petersburg	Lincoln-Marshall	750	760	681	463	423	10.1
Philadelphia	Loudon	670	670	507	554	(X)	32.1
Pigeon Forge	Sevier	2,730	2,600	1,822	1,361	(X)	49.8
Pikeville	Bledsoe	2,200	2,110	2,085	1,454	951	5.5
Piperton	Fayette	820	790	746	(X)	(X)	9.9
Pittman Center	Sevier	630	600	488	(X)	(X)	29.1
Pleasant Hill	Cumberland	480	470	371	293	267	29.4
Portland	Sumner	4,560	4,420	4,030	2,872	2,424	13.2
Powell's Crossroads	Marion	1,030	980	918	(X)	(X)	12.2
Pulaski	Giles	7,580	7,530	7,184	6,989	6,616	5.5
Puryear	Henry	610	690	624	458	408	-2.2

TABLE 1.13--LOCATION AND POPULATION, INCORPORATED URBAN PLACES, 1960–1980, DECENNIAL CENSUS YEARS, AND 1986 AND 1988 (Continued)

Incorporated urban place	County	1988	1986	1980	1970	1960	Percent change 1980–1988
Ramer	McNairy	430	390	429	347	358	0.2
Red Bank	Hamilton	13,020	12,910	13,129	12,715	10,777	-0.8
Red Boiling Springs	Macon	1,300	1,250	1,173	726	597	10.8
Rickman	Overton	850	830	798	(X)	(X)	6.5
Ridgely	Lake	1,560	1,590	1,932	1,657	1,464	-19.3
Ridgeside	Hamilton	480	460	417	458	448	15.1
Ridgetop	Davidson-Robertson	1,330	1,290	1,225	858	372	8.6
Ripley	Lauderdale	6,240	6,330	6,366	4,794	3,782	-2.0
Rives	Obion	360	400	386	385	291	-6.7
Rockford	Blount	630	600	567	(X)	(X)	11.1
Rockwood	Roane	5,640	5,670	5,695[a]	5,259	5,345	-1.0
Rogersville	Hawkins	4,080	4,180	4,368	4,076	3,121	-6.6
Rossville	Fayette	390	380	379	410	183	2.9
Rutherford	Gibson	1,180	1,230	1,378	1,385	983	-14.4
Rutledge	Grainger	1,030	1,060	1,058	863	793	-2.6
St. Joseph	Lawrence	670	710	897	637	547	-25.3
Saltillo	Hardin	410	410	434	423	397	-5.5
Samburg	Obion	560	410	465	463	451	20.4
Sardis	Henderson	290	300	301	350	274	-3.7
Saulsbury	Hardeman	170	150	156	156	141	9.0
Savannah	Hardin	6,890	6,900	6,992	5,576	4,315	-1.5
Scotts Hill	Henderson-Decatur	710	660	668	548	298	6.3
Selmer	McNairy	4,140	4,090	3,979	3,495	1,897	4.0
Sevierville	Sevier	7,420	6,420	5,444	2,661	2,890	36.3
Sharon	Weakley	990	1,010	1,134	1,188	966	-12.7
Shelbyville	Bedford	13,670	13,630	13,530	12,262	10,466	1.0
Signal Mountain	Hamilton	6,910	6,490	5,818	4,839	3,413	18.8
Silerton	Hardeman-Chester	110	110	100	88	84	10.0
Slayden	Dickson	60	60	69	95	101	-13.0
Smithville	DeKalb	4,150	4,050	3,839	2,997	2,348	8.1
Smyrna	Rutherford	16,730	13,610	9,441[a]	5,698	3,612	77.2
Sneedville	Hancock	1,140	1,160	1,110	874	799	2.7
Soddy-Daisy	Hamilton	9,150	8,440	8,388	7,569	(X)	9.1
Somerville	Fayette	2,200	2,120	2,264	1,816	1,820	-2.8
South Carthage	Smith	990	980	1,004	859	(X)	-1.4
South Fulton	Obion	3,480	3,450	2,980	3,122	2,512	16.8
South Pittsburg	Marion	3,500	3,480	3,636	3,613	4,130	-3.7
Sparta	White	5,160	5,010	4,864	4,930	4,510	6.1
Spencer	Van Buren	1,120	1,120	1,126	1,179	870	-0.5
Spring City	Rhea	2,130	2,050	1,951	1,756	1,800	9.2
Spring Hill	Williamson-Maury	1,210	1,130	989	685	689	22.3
Springfield	Robertson	11,570	10,790	10,814	9,720	9,221	7.0
Stanton	Haywood	620	570	540	372	458	14.8
Stantonville	McNairy	250	240	271	296	(X)	-7.7
Surgoinsville	Hawkins	1,460	1,480	1,536	1,285	1,132	-4.9
Sweetwater	Monroe	5,260	5,210	5,175	4,340	4,145	1.6
Tazewell	Claiborne	2,150	2,240	2,090	1,860	1,264	2.9
Tellico Plains	Monroe	670	690	698	773	794	-4.0

TABLE 1.13--LOCATION AND POPULATION, INCORPORATED URBAN PLACES, 1960–1980, DECENNIAL CENSUS YEARS, AND 1986 AND 1988 (Continued)

Incorporated urban place	County	1988	1986	1980	1970	1960	Percent change 1980–1988
Tennessee Ridge	Houston	1,500	1,330	1,325	664	324	13.2
Tiptonville	Lake	2,640	2,650	2,438	2,407	2,068	8.3
Toone	Hardeman	470	450	355	200	202	32.4
Townsend	Blount	370	330	351	267	283	5.4
Tracy City	Grundy	1,580	1,540	1,434	1,388	1,577	10.2
Trenton	Gibson	4,550	4,610	4,601	4,226	4,225	-1.1
Trezevant	Carroll	1,050	1,040	921	877	944	14.0
Trimble	Dyer-Obion	670	670	722	675	581	-7.2
Troy	Obion	1,030	1,070	1,093	826	587	-5.8
Tullahoma	Coffee-Franklin	17,150	16,780	15,800	15,311	12,242	8.5
Tusculum	Greene	2,110	2,140	2,190	1,180	1,433	-3.7
Union City	Obion	10,300	10,460	10,436	11,925	8,837	-1.3
Vanleer	Dickson	390	390	401	320	234	-2.7
Viola	Warren	180	170	149	193	206	20.8
Vonore	Monroe	570	570	528	524	(X)	8.0
Walden	Hamilton	1,440	1,380	1,293	(X)	(X)	11.4
Wartburg	Morgan	1,050	940	761	541	(X)	38.0
Wartrace	Bedford	520	530	540	616	545	-3.7
Watauga	Carter	480	440	376	314	(X)	27.7
Watertown	Wilson	1,390	1,310	1,300	1,061	919	6.9
Waverly	Humphreys	4,140	4,170	4,405	3,794	2,891	-6.0
Waynesboro	Wayne	2,170	2,130	2,109	1,983	1,343	2.9
Westmoreland	Sumner	1,960	1,960	1,754	1,423	865	11.7
White Bluff	Dickson	2,570	2,370	2,055	1,163	486	25.1
White House	Robertson-Sumner	4,490	3,870	2,225	(X)	(X)	101.8
White Pine	Jefferson	2,050	1,980	1,900	1,532	1,035	7.9
Whiteville	Hardeman	1,130	1,170	1,270	992	757	-11.0
Whitwell	Marion	1,780	1,760	1,783	1,669	1,857	-0.2
Williston	Fayette	390	400	395	(X)	(X)	-1.3
Winchester	Franklin	6,290	6,180	6,099[a]	5,256	4,760	3.1
Winfield	Scott	500	510	470	(X)	(X)	6.4
Woodbury	Cannon	2,340	2,280	2,160	1,725	1,562	8.3
Woodland Mills	Obion	490	500	526	396	(X)	-6.8
Yorkville	Gibson	230	240	272	243	(X)	-15.4

Note: Population is as counted in each Decennial Census year. No provision has been made for comparable land areas. Growth by annexation is reflected in the data.

(X) not applicable.

1. Beginning in 1980 includes Carter County.

2. Beginning in 1980 includes Henry County.

3. Beginning in 1970 includes metro Nashville-Davidson.

a. Changes in the 1980 base population figures are the result of census corrections or annexations.

Source: U.S. Department of Commerce, Bureau of the Census, *1980 Census of Population, Number of Inhabitants, Tennessee*; and direct correspondence.

TABLE 1.14--LAND AREA, POPULATION, AND AGE CHARACTERISTICS, SOUTHEASTERN STATES AND UNITED STATES, 1987

State	Land area (square miles)	Total population[1] (1,000)	Population per square mile	Percentage: Under 5 years of age	Percentage: 5 to 17 years of age	Percentage: 65 years of age or older
TENNESSEE	41,155	4,855	118.0	6.8	19.0	12.4
Alabama	50,767	4,083	80.4	7.2	20.1	12.4
Arkansas	52,078	2,388	45.9	7.2	19.9	14.6
Florida	54,153	12,023	222.0	6.8	15.7	17.8
Georgia	58,056	6,222	107.2	7.7	20.2	10.0
Kentucky	39,669	3,727	94.0	6.9	19.8	12.3
Louisiana	44,521	4,461	100.2	8.6	20.8	10.8
Mississippi	47,233	2,625	55.6	8.0	22.1	12.1
North Carolina	48,843	6,413	131.3	6.8	18.5	11.8
South Carolina	30,203	3,425	113.4	7.5	20.0	10.7
Virginia	39,704	5,904	148.7	7.1	17.6	10.6
West Virginia	24,119	1,897	78.7	6.2	19.7	13.9
UNITED STATES	3,539,289	243,400	68.8	7.5	18.6	12.3

Note: Percentages computed by the Center for Business and Economic Research.

1. Preliminary.

Source: U.S. Department of Commerce, Bureau of the Census, *Statistical Abstract of the United States, 1989.*

TABLE 1.15--POPULATION AND PERCENTAGE OF U.S. POPULATION, SOUTHEASTERN STATES AND UNITED STATES, 1950–1980, DECENNIAL CENSUS YEARS

	1980			1970		
State	Population	Decennial percent change	Percentage of U.S. population [1]	Population	Decennial percent change	Percentage of U.S. population [1]
TENNESSEE	4,591,120	16.9	2.0	3,926,018	10.1	1.9
Alabama	3,893,888	13.1	1.7	3,444,354	5.4	1.7
Arkansas	2,286,435	18.9	1.0	1,923,322	7.7	0.9
Florida	9,746,324	43.5	4.3	6,791,418	37.2	3.3
Georgia	5,463,105	19.1	2.4	4,587,930	16.4	2.3
Kentucky	3,660,777	13.7	1.6	3,220,711	6.0	1.6
Louisiana	4,205,900	15.4	1.9	3,644,637	12.0	1.8
Mississippi	2,520,638	13.7	1.1	2,216,994	1.8	1.1
North Carolina	5,881,766	15.7	2.6	5,084,411	11.6	2.5
South Carolina	3,121,820	20.5	1.4	2,590,713	8.7	1.3
Virginia	5,346,818	14.9	2.4	4,651,448	17.3	2.3
West Virginia	1,949,644	11.8	0.9	1,744,237	-6.2	0.9
UNITED STATES	226,545,805	11.4	100.0	203,302,031	11.4	100.0

	1960			1950		
State	Population	Decennial percent change	Percentage of U.S. population [1]	Population	Decennial percent change	Percentage of U.S. population [1]
TENNESSEE	3,567,089	8.4	2.0	3,291,718	12.9	2.2
Alabama	3,266,740	6.7	1.8	3,061,743	8.1	2.0
Arkansas	1,786,272	-6.5	1.0	1,909,511	-2.0	1.3
Florida	4,951,560	78.7	2.8	2,771,305	46.1	1.8
Georgia	3,943,116	14.5	2.2	3,444,578	10.3	2.3
Kentucky	3,038,156	3.2	1.7	2,944,806	3.5	1.9
Louisiana	3,257,022	21.4	1.8	2,683,516	13.5	1.8
Mississippi	2,178,141	0.0	1.2	2,178,914	-0.2	1.4
North Carolina	4,556,155	12.2	2.5	4,061,929	13.7	2.7
South Carolina	2,382,594	12.5	1.3	2,117,027	11.4	1.4
Virginia	3,966,949	19.5	2.2	3,318,680	23.9	2.2
West Virginia	1,860,421	-7.2	1.0	2,005,552	5.4	1.3
UNITED STATES	179,323,175	18.5	100.0	151,325,798	14.5	100.0

1. Percentages computed by the Center for Business and Economic Research.

Source: U.S. Department of Commerce, Bureau of the Census, *1980 Census of Population, Number of Inhabitants, United States Summary*, and earlier editions.

TABLE 1.16--POPULATION AND COMPONENTS OF CHANGE, SOUTHEASTERN STATES, 1980–1988, SELECTED YEARS [In thousands]

State	Population					
	1988	1987r	1986r	1985r	1984 r	1980
TENNESSEE	4,895	4,855	4,800	4,766	4,728	4,591
Alabama	4,102	4,084	4,051	4,021	3,991	3,894
Arkansas	2,395	2,388	2,371	2,360	2,346	2,286
Florida	12,335	12,022	11,688	11,367	11,053	9,746
Georgia	6,342	6,227	6,101	5,975	5,845	5,463
Kentucky	3,727	3,723	3,722	3,724	3,720	3,661
Louisiana	4,408	4,448	4,497	4,484	4,462	4,206
Mississippi	2,620	2,624	2,624	2,613	2,599	2,521
North Carolina	6,489	6,409	6,327	6,258	6,167	5,882
South Carolina	3,470	3,426	3,381	3,333	3,296	3,122
Virginia	6,015	5,914	5,798	5,704	5,635	5,347
West Virginia	1,876	1,898	1,917	1,936	1,952	1,950

	Change 1980–1988					
			Components of change			
	Net change				Net migration	
	Number	%	Births	Deaths	Number	%
TENNESSEE	304	6.6	553	352	103	2.3
Alabama	209	5.4	497	302	14	0.3
Arkansas	108	4.7	291	194	12	0.5
Florida	2,588	26.6	1,283	964	2,270	23.3
Georgia	879	16.1	781	390	488	8.9
Kentucky	66	1.8	449	282	-101	-2.8
Louisiana	202	4.8	664	300	-162	-3.9
Mississippi	99	3.9	364	199	-66	-2.6
North Carolina	607	10.3	724	428	311	5.3
South Carolina	348	11.2	427	221	142	4.5
Virginia	668	12.5	692	368	345	6.4
West Virginia	-73	-3.8	210	161	-122	-6.3

Note: 1980 population is as of April 1. Population estimates 1981--1988 are as of July 1.

r revised.

Source: U.S. Department of Commerce, Bureau of the Census, *Current Population Reports*, Series P-25, No. 1044.

TABLE 1.17--ESTIMATED NUMBER OF VETERANS, BY PERIOD OF SERVICE, SOUTHEASTERN STATES AND UNITED STATES, SEPTEMBER 30, 1988
[In thousands]

State	Total veterans	Veterans per 1,000 population [1]	Wartime veterans					Total peacetime veterans
			Total [2]	Vietnam era	Korean conflict	World War II	World War I	
TENNESSEE	522	145.6	403	167	91	171	2	119
Alabama	402	136.8	314	122	83	137	2	89
Arkansas	266	153.9	205	81	47	96	1	61
Florida	1,492	161.9	1,204	410	284	651	9	288
Georgia	652	147.7	496	233	120	193	2	157
Kentucky	363	134.6	284	109	66	123	2	79
Louisiana	429	137.5	331	137	75	143	1	97
Mississippi	232	128.3	180	66	45	85	1	52
North Carolina	684	146.2	534	208	126	241	2	150
South Carolina	352	145.3	273	118	68	117	1	79
Virginia	668	156.5	516	225	142	222	2	152
West Virginia	222	157.6	173	65	37	80	1	48
UNITED STATES	27,155	152.4	21,175	8,242	4,925	9,415	113	5,980

1. Veterans per 1,000 civilian population age 18 and over. Based on U.S. Department of Commerce, Bureau of the Census civilian population estimates for July 1, 1987.
2. Veterans who served in more than one wartime period are counted only once in the wartime total. This is not the case for the number shown for each specific war ; therefore, the sum of these numbers will be greater than the total.

Source: Veterans Administration, *Veteran Population, September 30, 1988.*

TABLE 1.18--PERSONS NATURALIZED, BY STATE OF RESIDENCE, SOUTHEASTERN STATES AND UNITED STATES, 1970–1987, SELECTED YEARS

State	1987	1986	1985	1984	1983	1980	1979	1975	1970
TENNESSEE	911	1,033	846	680	627	490	333	482	351
Alabama	506	664	609	926	452	414	367	357	393
Arkansas	540	605	456	290	248	163	139	135	82
Florida	8,041	20,366	10,362	19,855	12,617	11,417	11,757	10,576	11,556
Georgia	1,856	1,834	1,804	2,819	1,654	985	987	853	873
Kentucky	630	675	910	386	429	199	412	347	313
Louisiana	1,406	2,575	2,490	2,225	705	772	899	652	828
Mississippi	239	381	432	302	208	189	278	238	176
North Carolina	1,208	1,702	1,626	1,532	1,166	1,057	650	693	598
South Carolina	484	558	1,289	1,021	253	419	376	409	334
Virginia	3,335	4,892	5,147	4,038	2,206	1,653	2,171	2,207	1,509
West Virginia	241	235	278	217	293	281	240	178	118
UNITED STATES	227,008	280,623	244,717	197,023	178,948	157,938	164,150	141,537	110,399

Note: United States total includes territories.

Source: U.S. Department of Justice, Immigration and Naturalization Service, *1987 Statistical Yearbook of the Immigration and Naturalization Service*, and earlier editions.

TABLE 1.19--LARGEST CITY AND TOTAL STATE POPULATION DISTRIBUTION, BY CITY SIZE, SOUTHEASTERN STATES, 1980

State	Percentage urban of total state population	Population distribution by city size (%)							Largest city	
		100,000 or more	50,000 to 100,000	25,000 to 50,000	10,000 to 25,000	5,000 to 10,000	2,500 to 5,000	Other urban	Name	Popu-lation
TENNESSEE	60.4	31.3	1.2	5.7	8.9	6.0	4.4	2.9	Memphis	646,305
Alabama	60.0	20.6	1.9	9.2	11.2	8.5	5.2	3.4	Birmingham	284,413
Arkansas	51.6	6.9	8.4	8.1	12.4	6.7	7.1	2.0	Little Rock	158,461
Florida	84.3	19.9	7.2	15.2	17.3	10.8	4.1	9.7	Jacksonville	534,402
Georgia	62.4	15.6	2.3	7.7	11.0	6.5	5.4	13.9	Atlanta	425,022
Kentucky	50.9	13.5	1.5	7.0	11.9	6.0	5.4	5.6	Louisville	298,451
Louisiana	68.6	27.2	9.1	3.9	12.3	7.0	4.2	5.0	New Orleans	557,028
Mississippi	47.3	8.0	(X)	11.9	13.3	7.6	5.6	0.9	Jackson	202,895
North Carolina	48.0	14.5	3.0	7.4	7.2	4.8	5.9	5.3	Charlotte	314,447
South Carolina	54.1	3.2	6.1	4.4	13.7	10.5	6.4	9.8	Columbia	101,208
Virginia	66.0	29.5	1.2	8.3	12.7	6.8	2.7	4.7	Norfolk	266,979
West Virginia	36.2	(X)	6.5	5.7	8.9	4.7	6.2	4.2	Charleston	63,968

(X) not applicable.

Source: U.S. Department of Commerce, Bureau of the Census, *1980 Census of Population, Number of Inhabitants*.

TABLE 1.20--POPULATION, METROPOLITAN STATISTICAL AREAS, SOUTHEASTERN STATES, 1970 AND 1980 [In thousands]

Metropolitan statistical area	1980 Total	1980 Percentage Under 18 years old	1980 Percentage 65 years and over	1970	Percent change 1970–1980
Albany, GA	112	34.0	7.2	97	16.3
Anderson, SC	133	29.0	10.8	105	26.3
Anniston, AL	120	28.5	9.7	103	16.2
Asheville, NC	161	25.8	13.7	145	10.9
Athens, GA	130	25.5	8.9	108	20.7
Atlanta, GA	2,138	29.4	7.8	1,684	27.0
Augusta, GA-SC	346	30.0	8.4	291	18.8
Baton Rouge, LA	494	31.5	7.0	376	31.6
Biloxi-Gulfport, MS	182	30.7	9.1	152	19.9
Birmingham, AL	884	28.1	11.7	794	11.3
Bradenton, FL	148	20.9	27.1	97	52.9
Burlington, NC	99	26.3	11.5	97	2.9
Charleston, SC	430	30.5	6.9	336	28.1
Charleston, WV	270	26.8	11.5	257	4.8
Charlotte-Gastonia-Rock Hill, NC-SC	971	28.5	9.6	840	15.6
Charlottesville, VA	114	23.4	9.6	90	26.9
CHATTANOOGA, TN-GA	427	28.4	10.9	371	15.0
CLARKSVILLE-HOPKINSVILLE, TN-KY	150	29.1	8.1	119	26.3
Columbia, SC	410	27.9	7.3	323	27.0
Columbus, GA-AL	239	29.5	8.5	239	0.3
Danville, VA	112	27.0	12.7	105	6.3
Daytona Beach, FL	259	21.2	22.3	169	52.7
Dothan, AL	122	30.9	9.3	110	11.8
Fayetteville, NC	247	31.0	4.5	212	16.6
Fayetteville-Springdale, AR	100	25.7	10.7	77	29.9
Florence, AL	135	28.7	11.0	118	14.7
Florence, SC	110	32.3	8.6	90	22.9
Fort Lauderdale-Hollywood-Pompano Beach, FL	1,018	21.0	22.0	620	64.2
Fort Myers, FL	205	21.9	22.3	105	95.1
Fort Pierce, FL	151	23.9	20.1	79	91.7
Fort Smith, AR-OK	163	30.0	12.5	128	26.9
Fort Walton Beach, FL	110	30.2	5.8	88	24.6
Gadsden, AL	103	28.7	12.7	94	9.5
Gainesville, FL	171	24.0	7.5	119	43.5
Greensboro-Winston-Salem-High Point, NC	852	27.2	10.2	743	14.7
Greenville-Spartanburg, SC	569	28.0	9.8	473	20.2
Hickory, NC	203	28.8	9.7	171	18.8
Houma-Thibodaux, LA	177	34.9	6.7	145	22.0
Huntington-Ashland, WV-KY-OH	336	28.8	11.7	307	9.7
Huntsville, AL	197	29.4	7.2	187	5.6
Jackson, MS	362	31.1	9.4	289	25.4
Jacksonville, FL	722	29.2	9.7	613	17.9
Jacksonville, NC	113	26.8	3.7	103	9.4
JOHNSON CITY-KINGSPORT-BRISTOL, TN-VA	434	27.3	11.4	374	16.1
KNOXVILLE, TN	566	26.3	11.2	477	18.8
Lafayette, LA	190	31.9	7.1	144	32.0
Lake Charles, LA	167	31.5	8.7	145	15.0
Lakeland-Winter Haven, FL	322	27.2	14.3	229	40.8

TABLE 1.20--POPULATION, METROPOLITAN STATISTICAL AREAS, SOUTHEASTERN STATES, 1970 AND 1980 [In thousands] (Continued)

Metropolitan statistical area	1980 Total	1980 Percentage Under 18 years old	1980 Percentage 65 years and over	1970	Percent change 1970–1980
Lexington-Fayette, KY	318	27.1	9.2	267	19.1
Little Rock-North Little Rock, AR	474	29.7	9.9	381	24.5
Louisville, KY-IN	957	28.8	10.4	907	5.5
Lynchburg, VA	141	26.9	11.5	125	13.1
Macon-Warner Robins, GA	264	30.5	8.9	235	12.4
Melbourne-Titusville-Palm Bay, FL	273	24.9	12.7	230	18.7
MEMPHIS, TN-AR-MS	913	30.5	9.3	834	9.5
Miami-Hialeah, FL	1,626	24.0	15.7	1,268	28.2
Mobile, AL	444	31.3	10.2	377	17.7
Monroe, LA	139	32.0	10.0	115	20.7
Montgomery, AL	273	30.7	10.1	226	20.7
NASHVILLE, TN	851	27.5	10.4	699	21.6
New Orleans, LA	1,256	30.4	9.1	1,100	14.2
Norfolk-Virginia Beach-Newport News, VA	1,160	28.5	7.7	1,059	9.6
Ocala, FL	122	26.2	17.1	69	77.4
Orlando, FL	700	27.3	10.9	453	54.4
Owensboro, KY	86	30.2	10.9	79	8.1
Panama City, FL	98	29.1	9.5	75	29.8
Parkersburg-Marietta, WV-OH	158	29.0	11.7	144	9.7
Pascagoula, MS	118	34.6	6.3	88	34.1
Pensacola, FL	290	29.3	8.6	243	19.2
Pine Bluff, AR	91	31.2	12.2	85	6.3
Raleigh-Durham, NC	561	25.3	8.5	446	25.8
Richmond-Petersburg, VA	761	26.9	9.9	676	12.6
Roanoke, VA	220	25.6	12.8	200	10.4
Sarasota, FL	202	17.5	30.0	120	68.0
Savannah, GA	221	30.1	10.3	201	9.5
Shreveport, LA	333	30.8	10.4	296	12.5
Tallahassee, FL	190	27.1	7.8	142	33.7
Tampa-St. Petersburg-Clearwater, FL	1,614	22.3	21.5	1,106	46.0
Tuscaloosa, AL	138	27.1	9.7	116	18.5
West Palm Beach-Boca Raton-Delray Beach, FL	577	21.3	23.3	349	65.3
Wheeling, WV-OH	186	26.4	14.0	182	2.0
Wilmington, NC	103	27.8	10.1	83	24.7

Note: The Metropolitan Statistical Areas are as defined by the Office of Management and Budget as of June 30, 1983. Figures for 1970 include corrections. Table 20.2 gives 1988 population estimates.

Source: U.S. Department of Commerce, Bureau of the Census, *Statistical Abstract of the United States, 1984*.

TABLE 1.21--POPULATION, BY RACE, 1980, AND PERCENTAGE MINORITY POPULATION, 1970 AND 1980, SOUTHEASTERN CITIES OF 100,000 OR MORE

		Non-hispanic			Percentage minority	
City	Total	White	Black	Other	1980	1970
Alexandria, VA	103,200	72,100	22,800	4,400	30	17
Arlington, VA	152,600	120,300	13,900	9,600	21	10
Atlanta, GA	425,000	135,400	280,400	3,300	68	52
Baton Rouge, LA	219,400	133,000	79,300	3,000	39	29
Birmingham, AL	284,400	124,000	156,900	1,300	56	42
CHATTANOOGA, TN	169,600	114,100	53,200	1,000	33	36
Chesapeake, VA	114,500	80,800	31,400	1,200	29	23
Columbia, SC	101,200	57,500	40,200	1,200	43	32
Columbus, GA	169,400	106,100	57,400	2,500	37	28
Durham, NC	100,800	51,900	47,100	900	49	40
Ft. Lauderdale, FL	153,300	114,100	31,500	1,300	26	16
Greensboro, NC	155,600	101,700	50,900	1,800	35	29
Hampton, VA	122,600	77,400	41,700	1,800	37	27
Hialeah, FL	145,300	34,800	1,600	1,000	76	44
Hollywood, FL	121,300	109,200	4,800	1,000	10	6
Huntsville, AL	142,500	109,700	29,300	2,100	23	13
Jackson, MS	202,900	105,800	94,500	1,100	48	40
Jacksonville, FL	540,900	388,400	135,800	6,900	28	25
KNOXVILLE, TN	175,000	146,600	25,500	1,800	16	13
Lexington, KY	204,200	173,600	27,000	2,200	15	19
Little Rock, AR	158,500	104,600	50,700	1,800	34	26
Louisville, KY	298,500	210,900	83,600	1,900	29	25
Macon, GA	116,900	63,900	51,700	500	45	38
MEMPHIS, TN	646,400	331,800	305,000	4,400	49	40
Miami, FL	346,900	67,200	82,100	3,500	81	66
Mobile, AL	200,500	124,400	71,900	1,800	38	37
Montgomery, AL	177,900	106,000	69,000	1,200	40	35
NASHVILLE, TN	455,700	342,600	105,200	4,200	25	22
New Orleans, LA	557,500	224,700	304,700	8,900	60	48
Newport News, VA	144,900	94,600	45,200	2,500	35	30
Norfolk, VA	267,000	159,900	93,100	7,900	40	31
Orlando, FL	128,300	83,800	38,000	1,500	35	31
Portsmouth, VA	104,600	55,800	46,800	900	47	41
Raleigh, NC	150,300	105,200	41,000	2,700	30	24
Richmond, VA	219,200	103,900	111,200	1,900	53	43
Roanoke, VA	100,200	77,100	21,900	600	23	20
Savanna, GA	141,400	69,500	68,600	1,500	51	46
Shreveport, LA	205,800	118,200	83,600	1,300	43	34
St. Petersburg, FL	238,600	191,800	40,400	2,200	20	16
Tampa, FL	271,500	169,800	62,500	3,200	37	30
Virginia Beach, VA	262,200	223,900	26,000	7,200	15	11
Winston-Salem, NC	131,900	77,200	52,500	1,000	41	35

Source: American Demographics, Inc., Ithaca, N.Y., *American Demographics, November 1984*, used by special permission.

The measure most commonly used as a gauge of the United States' economy is gross national product, or GNP, defined as the market value of all goods and services produced over a given period of time. Tables 2.1 and 2.2 present analogous information for Tennessee gross state product from 1977-1986, specifying the contribution of some 11 different sectors to the level of state economic activity. Tennessee gross state product (GSP) information, formerly estimated by the Center for Business and Economic Research, is now estimated biennially by the U.S. Department of Commerce, Bureau of Economic Analysis (BEA). These estimates are part of a consistent series for all states in the U.S.

Personal income is also estimated by BEA for counties, states, regions, and the nation. Income is estimated for geographic areas, both as a place of work – wages, salary, and proprietors' income paid there – and as a place of residence – total income of all persons residing there, including dividends, rents, and transfer payments. Summary data are published in the April and August issues of the *Survey of Current Business*. Detailed data are published periodically in regional volumes. The latest of these is *Local Area Personal Income, 1982-1987*. Due to recent historical revision to this series, data users needing personal income data for the years 1969-1981 should request revised data from the BEA or the Center for Business and Economic Research.

As part of personal income estimates, BEA estimates transfer payments for each county in the U.S. These details of pension and veterans' and public assistance income are found in Table 2.18. Transfer payments reported in per capita amounts and as a percentage of total personal income are detailed in Table 2.19.

The Consumer Price Index (CPI) is used to measure changes in the cost of living for any specific location over a selected period of time. Though some 27 cities have a consumer price index specific to them, no index is computed specifically for Tennessee or any of its cities. The most commonly used measure is the U.S. City Average. Indexes are issued in monthly news releases by the Bureau of Labor Statistics (BLS), and published in *Monthly Labor Review* as well as in the *Survey of Current Business* and most newspapers. Beginning with 1978, data are reported for "Wage Earners and Clerical Workers" (CPI-W) and "All Urban Consumers" (CPI-U). CPI-W covers only about 32 percent of the population, but CPI-U covers 80 percent of all noninstitutional civilian population and includes professional, managerial, and technical workers, the self-employed, short-term workers, the unemployed, retirees, and others not in the labor force, in addition to wage earners and clerical workers.

TABLE OF CONTENTS

TABLE OF CONTENTS
(Continued)

Table Number Page Number

TABLE 2.1-- GROSS STATE PRODUCT, BY SECTOR, TENNESSEE, 1977, 1985, and 1986
[In millions of current dollars]

Sector	1986 Amount	1986 %	1985 Amount	1985 %	1977 Amount	1977 %
Total gross state product	72,326	100.0	67,561	100.0	33,198	100.0
Manufacturing	18,096	25.0	17,336	25.7	9,572	28.8
Durable goods	9,498	13.1	9,117	13.5	4,375	13.2
Nondurable goods	8,598	11.9	8,219	12.2	5,197	15.7
Construction	3,188	4.4	2,847	4.2	1,589	4.8
Mining	351	0.5	371	0.5	287	0.9
Wholesale and retail trade	13,464	18.6	12,550	18.6	6,309	19.0
Services	11,135	15.4	10,109	15.0	3,857	11.6
Finance, insurance, and real estate	10,326	14.3	9,189	13.6	3,778	11.4
Transportation, communications, and public utilities	5,614	7.8	5,254	7.8	2,409	7.3
Government	8,770	12.1	8,323	12.3	4,461	13.4
Federal	3,387	4.7	3,357	4.9	1,838	5.5
State and local	5,383	7.4	4,966	7.4	2,623	7.9
Agriculture	1,382	1.9	1,582	2.3	936	2.8

Source: U.S. Department of Commerce, Bureau of Economic Analysis, direct correspondence.

FIGURE 2.1
Tennessee Gross State Product and Percentage Change, 1977–1986

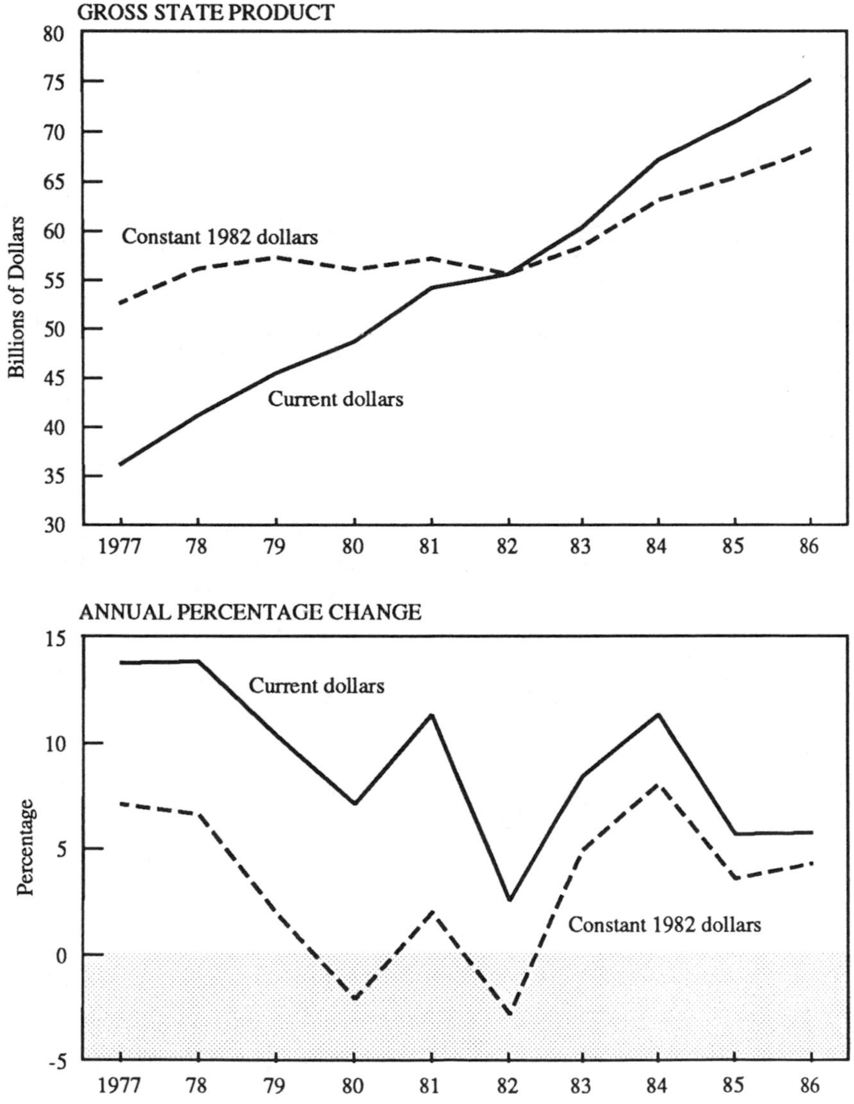

Source: U.S. Department of Commerce, Bureau of Economic Analysis, Direct Correspondence.

TABLE 2.2-- GROSS STATE PRODUCT, BY SECTOR, AND PERCENTAGE CHANGE, TENNESSEE, 1977–1986 [In millions of 1982 dollars]

Sector	1986	1985	1984	1983	1982	1981	1980	1979	1978	1977
GROSS STATE PRODUCT	64,123	61,337	58,808	54,214	51,966	52,805	51,810	52,757	51,627	47,941
Percentage change	4.5	4.3	8.5	4.3	-1.6	1.9	-1.8	2.2	7.7	5.8
Manufacturing	18,057	17,348	16,867	14,859	13,439	14,007	13,356	14,044	13,881	12,946
Percentage change	4.1	2.9	13.5	10.6	-4.1	4.9	-4.9	1.2	7.2	9.2
Durable goods	10,389	9,816	9,212	6,845	5,903	6,477	6,126	6,667	6,619	6,021
Percentage change	5.8	6.6	34.6	16.0	-8.9	5.7	-8.1	0.7	9.9	11.3
Nondurable goods	7,668	7,532	7,655	8,014	7,536	7,530	7,230	7,377	7,262	6,925
Percentage change	1.8	-1.6	-4.5	6.3	0.1	4.2	-2.0	1.6	4.9	7.4
Construction	2,711	2,535	2,394	2,170	2,111	2,153	2,443	2,767	2,929	2,680
Percentage change	6.9	5.9	10.3	2.8	-2.0	-11.9	-11.7	-5.5	9.3	2.9
Mining	371	380	370	355	365	418	418	422	423	394
Percentage change	-2.4	2.7	4.2	-2.7	-12.7	0.0	-1.0	-0.2	7.4	2.6
Trade	12,329	11,554	10,761	9,821	9,371	9,332	9,369	9,770	9,623	9,089
Percentage change	6.7	7.4	9.6	4.8	0.4	-0.4	-4.1	1.5	5.9	5.6
Services	9,048	8,556	8,117	7,523	7,182	7,161	6,831	6,631	6,373	5,909
Percentage change	5.8	5.4	7.9	4.8	0.3	4.8	3.0	4.1	7.9	4.5
Finance, insurance, real estate	8,263	7,777	7,543	7,271	7,058	6,692	6,519	6,353	6,045	5,588
Percentage change	6.3	3.1	3.7	3.0	5.5	2.7	2.6	5.1	8.2	1.9
Transportation, communications, public utilities	4,803	4,573	4,406	4,055	3,864	4,054	4,101	4,119	4,000	3,641
Percentage change	5.0	3.8	8.7	4.9	-4.7	-1.2	-0.4	3.0	9.9	7.8
Government	7,041	6,971	6,810	6,844	6,893	7,398	7,446	7,429	7,192	6,552
Percentage change	1.0	2.4	-0.5	-0.7	-6.8	-0.6	0.2	3.3	9.8	6.3
Federal	2,861	2,880	2,838	2,898	2,940	3,294	3,246	3,260	3,152	2,748
Percentage change	-0.7	1.5	-2.1	-1.4	-10.8	1.5	-0.4	3.4	14.7	5.6
State and local	4,180	4,091	3,972	3,946	3,953	4,104	4,200	4,169	4,040	3,804
Percentage change	2.2	3.0	0.7	-0.2	-3.7	-2.3	0.7	3.2	6.2	6.9
Agriculture	1,500	1,643	1,540	1,316	1,683	1,590	1,327	1,222	1,161	1,142
Percentage change	-8.7	6.7	17.0	-21.8	5.9	19.8	8.6	5.3	1.7	-3.2
PER CAPITA GROSS STATE PRODUCT (dollars)	13,359	12,870	12,438	11,560	11,137	11,383	11,256	11,638	11,570	10,891
Percentage change	3.8	3.5	7.6	3.8	-2.2	1.1	-3.3	0.6	6.2	4.1

Source: U.S. Department of Commerce, Bureau of Economic Analysis, direct correspondence.

TABLE 2.3-- PER CAPITA PERSONAL INCOME, TENNESSEE, 1929–1988, SELECTED YEARS

Year	Per capita personal income	Percentage of U.S. [1]	Percentage change [2]
1988[p]	$13,659	83.1	6.1
1987[r]	12,876	83.2	7.4
1986[r]	11,988	82.1	6.5
1985[r]	11,252	81.0	5.6
1984[r]	10,651	81.2	9.2
1983[r]	9,752	80.6	5.9
1982[r]	9,208	80.2	4.5
1981[r]	8,811	80.5	9.7
1980[r]	8,030	81.0	8.6
1979	7,392	81.8	10.5
1978	6,692	82.3	12.5
1977	5,948	81.5	9.0
1976	5,457	82.0	10.8
1975[r]	4,924	81.1	6.7
1974	4,615	81.8	8.9
1973	4,236	81.7	13.1
1972	3,745	80.3	10.3
1971	3,396	79.1	7.8
1970[r]	3,151	77.8	52.4
1965	2,067	74.6	31.2
1960	1,575	71.1	21.3
1955	1,298	69.3	27.8
1950	1,016	68.1	11.6
1945	910	74.3	170.0
1940	337	57.2	28.1
1935	263	55.6	-30.4
1929	378	54.2	(a)

Note: These data represent the most current revisions to personal income and differ slightly from detail shown in Table 2.4.

p preliminary.

r revised.

1. Computed by the Center for Business and Economic Research.

2. Computed by the Center for Business and Economic Research for five-year periods prior to 1970 except for the period 1929–1935.

a. Personal income was not estimated for years prior to 1929.

Source: U.S. Department of Commerce, Bureau of Economic Analysis, Regional Economics Information System, direct subscription.

TABLE 2.4-- PERSONAL INCOME BY MAJOR SOURCE, TENNESSEE, 1982–1987 [In millions of dollars]

Source	1987	1986	1985	1984	1983	1982
INCOME BY PLACE OF RESIDENCE						
Total personal income	62,522,270	57,550,432	53,636,509	50,359,948	45,744,807	42,968,986
Nonfarm personal income	61,875,036	57,110,137	53,107,847	49,650,331	45,489,663	42,366,993
Farm income[1]	647,234	440,295	528,662	709,617	255,144	601,993
Population (thousands)[2]	4,854.9	4,800.1	4,767.4	4,728.9	4,690.9	4,666.4
Per capita personal income (dollars)	12,878	11,989	11,251	10,649	9,752	9,208
Derivation of total personal income						
Earnings by place of work	47,945,772	43,811,445	40,652,412	38,171,509	34,297,891	32,273,770
Less: personal contributions for social insurance[3]	2,959,050	2,728,529	2,492,752	2,213,577	2,014,184	2,011,461
Plus: adjustment for residence	-689,939	-576,187	-523,823	-467,176	-440,712	-413,055
Equals: net earn. by place of residence	44,296,783	40,506,729	37,635,837	35,490,756	31,842,995	29,849,254
Plus: dividends, interest, and rent[4]	8,503,228	7,910,141	7,459,593	6,933,550	6,194,131	5,930,346
Plus: transfer payments	9,722,259	9,133,562	8,541,079	7,935,642	7,707,681	7,189,386
EARNINGS BY PLACE OF WORK						
Components of earnings						
Wages and salaries	38,502,448	35,260,852	32,836,492	30,584,171	27,843,610	26,168,911
Other labor income	3,568,106	3,311,577	3,083,537	3,007,782	2,853,924	2,663,624
Proprietors' income[5]	5,875,218	5,239,016	4,732,383	4,579,556	3,600,357	3,441,235
Farm	539,022	337,988	426,525	606,494	150,025	492,685
Nonfarm	5,336,196	4,901,028	4,305,858	3,973,062	3,450,332	2,948,550
Earnings by industry						
Farm	647,234	440,295	528,662	709,617	255,144	601,993
Nonfarm	47,298,538	43,371,150	40,123,750	37,461,892	34,042,747	31,671,777
Private	40,125,039	36,795,016	33,885,776	31,682,782	28,550,925	26,417,827
Ag. serv., for., fish., and other[6]	**157,987**	**138,979**	**146,015**	**146,935**	**147,753**	**116,520**
Agricultural services	142,372	124,655	133,024	133,523	132,968	111,199
Forestry, fisheries, and other[6]	15,615	14,324	12,991	13,412	14,785	5,321
Forestry	7,299	6,959	8,074	12,464	12,365	4,424
Fisheries	8,316	7,365	4,917	948	2,420	897
Mining	**229,967**	**217,156**	**274,479**	**260,499**	**250,168**	**275,088**
Coal mining	87,715	96,109	103,637	109,964	103,519	124,163
Oil and gas extraction	39,393	27,656	75,844	58,609	59,920	74,973
Metal mining	25,879	22,794	23,284	26,003	27,006	24,159
Nonmetallic minerals, except fuels	76,980	70,597	71,714	65,923	59,723	51,793
Construction	**3,169,065**	**2,867,794**	**2,492,557**	**2,267,451**	**1,951,911**	**1,864,993**
General building contractors	1,028,112	905,894	750,821	706,602	610,111	591,643

TABLE 2.4-- PERSONAL INCOME BY MAJOR SOURCE, TENNESSEE, 1982–1987 [In millions of dollars] (Continued)

Source	1987	1986	1985	1984	1983	1982
Heavy construction contractors	404,914	336,511	312,985	302,489	259,411	249,545
Special trade contractors	1,736,039	1,625,389	1,428,751	1,258,360	1,082,389	1,023,805
Manufacturing	**11,812,067**	**11,229,385**	**10,699,625**	**10,366,367**	**9,454,777**	**8,784,159**
Nondurable goods	5,625,085	5,348,813	5,145,341	5,058,953	5,158,059	4,859,985
Food and kindred products	961,748	917,493	866,644	820,648	772,186	759,934
Textile mill products	414,577	380,105	354,755	390,510	372,544	328,782
Apparel and other textile products	773,919	741,532	708,837	733,298	688,064	627,988
Paper and allied products	580,933	528,891	502,341	471,839	429,818	403,964
Printing and publishing	700,613	643,334	583,753	539,669	495,160	440,334
Chemicals and allied products	1,351,286	1,333,996	1,317,369	1,274,951	1,637,261	1,593,346
Petroleum and coal products	29,659	27,118	25,242	27,104	28,878	21,651
Tobacco manufactures	39,755	39,670	45,031	40,333	39,218	36,770
Rubber and misc. plastics products	635,984	604,412	595,179	572,812	497,800	433,526
Leather and leather products	136,611	132,262	146,190	187,789	197,130	213,690
Durable goods	6,186,982	5,880,572	5,554,284	5,307,414	4,296,718	3,924,174
Lumber and wood products	416,962	371,999	332,184	320,422	281,734	233,939
Furniture and fixtures	441,281	417,654	408,287	372,843	318,930	275,562
Primary metal industries	479,771	490,856	460,243	496,158	424,712	417,260
Fabricated metal products	1,043,590	1,032,854	1,000,947	927,733	594,015	570,233
Machinery, except electrical	973,626	918,933	896,313	854,053	694,033	669,603
Electric and electronic equipment	860,917	813,765	805,922	800,753	704,439	637,806
Trans. equip. excl. motor vehicles	491,805	445,086	384,277	342,306	309,340	261,738
Motor vehicles and equipment	567,092	541,093	475,225	433,234	314,061	265,066
Stone, clay, and glass products	437,874	409,354	379,283	371,258	307,979	274,839
Instruments and related products	231,355	222,777	209,778	189,648	171,080	159,948
Misc. manufacturing industries	242,709	216,201	201,825	199,006	176,395	158,180
Transportation and public utilities	**3,403,603**	**3,096,350**	**2,845,464**	**2,672,731**	**2,417,110**	**2,277,589**
Railroad transportation	265,476	286,341	307,297	316,171	296,583	284,617
Trucking and warehousing	1,338,011	1,201,241	1,116,192	1,087,504	948,452	901,401
Water transportation	23,626	23,656	27,454	24,047	21,635	23,947
Other transportation	889,375	776,468	626,236	536,752	443,363	380,297
Local & interurban passenger transit	87,542	87,426	76,968	81,647	74,366	77,109
Transportation by air	710,779	608,307	482,083	400,436	321,836	258,163
Pipelines, except natural gas	1,616	1,611	1,596	1,487	1,520	1,446
Transportation services	89,438	79,124	65,589	53,182	45,641	43,579
Communication	685,906	623,645	604,305	571,302	587,565	575,999
Electric, gas, and sanitary services	201,209	184,999	163,980	136,955	119,512	111,328
Wholesale trade	**3,227,083**	**2,968,563**	**2,774,694**	**2,557,795**	**2,318,962**	**2,225,222**
Retail trade	**5,019,216**	**4,575,621**	**4,267,379**	**3,995,670**	**3,706,773**	**3,386,915**

TABLE 2.4-- PERSONAL INCOME BY MAJOR SOURCE, TENNESSEE, 1982–1987 [In millions of dollars] (Continued)

Source	1987	1986	1985	1984	1983	1982
Building materials and garden equipment	308,126	270,212	259,740	243,513	185,452	192,072
General merchandise stores	592,628	561,993	524,918	485,524	452,460	427,032
Food stores	750,499	706,135	688,894	684,563	657,212	631,345
Automotive dealers & service stations	957,588	851,960	826,445	748,039	677,637	596,425
Apparel and accessory stores	259,943	233,930	235,621	213,539	200,117	174,075
Furniture and home furnishings stores	308,694	275,867	249,729	225,418	240,262	188,853
Eating and drinking places	1,052,608	945,053	862,252	774,992	729,532	661,811
Miscellaneous retail stores	789,130	730,471	619,780	620,082	564,101	515,302
Finance, insurance, and real estate	**2,615,863**	**2,355,642**	**2,080,517**	**1,896,200**	**1,733,993**	**1,524,947**
Banking and credit agencies	936,351	849,996	778,074	721,517	655,758	593,184
Other finance, insur., & real estate	1,679,512	1,505,646	1,302,443	1,174,683	1,078,235	931,763
Security & commodity brokers & serv.	263,265	251,767	195,526	166,229	169,871	109,309
Insurance carriers	584,150	527,583	487,517	443,762	427,411	401,247
Insurance agents, brokers, & services	419,092	365,075	306,551	280,082	233,545	227,540
Real estate	214,219	186,242	172,239	158,903	133,986	89,209
Combined real estate, insurance, etc.	3,645	3,432	13,745	9,951	7,611	3,683
Holding & other investment companies	195,141	171,547	126,865	115,756	105,811	100,775
Services	**10,490,188**	**9,345,526**	**8,305,046**	**7,519,134**	**6,569,478**	**5,962,394**
Hotels and other lodging places	398,297	363,724	341,491	320,278	279,316	282,820
Personal services	653,610	590,776	521,228	422,387	397,805	348,191
Private households	191,885	189,483	189,375	187,886	168,455	161,931
Business services	1,933,512	1,784,356	1,553,683	1,350,574	1,013,871	898,469
Auto repair, services, and garages	485,037	441,313	396,551	349,222	297,264	255,348
Miscellaneous repair services	198,900	185,516	155,959	166,593	140,374	111,311
Amusement and recreation services	238,646	215,258	183,430	160,117	154,899	154,172
Motion pictures	30,706	29,101	28,969	30,124	27,846	22,970
Health services	3,899,941	3,395,899	3,110,813	2,863,983	2,630,547	2,369,477
Legal services	606,635	527,873	455,577	421,008	344,831	308,341
Educational services	380,715	350,916	331,012	298,918	262,346	244,321
Social services	148,741	140,219	126,938	111,605	98,673	94,376
Museums, botanical, zoological gardens	5,111	4,083	3,628	2,783	2,561	2,110
Membership organizations	331,813	312,876	297,271	285,958	274,629	269,177
Miscellaneous services	986,639	814,133	609,121	547,698	476,061	439,380
Government and government enterprises	**7,173,499**	**6,576,134**	**6,237,974**	**5,779,110**	**5,491,822**	**5,253,950**
Federal, civilian	1,931,415	1,757,305	1,760,480	1,672,424	1,645,567	1,616,712
Military	334,544	314,979	315,009	306,055	289,734	277,467
State and local	4,907,540	4,503,850	4,162,485	3,800,631	3,556,521	3,359,771

Notes on following page.

TABLE 2.4-- PERSONAL INCOME BY MAJOR SOURCE, TENNESSEE, 1982–1987 [In millions of dollars] (Continued)

(D) Not shown to avoid disclosure of confidential information.

1. Farm income consists of proprietors' net farm income, the wages of hired farm labor, the pay-in-kind of hired farm labor, and the salaries of officers of corporate farms.
2. Midyear population estimates of the Bureau of the Census. Estimates for 1986–87 reflect revisions available as of September 1988. In some instances, estimates prior to 1986 are not consistent with those for 1986–87.
3. Personal contributions for social insurance are included in earnings by type and industry but excluded from personal income.
4. Includes the capital consumption adjustment for rental income of persons.
5. Includes the inventory valuation and capital consumption adjustments.
6. "Other" consists of the wages and salaries of U.S. residents employed by international organizations and foreign embassies and consulates in the United States.

a. Less than $50,000. Estimates are included in totals.

Source: U.S. Department of Commerce, Bureau of Economic Analysis, Regional Economics Information System, direct subscription.

TABLE 2.5-- TRANSFER PAYMENTS BY MAJOR SOURCE, TENNESSEE, 1982–1987 [In thousands of dollars]

Source	1987	1986	1985	1984	1983	1982
TOTAL TRANSFER PAYMENTS	9,722,259	9,133,562	8,541,079	7,935,642	7,707,681	7,189,386
Government payments to individuals	9,044,631	8,526,104	8,013,123	7,494,092	7,321,021	6,829,482
Retirement, disability & health insurance	5,206,861	4,960,101	4,731,691	4,419,688	4,212,103	3,902,708
Old-age, survivors & disability insurance	3,876,301	3,705,425	3,507,075	3,303,518	3,115,691	2,883,213
Railroad retirement & disability	128,202	125,959	121,782	119,115	119,625	115,094
Federal civilian employee retirement	385,028	352,988	337,023	313,904	298,098	277,541
Military retirement	353,919	343,395	334,410	291,142	310,341	293,092
State & local government employee retirement	369,683	339,164	336,480	298,577	275,913	244,494
Workers' compensation (federal & state)	43,278	42,343	43,894	38,708	36,058	34,851
Other government disability insurance & retirement[1]	50,450	50,827	51,027	54,724	56,377	54,423
Medical[2]	2,385,631	2,115,274	1,851,121	1,672,982	1,518,947	1,316,245
Income maintenance benefit	779,454	747,541	712,385	703,292	707,551	686,880
Supplemental security income (SSI)	315,016	293,209	278,330	269,872	245,403	232,632
Aid to families with dependent children (AFDC)	121,935	106,141	94,048	85,670	84,604	79,152
Food stamps	279,435	279,944	279,130	286,683	316,969	315,843
Other income maintenance[3]	63,068	68,247	60,877	61,067	60,575	59,253
Unemployment insurance benefit	201,494	207,822	210,174	194,637	372,912	453,598
State unemployment insurance compensation	181,664	189,391	196,083	186,262	347,951	422,088
Unemployment compensation for federal civilian employees (UCFE)	7,132	7,242	6,851	3,626	15,253	23,774
Unemployment compensation for railroad employees	2,844	2,776	2,477	3,018	5,576	4,453
Unemployment compensation for veterans (UCX)	2,378	2,278	2,349	1,086	3,255	1,831
Other unemployment compensation[4]	7,476	6,135	2,414	645	877	1,452
Veterans' benefit	377,274	394,139	403,835	400,502	403,982	382,293
Veterans' pensions & compensation	331,735	351,198	353,045	347,769	339,514	309,511
Educational assistance to veterans, dependents, & survivors[5]	14,580	18,763	25,596	30,071	40,296	48,357
Veterans' life insurance benefit	30,222	23,631	24,734	21,861	23,155	23,147
Other assistance to veterans[6]	737	547	460	801	1,017	1,278
Federal educational & training assistance (excluding veterans)[7]	88,264	96,784	100,606	101,248	103,497	85,842
Other payments to individuals[8]	5,653	4,443	3,311	1,743	2,029	1,916
Payments to nonprofit institutions	229,441	218,806	200,842	185,951	170,387	160,495
Federal government	75,081	72,138	61,736	64,421	59,198	53,016
State & local government[9]	87,615	82,299	76,113	63,995	58,691	62,569
Business	66,745	64,369	62,993	57,535	52,498	44,910
Business payments to individuals[10]	448,187	388,652	327,114	255,599	216,273	199,409

Notes on following page.

TABLE 2.5-- TRANSFER PAYMENTS BY MAJOR SOURCE, TENNESSEE, 1982–1987 [In thousands of dollars] (Continued)

1. Includes temporary disability payments and Black Lung payments.
2. Consists of Medicare payments, medical vendor payments, and CHAMPUS payments.
3. Includes general, emergency, refugee, and energy assistance, foster home care payments, and earned income tax credits.
4. Consists of trade readjustment allowance payments, Redwood Park benefit payments, public service employment benefit payments, and transitional benefit payments.
5. Includes Veterans' Readjustment benefit payments and Educational Assistance to spouses/children of disabled/deceased veterans.
6. Includes payments to paraplegics, payments for autos and conveyances for disabled veterans, veterans' aid & veterans' bonuses.
7. Includes federal fellowship payments (National Science Foundation, fellowships and traineeships, subsistence payments to State Maritime Academy cadets, and other federal fellowships), interest subsidy on higher education loans, Basic Educational Opportunity Grants, and Job Corps payments.
8. Includes Bureau of Indian Affairs payments, education exchange payments, compensation of survivors of public safety officers, compensation of victims of crime, and other special payments to individuals.
9. Consists of state and local government payments for foster home care supervised by private agencies, state and local government educational assistance payments to nonprofit institutions, and other state and local government payments to nonprofit institutions.
10. Includes consumer bad debts, personal injury payments to individuals other than employees, and other business transfer payments.

Source: U.S. Department of Commerce, Bureau of Economic Analysis, Regional Economics Information System, direct subscription.

TABLE 2.6-- PER CAPITA EARNINGS, PROPERTY INCOME, AND TRANSFER PAYMENTS, AND PERCENTAGE OF TOTAL PERSONAL INCOME, TENNESSEE AND METROPOLITAN STATISTICAL AREAS, 1987

Metropolitan statistical area	Earnings			Property income			Transfer payments		
	Per capita ($)	Percentage of total personal income	Percent change 1986–87	Per capita ($)	Percentage of total personal income	Percent change 1986–87	Per capita ($)	Percentage of total personal income	Percent change 1986–87
TENNESSEE	9,124	70.8	8.1	1,751	13.6	6.3	2,003	15.6	5.3
Chattanooga	9,469	70.5	9.0	1,892	14.1	7.0	2,068	15.4	5.1
Clarksville-Hopkinsville	8,049	72.6	7.7	1,238	11.2	6.4	1,800	16.2	5.6
Jackson	8,257	68.0	8.3	1,737	14.3	6.9	2,152	17.7	6.6
Johnson City-Kingsport-Bristol	7,881	68.3	5.8	1,667	14.4	7.1	1,999	17.3	5.5
Knoxville	9,153	69.6	8.1	1,952	14.9	6.5	2,038	15.5	5.5
Memphis	10,406	72.9	7.9	1,762	12.3	6.0	2,104	14.7	6.2
Nashville-Davidson	11,431	74.9	7.2	2,057	13.5	4.8	1,765	11.6	3.9

Source: U.S. Department of Commerce, Bureau of Economic Analysis, Regional Economics Information System, direct subscription.

TABLE 2.7-- PERSONAL INCOME BY MAJOR SOURCE, CHATTANOOGA METROPOLITAN STATISTICAL AREA, 1982–1987 [In thousands of dollars]

Source	1987	1986	1985	1984	1983	1982
INCOME BY PLACE OF RESIDENCE						
Total personal income	5,795,128	5,314,320	4,946,623	4,628,285	4,292,158	4,079,759
Nonfarm personal income	5,771,235	5,290,390	4,925,661	4,603,821	4,278,863	4,061,039
Farm income[1]	23,893	23,930	20,962	24,464	13,295	18,720
Population (thousands)[2]	431.5	427.9	424.7	425.1	422.9	427.8
Per capita personal income (dollars)	13,429	12,420	11,647	10,888	10,149	9,536
Derivation of total personal income						
Earnings by place of work	4,530,031	4,098,223	3,780,438	3,562,813	3,270,327	3,130,815
Less: personal contributions for social insurance[3]	279,248	254,636	232,058	208,001	192,177	195,629
Plus: adjustment for residence	-164,798	-127,211	-101,496	-101,354	-79,213	-76,450
Equals: net earn. by place of residence	4,085,985	3,716,376	3,446,884	3,253,458	2,998,937	2,858,736
Plus: dividends, interest, and rent[4]	816,599	756,382	713,098	647,997	590,593	563,064
Plus: transfer payments	892,544	841,562	786,641	726,830	702,628	657,959
EARNINGS BY PLACE OF WORK						
Components of earnings						
Wages and salaries	3,696,584	3,331,623	3,094,816	2,907,391	2,687,735	2,595,528
Other labor income	330,407	304,379	285,003	281,556	272,075	263,924
Proprietors' income[5]	503,040	462,221	400,619	373,866	310,517	271,363
Farm	21,624	21,734	18,699	22,117	10,921	16,262
Nonfarm	481,416	440,487	381,920	351,749	299,596	255,101
Earnings by industry						
Farm	23,893	23,930	20,962	24,464	13,295	18,720
Nonfarm	4,506,138	4,074,293	3,759,476	3,538,349	3,257,032	3,112,095
Private	3,671,658	3,342,465	3,071,704	2,885,189	2,645,056	2,523,020
Ag. serv., for., fish., and other[6]	**11,896**	**10,397**	**10,448**	**9,893**	**9,964**	**7,771**
Agricultural services	(D)	(D)	(D)	(D)	(D)	(D)
Forestry, fisheries, and other[6]	2,009	1,872	1,547	(D)	(D)	(D)
Forestry	(D)	(D)	(D)	(D)	(D)	(D)
Fisheries	(D)	1,273	899	217	450	139
Mining	**26,084**	**32,796**	**37,103**	**35,487**	**34,272**	**43,160**
Coal mining	(D)	(D)	(D)	(D)	(D)	(D)
Oil and gas extraction	3,298	2,008	7,885	5,643	5,613	7,209
Metal mining	0	0	0	0	0	(D)
Nonmetallic minerals, except fuels	(D)	(D)	(D)	(D)	(D)	(D)
Construction	**282,765**	**255,148**	**226,985**	**200,371**	**179,657**	**170,901**
General building contractors	87,321	69,424	(D)	57,479	46,526	36,508

TABLE 2.7-- PERSONAL INCOME BY MAJOR SOURCE, CHATTANOOGA METROPOLITAN STATISTICAL AREA, 1982–1987 [In thousands of dollars] (Continued)

Source	1987	1986	1985	1984	1983	1982
Heavy construction contractors	28,885	(D)	22,509	23,010	20,082	23,251
Special trade contractors	166,559	151,598	134,278	119,882	113,049	111,142
Manufacturing	**1,082,068**	**1,009,827**	**939,038**	**936,350**	**890,096**	**878,328**
Nondurable goods	638,741	575,416	518,447	508,977	494,932	482,697
Food and kindred products	155,011	138,913	115,298	111,364	108,470	101,909
Textile mill products	223,758	199,217	174,128	174,497	165,005	146,873
Apparel and other textile products	(D)	(D)	10,175	(D)	(D)	(D)
Paper and allied products	(D)	(D)	36,856	34,507	27,996	23,418
Printing and publishing	46,099	39,899	35,806	32,625	31,210	27,661
Chemicals and allied products	115,128	106,277	97,234	102,738	113,733	136,096
Petroleum and coal products	2,619	3,841	5,147	5,292	5,276	4,214
Rubber and misc. plastics products	18,088	16,659	15,477	13,958	12,534	12,084
Leather and leather products	6,185	6,844	8,506	8,128	7,463	8,919
Durable goods	443,327	434,411	420,591	427,373	392,035	393,030
Lumber and wood products	(D)	(D)	(D)	(D)	(D)	(D)
Furniture and fixtures	9,858	7,915	7,591	7,211	6,515	5,977
Primary metal industries	99,825	95,633	91,366	106,784	84,394	78,774
Fabricated metal products	101,655	109,702	121,748	128,452	135,018	147,421
Machinery, except electrical	63,183	58,994	55,823	52,280	49,655	52,034
Electric and electronic equipment	(D)	(D)	(D)	(D)	(D)	(D)
Trans. equip. excl. motor vehicles	(D)	(D)	(D)	(D)	1,163	725
Motor vehicles and equipment	(D)	(D)	(D)	(D)	(D)	(D)
Stone, clay, and glass products	40,933	44,452	46,601	47,195	39,429	40,811
Instruments and related products	15,769	14,561	12,528	11,326	9,786	9,344
Misc. manufacturing industries	15,714	14,889	13,838	(D)	10,875	9,170
Transportation and public utilities	**267,078**	**253,714**	**233,527**	**223,450**	**201,560**	**195,748**
Railroad transportation	44,325	45,503	47,345	46,095	39,594	38,179
Trucking and warehousing	122,859	113,305	99,657	97,613	82,673	81,139
Water transportation	2,665	2,861	2,740	2,363	(D)	(D)
Other transportation	21,549	20,017	17,453	15,559	(D)	(D)
Local & interurban passenger transit	8,090	8,274	7,075	7,909	6,849	6,700
Transportation by air	8,706	7,594	6,990	4,863	(D)	(D)
Transportation services	4,753	4,320	3,496	2,862	2,084	2,010
Communication	50,424	48,220	46,070	43,710	48,249	46,910
Electric, gas, and sanitary services	21,630	(D)	(D)	(D)	(D)	(D)
Wholesale trade	**305,220**	**285,872**	**264,129**	**246,974**	**215,419**	**197,987**
Retail trade	**467,184**	**417,713**	**395,511**	**373,080**	**336,611**	**319,251**
Building materials and garden equipment	24,604	19,046	(D)	17,216	13,596	14,574
General merchandise stores	42,132	37,142	(D)	30,083	29,727	30,573

TABLE 2.7-- PERSONAL INCOME BY MAJOR SOURCE, CHATTANOOGA METROPOLITAN STATISTICAL AREA, 1982–1987 [In thousands of dollars] (Continued)

Source	1987	1986	1985	1984	1983	1982
Food stores	63,665	59,807	69,286	63,529	58,019	61,752
Automotive dealers & service stations	81,187	70,652	68,220	63,304	56,331	57,354
Apparel and accessory stores	17,018	15,698	15,395	16,750	13,933	11,258
Furniture and home furnishings stores	23,828	20,521	(D)	(D)	15,733	13,336
Eating and drinking places	120,393	105,797	95,005	91,578	86,078	75,263
Miscellaneous retail stores	88,306	82,052	68,484	67,327	56,812	49,557
Finance, insurance, and real estate	**310,569**	**272,998**	**252,483**	**222,890**	**208,001**	**191,858**
Banking and credit agencies	(D)	(D)	(D)	48,768	(D)	(D)
Other finance, insur., & real estate	233,021	203,749	185,452	167,194	150,366	136,287
Security & commodity brokers & serv.	9,980	9,302	8,214	6,792	7,104	4,923
Insurance carriers	164,158	144,535	132,614	122,019	111,460	107,694
Insurance agents, brokers, & services	39,824	33,568	28,845	22,837	18,950	18,624
Real estate	11,437	8,358	8,432	7,836	7,000	1,353
Combined real estate, insurance, etc.	61	64	70	(a)	(a)	663
Holding & other investment companies	14,403	14,150	12,923	(D)	9,704	6,278
Services	**918,794**	**804,000**	**712,480**	**636,694**	**569,476**	**518,016**
Hotels and other lodging places	(D)	(D)	(D)	(D)	(D)	(D)
Personal services	80,345	72,065	69,067	61,740	59,698	53,911
Private households	15,139	14,936	14,911	14,773	13,218	12,692
Business services	149,784	128,003	106,350	84,155	72,781	65,046
Auto repair, services, and garages	49,344	45,185	40,351	35,564	29,482	25,589
Miscellaneous repair services	19,551	18,198	16,017	17,217	14,920	10,679
Amusement and recreation services	15,733	13,959	12,811	11,180	10,211	9,801
Motion pictures	2,822	3,053	2,865	1,988	1,759	1,532
Health services	316,334	268,209	246,144	226,603	205,133	185,802
Legal services	78,596	67,387	61,054	55,182	46,077	40,787
Educational services	(D)	(D)	(D)	(D)	(D)	16,197
Social services	12,827	10,686	8,646	8,084	6,999	(D)
Museums, botanical, zoological gardens	(D)	(D)	(D)	(D)	(D)	(D)
Membership organizations	29,984	28,825	27,581	26,999	26,312	26,147
Miscellaneous services	102,789	88,096	65,218	56,327	49,183	45,123
Government and government enterprises	**834,480**	**731,828**	**687,772**	**653,160**	**611,976**	**589,075**
Federal, civilian	368,412	303,915	283,770	277,482	257,214	253,732
Military	15,636	13,934	12,617	11,741	11,409	10,241
State and local	450,432	413,979	391,385	363,937	343,353	325,102

See Table 2.4 for notes.

Source: U.S. Department of Commerce, Bureau of Economic Analysis, Regional Economics Information System, direct subscription.

TABLE 2.8-- PERSONAL INCOME BY MAJOR SOURCE, CLARKSVILLE-HOPKINSVILLE METROPOLITAN STATISTICAL AREA, 1982–1987 [In thousands of dollars]

Source	1987	1986	1985	1984	1983	1982
INCOME BY PLACE OF RESIDENCE						
Total personal income	1,735,774	1,614,135	1,529,811	1,441,021	1,315,496	1,285,496
Nonfarm personal income	1,723,422	1,605,820	1,513,358	1,415,944	1,313,944	1,256,719
Farm income[1]	12,352	8,315	16,453	25,077	1,552	28,777
Population (thousands)[2]	156.6	156.1	153.9	151.8	153.7	154.7
Per capita personal income (dollars)	11,087	10,341	9,937	9,492	8,559	8,308
Derivation of total personal income						
Earnings by place of work	1,320,850	1,228,477	1,165,971	1,105,580	1,025,320	989,135
Less: personal contributions for social insurance[3]	73,069	68,204	62,915	57,358	53,795	52,473
Plus: adjustment for residence	12,311	6,016	4,571	2,637	-28,991	-8,137
Equals: net earn. by place of residence	1,260,092	1,166,289	1,107,627	1,050,859	942,534	928,525
Plus: dividends, interest, and rent[4]	193,829	181,731	170,938	159,759	147,495	144,342
Plus: transfer payments	281,853	266,115	251,246	230,403	225,467	212,629
EARNINGS BY PLACE OF WORK						
Components of earnings						
Wages and salaries	1,116,281	1,043,244	990,781	930,275	887,422	843,638
Other labor income	69,409	64,287	60,178	59,494	56,495	52,195
Proprietors' income[5]	135,160	120,946	115,012	115,811	81,403	93,302
Farm	6,974	3,209	11,341	19,925	-3,701	23,318
Nonfarm	128,186	117,737	103,671	95,886	85,104	69,984
Earnings by industry						
Farm	12,352	8,315	16,453	25,077	1,552	28,777
Nonfarm	1,308,498	1,220,162	1,149,518	1,080,503	1,023,768	960,358
Private	706,683	644,492	587,787	561,643	513,881	472,937
Ag. serv., for., fish., and other[6]	**3,538**	**3,148**	**3,194**	**(D)**	**(D)**	**(D)**
Agricultural services	3,412	3,038	3,109	(D)	(D)	(D)
Forestry, fisheries, and other[6]	126	110	85	72	121	(a)
Forestry	(a)	(a)	(a)	62	78	(a)
Fisheries	110	98	64	(a)	(a)	(a)
Mining	**5,028**	**3,356**	**2,346**	**(D)**	**2,078**	**(D)**
Coal mining	(D)	(D)	(D)	(D)	(D)	(D)
Oil and gas extraction	(D)	(D)	1,743	(D)	(D)	(D)
Metal mining	-122	292	-982	-1,914	-605	-5,402
Nonmetallic minerals, except fuels	(D)	(D)	(D)	(D)	(D)	(D)
Construction	**64,200**	**60,883**	**47,214**	**44,731**	**39,410**	**33,757**
General building contractors	16,430	15,151	(D)	(D)	(D)	(D)

TABLE 2.8-- PERSONAL INCOME BY MAJOR SOURCE, CLARKSVILLE-HOPKINSVILLE METROPOLITAN STATISTICAL AREA, 1982–1987
[In thousands of dollars] (Continued)

Source	1987	1986	1985	1984	1983	1982
Heavy construction contractors	10,081	9,849	(D)	(D)	(D)	(D)
Special trade contractors	37,689	35,883	28,177	24,288	22,300	19,995
Manufacturing	**220,925**	**209,502**	**197,729**	**192,814**	**174,317**	**161,374**
Nondurable goods	100,787	105,386	97,667	92,878	85,461	79,482
Food and kindred products	(D)	(D)	(D)	(D)	(D)	(D)
Textile mill products	(D)	(D)	(D)	(D)	(D)	(D)
Apparel and other textile products	(D)	(D)	(D)	(D)	(D)	(D)
Paper and allied products	(D)	(D)	(D)	(D)	(D)	(D)
Printing and publishing	(D)	19,324	(D)	14,880	12,942	12,464
Chemicals and allied products	(D)	(D)	(D)	(D)	(D)	(D)
Petroleum and coal products	5,716	5,060	4,170	4,732	4,176	3,844
Tobacco manufactures	(D)	15,225	15,884	14,352	13,356	11,326
Rubber and misc. plastics products	(D)	(D)	(D)	(D)	(D)	(D)
Leather and leather products	(D)	(D)	(D)	(D)	(D)	(D)
Durable goods	120,138	104,116	100,062	99,936	88,856	81,892
Lumber and wood products	6,074	5,235	4,796	4,397	3,789	2,788
Furniture and fixtures	(D)	(D)	(D)	(D)	(D)	(D)
Primary metal industries	(D)	(D)	(D)	(D)	(D)	(D)
Fabricated metal products	10,597	9,955	9,438	9,596	8,841	7,260
Machinery, except electrical	(D)	(D)	(D)	(D)	(D)	(D)
Electric and electronic equipment	(D)	(D)	(D)	(D)	(D)	(D)
Trans. equip. excl. motor vehicles	(D)	(D)	(D)	(D)	(D)	(D)
Motor vehicles and equipment	(D)	(D)	(D)	(D)	(D)	(D)
Stone, clay, and glass products	(D)	(D)	(D)	(D)	(D)	(D)
Instruments and related products	(D)	(D)	(D)	(D)	(D)	(D)
Misc. manufacturing industries	(D)	(D)	(D)	(D)	(D)	(D)
Transportation and public utilities	**40,439**	**37,102**	**35,020**	**34,392**	**31,477**	**30,436**
Railroad transportation	(D)	(D)	998	1,119	1,078	1,014
Trucking and warehousing	16,651	15,630	14,734	15,409	12,029	11,790
Water transportation	(D)	(D)	0	0	(D)	(D)
Other transportation	2,155	2,332	1,977	(D)	1,853	1,627
Local & interurban passenger transit	(D)	1,136	(D)	(D)	1,287	1,147
Transportation by air	430	(D)	(D)	(D)	(D)	(D)
Transportation services	576	538	385	(D)	(D)	(D)
Communication	14,282	12,324	11,789	10,929	11,920	11,706
Electric, gas, and sanitary services	6,378	5,843	5,522	(D)	(D)	(D)
Wholesale trade	**41,327**	**38,095**	**36,027**	**33,252**	**31,468**	**33,419**
Retail trade	**128,035**	**113,629**	**108,163**	**106,488**	**99,753**	**88,954**
Building materials and garden equipment	6,654	6,031	6,361	6,002	4,875	4,238

TABLE 2.8-- PERSONAL INCOME BY MAJOR SOURCE, CLARKSVILLE-HOPKINSVILLE METROPOLITAN STATISTICAL AREA, 1982–1987
[In thousands of dollars] (Continued)

Source	1987	1986	1985	1984	1983	1982
General merchandise stores	16,324	13,698	13,122	11,705	13,496	14,198
Food stores	14,193	13,285	13,182	12,552	11,361	10,422
Automotive dealers & service stations	30,785	28,211	27,117	26,206	22,687	19,303
Apparel and accessory stores	5,001	3,842	3,949	4,377	4,175	3,604
Furniture and home furnishings stores	8,673	8,116	6,971	6,560	7,228	5,725
Eating and drinking places	28,840	24,521	22,997	24,555	21,949	18,427
Miscellaneous retail stores	17,565	15,925	14,464	14,531	13,982	13,037
Finance, insurance, and real estate	**36,573**	**33,785**	**30,255**	**28,899**	**27,334**	**24,733**
Banking and credit agencies	20,452	19,071	17,398	16,878	16,087	14,717
Other finance, insur., & real estate	16,121	14,714	12,857	12,021	11,247	10,016
Security & commodity brokers & serv.	(D)	(D)	(D)	(D)	(D)	(D)
Insurance carriers	(D)	3,280	3,978	4,077	3,678	3,075
Insurance agents, brokers, & services	8,271	7,432	5,715	5,341	4,581	4,438
Real estate	2,117	1,712	1,887	1,686	1,956	1,173
Combined real estate, insurance, etc.	182	166	204	71	(D)	(D)
Holding & other investment companies	(D)	(D)	(D)	(D)	534	777
Services	**166,618**	**144,992**	**127,839**	**116,635**	**104,679**	**99,605**
Hotels and other lodging places	3,443	3,294	3,095	2,703	2,726	2,267
Personal services	16,013	15,228	13,764	11,148	10,304	9,104
Private households	5,904	5,858	5,876	5,851	5,261	5,050
Business services	18,286	15,482	13,302	11,974	9,636	8,791
Auto repair, services, and garages	17,063	15,615	13,033	12,155	9,721	8,518
Miscellaneous repair services	3,728	3,585	3,016	3,959	3,365	2,684
Amusement and recreation services	(D)	(D)	(D)	(D)	1,225	1,095
Health services	58,678	49,859	45,613	41,395	39,587	40,675
Legal services	10,131	8,535	7,326	6,676	5,668	5,306
Educational services	6,585	4,251	3,926	3,209	2,968	2,798
Social services	3,995	2,921	2,741	3,601	2,639	1,822
Museums, botanical, zoological gardens	(D)	(D)	(D)	(D)	0	0
Membership organizations	7,643	7,107	6,907	5,955	5,861	5,767
Miscellaneous services	12,930	11,196	7,499	6,498	5,718	5,728
Government and government enterprises	**601,815**	**575,670**	**561,731**	**518,860**	**509,887**	**487,421**
Federal, civilian	83,902	75,910	73,441	72,429	76,674	69,312
Military	390,935	383,145	379,713	347,072	339,000	329,894
State and local	126,978	116,615	108,577	99,359	94,213	88,215

See Table 2.4 for notes.

Source: U.S. Department of Commerce, Bureau of Economic Analysis, Regional Economics Information System, direct subscription.

TABLE 2.9-- PERSONAL INCOME BY MAJOR SOURCE, JACKSON METROPOLITAN STATISTICAL AREA, 1982–1987 [In thousands of dollars]

Source	1987	1986	1985	1984	1983	1982
INCOME BY PLACE OF RESIDENCE						
Total personal income	948,680	877,329	821,440	774,761	700,701	650,938
Nonfarm personal income	940,010	874,721	819,228	770,510	701,322	646,581
Farm income[1]	8,670	2,608	2,212	4,251	-621	4,357
Population (thousands)[2]	78.1	77.9	77.8	76.6	76.0	76.0
Per capita personal income (dollars)	12,145	11,268	10,561	10,112	9,222	8,567
Derivation of total personal income						
Earnings by place of work	833,632	768,640	709,701	674,600	593,196	544,006
Less: personal contributions for social insurance[3]	50,417	47,184	43,140	38,730	34,377	33,835
Plus: adjustment for residence	-138,261	-127,779	-115,407	-110,247	-94,356	-83,532
Equals: net earn. by place of residence	644,954	593,677	551,154	525,623	464,463	426,639
Plus: dividends, interest, and rent[4]	135,670	126,488	123,336	112,999	101,701	99,544
Plus: transfer payments	168,056	157,164	146,950	136,139	134,537	124,755
EARNINGS BY PLACE OF WORK						
Components of earnings						
Wages and salaries	670,812	623,278	579,520	547,981	483,870	444,084
Other labor income	65,291	61,322	55,404	54,743	50,477	46,027
Proprietors' income[5]	97,529	84,040	74,777	71,876	58,849	53,895
Farm	7,210	1,235	848	2,874	-2,025	2,895
Nonfarm	90,319	82,805	73,929	69,002	60,874	51,000
Earnings by industry						
Farm	8,670	2,608	2,212	4,251	-621	4,357
Nonfarm	824,962	766,032	707,489	670,349	593,817	539,649
Private	684,481	637,491	587,327	559,400	490,451	444,532
Ag. serv., for., fish., and other[6]	**2,127**	**1,441**	**1,421**	**1,576**	**1,645**	**2,057**
Agricultural services	2,002	1,359	1,357	1,518	1,570	2,056
Forestry, fisheries, and other[6]	125	82	64	58	75	(a)
Forestry	(a)	(a)	(a)	51	53	(a)
Fisheries	81	72	(a)	(a)	(a)	(a)
Mining	**828**	**412**	**999**	**702**	**627**	**760**
Coal mining	(a)	(a)	(a)	(a)	(a)	(a)
Oil and gas extraction	(D)	(D)	998	700	625	758
Nonmetallic minerals, except fuels	(D)	(D)	0	0	0	0
Construction	**57,386**	**52,003**	**41,862**	**40,915**	**33,677**	**30,885**
General building contractors	16,396	13,673	10,582	11,187	9,985	9,037
Heavy construction contractors	13,374	12,415	9,219	10,323	8,170	6,705

TABLE 2.9-- PERSONAL INCOME BY MAJOR SOURCE, JACKSON METROPOLITAN STATISTICAL AREA, 1982–1987 [In thousands of dollars] (Continued)

Source	1987	1986	1985	1984	1983	1982
Special trade contractors	27,616	25,915	22,061	19,405	15,522	15,143
Manufacturing	**233,826**	**225,366**	**202,228**	**196,880**	**169,481**	**151,768**
Nondurable goods	94,083	88,307	82,838	79,788	66,985	62,024
Food and kindred products	61,458	61,579	57,175	51,013	40,991	36,881
Textile mill products	(D)	(D)	(D)	(D)	(D)	(D)
Apparel and other textile products	(D)	(D)	(D)	2,947	2,226	2,602
Paper and allied products	8,926	7,796	7,526	7,657	6,115	5,190
Printing and publishing	7,289	6,493	5,401	4,341	3,645	3,371
Chemicals and allied products	2,168	(D)	(D)	(D)	(D)	(D)
Rubber and misc. plastics products	1,657	1,248	1,192	(D)	(D)	(D)
Durable goods	139,743	137,059	119,390	117,092	102,496	89,744
Lumber and wood products	25,882	22,211	20,541	19,368	16,300	13,443
Furniture and fixtures	(D)	(D)	(D)	(D)	(D)	(D)
Primary metal industries	(D)	(D)	(D)	24,910	(D)	(D)
Fabricated metal products	7,449	4,190	2,920	2,400	2,032	1,601
Machinery, except electrical	25,980	22,873	(D)	(D)	(D)	(D)
Electric and electronic equipment	(D)	(D)	(D)	(D)	(D)	(D)
Trans. equip. excl. motor vehicles	(D)	(D)	(D)	(D)	(D)	(D)
Motor vehicles and equipment	(D)	(D)	(D)	(D)	0	0
Stone, clay, and glass products	27,242	39,411	40,137	38,365	32,627	29,623
Instruments and related products	661	(D)	(D)	(D)	(D)	(D)
Misc. manufacturing industries	432	361	275	288	269	275
Transportation and public utilities	**53,478**	**51,999**	**49,305**	**46,615**	**43,105**	**41,280**
Railroad transportation	16,015	17,409	18,710	18,519	17,668	16,908
Trucking and warehousing	16,370	15,229	12,965	12,495	10,433	9,002
Other transportation	2,817	2,537	1,987	1,135	(D)	(D)
Local & interurban passenger transit	(D)	(D)	(D)	200	(D)	(D)
Transportation by air	(D)	(D)	(D)	122	186	180
Transportation services	2,560	2,294	1,765	813	717	813
Communication	17,801	16,349	15,325	14,344	13,842	14,162
Electric, gas, and sanitary services	475	475	318	122	(D)	(D)
Wholesale trade	**36,590**	**35,258**	**48,072**	**45,260**	**40,981**	**39,820**
Retail trade	**86,923**	**80,818**	**75,277**	**71,732**	**67,242**	**59,193**
Building materials and garden equipment	4,894	4,859	4,612	4,172	2,647	2,681
General merchandise stores	11,535	10,960	10,628	10,202	10,164	7,835
Food stores	10,486	9,463	9,589	11,119	10,446	10,854
Automotive dealers & service stations	16,079	14,927	13,465	12,246	11,076	9,685
Apparel and accessory stores	4,597	4,330	4,234	4,627	4,389	4,179
Furniture and home furnishings stores	6,647	6,244	5,457	4,912	5,405	4,394

TABLE 2.9-- PERSONAL INCOME BY MAJOR SOURCE, JACKSON METROPOLITAN STATISTICAL AREA, 1982–1987 [In thousands of dollars] (Continued)

Source	1987	1986	1985	1984	1983	1982
Eating and drinking places	17,897	17,354	16,473	13,153	12,395	10,106
Miscellaneous retail stores	14,788	12,681	10,819	11,301	10,720	9,459
Finance, insurance, and real estate	**30,904**	**26,879**	**24,238**	**23,408**	**21,810**	**19,424**
Banking and credit agencies	15,903	13,085	11,559	12,586	10,857	10,194
Other finance, insur., & real estate	15,001	13,794	12,679	10,822	10,953	9,230
Security & commodity brokers & serv.	(D)	(D)	(D)	(D)	(D)	(D)
Insurance carriers	(D)	(D)	(D)	(D)	(D)	(D)
Insurance agents, brokers, & services	5,359	4,610	3,970	3,946	3,356	3,267
Real estate	701	624	472	509	565	151
Combined real estate, insurance, etc.	206	192	205	56	73	63
Holding & other investment companies	1,339	1,092	1,110	618	951	626
Services	**182,419**	**163,315**	**143,925**	**132,312**	**111,883**	**99,345**
Hotels and other lodging places	4,533	3,541	2,951	2,620	3,086	2,820
Personal services	11,052	10,376	9,443	7,491	6,972	5,978
Private households	1,832	1,807	1,805	1,791	1,612	1,549
Business services	21,344	22,027	21,577	22,165	14,375	11,608
Auto repair, services, and garages	11,058	9,813	8,092	7,761	5,950	5,297
Miscellaneous repair services	5,938	4,913	3,958	3,787	(D)	(D)
Amusement and recreation services	1,862	1,718	1,454	1,240	976	875
Motion pictures	79	(a)	60	84	(D)	(D)
Health services	85,157	75,193	64,812	57,368	50,780	45,947
Legal services	10,543	8,215	7,061	6,946	5,737	5,121
Educational services	11,868	11,363	11,115	10,175	9,434	8,749
Social services	2,592	2,233	1,627	1,475	1,248	1,219
Membership organizations	5,681	5,003	4,812	4,705	4,583	4,501
Miscellaneous services	8,880	7,069	5,158	4,704	4,119	3,400
Government and government enterprises	**140,481**	**128,541**	**120,162**	**110,949**	**103,366**	**95,117**
Federal, civilian	15,212	14,223	14,057	13,077	13,363	13,604
Military	2,005	1,798	1,644	1,493	1,497	1,332
State and local	123,264	112,520	104,461	96,379	88,506	80,181

See Table 2.4 for notes.

Source: U.S. Department of Commerce, Bureau of Economic Analysis, Regional Economics Information System, direct subscription.

TABLE 2.10--PERSONAL INCOME BY MAJOR SOURCE, JOHNSON CITY-KINGSPORT-BRISTOL METROPOLITAN STATISTICAL AREA, 1982–1987
[In thousands of dollars]

Source	1987	1986	1985	1984	1983	1982
INCOME BY PLACE OF RESIDENCE						
Total personal income	5,110,783	4,805,036	4,516,472	4,271,009	3,992,722	3,788,195
Nonfarm personal income	5,054,652	4,763,866	4,469,175	4,210,913	3,956,339	3,729,690
Farm income[1]	56,131	41,170	47,297	60,096	36,383	58,505
Population (thousands)[2]	442.6	440.9	442.2	441.7	440.8	440.2
Per capita personal income (dollars)	11,547	10,898	10,215	9,669	9,058	8,606
Derivation of total personal income						
Earnings by place of work	3,779,211	3,525,689	3,301,879	3,095,084	2,904,539	2,796,071
Less: personal contributions for social insurance[3]	234,515	220,034	203,239	179,862	170,313	172,921
Plus: adjustment for residence	-56,403	-21,710	-14,623	10,399	3,419	4,612
Equals: net earn. by place of residence	3,488,293	3,283,945	3,084,017	2,925,621	2,737,645	2,627,762
Plus: dividends, interest, and rent[4]	737,749	685,856	644,196	610,444	547,626	503,876
Plus: transfer payments	884,741	835,235	788,259	734,944	707,451	656,557
EARNINGS BY PLACE OF WORK						
Components of earnings						
Wages and salaries	3,035,470	2,841,065	2,670,652	2,479,588	2,353,280	2,269,149
Other labor income	304,655	289,328	274,428	267,514	265,587	256,336
Proprietors' income[5]	439,086	395,296	356,799	347,982	285,672	270,586
Farm	46,138	31,735	37,863	50,650	26,749	48,478
Nonfarm	392,948	363,561	318,936	297,332	258,923	222,108
Earnings by industry						
Farm	56,131	41,170	47,297	60,096	36,383	58,505
Nonfarm	3,723,080	3,484,519	3,254,582	3,034,988	2,868,156	2,737,566
Private	3,229,185	3,020,771	2,825,023	2,637,696	2,487,013	2,373,503
Ag. serv., for., fish., and other[6]	**9,368**	**8,093**	**10,422**	**11,418**	**10,771**	**9,071**
Agricultural services	9,139	7,900	10,174	10,062	10,215	9,126
Forestry, fisheries, and other[6]	229	193	248	(D)	556	-55
Forestry	124	101	186	(D)	526	-66
Fisheries	105	92	62	(a)	(a)	(a)
Mining	**11,611**	**9,777**	**8,452**	**6,590**	**6,213**	**7,447**
Coal mining	(D)	(D)	(D)	(D)	(D)	(D)
Oil and gas extraction	(D)	5,465	5,051	3,200	2,967	3,619
Metal mining	(a)	(a)	(a)	(a)	(a)	-116
Nonmetallic minerals, except fuels	(D)	(D)	(D)	(D)	(D)	(D)
Construction	**203,823**	**180,627**	**170,130**	**155,953**	**162,767**	**177,847**
General building contractors	77,429	63,176	55,733	52,578	65,621	78,923
Heavy construction contractors	18,806	16,837	19,166	19,167	(D)	(D)
Special trade contractors	104,597	100,614	91,722	81,066	73,003	75,052

TABLE 2.10--PERSONAL INCOME BY MAJOR SOURCE, JOHNSON CITY-KINGSPORT-BRISTOL METROPOLITAN STATISTICAL AREA, 1982–1987
[In thousands of dollars] (Continued)

Source	1987	1986	1985	1984	1983	1982
Manufacturing	**1,462,081**	**1,384,840**	**1,315,012**	**1,223,735**	**1,143,898**	**1,100,053**
Nondurable goods	900,823	875,406	832,248	786,933	763,568	723,349
Food and kindred products	(D)	(D)	(D)	44,482	41,975	45,252
Textile mill products	(D)	(D)	(D)	(D)	(D)	(D)
Apparel and other textile products	47,035	46,305	42,487	42,497	(D)	37,038
Paper and allied products	(D)	50,286	(D)	(D)	(D)	(D)
Printing and publishing	(D)	(D)	(D)	(D)	(D)	(D)
Chemicals and allied products	(D)	482,808	463,872	(D)	(D)	(D)
Petroleum and coal products	612	653	343	922	676	657
Tobacco manufactures	(D)	(D)	(D)	(D)	(D)	(D)
Rubber and misc. plastics products	(D)	(D)	(D)	(D)	(D)	(D)
Leather and leather products	(D)	979	(D)	(D)	(D)	(D)
Durable goods	561,258	509,434	482,764	436,802	380,330	376,704
Lumber and wood products	19,945	17,679	15,964	14,887	12,962	11,017
Furniture and fixtures	(D)	(D)	(D)	(D)	(D)	(D)
Primary metal industries	(D)	(D)	(D)	(D)	(D)	(D)
Fabricated metal products	(D)	(D)	(D)	(D)	(D)	(D)
Machinery, except electrical	(D)	(D)	(D)	(D)	(D)	(D)
Electric and electronic equipment	(D)	(D)	(D)	(D)	(D)	(D)
Trans. equip. excl. motor vehicles	(D)	(D)	(D)	(D)	(D)	(D)
Motor vehicles and equipment	(D)	(D)	(D)	(D)	(D)	(D)
Stone, clay, and glass products	(D)	(D)	(D)	(D)	(D)	(D)
Instruments and related products	(D)	(D)	(D)	(D)	(D)	(D)
Misc. manufacturing industries	(D)	(D)	(D)	(D)	(D)	(D)
Transportation and public utilities	**186,344**	**181,395**	**168,910**	**166,514**	**162,771**	**156,774**
Railroad transportation	19,860	18,810	18,423	18,374	17,949	18,567
Trucking and warehousing	(D)	(D)	(D)	(D)	65,909	60,540
Water transportation	(D)	(D)	(D)	(D)	(D)	(D)
Other transportation	(D)	(D)	(D)	(D)	(D)	(D)
Local & interurban passenger transit	(D)	3,307	2,885	3,063	(D)	(D)
Transportation by air	4,470	(D)	(D)	(D)	(D)	(D)
Transportation services	2,390	(D)	(D)	1,347	1,151	1,137
Communication	(D)	(D)	(D)	(D)	55,965	54,608
Electric, gas, and sanitary services	(D)	(D)	(D)	(D)	(D)	(D)
Wholesale trade	**180,763**	**178,801**	**162,438**	**150,607**	**141,998**	**136,855**
Retail trade	**364,937**	**345,469**	**330,706**	**310,485**	**301,692**	**280,576**
Building materials and garden equipment	21,747	19,944	19,252	19,192	16,042	16,055
General merchandise stores	45,607	44,118	42,000	35,088	31,217	32,226

TABLE 2.10--PERSONAL INCOME BY MAJOR SOURCE, JOHNSON CITY-KINGSPORT-BRISTOL METROPOLITAN STATISTICAL AREA, 1982–1987
[In thousands of dollars] (Continued)

Source	1987	1986	1985	1984	1983	1982
Food stores	55,623	53,329	53,121	56,040	59,728	56,214
Automotive dealers & service stations	71,873	65,716	65,885	62,438	58,589	53,986
Apparel and accessory stores	15,815	14,321	15,569	15,944	19,893	17,285
Furniture and home furnishings stores	24,720	23,829	21,302	18,805	20,886	16,971
Eating and drinking places	76,559	68,660	66,036	58,572	56,778	52,474
Miscellaneous retail stores	52,479	55,169	47,211	43,927	38,154	34,781
Finance, insurance, and real estate	**113,047**	**105,269**	**91,952**	**84,230**	**80,386**	**71,824**
Banking and credit agencies	(D)	(D)	(D)	(D)	37,802	36,667
Other finance, insur., & real estate	61,692	56,757	45,678	41,700	39,339	32,407
Security & commodity brokers & serv.	5,480	(D)	(D)	(D)	(D)	(D)
Insurance carriers	(D)	(D)	(D)	(D)	(D)	(D)
Insurance agents, brokers, & services	22,088	19,628	17,257	16,854	14,609	14,078
Real estate	1,695	2,045	3,460	4,108	3,601	1,310
Combined real estate, insurance, etc.	321	383	716	(D)	(D)	(D)
Holding & other investment companies	(D)	12,241	(D)	(D)	3,104	2,060
Services	**697,211**	**626,500**	**567,001**	**528,164**	**476,517**	**433,056**
Hotels and other lodging places	11,292	10,840	8,825	8,370	8,958	8,985
Personal services	48,373	45,409	39,437	32,164	31,490	27,856
Private households	10,133	9,977	9,935	10,027	8,998	8,628
Business services	82,939	71,884	68,238	58,769	54,160	47,626
Auto repair, services, and garages	32,566	28,990	26,263	24,888	22,173	18,492
Miscellaneous repair services	14,412	13,719	11,495	12,403	10,700	8,970
Amusement and recreation services	8,746	(D)	(D)	(D)	5,484	5,577
Motion pictures	(D)	(D)	(D)	(D)	(D)	(D)
Health services	338,291	297,932	274,118	261,687	238,597	219,053
Legal services	40,139	32,683	28,712	26,932	21,904	20,293
Educational services	(D)	(D)	(D)	(D)	(D)	(D)
Social services	10,501	9,611	9,019	8,449	7,527	6,604
Museums, botanical, zoological gardens	(D)	(D)	(D)	(D)	(D)	(D)
Membership organizations	26,592	25,349	24,264	24,136	23,624	23,074
Miscellaneous services	52,988	54,820	42,463	38,305	28,845	25,089
Government and government enterprises	**493,895**	**463,748**	**429,559**	**397,292**	**381,143**	**364,063**
Federal, civilian	100,859	93,937	94,920	93,031	90,493	89,061
Military	13,204	12,126	10,890	9,746	9,159	8,539
State and local	379,832	357,685	323,749	294,515	281,491	266,463

See Table 2.4 for notes.

Source: U.S. Department of Commerce, Bureau of Economic Analysis, Regional Economics Information System, direct subscription.

TABLE 2.11--PERSONAL INCOME BY MAJOR SOURCE, KNOXVILLE METROPOLITAN STATISTICAL AREA, 1982–1987 [In thousands of dollars]

Source	1987	1986	1985	1984	1983	1982
INCOME BY PLACE OF RESIDENCE						
Total personal income	7,807,643	7,192,033	6,728,370	6,368,462	5,845,726	5,520,789
Nonfarm personal income	7,762,459	7,154,925	6,687,328	6,314,835	5,811,622	5,471,622
Farm income[1]	45,184	37,108	41,042	53,627	34,104	49,167
Population (thousands)[2]	594.0	587.9	589.1	589.3	586.1	582.3
Per capita personal income (dollars)	13,144	12,234	11,421	10,807	9,974	9,481
Derivation of total personal income						
Earnings by place of work	5,877,757	5,372,637	4,960,266	4,698,916	4,295,172	4,070,768
Less: personal contributions for social insurance[3]	359,983	331,792	302,677	272,114	250,406	254,052
Plus: adjustment for residence	-80,534	-61,534	-13,474	6,303	13,028	26,020
Equals: net earn. by place of residence	5,437,240	4,979,311	4,644,115	4,433,105	4,057,794	3,842,736
Plus: dividends, interest, and rent[4]	1,159,516	1,077,724	1,029,862	957,614	842,887	809,836
Plus: transfer payments	1,210,887	1,134,998	1,054,393	977,743	945,045	868,217
EARNINGS BY PLACE OF WORK						
Components of earnings						
Wages and salaries	4,712,895	4,302,915	3,991,781	3,759,589	3,476,228	3,318,332
Other labor income	424,776	397,144	371,796	365,692	352,086	333,106
Proprietors' income[5]	740,086	672,578	596,689	573,635	466,858	419,330
Farm	38,909	31,138	35,043	47,517	27,890	42,713
Nonfarm	701,177	641,440	561,646	526,118	438,968	376,617
Earnings by industry						
Farm	45,184	37,108	41,042	53,627	34,104	49,167
Nonfarm	5,832,573	5,335,529	4,919,224	4,645,289	4,261,068	4,021,601
Private	4,789,194	4,388,925	4,034,131	3,820,722	3,465,564	3,264,079
Ag. serv., for., fish., and other[6]	**14,177**	**12,546**	**12,641**	**12,078**	**12,826**	**10,828**
Agricultural services	12,061	10,664	10,826	10,379	11,060	9,648
Forestry, fisheries, and other[6]	(D)	(D)	(D)	(D)	(D)	(D)
Forestry	(D)	(D)	(D)	(D)	(D)	(D)
Fisheries	524	472	310	66	165	68
Mining	**59,552**	**52,999**	**56,314**	**60,583**	**54,521**	**61,827**
Coal mining	(D)	(D)	(D)	(D)	(D)	(D)
Oil and gas extraction	4,213	2,587	9,341	6,595	6,417	8,152
Metal mining	(D)	(D)	(D)	(D)	(D)	(D)
Nonmetallic minerals, except fuels	12,954	(D)	(D)	(D)	(D)	(D)
Construction	**433,096**	**373,077**	**327,379**	**319,457**	**275,045**	**258,434**
General building contractors	170,080	139,158	116,417	114,197	(D)	75,929

TABLE 2.11--PERSONAL INCOME BY MAJOR SOURCE, KNOXVILLE METROPOLITAN STATISTICAL AREA, 1982–1987 [In thousands of dollars] (Continued)

Source	1987	1986	1985	1984	1983	1982
Heavy construction contractors	(D)	39,424	35,953	37,408	(D)	(D)
Special trade contractors	191,389	194,495	175,009	167,852	144,733	144,945
Manufacturing	**1,267,640**	**1,277,371**	**1,233,479**	**1,200,643**	**1,063,093**	**969,060**
Nondurable goods	409,008	387,035	362,967	376,031	595,592	543,566
Food and kindred products	(D)	(D)	(D)	(D)	(D)	(D)
Textile mill products	(D)	(D)	(D)	(D)	(D)	(D)
Apparel and other textile products	(D)	(D)	(D)	(D)	(D)	(D)
Paper and allied products	(D)	(D)	(D)	(D)	(D)	(D)
Printing and publishing	68,700	61,667	56,500	48,458	41,963	40,140
Chemicals and allied products	(D)	(D)	(D)	(D)	(D)	(D)
Petroleum and coal products	530	564	2,366	1,640	1,273	1,011
Rubber and misc. plastics products	(D)	(D)	(D)	(D)	(D)	(D)
Leather and leather products	(D)	(D)	(D)	6,513	7,413	6,741
Durable goods	858,632	874,426	848,092	806,508	451,846	411,034
Lumber and wood products	49,381	38,287	32,339	29,957	27,261	22,038
Furniture and fixtures	34,598	29,468	28,242	(D)	(D)	(D)
Primary metal industries	142,623	(D)	164,803	196,309	(D)	(D)
Fabricated metal products	(D)	(D)	(D)	(D)	(D)	(D)
Machinery, except electrical	72,518	73,038	73,869	73,544	60,636	55,719
Electric and electronic equipment	59,050	62,308	70,761	(D)	(D)	(D)
Trans. equip. excl. motor vehicles	36,462	27,425	23,712	16,169	(D)	(D)
Motor vehicles and equipment	(D)	(D)	(D)	(D)	(D)	(D)
Stone, clay, and glass products	(D)	(D)	(D)	(D)	(D)	(D)
Instruments and related products	(D)	(D)	(D)	(D)	(D)	(D)
Misc. manufacturing industries	20,871	21,089	19,612	17,813	16,051	18,286
Transportation and public utilities	**325,986**	**283,602**	**264,197**	**261,240**	**244,534**	**238,259**
Railroad transportation	41,822	43,720	45,024	46,424	42,321	38,769
Trucking and warehousing	144,823	110,687	99,491	98,828	81,442	78,415
Water transportation	(D)	(D)	(D)	(D)	(D)	(D)
Other transportation	31,771	30,642	28,966	29,048	(D)	(D)
Local & interurban passenger transit	14,750	14,304	13,990	15,909	14,563	16,352
Transportation by air	12,057	11,643	11,288	10,347	10,257	9,969
Transportation services	6,201	5,888	4,484	3,926	3,165	3,195
Communication	(D)	81,005	(D)	67,221	83,379	82,783
Electric, gas, and sanitary services	(D)	(D)	(D)	(D)	(D)	(D)
Wholesale trade	**406,595**	**369,324**	**339,458**	**297,040**	**279,032**	**277,728**
Retail trade	**655,778**	**605,480**	**554,685**	**529,646**	**491,017**	**477,192**
Building materials and garden equipment	40,368	36,112	36,750	38,351	28,161	31,184
General merchandise stores	83,449	80,345	75,457	69,390	61,684	60,155

TABLE 2.11--PERSONAL INCOME BY MAJOR SOURCE, KNOXVILLE METROPOLITAN STATISTICAL AREA, 1982–1987 [In thousands of dollars] (Continued)

Source	1987	1986	1985	1984	1983	1982
Food stores	73,013	70,717	67,296	68,980	63,239	63,396
Automotive dealers & service stations	128,590	112,641	102,490	94,333	83,247	71,895
Apparel and accessory stores	25,422	23,736	23,434	25,663	23,932	22,137
Furniture and home furnishings stores	34,827	32,880	31,320	28,515	30,425	25,388
Eating and drinking places	151,796	147,116	131,112	119,971	115,960	124,873
Miscellaneous retail stores	105,814	96,201	81,062	84,443	83,934	77,408
Finance, insurance, and real estate	**232,230**	**205,892**	**184,311**	**173,991**	**170,182**	**154,301**
Banking and credit agencies	90,523	(D)	(D)	(D)	(D)	63,614
Other finance, insur., & real estate	137,130	(D)	(D)	97,997	92,038	79,527
Security & commodity brokers & serv.	18,684	21,581	19,365	16,988	17,633	12,386
Insurance carriers	32,494	30,857	29,404	28,531	27,117	25,132
Insurance agents, brokers, & services	47,066	38,019	31,583	28,823	24,549	23,273
Real estate	18,794	13,704	16,758	17,877	16,733	14,822
Combined real estate, insurance, etc.	610	584	616	270	361	324
Holding & other investment companies	20,919	15,386	8,924	11,570	10,334	7,308
Services	**1,394,140**	**1,208,634**	**1,061,667**	**966,044**	**875,314**	**816,450**
Hotels and other lodging places	61,859	56,915	52,150	53,329	50,498	59,388
Personal services	72,045	64,192	59,016	46,251	43,931	39,236
Private households	16,191	15,988	15,972	15,851	14,216	13,666
Business services	216,050	182,357	162,464	140,658	123,494	113,350
Auto repair, services, and garages	59,951	52,690	47,394	39,448	32,755	29,140
Miscellaneous repair services	23,953	23,361	20,261	19,227	16,715	14,195
Amusement and recreation services	31,977	26,095	19,569	17,485	16,669	31,664
Motion pictures	(D)	(D)	(D)	(D)	(D)	(D)
Health services	552,041	472,656	428,918	402,670	368,685	332,113
Legal services	96,386	84,993	69,992	62,707	49,853	44,861
Educational services	(D)	(D)	(D)	(D)	(D)	(D)
Social services	13,545	14,085	13,177	12,264	10,894	9,993
Museums, botanical, zoological gardens	(D)	(D)	(D)	(D)	(D)	(D)
Membership organizations	39,679	37,460	36,238	35,141	33,246	32,822
Miscellaneous services	(D)	148,868	111,142	97,434	93,181	76,654
Government and government enterprises	**1,043,379**	**946,604**	**885,093**	**824,567**	**795,504**	**757,522**
Federal, civilian	327,930	307,810	296,590	306,842	300,364	286,957
Military	18,294	16,783	15,935	14,571	13,324	12,225
State and local	697,155	622,011	572,568	503,154	481,816	458,340

See Table 2.4 for notes.

Source: U.S. Department of Commerce, Bureau of Economic Analysis, Regional Economics Information System, direct subscription.

TABLE 2.12--PERSONAL INCOME BY MAJOR SOURCE, MEMPHIS METROPOLITAN STATISTICAL AREA, 1982–1987 [In thousands of dollars]

Source	1987	1986	1985	1984	1983	1982
INCOME BY PLACE OF RESIDENCE						
Total personal income	13,870,288	12,754,237	11,909,606	11,193,265	10,224,793	9,523,454
Nonfarm personal income	13,824,089	12,731,743	11,880,837	11,152,349	10,212,081	9,478,984
Farm income[1]	46,199	22,494	28,769	40,916	12,712	44,470
Population (thousands)[2]	971.9	960.0	950.2	937.8	932.4	927.5
Per capita personal income (dollars)	14,271	13,285	12,534	11,935	10,966	10,268
Derivation of total personal income						
Earnings by place of work	11,189,908	10,226,918	9,534,950	8,906,124	8,068,650	7,516,766
Less: personal contributions for social insurance[3]	688,566	634,984	583,569	518,632	473,459	468,835
Plus: adjustment for residence	-387,796	-335,948	-308,810	-268,361	-239,296	-208,832
Equals: net earn. by place of residence	10,113,546	9,255,986	8,642,571	8,119,131	7,355,895	6,839,099
Plus: dividends, interest, and rent[4]	1,712,196	1,595,293	1,515,925	1,418,480	1,269,998	1,210,535
Plus: transfer payments	2,044,546	1,902,958	1,751,110	1,655,654	1,598,900	1,473,820
EARNINGS BY PLACE OF WORK						
Components of earnings						
Wages and salaries	9,276,094	8,485,378	7,960,392	7,423,855	6,744,436	6,298,567
Other labor income	833,407	766,583	710,731	688,390	646,201	597,496
Proprietors' income[5]	1,080,407	974,957	863,827	793,879	678,013	620,703
Farm	31,492	8,589	14,797	26,786	-1,674	29,517
Nonfarm	1,048,915	966,368	849,030	767,093	679,687	591,186
Earnings by industry						
Farm	46,199	22,494	28,769	40,916	12,712	44,470
Nonfarm	11,143,709	10,204,424	9,506,181	8,865,208	8,055,938	7,472,296
Private	9,313,163	8,508,301	7,876,878	7,326,210	6,622,947	6,134,163
Ag. serv., for., fish., and other[6]	**33,047**	**27,387**	**26,736**	**23,940**	**23,475**	**18,879**
Agricultural services	32,139	26,629	24,958	22,205	21,589	17,941
Forestry, fisheries, and other[6]	908	799	(D)	(D)	807	(D)
Forestry	142	121	(D)	(D)	615	(D)
Fisheries	766	678	440	66	204	74
Mining	**11,576**	**(D)**	**19,968**	**16,655**	**15,818**	**18,155**
Coal mining	1,658	1,625	1,574	2,234	2,115	1,871
Oil and gas extraction	6,907	4,544	15,620	11,556	11,088	14,029
Metal mining	(a)	(a)	(a)	(a)	(a)	-109
Nonmetallic minerals, except fuels	(D)	(D)	(D)	(D)	(D)	(D)
Construction	**688,404**	**629,378**	**564,155**	**508,861**	**435,975**	**391,190**
General building contractors	205,367	193,273	163,157	144,784	124,258	108,119
Heavy construction contractors	76,046	59,517	56,659	60,592	51,786	44,714
Special trade contractors	406,991	376,588	344,339	303,485	259,931	238,357

TABLE 2.12--PERSONAL INCOME BY MAJOR SOURCE, MEMPHIS METROPOLITAN STATISTICAL AREA, 1982–1987 [In thousands of dollars] (Continued)

Source	1987	1986	1985	1984	1983	1982
Manufacturing	**1,574,063**	**1,487,812**	**1,443,955**	**1,403,023**	**1,303,159**	**1,288,842**
Nondurable goods	919,817	865,369	827,324	788,663	768,032	768,183
Food and kindred products	234,255	221,088	222,863	212,341	205,689	212,877
Textile mill products	(D)	(D)	(D)	(D)	(D)	(D)
Apparel and other textile products	(D)	(D)	(D)	(D)	(D)	(D)
Paper and allied products	187,697	184,721	174,077	163,385	152,657	142,930
Printing and publishing	(D)	(D)	(D)	(D)	(D)	(D)
Chemicals and allied products	236,500	219,422	209,936	199,185	178,981	170,556
Petroleum and coal products	19,642	19,200	15,150	18,241	21,656	15,365
Tobacco manufactures	(D)	13,033	18,488	16,152	15,285	15,611
Rubber and misc. plastics products	31,854	31,859	(D)	(D)	42,121	77,703
Leather and leather products	(D)	(D)	(D)	(D)	(D)	(D)
Durable goods	654,246	622,443	616,631	614,360	535,127	520,659
Lumber and wood products	60,257	54,925	51,240	47,559	45,033	40,721
Furniture and fixtures	(D)	(D)	(D)	(D)	(D)	(D)
Primary metal industries	20,493	18,667	19,811	(D)	(D)	(D)
Fabricated metal products	122,574	114,522	111,821	104,301	103,982	113,301
Machinery, except electrical	140,906	136,416	144,452	(D)	(D)	(D)
Electric and electronic equipment	85,614	75,279	(D)	(D)	(D)	(D)
Trans. equip. excl. motor vehicles	(D)	(D)	6,401	(D)	(D)	5,321
Motor vehicles and equipment	55,695	57,642	57,721	(D)	42,283	36,774
Stone, clay, and glass products	(D)	(D)	(D)	27,268	23,737	(D)
Instruments and related products	47,681	42,349	34,347	29,144	26,378	24,160
Misc. manufacturing industries	22,853	20,164	19,151	27,943	23,057	19,560
Transportation and public utilities	**1,267,852**	**1,130,217**	**1,026,372**	**918,266**	**811,068**	**750,119**
Railroad transportation	58,309	(D)	(D)	(D)	72,374	74,382
Trucking and warehousing	336,680	306,775	311,170	299,579	267,396	267,294
Water transportation	10,804	8,780	9,577	10,399	9,872	(D)
Other transportation	699,889	(D)	(D)	(D)	325,944	265,197
Local & interurban passenger transit	30,199	31,139	26,921	26,929	25,769	28,070
Transportation by air	621,981	(D)	(D)	(D)	273,705	212,758
Pipelines, except natural gas	1,616	1,611	1,596	1,487	1,520	1,446
Transportation services	47,110	39,865	35,294	29,481	26,251	24,311
Communication	137,671	121,835	118,518	106,988	114,709	112,125
Electric, gas, and sanitary services	21,789	18,611	16,645	14,238	12,661	11,800
Wholesale trade	**1,155,955**	**1,059,808**	**1,001,781**	**928,784**	**832,685**	**807,633**
Retail trade	**1,225,071**	**1,117,006**	**1,043,854**	**978,535**	**915,300**	**817,810**
Building materials and garden equipment	58,054	49,224	45,023	41,235	34,275	35,000
General merchandise stores	141,265	133,474	128,494	120,307	118,574	108,005

TABLE 2.12--PERSONAL INCOME BY MAJOR SOURCE, MEMPHIS METROPOLITAN STATISTICAL AREA, 1982–1987 [In thousands of dollars] (Continued)

Source	1987	1986	1985	1984	1983	1982
Food stores	160,016	155,880	157,275	153,379	154,080	144,459
Automotive dealers & service stations	246,063	213,102	200,394	173,829	153,267	132,727
Apparel and accessory stores	70,703	63,693	61,123	62,573	54,792	50,017
Furniture and home furnishings stores	75,082	65,211	60,747	53,964	54,488	45,107
Eating and drinking places	266,920	240,079	214,845	199,002	187,474	156,591
Miscellaneous retail stores	202,628	196,343	175,953	167,951	158,350	145,904
Finance, insurance, and real estate	**770,101**	**722,993**	**619,295**	**575,196**	**508,540**	**410,710**
Banking and credit agencies	292,778	281,740	234,269	226,298	186,530	152,509
Other finance, insur., & real estate	470,847	430,292	371,630	343,797	319,569	255,443
Security & commodity brokers & serv.	163,919	152,303	119,263	102,080	101,786	63,330
Insurance carriers	97,857	91,092	85,073	80,449	77,595	75,282
Insurance agents, brokers, & services	96,572	89,437	76,420	71,557	59,106	54,158
Real estate	75,436	66,290	57,271	54,184	46,968	33,983
Combined real estate, insurance, etc.	1,183	1,033	2,057	1,071	1,082	1,156
Holding & other investment companies	41,197	36,060	39,924	38,334	34,077	28,481
Services	**2,576,189**	**2,314,383**	**2,121,680**	**1,964,829**	**1,769,258**	**1,624,760**
Hotels and other lodging places	175,158	154,902	149,746	146,000	130,991	126,299
Personal services	133,185	121,003	104,543	89,957	82,150	71,980
Private households	66,541	64,520	64,511	65,216	58,441	56,162
Business services	458,604	406,223	370,668	338,290	293,468	254,622
Auto repair, services, and garages	107,831	100,207	92,440	83,082	70,807	62,195
Miscellaneous repair services	46,897	43,882	37,058	39,935	30,947	27,328
Amusement and recreation services	(D)	(D)	38,007	34,532	27,566	25,351
Motion pictures	(D)	(D)	(D)	(D)	(D)	(D)
Health services	997,047	881,392	827,804	769,097	716,002	658,101
Legal services	154,686	135,019	117,459	109,429	91,552	82,411
Educational services	66,780	62,308	58,937	51,329	45,393	44,145
Social services	36,760	38,735	37,070	30,561	25,645	24,086
Museums, botanical, zoological gardens	(D)	(D)	(D)	(D)	(D)	(D)
Membership organizations	72,716	68,682	66,199	62,449	60,688	58,801
Miscellaneous services	206,023	184,433	143,457	129,836	117,183	116,719
Government and government enterprises	**1,830,546**	**1,696,123**	**1,629,303**	**1,538,998**	**1,432,991**	**1,338,133**
Federal, civilian	498,333	463,497	468,454	427,608	422,313	384,290
Military	210,370	200,893	209,368	209,238	200,790	197,203
State and local	1,121,843	1,031,733	951,481	902,152	809,888	756,640

See Table 2.4 for notes.

Source: U.S. Department of Commerce, Bureau of Economic Analysis, Regional Economics Information System, direct subscription.

TABLE 2.13--PERSONAL INCOME BY MAJOR SOURCE, NASHVILLE-DAVIDSON METROPOLITAN STATISTICAL AREA, 1982–1987 [In thousands of dollars]

Source	1987	1986	1985	1984	1983	1982
INCOME BY PLACE OF RESIDENCE						
Total personal income	14,583,856	13,334,536	12,187,266	11,092,052	9,951,790	9,212,403
Nonfarm personal income	14,511,948	13,282,899	12,116,981	10,989,639	9,916,890	9,121,073
Farm income[1]	71,908	51,637	70,285	102,413	34,900	91,330
Population (thousands)[2]	956.2	931.0	911.0	895.1	878.9	867.4
Per capita personal income (dollars)	15,253	14,322	13,378	12,392	11,323	10,621
Derivation of total personal income						
Earnings by place of work	11,934,758	10,857,799	9,873,842	8,923,253	7,909,056	7,266,352
Less: personal contributions for social insurance[3]	744,395	682,505	609,907	522,429	466,694	456,098
Plus: adjustment for residence	-260,687	-248,741	-227,624	-204,368	-148,478	-125,845
Equals: net earn. by place of residence	10,929,676	9,926,553	9,036,311	8,196,456	7,293,884	6,684,409
Plus: dividends, interest, and rent[4]	1,966,830	1,827,003	1,680,254	1,538,301	1,344,712	1,295,492
Plus: transfer payments	1,687,350	1,580,980	1,470,701	1,357,295	1,313,194	1,232,502
EARNINGS BY PLACE OF WORK						
Components of earnings						
Wages and salaries	9,750,620	8,873,335	8,086,997	7,266,774	6,488,880	5,955,933
Other labor income	893,616	820,124	750,712	707,390	656,679	598,569
Proprietors' income[5]	1,290,522	1,164,340	1,036,133	949,089	763,497	711,850
Farm	58,591	39,039	57,709	89,738	21,977	77,887
Nonfarm	1,231,931	1,125,301	978,424	859,351	741,520	633,963
Earnings by industry						
Farm	71,908	51,637	70,285	102,413	34,900	91,330
Nonfarm	11,862,850	10,806,162	9,803,557	8,820,840	7,874,156	7,175,022
Private	10,470,789	9,524,214	8,607,741	7,742,273	6,848,763	6,200,212
Ag. serv., for., fish., and other[6]	**36,133**	**33,015**	**32,216**	**30,201**	**28,609**	**23,079**
Agricultural services	34,527	31,557	31,063	27,203	25,499	21,290
Forestry, fisheries, and other[6]	1,686	1,458	1,153	781	1,097	118
Forestry	149	120	207	565	616	-80
Fisheries	1,537	1,338	946	217	484	199
Mining	**23,063**	**21,648**	**40,674**	**30,498**	**32,638**	**30,577**
Coal mining	1,392	1,354	1,366	1,371	(D)	(D)
Oil and gas extraction	8,643	(D)	(D)	(D)	(D)	(D)
Metal mining	(D)	114	-383	-746	(D)	(D)
Nonmetallic minerals, except fuels	(D)	(D)	(D)	(D)	(D)	(D)
Construction	**952,713**	**888,964**	**753,353**	**655,437**	**536,964**	**511,130**
General building contractors	292,395	276,506	221,846	204,140	160,945	158,496
Heavy construction contractors	133,320	113,443	101,033	92,620	81,122	79,323
Special trade contractors	526,998	499,015	430,474	358,677	294,897	273,311

TABLE 2.13--PERSONAL INCOME BY MAJOR SOURCE, NASHVILLE-DAVIDSON METROPOLITAN STATISTICAL AREA, 1982–1987 [In thousands of dollars]
(Continued)

Source	1987	1986	1985	1984	1983	1982
Manufacturing	**2,416,367**	**2,262,418**	**2,146,186**	**1,977,466**	**1,752,024**	**1,570,458**
Nondurable goods	908,244	837,139	811,619	809,445	756,866	693,915
Food and kindred products	191,131	188,997	174,513	169,007	168,424	160,679
Textile mill products	(D)	27,715	(D)	(D)	(D)	(D)
Apparel and other textile products	(D)	(D)	(D)	(D)	(D)	(D)
Paper and allied products	(D)	(D)	(D)	(D)	(D)	(D)
Printing and publishing	240,446	(D)	(D)	(D)	(D)	(D)
Chemicals and allied products	(D)	(D)	105,041	107,102	110,433	107,464
Petroleum and coal products	2,562	1,349	1,216	(D)	(D)	(D)
Tobacco manufactures	(D)	2,388	(D)	(D)	(D)	(D)
Rubber and misc. plastics products	(D)	(D)	(D)	(D)	(D)	(D)
Leather and leather products	(D)	(D)	(D)	(D)	(D)	(D)
Durable goods	1,468,503	1,386,350	1,294,852	1,128,027	957,954	840,206
Lumber and wood products	(D)	(D)	(D)	(D)	(D)	(D)
Furniture and fixtures	(D)	(D)	(D)	(D)	(D)	(D)
Primary metal industries	32,047	(D)	23,694	29,219	(D)	(D)
Fabricated metal products	167,825	165,487	147,855	144,094	124,199	116,207
Machinery, except electrical	153,506	143,827	149,013	102,561	89,035	90,281
Electric and electronic equipment	(D)	(D)	(D)	(D)	(D)	(D)
Trans. equip. excl. motor vehicles	(D)	(D)	(D)	(D)	(D)	(D)
Motor vehicles and equipment	(D)	(D)	(D)	(D)	(D)	(D)
Stone, clay, and glass products	153,398	145,858	133,582	120,305	99,893	86,825
Instruments and related products	(D)	(D)	(D)	(D)	(D)	(D)
Misc. manufacturing industries	(D)	(D)	(D)	(D)	(D)	(D)
Transportation and public utilities	**864,805**	**786,032**	**740,880**	**703,355**	**631,976**	**600,687**
Railroad transportation	43,027	48,597	52,482	57,009	55,208	48,457
Trucking and warehousing	402,044	365,889	338,880	320,430	282,720	268,790
Water transportation	(D)	(D)	(D)	8,904	7,620	8,748
Other transportation	(D)	(D)	(D)	(D)	(D)	(D)
Local & interurban passenger transit	(D)	(D)	(D)	19,767	18,186	18,508
Transportation by air	(D)	(D)	(D)	(D)	(D)	(D)
Transportation services	21,050	17,921	15,091	12,120	10,009	9,064
Communication	250,096	224,083	223,310	207,560	196,765	189,953
Electric, gas, and sanitary services	55,555	49,809	(D)	(D)	(D)	(D)
Wholesale trade	**885,697**	**801,437**	**731,008**	**665,173**	**593,806**	**545,030**
Retail trade	**1,332,137**	**1,218,045**	**1,124,548**	**1,011,041**	**910,486**	**808,563**
Building materials and garden equipment	63,512	(D)	(D)	46,443	36,957	33,498
General merchandise stores	172,617	167,686	153,016	149,386	138,819	126,806

TABLE 2.13--PERSONAL INCOME BY MAJOR SOURCE, NASHVILLE-DAVIDSON METROPOLITAN STATISTICAL AREA, 1982–1987 [In thousands of dollars]
(Continued)

Source	1987	1986	1985	1984	1983	1982
Food stores	247,033	230,830	214,630	205,627	192,554	174,005
Automotive dealers & service stations	231,971	210,161	207,845	185,739	166,209	144,100
Apparel and accessory stores	83,667	77,694	77,524	44,161	39,626	36,028
Furniture and home furnishings stores	81,817	68,917	60,350	52,354	51,635	37,854
Eating and drinking places	262,317	235,556	215,680	189,432	168,538	144,843
Miscellaneous retail stores	176,698	156,490	131,684	132,731	114,044	109,386
Finance, insurance, and real estate	**898,110**	**781,843**	**680,453**	**597,866**	**536,227**	**490,567**
Banking and credit agencies	246,324	202,653	(D)	(D)	(D)	(D)
Other finance, insur., & real estate	642,026	572,566	(D)	(D)	(D)	(D)
Security & commodity brokers & serv.	63,914	61,981	42,997	35,302	37,827	25,564
Insurance carriers	241,401	211,785	194,140	171,800	171,433	157,704
Insurance agents, brokers, & services	139,097	119,833	98,791	87,130	72,707	73,431
Real estate	97,711	87,315	77,027	63,289	47,255	37,437
Combined real estate, insurance, etc.	(D)	(D)	(D)	(D)	(D)	(D)
Holding & other investment companies	102,506	93,937	54,918	48,120	41,750	51,718
Services	**3,058,901**	**2,730,812**	**2,358,423**	**2,071,236**	**1,826,033**	**1,620,121**
Hotels and other lodging places	108,904	97,892	91,293	76,251	50,582	49,910
Personal services	148,789	138,223	122,341	97,895	90,782	81,732
Private households	47,985	46,454	46,433	47,003	42,103	40,478
Business services	548,341	498,055	396,218	320,712	259,217	223,881
Auto repair, services, and garages	116,729	106,073	96,610	81,880	71,171	62,097
Miscellaneous repair services	47,230	42,876	35,506	35,531	30,405	21,533
Amusement and recreation services	125,973	114,751	94,601	82,026	88,339	75,719
Motion pictures	(D)	10,935	11,940	12,114	10,520	8,573
Health services	1,129,547	968,705	863,893	768,873	711,928	626,258
Legal services	164,018	144,871	124,194	116,223	95,245	83,352
Educational services	193,934	179,449	167,967	153,161	132,712	120,031
Social services	45,146	40,729	35,203	32,050	27,988	26,126
Museums, botanical, zoological gardens	2,429	2,128	1,782	1,177	1,129	761
Membership organizations	83,147	77,707	70,481	67,992	63,912	62,141
Miscellaneous services	283,900	258,935	197,327	176,627	147,604	135,833
Government and government enterprises	**1,392,061**	**1,281,948**	**1,195,816**	**1,078,567**	**1,025,393**	**974,810**
Federal, civilian	311,903	292,983	287,085	258,567	253,115	245,874
Military	38,681	35,629	32,946	30,276	26,131	23,165
State and local	1,041,477	953,336	875,785	789,724	746,147	705,771

See Table 2.4 for notes.

Source: U.S. Department of Commerce, Bureau of Economic Analysis, Regional Economics Information System, direct subscription.

TABLE 2.14--POVERTY STATUS OF FAMILIES, METROPOLITAN STATISTICAL AREAS, TENNESSEE, 1979

Type of family	Chattanooga	Clarksville-Hopkinsville	Johnson City-Kingsport-Bristol
TOTAL FAMILIES	117,460	37,837	123,177
Families with incomes less than poverty level[1]	12,670	4,990	15,092
Percentage of all families	11	13	12
Female heads of household[2]	5,367	1,880	4,366
Percentage of poverty families	42	38	29
Percentage with children under age 18	85	92	76
Percentage with children under age 6	44	50	32
Heads of household aged 65 years and over	1,956	743	3,315
Percentage of poverty families	15	15	22

	Knoxville	Memphis	Nashville-Davidson
TOTAL FAMILIES	130,431	232,789	228,417
Families with incomes less than poverty level[1]	14,453	36,310	20,436
Percentage of all families	11	16	9
Female heads of household[2]	5,527	20,072	9,093
Percentage of poverty families	38	55	45
Percentage with children under age 18	85	90	87
Percentage with children under age 6	40	49	45
Heads of household aged 65 years and over	2,270	5,080	3,699
Percentage of poverty families	16	14	18

1. Classification of families by poverty status varies according to family size and place of residence. For example, in 1979, the national poverty threshold for a family of four was $7,412. See Table 2.17 for detail on poverty thresholds for 1988.

2. No husband present.

Source: U.S. Department of Commerce, Bureau of the Census, *1980 Census of Population, General Social and Economic Characteristics, Tennessee.*

TABLE 2.15--TOTAL PERSONAL INCOME, RESIDENCE ADJUSTED, COUNTIES, 1970–1987, SELECTED YEARS [In millions of dollars]

County	1987	1986[r]	1985[r]	1984	1983	1982	1980	1975	1970
Anderson	914.7	844.2	801.7	769.2	719.5	672.4	586.1	346.8	203.2
Bedford	365.3	332.9	308.9	294.1	258.0	244.2	213.5	118.7	79.7
Benton	155.4	146.1	141.3	134.2	119.8	117.7	106.7	58.1	32.2
Bledsoe	84.2	77.1	72.3	69.2	60.8	56.1	50.9	29.5	16.4
Blount	1,074.6	988.9	928.5	881.5	802.8	757.3	638.9	325.6	197.5
Bradley	886.8	812.4	763.1	708.9	650.1	588.1	499.7	263.9	159.5
Campbell	313.5	295.6	283.5	276.2	255.5	246.8	218.0	117.8	55.1
Cannon	117.6	108.7	101.2	96.2	84.2	81.7	67.3	38.3	21.1
Carroll	291.2	269.0	257.6	255.6	235.4	219.5	190.1	109.7	71.7
Carter	488.3	460.1	430.2	411.1	384.8	363.8	313.0	170.1	110.1
Cheatham	300.8	273.0	247.6	216.9	204.8	175.8	162.9	78.6	39.8
Chester	131.6	119.5	111.0	105.5	91.0	83.5	74.3	42.7	24.0
Claiborne	264.2	240.6	231.7	222.2	198.3	189.1	159.5	81.0	39.4
Clay	66.8	60.8	57.0	53.2	48.4	45.6	39.5	21.4	13.4
Cocke	247.5	227.2	215.1	211.8	196.5	192.4	168.2	101.4	56.3
Coffee	531.0	491.8	452.2	423.0	384.7	367.9	310.6	175.9	106.6
Crockett	150.0	133.3	126.5	119.3	100.2	104.0	89.1	57.8	40.6
Cumberland	348.2	315.9	288.7	269.8	238.1	217.6	184.0	92.6	47.3
Davidson	8,227.8	7,583.1	6,993.4	6,464.3	5,827.8	5,488.7	4,560.0	2,741.2	1,759.2
Decatur	100.9	94.3	91.6	90.5	81.5	78.3	68.4	38.7	23.4
DeKalb	160.8	141.6	130.3	130.6	110.4	103.7	93.2	49.1	28.0
Dickson	416.1	380.6	348.3	315.6	285.7	264.3	229.5	118.7	63.4
Dyer	400.6	363.7	352.4	336.0	297.2	278.3	250.2	150.3	88.4
Fayette	278.7	250.0	224.2	207.4	177.3	169.0	153.8	87.2	43.8
Fentress	114.3	106.2	102.7	98.5	87.9	81.1	71.5	39.9	23.0
Franklin	348.3	323.7	305.9	290.7	263.0	248.9	211.8	121.2	72.8
Gibson	553.3	502.1	488.7	474.9	419.8	389.6	344.4	219.6	144.4
Giles	287.0	265.4	255.9	261.9	230.3	216.5	188.3	101.2	62.1
Grainger	138.9	128.4	121.1	116.6	104.6	100.9	86.3	45.6	28.0
Greene	599.1	561.2	525.0	495.1	446.6	428.3	355.8	192.5	120.0
Grundy	122.2	113.2	106.8	105.4	94.2	93.0	81.1	43.5	22.9
Hamblen	547.6	507.7	477.4	451.4	415.8	393.2	333.1	196.5	115.4
Hamilton	4,254.8	3,891.8	3,631.9	3,397.3	3,159.3	3,012.6	2,598.8	1,574.8	960.9
Hancock	47.4	44.0	41.1	39.7	36.1	35.4	31.5	18.0	12.4
Hardeman	222.7	200.5	188.8	175.6	158.7	152.6	137.6	77.4	44.0
Hardin	222.7	204.5	191.3	180.6	164.2	159.8	144.1	73.9	40.2
Hawkins	427.6	400.8	376.8	358.8	331.4	314.4	263.6	151.1	81.9
Haywood	211.7	186.8	172.0	157.7	141.4	136.5	124.6	72.9	43.4
Henderson	225.5	208.3	198.1	188.7	164.8	155.1	136.6	77.9	45.8
Henry	306.9	291.4	287.7	294.4	256.9	242.7	218.1	117.3	62.1
Hickman	172.8	159.0	147.5	135.7	120.5	113.7	98.5	53.5	30.8
Houston	72.5	66.6	62.7	58.1	52.4	50.5	44.7	21.1	15.1
Humphreys	173.0	161.6	152.8	149.1	135.1	134.8	123.9	63.6	37.6
Jackson	77.0	71.4	68.5	65.5	57.8	57.2	47.4	25.1	15.6
Jefferson	336.5	311.0	293.0	279.3	256.3	239.4	205.0	104.7	60.1
Johnson	109.5	103.3	101.4	95.6	92.7	86.4	77.3	44.8	24.4
Knox	4,707.7	4,337.3	4,045.7	3,807.7	3,493.5	3,307.2	2,788.6	1,562.5	923.2
Lake	60.1	55.4	53.3	53.8	51.1	49.5	45.1	30.7	17.7
Lauderdale	244.9	219.3	209.0	199.6	177.4	162.6	143.9	83.2	45.9
Lawrence	381.6	347.1	338.2	332.2	290.5	270.6	252.4	136.1	71.7
Lewis	77.9	72.5	71.8	65.2	57.3	55.0	48.6	28.0	15.8
Lincoln	308.5	284.4	269.6	249.1	217.7	207.1	190.7	105.3	64.1
Loudon	337.6	311.4	293.0	284.5	256.6	247.5	218.8	117.2	66.9

TABLE 2.15--TOTAL PERSONAL INCOME, RESIDENCE ADJUSTED, COUNTIES, 1970–1987, SELECTED YEARS [In millions of dollars] (Continued)

County	1987	1986[r]	1985[r]	1984	1983	1982	1980	1975	1970
McMinn	468.3	441.1	416.5	393.9	363.4	338.4	292.6	162.6	97.2
McNairy	231.3	211.6	199.5	184.4	168.4	157.5	137.6	78.0	41.3
Macon	156.0	142.8	132.6	133.4	115.3	115.1	96.7	55.1	32.5
Madison	948.7	877.3	821.4	774.8	700.7	650.9	566.8	345.8	193.9
Marion	243.9	233.8	221.0	208.0	188.3	185.9	165.3	94.6	49.8
Marshall	256.2	236.1	223.4	222.1	187.2	168.7	149.4	82.0	51.7
Maury	647.6	606.4	554.0	529.7	471.3	456.2	395.3	232.6	137.9
Meigs	79.3	71.4	66.0	64.1	60.2	54.3	48.0	24.1	11.8
Monroe	288.2	263.0	244.9	229.5	209.1	195.4	168.3	90.1	53.9
Montgomery	1,057.2	974.2	907.9	842.6	767.4	730.9	606.9	372.4	205.6
Moore	44.7	43.2	42.1	41.7	36.7	35.7	31.3	15.5	9.4
Morgan	141.1	131.0	122.3	117.1	105.1	104.2	89.9	46.5	25.7
Obion	395.6	368.0	345.9	335.8	302.6	272.2	240.3	152.2	93.5
Overton	141.0	130.2	123.0	119.5	108.0	102.0	87.0	50.3	29.6
Perry	64.6	61.3	57.5	56.6	48.8	45.0	38.7	20.7	11.9
Pickett	31.4	29.1	28.3	26.9	25.0	23.7	20.7	12.5	8.6
Polk	138.9	132.8	123.9	117.8	106.3	97.8	87.6	55.6	32.3
Putnam	599.6	543.5	500.0	464.6	418.1	389.5	325.7	166.2	89.7
Rhea	285.8	263.8	245.1	230.3	213.3	195.2	172.7	103.0	41.0
Roane	599.0	556.4	527.8	507.8	472.8	456.5	395.6	199.2	110.5
Robertson	460.5	416.3	381.4	360.0	307.7	299.7	260.4	140.1	85.2
Rutherford	1,427.9	1,285.8	1,152.3	1,014.0	898.1	813.4	674.2	322.9	159.3
Scott	164.2	157.4	147.0	139.4	125.1	119.6	104.5	55.3	28.3
Sequatchie	79.2	72.6	67.6	64.2	58.4	55.2	51.1	28.1	14.1
Sevier	531.7	487.4	449.1	428.2	390.4	369.3	303.2	146.2	76.0
Shelby	12,177.8	11,218.9	10,477.4	9,859.0	9,008.3	8,391.5	7,316.6	4,363.8	2,593.5
Smith	170.8	157.4	147.7	142.2	126.4	125.8	111.7	54.9	32.7
Stewart	95.0	87.4	82.1	76.4	68.1	63.1	53.2	29.8	22.6
Sullivan	1,842.5	1,730.8	1,625.1	1,521.1	1,440.7	1,375.1	1,175.1	698.9	443.7
Sumner	1,375.2	1,253.4	1,145.5	1,035.0	926.5	851.4	725.5	344.7	184.6
Tipton	398.7	356.9	333.2	314.6	287.7	266.9	237.3	136.5	71.7
Trousdale	63.3	57.4	54.6	53.1	45.0	47.2	45.1	24.7	14.8
Unicoi	172.7	163.9	153.5	151.4	140.1	133.0	110.3	63.4	41.1
Union	103.7	94.8	89.3	86.0	78.7	74.4	64.7	32.1	18.4
Van Buren	42.0	38.8	36.2	35.1	31.2	28.9	26.5	13.2	6.8
Warren	356.2	325.4	304.8	308.5	265.2	258.6	245.7	126.4	77.0
Washington	1,162.2	1,092.3	1,018.0	966.5	899.8	844.1	719.7	394.6	233.4
Wayne	132.3	122.6	117.0	117.4	105.6	100.0	88.2	45.2	27.5
Weakley	350.5	324.3	303.1	291.0	260.4	250.6	217.7	131.9	78.3
White	215.7	200.5	193.4	184.8	165.8	159.1	140.6	72.1	39.3
Williamson	1,458.9	1,311.7	1,168.8	1,016.0	882.2	779.0	645.9	263.4	125.4
Wilson	916.5	830.6	749.9	670.3	618.9	540.0	484.4	217.3	115.4

r revised.

Source: U.S. Department of Commerce, Bureau of Economic Analysis, Regional Economics Information System, direct subscription.

FIGURE 2.2
Per Capita Personal Income, Tennessee Counties, 1987
(Tennessee Per Capita Personal Income = $12,878)

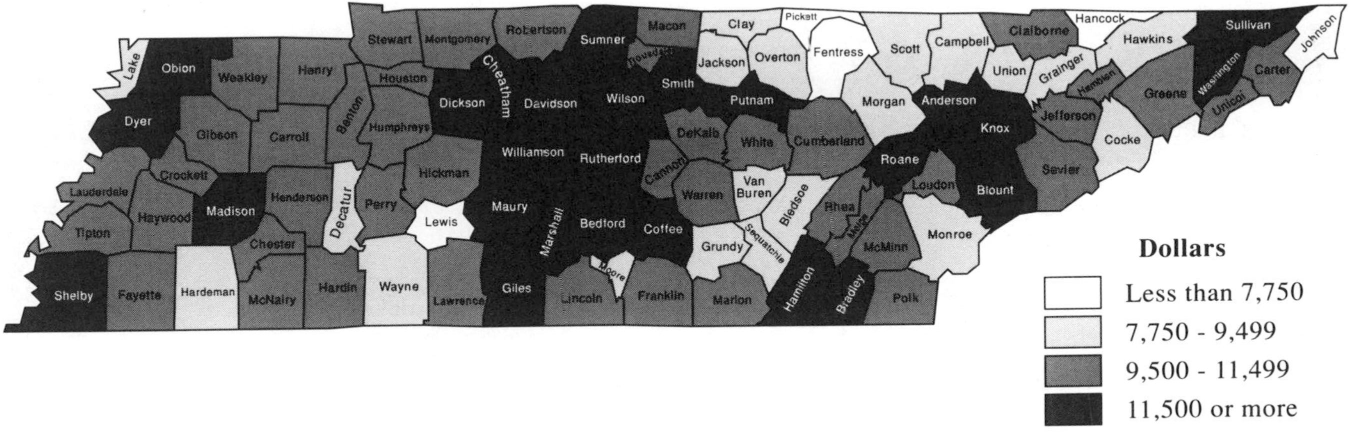

Source: U.S. Department of Commerce, Bureau of Economic Analysis.

TABLE 2.16--PER CAPITA PERSONAL INCOME, RESIDENCE ADJUSTED, COUNTIES, 1970–1987, SELECTED YEARS [In dollars]

County	1987	1986[r]	1985[r]	1984	1983	1982	1980	1975	1970
Anderson	13,105	12,209	11,634	11,111	10,462	9,844	8,684	5,612	3,357
Bedford	12,397	11,397	10,699	10,271	9,151	8,662	7,644	4,531	3,193
Benton	10,336	9,720	9,366	8,911	7,958	7,780	7,152	4,294	2,645
Bledsoe	8,759	8,060	7,521	7,283	6,537	5,992	5,376	3,345	2,155
Blount	12,819	11,954	11,372	10,894	9,961	9,542	8,197	4,728	3,095
Bradley	12,171	11,262	10,646	10,032	9,361	8,543	7,378	4,397	3,119
Campbell	8,845	8,316	7,967	7,776	7,190	6,992	6,227	3,788	2,095
Cannon	10,780	10,108	9,397	9,070	7,959	7,761	6,558	3,975	2,464
Carroll	10,386	9,611	9,126	9,017	8,401	7,795	6,720	3,977	2,780
Carter	9,508	8,977	8,375	7,941	7,508	7,115	6,216	3,565	2,536
Cheatham	11,665	11,000	10,326	9,339	9,088	8,023	7,527	4,472	2,990
Chester	10,051	9,348	8,653	8,305	7,210	6,658	5,853	3,742	2,414
Claiborne	9,947	9,159	8,636	8,407	7,637	7,405	6,465	3,824	2,008
Clay	8,569	7,737	7,221	6,717	6,152	5,938	5,140	3,148	2,012
Cocke	8,431	7,765	7,338	7,247	6,724	6,610	5,829	3,670	2,215
Coffee	12,746	11,920	11,092	10,505	9,546	9,205	8,064	4,951	3,265
Crockett	10,604	9,389	8,845	8,406	7,051	7,341	6,012	3,835	2,820
Cumberland	10,645	9,954	9,281	8,853	7,957	7,446	6,393	3,791	2,273
Davidson	16,263	15,232	14,214	13,234	12,014	11,450	9,540	5,925	3,925
Decatur	9,148	8,515	8,222	8,203	7,477	7,139	6,294	3,866	2,489
DeKalb	11,105	9,826	9,182	9,338	8,053	7,609	6,840	3,937	2,510
Dickson	12,310	11,576	10,921	10,040	9,253	8,697	7,617	4,358	2,874
Dyer	11,686	10,594	10,240	9,806	8,653	8,061	7,213	4,683	2,903
Fayette	10,610	9,650	8,747	8,230	7,163	6,834	6,071	3,521	1,947
Fentress	7,292	6,789	6,597	6,318	5,710	5,366	4,814	2,896	1,814
Franklin	10,175	9,551	9,159	8,709	7,997	7,657	6,610	4,172	2,659
Gibson	11,368	10,294	10,003	9,709	8,632	7,939	6,965	4,535	3,018
Giles	11,640	10,706	10,227	10,498	9,294	8,780	7,651	4,358	2,796
Grainger	7,974	7,393	6,983	6,767	6,103	5,925	5,144	2,916	1,991
Greene	10,604	9,921	9,299	8,810	8,043	7,806	6,519	3,770	2,517
Grundy	8,457	7,851	7,364	7,413	6,688	6,562	5,867	3,474	2,149
Hamblen	10,429	9,633	9,027	8,471	7,662	7,648	6,732	4,375	2,961
Hamilton	14,807	13,659	12,775	11,911	11,116	10,482	9,010	5,777	3,758
Hancock	7,005	6,499	5,973	5,758	5,268	5,225	4,577	2,726	1,851
Hardeman	9,154	8,318	7,887	7,444	6,759	6,504	5,776	3,338	1,968
Hardin	10,057	9,205	8,559	8,093	7,367	7,088	6,451	3,715	2,196
Hawkins	9,476	8,938	8,335	8,010	7,450	7,065	6,001	3,896	2,405
Haywood	10,165	8,902	8,290	7,685	6,894	6,697	6,129	3,628	2,208
Henderson	9,968	9,248	8,830	8,605	7,601	7,180	6,375	3,900	2,620
Henry	10,486	9,921	9,823	10,101	8,811	8,316	7,595	4,475	2,607
Hickman	10,466	9,808	9,256	8,647	7,629	7,450	6,488	3,930	2,531
Houston	10,195	9,437	8,944	8,312	7,494	7,135	6,478	3,310	2,572
Humphreys	10,811	10,073	9,606	9,395	8,522	8,302	7,750	4,243	2,736
Jackson	8,272	7,622	7,358	7,037	6,276	6,169	5,051	2,923	1,902
Jefferson	10,035	9,316	8,870	8,223	7,779	7,375	6,522	3,741	2,397
Johnson	7,742	7,298	7,216	6,762	6,563	6,178	5,611	3,488	2,096
Knox	14,292	13,293	12,283	11,544	10,602	10,043	8,695	5,215	3,326
Lake	8,072	7,394	6,783	6,600	6,385	6,382	6,027	4,011	2,202
Lauderdale	9,714	8,723	8,386	8,110	7,270	6,625	5,865	3,623	2,268
Lawrence	10,850	9,942	9,718	9,568	8,488	7,937	7,389	4,211	2,452
Lewis	7,458	6,988	6,901	6,255	5,583	5,369	4,970	3,355	2,334
Lincoln	11,329	10,516	10,009	9,344	8,304	7,915	7,209	4,014	2,620
Loudon	10,958	10,247	9,642	9,445	8,487	8,195	7,624	4,412	2,756

TABLE 2.16--PER CAPITA PERSONAL INCOME, RESIDENCE ADJUSTED, COUNTIES, 1970–1987, SELECTED YEARS [In dollars] (Continued)

County	1987	1986[r]	1985[r]	1984	1983	1982	1980	1975	1970
McMinn	10,818	10,211	9,644	9,165	8,477	7,934	6,963	4,099	2,735
McNairy	9,673	8,961	8,513	7,905	7,307	6,842	6,091	3,780	2,239
Macon	9,593	8,897	8,325	8,442	7,285	7,175	6,131	4,117	2,630
Madison	12,145	11,268	10,561	10,112	9,222	8,567	7,577	4,858	2,934
Marion	9,607	9,285	8,931	8,444	7,670	7,532	6,754	4,176	2,410
Marshall	12,152	11,353	10,824	10,909	9,526	8,528	7,572	4,432	2,983
Maury	11,894	11,235	10,402	10,135	9,147	8,835	7,719	4,914	3,140
Meigs	9,776	8,969	8,476	8,260	7,823	7,222	6,447	3,987	2,247
Monroe	9,407	8,639	8,100	7,664	7,101	6,677	5,849	3,480	2,286
Montgomery	11,247	10,539	10,107	9,681	8,702	8,233	7,251	5,119	3,267
Moore	9,401	8,891	8,455	8,600	7,848	7,820	6,931	3,891	2,621
Morgan	8,342	7,783	7,220	6,838	6,095	6,093	5,386	3,150	1,872
Obion	11,971	11,137	10,412	10,122	9,289	8,276	7,322	4,662	3,080
Overton	7,831	7,337	6,900	6,701	6,050	5,833	4,945	3,129	1,983
Perry	10,039	9,532	8,814	8,717	7,746	7,172	6,316	3,535	2,246
Pickett	6,934	6,346	6,265	5,967	5,531	5,277	4,736	2,950	2,302
Polk	10,120	9,619	9,074	8,571	7,820	7,206	6,428	4,485	2,756
Putnam	11,583	10,688	9,870	9,268	8,408	7,924	6,803	3,972	2,514
Rhea	11,293	10,555	9,926	9,278	8,644	7,999	7,118	5,000	2,373
Roane	12,086	11,245	10,615	10,201	9,558	9,309	8,156	4,703	2,837
Robertson	10,992	10,279	9,671	9,314	8,126	7,947	7,007	4,226	2,911
Rutherford	13,308	12,549	11,686	10,700	9,824	9,031	7,961	4,693	2,713
Scott	7,950	7,575	7,100	6,806	6,234	6,011	5,398	3,184	1,912
Sequatchie	8,865	8,152	7,625	7,334	6,679	6,326	5,927	3,762	2,205
Sevier	11,126	10,412	9,637	9,316	8,690	8,437	7,278	4,229	2,668
Shelby	14,869	13,839	13,037	12,406	11,393	10,657	9,391	5,879	3,583
Smith	11,627	10,731	10,163	9,732	8,625	8,572	7,478	3,948	2,580
Stewart	10,063	9,461	8,852	8,365	7,722	7,218	6,133	3,713	3,068
Sullivan	12,512	11,836	11,163	10,439	9,899	9,417	8,144	5,157	3,482
Sumner	13,812	12,964	12,201	11,286	10,383	9,594	8,417	4,646	3,253
Tipton	10,818	9,912	9,469	9,074	8,389	7,874	7,179	4,297	2,569
Trousdale	10,435	9,619	9,348	9,301	7,873	7,928	7,344	4,623	2,856
Unicoi	10,307	9,741	9,108	8,960	8,407	8,024	6,725	3,985	2,680
Union	8,454	7,784	7,316	7,071	6,445	6,182	5,504	3,135	1,988
Van Buren	8,766	8,050	7,414	7,262	6,515	6,073	5,591	3,119	1,803
Warren	10,640	9,730	9,099	9,251	7,984	7,787	7,520	4,232	2,843
Washington	12,700	11,980	10,998	10,524	9,824	9,313	8,075	4,817	3,144
Wayne	9,340	8,698	8,262	8,318	7,472	7,064	6,312	3,354	2,215
Weakley	10,669	9,903	9,119	8,765	7,839	7,647	6,609	4,228	2,701
White	10,620	9,922	9,723	9,324	8,442	8,074	7,158	3,985	2,403
Williamson	19,318	18,221	17,015	15,300	13,899	12,614	11,037	5,739	3,619
Wilson	13,812	13,011	12,004	11,087	10,601	9,401	8,610	4,649	3,097

r revised.

Source: U.S. Department of Commerce, Bureau of Economic Analysis, Regional Economics Information System, direct subscription.

TABLE 2.17--POVERTY STATUS OF FAMILIES, COUNTIES, 1979

	Anderson	Bedford	Benton	Bledsoe	Blount	Bradley	Campbell	Cannon
Total families	19,174	7,891	4,329	2,480	22,433	18,791	9,738	2,954
Families with incomes less than poverty level[1]	2,175	902	567	530	2,326	2,058	2,056	396
Percentage of all families	11.3	11.4	13.1	21.4	10.4	11.0	21.1	13.4
Female head of household	721	260	103	117	736	669	485	81
Percentage of poverty families	33.1	28.8	18.2	22.1	31.6	32.5	23.6	20.5
Percentage with children under 18 years	84.0	74.6	92.2	71.8	83.6	75.9	83.5	69.1
Percentage with children under 6 years	34.4	19.2	22.3	23.1	39.0	22.9	33.0	40.7
Householder age 65 years and over	396	229	156	109	410	309	419	94
Percentage of poverty families	18.2	25.4	27.5	20.6	17.6	15.0	20.4	23.7

	Carroll	Carter	Cheatham	Chester	Claiborne	Clay	Cocke	Coffee
Total families	8,341	14,364	6,075	3,381	6,889	2,218	8,076	10,942
Families with incomes less than poverty level[1]	1,154	2,125	555	640	1,711	520	1,887	1,231
Percentage of all families	13.8	14.8	9.1	18.9	24.8	23.4	23.4	11.3
Female head of household	285	593	139	141	307	87	488	323
Percentage of poverty families	24.7	27.9	25.0	22.0	17.9	16.7	25.9	26.2
Percentage with children under 18 years	82.5	78.4	92.8	69.5	65.5	81.6	79.5	83.9
Percentage with children under 6 years	36.1	33.2	32.4	21.3	26.4	27.6	27.9	49.2
Householder age 65 years and over	357	451	121	255	364	161	374	296
Percentage of poverty families	30.9	21.2	21.8	39.8	21.3	31.0	19.8	24.0

	Crockett	Cumber-land	Davidson	Decatur	DeKalb	Dickson	Dyer	Fayette
Total families	4,181	8,183	125,251	3,170	3,970	8,381	9,745	6,256
Families with incomes less than poverty level[1]	741	1,456	11,474	523	747	856	1,257	1,486
Percentage of all families	17.7	17.8	9.2	16.5	18.8	10.2	12.9	23.8
Female head of household	229	288	6,417	104	128	258	342	496
Percentage of poverty families	30.9	19.8	55.9	19.9	17.1	30.1	27.2	33.4
Percentage with children under 18 years	76.9	82.6	89.5	79.8	78.9	79.5	79.8	87.3
Percentage with children under 6 years	41.9	28.1	47.2	26.9	32.8	45.0	33.0	53.2
Householder age 65 years and over	236	307	1,579	225	172	251	341	408
Percentage of poverty families	31.8	21.1	13.8	43.0	23.0	29.3	27.1	27.5

TABLE 2.17--POVERTY STATUS OF FAMILIES, COUNTIES, 1979 (Continued)

	Fentress	Franklin	Gibson	Giles	Grainger	Greene	Grundy	Hamblen
Total families	4,106	8,833	14,170	7,049	4,888	15,275	3,774	14,099
Families with incomes less than poverty level[1]	1,221	1,159	2,053	944	994	2,277	801	1,827
Percentage of all families	29.7	13.1	14.5	13.4	20.3	14.9	21.2	13.0
Female head of household	188	282	720	248	190	526	177	580
Percentage of poverty families	15.4	24.3	35.1	26.3	19.1	23.1	22.1	31.7
Percentage with children under 18 years	73.9	75.2	83.1	83.5	60.5	81.6	80.8	84.8
Percentage with children under 6 years	25.5	31.6	37.5	37.9	24.7	40.7	29.9	30.0
Householder age 65 years and over	237	296	575	234	261	542	116	283
Percentage of poverty families	19.4	25.5	28.0	24.8	26.3	23.8	14.5	15.5

	Hamilton	Hancock	Hardeman	Hardin	Hawkins	Haywood	Hender-son	Henry
Total families	78,176	1,979	6,002	6,437	12,578	5,185	6,267	8,391
Families with incomes less than poverty level[1]	7,989	782	1,302	1,159	1,979	1,393	911	949
Percentage of all families	10.2	39.5	21.7	18.0	15.7	26.9	14.5	11.3
Female head of household	4,055	105	415	247	464	505	234	229
Percentage of poverty families	50.8	13.4	31.9	21.3	23.4	36.3	25.7	24.1
Percentage with children under 18 years	86.7	63.8	88.0	69.6	71.3	89.7	86.3	77.3
Percentage with children under 6 years	45.1	28.6	47.7	19.0	26.9	52.1	34.6	41.0
Householder age 65 years and over	999	200	372	425	457	299	260	327
Percentage of poverty families	12.5	25.6	28.6	36.7	23.1	21.5	28.5	34.5

	Hickman	Houston	Hum-phreys	Jackson	Jefferson	Johnson	Knox	Lake
Total families	4,184	1,937	4,585	2,692	8,820	4,011	85,435	2,012
Families with incomes less than poverty level[1]	481	293	488	604	1,192	959	9,244	479
Percentage of all families	11.5	15.1	10.6	22.4	13.5	23.9	10.8	23.8
Female head of household	97	63	160	89	307	250	3,902	159
Percentage of poverty families	20.2	21.5	32.8	14.7	25.8	26.1	42.2	33.2
Percentage with children under 18 years	46.4	79.4	80.0	73.0	78.2	64.8	85.6	82.4
Percentage with children under 6 years	17.5	38.1	45.6	30.3	30.9	31.2	42.4	39.0
Householder age 65 years and over	141	93	98	181	269	279	1,371	101
Percentage of poverty families	29.3	31.7	20.1	30.0	22.6	29.1	14.8	21.1

TABLE 2.17--POVERTY STATUS OF FAMILIES, COUNTIES, 1979 (Continued)

	Lauderdale	Lawrence	Lewis	Lincoln	Loudon	McMinn	McNairy	Macon
Total families	6,384	9,604	2,515	7,742	8,407	11,972	6,680	4,661
Families with incomes less than poverty level[1]	1,303	1,264	444	1,027	866	1,664	986	654
Percentage of all families	20.4	13.2	17.7	13.3	10.3	13.9	14.8	14.0
Female head of household	396	258	58	243	214	489	170	115
Percentage of poverty families	30.4	20.4	13.1	23.7	24.7	29.4	17.2	17.6
Percentage with children under 18 years	79.0	76.4	81.0	81.9	65.9	87.5	87.6	49.6
Percentage with children under 6 years	39.9	27.5	24.1	32.9	22.0	50.7	43.5	16.5
Householder age 65 years and over	419	364	93	302	248	389	338	247
Percentage of poverty families	32.2	28.8	20.9	29.4	28.6	23.4	34.3	37.8

	Madison	Marion	Marshall	Maury	Meigs	Monroe	Mont-gomery	Moore
Total families	19,942	6,841	5,608	14,469	2,075	7,979	22,012	1,292
Families with incomes less than poverty level[1]	2,639	1,114	566	1,895	255	1,290	2,425	162
Percentage of all families	13.2	16.3	10.1	13.1	12.3	16.2	11.0	12.5
Female head of household	1,197	274	189	744	20	312	863	15
Percentage of poverty families	45.4	24.6	33.4	39.3	7.8	24.2	35.6	9.3
Percentage with children under 18 years	87.4	85.8	76.7	84.4	90.0	78.5	84.5	100.0
Percentage with children under 6 years	48.7	44.5	49.2	36.0	35.0	31.1	44.7	0.0
Householder age 65 years and over	496	215	148	511	92	283	446	23
Percentage of poverty families	18.8	19.3	26.1	27.0	36.1	21.9	18.4	14.2

	Morgan	Obion	Overton	Perry	Pickett	Polk	Putnam	Rhea
Total families	4,512	9,304	5,191	1,793	1,337	3,832	13,021	6,640
Families with incomes less than poverty level[1]	973	1,134	1,126	205	306	641	1,665	1,035
Percentage of all families	21.6	12.2	21.7	11.4	22.9	16.7	12.8	15.6
Female head of household	238	343	197	26	36	116	362	276
Percentage of poverty families	24.5	30.2	17.5	12.7	11.8	18.1	21.7	26.7
Percentage with children under 18 years	72.3	82.5	69.0	50.0	80.6	81.9	84.5	92.0
Percentage with children under 6 years	21.4	28.0	34.0	30.8	44.4	26.7	37.6	40.2
Householder age 65 years and over	203	285	355	21	77	170	402	236
Percentage of poverty families	20.9	25.1	31.5	10.2	25.2	26.5	24.1	22.8

TABLE 2.17--POVERTY STATUS OF FAMILIES, COUNTIES, 1979 (Continued)

	Roane	Robertson	Rutherford	Scott	Sequatchie	Sevier	Shelby	Smith
Total families	13,895	10,275	22,109	5,181	2,440	12,054	197,394	4,383
Families with incomes less than poverty level[1]	1,404	1,183	1,937	1,239	501	1,572	30,242	482
Percentage of all families	10.1	11.5	8.8	23.9	20.5	13.0	15.3	11.0
Female head of household	391	333	657	320	143	317	17,763	124
Percentage of poverty families	27.8	28.1	33.9	25.8	28.5	20.2	58.7	25.7
Percentage with children under 18 years	80.8	68.5	83.7	83.8	81.8	82.3	89.8	69.4
Percentage with children under 6 years	37.6	35.1	44.0	46.3	32.2	32.2	49.0	29.8
Householder age 65 years and over	246	275	402	199	118	388	3,904	171
Percentage of poverty families	17.5	23.2	20.8	16.1	23.6	24.7	12.9	35.5

	Stewart	Sullivan	Sumner	Tipton	Trousdale	Unicoi	Union	Van Buren
Total families	2,545	41,862	24,114	8,627	1,836	4,814	3,389	1,390
Families with incomes less than poverty level[1]	430	4,222	2,007	1,381	131	570	708	193
Percentage of all families	16.9	10.1	8.3	16.0	7.1	11.8	20.9	13.9
Female head of household	61	1,354	528	473	33	151	168	33
Percentage of poverty families	14.2	32.1	26.3	34.3	25.2	26.5	23.7	17.1
Percentage with children under 18 years	83.6	77.0	79.2	83.5	84.8	81.5	88.7	48.5
Percentage with children under 6 years	21.3	33.2	31.8	46.7	21.2	24.5	16.7	48.5
Householder age 65 years and over	130	804	510	393	37	151	93	43
Percentage of poverty families	30.2	19.0	25.4	28.5	28.2	26.5	13.1	22.3

	Warren	Wash-ington	Wayne	Weakley	White	William-son	Wilson
Total families	9,315	23,934	3,914	8,901	5,731	16,393	15,819
Families with incomes less than poverty level[1]	1,340	2,520	647	1,107	773	1,111	1,313
Percentage of all families	14.4	10.5	16.5	12.4	13.5	6.8	8.3
Female head of household	306	831	95	200	182	266	495
Percentage of poverty families	22.8	33.0	14.7	18.1	23.5	23.9	37.7
Percentage with children under 18 years	83.7	79.8	70.5	75.0	78.0	83.1	80.6
Percentage with children under 6 years	31.0	40.6	26.3	34.0	26.9	38.3	42.4
Householder age 65 years and over	368	550	235	350	162	269	292
Percentage of poverty families	27.5	21.8	36.3	31.6	21.0	24.2	22.2

Notes on following page.

TABLE 2.17--POVERTY STATUS OF FAMILIES, COUNTIES, 1979 (Continued)

1. Classification of families by poverty status varies according to family size, age and place of residence. Data for state and substate levels are available only from the decennial census. The latest data are for 1979. However, poverty thresholds are updated annually to reflect changes in the annual average Consumer Price Index and are published in Current Population Reports, Consumer Income, Series P-60.

	Poverty thresholds for selected categories		
Year	Family of four	Single person 65 and over	Two persons, householder 65 and over
1988	$12,092	$5,674	$7,158
1987	11,612	5,447	6,872
1986	11,203	5,255	6,630
1985	10,989	5,156	6,503
1984	10,609	4,979	6,282
1983	10,178	4,775	6,023
1982	9,862	4,626	5,836
1981	9,287	4,359	5,498
1980	8,414	3,941	4,954
1979	7,412	3,479	4,390

Source: U.S. Department of Commerce, Bureau of the Census, *1980 Census of Population, General Social and Economic Characteristics, Tennessee.*

TABLE 2.18--TRANSFER PAYMENTS, BY TYPE, COUNTIES, 1987 [In thousands of dollars]

Type of payments	Anderson	Bedford	Benton	Bledsoe	Blount	Bradley	Campbell	Cannon
Total transfer payments	158,627	56,672	36,243	17,943	175,203	115,830	93,026	19,554
Retirement, disability & health insurance	100,696	32,841	20,398	8,167	106,433	65,639	49,998	10,711
Medical[1]	29,861	12,471	8,603	4,796	35,949	22,472	20,425	4,923
Income maintenance benefit	11,035	3,372	2,349	2,013	9,614	7,668	11,147	1,312
Unemployment insurance benefit	2,674	1,222	1,308	386	3,807	2,960	2,359	441
Veterans' benefit	4,007	2,687	1,492	1,376	6,486	5,155	4,051	762
Federal educational & training assistance[2]	342	166	64	(a)	748	1,655	213	(a)
Payments to nonprofit institutions	3,315	1,400	715	456	3,981	3,460	1,684	519
Business payments to individuals[3]	6,616	2,479	1,296	697	8,088	6,737	3,108	827

	Carroll	Carter	Cheatham	Chester	Claiborne	Clay	Cocke	Coffee
Total transfer payments	67,646	96,061	33,270	23,151	54,083	13,255	60,921	85,424
Retirement, disability & health insurance	37,965	54,050	18,552	12,021	27,082	6,092	26,190	50,670
Medical[1]	16,379	18,269	7,399	4,606	11,433	3,704	16,333	18,376
Income maintenance benefit	4,729	8,366	1,622	2,330	7,170	1,985	8,980	5,045
Unemployment insurance benefit	2,289	2,499	736	525	806	171	2,557	1,778
Veterans' benefit	2,183	5,887	1,690	1,309	3,339	343	2,813	3,164
Federal educational & training assistance[2]	413	490	109	698	955	(a)	125	422
Payments to nonprofit institutions	1,332	2,438	1,225	621	1,262	370	1,394	1,972
Business payments to individuals[3]	2,324	4,002	1,907	1,026	2,005	548	2,495	3,949

	Crockett	Cumber-land	Davidson	Decatur	DeKalb	Dickson	Dyer	Fayette
Total transfer payments	29,473	73,006	1,017,105	22,303	28,558	65,934	75,528	50,035
Retirement, disability & health insurance	15,406	43,108	540,792	12,276	14,963	36,790	39,120	18,664
Medical[1]	7,767	14,651	273,992	4,776	7,122	15,888	19,205	18,196
Income maintenance benefit	2,847	5,236	63,628	1,848	2,528	3,992	7,017	7,287
Unemployment insurance benefit	883	1,181	15,703	617	672	1,494	1,661	686
Veterans' benefit	722	4,119	32,469	1,281	1,350	3,005	3,302	1,952
Federal educational & training assistance[2]	59	164	12,040	(a)	62	174	395	111
Payments to nonprofit institutions	671	1,554	24,008	523	687	1,605	1,628	1,248
Business payments to individuals[3]	1,101	2,955	53,888	922	1,157	2,947	3,160	1,860

TABLE 2.18--TRANSFER PAYMENTS, BY TYPE, COUNTIES, 1987 [In thousands of dollars] (Continued)

Type of payments	Fentress	Franklin	Gibson	Giles	Grainger	Greene	Grundy	Hamblen
Total transfer payments	34,312	65,791	109,855	56,441	30,594	101,090	31,277	92,819
Retirement, disability & health insurance	14,623	37,634	60,346	29,009	15,307	56,100	15,575	48,603
Medical[1]	10,050	14,818	27,448	14,595	7,156	19,049	8,038	20,575
Income maintenance benefit	4,787	4,365	8,440	4,248	3,751	9,054	3,599	8,365
Unemployment insurance benefit	894	1,256	3,139	1,292	905	3,852	842	2,919
Veterans' benefit	1,853	2,895	3,554	3,492	1,361	4,634	1,311	3,742
Federal educational & training assistance[2]	66	310	341	401	74	605	62	916
Payments to nonprofit institutions	745	1,624	2,310	1,172	828	2,684	687	2,493
Business payments to individuals[3]	1,276	2,849	4,221	2,203	1,192	5,047	1,146	5,145

	Hamilton	Hancock	Hardeman	Hardin	Hawkins	Haywood	Henderson	Henry
Total transfer payments	626,767	15,192	56,876	45,728	78,239	46,308	43,476	71,325
Retirement, disability & health insurance	345,997	5,119	24,529	23,414	41,598	17,946	24,519	42,544
Medical[1]	156,585	4,862	18,683	10,283	16,896	14,895	8,742	13,757
Income maintenance benefit	42,801	3,460	7,391	5,410	8,452	7,217	3,725	4,430
Unemployment insurance benefit	9,408	255	1,052	1,393	1,635	1,068	1,477	3,075
Veterans' benefit	21,257	648	1,929	2,111	3,795	2,404	1,935	3,339
Federal educational & training assistance[2]	7,734	(a)	135	124	192	88	97	155
Payments to nonprofit institutions	13,644	320	1,155	1,052	2,142	990	1,075	1,388
Business payments to individuals[3]	29,009	491	1,974	1,916	3,477	1,676	1,880	2,603

	Hickman	Houston	Hum-phreys	Jackson	Jefferson	Johnson	Knox	Lake
Total transfer payments	31,042	17,056	33,520	17,578	65,353	32,370	674,364	17,431
Retirement, disability & health insurance	17,560	9,599	18,090	8,265	35,683	15,783	383,083	8,079
Medical[1]	7,264	4,095	8,225	4,422	14,682	8,027	152,470	5,148
Income maintenance benefit	2,112	1,255	2,165	2,076	4,990	4,171	43,913	2,410
Unemployment insurance benefit	717	511	1,440	400	2,011	1,011	11,990	247
Veterans' benefit	1,308	692	1,359	1,250	2,718	1,572	23,590	592
Federal educational & training assistance[2]	71	(a)	69	(a)	1,041	59	8,451	(a)
Payments to nonprofit institutions	784	338	760	443	1,592	671	15,637	354
Business payments to individuals[3]	1,207	528	1,393	672	2,597	1,059	34,849	560

TABLE 2.18--TRANSFER PAYMENTS, BY TYPE, COUNTIES, 1987 [In thousands of dollars] (Continued)

Type of payments	Lauderdale	Lawrence	Lewis	Lincoln	Loudon	McMinn	McNairy	Macon
Total transfer payments	54,617	68,986	18,932	56,158	62,639	81,745	50,485	27,032
Retirement, disability & health insurance	25,266	39,940	9,335	33,827	36,609	45,676	26,312	13,442
Medical[1]	17,643	13,585	4,868	11,828	13,164	17,790	11,542	6,644
Income maintenance benefit	6,794	5,529	1,734	3,716	4,285	6,439	5,603	2,570
Unemployment insurance benefit	930	3,101	800	898	1,410	2,243	1,389	912
Veterans' benefit	730	1,926	794	2,178	2,918	3,127	2,474	1,319
Federal educational & training assistance[2]	118	150	76	116	131	442	102	70
Payments to nonprofit institutions	1,198	1,671	495	1,294	1,464	2,056	1,136	772
Business payments to individuals[3]	1,909	3,043	818	2,269	2,623	3,922	1,899	1,284

Type of payments	Madison	Marion	Marshall	Maury	Meigs	Monroe	Mont-gomery	Moore
Total transfer payments	168,056	52,078	41,124	106,693	14,473	57,674	168,394	5,811
Retirement, disability & health insurance	89,336	27,049	22,717	59,013	8,091	30,354	104,625	3,484
Medical[1]	40,106	13,108	10,132	25,106	3,022	12,466	28,441	1,042
Income maintenance benefit	14,600	4,673	2,754	7,703	1,319	5,753	9,032	333
Unemployment insurance benefit	3,901	1,668	967	2,354	531	1,684	3,205	129
Veterans' benefit	5,584	2,124	1,612	4,531	484	2,869	9,537	246
Federal educational & training assistance[2]	2,803	108	89	506	(a)	478	1,648	(a)
Payments to nonprofit institutions	3,709	1,206	1,002	2,586	385	1,454	3,951	226
Business payments to individuals[3]	7,927	2,112	1,827	4,831	597	2,581	7,859	325

Type of payments	Morgan	Obion	Overton	Perry	Pickett	Polk	Putnam	Rhea
Total transfer payments	32,661	62,629	35,208	14,073	8,935	29,910	98,765	52,263
Retirement, disability & health insurance	15,940	36,018	17,457	7,385	4,045	17,156	56,745	27,217
Medical[1]	8,269	13,296	8,504	3,667	2,126	6,255	19,250	12,699
Income maintenance benefit	3,973	4,680	3,818	1,029	1,094	2,186	6,154	5,254
Unemployment insurance benefit	788	1,180	863	610	503	1,075	2,144	1,240
Veterans' benefit	1,660	2,685	2,171	580	572	1,516	4,581	2,184
Federal educational & training assistance[2]	72	140	114	(a)	(a)	58	2,592	414
Payments to nonprofit institutions	803	1,568	856	305	215	651	2,457	1,203
Business payments to individuals[3]	1,136	3,023	1,404	461	356	998	4,782	2,022

TABLE 2.18--TRANSFER PAYMENTS, BY TYPE, COUNTIES, 1987 [In thousands of dollars] (Continued)

Type of payments	Roane	Robertson	Rutherford	Scott	Sequatchie	Sevier	Shelby	Smith
Total transfer payments	103,318	68,858	158,853	46,109	15,942	85,102	1,793,275	26,895
Retirement, disability & health insurance	60,408	36,465	93,477	20,229	8,014	47,709	850,790	14,324
Medical[1]	22,131	18,171	28,588	12,570	4,410	16,619	545,561	6,590
Income maintenance benefit	7,651	4,385	7,404	6,886	1,696	5,632	179,768	1,964
Unemployment insurance benefit	2,123	1,708	3,358	1,625	429	4,100	24,106	842
Veterans' benefit	3,564	2,532	7,416	2,002	209	3,792	52,528	1,215
Federal educational & training assistance[2]	747	178	4,129	137	(a)	204	21,871	63
Payments to nonprofit institutions	2,353	1,990	5,091	981	423	2,270	38,356	697
Business payments to individuals[3]	4,284	3,380	9,266	1,655	714	4,721	79,303	1,183

Type of payments	Stewart	Sullivan	Sumner	Tipton	Trousdale	Unicoi	Union	Van Buren
Total transfer payments	23,882	286,154	146,399	71,174	10,542	38,959	21,644	7,465
Retirement, disability & health insurance	14,324	173,190	81,766	33,868	5,071	23,627	10,082	3,610
Medical[1]	4,563	53,551	33,165	20,430	2,919	7,217	5,533	1,684
Income maintenance benefit	1,526	18,158	7,399	8,093	808	2,968	2,713	840
Unemployment insurance benefit	398	5,639	4,111	1,356	290	1,086	687	271
Veterans' benefit	1,874	12,002	6,310	2,578	605	1,910	1,129	496
Federal educational & training assistance[2]	(a)	1,544	611	196	56	71	52	(a)
Payments to nonprofit institutions	448	6,993	4,728	1,729	288	795	582	228
Business payments to individuals[3]	699	14,907	8,194	2,882	498	1,265	852	310

Type of payments	Warren	Washington	Wayne	Weakley	White	Williamson	Wilson
Total transfer payments	64,422	193,462	25,409	62,794	41,674	97,526	99,405
Retirement, disability & health insurance	34,638	112,499	12,967	36,543	23,320	53,417	51,855
Medical[1]	15,777	36,279	5,578	12,270	9,628	22,789	26,694
Income maintenance benefit	4,587	12,157	2,665	3,347	3,069	3,956	5,050
Unemployment insurance benefit	1,628	3,723	1,132	1,150	959	1,357	2,687
Veterans' benefit	3,064	11,465	1,239	3,120	1,974	5,591	3,972
Federal educational & training assistance[2]	183	4,007	59	2,082	86	322	548
Payments to nonprofit institutions	1,589	4,345	672	1,560	966	3,587	3,151
Business payments to individuals[3]	2,917	8,881	1,080	2,684	1,649	6,420	5,371

Notes on following page.

TABLE 2.18--TRANSFER PAYMENTS, BY TYPE, COUNTIES, 1987 [In thousands of dollars] (Continued)

Note: Includes items not detailed separately.

1. Consists of Medicare payments, medical vendor payments, and CHAMPUS payments.

2. Includes federal fellowship payments (National Science Foundation, fellowships and traineeships, subsistence payments to State Maritime Academy cadets, and other federal fellowships), interest subsidy on higher education loans, Basic Educational Opportunity Grants, and Job Corps payments. Excludes veterans.

3. Includes consumer bad debts, personal injury payments to individuals other than employees, and other business transfer payments.

a. Less than $50,000. Estimates are included in totals.

Source: U.S. Department of Commerce, Bureau of Economic Analysis, Regional Economics Information System, direct subscription.

TABLE 2.19--TOTAL AND PER CAPITA TRANSFER PAYMENTS, AND TRANSFER PAYMENTS AS A PERCENTAGE OF PERSONAL INCOME, TENNESSEE AND COUNTIES, 1987

County	Total ($1,000)	Per capita ($)	Percentage of personal income	County	Total ($1,000)	Per capita ($)	Percentage of personal income
Anderson	158,627	2,273	17.3	Lewis	18,932	1,813	24.3
Bedford	56,672	1,923	15.5	Lincoln	56,158	2,062	18.2
Benton	36,243	2,410	23.3	Loudon	62,639	2,033	18.6
Bledsoe	17,943	1,866	21.3	McMinn	81,745	1,888	17.5
Blount	175,203	2,090	16.3	McNairy	50,485	2,112	21.8
Bradley	115,830	1,590	13.1	Macon	27,032	1,662	17.3
Campbell	93,026	2,624	29.7	Madison	168,056	2,152	17.7
Cannon	19,554	1,792	16.6	Marion	52,078	2,051	21.4
Carroll	67,646	2,413	23.2	Marshall	41,124	1,950	16.1
Carter	96,061	1,871	19.7	Maury	106,693	1,960	16.5
Cheatham	33,270	1,290	11.1	Meigs	14,473	1,783	18.3
Chester	23,151	1,768	17.6	Monroe	57,674	1,882	20.0
Claiborne	54,083	2,036	20.5	Montgomery	168,394	1,792	15.9
Clay	13,255	1,700	19.8	Moore	5,811	1,221	13.0
Cocke	60,921	2,076	24.6	Morgan	32,661	1,931	23.1
Coffee	85,424	2,050	16.1	Obion	62,629	1,895	15.8
Crockett	29,473	2,084	19.6	Overton	35,208	1,956	25.0
Cumberland	73,006	2,232	21.0	Perry	14,073	2,186	21.8
Davidson	1,017,105	2,010	12.4	Pickett	8,935	1,973	28.5
Decatur	22,303	2,022	22.1	Polk	29,910	2,180	21.5
DeKalb	28,558	1,972	17.8	Putnam	98,765	1,908	16.5
Dickson	65,934	1,950	15.8	Rhea	52,263	2,065	18.3
Dyer	75,528	2,203	18.9	Roane	103,318	2,085	17.2
Fayette	50,035	1,905	18.0	Robertson	68,858	1,644	15.0
Fentress	34,312	2,188	30.0	Rutherford	158,853	1,481	11.1
Franklin	65,791	1,922	18.9	Scott	46,109	2,232	28.1
Gibson	109,855	2,257	19.9	Sequatchie	15,942	1,785	20.1
Giles	56,441	2,289	19.7	Sevier	85,102	1,781	16.0
Grainger	30,594	1,757	22.0	Shelby	1,793,275	2,190	14.7
Greene	101,090	1,789	16.9	Smith	26,895	1,831	15.7
Grundy	31,277	2,164	25.6	Stewart	23,882	2,529	25.1
Hamblen	92,819	1,768	17.0	Sullivan	286,154	1,943	15.5
Hamilton	626,767	2,181	14.7	Sumner	146,399	1,470	10.6
Hancock	15,192	2,247	32.1	Tipton	71,174	1,931	17.9
Hardeman	56,876	2,338	25.5	Trousdale	10,542	1,739	16.7
Hardin	45,728	2,065	20.5	Unicoi	38,959	2,325	22.6
Hawkins	78,239	1,734	18.3	Union	21,644	2,713	20.9
Haywood	46,308	2,223	21.9	Van Buren	7,465	1,557	17.8
Henderson	43,476	1,922	19.3	Warren	64,422	1,924	18.1
Henry	71,325	2,437	23.2	Washington	193,462	2,114	16.6
Hickman	31,042	1,880	18.0	Wayne	25,409	1,794	19.2
Houston	17,056	2,397	23.5	Weakley	62,794	1,912	17.9
Humphreys	33,520	2,095	19.4	White	41,674	2,052	19.3
Jackson	17,578	1,889	22.8	Williamson	97,526	1,291	6.7
Jefferson	65,353	1,949	19.4	Wilson	99,405	1,498	10.8
Johnson	32,370	2,289	29.64	TENNESSEE	9,722,259	2,003	15.6
Knox	674,364	2,047	14.3				
Lake	17,431	2,340	29.0				
Lauderdale	54,617	2,166	22.3				
Lawrence	68,986	1,962	18.1				

Note: The per capita amounts are based on population as of July 1.

Source: U.S. Department of Commerce, Bureau of Economic Analysis, Regional Economics Information System.

TABLE 2.20--TOTAL GROSS STATE PRODUCT, SOUTHEASTERN STATES, 1977–1986 [In millions of dollars]

State	1986	1985	1984	1983	1982	1981	1980	1979	1978	1977
TENNESSEE	72,328	67,560	63,207	56,319	51,967	49,881	45,018	42,235	38,289	33,196
Alabama	55,007	51,919	48,710	43,918	40,328	38,829	34,969	32,769	29,607	25,768
Arkansas	31,633	29,926	28,716	25,394	23,462	22,885	20,123	18,911	17,154	14,665
Florida	177,729	164,340	149,554	132,590	118,301	110,787	97,830	86,060	75,367	64,830
Georgia	102,922	94,121	86,213	74,966	66,766	62,481	55,503	51,038	45,868	40,354
Kentucky	53,135	51,234	49,512	44,565	42,286	40,947	36,828	35,234	32,028	28,434
Louisiana	74,426	79,719	79,034	73,930	75,743	74,505	62,166	51,178	43,896	38,003
Mississippi	31,830	30,819	29,637	26,610	25,537	24,545	21,470	20,178	17,959	15,786
North Carolina	100,961	93,821	87,748	77,669	69,128	65,940	58,876	54,532	49,737	43,754
South Carolina	44,727	41,832	39,581	35,224	31,940	30,788	27,275	25,102	22,391	19,709
Virginia	104,155	95,369	87,599	78,506	70,375	65,816	58,634	53,415	48,434	42,880
West Virginia	24,096	23,541	22,885	21,619	21,370	20,702	19,197	17,722	16,172	14,477

Note: These estimates of gross state product are from a new series introduced by the Bureau of Economic Analysis, Spring 1988. The complete series includes all states and the District of Columbia for the years 1963–86.

Source: U.S Department of Commerce, Bureau of Economic Analysis, *Survey of Current Business*, May 1988.

TABLE 2.21--PERSONAL INCOME, SOUTHEASTERN STATES, 1935–1988, SELECTED YEARS [In millions of dollars]

State	1988^p	1987^r	1986^r	1985^r	1984^r	1983^r	1982^r	1981^r	1980^r	1979^r
TENNESSEE	67,909	63,003	57,870	53,637	50,360	45,745	42,969	40,872	36,958	33,508
Alabama	52,720	49,165	45,999	43,026	40,349	37,093	34,851	33,261	30,063	27,333
Arkansas	29,263	27,275	26,035	24,838	23,309	21,158	19,855	19,139	17,097	15,761
Florida	204,788	187,476	171,112	158,411	143,926	130,641	118,530	110,296	96,078	82,566
Georgia	96,779	89,595	82,410	75,394	68,920	61,211	55,787	51,842	45,805	41,025
Kentucky	47,784	44,663	41,955	40,102	38,732	35,340	34,281	32,738	29,401	26,912
Louisiana	54,179	51,176	50,658	50,679	48,798	46,456	44,863	42,211	36,697	31,740
Mississippi	29,123	27,032	25,386	24,174	23,159	21,431	20,551	19,489	17,500	16,150
North Carolina	92,822	85,582	78,786	72,987	67,851	60,722	55,867	52,891	47,180	42,336
South Carolina	44,855	41,372	38,331	35,780	33,476	30,329	28,048	26,676	23,790	21,267
Virginia	106,315	97,807	89,614	82,523	76,452	69,310	63,837	59,343	52,754	46,392
West Virginia	22,018	20,898	20,204	19,504	18,902	17,895	17,671	16,741	15,459	14,004
	1978^r	1975^r	1970^r	1965	1960	1955	1950	1945	1940	1935
TENNESSEE	29,859	20,978	12,405	7,849	5,632	4,434	3,367	2,616	989	737
Alabama	24,430	17,257	10,159	6,797	4,959	3,812	2,748	2,160	794	590
Arkansas	14,135	9,889	5,456	3,484	2,451	1,999	1,606	1,296	504	391
Florida	71,396	49,822	26,990	14,413	9,877	6,136	3,623	2,902	988	602
Georgia	36,440	25,942	15,551	9,540	6,561	5,078	3,644	2,705	1,042	790
Kentucky	24,024	16,926	10,148	6,491	4,843	3,836	2,871	2,062	910	729
Louisiana	27,919	19,048	11,209	7,339	5,389	4,029	2,968	2,126	850	640
Mississippi	14,264	9,938	5,768	3,709	2,636	2,122	1,661	1,303	464	365
North Carolina	38,073	27,351	16,503	10,226	7,282	5,691	4,331	2,880	1,148	897
South Carolina	18,874	13,429	7,806	4,774	3,358	2,654	1,932	1,434	581	404
Virginia	41,327	29,463	17,440	10,926	7,529	5,754	4,087	3,350	1,252	873
West Virginia	12,505	9,034	5,375	3,699	2,960	2,438	2,092	1,480	760	598

Note: Includes most current data revisions.

p preliminary.

r revised.

Source: U.S. Department of Commerce, Bureau of Economic Analysis, Regional Economics Information System, direct subscription.

TABLE 2.22--PER CAPITA PERSONAL INCOME, SOUTHEASTERN STATES AND UNITED STATES, 1940–1988, SELECTED YEARS [In dollars]

State	1988[p]	1987[r]	1986[r]	1985[r]	1984[r]	1983[r]	1982[r]	1980[r]	1970[r]	1960	1950	1940
TENNESSEE	13,873	12,977	12,056	11,253	10,652	9,753	9,208	8,030	3,151	1,575	1,016	337
Alabama	12,851	12,039	11,356	10,699	10,110	9,360	8,836	7,704	2,945	1,515	899	279
Arkansas	12,219	11,421	10,980	10,526	9,935	9,099	8,604	7,465	2,827	1,370	842	258
Florida	16,603	15,594	14,640	13,936	13,022	12,143	11,315	9,764	3,943	1,974	1,289	516
Georgia	15,260	14,387	13,508	12,618	11,792	10,672	9,867	8,348	3,377	1,658	1,054	334
Kentucky	12,822	11,996	11,271	10,769	10,413	9,518	9,278	8,022	3,141	1,593	978	318
Louisiana	12,292	11,506	11,264	11,303	10,937	10,460	10,235	8,682	3,071	1,653	1,101	359
Mississippi	11,116	10,301	9,674	9,250	8,912	8,297	8,006	6,926	2,597	1,208	764	213
North Carolina	14,304	13,353	12,453	11,664	11,002	9,990	9,284	7,999	3,236	1,592	1,065	321
South Carolina	12,926	12,078	11,336	10,734	10,157	9,326	8,710	7,589	3,004	1,404	914	305
Virginia	17,675	16,539	15,456	14,467	13,567	12,470	11,630	9,827	3,743	1,889	1,233	460
West Virginia	11,735	11,013	10,539	10,074	9,685	9,115	9,007	7,915	3,078	1,597	1,043	398
SOUTHEAST	14,462	13,531	12,716	12,045	11,368	10,485	9,877	8,484	3,293	1,632	1,032	340
UNITED STATES[1]	16,489	15,472	14,596	13,896	13,114	12,098	11,481	9,919	4,051	2,216	1,492	589
Southeast as a percentage of U.S. per capita income	87.7	87.5	87.1	86.7	86.7	86.7	86.0	85.5	81.3	73.6	69.2	57.7

Note: These data represent the most current revisions. Percentages were computed by the Center for Business and Economic Research.

p preliminary.

r revised.

1. Includes Alaska and Hawaii after 1960.

Source: U.S. Department of Commerce, Bureau of Economic Analysis, Regional Economics Information System, *Survey of Current Business*, August 1989, Volume 69, Number 8; and direct subscription.

TABLE 2.23--POVERTY STATUS OF PERSONS AND FAMILIES, SOUTHEASTERN STATES AND UNITED STATES, 1959, 1969, AND 1979 [In thousands]

	Number below poverty level					
	Persons			Families		
State	1979	1969	1959	1979	1969	1959
TENNESSEE	736	836	1,374	164	186	306
Alabama	720	857	1,374	154	181	292
Arkansas	424	523	843	94	115	190
Florida	1,287	1,088	1,371	268	229	309
Georgia	884	924	1,505	189	192	314
Kentucky	626	718	1,137	144	159	253
Louisiana	765	933	1,274	163	188	26
Mississippi	587	767	1,173	121	154	240
North Carolina	840	996	1,796	183	211	373
South Carolina	500	595	1,049	106	119	206
Virginia	611	691	1,164	129	143	245
West Virginia	287	380	637	62	82	139
UNITED STATES	27,393	27,209	38,685	5,670	5,481	8,315

	Poverty rate (%)					
	Persons			Families		
State	1979	1969	1959	1979	1969	1959
TENNESSEE	16.5	21.8	39.3	13.1	18.2	34.2
Alabama	18.9	25.4	42.5	14.8	20.7	36.9
Arkansas	19.0	27.8	47.5	14.9	22.8	42.1
Florida	13.5	16.4	28.4	9.9	12.7	23.8
Georgia	16.6	20.7	39.0	13.2	16.7	33.1
Kentucky	17.6	22.9	38.3	14.6	19.2	33.6
Louisiana	18.6	26.3	39.5	15.1	21.5	34.0
Mississippi	23.9	35.4	54.5	18.7	28.9	47.9
North Carolina	14.8	20.3	40.6	11.6	16.3	34.1
South Carolina	16.6	23.9	45.4	13.1	19.0	38.0
Virginia	11.8	15.5	30.6	9.2	12.3	25.7
West Virginia	15.0	22.2	35.6	11.7	18.0	30.2
UNITED STATES	12.4	13.7	22.1	9.6	10.7	18.4

Note: See Table 2.17 for detail on poverty thresholds for 1988.

Source: U.S. Department of Commerce, Bureau of the Census, *1980 Census of Population and Housing, General Social and Economic Characteristics*, individual states; and *Current Population Reports*, Series P-20, No. 334.

FIGURE 2.3
Consumer Price Index, Not Seasonally Adjusted, Urban Consumers, 12-Month Change, 1984–1988

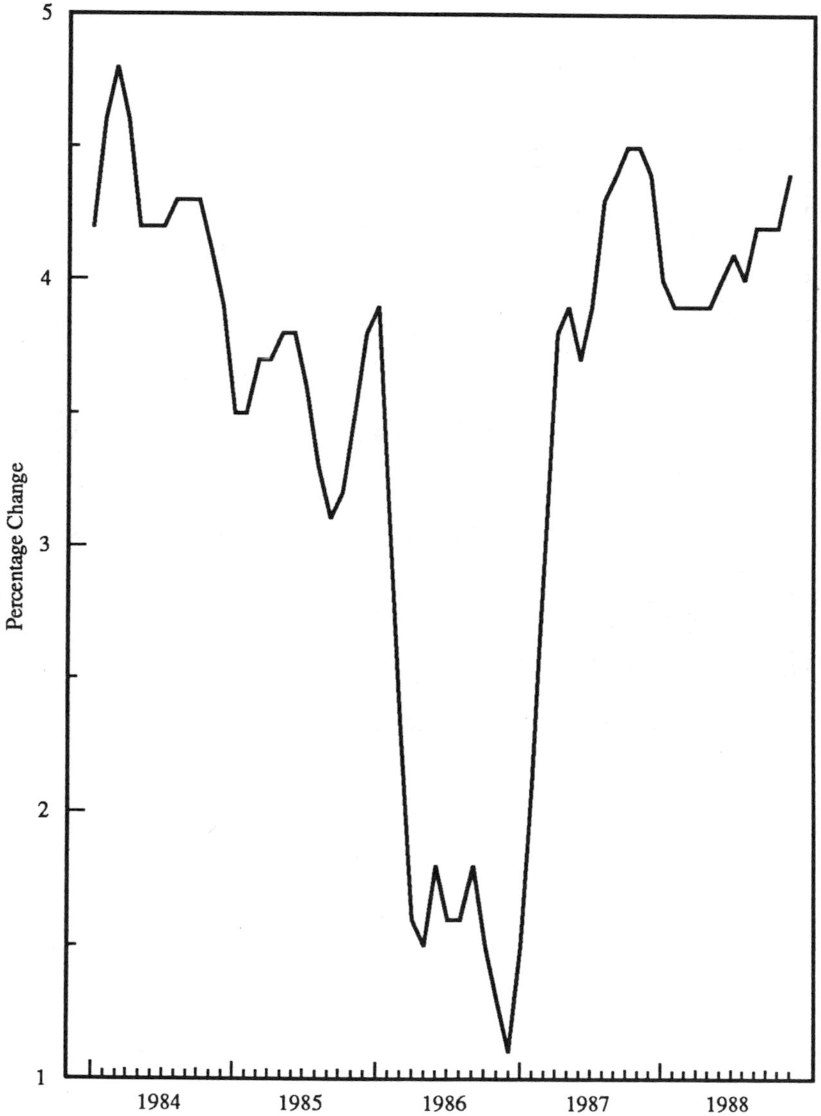

Note: Percentage change is from the same month one year earlier.
Source: U.S. Department of Labor, Bureau of Labor Statistics, monthly news releases.

TABLE 2.24--CONSUMER PRICE INDEX FOR URBAN WAGE EARNERS AND CLERICAL WORKERS AND FOR ALL URBAN CONSUMERS, U.S. CITY AVERAGE, NOT SEASONALLY ADJUSTED, 1970–1988, SELECTED YEARS [1982–84=100]

Year	Jan.	Feb.	March	April	May	June	July	August	Sept.	Oct.	Nov.	Dec.	Annual average	Annual change (%)
	Urban wage earners and clerical workers (CPI-W)													
1988	114.5	114.7	115.1	115.7	116.2	116.7	117.2	117.7	118.5	118.9	119.0	119.2	117.0	4.0
1987	110.0	110.5	111.0	111.6	111.9	112.4	112.7	113.3	113.8	114.1	114.3	114.2	112.5	3.6
1986	108.9	108.5	107.9	107.6	107.9	108.4	108.4	108.6	109.1	109.1	109.2	109.3	108.6	1.6
1985	104.9	105.4	105.9	106.3	106.7	107.0	107.1	107.3	107.6	107.9	108.3	108.6	106.9	3.5
1984	101.6	101.8	101.8	102.1	102.5	102.8	103.2	104.2	104.8	104.8	104.7	104.8	103.3	3.4
1983	98.1	98.1	98.4	99.0	99.5	99.8	100.1	100.5	101.0	101.2	101.2	101.2	99.8	3.0
1982	94.7	95.0	94.8	95.2	96.2	97.4	98.0	98.2	98.3	98.6	98.4	98.0	96.9	6.0
1981	87.5	88.5	89.0	89.6	90.3	91.1	92.2	92.8	93.7	93.9	94.1	94.4	91.4	10.3
1980	78.3	79.4	80.5	81.4	82.3	83.2	83.3	83.8	84.6	85.3	86.1	86.9	82.9	13.5
1979	68.7	69.5	70.3	71.1	71.9	72.8	73.7	74.4	75.1	75.7	76.4	77.2	73.1	11.4
1978	62.8	63.2	63.7	64.3	64.9	65.6	66.0	66.4	66.8	67.4	67.7	68.1	65.6	7.6
1977	58.9	59.5	59.8	60.3	60.6	61.0	61.3	61.5	61.8	61.9	62.2	62.5	60.9	6.5
1976	56.0	56.1	56.2	56.5	56.8	57.1	57.4	57.7	57.9	58.2	58.3	58.5	57.2	5.7
1975	52.4	52.8	53.0	53.2	53.5	53.9	54.5	54.7	54.9	55.3	55.6	55.8	54.1	9.2
1974	46.9	47.5	48.0	48.3	48.8	49.3	49.7	50.3	50.9	51.4	51.8	52.2	49.6	11.0
1973	42.9	43.2	43.6	43.9	44.1	44.4	44.5	45.4	45.5	45.9	46.2	46.5	44.7	6.2
1972	41.4	41.6	41.6	41.7	41.9	42.0	42.1	42.2	42.4	42.5	42.6	42.7	42.1	3.3
1971	40.0	40.1	40.2	40.4	40.6	40.8	40.9	41.0	41.0	41.1	41.2	41.3	40.7	4.3
1970	38.0	38.2	38.4	38.7	38.8	39.0	39.2	39.2	39.4	39.6	39.8	40.0	39.0	5.8

TABLE 2.24--CONSUMER PRICE INDEX FOR URBAN WAGE EARNERS AND CLERICAL WORKERS AND FOR ALL URBAN CONSUMERS, U.S. CITY AVERAGE, NOT SEASONALLY ADJUSTED, 1970–1988, SELECTED YEARS [1982–84=100] (Continued)

Year	Jan.	Feb.	March	April	May	June	July	August	Sept.	Oct.	Nov.	Dec.	Annual average	Annual change (%)
								All urban consumers (CPI-U)						
1988	115.7	116.0	116.5	117.1	117.5	118.0	118.5	119.0	119.8	120.2	120.3	120.5	118.3	4.1
1987	111.2	111.6	112.1	112.7	113.1	113.5	113.8	114.4	115.0	115.3	115.4	115.4	113.6	3.7
1986	109.6	109.3	108.8	108.6	108.9	109.5	109.5	109.7	110.2	110.3	110.4	110.5	109.6	1.9
1985	105.5	106.0	106.4	106.9	107.3	107.6	107.8	108.0	108.3	108.7	109.0	109.3	107.6	3.5
1984	101.9	102.4	102.6	103.1	103.4	103.7	104.1	104.5	105.0	105.3	105.3	105.3	103.9	4.3
1983	97.8	97.9	97.9	98.6	99.2	99.5	99.9	100.2	100.7	101.0	101.2	101.3	99.6	3.2
1982	94.3	94.6	94.5	94.9	95.8	97.0	97.5	97.7	97.9	98.2	98.0	97.6	96.5	6.1
1981	87.0	87.9	88.5	89.1	89.8	90.6	91.6	92.3	93.2	93.4	93.7	94.0	90.9	10.3
1980	77.8	78.9	80.1	81.0	81.8	82.7	82.7	83.3	84.0	84.8	85.5	86.3	82.4	13.5
1979	68.3	69.1	69.8	70.6	71.5	72.3	73.1	73.8	74.6	75.2	75.9	76.7	72.6	11.3
1978	62.5	62.9	63.4	63.9	64.5	65.2	65.7	66.0	66.5	67.1	67.4	67.7	65.2	7.6

Note: Beginning with the release of data for January 1988, CPI's were shifted from the old reference base period 1967=100 to the new reference base period 1982–84=100. Factors for conversion from the old base to the new base for CPI-U AND CPI-W are .3338279 and .3357176, respectively. When multiplied by the appropriate conversion factor, the January 1988 CPI-U of 346.7 becomes 115.7 and the CPI-W of 341.0 becomes 114.5. Because of rounding effects, there may be minor differences between the final rebased index and the result obtained using the conversion factor.

Source: U.S. Department of Labor, Bureau of Labor Statistics, *CPI Detailed Report*, monthly.

TABLE 2.25--PURCHASING POWER OF THE CONSUMER DOLLAR AND THE CONSUMER PRICE INDEX, ANNUAL AVERAGES, 1958–1988

Year	Purchasing power (1982–84=$1.00)	Consumer Price Index (1982–84=100)
1988	$0.846	118.3
1987	0.880	113.6
1986	0.912	109.6
1985	0.929	107.6
1984	0.962	103.9
1983	1.004	99.6
1982	1.036	96.5
1981	1.100	90.9
1980	1.214	82.4
1979	1.377	72.6
1978	1.534	65.2
1977	1.650	60.6
1976	1.757	56.9
1975	1.859	53.8
1974	2.028	49.3
1973	2.252	44.4
1972	2.392	41.8
1971	2.469	40.5
1970	2.577	38.8
1969	2.725	36.7
1968	2.874	34.8
1967	2.994	33.4
1966	3.077	32.5
1965	3.175	31.5
1964	3.226	31.0
1963	3.268	30.6
1962	3.300	30.3
1961	3.344	29.9
1960	3.378	29.6
1959	3.425	29.2
1958	3.460	28.9

Note: The Consumer Price Index used is that for All Urban Consumers.

Source: U.S. Department of Labor, Bureau of Labor Statistics, *CPI Detailed Report*, January 1989, and earlier editions.

TABLE 2.26--ANNUAL AVERAGE CONSUMER PRICE INDEX, UNITED STATES CITY AVERAGE AND SELECTED CITIES, 1988 [1982–84=100]

City	All urban consumers: Annual average 1988	All urban consumers: Percent change from 1987 to 1988	Urban wage earners and clerical workers: Annual average 1988	Urban wage earners and clerical workers: Percent change from 1987 to 1988
U.S. CITY AVERAGE	118.3	4.1	117.0	4.0
Anchorage, AK	108.6	0.4	108.3	0.4
Atlanta, GA	120.4	3.3	118.6	3.3
Baltimore, MD	119.3	4.5	118.9	4.5
Boston-Lawrence-Salem-MA-NH	124.2	6.1	124.1	6.0
Buffalo-Niagara Falls, NY	117.4	3.9	113.2	3.9
Chicago-Gary-Lake County, IL-IN-WI	119.0	3.9	115.3	3.8
Cincinnati-Hamilton, OH-KY-IN	116.1	3.8	114.0	3.8
Cleveland-Akron-Lorain, OH	116.7	3.5	111.8	3.5
Dallas-Fort Worth, TX	116.1	2.8	115.8	2.8
Denver-Boulder, CO	113.7	2.6	112.0	2.7
Detroit-Ann Arbor, MI	116.1	3.9	113.3	3.8
Honolulu, HI	121.7	5.9	122.8	6.0
Houston-Galveston-Brazoria, TX	109.5	2.8	109.7	3.1
Kansas City, MO-KS	117.4	3.8	114.4	3.8
Los Angeles-Anaheim-Riverside, CA	122.1	4.6	119.0	4.4
Miami-Fort Lauderdale, FL	116.8	4.5	115.9	4.3
Milwaukee, WI	115.9	3.9	118.6	3.9
Minneapolis-St. Paul, MN-WI	117.2	5.0	115.5	5.2
New Orleans, LA	102.7	2.7	103.3	3.3
N.Y.-Northern N.J.-Long Island, NY-NJ-CT	123.7	4.8	121.8	4.5
Philadelphia-Wilmington-Trenton, PA-NJ-DE-MD	122.4	4.8	122.2	4.7
Pittsburgh-Beaver Valley, PA	114.9	3.1	110.4	3.1
Portland-Vancouver, OR-WA	114.7	3.4	112.0	3.2
St. Louis-East St. Louis, MO-IL	115.7	3.1	115.4	3.2
San Diego, CA	123.4	5.0	116.5	4.9
San Francisco-Oakland-San Jose, CA	120.5	4.4	119.4	4.5
Seattle-Tacoma, WA	112.8	3.3	110.9	3.3
Tampa-St. Petersburg-Clearwater, FL	103.7	3.7	103.4	3.4
Washington, DC-MD-VA	121.0	4.1	120.3	4.2

Note: The sample used to compute the United States City Average includes 85 urban areas across the U.S., 29 of which have a Consumer Price Index specific to their areas. Consumer price indexes are meant to compare price changes in a given area over time, so the indexes should not be used to compare one city to another.

Source: U.S. Department of Labor, Bureau of Labor Statistics, *CPI Detailed Report*, January 1989.

TABLE 2.27--CONSUMER PRICE INDEX FOR CITIES IN THE SOUTH, BY POPULATION SIZE CLASS, 1988 [1982–84=100]

Population size	Jan.	Feb.	March	April	May	June	July	August	Sept.	Oct.	Nov.	Dec.	Annual Average	Annual Percent change
	Urban wage earners and clerical workers													
SOUTH[1]	113.6	113.8	114.2	114.7	114.9	115.5	116.1	116.5	117.2	117.7	117.8	118.0	115.8	3.5
Less than 50,000	113.5	113.4	113.4	114.2	114.4	115.3	115.8	116.2	116.8	116.8	117.0	117.0	115.3	3.4
50,000–450,000	113.6	113.8	114.3	114.9	115.0	115.3	116.1	116.4	117.0	117.7	117.9	118.1	115.8	3.4
450,000–1,200,000	112.9	113.0	113.6	114.1	114.0	114.7	115.2	115.8	116.6	117.5	117.7	117.8	115.2	3.7
More than 1,200,000	114.1	114.4	114.7	115.1	115.7	116.4	116.9	117.2	117.9	118.1	118.0	118.4	116.4	3.6
	All urban consumers													
SOUTH[1]	114.1	114.4	114.8	115.4	115.6	116.1	116.6	117.0	117.7	118.2	118.3	118.5	116.4	3.6
Less than 50,000	112.8	112.7	112.7	113.6	113.7	114.5	115.0	115.3	116.0	116.0	116.3	116.3	114.6	3.5
50,000–450,000	113.3	113.4	114.0	114.5	114.6	114.9	115.6	115.9	116.4	117.1	117.4	117.6	115.4	3.4
450,000–1,200,000	114.8	115.1	115.8	116.3	116.2	116.7	117.1	117.6	118.6	119.5	119.6	119.7	117.3	4.0
More than 1,200,000	114.9	115.2	115.5	116.0	116.7	117.2	117.7	118.0	118.7	118.9	118.9	119.2	117.2	3.5

Note: Indexes are not seasonally adjusted.

1. South includes Alabama, Arkansas, Delaware, District of Columbia, Florida, Georgia, Kentucky, Louisiana, Maryland, Mississippi, North Carolina, Oklahoma, South Carolina, Tennessee, Texas, Virginia, and West Virginia.

Source: U.S. Department of Labor, Bureau of Labor Statistics, *CPI Detailed Report*, monthly.

The Bureau of Labor Statistics (BLS) in the U.S. Department of Labor publishes state, regional, and national data on employment and earnings. Its monthly periodical, *Employment and Earnings*, is based on surveys taken across the U.S. The Employment Cost Index (ECI), a relatively new series from BLS, gives quarterly indices for national, regional, and metropolitan/nonmetropolitan areas. These indices measure change in employers' costs for employee compensation over time. Users should be cautioned that the ECI does not estimate wage or compensation levels, but rather the change in levels.

Each state's department of employment security coorperates with the BLS in the provision of employment statistics for its own state. The Tennessee Department of Employment Security (TDES) is the primary source of employment data at the state and county levels. Its annual report, *Tennessee Covered Employment and Wages by Industry*, provides summary payroll data on workers covered by unemployment insurance laws. These data, collected from employers, provide a count of jobs held by major industry groups. In another publication, *Annual Average Labor Force Estimates*, TDES uses sample surveys to estimate the size of the civilian labor force, employment and unemployment rates for the state, metropolitan statistical areas and nonmetropolitan counties. This report also details estimated nonagricultural employment or jobs by industry group. The Department of Employment Security also publishes a monthly newsletter, *The Labor Market Report*, which provides estimates of hours and earnings for manufacturing production workers (these estimates are reported in Chapter 4). In addition, the local offices of TDES can provide timely information for their areas, although they point out that even the best efforts may not be able to accurately track mobile employment such as construction crews.

The term "labor force" includes all those persons who are 16 years of age or over and classified as employed, unemployed, or members of the armed forces. Employed persons include those counted during the survey week who did any work for pay or profit or worked 15 or more hours unpaid in family enterprises and those who had jobs but were temporarily absent for noneconomic reasons. Unemployed persons are defined as those not at work during the survey week but who had attempted to find work within the previous four weeks and were still available for work. Those laid off or waiting to report to a new job within 30 days are also counted as unemployed.

TABLE OF CONTENTS

TABLE OF CONTENTS
(Continued)

Table Number | Page Number

TABLE 3.1-- EMPLOYMENT AND WAGES COVERED BY UNEMPLOYMENT INSURANCE, BY INDUSTRY, TENNESSEE, 1987

Industry	Number of employers	Average annual employment	Total wages	Average annual wages	Average premium rate	Total premiums due
TOTAL	102,641	1,914,976	$34,797,239,895	$18,171	$1.70	$199,340,861
Agriculture, forestry and fishing	1,536	11,297	131,618,454	11,650	1.93	1,539,015
Mining and quarrying	353	6,551	160,925,053	24,564	3.88	2,129,987
Contract construction	10,347	94,930	1,852,786,885	19,517	4.00	34,226,818
Manufacturing	7,403	495,100	10,305,868,677	20,815	1.94	73,720,517
Durable goods	4,366	244,155	5,336,201,377	21,855	2.00	38,463,435
Lumber and wood products	1,072	19,870	292,066,691	14,698	1.98	2,965,273
Furniture and fixtures	352	25,164	399,082,018	15,859	1.71	3,308,423
Stone, clay and glass products	369	15,133	383,842,071	25,364	2.78	3,446,535
Primary metal industries	158	15,281	402,366,213	26,331	1.63	1,952,478
Fabricated metal products	666	40,345	904,657,873	22,423	1.56	5,000,633
Machinery, except electrical	778	36,218	864,499,089	23,869	2.26	6,655,264
Electrical and electronic equipment	302	37,465	778,769,643	20,786	2.06	5,963,391
Transportation equipment	285	33,959	894,855,153	26,351	2.36	6,358,232
Instruments and related products	117	9,271	209,068,864	22,550	1.57	1,117,782
Miscellaneous manufacturing industries	267	11,449	206,993,762	18,079	1.89	1,695,424
Nondurable goods	3,037	250,945	4,969,667,300	19,803	1.88	35,257,082
Food and kindred products	379	38,605	841,985,338	21,810	1.28	3,754,610
Tobacco manufactures	10	1,402	32,411,381	23,117	3.46	355,314
Textile mill products	157	23,950	381,239,069	15,918	1.97	3,621,021
Apparel and other finished products	571	64,560	713,283,876	11,048	2.96	13,530,147
Paper and allied products	166	18,806	516,630,855	27,471	1.55	2,275,223
Printing, publishing and allied industries	1,150	30,918	618,596,138	20,007	1.16	2,597,722
Chemicals and allied products	244	38,346	1,162,139,032	30,306	0.73	2,151,059
Petroleum and coal products	28	861	21,226,367	24,653	2.74	187,316
Rubber and miscellaneous plastic products	256	24,227	560,552,335	23,137	1.54	2,966,617
Leather and leather products	76	9,271	121,602,909	13,116	5.57	3,818,053

TABLE 3.1-- EMPLOYMENT AND WAGES COVERED BY UNEMPLOYMENT INSURANCE, BY INDUSTRY, TENNESSEE, 1987 (Continued)

Industry	Number of employers	Average annual employment	Total wages	Average annual wages	Average premium rate	Total premiums due
Transportation, communications, and public utilities	4,068	97,058	2,392,343,976	24,648	1.23	9,344,895
Trade	34,835	477,431	6,673,349,661	13,977	1.22	38,273,788
Wholesale trade	10,845	123,312	2,830,409,045	22,953	1.23	11,737,483
Retail trade	23,990	354,120	3,842,940,616	10,852	1.21	26,536,305
Finance, insurance, and real estate	7,770	96,598	2,174,947,061	22,515	0.98	7,270,523
Services	34,325	381,591	6,568,197,461	17,212	1.42	30,373,527
State and local government	1,720	253,863	4,528,907,384	17,839	1.37	2,345,455
State government						
Education	51	27,582	586,776,896	21,273	1.35	3,014
Other	355	44,539	827,069,636	18,569	1.70	167,551
Local government						
Education	258	89,053	1,532,089,773	17,204	1.35	390,138
Other	1,056	92,689	1,582,971,079	17,078	1.35	1,784,752
Other	284	558	8,295,283	14,866	2.68	116,336

Source: Tennessee Department of Employment Security, Research and Statistics Section, *Tennessee Covered Employment and Wages by Industry, Statewide and by County, 1987.*

FIGURE 3.1
Distribution of Tennessee Insured Employment and Average Weekly Wages by Sector, 1987

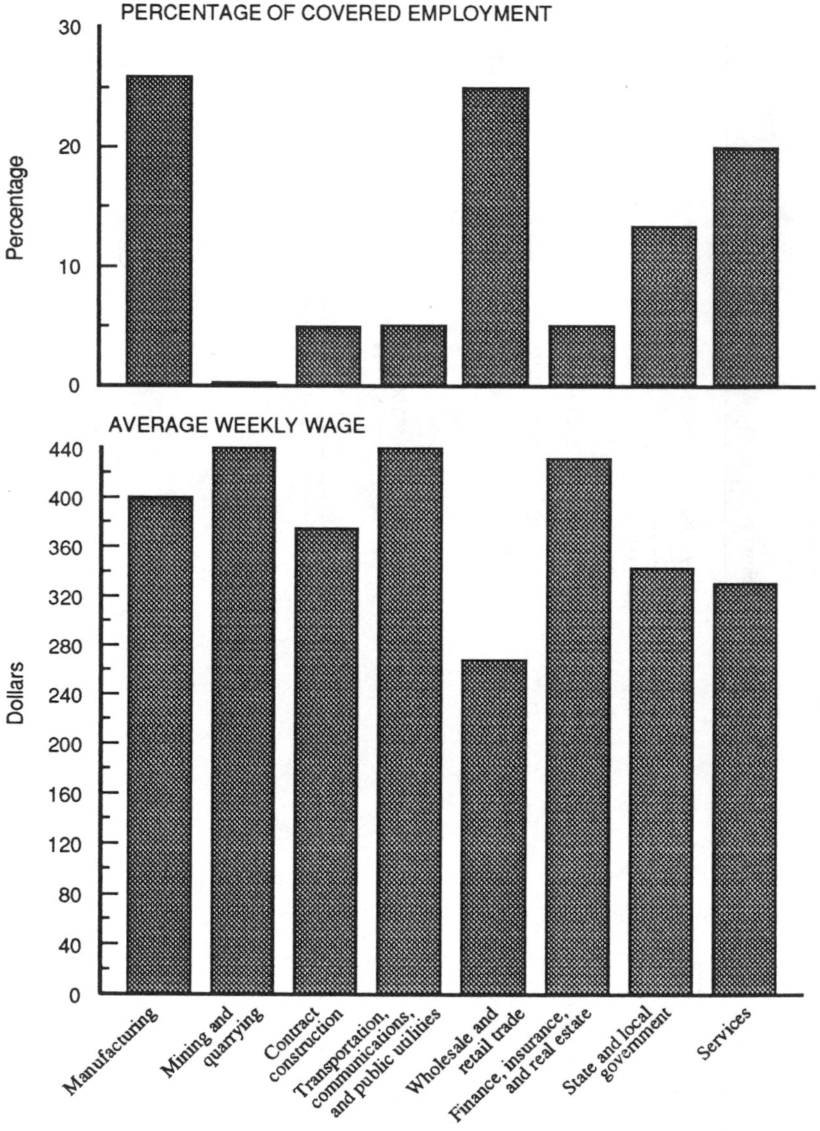

Source: Tennessee Department of Employment Security, *Tennessee Covered Employment and Wages by Industry, Statewide and by County, 1986–1987.*

TABLE 3.2-- EMPLOYMENT, BY OCCUPATION, BY SEX, AND BY RACE, TENNESSEE, 1980

		Female		White		Nonwhite	
Category	Total	Number	%	Number	%	Number	%
TOTAL	1,914,920	821,053	42.9	1,655,604	86.5	259,316	13.5
Executive, administrative, and managerial	171,064	50,507	29.5	159,911	93.5	11,153	6.5
Professional specialty	206,643	107,743	52.1	182,618	88.4	24,025	11.6
Technicians and related support	57,885	26,987	46.6	50,676	87.5	7,209	12.5
Sales	184,733	85,494	46.3	172,294	93.3	12,439	6.7
Administrative support, including clerical	294,347	223,268	75.9	258,599	87.9	35,748	12.1
Private household	14,280	13,793	96.6	5,033	35.2	9,247	64.8
Protective services	26,372	2,459	9.3	22,886	86.8	3,486	13.2
Service, except protective and household	190,642	123,324	64.7	140,482	73.7	50,160	26.3
Farming, forestry, and fishing	49,478	4,912	9.9	45,629	92.2	3,849	7.8
Precision production, craft, and repair	254,491	21,795	8.6	232,868	91.5	21,623	8.5
Machine operators, assemblers, and inspectors	262,451	132,497	50.5	220,590	84.0	41,861	16.0
Transportation and material moving	96,450	6,428	6.7	80,633	83.6	15,817	16.4
Handlers, cleaners, helpers, and laborers	106,084	21,846	20.6	83,385	78.6	22,699	21.4

Note: Percentages are of all employed persons aged 16 and over. These were computed by the Center for Business and Economic Research.

Source: U.S. Department of Commerce, Bureau of the Census, *1980 Census of Population, General Social and Economic Characteristics, Tennessee.*

TABLE 3.3-- UNEMPLOYMENT RATE, TENNESSEE AND UNITED STATES, MONTHLY, 1979–1988 [Not seasonally adjusted]

	Jan.	Feb.	March	April	May	June	July	August	Sept.	Oct.	Nov.	Dec.	Annual average
1988													
Tennessee	5.8	5.7	5.7	5.8	5.3	7.2	6.3	5.9	5.8	5.2	5.2	5.5	5.8
United States	6.3	6.2	5.9	5.3	5.4	5.5	5.5	5.4	5.2	5.0	5.2	5.0	5.5
1987[r]													
Tennessee	7.6	7.2	7.7	7.4	7.0	7.5	6.5	6.7	6.1	5.2	5.4	4.9	6.6
United States	7.3	7.2	6.9	6.2	6.1	6.3	6.1	5.8	5.7	5.7	5.6	5.4	6.2
1986[r]													
Tennessee	8.5	8.9	8.7	8.3	7.3	8.4	7.9	8.0	7.7	8.0	7.5	7.4	8.0
United States	7.3	7.8	7.5	7.0	7.0	7.3	7.0	6.7	6.8	6.6	6.6	6.3	7.0
1985[r]													
Tennessee	8.0	8.4	8.6	8.4	7.7	8.6	8.1	8.6	7.8	7.1	7.2	7.6	8.0
United States	8.0	7.8	7.5	7.1	7.0	7.5	7.4	6.9	6.9	6.8	6.7	6.7	7.2
1984[r]													
Tennessee	9.8	8.7	9.6	9.4	8.6	9.6	8.7	8.8	8.2	7.5	7.0	6.8	8.6
United States	8.8	8.4	8.1	7.6	7.2	7.4	7.5	7.3	7.1	7.0	6.9	7.0	7.5
1983[r]													
Tennessee	13.2	13.0	11.8	11.6	11.4	12.8	12.3	12.1	10.7	10.2	9.7	9.0	11.5
United States	11.4	11.3	10.8	10.0	9.8	10.2	9.4	9.2	8.8	8.4	8.1	8.0	9.6
1982[r]													
Tennessee	11.8	12.3	12.6	11.7	10.6	12.6	11.8	12.2	11.1	11.2	11.4	12.8	11.8
United States	9.4	9.6	9.5	9.2	9.1	9.8	9.8	9.6	9.7	9.9	10.4	10.5	9.7
1981[r]													
Tennessee	9.7	9.7	9.1	8.0	7.9	9.5	9.4	8.6	8.4	8.7	9.7	10.2	9.1
United States	8.2	8.0	7.7	7.0	7.1	7.7	7.3	7.2	7.3	7.5	7.9	8.3	7.6
1980[r]													
Tennessee	6.9	6.8	6.9	6.4	6.7	7.8	7.8	8.0	6.9	7.3	7.8	8.3	7.3
United States	6.9	6.8	6.6	6.7	7.1	7.8	7.9	7.6	7.2	7.1	7.1	6.9	7.1
1979													
Tennessee	7.1	6.7	5.3	4.7	5.2	6.8	6.3	6.2	5.2	4.9	5.5	5.6	5.8
United States	6.4	6.4	6.1	5.5	5.2	6.0	5.9	5.9	5.7	5.6	5.6	5.7	5.8

r revised.

Source: Tennessee Department of Employment Security, direct correspondence.

FIGURE 3.2
Unemployment Rate, Tennessee and the United States, Monthly, 1984–1988

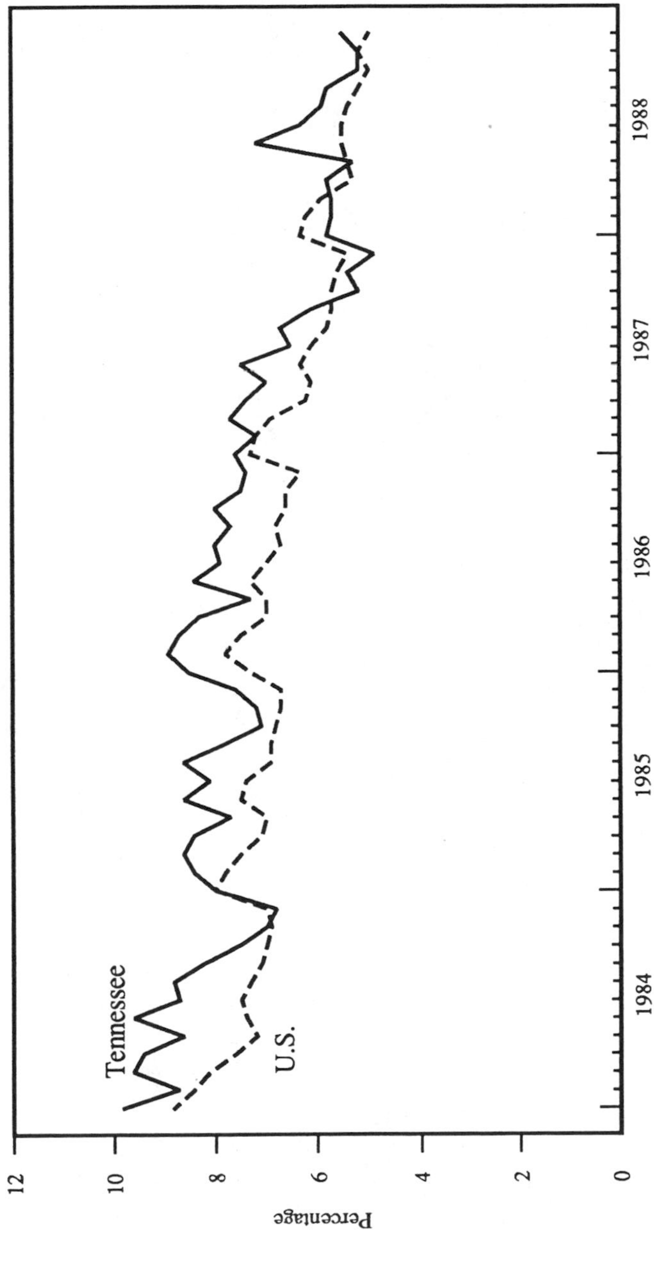

Source: Tennessee Department of Employment Security, direct correspondence.

TABLE 3.4-- FULL-TIME EQUIVALENT EMPLOYMENT AND PAYROLLS OF STATE AND LOCAL GOVERNMENTS, WITH RATES PER 10,000 POPULATION, BY FUNCTION, TENNESSEE, OCTOBER 1987

Function	State and local governments			State government only	
	Employ-ment	Employment per 10,000 population	Payroll ($1,000)	Employ-ment	Payroll ($1,000)
All functions	232,520	479.4	383,154	70,892	125,355
Education services					
Higher education	26,188	54.0	49,878	26,188	49,878
Instructional employees only	8,790	18.1	26,038	8,790	26,038
Elementary and secondary education	82,681	170.5	135,771	0	0
Instructional employees only	57,276	118.1	110,166	0	0
Libraries	929	1.9	1,264	0	0
Other education	1,896	3.9	3,570	1,896	3,570
Social services and income maintenance					
Public welfare	8,104	16.7	11,425	5,204	8,502
Hospitals	25,296	52.2	39,298	9,453	14,986
Health	5,955	12.3	10,297	4,027	7,484
Social insurance administration	1,528	3.2	2,692	1,528	2,692
Transportation					
Highways	11,550	23.8	15,880	5,021	8,241
Air and water transportation	567	1.2	1,103	0	0
Public safety					
Police protection	11,011	22.7	17,987	1,145	2,355
Police officers only	8,362	17.2	15,006	868	1,936
Fire protection	5,315	11.0	9,710	0	0
Firefighters only	4,752	9.8	8,820	0	0
Corrections	7,848	16.2	11,870	5,975	9,374
Environment and housing					
Natural resources	2,695	5.6	4,315	2,551	4,157
Parks and recreation	3,407	7.0	4,471	1,110	1,275
Housing and community development	2,735	5.6	3,898	0	0
Sewerage	1,675	3.5	2,536	0	0
Solid waste management	3,399	7.0	4,144	0	0

TABLE 3.4-- FULL-TIME EQUIVALENT EMPLOYMENT AND PAYROLLS OF STATE AND LOCAL GOVERNMENTS, WITH RATES PER 10,000 POPULATION, BY FUNCTION, TENNESSEE, OCTOBER 1987 (Continued)

Function	State and local governments			State government only	
	Employ-ment	Employment per 10,000 population	Payroll ($1,000)	Employ-ment	Payroll ($1,000)
Governmental administration					
Judicial and legal	3,661	7.5	7,141	1,118	2,856
Financial and other	7,919	16.3	13,020	3,108	5,461
Local utilities					
Water supply	3,909	8.1	6,240	0	0
Electric power and gas supply	7,419	15.3	15,405	0	0
Public transit	685	1.4	1,183	0	0
Other and unallocable	6,148	12.7	10,055	2,568	4,523

Source: U.S. Department of Commerce, Bureau of the Census, *Public Employment in 1987*.

TABLE 3.5-- GOVERNMENT EMPLOYMENT, BY LEVEL OF GOVERNMENT, TENNESSEE, 1945–1987, SELECTED YEARS [In thousands of employees]

Year	All governments [1]	Federal (civilian) [2]	State	Local[3]
1987	321	58	82	181
1986	314	58	81	175
1985	307	57	79	171
1984	307	58	78	171
1983	303	58	76	168
1982	310	66	77	168
1981	319	72	75	172
1980	325	70	74	180
1979	321	68	75	177
1978	315	68	73	174
1977	293	57	74	162
1976	283	55	69	158
1975	275	53	63	159
1974	265	50	64	151
1973	263	49	61	153
1972	248	48	60	140
1971	235	46	56	133
1970	221	42	55	124
1969	217	43	51	124
1968	217	44	47	126
1967	206	42	45	119
1966	198	45	41	113
1965	187	38	37	111
1964	179	38	34	108
1963	172	38	32	102
1962	170	38	30	101
1961	160	36	28	96
1960	151	36	26	89
1959	150	39	25	86
1955	132	42	21	69
1950	114	36	17	60
1945	93	42	n.a.	n.a.

Note: Detail may not add to total due to independent rounding.

n.a. not available.

1. Employment as of October 12, except for the years 1945 and 1957. Data for these years are as of April 12.

2. The month in which federal civilian employment is enumerated has varied.

3. Statistics for local governments are estimates subject to sampling variations.

Source: U.S. Department of Commerce, Bureau of the Census, *Public Employment in 1987*, and earlier editions.

TABLE 3.6-- CIVILIAN EMPLOYMENT IN THE FEDERAL GOVERNMENT, BY SELECTED AGENCIES, TENNESSEE, 1950–1986

Year	Total	Department of Defense	U.S. Postal Service	Veterans Adminis-tration	Other agencies
1986	57,950	7,211	13,615	7,188	29,936
1982	58,200	7,300	11,700	6,500	32,700
1981	67,300	8,100	11,800	6,300	41,100
1980	71,600	7,800	12,000	6,400	45,400
1979	69,900	7,800	12,000	6,200	43,900
1978	68,000	7,800	11,800	6,100	42,300
1977	63,700	8,100	11,900	6,200	37,500
1976	51,800	7,500	11,100	5,900	27,300
1975	55,400	8,000	12,100	5,900	27,000
1974	50,300	7,900	12,000	4,700	26,100
1973	49,300	7,600	11,100	5,300	25,300
1972	48,500	7,500	11,000	5,300	24,700
1971	46,900	7,100	11,200	5,100	23,600
1970	44,800	7,400	10,900	4,600	21,800
1969	42,400	8,000	11,200	4,500	18,700
1968	40,300	7,300	11,100	4,600	17,300
1967	40,100	7,200	10,800	4,600	17,500
1966	39,300	7,200	10,700	4,500	16,900
1965	40,700	6,100	12,500	4,500	17,500
1964	38,200	6,200	9,400	4,600	17,900
1963	36,300	6,300	9,400	4,700	15,900
1962	36,400	6,600	9,400	4,700	15,700
1961	35,600	6,700	9,200	4,900	14,700
1960	34,100	6,600	9,000	4,800	13,500
1959	36,300	7,700	9,000	4,900	14,700
1958	37,500	8,500	8,800	4,800	15,400
1957	37,400	8,000	9,700	5,000	14,600
1956	37,900	9,500	8,700	5,100	14,700
1955	37,800	9,500	7,900	5,000	15,300
1954	41,200	8,700	7,900	5,200	19,400
1953	41,200	9,700	8,200	5,400	18,000
1952	44,100	10,400	8,500	5,400	19,900
1951	44,500	12,700	8,100	5,600	18,100
1950	36,300	7,900	8,200	5,700	14,500

Note: Excludes members and employees of Congress, Central Intelligence Agency, temporary Christmas help of the U.S. Postal Service, and the National Security Agency.

Source: Tax Foundation, Inc., *Facts and Figures on Government Finance, 1988–1989*, and earlier editions; and U.S. Department of Commerce, Bureau of the Census, *Statistical Abstract of the United States, 1984*, and earlier editions.

TABLE 3.7-- NUMBER OF EMPLOYEES IN NONAGRICULTURAL ESTABLISHMENTS, BY SECTOR, TENNESSEE, 1950–1988, SELECTED YEARS
[In thousands of persons]

Sector[1]	1988	1987[r]	1986	1985	1984	1983	1982	1981	1980
Total	2,065.8	2,011.6	1,929.8	1,867.8	1,812.0	1,719.0	1,703.0	1,755.4	1,746.6
Manufacturing	508.2	497.4	490.5	492.4	497.1	468.6	466.7	506.9	502.1
Construction	94.4	95.2	90.0	85.6	78.3	69.6	72.2	76.2	81.2
Transportation and public utilities	108.8	103.4	97.6	93.0	89.1	83.6	84.0	86.7	86.6
Trade	488.2	477.2	452.1	435.3	413.3	389.9	380.5	379.9	379.7
Finance, insurance, and real estate	103.9	101.4	95.4	89.4	85.9	81.9	79.9	79.6	78.7
Services	430.0	408.9	384.7	360.2	344.3	323.4	313.1	304.4	291.0
Government	325.6	321.2	312.4	304.2	296.1	294.1	297.5	311.7	317.2
Other non-manufacturing	6.7	6.9	7.1	7.7	7.9[r]	7.9	9.2	10.0	10.1
		1979	1978	1977	1976	1975	1970	1960	1950
Total		1,777.3	1,737.0	1,648.1	1,577.4	1,505.7	1,327.6	925.4	759.3
Manufacturing		524.7	526.0	507.5	487.2	459.0	463.8	315.0	249.2
Construction		89.2	87.3	78.4	75.2	76.0	65.3	48.5	47.8
Transportation and public utilities		87.3	83.2	78.3	73.3	70.8	66.4	55.4	59.5
Trade		388.7	379.1	357.2	399.8	320.8	257.7	193.2	161.1
Finance, insurance, and real estate		77.6	74.3	71.1	69.8	68.9	56.5	39.2	24.6
Services		285.4	270.7	254.5	240.0	229.4	184.9	120.3	93.0
Government		313.9	305.6	291.2	282.7	271.3	225.9	146.3	111.2
Other non-manufacturing		10.5	10.8	9.9	9.4	9.5	7.1	7.5	12.9

r revised.

1. Classification is in accordance with the 1972 SIC manual.

Source: Tennessee Department of Employment Security, Research and Statistics Section, *Tennessee Labor Force Estimates, 1984–1988*, and earlier editions.

TABLE 3.8-- LABOR FORCE, EMPLOYMENT, AND UNEMPLOYMENT RATE, TENNESSEE AND METROPOLITAN STATISTICAL AREAS, 1987 AND 1988

Metropolitan statistical area	1988 Labor force	1988 Employed persons	1988 Unemployment rate	1987[r] Labor force	1987[r] Employed persons	1987[r] Unemployment rate
TENNESSEE	2,350,000	2,214,000	5.8	2,336,000	2,182,000	6.6
Chattanooga	212,600	200,900	5.5	208,200	196,400	5.7
Hamilton County	143,890	136,520	5.1	141,750	134,170	5.3
Marion County	10,320	9,330	9.6	10,390	9,170	11.7
Sequatchie County	3,600	3,360	6.7	3,640	3,300	9.3
Clarksville-Hopkinsville	53,700	50,100	6.7	53,200	49,300	7.3
Montgomery County	33,760	31,570	6.5	33,420	31,140	6.8
Jackson[1]	38,760	36,420	6.0	37,470	34,290	8.5
Johnson City-Kingsport-Bristol	215,000	202,900	5.6	214,700	200,100	6.8
Carter County	24,300	22,470	7.5	24,220	22,250	8.1
Hawkins County	19,830	18,700	5.7	19,760	18,520	6.3
Sullivan County	73,610	70,000	4.9	74,480	69,340	6.9
Unicoi County	7,710	7,160	7.1	7,780	7,090	8.9
Washington County	46,360	43,790	5.5	46,160	43,370	6.0
Knoxville	285,600	270,000	5.5	284,500	266,200	6.4
Anderson County	32,820	31,260	4.8	32,890	30,830	6.3
Blount County	38,250	36,060	5.7	38,080	35,560	6.6
Grainger County	7,170	6,670	7.0	7,180	6,580	8.4
Jefferson County	15,550	14,520	6.6	15,530	14,320	7.8
Knox County	163,310	155,660	4.7	162,170	153,510	5.3
Sevier County	23,130	20,820	10.0	23,280	20,530	11.8
Union County	5,350	5,000	6.5	5,400	4,930	8.7
Memphis	443,100	420,600	5.1	441,500	416,200	5.7
Shelby County	403,330	383,920	4.8	402,400	380,310	5.5
Tipton County	16,420	15,390	6.3	16,360	15,250	6.8
Nashville	523,700	500,900	4.4	522,700	499,800	4.4
Cheatham County	12,770	12,300	3.7	12,780	12,270	4.0
Davidson County	285,780	274,510	3.9	285,210	273,920	4.0

TABLE 3.8-- LABOR FORCE, EMPLOYMENT, AND UNEMPLOYMENT RATE, TENNESSEE AND METROPOLITAN STATISTICAL AREAS, 1987 AND 1988 (Continued)

Metropolitan statistical area	1988 Labor force	1988 Employed persons	1988 Unemploy-ment rate	1987[r] Labor force	1987[r] Employed persons	1987[r] Unemploy-ment rate
Dickson County	16,550	15,520	6.2	16,510	15,480	6.2
Robertson County	21,230	20,010	5.7	21,220	19,970	5.9
Rutherford County	58,350	55,600	4.7	58,370	55,480	5.0
Sumner County	52,310	49,320	5.7	52,090	49,220	5.5
Williamson County	41,310	40,140	2.8	41,170	40,060	2.7
Wilson County	35,360	33,460	5.4	35,320	33,390	5.5

Note: The Department of Employment Security makes its estimates for the components of the MSA located outside of Tennessee as well as for the Tennessee portions. The MSA total, therefore, will not equal the sum of the Tennessee counties for those MSA's located in more than one state. To identify nonstate counties within these MSA's, see Figure 0.1.

r revised using 1988 benchmark.

1. Jackson Metropolitan Statistical Area consists of Madison County.

Source: Tennessee Department of Employment Security, CPS Labor Force Estimates Summary, direct correspondence.

TABLE 3.9-- NUMBER OF EMPLOYEES IN NONAGRICULTURAL ESTABLISHMENTS, BY SECTOR, METROPOLITAN STATISTICAL AREAS, 1980–1988
[In thousands of persons]

MSA and sector[1]	1988	1987[r]	1986	1985	1984	1983	1982	1981	1980
CHATTANOOGA									
Total	195.9	190.3	179.7	174.9	171.3	166.2	164.6	171.2	168.7
Manufacturing	47.2	46.0	43.8	43.7	43.7	43.3	44.4	48.4	50.2
Construction	8.3	7.9	7.5	7.5	6.6	5.7	5.6	6.0	6.5
Transportation	9.1	9.0	8.7	8.3	7.8	7.2	7.6	7.7	7.3
Trade	45.2	43.9	41.2	40.1	39.2	36.6	35.1	36.5	33.0
Finance	12.5	12.0	11.1	10.5	10.0	9.8	10.1	10.0	9.6
Services	38.3	37.5	35.2	33.3	31.7	31.1	29.7	29.8	28.2
Government	34.6	33.3	31.2	30.5	31.3	31.4	30.8	31.5	32.7
Other non-manufacturing	0.7	0.7	0.9	1.0	1.0	1.1	1.3	1.3	1.2

MSA and sector[1]	1988	1987	1986	1985	1984	1983	1982	1981	1980
CLARKSVILLE-HOPKINSVILLE[2]									
Total	23.9	23.3	22.1	21.0	19.8	19.3	19.9	21.5	20.7
Manufacturing	5.5	5.3	4.9	4.8	4.7	4.7	5.4	6.7	6.1
Construction	1.4	1.4	1.0	0.7	0.6	0.6	0.6	0.8	0.8
Transportation	1.0	0.9	0.9	0.8	0.8	0.8	0.7	0.7	0.7
Trade	5.8	5.5	5.2	4.9	4.4	4.2	4.1	4.3	4.3
Finance	1.2	1.2	1.1	1.0	0.9	0.8	0.8	0.8	0.8
Services	3.2	3.2	3.3	3.2	2.9	2.8	2.7	2.7	2.5
Government	5.8	5.8	5.7	5.5	5.4	5.4	5.5	5.4	5.4
Other non-manufacturing	0.0	0.0	0.0	0.1	0.1	0.0	0.1	0.1	0.1

MSA and sector[1]	1988	1987	1986	1985	1984	1983	1982	1981	1980
JACKSON									
Total	37.2	34.5	33.6	32.7	33.2	30.4	29.2	29.5	30.3
Manufacturing	8.6	8.2	8.2	8.3	8.5	7.9	7.7	8.5	8.6
Construction	2.0	1.8	1.5	1.5	1.4	1.2	1.2	1.3	1.7
Transportation	1.5	1.6	1.5	1.4	1.4	1.5	1.3	1.3	1.3
Trade	8.9	7.8	7.5	7.6	7.6	7.1	7.0	6.4	6.7
Finance	1.2	1.0	1.2	1.0	1.0	1.0	0.9	1.0	1.1
Services	7.6	6.8	6.6	6.0	6.2	4.9	4.6	4.6	4.3
Government	7.3	7.3	7.1	6.8	7.0	6.8	6.5	6.4	6.5
Other non-manufacturing	0.1	0.0	0.0	0.1	0.1	0.0	0.0	0.1	0.1

TABLE 3.9-- NUMBER OF EMPLOYEES IN NONAGRICULTURAL ESTABLISHMENTS, BY SECTOR, METROPOLITAN STATISTICAL AREAS, 1980–1988
[In thousands of persons] (Continued)

MSA and sector[1]	1988	1987[r]	1986	1985	1984	1983	1982	1981	1980
JOHNSON CITY-KINGSPORT-BRISTOL									
Total	163.2	159.5	154.4	151.1	147.0	142.5	141.6	136.2	136.3
Manufacturing	53.0	53.2	52.8	52.7	53.1	51.1	51.7	53.0	53.1
Construction	7.0	6.7	5.9	6.2	5.6	5.7	6.9	6.7	7.0
Transportation	6.2	6.0	6.1	6.0	5.7	6.2	6.0	5.6	5.8
Trade	37.0	35.7	34.4	33.5	31.0	29.2	27.9	23.9	24.1
Finance	5.3	5.2	4.9	4.8	4.7	4.6	4.3	4.5	4.4
Services	30.1	28.7	27.0	25.3	24.0	22.5	21.8	18.3	17.1
Government	24.2	23.7	23.0	22.7	22.7	23.0	22.8	23.9	24.4
Other non-manufacturing	0.4	0.3	0.4	0.0	0.2	0.2	0.2	0.2	0.3
MSA and sector[1]	1988	1987[r]	1986	1985	1984	1983	1982	1981	1980
KNOXVILLE[2]									
Total	259.9	251.9	242.0	235.0	232.6	224.1	207.8	205.1	195.3
Manufacturing	53.6	50.6	51.0	50.9	50.9	48.2	49.0	51.5	52.4
Construction	12.9	12.4	11.9	11.1	10.9	9.8	9.0	9.7	9.5
Transportation	10.2	9.8	9.0	8.8	8.5	7.9	8.6	8.5	8.2
Trade	65.0	63.6	60.7	57.5	54.7	51.7	47.7	44.0	41.5
Finance	9.8	9.5	9.0	8.8	9.0	9.6	8.9	8.8	8.2
Services	56.4	53.4	50.1	48.8	49.8	47.7	38.5	34.3	32.4
Government	50.3	50.8	48.4	47.2	46.7	47.3	44.5	46.7	41.5
Other non-manufacturing	1.7	1.9	1.9	1.8	2.1	1.9	1.6	1.6	1.6
MSA and sector[1]	1988	1987[r]	1986	1985	1984	1983	1982	1981	1980
MEMPHIS[2]									
Total	433.3	422.0	403.0	388.7	374.8	355.7	349.2	359.4	359.4
Manufacturing	55.1	53.6	51.8	52.2	53.4	51.4	53.9	59.5	59.6
Construction	18.3	19.1	18.5	18.1	16.3	13.9	12.4	14.4	15.9
Transportation	40.7	38.8	35.5	33.3	30.4	27.4	26.6	27.6	27.5
Trade	117.1	116.3	111.2	108.2	103.4	97.8	96.5	97.4	97.1
Finance	24.9	24.2	22.9	21.9	21.4	20.3	19.4	19.9	19.8
Services	106.0	98.9	93.8	88.3	86.0	81.1	77.9	76.8	73.6
Government	71.2	71.1	69.2	66.6	63.8	63.7	62.3	63.6	65.7
Other non-manufacturing	0.1	0.1	0.1	0.1	0.1	0.1	0.2	0.2	0.2

TABLE 3.9-- NUMBER OF EMPLOYEES IN NONAGRICULTURAL ESTABLISHMENTS, BY SECTOR, METROPOLITAN STATISTICAL AREAS, 1980–1988
[In thousands of persons] (Continued)

MSA and sector[1]	1988	1987[r]	1986	1985	1984	1983	1982	1981	1980
NASHVILLE-DAVIDSON									
Total	483.5	476.7	456.1	434.1	407.5	380.6	366.3	370.5	360.2
Manufacturing	89.8	90.3	90.5	89.4	86.6	80.1	79.1	84.1	80.8
Construction	27.1	28.9	28.2	25.7	22.8	19.3	18.3	17.5	18.7
Transportation	24.2	24.2	22.7	22.2	21.7	20.0	19.8	20.3	19.5
Trade	118.8	116.9	111.5	105.5	98.2	89.9	87.1	85.2	82.0
Finance	34.4	33.6	31.4	29.0	27.3	26.6	25.6	25.1	24.5
Services	121.0	116.4	107.0	99.1	89.6	83.3	75.6	77.0	71.9
Government	67.4	65.7	64.2	62.4	60.7	60.8	60.8	61.3	62.8
Other non-manufacturing	0.8	0.7	0.6	0.7	0.6	0.6	0.1	(a)	(a)

Note: For area included in each MSA see figure 0.1. Detail may not add to total due to independent rounding.

r revised to 1988 benchmark.

1. Classification is in accordance with the 1972 SIC Manual.

2. Knoxville includes the counties of Knox, Anderson, Blount, and Union prior to 1983; Jefferson, Grainger and Sevier are added beginning in 1983. Memphis excludes the DeSoto County, Mississippi portion of the MSA; Clarksville includes only the Montgomery County, Tennessee portion of this MSA.

a. Included in services.

Source: Tennessee Department of Employment Security, Research and Statistics Section, *Tennessee Annual Average Labor Force Estimates, 1984–1988*, and earlier editions.

TABLE 3.10--PAYROLL AND FULL-TIME EQUIVALENT EMPLOYMENT OF CITY GOVERNMENTS, BY SELECTED FUNCTIONS, TENNESSEE CITIES WITH POPULATION OF 75,000 OR MORE, OCTOBER 1987

City	Average October earnings[3] ($)	Total	Education	Highways	Police	Fire	Utilities	Sanitation	Parks	Governmental administration
		Employment								
Chattanooga[1]		5,505	2,473	162	485	458	623	214	169	151
Knoxville		2,571	0	22	356	352	957	102	53	89
Memphis[2]		20,133	10,541	308	1,394	1,461	3,391	936	512	347
Nashville-Davidson[2]		16,965	7,476	328	1,300	984	1,884	338	399	877
		Payroll ($1,000)								
Chattanooga[1]	1,958	10,265	5,795	168	734	729	1,341	278	235	260
Knoxville	2,055	5,170	0	39	741	734	2,035	247	29	167
Memphis[2]	1,977	37,867	20,301	523	2,860	3,082	7,188	1,257	1,016	603
Nashville-Davidson[2]	2,024	33,396	18,292	456	2,246	1,837	3,836	401	662	1,605

Note: Total includes "All other" category not shown separately.
1. Noneducation data are for October 1984.
2. Noneducation data are for October 1985.
3. Full-time employees only.
Source: U.S. Department of Commerce, Bureau of the Census, *City Employment in 1987*.

TABLE 3.11--LABOR FORCE, EMPLOYMENT, AND UNEMPLOYMENT RATE, TENNESSEE AND COUNTIES, 1987 AND 1988

County	1988			1987[r]		
	Labor force	Employed persons	Unem- ploy- ment rate	Labor force	Employed persons	Unem- ploy- ment rate
TENNESSEE	2,350,000	2,214,000	5.8	2,336,000	2,182,000	6.6
Anderson	32,820	31,260	4.8	32,890	30,830	6.3
Bedford	13,610	12,720	6.5	12,950	11,990	7.4
Benton	6,990	6,510	6.9	6,750	5,990	11.3
Bledsoe	5,160	4,910	4.8	5,090	4,790	5.9
Blount	38,250	36,060	5.7	38,080	35,560	6.6
Bradley	37,920	35,940	5.2	36,980	34,760	6.0
Campbell	12,270	10,920	11.0	13,130	11,270	14.2
Cannon	3,950	3,600	8.9	3,730	3,350	10.2
Carroll	11,990	11,000	8.3	12,130	10,780	11.1
Carter	24,300	22,470	7.5	24,220	22,250	8.1
Cheatham	12,770	12,300	3.7	12,780	12,270	4.0
Chester	5,110	4,780	6.5	5,220	4,860	6.9
Claiborne	10,770	9,940	7.7	10,780	9,900	8.2
Clay	5,450	5,190	4.8	5,100	4,910	3.7
Cocke	13,060	11,250	13.9	13,330	11,420	14.3
Coffee	17,880	16,710	6.5	17,770	16,410	7.7
Crockett	7,050	6,610	6.2	6,560	5,900	10.1
Cumberland	13,810	12,800	7.3	13,160	12,030	8.6
Davidson	285,780	274,510	3.9	285,210	273,920	4.0
Decatur	4,570	4,200	8.1	4,310	3,820	11.4
DeKalb	6,480	5,890	9.1	6,110	5,610	8.2
Dickson	16,550	15,520	6.2	16,510	15,480	6.2
Dyer	15,860	14,850	6.4	15,230	13,910	8.7
Fayette	10,370	9,590	7.5	10,560	9,830	6.9
Fentress	5,930	5,330	10.1	6,150	5,440	11.5
Franklin	14,670	13,820	5.8	14,280	13,370	6.4
Gibson	22,170	20,320	8.3	22,380	20,150	10.0
Giles	9,930	9,120	8.2	9,890	9,000	9.0
Grainger	7,170	6,670	7.0	7,180	6,580	8.4
Greene	26,230	23,780	9.3	26,720	23,820	10.9
Grundy	5,070	4,590	9.5	5,250	4,590	12.6
Hamblen	25,170	23,390	7.1	25,260	23,200	8.2
Hamilton	143,890	136,520	5.1	141,750	134,170	5.3
Hancock	3,050	2,880	5.6	2,910	2,690	7.6
Hardeman	10,830	10,040	7.3	10,890	9,910	9.0
Hardin	9,990	9,110	8.8	9,960	9,020	9.4
Hawkins	19,830	18,700	5.7	19,760	18,520	6.3
Haywood	8,490	7,800	8.1	8,270	7,330	11.4
Henderson	10,630	9,840	7.4	10,250	9,260	9.7
Henry	12,210	11,020	9.7	12,800	10,660	16.7
Hickman	7,210	6,660	7.6	7,160	6,610	7.7
Houston	2,930	2,620	10.6	2,860	2,510	12.2
Humphreys	5,170	4,550	12.0	5,560	4,670	16.0
Jackson	3,760	3,370	10.4	3,910	3,570	8.7
Jefferson	15,550	14,520	6.6	15,530	14,320	7.8
Johnson	5,390	4,600	14.7	5,620	4,980	11.4
Knox	163,310	155,660	4.7	162,170	153,510	5.3
Lake	2,270	2,110	7.0	2,330	2,090	10.3

TABLE 3.11--LABOR FORCE, EMPLOYMENT, AND UNEMPLOYMENT RATE, TENNESSEE AND COUNTIES, 1987 AND 1988 (Continued)

	1988			1987[r]		
County	Labor force	Employed persons	Unem-ploy-ment rate	Labor force	Employed persons	Unem-ploy-ment rate
Lauderdale	11,270	10,490	6.9	10,680	9,880	7.5
Lawrence	14,800	12,900	12.8	14,980	13,260	11.5
Lewis	4,210	3,850	8.6	3,900	3,410	12.6
Lincoln	12,630	11,850	6.2	12,080	11,360	6.0
Loudon	14,300	13,500	5.6	13,790	12,750	7.5
McMinn	20,590	19,310	6.2	20,120	18,500	8.1
McNairy	10,750	9,820	8.7	11,050	9,860	10.8
Macon	8,300	7,550	9.0	8,230	7,590	7.8
Madison	38,760	36,420	6.0	37,470	34,290	8.5
Marion	10,320	9,330	9.6	10,390	9,170	11.7
Marshall	10,250	9,720	5.2	10,190	9,500	6.8
Maury	24,870	23,310	6.3	24,130	22,370	7.3
Meigs	3,760	3,350	10.9	4,050	3,650	9.9
Monroe	16,080	14,950	7.0	16,020	14,710	8.2
Montgomery	33,760	31,570	6.5	33,420	31,140	6.8
Moore	1,840	1,740	5.4	1,940	1,820	6.2
Morgan	5,780	5,320	8.0	5,550	4,950	10.8
Obion	15,070	14,180	5.9	15,170	14,150	6.7
Overton	7,270	6,670	8.3	6,650	5,930	10.8
Perry	3,100	2,880	7.1	2,960	2,580	12.8
Pickett	1,740	1,540	11.5	1,780	1,460	18.0
Polk	4,280	3,690	13.8	4,890	4,340	11.2
Putnam	28,420	26,930	5.2	25,940	24,340	6.2
Rhea	10,310	9,220	10.6	10,780	9,770	9.4
Roane	25,850	24,460	5.4	26,180	24,570	6.1
Robertson	21,230	20,010	5.7	21,220	19,970	5.9
Rutherford	58,350	55,600	4.7	58,370	55,480	5.0
Scott	7,020	6,250	11.0	7,260	6,080	16.3
Sequatchie	3,600	3,360	6.7	3,640	3,300	9.3
Sevier	23,130	20,820	10.0	23,280	20,530	11.8
Shelby	403,330	383,920	4.8	402,400	380,310	5.5
Smith	7,370	6,900	6.4	7,690	7,220	6.1
Stewart	4,870	4,520	7.2	4,900	4,550	7.1
Sullivan	73,610	70,000	4.9	74,480	69,340	6.9
Sumner	52,310	49,320	5.7	52,090	49,220	5.5
Tipton	16,420	15,390	6.3	16,360	15,250	6.8
Trousdale	3,860	3,680	4.7	3,560	3,380	5.1
Unicoi	7,710	7,160	7.1	7,780	7,090	8.9
Union	5,350	5,000	6.5	5,400	4,930	8.7
Van Buren	2,600	2,430	6.5	2,520	2,290	9.1
Warren	13,870	12,670	8.7	13,060	11,640	10.9
Washington	46,360	43,790	5.5	46,160	43,370	6.0
Wayne	7,350	6,600	10.2	7,280	6,540	10.2
Weakley	14,910	14,230	4.6	14,500	13,710	5.4
White	8,240	7,690	6.7	7,910	7,230	8.6
Williamson	41,310	40,140	2.8	41,170	40,060	2.7
Wilson	35,360	33,460	5.4	35,320	33,390	5.5

r revised using 1988 benchmark.

Source: Tennessee Department of Employment Security, CPS Labor Force Summary, direct correspondence.

FIGURE 3.3
Unemployment Rates by County, 1988
(Tennessee average = 5.8%)

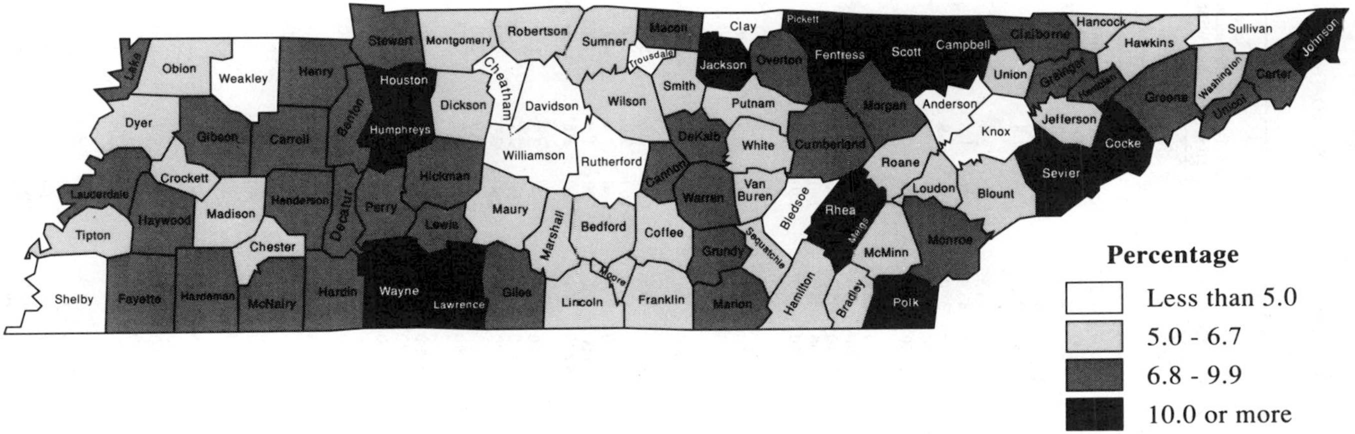

Note: Rates are benchmarked 1988.
Source: Tennessee Department of Employment Security, direct correspondence.

TABLE 3.12--NONAGRICULTURAL EMPLOYMENT, BY SECTOR, NON-MSA COUNTIES, 1988

		Manufacturing		Contract construction		Transportation, communications and utilities		Wholesale and retail trade	
County	Total	Em-ployed	%	Em-ployed	%	Em-ployed	%	Em-ployed	%
Bedford	10,990	5,480	49.9	450	4.1	400	3.6	1,690	15.4
Benton	3,540	1,160	32.8	120	3.4	110	3.1	780	22.0
Bledsoe	2,360	820	34.7	30	1.3	70	3.0	140	5.9
Bradley	29,480	12,150	41.2	1,380	4.7	400	1.4	5,400	18.3
Campbell	7,270	2,080	28.6	130	1.8	190	2.6	1,600	22.0
Cannon	2,010	870	43.3	50	2.5	100	5.0	250	12.4
Carroll	7,710	3,360	43.6	120	1.6	270	3.5	1,320	17.1
Chester	3,050	1,160	38.0	150	4.9	120	3.9	420	13.8
Claiborne	5,920	2,430	41.0	90	1.5	120	2.0	800	13.5
Clay	2,720	1,650	60.7	20	0.7	20	0.7	160	5.9
Cocke	6,250	2,410	38.6	150	2.4	50	0.8	1,190	19.0
Coffee	18,570	5,690	30.6	610	3.3	210	1.1	3,040	16.4
Crockett	3,120	1,410	45.2	90	2.9	70	2.2	640	20.5
Cumberland	9,080	2,300	25.3	280	3.1	170	1.9	2,140	23.6
Decatur	3,510	1,520	43.3	120	3.4	150	4.3	440	12.5
DeKalb	3,960	1,980	50.0	60	1.5	130	3.3	550	13.9
Dyer	13,020	5,100	39.2	840	6.5	380	2.9	2,710	20.8
Fayette	5,000	2,170	43.4	220	4.4	80	1.6	650	13.0
Fentress	3,430	1,580	46.1	90	2.6	60	1.7	430	12.5
Franklin	6,750	1,600	23.7	160	2.4	80	1.2	1,430	21.2
Gibson	16,880	8,530	50.5	680	4.0	590	3.5	2,870	17.0
Giles	7,380	3,530	47.8	160	2.2	90	1.2	1,290	17.5
Greene	19,290	9,140	47.4	650	3.4	400	2.1	2,830	14.7
Grundy	1,900	600	31.6	30	1.6	100	5.3	240	12.6
Hamblen	23,190	13,370	57.7	410	1.8	550	2.4	3,670	15.8
Hancock	920	380	41.3	30	3.3	0	0.0	70	7.6
Hardeman	7,140	2,570	36.0	190	2.7	100	1.4	1,280	17.9
Hardin	6,470	3,020	46.7	250	3.9	120	1.9	1,150	17.8
Haywood	5,270	2,300	43.6	160	3.0	220	4.2	920	17.5
Henderson	7,020	4,190	59.7	140	2.0	70	1.0	1,060	15.1
Henry	8,970	3,300	36.8	250	2.8	260	2.9	1,990	22.2
Hickman	3,400	1,420	41.8	100	2.9	80	2.4	320	9.4
Houston	1,590	450	28.3	(D)	(D)	(D)	(D)	190	11.9
Humphreys	4,720	1,940	41.1	260	5.5	(D)	(D)	550	11.7
Jackson	1,560	680	43.6	60	3.8	70	4.5	130	8.3
Johnson	3,060	1,460	47.7	140	4.6	(D)	(D)	300	9.8
Lake	1,550	420	27.1	10	0.6	20	1.3	250	16.1
Lauderdale	8,720	5,030	57.7	120	1.4	210	2.4	1,090	12.5
Lawrence	10,360	5,050	48.7	350	3.4	360	3.5	1,780	17.2
Lewis	2,390	1,060	44.4	50	2.1	40	1.7	400	16.7
Lincoln	7,210	2,850	39.5	400	5.5	140	1.9	1,450	20.1
Loudon	7,590	3,100	40.8	240	3.2	320	4.2	1,110	14.6
McMinn	16,960	8,760	51.7	360	2.1	750	4.4	2,870	16.9
McNairy	6,650	3,540	53.2	80	1.2	230	3.5	830	12.5
Macon	4,010	2,150	53.6	(D)	(D)	180	4.5	270	6.7
Marshall	9,460	6,080	64.3	190	2.0	170	1.8	1,110	11.7
Maury	19,350	5,720	29.6	1,440	7.4	560	2.9	4,290	22.2
Meigs	1,340	550	41.0	(D)	(D)	(D)	(D)	120	9.0
Monroe	8,040	3,610	44.9	250	3.1	220	2.7	1,450	18.0
Moore	1,090	420	38.5	(D)	(D)	10	0.9	40	3.7

TABLE 3.12--NONAGRICULTURAL EMPLOYMENT, BY SECTOR, NON-MSA COUNTIES, 1988
(Continued)

Finance, insurance and real estate		Services		Government		All other non-manufacturing		
Employed	%	Employed	%	Employed	%	Employed	%	County
300	2.7	1,160	10.6	1,480	13.5	30	0.3	Bedford
70	2.0	560	15.8	660	18.6	80	2.3	Benton
30	1.3	160	6.8	1,090	46.2	10	0.4	Bledsoe
820	2.8	5,600	19.0	3,630	12.3	100	0.3	Bradley
190	2.6	1,000	13.8	1,720	23.7	360	5.0	Campbell
110	5.5	280	13.9	350	17.4	0	0.0	Cannon
220	2.9	1,200	15.6	1,210	15.7	10	0.1	Carroll
60	2.0	(D)	0.0	480	15.7	660	21.6	Chester
190	3.2	820	13.9	1,060	17.9	410	6.9	Claiborne
30	1.1	430	15.8	390	14.3	20	0.7	Clay
200	3.2	820	13.1	1,370	21.9	60	1.0	Cocke
580	3.1	5,880	31.7	2,520	13.6	40	0.2	Coffee
100	3.2	290	9.3	520	16.7	0	0.0	Crockett
1,070	11.8	1,760	19.4	1,160	12.8	200	2.2	Cumberland
80	2.3	510	14.5	580	16.5	110	3.1	Decatur
120	3.0	560	14.1	550	13.9	10	0.3	DeKalb
420	3.2	1,700	13.1	1,840	14.1	30	0.2	Dyer
140	2.8	460	9.2	1,260	25.2	20	0.4	Fayette
100	2.9	440	12.8	650	19.0	80	2.3	Fentress
210	3.1	2,030	30.1	1,170	17.3	70	1.0	Franklin
360	2.1	1,750	10.4	2,080	12.3	20	0.1	Gibson
280	3.8	930	12.6	1,060	14.4	40	0.5	Giles
380	2.0	2,700	14.0	3,040	15.8	150	0.8	Greene
50	2.6	200	10.5	570	30.0	110	5.8	Grundy
580	2.5	2,470	10.7	1,970	8.5	170	0.7	Hamblen
(D)	(D)	(D)	(D)	310	33.7	130	14.1	Hancock
170	2.4	960	13.4	1,860	26.1	10	0.1	Hardeman
130	2.0	550	8.5	1,210	18.7	40	0.6	Hardin
220	4.2	520	9.9	920	17.5	10	0.2	Haywood
150	2.1	500	7.1	900	12.8	10	0.1	Henderson
240	2.7	980	10.9	1,700	19.0	250	2.8	Henry
90	2.6	240	7.1	1,150	33.8	0	0.0	Hickman
(D)	(D)	420	26.4	410	25.8	90	5.7	Houston
(D)	(D)	420	8.9	1,330	28.2	220	4.7	Humphreys
40	2.6	230	14.7	340	21.8	10	0.6	Jackson
(D)	(D)	180	5.9	640	20.9	340	11.1	Johnson
30	1.9	180	11.6	640	41.3	0	0.0	Lake
190	2.2	630	7.2	1,440	16.5	10	0.1	Lauderdale
200	1.9	1,050	10.1	1,540	14.9	30	0.3	Lawrence
110	4.6	260	10.9	470	19.7	0	0.0	Lewis
290	4.0	610	8.5	1,430	19.8	40	0.6	Lincoln
290	3.8	1,000	13.2	1,490	19.6	40	0.5	Loudon
410	2.4	1,720	10.1	2,040	12.0	50	0.3	McMinn
240	3.6	720	10.8	1,010	15.2	0	0.0	McNairy
160	4.0	590	14.7	610	15.2	50	1.2	Macon
170	1.8	660	7.0	1,040	11.0	40	0.4	Marshall
1,080	5.6	2,490	12.9	3,590	18.6	180	0.9	Maury
(D)	(D)	(D)	(D)	490	36.6	180	13.4	Meigs
200	2.5	980	12.2	1,250	15.5	80	1.0	Monroe
(D)	(D)	40	3.7	500	45.9	80	7.3	Moore

TABLE 3.12--NONAGRICULTURAL EMPLOYMENT, BY SECTOR, NON-MSA COUNTIES, 1988 (Continued)

County	Total	Manufacturing Em-ployed	Manufacturing %	Contract construction Em-ployed	Contract construction %	Transportation, communications and utilities Em-ployed	Transportation, communications and utilities %	Wholesale and retail trade Em-ployed	Wholesale and retail trade %
Morgan	2,690	1,120	41.6	10	0.4	80	3.0	180	6.7
Obion	14,200	6,870	48.4	700	4.9	240	1.7	2,730	19.2
Overton	4,470	2,330	52.1	100	2.2	90	2.0	590	13.2
Perry	2,130	1,340	62.9	10	0.5	50	2.3	150	7.0
Pickett	1,100	610	55.5	0	0.0	20	1.8	80	7.3
Polk	2,720	1,140	41.9	20	0.7	60	2.2	340	12.5
Putnam	24,640	8,160	33.1	820	3.3	890	3.6	4,940	20.0
Rhea	8,740	4,320	49.4	120	1.4	210	2.4	950	10.9
Roane	14,880	7,360	49.5	200	1.3	180	1.2	1,980	13.3
Scott	4,400	1,570	35.7	180	4.1	170	3.9	800	18.2
Smith	3,770	1,370	36.3	380	10.1	150	4.0	440	11.7
Stewart	2,620	660	25.2	(D)	(D)	(D)	(D)	200	7.6
Trousdale	2,290	1,050	45.9	(D)	(D)	(D)	(D)	500	21.8
Van Buren	1,170	780	66.7	10	0.9	0	0.0	10	0.9
Warren	11,470	5,800	50.6	310	2.7	340	3.0	1,970	17.2
Wayne	3,770	2,140	56.8	10	0.3	50	1.3	380	10.1
Weakley	9,890	3,780	38.2	130	1.3	130	1.3	1,640	16.6
White	5,970	3,490	58.5	180	3.0	140	2.3	970	16.2

TABLE 3.12--NONAGRICULTURAL EMPLOYMENT, BY SECTOR, NON-MSA COUNTIES, 1988
(Continued)

Finance, insurance and real estate		Services		Government		All other non-manufacturing		
Em-ployed	%	Em-ployed	%	Em-ployed	%	Em-ployed	%	County
50	1.9	200	7.4	960	35.7	90	3.3	Morgan
290	2.0	1,840	13.0	1,480	10.4	50	0.4	Obion
100	2.2	400	8.9	810	18.1	50	1.1	Overton
30	1.4	250	11.7	300	14.1	0	0.0	Perry
30	2.7	90	8.2	270	24.5	0	0.0	Pickett
130	4.8	280	10.3	750	27.6	0	0.0	Polk
520	2.1	4,410	17.9	4,790	19.4	110	0.4	Putnam
150	1.7	920	10.5	2,010	23.0	60	0.7	Rhea
290	1.9	1,640	11.0	3,160	21.2	70	0.5	Roane
140	3.2	250	5.7	1,010	23.0	280	6.4	Scott
120	3.2	460	12.2	540	14.3	310	8.2	Smith
100	3.8	110	4.2	1,400	53.4	140	5.3	Stewart
110	4.8	200	8.7	370	16.2	70	3.1	Trousdale
10	0.9	30	2.6	330	28.2	0	0.0	Van Buren
260	2.3	1,400	12.2	1,320	11.5	70	0.6	Warren
100	2.7	300	8.0	780	20.7	10	0.3	Wayne
230	2.3	1,110	11.2	2,720	27.5	150	1.5	Weakley
100	1.7	470	7.9	590	9.9	30	0.5	White

Note: Percentages were computed by the Center for Business and Economic Research.

(D) Included in "All other nonmanufacturing" to avoid disclosure of individual establishment data.

Source: Tennessee Department of Employment Security, Research and Statistics Section, *Annual Averages, Tennessee Labor Force Estimates, 1984–1988*.

TABLE 3.13--EMPLOYMENT, BY OCCUPATION, COUNTIES, 1980

County	Total employed	Executive, adminis-trative and managerial	Profes-sional specialty	Techni-cians and related support	Sales	Adminis-trative support, clerical	Private house-hold
Anderson	28,276	2,261	4,451	2,050	2,243	4,162	204
Bedford	12,522	920	859	225	1,000	1,640	121
Benton	5,572	336	340	194	430	510	39
Bledsoe	3,587	108	315	36	238	325	22
Blount	31,358	2,454	3,342	1,102	3,018	4,382	215
Bradley	29,417	2,230	3,036	681	2,442	4,061	175
Campbell	10,933	756	845	278	869	1,150	33
Cannon	4,383	219	250	79	321	539	17
Carroll	11,321	750	865	228	810	1,253	57
Carter	19,509	990	1,862	582	1,537	2,592	68
Cheatham	9,137	753	644	199	581	1,534	38
Chester	5,191	319	472	83	391	859	22
Claiborne	8,316	430	744	188	725	937	63
Clay	2,970	139	222	28	210	241	8
Cocke	10,074	515	709	146	605	967	32
Coffee	16,504	1,312	2,189	638	1,324	2,106	154
Crockett	5,671	384	370	108	418	657	21
Cumberland	10,181	750	916	333	956	1,230	7
Davidson	229,816	27,166	31,949	8,471	24,245	48,145	1,939
Decatur	4,288	299	251	97	256	420	17
DeKalb	5,490	328	349	60	304	598	22
Dickson	12,224	934	962	224	1,105	1,772	92
Dyer	14,036	1,026	921	290	1,322	1,915	184
Fayette	8,643	461	609	223	513	1,003	141
Fentress	4,990	266	425	91	359	416	5
Franklin	12,513	832	1,246	311	966	1,376	118
Gibson	19,608	1,400	1,313	448	1,736	2,373	150
Giles	10,485	597	749	190	699	1,344	72
Grainger	6,015	314	340	72	356	456	14
Greene	22,293	1,543	1,997	842	1,512	2,397	48
Grundy	4,401	162	266	54	243	337	24
Hamblen	20,579	1,873	1,807	400	1,821	2,619	117
Hamilton	125,720	13,219	15,918	4,239	13,046	21,026	830
Hancock	2,055	63	156	41	111	132	6
Hardeman	8,034	544	572	237	432	852	71
Hardin	8,714	524	613	159	654	697	5
Hawkins	16,100	764	1,273	398	961	2,156	103
Haywood	6,738	490	631	97	572	744	95
Henderson	8,508	569	569	140	645	804	27
Henry	11,197	833	789	269	1,008	1,356	108
Hickman	6,067	303	403	121	358	606	41
Houston	2,265	124	212	50	72	280	18
Humphreys	6,185	317	508	214	460	521	23
Jackson	3,564	201	280	59	226	366	24
Jefferson	12,701	872	1,242	303	785	1,462	38
Johnson	4,908	172	318	110	268	447	25
Knox	141,632	14,530	20,444	6,076	16,103	23,520	676
Lake	2,507	115	168	35	184	275	22
Lauderdale	8,540	363	746	115	600	835	86
Lawrence	13,079	703	1,011	166	983	1,443	66

TABLE 3.13--EMPLOYMENT, BY OCCUPATION, COUNTIES, 1980 (Continued)

Protective services	Service, except protective and household	Farming, forestry and fishing	Precision production, craft and repair	Machine operators, assemblers, inspectors	Transportation and material moving	Handlers, cleaners, helpers and laborers	County
521	2,568	279	4,524	2,774	996	1,243	Anderson
138	1,153	644	1,957	2,658	498	709	Bedford
51	589	225	1,060	1,090	334	374	Benton
108	312	405	556	740	238	184	Bledsoe
372	3,349	619	5,075	3,619	1,924	1,887	Blount
297	2,742	516	4,311	5,625	1,448	1,853	Bradley
198	1,265	199	1,979	1,563	967	831	Campbell
30	456	323	697	1,027	245	180	Cannon
157	1,005	486	1,636	2,728	519	827	Carroll
265	1,682	383	3,066	4,210	980	1,292	Carter
107	801	275	1,894	1,253	599	459	Cheatham
68	691	246	605	879	269	287	Chester
131	674	609	1,387	1,306	696	426	Claiborne
46	294	295	393	789	170	135	Clay
104	1,030	649	1,509	2,319	630	859	Cocke
286	1,427	601	2,325	2,730	642	770	Coffee
34	480	517	861	1,216	298	307	Crockett
145	1,241	421	1,496	1,494	602	590	Cumberland
4,112	23,779	1,421	23,198	16,221	8,812	10,358	Davidson
55	310	266	557	1,119	292	349	Decatur
63	473	553	869	1,299	270	302	DeKalb
181	1,236	414	2,205	1,783	658	658	Dickson
166	1,308	764	2,051	2,691	697	701	Dyer
126	928	882	1,245	1,459	539	514	Fayette
53	372	386	675	1,307	353	282	Fentress
174	1,282	653	1,887	2,144	754	770	Franklin
189	1,601	974	2,711	4,654	997	1,062	Gibson
126	955	643	1,351	2,638	547	574	Giles
56	513	477	1,075	1,321	480	541	Grainger
150	2,324	1,420	3,354	4,515	1,124	1,067	Greene
29	253	509	744	985	350	445	Grundy
195	1,730	429	3,222	3,991	1,320	1,055	Hamblen
1,900	13,488	738	15,471	13,676	5,512	6,657	Hamilton
20	194	353	264	497	114	104	Hancock
127	1,119	524	948	1,636	459	513	Hardeman
46	771	372	1,426	2,102	755	590	Hardin
167	1,218	520	2,749	3,405	1,043	1,343	Hawkins
62	827	531	752	1,186	355	396	Haywood
92	703	466	1,201	2,314	450	528	Henderson
76	1,094	515	1,629	2,211	603	706	Henry
115	457	301	895	1,660	459	348	Hickman
20	188	118	482	434	107	160	Houston
78	615	105	1,279	1,133	402	530	Humphreys
23	253	256	537	904	210	225	Jackson
115	1,350	467	2,319	2,120	795	833	Jefferson
62	353	392	701	1,479	252	329	Johnson
1,826	16,272	1,190	16,911	12,077	5,935	6,072	Knox
68	302	270	291	564	94	119	Lake
244	669	657	1,175	2,000	493	557	Lauderdale
89	1,144	654	1,981	3,204	834	801	Lawrence

TABLE 3.13--EMPLOYMENT, BY OCCUPATION, COUNTIES, 1980 (Continued)

County	Total employed	Executive, adminis-trative and managerial	Profes-sional specialty	Techni-cians and related support	Sales	Adminis-trative support, clerical	Private house-hold
Lewis	4,009	222	276	70	236	450	8
Lincoln	11,408	797	757	340	1,053	1,399	130
Loudon	12,119	618	1,076	347	822	1,466	52
McMinn	17,290	1,273	1,254	398	1,438	1,880	122
McNairy	8,723	476	585	151	595	942	55
Macon	6,545	223	363	94	349	713	5
Madison	31,574	2,727	3,497	913	3,823	4,469	213
Marion	8,253	463	597	165	580	813	45
Marshall	8,440	576	545	153	685	1,119	34
Maury	22,234	1,706	1,991	513	2,051	2,549	267
Meigs	2,848	148	145	37	213	264	40
Monroe	10,766	500	667	181	896	1,121	46
Montgomery	28,138	2,509	2,903	515	3,059	4,422	271
Moore	1,967	86	164	59	90	181	25
Morgan	5,197	264	369	75	283	529	19
Obion	13,389	1,025	918	287	1,215	1,519	171
Overton	6,764	383	460	109	444	567	15
Perry	2,312	121	117	27	171	201	19
Pickett	1,655	112	117	27	128	150	2
Polk	4,918	281	364	107	178	480	12
Putnam	20,105	1,704	2,244	495	2,049	2,958	160
Rhea	9,511	595	718	167	546	906	36
Roane	19,301	1,163	2,151	816	1,427	2,574	67
Robertson	15,674	1,037	1,007	331	1,115	2,271	95
Rutherford	38,612	3,351	4,147	1,119	3,912	6,114	288
Scott	5,504	441	502	117	308	721	7
Sequatchie	2,976	193	244	57	244	262	4
Sevier	16,915	1,534	1,391	320	1,906	1,968	44
Shelby	322,287	35,451	38,105	10,537	38,199	62,598	3,825
Smith	6,222	317	420	142	409	585	24
Stewart	2,980	102	208	49	177	321	10
Sullivan	60,788	5,237	7,539	2,148	6,196	8,948	265
Sumner	37,674	3,947	3,845	1,036	4,482	5,520	308
Tipton	12,167	838	901	360	1,117	1,601	116
Trousdale	2,943	155	262	58	204	327	21
Unicoi	6,210	330	503	162	365	707	30
Union	4,471	204	169	90	184	442	24
Van Buren	2,157	67	139	8	81	141	25
Warren	13,871	809	938	245	1,057	1,461	71
Washington	37,721	3,022	4,903	1,421	3,903	5,561	235
Wayne	5,402	233	278	112	294	458	28
Weakley	13,239	860	1,186	278	1,130	1,577	76
White	8,382	582	471	102	529	864	64
Williamson	27,380	4,431	3,509	746	3,275	4,381	246
Wilson	25,062	2,418	2,230	621	2,292	4,009	157

TABLE 3.13--EMPLOYMENT, BY OCCUPATION, COUNTIES, 1980 (Continued)

Protective services	Service except protective and household	Farming, forestry and fishing	Precision production, craft and repair	Machine operators, assemblers, inspectors	Transportation and material moving	Handlers, cleaners, helpers and laborers	County
20	282	245	690	1,099	249	162	Lewis
79	863	893	1,698	2,405	545	449	Lincoln
134	1,315	451	2,064	2,239	729	806	Loudon
189	1,495	565	2,678	3,704	1,223	1,071	McMinn
120	671	412	1,394	2,320	489	513	McNairy
45	452	516	972	1,781	427	605	Macon
463	3,575	597	3,736	4,065	1,584	1,912	Madison
111	759	178	1,600	1,570	676	696	Marion
104	670	654	1,228	1,760	418	494	Marshall
256	2,253	944	3,184	3,842	1,316	1,362	Maury
9	205	160	589	653	206	179	Meigs
62	897	602	1,700	2,723	592	779	Monroe
370	3,368	869	3,931	3,479	1,115	1,327	Montgomery
19	180	147	308	419	96	193	Moore
163	447	144	1,175	973	450	306	Morgan
130	1,221	821	1,814	2,600	710	958	Obion
86	591	474	1,029	1,820	370	416	Overton
49	154	53	304	726	232	138	Perry
28	89	104	238	476	76	108	Pickett
77	351	232	737	1,289	337	473	Polk
229	1,860	470	2,649	3,464	732	1,091	Putnam
145	921	152	1,804	2,373	469	679	Rhea
284	1,954	247	3,807	2,778	897	1,136	Roane
122	1,405	1,366	2,443	2,521	837	1,124	Robertson
549	4,359	887	5,190	4,898	1,807	1,991	Rutherford
53	469	188	1,025	720	564	389	Scott
39	286	126	514	590	185	232	Sequatchie
294	2,206	498	2,485	2,443	878	948	Sevier
5,545	34,418	2,148	33,341	23,580	16,270	18,270	Shelby
79	464	336	1,084	1,293	533	536	Smith
24	275	252	538	673	196	155	Stewart
599	5,298	841	8,706	8,612	3,033	3,366	Sullivan
366	2,893	892	6,148	4,766	1,632	1,839	Sumner
192	1,285	579	1,744	1,802	804	828	Tipton
18	210	164	523	604	158	239	Trousdale
121	557	137	1,117	1,323	466	392	Unicoi
26	385	208	865	1,166	412	296	Union
41	159	163	250	861	125	97	Van Buren
127	1,155	1,059	2,029	3,438	716	766	Warren
443	3,602	875	5,282	4,832	1,821	1,821	Washington
41	367	299	674	1,699	393	526	Wayne
119	1,411	725	1,585	2,746	726	820	Weakley
96	565	476	1,207	2,555	531	340	White
218	2,175	957	3,250	2,263	991	938	Williamson
225	2,285	460	3,676	3,759	1,314	1,616	Wilson

Source: U.S. Department of Commerce, Bureau of the Census, *1980 Census of Population, General Social and Economic Characteristics, Tennessee.*

TABLE 3.14--INSURED EMPLOYMENT AND AVERAGE WAGES, COUNTIES, 1987

County	Number of em-ployers	Annual average employ-ment	Annual average wages	Average weekly wages	Rank of average weekly wages	Taxable wages	Average premium rate [1]
Anderson	1,346	25,289	$22,338	$429	2	$170,045,774	1.50
Bedford	601	10,094	16,583	318	23	68,043,805	2.02
Benton	283	3,197	13,161	253	70	20,408,101	3.23
Bledsoe	104	1,553	12,371	237	81	9,122,594	1.75
Blount	1,442	21,760	18,405	353	13	132,297,666	1.74
Bradley	1,319	28,501	17,097	328	21	186,590,181	1.88
Campbell	525	7,544	13,461	258	67	40,710,529	3.20
Cannon	129	1,850	12,779	245	77	11,440,178	1.67
Carroll	494	7,379	12,177	234	86	41,519,061	2.81
Carter	608	9,692	14,252	274	49	56,898,332	2.16
Cheatham	288	3,632	17,137	329	20	22,278,652	1.54
Chester	181	2,605	14,205	273	51	15,151,214	1.99
Claibome	375	5,698	13,403	257	68	33,501,652	2.12
Clay	99	1,985	12,231	235	83	14,011,575	1.67
Cocke	411	6,246	13,930	267	60	35,981,703	2.98
Coffee	874	18,243	19,370	372	9	121,191,786	1.52
Crockett	232	2,466	13,103	251	72	15,550,219	3.26
Cumberland	653	9,050	14,089	270	57	52,587,163	2.31
Davidson	14,445	338,868	20,131	387	5	1,996,465,116	1.37
Decatur	210	3,288	12,422	238	80	21,789,099	2.16
DeKalb	256	4,341	14,435	277	48	27,744,011	2.19
Dickson	590	7,651	14,998	288	41	46,698,076	1.68
Dyer	753	11,701	17,267	332	19	72,227,698	1.86
Fayette	285	4,785	14,144	272	54	28,524,021	2.06
Fentress	250	3,540	10,190	195	94	20,918,159	2.62
Franklin	549	6,486	14,152	272	53	33,099,136	2.02
Gibson	947	15,958	15,735	302	33	105,290,554	2.28
Giles	483	7,425	15,596	299	34	47,087,468	1.66
Grainger	167	2,453	12,189	234	85	15,419,671	1.90
Greene	957	21,480	15,211	292	39	123,166,180	2.28
Grundy	151	1,770	10,497	201	93	11,049,199	2.41
Hamblen	1,093	24,456	16,766	322	22	161,591,562	1.47
Hamilton	6,779	136,634	18,426	354	12	846,802,727	1.42
Hancock	50	842	10,737	206	92	4,660,902	1.84
Hardeman	381	6,466	14,017	269	59	32,595,311	2.58
Hardin	420	6,558	14,222	273	50	39,969,833	3.14
Hawkins	436	7,450	18,209	350	14	45,099,347	1.84
Haywood	334	5,445	14,106	271	55	34,524,797	1.75
Henderson	376	6,773	13,690	263	64	43,339,438	2.56
Henry	608	8,403	15,396	296	37	54,280,248	2.48
Hickman	209	2,859	13,617	261	66	17,462,634	2.17
Houston	104	1,328	12,543	241	79	7,551,781	2.37
Humphreys	294	4,495	20,077	386	6	30,857,391	3.21
Jackson	100	1,587	12,872	247	75	10,153,863	1.79
Jefferson	492	7,670	15,002	288	40	46,254,221	1.83
Johnson	189	3,082	12,183	234	84	20,515,878	3.77
Knox	8,235	150,737	17,652	339	16	861,734,469	1.74
Lake	139	1,187	11,270	216	91	7,036,117	1.93
Lauderdale	356	7,710	14,586	280	46	51,314,437	1.53
Lawrence	666	10,096	15,903	305	30	64,393,862	3.66

TABLE 3.14--INSURED EMPLOYMENT AND AVERAGE WAGES, COUNTIES, 1987 (Continued)

County	Number of em- ployers	Annual average employ- ment	Annual average wages	Average weekly wages	Rank of average weekly wages	Taxable wages	Average premium rate[1]
Lewis	157	2,166	13,749	264	63	13,420,563	3.55
Lincoln	537	7,456	13,997	269	58	47,605,270	1.91
Loudon	509	7,723	16,207	311	28	50,999,042	1.94
McMinn	712	15,047	17,459	335	17	101,104,768	1.75
McNairy	379	7,172	13,734	264	62	45,607,569	2.51
Macon	231	4,196	12,936	248	74	29,927,254	2.15
Madison	1,901	33,751	17,397	334	18	194,726,088	1.77
Marion	341	4,802	14,816	284	44	30,370,300	1.50
Marshall	395	8,423	16,424	315	26	59,791,862	1.34
Maury	1,180	18,157	18,002	346	15	112,754,365	1.90
Meigs	64	1,314	14,971	287	43	7,871,771	2.09
Monroe	492	7,240	13,093	251	71	43,670,747	2.23
Montgomery	1,531	21,598	15,393	296	36	121,738,933	2.50
Moore	50	1,225	18,454	354	11	6,341,246	2.06
Morgan	150	2,085	13,001	250	73	12,481,544	2.52
Obion	682	13,814	19,988	384	7	93,922,440	1.77
Overton	269	3,881	11,416	219	90	25,703,456	2.16
Perry	110	1,830	12,772	245	76	12,812,492	1.61
Pickett	82	1,019	10,031	192	95	6,436,727	2.85
Polk	186	3,071	15,939	306	29	18,179,432	1.18
Putnam	1,200	22,657	15,235	292	38	138,171,741	1.91
Rhea	345	7,540	14,944	287	42	45,194,733	2.52
Roane	650	16,842	22,539	433	1	104,424,048	1.00
Robertson	621	8,605	15,438	296	35	50,984,393	2.11
Rutherford	1,897	38,027	20,316	390	4	238,912,496	1.62
Scott	281	4,549	14,552	279	47	29,387,756	2.89
Sequatchie	133	1,715	12,654	243	78	10,094,682	2.56
Sevier	1,527	17,552	12,100	232	88	109,390,393	3.17
Shelby	17,318	362,592	19,926	383	8	2,153,637,008	1.38
Smith	235	3,844	14,627	281	45	24,899,966	2.14
Stewart	107	1,412	12,240	235	82	9,612,963	1.44
Sullivan	2,813	61,488	21,372	411	3	388,578,602	1.25
Sumner	1,733	23,657	16,388	315	25	146,597,327	1.83
Tipton	494	5,985	14,048	270	56	35,457,883	1.50
Trousdale	103	1,838	12,082	232	87	11,438,490	2.34
Unicoi	238	3,925	15,767	303	31	23,539,756	1.73
Union	120	1,151	13,801	265	61	7,857,595	1.65
Van Buren	34	974	14,195	272	52	6,678,593	1.78
Warren	607	10,773	15,712	302	32	72,317,933	2.35
Washington	1,973	36,532	16,291	313	27	212,722,628	1.69
Wayne	196	3,540	11,771	226	89	23,645,158	2.42
Weakley	549	8,957	13,346	256	69	46,980,127	2.31
White	349	5,841	13,634	262	65	37,690,253	2.32
Williamson	2,128	22,170	18,876	363	10	153,830,793	1.96
Wilson	1,097	14,654	16,388	315	24	100,116,771	2.02

Note: Rankings were based on unrounded average weekly wages.

1. Average premium rate was computed by the Tennessee Department of Employment Security, taking total contributions as a percentage of taxable wages.

Source: Tennessee Department of Employment Security, Research and Statistics Section, *Tennessee Covered Employment and Wages by Industry, Statewide and by County, 1987*.

FIGURE 3.4
Average Weekly Wages of Covered Employment by County, 1987
(Tennessee average = $349)

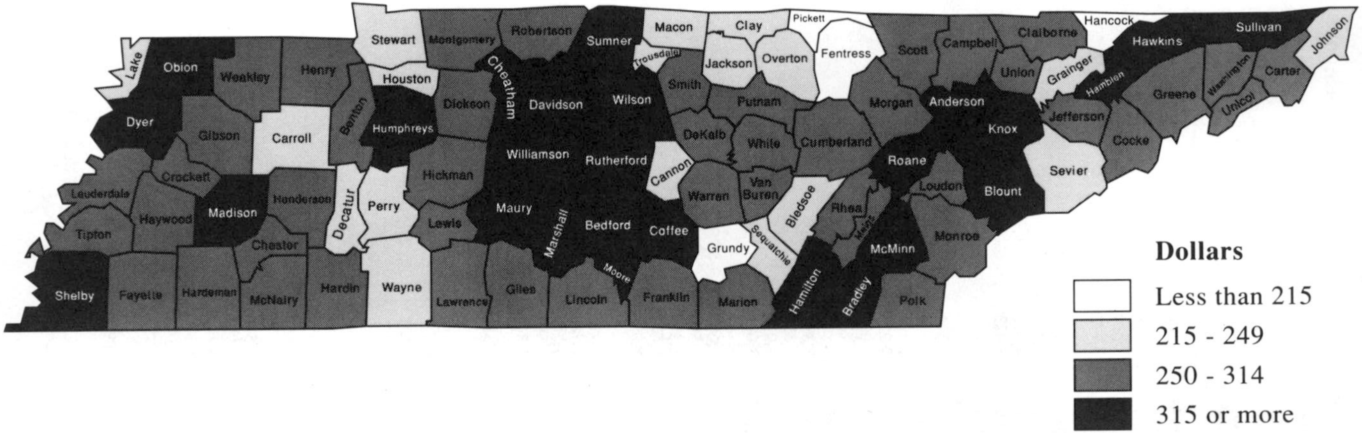

Source: Tennessee Department of Employment Security, *Tennessee Covered Employment and Wages by Industry, Statewide and by County*, 1986–1987.

TABLE 3.15--LOCAL GOVERNMENT EMPLOYMENT, BY SELECTED FUNCTION, COUNTIES, OCTOBER 1982

County	Total[1]	Edu-cation	Environ-ment and housing	High-ways	Public welfare	Health and hospi-tals	Fire and police	Govern-ment adminis-tration	Utilities, sanita-tion and sewerage control
Anderson	2,128	1,407	79	82	13	40	178	148	73
Bedford	1,077	494	75	48	0	305	84	15	47
Benton	683	307	9	4	0	254	22	23	42
Bledsoe	235	153	6	37	0	0	15	16	2
Blount	1,847	1,179	92	83	0	24	150	141	128
Bradley	2,148	1,040	52	73	0	568	141	79	152
Campbell	1,390	637	86	101	0	318	86	68	69
Cannon	221	137	3	29	0	10	10	27	0
Carroll	963	553	28	68	3	192	60	27	19
Carter	1,540	881	57	54	0	273	97	64	93
Cheatham	559	380	4	37	76	6	29	7	18
Chester	266	175	6	25	0	0	23	21	5
Claiborne	893	513	27	32	0	232	39	26	18
Clay	252	185	5	27	1	0	11	12	3
Cocke	762	434	47	60	0	118	57	25	0
Coffee	1,141	682	69	62	0	15	108	57	113
Crockett	364	249	6	34	0	0	27	12	20
Cumberland	772	542	40	68	0	4	55	35	14
Davidson (Metro)	16,153	6,602	1,643	391	285	1,582	2,281	971	1,455
Decatur	371	185	17	31	1	79	21	15	9
DeKalb	354	204	29	3	0	0	28	25	54
Dickson	812	467	36	62	7	4	61	50	100
Dyer	1,751	575	130	67	112	602	145	49	37
Fayette	759	503	13	62	95	1	32	26	10
Fentress	361	256	12	44	0	0	24	17	7
Franklin	1,102	493	48	48	0	335	73	66	31
Gibson	2,031	1,395	71	87	1	121	147	85	87
Giles	845	357	42	64	0	195	52	47	66
Grainger	323	244	9	31	0	0	15	18	1
Greene	1,413	1,015	85	76	0	16	104	45	31
Grundy	372	256	12	26	0	0	32	19	14
Hamblen	1,359	911	107	43	0	0	116	62	92
Hamilton	12,084	4,023	944	391	720	2,940	1,287	550	748
Hancock	270	157	2	12	1	79	7	8	1
Hardeman	649	453	19	51	2	1	54	31	20
Hardin	747	377	25	44	0	189	41	32	26
Hawkins	1,119	796	39	96	11	2	62	52	38
Haywood	593	394	34	47	2	0	47	18	38
Henderson	645	313	14	44	0	88	41	28	90
Henry	1,102	430	37	69	86	276	79	34	83
Hickman	433	227	6	44	0	77	21	17	10
Houston	211	124	8	27	0	0	17	25	6
Humphreys	435	263	17	39	0	0	44	33	25
Jackson	261	141	7	42	8	7	18	17	6
Jefferson	1,175	565	31	51	5	373	50	52	33
Johnson	366	261	10	40	3	0	26	13	8
Knox	9,563	4,807	745	157	24	207	1,114	349	1,135
Lake	209	127	10	19	0	0	21	21	8
Lauderdale	660	424	37	49	3	3	51	41	48
Lawrence	944	604	48	90	0	20	79	31	31

TABLE 3.15--LOCAL GOVERNMENT EMPLOYMENT, BY SELECTED FUNCTION, COUNTIES, OCTOBER 1982 (Continued)

County	Total[1]	Education	Environment and housing	Highways	Public welfare	Health and hospitals	Fire and police	Government administration	Utilities, sanitation and sewerage control
Lewis	248	135	11	47	0	0	16	26	4
Lincoln	957	441	24	64	5	233	57	36	81
Loudon	892	493	32	53	4	114	67	52	48
McMinn	1,317	667	101	78	5	152	106	57	104
McNairy	795	424	15	54	4	171	51	30	37
Macon	396	257	15	37	0	8	31	25	8
Madison	6,160	999	163	121	28	3,084	310	99	278
Marion	668	468	33	48	0	0	58	33	13
Marshall	595	347	37	39	0	0	47	28	76
Maury	1,953	827	118	95	3	513	152	74	103
Meigs	207	142	1	31	0	0	7	15	2
Monroe	722	482	27	27	2	22	62	50	35
Montgomery	2,603	1,292	88	137	60	532	245	66	149
Moore	105	82	1	8	1	1	5	5	1
Morgan	389	280	35	28	3	2	14	19	1
Obion	846	497	48	76	0	0	93	71	40
Overton	502	336	7	72	0	1	35	23	5
Perry	202	114	4	29	0	0	12	27	2
Pickett	123	79	2	23	0	0	9	8	1
Polk	551	250	9	48	0	111	33	72	7
Putnam	1,769	651	58	70	0	667	133	83	74
Rhea	795	426	34	39	0	167	50	38	26
Roane	1,417	754	67	83	0	218	109	84	75
Robertson	1,117	598	44	44	0	256	88	33	44
Rutherford	2,295	1,417	176	87	0	99	261	99	123
Scott	789	385	4	49	1	259	35	22	26
Sequatchie	251	175	9	20	0	0	13	19	6
Sevier	1,291	708	137	74	2	1	135	47	125
Shelby	31,361	13,255	2,744	1,031	839	2,436	4,130	1,290	3,452
Smith	303	219	12	3	1	0	25	21	10
Stewart	248	157	3	42	0	6	18	19	1
Sullivan	4,163	2,850	258	224	29	6	375	189	87
Sumner	2,565	1,329	89	176	16	405	227	135	126
Tipton	829	562	36	75	0	0	52	41	35
Trousdale	197	102	14	26	1	0	26	17	5
Unicoi	542	272	10	34	52	93	45	19	0
Union	188	126	4	21	2	2	13	13	2
Van Buren	149	67	2	31	0	5	8	32	2
Warren	954	516	53	42	0	160	75	39	56
Washington	2,823	1,397	119	141	18	1	238	91	712
Wayne	516	275	13	54	0	109	19	25	4
Weakley	859	434	42	68	95	0	64	33	82
White	487	357	10	38	0	0	30	21	28
Williamson	1,385	982	64	62	0	17	114	72	43
Wilson	1,207	803	58	34	0	0	108	91	74

Note: Data are full-time equivalent employment for all government functions.

1. Includes categories not shown separately.

Source: U.S. Department of Commerce, Bureau of the Census, *1982 Census of Governments, Compendium of Public Employment.*

TABLE 3.16--JOBS, PERCENTAGE CHANGE, AND COMPONENTS OF CHANGE, 1980–1986 [In thousands]

State	Total jobs, 1986[a]	Change, 1980–1986		Job change due to establishment:			
		Number	%	Births	Expansions	Deaths	Contractions
TENNESSEE	1,865.2	254.1	15.77	645.7	261.1	-501.3	-151.4
Alabama	1,241.2	98.4	8.61	443.4	170.7	-390.4	-125.2
Arkansas	782.4	61.9	8.60	242.4	102.6	-208.1	-74.9
Florida	4,169.8	924.9	28.50	1,780.1	617.7	-1,167.1	-305.8
Georgia	2,461.5	445.3	22.09	906.3	349.4	-638.8	-171.6
Kentucky	1,146.5	10.7	0.94	359.5	157.7	-378.7	-127.8
Louisiana	1,542.1	163.8	11.89	561.5	228.2	-464.7	-161.2
Mississippi	784.8	103.8	15.24	278.1	88.2	-203.2	-59.3
North Carolina	2,307.2	412.3	21.76	750.5	349.9	-513.5	-174.6
South Carolina	1,123.1	135.7	13.74	387.3	135.0	-283.4	-103.3
Virginia	2,079.9	384.1	22.65	771.4	292.3	-510.3	-169.3
West Virginia	500.6	-31.3	-5.88	135.7	59.6	-152.2	-74.4
UNITED STATES	91,247.7	10,470.0	12.96	31,846.5	12,684.5	-25,205.2	-8,855.8

a. Excludes government employment. Covers approximately 93 percent of full-time business activity, generally firms with at least one paid employee.

Source: U.S. Department of Commerce, Bureau of the Census, *Statistical Abstract of the United States, 1989.*

TABLE 3.17--NUMBER AND RATE OF UNEMPLOYED AND INSURED UNEMPLOYED, SOUTHEASTERN STATES, 1984–1987

	Total unemployed								Insured unemployed							
	Number (1,000)				Rate[1]				Number (1,000)				Rate[2]			
State	1987	1986	1985	1984	1987	1986	1985	1984	1987	1986	1985	1984	1987	1986	1985	1984
TENNESSEE	154	185	180	190	6.6	8.0	8.0	8.6	39.8	44.3	46.1	40.7	2.2	2.5	2.7	2.5
Alabama	147	185	160	200	7.8	9.8	8.9	11.1	36.9	42.7	42.5	42.5	2.7	3.2	3.3	3.5
Arkansas	88	94	91	93	8.1	8.7	8.7	8.9	26.6	27.5	27.3	24.9	3.4	3.6	3.7	3.5
Florida	312	320	319	325	5.3	5.7	6.0	6.3	51.7	59.0	56.6	54.6	1.1	1.4	1.4	1.4
Georgia	167	178	187	166	5.5	5.9	6.5	6.0	40.8	43.5	42.0	37.8	1.6	1.8	1.8	1.8
Kentucky	148	156	161	160	8.8	9.3	9.5	9.3	28.7	37.2	36.2	35.0	2.4	3.2	3.2	3.3
Louisiana	234	261	229	195	12.0	13.1	11.5	10.0	60.7	81.1	66.0	58.5	4.2	5.4	4.3	3.9
Mississippi	117	136	115	116	10.2	11.7	10.3	10.8	25.5	31.4	28.8	27.5	3.2	4.0	3.7	3.7
North Carolina	146	170	167	204	4.5	5.3	5.4	6.7	41.9	49.3	57.3	50.0	1.6	1.9	2.3	2.2
South Carolina	91	100	107	105	5.6	6.2	6.8	7.1	22.1	27.8	34.1	28.4	1.8	2.3	2.8	2.5
Virginia	126	145	161	143	4.2	5.0	5.6	5.0	21.0	23.2	25.5	23.9	0.9	1.0	1.2	1.2
West Virginia	81	88	100	115	10.8	11.8	13.0	15.0	19.8	23.6	25.8	26.7	3.6	4.3	4.7	5.0

1. Total unemployment as a percentage of civilian labor force.

2. Insured unemployment as a percentage of average covered employment in the previous year.

Source: U.S. Department of Commerce, Bureau of the Census, *Statistical Abstract of the United States, 1989*, and earlier editions.

TABLE 3.18--CIVILIAN LABOR FORCE AND PARTICIPATION RATES, BY SEX, SOUTHEASTERN STATES AND UNITED STATES, 1980 AND 1987 [Labor force in thousands]

State	Civilian labor force: Total	Civilian labor force: Male	Female: Total	Female: Percentage of labor force	Participation rate[1]: Male	Participation rate[1]: Female	Employed as a percentage of total population[2]
				1987			
TENNESSEE	2,336	1,274	1,062	45.5	73.4	54.5	59.2
Alabama	1,893	1,045	848	44.8	74.3	52.1	57.5
Arkansas	1,090	607	483	44.3	71.6	51.9	56.3
Florida	5,870	3,177	2,693	45.9	71.4	54.1	58.9
Georgia	3,053	1,642	1,411	46.2	77.9	57.6	63.3
Kentucky	1,686	955	731	43.4	73.5	49.5	55.4
Louisiana	1,955	1,119	836	42.8	73.8	49.4	53.6
Mississippi	1,151	643	508	44.1	72.6	51.3	55.1
North Carolina	3,276	1,751	1,525	46.6	77.3	59.9	65.1
South Carolina	1,632	889	743	45.5	75.2	56.6	61.7
Virginia	2,989	1,642	1,347	45.1	78.1	59.0	65.3
West Virginia	749	437	312	41.7	64.7	40.4	46.1
UNITED STATES	119,865	66,207	53,658	44.8	76.2	56.0	61.5
				1980			
TENNESSEE	2,015	1,159	856	42.5	74.3	49.5	56.9
Alabama	1,642	954	687	41.8	72.5	47.2	54.0
Arkansas	972	552	420	43.2	72.4	49.0	55.5
Florida	3,925	2,219	1,706	43.5	68.5	45.8	53.0
Georgia	2,385	1,335	1,050	44.0	77.4	53.1	60.3
Kentucky	1,620	939	681	42.0	76.6	50.0	57.5
Louisiana	1,723	1,015	708	41.1	75.3	46.6	56.1
Mississippi	1,024	579	445	43.5	73.1	48.5	55.4
North Carolina	2,741	1,531	1,210	44.1	78.8	55.6	62.2
South Carolina	1,306	735	571	43.7	75.6	51.2	58.3
Virginia	2,530	1,414	1,116	44.1	79.6	54.5	62.8
West Virginia	768	482	286	37.2	71.5	39.1	49.6
UNITED STATES	104,719	60,145	44,574	42.6	77.4	51.6	59.3

Note: Data are annual averages. Rates are based on civilian non-institutional population, 16 years and over. Detail may not add to total due to independent rounding.

1. Percentage of civilian noninstitutional population of each specified group in the civilian labor force.

2. Based on a survey and subject to sampling variability; changes should be interpreted with caution.

Source: U.S. Department of Commerce, Bureau of the Census, *Statistical Abstract of the United States, 1989*; and U.S. Department of Labor, Bureau of Labor Statistics, *Geographic Profile of Employment and Unemployment, 1980.*

TABLE 3.19--UNEMPLOYED, BY SEX, 1987, AND UNEMPLOYMENT RATE, BY SEX, 1980 AND 1987, SOUTHEASTERN STATES AND UNITED STATES

	1987 unemployed (1,000)			Rate of unemployment[1]					
				1987			1980		
State	Total	Male	Female	Total	Male	Female	Total	Male	Female
TENNESSEE	154	77	77	6.6	6.1	7.2	7.2	6.8	7.7
Alabama	147	73	74	7.8	7.0	8.7	8.8	7.6	10.4
Arkansas	88	43	45	8.1	7.1	9.3	7.6	7.2	8.2
Florida	312	157	155	5.3	5.0	5.8	6.0	5.3	6.8
Georgia	167	71	96	5.5	4.4	6.8	6.4	4.8	8.5
Kentucky	148	83	65	8.8	8.7	8.9	8.1	8.4	7.7
Louisiana	234	135	99	12.0	12.1	11.8	6.7	6.4	7.1
Mississippi	117	61	56	10.2	9.5	11.0	7.5	5.8	9.5
North Carolina	146	69	77	4.5	3.9	5.1	6.5	6.1	7.1
South Carolina	91	38	53	5.6	4.3	7.2	6.9	6.2	7.7
Virginia	126	61	65	4.2	3.8	4.8	5.1	4.3	6.1
West Virginia	81	53	28	10.8	12.2	8.9	9.4	9.8	8.6
UNITED STATES	7,425	4,101	3,324	6.2	6.2	6.2	7.1	6.9	7.4

Note: Data are annual averages. Detail may not add to total due to independent rounding.

1. Percentage unemployed of civilian labor force in specified group.

Source: U.S. Department of Commerce, Bureau of the Census, *Statistical Abstract of the United States, 1989*; and U.S. Department of Labor, Bureau of Labor Statistics, *Geographic Profile of Employment and Unemployment, 1980.*

TABLE 3.20--STATE AND LOCAL GOVERNMENT FULL-TIME EQUIVALENT EMPLOYMENT, SOUTHEASTERN STATES, OCTOBER 1987

	FTE employment			Number per 10,000 population		
State	Total	State	Local[1]	Total	Education	Other
TENNESSEE	232,520	70,892	161,628	479.4	228.4	251.0
Alabama	203,679	70,196	133,483	499.2	252.6	246.6
Arkansas	110,559	38,721	71,838	464.5	247.8	216.7
Florida	546,097	125,983	420,114	454.3	207.5	246.8
Georgia	343,417	95,460	247,957	552.1	253.6	298.5
Kentucky	169,122	64,471	104,651	454.6	255.0	199.6
Louisiana	236,292	84,990	151,302	529.8	261.2	268.6
Mississippi	141,997	44,382	97,615	542.0	283.5	258.5
North Carolina	323,088	99,778	223,310	504.0	273.6	230.5
South Carolina	180,308	69,837	110,471	527.2	276.8	250.4
Virginia	304,222	103,849	200,373	515.6	272.4	243.3
West Virginia	94,666	33,657	61,009	500.9	291.6	209.3

Note: Detail may not add to total due to independent rounding.

1. Statistics for local governments are estimates subject to sampling variations.

Source: U.S. Department of Commerce, Bureau of the Census, *Public Employment in 1987.*

TABLE 3.21--PAID CIVILIAN EMPLOYMENT IN THE FEDERAL GOVERNMENT, SOUTHEASTERN STATES, 1984 AND 1986

	1986			1984		
State	Total (1,000)	Rate per 10,000 population	Percentage defense	Total (1,000)	Rate per 10,000 population	Percentage defense
TENNESSEE	58	120.8	12.1	57	120.6	12.4
Alabama	59	145.6	45.8	60	150.4	45.3
Arkansas	19	80.1	26.3	18	76.7	24.4
Florida	101	86.5	31.7	91	82.4	33.1
Georgia	86	140.9	46.5	80	136.9	46.7
Kentucky	33	88.5	42.4	35	94.1	39.9
Louisiana	33	73.3	27.3	32	71.7	28.3
Mississippi	24	91.4	45.8	24	92.4	43.9
North Carolina	45	71.1	35.6	43	69.7	35.9
South Carolina	32	94.8	62.5	33	99.9	62.1
Virginia	156	269.6	67.9	155	275.0	68.5
West Virginia	15	78.2	13.3	15	76.9	10.5

Note: Rates are based on July 1 resident population for the corresponding years.

Source: U.S. Department of Commerce, Bureau of the Census, *Statistical Abstract of the United States, 1988*, and earlier editions.

TABLE 3.22--EMPLOYMENT COST INDEX, PRIVATE NONFARM WORKERS, REGIONS, 1987 AND 1988 [June 1981=100]

Region	1988 March	1988 June	1988 September	1988 December	Percent change Dec. 1987-Dec. 1988	1987 March	1987 June	1987 September	1987 December
					Compensation[1]				
All private industry workers[2]	138.1	139.8	141.2	142.6	4.9	132.9	133.8	135.1	136.0
Northeast	143.7	145.9	147.8	150.4	6.0	137.4	138.6	140.3	141.9
South	137.1	139.3	140.4	141.3	4.4	132.1	133.2	134.2	135.4
Midwest	134.4	135.5	136.7	138.0	4.8	129.1	130.2	131.2	131.7
West	138.3	139.5	140.6	141.5	3.8	134.1	134.2	135.8	136.3
Metropolitan areas	138.9	140.5	142.0	143.6	5.0	133.5	134.4	135.8	136.7
Nonmetropolitan areas	133.6	135.5	136.2	136.8	3.6	129.0	130.2	131.3	132.0
					Wages and salaries				
All private industry workers[2]	135.1	136.6	137.9	139.3	4.1	130.8	131.7	133.0	133.8
Northeast	140.9	142.9	144.6	147.3	5.4	135.4	136.6	138.3	139.7
South	134.0	136.1	137.1	137.8	3.6	130.1	131.1	132.1	133.0
Midwest	131.3	132.1	133.3	134.5	3.5	127.4	128.5	129.6	129.9
West	134.9	136.0	137.4	138.1	3.4	131.2	131.1	133.1	133.5
Metropolitan areas	135.8	137.3	138.7	140.2	4.2	131.6	132.4	133.7	134.6
Nonmetropolitan areas	130.9	133.0	133.5	133.7	3.0	126.6	127.8	129.1	129.8

1. Compensation consists of wages, salaries, and employer cost of employee benefits.
2. The indexes for the occupation and industry groups are calculated differently from those for regions.
Source: U.S. Department of Labor, Bureau of Labor Statistics, *Monthly Labor Review*, March 1989.

Nearly 25 percent of the nonagricultural jobs in Tennessee in 1988 were in manufacturing, as compared to a U.S. average of 18 percent. The manufacturing sector accounted for 25 percent of the total gross state product in Tennessee in 1988. Data on manufacturing – statistics on employment, payrolls, value added by manufacture, inventories, and new capital expenditures – are very important to decision-making processes in Tennessee. A major source of manufacturing industry data is the *Census of Manufactures*, compiled every five years by the U.S. Department of Commerce, Bureau of the Census. Since data from the 1987 Census will not be published until late 1990, most data included in this chapter are taken from the *1982 Census.*

For most sources, industrial data are given by Standard Industrial Classification (SIC). This code provides classifications for industries where industry is defined as a number of establishments producing a single product or a closely related group of products. An establishment is classified in a particular industry if its production of a product or product group exceeds in value its production of any other product group. Data reported in this edition of the *Abstract* are classified in accordance with the *1972 Standard Industrial Classification Manual*, its supplement of 1977, and 1982 revisions. A *1987 SIC Manual*, currently available, will be used to collect and report industry detail in the future.

Employment data for Tennessee's metropolitan areas are provided by the Tennessee Department of Employment Security in its monthly *Labor Market Report,* whose data are the most current available. In addition to providing employment by sector, it will provide estimates of weekly and hourly earnings and hours worked for production workers in selected categories.

In addition to those sources specifically concerned with manufacturing, virtually every source cited in the preface to Chapter 3 on Employment and Earnings will produce data for categories of manufacturing. Information regarding the quantities and types of fuels used by industry class is included in Chapter 10, Energy.

Intercensal data for states are published in the *Annual Survey of Manufactures* (ASM). These data supplement the census data in Tables 4.1 and 4.2. Export-related manufacturing data in Table 4.23 are also from the ASM. Another source of data on manufacturing establishments is *County Business Patterns.* This annual Census Bureau report is the only source of intercensal substate data for many industries.

TABLE OF CONTENTS

TABLE OF CONTENTS
(Continued)

Table Number Page Number

TABLE 4.1-- NUMBER OF MANUFACTURING ESTABLISHMENTS, EMPLOYEES, AND PRODUCTION WORKERS, AND VALUE ADDED BY MANUFACTURE, TENNESSEE, 1899–1986, SELECTED YEARS

Year	Total establishments	Total employees	Total production workers	Value added by manufacture ($1,000)
1986	n.a.	466,600	341,300	23,624,900
1985	n.a.	468,200	344,400	22,223,800
1984	n.a.	477,000	353,200	21,963,900
1983	n.a.	457,400	336,600	19,868,300
1982	6,417	461,600	337,500	17,822,900
1981[a]	5,753	493,583	n.a.	n.a.
1980[a]	5,739	509,694	n.a.	n.a.
1979[a]	5,765	524,443	n.a.	n.a.
1978	n.a.	509,900	389,000	14,045,800
1977	6,487	489,800	375,700	12,663,400
1976	n.a.	478,700	359,800	10,723,600
1975	n.a.	452,100	338,000	9,289,200
1974	n.a.	489,500	381,700	9,563,800
1973	n.a.	493,300	389,300	8,772,500
1972	5,647	467,400	367,000	7,662,000
1971	n.a.	444,200	346,900	6,728,900
1970	n.a.	447,900	348,200	6,297,000
1969	n.a.	456,300	360,500	5,982,100
1968	n.a.	434,100	345,100	5,542,000
1967	5,040	418,000	333,600	4,921,100
1966	n.a.	401,100	320,800	4,627,800
1965	n.a.	373,400	299,200	4,139,400
1964	n.a.	344,900	273,945	3,577,187
1963	4,787	334,900	266,969	3,299,300
1958	4,508	279,300	220,823	2,207,073
1954	4,058	267,496	214,027	1,678,786
1947	3,345	222,300	193,197	961,385
1939	2,225	152,179	131,024	318,378
1929	2,855	142,020	128,400	322,898
1919	4,426	107,725	94,564	210,201
1909	4,609	82,257	73,840	76,201
1899	3,116	49,292	45,963	38,190

n.a. not available.

a. Data are from *County Business Patterns* and do not provide direct comparison with economic census data.

Source: U.S. Department of Commerce, Bureau of the Census, *1986 Annual Survey of Manufactures, Geographic Area Statistics*, and earlier editions; *1982 Census of Manufactures, Geographic Area Series, Tennessee*, and earlier editions; and *County Business Patterns, 1979–1981*.

TABLE 4.2-- MANUFACTURING STATISTICS, BY SECTOR, TENNESSEE, 1982 AND 1986 [Dollar amounts in millions]

Sector	1986: Total employees (1,000)	1986: Value added by manufacture	1982: Number of establishments: Total	1982: Number of establishments: With 20 or more employees	1982: All employees: Number (1,000)	1982: All employees: Payroll	1982: Production workers: Number (1,000)	1982: Production workers: Wages	1982: Value added by manufacture	1982: Value of shipments	1982: New capital expenditures
All industries, total	466.6	$23,624.9	6,417	2,617	461.6	$7,377.7	337.5	$4,602.9	$17,822.9	$40,776.5	$2,061.5
Food and kindred products	36.0	3,076.4	431	245	36.3	618.0	23.4	335.3	2,160.8	6,557.2	321.5
Tobacco products	1.1	284.0	9	8	1.3	19.8	1.0	12.8	203.8	345.7	3.6
Textile mill products	21.2	639.2	139	103	24.1	278.5	21.2	222.4	557.7	1,378.4	37.4
Apparel, other textile products	55.9	1,215.8	458	329	58.8	525.1	51.0	402.1	1,142.3	2,135.3	31.0
Lumber and wood products	14.9	441.4	836	163	14.1	155.2	12.1	119.7	266.0	699.7	19.2
Furniture and fixtures	23.8	813.4	303	150	21.0	240.4	17.6	171.3	516.5	1,032.3	15.9
Paper and allied products	17.0	1,298.6	141	104	17.1	339.7	12.9	238.1	1,054.7	2,278.1	109.2
Printing and publishing	33.0	1,509.6	963	200	27.7	412.2	16.1	224.7	906.4	1,494.8	49.5
Chemicals and allied products	43.3	3,576.7	235	106	50.3	1,180.9	30.8	626.5	3,024.0	6,697.6	471.4
Petroleum and coal products	1.1	59.1	44	14	1.2	24.3	0.8	15.9	47.8	809.6	22.8
Rubber, miscellaneous plastics products	21.4	1,316.1	222	118	19.2	338.1	14.9	238.1	943.3	1,937.7	53.2
Leather and leather products	8.5	252.6	88	61	15.2	147.0	13.1	105.9	396.4	702.7	10.5
Stone, clay, glass products	13.5	867.6	305	95	13.7	251.6	11.0	188.9	574.6	1,067.8	64.0
Primary metal industries	13.9	562.7	117	77	14.4	325.3	11.7	247.9	430.4	1,935.7	96.2
Fabricated metal products	33.2	1,475.9	567	248	30.5	512.3	23.2	339.1	1,063.5	2,195.2	59.3
Machinery, except electrical	38.3	2,143.7	677	197	29.4	492.7	21.4	324.0	1,672.6	2,958.6	92.4
Electric, electronic equipment	30.8	1,496.1	237	126	36.7	567.8	27.1	360.9	1,511.8	3,533.7	107.6
Transportation equipment	29.1	1,773.6	174	86	24.2	460.9	18.1	307.5	783.1	1,992.4	469.4
Instruments, related products	6.7	383.3	71	25	5.0	87.8	2.9	37.7	224.0	337.6	10.9
Miscellaneous manufacturing industries	10.1	439.2	247	77	10.1	137.2	7.4	84.4	343.1	686.3	16.6
Auxiliaries	13.8	0.0	153	85	11.3	262.9	0.0	0.0	0.0	0.0	0.0

Note: Individual columns may not add to totals due to independent rounding.

Source: U.S. Department of Commerce, Bureau of the Census, *1986 Annual Survey of Manufactures, Geographic Area Statistics*; and *1982 Census of Manufactures, Geographic Area Series, Tennessee*.

FIGURE 4.1
Manufacturing Employment and Value Added, Distribution by Sector, Tennessee, 1986

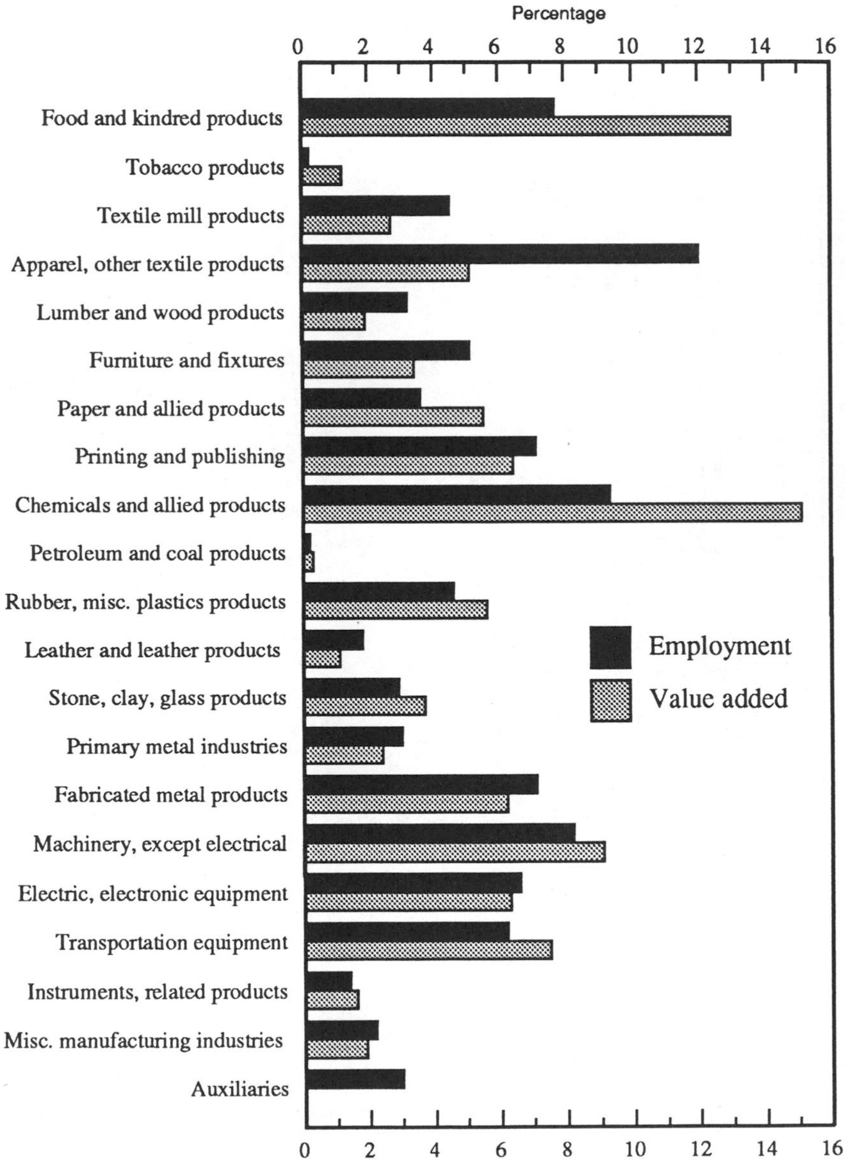

Source: U.S. Department of Commerce, Bureau of the Census, *1986 Annual Survey of Manufactures*, Geographic Area Statistics.

TABLE 4.3-- NUMBER OF MANUFACTURING ESTABLISHMENTS, BY SECTOR AND BY EMPLOYMENT-SIZE CLASS, TENNESSEE, 1986

Sector	Total	Employment-size class								
		1–4	5–9	10–19	20–49	5–99	100–249	250–499	500–999	1,000 or more
All industries, total	6,451	1,792	962	934	1,044	653	608	291	117	50
Food and kindred products	374	88	40	33	68	46	58	29	10	2
Tobacco products	9	0	0	0	2	2	3	1	1	0
Textile mill products	131	21	6	9	22	21	27	12	11	2
Apparel, other textile products	447	73	25	25	53	88	108	60	13	2
Lumber and wood products	792	308	163	135	99	49	34	3	1	0
Furniture and fixtures	297	66	40	38	54	40	33	18	6	2
Paper and allied products	145	8	10	18	29	34	33	8	3	2
Printing and publishing	1,024	425	213	143	125	65	32	10	6	5
Chemicals and allied products	251	70	29	46	37	22	20	11	4	12
Petroleum and coal products	44	11	18	5	5	3	1	1	0	0
Rubber, plastics products	253	56	29	37	50	23	33	19	4	2
Leather and leather products	69	14	3	5	12	9	9	14	3	0
Stone, clay, and glass products	308	68	54	64	68	25	18	6	4	1
Primary metal industries	112	15	6	18	25	19	16	8	4	1
Fabricated metal products	583	125	83	93	138	61	56	19	6	2
Machinery, except electrical	664	177	121	146	116	45	34	12	6	7
Electric, electronic equipment	247	77	24	25	35	23	20	23	16	4
Transportation equipment	198	38	27	27	31	20	23	17	10	5
Instruments, related products	90	31	20	8	8	11	3	7	1	1
Miscellaneous manufacturing	254	99	42	43	24	20	18	3	5	0
Administrative and auxiliary	159	22	9	16	43	27	29	10	3	0

Source: U.S. Department of Commerce, Bureau of the Census, *County Business Patterns, 1986, Tennessee.*

TABLE 4.4-- AVERAGE WEEKLY HOURS AND AVERAGE WEEKLY AND HOURLY EARNINGS FOR MANUFACTURING PRODUCTION WORKERS, BY SECTOR, TENNESSEE, 1985–1988

	Average weekly earnings				Average hourly earnings				Average weekly hours			
Sector	1988	1987	1986	1985	1988	1987	1986	1985	1988	1987	1986	1985
All manufacturing	$372.74	$364.90	$353.50	$339.72	$8.96	$8.78	$8.58	$8.29	41.6	41.6	41.2	41.0
Durable goods	398.79	393.48	376.48	359.20	9.45	9.38	9.05	8.66	42.2	41.9	41.6	41.4
Lumber and wood products	261.65	249.23	234.55	222.47	6.32	6.12	5.82	5.64	41.4	40.7	40.3	39.4
Furniture and fixtures	295.46	297.49	287.34	278.43	7.48	7.41	7.33	7.09	39.5	40.2	39.2	39.3
Stone, clay, and glass products	548.42	529.95	508.24	495.91	12.16	11.55	11.17	10.77	45.1	45.8	45.5	46.0
Primary metal products	500.25	502.23	464.61	445.14	11.50	11.68	10.83	10.74	43.5	43.0	42.9	41.4
Fabricated metal products	415.65	394.36	388.44	380.89	9.92	9.47	9.36	9.09	41.9	41.6	41.5	41.9
Machinery, including electric	390.35	385.90	365.47	339.82	9.25	9.07	8.64	8.22	42.2	42.5	42.3	41.3
Instruments and related products	393.96	362.25	342.66	340.88	9.38	8.97	8.44	8.09	42.0	40.4	40.6	42.2
Nondurable goods	345.63	336.16	329.66	320.02	8.43	8.16	8.08	7.90	41.0	41.2	40.8	40.5
Food and kindred products	346.42	343.64	337.40	326.30	8.47	8.40	8.29	8.13	40.9	40.9	40.7	40.1
Textile mill products	288.16	286.00	271.58	252.06	7.08	6.79	6.56	6.32	40.7	42.1	41.4	39.9
Apparel	213.74	208.79	198.38	192.54	5.61	5.46	5.29	5.17	38.1	38.3	37.5	37.2
Paper and allied products	508.90	484.45	467.28	442.83	11.16	10.81	10.62	10.18	45.6	44.8	44.0	43.5
Chemical and allied products	485.06	460.20	442.54	432.84	11.44	11.01	10.82	10.52	42.4	41.8	40.9	41.2
Rubber and plastic products	442.83	425.79	416.02	409.60	10.18	9.65	9.52	9.30	43.5	44.1	43.7	44.1
Leather and leather products	244.00	252.76	232.05	239.87	6.10	6.17	5.95	5.81	40.0	41.0	39.0	41.2

Source: Tennessee Department of Employment Security, direct correspondence.

TABLE 4.5-- POLLUTION ABATEMENT OPERATING COSTS, BY INDUSTRY GROUP AND BY TYPE OF POLLUTION, TENNESSEE, 1985 [In millions of dollars]

Industry group	Total gross annual cost	Payments to government units			Operating costs by form of pollutant abated			
		Total	Use of public sewage	Solid waste collection and disposal	Total	Air	Water	Solid waste
TOTAL	309.8	28.5	25.0	3.5	281.3	99.2	102.3	79.8
Food and kindred products	21.4	8.7	7.8	0.9	12.8	5.1	4.1	3.5
Textile mill products	2.8	1.2	1.1	0.1	1.6	0.8	0.5	0.3
Lumber and wood products	2.1	0.2	0.2	(a)	1.9	0.8	0.0	1.1
Paper and allied products	27.9	5.2	5.1	0.1	22.6	9.4	8.3	4.9
Printing and publishing	7.4	0.6	0.5	0.1	6.8	5.2	0.5	1.2
Chemicals and allied products	159.6	4.1	3.8	0.2	155.5	41.3	73.3	40.9
Rubber and miscellaneous plastics products	8.5	1.1	0.7	0.5	7.3	1.9	1.6	3.9
Stone, clay, and glass products	13.7	0.4	0.3	0.1	13.4	4.4	(D)	2.6
Primary metal industries	25.4	1.0	0.6	0.3	24.4	17.1	3.6	3.8
Fabricated metal products	5.6	0.7	0.7	0.1	4.8	0.8	1.6	2.4
Machinery, except electrical	9.3	1.0	0.8	0.2	8.2	3.9	1.9	2.4
Electric and electronic equipment	10.2	1.2	0.9	0.2	9.1	3.6	2.1	3.3
Transportation equipment	8.0	1.4	1.4	0.1	6.5	1.6	2.7	2.2
Miscellaneous manufacturing industries	1.2	0.4	0.4	(a)	0.8	0.3	0.1	0.4

Note: Detail may not add to total due to independent rounding. Data exclude industry group 23, apparel and other textile products, and cover only establishments with 20 or more employees.

(D) withheld to avoid disclosing operations of individual companies.

a. Represents a value of less than $50,000.

Source: U.S. Department of Commerce, Bureau of the Census, *Current Industrial Reports, Pollution Abatement Cost and Expenditures, 1985*.

TABLE 4.6-- POLLUTION ABATEMENT CAPITAL EXPENDITURES AND COSTS, BY TYPE OF POLLUTION, TENNESSEE, 1978–1985 [In millions of dollars]

	Pollution abatement capital expenditures					Pollution abatement gross annual costs[1]				
	Total	Air	Water	Solid waste	Percent change from prior year	Total	Air	Water	Solid waste	Percent change from prior year
1985	88.9	37.7	38.6	12.6	55	309.8	99.2	127.3	83.4	13
1984	57.4	29.7	15.6	12.0	-8	274.3	89.4	117.3	67.6	23
1983	62.6	33.4	24.9	4.4	-45	222.3	78.9	99.5	43.8	29
1982	112.9	71.1	32.6	9.2	26	172.2	49.5	89.3	33.2	-8
1981	89.8	57.5	28.6	3.7	14	187.9	51.2	103.6	33.0	9
1980	78.7	32.6	41.1	5.0	-5	172.8	56.9	78.7	37.1	6
1979	83.1	36.7	38.4	8.0	5	163.5	47.3	86.0	30.2	17
1978	79.1	41.6	29.8	7.6	-27	139.3	41.6	73.6	24.0	5

Note: Detail may not add to total due to independent rounding. Data exclude industry group 23, apparel and other textile products, and cover only establishments with 20 or more employees.

1. Includes payments to government units.

Source: U.S. Department of Commerce, Bureau of the Census, *Current Industrial Reports, Pollution Abatement Costs and Expenditures, 1985*, and earlier editions.

TABLE 4.7-- EXPORT-RELATED MANUFACTURING SHIPMENTS AND EMPLOYMENT, TENNESSEE, 1986 [Shipments in millions of dollars and employment in thousands of jobs]

Industry	Value of shipments: Total: Amount	Value of shipments: Total: Percentage of total manufacturing shipments	Value of shipments: Direct exports	Value of shipments: Supporting exports	Employment: Total: Amount	Employment: Total: Percentage of total manufacturing employment	Employment: Direct exports	Employment: Supporting exports
Total	5,760.5	10.9	2,910.4	2,850.1	42.2	9.0	17.9	24.3
Food and kindred products	439.4	5.4	287.4	152.0	1.2	3.3	0.7	0.5
Tobacco products	109.7	23.0	108.2	1.5	0.4	36.4	0.4	(a)
Textile mill products	100.1	6.1	23.2	76.9	0.9	4.2	0.1	0.8
Apparel and other textile products	59.5	2.7	45.4	14.1	0.9	1.6	0.6	0.3
Lumber and wood products	60.8	6.3	18.8	42.0	0.8	5.4	0.1	0.7
Furniture and fixtures	51.7	3.4	29.5	22.2	0.7	2.9	0.3	0.4
Paper and allied products	274.7	9.9	50.2	224.5	1.6	9.4	0.2	1.4
Printing and publishing	83.2	3.6	10.1	73.1	1.0	3.0	(a)	1.0
Chemicals and allied products	1,535.0	20.8	907.5	627.5	8.8	20.3	5.1	3.7
Petroleum and coal products	40.4	6.8	8.3	32.1	(a)	(a)	(a)	(a)
Rubber, miscellaneous plastics products	268.6	10.5	66.7	201.9	2.3	10.7	0.5	1.8
Leather and leather products	21.1	4.2	15.4	5.7	0.4	4.7	0.3	0.1
Stone, clay, and glass products	172.4	10.9	99.9	72.5	1.4	10.3	0.7	0.7
Primary metal industries	528.9	24.7	74.8	454.1	3.3	23.7	0.3	3.0
Fabricated metal products	314.5	10.9	81.9	232.6	3.7	11.1	0.9	2.8
Machinery, except electrical	672.5	15.2	454.5	218.0	4.8	12.5	2.8	2.0
Electric and electronic equipment	498.1	10.5	226.1	272.0	3.9	12.7	1.3	2.6
Transportation equipment	383.0	8.6	301.0	82.0	2.4	8.2	1.9	0.5
Instruments and related products	90.3	15.8	71.5	18.8	1.1	16.7	0.9	0.2
Miscellaneous manufacturing	55.8	6.9	29.1	26.7	0.5	5.0	0.2	0.3
Auxiliaries	0.0	0.0	0.0	0.0	1.7	12.3	0.0	1.7

a. Less than 0.05.

Source: U.S. Department of Commerce, Bureau of the Census, *Exports from Manufacturing Establishments: 1985 and 1986.*

TABLE 4.8-- AVERAGE WEEKLY HOURS AND AVERAGE WEEKLY AND HOURLY EARNINGS FOR MANUFACTURING PRODUCTION WORKERS, METROPOLITAN STATISTICAL AREAS, 1955–1988, SELECTED YEARS [Earnings in dollars]

	Chattanooga			Johnson City–Kingsport–Bristol			Knoxville			Memphis			Nashville–Davidson		
	Earnings			Earnings			Earnings			Earnings			Earnings		
Year	Weekly	Hourly	Hours	Weekly	Hourly	Hours	Weekly	Hourly	Hours	Weekly	Hourly	Hours	Weekly	Hourly	Hours
1988	348.30	8.10	43.0	414.42	9.44	43.9	366.79	8.99	40.8	387.23	9.09	42.6	434.72	10.45	41.6
1987	334.68	7.90	42.4	403.47	9.21	43.8	369.58	9.08	40.7	379.14	8.84	42.9	433.51	10.23	42.4
1986	320.04	7.62	42.0	396.36	9.07	43.7	352.63	8.95	39.4	377.54	8.78	43.0	378.58	9.56	39.6
1985	307.93	7.42	41.5	374.85	8.82	42.5	360.93	8.89	40.6	361.15	8.64	41.8	376.65	9.30	40.5
1984	309.86	7.36	42.1	352.49	8.44	41.8	353.76	8.80	40.2	339.49	8.26	41.1	368.74	8.95	41.2
1983	296.31	7.14	41.5	n.a.	n.a.	n.a.	358.27	8.39	40.3	324.69	7.90	41.1	338.65	8.28	40.9
1982	272.84	7.05	38.7	n.a.	n.a.	n.a.	324.24	8.40	38.6	311.22	7.80	39.9	307.72	7.87	39.1
1981	265.36	6.52	40.7	n.a.	n.a.	n.a.	296.56	7.47	39.7	302.25	7.50	40.3	298.00	7.34	40.6
1980	247.25	6.09	40.6	n.a.	n.a.	n.a.	274.51	6.88	39.9	275.77	6.86	40.2	256.89	6.52	39.4
1979	224.62	5.56	40.4	n.a.	n.a.	n.a.	260.98	6.46	40.4	250.22	6.24	40.1	237.21	5.96	39.8
1978	209.44	5.21	40.2	n.a.	n.a.	n.a.	238.58	5.92	40.3	237.55	5.88	40.4	220.70	5.49	40.2
1975	168.05	4.17	40.3	n.a.	n.a.	n.a.	176.91	4.49	39.4	187.80	4.66	40.3	163.80	4.20	39.0
1970	116.91	2.93	39.9	n.a.	n.a.	n.a.	120.87	3.06	39.5	122.31	3.02	40.5	117.20	2.93	40.0
1965	92.74	2.24	41.4	n.a.	n.a.	n.a.	96.63	2.38	40.6	97.11	2.34	41.5	92.74	2.24	41.4
1960	74.48	1.90	39.2	n.a.	n.a.	n.a.	84.38	2.12	39.8	81.81	2.01	40.7	78.58	1.95	40.3
1955	62.37	1.54	40.5	n.a.	n.a.	n.a.	69.20	1.73	40.0	69.01	1.62	42.6	n.a.	n.a.	n.a.

Note: Data are given for MSA's according to their boundaries at the time. See the "area definitions" in the source to see when area changes occurred. Memphis data exclude the DeSoto, Mississippi component. For state level data see Table 4.4.

n.a. not available.

Source: Tennessee Department of Employment Security, direct correspondence and *Tennessee and Standard Metropolitan Statistical Areas, Employment Estimates, 1981*, and earlier editions; and direct correspondence; U.S. Department of Labor, Bureau of Labor Statistics, *Employment and Earnings, May 1979*, Vol. 26, No. 5, and earlier editions since 1975; *Employment and Earnings, States and Areas, 1939–1974*.

TABLE 4.9-- MANUFACTURING STATISTICS, METROPOLITAN STATISTICAL AREAS, 1977 AND 1982 [Dollar amounts in millions]

MSA's	1982									1977	
	Establishments		Employees		Production workers						
	Total	With 20 or more employees	Number (1,000)	Payroll	Number (1,000)	Wages	Value added by manu-facture	Value of shipments	New capital expend-itures	Em-ployees (1,000)	Value added by manu-facture
TENNESSEE	6,417	2,617	461.6	$7,377.7	337.5	$4,602.9	$17,841.6	$40,795.2	$2,061.5	489.8	$12,663.4
Chattanooga, TN–GA	656	284	45.8	763.5	33.9	487.5	1,703.2	4,479.6	116.3	53.9	1,290.0
Portion in Georgia	137	59	8.0	108.4	6.4	73.4	301.5	1,041.7	17.6	9.9	199.8
Portion in Tennessee	519	225	37.8	655.0	27.4	414.2	1,401.7	3,438.0	98.7	43.9	1,090.2
Clarksville-Hopkinsville, TN–KY	114	50	9.4	131.1	6.5	79.8	291.6	676.5	25.8	9.4	233.3
Portion in Kentucky	53	26	3.1	41.8	2.4	27.5	85.5	233.2	6.9	3.7	89.3
Portion in Tennessee	61	24	6.2	89.3	4.1	52.3	206.0	443.3	18.9	5.6	144.0
Johnson City-Kingsport–Bristol, TN–VA	445	196	52.9	965.8	37.3	580.0	2,227.4	5,102.7	401.7	54.5	1,505.0
Portion in Virginia	110	50	8.9	128.4	6.7	89.6	351.9	928.0	14.0	8.7	217.4
Portion in Tennessee	335	146	44.0	837.4	30.6	490.4	1,875.4	4,174.7	387.8	45.8	1,287.6
Knoxville	580	203	39.3	713.8	28.0	443.8	1,625.0	3,497.3	93.9	39.6	1,174.8
Memphis, TN–MS–AR	1,096	474	60.5	1,100.8	40.2	619.1	3,026.6	7,644.1	235.1	64.1	2,159.7
Portion in Tennessee	978	412	54.3	1,006.4	35.9	561.5	2,780.9	7,055.7	215.8	59.2	2,054.8
Portion in Mississippi	72	39	4.4	69.8	3.0	41.1	198.3	421.4	15.7	3.4	66.4
Portion in Arkansas	46	23	1.8	24.7	1.4	16.4	47.4	167.0	3.6	1.6	38.6
Nashville–Davidson	1,357	510	79.0	1,350.3	51.9	750.8	2,707.0	6,327.8	603.2	80.5	1,935.3

Source: U.S. Department of Commerce, Bureau of the Census, *1982 Census of Manufactures, Geographic Area Series, Tennessee*, and *1977*.

TABLE 4.10--MANUFACTURING STATISTICS, BY SECTOR, CHATTANOOGA METROPOLITAN STATISTICAL AREA, 1977 AND 1982 [Dollar amounts in millions]

Sector	1982									1977	
	Establishments		Employees		Production workers						
	Total	With 20 or more employees	Number (1,000)	Payroll	Number (1,000)	Wages	Value added by manu-facture	Value of shipments	New capital expend-itures	Em-ployees (1,000)	Value added by manu-facture
All industries, total	656	284	45.8	$763.5	33.9	$487.5	$1,703.2	$4,479.6	$116.3	53.9	$1,290.0
Food and kindred products	47	23	5.4	87.4	3.3	42.0	341.3	996.8	32.3	5.0	158.8
Textile mill products	65	50	9.8	120.9	8.7	95.8	333.0	1,142.0	10.1	12.4	220.9
Apparel, other textile products	32	14	1.0	7.8	0.9	6.2	12.2	23.4	0.3	1.9	22.8
Lumber and wood products	45	5	0.5	5.3	0.4	3.9	12.9	28.0	0.5	0.7	12.7
Furniture and fixtures	15	8	0.6	6.1	0.5	4.1	9.6	22.3	0.4	0.6	9.6
Paper and allied products	22	15	1.4	24.8	1.1	17.7	60.5	147.5	6.9	1.1	27.5
Printing and publishing	81	20	1.6	21.9	0.9	12.2	47.8	77.7	3.4	1.4	27.7
Chemicals and allied products	39	19	5.0	116.7	3.4	68.0	274.1	687.4	17.0	6.2	243.4
Rubber and miscellaneous plastics products	13	9	0.4	7.4	0.3	4.8	17.6	47.2	1.5	0.6	22.0
Leather and leather products	10	8	0.8	7.7	0.7	4.8	21.5	39.9	0.5	1.1	19.7
Stone, clay and glass products	30	9	2.8	52.3	2.5	43.8	106.8	205.8	7.8	1.6	48.9
Primary metal industries	19	12	3.4	58.1	2.8	43.7	110.9	237.8	8.0	5.2	103.7
Fabricated metal products	75	34	6.3	126.7	4.6	84.5	190.1	422.4	8.6	8.1	195.4
Machinery, except electrical	78	21	2.9	52.3	2.0	32.7	80.2	185.9	5.4	3.5	84.3
Electric, electronic equipment	16	11	1.8	30.2	1.2	15.1	56.7	154.8	4.2	2.7	73.3
Instruments and related products	4	2	(a)	(D)	(D)	(D)	(D)	(D)	(D)	n.a.	n.a.
Miscellaneous manufacturing industries	17	7	0.5	5.4	0.4	3.9	12.4	25.4	0.6	0.4	8.0
Auxiliaries	34	15	1.1	25.4	0.0	0.0	0.0	0.0	0.0	0.8	0.0

Note: Totals include categories not shown separately.

n.a. not available.

(D) withheld to avoid disclosure.

a. Range is from 250 to 499 employees. Actual data is withheld to avoid disclosure.

Source: U.S. Department of Commerce, Bureau of the Census, *1982 Census of Manufactures, Geographic Area Series, Tennessee*, and *1977*.

TABLE 4.11--MANUFACTURING STATISTICS, BY SECTOR, CLARKSVILLE–HOPKINSVILLE METROPOLITAN STATISTICAL AREA, 1977 AND 1982
[Dollar amounts in millions]

	1982									1977	
	Establishments		Employees		Production workers						
Sector	Total	With 20 or more employees	Number (1,000)	Payroll	Number (1,000)	Wages	Value added by manu-facture	Value of shipments	New capital expend-itures	Em-ployees (1,000)	Value added by manu-facture
All industries, total	114	50	9.4	$131.1	6.5	$79.8	$291.6	$676.5	$25.8	9.4	$233.3
Food and kindred products	10	6	0.3	4.2	0.1	1.7	8.7	28.5	0.5	0.8	8.7
Apparel, other textile products	10	4	1.2	11.2	1.1	8.9	20.2	36.0	0.8	1.3	11.8
Printing and publishing	17	6	1.1	15.0	0.7	8.7	37.9	57.6	2.6	0.6	13.3
Rubber and miscellaneous plastics products	4	2	(a)	(D)	(D)	(D)	(D)	(D)	(D)	n.a.	n.a.
Leather and leather products	3	3	1.3	11.1	1.1	9.5	12.5	29.6	(D)	1.3	13.1
Primary metal industries	5	4	(b)	(D)	(D)	(D)	(D)	(D)	(D)	n.a.	n.a.
Fabricated metal products	9	4	0.4	4.8	0.3	3.4	9.1	18.0	0.5	0.5	10.5
Machinery, except electrical	5	4	(c)	(D)	(D)	(D)	(D)	(D)	(D)	n.a.	n.a.
Electric and electronic equipment	4	2	(a)	(D)	(D)	(D)	(D)	(D)	(D)	n.a.	n.a.
Auxiliaries	6	2	0.5	11.3	0.0	0.0	0.0	0.0	0.0	n.a.	n.a.

Note: Totals include categories not shown separately.

n.a. not available.

(D) withheld to avoid disclosing figures of individual companies.

a. Range is 250–499. Actual is withheld to avoid disclosure.

b. Range is 500–999. Actual is withheld to avoid disclosure.

c. Range is 1,000–2,499. Actual is withheld to avoid disclosure.

Source: U.S. Department of Commerce, Bureau of the Census, *1982 Census of Manufactures, Geographic Area Series, Tennessee*; and *1977*.

TABLE 4.12--MANUFACTURING STATISTICS, BY SECTOR, JOHNSON CITY-KINGSPORT-BRISTOL METROPOLITAN STATISTICAL AREA, 1977 AND 1982
[Dollar amounts in millions]

	1982									1977	
	Establishments		Employees		Production workers						
Sector	Total	With 20 or more employees	Number (1,000)	Payroll	Number (1,000)	Wages	Value added by manu- facture	Value of shipments	New capital expend- itures	Em- ployees (1,000)	Value added by manu- facture
All industries, total	445	196	52.9	$965.8	37.3	$580.0	$2,227.4	$5,102.7	$401.7	54.5	$1,505.0
Food and kindred products	31	18	2.9	44.4	1.5	19.9	127.7	366.3	6.2	2.8	78.4
Textile mill products	16	13	3.0	39.4	2.7	32.7	64.0	190.8	(D)	3.7	63.8
Apparel, other textile products	30	24	4.1	34.4	3.6	28.0	73.4	117.3	(D)	4.6	61.1
Lumber and wood products	60	8	0.9	8.6	0.8	6.5	13.8	39.0	(D)	1.1	14.8
Furniture and fixtures	9	4	0.8	7.5	0.7	5.5	15.1	24.4	(D)	1.5	19.2
Paper and allied products	6	5	1.6	38.6	1.3	31.1	74.3	169.7	(D)	n.a.	n.a.
Printing and publishing	68	17	4.5	69.5	3.4	49.6	136.2	233.4	11.8	4.5	97.4
Chemicals and allied products	17	13	(a)	(D)	(D)	(D)	(D)	(D)	(D)	n.a.	n.a.
Rubber and miscellaneous plastic products	13	9	1.0	14.2	0.7	8.5	48.3	114.1	(D)	0.8	20.1
Stone, clay and glass products	32	16	1.7	28.4	1.4	21.5	90.3	164.0	(D)	2.4	57.0
Primary metal industries	12	8	1.2	21.0	0.9	14.0	31.7	110.1	(D)	1.2	31.8
Fabricated metal products	36	18	2.8	48.4	2.2	36.7	141.0	368.0	(D)	4.7	134.3
Machinery, except electrical	55	18	4.7	76.9	3.4	50.6	583.2	847.3	(D)	3.4	335.5
Electric, electronic equipment	16	11	5.3	96.9	3.4	48.6	127.7	322.2	9.7	4.9	118.7
Transportation equipment	11	5	1.0	18.5	0.8	13.0	55.7	111.1	3.0	0.5	15.5
Instruments and related products	6	1	(b)	(D)	(D)	(D)	(D)	(D)	(D)	n.a.	n.a.
Miscellaneous manufacturing industries	15	2	0.3	4.6	0.2	3.3	8.1	17.1	(D)	n.a.	n.a.
Auxiliaries	8	4	0.6	13.1	0.0	0.0	0.0	0.0	0.0	0.5	0.0

Note: Totals include categories not shown separately.

n.a. not available.

(D) withheld to avoid disclosing figures for individual companies.

a. Range is 2,500 or more. Actual is withheld to avoid disclosure.

b. Range is 1,000-2,499. Actual is withheld to avoid disclosure.

Source: U.S. Department of Commerce, Bureau of the Census, *1982 Census of Manufactures, Geographic Area Series, Tennessee*; and *1977*.

TABLE 4.13--MANUFACTURING STATISTICS, BY SECTOR, KNOXVILLE METROPOLITAN STATISTICAL AREA, 1977 AND 1982 [Dollar amounts in millions]

	1982										1977	
	Establishments		Employees		Production workers							
Sector	Total	With 20 or more employees	Number (1,000)	Payroll	Number (1,000)	Wages	Value added by manu-facture	Value of shipments	New capital expend-itures		Em-ployees (1,000)	Value added by manu-facture
All industries, total	580	203	39.3	$713.8	28.0	$443.8	$1,625.0	$3,497.3	$93.9		39.6	$1,174.8
Food and kindred products	42	26	3.7	53.6	2.3	28.6	183.3	504.9	13.9		3.8	96.3
Textile mill products	11	4	(a)	(D)	(D)	(D)	(D)	(D)	(D)		2.6	34.5
Apparel, other textile products	38	22	6.8	68.9	5.7	46.6	247.9	426.7	4.8		9.4	203.5
Lumber and wood products	34	9	0.7	7.5	0.6	5.3	12.2	30.0	0.2		0.6	9.7
Furniture and fixtures	23	8	0.6	6.5	0.5	4.0	11.0	28.3	0.3		0.6	9.1
Paper and allied products	7	5	(b)	(D)	(D)	(D)	(D)	(D)	(D)		0.3	7.6
Printing and publishing	121	21	2.1	35.0	1.1	14.1	79.7	118.4	4.0		1.5	39.9
Chemicals and allied products	19	6	(c)	(D)	(D)	(D)	(D)	(D)	(D)		n.a.	n.a.
Rubber and miscellaneous plastic products	20	10	1.4	23.4	1.1	16.0	39.3	88.9	1.7		1.1	32.6
Stone, clay and glass products	31	14	1.0	16.7	0.8	12.0	33.8	65.6	2.9		1.2	29.5
Primary metal industries	10	5	(c)	(D)	(D)	(D)	(D)	(D)	(D)		n.a.	n.a.
Fabricated metal products	57	22	2.0	33.9	1.6	23.2	67.0	152.3	3.3		1.3	33.5
Machinery, except electrical	67	21	1.8	31.3	1.2	20.4	64.5	111.5	6.3		1.6	41.8
Electric, electronic equipment	17	3	0.6	7.4	0.4	4.5	12.5	26.8	(D)		0.8	16.1
Transportation equipment	15	6	1.9	34.4	1.5	24.1	58.7	123.7	0.8		2.1	44.3
Instruments and related products	20	6	0.7	12.8	0.4	5.5	31.8	46.7	1.2		n.a.	n.a.
Miscellaneous manufacturing industries	30	9	1.0	15.7	0.7	8.4	22.8	50.2	(D)		1.2	22.8
Auxiliaries	9	4	0.4	9.5	0.0	0.0	0.0	0.0	0.0		n.a.	n.a.

Note: Totals include categories not shown separately.

n.a. not available.

(D) withheld to avoid disclosing figures for individual companies.

a. Range is 1,000–2,499. Actual is withheld to avoid disclosure.

b. Range is 250–499. Actual data withheld to avoid disclosure.

c. Range is 2,500 or more. Actual data withheld to avoid disclosure.

Source: U.S. Department of Commerce, Bureau of the Census, *1982 Census of Manufactures, Geographic Area Series, Tennessee*; and *1977*.

TABLE 4.14--MANUFACTURING STATISTICS, BY SECTOR, MEMPHIS METROPOLITAN STATISTICAL AREA, 1977 AND 1982 [Dollar amounts in millions]

	1982										1977	
	Establishments		Employees		Production workers							
Sector	Total	With 20 or more employees	Number (1,000)	Payroll	Number (1,000)	Wages	Value added by manu-facture	Value of shipments	New capital expend-itures		Em-ployees (1,000)	Value added by manu-facture
All industries, total	1,096	474	60.5	$1,100.8	40.2	$619.1	$3,026.6	$7,644.1	$235.1		64.1	$2,159.7
Food and kindred products	84	58	8.4	174.5	5.6	105.4	600.6	2,001.1	35.5		10.5	448.7
Tobacco products	1	1	(a)	(D)	(D)	(D)	(D)	(D)	(D)		n.a.	n.a.
Textile mill products	9	5	0.5	6.1	0.4	3.9	12.0	23.4	(D)		0.5	8.2
Apparel, other textile products	34	20	2.2	22.3	2.0	16.7	55.0	120.5	1.4		2.3	36.0
Lumber and wood products	77	30	2.4	29.0	2.1	22.3	43.0	123.2	1.5		3.4	44.5
Furniture and fixtures	56	27	3.3	39.7	2.5	22.4	80.9	179.4	3.0		3.0	50.7
Paper and allied products	39	31	5.8	114.9	4.3	78.5	437.1	865.2	37.8		4.7	167.0
Printing and publishing	177	35	4.2	74.8	2.6	41.4	166.0	258.5	9.2		3.7	94.2
Chemicals and allied products	78	41	6.2	130.2	3.7	67.5	629.2	1,234.3	53.5		5.7	404.2
Petroleum and coal products	19	5	(b)	(D)	(D)	(D)	(D)	(D)	(D)		0.7	95.3
Rubber and miscellaneous plastic products	32	14	2.4	57.5	1.8	43.0	91.1	252.3	7.2		3.9	123.1
Leather and leather products	3	2	(a)	(D)	(D)	(D)	(D)	(D)	(D)		n.a.	n.a.
Stone, clay and glass products	48	18	1.2	18.6	0.9	12.4	37.7	88.7	3.1		1.5	38.1
Primary metal industries	17	11	1.0	15.9	0.8	11.2	29.7	94.0	3.2		1.3	28.3
Fabricated metal products	139	65	5.2	89.6	3.8	55.4	173.6	400.2	11.4		5.5	152.3
Machinery, except electrical	108	33	5.1	95.1	3.3	53.9	227.6	462.8	24.5		5.7	186.9
Electric, electronic equipment	25.0	17.0	3.3	55.5	2.2	29.3	214.2	432.5	14.0		2.6	86.9
Instruments and related products	14	6	1.1	21.6	0.6	9.4	63.6	87.1	2.6		0.7	29.8
Transportation equipment	33	16	1.6	22.6	1.2	15.7	42.3	103.1	3.0		0.7	15.0
Miscellaneous manufacturing industries	52	16	1.6	19.8	1.3	13.2	37.3	80.1	0.7		2.0	34.7
Auxiliaries	51	23	3.4	87.5	0.0	0.0	0.0	0.0	0.0		2.0	0.0

n.a. not available.

(D) withheld to avoid disclosing data for individual companies.

a. Range is 250–499. Actual data is withheld to avoid disclosure.

b. Range is 500–999. Actual data is withheld to avoid disclosure.

Source: U.S. Department of Commerce, Bureau of the Census, *1982 Census of Manufactures, Geographic Area Series, Tennessee*; and *1977*.

TABLE 4.15--MANUFACTURING STATISTICS, BY SECTOR, NASHVILLE-DAVIDSON METROPOLITAN STATISTICAL AREA, 1977 AND 1982
[Dollar amounts in millions]

	1982									1977	
	Establishments		Employees		Production workers						
Sector	Total	With 20 or more employees	Number (1,000)	Payroll	Number (1,000)	Wages	Value added by manufacture	Value of shipments	New capital expenditures	Employees (1,000)	Value added by manufacture
All industries, total	1,357	510	79.0	$1,350.3	51.9	$750.8	$2,707.0	$6,327.8	$603.2	80.5	$1,935.3
Food and kindred products	85	55	7.0	126.6	4.1	61.3	321.5	1,178.5	15.8	6.4	231.4
Tobacco products	5	5	(a)	(D)	(D)	(D)	(D)	(D)	(D)	n.a.	n.a.
Textile mill products	10	5	1.3	15.3	1.0	10.8	31.1	73.5	(D)	2.0	27.4
Apparel, other textile products	43	25	4.5	48.3	3.8	33.1	135.5	241.2	8.9	5.2	92.4
Lumber and wood products	91	13	1.5	17.2	1.2	13.1	38.8	98.1	2.5	1.8	37.2
Furniture and fixtures	50	26	3.9	56.6	3.0	36.4	138.2	239.5	5.3	3.7	81.5
Paper and allied products	25	16	2.2	35.2	1.5	21.8	81.7	184.9	2.9	2.3	58.0
Printing and publishing	309	73	11.4	166.6	5.7	82.8	378.0	652.1	19.0	10.4	199.8
Chemicals and allied products	49	13	3.7	94.0	2.4	50.8	184.1	575.6	23.8	4.6	181.1
Rubber, miscellaneous plastics products	49	18	2.9	54.2	2.1	34.4	113.3	249.9	10.1	3.7	91.3
Leather and leather products	19	10	3.7	44.3	2.7	22.4	106.3	182.9	4.0	3.9	84.4
Stone, clay and glass products	57	23	4.0	86.6	3.2	63.9	171.1	324.8	(D)	5.2	189.5
Primary metal industries	23	14	0.9	16.7	0.7	11.3	30.4	117.9	2.5	0.8	20.2
Fabricated metal products	139	58	6.5	102.5	4.7	60.2	241.6	468.4	12.6	6.3	140.8
Machinery, except electrical	158	46	3.4	57.6	2.4	37.1	106.6	199.6	12.2	2.6	58.2
Electric, electronic equipment	85	34	7.2	102.7	6.0	73.1	304.4	685.5	12.8	6.8	170.7
Transportation equipment	55	28	8.0	191.7	5.3	113.1	188.5	608.1	(D)	7.9	225.8
Instruments and related products	10	2	0.8	11.1	0.6	7.1	14.9	29.0	0.4	0.9	13.2
Miscellaneous manufacturing industries	46	11	0.9	12.2	0.7	8.1	30.4	63.0	1.1	1.2	16.1
Auxiliaries	42	30	4.3	97.0	0.0	0.0	0.0	0.0	0.0	4.1	0.0

Note: Totals include categories not shown separately.

n.a. not available.

(D) withheld to avoid disclosing figures of individual companies.

a. Range is 500–999. Actual data is withheld to avoid disclosure.

Source: U.S. Department of Commerce, Bureau of the Census, *1982 Census of Manufactures, Geographic Area Series, Tennessee*; and *1977*.

TABLE 4.16--MANUFACTURING EMPLOYEES AND PAYROLL, AND NUMBER OF ESTABLISHMENTS BY EMPLOYMENT-SIZE CLASS, COUNTIES, 1986

County	Number of employees[1]	Annual payroll ($1,000)	Employment-size class: Total	1–4	5–9	10–19	20–49	50–99	100–249	250–499	500–999	1,000 or more
Anderson	11,499	316,456	87	34	13	13	14	2	5	5	0	1
Bedford	4,533	80,185	54	12	6	7	10	9	3	5	2	0
Benton	575	10,813	16	5	5	0	2	2	2	0	0	0
Bledsoe	665	8,850	14	4	3	3	2	0	1	1	0	0
Blount	6,413	173,672	72	30	5	16	9	5	3	1	2	1
Bradley	12,734	229,449	136	43	20	12	19	14	13	9	5	1
Campbell	2,512	33,575	37	10	4	7	8	2	3	2	1	0
Cannon	1,027	11,825	14	5	1	2	1	1	3	1	0	0
Carroll	2,834	40,369	40	18	5	2	4	3	3	4	1	0
Carter	3,556	59,401	40	9	11	4	3	2	9	1	0	1
Cheatham	(a)	(D)	20	6	5	4	3	1	0	0	0	1
Chester	1,123	14,610	20	5	1	6	3	2	2	1	0	0
Claiborne	2,279	25,626	30	14	4	2	1	3	2	3	1	0
Clay	1,314	16,814	14	2	1	1	4	2	2	2	0	0
Cocke	2,254	36,016	37	15	5	1	3	5	6	2	0	0
Coffee	5,866	93,750	68	15	11	8	11	7	7	7	2	0
Crockett	893	15,928	13	3	1	3	1	1	3	1	0	0
Cumberland	2,002	32,738	44	16	5	7	5	4	5	2	0	0
Davidson	50,648	1,209,487	824	269	124	120	137	74	60	25	9	6
Decatur	1,319	13,160	18	5	4	2	1	4	1	0	1	0
DeKalb	1,840	22,506	24	6	3	2	3	4	3	3	0	0
Dickson	1,993	31,176	39	16	3	7	4	4	2	3	0	0
Dyer	4,004	83,579	37	7	11	5	3	2	5	2	1	1
Fayette	1,643	26,803	29	4	7	5	5	3	4	0	1	0
Fentress	1,865	13,160	37	8	9	4	6	4	4	2	0	0
Franklin	1,456	19,248	33	10	6	2	7	2	5	1	0	0
Gibson	7,934	144,074	68	18	9	6	5	7	15	6	1	1
Giles	3,751	62,352	36	8	5	5	6	3	6	1	1	1
Grainger	666	8,093	17	5	3	2	3	1	3	0	0	0
Greene	9,374	170,365	76	16	10	14	15	4	9	2	5	1

TABLE 4.16--MANUFACTURING EMPLOYEES AND PAYROLL, AND NUMBER OF ESTABLISHMENTS BY EMPLOYMENT–SIZE CLASS, COUNTIES, 1986 (Continued)

County	Number of employees[1]	Annual payroll ($1,000)	Employment–size class									
			Total	1–4	5–9	10–19	20–49	50–99	100–249	250–499	500–999	1,000 or more
Grundy	550	3,816	10	4	0	2	0	1	3	0	0	0
Hamblen	12,975	216,641	117	23	14	11	19	24	14	7	2	3
Hamilton	30,835	657,224	435	102	68	62	76	56	47	12	9	3
Hancock	(b)	(D)	3	2	0	0	0	1	0	0	0	0
Hardeman	2,504	43,498	32	9	7	5	3	3	1	3	1	0
Hardin	2,727	45,003	42	16	4	6	5	5	1	5	0	0
Hawkins	4,743	125,175	29	7	5	6	2	1	1	3	3	1
Haywood	2,069	31,862	23	3	1	6	4	3	3	3	0	0
Henderson	3,520	49,751	31	4	6	3	6	4	3	3	2	0
Henry	3,789	62,774	44	8	6	10	5	4	7	3	0	1
Hickman	1,288	17,590	21	8	2	2	3	4	0	1	1	0
Houston	507	7,397	13	4	1	3	2	1	2	0	0	0
Humphreys	2,408	58,389	22	6	3	2	3	0	5	2	1	0
Jackson	932	10,356	23	5	9	0	2	4	2	1	0	0
Jefferson	2,246	32,584	43	11	5	10	7	6	2	1	1	0
Johnson	1,803	19,743	20	6	3	5	1	1	1	2	1	0
Knox	25,268	483,921	444	146	66	63	80	37	28	13	8	3
Lake	480	6,214	6	2	1	0	0	1	2	0	0	0
Lauderdale	4,284	68,303	28	3	4	3	2	4	8	1	3	0
Lawrence	5,518	91,259	55	17	9	6	7	6	8	1	0	1
Lewis	1,390	19,278	21	8	5	3	1	1	0	3	0	0
Lincoln	2,308	34,970	32	10	5	8	1	2	3	2	1	0
Loudon	3,130	64,763	37	14	2	1	7	4	4	4	1	0
McMinn	9,378	187,513	75	18	10	6	10	7	11	9	3	1
McNairy	2,926	38,613	50	20	5	5	4	10	2	3	1	0
Macon	1,269	19,120	25	7	2	6	3	2	5	0	0	0
Madison	8,251	177,683	92	20	16	16	13	11	7	3	6	0
Marion	1,050	19,068	20	4	4	2	3	4	3	0	0	0

TABLE 4.16--MANUFACTURING EMPLOYEES AND PAYROLL, AND NUMBER OF ESTABLISHMENTS BY EMPLOYMENT–SIZE CLASS, COUNTIES, 1986
(Continued)

County	Number of employees[1]	Annual payroll ($1,000)	Employment–size class									
			Total	1–4	5–9	10–19	20–49	50–99	100–249	250–499	500–999	1,000 or more
Marshall	5,718	107,871	47	7	5	9	10	8	2	3	2	1
Maury	4,833	106,522	72	15	10	8	23	5	5	5	1	0
Meigs	521	7,669	8	1	1	1	3	0	1	1	0	0
Monroe	3,025	45,120	58	16	9	11	7	6	4	5	0	0
Montgomery	5,217	97,127	66	21	10	8	13	4	5	2	2	1
Moore	(c)	(D)	7	4	0	0	0	2	0	0	1	0
Morgan	887	8,770	17	7	3	1	1	1	3	1	0	0
Obion	6,364	177,201	40	8	5	6	9	1	4	5	1	1
Overton	894	10,443	30	8	8	4	4	3	3	0	0	0
Perry	1,096	14,495	16	5	3	2	2	0	2	2	0	0
Pickett	400	3,368	12	5	0	1	4	1	1	0	0	0
Polk	(a)	(D)	17	5	3	2	1	5	0	0	0	1
Putnam	7,593	123,392	108	23	21	15	22	7	12	6	1	1
Rhea	4,850	67,163	32	8	2	5	5	4	3	2	2	1
Roane	4,388	91,199	29	13	1	1	5	3	3	1	0	2
Robertson	3,420	55,902	44	11	5	6	7	7	5	1	2	0
Rutherford	14,548	348,706	139	32	20	23	18	17	14	9	4	2
Scott	1,396	21,590	29	6	8	6	3	2	2	2	0	0
Sequatchie	531	4,299	13	5	0	3	1	1	3	0	0	0
Sevier	2,398	37,113	62	28	9	6	10	4	2	2	1	0
Shelby	49,031	1,087,191	958	213	152	162	204	110	84	22	7	4
Smith	1,335	18,691	11	0	2	3	0	1	4	1	0	0
Stewart	543	6,760	11	2	1	6	1	0	0	1	0	0
Sullivan	22,499	615,264	136	45	20	22	18	8	10	4	3	6
Sumner	8,238	143,234	170	60	25	23	26	14	15	4	3	0
Tipton	1,950	29,653	24	1	6	1	4	5	5	2	0	0
Trousdale	1,046	12,744	10	1	0	2	1	1	4	1	0	0

TABLE 4.16--MANUFACTURING EMPLOYEES AND PAYROLL, AND NUMBER OF ESTABLISHMENTS BY EMPLOYMENT-SIZE CLASS, COUNTIES, 1986
(Continued)

County	Number of employees[1]	Annual payroll ($1,000)	Employment-size class									
			Total	1-4	5-9	10-19	20-49	50-99	100-249	250-499	500-999	1,000 or more
Unicoi	1,554	34,360	21	5	2	3	3	2	4	2	0	0
Union	499	7,836	11	4	0	2	1	3	1	0	0	0
Van Buren	904	10,142	10	2	0	2	0	3	2	1	0	0
Warren	5,043	91,233	53	13	7	5	13	4	8	1	1	1
Washington	10,186	198,596	118	24	17	22	14	16	13	10	1	1
Wayne	1,736	19,370	25	5	4	5	5	0	3	3	0	0
Weakley	2,793	36,762	47	16	7	5	8	4	3	3	1	0
White	3,378	44,543	32	6	5	2	4	6	5	2	2	0
Williamson	5,219	93,088	91	35	12	15	11	3	7	7	1	0
Wilson	5,624	91,190	89	26	16	12	16	8	4	3	4	0

(D) Withheld to avoid disclosing data of individual operations.

1. Number of employees for week including March 12.

a. 1,000–2,499 employees.

b. 20–99 employees.

c. 500–999 employees.

Source: U.S. Department of Commerce, Bureau of the Census, *County Business Patterns, 1986.*

TABLE 4.17--MANUFACTURING STATISTICS, COUNTIES, 1977 AND 1982 [Dollar amounts in millions]

County	1982									1977	
	Establishments		Employees		Production workers						
	Total	With 20 or more employees	Number (1,000)	Payroll	Number (1,000)	Wages	Value added by manu-facture	Value of shipments	New capital expend-itures	Em-ployees (1,000)	Value added by manu-facture
Anderson	83	28	10.0	$219.0	5.8	$111.2	$637.9	$748.3	$5.8	(D)	(D)
Bedford	60	28	3.7	49.1	3.0	33.1	124.5	279.2	9.3	4.7	$124.2
Benton	16	6	0.6	7.2	0.5	5.4	14.2	26.8	0.9	0.9	18.4
Bledsoe	18	2	0.3	3.0	0.3	2.5	9.9	22.6	0.7	(D)	(D)
Blount	69	18	(D)	(D)	(D)	(D)	(D)	(D)	(D)	(D)	(D)
Bradley	137	59	12.4	171.1	9.6	114.5	437.4	966.6	27.0	11.7	277.4
Campbell	30	16	2.0	21.4	1.8	17.0	44.7	100.0	1.3	2.1	29.9
Cannon	13	8	(D)	(D)	(D)	(D)	(D)	(D)	(D)	(D)	(D)
Carroll	35	12	2.8	29.2	2.3	21.5	66.7	158.1	4.6	3.0	46.4
Carter	40	15	3.2	44.5	2.5	29.7	70.3	137.8	4.3	3.5	58.7
Cheatham	27	6	2.0	30.3	1.7	22.9	121.2	210.1	1.7	2.0	59.3
Chester	19	7	1.0	11.7	0.8	8.7	25.6	50.7	0.9	1.0	17.5
Claiborne	28	11	1.8	17.7	1.5	13.5	27.1	82.8	1.4	2.0	25.8
Clay	14	6	0.9	7.7	0.8	6.8	17.5	31.6	0.5	0.5	9.5
Cocke	39	18	2.5	35.5	1.9	25.8	77.2	211.8	6.5	3.3	88.4
Coffee	60	32	4.9	65.7	3.9	45.8	177.2	293.1	11.7	4.5	84.6
Crockett	15	7	1.1	14.0	0.7	6.2	34.0	59.5	17.9	1.8	42.0
Cumberland	45	15	1.7	20.3	1.3	14.3	46.9	107.1	3.2	2.0	35.9
Davidson	817	287	45.5	849.4	27.2	445.6	1,577.7	3,852.1	142.5	50.1	1,237.6
Decatur	26	8	1.9	18.5	1.5	13.9	24.0	60.1	0.7	2.1	19.9
DeKalb	21	12	1.6	14.3	1.4	11.7	47.1	75.1	0.9	1.8	21.6
Dickson	41	14	2.4	28.7	2.0	19.9	60.7	105.5	2.7	3.0	62.6
Dyer	43	16	3.8	59.4	3.1	42.6	141.4	364.3	12.0	4.6	109.4
Fayette	26	11	1.6	20.2	1.3	15.0	29.6	91.4	4.2	1.5	17.7
Fentress	35	12	1.5	11.8	1.3	10.3	13.7	44.9	1.1	1.2	17.9
Franklin	34	14	1.6	17.9	1.4	13.6	32.9	92.7	2.4	2.1	28.3
Gibson	70	38	7.7	108.3	6.1	76.2	234.9	546.1	20.1	8.0	152.6
Giles	41	20	4.1	52.3	3.6	42.3	181.5	320.3	8.8	3.7	110.6

TABLE 4.17--MANUFACTURING STATISTICS, COUNTIES, 1977 AND 1982 [Dollar amounts in millions] (Continued)

County	1982									1977	
	Establishments		Employees		Production workers						
	Total	With 20 or more employees	Number (1,000)	Payroll	Number (1,000)	Wages	Value added by manu-facture	Value of shipments	New capital expend-itures	Em-ployees (1,000)	Value added by manu-facture
Grainger	19	7	0.9	9.0	0.8	7.1	22.9	49.8	0.6	0.7	13.4
Greene	77	36	8.4	123.7	5.7	76.3	503.2	1,262.7	42.8	7.5	198.9
Grundy	13	4	0.7	4.6	0.6	3.8	5.9	7.2	0.1	0.5	3.5
Hamblen	110	55	11.5	162.4	9.0	113.3	336.8	830.9	24.4	13.0	272.4
Hamilton	485	211	36.1	635.9	26.0	398.1	1,352.2	3,330.1	97.1	41.3	1,045.5
Hancock	2	1	(D)	(D)	(D)	(D)	(D)	(D)	(D)	(D)	(D)
Hardeman	28	12	2.0	28.8	1.7	21.1	68.3	148.0	1.7	1.4	26.5
Hardin	46	17	2.8	38.4	2.4	27.9	104.0	256.4	6.5	3.2	76.0
Hawkins	21	9	4.2	81.7	3.2	57.9	198.1	376.7	11.9	3.8	104.9
Haywood	27	14	1.4	19.4	1.1	12.5	67.0	144.1	5.3	1.2	20.4
Henderson	31	16	3.1	35.6	2.5	28.2	80.8	154.9	4.4	3.0	66.1
Henry	46	19	3.7	53.8	2.9	36.5	132.3	278.0	7.0	4.2	109.1
Hickman	16	8	1.1	12.9	0.9	8.1	46.5	78.6	1.2	1.3	33.8
Houston	13	4	0.4	6.2	0.4	4.8	10.5	16.8	(D)	0.4	6.2
Humphreys	18	10	2.0	48.1	1.4	27.9	142.2	351.9	14.2	2.7	157.3
Jackson	18	9	1.4	21.2	0.9	10.4	39.8	88.9	2.9	(D)	(D)
Jefferson	40	14	3.0	35.1	2.6	28.4	70.4	213.1	3.9	(D)	(D)
Johnson	19	7	2.1	19.9	1.8	16.1	37.3	124.3	3.6	(D)	(D)
Knox	418	154	22.9	331.8	16.8	201.4	778.8	1,759.5	38.7	25.4	553.1
Lake	11	3	0.4	4.0	0.3	2.7	7.6	36.4	0.6	0.6	12.2
Lauderdale	35	19	3.6	42.5	3.1	34.3	172.5	264.0	3.9	3.8	91.7
Lawrence	59	18	4.4	69.3	3.8	56.1	116.2	355.6	8.0	5.3	120.0
Lewis	25	6	1.3	14.6	1.1	10.6	29.8	55.9	1.7	1.2	21.5
Lincoln	27	10	2.1	21.5	1.7	15.5	52.7	154.1	1.4	3.3	61.9
Loudon	30	17	2.9	44.3	2.3	34.5	133.2	221.4	(D)	3.4	101.0
McMinn	84	44	8.1	134.5	6.1	89.0	344.0	737.1	47.7	8.5	201.1
McNairy	44	18	3.6	41.5	2.6	22.8	113.2	192.4	4.3	3.4	61.3

TABLE 4.17--MANUFACTURING STATISTICS, COUNTIES, 1977 AND 1982 [Dollar amounts in millions] (Continued)

County	1982									1977	
	Establishments		Employees		Production workers		Value added by manu-facture	Value of shipments	New capital expend-itures	Em-ployees (1,000)	Value added by manu-facture
	Total	With 20 or more employees	Number (1,000)	Payroll	Number (1,000)	Wages					
Macon	28	10	1.7	17.8	1.5	14.2	37.7	62.2	0.9	1.7	22.6
Madison	100	42	8.1	129.1	6.3	87.5	356.2	849.5	36.6	8.3	208.6
Marion	24	9	1.3	15.9	1.1	13.5	44.1	98.7	1.5	1.6	38.7
Marshall	45	24	4.5	55.7	3.6	38.3	154.7	342.7	9.4	4.3	101.5
Maury	79	37	5.0	85.4	3.9	57.5	241.9	569.5	23.9	6.2	220.8
Meigs	9	4	(D)	(D)	(D)	(D)	(D)	(D)	(D)	0.4	4.4
Monroe	61	21	2.5	23.9	2.1	18.2	44.5	85.2	1.6	2.3	36.3
Montgomery	61	24	6.2	89.3	4.1	52.3	206.0	443.3	18.9	5.6	144.0
Moore	3	2	(D)	(D)	(D)	(D)	(D)	(D)	(D)	(D)	(D)
Morgan	14	5	0.8	7.2	0.7	5.9	32.3	43.5	(D)	1.0	14.6
Obion	40	19	5.2	92.4	4.3	69.6	378.8	746.6	9.2	5.9	203.5
Overton	31	7	1.1	9.6	0.9	7.6	10.7	29.1	0.2	1.3	12.9
Perry	21	6	0.7	7.1	0.6	5.6	15.5	26.3	0.5	1.0	12.3
Pickett	9	6	0.7	5.7	0.7	4.9	8.1	15.2	0.1	(D)	(D)
Polk	16	6	(D)	(D)	(D)	(D)	(D)	(D)	(D)	(D)	(D)
Putnam	101	46	5.7	66.1	4.5	44.4	186.9	354.9	5.8	5.9	107.1
Rhea	40	17	3.7	43.2	3.2	34.9	122.0	227.8	2.5	4.2	96.0
Roane	31	11	(D)	(D)	(D)	(D)	(D)	(D)	(D)	9.5	382.0
Robertson	46	23	3.3	41.0	2.3	23.2	111.8	237.6	9.5	3.1	67.6
Rutherford	129	64	9.1	166.5	6.1	88.3	322.0	795.8	(D)	8.4	209.4
Scott	25	5	0.6	9.2	0.5	6.9	19.6	48.0	0.6	0.9	14.0
Sequatchie	10	5	0.4	3.2	0.4	2.5	5.4	9.2	0.1	1.0	6.1
Sevier	61	14	2.4	33.5	2.0	24.1	62.8	118.9	5.7	1.9	38.5
Shelby	958	401	53.0	989.8	34.9	550.5	2,732.9	6,931.8	212.5	58.2	2,023.7
Smith	13	6	1.6	12.2	1.4	10.0	33.8	74.1	(D)	1.3	19.1
Stewart	7	0	0.1	0.5	(a)	0.4	1.2	2.4	0.2	(D)	(D)
Sullivan	143	55	24.1	512.4	16.4	299.9	1,222.8	2,867.6	(D)	25.5	847.0
Sumner	143	58	6.8	99.1	5.2	66.7	223.6	515.0	18.7	5.0	116.7

TABLE 4.17--MANUFACTURING STATISTICS, COUNTIES, 1977 AND 1982 [Dollar amounts in millions] (Continued)

County	1982									1977	
	Establishments		Employees		Production workers		Value added by manu- facture	Value of shipments	New capital expend- itures	Em- ployees (1,000)	Value added by manu- facture
	Total	With 20 or more employees	Number (1,000)	Payroll	Number (1,000)	Wages					
Tipton	20	11	1.3	16.6	1.0	11.1	48.0	124.0	3.3	1.0	31.0
Trousdale	8	5	1.0	8.4	0.9	6.1	19.3	27.9	1.3	1.4	24.3
Unicoi	22	9	1.4	25.7	1.0	16.5	64.5	93.6	10.8	1.4	33.1
Union	10	3	(D)	(D)	(D)	(D)	(D)	(D)	(D)	0.2	3.9
Van Buren	9	6	0.6	8.8	0.5	6.8	8.9	20.2	(D)	0.6	3.7
Warren	63	25	5.4	73.2	4.4	54.1	235.3	487.7	11.4	6.5	151.8
Washington	109	58	11.2	173.0	7.5	86.3	319.8	699.0	(D)	11.7	244.0
Wayne	30	12	1.8	16.8	1.6	12.4	42.4	81.1	0.9	1.8	26.1
Weakley	46	15	3.1	32.0	2.6	23.5	61.7	129.1	2.8	3.5	45.2
White	34	20	3.0	33.6	2.5	25.3	65.5	137.6	2.3	3.4	48.8
Williamson	82	29	4.3	59.7	2.9	30.1	118.7	250.9	9.3	3.6	70.5
Wilson	72	29	5.7	75.6	4.6	54.1	171.3	360.8	8.4	5.4	111.8

(D) withheld to avoid disclosing figures for individual companies.

a. Less than 500.

Source: U.S. Department of Commerce, Bureau of the Census, *1982 Census of Manufactures, Geographic Area Series, Tennessee*, and *1977*.

TABLE 4.18--MANUFACTURING STATISTICS, CITIES WITH 450 OR MORE MANUFACTURING EMPLOYEES, 1977 AND 1982 [Dollar amounts in millions]

	1982									1977	
	Establishments		Employees		Production workers						
City	Total	With 20 or more employees	Number (1,000)	Payroll	Number (1,000)	Wages	Value added by manu-facture	Value of shipments	New capital expend-itures	Em-ployees (1,000)	Value added by manu-facture
Alamo	6	3	(D)	(D)	(D)	(D)	(D)	(D)	(D)	n.a.	n.a.
Alcoa	10	3	(D)	(D)	(D)	(D)	(D)	(D)	(D)	(D)	(D)
Athens	37	19	4.1	$57.5	3.1	$37.8	$124.8	$272.3	$7.0	4.0	$77.9
Bolivar	9	5	1.1	16.3	0.9	11.8	30.0	66.2	0.6	0.6	7.8
Bristol	51	17	(D)	(D)	(D)	(D)	(D)	(D)	(D)	(D)	(D)
Brownsville	21	13	1.4	18.7	1.0	12.1	65.9	141.4	5.0	1.2	20.4
Centerville	9	6	(D)	(D)	(D)	(D)	(D)	(D)	(D)	1.2	31.7
Chattanooga	407	186	32.1	575.9	23.4	369.5	1,219.7	3,040.4	74.3	38.1	969.6
Church Hill	1	1	(D)	(D)	(D)	(D)	(D)	(D)	(D)	n.a.	n.a.
Clarksville	49	19	(D)	(D)	(D)	(D)	(D)	(D)	(D)	(D)	(D)
Cleveland	105	46	10.1	135.3	7.9	90.4	282.2	713.6	16.9	9.9	185.5
Clinton	19	9	1.7	25.1	1.4	18.6	44.8	111.0	3.4	0.9	34.8
Collegedale	7	5	(D)	(D)	(D)	(D)	(D)	(D)	(D)	(D)	(D)
Collierville	23	13	2.0	31.2	1.6	21.8	109.8	286.6	(D)	1.8	79.7
Columbia	50	23	3.1	45.4	2.4	30.3	109.0	276.4	9.9	4.6	153.5
Cookeville	79	37	5.0	59.6	3.9	39.5	177.6	337.4	5.5	5.0	95.8
Covington	16	9	(D)	(D)	(D)	(D)	(D)	(D)	(D)	(D)	(D)
Crossville	31	12	1.5	18.0	1.1	12.8	43.7	99.8	3.1	1.9	35.4
Dayton	21	10	2.7	29.1	2.3	23.2	79.5	159.8	1.6	(D)	(D)
Dickson	16	6	1.9	22.6	1.6	15.7	47.6	74.9	2.1	2.4	51.2
Dyersburg	32	8	2.8	48.6	2.4	35.5	97.1	242.0	11.1	3.8	99.7
Elizabethton	25	13	2.9	41.4	2.3	27.2	67.1	128.5	(D)	3.5	58.4
Erwin	10	5	(D)	(D)	(D)	(D)	(D)	(D)	(D)	(D)	(D)
Etowah	16	10	(D)	(D)	(D)	(D)	(D)	(D)	(D)	1.7	18.5
Fayetteville	19	9	2.0	20.9	1.6	15.0	51.5	151.8	1.4	3.3	61.8
Franklin	60	21	3.7	51.1	2.6	26.6	111.1	224.2	8.8	3.5	69.3
Gallatin	45	22	3.1	48.6	2.4	33.5	123.1	306.3	10.5	2.3	58.5
Goodlettsville	33	11	1.6	32.8	1.0	18.0	39.2	215.9	1.5	1.5	34.0

TABLE 4.18--MANUFACTURING STATISTICS, CITIES WITH 450 OR MORE MANUFACTURING EMPLOYEES, 1977 AND 1982 [Dollar amounts in millions] (Continued)

	1982									1977	
	Establishments		Employees		Production workers						
City	Total	With 20 or more employees	Number (1,000)	Payroll	Number (1,000)	Wages	Value added by manufacture	Value of shipments	New capital expenditures	Employees (1,000)	Value added by manufacture
Greeneville	54	33	7.2	106.3	4.9	66.9	462.5	1,164.2	28.2	(D)	(D)
Harriman	11	6	2.3	23.4	2.0	18.1	71.2	116.7	(D)	(D)	(D)
Hartsville	6	4	(D)	(D)	(D)	(D)	(D)	(D)	(D)	n.a.	n.a.
Henderson	13	5	0.9	10.3	0.7	7.8	23.7	46.7	0.9	(D)	(D)
Hendersonville	44	13	1.6	24.8	1.1	15.1	48.6	93.8	4.2	0.8	27.9
Hohenwald	12	6	1.3	14.1	1.1	10.1	28.9	53.9	1.7	1.2	21.5
Humboldt	19	11	2.0	28.8	1.6	20.6	59.9	175.8	11.6	1.9	35.2
Huntingdon	9	3	(D)	(D)	(D)	(D)	(D)	(D)	(D)	(D)	(D)
Jackson	87	38	7.7	123.2	6.0	83.8	348.9	815.5	35.8	5.1	129.4
Johnson City	77	46	8.3	121.3	5.9	68.7	262.0	514.4	18.8	10.7	232.2
Kingsport	52	24	17.1	404.3	11.3	229.7	570.4	1,906.6	(D)	18.5	436.3
Knoxville	309	106	17.9	258.1	13.2	158.4	625.9	1,403.0	30.3	18.5	404.4
Lafayette	13	7	1.4	14.6	1.2	11.6	28.7	48.6	0.7	1.3	18.3
LaFollette	19	8	0.9	9.3	0.7	7.3	20.7	39.4	0.6	1.3	12.3
LaVergne	21	11	1.5	31.1	1.0	18.0	46.2	177.5	5.7	2.0	52.4
Lawrenceburg	30	8	(D)	(D)	(D)	(D)	(D)	(D)	(D)	4.6	109.8
Lebanon	45	23	5.3	71.4	4.4	50.9	164.3	342.1	8.2	5.0	108.0
Lenoir City	10	8	1.0	15.0	0.8	11.0	31.9	63.9	2.6	0.6	6.7
Lewisburg	39	22	(D)	(D)	(D)	(D)	(D)	(D)	(D)	(D)	(D)
Lexington	21	14	2.6	32.0	2.2	25.5	75.8	147.6	4.2	2.9	65.1
Livingston	19	4	0.8	7.5	0.7	5.9	8.5	21.5	0.2	1.2	11.4
Loudon	11	7	(D)	(D)	(D)	(D)	(D)	(D)	(D)	(D)	(D)
McKenzie	13	8	1.3	12.0	1.0	7.3	32.2	75.4	3.4	1.4	17.2
McMinnville	33	19	5.0	67.1	4.0	49.3	221.1	463.2	10.4	6.1	145.5
Manchester	17	9	1.8	18.9	1.5	15.9	80.8	127.0	2.3	1.2	31.7
Maryville	30	8	0.8	13.2	0.6	7.6	27.2	55.1	3.5	0.6	14.8
Memphis	844	355	47.1	867.4	30.6	474.3	2,324.5	5,866.1	160.5	51.7	1,725.4

TABLE 4.18--MANUFACTURING STATISTICS, CITIES WITH 450 OR MORE MANUFACTURING EMPLOYEES, 1977 AND 1982 [Dollar amounts in millions] (Continued)

City	1982									1977	
	Establishments		Employees		Production workers		Value added by manu-facture	Value of shipments	New capital expend-itures	Em-ployees (1,000)	Value added by manu-facture
	Total	With 20 or more employees	Number (1,000)	Payroll	Number (1,000)	Wages					
Milan	15	10	1.8	27.1	1.4	18.3	76.3	156.7	3.8	3.9	81.9
Morristown	85	47	(D)	(D)	(D)	(D)	(D)	(D)	(D)	(D)	(D)
Mount Carmel	2	2	(D)	(D)	(D)	(D)	(D)	(D)	(D)	n.a.	n.a.
Mount Pleasant	10	7	0.9	16.9	0.6	10.9	60.8	123.1	7.3	0.5	13.4
Murfreesboro	81	42	5.5	89.0	3.8	56.0	228.6	513.5	7.2	5.3	136.7
Nashville-Davidson	785	276	43.9	816.9	62.2	427.7	1,538.8	3,636.4	141.1	48.4	1,193.9
Newbern	6	5	0.8	9.1	0.6	6.1	41.6	116.0	0.5	n.a.	n.a.
Newport	23	15	(D)	(D)	(D)	(D)	(D)	(D)	(D)	(D)	(D)
Oak Ridge	56	19	(D)	(D)	(D)	(D)	(D)	(D)	(D)	(D)	(D)
Oneida	11	3	0.5	7.5	0.4	5.4	16.9	42.4	0.4	0.7	11.6
Paris	28	10	2.8	40.6	2.2	27.1	110.8	214.4	5.3	3.8	100.1
Portland	25	15	1.3	16.7	1.0	11.4	35.1	75.0	3.8	1.3	21.8
Pulaski	16	10	1.7	19.8	1.5	16.0	83.5	118.3	2.3	1.6	24.8
Ripley	15	8	1.5	17.8	1.2	14.4	55.0	98.5	1.5	1.7	23.7
Rockwood	6	3	(D)	(D)	(D)	(D)	(D)	(D)	(D)	(D)	(D)
Rogersville	9	2	(D)	(D)	(D)	(D)	(D)	(D)	(D)	(D)	(D)
Savannah	21	7	(D)	(D)	(D)	(D)	(D)	(D)	(D)	1.9	22.1
Selmer	12	7	1.9	26.4	1.2	13.1	60.9	108.8	3.2	1.9	36.3
Sevierville	21	8	1.1	15.6	0.9	10.1	27.1	52.7	0.5	1.0	20.6
Shelbyville	42	24	3.3	43.0	2.6	28.6	107.3	248.5	9.1	4.6	122.4
Smithville	15	8	1.3	11.8	1.2	9.8	43.3	69.6	0.8	(D)	(D)
Smyrna	16	8	1.7	40.7	1.0	11.0	34.7	76.7	(D)	(D)	(D)
South Pittsburg	11	5	1.0	11.5	0.9	9.8	20.2	60.3	(D)	1.1	23.2
Sparta	21	13	2.6	29.8	2.2	23.0	61.3	127.4	2.1	(D)	(D)
Springfield	25	16	2.7	36.6	1.8	19.7	99.4	213.6	9.0	3.0	64.9

TABLE 4.18--MANUFACTURING STATISTICS, CITIES WITH 450 OR MORE MANUFACTURING EMPLOYEES, 1977 AND 1982 [Dollar amounts in millions] (Continued)

City	1982									1977	
	Establishments		Employees		Production workers		Value added by manu-facture	Value of shipments	New capital expend-itures	Em-ployees (1,000)	Value added by manu-facture
	Total	With 20 or more employees	Number (1,000)	Payroll	Number (1,000)	Wages					
Sweetwater	20	8	1.0	12.8	0.8	9.3	24.0	45.0	0.8	1.1	23.5
Trenton	10	6	0.9	11.6	0.7	6.8	5.2	25.0	1.6	(D)	(D)
Tullahoma	33	22	3.0	43.6	2.2	27.4	82.9	142.7	9.0	(D)	(D)
Union City	17	9	4.1	81.3	3.3	61.7	353.8	700.9	7.6	4.6	186.1
Winchester	10	5	(D)	(D)	(D)	(D)	(D)	(D)	(D)	0.7	9.7

n.a. not available.

(D) withheld to avoid disclosing figures for individual companies.

Source: U.S. Department of Commerce, Bureau of the Census, *1982 Census of Manufactures, Geographic Area Series, Tennessee*; and *1977*.

TABLE 4.19--MANUFACTURING STATISTICS, SOUTHEASTERN STATES, 1972–1982, CENSUS YEARS

State	Total establishments			Total employees (1,000)			Total payroll ($1,000,000)			Value added by manufacture ($1,000,000)			Index of employment change 1982 (1977=100)
	1982	1977	1972	1982	1977	1972	1982	1977	1972	1982	1977	1972	
TENNESSEE	6,417	6,487	5,647	461.6	489.8	467.4	7,377.7	5,218.7	3,351.7	17,842	12,663	7,662	94
Alabama	5,528	5,863	4,984	329.6	341.0	322.6	5,234.4	3,773.2	2,396.8	12,046	8,406	5,065	97
Arkansas	3,313	3,595	2,897	189.8	197.1	180.9	2,823.7	1,932.4	1,151.7	7,755	4,882	2,800	96
Florida	13,723	12,399	10,275	454.4	358.0	342.9	7,773.2	4,133.1	2,750.3	18,112	9,255	5,787	127
Georgia	8,535	8,623	7,627	503.2	484.7	467.5	7,912.2	5,124.5	3,336.0	19,212	12,549	7,386	104
Kentucky	3,502	3,548	3,167	246.6	277.5	258.7	4,638.8	3,452.2	2,160.0	11,820	9,546	5,682	89
Louisiana	4,107	4,276	3,651	202.0	194.8	179.4	4,304.2	2,682.7	1,601.4	11,755	9,418	4,273	104
Mississippi	3,126	3,289	2,727	201.7	219.4	200.4	2,880.8	2,061.5	1,302.4	7,825	5,619	2,825	92
North Carolina	10,134	9,954	8,632	799.1	765.3	743.7	11,723.5	7,518.5	4,929.1	28,510	18,231	11,015	104
South Carolina	4,205	4,229	3,719	367.4	374.2	345.1	5,538.6	3,804.9	2,344.5	12,217	8,186	4,966	98
Virginia	5,568	5,519	4,837	391.1	395.2	375.4	6,649.0	4,442.4	2,826.0	17,256	10,882	6,178	99
West Virginia	1,662	1,857	1,733	95.8	117.0	120.8	2,007.0	1,620.5	1,097.6	4,049	3,880	2,647	82

Note: The United States index of employment change for 1982 was 98 (1977=100).

Source: U.S. Department of Commerce, Bureau of the Census, *1982 Census of Manufactures, Geographic Area Series*, individual states, and 1977.

TABLE 4.20--WATER USED AND DISCHARGED BY METHOD OF TREATMENT, MANUFACTURING ESTABLISHMENTS REPORTING WATER INTAKE OF 20 MILLION GALLONS OR MORE, SOUTHEASTERN STATES, 1983 [In billions of gallons]

State	Gross water used			Water discharged										
					Treated, by method[1]									
	Total	Intake	Recirculated and reused	Untreated	Total[2]	Surface skimming	Neutralization	Coagulation	Flotation	Primary settling	Biological oxidation	Secondary settling	Filtration	Chlorination
TENNESSEE	1,111.4	437.1	674.3	262.2	82.7	10.8	46.7	5.1	0.8	45.1	53.2	(D)	3.1	2.9
Alabama	709.3	293.3	416.0	73.1	204.5	107.5	102.0	7.4	2.7	141.1	155.2	106.8	1.7	(D)
Arkansas	450.5	79.6	370.8	7.9	62.1	3.0	20.6	2.4	3.0	41.8	52.2	18.8	2.1	0.3
Florida	895.0	239.9	655.1	81.2	86.1	13.0	32.4	1.1	(D)	71.6	66.5	45.7	(D)	5.8
Georgia	707.2	206.8	500.4	51.5	140.4	17.3	39.4	5.5	3.5	92.4	100.8	35.8	5.6	4.2
Kentucky	297.1	115.1	182.0	63.4	37.1	15.3	13.3	(D)	3.7	27.7	15.7	15.2	0.9	1.0
Louisiana	3,313.0	855.5	2,457.5	426.2	375.3	89.5	278.9	22.3	19.7	100.7	116.8	58.5	3.8	3.2
Mississippi	319.9	79.4	240.5	21.5	51.5	14.3	25.3	(D)	4.6	27.9	37.1	23.4	(D)	1.4
North Carolina	681.2	188.6	492.7	61.3	90.9	41.0	26.2	19.7	1.6	60.3	81.2	48.4	3.9	19.0
South Carolina	904.2	412.0	492.2	304.9	92.4	21.5	32.5	11.7	1.4	40.2	52.1	30.3	2.8	5.1
Virginia	764.5	262.0	502.6	175.4	64.6	14.0	27.1	5.9	1.9	31.1	50.5	30.6	3.2	5.0
West Virginia	403.0	288.3	114.7	140.7	134.6	(D)	112.7	(D)	(D)	(D)	(D)	(D)	2.4	(D)

(D) Withheld to avoid disclosing data for individual companies.

1. Water discharged may be treated by one or more methods.

2. Total includes categories not shown separately.

Source: U.S. Department of Commerce, Bureau of the Census, *1982 Census of Manufactures, Subject Series, Water Use in Manufactures.*

TABLE 4.21--AVERAGE HOURLY EARNINGS FOR MANUFACTURING PRODUCTION WORKERS, SOUTHEASTERN STATES AND UNITED STATES, 1975–1987, SELECTED YEARS
[In dollars]

State	1987	1986	1985	1984	1983	1982	1981	1980	1975
TENNESSEE	8.78	8.58	8.29	7.93	7.49	7.16	6.72	6.08	3.93
Alabama	8.76	8.64	8.48	7.97	7.58	7.33	7.01	6.49	4.10
Arkansas	7.88	7.76	7.57	7.31	7.05	6.69	6.26	5.71	3.69
Florida	8.16	8.02	7.86	7.62	7.33	7.02	6.53	5.98	4.11
Georgia	8.51	8.35[r]	8.10	7.58	7.13	6.75	6.37	5.77	3.80
Kentucky	10.04	9.86	9.53	9.28	8.79	8.38	7.86	7.34	4.77
Louisiana	10.90	10.60	10.43	10.06	9.79	9.38	8.58	7.74	4.88
Mississippi	7.59	7.46	7.22	6.95	6.70	6.41	6.01	5.44	3.58
North Carolina	7.83	7.54	7.29	7.01	6.68	6.35	5.94	5.37	3.52
South Carolina	8.10	7.92	7.61	7.28	7.03	6.68	6.18	5.59	3.59
Virginia	9.15	8.83[r]	8.51	8.10	7.79	7.37	6.84	6.22	3.99
West Virginia	10.56	10.38	10.24	9.93	9.74	9.40	8.80	8.08	4.93
UNITED STATES	9.91	9.73	9.54[r]	9.19	8.83	8.49	7.99	7.27	4.83

r revised.

Source: U.S. Department of Commerce, Bureau of the Census, *Statistical Abstract of the United States, 1989*, and earlier editions.

TABLE 4.22--NUMBER OF EMPLOYEES IN MANUFACTURING ESTABLISHMENTS, SOUTHEASTERN STATES, 1950–1987, SELECTED YEARS [In thousands of persons]

State	1987	1986	1985	1984	1983	1982	1981	1980	1979	1978	1977
TENNESSEE	495	492	489	498	470	468	509	503	525	526	508
Alabama	368	358	357	358	338	337	362	363	375	369	354
Arkansas	220	212	210	214	200	196	210	209	217	218	209
Florida	530	517	515	502	464	460	472	456	438	416	381
Georgia	569	565	554	545	509	501	525	519	527	516	494
Kentucky	260	253	256	258	241	247	270	276	295	292	285
Louisiana	164	167	178	182	180	206	222	214	213	210	203
Mississippi	228	223	221	219	203	204	220	222	235	235	230
North Carolina	855	832	827	831	789	781	821	820	824	807	781
South Carolina	373	364	365	378	362	362	390	392	399	391	380
Virginia	429	424	423	420	400	398	414	414	413	409	401
West Virginia	86	87	90	91	90	99	112	117	126	127	124

	1976	1975	1974	1973	1972	1971	1970	1965	1960	1950
TENNESSEE	487	459	513	519	489	460	464	387	315	249
Alabama	340	322	354	351	333	323	327	279	239	218
Arkansas	195	179	204	200	185	172	169	136	103	n.a.
Florida	354	339	376	381	351	323	323	253	208	103
Georgia	476	439	484	495	477	462	467	404	342	287
Kentucky	273	260	291	288	268	253	255	208	173	141
Louisiana	195	186	193	191	183	178	179	161	145	n.a.
Mississippi	219	202	220	221	208	190	182	153	120	87
North Carolina	756	716	790	797	757	716	713	591	505	414
South Carolina	371	340	376	375	354	337	340	293	245	210
Virginia	388	372	402	402	388	366	366	323	275	230
West Virginia	124	121	132	129	123	123	127	129	125	131

Note: All data are based on 1972 *Standard Industrial Classification Manual.*

n.a. not available.

Source: U.S. Department of Commerce, Bureau of the Census, *Statistical Abstract of the United States, 1989*; U.S. Department of Labor, Bureau of Labor Statistics, *Employment and Earnings, May 1983*, and earlier editions; *Employment and Earnings, States and Areas, 1939–1978*; and *Tennessee Department of Employment Security, Tennessee and Standard Metropolitan Statistical Areas Employment Estimates, 1979, 1980, 1981.*

TABLE 4.23--EXPORT STATISTICS, SOUTHEASTERN STATES AND UNITED STATES, 1985 AND 1986

	Value of shipments ($ million)						Manufacturing employment (1,000)					
	Total		Export-related		Export shipments as a percentage of total		Total		Export-related		Export employment as a percentage of total	
State	1986	1985	1986	1985	1986	1985	1986	1985	1986	1985	1986	1985
TENNESSEE	52,717.0	50,610.4	5,760.5	5,370.6	10.9	10.6	466.4	468.2	42.2	42.8	9.0	9.1
Alabama	36,537.2	36,634.7	4,409.9	4,457.6	12.1	12.2	328.9	330.7	31.7	31.8	9.6	9.6
Arkansas	22,131.2	21,839.8	2,343.8	2,353.7	10.6	10.8	193.6	190.4	17.8	16.6	9.2	8.7
Florida	50,322.3	49,690.7	6,215.1	6,356.2	12.4	12.8	479.7	475.6	52.5	53.0	10.9	11.1
Georgia	67,848.2	63,057.4	5,864.0	4,925.4	8.6	7.8	543.3	539.2	42.5	40.2	7.8	7.5
Kentucky	37,348.9	38,403.7	4,147.3	4,358.5	11.1	11.3	237.9	246.6	24.4	24.5	10.3	9.9
Louisiana	43,861.1	52,827.8	5,977.3	6,739.7	13.6	12.8	158.5	171.0	16.7	18.1	10.5	10.6
Mississippi	21,719.1	22,723.2	2,459.4	2,363.1	11.3	10.4	204.7	203.9	16.7	15.5	8.2	7.6
North Carolina	84,934.9	81,984.6	9,713.7	8,778.2	11.4	10.7	802.9	812.1	75.5	70.2	9.4	8.6
South Carolina	36,119.2	33,869.4	4,944.9	4,307.5	13.7	12.7	352.5	350.7	39.1	36.5	11.1	10.4
Virginia	47,346.0	45,553.5	5,083.4	4,999.8	10.7	11.0	406.5	408.7	38.4	37.0	9.4	9.1
West Virginia	10,736.2	10,602.9	2,106.7	1,906.6	19.6	18.0	85.9	84.5	12.4	11.6	14.4	13.7
UNITED STATES	2,260,314.6	2,278,860.0	294,339.5	286,703.6	13.0	12.6	18,371.2	18,787.8	2,318.2	2,294.8	12.6	12.2

Source: U.S. Department of Commerce, Bureau of the Census, *Exports from Manufacturing Establishments: 1985 and 1986.*

According to information compiled by the U.S. Bureau of the Census from data published by the U.S. Bureau of Mines and the U.S. Energy Information Administration, coal is the principal mineral produced in Tennessee, followed by stone and zinc. Also noteworthy is the fact that Tennessee leads the nation in the quantities of zinc and pyrites produced. These and other mineral statistics are available from three principal sources: the U.S. Department of Commerce, Bureau of the Census *Census of Mineral Industries*, published every five years; the U.S. Department of the Interior, Bureau of Mines, *Minerals Yearbook*, issued annually, and numerous publications of the U.S. Department of Energy, Energy Information Administration, also issued annually.

The *Geographic Area Report* from the 1982 Census provides information on the number of mineral establishments for each Tennessee county. These data are presented in Table 5.3. Tables featuring state and county data on the value of nonfuel mineral production are from the *Minerals Yearbook*, *Volume II*, and are currently available for 1986.

Data on fuel minerals are excluded from the *Minerals Yearbook* beginning in 1978. Since the establishment of the U.S. Department of Energy, Energy Information Administration (EIA) in 1977, data on the mining of fuel minerals have been detailed in EIA publications, *Coal Production*, *Petroleum Supply Annual*, and the *Natural Gas Annual*. The most current data from these sources are for 1987. An alternative source for gas data is *Gas Facts*, an annual yearbook published by the American Gas Association. Each of these publications provides data on the utilization of fuels as well as their production. However, utilization data have been reserved for Chapter 10 in order to present a complete picture of energy consumption. Therefore, the reader should turn to the Energy chapter for more information on fuel minerals.

Part of the difficulty in providing minerals data is the nature of the industry itself. Much of the production is characterized by small, independent companies, with frequent entry and exit of firms or turnover in management. The data, when they can be obtained, are not always consistent or accurate. In many cases, data for local areas must be suppressed to avoid disclosing data for any individual firm.

TABLE OF CONTENTS

FIGURE 5.1
Principal Mineral-Producing Counties in Tennessee

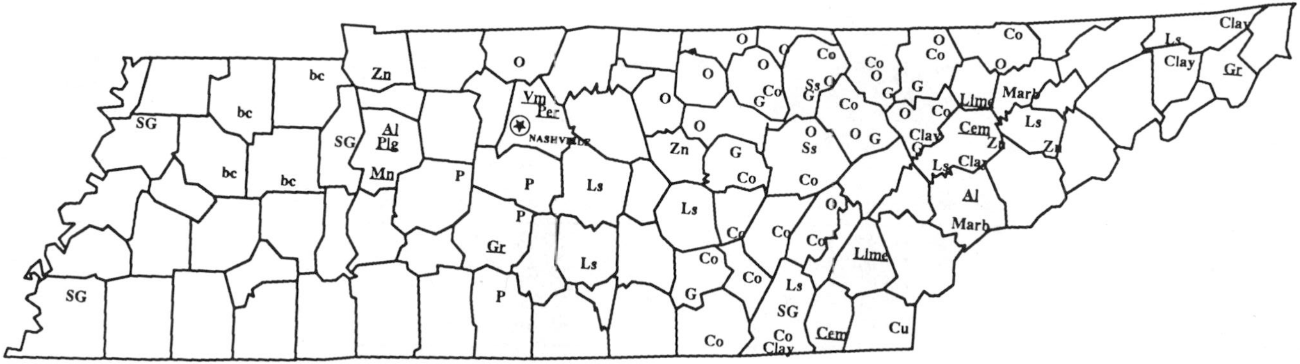

Non-fuel Minerals

Al	Aluminum plant	Gr	Graphite products	P	Phosphate rock	Ss	Sandstone
bc	Ball clay	Lime	Lime plant	Per	Perlite plant	Vm	Vermiculite plant
Cem	Cement plant	Ls	Limestone	Pig	Titanium dioxide pigments	Zn	Zinc
Clay	Clay	Marb	Marble-dimension			Zn	Zinc smelter
Cu	Copper	Mn	Manganese plant	SG	Sand and gravel		

Fuel Minerals

Co	Coal
G	Natural Gas
O	Crude Oil

Note: Underscoring represents a manufacturing operation.
Source: U.S. Department of Interior, Bureau of Mines, *Minerals Yearbook, 1985*; and Tennessee Department of Economic and Community Development, Energy Division, *Tennessee Energy Statistics Quarterly*, Fourth Quarter 1985.

TABLE 5.1-- PRODUCTION AND VALUE OF PRODUCTION OF SELECTED NON-FUEL MINERALS, TENNESSEE, 1950–1986, SELECTED YEARS

Mineral and units of measure	1986	1985	1984	1980	1975	1970	1965	1960	1955	1950
	Production									
Clays (1,000 short tons)[1]	1,164	1,244	1,165	1,188	1,310	1,401	1,495	1,270	1,208	787
Phosphate rock (1,000 metric tons)	1,232	1,233	1,368	1,582	2,291	3,073[a]	2,637	1,939	1,466	1,384
Sand and gravel (1,000 short tons)	7,848	7,769[e]	6,954	8,921	10,909	6,715	8,193	6,293	5,137	4,153
Stone (1,000 short tons)	40,706[e]	37,945[r]	36,206[e,r]	38,594	38,439	35,374	28,888	20,074	14,381[b]	7,979
Zinc, recoverable content of ores (metric tons)	102,118	104,471	116,526	111,754	83,293	118,260	122,387	91,394	40,216	35,326
	Value ($1,000)									
	1986	1985	1984	1980	1975	1970	1965	1960	1955	1950
Clays[1]	25,228	25,913	21,690	22,844	9,008	7,123	6,103	4,537	4,170	3,094
Phosphate rock	27,000	27,000[r]	33,275	12,765	28,803	15,005	22,296	15,424	10,526	10,028
Sand and gravel	30,115	28,156[e]	26,733	24,930	22,102	10,639	10,690	7,655	5,814	4,411
Stone	177,153[e]	157,616[r]	139,849[e,r]	127,876	81,187	50,013	38,859	29,942	22,276	13,802
Zinc	85,550	92,971	124,854	92,218	64,968	36,233	35,737	23,580	9,893	10,033

Note: Production is as measured by mine shipments, sales, or marketable production (including consumption by producers). Beginning in 1985, stone excludes granite.

r revised.

e estimated.

1. Excludes fuller's earth.

a. Measurement in thousand short tons.

b. Excludes granite.

Source: U.S. Department of the Interior, Bureau of Mines, *Minerals Yearbook, 1986, Volume II, Area Reports: Domestic,* and earlier editions.

TABLE 5.2-- COAL PRODUCTION AND NUMBER OF COAL MINES, BY TYPE OF MINING, AND AVERAGE MINE PRICE, TENNESSEE, 1960–1987 [Production in thousands of short tons]

	Total			Underground		Surface	
Year	Number	Production	Average mine price ($ per short ton)	Number	Production	Number	Production
1987	72	6,351	27.65	47	4,813	25	1,538
1986	75	6,749	28.00	49	5,232	26	1,516
1985	90	7,339	28.54	54	5,147	36	2,192
1984	90	7,211	28.99	55	5,196	35	2,014
1983	95	6,565	29.02	48	4,358	47	2,208
1982	105	7,287	29.49	51	4,518	54	2,769
1981	115	9,706	29.45	46	5,058	69	4,648
1980	117	9,157	27.54	54	4,682	63	4,474
1979	122	9,303	26.94	54	4,760	68	4,543
1978	231	10,032	23.21	85	4,150	146	5,882
1977	183	9,433	21.86	64	3,858	121	5,575
1976	185	9,283	16.31	75	4,428	110	4,855
1975	166	8,206	17.10	62	3,806	104	4,400
1974	125	7,541	18.02	50	3,106	75	4,435
1973	119	8,220	8.13	46	3,636	73	4,584
1972	211	11,260	7.23	108	5,866	103	5,394
1971	186	9,271	6.40	78	3,543	108	5,728
1970	203	8,236	4.90	116	4,350	87	3,886
1969	185	8,082	3.80	112	4,473	73	3,609
1968	182	8,148	3.64	114	4,624	68	3,524
1967	193	6,833	3.95	126	3,954	67	2,879
1966	203	6,308	3.77	144	3,730	59	2,578
1965	230	5,865	3.57	180	3,581	50	2,284
1964	253	5,990	3.79	199	3,664	54	2,326
1963	266	6,121	3.71	200	3,379	66	2,742
1962	353	6,214	3.63	289	3,721	64	2,493
1961	391	5,860	3.53	314	3,835	77	2,024
1960	415	5,931	3.57	332	3,939	83	1,992

Note: Data exclude mines producing less than 10,000 short tons of coal during the year.

Source: U.S. Department of Energy, Energy Information Administration, Office of Coal, Nuclear, Electric and Alternate Fuels, *Coal Production, 1987*, and earlier editions; and The Tennessee Energy Authority, *Tennessee Energy Profiles, 1960–1980*.

TABLE 5.3-- NUMBER OF MINERAL ESTABLISHMENTS, BY MAJOR ACTIVITY, SELECTED COUNTIES, 1982

County	All mineral industries	Metal mining	Bituminous coal and lignite mining	Oil and gas extraction	Nonmetallic minerals mining
Anderson	46	0	31	14	1
Bedford	1	0	0	0	1
Benton	5	0	0	0	5
Bledsoe	2	0	2	0	0
Blount	6	0	1	1	4
Bradley	2	0	1	0	1
Campbell	48	0	43	2	3
Carter	1	0	0	0	1
Cheatham	3	0	1	1	1
Claiborne	15	0	13	2	0
Clay	3	0	0	2	1
Coffee	5	0	0	3	2
Crockett	2	0	1	1	0
Cumberland	28	0	3	18	7
Davidson	37	1	8	15	13
Decatur	4	0	0	0	4
Dickson	1	0	0	0	1
Dyer	1	0	0	0	0
Fayette	1	1	0	0	1
Fentress	23	0	8	13	2
Franklin	3	0	0	0	3
Greene	3	0	0	1	2
Grundy	6	0	6	0	0
Hamblen	1	0	0	0	1
Hamilton	18	0	7	4	7
Hancock	3	0	0	2	1
Hardin	4	0	0	1	3
Hawkins	3	0	0	3	0
Haywood	1	0	0	1	0
Henry	5	0	0	1	4
Hickman	1	0	0	0	1
Jackson	3	0	0	3	0
Jefferson	12	6	3	2	1
Johnson	1	0	0	0	1
Knox	38	3	18	4	13
Lake	1	0	0	0	1
Lincoln	1	0	0	1	0
Loudon	1	0	0	0	1
McMinn	2	0	0	1	1
Marion	7	0	5	1	1
Maury	6	0	0	1	5
Meigs	1	0	0	0	1
Monroe	6	0	0	1	5
Montgomery	1	0	0	0	1
Moore	1	0	0	0	1
Morgan	25	0	11	14	0
Obion	1	0	0	0	1
Overton	9	0	0	8	1
Pickett	2	0	0	2	0
Polk	1	1	0	0	0

TABLE 5.3-- NUMBER OF MINERAL ESTABLISHMENTS, BY MAJOR ACTIVITY, SELECTED COUNTIES, 1982 (Continued)

County	All mineral industries	Metal mining	Bituminous coal and lignite mining	Oil and gas extraction	Nonmetallic minerals mining
Rhea	5	0	1	1	3
Roane	14	0	6	5	3
Robertson	3	0	0	1	2
Rutherford	3	0	0	1	2
Scott	46	0	29	17	0
Sequatchie	14	0	12	1	1
Sevier	3	0	0	2	1
Shelby	21	0	3	9	9
Smith	2	1	0	0	1
Sullivan	9	0	5	1	3
Sumner	3	0	1	1	1
Union	2	1	0	0	1
Van Buren	1	0	0	1	0
Warren	4	0	0	2	2
Washington	4	0	3	0	1
Weakley	2	0	0	0	2
White	4	0	1	1	2
Williamson	4	0	0	2	2
Wilson	2	0	0	0	2

Note: County data shown in this table are limited to counties or industry groups with a value of shipments and receipts greater than $5 million.

Source: U.S. Department of Commerce, Bureau of the Census, *1982 Census of Mineral Industries, Geographic Area Series, East South Central States.*

TABLE 5.4-- COAL PRODUCTION AND NUMBER OF COAL MINES, BY TYPE OF MINING, AND AVERAGE MINE PRICE, TENNESSEE AND SELECTED COUNTIES, 1987
(Production in thousands of short tons)

County	Total			Underground		Surface	
	Number	Production	Avg. mine price ($ per short ton)	Number	Production	Number	Production
TENNESSEE	72	6,351	27.65	47	4,813	25	1,538
Anderson	10	1,263	26.96	6	1,129	4	133
Campbell	17	1,176	24.73	8	816	9	360
Claiborne	7	1,594	33.50	4	1,324	3	269
Fentress	1	216	(D)	0	0	1	216
Grundy	1	47	(D)	0	0	1	47
Marion	4	294	24.75	3	269	1	25
Morgan	3	214	(D)	1	73	2	140
Rhea	2	80	(D)	2	80	0	0
Scott	6	464	26.66	6	464	0	0
Sequatchie	21	1,005	26.72	17	657	4	348

Note: Excludes silt, culm, refuse bank, slurry dam and dredge production. Excludes mines producing less than 10,000 short tons of coal during the year.

(D) withheld to avoid disclosure of individual company data.

Source: U. S. Department of Energy, Energy Information Administration, Office of Coal, Nuclear, Electric and Alternate Fuels, *Coal Production, 1987.*

TABLE 5.5-- PRINCIPAL NON-FUEL MINERALS AND VALUE OF NON-FUEL MINERAL PRODUCTION, SOUTHEASTERN STATES, 1986

State	Value ($1,000)	Rank in U.S.	Percentage of U.S. production	Principal minerals in order of value
TENNESSEE	481,656	15	2.05	Stone, zinc, cement, pyrites
Alabama	405,216	19	1.73	Cement, stone, lime, sand and gravel
Arkansas	263,007	29	1.12	Bromine, stone, cement, sand and gravel
Florida	1,295,153	4	5.52	Phosphate rock, stone, cement, sand and gravel
Georgia	1,091,455	7	4.65	Clays, stone, cement, sand and gravel
Kentucky	267,265	28	1.14	Stone, lime, cement, sand and gravel
Louisiana	446,798	18	1.91	Sulfur, salt, sand and gravel, stone
Mississippi	101,095	40	0.43	Sand and gravel, clays, cement, stone
North Carolina	466,423	17	1.99	Stone, phosphate rock, lithium minerals, sand and gravel
South Carolina	295,889	27	1.26	Cement, stone, clays, sand and gravel
Virginia	393,037	20	1.68	Stone, cement, sand and gravel, lime
West Virginia	129,809	38	0.55	Cement, stone, salt, sand and gravel (industrial)

Note: Unless otherwise noted, stone is crushed stone; sand and gravel is for construction; cement is portland; and sulfur is Frasch.

Source: U.S. Department of the Interior, Bureau of Mines, *Minerals Yearbook, 1986, Volume II, Area Reports: Domestic.*

TABLE 5.6-- VALUE OF PRODUCTION OF MINERALS,[1] SOUTHEASTERN STATES AND UNITED STATES, 1930–1986, SELECTED YEARS [In thousands of dollars]

State	1986	1985	1984	1983	1980	1970	1960	1950	1940	1930
TENNESSEE	481,656	472,287	478,321	407,051	407,837	220,465	145,538	90,405	42,683	32,499
Alabama	405,216	405,915	409,841	361,326	328,633	323,245	221,802	158,975	64,998	55,462
Arkansas	263,007	256,697	272,628	246,430	286,631	225,625	159,519	119,642	37,479	34,901
Florida	1,295,153	1,559,266	1,510,364	1,274,979	1,508,754	300,042	180,286	70,717	14,854	15,484
Georgia	1,091,455	946,075	940,492	850,224	770,688	203,225	92,305	43,394	16,932	12,831
Kentucky	267,265	267,558	256,998	224,517	204,300	847,465	414,553	459,956	131,974	111,691
Louisiana	446,798	522,268	511,470	446,761	583,766	5,102,321	1,990,895	693,607	189,153	71,929
Mississippi	101,095	102,793	94,178	89,705	103,940	249,973	199,210	102,945	7,240	1,775
North Carolina	466,423	432,756	451,480	399,158	379,366	98,365	45,096	26,338	21,113	7,462
South Carolina	295,889	275,929	275,850	230,594	194,779	56,365	30,987	11,394	5,306	3,341
Virginia	393,037	381,276	341,589	289,344	305,306	374,321	208,880	137,806	50,004	34,603
West Virginia	129,809	105,409	112,187	103,973	106,286	1,285,364	722,628	829,633	329,892	290,119
TENNESSEE as percentage of U.S.	2.05	2.03	2.07	1.93	1.62	0.74	0.81	0.76	0.76	0.67
SOUTHEAST as percentage of U.S.	24.04	24.66	24.43	23.30	20.63	31.17	24.47	23.14	16.25	14.10

Note: Percentages computed by the Center for Business and Economic Research.

1. Beginning in 1978 fuel minerals are excluded from this data source.

Source: U.S. Department of the Interior, Bureau of Mines, *Minerals Yearbook, 1986, Volume II, Area Reports: Domestic*, and earlier editions; and *Mineral Resources of the United States, 1931, Part 1 - Metals, Summary.*

TABLE 5.7-- AVERAGE DAILY PRODUCTION, DAILY PRODUCTIVE CAPACITY, AND PERCENT UTILIZATION OF COAL MINES, BY TYPE OF MINING, SELECTED SOUTHEASTERN STATES AND UNITED STATES, 1986 [In thousands of short tons]

State	Total			Underground			Surface		
	Average daily production[1]	Daily productive capacity at end of year[2]	Percentage utilization[3]	Average daily production[1]	Daily productive capacity at end of year[2]	Percentage utilization[3]	Average daily production[1]	Daily productive capacity at end of year[2]	Percentage utilization[3]
TENNESSEE	29	31	96.18	22	23	96.59	7	8	94.99
Alabama	107	112	95.32	57	61	93.49	49	50	97.55
Arkansas	1	(D)	(D)	0	0	0.00	1	(D)	(D)
Kentucky	718	761	94.40	413	445	92.72	305	316	96.76
Louisiana	7	(D)	(D)	0	0	0.00	7	(D)	(D)
Virginia	202	206	98.22	168	171	98.10	34	35	98.85
West Virginia	623	664	93.75	493	528	93.36	130	136	95.24
UNITED STATES	3,768	4,040	93.27	1,675	1,810	92.55	2,093	2,230	93.84

Note: Includes only those states producing significant amounts of coal; excludes silt, culm, refuse bank, slurry dam, and dredge production, and excludes mines producing less than 10,000 short tons of coal during the year.

(D) withheld to avoid disclosure of individual company data.

1. Computed at the mine level by dividing the mine production by the total number of days worked at the mine during the year.

2. Maximum amount of coal that can be produced on a daily basis as reported by mining companies on government forms.

3. Computed by dividing average daily production by daily productive capacity and multiplying by 100.

Source: U.S. Department of Energy, Energy Information Administration, Office of Coal, Nuclear, Electric and Alternate Fuels, *Coal Production, 1986.*

TABLE 5.8-- RECOVERABLE COAL RESERVES AND AVERAGE RECOVERY PERCENTAGE AT COAL MINES, BY TYPE OF MINING, SELECTED SOUTHEASTERN STATES AND UNITED STATES, 1987 [In millions of short tons]

	Total		Underground		Surface	
State	Recoverable coal reserves [1]	Average recovery percentage [2]	Recoverable coal reserves [1]	Average recovery percentage [2]	Recoverable coal reserves [1]	Average recovery percentage [2]
TENNESSEE	102.7	67.78	(D)	(D)	(D)	(D)
Alabama	537.6	78.97	361.3	54.00	176.3	84.57
Arkansas	(D)	(D)	0.0	0.00	(D)	(D)
Kentucky	1,739.1	70.92	1,256.6	63.50	482.5	82.90
Louisiana	(D)	(D)	0.0	0.00	(D)	(D)
Virginia	507.5	67.60	437.5	62.43	70.0	82.82
West Virginia	2,547.6	66.82	2,127.6	61.04	420.0	80.13
UNITED STATES	24,241.2	71.58	8,171.2	61.58	16,070.0	81.66

Note: Includes only those states producing significant amounts of coal; excludes silt, culm, refuse bank, slurry dam, and dredge production, and excludes mines producing less than 10,000 short tons of coal during the year.

(D) withheld to avoid disclosure of individual company data.

1. Represents the quantity of coal that can be recovered from existing coal reserves at reporting mines.

2. Represents the percentage of coal that can be recovered from coal reserves at reporting mines, averaged for all mines in the reported geographic area.

Source: U.S. Department of Energy, Energy Information Administration, Office of Coal, Nuclear, Electric and Alternate Fuels, *Coal Production, 1987.*

TABLE 5.9-- COAL PRODUCTION AND NUMBER OF COAL MINES, BY TYPE OF MINING, SELECTED SOUTHEASTERN STATES AND UNITED STATES, 1987 [In thousands of short tons]

	Total		Underground		Surface	
State	Number	Production	Number	Production	Number	Production
TENNESSEE	72	6,351	47	4,813	25	1,538
Alabama	77	25,461	11	14,329	66	11,132
Arkansas	4	67	0	0	4	67
Kentucky	1,034	163,718	635	92,143	399	71,575
Louisiana	1	2,751	0	0	1	2,751
Virginia	374	44,179	287	36,731	87	7,448
West Virginia	614	135,933	417	107,169	197	28,764
UNITED STATES	3,030	914,659	1,563	371,263	1,467	543,396

Note: Includes only those states producing significant amounts of coal; excludes silt, culm, refuse bank, slurry dam, and dredge production and excludes mines producing less than 10,000 short tons of coal during the year.

Source: U.S. Department of Energy, Energy Information Administration, Office of Coal, Nuclear, Electric and Alternate Fuels, *Coal Production, 1987*.

TABLE 5.10--COAL STOCKS AT COAL MINES, SELECTED SOUTHEASTERN STATES AND UNITED STATES, 1987 [In thousands of short tons]

State	Coal stocks at end of 1987	Coal stocks at end of 1986	Net change in coal stocks during year	Percent change in coal stocks during year
TENNESSEE	84	359	-275	-76.56
Alabama	2,388	2,597	-209	-8.05
Arkansas	2	3	-2	-50.00
Kentucky	4,010	3,914	96	2.46
Louisiana	0	0	0	0.00
Virginia	2,211	2,618	-407	-15.55
West Virginia	3,437	3,979	-542	-13.62
UNITED STATES	26,917	30,609	-3,691	-12.06

Note: Includes only those states producing significant amounts of coal; excludes silt, culm, refuse bank, slurry dam, and dredge production and excludes mines producing less than 10,000 short tons of coal during the year. Total may not equal sum of components due to independent rounding.

Source: U.S. Department of Energy, Energy Information Administration, Office of Coal, Nuclear, Electric and Alternate Fuels, *Coal Production, 1987*.

TABLE 5.11--COAL MINING PRODUCTIVITY, BY TYPE OF MINING, SELECTED SOUTHEASTERN STATES AND UNITED STATES, 1987

	Total			Underground			Surface		
State	Average number of miners working daily [1]	Average number of days worked during year	Average production per miner per hour [2] (short tons)	Average number of miners working daily [1]	Average number of days worked during year	Average production per miner per hour [2] (short tons)	Average number of miners working daily [1]	Average number of days worked during year	Average production per miner per hour [2] (short tons)
TENNESSEE	1,998	222	1.67	1,552	224	1.58	446	219	2.04
Alabama	6,718	222	1.97	4,461	238	1.68	2,257	219	2.53
Arkansas	19	214	1.80	0	0	0.00	19	214	1.80
Kentucky	32,590	197	2.69	21,505	198	2.40	11,085	195	3.18
Louisiana	81	286	15.26	0	0	0.00	81	286	15.26
Virginia	12,047	197	2.08	10,228	197	2.01	1,819	197	2.52
West Virginia	29,458	200	2.47	24,513	199	2.31	4,945	202	3.29
UNITED STATES	142,667	207	3.30	89,857	202	2.20	52,810	212	4.98

Note: See Table 5.9 for total production, by type of mining, for the Southeastern states and United States.

1. Includes all employees engaged in production, preparation, processing, development, maintenance, repair, shop or yard work at mining operations. Excludes office workers. Includes mining operations management and all technical and engineering personnel.

2. Calculated by dividing total coal production by the total direct labor hours worked by all mine employees identified in footnote 1.

Source: U.S. Department of Energy, Energy Information Administration, Office of Coal, Nuclear, Electric and Altemate Fuels, *Coal Production, 1987*.

TABLE 5.12--COAL PRODUCTION AND AVERAGE MINE PRICE, BY DISPOSITION, SELECTED SOUTHEASTERN STATES AND UNITED STATES, 1987

State	Total[1]		Open market[2]		Captive[3]	
	Production (1,000 short tons)	Average mine price ($ per short ton)	Production (1,000 short tons)	Average mine price ($ per short ton)	Production (1,000 short tons)	Average mine price ($ per short ton)
TENNESSEE	6,351	27.65	6,318	(D)	33	(D)
Alabama	25,461	41.42	25,100	41.58	362	30.50
Arkansas	67	(D)	67	(D)	0	0.00
Kentucky	163,718	26.15	160,297	25.95	3,421	35.71
Louisiana	2,751	(D)	0	0.00	2,751	(D)
Virginia	44,179	27.42	44,177	27.42	2	41.60
West Virginia	135,933	29.15	127,625	28.73	8,308	35.56
UNITED STATES	914,659	23.07	812,833	23.26	101,826	21.51

Note: Includes only those states producing significant amounts of coal; excludes silt, culm, refuse bank, slurry dam, and dredge production, and excludes mines producing less than 10,000 short tons of coal during the year. Average mine price is calculated by dividing the total f.o.b. mine value of the coal produced by the total production.

(D) withheld to avoid disclosure of individual company data.

1. Total may not equal sum of components due to independent rounding.

2. Open market includes all coal sold on the open market to other coal companies or consumers.

3. Captive includes all coal used by the producing company or sold to affiliated or parent companies.

Source: U.S. Department of Energy, Energy Information Administration, Office of Coal, Nuclear, Electric and Alternate Fuels, *Coal Production, 1987*.

TABLE 5.13--NUMBER OF PRODUCING GAS WELLS AND NET WELLHEAD PRODUCTION OF NATURAL GAS, SOUTHEASTERN STATES AND UNITED STATES, 1970–1987, SELECTED YEARS

	Number of producing gas wells[1]							
State	1987	1986	1985	1984	1983	1982	1980	1970
TENNESSEE	840	921	988	780	540	340	177	15
Alabama	1,135	1,029	863	690	461	489	314	2
Arkansas	2,847	2,719	2,623	2,371	1,763	1,959	1,114	1,008
Florida	n.a.	n.a.	n.a.	n.a.	n.a.	0	0	0
Georgia	0	0	0	0	0	0	0	0
Kentucky	10,366	9,747	9,285	8,798	8,532	8,219	7,984	6,913
Louisiana	15,890	15,313	16,716	17,124	16,700	16,586	16,190	9,690
Mississippi	775	414	710	683	552	596	447	325
North Carolina	0	0	0	0	0	0	0	0
South Carolina	0	0	0	0	0	0	0	0
Virginia	689	573	495	425	299	298	258	115
West Virginia	34,300	33,400	32,475	31,150	29,675	27,450	25,900	20,702
UNITED STATES	249,225	241,527	243,344	233,853	221,952	210,753	182,004	117,483

	Net wellhead production[2] (1,000,000 cubit feet)							
	1987	1986	1985	1984	1983	1982	1980	1970
TENNESSEE	2,707	3,464	4,686	5,022	3,950	2,976	1,241	(a)
Alabama	137,293	127,387	128,651	123,870	114,847	124,994	108,702	(a)
Arkansas	142,219	132,836	155,923	137,385	128,535	125,584	112,202	181,577
Florida	9,132	9,766	11,604	13,867	23,356	25,303	46,421	(a)
Georgia	0	0	0	0	0	0	0	0
Kentucky	70,125	80,195	73,126	61,518	46,720	51,924	57,180	77,892
Louisiana	5,147,799	4,919,567	5,038,715	5,850,063	5,357,763	6,191,409	6,962,775	7,942,365
Mississippi	202,892	191,173	184,346	201,480	194,936	212,929	202,096	133,264
North Carolina	0	0	0	0	0	0	0	0
South Carolina	0	0	0	0	0	0	0	0
Virginia	19,520	15,427	15,041	8,928	4,346	6,880	7,812	2,805
West Virginia	160,000	135,431	144,883	143,730	130,078	150,850	156,551	242,452
UNITED STATES	17,848,276	17,225,395	17,619,278	18,561,668	17,139,041	18,821,536	20,504,238	22,410,102

1. Data pertain only to dry gas and condensate wells. Data are as of December 31.

2. As defined by American Gas Association "Net Wellhead Production" equals "Gross Production" less gas for repressuring and therefore includes natural gas liquids.

a. Included in U.S. total.

Source: Energy Information Administration, *Natural Gas Annual, Volume I, 1987,* and earlier editions.

TABLE 5.14--WELLS AND DRY HOLES DRILLED AS EXPLORATORY TESTS, BY TYPE OF WELL, SOUTHEASTERN STATES, 1986

State	Total drilled	Dry holes	Producers Total	Producers Oil	Producers Gas
TENNESSEE	52	31	21	7	14
Alabama	78	51	27	6	21
Arkansas	83	65	18	10	8
Florida	6	5	1	1	0
Georgia	2	2	0	0	0
Kentucky	163	138	25	9	16
Louisiana	404	336	68	20	48
Mississippi	109	90	19	16	3
North Carolina	0	0	0	0	0
South Carolina	0	0	0	0	0
Virginia	7	6	1	0	1
West Virginia	9	2	7	0	7

Source: American Gas Association, *Gas Facts, 1986*.

TABLE 5.15--PRODUCTION OF CRUDE OIL (INCLUDING LEASE CONDENSATE), SELECTED SOUTHEASTERN STATES AND UNITED STATES, 1988 [In thousands of barrels]

State	Production[1]	Daily average
TENNESSEE	601	2
Alabama	20,797	57
Arkansas	13,606	37
Florida	7,746	21
Kentucky	5,458	15
Louisiana	165,006	451
Mississippi	27,553	75
Virginia	25	(a)
West Virginia	2,621	7
UNITED STATES	2,979,123	8,140

Note: Includes only those states which produce over 10,000 barrels per month.

1. Includes offshore production.

a. Less than 500 barrels.

Source: U.S. Department of Energy, Energy Information Administration, Office of Oil and Gas, *Petroleum Supply Annual, 1988, Volume 1*.

The only complete assessment of the United States' housing stock occurs in each decennial census. Characteristics of the physical structure, including plumbing and heating, are reported along with market value or rent paid and number of persons per unit. The 1980 Census also reports on housing ownership and the use of mobile homes as well as single- and multi-family units.

Between decennial census years, the Bureau of the Census monitors additions to the national housing stock in 17,000 permit-issuing counties and places; 203 are in Tennessee. The sample size for this survey has been increased twice in the last ten years: from 14,000 to 16,000 in 1978 and then from 16,000 to 17,000 in 1984. These permits for housing stock additions are published in the Bureau's monthly *Construction Reports, Housing Authorized by Building Permits and Public Contracts.* Permit data are collected for approximately 25 types of residential and nonresidential structures. While the volume of such information precludes regular publication, monthly reports for specified regions are available upon request from Construction Statistics Division at the Bureau. *Construction Reports* are also published on *Housing Starts* (including new mobile homes put in place), *Characteristics of New Housing* and *One-Family Houses Sold and for Sale.*

Within Tennessee, the Tennessee Housing Development Agency (THDA) publishes annually a *Report on the Need for Housing in Tennessee.* These survey data on public and private additions to the housing stock, and prices, rents, and vacancy rates are the most comprehensive annual data available at the county levels. Volume I of the 1989 *Report* projects for each county the number of housing units needed annually through 2000 for new household formation, in-migration, future vacancy needs, and replacement of permanent losses to the housing stock. Volume II, last published in 1986, provides information on apartment rents and vacancy rates. Median sales price and size of new and existing single family homes sold are also included in this report.

Nonresidential construction information at the local level is not widely available. F. W. Dodge, McGraw-Hill, Inc., provides estimates of construction contract valuations by states; however, such data are proprietary and are published here by special permission.

Additional information on the construction industry may be found in Chapters 2 and 3. Tables 2.1 and 2.2 provide information on the construction industry's contribution to gross state product, while other tables in this chapter include personal income from construction employment. For additional information on employment and earnings, the reader should turn to Chapter 3.

TABLE OF CONTENTS

TABLE 6.1-- ESTIMATED CONSTRUCTION CONTRACT VALUATIONS, BY TYPE OF CONSTRUCTION, TENNESSEE, 1967–1987 [In thousands of dollars]

Year	Total	Nonbuilding[1]	Residential	Nonresidential
1987	5,112,000	745,000	2,407,000	1,960,000
1986[a]	4,568,000	694,342	2,423,080	1,435,908
1985[a]	4,394,000	686,798	2,383,811	1,385,569
1984	4,238,431	671,176	2,160,211	1,407,044
1983	3,531,869	589,679	1,816,036	1,126,154
1982	2,541,742	520,738	1,127,555	893,449
1981	2,520,206	554,618	945,782	1,019,806
1980[a]	2,789,000	559,319	1,190,349	1,041,142
1979	4,880,482	2,425,089	1,362,367	1,093,026
1978	3,084,033	649,570	1,601,226	833,237
1977	6,219,038	4,193,985	1,291,950	733,103
1976	1,781,294	281,369	849,854	650,071
1975	1,673,873	433,454	654,531	585,888
1974	2,026,559	530,128	738,059	758,372
1973	2,219,007	333,973	1,166,880	718,154
1972	1,840,944	281,551	1,059,803	499,590
1971	1,530,737	244,116	763,896	522,725
1970	1,562,621	354,334	526,169	682,118
1969	1,480,916	520,033	494,148	466,735
1968	1,227,739	209,049	573,285	445,405
1967	1,043,884	171,761	522,278	349,845

1. Nonbuilding construction includes streets and highways, bridges, dams and reservoirs, water supply systems, etc.

a. Total has been revised; revisions for subcategories are not available.

Source: Data for 1987 and revised data are from the *Statistical Abstract of the United States, 1989*; original source is F. W. Dodge; proprietary data reprinted by special permission. Reproduction or dissemination of this information is granted only by contract or prior written permission from F. W. Dodge, McGraw-Hill, Inc., 24 Hartwell Avenue, Lexington, MA 02173, (617) 863-5100.

TABLE 6.2-- RESIDENTIAL BUILDING PERMITS, TENNESSEE, 1970–1987

Year	Total housing units[1]	Public units	Private units: Total	Private units: Single-family	Private units: Multi-family
1987	30,145	226	29,919	21,686	8,233
1986	34,406	50	34,356	21,607	12,749
1985	38,126	0	38,126	17,310	20,816
1984	37,085	321	36,764	13,769	22,995
1983	26,960	407	26,553	13,548	13,005
1982	15,008	209	14,799	7,328	7,471
1981	11,839	164	11,675	7,531	4,144
1980	19,746	357	19,389	12,334	7,055
1979	23,340	0	23,340	15,484	7,856
1978	28,811	200	28,611	18,947	9,664
1977	26,467	205	26,262	16,914	9,348
1976	19,136	230	18,906	14,436	4,470
1975	14,484	459	14,025	10,711	3,314
1974	18,032	121	17,911	10,908	7,003
1973	39,000	166	38,834	14,829	24,005
1972	45,997	509	45,488	17,506	27,982
1971	36,852	1,253	35,599	17,072	18,527
1970	24,769	2,270	22,499	14,157	8,342

1. Excluding mobile homes.

Source: U.S. Department of Commerce, Bureau of the Census, *Construction Reports, Housing Authorized by Building Permits and Public Contracts, 1987*, and earlier editions.

FIGURE 6.1
Residential Building Permits in Tennessee, Private Units, 1978–1987

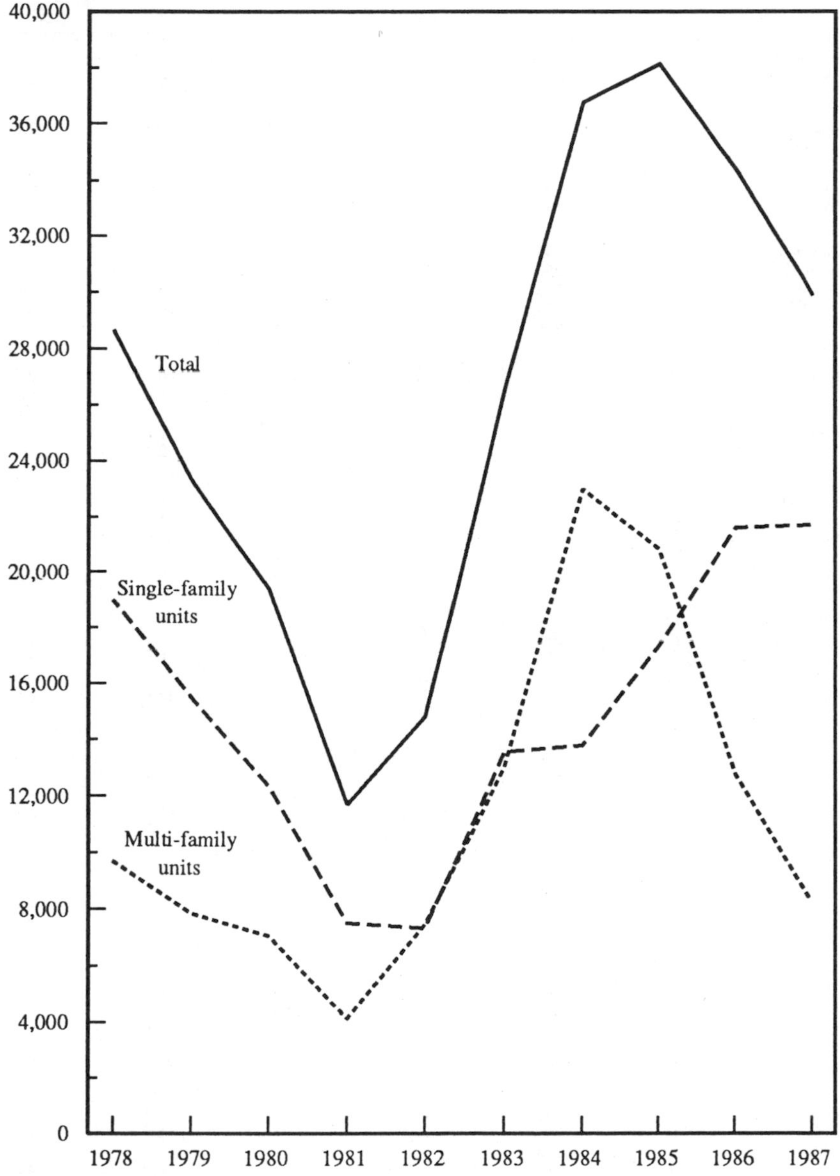

Source: U.S. Department of Commerce, Bureau of the Census, *Construction Reports: Housing Authorized by Building Permits and Public Contracts, 1987.*

TABLE 6.3-- APARTMENT VACANCY RATES AND MEDIAN RENTS, BY NUMBER OF BEDROOMS, TENNESSEE AND SELECTED COUNTIES, SPRING 1986

	Median rent ($)			Vacancy rate (%)		
County	All units[1]	One bedroom	Two bedroom	All units[1]	One bedroom	Two bedroom
TENNESSEE	315	285	325	5.2	5.6	4.9
Anderson	285	260	390	20.7	20.3	22.1
Bedford	250	200	280	1.4	2.8	0.0
Benton	185	n.a.	n.a.	0.0	n.a.	n.a.
Bledsoe	125	n.a.	125	0.0	n.a.	0.0
Blount	265	205	275	6.7	11.7	5.4
Bradley	261	235	281	3.9	3.0	5.0
Campbell	220	250	220	3.5	1.1	4.7
Cannon	225	225	n.a.	3.7	3.7	n.a.
Carroll	200	184	200	21.9	29.7	6.3
Carter	210	205	235	2.4	1.9	3.0
Cheatham	260	245	270	0.0	0.0	0.0
Chester	175	n.a.	n.a.	0.0	n.a.	n.a.
Claiborne	170	n.a.	175	1.6	n.a.	2.0
Cocke	150	n.a.	150	1.3	n.a.	1.3
Coffee	305	253	320	1.7	2.1	1.6
Cumberland	275	250	300	5.6	2.2	7.1
Davidson	370	325	390	1.4	1.3	1.4
DeKalb	225	n.a.	225	8.3	n.a.	8.3
Dickson	300	260	350	0.0	0.0	0.0
Dyer	190	160	195	0.9	0.0	1.1
Fayette	213	n.a.	n.a.	0.0	n.a.	n.a.
Gibson	215	215	215	2.1	4.2	1.8
Giles	291	256	291	1.3	0.0	2.1
Grainger	187	n.a.	187	6.7	n.a.	10.5
Greene	240	210	240	9.7	18.6	6.5
Grundy	90	75	90	0.0	0.0	0.0
Hamblen	185	170	300	4.1	3.3	5.2
Hamilton	320	285	330	5.9	8.4	3.4
Hardeman	240	210	240	0.0	0.0	0.0
Hardin	200	n.a.	200	0.0	n.a.	0.0
Hawkins	275	245	275	3.6	10.2	1.3
Haywood	240	n.a.	240	2.3	n.a.	2.3
Henry	200	200	225	4.2	0.0	7.1
Hickman	322	n.a.	322	0.0	n.a.	0.0
Humphreys	225	354	225	10.1	5.7	13.6
Jefferson	190	180	193	4.5	0.0	6.4
Knox	294	270	335	5.8	5.5	5.8
Lake	113	n.a.	n.a.	0.0	n.a.	n.a.
Lauderdale	235	215	265	9.1	8.8	9.2
Lawrence	220	205	225	14.7	37.5	7.7
Lincoln	195	191	195	1.7	2.8	1.2
Loudon	392	392	200	4.7	0.0	11.1
McMinn	330	275	330	2.9	0.0	3.3
McNairy	180	180	200	1.9	0.0	4.0
Macon	225	200	235	1.8	3.6	0.0

TABLE 6.3-- APARTMENT VACANCY RATES AND MEDIAN RENTS, BY NUMBER OF BEDROOMS, TENNESSEE AND SELECTED COUNTIES, SPRING 1986 (Continued)

	Median rent ($)			Vacancy rate (%)		
County	All units[1]	One bedroom	Two bedroom	All units[1]	One bedroom	Two bedroom
Madison	295	250	325	9.5	7.3	11.4
Marion	200	n.a.	200	3.0	n.a.	3.7
Marshall	195	218	195	4.8	6.3	3.8
Maury	329	285	335	7.3	6.9	8.0
Monroe	215	n.a.	240	3.4	n.a.	5.3
Montgomery	295	270	325	3.2	3.9	3.0
Morgan	220	n.a.	n.a.	5.9	n.a.	n.a.
Obion	220	215	218	1.2	0.0	0.8
Putnam	250	225	250	1.9	0.6	1.9
Rhea	195	195	210	6.6	7.8	5.0
Roane	260	412	250	4.2	2.6	6.8
Robertson	325	285	325	2.7	4.2	2.7
Rutherford	295	285	310	3.3	2.8	3.2
Scott	225	190	225	5.6	5.6	6.3
Sequatchie	175	n.a.	170	0.0	n.a.	0.0
Sevier	200	180	200	7.7	13.3	5.0
Shelby	295	270	305	7.7	8.7	7.1
Smith	225	n.a.	225	0.0	n.a.	0.0
Sullivan	230	190	265	3.4	3.6	3.2
Sumner	390	305	395	2.2	1.3	2.8
Tipton	346	346	n.a.	0.0	0.0	n.a.
Trousdale	230	230	n.a.	0.0	0.0	n.a.
Unicoi	240	180	240	9.5	5.0	5.1
Union	190	n.a.	190	0.0	n.a.	0.0
Warren	250	175	250	5.7	3.9	5.9
Washington	250	190	275	4.5	4.6	4.0
Weakley	225	160	225	0.0	0.0	0.0
White	275	n.a.	275	5.0	n.a.	5.0
Williamson	340	280	340	0.6	2.3	0.4
Wilson	350	240	350	2.9	8.3	1.3

Note: Survey limited to conventional apartments in buildings with at least four units.

n.a. not available.

1. Includes categories not shown separately.

Source: Tennessee Housing Development Agency, *Report on the Need for Housing in Tennessee, 1986*, Volume II.

TABLE 6.4-- ESTIMATED MEDIAN PRICES AND SIZES OF SINGLE FAMILY HOMES SOLD, COUNTIES, 1985

	All sales		New homes		Existing homes	
County	Median price ($)	Median size (sq. ft.)	Median price ($)	Median size (sq. ft.)	Median price ($)	Median size (sq. ft.)
Anderson	45,100	1,126	49,500	1,048	43,075	1,140
Bedford	36,975	1,240	38,250	1,040	36,950	1,250
Benton	22,250	1,132	n.a.	n.a.	22,250	1,132
Bledsoe	37,000	1,300	47,500	1,700	36,500	1,300
Blount	48,500	1,101	49,950	1,028	45,750	1,115
Bradley	44,000	1,600	58,450	2,000	43,450	1,600
Campbell	32,250	1,135	n.a.	n.a.	32,250	1,135
Cannon	34,000	1,100	n.a.	n.a.	34,000	1,100
Carroll	28,700	1,305	n.a.	n.a.	28,700	1,305
Carter	45,500	1,187	45,500	1,260	45,500	1,175
Cheatham	42,373	1,191	35,500	1,648	42,373	1,181
Chester	36,000	1,282	42,000	1,200	34,000	1,300
Claiborne	30,000	1,020	n.a.	n.a.	30,000	1,020
Clay	32,000	1,134	n.a.	n.a.	32,000	1,134
Cocke	37,500	1,120	n.a.	n.a.	37,500	1,120
Coffee	38,250	1,224	47,000	1,304	37,427	1,216
Crockett	31,000	1,176	n.a.	n.a.	31,000	1,176
Cumberland	45,000	1,156	46,600	1,096	45,000	1,196
Davidson	67,000	1,276	58,900	1,066	67,000	1,300
Decatur	34,250	1,277	40,200	1,233	32,500	1,282
DeKalb	33,000	1,202	42,000	1,350	33,000	1,200
Dickson	38,650	1,176	57,000	925	38,200	1,182
Dyer	30,000	1,262	n.a.	n.a.	30,000	1,262
Fayette	39,750	1,381	n.a.	n.a.	39,750	1,381
Fentress	31,250	1,092	34,750	1,030	30,000	1,142
Franklin	35,000	1,260	41,950	1,254	33,500	1,274
Gibson	25,000	1,282	n.a.	n.a.	25,000	1,282
Giles	35,000	1,235	47,325	1,257	35,000	1,227
Grainger	28,000	1,040	n.a.	n.a.	28,000	1,040
Greene	42,500	1,351	43,250	1,092	42,500	1,380
Grundy	42,000	1,400	52,950	1,700	41,000	1,400
Hamblen	40,000	1,263	n.a.	n.a.	40,000	1,263
Hamilton	52,600	1,650	65,900	2,000	50,450	1,500
Hancock	31,500	984	36,500	1,260	30,550	935
Hardeman	37,250	1,422	36,250	911	37,500	1,529
Hardin	35,750	1,362	43,750	1,342	35,000	1,362
Hawkins	40,729	1,173	53,000	1,562	40,458	1,163
Haywood	36,250	1,408	45,500	1,246	36,000	1,429
Henderson	37,000	1,385	36,500	1,144	37,000	1,412
Henry	38,798	1,387	n.a.	n.a.	38,798	1,387
Hickman	29,900	1,129	31,564	1,000	29,900	1,130
Houston	27,250	1,086	45,000	1,196	27,125	1,076
Humphreys	30,000	1,107	n.a.	n.a.	30,000	1,107
Jackson	35,250	1,238	36,750	1,075	33,750	1,297
Jefferson	32,300	1,068	60,000	1,080	32,000	1,056
Johnson	38,000	1,148	33,800	1,008	38,950	1,151
Knox	50,804	1,447	67,500	1,700	46,441	1,400
Lake	20,000	1,214	n.a.	n.a.	20,000	1,214
Lauderdale	27,500	1,188	46,000	1,956	27,500	1,188
Lawrence	33,375	1,253	33,500	1,125	33,250	1,256

TABLE 6.4-- ESTIMATED MEDIAN PRICES AND SIZES OF SINGLE FAMILY HOMES SOLD, COUNTIES, 1985 (Continued)

	All sales		New homes		Existing homes	
County	Median price ($)	Median size (sq. ft.)	Median price ($)	Median size (sq. ft.)	Median price ($)	Median size (sq. ft.)
Lewis	25,000	1,188	32,500	1,128	23,500	1,210
Lincoln	34,250	1,250	48,750	1,322	33,958	1,240
Loudon	34,100	1,131	38,000	1,260	33,200	1,127
McMinn	43,000	1,600	56,200	1,900	39,000	1,500
McNairy	39,410	1,429	44,650	1,362	38,100	1,435
Macon	31,250	1,220	33,500	1,242	31,000	1,215
Madison	57,000	1,650	58,000	1,656	57,000	1,650
Marion	42,200	1,400	49,450	1,650	40,400	1,350
Marshall	33,750	1,244	60,125	1,391	32,400	1,185
Maury	45,500	1,300	90,450	2,018	44,900	1,300
Meigs	41,800	1,500	53,000	2,250	39,000	1,463
Monroe	29,750	1,113	n.a.	n.a.	29,750	1,113
Montgomery	43,500	1,284	54,425	1,387	42,831	1,279
Moore	38,500	1,380	28,000	824	38,750	1,390
Morgan	32,900	1,020	44,900	1,356	30,000	1,000
Obion	32,250	1,223	40,750	1,168	32,250	1,230
Overton	30,000	1,204	30,000	1,750	30,000	1,202
Perry	23,000	1,080	15,000	918	28,000	1,088
Pickett	27,050	942	15,000	728	27,600	960
Polk	40,450	1,600	55,900	2,000	38,000	1,500
Putnam	45,500	1,396	51,250	1,452	45,500	1,392
Rhea	41,000	1,600	56,000	2,300	38,000	1,475
Roane	56,320	1,348	67,000	1,509	53,500	1,341
Robertson	38,000	1,152	36,375	1,089	38,000	1,155
Rutherford	48,375	1,276	n.a.	n.a.	48,375	1,276
Scott	35,000	1,200	52,000	1,414	35,000	1,104
Sequatchie	39,900	1,400	59,900	1,900	39,000	1,380
Sevier	48,500	1,236	51,500	1,266	48,500	1,230
Shelby	59,200	1,494	69,900	1,700	55,000	1,492
Smith	35,000	1,325	n.a.	n.a.	35,000	1,325
Stewart	27,000	1,066	44,000	1,454	26,500	1,066
Sullivan	44,450	1,324	n.a.	n.a.	44,450	1,324
Sumner	48,263	1,274	74,500	1,625	48,000	1,256
Tipton	45,231	1,329	46,011	1,200	45,000	1,349
Trousdale	33,500	1,248	n.a.	n.a.	33,500	1,248
Unicoi	44,253	1,344	53,000	1,920	42,750	1,344
Union	42,500	1,248	n.a.	n.a.	42,500	1,248
Van Buren	33,250	1,105	n.a.	n.a.	33,250	1,105
Warren	33,500	1,325	48,800	2,047	33,500	1,294
Washington	44,500	1,352	45,450	1,120	44,500	1,371
Wayne	24,450	1,189	38,750	1,177	23,850	1,189
Weakley	22,000	1,198	21,000	900	22,151	1,201
White	32,000	1,217	28,500	1,187	32,000	1,217
Williamson	85,155	1,554	38,000	1,979	86,750	1,506
Wilson	47,907	1,250	45,950	1,248	48,000	1,250

n.a. not available.

Source: Tennessee Housing Development Agency, *Report on the Need for Housing in Tennessee, 1986*, Volume II.

TABLE 6.5-- NUMBER OF HOUSING UNITS, BY TENURE AND VACANCY STATUS AND BY NUMBER OF PERSONS PER ROOM, AND MEDIAN NUMBER OF ROOMS PER HOUSING UNIT, COUNTIES, 1980

			Year-round housing units			Number of occupied housing units by persons per room			Median number of rooms per housing unit
County	Total	Total occupied	Owner-occupied	Renter-occupied	Vacant	1.00 or less	1.01-1.50	1.51 or more	
Anderson	25,849	24,616	17,667	6,949	1,213	23,692	753	171	5.1
Bedford	10,814	9,943	7,189	2,754	856	9,543	338	62	5.2
Benton	6,526	5,577	4,538	1,039	914	5,394	150	33	5.0
Bledsoe	3,406	2,979	2,328	651	350	2,804	133	42	5.0
Blount	30,836	28,177	21,112	7,065	2,340	27,358	698	121	5.3
Bradley	24,705	23,026	16,104	6,922	1,628	22,087	777	162	5.1
Campbell	13,250	12,087	8,981	3,106	1,046	11,290	629	168	5.0
Cannon	4,002	3,625	2,926	699	353	3,465	118	42	5.1
Carroll	11,306	10,321	8,207	2,114	967	9,959	289	73	5.1
Carter	19,315	17,868	13,947	3,921	1,229	17,172	589	107	5.1
Cheatham	7,481	7,063	5,864	1,199	370	6,700	292	71	5.2
Chester	4,470	4,210	3,206	1,004	247	4,026	148	36	5.1
Claiborne	9,385	8,295	6,328	1,967	944	7,844	340	111	5.1
Clay	3,015	2,731	2,209	522	237	2,610	98	23	5.0
Cocke	11,305	10,154	7,282	2,872	1,106	9,501	513	140	4.8
Coffee	14,992	13,649	9,738	3,911	1,318	13,193	380	76	5.3
Crockett	5,655	5,380	4,070	1,310	249	5,108	203	69	5.2
Cumberland	10,998	9,887	7,718	2,169	873	9,359	434	94	5.2
Davidson	187,430	177,737	102,140	75,597	9,602	171,603	4,627	1,507	5.1
Decatur	4,877	4,081	3,259	822	758	3,949	110	22	5.0
DeKalb	6,080	4,956	3,887	1,069	953	4,770	155	31	5.1
Dickson	11,140	10,468	8,358	2,110	651	10,074	309	85	5.3
Dyer	13,332	12,696	8,604	4,092	617	12,144	434	118	5.1
Fayette	8,152	7,431	5,299	2,132	709	6,427	604	400	5.1
Fentress	5,606	5,027	3,910	1,117	540	4,721	247	59	5.2

TABLE 6.5-- NUMBER OF HOUSING UNITS, BY TENURE AND VACANCY STATUS AND BY NUMBER OF PERSONS PER ROOM, AND MEDIAN NUMBER OF ROOMS PER HOUSING UNIT, COUNTIES, 1980 (Continued)

			Year-round housing units			Number of occupied housing units by persons per room			Median
County	Total	Total occupied	Owner-occupied	Renter-occupied	Vacant	1.00 or less	1.01-1.50	1.51 or more	number of rooms per housing unit
Franklin	11,583	10,792	8,273	2,519	778	10,336	375	81	5.4
Gibson	19,577	18,202	13,440	4,762	1,312	17,473	555	174	5.2
Giles	9,557	8,825	6,391	2,434	691	8,466	289	70	5.1
Grainger	7,082	5,694	4,658	1,036	779	5,361	264	69	5.0
Greene	21,132	19,157	14,581	4,576	1,904	18,397	628	132	5.2
Grundy	5,137	4,510	3,809	701	378	4,144	273	93	5.0
Hamblen	18,464	17,257	12,478	4,779	1,153	16,615	524	118	5.2
Hamilton	110,319	103,319	66,675	36,644	6,650	99,458	3,171	690	5.2
Hancock	2,686	2,351	1,817	534	323	2,166	133	52	4.9
Hardeman	8,405	7,623	5,510	2,113	731	6,913	475	235	5.1
Hardin	8,947	7,970	6,175	1,795	664	7,583	309	78	5.1
Hawkins	17,016	15,288	11,838	3,450	1,575	14,583	578	127	5.1
Haywood	7,045	6,513	4,336	2,177	499	5,813	464	236	5.1
Henderson	8,297	7,686	6,109	1,577	562	7,381	244	61	5.1
Henry	13,494	10,914	8,326	2,588	1,200	10,583	264	67	5.0
Hickman	5,634	5,094	4,190	904	507	4,837	201	56	5.2
Houston	2,799	2,410	1,892	518	377	2,319	72	19	5.2
Humphreys	6,512	5,634	4,422	1,212	649	5,411	190	33	5.2
Jackson	3,704	3,363	2,696	667	337	3,210	125	28	5.1
Jefferson	12,230	10,623	8,244	2,379	1,215	10,186	370	67	5.1
Johnson	5,385	4,840	3,973	867	487	4,580	205	55	5.2
Knox	125,883	117,951	74,569	43,382	7,826	114,750	2,545	656	5.1
Lake	3,000	2,575	1,415	1,160	312	2,376	143	56	4.8
Lauderdale	9,269	8,281	5,430	2,851	828	7,682	432	167	4.9
Lawrence	12,540	11,867	9,088	2,779	662	11,400	376	91	5.3

TABLE 6.5-- NUMBER OF HOUSING UNITS, BY TENURE AND VACANCY STATUS AND BY NUMBER OF PERSONS PER ROOM, AND MEDIAN NUMBER OF ROOMS PER HOUSING UNIT, COUNTIES, 1980 (Contineud)

			Year-round housing units			Number of occupied housing units by persons per room			Median number of rooms per housing unit
County	Total	Total occupied	Owner-occupied	Renter-occupied	Vacant	1.00 or less	1.01-1.50	1.51 or more	
Lewis	3,249	3,055	2,342	713	180	2,868	136	51	5.1
Lincoln	10,292	9,533	6,930	2,603	730	9,170	294	69	5.3
Loudon	10,835	10,289	8,077	2,212	525	9,924	299	66	5.3
McMinn	15,797	14,727	11,267	3,460	1,047	14,155	474	98	5.2
McNairy	9,016	8,179	6,597	1,582	804	7,886	235	58	5.1
Macon	6,096	5,645	4,589	1,056	433	5,416	182	47	5.1
Madison	28,834	26,713	17,547	9,166	2,100	25,542	850	321	5.2
Marion	9,031	8,270	6,531	1,739	709	7,837	328	105	5.0
Marshall	7,646	7,144	5,111	2,033	483	6,835	246	63	5.2
Maury	19,540	18,180	12,970	5,210	1,337	17,411	596	173	5.2
Meigs	2,996	2,520	2,006	514	290	2,354	122	44	4.9
Monroe	11,002	9,637	7,754	1,883	1,117	9,074	456	107	5.1
Montgomery	29,724	27,198	17,184	10,014	2,510	26,184	793	221	5.2
Moore	1,669	1,534	1,252	282	131	1,465	56	13	5.5
Morgan	5,924	5,389	4,327	1,062	504	5,088	249	52	5.2
Obion	13,059	12,079	8,749	3,330	900	11,654	353	72	5.1
Overton	6,526	6,122	4,916	1,206	383	5,848	222	52	5.0
Perry	2,842	2,240	1,834	406	322	2,134	78	28	4.9
Pickett	1,867	1,542	1,311	231	150	1,464	65	13	5.1
Polk	5,090	4,607	3,694	913	423	4,312	233	62	5.0
Putnam	17,801	16,706	11,325	5,381	1,060	16,248	380	78	5.2
Rhea	9,382	8,285	6,175	2,110	793	7,858	345	82	5.0
Roane	18,732	17,078	13,229	3,849	1,448	16,421	545	112	5.3
Robertson	13,308	12,532	9,202	3,330	732	11,901	498	133	5.2
Rutherford	30,541	28,002	18,591	9,411	2,463	26,868	896	238	5.2

TABLE 6.5-- NUMBER OF HOUSING UNITS, BY TENURE AND VACANCY STATUS AND BY NUMBER OF PERSONS PER ROOM, AND MEDIAN NUMBER OF ROOMS PER HOUSING UNIT, COUNTIES, 1980 (Continued)

			Year-round housing units			Number of occupied housing units by persons per room			Median number of rooms per housing unit
County	Total	Total occupied	Owner-occupied	Renter-occupied	Vacant	1.00 or less	1.01-1.50	1.51 or more	
Scott	6,608	6,200	4,619	1,581	333	5,672	432	96	5.0
Sequatchie	3,162	2,891	2,253	638	234	2,716	140	35	5.0
Sevier	17,504	14,741	11,478	3,263	1,932	14,160	457	124	5.1
Shelby	286,381	269,186	158,171	111,015	16,988	252,764	11,641	4,781	5.2
Smith	6,051	5,392	4,159	1,233	640	5,179	177	36	5.2
Stewart	3,581	3,104	2,606	498	359	2,997	84	23	5.2
Sullivan	54,976	52,022	39,241	12,781	2,790	50,550	1,248	224	5.3
Sumner	30,153	28,557	22,132	6,425	1,550	27,603	799	155	5.5
Tipton	11,574	10,778	7,453	3,325	753	9,993	556	229	5.1
Trousdale	2,496	2,227	1,545	682	254	2,120	83	24	4.9
Unicoi	6,400	5,948	4,719	1,229	413	5,736	177	35	5.2
Union	4,642	3,947	3,162	785	516	3,681	201	65	4.9
Van Buren	1,753	1,590	1,366	224	138	1,498	74	18	5.1
Warren	12,968	11,869	8,887	2,982	1,043	11,492	316	61	5.3
Washington	33,673	31,191	21,369	9,822	2,395	30,167	851	173	5.2
Wayne	5,175	4,792	3,899	893	356	4,553	182	57	5.1
Weakley	12,463	11,567	8,442	3,125	873	11,201	296	70	5.1
White	7,585	6,988	5,674	1,314	570	6,690	247	51	5.2
Williamson	19,719	18,723	15,156	3,567	981	18,089	509	125	6.1
Wilson	20,135	18,863	15,027	3,836	1,181	18,167	565	131	5.5

Note: The difference between the sum of owner-occupied, renter-occupied and vacant year-round housing units and the total number of housing units is the number of vacant seasonal and migratory housing units.

Source: U.S. Department of Commerce, Bureau of the Census, *1980 Census of Housing, General Housing Characteristics, Tennessee.*

TABLE 6.6-- HOUSING UNITS, BY TYPE, POPULATION, AND MEDIAN VALUE, TENNESSEE AND COUNTIES, 1980

County	Population in housing units	Population per household [1]	Type of structure: Single-family	Multi-family: 2 to 9 units	Multi-family: 10 or more units	Mobile home or trailer	Median value of owner-occupied units [2]	Median rent of renter-occupied units [3]
TENNESSEE	4,479,136	2.77	1,373,214	162,858	95,663	105,112	$35,600	$148
Anderson	66,478	2.70	20,914	1,706	1,170	2,039	36,200	151
Bedford	27,568	2.77	9,029	725	226	819	30,400	102
Benton	14,710	2.64	5,231	245	60	955	29,500	102
Bledsoe	8,594	2.88	2,746	108	7	468	21,300	85
Blount	76,718	2.72	24,803	2,200	1,108	2,406	37,500	140
Bradley	66,117	2.87	19,245	2,784	1,019	1,606	35,500	144
Campbell	34,785	2.88	10,541	694	386	1,512	23,300	100
Cannon	10,132	2.80	3,570	131	24	253	28,400	85
Carroll	27,854	2.70	9,702	672	16	898	26,200	90
Carter	49,396	2.76	15,343	1,518	274	1,962	27,400	110
Cheatham	21,498	3.04	6,029	230	74	1,100	36,200	133
Chester	11,587	2.75	3,777	285	20	375	27,600	99
Claiborne	24,173	2.91	7,881	313	21	1,024	30,400	93
Clay	7,607	2.79	2,486	139	4	339	26,200	61
Cocke	28,705	2.83	8,943	680	102	1,535	25,800	89
Coffee	37,854	2.77	12,198	945	522	1,302	35,200	129
Crockett	14,841	2.76	5,037	257	30	305	24,700	69
Cumberland	28,481	2.88	9,327	359	216	858	30,600	110
Davidson	457,691	2.58	129,100	24,224	30,399	3,616	44,900	196
Decatur	10,781	2.64	4,164	204	53	418	27,300	82
DeKalb	13,489	2.72	5,167	259	41	442	26,400	99
Dickson	29,869	2.85	9,319	680	239	881	31,600	125
Dyer	34,429	2.71	11,219	1,207	235	652	26,700	117
Fayette	24,930	3.35	6,880	430	16	814	28,900	60
Fentress	14,788	2.94	4,992	158	9	408	21,000	76

TABLE 6.6-- HOUSING UNITS, BY TYPE, POPULATION, AND MEDIAN VALUE, TENNESSEE AND COUNTIES, 1980 (Continued)

County	Population in housing units	Population per household [1]	Type of structure: Single-family	Multi-family: 2 to 9 units	Multi-family: 10 or more units	Mobile home or trailer	Median value of owner-occupied units [2]	Median rent of renter-occupied units [3]
Franklin	31,015	2.87	10,089	659	89	733	32,300	104
Gibson	48,914	2.69	16,954	1,400	139	1,021	26,300	91
Giles	24,227	2.75	8,038	675	169	634	27,700	102
Grainger	16,606	2.92	5,315	200	19	939	25,900	101
Greene	52,952	2.76	17,377	1,126	245	2,313	30,200	109
Grundy	13,753	3.05	4,103	145	11	629	19,400	75
Hamblen	48,959	2.84	15,093	1,588	462	1,267	33,100	127
Hamilton	279,652	2.71	83,254	14,900	7,566	4,249	37,000	154
Hancock	6,882	2.93	2,398	72	3	201	21,000	53
Hardeman	22,852	3.00	7,177	392	95	690	25,400	73
Hardin	22,106	2.77	7,589	195	21	829	28,200	87
Hawkins	43,688	2.86	13,905	668	426	1,864	32,200	127
Haywood	20,214	3.10	6,227	459	117	209	26,700	68
Henderson	21,209	2.76	6,676	408	3	1,161	27,400	101
Henry	28,386	2.60	9,781	882	114	1,337	29,300	102
Hickman	14,463	2.84	4,854	175	27	545	26,000	106
Houston	6,820	2.83	2,321	111	13	342	25,600	108
Humphreys	15,882	2.82	5,327	283	60	613	31,700	120
Jackson	9,355	2.78	3,201	112	2	385	27,700	63
Jefferson	29,814	2.81	9,546	527	196	1,569	30,400	102
Johnson	13,719	2.83	4,463	156	25	683	25,700	100
Knox	307,939	2.61	94,700	12,217	13,742	5,118	39,900	159
Lake	7,302	2.84	2,501	177	26	183	24,600	55
Lauderdale	23,699	2.86	7,848	648	91	522	25,200	79
Lawrence	33,799	2.85	10,900	701	125	803	30,400	103
Lewis	8,686	2.84	2,638	124	8	465	23,000	84
Lincoln	26,259	2.75	8,885	657	71	650	27,000	87

TABLE 6.6-- HOUSING UNITS, BY TYPE, POPULATION, AND MEDIAN VALUE, TENNESSEE AND COUNTIES, 1980 (Continued)

County	Population in housing units	Population per household [1]	Type of structure: Single-family	Type of structure: Multi-family: 2 to 9 units	Type of structure: Multi-family: 10 or more units	Type of structure: Mobile home or trailer	Median value of owner-occupied units [2]	Median rent of renter-occupied units [3]
Loudon	28,263	2.75	9,142	536	179	957	31,500	103
McMinn	41,453	2.81	13,099	841	463	1,371	30,300	106
McNairy	22,349	2.73	7,938	277	50	718	25,200	79
Macon	15,534	2.75	5,163	295	31	589	27,800	108
Madison	72,363	2.71	22,654	3,798	1,226	1,135	36,200	127
Marion	24,230	2.93	7,142	394	125	1,318	25,800	107
Marshall	19,432	2.72	6,527	531	189	380	26,700	86
Maury	50,438	2.78	15,931	1,799	557	1,230	31,700	121
Meigs	7,427	2.95	2,186	117	20	487	33,500	113
Monroe	28,226	2.93	9,065	465	91	1,133	26,400	102
Montgomery	78,113	2.87	22,244	3,248	1,563	2,653	37,400	175
Moore	4,510	2.94	1,460	47	1	157	33,300	103
Morgan	16,143	3.00	4,821	221	33	818	23,900	91
Obion	32,580	2.70	10,607	1,405	91	876	28,800	103
Overton	17,437	2.85	5,415	376	23	691	24,900	82
Perry	6,063	2.71	2,133	74	0	355	22,300	77
Pickett	4,346	2.82	1,473	50	25	144	24,800	78
Polk	13,577	2.95	4,193	156	14	667	21,000	82
Putnam	44,285	2.65	13,726	1,584	910	1,546	36,900	129
Rhea	23,602	2.85	7,038	713	99	1,228	28,100	123
Roane	48,124	2.82	14,979	1,192	522	1,833	33,100	106
Robertson	36,707	2.93	11,365	888	95	916	35,000	105
Rutherford	79,579	2.84	23,069	2,815	2,342	2,239	42,800	181
Scott	19,167	3.09	5,346	303	7	877	21,800	83
Sequatchie	8,473	2.93	2,448	91	10	576	25,100	118
Sevier	41,145	2.79	13,859	863	251	1,700	37,700	133

TABLE 6.6-- HOUSING UNITS, BY TYPE, POPULATION, AND MEDIAN VALUE, TENNESSEE AND COUNTIES, 1980 (Continued)

County	Population in housing units	Population per household[1]	Type of structure: Single-family	Multi-family: 2 to 9 units	Multi-family: 10 or more units	Mobile home or trailer	Median value of owner-occupied units[2]	Median rent of renter-occupied units[3]
Shelby	756,448	2.81	220,127	43,223	20,047	2,777	38,600	155
Smith	14,865	2.76	5,124	288	28	592	31,200	106
Stewart	8,656	2.79	2,953	87	1	422	25,600	100
Sullivan	142,911	2.75	43,984	4,153	1,756	4,919	36,700	133
Sumner	85,246	2.99	24,863	1,819	1,182	2,243	46,800	193
Tipton	32,779	3.04	9,820	589	47	1,075	34,100	104
Trousdale	6,085	2.73	1,889	151	91	350	30,100	149
Unicoi	16,288	2.74	5,309	299	103	650	30,600	108
Union	11,701	2.96	3,699	153	14	597	27,400	104
Van Buren	4,715	2.97	1,517	53	1	157	25,000	72
Warren	32,508	2.74	10,757	896	426	833	28,700	120
Washington	84,554	2.71	25,787	3,377	1,882	2,540	37,300	148
Wayne	13,788	2.88	4,520	190	19	419	22,800	79
Weakley	30,116	2.60	10,301	982	289	868	27,100	112
White	19,443	2.78	6,633	278	51	596	28,900	90
Williamson	57,691	3.08	17,217	1,004	451	1,032	71,800	161
Wilson	55,504	2.94	16,888	1,427	222	1,507	48,000	155

1. Population per household equals population per occupied housing unit.
2. Value data are limited to owner-occupied and vacant for-sale one-family houses on fewer than ten acres, without a commercial establishment or medical office on the property. Mobile homes, boats, trailers, and owner-occupied non-condominium units in multi-family buildings are excluded.
3. Contract rent data are tabulated for specified renter-occupied and specified vacant for-rent housing units, and exclude one-family houses on ten acres or more.

Source: U.S. Department of Commerce, Bureau of the Census, *1980 Census of Housing, General Housing Characteristics, Tennessee.*

FIGURE 6.2
Median Value of Owner-Occupied Housing Units, by County, 1980

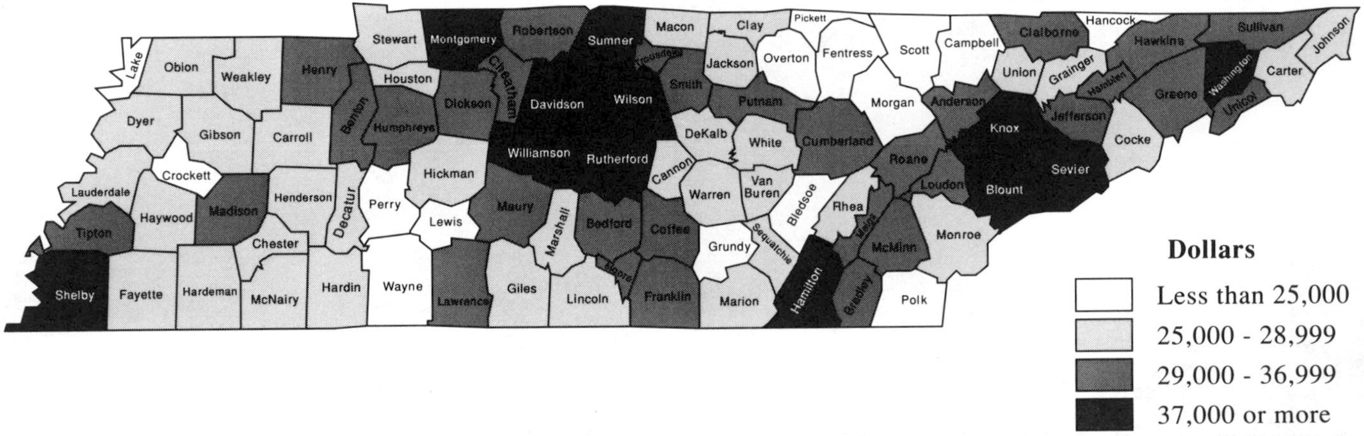

Source: U.S. Department of Commerce, Bureau of the Census, *Census of Housing, 1980*. General Housing Characteristics, Tennessee.

TABLE 6.7-- ESTIMATED HOUSING UNITS, 1988, AND PROJECTED HOUSING NEEDS, 1989 AND 2000, TENNESSEE AND COUNTIES

Counties	Estimated existing housing units 1988	Projected housing units needed 1989	Projected deficit (excess) 1989	Projected housing units needed 2000	Annual construction needed 1990–2000
TENNESSEE	1,929,565	2,083,068	153,589	2,497,850	51,437
Anderson	28,378	30,307	1,929	37,551	834
Bedford	11,755	12,360	605	13,351	145
Benton	6,809	7,014	205	7,841	94
Bledsoe	3,980	4,133	153	5,541	142
Blount	33,139	35,418	2,279	44,641	1,046
Bradley	27,793	30,770	2,977	38,020	930
Campbell	14,116	15,770	1,654	21,717	691
Cannon	4,203	4,510	307	5,199	90
Carroll	11,629	12,806	1,177	13,615	180
Carter	20,505	21,894	1,389	26,759	568
Cheatham	9,046	10,171	1,125	13,621	416
Chester	5,170	5,938	813	7,354	198
Claiborne	10,534	10,627	93	13,825	299
Clay	3,648	3,254	-394	3,941	27
Cocke	12,837	12,169	-668	14,825	181
Coffee	16,170	17,262	1,092	20,335	379
Crockett	5,887	6,400	513	6,932	95
Cumberland	13,267	12,773	-494	17,709	404
Davidson	222,670	227,853	5,183	263,648	3,724
Decatur	5,055	5,000	-55	5,703	59
DeKalb	6,194	6,258	64	7,406	110
Dickson	12,140	13,801	1,661	16,831	426
Dyer	13,711	15,912	2,201	17,849	376
Fayette	9,232	9,326	94	12,647	310
Fentress	6,252	6,103	-149	8,521	206
Franklin	12,747	13,653	906	16,221	316
Gibson	19,713	21,945	2,232	22,655	267
Giles	10,261	11,125	864	12,832	234
Grainger	7,423	7,127	-296	8,769	122
Greene	22,952	23,871	919	27,636	425
Grundy	5,793	5,798	-5	7,530	156
Hamblen	19,615	22,061	2,446	26,722	646
Hamilton	120,422	132,371	11,949	151,675	2,841
Hancock	3,057	2,737	-320	3,336	25
Hardeman	8,896	9,781	885	11,837	267
Hardin	9,289	9,954	665	12,086	254
Hawkins	17,819	19,218	1,399	24,562	613
Haywood	7,404	7,972	568	10,136	248
Henderson	8,638	9,767	1,129	11,755	283
Henry	12,689	13,896	1,207	15,629	267
Hickman	5,801	6,695	894	7,948	195
Houston	2,988	2,923	-65	3,260	25
Humphreys	6,657	7,098	441	8,173	138
Jackson	4,150	4,001	-149	4,699	50
Jefferson	13,223	13,965	742	16,598	307
Johnson	6,057	5,954	-103	7,411	123
Knox	134,456	150,530	16,074	176,887	3,857
Lake	2,940	3,035	95	3,324	35

TABLE 6.7-- ESTIMATED HOUSING UNITS, 1988, AND PROJECTED HOUSING NEEDS, 1989 AND 2000, TENNESSEE AND COUNTIES (Continued)

Counties	Estimated existing housing units 1988	Projected housing units needed 1989	Projected deficit (excess) 1989	Projected housing units needed 2000	Annual construction needed 1990–2000
Lauderdale	9,297	11,051	1,772	13,919	420
Lawrence	13,586	14,720	1,134	17,574	362
Lewis	3,700	4,757	1,057	6,564	260
Lincoln	11,261	11,603	342	13,053	163
Loudon	11,943	12,796	853	15,415	316
Macon	6,481	7,354	873	9,076	236
Madison	31,776	34,640	2,864	40,086	755
McMinn	17,030	18,356	1,326	21,370	394
McNairy	9,808	10,545	737	13,054	295
Marion	10,632	10,241	-391	12,861	203
Marshall	8,402	8,895	493	10,001	145
Maury	21,630	23,290	1,660	27,274	513
Meigs	3,612	3,267	-345	4,684	97
Monroe	11,017	12,172	1,155	15,604	417
Montgomery	34,817	39,869	5,052	53,622	1,710
Moore	1,926	2,000	74	2,353	30
Morgan	6,473	6,944	471	9,283	255
Obion	13,287	14,916	1,629	15,693	219
Overton	7,206	7,563	357	9,326	193
Perry	3,142	2,768	-374	3,296	14
Pickett	1,872	1,982	110	2,652	71
Polk	5,701	5,650	-51	6,894	108
Putnam	20,365	23,327	2,962	30,244	898
Rhea	10,476	11,232	756	15,000	411
Roane	18,607	21,302	2,695	26,679	734
Robertson	14,908	16,291	1,383	21,340	585
Rutherford	41,352	40,068	-1,284	52,760	1,037
Scott	7,296	7,962	666	11,253	351
Sequatchie	3,888	3,724	-164	4,958	97
Sevier	20,860	19,791	-1,069	26,935	552
Shelby	311,586	347,250	35,664	402,093	8,228
Smith	6,320	6,751	431	7,382	96
Stewart	3,795	3,713	-82	4,253	42
Sullivan	56,663	62,651	5,988	73,060	1,491
Sumner	37,355	40,426	3,071	50,872	1,229
Tipton	12,744	13,473	729	16,911	379
Trousdale	2,612	2,958	346	3,632	93
Unicoi	6,840	6,954	115	8,099	114
Union	5,014	5,104	90	6,787	161
Van Buren	1,877	2,057	170	2,878	90
Warren	13,405	14,934	1,529	17,700	390
Washington	35,715	40,472	4,757	49,483	1,252
Wayne	5,814	5,781	-33	6,868	96
Weakley	12,838	15,527	2,689	16,555	338
White	7,930	8,599	669	9,858	175
Williamson	25,185	27,374	2,189	38,536	1,214
Wilson	24,401	26,685	2,284	32,994	781

Source: Tennessee Housing Development Agency, *Report on the Need for Housing in Tennessee, 1989: The Need for Housing Based on Changes in the Population.*

TABLE 6.8-- NUMBER OF HOUSING UNITS, BY TENURE AND VACANCY STATUS AND BY NUMBER OF PERSONS PER ROOM, AND MEDIAN NUMBER OF ROOMS PER HOUSING UNIT, TENNESSEE, METROPOLITAN STATISTICAL AREAS, AND INCORPORATED MUNICIPALITIES WITH 10,000 OR MORE INHABITANTS, 1980

MSA or municipality	Year-round housing units					Number of occupied housing units by persons per room			Median number of rooms per housing unit
	Total	Total occupied	Owner-occupied	Renter-occupied	Vacant	1.00 or less	1.01-1.50	1.51 or more	
TENNESSEE	1,747,422	1,618,505	1,110,074	508,431	118,342	1,547,761	54,539	16,205	5.2
Metropolitan Statistical Areas:									
Chattanooga	161,124	150,760	104,097	46,663	9,855	144,680	4,990	1,090	5.2
Clarksville-Hopkinsville	50,919	46,844	28,373	18,471	4,039	44,796	1,553	495	5.2
Johnson City-Kingsport-Bristol	166,786	154,169	115,199	38,970	11,684	148,754	4,522	893	5.2
Knoxville	187,210	174,691	116,510	58,181	11,895	169,481	4,197	1,013	5.2
Memphis	332,079	311,996	188,191	123,805	19,385	292,066	13,973	5,957	5.3
Nashville-Davidson	319,907	301,945	196,470	105,475	17,530	291,005	8,495	2,445	5.3
Municipalities with 10,000 or more inhabitants:									
Athens	4,784	4,445	2,914	1,531	338	4,318	106	21	5.2
Bartlett	5,369	5,110	4,641	469	259	5,071	33	6	6.5
Bristol	9,878	9,305	6,254	3,051	567	9,058	205	42	5.2
Chattanooga	66,630	62,139	34,920	27,219	4,444	59,265	2,320	554	5.0
Clarksville	19,412	17,817	9,527	8,290	1,590	17,187	496	134	5.1
Cleveland	10,605	9,946	5,630	4,316	656	9,587	284	75	5.0
Columbia	10,224	9,666	6,452	3,214	551	9,310	268	88	5.3
Cookeville	7,583	7,087	3,663	3,424	490	6,934	122	31	5.0
Dyersburg	6,423	6,089	3,672	2,417	329	5,844	177	68	5.0
East Ridge	8,613	8,377	5,776	2,601	234	8,276	90	11	5.4
Elizabethton	5,081	4,763	3,283	1,480	315	4,639	111	13	5.2
Franklin	4,558	4,351	2,564	1,787	207	4,114	183	54	5.0
Gallatin	6,588	6,107	4,028	2,079	480	5,862	192	53	5.7
Germantown	6,811	6,209	5,346	863	590	6,190	17	2	7.9
Greeneville	5,783	5,447	3,530	1,917	325	5,296	128	23	5.2

TABLE 6.8-- NUMBER OF HOUSING UNITS, BY TENURE AND VACANCY STATUS AND BY NUMBER OF PERSONS PER ROOM, AND MEDIAN NUMBER OF ROOMS PER HOUSING UNIT, TENNESSEE, METROPOLITAN STATISTICAL AREAS, AND INCORPORATED MUNICIPALITIES WITH 10,000 OR MORE INHABITANTS, 1980 (Continued)

			Year-round housing units			Number of occupied housing units by persons per room			Median number of rooms per housing unit
MSA or municipality	Total	Total occupied	Owner-occupied	Renter-occupied	Vacant	1.00 or less	1.01-1.50	1.51 or more	
Hendersonville	8,741	8,406	6,705	1,701	329	8,266	126	14	6.1
Humboldt	3,855	3,676	2,470	1,206	178	3,476	137	63	5.1
Jackson	19,383	18,132	10,676	7,456	1,241	17,372	537	223	5.2
Johnson City	15,032	14,031	8,171	5,860	989	13,587	369	75	5.1
Kingsport	13,289	12,665	8,046	4,619	618	12,378	243	44	5.2
Knoxville	73,263	68,574	35,075	33,499	4,659	66,504	1,578	492	4.8
Lawrenceburg	4,094	3,929	2,648	1,281	165	3,829	86	14	5.3
Lebanon	4,598	4,334	2,482	1,852	262	4,126	169	39	5.0
McMinnville	4,525	4,244	2,672	1,572	278	4,129	92	23	5.2
Maryville	7,156	6,685	4,241	2,444	467	6,537	123	25	5.3
Memphis	244,470	230,474	129,662	100,812	13,841	215,219	10,777	4,478	5.3
Millington	4,044	3,732	1,207	2,525	310	3,562	131	39	4.9
Morristown	7,838	7,376	4,427	2,949	455	7,091	229	56	4.9
Murfreesboro	12,435	11,517	5,870	5,647	916	11,123	277	117	5.1
Nashville-Davidson	179,129	169,674	95,640	74,034	9,367	163,615	4,563	1,496	5.1
Oak Ridge	11,487	11,021	7,082	3,939	466	10,835	150	36	5.3
Paris	4,699	4,397	2,869	1,528	298	4,271	99	27	5.0
Red Bank	5,594	5,611	3,113	2,498	342	5,536	68	7	4.9
Shelbyville	5,409	5,031	3,195	1,836	373	4,827	176	28	5.1
Springfield	3,934	3,792	2,201	1,591	140	3,527	199	66	5.0
Tullahoma	6,236	5,787	3,857	1,930	442	5,623	133	31	5.5
Union City	4,276	4,027	2,439	1,588	246	3,904	100	23	5.1

Note: The difference between the sum of owner-occupied, renter-occupied and vacant year-round units and the total number of housing units is the number of vacant seasonal and migratory housing units.

Source: U.S. Department of Commerce, Bureau of the Census, *1980 Census of Housing, General Housing Characteristics, Tennessee.*

TABLE 6.9-- HOUSING UNITS, BY TYPE, POPULATION, AND MEDIAN VALUE, TENNESSEE, METROPOLITAN STATISTICAL AREAS AND INCORPORATED MUNICIPALITIES WITH 10,000 OR MORE INHABITANTS, 1980

MSA or municipality	Population in housing units	Population per household[1]	Type of structure: Single-family	Multi-family: 2 to 9 units	Multi-family: 10 or more units	Mobile home or trailer	Median value of owner-occupied units[2]	Median rent of renter-occupied units[3]
TENNESSEE	4,479,136	2.77	1,373,214	162,858	95,663	105,112	$35,600	$148
Metropolitan Statistical Areas:								
Clarksville-Hopkinsville	136,010	2.90	37,083	7,065	2,234	4,501	35,400	171
Chattanooga	417,346	2.77	123,825	17,823	8,294	10,673	34,300	150
Johnson City-Kingsport-Bristol	425,703	2.76	133,045	12,240	5,344	15,224	34,200	129
Knoxville	462,836	2.65	144,116	16,276	16,034	10,160	38,700	156
Memphis	892,232	2.86	257,440	46,365	20,973	6,603	38,100	153
Nashville-Davidson	823,785	2.73	237,850	33,087	35,004	13,534	44,800	187
Municipalities:								
Athens	11,738	2.64	3,847	434	394	108	29,600	107
Bartlett	16,922	3.31	5,202	157	6	4	58,100	230
Bristol	23,589	2.54	7,512	1,311	479	570	32,700	139
Chattanooga	163,390	2.63	48,429	11,223	5,795	1,136	33,300	139
Clarksville	50,068	2.81	13,536	2,852	1,524	1,495	38,300	179
Cleveland	26,961	2.61	7,621	1,981	745	255	36,400	141
Columbia	25,793	2.67	7,946	1,370	466	435	33,100	125
Cookeville	17,262	2.44	5,151	1,184	839	403	42,600	141
Dyersburg	15,622	2.57	5,096	917	223	182	27,300	125
East Ridge	21,079	2.52	6,920	1,049	568	74	35,500	216
Elizabethton	12,161	2.55	3,932	756	187	203	27,900	101
Franklin	12,107	2.78	3,388	525	388	257	41,700	164
Gallatin	16,771	2.75	5,041	742	394	410	39,000	154
Germantown	20,459	3.30	6,405	323	69	2	92,400	317
Greeneville	13,743	2.52	4,680	729	197	166	32,700	109
Hendersonville	26,530	3.16	7,449	418	714	154	53,900	238
Humboldt	10,084	2.74	3,297	341	46	170	25,400	95

TABLE 6.9-- HOUSING UNITS, BY TYPE, POPULATION, AND MEDIAN VALUE, TENNESSEE, METROPOLITAN STATISTICAL AREAS AND INCORPORATED MUNICIPALITIES WITH 10,000 OR MORE INHABITANTS, 1980 (Continued)

MSA or municipality	Population in housing units	Population per household[1]	Type of structure: Single-family	Type of structure: Multi-family 2 to 9 units	Type of structure: Multi-family 10 or more units	Type of structure: Mobile home or trailer	Median value of owner-occupied units[2]	Median rent of renter-occupied units[3]
Jackson	47,032	2.59	14,316	3,507	1,201	349	35,900	128
Johnson City	35,766	2.55	11,048	2,295	1,216	461	36,400	133
Kingsport	31,694	2.50	10,451	1,506	1,171	155	36,100	132
Knoxville	164,246	2.40	50,557	9,621	12,349	706	32,600	156
Lawrenceburg	9,988	2.54	3,407	445	114	128	33,100	111
Lebanon	11,356	2.62	3,550	789	157	100	33,700	143
McMinnville	10,547	2.49	3,583	595	298	46	26,900	103
Maryville	16,566	2.48	5,384	1,040	577	151	40,300	130
Memphis	635,259	2.76	182,742	40,420	19,556	1,597	35,200	152
Millington	11,664	3.13	2,848	643	263	288	40,000	160
Morristown	19,342	2.62	6,124	1,039	415	253	26,500	123
Murfreesboro	29,276	2.54	8,324	1,776	2,008	325	44,800	185
Nashville-Davidson	435,645	2.57	121,970	23,617	29,999	3,455	43,800	195
Oak Ridge	27,514	2.50	9,339	1,108	1,031	9	42,100	164
Paris	10,573	2.40	3,679	663	68	285	28,300	99
Red Bank	13,124	2.34	4,030	928	949	46	34,500	189
Shelbyville	13,208	2.63	4,278	546	206	374	30,600	102
Springfield	10,588	2.79	3,234	508	61	129	31,200	95
Tullahoma	15,530	2.68	5,118	460	424	227	37,100	124
Union City	10,283	2.55	3,119	970	52	132	32,600	120

1. Population per household equals population per-occupied housing unit.

2. Value data are limited to owner-occupied and vacant for-sale one-family houses on fewer than ten acres, without a commercial establishment or medical office on the property. Mobile homes, boats, trailers, and owner-occupied noncondominium units in multi-family buildings are excluded.

3. Contract rent data are tabulated for specified renter-occupied and specified vacant for-rent housing units, and exclude one-family houses on ten acres or more.

Source: U.S. Department of Commerce, Bureau of the Census, *1980 Census of Housing, General Housing Characteristics, Tennessee.*

TABLE 6.10--NUMBER OF NEW HOUSING UNITS AUTHORIZED BY BUILDING PERMITS, SELECTED CITIES, TENNESSEE, 1960–1987, SELECTED YEARS

Year	Chattanooga	Clarksville	Jackson	Johnson City	Kingsport	Knoxville	Memphis	Nashville-Davidson County [1]	Oak Ridge
1987	1,228	971	263	192	136	971	n.a.	3,557	111
1986	1,327	917	412	253	172	418	n.a.	8,127	40
1985	1,910	769	351	170	110	510	n.a.	10,095	177
1984	581	717	346	139	592	179	n.a.	12,422	148
1983	995	914	351	222	275	484	932	6,698	169
1982	423	741	109	294	198	1,048	432	2,284	178
1981	297	157	214	97	98	646	564	1,333	136
1980	1,064	553	344	210	393	1,149	1,324	1,892	116
1979	632	494	416	219	250	1,024	1,367	3,253	122
1978	634[a]	565	497	245	316	1,957	1,565	3,532	137
1977	893	641	315	295	82	929	2,381	5,133	244
1976	1,140	876	128	101	94	928	577	3,505	158
1975	906	417	127	118	72	373	1,000	1,900	182
1974	711	400	266	285	159	536	869	4,425	120
1973	1,878	1,211	246	247	840	2,796	6,609	6,001	331
1972	940	1,042	257	307	260	2,730	9,451	8,165	88
1971	878	483	632	186	163	2,313	7,249	6,867	110
1970	1,016	258	522	124[a]	178[a]	1,413	4,458	3,655	92
1969	355	127	294	304	99	1,071	3,641	5,006	206
1968	749	358	277	406	266	2,120	4,047	6,418	156
1967	229	294	200	190	92	1,962	3,809	4,871	143
1966	189	189	246	142	256	1,220	3,952	3,979	111
1965	229	258	199	200	112	1,911	4,605	4,224	126
1964	621	242	402	197	117	1,201	2,917	4,751	165
1960	785	207	66	151	87	303	2,266	3,039	269

Note: Data include both private and public new housing units.

n.a. not available.

1. Permit system covers entire unincorporated area of the county and Nashville city.

a. Data shown are for 11 months.

Source: U.S. Department of Commerce, Bureau of the Census, *Construction Reports, Housing Units Authorized by Building Permits and Public Contracts*, 1987, and earlier editions.

TABLE 6.11--NUMBER OF HOUSING UNITS, BY VALUE, TENNESSEE AND METROPOLITAN STATISTICAL AREAS, 1980

		Metropolitan Statistical Area					
	TENNESSEE	Chattanooga	Clarksville-Hopkinsville	Kingsport-Bristol-Johnson City	Knoxville	Memphis	Nashville
Value of owner-occupied and vacant-for-sale housing units[1]							
Less than $10,000	49,536	4,928	1,222	5,063	4,912	5,200	4,051
$10,000 - $14,999	51,201	5,126	1,175	5,840	5,237	7,082	4,844
$15,000 - $19,999	65,806	6,990	1,578	7,512	6,153	11,714	6,906
$20,000 - $24,999	79,442	8,411	1,933	8,817	8,069	14,686	9,285
$25,000 - $29,999	80,427	8,444	2,148	8,302	7,939	16,348	10,994
$30,000 - $34,999	83,507	9,032	2,723	8,681	9,120	17,210	13,138
$35,000 - $39,999	73,708	8,037	2,685	7,452	8,225	15,471	13,592
$40,000 - $49,999	120,014	12,008	3,899	11,958	14,251	24,491	26,438
$50,000 - $59,999	81,922	7,444	1,920	8,104	10,894	17,273	20,023
$60,000 - $79,999	90,342	8,098	1,719	8,917	12,621	19,242	23,645
$80,000 - $99,999	31,941	2,548	525	2,739	4,058	7,859	9,745
$100,000 or more	30,966	2,515	433	2,454	3,902	7,937	9,933
Median value, owner-occupied	$35,600	$34,300	$35,400	$34,200	$38,700	$38,100	$44,800
Median price asked, vacant-for-sale	$40,900	$40,300	$35,500	$39,800	$48,700	$51,000	$48,000

1. The value data are limited to owner-occupied and vacant for-sale one-family houses on fewer than ten acres, without a commercial establishment or medical office on the property. All condominiums, owner-occupied noncondominiums in multi- family buildings, mobile homes, boats, and trailers are excluded.

Source: U.S. Department of Commerce, Bureau of the Census, *1980 Census of Housing, General Housing Characteristics, Tennessee.*

TABLE 6.12--NUMBER OF HOUSING UNITS, BY CONTRACT RENT, TENNESSEE AND METROPOLITAN STATISTICAL AREAS, 1980

	TENNESSEE	Metropolitan Statistical Area					
		Chattanooga	Clarksville-Hopkinsville	Kingsport-Bristol-Johnson City	Knoxville	Memphis	Nashville
Monthly contract rent of renter-occupied and vacant-for-rent housing units [1]							
Less than $50	38,204	2,690	810	2,855	3,455	9,268	5,050
$ 50 - $ 59	23,582	1,972	515	1,727	2,393	6,160	3,383
$ 60 - $ 79	42,351	3,563	833	3,203	3,902	12,203	5,418
$ 80 - $ 99	32,754	3,171	679	2,476	3,036	10,102	4,313
$100 - $119	40,417	4,693	1,124	3,833	4,641	7,705	6,029
$120 - $149	56,846	6,200	1,907	5,773	7,689	11,907	9,459
$150 - $169	50,784	5,341	2,545	4,546	6,914	13,119	9,277
$170 - $199	51,340	4,748	3,233	3,536	7,019	15,608	11,875
$200 - $249	69,996	6,641	3,504	3,452	9,124	19,010	23,000
$250 or more	59,159	6,164	1,609	2,329	7,856	15,264	23,215
No cash rent	33,046	2,941	2,110	3,571	3,523	4,182	4,319
Median rent, renter-occupied	$148	$150	$171	$129	$156	$153	$187
Median rent asked, vacant-for-rent	$156	$159	$161	$140	$170	$167	$208

1. The contract rent data exclude one-family houses on ten acres or more.

Source: U.S. Department of Commerce, Bureau of the Census, *1980 Census of Housing, General Housing Characteristics, Tennessee.*

TABLE 6.13--NUMBER OF CONTRACT CONSTRUCTION EMPLOYEES, TENNESSEE AND METROPOLITAN STATISTICAL AREAS, 1970–1988, SELECTED YEARS
[In thousands of persons]

		Metropolitan Statistical Area						
Year	TENNESSEE	Chattanooga	Clarksville-Hopkinsville[1]	Jackson	Kingsport-Bristol-Johnson City	Knoxville[2]	Memphis[3]	Nashville-Davidson
1988	94.4	8.3	1.4	2.0	7.0	12.9	18.3	27.1
1987	95.2[r]	7.9[r]	1.4	1.8	6.7[r]	12.4[r]	19.1[r]	28.9[r]
1986	90.0	7.5	1.0	1.5	5.9	11.9	18.5	28.2
1985	85.6	7.5	0.7	1.5	6.2	11.1	18.1	25.7
1984	78.3	6.6	0.6	1.4	5.6	10.9	16.3	22.8
1983	69.6	5.7	0.6	1.2	5.7	9.8	13.9	19.3
1982	72.2	5.6	0.6	1.2	6.9	9.5	12.4	18.3
1981	76.2	6.0	0.8	1.3	6.7	9.7	14.4	17.5
1980	81.2	6.5	0.8	1.7	7.0	9.5	15.9	18.7
1979	89.2	6.7	0.9	1.9	7.8	12.1	16.6	20.7
1978	87.3	7.3	1.0	1.8	7.0	12.2	15.6	20.2
1977	78.4	6.1	1.0	1.9	6.2	11.1	14.4	18.1
1976	75.2	6.1	1.0	2.0	6.6	9.7	15.0	17.0
1975	76.0	6.0	0.9	n.a.	7.1	9.9	16.1	17.6
1970	65.3	6.6	n.a.	n.a.	n.a.	7.6	14.0	15.1

Note: Data are revised to reflect the changes in *The Standard Industrial Classification Manual* in 1972, and the Metropolitan Statistical Area geographic boundaries through 1983. Data are comparable across all years for each MSA, with the exception of Knoxville (see footnote 2).

n.a. not available.

r revised.

1. Includes Montgomery County only.

2. Data for 1970–1982 are comparable. Beginning in 1983 Grainger, Jefferson, and Sevier counties have been added to the Knoxville MSA.

3. Includes Shelby and Tipton Counties in Tennessee and Crittenden County, Arkansas.

Source: Tennessee Department of Employment Security, *Annual Averages, Tennessee Labor Force Estimates, 1984–1988*, and earlier editions; and *Tennessee and Standard Metropolitan Statistical Areas, Employment Estimates, Revised Historical Series, 1972–1977*; U.S. Department of Labor, Bureau of Labor Statistics, *Employment and Earnings, States and Areas, 1939–1978*; and direct correspondence.

TABLE 6.14--ESTIMATED CONSTRUCTION CONTRACT VALUATIONS, SOUTHEASTERN STATES, 1983–1987 [In thousands of dollars]

	1987		1986		1985		1984		1983	
State	Residential	Nonresidential	Residential	Nonresidential	Residential	Nonresidential	Residential	Nonresidential	Residential	Nonresidential
TENNESSEE	2,407,000	1,960,000	2,423,080	1,435,908	2,383,811	1,385,569	2,160,211	1,407,044	1,816,036	1,126,154
Alabama	1,358,000	1,030,000	1,453,228	990,743	1,247,506	1,068,943	1,238,669	919,983	1,286,524	1,024,800
Arkansas	670,000	406,000	738,762	423,062	783,151	453,344	915,127	454,199	898,398	358,821
Florida	11,174,000	5,443,000	10,852,029	5,290,485	10,329,715	5,576,924	10,032,241	5,170,753	8,604,123	4,355,216
Georgia	4,787,000	2,851,000	4,865,262	2,764,715	3,988,135	2,674,822	3,690,916	2,128,998	3,314,279	1,756,543
Kentucky	1,354,000	1,225,000	1,306,938	1,098,649	1,157,428	986,149	1,240,567	711,596	1,233,448	750,805
Louisiana	1,049,000	1,017,000	1,092,225	1,100,262	1,414,749	1,394,675	1,856,831	1,462,061	1,895,400	1,330,971
Mississippi	604,000	647,000	697,773	495,118	698,191	472,265	858,110	406,099	838,485	342,008
North Carolina	3,756,000	2,621,000	3,900,892	2,165,558	3,822,114	2,205,805	3,213,123	1,666,121	2,879,661	1,418,776
South Carolina	1,796,000	1,270,000	1,743,533	1,027,432	1,863,605	1,000,595	1,776,169	753,655	1,538,935	787,678
Virginia	4,513,000	3,071,000	4,546,955	3,034,646	3,845,121	2,642,256	3,279,091	2,286,131	2,813,677	1,632,490
West Virginia	227,000	318,000	238,153	310,115	209,813	291,915	255,944	202,923	286,358	176,444

Note: Represents value of construction in states in which work was done. Includes new structures, additions to existing structures, and major alterations. Excludes nonbuilding construction.

Source: Data for 1987 are from the *Statistical Abstract of the United States, 1989*; original source is F. W. Dodge, proprietary data reprinted by special permission. Reproduction or dissemination of this information is granted only by contract or prior written permission from F.W. Dodge, McGraw-Hill, Inc., 24 Hartwell Avenue, Lexington, MA 02173, (617) 863-5100.

TABLE 6.15--HOUSING PRICE INDEX AND MEDIAN AND AVERAGE SALES PRICES OF NEW ONE-FAMILY HOMES IN THE SOUTH, 1963–1988

	Median sales price	Average sales price	Housing price index (1982 = 100)
1988	$92,000[p]	$114,400[p]	108.8
1987	88,000	106,600[r]	109.6
1986	80,200	95,300	109.2
1985	75,000	88,900	109.0
1984	72,000	86,000	105.7
1983	70,900	83,000	102.6
1982	66,100	78,300	100.0
1981	64,400	75,600	95.5
1980	59,600	69,100	86.8
1979	57,300	63,800	77.6
1978	50,300	55,600	68.4
1977	44,100	48,100	60.8
1976	40,500	43,800	55.5
1975	37,300	39,600	51.7
1974	34,500	36,800	47.1
1973	30,900	33,200	42.8
1972	25,800	28,500	40.1
1971	22,500	25,900	37.7
1970	20,300	24,000	35.1
1969	22,800	25,300	33.9
1968	21,500	23,600	32.1
1967	19,400	21,100	30.8
1966	18,200	20,200	30.4
1965	17,500	18,900	28.9
1964	16,700	18,100	28.8
1963	16,100	16,800	28.0

Note: Median and average sales prices are collected from a sample of all new one-family house sales and include the value of land. The price index presented here is intended to reflect the changing cost of a typical house sold in the base weighting period of 1982 and is calculated from a sample of houses with similar characteristics with respect to lot size, square footage, presence of a garage, and seven other characteristics.

p preliminary.

r revised.

Source: U.S. Department of Commerce and U.S. Department of Housing and Urban Development, *Construction Reports, Price Index of New One-Family Houses Sold*, Fourth Quarter 1988; and *New One-Family Houses Sold and for Sale*, December 1988; and U.S. Department of Commerce, Bureau of Industrial Economics, Construction and Building Products Division, *Construction Review*, Vol. 29, No. 4.

TABLE 6.16--MORTGAGE LOANS HELD BY INSURED SAVINGS ASSOCIATIONS, SOUTHEASTERN STATES, 1986 [In thousands of dollars]

State	Total loans[1]	Conventional: Amount	Conventional: Percentage of total	VA-guaranteed and FHA-HD insured: Amount	VA-guaranteed and FHA-HD insured: Percentage of total
TENNESSEE	6,543,754	6,288,238	96.1	192,008	2.9
Alabama	5,073,598	4,668,710	92.0	341,558	6.7
Arkansas	4,492,528	4,261,026	94.8	137,198	3.1
Florida	48,151,873	46,002,018	95.5	1,590,034	3.3
Georgia	9,983,810	9,717,812	97.3	140,482	1.4
Kentucky	4,440,633	4,307,151	97.0	90,357	2.0
Louisiana	10,264,700	9,869,634	96.2	248,415	2.4
Mississippi	2,433,746	2,152,696	88.5	240,599	9.9
North Carolina	13,317,066	12,995,516	97.6	218,237	1.6
South Carolina	6,867,272	6,701,984	97.6	96,242	1.4
Virginia	15,045,724	14,213,648	94.5	651,486	4.3
West Virginia	1,329,951	1,275,453	95.9	39,830	3.0

Note: Percentages were computed by the Center for Business and Economic Research.

1. Total includes advances for taxes, insurance, and accrued interest, not shown separately.

Source: Federal Home Loan Bank Board, *Combined Financial Statements FSLIC-Insured Savings and Loan Associations*, 1986.

TABLE 6.17--MORTGAGE LOANS MADE BY INSURED SAVINGS ASSOCIATIONS, BY PURPOSE, SOUTHEASTERN STATES, 1987 [In millions of dollars]

State	Total loans closed[1]	Construction: Residential	Construction: Non-residential	Permanent[2]: Residential	Permanent[2]: Non-residential	Permanent[2]: Land	Refinancing loans[3]
TENNESSEE	2,028	421	91	1,282	145	91	465
Alabama	1,690	256	46	1,295	80	14	249
Arkansas	793	73	14	617	71	17	258
Florida	12,797	2,857	678	7,397	1,264	602	2,351
Georgia	5,378	1,066	208	3,544	392	168	1,067
Kentucky	1,618	141	30	1,345	93	10	368
Louisiana	2,281	98	21	1,469	395	298	417
Mississippi	1,167	183	14	844	94	32	296
North Carolina	5,202	1,088	323	3,305	343	145	1,128
South Carolina	2,433	485	93	1,546	241	68	609
Virginia	7,890	1,056	608	5,334	590	302	1,644
West Virginia	384	18	5	345	13	3	88

Note: All activity reported on a gross basis (i.e., the entire amount of the loan) including refinancing.

1. Detail may not add to total due to independent rounding.

2. Loans and contracts to finance the acquisition of property where construction has been completed, farm land, developed building lots and vacant land.

3. Included in construction and permanent categories.

Source: Federal Home Loan Bank Board, *Savings and Home Financing Source Book*, 1987.

TABLE 6.18--NUMBER AND AVERAGE SALES PRICE OF NEW MOBILE HOMES PLACED FOR RESIDENTIAL USE, SOUTHEASTERN STATES, 1987 AND 1988
[Number in thousands]

	1988						1987					
	Total		Single-wide		Double-wide		Total		Single-wide		Double-wide	
State	Number	Price	Number	Price	Number	Price	Number	Price	Number	Price	Number	Price
TENNESSEE	9.2	$20,100	6.7	$16,600	2.5	$29,200	9.0	$19,500	6.4	$15,400	2.6	$29,600
Alabama	11.9	20,200	8.8	17,100	3.1	29,000	11.2	18,800	9.1	16,800	2.1	27,400
Arkansas	4.0	19,800	3.2	17,800	0.8	27,800	5.4	19,600	4.5	17,800	0.9	29,000
Florida	23.3	27,800	8.2	16,000	15.0	34,500	25.6	26,600	9.5	17,100	16.0	32,800
Georgia	14.7	20,800	8.2	15,400	6.5	27,700	15.2	19,900	8.8	15,300	6.4	26,100
Kentucky	5.8	18,700	4.6	16,500	1.1	27,300	5.4	19,500	4.0	16,100	1.4	29,300
Louisiana	1.7	21,500	1.5	20,100	0.2	30,000	3.0	19,000	2.8	18,000	0.3	29,400
Mississippi	4.4	18,400	3.5	15,900	0.9	27,700	5.0	19,400	3.8	16,200	1.2	29,700
North Carolina	23.5	22,800	16.1	18,200	7.3	32,900	24.2	21,400	16.7	17,400	7.5	30,300
South Carolina	13.9	21,900	8.6	17,400	5.3	29,200	15.1	20,800	10.7	17,400	4.4	29,200
Virginia	4.7	22,800	3.1	17,300	1.6	34,000	7.4	21,100	5.4	17,500	2.0	30,900
West Virginia	3.8	23,000	2.3	17,000	1.4	32,900	3.8	21,600	2.8	18,200	0.9	31,900

Note: Detail may not add to total due to rounding.
Source: U.S. Department of Commerce, Bureau of the Census, *Construction Reports, Housing Starts, May 1989.*

The historical order of appearance of the economic censuses is an indicator of increasing diversity in the American economy. The first population census was conducted in 1790, and the first official measures of the economy appeared with the *Census of Manufacturing* in 1810, no doubt as a result of the belief that an independent nation must develop its own manufactures. The *Census of Agriculture* did not appear until 1840. For nearly a century, these two sources were the only measures of the U.S. economy. The first *Census of Business*, covering only retail and wholesale concerns, was not taken until 1929. Then, in 1933, a few service activities were added.

As trade and services have come to account for an increasing share of the economy, the data collected have been more detailed, and in 1972 the *Census of Business* was replaced by three separate reports: *The Census of Retail Trade*, *The Census of Wholesale Trade*, and the *Census of Selected Service Industries*. In 1977 a report on *Major Retail Centers* was added, providing information on major shopping areas within the Metropolitan Statistical Areas. The reports on *Minority-Owned Business Enterprises* and *Women-Owned Businesses* are other recent additions.

The *Census of Retail Trade* includes all establishments primarily engaged in selling for personal or household consumption, including liquor stores operated by governments and post exchanges and other military retail operations of the federal government. Data by type of retail establishment are available by county and place where detail does not disclose the operation of an individual business. The *Census of Wholesale Trade* covers establishments primarily engaged in selling goods to dealers and distributors for resale or to purchasers who buy for business and farm uses. Since wholesale establishments are fewer in number, data are not broken down by category; yet data are more frequently surpressed to avoid disclosure. The *Census of Service Industries* covers a wide variety of establishments providing selected personal and business services.

Trade and service industry data for 1987 are presented using both the 1987 Standard Industrial Classification (SIC) and the 1972 SIC and its 1977 Supplement. The 1972 SIC codes were used to produce comparative tables, 7.3, 7.5, and 7.7, as it was not possible to retabulate the 1982 data using the new 1987 classifications.

Also, 1982 data were revised to show the number of establishments in business at any time during 1982. This revision provides a comparable count of firms for 1982 and 1987. In censuses prior to 1987, the count of establishments had been restricted to those in business at the end of the year.

TABLE OF CONTENTS

Table Number — Page Number

TABLE 7.1-- MONTHLY RETAIL SALES, TENNESSEE, 1979–1988 [In millions of dollars]

Year	Jan.	Feb.	March	April	May	June	July	August	Sept.	Oct.	Nov.	Dec.	Annual
1988	1,903	2,075	2,395	2,380	2,469	2,442	2,437	2,598	2,348	2,455	2,514	3,034	29,050
1987[r]	1,818	1,863	2,187	2,321	2,430	2,375	2,398	2,499	2,244	2,321	2,291	2,754	27,501
1986[r]	1,746	1,622	1,990	2,049	2,179	2,069	2,146	2,120	2,066	2,133	2,047	2,586	24,753
1985[r]	1,535	1,487	1,810	1,841	1,926	1,865	1,937	2,010	1,913	1,988	1,973	2,403	22,688
1984[r]	1,490	1,450	1,719	1,677	1,762	1,778	1,715	1,756	1,711	1,803	1,865	2,158	20,884
1983[r]	1,246	1,235	1,525	1,505	1,523	1,607	1,654	1,623	1,611	1,648	1,670	1,991	18,838
1982	1,169	1,139	1,334	1,372	1,412	1,407	1,456	1,436	1,384	1,432	1,463	1,782	16,786
1981	1,201	1,150	1,368	1,383	1,390	1,396	1,393	1,455	1,368	1,396	1,374	1,736	16,610
1980	1,091	1,083	1,223	1,206	1,281	1,266	1,289	1,314	1,284	1,362	1,382	1,688	15,469
1979	966	953	1,266	1,221	1,252	1,247	1,218	1,295	1,215	1,219	1,300	1,533	14,685

Note: Not adjusted for seasonal variations.
r revised.
Source: U.S. Department of Commerce, Bureau of the Census, *Current Business Reports, Revised Monthly Retail Sales and Inventories: January 1979 through December 1988.*

TABLE 7.2-- RETAIL TRADE DATA, BY TYPE OF ESTABLISHMENT, TENNESSEE, 1987
[Dollar amounts in thousands]

Type of establishment	Number of establish-ments	Sales	Annual payroll	Number of paid employees [1]
TOTAL	29,373	$28,532,933	$3,198,060	338,168
Building materials and garden supply stores	1,537	1,652,247	181,963	12,878
General merchandise stores	953	3,805,353	392,120	42,089
Food stores	4,214	5,654,155	515,427	58,735
Automotive dealers	2,435	7,140,596	581,616	29,169
Gasoline service stations	2,491	2,206,641	136,210	15,532
Apparel and accessory stores	2,943	1,333,823	161,806	19,755
Furniture and home furnishings stores	2,244	1,347,652	176,463	13,517
Eating and drinking places	6,209	2,595,902	667,377	108,720
Drug and proprietary stores	1,228	1,019,097	126,883	11,176
Miscellaneous retail stores	5,119	1,777,467	258,195	26,597

Note: Includes only establishments with payroll.

1. Survey taken during week of March 12.

Source: U.S. Department of Commerce, Bureau of the Census, *1987 Census of Retail Trade, Geographic Area Series, Tennessee.*

TABLE 7.3-- RETAIL STORES, COMPARATIVE STATISTICS BASED ON 1972 STANDARD INDUSTRIAL CLASSIFICATION, BY TYPE OF ESTABLISHMENT, TENNESSEE, 1982 AND 1987 [Dollar amounts in thousands]

Type of establishment	1987				1982			
	Number of establish-ments	Sales	Annual payroll	Number of paid employees [1]	Number of establish-ments	Sales	Annual payroll	Number of paid employees [1]
TOTAL	29,410	$28,540,008	$3,199,140	338,295	28,357	$18,825,999	$2,111,501	260,627
Building materials and garden supply stores	1,537	1,652,247	181,963	12,878	1,407	864,917	103,450	9,330
General merchandise stores	953	3,805,353	392,120	42,089	1,001	2,432,635	293,844	38,942
Food stores	4,214	5,654,155	515,427	58,735	4,363	4,548,049	404,158	45,556
Automotive dealers	2,435	7,140,596	581,616	29,169	2,187	3,716,102	301,496	20,489
Gasoline service stations	2,491	2,206,641	136,210	15,532	2,783	1,957,688	92,960	11,607
Apparel and accessory stores	2,943	1,333,823	161,806	19,755	2,975	915,838	123,211	17,866
Furniture and home furnishings stores	2,244	1,347,652	176,463	13,517	2,031	772,749	106,523	9,849
Eating and drinking places	6,209	2,595,902	667,377	108,720	5,519	1,642,839	413,447	74,264
Drug and proprietary stores	1,228	1,019,097	126,883	11,176	1,220	639,664	82,643	9,632
Miscellaneous retail stores	5,156	1,784,542	259,275	26,724	4,871	1,335,518	189,769	23,092

Note: Includes only establishments with payroll. There were several differences between the 1982 and 1987 censuses that would affect the comparability:

a) In 1982, classifications were based on the 1972 Standard Industrial Classification Manual. For 1987, classifications are based on the 1987 SIC Manual.

b) In 1982 and prior censuses, the count of establishments represented the number in business at the end of the year. For 1987, the count of establishments represents those in business at any time during the year.

Table 7.2 shows the 1987 data with these differences. In the above table, the data have been revised for comparative purposes:

a) The 1987 data have been reclassified using the 1972 SIC manual.

b) The 1982 data have also been revised to represent all establishments in business at any time during the year.

1. Survey taken during week of March 12.

Source: U.S. Department of Commerce, Bureau of the Census, *1987 Census of Retail Trade, Geographic Area Series, Tennessee.*

FIGURE 7.1
Retail Sales and Percentage Change, by Type of Business, Establishments with Payroll, Tennessee, 1982 and 1987

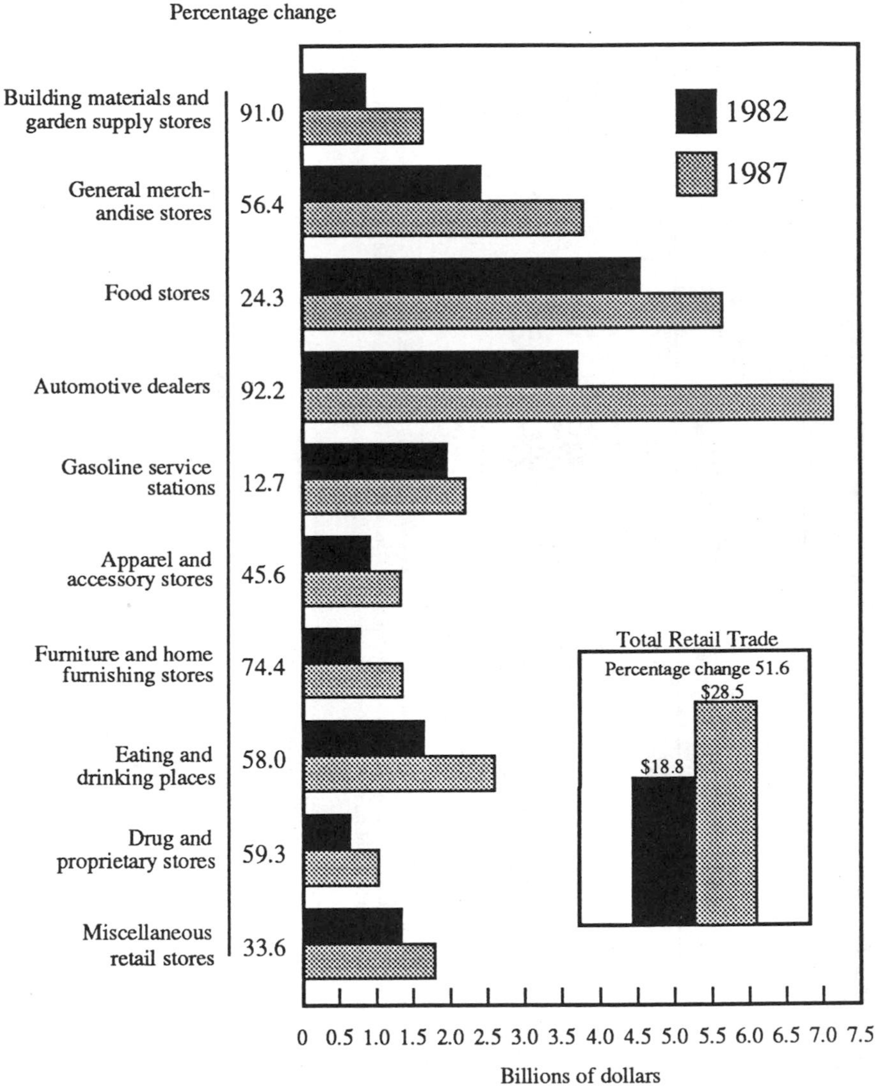

Note: Comparative statistics based on 1972 SIC. Includes only establishments with payroll.
Source: U.S. Department of Commerce, Bureau of the Census, 1987 *Census of Retail Trade, Tennessee.*

TABLE 7.4-- WHOLESALE TRADE DATA, BY TYPE OF OPERATION, TENNESSEE, 1987 [Dollar amounts in thousands]

Kind of business	Number of establish-ments	Sales	Annual payroll	Number of paid employees[1]	Operating expenses	End-of-1986 inventories	End-of-1987 inventories
Total	8,782	$48,278,891	$2,518,097	115,927	$5,171,868	$3,092,312	$3,428,029
Merchant wholesalers	7,237	25,707,687	1,880,233	93,186	3,836,643	2,632,295	2,946,289
Wholesale distributors and jobbers	6,954	22,336,474	1,798,208	89,470	3,610,357	2,241,193	2,490,759
Importers	155	1,657,285	58,419	2,428	143,066	204,321	253,082
Exporters	42	674,422	9,359	393	20,778	25,973	30,113
Terminal grain elevators	5	(D)	(D)	(D)	(D)	(D)	(D)
Country grain elevators	42	(D)	(D)	(D)	(D)	(D)	(D)
Assemblers of farm products, except country grain elevators	39	787,903	7,381	459	45,695	147,060	159,852
Manufacturers' sales branches and sales offices	742	17,514,804	532,576	17,310	1,122,854	441,642	458,874
Sales branches with stock	463	7,016,520	334,543	12,005	663,388	441,642	458,874
Sales offices without stock	279	10,498,284	198,033	5,305	459,466	0	0
Agents, brokers, and commission merchants	803	5,056,400	105,288	5,431	212,371	18,375	22,866
Auction companies	55	687,302	6,136	1,015	14,140	1,206	1,751
Brokers	209	2,174,114	33,333	1,567	66,404	1,711	1,648
Commission merchants	115	467,378	14,074	851	29,788	6,147	5,766
Import agents	9	171,877	3,967	107	12,594	2,886	6,272
Export agents	4	17,912	105	27	719	0	0
Manufacturers' agents	411	1,537,817	47,573	1,864	88,726	6,425	7,429

(D) withheld to avoid disclosure.

1. Survey taken during week of March 12.

Source: U.S. Department of Commerce, Bureau of the Census, *1987 Census of Wholesale Trade, Geographic Area Series, Tennessee.*

TABLE 7.5-- WHOLESALE ESTABLISHMENTS, COMPARATIVE STATISTICS BASED ON 1972 STANDARD INDUSTRIAL CLASSIFICATION, BY TYPE OF ESTABLISHMENT, TENNESSEE, 1982 AND 1987

Item	1987	1982
Total establishments		
Number of establishments	8,745	8,229
Sales ($1,000)	48,271,816	37,833,180
Annual payroll ($1,000)	2,517,017	1,761,269
Number of paid employees[1]	115,800	101,783
Type of operation		
Merchant wholesalers		
Number of establishments	7,200	6,621
Sales ($1,000)	25,700,612	19,443,542
Annual payroll ($1,000)	1,879,153	1,262,588
Number of paid employees[1]	93,059	79,561
Manufacturers' sales branches and sales offices		
Number of establishments	742	813
Sales ($1,000)	17,514,804	14,690,898
Annual payroll ($1,000)	532,576	428,828
Number of paid employees[1]	17,310	17,814
Agents, brokers, and commission merchants		
Number of establishments	803	795
Sales ($1,000)	5,056,400	3,698,740
Annual payroll ($1,000)	105,288	69,853
Number of paid employees[1]	5,431	4,408

See Table 7.3 for note on comparability.

1. Survey taken during week of March 12.

Source: U.S. Department of Commerce, Bureau of the Census, *1987 Census of Wholesale Trade, Geographic Area Series, Tennessee.*

TABLE 7.6-- SERVICE INDUSTRY ESTABLISHMENTS, RECEIPTS, PAYROLL AND EMPLOYMENT, BY TYPE OF ESTABLISHMENT, 1987 [Dollar amounts in thousands]

Kind of business	Number of establishments			Receipts	Annual payroll	Number of paid employees [1]
	Total	Unincorporated businesses				
		Individual proprietor-ships	Partner-ships			
TOTAL	27,829	11,761	2,838	$12,010,161	$4,486,948	282,908
Hotels, motels, and other lodging places	993	310	213	814,385	210,756	24,580
Personal services	3,500	1,928	366	646,984	226,989	23,420
Business services	4,046	1,110	263	2,009,604	811,020	74,268
Automotive repair, services, and parking	2,718	1,292	268	892,497	188,564	13,088
Miscellaneous repair services	1,176	606	97	299,711	87,235	5,444
Amusement and recreation services	1,905	590	244	675,592	168,298	15,293
Health services	7,399	3,410	433	3,797,943	1,648,366	75,344
Legal services	2,018	1,134	564	605,799	192,545	8,523
Selected educational services	160	37	9	50,311	19,106	1,250
Social services	769	342	46	106,577	42,028	5,476
Engineering, accounting, research, management, and related services	2,878	970	311	2,081,243	882,352	35,506
Other services	267	32	24	29,515	9,689	716

Note: Includes only those establishments with payroll that were subject to Federal Income Tax.

1. Survey taken during week of March 12.

Source: U.S. Department of Commerce, Bureau of the Census, *1987 Census of Service Industries, Geographic Area Series, Tennessee.*

TABLE 7.7-- SERVICE INDUSTRY COMPARATIVE STATISTICS, BASED ON 1972 STANDARD INDUSTRIAL CLASSIFICATION, TENNESSEE, 1982 AND 1987

Kind of business	Number of establishments			Receipts ($1,000)			Number of paid employees[1]		
	1987	1982	Percent change	1987	1982	Percent change	1987	1982	Percent change
TOTAL, except hospitals	27,763	22,903	21.2	11,225,076	6,343,907	76.9	267,749	177,325	51.0
Hotels, motels, and other lodging	993	980	1.3	814,385	592,457	37.5	24,580	20,882	17.7
Personal services	3,758	3,559	5.6	701,899	445,524	57.5	25,075	19,744	27.0
Business services	5,271	3,288	60.3	3,117,978	1,503,624	107.4	93,091	47,294	96.8
Automotive repair, services, and parking	2,718	2,252	20.7	892,497	509,306	75.2	13,088	9,312	40.5
Miscellaneous repair services	1,176	1,056	11.4	299,711	202,677	47.9	5,444	4,482	21.5
Amusement and recreation services	1,344	1,388	-3.2	604,580	406,525	48.7	12,641	11,065	14.2
Health services, except hospitals	7,333	6,293	16.5	3,012,858	1,727,932	74.4	60,185	42,611	41.2
Legal services	2,018	1,896	6.4	605,799	338,780	78.8	8,523	6,473	31.7
Selected educational services	160	91	75.8	50,311	18,664	169.6	1,250	544	129.8
Social services	769	477	61.2	106,577	37,717	182.6	5,476	3,596	52.3
Engineering, architectural, and surveying services	947	741	27.8	695,305	377,132	84.4	11,687	6,920	68.9
Accounting, auditing, and bookkeeping services	1,009	829	21.7	293,661	177,281	65.6	5,993	4,249	41.0
Other services	267	(a)	(X)	29,515	(a)	(X)	716	(a)	(X)

See Table 7.3 for note on comparability.

Note: Includes only those establishments with payroll that were subject to Federal Income Tax.

(X) not applicable.

1. Survey taken during week of March 12.

a. not comparable.

Source: U.S. Department of Commerce, Bureau of the Census, *1987 Census of Service Industries, Geographic Area Series, Tennessee.*

TABLE 7.8-- NUMBER AND LIABILITIES OF BUSINESS FAILURES, TENNESSEE, 1955–1988, SELECTED YEARS [Liabilities in thousands of dollars]

Year	Number of failures [1]	Current liabilities [2]
1988[p]	1,169	415,668
1987[r]	1,134	324,557
1986	1,180	321,114
1985	1,217	442,025
1984	1,326	1,044,724
1983	989	252,874
1982	814	226,795
1981	603	129,000
1980	449	115,000
1979	234	47,123
1978	155	28,369
1977	150	65,936
1976	214	52,281
1975	190	81,625
1974	147	25,025
1973	118	13,499
1972	130	13,990
1971	119	18,283
1970	170	48,090
1969	123	23,024
1968	115	9,486
1967	145	13,513
1966	134	13,802
1965	188	19,938
1960	172	10,850
1955	129	8,717

Note: Data are for commercial and industrial failures only through 1983, excluding failures of banks, railroads, real estate, insurance, holding and financial companies, steamship lines, travel agencies, etc. Beginning in 1984, data are based on expanded coverage and new methodology and are, therefore, not comparable with earlier years.

p preliminary.

r revised.

1. Includes concerns discontinuing following assignment, voluntary or involuntary petition in bankruptcy, attachment, execution, foreclosure, etc.; voluntary withdrawals from business with known loss to creditors; also enterprises involved in court action, such as receivership and reorganization or arrangement which may or may not lead to discontinuance; and businesses making voluntary compromise with creditors out of court.

2. Liabilities exclude long-term publicly held obligations; offsetting assets are not taken into account.

Source: Printed by permission from The Dun and Bradstreet Corporation, *Business Failure Record*, corresponding years, and direct correspondence.

TABLE 7.9-- DEPARTMENT STORES AND MONTHLY SALES, SELECTED METROPOLITAN STATISTICAL AREAS, 1986 AND 1987 [Sales in thousands of dollars]

	Chattanooga		Johnson City–Kingsport–Bristol		Knoxville		Memphis		Nashville	
Detail	1987	1986	1987	1986	1987	1986	1987	1986	1987	1986
Number of stores[1]	27	26	29	29	41	41	41	39	52	53
Sales[2]										
January	15,837	13,624	16,207	15,377	23,316	22,531	37,199	34,371	41,172	36,864
February	15,935	14,019	16,105	14,497	24,962	21,933	37,810	36,167	42,168	36,215
March	21,652	20,123	21,370	21,332	32,106	31,744	50,851	49,932	56,907	54,778
April	22,877	19,788	23,067	21,217	33,760	30,465	53,437	49,320	60,964	53,067
May	23,878	21,802	24,809	23,060	37,214	34,846	56,087	53,978	63,761	56,660
June	22,001	19,922	22,635	21,623	33,518	31,239	49,535	47,750	55,692	52,864
July	21,852	19,869	22,640	21,805	33,764	31,560	48,502	48,291	55,160	51,455
August	24,043	21,864	24,760	23,592	37,297	34,277	57,642	54,486	61,920	59,395
September	21,728	19,982	22,938	21,407	34,437	31,990	49,185	46,718	56,803	52,238
October	25,344	23,039	27,698	24,437	40,872	35,472	57,973	54,397	66,811	60,058
November	29,382	27,326	33,162	30,173	48,803	44,360	67,504	64,515	77,250	77,237
December	46,025	42,982	48,801	44,526	73,900	65,974	110,502	98,241	120,609	111,503
Annual	290,554	264,340	304,192	283,046	453,949	416,391	676,227	638,166	759,217	702,334
Percentage change 1986–1987	9.9		7.5		9.0		6.0		8.1	

Note: These data are currently available from the International Council of Shopping Centers for a fee. Address: 665 Fifth Avenue, New York, NY 10022; or phone (212)421-8181.

1. As of January 1988 for 1987 and as of January 1987 for 1986.

2. Not adjusted for seasonal variations. Includes sales for leased departments operated within department stores.

Source: U.S. Department of Commerce, Bureau of the Census, *Current Business Reports, Monthly Retail Trade*, January 1988.

TABLE 7.10--RETAIL TRADE DATA, BY TYPE OF ESTABLISHMENT, METROPOLITAN STATISTICAL AREAS, 1987 [Dollar amounts in thousands]

MSA and type of establishment	Number of establish-ments	Sales	Annual payroll	Number of paid employees [1]
CHATTANOOGA				
Total retail trade	2,702	$2,661,888	$307,524	31,288
Building materials and garden supply stores	139	150,264	16,852	1,003
General merchandise stores	80	327,912	37,861	3,902
Food stores	287	561,625	47,887	5,120
Automotive dealers	195	592,607	52,617	2,444
Gasoline service stations	271	234,569	14,011	1,436
Apparel and accessory stores	287	135,747	16,384	1,956
Furniture and home furnishings stores	216	134,611	17,874	1,444
Eating and drinking places	614	245,332	61,919	10,185
Drug and proprietary stores	102	78,169	10,894	988
Miscellaneous retail stores	511	201,052	31,225	2,810
CLARKSVILLE-HOPKINSVILLE				
Total retail trade	970	881,628	103,284	11,032
Building materials and garden supply stores	51	63,387	7,066	474
General merchandise stores	28	119,819	14,058	1,661
Food stores	110	144,510	14,346	1,539
Automotive dealers	76	265,583	22,191	1,223
Gasoline service stations	69	55,364	3,405	439
Apparel and accessory stores	103	36,114	4,378	563
Furniture and home furnishings stores	74	40,281	5,284	416
Eating and drinking places	232	82,148	22,139	3,647
Drug and proprietary stores	38	24,123	3,316	262
Miscellaneous retail stores	189	50,299	7,101	808
JACKSON				
Total retail trade	584	589,142	64,282	6,882
Building materials and garden supply stores	32	50,296	4,864	287
General merchandise stores	20	112,907	11,654	1,307
Food stores	74	110,358	9,306	1,127
Automotive dealers	51	112,945	9,157	465
Gasoline service stations	56	49,698	3,235	384
Apparel and accessory stores	62	29,161	4,066	518
Furniture and home furnishings stores	49	26,071	3,757	319
Eating and drinking places	107	42,457	10,520	1,696
Drug and proprietary stores	20	16,262	1,895	170
Miscellaneous retail stores	113	38,987	5,828	609
JOHNSON CITY-KINGSPORT-BRISTOL				
Total retail trade	2,459	2,256,191	247,716	27,664
Building materials and garden supply stores	133	160,844	14,250	1,079
General merchandise stores	81	336,470	36,854	4,007
Food stores	327	474,047	40,077	4,643
Automotive dealers	219	554,181	43,061	2,580
Gasoline service stations	203	141,729	8,156	997
Apparel and accessory stores	235	91,453	10,606	1,340
Furniture and home furnishings stores	207	95,279	11,989	1,086
Eating and drinking places	515	203,678	53,567	8,856
Drug and proprietary stores	123	85,259	11,970	993
Miscellaneous retail stores	416	113,251	17,186	2,083

TABLE 7.10--RETAIL TRADE DATA, BY TYPE OF ESTABLISHMENT, METROPOLITAN STATISTICAL AREAS, 1987 [Dollar amounts in thousands] (Continued)

MSA and type of establishment	Number of establishments	Sales	Annual payroll	Number of paid employees [1]
KNOXVILLE				
Total retail trade	4,296	4,216,793	482,421	50,694
Building materials and garden supply stores	216	239,570	27,217	1,803
General merchandise stores	104	525,797	56,071	5,571
Food stores	599	794,861	75,253	9,032
Automotive dealers	307	1,041,630	83,372	4,096
Gasoline service stations	345	366,895	22,106	2,587
Apparel and accessory stores	446	218,162	23,834	2,877
Furniture and home furnishings stores	334	203,944	25,087	2,074
Eating and drinking places	948	441,247	115,862	17,252
Drug and proprietary stores	167	132,863	17,125	1,443
Miscellaneous retail stores	830	251,824	36,494	3,959
MEMPHIS				
Total retail trade	5,404	6,280,063	712,253	72,495
Building materials and garden supply stores	215	261,736	32,806	2,422
General merchandise stores	181	861,738	87,331	9,368
Food stores	765	1,124,401	104,811	12,407
Automotive dealers	427	1,655,584	143,791	6,593
Gasoline service stations	434	527,821	32,797	3,477
Apparel and accessory stores	623	337,987	44,068	5,075
Furniture and home furnishings stores	405	320,462	42,336	2,903
Eating and drinking places	1,159	531,050	138,673	22,043
Drug and proprietary stores	160	245,823	25,805	2,291
Miscellaneous retail stores	1,035	413,461	59,835	5,916
NASHVILLE-DAVIDSON				
Total retail trade	5,840	6,893,335	808,691	83,116
Building materials and garden supply stores	274	376,687	40,479	2,894
General merchandise stores	139	952,190	96,468	9,483
Food stores	740	1,228,077	124,842	12,661
Automotive dealers	440	1,736,361	142,687	6,634
Gasoline service stations	445	527,317	34,400	3,846
Apparel and accessory stores	628	321,611	39,913	4,778
Furniture and home furnishings stores	481	363,496	48,080	3,312
Eating and drinking places	1,371	717,042	186,516	30,233
Drug and proprietary stores	240	207,070	26,464	2,403
Miscellaneous retail stores	1,082	463,484	68,842	6,872

Note: Includes only establishments with payroll.

1. Survey taken during week March 12.

Source: U.S. Department of Commerce, Bureau of the Census, *1987 Census of Retail Trade, Geographic Area Series, Tennessee.*

TABLE 7.11--WHOLESALE TRADE DATA, BY TYPE OF BUSINESS ESTABLISHMENT, METROPOLITAN STATISTICAL AREAS, 1987 [Dollar amounts in thousands]

Metropolitan Statistical Area	Total				Merchant wholesalers			
	Number of establish-ments	Sales	Annual payroll	Number of paid employees [1]	Number of establish-ments	Sales	Annual payroll	Number of paid employees [1]
Chattanooga	944	$4,213,833	$248,854	11,937	790	$2,182,896	$198,229	9,926
Clarksville–Hopkinsville	195	468,871	29,384	1,824	176	405,360	26,617	1,548
Jackson	167	453,130	34,171	1,922	155	419,715	31,630	1,832
Johnson City–Kingsport–Bristol	605	3,622,213	191,030	9,230	528	1,396,322	105,618	6,524
Knoxville	1,178	4,637,599	352,233	15,264	975	(D)	(D)	(D)
Memphis	2,241	22,205,695	848,663	35,802	1,706	10,603,471	593,006	26,885
Nashville	2,101	10,742,878	679,133	29,652	1,662	6,098,910	541,037	24,707

(D) withheld to avoid disclosure.

1. Survey taken during week of March 12.

Source: U.S. Department of Commerce, Bureau of the Census, *1987 Census of Wholesale Trade, Geographic Area Series, Tennessee.*

TABLE 7.12--SERVICE INDUSTRIES DATA, BY TYPE OF ESTABLISHMENT, METROPOLITAN STATISTICAL AREAS, 1987 [Dollar amounts in thousands]

Metropolitan Statistical Area	Number of establish-ments	Receipts	Annual payroll	Number of paid employees [1]
CHATTANOOGA				
TOTAL	2,565	$1,120,612	$419,745	26,871
Hotels, motels, and other lodging places	74	63,852	16,831	2,171
Personal services	335	66,158	24,258	2,318
Business services	409	180,421	75,299	8,064
Automotive repair, services, and parking	268	86,313	19,690	1,274
Miscellaneous repair services	98	30,222	9,242	585
Amusement and recreation services, including motion pictures	135	46,803	11,720	1,027
Health services	711	446,780	183,063	7,770
Legal services	168	73,826	26,949	1,008
Selected educational services	15	5,504	1,994	137
Social services	61	15,872	4,780	603
Engineering, accounting, research, management, and related services	260	101,308	44,872	1,812
Other services	31	3,553	1,047	102
CLARKSVILLE-HOPKINSVILLE				
TOTAL	700	155,200	54,207	4,361
Hotels, motels, and other lodging places	29	10,765	2,449	433
Personal services	126	14,930	5,262	629
Business services	77	18,997	7,099	715
Automotive repair, services, and parking	92	18,080	4,137	352
Miscellaneous repair services	30	4,275	1,243	93
Amusement and recreation services, including motion pictures	40	6,283	1,326	184
Health services	176	55,012	23,443	1,209
Legal services	48	11,196	2,792	185
Selected educational services	3	2,186	766	39
Social services	23	4,055	1,614	232
Engineering, accounting, research, management, and related services	50	9,243	4,031	281
Other services	6	178	45	9
JACKSON				
TOTAL	542	208,938	96,318	5,101
Hotels, motels, and other lodging places	24	9,465	2,094	284
Personal services	68	12,355	4,201	489
Business services	76	26,502	12,381	1,200
Automotive repair, services, and parking	59	(D)	(D)	(D)
Miscellaneous repair services	26	6,115	2,347	141
Amusement and recreation services, including motion pictures	38	(D)	(D)	(D)
Health services	133	113,622	60,299	2,037
Legal services	43	10,114	4,156	166
Selected educational services	3	(D)	(D)	(D)
Social services	18	1,437	607	84
Engineering, accounting, research, management, and related services	53	8,903	4,734	215
Other services	1	(D)	(D)	(D)
JOHNSON CITY-KINGSPORT-BRISTOL				
TOTAL	2,184	681,869	261,573	16,841
Hotels, motels, and other lodging places	67	45,825	11,394	1,359
Personal services	345	50,648	18,529	1,934
Business services	230	89,718	37,246	3,277
Automotive repair, services, and parking	212	50,372	11,235	889
Miscellaneous repair services	91	14,879	4,353	336
Amusement and recreation services, including motion pictures	151	25,699	5,650	749
Health services	628	320,144	140,826	6,460
Legal services	195	40,922	13,686	680

TABLE 7.12--SERVICE INDUSTRIES DATA, BY TYPE OF ESTABLISHMENT, METROPOLITAN STATISTICAL AREAS, 1987 [Dollar amounts in thousands] (Continued)

Metropolitan Statistical Area	Number of establish-ments	Receipts	Annual payroll	Number of paid employees[1]
Selected educational services	3	(D)	(D)	(D)
Social services	59	7,389	3,245	393
Engineering, accounting, research, management, and related services	187	35,463	15,187	742
Other services	16	(D)	(D)	(D)
KNOXVILLE				
TOTAL	4,209	2,136,442	746,209	41,410
Hotels, motels, and other lodging places	262	175,287	40,383	4,174
Personal services	488	83,613	28,053	3,046
Business services	583	235,662	97,294	7,722
Automotive repair, services, and parking	370	116,546	25,106	1,712
Miscellaneous repair services	172	37,017	12,148	798
Amusement and recreation services, including motion pictures	285	99,112	24,500	2,569
Health services	1,122	531,064	239,914	9,822
Legal services	250	90,262	29,148	1,262
Selected educational services	30	5,418	1,947	131
Social services	92	14,875	6,063	761
Engineering, accounting, research, management, and related services	507	743,244	240,283	9,298
Other services	48	4,342	1,371	115
MEMPHIS				
TOTAL	5,810	2,672,602	1,031,415	66,574
Hotels, motels, and other lodging places	149	171,018	46,930	5,008
Personal services	705	148,886	56,656	5,799
Business services	1,021	592,517	254,026	23,730
Automotive repair, services, and parking	613	292,724	59,012	3,887
Miscellaneous repair services	288	88,246	27,497	1,568
Amusement and recreation services, including motion pictures	264	139,417	31,223	3,051
Health services	1,484	729,973	343,502	12,917
Legal services	445	149,400	49,470	2,059
Selected educational services	35	8,265	3,593	237
Social services	146	17,884	7,814	1,070
Engineering, accounting, research, management, and related services	613	328,638	150,396	7,149
Other services	47	5,634	1,296	99
NASHVILLE-DAVIDSON				
TOTAL	7,107	3,505,767	1,275,052	81,033
Hotels, motels, and other lodging places	195	295,748	81,097	9,596
Personal services	727	149,421	55,771	5,368
Business services	1,228	687,468	256,486	22,958
Automotive repair, services, and parking	611	236,861	52,382	3,404
Miscellaneous repair services	286	87,912	22,925	1,350
Amusement and recreation services, including motion pictures	630	325,655	86,647	6,234
Health services	1,686	994,862	429,681	18,877
Legal services	489	183,153	56,018	2,377
Selected educational services	49	17,232	6,902	406
Social services	233	38,261	16,117	2,014
Engineering, accounting, research, management, and related services	881	476,312	206,318	8,198
Other services	92	12,882	4,708	251

Note: Includes only those establishments with payroll that were subject to Federal Income Tax.

(D) withheld to avoid disclosure.

1. Survey taken during week March 12.

Source: U.S. Department of Commerce, Bureau of the Census, *1987 Census of Service Industries, Geographic Area Series, Tennessee.*

TABLE 7.13--RETAIL SALES OF ESTABLISHMENTS WITH PAYROLL, BY TYPE OF ESTABLISHMENT, TENNESSEE, COUNTIES, AND MUNICIPALITIES WITH POPULATION OF 2,500 OR MORE, 1987 [In thousands of dollars]

County and municipality	Total	Building material dealers, etc. [1]	General merchandise stores	Food stores	Automotive dealers
TENNESSEE	28,532,933	1,652,247	3,805,353	5,654,155	7,140,596
Anderson	400,905	17,817	51,311	92,250	123,429
Clinton	97,506	3,646	(D)	20,384	46,035
Oak Ridge (part)[2]	254,592	11,294	39,742	54,280	75,409
Oliver Springs (part)[2]	11,746	(D)	(D)	(D)	(D)
Bedford	121,605	6,865	13,846	33,653	25,868
Shelbyville	118,130	(D)	13,846	32,675	25,868
Benton	50,389	2,986	(D)	10,963	9,222
Camden	38,305	(D)	(D)	6,969	9,222
Bledsoe	15,851	2,311	899	4,891	(D)
Blount	607,203	35,477	70,747	112,392	254,801
Alcoa	321,300	10,146	(D)	30,108	224,961
Maryville	244,136	18,787	45,904	68,310	(D)
Bradley	419,759	36,312	51,589	96,607	102,511
Cleveland	362,906	18,240	(D)	75,460	96,847
Campbell	139,871	5,915	11,667	41,118	26,963
Jellico	16,344	(D)	(D)	(D)	(D)
LaFollette	88,475	4,915	10,962	25,159	23,809
Cannon	20,794	1,430	1,108	7,318	(D)
Carroll	101,390	6,568	9,843	26,350	29,175
Huntingdon	40,600	3,082	(D)	11,043	(D)
McKenzie (part)[2]	(D)	(D)	(D)	(D)	(D)
Carter	153,386	15,586	23,648	40,684	(D)
Elizabethton	136,974	13,169	(D)	33,803	25,113
Johnson City (part)[2]	0	0	0	0	0
Cheatham	52,401	6,278	1,034	22,134	(D)
Chester	34,596	(D)	1,339	6,912	(D)
Henderson	24,516	(D)	1,339	(D)	(D)
Claiborne	48,632	5,855	2,121	19,345	2,648
Clay	10,168	1,724	185	4,166	(D)
Cocke	127,290	6,430	(D)	33,432	18,269
Newport	101,054	(D)	(D)	29,138	(D)
Coffee	257,230	18,062	42,296	50,407	54,998
Manchester	91,043	(D)	(D)	19,992	(D)
Tullahoma (part)[2]	157,409	12,647	(D)	25,096	39,157
Crockett	46,070	2,015	(D)	11,186	(D)
Alamo	35,345	(D)	(D)	7,941	(D)
Cumberland	168,771	13,338	(D)	53,216	34,988
Crossville	152,592	12,636	(D)	47,923	34,988
Davidson	4,673,218	191,216	766,877	697,420	1,159,886
Belle Meade	35,523	(D)	0	(D)	0
Forest Hills	538	0	0	(D)	0
Goodlettsville (part)[2]	239,477	(D)	111,882	16,331	(D)
Nashville-Davidson	4,397,418	185,536	654,995	663,916	(D)
Oak Hill	262	0	0	0	0
Decatur	45,296	2,224	(D)	13,546	12,417
DeKalb	40,544	1,390	2,479	13,407	10,653
Smithville	34,591	(D)	2,479	9,671	(D)
Dickson	177,479	13,907	(D)	49,731	(D)
Dickson	146,710	(D)	(D)	30,692	35,283

TABLE 7.13--RETAIL SALES OF ESTABLISHMENTS WITH PAYROLL, BY TYPE OF ESTABLISHMENT, TENNESSEE, COUNTIES, AND MUNICIPALITIES WITH POPULATION OF 2,500 OR MORE, 1987 [In thousands of dollars]

Gasoline service stations	Apparel, accessory stores	Furniture, equipment stores	Eating, drinking places	Drug stores	Miscellaneous retail stores	County and municipality
2,206,641	1,333,823	1,347,652	2,595,902	1,019,097	1,777,467	TENNESSEE
26,947	14,643	8,713	31,118	15,097	19,580	Anderson
4,990	(D)	876	3,634	4,321	(D)	Clinton
9,245	12,567	7,225	20,288	7,450	17,092	Oak Ridge (part)[2]
2,392	(D)	(D)	570	1,554	(D)	Oliver Springs (part)[2]
10,155	2,983	5,092	9,535	6,550	7,058	Bedford
(D)	2,983	(D)	9,193	6,550	(D)	Shelbyville
10,353	842	(D)	3,860	2,098	1,245	Benton
3,920	842	(D)	(D)	2,098	1,245	Camden
(D)	0	(D)	978	(D)	(D)	Bledsoe
28,677	11,509	24,672	38,320	17,303	13,305	Blount
5,207	2,334	923	18,026	(D)	(D)	Alcoa
21,250	8,554	22,668	18,225	11,813	(D)	Maryville
30,554	18,455	17,426	36,577	15,564	14,164	Bradley
20,746	18,455	(D)	36,170	(D)	(D)	Cleveland
24,758	4,996	3,500	10,399	5,178	5,377	Campbell
4,152	(D)	(D)	1,435	(D)	(D)	Jellico
4,992	(D)	2,831	5,683	(D)	(D)	LaFollette
2,382	448	(D)	536	(D)	873	Cannon
9,450	3,411	5,276	3,941	5,043	2,333	Carroll
4,430	(D)	(D)	1,567	2,309	(D)	Huntingdon
3,955	2,118	2,796	1,917	(D)	(D)	McKenzie (part)[2]
13,277	2,465	4,496	15,610	6,888	(D)	Carter
11,320	(D)	4,291	13,797	(D)	(D)	Elizabethton
0	0	0	0	0	0	Johnson City (part)[2]
8,367	(D)	(D)	3,285	3,161	(D)	Cheatham
3,216	1,303	2,552	2,222	(D)	536	Chester
(D)	(D)	(D)	2,222	(D)	536	Henderson
3,786	995	2,256	3,273	3,092	5,261	Claiborne
(D)	0	0	735	(D)	1,648	Clay
14,488	4,576	2,482	12,696	6,199	(D)	Cocke
10,672	(D)	2,482	11,316	6,199	(D)	Newport
17,595	9,532	9,114	25,833	10,782	18,611	Coffee
10,762	(D)	(D)	12,920	4,702	(D)	Manchester
5,612	8,572	4,535	12,686	6,080	(D)	Tullahoma (part)[2]
4,817	(D)	1,323	1,104	2,274	(D)	Crockett
(D)	(D)	(D)	707	(D)	(D)	Alamo
9,737	6,073	2,975	14,057	6,244	(D)	Cumberland
5,442	(D)	(D)	11,331	(D)	(D)	Crossville
304,882	247,126	281,435	534,260	134,657	355,459	Davidson
(D)	(D)	(D)	(D)	3,691	(D)	Belle Meade
0	(D)	0	(D)	0	(D)	Forest Hills
(D)	15,752	9,462	26,910	3,150	(D)	Goodlettsville (part)[2]
279,912	224,460	271,625	505,548	127,816	(D)	Nashville-Davidson
0	(D)	(D)	(D)	0	0	Oak Hill
7,435	341	785	1,901	2,038	(D)	Decatur
3,476	1,158	1,192	2,736	2,669	1,384	DeKalb
3,476	1,158	1,192	(D)	(D)	(D)	Smithville
10,561	5,504	8,113	12,410	5,917	(D)	Dickson
4,616	5,504	(D)	11,092	(D)	(D)	Dickson

TABLE 7.13--RETAIL SALES OF ESTABLISHMENTS WITH PAYROLL, BY TYPE OF ESTABLISHMENT, TENNESSEE, COUNTIES, AND MUNICIPALITIES WITH POPULATION OF 2,500 OR MORE, 1987 [In thousands of dollars] (Continued)

County and municipality	Total	Building material dealers, etc.[1]	General merchandise stores	Food stores	Automotive dealers
Dyer	243,101	17,180	34,513	47,550	70,114
Dyersburg	233,886	(D)	(D)	42,460	(D)
Newbern	5,461	(D)	(D)	3,905	(D)
Fayette	44,226	4,744	4,979	14,466	7,498
Fentress	37,326	7,453	2,316	15,431	1,470
Franklin	130,560	11,446	14,360	37,372	29,348
Tullahoma (part)[2]	0	0	0	0	0
Winchester	69,434	(D)	(D)	6,875	(D)
Gibson	210,336	6,856	25,940	36,974	66,882
Humboldt	72,443	948	(D)	9,076	26,142
Milan	49,898	(D)	(D)	11,393	6,591
Trenton	47,249	1,544	3,155	11,105	14,452
Giles	107,534	5,288	(D)	27,896	21,805
Pulaski	90,237	4,711	(D)	25,064	(D)
Grainger	24,895	(D)	0	7,185	10,921
Greene	246,460	20,530	26,810	61,837	51,834
Greeneville	227,557	18,890	26,056	55,141	51,469
Grundy	35,282	(D)	1,137	9,143	2,777
Hamblen	328,771	23,094	36,617	71,910	101,679
Morristown	316,326	23,094	36,617	66,341	(D)
Hamilton	2,110,182	110,567	275,800	387,697	515,184
Chattanooga	1,735,866	85,062	241,706	286,760	494,271
Collegedale	11,020	0	0	(D)	0
East Ridge	154,592	16,248	(D)	33,494	15,403
Red Bank	59,214	3,421	0	22,260	2,959
Signal Mountain	7,165	(D)	0	(D)	0
Soddy-Daisy	36,842	(D)	(D)	(D)	1,097
Hancock	7,920	(D)	0	(D)	(D)
Hardeman	95,871	10,124	(D)	22,434	15,473
Bolivar	51,461	2,468	(D)	11,830	12,769
Hardin	99,367	5,277	(D)	25,896	26,043
Savannah	87,969	(D)	(D)	21,754	(D)
Hawkins	116,120	10,163	8,660	41,047	18,591
Church Hill	21,439	(D)	(D)	(D)	(D)
Kingsport (part)[2]	21,185	(D)	(D)	(D)	(D)
Mount Carmel	4,831	(D)	0	(D)	(D)
Rogersville	60,614	1,370	6,767	19,577	15,254
Haywood	76,206	4,934	(D)	17,898	23,801
Brownsville	69,895	(D)	(D)	(D)	23,801
Henderson	92,548	8,163	11,258	19,564	23,446
Lexington	81,206	3,934	(D)	16,900	22,797
Henry	140,750	10,906	16,312	33,160	29,640
McKenzie (part)[2]	0	0	0	0	0
Paris	128,792	(D)	(D)	31,337	(D)
Hickman	25,817	(D)	805	8,564	3,407
Centerville	20,190	(D)	805	(D)	3,407
Houston	12,327	(D)	(D)	5,986	(D)
Humphreys	64,025	6,715	(D)	18,766	9,510
Waverly	42,628	4,112	(D)	9,197	9,510
Jackson	24,813	(D)	(D)	11,886	784
Jefferson	112,205	7,353	(D)	34,686	21,066
Jefferson City	61,216	2,361	(D)	19,871	9,968

TABLE 7.13--RETAIL SALES OF ESTABLISHMENTS WITH PAYROLL, BY TYPE OF ESTABLISHMENT, TENNESSEE, COUNTIES, AND MUNICIPALITIES WITH POPULATION OF 2,500 OR MORE, 1987 [In thousands of dollars] (Continued)

Gasoline service stations	Apparel, acces-sory stores	Furniture, equip-ment stores	Eating, drinking places	Drug stores	Miscel-laneous retail stores	County and municipality
14,806	11,504	10,015	16,856	6,685	13,878	Dyer
(D)	(D)	(D)	15,612	(D)	13,878	Dyersburg
0	(D)	(D)	288	0	0	Newbern
3,734	(D)	(D)	2,322	1,943	1,774	Fayette
908	4,026	418	2,215	(D)	(D)	Fentress
5,362	1,503	4,364	8,872	6,267	11,666	Franklin
0	0	0	0	0	0	Tullahoma (part)[2]
4,134	(D)	2,145	4,547	3,641	(D)	Winchester
21,769	8,012	6,157	15,704	12,869	9,173	Gibson
8,780	4,057	2,270	3,615	3,957	(D)	Humboldt
2,618	1,128	1,793	9,060	4,763	2,412	Milan
5,681	1,273	1,753	1,879	1,873	4,534	Trenton
13,952	3,825	4,460	5,089	5,777	(D)	Giles
5,624	3,825	(D)	4,109	(D)	(D)	Pulaski
(D)	0	(D)	1,246	(D)	(D)	Grainger
22,362	8,169	8,385	18,885	11,090	16,558	Greene
13,887	8,169	(D)	18,044	11,090	(D)	Greeneville
11,137	(D)	(D)	3,517	1,340	1,238	Grundy
17,682	13,973	6,336	26,491	12,134	18,855	Hamblen
16,203	(D)	(D)	(D)	12,134	(D)	Morristown
164,757	112,935	112,994	209,152	60,239	160,857	Hamilton
110,305	101,657	81,017	154,460	39,723	140,905	Chattanooga
(D)	0	(D)	(D)	(D)	(D)	Collegedale
17,097	3,745	20,690	28,013	7,765	(D)	East Ridge
5,349	2,312	2,505	12,061	3,765	4,582	Red Bank
610	(D)	(D)	(D)	(D)	(D)	Signal Mountain
(D)	(D)	(D)	1,765	(D)	(D)	Soddy-Daisy
1,816	(D)	(D)	(D)	(D)	(D)	Hancock
10,088	747	1,867	4,804	2,796	(D)	Hardeman
4,327	747	(D)	4,275	(D)	(D)	Bolivar
5,188	1,577	4,875	6,952	4,149	(D)	Hardin
3,415	(D)	4,875	5,037	(D)	(D)	Savannah
6,905	1,626	3,846	10,414	7,407	7,461	Hawkins
(D)	(D)	(D)	(D)	2,067	(D)	Church Hill
(D)	(D)	0	2,770	(D)	(D)	Kingsport (part)[2]
0	0	(D)	(D)	0	0	Mount Carmel
2,086	(D)	(D)	5,600	3,798	(D)	Rogersville
6,472	3,404	3,070	4,083	3,300	(D)	Haywood
(D)	3,404	(D)	(D)	3,300	(D)	Brownsville
11,333	2,602	3,895	5,233	3,351	3,703	Henderson
9,425	(D)	3,895	(D)	3,351	(D)	Lexington
11,562	7,038	6,171	9,873	6,146	9,942	Henry
0	0	0	0	0	0	McKenzie (part)[2]
(D)	7,038	(D)	8,383	6,146	(D)	Paris
2,208	(D)	1,011	1,165	(D)	599	Hickman
1,596	(D)	(D)	685	(D)	(D)	Centerville
888	(D)	(D)	759	(D)	197	Houston
6,257	(D)	1,347	3,858	2,580	2,161	Humphreys
2,701	(D)	1,114	1,665	(D)	(D)	Waverly
(D)	0	253	733	(D)	2,525	Jackson
13,614	(D)	4,209	11,209	5,927	(D)	Jefferson
3,148	501	(D)	9,171	3,528	(D)	Jefferson City

TABLE 7.13--RETAIL SALES OF ESTABLISHMENTS WITH PAYROLL, BY TYPE OF ESTABLISHMENT, TENNESSEE, COUNTIES, AND MUNICIPALITIES WITH POPULATION OF 2,500 OR MORE, 1987 [In thousands of dollars] (Continued)

County and municipality	Total	Building material dealers, etc.[1]	General merchandise stores	Food stores	Automotive dealers
Johnson	30,837	2,511	1,791	11,852	3,692
Knox	2,710,025	165,740	367,214	475,024	598,885
Farragut	14,690	0	(D)	0	0
Knoxville	2,185,306	143,763	308,913	373,460	469,145
Lake	12,352	(D)	(D)	5,758	(D)
Lauderdale	67,183	2,829	10,293	17,953	12,186
Ripley	52,985	(D)	(D)	13,198	9,667
Lawrence	152,179	10,108	(D)	39,144	38,593
Lawrenceburg	124,802	(D)	(D)	29,146	37,790
Lewis	24,072	1,953	1,952	8,249	5,325
Hohenwald	23,896	1,953	1,952	8,249	5,325
Lincoln	112,091	7,200	(D)	26,832	31,236
Fayetteville	95,455	(D)	(D)	22,841	(D)
Loudon	135,146	7,214	(D)	31,063	52,205
Lenoir City	101,581	5,190	(D)	19,052	43,141
Loudon	22,211	(D)	(D)	7,623	(D)
McMinn	198,526	16,343	22,405	48,135	35,564
Athens	156,972	(D)	21,342	35,020	23,280
Etowah	23,033	(D)	1,063	9,542	(D)
McNairy	63,284	4,146	(D)	18,472	13,154
Selmer	34,132	2,458	(D)	(D)	3,112
Macon	42,661	4,610	7,831	13,492	3,238
Lafayette	36,048	(D)	(D)	(D)	(D)
Madison	589,142	50,296	112,907	110,358	112,945
Jackson	568,969	(D)	(D)	107,360	(D)
Marion	100,295	(D)	(D)	30,219	15,236
Jasper	18,600	(D)	(D)	(D)	(D)
South Pittsburg	46,960	2,045	6,826	(D)	13,065
Marshall	104,082	4,292	(D)	31,185	31,587
Lewisburg	91,965	4,292	(D)	24,236	31,587
Maury	298,439	26,029	37,249	64,681	66,376
Columbia	271,279	16,425	(D)	58,207	(D)
Mount Pleasant	10,253	(D)	(D)	3,644	(D)
Meigs	8,148	(D)	(D)	3,808	1,034
Monroe	115,840	13,391	14,615	33,363	19,053
Madisonville	48,338	(D)	(D)	13,593	7,605
Sweetwater	52,205	4,797	(D)	14,809	11,068
Montgomery	582,525	43,960	86,072	88,604	193,161
Clarksville	551,694	(D)	(D)	74,742	192,778
Moore	3,022	0	(D)	(D)	(D)
Morgan	18,848	313	(D)	7,809	(D)
Oliver Springs (part)[2]	0	0	0	0	0
Obion	170,454	17,149	20,536	32,634	46,370
South Fulton	10,708	(D)	0	(D)	3,374
Union City	139,813	11,369	(D)	23,250	39,455
Overton	38,245	4,378	3,778	14,089	5,085
Livingston	32,800	(D)	(D)	11,083	(D)
Perry	12,930	(D)	(D)	6,971	601
Pickett	7,747	(D)	(D)	(D)	2,171
Polk	22,450	753	2,241	11,485	2,694

TABLE 7.13--RETAIL SALES OF ESTABLISHMENTS WITH PAYROLL, BY TYPE OF ESTABLISHMENT, TENNESSEE, COUNTIES, AND MUNICIPALITIES WITH POPULATION OF 2,500 OR MORE, 1987 [In thousands of dollars] (Continued)

Gasoline service stations	Apparel, acces-sory stores	Furniture, equip-ment stores	Eating, drinking places	Drug stores	Miscel-laneous retail stores	County and municipality
3,779	629	585	1,215	2,877	1,906	Johnson
264,528	157,250	148,205	273,928	82,066	177,185	Knox
0	(D)	0	(D)	0	0	Farragut
181,995	130,343	135,748	226,147	64,518	151,274	Knoxville
1,602	(D)	0	1,021	(D)	381	Lake
7,348	1,482	2,822	4,091	4,805	3,374	Lauderdale
4,923	(D)	(D)	2,219	(D)	(D)	Ripley
8,639	3,597	12,460	7,333	7,997	(D)	Lawrence
5,409	(D)	(D)	6,765	7,234	(D)	Lawrenceburg
1,431	(D)	(D)	1,695	(D)	987	Lewis
1,431	(D)	(D)	(D)	(D)	987	Hohenwald
9,858	3,118	3,110	8,388	5,369	(D)	Lincoln
(D)	3,118	(D)	7,322	5,369	(D)	Fayetteville
9,834	(D)	4,572	10,413	6,024	3,982	Loudon
7,052	(D)	2,522	8,652	3,807	(D)	Lenoir City
(D)	(D)	(D)	1,175	(D)	746	Loudon
14,279	11,804	6,880	17,648	10,597	14,871	McMinn
10,578	10,147	6,297	15,213	8,507	(D)	Athens
2,585	1,657	(D)	(D)	1,635	2,944	Etowah
4,975	1,136	2,957	2,654	2,872	(D)	McNairy
1,767	(D)	(D)	2,310	(D)	(D)	Selmer
4,307	714	977	1,878	2,921	2,693	Macon
4,009	714	(D)	1,738	(D)	(D)	Lafayette
49,698	29,161	26,071	42,457	16,262	38,987	Madison
36,170	(D)	24,438	(D)	16,262	(D)	Jackson
11,551	(D)	(D)	5,427	(D)	(D)	Marion
1,348	(D)	(D)	1,253	(D)	(D)	Jasper
(D)	2,723	(D)	1,354	(D)	1,168	South Pittsburg
8,888	1,631	3,852	4,514	4,985	(D)	Marshall
(D)	(D)	(D)	(D)	(D)	(D)	Lewisburg
24,183	16,846	11,962	22,282	10,211	18,620	Maury
21,813	15,913	10,876	20,178	8,883	(D)	Columbia
(D)	(D)	(D)	(D)	(D)	515	Mount Pleasant
663	0	(D)	799	(D)	(D)	Meigs
9,992	4,061	3,073	10,302	4,995	2,995	Monroe
5,168	(D)	(D)	1,995	(D)	(D)	Madisonville
2,645	1,427	(D)	6,291	2,035	(D)	Sweetwater
30,350	24,341	28,015	51,593	12,416	24,013	Montgomery
(D)	22,759	(D)	46,579	(D)	(D)	Clarksville
(D)	0	0	(D)	(D)	0	Moore
1,037	(D)	0	587	(D)	(D)	Morgan
0	0	0	0	0	0	Oliver Springs (part)[2]
9,934	6,836	4,986	13,217	6,148	12,644	Obion
1,014	(D)	(D)	1,423	(D)	(D)	South Fulton
6,964	6,052	4,758	10,356	5,314	(D)	Union City
2,386	797	2,617	2,474	1,716	925	Overton
2,386	(D)	2,617	(D)	1,716	925	Livingston
946	(D)	(D)	1,087	(D)	(D)	Perry
1,237	(D)	(D)	402	(D)	(D)	Pickett
(D)	(D)	(D)	2,144	1,531	(D)	Polk

TABLE 7.13--RETAIL SALES OF ESTABLISHMENTS WITH PAYROLL, BY TYPE OF ESTABLISHMENT, TENNESSEE, COUNTIES, AND MUNICIPALITIES WITH POPULATION OF 2,500 OR MORE, 1987 [In thousands of dollars] (Continued)

County and municipality	Total	Building material dealers, etc.[1]	General merchandise stores	Food stores	Automotive dealers
Putnam	332,107	28,901	47,386	77,697	65,608
Cookeville	311,068	25,116	(D)	68,612	(D)
Monterey	8,077	(D)	(D)	3,004	(D)
Rhea	90,367	3,567	9,161	32,760	21,339
Dayton	70,069	(D)	(D)	25,684	18,933
Roane	191,853	9,046	19,961	55,434	61,590
Harriman	98,769	5,065	(D)	20,931	36,182
Kingston	26,488	1,998	(D)	12,250	(D)
Oak Ridge (part)[2]	0	0	0	0	0
Oliver Springs (part)[2]	7,933	0	0	(D)	(D)
Rockwood	42,002	(D)	2,527	10,803	17,689
Robertson	168,990	10,465	(D)	46,714	53,455
Greenbrier	4,593	(D)	0	(D)	(D)
Springfield	143,994	(D)	(D)	33,264	52,654
Rutherford	609,552	56,616	58,208	125,171	154,897
LaVergne	21,834	(D)	0	2,122	(D)
Murfreesboro	488,853	(D)	(D)	87,369	142,579
Smyrna	89,052	(D)	(D)	32,125	10,446
Scott	46,182	(D)	(D)	13,525	6,313
Oneida	36,889	(D)	(D)	8,213	4,572
Sequatchie	30,811	(D)	(D)	12,579	8,124
Dunlap	26,441	(D)	(D)	11,229	(D)
Sevier	348,358	12,320	24,029	67,770	29,500
Gatlinburg	83,113	(D)	(D)	10,847	(D)
Sevierville	130,021	6,066	22,484	24,144	27,568
Shelby	5,635,313	218,245	785,443	956,993	1,541,529
Bartlett	103,982	14,683	(D)	43,421	(D)
Collierville	59,314	6,561	2,433	(D)	4,651
Germantown	158,517	3,398	(D)	59,015	(D)
Memphis	4,811,298	171,275	642,606	745,835	1,423,491
Millington	105,340	(D)	19,951	18,717	32,681
Smith	58,623	(D)	(D)	13,662	9,854
Carthage	48,339	(D)	(D)	9,904	9,854
Stewart	18,403	(D)	1,137	9,507	(D)
Sullivan	974,339	44,032	185,931	157,061	286,784
Bristol	299,712	(D)	(D)	48,322	120,903
Kingsport (part)[2]	590,761	(D)	(D)	(D)	(D)
Sumner	436,571	46,112	40,529	124,741	89,590
Gallatin	197,178	19,695	23,142	41,406	70,733
Goodlettsville (part)[2]	4,483	(D)	0	0	(D)
Hendersonville	166,812	19,212	(D)	56,152	16,590
Portland	29,751	(D)	(D)	10,345	(D)
Tipton	105,303	11,108	14,457	26,787	21,952
Covington	76,143	(D)	(D)	19,265	20,599
Trousdale	22,351	(D)	(D)	8,298	568
Hartsville	20,928	0	(D)	(D)	(D)
Unicoi	41,216	2,306	2,509	12,209	(D)
Erwin	37,394	(D)	2,509	11,765	(D)
Union	13,202	(D)	(D)	5,554	3,028
Van Buren	439	0	0	(D)	0

TABLE 7.13--RETAIL SALES OF ESTABLISHMENTS WITH PAYROLL, BY TYPE OF ESTABLISHMENT, TENNESSEE, COUNTIES, AND MUNICIPALITIES WITH POPULATION OF 2,500 OR MORE, 1987 [In thousands of dollars] (Continued)

Gasoline service stations	Apparel, acces-sory stores	Furniture, equip-ment stores	Eating, drinking places	Drug stores	Miscel-laneous retail stores	County and municipality
22,528	16,159	12,722	29,717	8,599	22,790	Putnam
20,004	(D)	12,032	27,901	7,369	(D)	Cookeville
1,141	(D)	(D)	1,414	0	(D)	Monterey
5,675	2,760	1,320	5,516	4,655	3,614	Rhea
2,611	(D)	(D)	3,368	2,242	(D)	Dayton
8,500	4,897	5,857	12,453	10,155	3,960	Roane
2,818	1,678	1,100	8,192	4,247	(D)	Harriman
2,535	(D)	709	1,659	2,388	(D)	Kingston
0	0	0	0	0	0	Oak Ridge (part)[2]
0	0	(D)	0	0	(D)	Oliver Springs (part)[2]
(D)	(D)	(D)	1,846	3,520	282	Rockwood
17,300	(D)	(D)	8,525	6,405	(D)	Robertson
0	0	0	0	(D)	0	Greenbrier
8,681	(D)	4,257	8,157	5,638	(D)	Springfield
56,221	23,939	29,845	57,008	16,792	30,855	Rutherford
9,123	0	(D)	(D)	(D)	889	LaVergne
40,927	22,924	26,854	45,376	11,535	(D)	Murfreesboro
(D)	1,015	662	9,898	(D)	(D)	Smyrna
1,490	950	(D)	5,028	4,136	1,218	Scott
(D)	(D)	(D)	(D)	(D)	1,218	Oneida
3,463	(D)	(D)	1,580	(D)	(D)	Sequatchie
(D)	(D)	0	(D)	(D)	294	Dunlap
30,352	32,896	15,989	85,141	10,282	40,079	Sevier
3,023	7,772	2,012	37,977	(D)	17,681	Gatlinburg
17,418	3,779	2,593	13,105	6,112	6,752	Sevierville
403,554	324,876	308,142	487,642	221,268	387,621	Shelby
10,407	(D)	7,249	10,985	6,929	(D)	Bartlett
9,916	(D)	1,217	7,946	3,523	(D)	Collierville
11,564	27,633	4,637	16,107	(D)	(D)	Germantown
346,105	256,971	279,384	416,565	186,230	342,836	Memphis
7,636	2,520	3,956	12,127	3,532	(D)	Millington
9,838	1,083	7,397	2,215	2,757	1,116	Smith
(D)	1,083	7,397	1,152	(D)	(D)	Carthage
424	(D)	(D)	1,227	(D)	498	Stewart
58,670	41,841	36,806	84,308	31,215	47,691	Sullivan
13,731	(D)	11,605	26,446	8,879	(D)	Bristol
(D)	(D)	22,521	52,130	(D)	(D)	Kingsport (part)[2]
40,190	11,428	10,208	37,742	17,352	18,679	Sumner
4,904	4,286	4,365	14,336	6,911	7,400	Gallatin
(D)	0	0	0	0	(D)	Goodlettsville (part)[2]
14,061	(D)	3,688	18,844	7,202	(D)	Hendersonville
(D)	(D)	1,179	2,103	(D)	(D)	Portland
9,328	2,284	2,668	6,476	3,754	6,489	Tipton
5,059	2,284	(D)	5,676	(D)	4,316	Covington
7,351	(D)	315	(D)	(D)	3,412	Trousdale
7,351	(D)	315	(D)	(D)	(D)	Hartsville
1,920	64	1,381	6,003	3,243	(D)	Unicoi
972	64	1,381	4,992	3,243	(D)	Erwin
(D)	(D)	(D)	285	(D)	(D)	Union
(D)	0	0	(D)	0	0	Van Buren

TABLE 7.13--RETAIL SALES OF ESTABLISHMENTS WITH PAYROLL, BY TYPE OF ESTABLISHMENT, TENNESSEE, COUNTIES, AND MUNICIPALITIES WITH POPULATION OF 2,500 OR MORE, 1987 [In thousands of dollars] (Continued)

County and municipality	Total	Building material dealers, etc.[1]	General merchan-dise stores	Food stores	Auto-motive dealers
Warren	150,310	11,853	19,925	43,342	27,679
McMinnville	131,287	(D)	19,925	31,959	(D)
Washington	528,121	44,870	(D)	103,860	118,369
Johnson City (part)[2]	473,397	39,031	(D)	83,040	113,980
Jonesborough	16,104	(D)	(D)	8,165	1,908
Wayne	34,738	8,335	1,732	15,231	(D)
Weakley	116,716	8,437	(D)	27,336	22,414
McKenzie (part)[2]	(D)	0	0	(D)	0
Martin	73,629	3,734	(D)	9,577	(D)
White	83,931	4,090	(D)	19,608	34,409
Sparta	73,104	(D)	(D)	16,593	(D)
Williamson	488,610	28,979	(D)	105,006	157,341
Brentwood	138,037	7,455	0	36,361	(D)
Fairview	13,075	(D)	0	9,284	(D)
Franklin	321,574	16,975	(D)	54,381	135,103
Wilson	286,514	23,114	(D)	57,160	77,780
Lebanon	245,177	18,599	(D)	44,296	(D)
Mt. Juliet	20,856	1,581	0	7,415	(D)

TABLE 7.13--RETAIL SALES OF ESTABLISHMENTS WITH PAYROLL, BY TYPE OF ESTABLISHMENT, TENNESSEE, COUNTIES, AND MUNICIPALITIES WITH POPULATION OF 2,500 OR MORE, 1987 [In thousands of dollars] (Continued)

Gasoline service stations	Apparel, acces-sory stores	Furniture, equip-ment stores	Eating, drinking places	Drug stores	Miscel-laneous retail stores	County and municipality
5,544	9,361	5,578	9,817	6,601	10,610	Warren
(D)	(D)	(D)	(D)	6,601	(D)	McMinnville
31,558	24,783	25,869	54,242	21,221	24,940	Washington
23,516	(D)	(D)	50,616	17,328	(D)	Johnson City (part)[2]
1,491	(D)	0	1,368	1,983	(D)	Jonesborough
(D)	220	101	491	2,032	692	Wayne
8,195	5,272	5,808	9,729	5,346	(D)	Weakley
0	0	0	0	0	0	McKenzie (part)[2]
3,464	2,658	4,665	7,545	2,642	(D)	Martin
3,224	2,036	1,022	4,151	3,597	(D)	White
(D)	(D)	(D)	(D)	3,597	1,627	Sparta
46,546	21,248	21,343	37,473	14,753	(D)	Williamson
11,843	(D)	10,650	13,842	5,069	(D)	Brentwood
(D)	0	0	197	(D)	(D)	Fairview
29,629	10,755	(D)	22,506	8,509	(D)	Franklin
43,250	9,570	7,555	26,339	8,033	(D)	Wilson
35,154	(D)	7,078	21,633	6,291	(D)	Lebanon
(D)	(D)	(D)	(D)	(D)	2,201	Mt. Juliet

(D) withheld to avoid disclosure.

1. Includes building materials, hardware, garden supply, mobile home dealers.

2. Municipalities located in more than one county.

Source: U.S. Department of Commerce, Bureau of the Census, *1987 Census of Retail Trade, Geographic Area Series, Tennessee.*

TABLE 7.14--WHOLESALE TRADE DATA, TENNESSEE, COUNTIES AND MUNICIPALITIES WITH POPULATION OF 2,500 OR MORE, 1987 [Dollar amounts in thousands]

County and municipality	Number of establishments			Sales	Annual payroll	Number of paid employees[1]
	Total	Merchant wholesalers	Other operating types			
TENNESSEE	8,782	7,237	1,545	$48,278,891	$2,518,097	115,927
Anderson	56	47	9	133,172	15,666	723
Clinton	11	11	0	(D)	(D)	(D)
Oak Ridge (part)[2]	31	26	5	29,316	2,632	155
Oliver Springs (part)[2]	1	1	0	(D)	(D)	(D)
Bedford	39	36	3	(D)	(D)	(D)
Shelbyville	30	28	2	81,214	5,135	278
Benton	18	17	1	18,248	1,475	104
Camden	15	14	1	(D)	(D)	(D)
Bledsoe	2	2	0	(D)	(D)	(D)
Blount	85	74	11	350,836	23,479	1,258
Alcoa	20	17	3	55,669	3,345	245
Maryville	37	33	4	182,884	11,564	599
Bradley	97	90	7	582,046	20,865	1,234
Cleveland	82	76	6	570,179	20,251	1,184
Campbell	27	27	0	(D)	(D)	(D)
Jellico	3	3	0	(D)	(D)	(D)
LaFollette	11	11	0	31,592	2,484	130
Cannon	4	4	0	(D)	(D)	(D)
Carroll	34	31	3	(D)	(D)	(D)
Huntingdon	14	13	1	38,096	1,336	98
McKenzie (part)[2]	11	9	2	6,553	712	52
Carter	23	23	0	(D)	(D)	(D)
Elizabethton	17	17	0	20,055	2,031	135
Johnson City (part)[2]	0	0	0	0	0	0
Cheatham	7	7	0	(D)	(D)	(D)
Chester	14	14	0	19,769	1,062	73
Henderson	12	12	0	(D)	(D)	(D)
Claiborne	19	15	4	(D)	(D)	(D)
Clay	4	4	0	(D)	(D)	(D)
Cocke	26	21	5	52,613	1,558	146
Newport	17	15	2	25,652	1,138	89
Coffee	55	52	3	(D)	(D)	(D)
Manchester	16	15	1	37,169	1,583	135
Tullahoma (part) 2	23	22	1	46,960	4,266	218
Crockett	16	15	1	(D)	(D)	(D)
Alamo	3	3	0	(D)	(D)	(D)
Cumberland	33	32	1	(D)	(D)	(D)
Crossville	22	22	0	(D)	(D)	(D)
Davidson	1,506	1,179	327	8,818,393	575,227	24,329
Belle Meade	6	3	3	(D)	(D)	(D)
Forest Hills	5	2	3	9,386	476	11
Goodlettsville (part)[2]	38	31	7	(D)	(D)	(D)
Nashville-Davidson[3]	1,454	1,141	313	8,124,514	552,492	23,360
Oak Hill	3	2	1	(D)	(D)	(D)
Decatur	10	8	2	(D)	(D)	(D)
DeKalb	11	11	0	9,144	930	75
Smithville	8	8	0	(D)	(D)	(D)
Dickson	34	30	4	(D)	(D)	(D)
Dickson	24	22	2	(D)	(D)	(D)

TABLE 7.14--WHOLESALE TRADE DATA, TENNESSEE, COUNTIES AND MUNICIPALITIES WITH POPULATION OF 2,500 OR MORE, 1987 [Dollar amounts in thousands] (Continued)

County and municipality	Number of establishments: Total	Merchant whole-salers	Other operating types	Sales	Annual payroll	Number of paid employees[1]
Dyer	68	61	7	176,343	8,920	573
Dyersburg	51	46	5	143,842	7,898	510
Newbern	6	5	1	14,673	694	43
Fayette	16	16	0	41,868	3,231	204
Fentress	6	6	0	6,286	421	33
Franklin	24	22	2	45,563	3,139	217
Tullahoma (part)[2]	0	0	0	0	0	0
Winchester	7	7	0	(D)	(D)	(D)
Gibson	67	63	4	140,669	7,608	467
Humboldt	14	14	0	16,890	1,073	74
Milan	19	17	2	45,337	2,212	124
Trenton	21	20	1	63,699	2,811	189
Giles	38	35	3	60,272	4,338	283
Pulaski	23	21	2	48,912	3,478	210
Grainger	10	10	0	11,520	1,139	68
Greene	67	49	18	170,180	8,532	718
Greeneville	51	35	16	155,906	6,614	542
Grundy	9	9	0	6,510	683	53
Hamblen	86	75	11	275,508	19,542	1,135
Morristown	70	63	7	(D)	(D)	(D)
Hamilton	816	670	146	3,957,120	226,165	10,530
Chattanooga	717	594	123	(D)	(D)	(D)
Collegedale	2	1	1	(D)	(D)	(D)
East Ridge	26	23	3	34,829	1,862	152
Red Bank	15	14	1	13,429	2,229	101
Signal Mountain	9	5	4	8,495	512	40
Soddy-Daisy	7	6	1	5,977	546	35
Hancock	5	5	0	2,635	184	24
Hardeman	23	21	2	31,596	2,134	195
Bolivar	10	9	1	17,739	986	94
Hardin	21	20	1	44,236	2,348	135
Savannah	13	13	0	(D)	(D)	(D)
Hawkins	20	18	2	(D)	(D)	(D)
Church Hill	1	0	1	(D)	(D)	(D)
Kingsport (part)[2]	0	0	0	0	0	0
Mount Carmel	1	1	0	(D)	(D)	(D)
Rogersville	11	10	1	(D)	(D)	(D)
Haywood	20	16	4	26,259	1,583	139
Brownsville	17	14	3	(D)	(D)	(D)
Henderson	22	21	1	59,037	3,137	252
Lexington	14	14	0	(D)	(D)	(D)
Henry	50	45	5	99,594	8,036	547
McKenzie (part)[2]	0	0	0	0	0	0
Paris	34	30	4	80,592	6,283	403
Hickman	10	9	1	6,693	467	40
Centerville	7	6	1	(D)	(D)	(D)
Houston	9	8	1	3,628	281	27
Humphreys	16	15	1	37,991	1,687	101
Waverly	11	11	0	(D)	(D)	(D)
Jackson	9	7	2	(D)	(D)	(D)
Jefferson	24	21	3	22,729	2,289	169
Jefferson City	6	6	0	4,584	439	36

TABLE 7.14--WHOLESALE TRADE DATA, TENNESSEE, COUNTIES AND MUNICIPALITIES WITH POPULATION OF 2,500 OR MORE, 1987 [Dollar amounts in thousands] (Continued)

County and municipality	Number of establishments: Total	Merchant whole-salers	Other operating types	Sales	Annual payroll	Number of paid employees [1]
Johnson	11	11	0	9,586	749	65
Knox	956	780	176	4,066,833	305,605	12,780
Farragut	1	1	0	(D)	(D)	(D)
Knoxville	753	627	126	3,128,958	203,653	9,568
Lake	14	12	2	42,499	2,029	211
Lauderdale	30	30	0	50,191	3,027	212
Ripley	13	13	0	28,762	1,524	108
Lawrence	40	35	5	74,573	3,887	271
Lawrenceburg	31	27	4	64,607	3,415	222
Lewis	9	9	0	19,496	1,277	109
Hohenwald	9	9	0	19,496	1,277	109
Lincoln	43	39	4	72,192	4,813	383
Fayetteville	31	27	4	59,042	3,717	319
Loudon	26	23	3	48,697	3,436	228
Lenoir City	11	9	2	27,671	1,485	112
Loudon	6	5	1	14,448	1,342	69
McMinn	51	50	1	91,859	6,790	453
Athens	31	31	0	(D)	(D)	(D)
Etowah	2	2	0	(D)	(D)	(D)
McNairy	27	25	2	87,452	11,440	540
Selmer	14	12	2	63,637	10,037	468
Macon	12	12	0	15,134	631	66
Lafayette	9	9	0	14,439	578	61
Madison	167	155	12	453,130	34,171	1,922
Jackson	149	138	11	420,418	30,821	1,680
Marion	19	18	1	28,378	2,093	132
Jasper	5	4	1	14,415	982	56
South Pittsburg	4	4	0	9,555	538	43
Marshall	14	13	1	18,072	1,922	121
Lewisburg	10	10	0	(D)	(D)	(D)
Maury	83	78	5	135,677	10,496	636
Columbia	66	63	3	100,392	8,819	514
Mount Pleasant	7	6	1	14,614	876	42
Meigs	0	0	0	0	0	0
Monroe	36	31	5	102,805	4,253	321
Madisonville	10	10	0	7,179	1,159	96
Sweetwater	13	10	3	20,362	1,532	104
Montgomery	90	85	5	169,871	11,798	726
Clarksville	81	76	5	151,707	9,940	660
Moore	2	2	0	(D)	(D)	(D)
Morgan	10	10	0	9,965	616	43
Oliver Springs (part)[2]	0	0	0	0	0	0
Obion	64	58	6	161,251	8,324	553
South Fulton	9	7	2	8,124	506	37
Union City	35	31	4	124,922	6,126	389
Overton	18	18	0	23,904	1,053	80
Livingston	11	11	0	18,999	586	45
Perry	5	5	0	11,606	1,532	97
Pickett	5	5	0	3,873	348	32
Polk	12	12	0	40,537	2,207	98

TABLE 7.14--WHOLESALE TRADE DATA, TENNESSEE, COUNTIES AND MUNICIPALITIES WITH POPULATION OF 2,500 OR MORE, 1987 [Dollar amounts in thousands] (Continued)

County and municipality	Number of establishments: Total	Merchant wholesalers	Other operating types	Sales	Annual payroll	Number of paid employees[1]
Putnam	101	94	7	206,970	15,492	1,033
Cookeville	96	89	7	(D)	(D)	(D)
Monterey	0	0	0	0	0	0
Rhea	11	10	1	14,310	568	54
Dayton	8	7	1	(D)	(D)	(D)
Roane	29	26	3	98,349	6,507	392
Harriman	11	11	0	(D)	(D)	(D)
Kingston	4	4	0	(D)	(D)	(D)
Oak Ridge (part)[2]	0	0	0	0	0	0
Oliver Springs (part)[2]	0	0	0	0	0	0
Rockwood	10	8	2	53,543	3,929	227
Robertson	46	37	9	105,086	6,157	471
Greenbrier	2	2	0	(D)	(D)	(D)
Springfield	31	25	6	78,334	4,781	346
Rutherford	146	132	14	432,465	40,024	1,956
LaVergne	23	21	2	210,649	19,793	783
Murfreesboro	95	85	10	173,395	15,716	866
Smyrna	17	16	1	36,906	4,135	254
Scott	15	13	2	21,007	1,229	115
Oneida	10	8	2	19,795	1,080	96
Sequatchie	5	5	0	8,671	343	26
Dunlap	5	5	0	8,671	343	26
Sevier	42	38	4	44,355	3,595	225
Gatlinburg	3	3	0	(D)	(D)	(D)
Sevierville	17	16	1	28,968	2,346	130
Shelby	2,081	1,562	519	21,108,532	803,832	33,584
Bartlett	30	21	9	102,332	4,600	189
Collierville	16	13	3	68,599	3,475	244
Germantown	87	43	44	1,352,674	29,003	928
Memphis	1,840	1,400	440	18,447,612	721,381	30,227
Millington	5	5	0	2,692	445	24
Smith	19	16	3	33,430	1,504	199
Carthage	11	10	1	14,150	491	68
Stewart	4	3	1	(D)	(D)	(D)
Sullivan	253	212	41	(D)	(D)	(D)
Bristol	82	64	18	267,868	56,704	2,070
Kingsport (part)[2]	114	94	20	2,028,762	47,210	1,709
Sumner	123	94	29	219,076	14,779	834
Gallatin	32	28	4	(D)	(D)	(D)
Goodlettsville (part)[2]	1	1	0	(D)	(D)	(D)
Hendersonville	62	38	24	74,844	5,757	299
Portland	14	14	0	18,046	2,085	138
Tipton	26	24	2	60,475	2,433	204
Covington	21	19	2	(D)	(D)	(D)
Trousdale	12	10	2	21,904	559	93
Hartsville	11	9	2	(D)	(D)	(D)
Unicoi	5	5	0	(D)	(D)	(D)
Erwin	3	3	0	(D)	(D)	(D)
Union	5	5	0	8,154	460	41
Van Buren	5	5	0	(D)	(D)	(D)

TABLE 7.14--WHOLESALE TRADE DATA, TENNESSEE, COUNTIES AND MUNICIPALITIES WITH POPULATION OF 2,500 OR MORE, 1987 [Dollar amounts in thousands] (Continued)

County and municipality	Number of establishments: Total	Merchant whole-salers	Other operating types	Sales	Annual payroll	Number of paid employees[1]
Warren	49	44	5	84,731	6,453	449
McMinnville	28	26	2	43,382	3,726	199
Washington	177	157	20	597,450	43,430	2,783
Johnson City (part)[2]	142	126	16	501,252	35,699	2,122
Jonesborough	4	4	0	(D)	(D)	(D)
Wayne	11	11	0	12,804	695	70
Weakley	50	49	1	88,395	6,454	372
McKenzie (part)[2]	0	0	0	0	0	0
Martin	17	17	0	(D)	(D)	(D)
White	28	25	3	55,731	2,905	251
Sparta	16	14	2	38,823	2,264	174
Williamson	168	119	49	839,611	24,371	1,076
Brentwood	77	47	30	(D)	(D)	(D)
Fairview	3	3	0	(D)	(D)	(D)
Franklin	67	54	13	151,858	8,390	441
Wilson	71	64	7	235,192	11,821	631
Lebanon	39	36	3	115,481	8,222	433
Mt. Juliet	15	14	1	22,276	2,220	119

(D) withheld to avoid disclosure.

1. Survey taken during week of March 12.

2. Municipalities located in more than one county.

3. Consists of the Metropolitan Government of Nashville and Davidson County.

Source: U.S. Department of Commerce, Bureau of the Census, *1987 Census of Wholesale Trade, Geographic Area Series, Tennessee.*

TABLE 7.15--SERVICE INDUSTRIES DATA, COUNTIES AND MUNICIPALITIES WITH POPULATION OF 2,500 OR MORE, 1987 [Dollar amounts in thousands]

County and municipality	Number of establish-ments	Receipts	Annual payroll	Number of paid employees[1]
Anderson	447	$683,054	$200,812	8,439
Clinton	50	14,837	3,721	383
Oak Ridge (part)[2]	324	(D)	(D)	(D)
Oliver Springs (part)[2]	16	(D)	(D)	(D)
Bedford	134	34,491	12,224	1,093
Shelbyville	119	32,183	11,442	1,006
Benton	61	19,096	5,910	514
Camden	45	14,219	5,124	419
Bledsoe	29	7,324	2,349	180
Blount	442	132,163	48,403	3,139
Alcoa	61	22,076	6,103	583
Maryville	274	77,107	30,816	1,794
Bradley	388	179,674	64,743	5,329
Cleveland	342	141,576	50,288	3,720
Campbell	108	21,327	6,353	679
Jellico	15	2,162	807	60
LaFollette	66	13,398	3,947	459
Cannon	27	8,934	3,307	239
Carroll	107	17,289	5,681	508
Huntingdon	42	8,128	2,881	282
McKenzie (part)[2]	35	(D)	(D)	(D)
Carter	157	41,363	15,030	1,055
Elizabethton	132	37,678	13,237	967
Johnson City (part)[2]	0	0	0	0
Cheatham	41	4,136	967	95
Chester	22	3,067	953	123
Henderson	19	2,898	903	105
Claiborne	65	15,226	4,134	465
Clay	26	12,190	4,816	317
Cocke	90	20,144	6,104	594
Newport	69	16,948	4,863	462
Coffee	257	387,307	219,824	8,153
Manchester	82	(D)	(D)	(D)
Tullahoma (part)[2]	146	(D)	(D)	(D)
Crockett	35	5,942	2,387	197
Alamo	19	4,373	1,978	158
Cumberland	145	29,898	10,546	898
Crossville	125	25,123	9,099	728
Davidson	4,843	2,786,669	1,006,911	63,282
Belle Meade	72	66,424	32,565	506
Forest Hills	11	903	421	17
Goodlettsville (part)[2]	116	39,747	17,261	1,570
Nashville-Davidson[3]	4,633	2,678,407	956,334	61,156
Oak Hill	11	1,188	330	33
Decatur	39	9,324	2,966	316
DeKalb	54	19,919	6,743	391
Smithville	42	17,429	5,920	316
Dickson	130	31,142	12,296	975
Dickson	87	24,377	10,554	819
Dyer	181	37,279	11,385	829
Dyersburg	162	34,801	10,589	746
Newbern	8	838	242	22
Fayette	44	6,790	2,207	212

TABLE 7.15--SERVICE INDUSTRIES DATA, COUNTIES AND MUNICIPALITIES WITH POPULATION OF 2,500 OR MORE, 1987 [Dollar amounts in thousands] (Continued)

County and municipality	Number of establish-ments	Receipts	Annual payroll	Number of paid employees [1]
Fentress	52	16,240	5,970	466
Franklin	122	18,451	6,148	439
Tullahoma (part)[2]	1	(D)	(D)	(D)
Winchester	82	12,925	4,150	332
Gibson	212	46,748	15,142	1,383
Humboldt	62	13,593	4,282	392
Milan	59	12,836	4,849	377
Trenton	51	15,826	4,889	497
Giles	100	35,083	12,629	910
Pulaski	76	29,259	10,406	654
Grainger	27	4,798	1,443	177
Greene	249	58,027	20,158	1,517
Greeneville	214	49,482	17,150	1,238
Grundy	26	5,544	1,545	229
Hamblen	275	82,751	28,013	1,869
Morristown	254	80,058	27,100	1,780
Hamilton	2,147	1,005,624	377,696	23,946
Chattanooga	1,710	878,848	335,856	20,854
Collegedale	15	8,075	2,940	230
East Ridge	157	59,759	18,949	1,401
Red Bank	95	24,522	8,805	557
Signal Mountain	42	4,536	1,728	103
Soddy-Daisy	23	1,626	401	42
Hancock	13	2,024	653	89
Hardeman	66	14,635	4,169	416
Bolivar	41	8,401	2,932	287
Hardin	78	13,924	4,018	352
Savannah	66	12,259	3,542	310
Hawkins	95	17,248	5,507	494
Church Hill	21	4,961	1,582	148
Kingsport (part)[2]	5	364	159	20
Mount Carmel	3	159	38	9
Rogersville	44	6,362	1,746	154
Haywood	65	15,969	4,971	361
Brownsville	60	15,003	4,786	336
Henderson	76	9,142	2,860	262
Lexington	56	7,790	2,528	223
Henry	148	37,759	10,757	705
McKenzie (part)[2]	0	0	0	0
Paris	122	32,189	9,312	589
Hickman	46	6,906	2,057	212
Centerville	30	5,755	1,784	181
Houston	16	6,308	2,362	172
Humphreys	61	15,955	4,673	373
Waverly	43	13,240	4,056	297
Jackson	30	7,702	2,501	227
Jefferson	88	15,116	4,455	430
Jefferson City	43	8,096	2,645	280
Johnson	35	7,242	2,278	196
Knox	2,715	1,111,249	441,485	25,018
Farragut	1	(D)	(D)	(D)
Knoxville	2,142	838,374	325,327	19,451
Lake	24	3,489	1,244	178

TABLE 7.15--SERVICE INDUSTRIES DATA, COUNTIES AND MUNICIPALITIES WITH POPULATION OF 2,500 OR MORE, 1987 [Dollar amounts in thousands] (Continued)

County and municipality	Number of establish-ments	Receipts	Annual payroll	Number of paid employees [1]
Lauderdale	67	11,422	3,655	374
Ripley	52	8,623	2,847	279
Lawrence	133	29,742	9,257	777
Lawrenceburg	102	17,860	4,827	419
Lewis	32	8,891	3,421	299
Hohenwald	26	8,034	2,901	279
Lincoln	122	18,717	5,495	563
Fayetteville	94	16,489	4,755	495
Loudon	106	22,054	7,510	703
Lenoir City	43	7,582	2,545	235
Loudon	38	11,447	3,982	386
McMinn	172	60,639	19,332	1,597
Athens	124	49,826	15,725	1,293
Etowah	30	6,024	2,474	200
McNairy	70	29,121	13,440	953
Selmer	42	6,425	1,770	144
Macon	47	8,016	2,352	234
Lafayette	38	5,328	1,534	120
Madison	542	208,938	96,318	5,101
Jackson	517	205,860	95,525	5,026
Marion	70	22,278	7,906	625
Jasper	24	3,144	1,248	79
South Pittsburg	27	10,453	3,845	324
Marshall	88	25,384	8,745	972
Lewisburg	71	23,467	8,265	919
Maury	310	96,157	32,253	2,276
Columbia	262	89,549	30,151	2,083
Mount Pleasant	25	4,239	1,260	129
Meigs	13	2,197	897	82
Monroe	83	18,901	5,957	524
Madisonville	19	2,617	761	67
Sweetwater	42	9,059	3,111	266
Montgomery	418	93,041	30,720	2,501
Clarksville	386	87,021	28,620	2,300
Moore	3	(D)	(D)	(D)
Morgan	17	3,536	1,269	146
Oliver Springs (part)[2]	0	0	0	0
Obion	161	41,320	12,799	901
South Fulton	23	2,082	494	58
Union City	108	36,644	11,504	764
Overton	49	16,053	4,849	378
Livingston	43	15,121	4,673	358
Perry	22	8,537	2,880	244
Pickett	12	2,267	677	88
Polk	44	7,423	2,279	201
Putnam	320	91,189	36,137	2,968
Cookeville	293	83,401	33,480	2,702
Monterey	8	2,129	852	94
Rhea	73	10,060	3,097	235
Dayton	45	5,539	1,656	134
Roane	167	32,086	10,412	791
Harriman	65	13,604	4,914	415
Kingston	35	6,622	1,888	133
Oak Ridge (part)[2]	3	(D)	(D)	(D)

TABLE 7.15--SERVICE INDUSTRIES DATA, COUNTIES AND MUNICIPALITIES WITH POPULATION OF 2,500 OR MORE, 1987 [Dollar amounts in thousands] (Continued)

County and municipality	Number of establish-ments	Receipts	Annual payroll	Number of paid employees[1]
Oliver Springs (part)[2]	1	(D)	(D)	(D)
Rockwood	37	6,695	2,126	128
Robertson	128	22,605	7,250	664
Greenbrier	8	1,165	445	35
Springfield	92	17,552	5,776	510
Rutherford	538	180,466	67,559	4,350
LaVergne	32	20,559	10,545	365
Murfreesboro	403	136,073	48,741	3,319
Smyrna	77	21,120	7,581	583
Scott	44	8,265	2,919	229
Oneida	33	4,704	1,872	127
Sequatchie	32	8,745	3,214	249
Dunlap	22	7,149	2,860	218
Sevier	470	185,749	48,405	4,061
Gatlinburg	142	67,871	17,234	1,756
Sevierville	129	20,160	6,683	558
Shelby	5,289	2,517,776	984,817	63,148
Bartlett	125	29,591	11,419	881
Collierville	71	12,258	4,070	368
Germantown	295	114,481	55,130	2,139
Memphis	4,475	2,255,617	877,757	56,983
Millington	54	11,638	4,211	340
Smith	55	14,266	4,469	375
Carthage	42	9,119	2,875	269
Stewart	14	1,706	453	42
Sullivan	893	346,288	135,537	7,374
Bristol	245	93,987	39,361	1,859
Kingsport (part)[2]	516	203,813	81,265	4,412
Sumner	521	163,826	61,262	4,305
Gallatin	153	44,389	16,934	1,306
Goodlettsville (part)[2]	3	311	104	10
Hendersonville	282	108,033	40,897	2,691
Portland	27	3,975	1,491	99
Tipton	103	15,365	4,137	361
Covington	65	11,082	3,001	249
Trousdale	23	5,637	2,025	155
Hartsville	19	5,203	1,915	142
Unicoi	60	10,927	4,308	326
Erwin	50	(D)	(D)	(D)
Union	20	4,313	1,206	146
Van Buren	3	(D)	(D)	(D)
Warren	151	40,473	13,142	996
McMinnville	127	38,474	12,557	914
Washington	588	173,566	67,289	5,117
Johnson City (part)[2]	480	157,832	61,691	4,551
Jonesborough	30	5,915	2,290	199
Wayne	30	7,415	2,685	208
Weakley	111	33,003	11,936	1,114
McKenzie (part)[2]	1	(D)	(D)	(D)
Martin	51	24,223	9,527	884
White	71	12,367	3,740	323
Sparta	59	10,954	3,475	305

TABLE 7.15--SERVICE INDUSTRIES DATA, COUNTIES AND MUNICIPALITIES WITH POPULATION OF 2,500 OR MORE, 1987 [Dollar amounts in thousands] (Continued)

County and municipality	Number of establish-ments	Receipts	Annual payroll	Number of paid employees [1]
Williamson	601	213,404	85,546	4,756
Brentwood	284	120,278	52,669	2,598
Fairview	10	975	233	23
Franklin	255	76,712	27,667	1,973
Wilson	305	103,519	33,261	2,606
Lebanon	214	88,689	27,861	2,238
Mt. Juliet	49	7,374	2,172	171

Note: Includes only those establishments with payroll that were subject to Federal Income Tax.

1. Survey taken during week of March 12.

2. Municipalities located in more than one county.

3. Includes the metropolitan government of Nashville and Davidson County.

Source: U.S. Department of Commerce, Bureau of the Census, *1987 Census of Service Industries, Geographic Area Series, Tennessee.*

TABLE 7.16--RETAIL TRADE STATISTICS, SOUTHEASTERN STATES, 1987 [Dollar amounts in thousands]

State	Number of establishments					
	Total	Individual proprietor-ships	Partner-ships	Sales	Annual payroll	Number of paid employees [1]
TENNESSEE	29,373	10,123	2,761	$28,532,933	$3,198,060	338,168
Alabama	24,092	7,936	1,558	21,260,901	2,357,486	249,847
Arkansas	15,096	5,692	1,111	11,631,735	1,245,802	138,671
Florida	83,808	13,814	2,964	87,925,609	10,297,035	1,022,862
Georgia	39,782	10,836	2,169	39,994,882	4,791,594	486,992
Kentucky	21,731	6,663	1,798	18,939,911	2,132,223	243,641
Louisiana	24,262	6,459	1,048	21,627,111	2,569,763	277,708
Mississippi	15,729	6,062	1,312	11,357,667	1,264,565	140,361
North Carolina	42,991	11,846	2,676	39,051,791	4,422,835	464,862
South Carolina	21,859	6,300	1,245	18,949,588	2,177,453	237,122
Virginia	34,916	7,704	1,643	38,960,210	4,556,660	453,325
West Virginia	10,737	3,405	595	9,029,979	994,297	109,220

Note: Includes only establishments with payroll.

1. Survey taken during week of March 12.

Source: U.S. Department of Commerce, Bureau of the Census, 1987 *Census of Retail Trade, Geographic Area Series*, individual states.

TABLE 7.17--WHOLESALE TRADE DATA, SOUTHEASTERN STATES, 1987 [Dollar amounts in thousands]

State	Number of establish-ments	Sales	Annual payroll	Number of paid employees[1]	Operating expenses
TENNESSEE	8,782	$48,278,891	$2,518,097	115,927	$5,171,868
Alabama	6,671	24,343,595	1,548,477	77,559	3,196,662
Arkansas	4,024	12,780,741	705,452	38,940	1,495,469
Florida	25,636	97,360,044	5,554,657	261,765	11,638,571
Georgia	13,678	86,853,971	4,116,577	178,235	8,529,135
Kentucky	5,650	24,461,486	1,240,003	63,606	2,538,774
Louisiana	7,643	31,477,276	1,652,536	80,533	3,459,995
Mississippi	3,850	12,249,754	733,066	39,936	1,563,650
North Carolina	12,109	57,027,579	3,064,076	140,158	6,051,686
South Carolina	5,271	17,084,415	1,064,842	54,551	2,221,689
Virginia	8,446	44,758,793	2,625,045	115,126	5,409,943
West Virginia	2,444	5,935,356	476,934	24,217	963,763

1. Survey taken during week of March 12.

Source: U.S. Department of Commerce, Bureau of the Census, *1987 Census of Wholesale Trade, Geographic Area Series*, individual states.

TABLE 7.18--SERVICE INDUSTRIES DATA, SOUTHEASTERN STATES, 1987 [Dollar amounts in thousands]

State	Number of establish-ments	Receipts	Annual payroll	Number of paid employees[1]
TENNESSEE	27,829	$12,010,161	$4,486,948	282,908
Alabama	20,474	8,397,181	3,066,890	189,566
Arkansas	12,437	3,703,250	1,365,908	93,960
Florida	98,713	45,530,941	16,909,560	974,746
Georgia	39,189	18,645,815	6,908,896	414,969
Kentucky	18,415	6,325,252	2,315,487	166,228
Louisiana	25,513	10,243,284	3,788,155	240,551
Mississippi	11,663	3,331,645	1,208,449	84,293
North Carolina	36,016	12,829,836	4,928,270	331,402
South Carolina	18,810	6,354,990	2,396,984	169,535
Virginia	38,337	20,414,594	8,128,443	438,728
West Virginia	8,909	2,917,003	1,030,947	67,281

Note: Includes only those establishments with payroll that were subject to Federal Income Tax.

1. Survey taken during week of March 12.

Source: U.S. Department of Commerce, Bureau of the Census, *1987 Census of Service Industries, Geographic Area Series*, individual states.

TABLE 7.19--NUMBER OF BUSINESS STARTS, BY INDUSTRY SECTOR, SOUTHEASTERN STATES, 1987

State	Total[1]		Agri-culture, forestry and fishing	Mining	Construc-tion	Manufac-turing	Transpor-tation and public utilities	Wholesale and retail trade	Finance, insurance and real estate	Ser-vices
	Firms	Employees								
TENNESSEE	3,852	21,784	47	9	495	326	122	1,716	232	802
Alabama	3,015	16,019	59	8	369	220	79	1,367	119	644
Arkansas	1,732	9,829	40	18	195	149	79	850	61	318
Florida	15,088	80,027	210	12	2,353	1,113	555	6,338	1,133	3,236
Georgia	6,972	36,341	96	8	881	556	233	2,737	433	1,591
Kentucky	2,876	14,212	49	92	345	202	108	1,270	130	603
Louisiana	3,490	19,687	44	85	380	187	127	1,580	219	833
Mississippi	1,743	8,625	50	15	160	127	64	876	84	345
North Carolina	5,072	26,881	69	2	733	509	126	2,235	292	962
South Carolina	2,843	18,335	44	5	335	212	96	1,290	197	567
Virginia	5,519	26,763	100	43	1,136	305	166	1,788	393	1,277
West Virginia	1,197	5,015	15	91	160	37	33	519	53	262

1. Total includes categories not shown separately.

Source: Printed by permission from The Dun and Bradstreet Corporation, *Business Starts Record, 1986/1987*.

TABLE 7.20--FAILURE RATES PER 10,000 BUSINESSES, SOUTHEASTERN STATES AND UNITED STATES, 1940–1988, SELECTED YEARS

State	1988 p	1987 r	1986	1985	1984	1980	1970	1960	1950	1940
TENNESSEE	117	114	142	149	164	101	41	40	15	36
Alabama	82	63	60	97	124	45	21	24	17	31
Arkansas	65	76	77	130	120	39	19	28	13	43
Florida	103	105	129	113	106	25	38	94	31	58
Georgia	100	90	54	87	64	46	34	46	22	70
Kentucky	87	113	138	142	119	46	25	22	11	29
Louisiana	156	178	213	163	103	32	32	44	18	14
Mississippi	95	116	117	112	92	39	18	25	17	36
North Carolina	50	44	55	65	75	34	15	25	18	45
South Carolina	59	42	49	45	47	n.a.	9	60	5	31
Virginia	78	73	70	106	97	52	29	31	21	63
West Virginia	62	68	78	130	120	25	33	35	20	26
UNITED STATES	98	102	120	115	107	42	44	57	34	63

Note: Businesses are those listed by The Dun and Bradstreet Corporation. Data are for commercial and industrial failures only through 1983, excluding failures of banks, railroads, real estate, insurance, holding and financial companies, steamship lines, travel agencies, etc. Beginning in 1984 data are based on expanded coverage and new methodology and are, therefore, not comparable with earlier years.

p preliminary.

r revised.

n.a. not available.

Source: Printed by permission from Dun and Bradstreet Corporation, *The Business Failure Record, 1987/1988*, and earlier editions; and direct correspondence.

The communications media covered in this section include newspapers, post offices, telephones, radio and television stations, and the cable television industry.

The Federal Communications Commission's (FCC) annual *Statistics of Communications Common Carriers* was the source for statistics on the telephone industry until 1982. Reports submitted by the American Telephone and Telegraph Company and other independent companies were compiled in this publication. However, due to recent industry changes, these data are no longer published. The Tennessee Telephone Association currently provides information on telephone companies serving each county in Tennessee. Sometimes as many as five companies serve one county. The *1980 Census of Housing* also provides data on telephone availability in occupied housing units. These data have been added to the *Abstract* to provide information on this industry.

Earlier data for the cable television industry were also from the FCC's *Annual Report*. The current source for statistics on cable television is *Television and Cable Factbook*, published by Warren Publishing, Inc. The previous publisher of this report was *Television Digest, Inc.*

Comprehensive data for Tennessee newspapers are detailed in the *Tennessee Newspaper Directory*, a semi-annual publication of the Tennessee Press Association. Included are data on paid circulation and publication of both daily and nondaily newspapers in Tennessee. Figure 8.1, also from the *Tennessee Newspaper Directory*, shows the location of newspaper publishers across the state.

Data on FM and AM radio stations for each Tennessee town and city are given in Table 8.8. These data are available in the yearbook issue of *Broadcasting Cablecasting*. Television data in Table 8.9 are also from this source.

In 1971 the U.S. Post Office Department became an independent agency, the U.S. Postal Service. Its method of reporting and publishing data has subsequently changed, especially with regard to local areas. Until 1987, the original data series was maintained through correspondence with the U.S. Postal Service in Memphis. The current source of data is the U.S. Postal Service, Washington, D.C. These data are developed from sample data.

TABLE OF CONTENTS

Table Number Page Number

TABLE 8.1-- TENNESSEE TELEPHONE COMPANIES, COUNTY SERVICE AREAS, 1987

County	Telephone company	Location of telephone company offices
Anderson	South Central Bell Telephone Company	Nashville
	Highland Telephone Cooperative, Inc.	Sunbright
	ALLTEL Tennessee, Inc.	Powell
Bedford	South Central Bell Telephone Company	Nashville
	Ben Lomand Rural Telephone Cooperative, Inc.	McMinnville
	United Telephone Company, Inc.	Chapel Hill
Benton	South Central Bell Telephone Company	Nashville
Bledsoe	Bledsoe Telephone Cooperative	Pikeville
Blount	South Central Bell Telephone Company	Nashville
Bradley	South Central Bell Telephone Company	Nashville
	Ooltewah-Collegedale Telephone Company, Inc.	Chickamauga, Ga.
Campbell	South Central Bell Telephone Company	Nashville
Cannon	DeKalb Telephone Cooperative	Alexandria
Carroll	South Central Bell Telephone Company	Nashville
	Peoples Telephone Company, Inc.	Erin
	Tennessee Telephone Company	Knoxville
	West Tennessee Telephone Company	Bradford
Carter	United Inter-Mountain Telephone Company	Bristol
Cheatham	South Central Bell Telephone Company	Nashville
Chester	South Central Bell Telephone Company	Nashville
	Adamsville Telephone Company, Inc.	Adamsville
Claiborne	South Central Bell Telephone Company	Nashville
	Claiborne Telephone Company, Inc.	New Tazewell
Clay	Twin Lakes Telephone Cooperative Corporation	Gainesboro
Cocke	South Central Bell Telephone Company	Nashville
Coffee	South Central Bell Telephone Company	Nashville
	Ben Lomand Rural Telephone Cooperative, Inc.	McMinnville
Crockett	South Central Bell Telephone Company	Nashville
	Crockett Telephone Company	Friendship
Cumberland	General Telephone Company of the Southeast	Cookeville
Davidson	South Central Bell Telephone Company	Nashville
	Tennessee Telephone Company	Knoxville
	United Telephone Company, Inc.	Chapel Hill
Decatur	Tennessee Telephone Company	Knoxville
DeKalb	DeKalb Telephone Cooperative	Alexandria
	Twin Lakes Telephone Cooperative Corporation	Gainesboro
Dickson	South Central Bell Telephone Company	Nashville
Dyer	South Central Bell Telephone Company	Nashville
	Yorkville Telephone Cooperative, Inc.	Yorkville
Fayette	South Central Bell Telephone Company	Nashville
	Millington Telephone Company, Inc.	Millington
Fentress	Twin Lakes Telephone Cooperative Corporation	Gainesboro
Franklin	South Central Bell Telephone Company	Nashville
	United Telephone Company, Inc.	Chapel Hill
Gibson	South Central Bell Telephone Company	Nashville
	West Tennessee Telephone Company	Bradford
	Yorkville Telephone Cooperative, Inc.	Yorkville
Giles	South Central Bell Telephone Company	Nashville
	Ardmore Telephone Company, Inc.	Ardmore
	Tennessee Telephone Company	Knoxville
Grainger	South Central Bell Telephone Company	Nashville
	ALLTEL Tennessee, Inc.	Powell

TABLE 8.1-- TENNESSEE TELEPHONE COMPANIES, COUNTY SERVICE AREAS, 1987 (Continued)

County	Telephone company	Location of telephone company offices
Greene	United Inter-Mountain Telephone Company	Bristol
Grundy	Ben Lomand Rural Telephone Cooperative, Inc.	McMinnville
Hamblen	South Central Bell Telephone Company	Nashville
Hamilton	South Central Bell Telephone Company	Nashville
	Ooltewah-Collegedale Telephone Company, Inc.	Chickamauga, Ga.
Hancock	South Central Bell Telephone Company	Nashville
	United Inter-Mountain Telephone Company	Bristol
Hardeman	South Central Bell Telephone Company	Nashville
Hardin	South Central Bell Telephone Company	Nashville
	Adamsville Telephone Company, Inc.	Adamsville
	Tennessee Telephone Company	Knoxville
Hawkins	South Central Bell Telephone Company	Nashville
	United Inter-Mountain Telephone Company	Bristol
Haywood	South Central Bell Telephone Company	Nashville
	Millington Telephone Company, Inc.	Millington
Henderson	South Central Bell Telephone Company	Nashville
	Tennessee Telephone Company	Knoxville
Henry	South Central Bell Telephone Company	Nashville
	Peoples Telephone Company, Inc.	Erin
	West Kentucky Rural Telephone Cooperative Corporation, Inc.	Mayfield, Ky.
Hickman	South Central Bell Telephone Company	Nashville
Houston	South Central Bell Telephone Company	Nashville
	Peoples Telephone Company, Inc.	Erin
Humphreys	South Central Bell Telephone Company	Nashville
	Humphreys County Telephone Company	New Johnsonville
Jackson	Twin Lakes Telephone Cooperative Corporation	Gainesboro
Jefferson	South Central Bell Telephone Company	Nashville
Johnson	United Inter-Mountain Telephone Company	Bristol
Knox	South Central Bell Telephone Company	Nashville
	ALLTEL Tennessee, Inc.	Powell
	Tennessee Telephone Company	Knoxville
Lake	South Central Bell Telephone Company	Nashville
Lauderdale	South Central Bell Telephone Company	Nashville
Lawrence	South Central Bell Telephone Company	Nashville
	Loretto Telephone Company, Inc.	Loretto
Lewis	South Central Bell Telephone Company	Nashville
Lincoln	South Central Bell Telephone Company	Nashville
	Ardmore Telephone Company, Inc.	Ardmore
Loudon	South Central Bell Telephone Company	Nashville
McMinn	South Central Bell Telephone Company	Nashville
	Englewood Telephone Company, Inc.	Englewood
	Tellico Telephone Company, Inc.	Tellico Plains
McNairy	South Central Bell Telephone Company	Nashville
	Adamsville Telephone Company, Inc.	Adamsville
Macon	North Central Telephone Cooperative, Inc.	Lafayette
Madison	South Central Bell Telephone Company	Nashville
Marion	South Central Bell Telephone Company	Nashville
	Ben Lomand Rural Telephone Cooperative, Inc.	McMinnville
	Bledsoe Telephone Cooperative	Pikeville
Marshall	South Central Bell Telephone Company	Nashville
	Tennessee Telephone Company	Knoxville
	United Telephone Company, Inc.	Chapel Hill

TABLE 8.1-- TENNESSEE TELEPHONE COMPANIES, COUNTY SERVICE AREAS, 1987 (Continued)

County	Telephone company	Location of telephone company offices
Maury	South Central Bell Telephone Company	Nashville
Meigs	South Central Bell Telephone Company	Nashville
Monroe	South Central Bell Telephone Company	Nashville
	Englewood Telephone Company, Inc.	Englewood
	Tellico Telephone Company, Inc.	Tellico Plains
Montgomery	South Central Bell Telephone Company	Nashville
Moore	South Central Bell Telephone Company	Nashville
Morgan	Highland Telephone Cooperative, Inc.	Sunbright
Obion	South Central Bell Telephone Company	Nashville
	Yorkville Telephone Cooperative, Inc.	Yorkville
Overton	Twin Lakes Telephone Cooperative Corporation	Gainesboro
Perry	Tennessee Telephone Company	Knoxville
Pickett	Twin Lakes Telephone Cooperative Corporation	Gainesboro
Polk	South Central Bell Telephone Company	Nashville
Putnam	General Telephone Company of the Southeast	Cookeville
	Twin Lakes Telephone Cooperative Corporation	Gainesboro
Rhea	South Central Bell Telephone Company	Nashville
Roane	South Central Bell Telephone Company	Nashville
Robertson	South Central Bell Telephone Company	Nashville
Rutherford	South Central Bell Telephone Company	Nashville
	Ben Lomand Rural Telephone Cooperative, Inc.	McMinnville
Scott	South Central Bell Telephone Company	Nashville
	Highland Telephone Cooperative, Inc.	Sunbright
Sequatchie	South Central Bell Telephone Company	Nashville
	Bledsoe Telephone Cooperative	Pikeville
Sevier	South Central Bell Telephone Company	Nashville
Shelby	South Central Bell Telephone Company	Nashville
	Millington Telephone Company, Inc.	Millington
Smith	South Central Bell Telephone Company	Nashville
	DeKalb Telephone Cooperative	Alexandria
	North Central Telephone Cooperative, Inc.	Lafayette
	Twin Lakes Telephone Cooperative Corporation	Gainesboro
Stewart	South Central Bell Telephone Company	Nashville
Sullivan	United Inter-Mountain Telephone Company	Bristol
Sumner	South Central Bell Telephone Company	Nashville
	North Central Telephone Cooperative, Inc.	Lafayette
Tipton	South Central Bell Telephone Company	Nashville
	Millington Telephone Company, Inc.	Millington
Trousdale	South Central Bell Telephone Company	Nashville
	North Central Telephone Cooperative, Inc.	Lafayette
Unicoi	United Inter-Mountain Telephone Company	Bristol
Union	South Central Bell Telephone Company	Nashville
	Claiborne Telephone Company, Inc.	New Tazewell
	ALLTEL Tennessee, Inc.	Powell
Van Buren	Ben Lomand Rural Telephone Cooperative, Inc.	McMinnville
	Bledsoe Telephone Cooperative	Pikeville
Warren	Ben Lomand Rural Telephone Cooperative, Inc.	McMinnville
	General Telephone Company of the Southeast	Cookeville
Washington	United Inter-Mountain Telephone Company	Bristol

TABLE 8.1-- TENNESSEE TELEPHONE COMPANIES, COUNTY SERVICE AREAS, 1987 (Continued)

County	Telephone company	Location of telephone company offices
Wayne	Tennessee Telephone Company	Knoxville
Weakley	South Central Bell Telephone Company	Nashville
	General Telephone Company of the Southeast	Cookeville
White	Ben Lomand Rural Telephone Cooperative, Inc.	McMinnville
	General Telephone Company of the Southeast	Cookeville
Williamson	South Central Bell Telephone Company	Nashville
	United Telephone Company, Inc.	Chapel Hill
Wilson	South Central Bell Telephone Company	Nashville
	Tennessee Telephone Company	Knoxville

Source: Tennessee Telephone Association, *1986–87 Membership Directory.*

TABLE 8.2-- NUMBER AND PAID CIRCULATION OF NEWSPAPERS PUBLISHED, TENNESSEE, 1955–1987

	Number of newspapers published						Net paid circulation (1,000)		
Year	Total [1]	Daily morning	Daily evening	Sunday edition	Weekly	Others [2]	Daily morning	Daily evening	Sunday edition [3]
1987	132	10	18	15	90	13	603.2	387.7	1,109.7
1986	135	9	18	16	93	13	594.4	400.6	1,099.5
1985	135	8	18	15	93	14	550.6	434.8	1,080.4
1984	143	8	19	16	96	17	585.2	448.3	1,083.4
1983	139	7	19	15	93	17	494.7	448.9	1,046.2
1982	153	7	22	16	104	18	494.0	564.9	1,061.9
1981	153	7	22	16	105	17	492.7	558.6 [a]	1,044.6
1980	154	7	22	16	106	17	500.4	578.4	1,038.7
1979	154	7	22	16	105	18	515.5	588.5	1,062.3
1978	163	7	25	14	118	13	454.6	594.1	968.0
1977	160	7	25	14	116	12	450.7	611.8	950.1
1976	158	6	25	14	115	12	448.5	609.2	948.2
1975	158	6	25	14	116	11	473.3	627.8	972.5
1974	160	6	25	14	118	11	496.5	625.2	952.3
1973	160	6	24	14	120	10	493.8	626.5	939.8
1972	164	6	23	14	122	13	494.9	604.5	881.8
1971	159	6	24	13	122	7	492.7	607.9	900.5
1970	159	6	23	13	123	7	492.0	638.0	901.3
1969	162	6	23	13	126	7	500.1	622.9	896.4
1968	160	6	23	13	123	8	498.0	601.7	874.4
1967	162	6	23	12	125	8	497.9	573.8	832.5
1966	162	6	21	10	127	8	486.8	568.3	819.3
1965	161	6	21	10	128	6	489.2	559.8	800.3
1964	159	6	21	10	126	6	481.6	557.5	788.7
1963	160	6	22	10	126	6	478.6	551.6	771.0
1962	158	6	22	9	124	6	487.0	562.5	765.3
1961	156	6	21	7	122	7	475.9	558.2	763.4
1960	156	6	21	10	123	6	462.8	546.5	753.5
1959	156	6	21	10	121	8	456.7	527.4	731.2
1958	156	6	21	10	120	9	462.7	535.0	706.1
1957	160	6	21	9	124	9	471.2	523.4	810.9
1956	158	7	21	12	121	9	469.7	517.2	807.8
1955	159	7	21	13	123	8	468.4	509.4	796.6

Note: Data for 1979–1987 were compiled by the Center for Business and Economic Research from data for individual newspaper publishers listed in the sources cited.

1. The difference between "total" column and the sum of "daily," "weekly," and "others" columns represents the number of all-day daily newspapers.

2. Newspapers published more than once per week; computed by the Center for Business and Economic Research.

3. Where source did not give separate figure for Sunday edition, daily circulation was counted.

a. Excludes Union City data which were not available.

Source: Tennessee Press Service, Inc., *Tennessee Newspaper Directory, 1988*, and earlier editions; and IMS Press, *IMS/Ayer Directory of Publications, 1955–1978*, used by special permission.

TABLE 8.3-- SELECTED DATA ON TENNESSEE POST OFFICE FACILITIES, 1960–1988, SELECTED YEARS

Item	1988	1987	1986	1985	1984	1980	1975	1970	1960
Number of post offices by CAG[1]									
Total	559	559	562	561	562	566	592	610	651
CAG A-G	134	131	128	121	114	108	100	87	69
CAG H-J	142	141	140	133	133	127	120	132	103
CAG K	229	229	233	238	237	243	263	256	257
CAG L	54	58	61	69	78	88	109	135	222
Number of branches and stations	128	144	144	144	140	151	163	174	145
Total post offices, branches and stations	687	703	706	705	702	717	755	784	796
Rural routes									
Number	1,522	1,477	1,421	1,500	1,478	1,344	1,234	1,189	1,170
Mileage	n.a.	89,380	n.a.	95,068	94,452	87,052	79,889	74,144	62,241

n.a. not available.

1. CAG refers to a post office's cost ascertainment grouping, which is determined by the revenue produced by the post office. A revenue unit is calculated by a formula. Using this unit and the revenue produced, the post office is categorized into a CAG. CAG's A-G equate to 1st class offices; H-J to 2nd class offices; K's are 3rd class offices; and L's are 4th class.

Source: United States Postal Service, direct correspondence; and United States Post Office Department, *Annual Report of the Postmaster General, 1960–1970.*

TABLE 8.4-- TOTAL REVENUE OF SELECTED TENNESSEE POST OFFICES, 1960–1987
[In thousands of dollars]

Year	Chattanooga	Kingsport	Knoxville	Memphis	Nashville
1987	35,234	18,266	26,405	115,386	127,539
1986	33,905	17,433	28,075	117,196	118,850
1985	30,296	17,603	25,701	108,886	98,766
1984	27,731	16,228	23,511	98,770	86,113
1983	26,481	15,232	22,782	92,227	78,473
1982	25,284	13,968	23,665	80,547	80,192
1981	20,875	13,555	19,060	66,358	71,283
1980	18,511	13,438	16,640	63,345	64,826
1979	18,095	13,499	15,848	63,527	57,167
1978	15,698	12,316	14,004	60,630	50,562
1977	13,908	10,585	13,524	51,654	44,387
1976	12,011	8,105	10,891	47,741	37,864
1975	10,025	6,097	9,055	44,028	31,470
1974	9,681	5,946	8,488	38,048	29,111
1973	9,132	6,032	7,560	34,504	26,910
1972	8,618	4,677	7,187	31,377	26,145
1971	6,881	4,193	6,101	26,289	22,143
1970	6,524	4,224	5,846	24,586	20,854
1969	5,800	3,184	5,149	20,288	18,100
1968	5,484	2,787	4,760	18,068	16,288
1967	5,472	3,258	4,659	16,969	16,049
1966	5,225	2,554	4,492	16,145	14,974
1965	4,859	2,009	4,250	15,221	13,779
1964	3,328	1,262	2,841	10,186	9,320
1963	3,203	1,477	2,800	10,048	9,346
1962	3,136	1,533	2,662	9,774	8,947
1961	3,004	1,482	2,592	9,587	8,735
1960	2,801	1,190	2,477	8,932	8,076

Source: United States Postal Service, direct correspondence; United States Post Office Department, *Revenues and Classes of Post Offices, 1965–1969*, Post Office Department Publication No. 4; *Receipts and Classes of Post Offices, 1958–1964*, Post Office Department Publication No. 4.

TABLE 8.5-- TELEPHONE AVAILABILITY IN OCCUPIED HOUSING UNITS, COUNTIES, 1980

County	Occupied housing units	Units lacking telephone	Percentage lacking telephone
Anderson	24,616	2,289	9.3
Bedford	9,943	969	9.7
Benton	5,577	632	11.3
Bledsoe	2,979	505	17.0
Blount	28,177	2,177	7.7
Bradley	23,026	2,322	10.1
Campbell	12,087	1,826	15.1
Cannon	3,625	533	14.7
Carroll	10,321	1,058	10.3
Carter	17,868	2,913	16.3
Cheatham	7,063	788	11.2
Chester	4,210	492	11.7
Claiborne	8,295	1,369	16.5
Clay	2,731	595	21.8
Cocke	10,154	1,950	19.2
Coffee	13,649	1,390	10.2
Crockett	5,380	617	11.5
Cumberland	9,887	1,626	16.4
Davidson	177,737	10,216	5.7
Decatur	4,081	716	17.5
DeKalb	4,956	967	19.5
Dickson	10,468	1,029	9.8
Dyer	12,696	1,389	10.9
Fayette	7,431	1,395	18.8
Fentress	5,027	1,089	21.7
Franklin	10,792	1,216	11.3
Gibson	18,202	1,548	8.5
Giles	8,825	957	10.8
Grainger	5,694	1,331	23.4
Greene	19,157	3,003	15.7
Grundy	4,510	802	17.8
Hamblen	17,257	1,966	11.4
Hamilton	103,319	6,803	6.6
Hancock	2,351	557	23.7
Hardeman	7,623	1,005	13.2
Hardin	7,970	1,257	15.8
Hawkins	15,288	2,332	15.3
Haywood	6,513	1,020	15.7
Henderson	7,686	1,100	14.3
Henry	10,914	1,154	10.6
Hickman	5,094	647	12.7
Houston	2,410	374	15.5
Humphreys	5,634	551	9.8
Jackson	3,363	632	18.8
Jefferson	10,623	1,466	13.8
Johnson	4,840	977	20.2
Knox	117,951	8,366	7.1
Lake	2,575	509	19.8
Lauderdale	8,281	1,283	15.5
Lawrence	11,867	1,331	11.2

TABLE 8.5-- TELEPHONE AVAILABILITY IN OCCUPIED HOUSING UNITS, COUNTIES, 1980 (Continued)

County	Occupied housing units	Units lacking telephone	Percentage lacking telephone
Lewis	3,055	410	13.4
Lincoln	9,533	1,082	11.4
Loudon	10,289	1,181	11.5
McMinn	14,727	1,606	10.9
McNairy	8,179	1,036	12.7
Macon	5,645	971	17.2
Madison	26,713	2,357	8.8
Marion	8,270	1,267	15.3
Marshall	7,144	908	12.7
Maury	18,180	1,632	9.0
Meigs	2,520	345	13.7
Monroe	9,637	1,487	15.4
Montgomery	27,198	2,456	9.0
Moore	1,534	216	14.1
Morgan	5,389	994	18.4
Obion	12,079	1,004	8.3
Overton	6,122	1,187	19.4
Perry	2,240	437	19.5
Pickett	1,542	328	21.3
Polk	4,607	860	18.7
Putnam	16,706	2,139	12.8
Rhea	8,285	1,231	14.9
Roane	17,078	1,822	10.7
Robertson	12,532	1,265	10.1
Rutherford	28,002	2,494	8.9
Scott	6,200	1,258	20.3
Sequatchie	2,891	555	19.2
Sevier	14,741	2,021	13.7
Shelby	269,186	17,820	6.6
Smith	5,392	625	11.6
Stewart	3,104	407	13.1
Sullivan	52,022	5,429	10.4
Sumner	28,557	2,607	9.1
Tipton	10,778	1,264	11.7
Trousdale	2,227	394	17.7
Unicoi	5,948	835	14.0
Union	3,947	824	20.9
Van Buren	1,590	354	22.3
Warren	11,869	1,599	13.5
Washington	31,191	4,060	13.0
Wayne	4,792	1,078	22.5
Weakley	11,567	1,157	10.0
White	6,988	960	13.7
Williamson	18,723	1,100	5.9
Wilson	18,863	1,790	9.5

Source: U.S. Department of Commerce, Bureau of the Census, *1980 Census of Housing, Detailed Housing Characteristics, Tennessee.*

FIGURE 8.1
Percentage of Occupied Housing Units Lacking Telephone, Tennessee Counties, 1980
(Tennessee percentage = 9.1)

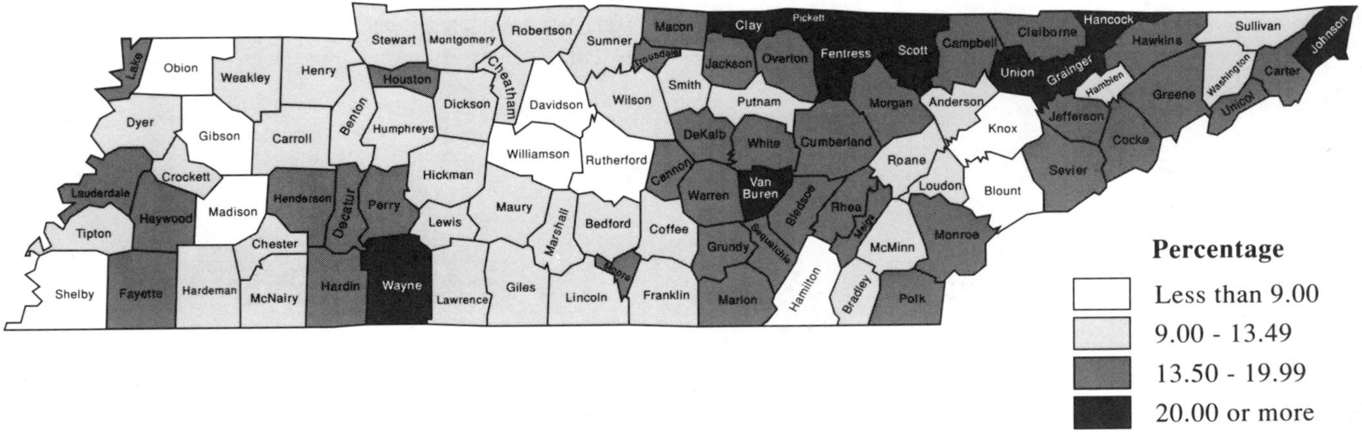

Source: U.S. Department of Commerce, Bureau of the Census, *1980 Census of Housing, Detailed Housing Characteristics*, Tennessee.

TABLE 8.6-- PAID CIRCULATION OF NON-DAILY NEWSPAPERS, COUNTIES, 1987

County	City	Newspaper	Paid circulation
Anderson	Clinton	Clinton Courier-News	7,371
	Lake City	The Town Crier	1,453
Benton	Camden	The Camden Chronicle	4,042
Bledsoe	Pikeville	The Bledsonian-Banner	2,342
Campbell	Jellico	The Advance-Sentinel	663
	LaFollette	The LaFollette Press	7,288
Cannon	Woodbury	Cannon Courier	3,380
Carroll	Huntingdon	Carroll County News	3,660
	Huntingdon	Tennessee Republican	4,881
	McKenzie	The McKenzie Banner	4,850
Cheatham	Ashland City	Ashland City Times	3,745
Chester	Henderson	Chester County Independent	3,603
Claiborne	Tazewell	The Claiborne Progress	6,281
Clay	Celina	Citizen-Statesman	2,902
Cocke	Newport	The Newport Plain Talk	9,279
Coffee	Manchester	Manchester Times	5,979
	Tullahoma	The Tullahoma News	7,720
Crockett	Alamo	The Crockett Times	3,831
Cumberland	Crossville	Crossville Chronicle	4,470
Davidson	Nashville	Nashville Record	1,476
	Nashville	Westview	2,479
Decatur	Parsons	The News Leader	3,766
DeKalb	Smithville	Smithville Review	4,106
Dickson	Dickson	The Dickson Herald	6,735
Fayette	Somerville	Fayette County Review	2,109
	Somerville	The Fayette Falcon	2,892
Fentress	Jamestown	Fentress Courier	4,532
Franklin	Winchester	The Herald-Chronicle	7,930
Gibson	Dyer	The Tri-City Reporter	3,409
	Humboldt	The Courier-Chronicle	4,500
	Milan	The Milan Mirror-Exchange	5,100
	Trenton	The Herald Gazette	3,860
Giles	Pulaski	The Giles Free Press	6,683
	Pulaski	The Pulaski Citizen	6,819
Grainger	Rutledge	Grainger County News	2,709
Grundy	Tracy City	Grundy County Herald	4,315
Hamilton	Chattanooga	Hamilton County Herald	381
Hardeman	Bolivar	The Bolivar Bulletin-Times	5,360
Hardin	Savannah	The Courier	8,635
Hawkins	Rogersville	Rogersville Review	6,768
Haywood	Brownsville	The States-Graphic	4,187
Henderson	Lexington	The Lexington Progress	6,782
Hickman	Centerville	Hickman County Times	4,700
Houston	Erin	The Stewart-Houston Times	4,544
Humphreys	Waverly	The News-Democrat	3,640
Jackson	Gainesboro	Jackson County Sentinel	2,961
Jefferson	Jefferson City	Jefferson County Standard-Banner	5,225
Johnson	Mountain City	The Tomahawk	5,189
Knox	Knoxville	West Side Story	1,147
Lake	Tiptonville	The Lake County Banner	3,020
Lauderdale	Ripley	The Lauderdale County Enterprise	4,427
	Ripley	The Lauderdale Voice	3,758
Lawrence	Lawrenceburg	The Democrat-Union	6,821
Lewis	Hohenwald	Lewis County Herald	2,911
Lincoln	Fayetteville	Elk Valley Times	6,358
Loudon	Lenoir City	The News-Herald	7,313

TABLE 8.6-- PAID CIRCULATION OF NON-DAILY NEWSPAPERS, COUNTIES, 1987 (Continued)

County	City	Newspaper	Paid circulation
McMinn	Etowah	The Etowah Enterprise	1,600
McNairy	Selmer	Independent-Appeal	6,214
Macon	Lafayette	Macon County Times	5,960
Marion	Jasper	The Jasper Journal	3,972
	South Pittsburg	South Pittsburg Hustler	3,360
Marshall	Lewisburg	Lewisburg Tribune	5,617
	Lewisburg	Marshall Gazette	5,663
Maury	Mt. Pleasant	The Record	933
Monroe	Madisonville	The Democrat	4,087
	Sweetwater	Monroe County Advocate	3,724
Moore	Lynchburg	The Moore County News	1,411
Morgan	Wartburg	The Morgan County News	4,205
Overton	Livingston	Livingston Enterprise	5,078
	Livingston	Overton County News	3,900
Perry	Linden	Buffalo River Review	2,547
Pickett	Byrdstown	Pickett County Press	1,560
Polk	Benton	The Polk County News/Citizen Advance	3,026
Rhea	Dayton	The Herald-News	4,581
Roane	Harriman	The Harriman Record	1,093
	Kingston	The Roane County News	6,898
	Rockwood	The Rockwood Times	1,193
Robertson	Springfield	Robertson County Times	9,488
Rutherford	Smyrna	The Rutherford Courier	3,735
Scott	Oneida	Independent Herald	3,922
	Oneida	Scott County News	6,490
Sequatchie	Dunlap	The Dunlap Tribune	2,319
Sevier	Pigeon Forge	Weekly Star	1,816
Shelby	Bartlett	Bartlett Express	2,867
	Collierville	Collierville Independent	2,046
	Germantown	Germantown News	6,293
	Millington	The Millington Star	3,529
Smith	Carthage	Carthage Courier	4,425
Stewart	Dover	The Stewart-Houston Times	4,544
Sullivan	Blountville	Sullivan County News	1,599
Sumner	Gallatin	The News-Examiner	8,520
	Portland	The Portland Leader	2,682
	Westmoreland	Westmoreland World	826
Tipton	Covington	The Covington Leader	6,924
Trousdale	Hartsville	The Hartsville Vidette	1,839
Unicoi	Erwin	The Erwin Record	4,911
Warren	McMinnville	Southern Standard	7,690
Washington	Jonesborough	Herald and Tribune	3,725
Wayne	Waynesboro	The Wayne County News	6,203
Weakley	Dresden	Dresden Enterprise	5,205
	Martin	Weakley County Press	5,324
Williamson	Franklin	The Review-Appeal	10,654
	Franklin	The Williamson Leader	4,000
Wilson	Lebanon	The Wilson World	4,223

Note: Paid circulation is that reported to the U.S. Postal Service in 1987 annual statement or the Publisher's Statement for Audit Bureau of Circulation (ABC) members, as of September 30, 1987.

Source: Tennessee Press Service, Inc., *Tennessee Newspaper Directory, 1988.*

FIGURE 8.2
Newspapers Published in Tennessee, by Frequency of Publication, by County, 1987

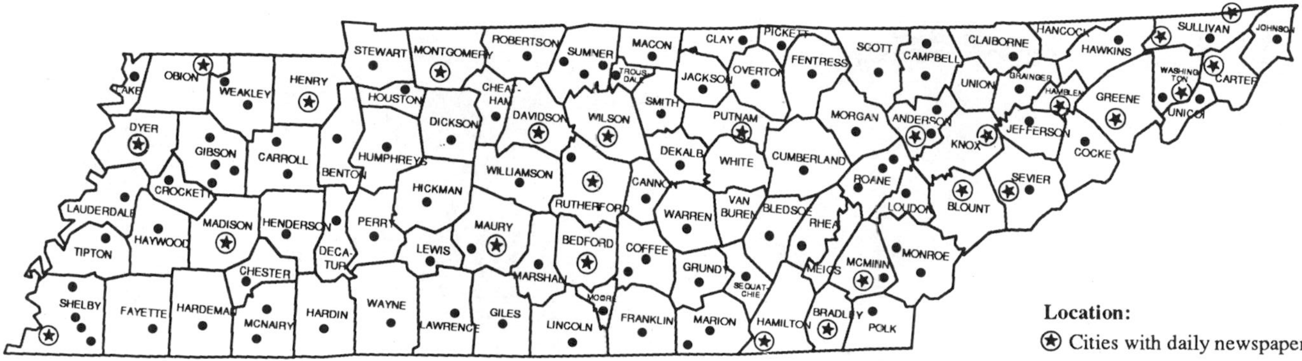

Location:

⊛ Cities with daily newspapers

• Cities with non-daily newspapers

Note: Where more than one newspaper is published, both are represented by one symbol. The following cities have both daily and non-daily newspapers: Chattanooga, Knoxville, Lebanon, and Nashville. See Tables 8.6 and 8.7 for circulation detail.
Source: Tennessee Press Association, Inc., *1988 Tennessee Newspaper Directory*.

TABLE 8.7-- PAID CIRCULATION OF DAILY AND SUNDAY NEWSPAPERS, CITIES, 1987

City	County	Newspaper name	Paid daily circulation	Sunday circulation
Athens	McMinn	The Daily Post-Athenian	10,205	0
Bristol	Sullivan	Bristol Herald Courier/ Virginia-Tennessean	42,352	43,903
Chattanooga	Hamilton	Chattanooga News-Free Press	64,675	112,888
		The Chattanooga Times	47,760	0
Clarksville	Montgomery	The Leaf-Chronicle	19,272	21,829
Cleveland	Bradley	Cleveland Daily Banner	16,554	17,601
Columbia	Maury	The Daily Herald	13,150	13,683
Cookeville	Putnam	Cookeville Herald-Citizen	8,632	9,807
Dyersburg	Dyer	State Gazette	8,236	0
Elizabethton	Carter	Elizabethton Star	7,910	7,910[a]
Greeneville	Greene	The Greeneville Sun	14,752	0
Jackson	Madison	The Jackson Sun	36,420	39,405
Johnson City	Washington	Johnson City Press	29,485	32,787
Kingsport	Sullivan	Kingsport Times-News[1]	46,654	47,492
Knoxville	Knox	The Knoxville Journal	44,016	0
		The Knoxville News-Sentinel	100,603	165,467
Lebanon	Wilson	The Lebanon Democrat	8,501	0
Maryville	Blount	The Daily Times	20,864	0
Memphis	Shelby	The Commercial Appeal	223,464	296,235
		The Daily News	1,977	0
Morristown	Hamblen	Citizen Tribune	21,860	23,758
Murfreesboro	Rutherford	The Daily News Journal	15,925	16,738
Nashville	Davidson	Nashville Banner	67,396	0
		The Tennessean	122,751	260,161
Oak Ridge	Anderson	The Oak Ridger	12,072	0
Paris	Henry	The Paris Post-Intelligencer	8,052	0
Sevierville	Sevier	The Mountain Press	7,013	0
Shelbyville	Bedford	Shelbyville Times-Gazette	8,101	0
Union City	Obion	Union City Daily Messenger	8,890	0

Note: Paid circulation is that reported to the U.S. Postal Service in 1987 annual statement or the Publisher's Statement for Audit Bureau of Circulation (ABC) members, as of September 30, 1987.

1. These papers have both morning and evening editions.

a. Separate circulation not listed for daily and Sunday editions.

Source: Tennessee Press Service, Inc., *Tennessee Newspaper Directory, 1988.*

TABLE 8.8-- SELECTED DATA ON AM AND FM RADIO STATIONS, MUNICIPALITIES, 1988

	AM stations			FM stations		
Municipality	Call letters	Frequency (khz)	Air date	Call letters	Frequency (mhz)	Air date
Adamsville	WEAB	960	1978			
Alamo	WCTA	810	1983			
Alcoa	WMDR	1470	1957	WYLV[1]	89.1	(a)
Algood	WWRT	1590	1981			
Ardmore	WSLV	1110	1968			
Ashland City	WAJN	790	1982			
Athens	WLAR	1450	1946	WJSQ	101.7	1979
	WYXI	1390	1966			
Benton	WBIN	1540	1977			
Berry Hill	WVOL	1470	1951			
Blountville	WJTZ	640	(a)			
Bolivar	WBOL	1560	1962	WQKZ	96.7	1975
Brentwood	WYOR	560	1985			
Bristol	WBCV	1550	1962	WHCB[1]	91.5	1984
	WOPI	1490	1929	WXBQ	96.9	1945
Brownsville	WBHT	1520	1963	WTBG	95.3	1965
Camden	WFWL	1220	1956	WRJB	98.3	1976
Carthage	WRKM	1350	1959	WRKM	102.3	1975
Centerville	WHLP	1570	1955	WCQT	96.7	1974
Chattanooga	WDEF	1370	1941	WDEF	92.3	1964
	WDOD	1310	1925	WDOD	96.5	1960
	WDXB	1490	1948	WDYN[1]	89.7	1968
	WGOW	1150	1936	WSKZ	106.5	1960
	WMOC	1450	1961	WMBW[1]	88.9	1969
	WNOO	1260	1951	WNOO	102.3	1977
				WUTC[1]	88.1	1980
Church Hill	WMCH	1260	1954			
Clarksville	WDXN	540	1954	WAPX[1]	91.7	1984
	WJZM	1400	1941			
	WKVL	1550	1980			
Cleveland	WBAC	1340	1945	WALV	95.3	1980
	WCLE	1570	1957	WUSY	100.7	1961
Clinton	WYSH	1380	1960	WTNZ	95.3	1966
Collegedale				WSMC[1]	90.5	1961
Collierville	WCRV	640	1966			
	WWEE	1170	(a)			
Colonial Heights	WPRQ	870	1984			
Columbia	WKRM	1340	1946	WKOM	101.7	1967
	WMCP	1280	1956			
Cookeville	WHUB	1400	1940	WHUB	98.3	1964
	WPTN	780	1962	WGSQ	94.3	1963
				WTTU[1]	88.5	1972
Copperhill	WLSB	1400	1958			
Covington	WKBL	1250	1954	WKBL	93.5	1965
Cowan	WZYX	1440	1957			
Crossville	WAEW	1330	1952	WXVL	99.3	1967
	WCSV	1490	1968			
Dayton	WDNT	1280	1957	WTCX	104.9	1976
	WREA	1520	1979			
Dickson	WDKN	1260	1955	WQZQ	102.5	1964
Dunlap	WSDQ	1190	1980			
Dyersburg	WDSG	1450	1946	WASL	100.1	1968
	WTRO	1330	1957			
Elizabethton	WBEJ	1240	1946	WUSJ	99.3	1968
	WIDD	1520	1964			
Englewood	WENR	1090	1967			
Erwin	WEMB	1420	1956	WXIS	103.9	1968

TABLE 8.8-- SELECTED DATA ON AM AND FM RADIO STATIONS, MUNICIPALITIES, 1988 (Continued)

	AM stations			FM stations		
Municipality	Call letters	Frequency (khz)	Air date	Call letters	Frequency (mhz)	Air date
Etowah	WCPH	1220	1955	WVKS	103.1	1977
Fairview	WPFD	850	1982			
Farragut	WTTN	670	(a)			
Fayetteville	WEKR	1240	1948	WYTM	105.5	1970
Franklin	WAKM	950	1953	WWRB	100.1	1961
	WIZO	1380	1969			
Gallatin	WAMG	1130	1966	WGFX	104.5	1960
	WHIN	1010	1948	WVCP[1]	88.5	1979
Gatlinburg	WSMM	1230	(a)	WSEV	105.5	1983
Greeneville	WGRV	1340	1946	WIKQ	94.9	1956
	WSMG	1450	1961			
Harriman	WKCE	1230	1983	WRGZ	92.7	1981
	WWBR	1600	1947			
Harrogate	WSVQ	740	1980	WLMU[1]	90.5	(a)
Hartsville	WJKM	1090	1966			
Henderson	WHHM	1580	1967	WFHC[1]	91.5	1967
				WFKX	95.9	1984
Hendersonville				WQQK	92.1	1970
Hohenwald	WMLR	1230	1970			
Humboldt	WHMT	1190	1972	WZDQ	102.3	1964
	WIRJ	740	1949			
Huntingdon	WJPJ	1530	1975	WHZZ	100.9	1979
Jackson	WDXI	1310	1948	WMXX	103.1	1979
	WJAK	1460	1954	WTNV	104.1	1947
	WTJS	1390	1931			
Jamestown	WCLC	1260	1957	WCLC	103.1	1985
	WDEB	1500	1968	WDEB	103.9	1972
Jasper	WAPO	820	(a)			
Jefferson City	WJFC	1480	1961	WJFC	99.3	1976
Jellico	WJJT	1540	1972			
Johnson City	WETB	790	1947	WETS[1]	89.5	1974
	WJCW	910	1938	WQUT	101.5	1948
Jonesborough	WUSJ	1590	1958			
Kingsport	WGOC	640	1967	WCSK[1]	90.3	1984
	WKIN	1320	1951	WZXY	104.9	1970
	WKPT	1400	1940	WTFM	98.5	1948
Kingston	WBBX	1410	1978			
Knoxville	WEMG	1430	1960	WEZK	97.5	1967
	WHJM	1180	(a)	WHGG[1]	88.3	(a)
	WIMZ	1240	1941	WIMZ	103.5	1949
	WITA	1490	1960	WIVK	107.7	1965
	WIVK	850	1953	WKCS[1]	91.1	1952
	WKXV	900	1953	WUOT[1]	91.9	1949
	WLIQ	1340	1946	WOKI	100.3	1974
	WMRE	1580	1961	WUTK[1]	90.3	1982
	WNOX	990	1921			
	WRJZ	620	1927			
Lafayette	WEEN	1460	1958			
LaFollette	WLAF	1450	1953	WQLA	104.9	1982
	WWGR	960	1983			
Lawrenceburg	WCMG	910	1982	WDXE	95.9	1964
	WDXE	1370	1951			
	WWLX	590	1987			
Lebanon	WCOR	900	1949	WFMQ[1]	91.5	1966
	WQDQ	1600	1979	WYHY	107.5	1962
Lenoir City	WBLC	1360	1965	WLIL	93.5	1967
	WLIL	730	1950			

TABLE 8.8-- SELECTED DATA ON AM AND FM RADIO STATIONS, MUNICIPALITIES, 1988 (Continued)

Municipality	AM stations Call letters	Frequency (khz)	Air date	FM stations Call letters	Frequency (mhz)	Air date
Lewisburg	WAXO	1220	1980	WJJM	94.3	1969
	WJJM	1490	1947			
Lexington	WDXL	1490	1954	WZLT	99.3	1964
Livingston	WLIV	920	1956	WXKG	95.9	1966
Lobelville				WIST	94.3	1974
Lookout Mountain	WFLI	1070	1961			
Loudon	WLOD	1140	1983			
Lynchburg	WTNX	1290	1981			
McKenzie	WHDM	1440	1954	WWYN	106.9	1963
McMinnville	WAKI	1230	1947	WTRZ	103.9	1964
	WBMC	960	1955			
Madison	WNKZ	1430	1958			
Madisonville	WRKQ	1250	1967			
Manchester	WMSR	1320	1957	WMSR	99.7	1962
Martin	WCMT	1410	1957	WCMT	101.7	1968
				WUTM[1]	90.3	1971
Maryville	WCGM	1120	(a)			
	WGAP	1400	1947			
Memphis	KWAM	990	1946	KRNB	101.1	1965
				KWLN	98.1	1960
	WDIA	1070	1947	WHRK	97.1	1961
	WEZI	1430	1955	WEVL[1]	89.9	1976
	WGSF	1210	1987	WEZI	94.3	1977
	WHBQ	560	1925	WGKX	105.9	1968
	WLOK	1340	1956	WKNO[1]	91.1	1972
	WMC	790	1923	WLYX[1]	89.3	1972
	WMQM	1480	1964	WMC	99.7	1947
	WREC	600	1922	WQOX[1]	88.5	1974
	WRVR	680	1925	WEGR	102.7	1967
	WXSS	1030	(a)	WRVR	104.5	1968
				WSMS[1]	91.7	1975
Milan	WKBJ	1600	1955	WYNU	92.3	1964
	WXKY	1360	1983			
Millington	WMPS	1380	1962			
Minor Hill				WLLX	92.1	1983
Monterey				WRJT	107.1	1986
Morristown	WCRK	1150	1947	WAZI	95.9	1964
	WMTN	1300	1957			
Mountain City	WMCT	1390	1967			
Mt. Carmel	WRVX	1200	(a)			
Mt. Pleasant	WXRQ	1460	1981			
Murfreesboro	WGNS	1450	1947	WMOT[1]	89.5	1969
	WMTS	810	1953	WTMG	96.3	1963
Nashville	WAMB	1160	1971	WFSK[1]	88.1	1973
	WJRR	760	1988	WKDF	103.3	1967
	WKDA	1240	1948	WLAC	105.9	1953
	WLAC	1510	1926	WNAZ[1]	89.1	1967
	WMDB	880	1983	WPLN[1]	90.3	1962
	WNAH	1360	1949			
	WNQM	1300	1948	WRVU[1]	91.1	1971
	WSIX	980	1927	WSIX	97.9	1948
	WSM	650	1925	WSM	95.5	1962
	WWGM	1560	1967	WZEZ	92.9	1976
Newport	WLIK	1270	1954			
	WNPC	1060	1978			
Oak Ridge	WATO	1290	1948	WKNF	94.3	1967
	WORI	1550	1973			

TABLE 8.8-- SELECTED DATA ON AM AND FM RADIO STATIONS, MUNICIPALITIES, 1988 (Continued)

	AM stations			FM stations		
Municipality	Call letters	Frequency (khz)	Air date	Call letters	Frequency (mhz)	Air date
Olive Hill				WDNX[1]	89.1	1975
Oneida	WBNT	1310	1959	WBNT	105.5	1965
Paris	WMUF	1000	1980	WAKQ	105.5	1967
	WTPR	710	1947			
Parsons	WTBP	1550	1970			
Pikeville	WUAT	1110	1972	WIKU[1]	91.3	(a)
Portland	WHRP	1270	1980			
Powell	WBZW	1040	1984			
Pulaski	WKSR	1420	1947	WINJ	98.3	1970
Red Bank				WJTT	94.3	1972
Ripley	WTRB	1570	1954			
Rockwood	WOFE	580	1957			
Rogersville	WRGS	1370	1954			
St. Joseph	WJOR	1040	1986			
Savannah	WORM	1010	1956	WKWX	93.5	1980
				WORM	101.7	1966
Selmer	WDTM	1150	1967	WXOQ	105.5	1986
Sevierville	WSEV	930	1955	WMYU	102.1	1961
Sewanee				WUTS[1]	91.5	1972
Shelbyville	WHAL	1400	1946	WYCQ	102.9	1962
	WLIJ	1580	1959			
Signal Mountain				WAWL[1]	91.5	1980
Smithville	WJLE	1480	1964	WJLE	101.7	1970
Smyrna	WSVT	710	1981			
Soddy-Daisy	WCHU	1550	1970			
	WSDT	1240	1970			
Somerville	WSTN	1410	1982			
South Pittsburg	WEPG	910	1954			
Sparta	WSMT	1050	1953	WSMT	105.5	1964
	WTZX	860	1971			
Spring City	WXQK	970	1979			
Springfield	WDBL	1590	1950	WDBL	94.3	1964
	WSGI	1190	1982			
Static	WSBI	1210	1986			
Summertown				WUTZ[1]	88.3	1979
Sweetwater	WDEH	800	1955	WDEH	98.3	1967
Tazewell	WNTT	1250	1960			
Thompson Station	WQDQ	1100	1983			
Trenton	WTNE	1500	1966	WLOT	97.7	1980
Tullahoma	WKQD	740	1947	WKQD	93.3	1962
Union City	WENK	1240	1946	WKWT	104.9	1974
Wartburg	WECO	940	1970	(b)	101.3	(a)
Waverly	WPHC	1060	1963	WVRY	104.9	1972
Waynesboro	WTNR	930	1970			
White Bluff	WBDX	1030	1982			
Winchester	WCDT	1340	1948			
Woodbury	WBRY	1540	1963			

Note: Stations are listed in the municipality in which they are located.

1. Non-commercial.

a. Air date unavailable.

b. New station; no call letters available yet.

Source: Broadcasting Publications, Inc., *Broadcasting/Cablecasting Yearbook, 1988*. Used by special permission.

TABLE 8.9-- SELECTED DATA ON TELEVISION STATIONS, CITIES, 1988

City	Channel	Call letters	Air date	Major network affiliation
Chattanooga	12	WDEF-TV	1954	CBS
	61	WDSI-TV	1972	Ind.; Fox
	3	WRCB-TV (Stereo)	1956	NBC
	45	WTCI[1]	1970	PBS
	9	WTVC	1958	ABC
Cleveland	53	WFLI-TV	1987	Ind.
Cookeville	22	WCTE[1]	1978	PBS
	28	WSJA	(a)	n.a.
Crossville	20	WINT-TV	1980	Ind.
Greeneville	39	WETO (Stereo)	1985	Ind.; Fox
Hendersonville	50	WPQD	(a)	n.a.
Jackson	7	WBBJ-TV	1955	ABC
	16	WJWT	1985	Ind.; Fox
Jellico	54	WPMC	(a)	n.a.
Johnson City	11	WJHL-TV	1953	CBS
Kingsport	19	WKPT-TV (Stereo)	1969	ABC
Knoxville	6	WATE-TV (Stereo)	1953	ABC
	10	WBIR-TV	1956	CBS
	43	WKCH-TV	1983	Ind.
	26	WTVK	1953	NBC
	15	(b)	(a)	n.a.
Lexington	11	WLJT-TV[1]	1968	PBS
Memphis	13	WHBQ-TV	1953	ABC
	10	WKNO-TV[1]	1956	PBS
	5	WMC-TV (Stereo)	1948	NBC
	30	WMKW-TV	1983	Ind.; Fox
	24	WPTY-TV	1978	Ind.
	3	WREG-TV	1956	CBS
Murfreesboro	39	WHTN	1983	Ind.
Nashville	30	WCAY-TV	1984	Ind.; Fox
	8	WDCN[1] (Stereo)	1962	PBS
	2	WKRN-TV	1953	ABC
	58	WNAB	(a)	n.a.
	4	WSMV (Stereo)	1950	NBC
	5	WTVF (Stereo)	1954	CBS
	17	WZTV	1976	Ind.
Sneedville	2	WSJK-TV[1]	1967	PBS

ABC - American Broadcasting Company
CBS - Columbia Broadcasting System
NBC - National Broadcasting Company
Ind. - Independent
PBS - Public Broadcasting System
n.a. not available.
1. Non-commercial.
a. Not on air, target date unknown.
b. New station; call letters not available.
Source: Broadcasting Publications, Inc., *Broadcasting/Cablecasting Yearbook 1988*. Used by special permission.

TABLE 8.10--NET REVENUE OF POST OFFICES, TENNESSEE MUNICIPALITIES WITH 1980 POPULATION OF 10,000 OR MORE, 1980–1987, SELECTED YEARS [In dollars]

Office	1987	1986	1985	1980
Athens	1,275,354	1,172,259	1,076,531	713,990
Chattanooga	35,234,082	33,904,751	30,295,686	18,511,074
Clarksville	3,795,704	3,568,820	3,275,349	2,403,136
Cleveland	4,820,322	4,679,617	4,203,247	2,500,533
Columbia	3,091,994	3,012,899	2,752,866	1,553,497
Cookeville	3,372,676	3,137,509	2,766,051	1,808,695
Dyersburg	2,954,564	1,322,197	1,169,729	763,713
Elizabethton	1,095,560	1,053,432	1,004,283	636,345
Franklin	2,831,606	2,529,519	2,161,328	1,014,432
Gallatin	36,474,255	33,589,765	25,265,632	18,512,082
Greeneville	2,126,588	2,137,871	1,979,497	1,360,086
Hendersonville	1,888,822	1,756,380	1,570,744	815,350
Humboldt	519,417	480,498	447,628	333,420
Jackson	5,658,863	5,422,905	5,066,353	3,340,969
Johnson City	5,368,731	5,085,266	4,714,498	2,957,547
Kingsport	18,265,673	17,433,357	17,603,438	13,438,352
Knoxville	26,404,930	28,075,348	25,701,164	16,640,143
Lawrenceburg	937,726	901,584	784,785	519,425
Lebanon	1,668,776	1,571,327	1,363,063	899,075
McMinnville	1,524,245	1,411,382	1,370,578	972,877
Maryville	1,910,032	1,892,290	1,655,959	1,145,140
Memphis	115,386,039	117,195,778	108,886,263	63,345,330
Millington	1,148,813	1,004,729	971,179	618,611
Morristown	2,164,812	2,140,962	2,029,129	1,322,807
Murfreesboro	6,142,540	6,021,620	5,341,249	3,529,423
Nashville	127,539,332	118,849,606	98,765,713	64,825,949
Oak Ridge	3,506,448	3,387,471	3,137,805	2,284,404
Paris	1,263,496	1,169,496	1,046,669	665,843
Shelbyville	1,991,332	1,776,651	1,432,550	822,430
Springfield	945,546	890,429	830,004	510,313
Tullahoma	1,808,667	1,779,138	1,556,468	861,558
Union City	1,065,757	1,012,824	946,311	691,179

Note: Data are not given for the following municipalities: Bartlett, Bristol, East Ridge, Germantown, and Red Bank.

Source: United States Postal Service, direct correspondence.

TABLE 8.11--TELEPHONE AVAILABILITY IN OCCUPIED HOUSING UNITS, SOUTHEASTERN STATES AND UNITED STATES, 1980

State	Occupied housing units	Units lacking telephone	Percentage lacking telephone
TENNESSEE	1,618,505	159,891	9.9
Alabama	1,341,856	173,225	12.9
Arkansas	816,065	102,368	12.5
Florida	3,744,254	367,641	9.8
Georgia	1,871,652	220,536	11.8
Kentucky	1,263,355	149,841	11.9
Louisiana	1,411,788	153,355	10.9
Mississippi	827,169	137,564	16.6
North Carolina	2,043,291	223,912	11.0
South Carolina	1,029,981	129,431	12.6
Virginia	1,863,073	154,057	8.3
West Virginia	686,311	73,278	10.7
UNITED STATES	80,389,673	5,669,677	7.1

Source: U.S. Department of Commerce, Bureau of the Census, *1980 Census of Housing, Detailed Housing Characteristics, United States Summary.*

TABLE 8.12--SELECTED STATISTICS ON THE CABLE TELEVISION INDUSTRY, SOUTHEASTERN STATES, 1980–1987, SELECTED YEARS

State	1987			1986			1985			1980		
	No. of cable systems	No. of commu-nities	No. of sub-scribers	No. of cable systems	No. of commu-nities	No. of sub-scribers	No. of cable systems	No. of commu-nities	No. of sub-scribers	No. of cable systems	No. of cummu-nities	No. of sub-scribers
TENNESSEE	147	394	798,535	139	377	734,909	146	323	702,415	57	111	250,489
Alabama	172	400	655,719	154	338	605,601	140	306	585,140	53	128	330,840
Arkansas	231	386	403,081	210	343	389,683	167	295	374,182	76	128	209,609
Florida	230	659	2,604,536	221	623	2,445,844	196	502	2,362,940	91	342	876,132
Georgia	198	535	1,049,666	184	460	948,512	174	389	897,081	67	175	387,961
Kentucky	236	811	695,704	207	727	659,224	214	668	626,396	97	239	234,212
Louisiana	146	312	766,706	138	291	727,320	135	270	725,699	38	97	294,539
Mississippi	124	242	382,904	110	219	375,828	109	213	444,703	41	107	241,471
North Carolina	178	573	1,012,009	169	517	964,216	152	429	920,082	54	135	339,051
South Carolina	103	271	503,511	88	247	457,449	81	208	430,300	33	104	176,649
Virginia	145	370	1,085,907	130	337	1,061,738	128	315	927,730	48	144	320,801
West Virginia	212	809	433,365	199	752	428,281	192	660	410,824	73	278	191,136

Note: Number of subscribers refers to number of basic subscribers.

Source: Warren Publishing, Inc., 2115 Ward Court, N.W., Washington, D.C. 20037, (202)872-9200, *Television and Cable Fact Book, 1988* (by special permission), and earlier editions; and U.S. Federal Communications Commission, *47th Annual Report, Fiscal Year 1981*.

Tennessee is fortunate in having not only a well-developed system of highways and railroads connecting its metropolitan areas and traversing the state, but also an extensive water transport system. Figure 9.1 shows the location of Tennessee's interstate highways, while Figure 9.2 provides the network of railway routes, including the latest changes in lines. Data on the location and facilities of Tennessee's riverports and airports are provided in Table 9.12 and Table 9.7, respectively.

Comprehensive statistics on public roads are provided by the U.S. Department of Transportation, Federal Highway Administration, Highway Statistics Division. That agency's annual publication, *Highway Statistics*, includes data on mileage, construction, maintenance, motor vehicle registrations, and tax collections for each state. The Federal Aviation Administration issues a variety of publications which have provided data for this chapter, including the *FAA Statistical Handbook of Aviation*, *Census of U.S. Civil Aircraft*, and *Airport Activity Statistics of Certificated Route Air Carriers*. Reports on Tennessee airports and roads are also issued by the State Department of Transportation.

The Bureau of the Census of the U.S. Department of Commerce publishes its *Census of Transportation* every five years. Data from the most recent Truck Inventory and Use Survey from the 1982 Census describe the size and type of trucks registered in Tennessee and truck use by industry. The number of trucks and truck miles is reported for each of the southeastern states. Table 9.24, also from this survey, presents information on the transportation of hazardous materials. Transportation questions were also included in the 1980 Census of Population. These data tell us how Tennesseans travel to work and provide information on the number of persons with public transportation disabilities.

County-specific data detail motor vehicle registrations and highway systems throughout the state. These data are collected by the Motor Vehicle Division of the Department of Revenue and the Tennessee Department of Transportation. The Tennessee Valley Authority's Economic Development and Analysis Branch provides information on waterfront development and river freight traffic on the Tennessee River. TVA's Navigation Development Branch issues information on the location and shipping characteristics of Tennessee's public river terminals.

Another important component of the transportation industry in Tennessee is the liquid petroleum pipelines. These are regulated as common carriers. However, the petroleum pipeline is featured with the natural gas pipeline in Figure 10.2. Readers should consult the Energy chapter for information on the transportation of petroleum.

TABLE OF CONTENTS

TABLE OF CONTENTS
(Continued)

Table Number Page Number

FIGURE 9.1
Principal Highways in Tennessee

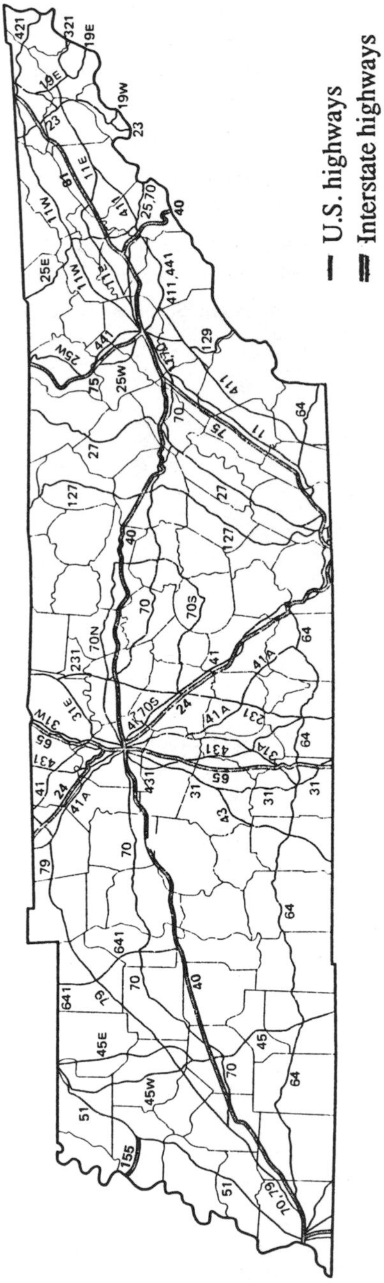

Source: Official Tourist Development Map of Tennessee.

TABLE 9.1-- EXPENDITURES FOR CONSTRUCTION AND MAINTENANCE OF STATE-ADMINISTERED HIGHWAYS, TENNESSEE AND UNITED STATES, 1925–1987, SELECTED YEARS
[In thousands of dollars]

	Construction[1]		Maintenance[2]	
Year	Tennessee	United States[3]	Tennessee	United States[3]
1987	355,074	21,221,467	154,738	7,179,665
1986	319,414	20,426,870	131,783	6,646,641
1985	332,400	18,882,214	136,447	6,385,453
1984	295,641	15,757,546	109,025	5,824,109
1983	337,126	13,713,084	79,878	5,487,063
1982	241,139	12,398,955	90,688	5,266,909
1981	282,881	12,430,807	76,477	4,866,185
1980	341,813	14,013,201	60,503	4,566,982
1979	310,544	11,798,070	48,204	4,352,592
1978	232,310	10,015,634	50,585	4,037,821
1977	200,799	8,882,863	42,241	3,465,798
1976	234,081	9,676,656	35,764	3,116,821
1975	258,952	10,168,550	34,532	2,946,178
1974	192,254	9,390,755	36,788	2,656,449
1973	163,971	8,981,484	31,966	2,458,251
1972	183,169	9,383,859	26,284	2,236,190
1971	162,960	9,416,682	25,372	2,086,947
1970	155,363	8,866,017	26,432	1,928,819
1969	149,341	7,876,135	22,473	1,723,160
1968	132,908	7,866,362	18,522	1,593,652
1967	129,301	7,339,818	18,157	1,513,502
1966	146,985	7,056,353	18,055	1,402,296
1965	143,548	6,458,214	15,017	1,309,786
1964	146,360	6,362,372	14,787	1,054,199
1963	135,023	5,649,619	14,045	992,117
1962	119,892	5,608,404	13,583	1,093,279
1961	103,164	5,105,084	10,998	1,019,839
1960	93,739	4,669,349	10,144	985,648
1955	29,373	3,102,994	8,184	675,629
1950	24,675	1,533,859	9,114	501,487
1945	5,910	210,467	2,491	289,368
1940	5,712	563,074	2,442	218,776
1935	6,243	438,306	2,070	187,122
1930	29,915	728,887	5,060	193,928
1925	9,243	403,843	1,560	119,304

1. Includes acquisition of right-of-way, engineering, construction of roads and major structures, and installation of traffic service facilities.

2. Includes physical maintenance and traffic services.

3. U.S. data through 1958 are for 48 states; after 1958 data include Alaska and Hawaii.

Source: U.S. Department of Transportation, Federal Highway Administration, Highway Statistics Division, *Highway Statistics, 1987*, and earlier editions; *Summary to 1955*.

TABLE 9.2-- MEANS OF TRANSPORTATION TO WORK AND PUBLIC TRANSPORTATION DISABILITY STATUS, PERSONS 16 YEARS AND OVER, TENNESSEE, 1980 [In thousands of persons]

		Urban population			
	Total	Total	Inside urbanized areas	Outside urbanized areas	Rural popu-lation
MEANS OF TRANSPORTATION TO WORK					
Workers 16 years and over	1,891.7	1,188.0	904.2	283.7	703.7
Private vehicle	1,727.8	1,073.6	817.7	255.9	654.2
Drive alone: Car	1,045.7	712.8	555.7	157.1	333.0
Truck or Van	243.8	114.6	80.0	34.5	129.2
Carpool: Car	348.3	210.2	157.4	52.8	138.1
Truck or Van	90.0	36.1	24.6	11.6	53.9
Public transportation	46.6	42.6	40.3	2.4	4.0
Bicycle	2.1	1.8	1.2	0.6	0.3
Motorcycle	3.8	2.6	2.1	0.5	1.2
Walked only	66.6	48.0	29.1	18.8	18.6
Other means	12.5	6.7	4.7	2.0	5.9
Worked at home	32.2	12.7	9.2	3.5	19.5
TRAVEL TIME TO WORK	1,863.1	1,177.9	896.8	281.1	685.2
Less than 10 minutes	297.9	205.7	115.9	89.9	92.2
10 to 19 minutes	646.5	438.5	326.3	112.1	208.0
20 to 29 minutes	398.7	258.0	228.3	29.7	140.7
30 to 44 minutes	340.4	194.7	166.7	28.0	145.7
45 or more minutes	179.5	81.0	59.6	21.4	98.5
Mean (in minutes)	21.2	19.5	20.6	n.a.	24.1
Workers traveling 45 or more minutes	59.1	59.4	59.5	n.a.	58.9
PUBLIC TRANSPORTATION DISABILITY STATUS OF NONINSTITUTIONAL PERSONS					
Persons 16 to 64 years	2,924.8	1,791.6	1,359.8	431.8	1,133.2
With a public transportation disability	68.5	39.4	28.8	10.6	29.1
Persons 65 years or over	494.3	295.6	209.1	86.5	198.7
With a public transportation disability	92.3	54.8	39.7	15.1	37.5

Note: Detail may not add to total due to independent rounding. For definitions of urban and rural population, see Table 1.1.

n.a. not available.

Source: U.S. Department of Commerce, Bureau of the Census, *1980 Census of Population, General Social and Economic Characteristics, Tennessee.*

TABLE 9.3-- MOTOR VEHICLE REGISTRATIONS, BY TYPE OF VEHICLE, TENNESSEE, 1925-1987, SELECTED YEARS

Year	Total	Automobiles	Buses	Trucks
1987	4,026,565	3,194,605	12,078	819,882
1986	3,932,220	3,097,473	12,499	822,248
1985	3,753,926	2,944,971	12,049	796,906
1984	3,568,661	2,822,315	11,555	734,791
1983	3,537,012	2,904,367	11,228	621,417
1982	3,381,216	2,765,974	11,624	603,618
1981	3,533,299	2,870,407	10,475	652,147
1980	3,271,345	2,564,551	10,374	696,420
1979	2,995,305	2,337,221	9,424	648,660
1978	2,911,222	2,351,910	9,175	550,137
1977	2,996,157	2,307,783	8,774	679,600
1976	2,804,840	2,153,922	8,705	642,213
1975	2,725,569	2,092,996	8,303	624,270
1974	2,568,381	1,987,890	7,906	572,585
1973	2,466,821	1,938,735	7,796	520,290
1972	2,293,635	1,819,121	7,608	466,906
1971	2,135,635	1,703,756	7,527	424,352
1970	2,049,992	1,638,268	7,432	404,292
1969	1,971,160	1,583,187	7,185	380,788
1968	1,906,774	1,543,887	6,498	356,389
1967	1,869,918	1,523,452	6,268	340,198
1966	1,757,575	1,426,481	5,415	325,679
1965	1,654,682	1,353,463	5,340	295,879
1964	1,573,437	1,288,397	5,301	279,739
1963	1,500,566	1,231,600	5,115	263,851
1962	1,429,055	1,175,489	4,793	248,773
1961	1,362,868	1,118,664	6,295	237,909
1960	1,307,010	1,070,432	5,537	231,041
1959	1,264,255	1,032,023	5,519	226,713
1958	1,203,405	980,438	5,739	217,228
1957	1,160,042	941,346	5,801	212,895
1956	1,131,437	914,470	5,666	211,301
1955	1,168,295	925,292	4,578	238,425
1950	858,111	672,966	4,092	181,053
1945	466,677	378,121	4,174	84,382
1940	461,183	380,210	2,154	78,819
1935	359,618	310,520	1,312	47,786
1930	373,534	330,978	1,179	41,377
1925	246,511	221,707	720	24,084

Note: The automobile classification includes taxicabs.

Source: U.S. Department of Transportation, Federal Highway Administration, Highway Statistics Division, *Highway Statistics, 1987*, and earlier editions; Summary to 1955.

TABLE 9.4-- LOCATION AND NUMBER OF MOTOR FREIGHT TERMINALS, TENNESSEE, 1990

City	County	Number of terminals	City	County	Number of terminals
Adamsville	McNairy	1	Hendersonville	Sumner	1
Alamo	Crockett	1	Henning	Lauderdale	1
Athens	McMinn	2	Humboldt	Gibson	1
Atwood	Carroll	1	Huntingdon	Carroll	1
Bells	Crockett	1	Jackson	Madison	12
Bluff City	Sullivan	1	Johnson City	Washington/Carter	8
Bradford	Gibson	1	Jonesborough	Washington	1
Brentwood	Williamson	1	Kenton	Gibson/Obion	1
Bristol	Sullivan	1	Kingsport	Hawkins/Sullivan	10
Brownsville	Haywood	1	Knoxville	Knox	22
Bruceton	Carroll	1	La Grange	Fayette	1
Calhoun	McMinn	1	LaVergne	Rutherford	1
Carthage	Smith	1	Lawrenceburg	Lawrence	3
Centerville	Hickman	1	Lebanon	Wilson	2
Charleston	Bradley	1	Lexington	Henderson	2
Chattanooga	Hamilton	30	McKenzie	Carroll/Henry/Weakley	1
Church Hill	Hawkins	1	McMinnville	Warren	3
Clarksville	Montgomery	1	Martin	Weakley	1
Cleveland	Bradley	4	Maryville	Blount	2
Clinton	Anderson	1	Maury City	Crockett	1
Collegedale	Hamilton	1	Medina	Gibson	1
Columbia	Maury	3	Memphis	Shelby	52
Cookeville	Putnam	7	Milan	Gibson	1
Covington	Tipton	1	Morristown	Hamblen	6
Cowan	Franklin	1	Mountain City	Johnson	1
Dayton	Rhea	1	Mount Carmel	Hawkins	1
Decaturville	Decatur	1	Mount Juliet	Wilson	1
Decherd	Franklin	1	Murfreesboro	Rutherford	5
Dresden	Weakley	2	Nashville	Davidson	42
Dyer	Gibson	1	Newbern	Dyer	1
Dyersburg	Dyer	6	Oak Ridge	Anderson/Roane	2
East Ridge	Hamilton	1	Obion	Obion	1
Elizabethton	Carter	1	Paris	Henry	3
Englewood	McMinn	1	Parsons	Decatur	1
Erwin	Unicoi	1	Portland	Sumner	2
Fairview	Williamson	1	Pulaski	Giles	2
Fayetteville	Lincoln	1	Red Bank	Hamilton	1
Franklin	Williamson	1	Ridgeside	Hamilton	1
Friendship	Crockett	1	Ripley	Lauderdale	1
Gadsden	Crockett	1	Rives	Obion	1
Gallatin	Sumner	3	Rutherford	Gibson	1
Gallaway	Fayette	1	Savannah	Hardin	1
Gates	Lauderdale	1	Scotts Hill	Decatur/Henderson	1
Gibson	Gibson	1	Selmer	McNairy	1
Gleason	Weakley	1	Sharon	Weakley	1
Goodlettsville	Davidson/Sumner	1	Shelbyville	Bedford	3
Greeneville	Greene	1	Signal Mountain	Hamilton	1
Greenfield	Weakley	1	Smyrna	Rutherford	1
Halls	Lauderdale	1	Soddy Daisy	Hamilton	1
Henderson	Chester	1	Somerville	Fayette	1

TABLE 9.4-- LOCATION AND NUMBER OF MOTOR FREIGHT TERMINALS, TENNESSEE, 1990 (Continued)

City	County	Number of terminals	City	County	Number of terminals
Sparta	White	2	Union City	Obion	3
Springfield	Robertson	1	Watauga	Carter	1
Spring Hill	Maury/Williamson	1	Watertown	Wilson	1
Surgoinsville	Hawkins	1	White House	Robertson/Sumner	1
Toone	Hardeman	1	Winchester	Franklin	1
Trenton	Gibson	1	Yorkville	Gibson	1
Trezevant	Carroll	1			
Trimble	Dyer/Obion	1			
Troy	Obion	1			
Tullahoma	Franklin/Coffee	2			

Source: International Thomson Transport Press, *American Motor Carrier Directory*, Spring 1990. Copyright material presented here with permission of the publisher.

TABLE 9.5-- SIZE AND WEIGHT LIMITATIONS FOR TRUCKS, TENNESSEE, 1989

Maximum overall height: 8 feet[1]

Maximum overall length, single truck: 13 feet 6 inches

Maximum overall length tractor and semi-trailer combination:[2]
Straight truck and semi-trailer or combination: 65 feet
Combination transporting poles or logs (in single length pieces): 75 feet
Twin trailer combination: There is no maximum overall length.

Maximum length of semi-trailers used in twin trailer combination:
Neither trailer shall exceed twenty-eight feet six inches.

Maximum gross weight:
Two axle single truck: 40,000 pounds
Three axle single truck: 54,000 pounds
Four axle single truck: 74,000 pounds
Three axle tractor and semi-trailer combination: 60,000 pounds
Four axle tractor and semi-trailer combination: 74,000 pounds
Five axle tractor and semi-trailer combination or five axle tractor,
Semi-trailers and converter gear (twin trailers): 80,000 pounds

Maximum gross axle weight:
Steering axle for single truck: 20,000 pounds
Steering axle for tractor: 20,000 pounds
Single axle for single truck, tractor, semi-trailer or converter gear: 20,000 pounds
Tandem axle for single truck, tractor or semi-trailer: 34,000 pounds

Note: Data are meant to give basic information pertaining to the trucking rules in Tennessee. They are not meant to provide all the requirements. For further information, contact Tennessee Department of Revenue, Motor Vehicle Enforcement.

1. 102 inches authorized on Interstate system and other designated routes.

2. When a motor vehicle consists of a truck-tractor and semi-trailer or trailer combination, the towed vehicle shall not exceed forty-eight feet in length from the point of attachment to the tractor except that this length may be increased to fifty-two feet when the load on such vehicle consists of livestock or automobiles and/or motor vehicles.

Source: Tennessee Department of Revenue, Motor Vehicle Division, *Proportional Registration Manual, 1988*.

TABLE 9.6-- TRUCKS COMPARATIVE USE SUMMARY, TENNESSEE, 1967–1982, CENSUS YEARS

	Percentage of trucks registered in Tennessee			
	1982	1977	1972	1967
Major use				
Agriculture	10.5	18.0	24.8	39.0
Forestry and lumbering	0.6	0.3	(a)	(a)
Mining and quarrying	0.1	0.4	(a)	(a)
Construction	7.2	4.8	7.0	8.6
Manufacturing	1.9	1.7	2.7	3.3
Wholesale, retail trade	5.5	8.1	9.7	9.2
For hire, transportation	2.4	2.3	3.3	2.4
Utilities, service	5.0	4.0	6.2	5.8
Personal transportation	66.5	58.2	44.4	27.1
Other	0.3	2.1	1.8	4.6
Body type				
Pickup, panel[1]	88.0	88.1	75.7	74.0
Platform, cattle rack	5.1	4.9	12.1	13.8
Van[1]	3.5	3.9	6.7	5.4
Utility	0.1	0.2	0.9	1.2
Other	3.3	2.8	4.4	5.6
Vehicle size				
Light (10,000 lbs. or less)	91.2	89.9	82.0	77.1
Medium (10,001–19,500 lbs.)	3.3	4.6	8.5	14.8
Light-heavy (19,501–26,000 lbs.)	1.7	2.0	2.1	2.6
Heavy-heavy (26,001 lbs. or more)	3.9	3.5	7.4	5.5
Year model				
1 to 2 years old	10.1	8.2	16.9	12.6
3 to 4 years old	15.9	17.9	19.6	20.1
Over 4 years old	74.0	73.9	63.6	67.3

Note: Detail may not add to total due to independent rounding.

1. Vans similar to panel trucks are included in pickup, panel category.

a. Less than 0.05 percent.

Source: U.S. Department of Commerce, Bureau of the Census, *1982 Census of Transportation, Truck Inventory and Use Survey, Tennessee.*

TABLE 9.7-- SELECTED AIRPORT STATISTICS, TENNESSEE, 1989

City	County	Airport name	Class[1]	Runway length (in feet)
Arlington	Shelby	Municipal	General Utility	3,800
Athens	McMinn	McMinn County	General Utility	4,700
Bolivar	Hardeman	Bolivar-Hardeman County	General Utility	4,000
Bristol	Sullivan	Tri-City Airport	Air Carrier	8,000
Camden	Benton	Benton County	Basic Utility II	3,500
Centerville	Hickman	Municipal	General Utility	4,000
Chattanooga	Hamilton	Dallas Bay Sky Park	Basic Utility	3,100
Chattanooga	Hamilton	Lovell Field	Air Carrier	7,400
Clarksville	Montgomery	Outlaw Field	Basic Transport	6,000
Cleveland	Bradley	Hardwick Field	Basic Utility I	3,300
Clifton	Wayne	Hassell Field	General Utility	4,600
Collegedale	Hamilton	Municipal	Basic Utility I	4,700
Columbia-Mt. Pleasant	Maury	Maury County	Basic Transport	5,000
Cookeville	Putnam	Putnam County	General Utility	3,800
Copper Hill	Polk	Martin Campbell	Basic Utility	3,500
Covington	Tipton	Municipal	General Utility	4,000
Crossville	Cumberland	Memorial	Basic Transport	5,400
Dayton	Rhea	Mark Anton	General Utility	4,500
Dickson	Dickson	Municipal	General Utility	4,000
Dyersburg	Dyer	Municipal	Basic Transport	5,000
Elizabethton	Carter	Municipal	Basic Utility II	4,000
Fayetteville	Lincoln	Municipal	Basic Transport	4,900
Gainesboro	Jackson	Jackson County	Basic Utility II	3,500
Gallatin	Sumner	Municipal	Basic Transport	5,000
Greeneville	Greene	Municipal	Basic Transport	6,300
Halls	Lauderdale	Arnold Field	General Utility	4,700
Hohenwald	Lewis	John A. Baker Field	General Utility	4,000
Humboldt	Gibson	Municipal	General Utility	4,000
Huntingdon-McKenzie	Carroll	Carroll County	Basic Transport	5,000
Jacksboro	Campbell	Campbell County	Basic Utility	3,500
Jackson	Madison	McKellar Field	General Transport	6,000
Jamestown	Fentress	Municipal	Basic Utility II	3,500
Jasper	Marion	Marion County	Basic Utility II	3,500
Johnson City	Carter	Johnson City (STOL)	Basic Utility I	3,000
Knoxville	Knox	Downtown Island	Basic Utility II	3,500
Knoxville	Blount	McGhee Tyson	Air Carrier	9,000
Lafayette	Macon	Municipal	General Utility	4,000
Lawrenceburg	Lawrence	Municipal	Basic Transport	5,000
Lebanon	Wilson	Municipal	Basic Utility II	4,000
Lewisburg	Marshall	Ellington Airport	Basic Transport	5,000
Lexington	Henderson	Franklin-Wilkins	General Utility	4,500
Linden	Perry	Perry County	Basic Utility II	3,600
Livingston	Overton	Municipal	General Utility	4,000
McKinnon	Houston	Houston County	Basic Utility I	3,000
McMinnville	Warren	Warren County Memorial	Basic Tranport	5,000
Madisonville	Monroe	Monroe County	Basic Utility II	3,500
Memphis	Shelby	General de Witt Spain	General Utility	3,800
Memphis	Shelby	International	Air Carrier	9,300
Milan-Trenton	Gibson	Gibson County	Basic Transport	4,800
Millington	Shelby	Charles W. Baker	Basic Utility II	3,500
Morristown	Hamblen	Moore-Murrell	General Transport	5,700
Mountain City	Johnson	Johnson County	General Utility	4,500

TABLE 9.7-- SELECTED AIRPORT STATISTICS, TENNESSEE, 1989 (Continued)

City	County	Airport name	Class[1]	Runway length (in feet)
Murfreesboro	Rutherford	Municipal	General Utility	3,900
Nashville	Davidson	Cornelia Fort	Basic Utility	2,800
Nashville	Davidson	John C. Tune	Basic Transport	5,000
Nashville	Davidson	Municipal	Air Carrier	8,500
Oneida	Scott	Scott Municipal	Basic Transport	5,500
Paris	Henry	Henry County	Basic Transport	5,000
Parsons	Decatur	Scott Field	General Utility	4,000
Portland	Sumner	Municipal	General Utility	4,000
Powell	Knox	Powell (STOL)	Basic Utility I	2,600
Pulaski	Giles	Abernathy Field	Basic Transport	5,000
Reelfoot Lake	Obion	Reelfoot Lake Airpark	Basic Utility II	3,500
Rockwood	Roane	Municipal	Basic Transport	5,000
Rogersville	Hawkins	Hawkins County	Basic Utility II	3,500
Savannah	Hardin	Savannah	Basic Transport	5,000
Selmer	McNairy	Robert Sibley Airport	General Utility	4,300
Sevierville	Sevier	Gatlinburg-Pigeon Forge	General Transport	5,500
Sewanee	Franklin	University of the South-Franklin County	Basic Utility I	3,300
Shelbyville	Bedford	Bomar	Basic Transport	5,000
Smithville	DeKalb	Municipal	Basic Utility II	4,100
Smyrna	Rutherford	Symrna	General Transport	8,000
Somerville	Fayette	Fayette County	Basic Utility II	3,500
Sparta	White	Sparta-White County	Basic Transport	5,000
Springfield	Robertson	Springfield-Robertson County	Basic Utility II	3,700
Tazewell	Claiborne	Tazewell Claiborne County	Basic Utility I	3,000
Tullahoma	Coffee	Soesbe-Martin	Basic Transport	5,000
Union City	Obion	Everett-Stewart Field	Basic Transport	5,000
Waverly	Humphreys	Humphreys County	General Utility	4,000
Winchester	Franklin	Municipal	General Utility	5,000

Note: Only airports with paved runways are listed. Military airports have been excluded.

1. Basic Utility I: Airport accommodating about 75 percent of propeller airplanes under 12,500 pounds.
   Basic Utility II: Airport accommodating about 95 percent of propeller airplanes under 12,500 pounds.
   General Utility: Accommodates all propeller airplanes under 12,500 pounds.
   Basic Transport: Accommodates turbojets up to 60,000 pounds.
   General Transport: Accommodates airplanes up to 175,000 pounds.
   Air Carrier: Airport serving regularly scheduled commercial airlines.

Source: Tennessee Department of Transportation, *Tennessee Airport Directory, 1982*, and direct correspondence; and Tennessee Department of Economic and Community Development, Industrial Development Division, *Transportation in Tennessee, 1979*.

TABLE 9.8-- STATUS OF THE AIRPORT IMPROVEMENT PROGRAM, BY TYPE OF AIRPORT, TENNESSEE, 1971–1986

	Air carriers		General aviation	
Year	Total federal funds ($1,000)	Total projects	Total federal funds ($1,000)	Total projects
1986	15,322	13	1,809	6
1985	14,236	10	1,718	5
1984	11,470	16	2,627	8
1983	12,377	16	1,827	9
1982	6,948	6	1,275	5
1981	74,305	86	8,337	35
1980	65,733	80	7,912	32
1979	60,401	72	6,833	28
1978	56,271	66	6,197	23
1977	46,699	58	5,739	20
1976	32,802	46	4,469	16
1975	26,685	42	2,974	10
1974	25,908	38	2,505	9
1973	1,580	8	17,124	30
1972	10,751	19	581	5
1971	4,026	8	502	4

Note: Beginning in 1982, air carriers refer to primary, commercial, and reliever airports. This reclassification of data resulted from the Airport and Airway Improvement Act of 1982.

Source: U.S. Department of Transportation, Federal Aviation Administration, *FAA Statistical Handbook of Aviation, Calendar Year 1986*, and earlier editions.

TABLE 9.9-- NUMBER OF AIRPORTS, BY LENGTH OF LONGEST RUNWAY, TENNESSEE, AS OF DECEMBER 31, 1986

Length of runway	Number
Total	186
Less than 3,000 feet	101
3,000–3,999	31
4,000–4,999	27
5,000–5,999	16
6,000–6,999	3
7,000–7,999	2
8,000–8,999	3
9,000–9,999	2
10,000 and over	1

Note: Includes seaplane bases, heliports, and military fields having joint civil-military use.

Source: U.S. Department of Transportation, Federal Aviation Administration, *FAA Statistical Handbook of Aviation, 1986*.

TABLE 9.10--AIRCRAFT DEPARTURES AND REVENUE TRAFFIC AT ON-LINE AIRPORTS, SELECTED TENNESSEE COMMUNITIES, DECEMBER 31, 1987

	TENNESSEE	Bristol–Johnson City–Kingsport	Chattanooga	Knoxville	Memphis	Nashville
Aircraft Departures	183,922	3,290	5,313	11,545	107,295	56,471
Scheduled	183,756	3,283	5,311	11,513	107,204	56,438
Nonscheduled	166	7	2	32	91	33
Passenger enplanements	8,947,174	140,131	276,100	520,482	5,023,047	2,987,233
Revenue Tons						
Enplaned[1]	557,350.00	1,155.52	1,625.96	7,009.47	534,311.96	13,240.19
Freight	524,767.90	317.52	699.57	5,442.30	513,305.28	4,996.33
Express	0.00	0.00	0.00	0.00	0.00	0.00
U.S. mail	32,580.57	838.00	926.39	1,566.26	21,006.06	8,243.86

1. Includes foreign mail not shown separately.

Source: U.S. Department of Transportation, Federal Aviation Administration, *Airport Activity Statistics of Certificated Route Air Carriers, 12 Months Ending December 31, 1987*.

TABLE 9.11--AIRCRAFT DEPARTURES AND PASSENGER ENPLANEMENTS AT ON-LINE AIRPORTS, TENNESSEE AND SELECTED COMMUNITIES, 1965–1987, SELECTED YEARS

Year	TENNESSEE	Bristol–Johnson City–Kingsport	Chattanooga	Knoxville	Memphis	Nashville
1987						
Departures	183,922	3,290	5,313	11,545	107,295	56,471
Enplanements	8,947,174	140,131	276,100	520,482	5,023,047	2,987,233
1986						
Departures	171,551	3,869	5,483	11,043	104,695	46,461
Enplanements	7,215,559	144,941	250,389	477,252	4,177,169	2,165,808
1985						
Departures	126,632	4,679	4,556	9,132	77,942	30,313
Enplanements	5,663,875	157,005	216,862	425,203	3,469,318	1,395,487
1984						
Departures	105,715	4,932	4,493	10,161	57,528	28,801
Enplanements	4,265,622	150,213	207,552	408,244	2,283,425	1,216,188
1983						
Departures	99,619	5,023	4,812	9,386	56,248	24,150
Enplanements	4,232,731	150,907	219,190	394,620	2,359,442	1,108,572
1982						
Departures	96,162	5,712	4,941	9,651	51,153	24,735
Enplanements	4,019,261	156,308	180,715	413,512	2,189,650	1,079,076
1981						
Departures	96,738	6,817	4,765	8,301	50,377	25,943
Enplanements	3,732,147	173,326	212,086	364,338	1,945,933	1,033,206
1980						
Departures	108,233	7,983	5,571	9,195	55,840	28,315
Enplanements	4,174,472	211,280	252,245	430,153	2,148,730	1,122,084
1979						
Departures	123,231	8,658	6,620	11,049	64,275	30,094
Enplanements	4,829,801	236,473	291,335	487,724	2,576,902	1,223,219
1978						
Departures	127,836	9,567	9,137	12,145	62,406	31,390
Enplanements	4,534,079	228,945	307,600	476,799	2,344,531	1,156,836
1977						
Departures	120,790	9,177	9,589	13,387	57,003	29,195
Enplanements	4,014,837	206,952	281,791	443,202	2,072,202	987,193
1976						
Departures	118,835	9,172	10,105	13,716	54,696	28,271
Enplanements	3,801,264	191,304	259,578	406,522	2,015,073	904,325
1975						
Departures	115,732	9,696	9,557	13,580	51,867	27,909
Enplanements	3,519,249	185,695	237,266	375,442	1,857,207	840,438
1965						
Departures	85,383	10,095	10,119	14,888	28,898	16,815
Enplanements	1,622,057	112,616	121,562	225,972	761,919	386,184

Source: U.S. Department of Transportation, Federal Aviation Administration, *Airport Activity Statistics of Certificated Route Air Carriers, 12 Months Ended December 31, 1987*, and earlier editions.

TABLE 9.12--PUBLIC RIVER TERMINALS, LOCATION AND FACILITIES, TENNESSEE RIVER AND ITS TRIBUTARIES, TENNESSEE, 1990

River	County	River mile	Facility name	Handling equipment[1]	Storage facility[2]	Transport access: Rail	Transport access: Major highway[3]
			TENNESSEE RIVER				
Tennessee	Humphreys	100.3R	Herbert Sangravel Co., Inc.	A,C,D,E	III	CSX	U.S. 70
	Humphreys	100.3R	Merchants Grain, Inc.	A,C	IV	CSX	U.S. 70
	Perry	135.5	Tinker Sand & Gravel, Inc.	A,C,D,E	III	None	TN. 100
	Marion	421.6R	Jasper Bulk Terminals, Inc.	None	None	None	I-24
	Marion	424.0L	Port of Nickajack	F	III	None	I-24
	Marion	430.3L	Serodino, Inc.	F	III,VI	None	I-24
	Hamilton	456.1R	Mid-South Terminals, Inc.	F	III,IV	Norfolk Southern	I-24
	Hamilton	456.1R	Ergon, Inc.	B	VI	Norfolk Southern	I-24
	Hamilton	462.0L	Combustion Engineering Co.	F	III	CSX	I-124
	Hamilton	463.1R	Southern Electric Fleeting Co.	F	III	None	I-124
	Hamilton	463.6R	Concrete Service Co.	F	III	Norfolk Southern	I-124
	Hamilton	463.8R	JIT Terminals, Inc.	B,F	II,VI,VIb (humidity controlled)	Norfolk Southern	I-124
	Loudon	600.2R	Fort Loudon Terminal	D,E	II,III	Norfolk Southern	I-40, I-75
	Knox	647.8L	Southern States Asphalt	B	II,III,IV	Norfolk Southern	I-40, I-75
	Knox	652.2R	Burkhart Enterprises	D,E,F	III	Norfolk Southern	I-40, I-75
			TENNESSEE RIVER TRIBUTARIES				
Little Tennessee	Monroe	18.9L	Burkhart Enterprises	F	III	CSX	U.S. 411
Emory	Monroe	11.0L	Harbert International	F	II,III,V	Norfolk Southern	I-40
Hiwassee	Monroe	18.2R	Hiwassee River Terminal	F	III,IV	Norfolk Southern	U.S. 11
Hiwassee	Monroe	17.2L	AKZO Salt, Inc.	F	II,III,V	Norfolk Southern	U.S. 11

1. Codes: Type of Handling Equipment
A. Conveyor system
B. Pipeline
C. Hopper facilities
D. Clamshell bucket
E. Fixed crane or derrick
F. Mobile crane or derrick
G. Floating crane/derrick
H. Hoists (fixed or mobile)

2. Codes: Type of Storage Facilities
I. Covered shed
II. Enclosed shed (warehouse)
III. Open storage area
IV. Grain elevators
V. Bins
VI. Liquid storage tanks
VI.a. Petroleum
VI.b. Other

3. Highway is within 10-mile radius.

Source: Tennessee Valley Authority, Navigation Development, direct correspondence.

TABLE 9.13--PRIVATE INVESTMENT IN WATERFRONT PLANTS AND TERMINALS ON THE TENNESSEE RIVER, 1933–1988 [In thousands of dollars]

Year	Investment in new and expanded plants		Cumulative investment in new and expanded plants		Cumulative percentage of total	
	Current $	1982 $	Current $	1982 $	Current $	1982 $
1988	460,500	378,079	5,752,846	11,262,952	100.0	100.0
1987	204,400	174,106	5,292,346	10,884,873	92.0	96.6
1986	146,350	128,265	5,087,946	10,710,767	88.4	95.1
1985	150,000	134,892	4,941,596	10,582,502	85.9	94.0
1984	211,065	195,975	4,791,596	10,447,610	83.3	92.8
1983	147,775	142,228	4,580,531	10,251,635	79.6	91.0
1982	40,000	40,000	4,432,756	10,109,407	77.1	89.8
1981	317,872	338,162	4,392,756	10,069,407	76.4	89.4
1980	316,886	369,762	4,074,884	9,731,245	70.8	86.4
1979	156,243	198,782	3,757,998	9,361,483	65.3	83.1
1978	97,523	135,073	3,601,755	9,162,701	62.6	81.4
1977	437,248	649,700	3,504,232	9,027,628	60.9	80.2
1976	71,632	113,521	3,066,984	8,377,928	53.3	74.4
1975	300,488	506,725	2,995,352	8,264,407	52.1	73.4
1974	162,273	300,506	2,694,864	7,757,682	46.8	68.9
1973	365,915	739,222	2,532,591	7,457,176	44.0	66.2
1972	46,195	99,344	2,166,676	6,717,954	37.7	59.6
1971	27,895	62,827	2,120,481	6,618,610	36.9	58.8
1970	78,943	187,960	2,092,586	6,555,783	36.4	58.2
1969	133,050	334,296	2,013,643	6,367,823	35.0	56.5
1968	311,251	825,599	1,880,593	6,033,527	32.7	53.6
1967	95,876	267,064	1,569,342	5,207,928	27.3	46.2
1966	180,755	516,443	1,473,466	4,940,864	25.6	43.9
1965	214,620	634,970	1,292,711	4,424,421	22.5	39.3
1964	62,157	188,927	1,078,091	3,789,451	18.7	33.6
1963	83,529	257,806	1,015,934	3,600,524	17.7	32.0
1962	110,050	344,984	932,405	3,342,718	16.2	29.7
1961	67,961	217,824	822,355	2,997,734	14.3	26.6
1960	27,937	90,411	754,394	2,779,910	13.1	24.7
1959	57,471	189,049	726,457	2,689,499	12.6	23.9
1958	21,788	73,360	668,986	2,500,450	11.6	22.2
1957	159,449	547,935	647,198	2,427,090	11.3	21.5
1956	169,703	603,925	487,749	1,879,155	8.5	16.7
1955	56,633	208,210	318,046	1,275,230	5.5	11.3
1954	94,985	361,160	261,413	1,067,020	4.5	9.5
1953	37,792	145,915	166,428	705,860	2.9	6.3
1952	44,805	175,706	128,636	559,945	2.2	5.0
1951	24,491	97,574	83,831	384,239	1.5	3.4
1950	3,506	14,669	59,340	286,665	1.0	2.5
1949	10,012	42,604	55,834	271,996	1.0	2.4
1948	32,767	138,843	45,822	229,392	0.8	2.0
1947	1,768	8,000	13,055	90,549	0.2	0.8
1946	729	3,758	11,287	82,549	0.2	0.7
1933–1945	10,558	78,791	10,558	78,791	0.2	0.7

Source: Tennessee Valley Authority, Economic Development and Analysis Branch, *Waterfront Industry on the Tennessee River, 1988.*

TABLE 9.14--NET TONS OF RIVER FREIGHT TRAFFIC, BY COMMODITY, MAINSTREAM OF TENNESSEE RIVER, 1935–1987, SELECTED YEARS [In thousands of tons]

Year	Total	Chemicals	Coal and coke	Forest products	Grains and products	Iron and steel	Petroleum products	Stone, sand, and gravel[1]	All other
1987	41,788.9	2,233.4	20,694.2	593.9	3,970.9	1,285.1	2,385.1	8,190.0	2,436.1
1986	39,998.9	2,215.0	21,884.4	519.4	4,340.8	1,187.5	2,079.7	5,248.9	2,519.0
1985	36,683.3	2,313.4	19,144.2	547.7	3,911.8	1,114.8	1,788.8	5,591.1	2,271.6
1984	33,182.0	2,440.0	16,275.9	548.2	4,604.8	1,334.3	1,677.3	4,214.4	2,087.1
1983	27,988.0	1,800.0	13,450.0	627.0	3,776.0	916.0	2,259.0	3,547.0	1,613.0
1982	25,513.0	1,752.0	14,081.0	583.0	3,285.0	690.0	1,598.0	2,051.0	1,473.0
1981	26,006.0	2,095.0	13,197.0	697.0	2,915.0	1,073.0	1,503.0	2,534.0	1,992.0
1980	29,397.0	2,488.0	15,651.0	591.0	2,895.0	937.0	1,918.0	3,158.0	1,759.0
1979	31,398.0	2,765.2	15,029.1	476.5	2,453.9	1,156.5	2,414.8	5,608.9	1,493.1
1978	31,634.5	2,829.8	13,412.4	449.5	2,506.5	1,270.9	3,303.1	6,099.4	1,683.0
1977	26,583.2	2,730.8	10,114.7	361.2	2,255.5	1,086.5	3,544.8	4,901.2	1,688.5
1976	26,254.2	2,619.8	9,354.3	320.5	1,921.7	1,132.2	3,472.2	5,839.1	1,590.4
1975	28,316.5	2,142.5	12,110.9	302.7	1,885.8	835.6	2,820.6	6,824.2	1,394.3
1974	27,123.6	2,513.3	9,329.1	336.5	1,963.3	1,193.2	2,140.9	8,146.5	1,500.8
1973	29,346.6	2,395.4	11,689.6	375.8	1,990.9	1,099.0	2,425.1	7,816.9	1,554.0
1972	28,529.7	2,204.0	12,021.7	372.8	1,918.9	1,079.3	3,185.5	6,352.1	1,395.4
1971	27,685.2	1,836.6	10,802.9	342.9	2,927.1	1,080.5	3,328.6	5,994.1	1,372.4
1970	25,489.2	1,609.8	9,714.1	328.2	2,939.0	868.6	2,927.8	5,506.7	1,595.1
1969	24,530.3	1,651.0	9,593.9	341.3	2,565.8	962.2	2,739.7	5,386.6	1,289.6
1968	23,018.3	1,280.6	8,827.5	297.7	1,815.4	810.3	2,651.8	5,929.6	1,405.4
1967	21,511.7	1,019.9	8,123.8	252.2	2,065.8	462.9	1,983.5	6,356.2	1,247.5
1966	19,709.1	581.4	7,892.6	245.4	2,200.1	515.8	1,082.8	6,292.8	898.2
1965	17,395.9	401.6	6,640.8	212.8	1,724.3	438.6	1,097.7	6,014.9	865.2
1964	15,373.9	352.6	6,328.3	202.3	1,784.2	375.8	875.9	4,723.1	731.8
1963	14,432.7	286.9	5,917.3	195.5	2,203.4	340.6	846.7	3,943.6	698.7
1962	13,115.4	311.7	4,655.1	168.3	2,908.3	259.7	790.4	3,531.3	490.5
1961	11,614.7	305.1	4,664.0	161.7	2,099.2	250.3	604.4	3,155.9	374.0
1960	12,440.7	345.8	5,177.4	183.1	2,261.4	306.5	794.2	3,000.5	371.7
1959	12,036.9	245.0	5,206.3	168.5	1,901.1	353.7	717.8	3,089.5	354.9
1958	12,040.8	246.3	5,052.8	176.0	1,773.0	286.3	787.4	2,879.2	839.8
1957	12,742.2	171.3	6,725.6	149.4	1,079.4	325.8	731.7	2,799.3	759.6
1956	12,299.4	86.8	7,473.8	109.2	649.8	293.0	826.3	2,162.3	698.2
1955	9,975.0	111.2	5,661.9	112.0	736.1	258.2	914.8	1,881.7	299.1
1950	3,051.2	(a)	207.2	29.3	160.7	117.5	754.3	1,657.1	125.0
1945	2,163.4	0.0	505.3	62.9	122.9	17.5	215.6	1,198.3	40.9
1940	2,206.9	0.0	(a)	141.9	43.1	20.6	102.9	1,842.1	56.3
1935	1,899.3	0.0	(a)	111.0	(a)	34.9	0.0	1,598.7	154.7

1. Includes waterway improvement material.

a. Included in all other category.

Source: Tennessee Valley Authority and U.S. Department of the Army, Corps of Engineers, direct correspondence.

TABLE 9.15--TON-MILES OF RIVER FREIGHT TRAFFIC, BY COMMODITY, MAINSTREAM OF TENNESSEE RIVER, 1935–1984, SELECTED YEARS [In millions of ton miles]

Year	Total	Chemicals	Coal and coke	Forest products	Grains and products	Iron and steel	Petroleum products	Stone, sand, and gravel[1]	All other
1984	6,127.0	400.0	2,913.2	72.8	1,726.2	214.1	253.0	142.4	405.3
1983	5,405.2	302.7	2,742.9	71.6	1,341.3	161.1	372.7	116.9	295.9
1982	5,101.9	329.5	2,947.6	76.2	1,045.6	148.0	265.2	82.7	207.1
1981	4,842.3	395.0	2,523.0	85.9	969.3	216.2	280.3	101.6	271.0
1980	5,330.0	502.6	2,967.1	60.9	932.9	169.3	313.0	102.8	281.3
1979	5,061.9	529.2	2,501.7	53.7	818.8	201.9	584.0	142.8	229.8
1978	4,416.6	583.4	1,535.0	50.4	904.8	221.5	712.0	149.0	260.6
1977	3,747.6	581.7	1,073.7	40.0	805.0	191.7	695.7	126.8	233.0
1976	3,663.7	522.2	1,099.2	33.0	728.6	214.6	705.5	159.2	201.6
1975	3,915.8	434.4	1,590.9	30.8	730.2	152.6	601.0	181.4	194.4
1974	3,578.8	437.9	1,259.1	36.5	769.9	202.8	497.0	205.2	170.4
1973	3,954.3	454.8	1,576.7	40.9	772.6	193.1	438.5	268.4	209.3
1972	3,755.9	412.7	1,404.0	36.9	739.7	175.2	540.1	234.6	212.8
1971	3,960.5	317.2	1,247.5	32.4	1,144.6	196.6	545.1	230.3	246.8
1970	3,667.7	256.2	1,173.6	33.2	1,145.2	144.3	447.3	208.8	259.2
1969	3,341.9	288.8	1,038.9	36.6	999.0	128.9	403.5	203.6	242.7
1968	2,757.8	242.7	848.8	35.5	706.7	138.9	374.9	186.6	223.7
1967	2,598.8	191.0	840.2	31.2	798.7	72.8	222.6	218.1	224.2
1966	2,556.4	142.6	874.0	28.9	855.0	77.4	203.0	206.5	169.1
1965	2,190.1	91.3	664.5	23.9	672.5	74.8	295.0	204.4	163.7
1964	2,053.9	71.0	604.8	22.6	699.2	71.2	280.7	153.5	150.8
1963	2,218.1	58.1	534.5	22.4	880.5	57.6	398.1	133.5	133.5
1962	2,268.8	66.4	423.7	19.0	1,171.9	43.8	347.7	85.2	111.2
1961	1,875.8	61.3	538.5	19.3	814.4	38.0	240.3	98.3	65.7
1960	2,312.7	62.7	712.2	25.3	923.9	73.7	359.8	76.9	78.2
1959	2,164.0	37.7	745.3	25.8	793.6	86.7	334.2	67.4	73.4
1958	2,103.3	48.0	712.0	28.2	744.9	85.2	343.0	80.8	61.1
1957	2,112.8	37.8	1,056.8	24.4	461.2	90.8	312.6	76.0	53.2
1956	2,003.4	22.9	1,130.3	17.4	273.0	83.5	342.1	55.1	79.3
1955	1,631.3	23.0	702.3	16.9	292.6	70.2	400.5	44.3	81.5
1950	589.4	(a)	54.2	4.6	57.1	42.5	359.8	49.0	22.2
1945	258.5	0.0	148.5	9.4	46.9	4.4	24.8	20.1	4.4
1940	97.4	0.0	(a)	21.4	17.9	4.9	33.5	15.3	4.4
1935	69.4	0.0	(a)	15.9	(a)	1.8	0.0	43.5	8.2

1. Includes waterway improvement material.

a. Included in all other category.

Source: U.S. Department of the Army, Corps of Engineers and Tennessee Valley Authority, direct correspondence.

TABLE 9.16--MOTOR VEHICLE REGISTRATIONS, BY TYPE OF VEHICLE, COUNTIES, 1988

County	Total [1]	Auto-mobiles	Motor-cycles	Buses	Taxis	Trucks	Semi-trailers
Anderson	81,325	76,730	1,789	7	16	2,134	648
Bedford	28,791	25,733	736	0	2	1,706	614
Benton	15,368	14,001	386	0	2	712	267
Bledsoe	7,535	6,889	142	0	0	397	107
Blount	87,351	81,582	1,901	3	12	3,279	572
Bradley	72,322	66,259	1,983	2	7	2,717	1,353
Campbell	27,032	24,746	376	0	11	1,115	784
Cannon	8,427	7,885	126	0	0	316	100
Carroll	22,723	21,312	342	0	6	796	267
Carter	42,891	39,997	1,057	1	9	1,393	434
Cheatham	19,420	17,485	585	0	0	989	358
Chester	9,818	8,981	179	0	2	457	199
Claiborne	24,849	22,667	476	0	0	1,173	507
Clay	6,878	6,376	125	0	0	236	141
Cocke	27,709	26,076	428	3	6	944	252
Coffee	39,604	36,320	1,023	1	4	1,750	506
Crockett	11,420	10,253	158	0	0	680	329
Cumberland	29,667	26,783	520	0	4	1,744	615
Davidson	479,085	373,587	9,298	139	260	27,973	67,713
Decatur	11,495	10,495	164	0	0	548	288
DeKalb	13,784	12,767	203	0	0	657	157
Dickson	32,277	29,442	765	0	4	1,768	297
Dyer	30,039	27,059	722	0	12	1,697	545
Fayette	17,840	16,598	253	0	0	659	330
Fentress	13,311	12,174	154	0	0	701	281
Franklin	29,315	26,512	612	0	1	1,213	977
Gibson	38,548	35,435	761	0	4	1,701	646
Giles	23,611	21,529	544	0	5	1,144	389
Grainger	13,254	12,309	207	0	0	578	160
Greene	47,329	43,743	838	9	6	2,044	689
Grundy	11,451	10,579	138	0	0	442	292
Hamblen	55,554	50,760	1,404	0	14	2,215	1,151
Hamilton	278,798	222,437	4,032	29	103	12,851	39,344
Hancock	4,594	4,301	69	0	0	205	19
Hardeman	17,822	16,633	289	0	0	692	208
Hardin	19,044	17,441	260	0	1	890	449
Hawkins	33,686	31,797	751	3	1	962	172
Haywood	13,706	12,523	217	0	2	759	205
Henderson	18,253	16,827	358	0	2	880	185
Henry	24,812	22,548	519	0	4	1,280	461
Hickman	13,279	12,215	270	0	0	661	133
Houston	5,745	5,407	105	0	1	159	73
Humphreys	15,067	13,754	239	0	2	732	338
Jackson	6,807	6,346	125	0	0	294	42
Jefferson	25,162	20,511	378	6	1	917	3,349
Johnson	12,550	11,845	263	0	0	351	91
Knox	277,424	251,798	5,232	32	68	15,006	5,279
Lake	4,795	4,434	94	0	0	195	72
Lauderdale	18,621	17,063	395	0	2	768	393
Lawrence	27,971	25,868	467	3	2	1,167	463
Lewis	8,180	7,331	253	0	0	382	214
Lincoln	23,603	21,636	323	0	2	1,195	446
Loudon	29,000	27,253	494	0	4	1,017	232

TABLE 9.16--MOTOR VEHICLE REGISTRATIONS, BY TYPE OF VEHICLE, COUNTIES, 1988 (Continued)

County	Total [1]	Auto-mobiles	Motor-cycles	Buses	Taxis	Trucks	Semi-trailers
McMinn	37,757	35,021	706	0	7	1,554	469
McNairy	22,349	20,761	338	1	0	970	277
Macon	14,771	13,599	341	0	1	626	203
Madison	67,394	61,202	957	4	21	4,159	1,048
Marion	22,965	21,344	412	1	1	920	287
Marshall	17,295	15,738	318	0	5	714	520
Maury	50,344	45,534	1,239	5	15	2,824	727
Meigs	7,297	6,739	157	0	0	333	68
Monroe	27,558	25,591	455	4	0	1,154	354
Montgomery	95,306	89,145	2,238	0	28	3,315	576
Moore	5,719	5,087	124	0	0	395	113
Morgan	11,919	11,096	177	0	0	561	85
Obion	27,186	24,760	407	0	4	1,334	681
Overton	12,424	11,463	104	0	4	596	256
Perry	5,992	5,511	97	0	0	287	97
Pickett	4,244	3,905	57	0	0	206	76
Polk	13,085	12,230	291	0	0	401	163
Putnam	47,481	42,791	993	7	4	2,633	1,053
Rhea	30,546	28,413	731	0	0	1,124	278
Roane	38,589	36,216	782	4	6	1,137	444
Robertson	30,531	27,991	664	0	6	1,550	311
Rutherford	91,973	83,918	2,290	5	26	4,230	1,493
Scott	16,446	14,955	322	0	1	834	334
Sequatchie	11,305	10,329	200	0	0	641	135
Sevier	45,669	42,173	964	8	6	2,372	146
Shelby	642,461	563,820	7,679	99	305	25,472	45,077
Smith	10,792	9,985	158	0	1	449	199
Stewart	9,553	8,886	230	0	12	362	63
Sullivan	144,616	131,165	3,271	6	62	6,056	4,056
Sumner	89,165	81,585	2,040	1	17	4,165	1,324
Tipton	28,669	26,625	421	0	3	1,337	283
Trousdale	7,032	6,423	179	0	0	339	91
Unicoi	16,453	15,427	374	0	0	571	81
Union	18,590	17,190	441	9	0	869	81
Van Buren	3,405	3,177	71	0	0	128	29
Warren	31,036	27,751	687	0	6	1,896	696
Washington	87,957	79,006	1,955	0	20	4,256	2,720
Wayne	12,280	11,408	161	0	0	507	204
Weakley	25,213	23,011	557	0	1	1,133	511
White	19,151	17,454	316	0	4	784	592
Williamson	72,456	66,325	1,615	15	8	3,662	819
Wilson	66,410	60,121	1,716	1	13	3,680	872
Unassigned	225,113	63,339	1,965	12	22	15,419	144,344

Note: Data are as of February 28, 1988. With the exception of automobiles, all registrations are renewable by March 1. Automobile registrations include all renewals from March 1, 1987, through February 28, 1988.

1. Totals include mobile homes and Music City buses not shown separately.

Source: Tennessee Department of Revenue, Motor Vehicle Division, direct correspondence.

TABLE 9.17--ROAD MILEAGE, BY TYPE, TENNESSEE AND COUNTIES, AS OF DECEMBER 31, 1988
[In miles]

County	Total	Inter-state system	State highway system	Local county roads	Local city streets	State park roads
TENNESSEE	83,638.48	1,062.12	12,408.02	53,666.59	15,365.54	373.27
Anderson	813.00	12.12	125.18	419.93	248.58	5.58
Bedford	919.40	0.46	159.12	661.90	97.92	0.00
Benton	723.68	8.77	91.84	570.23	40.35	12.49
Bledsoe	490.21	0.00	62.94	392.64	21.47	13.16
Blount	1,206.90	0.00	160.86	808.48	214.45	0.00
Bradley	1,027.57	19.35	113.78	689.98	203.24	1.22
Campbell	810.37	31.64	84.00	579.31	114.57	0.85
Cannon	455.47	0.00	80.68	360.42	14.37	0.00
Carroll	1,028.87	0.66	211.49	687.35	114.66	14.71
Carter	749.21	0.00	121.11	495.22	128.81	4.07
Cheatham	571.51	11.31	96.77	413.60	43.25	2.78
Chester	541.24	0.00	91.81	408.99	33.82	6.62
Claiborne	816.10	0.00	99.65	665.43	49.48	0.00
Clay	405.81	0.00	70.50	320.12	15.19	0.00
Cocke	849.47	21.95	120.09	456.56	54.82	0.00
Coffee	972.93	30.12	111.04	642.90	181.03	3.42
Crockett	535.71	0.00	101.32	393.04	41.35	0.00
Cumberland	935.57	36.05	148.55	663.21	82.05	5.71
Davidson	2,661.88	88.65	263.72	63.86	2,240.13	5.52
Decatur	618.07	5.67	103.93	471.54	36.93	0.00
DeKalb	599.90	0.00	100.96	437.36	52.60	8.98
Dickson	1,016.16	17.86	154.74	724.65	107.23	11.48
Dyer	881.18	15.93	157.25	593.07	114.93	0.00
Fayette	916.80	16.09	187.87	668.89	43.95	0.00
Fentress	554.78	0.00	112.71	412.53	26.67	2.87
Franklin	881.82	0.00	154.99	595.07	127.82	3.94
Gibson	1,249.08	0.00	225.92	851.27	171.89	0.00
Giles	1,105.77	22.40	151.71	854.55	77.11	0.00
Grainger	629.52	0.00	94.13	519.48	15.91	0.00
Greene	1,521.32	32.16	191.14	1,151.99	144.02	2.01
Grundy	443.90	7.31	93.33	247.86	92.43	2.97
Hamblen	622.51	9.92	79.02	393.76	136.06	2.93
Hamilton	2,234.89	32.39	232.98	542.35	1,415.94	11.23
Hancock	409.81	0.00	64.43	335.46	9.92	0.00
Hardeman	893.04	0.00	149.96	663.91	69.73	9.44
Hardin	919.43	0.00	165.44	665.87	68.37	5.26
Hawkins	1,047.29	0.00	162.36	754.71	130.22	0.00
Haywood	742.91	23.89	139.91	524.65	54.46	0.00
Henderson	945.30	24.64	160.83	657.50	47.30	55.03
Henry	1,061.41	0.00	171.45	805.92	78.27	5.77
Hickman	905.10	14.45	128.07	735.18	27.40	0.00
Houston	357.21	0.00	63.04	263.23	30.94	0.00
Humphreys	798.27	14.12	77.90	631.66	74.59	0.00
Jackson	599.79	0.00	126.59	455.15	18.05	0.00
Jefferson	860.33	27.69	121.56	626.03	85.05	0.00
Johnson	448.34	0.00	95.54	325.48	20.14	0.00
Knox	2,584.45	59.86	225.92	1,392.92	905.75	0.00
Lake	279.17	0.00	58.05	194.18	21.94	5.00
Lauderdale	706.99	0.00	133.35	507.58	60.67	5.39
Lawrence	1,250.01	0.00	150.30	969.67	123.78	6.26

TABLE 9.17--ROAD MILEAGE, BY TYPE, TENNESSEE AND COUNTIES, AS OF DECEMBER 31, 1988
[In miles] (Continued)

County	Total	Inter-state system	State highway system	Local county roads	Local city streets	State park roads
Lewis	391.06	0.00	69.87	266.05	29.29	0.00
Lincoln	1,006.88	0.00	181.47	775.63	49.78	0.00
Loudon	645.39	23.97	81.02	445.50	90.95	0.00
McMinn	1,117.23	24.99	138.29	789.17	164.78	0.00
McNairy	991.86	0.00	166.98	713.05	106.62	5.21
Macon	686.76	0.00	99.99	544.25	42.52	0.00
Madison	1,091.93	27.94	163.36	694.66	203.08	2.89
Marion	585.57	32.28	155.45	285.35	112.49	0.00
Marshall	739.44	12.77	141.41	496.80	83.42	5.04
Maury	1,170.69	17.68	195.15	767.58	180.73	0.00
Meigs	412.61	0.00	74.73	322.39	10.46	0.00
Monroe	1,105.49	6.51	153.23	763.69	110.01	1.22
Montgomery	1,121.95	17.20	166.65	669.93	267.55	0.62
Moore	258.59	0.00	42.06	213.07	3.46	0.00
Morgan	575.15	0.00	108.66	448.89	15.77	1.83
Obion	1,010.46	0.00	184.70	698.07	127.69	0.00
Overton	766.16	0.00	142.16	580.72	32.31	10.97
Perry	490.36	0.00	97.32	368.37	23.18	1.49
Pickett	272.70	0.00	46.05	196.49	12.28	17.88
Polk	705.02	0.00	108.26	378.40	23.25	1.89
Putnam	1,012.99	37.06	140.64	621.04	212.78	0.76
Rhea	596.84	0.00	91.29	433.94	71.61	0.00
Roane	929.10	22.98	128.01	603.46	174.65	0.00
Robertson	1,039.89	28.27	151.68	729.60	130.34	0.00
Rutherford	1,328.56	33.29	202.14	814.47	277.51	1.15
Scott	533.02	0.00	70.18	420.86	41.98	0.00
Sequatchie	321.89	0.00	56.60	218.64	46.65	0.00
Sevier	1,238.33	4.76	155.34	912.01	132.90	0.00
Shelby	3,499.64	62.18	277.44	696.18	2,432.25	31.59
Smith	584.92	17.17	103.99	429.78	33.98	0.00
Stewart	639.05	0.00	100.12	386.03	29.01	0.00
Sullivan	1,544.78	31.94	178.96	947.55	379.75	6.58
Sumner	1,360.47	5.93	217.11	803.86	331.56	2.01
Tipton	760.50	0.00	125.66	563.74	71.10	0.00
Trousdale	222.70	0.00	43.37	159.89	19.44	0.00
Unicoi	309.25	0.00	67.22	197.09	31.02	0.00
Union	478.17	0.00	71.95	376.06	26.58	3.58
Van Buren	294.79	0.00	75.50	177.73	18.66	22.90
Warren	901.54	0.00	162.29	644.48	88.58	6.19
Washington	1,193.72	17.91	138.08	724.40	313.33	0.00
Wayne	938.21	0.00	145.80	725.71	37.25	0.00
Weakley	1,169.22	0.00	188.95	867.04	113.02	0.21
White	743.29	0.00	101.82	593.89	47.58	0.00
Williamson	1,116.12	24.48	181.12	750.04	160.48	0.00
Wilson	1,136.74	27.35	166.12	784.40	124.30	34.57

Note: Federal reservation roads are not listed separately but are included in the total.

Source: Tennessee Department of Transportation, Office of Research and Planning, Research and Statistics Division, direct correspondence.

TABLE 9.18--MILEAGE OF EXISTING PUBLIC ROADS AND STREETS, BY FUNCTIONAL CLASSIFICATION, SOUTHEASTERN STATES AND UNITED STATES, 1987

		Rural					Urban				
State	Total	Total	Inter-state	Other arterial	Collector	Local	Total	Inter-state	Other arterial[1]	Collector	Local
TENNESSEE	83,691	68,559	788	5,208	16,263	46,300	15,132	274	2,209	1,774	10,875
Alabama	88,166	73,493	622	5,866	18,441	48,564	14,673	258	2,611	1,709	10,095
Arkansas	77,087	69,457	419	5,099	18,970	44,969	7,630	123	1,722	1,000	4,785
Florida	100,423	68,398	966	6,112	9,946	51,374	32,025	388	4,524	4,676	22,437
Georgia	106,767	86,594	884	8,573	21,333	55,804	20,173	359	3,641	1,829	14,344
Kentucky	69,629	62,078	579	3,320	16,570	41,609	7,551	173	1,571	893	4,914
Louisiana	58,272	46,061	532	2,671	11,653	31,205	12,211	177	2,125	1,142	8,767
Mississippi	72,065	64,940	563	5,642	14,666	44,069	7,125	123	1,309	750	4,943
North Carolina	93,234	74,928	599	4,102	19,617	50,610	18,306	206	4,035	1,362	12,703
South Carolina	63,420	54,104	673	4,959	12,535	35,937	9,316	117	1,609	1,151	6,439
Virginia	66,125	51,631	767	5,079	12,586	33,199	14,494	292	2,761	1,348	10,093
West Virginia	35,173	32,202	389	2,252	8,537	21,024	2,971	90	578	402	1,901
UNITED STATES	3,874,026	3,163,838	33,111	227,973	730,212	2,172,542	710,188	11,217	132,857	76,860	489,254

Note: Data are mileages of routes that were serving traffic as of December 31.

1. Includes other freeways and expressways.

Source: U.S. Department of Transportation, Federal Highway Administration, Highway Statistics Division, *Highway Statistics, 1987*.

TABLE 9.19--MOTOR VEHICLE REGISTRATIONS, BY OWNERSHIP AND BY TYPE OF VEHICLE, SOUTHEASTERN STATES, 1987

State	Total		Ownership		Type of vehicle		
	Registrations	Percent change 1986–87	Private and commercial	Publicly owned	Automobiles	Buses	Trucks
TENNESSEE	4,026,565	2.4	3,967,031	59,534	3,194,605	12,078	819,882
Alabama	3,546,583	2.6	3,504,551	42,032	2,633,403	8,402	904,778
Arkansas	1,444,991	1.3	1,424,737	20,254	935,599	5,257	504,135
Florida	10,683,590	3.1	10,464,480	219,110	8,521,630	34,845	2,127,115
Georgia	5,026,220	3.8	4,961,180	65,040	3,597,364	16,938	1,411,918
Kentucky	2,720,197	1.3	2,650,045	70,152	1,811,098	9,712	899,387
Louisiana	2,891,234	0.1	2,847,474	43,760	1,953,327	19,448	918,459
Mississippi	1,760,866	-0.5	1,734,097	26,769	1,344,842	8,244	407,780
North Carolina	4,870,224	2.8	4,775,762	94,462	3,491,660	32,883	1,345,681
South Carolina	2,366,144	2.7	2,329,854	36,290	1,782,844	13,633	569,667
Virginia	4,627,987	2.1	4,558,014	69,973	3,614,251	15,477	998,259
West Virginia	1,193,993	2.0	1,136,812	57,181	821,035	3,710	369,248

Source: U.S. Department of Transportation, Federal Highway Administration, Highway Statistics Division, *Highway Statistics, 1987*.

TABLE 9.20--MOTOR TRUCK REGISTRATIONS, SOUTHEASTERN STATES, 1960–1987, SELECTED YEARS

State	Total registered	Private and commercial	Federal	State, county, and municipal	Total registered	Private and commercial	Federal	State, county, and municipal
	1987				1980			
TENNESSEE	819,882	783,917	6,578	29,387	696,420	666,054	6,697	23,669
Alabama	904,778	881,940	3,257	19,581	823,846	801,957	3,283	18,606
Arkansas	504,135	494,614	1,811	7,710	531,726	522,374	1,687	7,665
Florida	2,127,115	2,015,757	9,654	101,704	1,387,642	1,294,734	7,661	85,247
Georgia	1,411,918	1,374,780	4,692	32,446	873,420	836,610	3,847	32,963
Kentucky	899,387	857,215	2,976	39,196	777,278	753,117	2,448	21,713
Louisiana	918,459	901,815	3,196	13,448	791,628	776,511	2,931	12,186
Mississippi	407,780	393,883	2,407	11,490	349,075	339,199	2,337	7,539
North Carolina	1,345,681	1,297,981	3,542	44,158	1,109,666	1,048,977	3,221	57,468
South Carolina	569,667	550,283	3,470	15,914	451,888	436,593	2,272	13,023
Virginia	998,259	970,276	5,549	22,434	541,128	517,411	4,583	19,134
West Virginia	369,248	333,301	1,345	34,602	387,313	362,798	1,296	23,219
	1970				1960			
TENNESSEE	404,292	385,045	4,592	14,655	231,041	219,926	3,056	8,059
Alabama	399,028	382,743	2,418	13,867	233,673	223,229	1,313	9,131
Arkansas	310,754	304,352	1,213	5,189	202,523	197,485	849	4,189
Florida	556,210	518,897	5,060	32,253	312,292	294,261	1,988	16,043
Georgia	510,886	493,432	2,604	14,850	283,266	271,386	1,614	10,266
Kentucky	380,867	367,978	1,559	11,330	241,590	232,106	947	8,537
Louisiana	365,228	352,455	1,825	10,948	228,195	219,693	1,233	7,269
Mississippi	290,301	279,571	1,838	8,892	188,539	180,867	1,147	6,525
North Carolina	578,302	533,156	2,146	43,000	325,357	305,022	1,619	18,716
South Carolina	250,518	238,363	1,512	10,643	150,308	141,448	1,294	7,566
Virginia	359,090	340,257	2,998	15,835	221,614	211,281	1,665	8,668
West Virginia	173,437	166,325	910	6,202	119,404	113,735	574	5,095

Source: U.S. Department of Transportation, Federal Highway Administration, Highway Statistics Division, *Highway Statistics, 1987*, and earlier editions.

TABLE 9.21--MOTOR FUEL CONSUMPTION AND TAXES, SOUTHEASTERN STATES, 1987

State	Gross gallons reported[1] (1,000)	Net total gallons taxed (1,000)	Gasoline tax rate (¢ per gallon)	Diesel tax rate (¢ per gallon)	Gross receipts from motor fuel taxes[2] ($1,000)
TENNESSEE	3,319,542	3,193,869	17.0 [a]	15.0 [a]	470,567
Alabama	2,492,332	2,481,895	13.0 [a]	14.0 [a]	252,539
Arkansas	1,570,455	1,545,110	13.5	12.5	203,601
Florida	6,700,630	6,653,016	9.7 [b]	9.7 [b]	651,405
Georgia	4,203,951	4,202,233	7.5	7.5	314,105
Kentucky	2,212,797	2,190,646	15.0 [c, d]	12.0 [c, d]	315,045
Louisiana	2,409,511	2,291,445	16.0	16.0	384,107
Mississippi	1,569,703	1,555,859	15.0	15.0	137,125
North Carolina	3,905,577	3,834,027	15.5 [c]	15.5 [c]	592,017
South Carolina	1,966,925	1,948,156	15.0	15.0	282,080
Virginia	3,534,299	3,444,011	17.5 [d]	16.0 [d]	557,194
West Virginia	979,480	974,895	10.5 [e]	10.5 [e]	106,406

Note: Tax rates are as of December 31.

1. Export sales and other amounts not consumed as motor fuel in state have been excluded wherever possible.

2. Includes revenues from state taxes on all motor-vehicle fuels and, for most states, only the portion of the tax on special fuels that is applicable to the gallonage used on the highways.

a. Includes 1 cent per gallon inspection fee in Tennessee and 2 cents per gallon inspection fee in Alabama.

b. Consists of a fixed rate of 4 cents per gallon plus a 5 percent sales tax applied to the average retail price of motor fuel established annually, with a minimum tax of 5.7 cents per gallon.

c. Variable tax rates are determined at various times of the year.

d. Two percent surtax on fuel purchased for any vehicle with 3 or more axles in Kentucky and 3.5 cents per gallon surtax on vehicle with 3 or more axles in Virginia.

e. There is also a consumer sales and service tax of 4.85 cents per gallon.

Source: U.S. Department of Transportation, Federal Highway Administration, Highway Statistics Division, *Highway Statistics, 1987*.

TABLE 9.22--STATE MOTOR FUEL TAX RATE AND REVENUE, SOUTHEASTERN STATES, 1960–1987, SELECTED YEARS

State	1987 Gasoline tax rate per gallon (¢)	1987 Gross tax collect-tions[1] ($1,000)	1986 Gasoline tax rate per gallon (¢)	1986 Gross tax collect-tions[1] ($1,000)	1980 Gasoline tax rate per gallon (¢)	1980 Gross tax collect-tions[1] ($1,000)	1970 Gasoline tax rate per gallon (¢)	1970 Gross tax collect-tions[1] ($1,000)	1960 Gasoline tax rate per gallon (¢)	1960 Gross tax collect-tions[1] ($1,000)
TENNESSEE	17.0	476,842	17.0	410,792	7.0	198,506	7.0	136,877	7.0	83,700
Alabama	13.0	255,686	13.0	256,505	11.0	189,504	7.0	118,032	7.0	72,850
Arkansas	13.5	207,714	13.5	200,610	9.5	135,031	7.5	77,191	6.5	39,862
Florida	9.7	653,201	9.7	606,244	8.0	417,685	7.0	236,148	7.0	125,731
Georgia	7.5	317,550	7.5	301,041	7.0	253,457	6.5	164,573	6.5	88,867
Kentucky	15.0	315,045	15.0	240,259	9.0	192,146	7.0	110,325	7.0	66,282
Louisiana	16.0	384,724	16.0	362,955	8.0	185,278	8.0	124,172	7.0	67,133
Mississippi	15.0	137,125	9.0	138,312	9.0	126,351	8.0	90,195	7.0	47,432
North Carolina	15.5	592,017	15.5	496,779	9.0	293,202	9.0	227,255	7.0	104,653
South Carolina	15.0	284,009	13.0	257,413	11.0	179,043	7.0	92,387	7.0	53,317
Virginia	17.5	558,557	15.0	446,024	11.0	289,784	7.0	158,234	7.0	86,745
West Virginia	10.5	106,406	10.5	103,278	10.0	100,034	8.5	59,425	7.0	35,021

Note: Data are on a calendar year basis. Tax rates are as of December 31. See footnotes, Table 9.21 for more detail regarding tax rates.

1. Includes revenues from state taxes on motor vehicle fuels and for most states, only the portion of the tax on special fuels that is applicable to gallonage used on highways. Includes in some states receipts in the form of tax credits for refund claims accepted by distributors acting as agents of the state and refund credits to users who are licensed as distributors.

Source: U.S. Department of Transportation, Federal Highway Administration, Highway Statistics Division, *Highway Statistics, 1987*, and earlier editions.

TABLE 9.23--NUMBER OF TRUCKS AND TRUCK-MILES, SOUTHEASTERN STATES, 1982

	All trucks			Trucks and truck miles, excluding pickups, panels, utilities, and station wagons		
State	Number of trucks (1,000)	Truck-miles (1,000,000)	Average miles per truck (1,000)	Trucks (1,000)	Truck-miles (1,000,000)	Average miles per truck (1,000)
TENNESSEE	767.2	8,479.0	11.1	93.6	2,091.2	21.7
Alabama	686.1	7,664.3	11.2	102.0	2,199.5	21.6
Arkansas	539.6	6,718.7	12.5	59.6	1,688.4	28.3
Florida	992.9	12,687.8	12.8	108.6	2,337.8	21.5
Georgia	n.a.	n.a.	n.a.	n.a.	n.a.	n.a.
Kentucky	648.0	5,818.2	9.0	93.0	1,061.9	11.4
Louisiana	n.a.	n.a.	n.a.	n.a.	n.a.	n.a.
Mississippi	n.a.	n.a.	n.a.	n.a.	n.a.	n.a.
North Carolina	n.a.	n.a.	n.a.	n.a.	n.a.	n.a.
South Carolina	463.4	5,187.3	11.2	49.4	989.6	20.0
Virginia	777.6	8,079.7	10.4	115.0	2,123.9	16.8
West Virginia	330.7	3,353.1	10.1	34.2	454.6	13.3

n.a. not available.

Source: U.S. Department of Commerce, Bureau of the Census, *1982 Census of Transportation, Truck Inventory and Use Survey*, individual states.

TABLE 9.24--TRUCK MILES FOR TRANSPORTATION OF HAZARDOUS MATERIALS, BY STATE OF TRUCK REGISTRATION, SOUTHEASTERN STATES, 1982
[In millions of truck miles]

State	Hazardous materials transported								
	By percentage of time carried				By type of material[1]				
	Less than 25	25 to 49	50 to 74	75 to 100	Flammables, combustibles	Acids, poisons, caustics	Explosives	Radioactive materials	Other
TENNESSEE	207.6	30.8	6.5	23.3	256.0	162.7	53.4	59.6	142.1
Alabama	263.3	32.1	19.7	39.8	306.5	207.0	86.8	76.7	107.9
Arkansas	368.4	30.7	21.6	7.0	391.2	309.9	1.4	7.8	12.1
Florida	223.2	64.9	10.8	55.5	265.9	146.4	29.7	23.0	38.7
Georgia	n.a.	n.a.	n.a.	n.a.	n.a.	n.a	n.a	n.a	n.a
Kentucky	86.1	44.4	11.2	17.6	140.0	72.1	12.3	0.1	21.0
Louisiana	n.a.	n.a.	n.a.	n.a.	n.a.	n.a	n.a	n.a	n.a
Mississippi	n.a.	n.a.	n.a.	n.a.	n.a.	n.a	n.a	n.a	n.a
North Carolina	n.a.	n.a.	n.a.	n.a.	n.a.	n.a	n.a	n.a	n.a
South Carolina	132.3	11.3	1.5	55.7	181.8	122.5	8.0	8.2	35.9
Virginia	219.1	68.4	9.2	51.8	329.2	142.5	30.4	91.4	90.2
West Virginia	15.4	18.9	8.0	9.7	44.2	21.1	12.0	10.6	14.6

Note: Detail may not add to total due to independent rounding.

n.a. not available.

1. Detail exceeds total as multiple responses were possible.

Source: U.S. Department of Commerce, Bureau of the Census, *1982 Census of Transportation, Truck Inventory and Use Survey*, individual states.

TABLE 9.25--NUMBER OF ACTIVE CIVILIAN PILOTS AND ACTIVE CIVIL GENERAL AVIATION AIRCRAFT, SOUTHEASTERN STATES, 1987

State	Total active civilian pilots	General aviation aircraft								
			Fixed wing aircraft							
			Piston		Turboprop		Turbojet			
		Total	Single-engine	Multi-engine	Single-engine	Multi-engine	Single-engine	Multi-engine	Roto-craft	Other
TENNESSEE	11,911	3,989	2,919	575	2	147	2	75	129	140
Alabama	9,271	3,954	3,078	472	0	125	1	69	142	67
Arkansas	6,266	3,154	2,467	435	7	93	1	39	78	34
Florida	45,095	16,506	11,166	3,318	5	401	12	347	806	451
Georgia	18,047	5,937	4,567	732	6	178	1	133	161	159
Kentucky	5,848	2,093	1,513	246	0	63	0	47	92	132
Louisiana	8,694	4,122	3,030	437	1	105	3	30	468	48
Mississippi	4,789	2,438	1,985	266	8	59	1	24	49	46
North Carolina	14,784	5,991	4,494	770	8	257	1	148	145	168
South Carolina	6,916	2,327	1,740	308	0	82	1	28	82	86
Virginia	15,374	3,950	3,032	391	1	139	0	84	116	187
West Virginia	2,533	1,237	970	139	0	41	1	7	47	32

Source: U.S. Department of Transportation, Federal Aviation Administration, Office of Management Systems, *Census of U.S. Civil Aircraft, Calendar Year 1987.*

FIGURE 9.2
Principal Railroads in Tennessee as of March, 1988

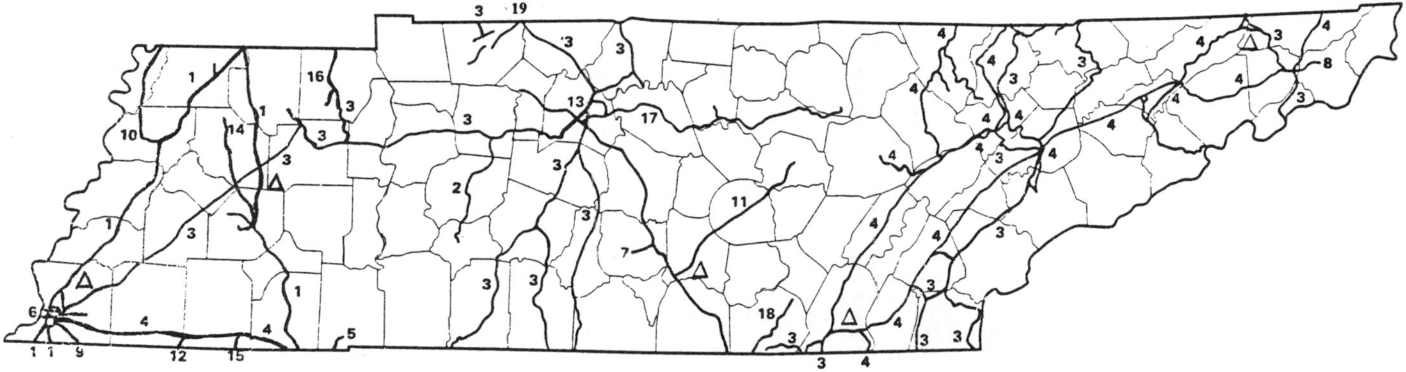

1	Illinois Central R.R.	8	East Tennessee Railway	15	South Rail Corporation
2	South Central Tennessee R.R.	9	Burlington Northern R.R.	16	KWT R.R.
3	CSXT R.R.	10	Tennken R.R.	17	Nashville and Eastern R.R.
4	Norfolk Southern R.R.	11	Caney Fork and Western R.R.	18	Sequatchie Valley R.R.
5	Corinth and Counce R.R.	12	Natchez Trace R.R.	19	Corman R.R.
6	Union Pacific R.R.	13	Nashville and Ashland City R.R.		
7	Walking Horse and Eastern R.R.	14	West Tennessee R.R.	Δ	U.S. Government

Source: Prepared from data supplied by the Tennessee Department of Transportation, Office of Public Transportation.

TABLE 9.26--RAILROAD MILEAGE OPERATED, SOUTHEASTERN STATES AND UNITED STATES, 1979–1987, SELECTED YEARS

State	1987	1986	1985	1981	1980	1979
TENNESSEE	2,234	2,537	2,597	3,035	3,136	3,136
Alabama	3,600	3,650	3,832	4,322	4,455	4,497
Arkansas	2,539	2,594	2,712	2,720	2,763	2,749
Florida	2,976	3,085	3,230	3,421	3,681	3,698
Georgia	4,954	5,031	5,119	4,747	5,468	5,471
Kentucky	2,521	2,846	3,175	3,569	3,515	3,572
Louisiana	2,691	2,785	3,050	3,310	3,373	3,452
Mississippi	1,496	1,510	1,744	2,823	3,063	3,161
North Carolina	3,090	3,217	3,334	2,845	3,577	3,640
South Carolina	2,490	2,533	2,579	2,558	2,736	2,772
Virginia	3,430	3,729	3,766	3,451	3,503	3,511
West Virginia	3,149	3,156	3,209	3,534	3,565	3,513
UNITED STATES	146,584	154,657	159,360	173,809	183,077	188,304

Note: Beginning in 1981, the miles of line shown represents mileage operated by Class I roads only. Prior to 1981, the miles shown represents mileage operated by Class I and Class II roads. Miles operated jointly by two or more railroads and two or more parallel tracks are not duplicated in this listing. Mileage of yard tracks and sidings are also excluded from these totals.

Source: Association of American Railroads, *Railroad Facts, 1988 Edition*, and earlier editions.

The U.S. Department of Energy was created in October 1977 to centralize the responsibilities of the Federal Power Commission, the U.S. Bureau of Mines, the Federal Energy Administration, and the U.S. Energy Research Administration. Data from publications of the U.S. Department of Energy, Energy Information Administration (EIA), provide information on energy consumption by type of fuel and consuming sector. At the present time, data on traditional energy sources are abundant. Not only are statistics on the many phases of production and utilization available, but in addition, a historical time series has been constructed in order to provide a reference for current and future changes in the energy picture. Publications of EIA include the *State Energy Data Report, 1960-1986*, the *Electric Power Annual*, the *Petroleum Supply Annual*, and *Coal Production*. While the utilization of fuel minerals is presented as "energy" data, information on mineral production and reserves is included in Chapter 5 on Mining.

In addition to reports published by the U.S. Department of Energy, the American Gas Association provides a comprehensive collection of data on sales, customers, consumption and prices of gas at state, national and international levels. These data are published in a yearbook titled *Gas Facts*.

The U.S. Department of Commerce, Bureau of the Census, includes energy data by industry group in the *1982 Census of Manufactures, Fuels and Electric Energy Consumed*. Data from this publication are presented in Tables 10.7 and 10.8. The next update for these data will be for the *1987 Census* published in late 1990.

Data on the electric utility industry, previously reported by the Federal Power Commission, are now reported in the *Electric Power Annual*. This report is an annual version of the *Electric Power Monthly*. For the TVA region and its local power distributors, major sources of data are *Electricity Sales Statistics*, published monthly, and the annual *Power Program Summary*. An important component of the energy picture is the climate of the area. TVA issues degree-day heating and cooling requirements for weather stations across Tennessee. These data are also published in *Electricity Sales Statistics* and reprinted with other climatic data in Chapter 12.

The production capability and generation of nuclear power plants in each of the southeastern states is reported in the EIA's *Electric Power Annual*. The *State Energy Data Book* also reports on nuclear energy consumption. Because other newer energy sources–such as solar and geothermal–are not in wide use and the technology is still largely experimental on any scale appropriate to public use, consistent and accessible statistics are not available.

TABLE OF CONTENTS

TABLE OF CONTENTS
(Continued)

FIGURE 10.1
Tennessee Energy Consumption by Sector and Fuel Type, 1986

CONSUMPTION BY SECTOR

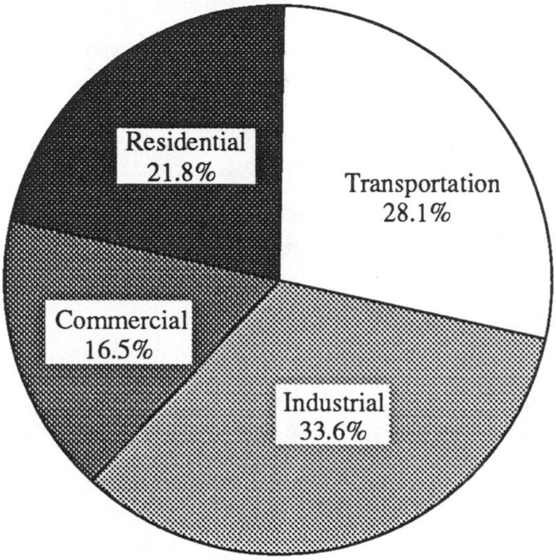

CONSUMPTION BY TYPE

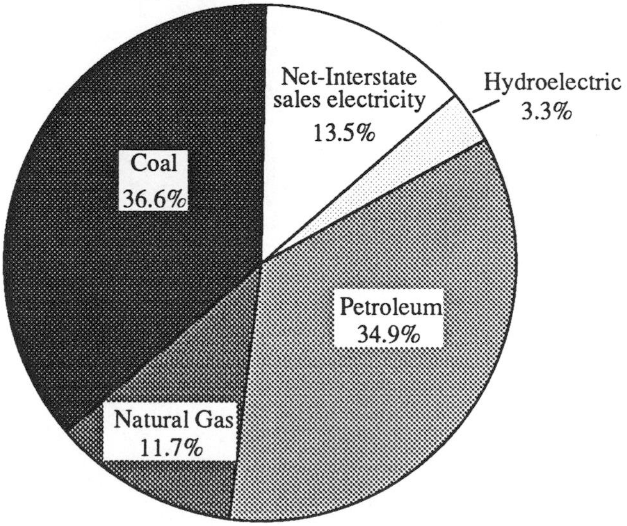

Source: U.S. Department of Energy, Energy Information Administration, Office of Energy Markets and End Use, *State Energy Data Report, 1960–1986.*

TABLE 10.1-- CONSUMPTION OF ENERGY, BY TYPE, TENNESSEE, 1960–1986 [In trillions of Btu]

Year	Total	Coal	Natural gas[1]	Petroleum	Nuclear	Hydro-electric[2]	Net interstate sales of electricity[3]
1986	1,657.3	607.4	194.0	578.1	-1.1	55.0	223.9
1985	1,649.8	599.7	196.7	562.0	104.5	67.6	119.2
1984	1,675.8	555.3	211.3	546.9	135.6	104.0	122.9
1983	1,601.2	547.1	199.1	493.9	153.2	104.0	104.0
1982	1,557.5	470.7	212.1	503.2	111.9	101.8	157.8
1981	1,654.6	565.9	227.1	518.8	51.9	61.8	229.1
1980	1,692.8	576.9	233.3	530.9	5.7	91.0	255.0
1979	1,756.3	542.3	233.9	596.1	0.0	127.4	256.7
1978	1,718.0	564.7	189.2	631.0	0.0	91.0	242.1
1977	1,736.3	553.7	208.4	601.0	0.0	108.5	264.6
1976	1,676.8	561.5	218.5	566.2	0.0	98.3	232.3
1975	1,574.3	471.9	224.1	504.2	0.0	122.9	251.3
1974	1,538.5	470.3	265.4	483.7	0.0	122.9	196.2
1973	1,572.5	532.9	300.1	498.8	0.0	119.0	121.7
1972	1,430.7	444.3	283.4	456.3	0.0	115.5	131.2
1971	1,328.5	370.0	270.8	413.6	0.0	98.7	175.4
1970	1,330.7	403.7	261.8	407.4	0.0	84.7	173.2
1969	1,304.9	436.7	257.5	400.7	0.0	78.1	131.8
1968	1,249.9	439.3	243.4	377.7	0.0	80.3	109.2
1967	1,204.5	352.0	242.0	348.2	0.0	100.4	161.9
1966	1,196.4	363.7	236.8	339.4	0.0	79.5	177.1
1965	1,101.0	338.8	211.1	301.5	0.0	91.5	158.1
1964	1,053.7	336.1	191.2	284.4	0.0	95.2	146.8
1963	1,025.9	386.3	179.2	273.0	0.0	80.9	106.5
1962	973.4	347.2	174.0	254.9	0.0	101.7	95.6
1961	935.9	354.2	166.7	236.9	0.0	93.2	85.0
1960	919.5	374.4	151.7	228.6	0.0	93.4	71.4

Note: Some changes in methodology were made and, where necessary, revisions were applied to the entire historical series. Totals may not equal sum of components due to independent rounding. Excludes small quantities of other energy sources for which consistent historical data are not available.

1. Includes supplemental gaseous fuels.

2. Includes industrial and utility production, and net imports of electricity.

3. Net interstate sales of electricity is the difference between the amounts of energy in the electricity sold within a state (including associated losses) and the energy input at the electric utilities within the state. The net interstate sales, therefore, include associated electrical system energy losses. A positive number indicates that more electricity (including associated losses) came into the state than went out of the state during the year.

Source: U.S. Department of Energy, Energy Infomation Administration, Office of Energy Markets and End Use, *State Energy Data Report, 1960 through 1986*.

TABLE 10.2-- TOTAL ENERGY CONSUMPTION, BY SECTOR, TENNESSEE, 1960–1986 [In trillions of Btu]

Year	Residential	Commercial	Industrial	Transportation
1986	361.3	274.1	556.7	465.2
1985	349.6	271.2	596.7	432.3
1984	352.6	253.1	638.8	431.3
1983	342.5	255.9	607.7	395.1
1982	339.7	236.0	583.5	398.2
1981	338.7	234.2	673.1	408.6
1980	364.8	225.1	694.0	408.9
1979	352.9	218.9	734.4	450.1
1978	367.1	206.3	701.7	443.0
1977	375.3	173.5	769.2	418.3
1976	343.0	146.7	781.0	406.0
1975	335.4	144.3	704.4	390.2
1974	298.8	153.4	705.3	380.9
1973	308.5	156.0	719.8	388.2
1972	300.6	149.5	625.0	355.6
1971	286.4	142.1	574.7	325.3
1970	282.9	134.6	604.9	308.3
1969	269.1	129.2	610.7	295.9
1968	246.8	119.2	606.7	277.2
1967	219.9	108.3	618.7	257.6
1966	214.8	102.0	630.9	248.8
1965	195.0	94.3	581.1	230.7
1964	185.8	89.7	556.5	221.7
1963	182.8	86.4	541.0	215.7
1962	169.3	94.0	508.3	201.8
1961	155.3	84.6	506.6	189.5
1960	155.1	77.2	513.3	173.9

Note: Some changes in methodology were made and, where necessary, revisions were applied to the entire historical series.

Source: U.S. Department of Energy, Energy Information Administration, Office of Energy Markets and End Use, *State Energy Data Report, 1960 through 1986.*

TABLE 10.3-- CONSUMPTION OF COAL, BY SECTOR, TENNESSEE, 1960–1986

Year	Residential		Commercial		Industrial	
	Trillion Btu	Thousand short tons	Trillion Btu	Thousand short tons	Trillion Btu	Thousand short tons
1986	0.7	28	1.2	51	104.2	4,205
1985	1.4	59	2.7	110	102.2	4,145
1984	2.6	108	4.9	200	96.7	3,941
1983	4.1	168	7.7	312	95.5	3,936
1982	1.5	62	2.7	114	75.9	3,122
1981	1.2	50	2.2	92	86.4	3,573
1980	2.0	82	3.6	152	67.2	2,774
1979	1.5	66	2.8	122	74.4	3,092
1978	1.8	75	3.2	139	71.8	3,018
1977	2.0	83	3.6	154	66.6	2,821
1976	2.1	86	3.8	159	54.1	2,270
1975	2.7	114	5.0	211	49.9	2,134
1974	2.8	120	5.1	222	56.6	2,450
1973	3.2	134	5.8	248	59.5	2,551
1972	3.6	152	6.6	280	53.2	2,286
1971	4.8	204	8.9	377	45.7	1,947
1970	4.5	191	8.4	352	58.0	2,452
1969	5.4	225	10.1	416	66.8	2,747
1968	4.5	184	8.3	339	82.7	3,365
1967	4.5	183	8.3	338	76.9	3,127
1966	5.2	214	9.7	395	79.4	3,203
1965	5.7	233	10.6	430	71.4	2,862
1964	5.7	230	10.4	423	63.8	2,550
1963	7.1	288	13.1	531	64.6	2,575
1962	7.6	308	14.0	568	59.3	2,355
1961	7.1	288	13.1	530	63.5	2,522
1960	8.3	336	15.3	618	58.1	2,307

Note: Some changes in methodology were made and, where necessary, revisions were applied to the entire historical series.

Source: U.S. Department of Energy, Energy Information Administration, Office of Energy Markets and End Use, *State Energy Data Report, 1960 through 1986*.

FIGURE 10.2
Natural Gas and Petroleum Products Pipelines, Tennessee, 1987

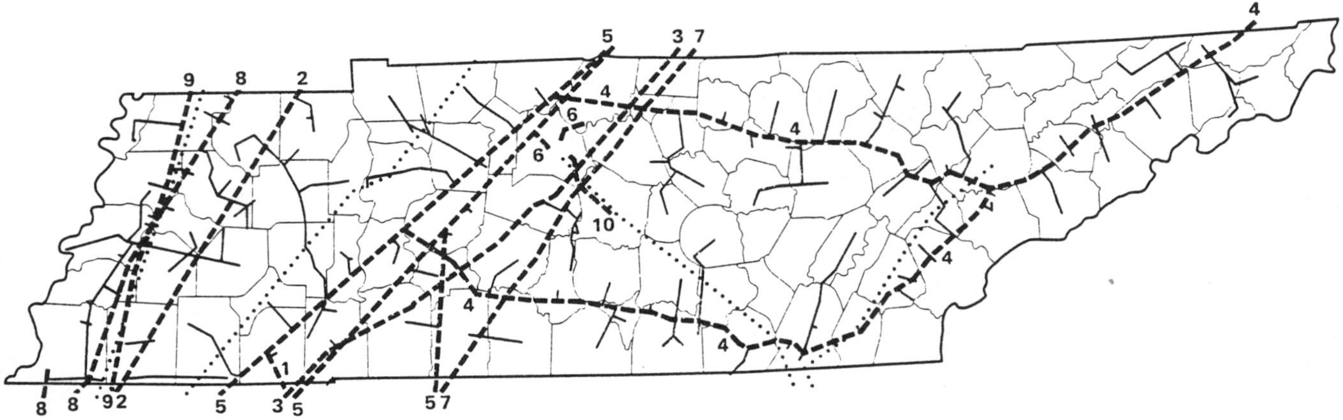

1	Alabama-Tennessee Natural Gas Company	6	Tennessee Natural Gas Lines, Incorporated	▬ ▬ ▬ Interstate Natural Gas Pipelines
2	Michigan-Wisconsin Pipe Line Company	7	Texas Eastern Transmission Corporation	—— Intrastate Natural Gas Pipelines
3	Columbia Gulf Transmission Company	8	Texas Gas Transmission Corporation	• • • Petroleum Products Pipelines
4	East Tennessee Natural Gas Company	9	Trunkline Gas Company	
5	Tennessee Gas Pipeline Company	10	Tennessee Gas Pipe Line Company	

Note: The four large metropolitan areas contain several satellite communities which are served by natural gas lines, but are not detailed here.
Source: Tennessee Public Service Commission, direct correspondence.

TABLE 10.4-- CONSUMPTION OF NATURAL GAS,[1] BY SECTOR, TENNESSEE, 1960–1986

	Residential		Commercial		Industrial		Transportation	
Year	Trillion Btu	Billion cubic feet	Trillion Btu	Billion cubic feet	Trillion Btu	Billion cubic feet	Trillion Btu	Billion cubic feet
1986	41.5	40	44.0	43	94.5	92	14.0	14
1985	40.8	39	44.9	43	100.6	97	10.5	10
1984	45.1	44	47.7	47	105.5	103	13.0	13
1983	41.5	41	43.9	43	102.4	100	11.1	11
1982	43.0	42	39.6	39	112.5	110	17.0	17
1981	42.5	42	43.4	43	123.1	121	17.8	18
1980	45.6	45	44.7	44	125.1	123	16.8	16
1979	46.6	45	44.1	43	122.3	118	20.8	20
1978	40.9	40	31.8	31	101.7	99	14.8	14
1977	44.9	44	36.2	35	113.0	110	14.3	14
1976	45.0	44	39.4	38	118.4	115	15.5	15
1975	45.4	44	43.8	42	115.1	112	19.7	19
1974	44.5	44	45.5	45	150.9	148	24.5	24
1973	46.9	46	46.9	46	164.5	161	29.0	28
1972	54.9	54	46.6	46	139.1	136	25.9	25
1971	48.0	47	45.0	44	132.1	129	27.2	27
1970	47.6	47	43.7	43	125.9	123	27.0	26
1969	47.2	45	42.7	41	122.8	118	25.9	25
1968	45.5	44	39.8	38	112.4	108	23.3	22
1967	43.4	42	35.8	34	113.5	109	23.2	22
1966	42.7	41	32.8	31	114.6	109	23.0	22
1965	38.9	37	29.6	28	101.9	97	23.7	23
1964	38.4	37	29.7	28	95.6	91	19.9	19
1963	42.8	41	28.6	27	83.7	79	19.3	18
1962	36.8	36	39.3	38	73.1	71	16.7	16
1961	35.1	34	34.2	33	74.4	72	16.0	15
1960	35.1	34	25.1	24	78.6	76	5.5	5

Note: Some changes in methodology were made and, where necessary, revisions were applied to the entire historical series.

1. Includes supplemental gaseous fuels.

Source: U.S. Department of Energy, Energy Information Administration, Office of Energy Markets and End Use, *State Energy Data Report, 1960 through 1986.*

TABLE 10.5-- CONSUMPTION OF PETROLEUM, BY SECTOR, TENNESSEE, 1960–1986

Year	Residential		Commercial		Industrial		Transportation	
	Trillion Btu	Thousand barrels	Trillion Btu	Thousand barrels	Trillion Btu	Thousand barrels	Trillion Btu	Thousand barrels
1986	11.1	2,760	13.3	2,458	101.2	17,335	451.2	83,621
1985	15.1	3,380	23.2	4,147	100.6	17,169	421.8	78,306
1984	13.3	3,001	18.6	3,365	95.6	16,373	418.3	77,589
1983	10.3	2,282	17.0	3,060	80.9	13,706	383.9	71,281
1982	9.3	2,030	11.2	2,031	99.7	17,000	381.3	70,884
1981	10.6	2,139	10.5	1,901	105.0	17,992	390.8	72,528
1980	10.4	2,358	10.2	1,897	115.7	19,934	392.1	72,830
1979	12.4	2,728	9.6	1,795	140.7	23,957	429.3	79,486
1978	18.9	4,148	11.0	2,101	142.8	23,950	428.2	79,500
1977	19.9	4,372	11.1	2,119	144.3	24,068	404.0	75,107
1976	21.2	4,663	11.7	2,222	128.4	21,551	390.5	72,619
1975	19.1	4,320	8.9	1,757	98.1	16,492	370.4	68,945
1974	19.3	4,244	8.6	1,674	97.6	16,461	356.4	66,355
1973	22.2	4,843	9.4	1,841	106.4	17,809	359.1	66,882
1972	20.1	4,425	8.5	1,666	97.1	16,311	329.6	61,413
1971	21.4	4,551	8.2	1,607	85.9	14,461	298.0	55,605
1970	21.2	4,512	8.3	1,622	96.6	16,383	281.2	52,452
1969	20.5	4,366	8.1	1,574	102.2	17,361	269.8	50,384
1968	19.7	4,063	8.1	1,559	96.2	16,328	253.8	47,405
1967	17.9	3,699	7.5	1,429	88.7	15,059	234.2	43,865
1966	13.3	2,780	6.1	1,171	94.4	15,925	225.6	42,235
1965	10.1	2,117	4.7	899	79.9	13,535	206.7	38,788
1964	8.5	1,811	4.3	822	70.1	11,964	201.6	37,789
1963	10.1	2,121	4.5	861	62.3	10,592	196.1	36,761
1962	9.1	1,889	4.3	821	56.5	9,488	184.9	34,728
1961	8.2	1,707	4.0	764	51.3	8,647	173.3	32,580
1960	8.4	1,740	3.6	682	49.2	8,347	167.4	31,495

Note: Some changes in methodology were made and, where necessary, revisions were applied to the entire historical series.

Source: U.S. Department of Energy, Energy Information Administration, Office of Energy Markets and End Use, *State Energy Data Report, 1960 through 1986.*

TABLE 10.6-- NET ELECTRIC ENERGY GENERATION, BY TYPE, TENNESSEE, 1980–1987, SELECTED YEARS [In gigawatt hours]

Type of generation	1987	1986	1985	1984	1983	1982	1980
Total	58,312	56,455	66,581	68,764	69,441	59,505	60,211
Coal-fired steam	50,730	51,108	50,242	45,963	45,279	39,479	50,617
Petroleum-fired steam	106	109	108	117	115	125	122
Gas-fired steam	(a)	(a)	(a)	(a)	(a)	(a)	114
Petroleum-fired turbine	18	17	20	1	38	28	76
Gas-fired turbine	0	0	0	0	7	(a)	0
Nuclear	-108	-105	9,672	12,501	14,051	10,104	519
Hydroelectric	7,566	5,326	6,539	10,181	9,952	9,769	8,764

Note: Negative generation denotes that electric power consumed for plant use exceeds gross generation. Totals may not equal sum of components because of independent rounding.

a. Less than 0.5 gigawatt hours.

Source: U.S. Department of Energy, Energy Information Administration, Office of Coal, Nuclear, Electric, and Alternate Fuels, *Electric Power Annual, 1987*, and earlier editions.

TABLE 10.7-- PURCHASED FUELS AND ELECTRIC ENERGY USED FOR HEAT AND POWER, BY INDUSTRY GROUP, TENNESSEE, 1981

Industry	Total fuels and electricity		Electricity		Total fuels	
	Btu (tril-lions)	Dollars (millions)	Kwh (mil-lions)	Dollars (millions)	Btu (tril-lions)	Dollars (millions)
Total manufacturing[1]	306.5	1,552.1	29,660.8	1,015.2	205.3	536.9
Food and kindred products	19.7	94.5	1,150.7	45.1	15.7	49.4
Textile mill products	5.2	35.7	680.8	26.1	2.9	9.6
Apparel	2.7	22.1	432.4	18.8	1.2	3.4
Lumber and wood products	2.3	17.9	228.9	11.3	1.5	6.6
Furniture and fixtures	1.8	14.0	207.8	9.9	1.1	4.1
Paper and allied products	32.4	148.4	2,261.3	78.3	24.7	70.1
Printing and publishing	2.2	15.9	263.3	11.2	1.3	4.7
Chemicals	142.0	611.8	12,264.7	417.0	100.2	194.8
Rubber and plastics	9.3	57.1	844.6	33.4	6.4	23.6
Leather and leather products	0.9	7.3	128.9	5.7	0.5	1.6
Stone, clay and glass	20.3	89.1	852.2	31.4	17.4	57.7
Primary metal industries	38.8	249.5	7,225.4	200.5	14.2	49.0
Fabricated metal products	6.5	42.0	648.4	27.0	4.3	15.0
Machinery, except electric	4.4	31.4	521.2	22.2	2.6	9.2
Electric and electronic equipment	9.1	61.2	1,122.0	42.3	5.3	18.8
Transportation	3.7	26.6	433.1	18.7	2.2	7.8
Instruments	0.3	2.7	53.3	2.2	0.2	0.5

TABLE 10.7-- PURCHASED FUELS AND ELECTRIC ENERGY USED FOR HEAT AND POWER, BY INDUSTRY GROUP, TENNESSEE, 1981 (Continued)

Industry	Fuel oil: Distillate (1,000 barrels)	Fuel oil: Residual (1,000 barrels)	Coal (1,000 short tons)	Natural gas (billion cubic ft.)	Liquefied petroleum (million pounds)
Total manufacturing[1]	754.9	583.2	3,019.9	93.0	42.7
Food and kindred products	31.5	164.4	(D)	10.8	4.8
Textile mill products	13.1	28.0	(D)	2.4	0.2
Apparel	2.7	1.3	(D)	1.2	(a)
Lumber and wood products	36.8	(D)	0.0	(D)	(D)
Furniture and fixtures	2.9	(D)	(D)	1.0	2.1
Paper and allied products	38.3	194.3	(D)	15.2	1.4
Printing and publishing	(D)	(D)	0.0	0.9	(D)
Chemicals	203.5	47.9	2,706.6	23.9	1.1
Rubber and plastics	23.1	48.7	(D)	4.2	4.4
Leather and leather products	(D)	0.0	(D)	0.4	0.0
Stone, clay and glass	148.9	(D)	(D)	10.7	1.7
Primary metal industries	110.3	(D)	27.5	9.8	4.2
Fabricated metal products	26.6	(D)	(D)	2.6	4.4
Machinery, except electric	9.4	9.0	0.0	1.8	2.4
Electric and electronic equipment	(D)	(D)	0.0	4.1	5.5
Transportation	13.9	(D)	0.0	1.9	6.9
Instruments	(D)	(D)	0.0	(D)	0.0

Note: Electricity purchased does not include 1,905.9 million kwh of electricity generated, of which 1,382.8 million kwh was in the chemical industrial sector.

(D) Withheld to avoid disclosing figures for individual companies.

1. Includes categories not shown separately.

a. Withheld because estimate did not meet publication standards.

Source: U.S. Department of Commerce, Bureau of the Census, *1982 Census of Manufactures, Fuels and Electric Energy Consumed.*

TABLE 10.8-- PURCHASED FUELS AND ELECTRIC ENERGY USED FOR HEAT AND POWER, BY MAJOR INDUSTRY GROUP, METROPOLITAN STATISTICAL AREAS, 1981

MSA and industry	Total fuels and electricity		Electricity		Fuels	
	Btu (trillions)	Dollars (millions)	Kwh (millions)	Dollars (millions)	Btu (trillions)	Dollars (millions)
CHATTANOOGA	28.1	149.4	2,162.0	81.4	20.7	68.0
Food and kindred products	2.7	13.0	167.5	6.3	2.2	6.7
Textile mill products	4.9	25.7	343.0	14.0	3.7	11.7
Apparel and textile products	0.2	1.5	35.1	1.3	0.1	0.2
Lumber and wood products	0.2	0.8	10.5	0.4	0.1	0.4
Paper and allied products	2.1	8.9	76.3	3.1	1.8	5.8
Chemicals and allied products	6.9	35.0	620.6	21.4	4.7	13.7
Stone, clay, and glass products	2.9	13.3	186.0	6.6	2.3	6.7
Primary metal industries	4.6	29.9	456.1	16.7	3.1	13.3
Fabricated metal products	1.9	10.7	140.4	5.9	1.4	4.8
Machinery, except electrical	0.4	2.5	36.3	1.6	0.3	0.9
Electric, electronic equipment	0.6	3.6	43.4	1.9	0.5	1.7
CLARKSVILLE	3.5	28.0	611.0	22.5	1.5	5.5
Fabricated metal products	0.2	0.7	7.2	0.3	0.1	0.5
JOHNSON CITY-KINGSPORT-BRISTOL	69.2	159.2	1,069.0	41.4	65.6	117.8
Food and kindred products	0.7	3.7	54.6	2.0	0.5	1.7
Textile mill products	1.1	7.5	130.4	5.0	0.7	2.5
Apparel and textile products	0.1	1.1	16.2	0.9	0.1	0.3
Printing and publishing	0.5	3.1	(D)	(D)	(D)	(D)
Rubber and plastic products	0.5	2.8	29.3	1.2	0.4	1.6
Primary metal industries	0.9	4.9	67.3	2.6	0.7	2.3
Fabricated metal products	0.6	5.4	104.8	4.4	0.2	0.9
Machinery, except electrical	0.6	4.8	100.5	3.7	0.2	1.1
Electric, electronic equipment	0.6	4.6	(D)	(D)	(D)	(D)
Transportation equipment	0.1	1.2	23.1	1.0	0.1	0.2
KNOXVILLE	31.5	161.9	4,611.2	117.6	15.8	44.3
Food and kindred products	1.2	6.1	75.2	3.0	0.9	3.1
Textile mill products	0.3	2.0	30.6	1.2	0.2	0.8
Apparel and textile products	0.4	3.3	60.5	2.5	0.2	0.8
Lumber and wood products	0.1	0.9	15.1	0.7	0.1	0.3
Furniture and fixtures	0.1	0.8	10.2	0.5	0.1	0.3

TABLE 10.8-- PURCHASED FUELS AND ELECTRIC ENERGY USED FOR HEAT AND POWER, BY MAJOR INDUSTRY GROUP, METROPOLITAN STATISTICAL AREAS, 1981 (Continued)

MSA and industry	Total fuels and electricity		Electricity		Fuels	
	Btu (trillions)	Dollars (millions)	Kwh (millions)	Dollars (millions)	Btu (trillions)	Dollars (millions)
Paper and allied products	0.7	2.4	24.8	1.0	0.6	1.4
Printing and publishing	0.1	0.7	12.9	0.6	(a)	0.2
Petroleum and coal products	0.2	0.8	2.7	0.1	0.2	0.6
Rubber and plastic products	0.5	3.0	48.5	1.9	0.3	1.1
Stone, clay, and glass products	2.3	8.5	65.6	2.5	2.1	6.0
Fabricated metal products	0.4	2.2	24.0	1.1	0.3	1.2
Machinery, except electric	0.3	1.7	27.4	1.1	0.2	0.6
Electric, electronic equipment	0.1	0.8	17.6	0.7	(a)	0.1
Miscellaneous manufacturing	0.1	0.8	(D)	(D)	(D)	(D)
MEMPHIS	39.2	183.4	2,112.5	84.1	32.0	99.3
Food and kindred products	10.0	42.0	452.7	17.7	8.4	24.4
Apparel and textile products	0.1	1.3	28.5	1.1	(a)	0.2
Lumber and wood products	0.6	3.6	31.6	1.7	0.5	1.9
Furniture and fixtures	0.2	1.8	31.5	1.4	0.1	0.4
Paper and allied products	4.2	21.1	320.4	12.2	3.1	9.0
Chemicals and allied products	14.3	58.2	502.4	18.5	12.6	39.8
Rubber and plastic products	2.2	11.6	135.2	5.3	1.7	6.4
Stone, clay, and glass products	1.8	6.5	46.8	1.9	1.7	4.7
Primary metal industries	0.6	4.7	(D)	(D)	(D)	(D)
Fabricated metal products	1.4	9.0	110.1	5.0	1.0	4.0
Machinery, except electrical	0.9	6.4	90.0	4.3	0.6	2.2
Electric, electronic equipment	0.4	2.8	48.2	2.2	0.2	0.6
Transportation equipment	0.1	0.8	12.7	0.6	0.1	0.3
Miscellaneous manufacturing	0.2	1.4	24.4	1.1	0.1	0.3
NASHVILLE-DAVIDSON	27.6	137.6	2,004.9	77.5	20.8	60.1
Food and kindred products	1.3	8.7	148.8	5.8	0.8	2.9
Apparel and textile products	0.2	2.0	39.6	1.9	(a)	0.2
Furniture and fixtures	0.6	3.5	51.0	2.2	0.4	1.3
Paper and allied products	0.5	3.7	68.0	2.8	0.3	0.9
Printing and publishing	1.1	7.1	121.0	4.6	0.7	2.4
Petroleum and coal products	0.3	1.4	(D)	(D)	(D)	(D)
Rubber and plastic products	1.4	10.3	(D)	(D)	(D)	(D)

TABLE 10.8-- PURCHASED FUELS AND ELECTRIC ENERGY USED FOR HEAT AND POWER, BY MAJOR INDUSTRY GROUP, METROPOLITAN STATISTICAL AREAS, 1981 (Continued)

MSA and industry	Total fuels and electricity		Electricity		Fuels	
	Btu (trillions)	Dollars (millions)	Kwh (millions)	Dollars (millions)	Btu (trillions)	Dollars (millions)
Leather and leather products	0.1	1.0	22.3	1.0	(a)	0.1
Stone, clay, and glass products	6.4	27.9	220.7	8.3	5.7	19.7
Primary metal industries	0.5	2.9	47.0	1.8	0.3	1.1
Fabricated metal products	0.8	5.7	95.8	4.2	0.4	1.5
Machinery, except electric	0.5	3.5	59.3	2.4	0.3	1.2
Electric and electronic equipment	1.3	8.1	139.0	5.5	0.8	2.6
Transportation equipment	1.4	9.4	139.7	5.9	1.0	3.5
Instruments and related products	0.1	0.5	(D)	(D)	(D)	(D)

(D) Withheld to avoid disclosing figures for individual companies.

a. Less than half of the unit of measure.

Source: U.S. Department of Commerce, Bureau of the Census, *1982 Census of Manufactures, Fuels and Electric Energy Consumed.*

TABLE 10.9-- FUEL CONSUMPTION FOR ELECTRIC ENERGY, TENNESSEE, 1976–1987

Year	Coal (1,000 short tons)	Petroleum (1,000 barrels)	Gas (million cubic feet)
1987	20,697	222	0
1986	21,051	232	0
1985	20,853	237	0
1984	19,106	207	0
1983	18,672	291	107
1982	16,532	287	0
1981	20,497	322	316
1980	21,679	406	1,105
1979	20,173	700	0
1978	21,621	5,177	0
1977	21,694	3,739	0
1976	22,362	2,486	176

Source: U.S. Department of Energy, Energy Information Administration, Office of Coal, Nuclear, Electric, and Alternate Fuels, *Electric Power Annual, 1987*, and earlier editions.

TABLE 10.10--FUEL COSTS AT ELECTRIC UTILITIES, TENNESSEE, 1977–1987

	Coal							
	Total		Contract		Spot		Petroleum, total	
Year	Cents per million Btu	Dollars per ton	Cents per million Btu	Dollars per ton	Cents per million Btu	Dollars per ton	Cents per million Btu	Dollars per barrel
1987	136.7	32.74	141.4	33.81	124.0	29.84	392.8	22.82
1986	141.9	33.79	149.7	35.63	117.0	27.94	336.8	19.57
1985	153.6	36.34	160.1	38.03	127.4	29.69	585.1	33.95
1984	162.2	38.30	170.8	40.65	139.8	32.36	611.3	35.58
1983	172.0	40.51	179.0	42.38	113.5	25.60	650.2	37.80
1982	174.5	41.22	178.0	42.14	121.8	27.89	810.2	47.15
1981	173.5	40.29	173.8	40.36	157.7	36.45	823.7	47.86
1980	155.7	36.21	155.7	36.22	134.6	32.07	639.0	37.28
1979	136.0	31.25	137.0	31.47	108.2	25.22	452.8	26.39
1978	119.6	26.99	116.2	26.08	129.6	29.74	264.8	15.47
1977	103.1	22.88	103.1	22.84	102.8	23.31	264.1	15.51

Note: Data are for plants with a capacity of 25 megawatts or greater prior to 1979. Beginning in 1979, data are for plants with a capacity of 50 megawatts or greater.

Source: U.S. Department of Energy, Energy Information Administration, Office of Coal, Nuclear, Electric, and Alternative Fuels, *Electric Power Annual, 1987*, and earlier editions.

FIGURE 10.3
TVA Generating Plants in Tennessee

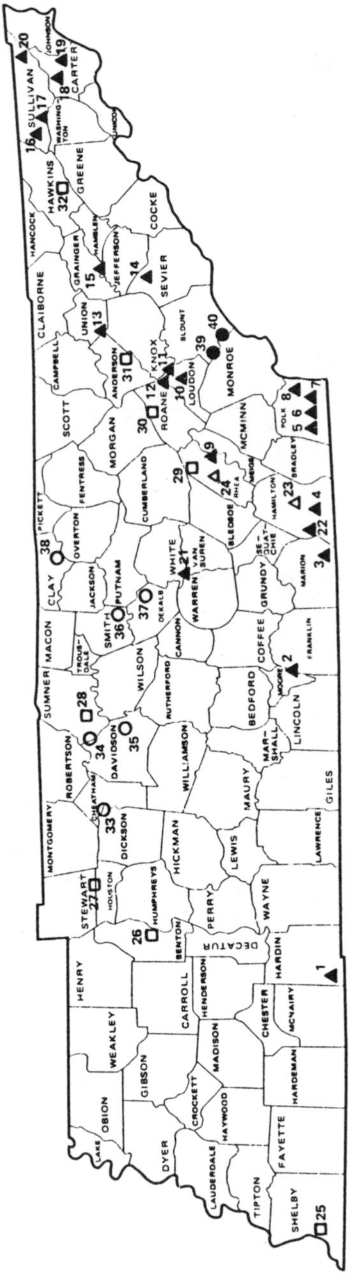

Please see legend on facing page

Legend for Figure 10.3

No.	TVA HYDRO PLANTS	
1.	Pickwick Landing	224,080
2.	Tims Ford	45,000
3.	Nickajack	103,950
4.	Chickamauga	120,000
5.	Ocoee 1	18,000
6.	Ocoee 2	21,000
7.	Ocoee 3	28,800
8.	Appalachia	82,800
9.	Watts Bar	166,500
10.	Tellico	(a)
11.	Fort Loudon	139,140
12.	Melton Hill	72,000
13.	Norris	100,800
14.	Douglas	120,600
15.	Cherokee	135,180
16.	Ft. Patrick Henry	36,000
17.	Boone	76,400
18.	Wilbur	10,700
19.	Watauga	57,600
20.	South Holston	38,500
21.	Great Falls	31,860
22.	Raccoon Mtn. Pumped Storage Station	1,530,000

No.	TVA NUCLEAR	
23.	Sequoyah Nuclear	2,441,160
24.	Watts Bar Nuclear (under construction)	2,539,800
	TVA COAL-FIRED, STEAM ELECTRIC	Kw Capacity
25.	Thomas H. Allen	990,000
26.	Johnsonville	1,485,200
27.	Cumberland	2,600,000
28.	Gallatin	1,255,200
29.	Watts Bar ("mothballed" in 1983)	240,000
30.	Kingston	1,700,000
31.	Bull Run	950,000
32.	John Sevier	800,000
	CORPS ENGINEER DAMS	
33.	Cheatham	36,000
34.	Old Hickory	100,000
35.	J. Percy Priest	28,000
36.	Cordell Hull	100,000
37.	Center Hill	135,000
38.	Dale Hollow	54,000

Note: In addition, combustion turbine peaking units have been installed at Allen (620,800 Kw), Johnsonville (1,088,000 Kw), and Gallatin (325,200 Kw).

a. Tellico Dam does not have generating capacity. Water from the Tellico Reservoir is used to increase flow through Fort Loudon generators via a canal linking the two reservoirs, resulting in an average annual energy increase of 200 million Kwh.

Source: Tennessee Valley Authority, Information Office, direct correspondence.

TABLE 10.11--TOTAL ELECTRICITY SALES TO FINAL CUSTOMERS, AND RELATED STATISTICS, TVA AND LOCAL DISTRIBUTORS, 1980–1989, SELECTED FISCAL YEARS

Item	1989	1988	1987	1986	1985	1984	1983	1982	1980
Customers served–June (1,000)									
Total	3,302	3,231	3,165	3,086	3,005	2,946	2,887	2,842	2,757
Residential	2,902	2,846	2,796	2,733	2,665	2,614	2,565	2,531	2,455
Commercial and industrial	391	377	360	346	332	325	317	308	299
Other	9	9	8	8	7	7	4	4	3
Electricity sales (1,000,000 kwh)									
Total	88,217	85,817	83,042	78,466	76,697	76,982	69,971	71,863	71,331
Residential	40,219	39,655	38,968	36,439	35,958	37,369	33,497	34,989	34,977
Commercial and industrial	46,885	45,054	42,991	40,943	39,658	38,513	35,331	35,734	35,275
Street and outdoor lighting	1,113	1,108	1,083	1,084	1,081	1,100	1,143	1,140	1,079
Revenue from electricity sales ($1,000,000)									
Total	4941.6	4858.0	4,605.9	4,080.1	3,812.1	3,761.4	3,385.0	3,351.7	2,368.7
Residential	2239.6	2280.2	2,132.3	1,831.2	1,725.2	1,764.2	1,568.3	1,581.5	1,121.1
Commercial and industrial	2561.7	2493.4	2,330.0	2,113.5	1,960.5	1,874.8	1,706.2	1,665.7	1,167.5
Street and outdoor lighting	86.3	84.4	80.2	77.4	73.9	72.1	64.6	61.4	47.6
Other	54.0	(a)	63.4	58.0	52.5	50.3	45.9	43.1	32.5

Note: Totals may not equal sum of components due to independent rounding.

a. Less than 0.05.

Source: Tennessee Valley Authority, *Electricity Sales Statistics*, Monthly Report 653, July 1989, and earlier editions.

TABLE 10.12--TVA AVERAGE ANNUAL ELECTRICAL USE, BILLS, AND RATES FOR RETAIL COMMERCIAL AND INDUSTRIAL CONSUMERS, DISTRIBUTORS SERVING TENNESSEE, CALENDAR YEAR 1988

	Demand under 50 Kw			Demand 50 Kw and over	
Distributor	Average annual Kwh use [1]	Average annual bill	Average rate (¢/Kwh)	Total consumption (1,000 Kwh)	Average rate (¢/Kwh)
Cities					
Alcoa	19,624	$1,290.33	6.58	99,068	5.53
Athens	22,547	1,435.92	6.37	287,544	5.04
Bolivar	19,507	1,250.50	6.41	70,235	5.38
Bristol	19,320	1,214.86	6.29	274,664	5.37
Brownsville	22,266	1,352.85	6.08	89,571	5.22
Chattanooga	29,438	1,898.52	6.45	2,670,571	5.12
Clarksville	31,259	1,956.87	6.26	175,084	5.62
Cleveland	27,942	1,726.33	6.18	380,593	5.26
Clinton	21,855	1,402.45	6.42	139,522	5.80
Columbia	24,963	1,552.17	6.22	183,228	5.17
Cookeville	24,805	1,568.31	6.32	216,423	5.25
Covington	26,404	1,679.24	6.36	92,413	5.33
Dayton	25,013	1,553.08	6.21	66,494	5.27
Dickson	19,424	1,284.77	6.61	111,950	5.63
Dyersburg	26,380	1,737.20	6.59	285,421	5.18
Elizabethton	19,699	1,261.86	6.41	141,553	5.48
Erwin	21,646	1,359.45	6.28	88,921	4.90
Etowah	22,016	1,400.28	6.36	69,777	4.83
Fayetteville	16,407	1,102.48	6.72	105,674	5.53
Gallatin	27,429	1,655.28	6.03	226,789	5.00
Greeneville	22,689	1,443.70	6.36	364,099	5.35
Harriman	20,568	1,434.20	6.97	73,983	6.02
Humboldt	22,324	1,297.61	5.81	110,208	5.18
Jackson	29,109	1,749.41	6.01	559,704	5.05
Jellico	17,091	1,111.28	6.50	17,103	6.50
Johnson City	28,448	1,710.46	6.01	509,438	5.05
Knoxville	28,213	1,812.30	6.42	1,804,722	5.26
LaFollette	19,283	1,258.95	6.53	105,540	5.86
Lawrenceburg	16,590	1,067.22	6.43	141,702	5.48
Lebanon	27,657	1,714.82	6.20	146,768	5.30
Lenoir City	22,054	1,465.46	6.64	241,796	5.66
Lewisburg	26,130	1,694.94	6.49	156,351	5.40
Lexington	19,787	1,262.30	6.38	114,516	5.67
Loudon	18,125	1,255.16	6.93	101,472	5.30
McMinnville	20,497	1,319.97	6.44	104,688	5.48
Maryville	26,226	1,629.23	6.21	143,287	5.16
Memphis	30,798	2,027.90	6.58	5,374,450	5.19
Milan	20,301	1,228.15	6.05	85,866	5.29
Morristown	29,698	1,877.24	6.32	337,246	5.46
Mount Pleasant	21,420	1,397.90	6.53	32,093	5.20
Murfreesboro	30,966	1,878.42	6.07	340,802	5.12
Nashville	33,692	2,113.36	6.27	4,757,772	5.01
Newbern	23,392	1,414.18	6.05	20,708	5.77
Newport	21,302	1,416.55	6.65	150,570	5.35
Oak Ridge	30,330	1,818.18	5.99	153,928	5.16
Paris	22,770	1,387.73	6.09	125,753	5.29
Pulaski	23,688	1,483.56	6.26	148,685	5.35

TABLE 10.12--TVA AVERAGE ANNUAL ELECTRICAL USE, BILLS, AND RATES FOR RETAIL COMMERCIAL AND INDUSTRIAL CONSUMERS, DISTRIBUTORS SERVING TENNESSEE, CALENDAR YEAR 1988 (Continued)

	Demand under 50 Kw			Demand 50 Kw and over	
Distributor	Average annual Kwh use [1]	Average annual bill	Average rate (¢/Kwh)	Total consumption (1,000 Kwh)	Average rate (¢/Kwh)
Ripley	21,109	1,300.14	6.16	156,191	4.86
Rockwood	18,877	1,253.23	6.64	59,633	5.60
Sevierville	22,957	1,543.87	6.73	274,385	5.68
Shelbyville	28,304	1,771.60	6.26	156,470	5.26
Smithville	25,278	1,592.45	6.30	31,615	5.42
Somerville	25,353	1,625.82	6.41	8,477	6.23
Sparta	24,589	1,606.97	6.54	37,109	5.53
Springfield	30,662	1,986.76	6.48	68,093	6.24
Sweetwater	21,130	1,292.78	6.12	72,530	5.57
Trenton	24,438	1,562.12	6.39	45,954	5.08
Tullahoma	26,679	1,680.65	6.30	95,378	5.45
Union City	27,984	1,649.61	5.89	263,021	4.16
Winchester	24,870	1,617.44	6.50	33,304	5.51
Counties					
Benton	20,826	1,332.77	6.40	80,636	5.75
Carroll	20,762	1,360.04	6.55	103,940	5.34
Weakley	15,909	1,022.78	6.43	145,964	5.45
Cooperatives					
Appalachian	20,018	1,386.98	6.93	176,452	5.82
Caney Fork	12,043	775.70	6.44	92,279	5.83
Chickasaw	15,484	1,019.00	6.58	50,709	5.69
Cumberland	19,219	1,278.03	6.65	221,994	5.94
Duck River	21,783	1,514.04	6.95	174,897	6.52
Forked Deer	15,507	1,089.32	7.02	28,522	6.26
Fort Loudoun	15,471	1,105.02	7.14	50,365	6.08
Gibson County	17,435	1,125.03	6.45	132,369	5.68
Holston	21,097	1,394.22	6.61	230,398	5.18
Meriwether Lewis	15,787	1,102.57	6.98	300,755	5.21
Middle Tennessee	20,491	1,314.17	6.41	674,630	5.00
Mountain	17,841	1,196.54	6.71	107,870	5.98
Pickwick	20,217	1,331.70	6.59	91,593	5.88
Plateau	18,359	1,353.11	7.37	64,952	6.40
Powell Valley, VA.	15,820	1,254.22	7.93	65,114	7.35
Sequachee Valley	20,803	1,407.25	6.76	171,248	5.89
Southwest Tennessee	12,863	922.74	7.17	113,695	6.16
Tennessee Valley	19,757	1,354.19	6.85	57,205	6.60
Tippah, MS.	15,426	1,002.33	6.50	91,850	5.66
Tri-County	17,797	1,214.27	6.82	305,413	5.37
Tri-State, GA.	16,008	1,190.77	7.44	28,401	6.68
Upper Cumberland	18,239	1,266.84	6.95	185,727	6.02
Volunteer	19,929	1,379.98	6.92	260,522	5.93

1. Annual Kwh per consumer; this is derived by dividing total consumption during the year by the average number of consumers.

Source: Tennessee Valley Authority, Division of Power Utilization, *Electricity Sales Statistics, Calendar Year 1988.*

TABLE 10.13--ELECTRIC POWER CONSUMPTION, SELECTED DATA, DISTRIBUTORS SERVING TENNESSEE USING TVA POWER, FISCAL YEAR 1987

Distributor	Number of consumers June 1987 Total	Number of consumers June 1987 Residential	Sales volume (1,000 Kwh) Total	Sales volume (1,000 Kwh) Residential	Average annual Kwh use, residential	Average annual bill, residential
Cities						
Alcoa	17,095	15,264	350,270	218,125	14,415	775
Athens	10,813	9,275	442,489	127,481	13,869	736
Bolivar	9,233	8,091	201,294	104,960	13,118	696
Bristol	25,990	22,763	641,511	333,869	14,778	766
Brownsville	4,410	3,729	144,948	50,040	13,532	690
Chattanooga	135,902	121,195	4,972,736	1,899,129	15,842	850
Clarksville	24,226	21,332	554,309	313,401	15,138	814
Cleveland	20,378	17,576	693,239	273,356	15,611	818
Clinton	21,806	19,817	458,104	288,792	14,683	794
Columbia	16,713	14,414	439,193	209,026	14,613	753
Cookeville	10,381	8,322	353,024	108,577	13,439	714
Covington	3,165	2,514	129,160	32,896	13,054	701
Dayton	6,742	5,983	169,210	71,929	12,158	639
Dickson	19,443	16,965	389,335	244,747	14,705	803
Dyersburg	10,301	8,720	372,931	108,633	12,505	683
Elizabethton	19,970	17,857	431,765	244,464	13,780	717
Erwin	7,097	6,375	172,058	78,331	12,349	651
Etowah	4,306	3,889	126,776	52,410	13,463	710
Fayetteville	13,807	12,117	284,596	156,617	13,060	718
Gallatin	8,506	7,222	353,308	116,699	16,724	854
Greeneville	26,446	23,643	714,481	316,585	13,492	721
Harriman	9,373	8,333	189,258	109,538	13,223	768
Humboldt	4,413	3,751	163,870	48,609	12,931	628
Jackson	25,481	21,735	949,397	276,072	12,816	654
Jellico	4,283	3,783	69,858	41,593	10,998	594
Johnson City	48,749	43,657	1,250,182	631,693	14,592	747
Knoxville	141,367	125,402	4,167,528	1,962,479	15,767	858
LaFollette	15,236	13,314	297,557	157,915	11,979	654
Lawrenceburg	15,079	12,900	332,578	174,465	13,640	710
Lebanon	7,081	5,720	259,532	90,502	15,861	839
Lenoir City	29,946	26,303	752,580	467,934	18,186	1,002
Lewisburg	4,609	3,870	211,147	53,974	13,997	765
Lexington	16,346	14,443	305,977	167,670	11,644	605
Loudon	4,819	4,317	165,646	56,325	13,206	752
McMinnville	6,286	5,097	181,940	69,995	13,789	722
Maryville	14,768	12,891	361,931	176,136	13,812	717
Memphis	326,676	294,820	10,089,477	4,116,701	14,091	774
Milan	6,876	5,962	192,063	87,857	14,848	757
Morristown	11,053	9,158	469,669	118,176	12,928	703
Mount Pleasant	3,210	2,747	82,151	37,426	13,709	736
Murfreesboro	19,365	16,755	649,344	245,332	15,028	777
Nashville	263,533	234,832	9,094,195	3,709,081	16,097	868
Newbern	1,375	1,159	38,007	15,684	13,603	712
Newport	14,664	12,922	324,568	148,883	11,562	637
Oak Ridge	13,166	11,653	359,457	171,847	14,880	762
Paris	16,040	14,442	350,577	186,184	12,963	665
Pulaski	11,097	9,820	286,995	128,461	13,154	700
Ripley	5,680	4,721	216,392	58,809	12,507	640

TABLE 10.13--ELECTRIC POWER CONSUMPTION, SELECTED DATA, DISTRIBUTORS SERVING TENNESSEE USING TVA POWER, FISCAL YEAR 1987 (Continued)

Distributor	Number of consumers June 1987 Total	Number of consumers June 1987 Residential	Sales volume (1,000 Kwh) Total	Sales volume (1,000 Kwh) Residential	Average annual Kwh use, residential	Average annual bill, residential
Rockwood	10,422	9,219	217,100	134,398	14,663	791
Sevierville	24,045	18,217	606,677	237,226	13,295	747
Shelbyville	6,898	5,885	241,394	79,795	13,659	724
Smithville	2,192	1,757	62,827	22,748	12,874	687
Somerville	1,308	983	29,051	13,937	14,280	769
Sparta	2,548	1,953	74,020	24,552	12,482	686
Springfield	4,993	4,275	142,165	60,660	14,361	815
Sweetwater	5,831	5,070	153,648	66,213	13,166	676
Trenton	2,519	1,990	81,779	26,418	13,316	729
Tullahoma	8,092	6,941	219,422	101,706	14,800	785
Union City	5,516	4,745	327,530	57,694	12,288	615
Winchester	3,878	3,228	92,065	47,165	14,836	809
Counties						
Benton	8,262	7,279	177,203	85,659	11,828	625
Carroll	13,499	11,882	289,077	160,543	13,567	731
Weakley	16,818	14,026	393,861	218,511	15,618	814
Cooperatives						
Appalachian	26,984	24,640	542,889	332,448	13,580	774
Caney Fork	20,722	17,932	347,017	238,581	13,463	707
Chickasaw	8,972	8,026	189,260	119,837	15,051	799
Cumberland	51,816	46,848	1,063,814	755,010	16,376	929
Duck River	40,916	37,374	767,364	530,031	14,346	830
Forked Deer	7,754	7,327	130,943	96,779	13,358	761
Fort Loudoun	16,581	15,370	269,197	195,031	12,857	750
Gibson County	28,801	25,569	539,577	361,647	14,161	761
Holston	19,693	18,149	474,103	223,744	12,439	689
Meriwether Lewis	24,355	20,477	577,497	252,169	12,419	693
Middle Tennessee	72,978	66,280	1,907,456	1,138,033	17,658	936
Mountain	22,925	20,421	372,804	194,992	9,605	543
Pickwick	15,346	13,553	288,005	168,900	12,577	678
Plateau	11,797	10,252	196,470	100,910	9,924	652
Powell Valley, VA.	20,546	18,732	280,363	188,429	10,092	664
Sequachee Valley	23,096	20,077	481,250	256,733	12,873	737
Southwest Tennessee	30,862	26,399	579,870	407,599	15,632	880
Tennessee Valley	14,311	12,480	238,305	148,584	12,020	686
Tippah, MS.	10,601	8,922	220,169	109,802	12,339	645
Tri-County	37,754	33,450	602,870	361,061	10,931	617
Tri-State, GA.	10,217	8,941	145,068	93,133	10,520	647
Upper Cumberland	30,804	27,971	566,912	343,561	12,288	703
Volunteer	65,122	59,334	1,097,043	743,329	12,780	734

Source: Tennessee Valley Authority, *1987 Power Program Summary, Volume II, Financial and Statistical Report for Municipal and Cooperative Distributors of TVA Power.*

TABLE 10.14--ENERGY CONSUMPTION, BY SOURCE, SOUTHEASTERN STATES, 1980 AND 1986 [In trillions of Btu]

State	Total		Coal		Natural gas[1]		Petroleum		Nuclear		Hydroelectric[2]	
	1986	1980[r]	1986	1980[r]	1986	1980	1986	1980[r]	1986	1980	1986	1980
TENNESSEE	1,657.3	1,692.8	607.4	576.9	194.0	233.3	578.1	530.9	-1.1	5.7	55.0	91.0
Percentage	100.0	100.0	36.6	34.1	11.7	13.8	34.9	31.4	-0.1	0.3	3.3	5.4
Alabama	1,454.4	1,516.2	660.5	661.0	210.2	278.4	508.3	457.7	124.9	256.3	54.2	97.7
Percentage	100.0	100.0	45.4	43.6	14.5	18.4	34.9	30.2	8.6	16.9	3.7	6.4
Arkansas	750.5	821.7	224.5	36.6	203.0	274.0	318.7	312.0	95.9	85.4	29.0	17.6
Percentage	100.0	100.0	29.9	4.5	27.0	33.3	42.5	38.0	12.8	10.4	3.9	2.1
Florida	2,666.4	2,444.1	459.4	225.5	298.9	329.6	1,476.6	1,661.6	238.1	182.6	2.2	2.2
Percentage	100.0	100.0	17.2	9.2	11.2	13.5	55.4	68.0	8.9	7.5	0.1	0.1
Georgia	1,828.1	1,638.4	692.5	521.5	286.6	325.3	756.8	706.4	78.2	92.0	22.2	45.9
Percentage	100.0	100.0	37.9	31.8	15.7	19.9	41.4	43.1	4.3	5.6	1.2	2.8
Kentucky	1,300.7	1,384.0	749.9	641.7	173.5	204.1	464.8	517.3	0.0	0.0	28.2	30.5
Percentage	100.0	100.0	57.7	46.4	13.3	14.7	35.7	37.4	0.0	0.0	2.2	2.2
Louisiana	3,229.0	3,594.3	171.9	2.5	1,496.1	1,862.2	1,359.4	1,604.4	115.0	0.0	0.0	0.0
Percentage	100.0	100.0	5.3	0.1	46.3	51.8	42.1	44.6	3.6	0.0	0.0	0.0
Mississippi	883.0	794.8	108.8	75.0	220.2	270.9	405.1	379.3	44.2	0.0	0.0	0.0
Percentage	100.0	100.0	12.3	9.4	24.9	34.1	45.9	47.7	5.0	0.0	0.0	0.0
North Carolina	1,749.6	1,603.7	583.2	624.7	140.3	155.2	704.3	667.7	219.2	63.0	26.0	57.0
Percentage	100.0	100.0	33.3	39.0	8.0	9.7	40.3	41.6	12.5	3.9	1.5	3.3
South Carolina	1,080.8	977.2	263.9	245.8	101.5	146.9	356.6	366.5	385.0	189.8	13.1	31.4
Percentage	100.0	100.0	24.4	25.2	9.4	15.0	33.0	37.5	35.6	19.4	1.2	2.9
Virginia	1,670.6	1,499.7	303.2	231.8	146.7	161.0	729.2	778.1	229.3	125.1	0.8	9.3
Percentage	100.0	100.0	18.1	15.5	8.8	10.7	43.6	51.9	13.7	8.3	0.0	0.6
West Virginia	720.3	872.3	877.2	857.8	121.1	147.6	250.0	311.5	0.0	0.0	10.8	11.6
Percentage	100.0	100.0	121.8	98.3	16.8	16.9	34.7	35.7	0.0	0.0	1.5	1.6

Note: Total includes net interstate sales of electricity not shown separately. A negative figure for net interstate sales of electricity will account for the sum of individual percentages being greater than 100 percent, while a positive figure will result in a sum less than 100 percent. Percentages were computed by the Center for Business and Economic Research.

r revised.

1. Includes supplemental gaseous fuels.

2. May include small quantities of electricity generated at industrial hydropower sites.

Source: U.S. Department of Energy, Energy Information Administration, Office of Energy Markets and End Use, *State Energy Data Report, 1960 through 1986.*

TABLE 10.15--NET ELECTRIC ENERGY GENERATION, BY TYPE, SOUTHEASTERN STATES, 1987 [In gigawatt hours]

State	Total	Coal-fired steam	Petroleum-fired steam	Gas-fired steam	Petroleum and gas-fired turbine/ internal combustion	Nuclear	Hydro-electric
TENNESSEE	58,312	50,730	106	(a)	18	-108	7,566
Alabama	69,336	50,501	31	97	11	11,248	7,449
Arkansas	36,287	19,373	5	3,131	1	11,369	2,407
Florida	110,765	54,640	20,304	16,079	752	18,773	217
Georgia	85,806	67,185	180	56	5	15,259	3,121
Kentucky	67,454	64,352	122	32	1	0	2,948
Louisiana	51,309	15,102	60	23,820	3	12,324	0
Mississippi	22,388	11,094	80	3,245	252	7,717	0
North Carolina	78,825	44,836	199	0	91	28,600	5,098
South Carolina	64,410	22,861	70	21	8	39,290	2,160
Virginia	42,697	20,621	2,930	155	39	18,145	807
West Virginia	78,372	77,773	262	22	(a)	0	315

Note: Negative generation denotes that electric power consumed for plant use exceeds gross generation. Totals may not equal sum of components because of independent rounding.

a. Less than 0.5 gigawatt hours.

Source: U.S. Department of Energy, Energy Information Administration, Office of Coal, Nuclear, Electric, and Alternate Fuels, *Electric Power Annual, 1987*.

TABLE 10.16--FUEL CONSUMPTION FOR ELECTRIC ENERGY, SOUTHEASTERN STATES AND UNITED STATES, 1987

State	Coal (1,000 short tons)	Petroleum (1,000 barrels)	Gas (million cubic feet)
TENNESSEE	20,697	222	0
Alabama	20,746	58	1,474
Arkansas	11,764	10	32,057
Florida	22,598	33,694	175,675
Georgia	27,130	361	826
Kentucky	28,569	225	336
Louisiana	10,029	118	246,912
Mississippi	4,562	188	41,119
North Carolina	17,255	435	1,162
South Carolina	9,019	116	538
Virginia	8,297	4,599	1,724
West Virginia	30,605	383	239
UNITED STATES	717,894	199,378	2,844,051

Source: U.S. Department of Energy, Energy Information Administration, Office of Coal, Nuclear, Electric, and Alternate Fuels, *Electric Power Annual, 1987.*

TABLE 10.17--FUEL COSTS AT ELECTRIC UTILITIES, SOUTHEASTERN STATES AND UNITED STATES, 1987

State	Coal		Petroleum		Gas	
	Cents per million Btu	Dollars per ton	Cents per million Btu	Dollars per barrel	Cents per million Btu	Dollars per million cubic feet
TENNESSEE	136.7	32.74	392.8	22.82	(X)	(X)
Alabama	192.4	47.04	403.1	23.38	210.2	2.22
Arkansas	155.2	26.94	386.0	22.20	152.2	1.57
Florida	181.5	45.01	292.0	18.69	271.4	2.73
Georgia	178.9	43.56	344.9	20.68	371.5	3.80
Kentucky	125.8	28.94	407.3	23.78	278.1	2.84
Louisiana	164.4	26.84	340.5	20.45	160.0	1.67
Mississippi	195.5	49.56	237.6	14.72	185.1	1.90
North Carolina	179.0	44.92	390.8	22.67	(X)	(X)
South Carolina	174.0	44.01	400.0	23.29	334.5	3.44
Virginia	158.1	40.52	309.3	19.13	243.0	2.52
West Virginia	142.2	35.38	436.1	25.53	393.6	3.94
UNITED STATES	150.6	31.83	301.1	18.98	223.5	2.31

Note: Data are for plants with a capacity of 50 megawatts or greater.

(X) not applicable.

Source: U.S. Department of Energy, Energy Information Administration, Office of Coal, Nuclear, Electric, and Alternate Fuels, *Electric Power Annual, 1987.*

TABLE 10.18--SALES OF ELECTRIC ENERGY TO ULTIMATE CUSTOMERS, BY CLASS OF SERVICE, SOUTHEASTERN STATES, 1987, AND TOTAL SALES, 1980–1987, SELECTED YEARS
[In gigawatt hours]

State	Total	Class of service: Residential	Commercial	Industrial	Other
TENNESSEE	70,545	27,668	18,626	23,397	853
Alabama	56,002	19,848	11,585	24,030	538
Arkansas	23,573	9,552	5,578	7,885	558
Florida	122,111	60,225	41,169	16,793	3,923
Georgia	68,862	25,277	18,257	24,586	742
Kentucky	51,332	16,258	8,930	23,783	2,362
Louisiana	59,125	19,802	12,650	23,063	3,610
Mississippi	27,844	11,197	7,144	8,877	625
North Carolina	78,900	29,633	19,486	28,229	1,552
South Carolina	51,795	16,806	10,260	24,028	700
Virginia	66,911	26,613	17,745	14,543	8,009
West Virginia	21,074	7,262	4,641	9,079	92

State	Total sales: 1987	1986	1985	1984	1983	1982	1980
TENNESSEE	70,545	68,893	68,457	71,751	69,366	65,824	73,391
Alabama	56,002	52,844	49,662	49,649	45,087	45,051	50,367
Arkansas	23,573	22,194	23,064	24,584	23,198	22,277	26,499
Florida	122,111	116,443	108,665	101,458	96,488	92,539	90,766
Georgia	68,862	66,056	59,972	57,042	54,243	52,609	51,209
Kentucky	51,332	50,493	39,325	41,352	47,161	47,091	49,787
Louisiana	59,125	57,499	58,809	59,639	55,266	56,694	52,877
Mississippi	27,844	27,385	25,725	25,166	23,699	22,974	23,258
North Carolina	78,900	74,216	70,959	70,535	66,218	62,343	58,737
South Carolina	51,795	49,198	42,507	41,769	41,771	40,272	37,264
Virginia	66,911	62,823	58,513	55,586	53,543	51,172	48,369
West Virginia	21,074	20,600	21,844	22,022	20,712	20,756	20,831

Note: Totals may not equal sum of components because of independent rounding.

Source: U.S. Department of Energy, Energy Information Administration, Office of Coal, Nuclear, Electric, and Alternate Fuels, *Electric Power Annual, 1987*, and earlier editions.

TABLE 10.19--RETAIL PRICES OF ELECTRICITY, BY TYPE OF USER, SELECTED SOUTHEASTERN CITIES, 1982 and 1986 [In cents per kilowatt-hour]

City	Residential[1] 1986	Residential[1] 1982	Residential[1] Percent change	Commercial[2] 1986	Commercial[2] 1982	Commercial[2] Percent change	Industrial[3] 1986	Industrial[3] 1982	Industrial[3] Percent change
Nashville, TN	5.46	4.35	25.5	5.73	5.28	8.5	5.10	4.43	15.1
Atlanta, GA	6.69	5.93	12.8	8.54	7.98	7.0	5.44	4.94	10.1
Louisville, KY	6.90	5.75	20.0	6.79	5.56	22.1	4.68	3.87	20.9
Miami, FL	9.11	7.44	22.4	8.02	6.32	26.9	6.91	5.66	22.1
New Orleans, LA[4]	6.60	6.64	-0.6	8.61	n.a.	n.a.	5.54	n.a.	n.a.
Richmond, VA	8.90	8.49	4.8	7.21	6.97	3.4	5.00	5.11	-2.2
Tampa, FL	9.82	7.94	23.7	8.28	n.a.	n.a.	6.87	n.a.	n.a.
Selected Cities[5]									
Low	2.26	1.30	73.8	2.98	1.76	69.3	2.42	1.31	84.7
Median	8.17	7.29	12.1	8.26	7.41	11.5	6.18	5.66	9.2
High	14.61	15.00	-2.6	14.25	14.20	0.4	10.86	11.39	-4.7

Note: Percentage change computed by the Center for Business and Economic Research.

n.a. not available.

1. Based on 500 kilowatt-hours.

2. Based on 10,000 kilowatt-hours at 40-kilowatt demand.

3. Based on 200,000 kilowatt-hours at 500-kilowatt demand.

4. Majority of customers served at this rate.

5. Average prices for 40 selected cities across the U.S.

Source: U.S. Department of Energy, Energy Information Administration, Office of Coal, Nuclear, Electric, and Alternate Fuels, *Electric Power Annual, 1986.*

TABLE 10.20--GAS UTILITY INDUSTRY SALES, BY CLASS OF SERVICE, SOUTHEASTERN STATES, 1986, AND TOTAL SALES, 1960–1986, SELECTED YEARS [In trillions of BTU]

State	Total	Class of service: Residential	Commercial	Industrial	Other[1]
TENNESSEE	145.0	40.8	42.7	60.2	1.3
Alabama	155.3	45.9	26.5	82.1	0.8
Arkansas	111.6	37.5	24.8	43.3	6.0
Florida	239.8	13.9	32.9	55.4	137.6
Georgia	237.3	89.7	51.7	91.0	4.9
Kentucky	119.7	60.8	27.9	26.0	5.0
Louisiana	207.3	57.5	22.7	75.0	52.1
Mississippi	103.3	25.2	12.5	38.2	27.4
North Carolina	130.4	32.1	26.5	70.7	1.1
South Carolina	93.2	17.6	15.7	59.4	0.5
Virginia	124.7	47.3	39.8	35.8	1.8
West Virginia	72.1	40.4	19.6	11.8	0.3

	Total sales: 1986	1985	1984	1983	1980	1970	1960
TENNESSEE	145.0	163.5	197.5	184.7	216.0	249.9	147.0
Alabama	155.3	179.2	193.7	183.8	224.6	290.0	180.3
Arkansas	111.6	142.9	174.5	182.7	207.4	339.9	177.3
Florida	239.8	232.9	238.5	223.2	232.2	218.7	91.1
Georgia	237.3	270.5	295.3	280.3	299.7	333.8	188.5
Kentucky	119.7	141.7	158.8	149.1	175.9	189.9	126.6
Louisiana	207.3	285.2	302.2	319.2	515.2	742.1	536.8
Mississippi	103.3	140.9	161.8	145.4	191.5	265.6	146.2
North Carolina	130.4	125.3	138.4	132.9	143.2	151.2	41.6
South Carolina	93.2	94.5	104.6	96.9	112.3	120.1	40.6
Virginia	124.7	124.3	136.3	133.5	134.8	133.9	64.3
West Virginia	72.1	78.4	91.2	100.2	128.6	156.9	130.4

Note: Excludes sales for resale. Totals may not be equal to sum of components due to independent rounding.

1. Includes electric generation.

Source: American Gas Association, *Gas Facts, 1986*, and earlier editions.

TABLE 10.21--GAS UTILITY INDUSTRY AVERAGE NUMBER OF CUSTOMERS, BY CLASS OF SERVICE, SOUTHEASTERN STATES AND UNITED STATES, 1986, AND AVERAGE CUSTOMERS, 1960–1986, SELECTED YEARS [In thousands]

State	Total	Class of service: Residential	Commercial	Industrial	Other
TENNESSEE	564.1	487.7	69.1	1.8	5.5
Alabama	697.8	643.9	49.3	2.0	2.6
Arkansas	532.8	471.0	60.1	1.6	0.1
Florida	462.7	421.1	40.3	0.6	0.7
Georgia	1,247.4	1,154.1	87.4	2.7	3.2
Kentucky	647.9	587.1	58.3	1.3	1.2
Louisiana	990.1	923.4	64.1	1.3	1.3
Mississippi	405.1	364.2	37.9	1.1	1.9
North Carolina	466.8	411.8	52.1	2.8	0.1
South Carolina	325.0	290.7	32.6	1.3	0.4
Virginia	585.4	527.1	51.5	2.4	4.4
West Virginia	386.8	354.8	31.6	0.3	0.1
UNITED STATES	50,710.3	46,588.1	3,892.6	177.1	52.5[a]

	Average number of customers: 1986	1985	1984	1983	1980	1970	1960
TENNESSEE	564.1	549.4	540.4	527.3	509.3	428.1	313.5
Alabama	697.8	688.4	686.4	683.3	679.0	588.8	453.3
Arkansas	332.8	530.9	525.4	520.4	489.9	419.3	299.1
Florida	462.7	460.5	455.6	454.4	433.0	370.1	244.1
Georgia	1,247.4	1,195.6	1,149.8	1,113.8	1,025.9	804.4	534.9
Kentucky	647.9	643.7	642.1	642.0	626.7	583.0	432.9
Louisiana	990.1	995.8	1,001.8	1,006.8	1,002.3	871.3	701.2
Mississippi	405.1	403.7	401.4	399.6	396.7	347.3	271.2
North Carolina	466.8	444.5	429.2	416.4	366.7	285.2	121.6
South Carolina	325.9	319.3	315.4	312.1	296.2	233.3	87.0
Virginia	585.4	563.8	553.2	547.0	523.2	497.3	361.8
West Virginia	386.8	387.3	389.4	391.0	393.6	381.9	357.2
UNITED STATES	50,710.3	49,970.7	49,324.8	48,799.2	47,225.1	41,482.1	33,053.8

Note: Excludes customers purchasing for resale.

a. Includes electric generation.

Source: American Gas Association, *Gas Facts, 1986*, and earlier editions.

TABLE 10.22--GAS UTILITY INDUSTRY AVERAGE ANNUAL CONSUMPTION PER CUSTOMER, BY CLASS OF SERVICE, SOUTHEASTERN STATES AND UNITED STATES, 1986, AND AVERAGE RESIDENTIAL CONSUMPTION, 1960–1986, SELECTED YEARS
[In millions of Btu]

State	Average total	Class of service: Residential	Commercial	Industrial	Electric generation	Other
TENNESSEE	257.1	83.6	617.1	33,201.7	(a)	237.6
Alabama	222.6	71.3	538.5	40,499.8	57,350.0	269.1
Arkansas	209.5	79.7	411.9	27,382.0	484,383.3	2,409.1
Florida	518.3	32.9	815.6	98,935.4	7,089,689.5	4,044.0
Georgia	190.2	77.7	591.3	33,367.3	752,566.7	140.8
Kentucky	184.7	103.5	477.9	20,687.3	(a)	4,017.7
Louisiana	209.4	62.3	354.7	58,042.4	1,884,472.2	14,584.9
Mississippi	255.0	69.2	330.9	34,769.4	1,927,841.7	2,266.3
North Carolina	279.3	78.0	508.1	25,004.4	1,015,200.0	841.8
South Carolina	286.9	60.7	482.2	46,211.4	151,200.0	606.0
Virginia	213.1	89.6	773.1	15,043.1	199,900.0	365.4
West Virginia	186.4	113.9	621.4	40,685.1	107,550.0	655.9
UNITED STATES	219.4	94.0	575.0	16,330.3	3,191,022.9	3,215.2

	Average annual residential consumption per customer: 1986	1985	1984	1983	1980	1970	1960
TENNESSEE	83.6	85.5	97.1	90.4	101.7	126.5	118.6
Alabama	71.3	73.6	81.7	78.7	86.9	106.9	96.6
Arkansas	79.7	87.2	100.7	93.1	95.6	133.0	121.7
Florida	32.9	32.5	37.4	36.1	40.0	48.2	19.6
Georgia	77.7	81.7	92.6	89.2	96.9	123.9	110.9
Kentucky	103.5	104.2	116.0	108.5	130.4	157.4	153.3
Louisiana	62.3	66.1	74.2	72.1	77.0	95.9	87.4
Mississippi	69.2	73.5	79.3	77.4	85.9	105.5	97.7
North Carolina	78.0	76.6	88.8	86.7	97.1	112.1	78.2
South Carolina	60.7	58.1	67.6	67.0	77.3	91.1	68.8
Virginia	89.6	84.3	93.9	90.8	99.7	111.1	83.4
West Virginia	113.9	108.9	120.4	116.5	131.0	161.0	163.5
UNITED STATES	94.0	98.3	102.0	99.1	111.0	129.2	104.8

Note: Customer data are based on yearly averages. They exclude customers purchasing for resale and sales for resale.

a. No sales reported.

Source: American Gas Association, *Gas Facts, 1986*, and earlier editions.

TABLE 10.23--GAS UTILITY INDUSTRY AVERAGE PRICES, BY CLASS OF SERVICE, SOUTHEASTERN STATES AND UNITED STATES, 1986, AND AVERAGE PRICES, 1960–1986, SELECTED YEARS [In dollars per million Btu]

State	Total	Class of service: Residential	Commercial	Industrial	Other
TENNESSEE	4.24	4.83	4.50	3.66	4.50
Alabama	4.63	6.28	5.12	3.54	4.62
Arkansas	3.68	4.27	3.83	3.20	3.57
Florida	2.92	7.08	4.56	2.89	3.30
Georgia	5.15	6.46	5.37	3.88	5.35
Kentucky	4.56	4.83	4.66	3.87	4.24
Louisiana	3.77	5.50	5.10	2.68	2.72
Mississippi	4.01	5.48	5.08	3.41	4.39
North Carolina	4.67	6.40	5.39	3.64	5.52
South Carolina	4.52	6.44	5.49	3.70	5.02
Virginia	5.36	6.47	5.41	3.89	5.13
West Virginia	5.55	5.97	5.32	4.51	6.05
UNITED STATES	4.60	5.65	5.03	3.65	4.02

	Average prices: 1986	1984	1983	1980	1970	1960
TENNESSEE	4.24	4.35	4.58	2.69	0.53	0.54
Alabama	4.63	4.85	4.92	3.11	0.52	0.52
Arkansas	3.68	3.96	3.87	1.97	0.37	0.33
Florida	2.92	4.00	3.90	2.63	0.55	0.52
Georgia	5.15	5.23	5.03	3.17	0.57	0.55
Kentucky	4.56	4.82	4.98	2.90	0.67	0.63
Louisiana	3.77	4.18	4.32	2.36	0.30	0.26
Mississippi	4.01	4.00	4.58	2.71	0.38	0.41
North Carolina	4.67	5.58	5.50	3.46	0.70	0.74
South Carolina	4.52	5.24	5.14	3.16	0.62	0.57
Virginia	5.36	6.02	6.03	3.58	0.95	1.05
West Virginia	5.55	5.48	5.58	3.27	0.64	0.60
UNITED STATES	4.60	5.13	5.12	3.13	0.64	0.60

Note: Prices are based on sales to final consumers.

Source: American Gas Association, *Gas Facts, 1986*, and earlier editions.

TABLE 10.24--NUMBER AND CAPACITY OF OPERABLE PETROLEUM REFINERIES, SOUTHEASTERN STATES AND UNITED STATES, AS OF JANUARY 1, 1989

	Number of operable refineries			Crude capacity (in barrels per calendar day)		
State	Total	Operating	Idle[1]	Total	Operating	Idle[1]
TENNESSEE	1	1	0	58,000	58,000	0
Alabama	5	4	1	153,600	144,100	9,500
Arkansas	3	3	0	58,400	51,400	7,000
Georgia	2	1	1	33,079	5,079	28,000
Kentucky	2	2	0	218,900	218,900	0
Louisiana	22	20	2	2,627,147	2,286,147	341,000
Mississippi	6	6	0	368,400	368,400	0
North Carolina	2	1	1	13,000	3,000	10,000
Virginia	2	2	0	54,700	54,700	0
West Virginia	2	2	0	16,808	16,808	0
UNITED STATES	204	193	11	15,654,874	15,011,824	643,050

1. Refineries where distillation units are completely idle but not permanently shut down on January 1, 1989.

Source: U.S. Department of Energy, Energy Information Administration, Office of Oil and Gas, *Petroleum Supply Annual, 1988, Volume 1.*

TABLE 10.25--SELECTED STATISTICS ON NUCLEAR POWER PLANTS, SOUTHEASTERN STATES AND UNITED STATES, 1987

		Net summer capability		Net generation	
State	Number of units	Nuclear (million kW)	Percentage of total	Nuclear (million kWh)	Percentage of total
TENNESSEE	2	2.3	13.5	-108[a]	(X)
Alabama	5	4.9	25.8	11,248	16.2
Arkansas	2	1.7	17.8	11,369	31.3
Florida	5	3.7	11.7	18,773	16.9
Georgia	3	2.6	13.9	15,259	17.8
Kentucky	0	0.0	0.0	0	0.0
Louisiana	2	2.0	11.8	12,324	24.0
Mississippi	1	1.1	16.5	7,717	34.5
North Carolina	5	4.7	23.7	28,600	36.3
South Carolina	7	6.4	43.0	39,290	61.0
Virginia	4	3.4	26.4	18,145	42.5
West Virginia	0	0.0	0.0	0	0.0
UNITED STATES	107	93.6	13.9	455,270	17.7

(X) not applicable.

a. Negative generation denotes that electric power consumed for plant use exceeds gross generation.

Source: U.S. Department of Commerce, Bureau of the Census, *Statistical Abstract of the United States, 1989.*

A principal source of data on agriculture is the *Census of Agriculture*, conducted by the U.S. Department of Commerce, Bureau of the Census, in five-year intervals beginning in 1840. The four-year intervals seen in the 1978 and 1982 agricultural censuses were used to put this census on the same schedule as the other economic censuses conducted by the Bureau. Data from the 1987 census are presented in this chapter.

Another comprehensive set of agricultural data, published annually, is the United States Department of Agriculture (USDA) Statistical Reporting Service's *Agricultural Statistics*, which provides estimates on crop production, livestock inventory, farm income, and prices received. Tennessee Agricultural Statistics Service, in cooperation with the USDA, publishes a similar annual state report, *Tennessee Agricultural Statistics, Annual Bulletin*, and a monthly bulletin, *Farm Facts.*

Agricultural Prices, Annual Summary, another publication of the USDA Statistical Reporting Service, provides indexes of prices received by farmers and prices paid by farmers for major production items. Price indexes for Tennessee and the U.S. are reported in Tables 11.10 and 11.24, respectively.

Farm income is reported by the USDA, Economic Research Service (ERS), in an annual bulletin titled *Economic Indicators of the Farm Sector*, which provides information on cash receipts by commodity, as shown in Table 11.4. This source also provides data on the various farm programs by state. Time-series data on farm debt outstanding for southeastern states and current information on agricultural cooperative membership and business volume in southeastern states are also reported by USDA Services.

County-level farm data are issued by the U.S. Department of Commerce, Bureau of the Census and Bureau of Economic Analysis (BEA). Rural farm populations, detailed in Table 11.16 and 11.17, are from the Census Bureau's decennial *Census of Population*. The *Census of Agriculture*, taken every five years, is a principal source of county data, whereas annual estimates of farm income are produced by BEA. These income data are provided on computer tape for secondary distribution by the Center for Business and Economic Research and other members of the BEA User Group.

Forestry data are gathered and published by the USDA, Forest Service, on a 10-year cycle. Data for this edition of the *Abstract* are from the Southern Forest Experiment Station, New Orleans.

TABLE OF CONTENTS

TABLE OF CONTENTS
(Continued)

TABLE 11.1-- NUMBER OF FARMS AND SUMMARY FARM STATISTICS, TENNESSEE, 1930–1987, SELECTED YEARS

Year	Number of farms	Total land in farms (1,000 acres)	Average size of farm (acres)	Average dollar value of land and buildings	
				Per farm	Per acre
1987	79,711	11,731	147	146,126	1,001
1982	90,565	12,475	138	139,141	1,014
1978[r]	86,910[a]	12,681	146	125,238	856
1974	93,659[a]	13,103	140	65,308	467
1969	121,406	15,057	124	33,176	268
1964	133,446	15,266	114	20,509	179
1959	157,688	16,081	102	13,288	130
1954	203,149	17,654	87	8,049	93
1950	231,631	18,534	80	6,182	77
1945	234,431	17,789	76	3,715	49
1940	247,617	18,493	75	2,683	36
1935	273,783	19,086	70	2,030	29
1930	245,657	18,003	73	3,025	41

Note: Beginning with the 1974 Census, a farm is defined as any place having annual sales of agricultural products of $1,000 or more. Earlier data include places of 10 or more acres that had annual sales of agricultural products of $50 or more and places of less than 10 acres that had annual sales of $250 or more.

r Data are revised so as to be comparable with later years. Beginning in 1982, the area sample survey was discontinued; thus data represent only farms on the mail list. The adjustment to the 1978 data was made by subtracting the area sample results from the 1978 totals.

a. Number of farms adjusted to 1969 definition:

1974 = 103,219

1978 = 117,233

Source: U.S. Department of Commerce, Bureau of the Census, *1987 Census of Agriculture, Tennessee*, and earlier editions.

TABLE 11.2-- FARM LAND USE PATTERN, TENNESSEE, 1945–1987, CENSUS YEARS [In acres]

Land use	1987	1982	1978 r	1974	1969
Total land in use for farms	11,731,386	12,474,931	12,680,809	13,103,224	15,056,907
Cropland total	7,185,903	7,602,106	7,786,086	7,756,516	8,403,509
Harvested	3,854,302	4,548,895	4,409,331	3,746,117	3,472,039
Pastured	2,472,453	2,608,138	2,886,362	3,500,924	3,780,947
Other	859,148	445,073	490,393	509,475	1,150,523
Woodland including woodland pastures	2,957,874	3,248,631	3,362,986	3,410,625	4,375,196
All other land[1]	1,587,609	1,624,194	1,531,737	1,936,083	2,278,202
Irrigated land	37,776	17,745	13,163	9,860	12,158

Land use	1964	1959	1954	1950	1945
Total land in use for farms	15,266,213	16,081,285	17,654,324	18,534,380	17,788,997
Cropland total	7,855,209	8,499,211	9,016,141	9,920,008	9,273,021
Harvested	3,617,961	4,116,418	4,860,793	5,575,106	5,843,567
Pastured	3,059,139	3,216,771	3,094,755	2,855,786	2,259,571
Other	1,178,109	1,166,022	1,060,593	1,489,116	1,169,883
Woodland including woodland pastures	4,859,186	5,201,315	5,935,369	5,868,607	5,053,051
All other land[1]	2,551,818	2,380,759	2,702,814	2,745,765	3,462,925
Irrigated land	10,737	10,979	22,548	1,012	393

Note: Total land area in Tennessee is 26,728,000 acres.

r Revised data, comparable to later years. See Table 11.1 for details.

1. Includes pastureland other than cropland and woodland pasture, rangeland, and land in house lots, ponds, roads, wasteland, etc.

Source: U.S. Department of Commerce, Bureau of the Census, *1987 Census of Agriculture, Tennessee*, and earlier editions.

TABLE 11.3-- GROSS AND NET INCOME FROM FARMING, TENNESSEE, 1950–1988, SELECTED YEARS [In millions of dollars]

Year	Agricultural cash receipts	Government payments	Non-cash income[1]	Other farm income[2]	Net inventory adjustment[3]	Gross farm income	Production expenses[4]	Net farm income
1988	2,045.7	140.4	492.8	122.5	20.7	2,822.1	2,052.8	769.3
1987	1,983.5	156.7	462.0	103.3	-41.8	2,663.7	2,024.3	639.4
1986	1,866.7	98.4	464.3	87.0	-151.5	2,365.0	1,958.7	406.3
1985r	2,028.9	61.7	463.4	83.7	-42.0	2,595.8	2,129.9	465.9
1984r	2,118.1	76.6	509.2	85.4	89.6	2,878.8	2,261.6	617.2
1983r	1,803.4	65.8	489.6	78.2	-122.8	2,314.2	2,178.5	135.7
1982r	1,949.2	28.1	509.5	57.6	98.2	2,642.6	2,176.1	466.5
1981	1,933.0	20.7	501.9	58.9	124.0	2,638.5	2,124.8	513.7
1980	1,849.5	18.7	439.5	68.0	-101.8	2,273.9	1,977.1	296.8
1979	1,776.5	8.4	375.0	30.6	-19.2	2,171.3	1,769.3	402.0
1978	1,578.6	15.5	276.2	31.7	-29.5	1,872.5	1,532.9	339.5
1977	1,391.7	12.4	266.3	17.1	-53.3	1,634.2	1,363.5	270.4
1976	1,289.3	11.4	229.2	15.7	57.9	1,603.5	1,261.8	341.7
1975	1,116.3	16.6	171.1	15.8	-4.6	1,315.2	1,131.8	183.4
1970	702.5	71.0	114.4	9.8	8.6	906.3	676.6	229.8
1965	603.3	36.7	112.9	6.4	-4.0	755.3	514.3	240.9
1960	503.3	14.9	102.5	3.8	-0.3	624.2	406.0	218.2
1955	440.4	5.6	121.0	1.2	46.0	614.2	325.0	289.3
1950	431.3	6.7	130.4	0.2	5.2	573.8	271.4	302.4

r revised.

1. Includes the value of farm products consumed directly in farm households and the rental value of housing provided by farm dwellings.
2. Includes cash income from recreation, machine hire, custom work and other farm-related income and forest product sales.
3. The estimated physical change in livestock and crops owned by farmers, valued at average prices prevailing during the year.
4. Includes operator households.

Source: U.S. Department of Agriculture and Tennessee Department of Agriculture, Tennessee Agricultural Statistics Service, *Farm Facts*, Vol. 89, No. 8, 1989; *Tennessee Agricultural Statistics, Annual Bulletin, 1988*, and earlier editions; and *Agricultural Trends in Tennessee*.

FIGURE 11.1
Cash Receipts: Livestock and Crops, Tennessee, 1979–1987

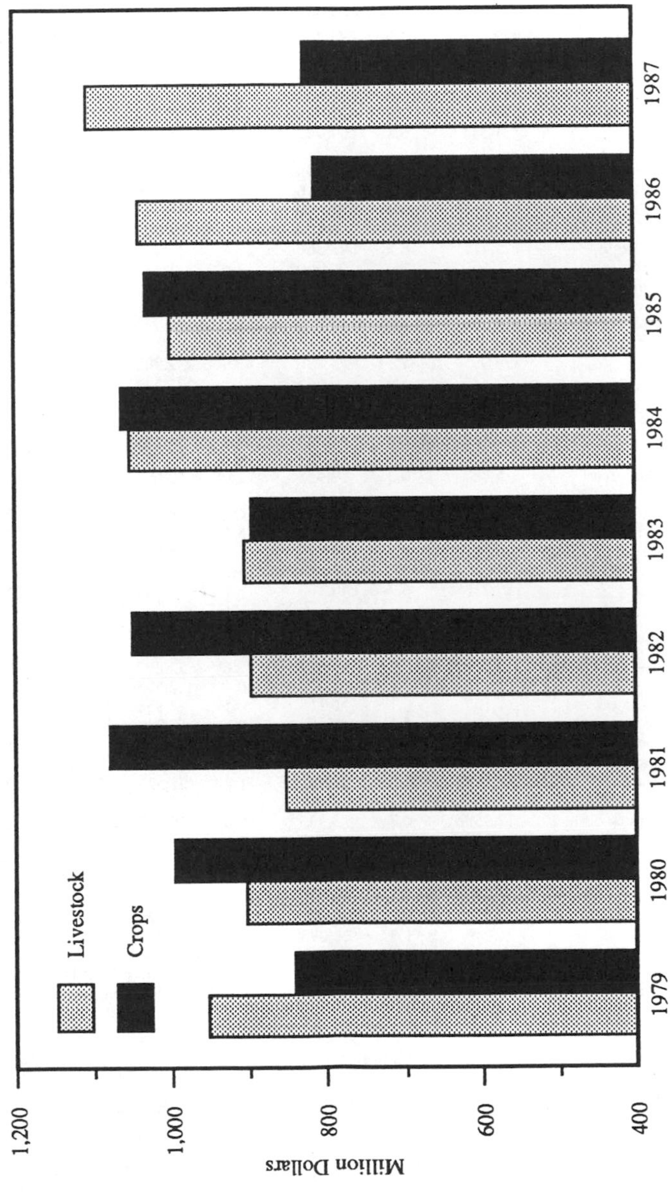

Source: U.S. Department of Agriculture, Economic Research Service, *Economic Indicators of the Farm Sector, State Financial Summary, 1986*, and earlier editions.

TABLE 11.4-- CASH RECEIPTS, BY COMMODITY, TENNESSEE, 1984–1987 [In thousands of dollars]

Commodity	1987 Value	1987 Percentage of total	1986[r] Value	1986[r] Percentage of total	1985[r] Value	1985[r] Percentage of total	1984 Value	1984 Percentage of total
All commodities	1,932,695	100.0	1,854,308	100.0	2,032,593	100.0	2,118,051	100.0
Livestock products	1,106,790	57.3	1,041,019	56.1	1,000,088	49.2	1,053,683	49.7
Meat animals	689,059	35.7	604,667	32.6	584,516	28.8	624,457	29.5
Cattle, calves	557,032	28.8	435,028	23.5	425,838	21.0	477,099	22.5
Hogs	131,555	6.8	169,417	9.1	158,461	7.8	147,137	6.9
Dairy products	273,076	14.1	274,596	14.8	281,851	13.9	275,856	13.0
Milk, retail	1,726	0.1	2,116	0.1	1,726	0.1	1,856	0.1
Milk, wholesale	271,350	14.0	272,480	14.7	280,125	13.8	274,000	12.9
Poultry and eggs	125,411	6.5	143,866	7.8	117,241	5.8	132,340	6.2
Chickens, farm	660	(a)	960	(a)	1,589	0.1	1,763	0.1
Eggs, chicken	25,683	1.3	33,758	1.8	35,721	1.8	43,428	2.1
Miscellaneous livestock[1]	19,244	1.0	17,889	1.0	16,480	0.8	21,030	1.0
Crops	825,905	42.7	813,290	43.9	1,032,505	50.8	1,064,368	50.3
Wheat	27,546	1.4	20,645	1.1	25,535	1.3	61,420	2.9
Feed crops	71,247	3.7	112,551	6.1	180,993	8.9	110,546	5.2
Corn	53,559	2.8	81,366	4.4	124,555	6.1	77,448	3.7
Hay	11,951	0.6	11,727	0.6	13,730	0.7	11,631	0.5
Sorghum, grain	5,737	0.3	19,458	1.0	42,698	2.1	21,281	1.0
Cotton	178,157	9.2	119,179	6.4	108,460	5.3	102,213	4.8
Cotton lint	160,989	8.3	108,846	5.9	100,164	4.9	90,408	4.3
Cottonseed	17,168	0.9	10,333	0.6	8,296	0.4	11,805	0.6
Tobacco	129,258	6.7	150,163	8.1	221,630	10.9	253,069	11.9
Soybean	163,911	8.5	163,100	8.8	261,146	12.8	263,380	12.4
Vegetables	43,894	2.3	47,487	2.6	52,212	2.6	50,606	2.4
Potatoes	1,910	0.1	1,910	0.1	2,508	0.1	2,200	0.1
Sweet potatoes	1,157	0.1	1,118	0.1	958	(a)	1,003	(a)
Snap beans	2,106	0.1	1,508	0.1	2,284	0.1	2,313	0.1
Tomatoes	19,044	1.0	21,000	1.1	23,940	1.2	19,320	0.9
Miscellaneous vegetables	19,677	1.0	21,951	1.2	22,522	1.1	25,770	1.2
Fruits and nuts	12,959	0.7	13,993	0.8	10,692	0.5	11,697	0.6
Apples	1,820	0.1	1,572	0.1	1,360	0.1	1,845	0.1
Other fruits and nuts	11,139	0.6	12,421	0.7	9,332	0.5	9,852	0.5
All other crops	198,933	10.3	186,172	10.0	171,837	8.5	211,437	10.0
Greenhouse nursery	173,984	9.0	162,077	8.7	152,124	7.5	193,772	9.1
Other crops	24,949	1.3	24,095	1.3	19,713	1.0	17,665	0.8

Note: "Other" and "miscellaneous" categories include commodities which are not enumerated separately for the state, as well as items protected for reasons of confidentiality. Percentages were computed by the Center for Business and Economic Research.

r revised.

1. Cash receipts include value of home consumption.

a. Less than 0.05 percent.

Source: U.S. Department of Agriculture, Economic Research Service, *Economic Indicators of the Farm Sector, State Financial Summary, 1987.*

TABLE 11.5-- PRODUCTION OF SELECTED CROPS, TENNESSEE, 1950–1987, SELECTED YEARS

Commodity	1987	1986	1985	1984	1983	1980	1970	1960	1950
Hay (all types)									
Production (1,000 tons)	2,644	2,092	3,156	2,678	2,044	1,764	1,718	1,717	1,965
Average yield per acre (tons)	1.68	1.52	1.95	1.79	1.51	1.49	1.55	1.29	1.25
Soybeans (for beans)									
Production (1,000 bu.)	28,750	35,500 r	45,260	48,100	31,520	45,900	26,450	8,865	3,822
Average yield per acre (bu.)	23.0	25.0	31.0	26.0	16.0	18.0	23.0	22.5	21.0
Corn (for grain)									
Production (1,000 bu.)	52,780	56,980	79,380	65,550	23,040	29,440	25,605	52,806	66,170
Average yield per acre (bu.)	91.0	74.0	98.0	95.0	48.0	46.0	45.0	39.0	32.5
Cotton									
Lint–production[1] (1,000 bales)	634	396	419	337	151	200	392	583	409
Seed–production (1,000 tons)	235	157	160	133	60	82	160	238	165
Average yield per acre, lint (lbs.)	700	567	600	498	337	349	483	545	310
Wheat									
Production (1,000 bu.)	14,350	10,725	8,000	21,400	19,800	18,620	6,545	3,288	3,050
Average yield per acre (bu.)	41.0	33.0	32.0	40.0	33.0	38.0	35.0	24.0	12.5
Tobacco (all types)									
Production (1,000 lbs.)	87,291	82,821	127,403	154,646	118,197	111,931	114,269	115,336	132,385
Average yield per acre (lbs.)	1,766	1,682	2,065	2,062	1,621	1,728	2,123	1,561	1,284
Oats									
Production (1,000 bu.)	n.a.	n.a.	n.a.	235	308	552	1,940	3,500	4,500
Average yield per acre (bu.)	n.a.	n.a.	n.a.	47.0	44.0	46.0	48.5	35.0	25.0
Snap beans									
Production (tons)	10,800	7,580	11,250	11,340	8,920	12,710	26,850	20,400	13,700
Average yield per acre (tons)	2.00	1.43	2.25	2.14	1.82	1.05	2.20	2.20	1.91
Sorghum (for silage)									
Production (1,000 tons)	100	96	84	78	72	132	88	180	n.a.
Average yield per acre (tons)	10	12	14	13	12	11	11	9	n.a.

TABLE 11.5-- PRODUCTION OF SELECTED CROPS, TENNESSEE, 1950–1987, SELECTED YEARS (Continued)

Commodity	1987	1986	1985	1984	1983	1980	1970	1960	1950
Sorghum (for grain)									
Production (1,000 bu.)	6,000	10,725	37,200	20,800	5,035	1,750	1,224	1,088	n.a.
Average yield per acre (bu.)	80	65	80	80	53	50	51	34	n.a.
Irish potatoes									
Production (1,000 cwt.)	144	234	375	270	175	196	361	584	1,449
Average yield per acre (cwt.)	80	90	150	90	70	70	95	80	63
Tomatoes									
Production (1,000 cwt.)	828	1,050	1,260	840	420	407	242	230	441
Average yield per acre (cwt.)	180	210	280	200	100	110	115	85	76
Sweet potatoes									
Production (1,000 cwt.)	88	99	165	95	112	160	266	490	972
Average yield per acre (cwt.)	110	110	150	95	80	80	95	89	54

n.a. not available.

r revised.

1. Bales of 500 pounds gross weight through 1963. Beginning with 1964, production is given in 480 pound net weight bales.

Source: U.S. Department of Agriculture and Tennessee Department of Agriculture, Tennessee Agricultural Statistics Service, *Tennessee Agricultural Statistics, Annual Bulletin, 1988*, and earlier editions; and *Agricultural Trends in Tennessee.*

TABLE 11.6-- NUMBER AND VALUE OF LIVESTOCK ON FARMS, TENNESSEE, JANUARY 1, 1930–1988, SELECTED YEARS [In thousands]

Year	Cattle		Milk cows, number[1]	Hogs[2]		Sheep and lambs	
	Number	Value		Number	Value	Number	Value
1988	2,300	$1,069,500	204	800	$64,000	12	$876
1987	2,400	804,000	203	770	70,070	13	988
1986	2,500	800,000	210	950	65,550	10	670
1985	2,535	823,875	210	1,100	78,100	9	572
1984	2,750	866,250	214	950	50,825	6	348
1983	2,675	949,625	217	750	64,875	8	508
1982	2,500	862,500	215	900	59,850	10	560
1981	2,350	951,750	215	1,140	77,520	11	583
1980	2,300	1,081,000	214	920	67,620	12	504
1975	3,300	445,500	217	1,395	30,690	21	599
1970	2,308	369,280	296	922	20,007	50	975
1965	2,240	215,040	437	1,453	23,539	95	1,216
1960	1,858	219,244	532	970	24,929	245	3,944
1955	1,771	116,886	695	1,371	30,573	286	4,376
1950	1,490	150,490	668	1,316	17,371	251	4,317
1945	1,483	73,112	666	1,450	8,410	333	3,330
1940	1,211	39,236	564	1,002	5,592	402	2,653
1935	1,233	19,632	594	982	9,525	411	1,877
1930	992	44,045	468	1,035	8,901	368	3,533

1. In years prior to 1970 the definition is "cows and heifers 2 years and older kept for milk." Beginning in 1970 the definition is "milk cows that have calved."

2. Data are as of December 1 of the previous year.

Source: U.S. Department of Agriculture and Tennessee Department of Agriculture, Tennessee Agricultural Statistics Service, *Tennessee Agricultural Statistics, Annual Bulletin, 1988*, and earlier editions; and *Agricultural Trends in Tennessee.*

TABLE 11.7-- MANUFACTURED DAIRY PRODUCTS, TENNESSEE, 1970–1987, SELECTED YEARS

Year	Creamery butter	American cheese made from whole milk	Cottage cheese curd	Cottage cheese creamed
	(1,000 pounds)			
1987	(D)	(D)	7,128	8,284
1986	(D)	(D)	(D)	(D)
1985	(D)	(D)	7,099	9,625
1984	(D)	10,613	6,970	9,297
1983	28,463	21,696	6,768	9,173
1982	27,329	19,274	5,981	8,896
1981	26,785	20,834	3,961	6,034
1980	23,285	21,826	4,439	6,357
1979	21,697	20,279	4,846	7,292
1978	20,675	18,892	4,898	6,961
1977	21,263	20,509	4,458	6,831
1976	18,277	20,536	4,787	7,002
1975	19,121	21,389	4,994	7,726
1974	16,839	27,051	5,257	7,555
1970	12,762	36,253	7,971	11,523

Year	Total ice cream	Sherbet (milk)	Ice milk	Ice cream mix	Ice milk mix	Milk sherbet mix
	(1,000 gallons)					
1987	21,267	1,005	6,794	11,049	2,900	622
1986	21,075	909	6,023	10,468	2,710	640
1985	19,119	918	6,636	9,702	2,769	590
1984	19,135	933	5,536	9,823	2,397	601
1983	18,633	916	5,413	9,507	2,379	588
1982	19,053	899	4,912	9,577	2,293	587
1981	18,095	1,031	5,164	9,236	2,501	670
1980	18,751	1,141	5,772	9,592	3,000	746
1979	18,371	1,114	6,446	9,360	3,183	741
1978	19,417	1,247	7,496	9,614	3,676	815
1977	18,008	1,454	7,665	9,562	4,053	858
1976	17,441	1,115	7,823	8,860	4,044	720
1975	18,465	1,261	8,892	9,353	4,532	813
1974	16,713	1,324	8,849	10,580	5,008	854
1970	15,827	1,465	9,829	9,539	6,320	908

(D) withheld to avoid disclosing data of individual operations.

Source: U.S. Department of Agriculture and Tennessee Department of Agriculture, Tennessee Agricultural Statistics Service, *Tennessee Agricultural Statistics, Annual Bulletin, 1988.*

TABLE 11.8-- EGG PRODUCTION, PRICE, AND VALUE OF PRODUCTION, TENNESSEE, 1960–1987

Year	Average number of layers during year (1,000 birds)	Eggs per layer (number)	Eggs produced (millions)	Price per dozen (¢)	Value of production[1] ($1,000)
1987	2,684	250	670	46.0	25,683
1986	2,637	251	663	61.1	33,758
1985	2,948	256	756	56.7	35,721
1984	2,901	256	744	71.0	44,020
1983	3,232	254	822	59.6	40,826
1982	3,649	242	884	63.3	46,631
1981	3,747	246	922	67.0	51,479
1980	3,961	243	962	56.5	45,294
1979	4,050	247	999	58.6	48,785
1978	4,016	243	974	53.4	43,343
1977	4,178	238	993	57.8	47,829
1976	4,136	235	974	59.0	47,889
1975	4,238	235	1,002	55.2	46,092
1974	4,295	237	1,028	58.2	49,858
1973	4,697	231	1,088	56.4	51,136
1972	4,832	230	1,113	37.0	34,318
1971	4,725	213	1,010	37.0	31,142
1970	5,228	203	1,064	43.0	38,127
1969	4,673	207	965	42.4	34,097
1968	5,013	205	1,029	36.6	31,385
1967	5,289	199	1,052	32.9	28,843
1966	4,900	198	972	39.9	32,319
1965	4,982	193	963	36.7	29,451
1964	5,058	194	979	36.3	29,614
1963	4,853	190	922	37.6	28,889
1962	4,916	189	927	36.1	27,888
1961	4,871	187	909	37.6	28,482
1960	5,228	183	957	38.0	30,305

Note: Annual estimates cover the period December 1 previous year through November 30 current year.

1. Includes home consumption by producers.

Source: U.S. Department of Agriculture and Tennessee Department of Agriculture, Tennessee Agricultural Statistics Service, *Tennessee Agricultural Statistics, Annual Bulletin, 1988*, and earlier editions.

TABLE 11.9-- FARM PRODUCTION EXPENSES, TENNESSEE, 1983–1988 [In millions of dollars]

Item	1988	1987	1986	1985	1984	1983
Total	2,052.8	2,024.3	1,958.7	2,129.9	2,261.6	2,178.5
Feed	267.7	213.8	208.1	238.3	251.8	273.6
Livestock	127.3	184.3	135.7	112.5	97.6	70.7
Seed	40.0	38.4	38.1	42.7	44.0	38.2
Fertilizer and lime	134.6	120.5	103.8	127.3	128.5	132.7
Pesticides	63.7	62.0	60.6	67.5	64.4	56.1
Fuel and oil	61.9	60.5	65.2	89.6	97.2	102.1
Electricity	24.0	22.3	18.1	20.1	20.2	20.0
Repair and maintenance	204.9	196.7	190.4	185.9	172.4	166.0
Other operations[1]	192.4	199.9	187.1	202.3	225.0	202.3
Interest						
Real estate	114.3	111.4	127.0	137.4	175.8	177.1
Nonreal estate	99.0	106.0	108.7	121.2	171.3	183.1
Labor expenses[2]	137.2	132.5	121.3	120.4	119.3	119.8
Net rent to landlords[3]	80.5	68.2	49.7	79.5	101.3	51.3
Capital consumption[4]	452.5	453.9	494.5	535.1	545.1	533.4
Property taxes	52.8	53.9	50.5	50.0	47.6	52.0

Note: Includes operator households.

1. Includes machine hire and custom work expenses; marketing, storage, and transportation expenses; and miscellaneous expenses.

2. Includes contract labor expenses, hired labor wages, perquisites, and Social Security payments.

3. Uses different data sources for years prior to 1984. Estimates are not directly comparable across years.

4. Includes depreciation, wear and tear, obsolescence and accidental damage of capital stock.

Source: U.S. Department of Agriculture and Tennessee Department of Agriculture, Tennessee Agricultural Statistics Service, *Tennessee Farm Facts*, Vol. 89, No. 8, 1989.

TABLE 11.10--INDEX NUMBERS OF PRICES RECEIVED BY FARMERS, TENNESSEE, 1980–1987, MONTHLY [1977 = 100]

Year	Jan.	Feb.	March	April	May	June	July	August	Sept.	Oct.	Nov.	Dec.	Average
							All farm products						
1987	119	121	122	124	125	129	129	131	131	128	127	128	126
1986	118	118	118	115	115[r]	117	119	121	119	118	118	119	118
1985	128	128	128	129	126	125	121	119	118	118	118	117	123
1984	136	135	140	140	139	136	133	132	130	126	128	128	134
1983	126	130	130	132	131	130	130	134	135	134	134	135	132
1982	125	128	128	130	131	129	129	128	125	123	124	123	127
1981	139	140	135	136	134	135	132	132	129	126	124	123	132
1980	133	135	129	123	122	125	130	135	137	138	141	139	132
							All crops						
1987	90	90	91	92	95	97	96	95	95	96	99	103	95
1986	100	99	100	100	101	100	97	95	90	91	92	92	96
1985	124	111	112	112	111	111	108	104	101	100	97	99	108
1984	128	121	130	133	135	134	124	122	119	114	112	111	124
1983	105	108	109	114	114	114	118	131	134	131	132	130	120
1982	111	112	112	114	114	113	111	107	104	103	106	106	109
1981	130	130	126	124	125	123	122	118	111	108	109	110	120
1980	110	110	107	105	105	106	112	117	123	124	131	127	115
							All livestock						
1987	146	149	150	154	152	159	159	163	163	157	152	151	155
1986	135	135	135	129	129	133	140	145	147	144	142	143	138
1985	145	144	143	143	140	139	132	133	133	134	137	134	138
1984	144	148	149	147	142	142	145	142	140	137	142	143	143
1983	145	151	150	148	146	144	140	137	136	136	136	140	142
1982	138	143	143	145	146	144	145	147	144	141	141	139	143
1981	147	149	145	148	143	145	141	144	146	142	138	135	144
1980	153	157	149	139	139	142	146	151	151	151	150	149	148

r revised.

Source: U.S. Department of Agriculture and Tennessee Department of Agriculture, Tennessee Agricultural Statistics Service, *Tennessee Agricultural Statistics, Annual Bulletin, 1988.*

TABLE 11.11--AVERAGE PRICES RECEIVED BY FARMERS FOR SELECTED CROPS, LIVESTOCK, AND POULTRY PRODUCTS, BY TYPE OF PRODUCT, TENNESSEE, 1960–1987, SELECTED YEARS

Commodity	1987	1986	1985	1984	1983	1980	1970	1960
Crops								
Cotton								
Lint (¢ per lb.)	63.30	49.00 r	53.60 r	56.70	68.50	78.40	22.07	31.40
Seed ($ per ton)	77.00	66.50	53.00	90.50	161.00	128.00	53.80	41.70
Tobacco ($ per lb.)	1.55	1.52	1.57	1.79	1.80	1.61	0.70	0.61
Corn ($ per bushel)	1.80	1.65 r	2.30	2.90	3.65	3.50	1.55	1.12
Hay ($ per ton)	54.00	61.00	52.00	52.00	49.50	46.00	29.00	25.60
Soybeans ($ per bushel)	5.50	4.87 r	5.08	5.97	7.96	7.88	2.79	2.04
Wheat ($ per bushel)	2.60	2.50	3.00	3.30	3.30	3.80	1.34	1.77
Oats ($ per bushel)	n.a.	n.a.	n.a.	2.40	2.15	2.00	0.78	0.79
Sorghum ($ per bushel)	1.48	1.34 r	1.88	2.24	2.97	2.97	1.20	1.00
Snap beans ($ per ton)	195.00	199.00	203.00	204.00	200.00	211.00	113.80	122.00
Tomatoes ($ per cwt.)	23.00	20.00	19.00	23.00	20.00	21.20	10.40	6.89
Irish potatoes ($ per cwt.)	10.30	9.55	7.60	9.40	8.50	7.60	4.30	3.00
Sweet potatoes ($ per cwt.)	14.50	11.70	11.60	13.90	14.20	14.80	5.62	4.48
Apples (¢ per lb.)	14.10	18.50 r	13.60	16.10	14.50	16.40	5.66	4.29
Peaches (¢ per lb.)	34.60	24.00	(a)	21.00	22.00	17.80	6.77	4.89
Livestock								
Cattle ($ per cwt.)	52.20	42.50	44.50	44.60	45.40	52.00	24.30	17.70
Calves ($ per cwt.)	72.60	56.30	56.50	54.10	55.90	70.40	35.00	22.60
Milk–Wholesale[1] ($ per cwt.)	13.40	13.10 r	13.50	13.70	13.60	13.30	5.69	4.23
Hogs ($ per cwt.)	50.40	45.70	43.20	47.10	46.70	38.20	22.50	15.20
Sheep ($ per cwt.)	28.50	21.00	21.20	20.50	18.10	19.50	7.70	5.10
Lambs ($ per cwt.)	81.80	67.80	62.80	59.00	56.40	62.10	26.00	18.90
Wool (¢ per lb.)	57.00	61.00	52.00	73.00	47.00	73.00	43.00	50.00
Poultry								
Eggs (¢ per doz.)	46.00	61.10	56.70	71.00	59.60 r	56.50	43.00	38.00
Commercial broilers (¢ per lb.)	25.50	31.50	27.50	31.00	27.50	25.00	14.10	16.10

Note: Prices are season or marketing year averages. See original source for specific time periods for each commodity.

r revised.

n.a. not available.

1. Prices are annual averages.

a. No significant production due to frost.

Source: U.S. Department of Agriculture and Tennessee Department of Agriculture, Tennessee Agricultural Statistics Service, *Tennessee Agricultural Statistics, Annual Bulletin, 1988*, and earlier editions; and *Agricultural Trends in Tennessee*.

TABLE 11.12--SELECTED FARM STATISTICS, COUNTIES, 1987

County	Number of farms	Average size (acres)	Average dollar value of land and buildings per farm	Value of farm products sold: Amount ($1,000)	Value of farm products sold: Average per farm ($)	Operators with major occupation farming
Anderson	463	87	148,505	5,420	11,706	129
Bedford	1,244	178	153,726	42,735	34,353	531
Benton	392	165	97,872	4,730	12,067	125
Bledsoe	482	184	160,295	10,427	21,632	220
Blount	1,185	86	169,544	13,689	11,552	422
Bradley	738	125	153,934	34,370	46,572	266
Campbell	470	74	94,277	3,544	7,541	150
Cannon	694	145	110,038	10,406	14,994	237
Carroll	848	196	127,583	16,963	20,004	347
Carter	686	55	72,797	5,719	8,336	182
Cheatham	567	118	151,044	5,495	9,691	187
Chester	387	189	122,614	6,860	17,727	158
Claiborne	1,528	93	84,164	14,864	9,728	630
Clay	528	143	80,405	4,480	8,484	207
Cocke	1,081	83	91,179	12,557	11,616	427
Coffee	887	162	161,977	21,464	24,199	366
Crockett	506	364	345,069	40,373	79,789	279
Cumberland	622	151	131,474	10,394	16,711	226
Davidson	561	103	229,569	8,082	14,407	160
Decatur	474	193	93,374	6,837	14,423	177
DeKalb	823	123	113,981	12,746	15,487	299
Dickson	1,068	139	120,788	9,295	8,703	374
Dyer	603	390	286,973	33,695	55,879	393
Fayette	765	354	281,354	51,754	67,652	345
Fentress	454	173	126,562	15,600	34,362	182
Franklin	1,126	136	151,590	34,876	30,973	492
Gibson	1,057	265	180,101	48,272	45,669	565
Giles	1,551	170	135,406	25,848	16,665	558
Grainger	1,219	89	91,657	9,991	8,196	485
Greene	3,580	74	95,009	42,233	11,797	1,459
Grundy	333	113	91,575	21,263	63,851	146
Hamblen	843	69	112,133	9,481	11,246	278
Hamilton	587	98	156,092	11,792	20,089	165
Hancock	760	101	82,913	5,767	7,588	377
Hardeman	488	384	185,133	15,839	32,457	210
Hardin	570	212	142,452	10,543	18,496	258
Hawkins	1,985	85	98,114	13,486	6,794	689
Haywood	527	422	339,651	46,564	88,357	316
Henderson	849	193	123,776	20,052	23,619	312
Henry	805	232	152,358	23,042	28,623	384
Hickman	650	199	128,663	8,257	12,703	238
Houston	245	186	114,245	2,562	10,455	88
Humphreys	506	238	146,881	7,579	14,979	186
Jackson	732	135	86,111	4,739	6,474	268
Jefferson	1,326	83	116,181	16,670	12,572	492
Johnson	888	70	72,508	6,163	6,940	328
Knox	1,253	76	175,590	11,382	9,084	396
Lake	85	1,082	954,576	14,704	172,991	67

TABLE 11.12--SELECTED FARM STATISTICS, COUNTIES, 1987 (Continued)

County	Number of farms	Average size (acres)	Average dollar value of land and buildings per farm	Value of farm products sold: Amount ($1,000)	Value of farm products sold: Average per farm ($)	Operators with major occupation farming
Lauderdale	572	345	242,032	30,881	53,989	290
Lawrence	1,428	141	119,076	24,056	16,846	475
Lewis	223	171	127,395	1,773	7,951	71
Lincoln	1,628	172	140,281	32,584	20,015	630
Loudon	760	102	151,299	31,486	41,429	247
McMinn	1,076	128	138,580	32,471	30,178	394
McNairy	715	209	138,761	17,137	23,968	278
Macon	1,242	101	71,592	9,527	7,671	424
Madison	614	261	212,954	23,084	37,597	288
Marion	310	181	188,026	5,835	18,824	98
Marshall	1,013	171	163,817	20,997	20,727	396
Maury	1,575	163	199,801	22,734	14,434	618
Meigs	322	171	171,894	5,195	16,134	110
Monroe	930	113	136,174	17,219	18,515	330
Montgomery	998	188	161,344	22,398	22,443	428
Moore	427	135	129,304	6,822	15,977	110
Morgan	304	145	106,388	3,894	12,811	79
Obion	761	340	253,298	41,114	54,026	392
Overton	842	131	98,127	9,709	11,531	314
Perry	220	265	113,823	3,178	14,443	84
Pickett	369	100	70,605	3,137	8,503	122
Polk	260	143	185,265	14,762	56,776	93
Putnam	1,072	98	99,260	10,021	9,348	401
Rhea	374	150	151,227	8,687	23,226	142
Roane	542	108	127,998	4,377	8,076	181
Robertson	1,543	165	210,762	43,376	28,112	725
Rutherford	1,562	144	215,859	21,798	13,955	503
Scott	239	145	131,421	4,221	17,662	66
Sequatchie	156	162	128,090	3,057	19,597	49
Sevier	953	82	134,187	8,174	8,577	338
Shelby	733	190	266,308	24,762	33,782	272
Smith	1,123	130	96,760	11,704	10,422	440
Stewart	371	150	101,105	3,028	8,162	121
Sullivan	1,432	68	143,524	13,893	9,702	495
Sumner	1,864	110	170,045	28,798	15,450	648
Tipton	650	293	282,132	32,983	50,742	313
Trousdale	439	133	128,911	6,317	14,389	206
Unicoi	266	39	62,139	1,125	4,228	92
Union	612	87	77,975	3,674	6,003	237
Van Buren	217	140	102,184	3,704	17,070	86
Warren	1,238	133	153,871	54,988	44,417	525
Washington	1,909	65	141,365	31,073	16,277	711
Wayne	698	194	102,903	7,113	10,190	210
Weakley	926	225	140,283	37,706	40,720	422
White	1,006	132	118,590	16,147	16,050	361
Williamson	1,421	155	288,145	25,821	18,171	460
Wilson	1,755	123	138,348	17,489	9,965	694

Source: U.S. Department of Commerce, Bureau of the Census, *1987 Census of Agriculture, Tennessee.*

TABLE 11.13--FARM OPERATOR CHARACTERISTICS, COUNTIES, 1987

County	All farms: Number	All farms: Percentage full owners	All farms: Percentage with nonfarm principal occupation[1]	Type of organization[2] (%): Individual or family	Type of organization[2] (%): Partnership	Type of organization[2] (%): Corporation
Anderson	463	70.2	72.1	93.3	5.8	0.9
Bedford	1,244	74.9	57.3	91.6	6.8	1.4
Benton	392	71.7	68.1	93.4	5.6	1.0
Bledsoe	482	72.0	54.4	93.4	5.8	0.4
Blount	1,185	66.9	64.4	91.4	7.6	0.6
Bradley	738	73.0	64.0	90.7	8.1	0.9
Campbell	470	78.7	68.1	92.6	7.0	0.0
Cannon	694	75.2	65.9	92.1	7.5	0.1
Carroll	848	70.5	59.1	89.4	9.4	0.5
Carter	686	70.6	73.5	93.3	6.4	0.1
Cheatham	567	68.1	67.0	87.8	9.9	1.9
Chester	387	64.1	59.2	90.2	9.0	0.8
Claiborne	1,528	75.0	58.8	88.8	10.7	0.2
Clay	528	77.5	60.8	89.0	10.2	0.4
Cocke	1,081	73.5	60.5	90.1	9.7	0.1
Coffee	887	72.6	58.7	91.5	7.6	0.6
Crockett	506	45.7	44.9	88.7	10.7	0.6
Cumberland	622	73.2	63.7	93.6	5.9	0.3
Davidson	561	73.1	71.5	87.0	10.0	2.3
Decatur	474	71.7	62.7	91.4	8.4	0.0
DeKalb	823	77.2	63.7	92.1	7.2	0.6
Dickson	1,068	75.2	65.0	90.5	9.2	0.0
Dyer	603	47.9	34.8	85.9	13.1	0.8
Fayette	765	60.5	54.9	89.4	9.2	0.9
Fentress	454	73.8	59.9	93.0	5.5	1.3
Franklin	1,126	69.4	56.3	88.7	9.6	1.2
Gibson	1,057	60.2	46.5	90.5	9.0	0.1
Giles	1,551	76.9	64.0	91.0	8.4	0.5
Grainger	1,219	76.2	60.2	90.6	8.9	0.2
Greene	3,580	73.7	59.2	89.2	10.3	0.3
Grundy	333	77.5	56.2	91.6	7.2	0.9
Hamblen	843	75.8	67.0	91.1	8.2	0.1
Hamilton	587	73.8	71.9	92.3	6.0	1.5
Hancock	760	72.9	50.4	91.4	8.6	0.0
Hardeman	488	62.1	57.0	90.0	8.2	1.6
Hardin	570	64.9	54.7	90.4	8.8	0.9
Hawkins	1,985	77.2	65.3	90.9	8.2	0.1
Haywood	527	46.7	40.0	84.8	13.1	1.5
Henderson	849	69.0	63.3	87.8	11.4	0.6
Henry	805	66.6	52.3	88.2	10.8	0.7
Hickman	650	76.0	63.4	92.6	6.6	0.3
Houston	245	74.3	64.1	92.7	7.3	0.0
Humphreys	506	68.8	63.2	91.3	7.5	1.0
Jackson	732	74.3	63.4	90.8	8.9	0.0
Jefferson	1,326	74.7	62.9	90.6	8.5	0.5
Johnson	888	79.5	63.1	90.8	9.0	0.2
Knox	1,253	72.9	68.4	93.0	5.9	0.6
Lake	85	17.6	21.2	76.5	11.8	11.8
Lauderdale	572	51.7	49.3	86.5	11.2	1.7
Lawrence	1,428	76.2	66.7	91.9	7.3	0.5

TABLE 11.13--FARM OPERATOR CHARACTERISTICS, COUNTIES, 1987 (Continued)

County	All farms			Type of organization[2] (%)		
	Number	Percent-age full owners	Percent-age with nonfarm principal occupation[1]	Individual or family	Partner-ship	Corpo-ration
Lewis	223	75.8	68.2	95.1	4.5	0.0
Lincoln	1,628	74.0	61.3	88.9	10.7	0.2
Loudon	760	74.2	67.5	90.5	8.0	0.8
McMinn	1,076	73.8	63.4	91.7	7.7	0.4
McNairy	715	67.8	61.1	92.9	7.1	0.0
Macon	1,242	76.4	65.9	89.0	10.3	0.2
Madison	614	64.8	53.1	90.6	7.3	1.0
Marion	310	67.7	68.4	91.3	8.7	0.0
Marshall	1,013	77.4	60.9	90.7	8.4	0.1
Maury	1,575	72.6	60.8	91.0	8.2	0.3
Meigs	322	73.6	65.8	90.4	9.0	0.6
Monroe	930	72.7	64.5	92.8	6.3	0.5
Montgomery	998	70.2	57.1	83.6	15.7	0.4
Moore	427	77.8	74.2	92.0	6.6	0.9
Morgan	304	66.8	74.0	93.8	5.9	0.0
Obion	761	55.8	48.5	82.1	15.5	1.7
Overton	842	77.6	62.7	91.4	6.7	1.4
Perry	220	63.6	61.8	89.5	10.0	0.0
Pickett	369	72.4	66.9	96.2	3.5	0.0
Polk	260	78.5	64.2	94.6	5.0	0.4
Putnam	1,072	75.0	62.6	93.5	6.0	0.2
Rhea	374	67.6	62.0	91.4	7.2	1.1
Roane	542	73.4	66.6	93.7	5.7	0.6
Robertson	1,543	70.1	53.0	86.2	12.6	0.6
Rutherford	1,562	73.6	67.8	93.0	6.4	0.3
Scott	239	65.3	72.4	92.1	5.4	2.5
Sequatchie	156	71.8	68.6	91.7	7.7	0.6
Sevier	953	70.4	64.5	93.3	5.4	0.8
Shelby	733	58.7	62.9	85.4	8.5	4.1
Smith	1,123	72.8	60.8	87.1	12.3	0.4
Stewart	371	67.7	67.4	93.3	6.5	0.0
Sullivan	1,432	72.4	65.4	91.5	7.5	0.4
Sumner	1,864	76.1	65.2	88.6	10.5	0.6
Tipton	650	54.6	51.8	85.8	11.8	2.0
Trousdale	439	66.3	53.1	85.0	14.6	0.0
Unicoi	266	77.1	65.4	93.6	4.9	0.8
Union	612	77.5	61.3	95.1	4.6	0.2
Van Buren	217	79.3	60.4	87.6	12.4	0.0
Warren	1,238	70.6	57.6	88.4	9.5	1.9
Washington	1,909	72.3	62.8	91.0	8.3	0.2
Wayne	698	79.9	69.9	89.8	9.0	0.4
Weakley	926	61.7	54.4	89.7	9.5	0.5
White	1,006	76.1	64.1	91.2	7.8	0.6
Williamson	1,421	73.9	67.6	87.9	9.7	1.7
Wilson	1,755	77.1	60.5	91.6	7.4	0.7

Note: Percentages were computed by the Center for Business and Economic Research.

1. Farms whose operators spent 50 percent or more of their time at nonfarm occupations. Does not apply to corporate farms.

2. Percentages representing cooperative, estate or trust, and institutional farms are not shown.

Source: U.S. Department of Commerce, Bureau of the Census, *1987 Census of Agriculture, Tennessee.*

TABLE 11.14--FARM INCOME, BY SOURCE, COUNTIES, 1987 [In thousands of dollars]

County	Receipts from marketing	Govern-ment pay-ments	Other income	Total income	Expenses	Inventory change	Net income
Anderson	5,552	147	2,984	8,683	6,296	-78	2,309
Bedford	37,500	1,503	7,641	46,644	35,360	-742	10,542
Benton	5,212	1,135	3,015	9,362	5,610	-199	3,553
Bledsoe	12,017	785	3,733	16,535	14,176	-285	2,074
Blount	21,020	340	7,533	28,893	18,319	-323	10,251
Bradley	33,915	908	4,366	39,189	28,194	-326	10,669
Campbell	3,255	69	2,061	5,385	3,267	-33	2,085
Cannon	13,382	721	4,992	19,095	12,946	-307	5,842
Carroll	19,660	4,298	6,290	30,248	27,765	1	2,484
Carter	6,430	159	3,005	9,594	5,811	-39	3,744
Cheatham	5,802	180	3,508	9,490	5,337	6	4,159
Chester	7,707	1,982	3,518	13,207	10,604	27	2,630
Claiborne	20,229	359	6,241	26,829	14,946	60	11,943
Clay	6,064	369	2,776	9,209	6,376	-80	2,753
Cocke	15,074	452	4,075	19,601	16,102	-85	3,414
Coffee	29,508	1,469	7,015	37,992	32,207	-491	5,294
Crockett	37,187	8,487	7,431	53,105	44,708	5,222	13,619
Cumberland	17,213	573	4,667	22,453	16,821	-217	5,415
Davidson	18,830	157	4,317	23,304	15,082	-225	7,997
Decatur	8,391	670	4,855	13,916	10,069	-162	3,685
DeKalb	21,628	555	4,048	26,231	19,084	-165	6,982
Dickson	13,653	259	7,386	21,298	15,299	-257	5,742
Dyer	38,082	6,298	10,657	55,037	50,870	-1,272	2,895
Fayette	73,884	7,554	10,381	91,819	79,663	2,199	14,355
Fentress	12,997	621	3,688	17,306	14,429	-206	2,671
Franklin	45,338	1,140	6,722	53,200	42,963	-305	9,932
Gibson	54,196	11,140	12,435	77,771	66,449	1,152	12,474
Giles	37,130	2,083	9,027	48,240	40,323	-649	7,268
Grainger	11,674	233	4,964	16,871	10,102	-64	6,705
Greene	47,032	2,037	13,159	62,228	55,371	-161	6,696
Grundy	16,361	307	2,006	18,674	10,997	-141	7,536
Hamblen	13,071	180	4,384	17,635	15,273	-198	2,164
Hamilton	17,137	308	4,085	21,530	15,768	-122	5,640
Hancock	6,031	200	2,317	8,548	4,201	5	4,352
Hardeman	17,419	3,589	8,598	29,606	23,710	748	6,644
Hardin	14,856	2,132	6,214	23,202	16,431	-403	6,368
Hawkins	17,674	591	7,694	25,959	19,466	-79	6,414
Haywood	42,474	9,619	8,704	60,797	52,836	5,442	13,403
Henderson	19,652	4,832	6,825	31,309	19,824	-353	11,132
Henry	22,033	3,928	9,201	35,162	34,164	-527	471
Hickman	9,661	428	4,757	14,846	10,791	-231	3,824
Houston	3,155	196	1,878	5,229	3,152	-55	2,022
Humphreys	9,015	562	3,899	13,476	9,948	-262	3,266
Jackson	5,641	213	3,126	8,980	5,463	-49	3,468
Jefferson	20,999	802	7,159	28,960	22,022	-326	6,612
Johnson	8,967	134	4,383	13,484	9,665	-18	3,801
Knox	22,887	288	8,318	31,493	24,322	-283	6,888
Lake	14,506	1,813	4,530	20,849	19,748	-624	477
Lauderdale	35,163	6,001	7,735	48,899	41,361	680	8,218
Lawrence	29,086	2,852	9,426	41,364	35,103	-723	5,538

TABLE 11.14--FARM INCOME, BY SOURCE, COUNTIES, 1987 [In thousands of dollars] (Continued)

County	Receipts from marketing	Government payments	Other income	Total income	Expenses	Inventory change	Net income
Lewis	1,684	189	1,264	3,137	1,885	-68	1,184
Lincoln	42,584	2,197	10,313	55,094	45,096	-971	9,027
Loudon	29,791	549	4,834	35,174	27,331	-201	7,642
McMinn	41,932	1,274	6,835	50,041	45,661	-391	3,989
McNairy	16,280	3,075	6,161	25,516	22,925	-172	2,419
Macon	13,366	623	5,533	19,522	12,447	-10	7,065
Madison	26,651	5,265	7,862	39,778	34,878	2,374	7,274
Marion	6,502	372	3,154	10,028	7,326	-164	2,538
Marshall	28,089	939	6,358	35,386	28,739	-508	6,139
Maury	28,495	1,159	10,732	40,386	34,548	-656	5,182
Meigs	5,563	463	2,103	8,129	5,661	-92	2,376
Monroe	20,730	519	5,655	26,904	22,078	-233	4,593
Montgomery	24,181	2,702	9,222	36,105	31,062	-60	4,983
Moore	14,791	112	2,232	17,135	13,980	-210	2,945
Morgan	5,441	200	2,235	7,876	4,766	-87	3,023
Obion	44,826	8,383	12,634	65,843	60,750	-1,501	3,592
Overton	13,197	721	5,991	19,909	13,331	-264	6,314
Perry	4,711	479	3,835	9,025	5,390	-108	3,527
Pickett	3,487	306	2,364	6,157	5,225	-18	914
Polk	16,591	599	1,869	19,059	14,076	-164	4,819
Putnam	13,074	363	6,253	19,690	12,087	-241	7,362
Rhea	10,752	640	2,216	13,608	9,339	-99	4,170
Roane	7,568	183	3,471	11,222	7,661	-124	3,437
Robertson	57,343	3,357	14,087	74,787	71,463	-326	2,998
Rutherford	28,336	1,414	9,552	39,302	29,144	-627	9,531
Scott	5,014	80	1,524	6,618	5,175	-72	1,371
Sequatchie	3,129	206	1,165	4,500	3,067	-98	1,335
Sevier	9,077	230	4,642	13,949	9,932	-139	3,878
Shelby	36,125	3,278	11,282	50,685	37,884	555	13,356
Smith	15,046	305	4,644	19,995	15,360	-272	4,363
Stewart	4,875	100	2,895	7,870	4,872	-42	2,956
Sullivan	18,018	181	7,576	25,775	18,894	-120	6,761
Sumner	34,013	1,231	12,178	47,422	37,305	-296	9,821
Tipton	36,979	5,044	9,079	51,102	46,092	2,413	7,423
Trousdale	6,160	150	2,080	8,390	5,790	52	2,652
Unicoi	1,355	61	915	2,331	1,343	47	1,035
Union	4,251	81	3,150	7,482	4,667	42	2,857
Van Buren	7,926	113	1,182	9,221	4,866	-126	4,229
Warren	114,821	1,459	9,211	125,491	105,088	-443	19,960
Washington	35,271	1,148	10,254	46,673	34,291	-248	12,134
Wayne	7,832	623	4,079	12,534	7,952	-233	4,349
Weakley	37,741	8,472	8,380	54,593	49,086	-826	4,681
White	19,387	907	7,860	28,154	19,803	-309	8,042
Williamson	32,736	930	14,889	48,555	37,905	-543	10,107
Wilson	23,399	405	8,821	32,625	23,255	-494	8,876

Source: U.S. Department of Commerce, Bureau of Economic Analysis, Regional Economic Information System, direct subscription.

FIGURE 11.2
Cash Receipts from Farm Marketings, Tennessee Counties, 1987

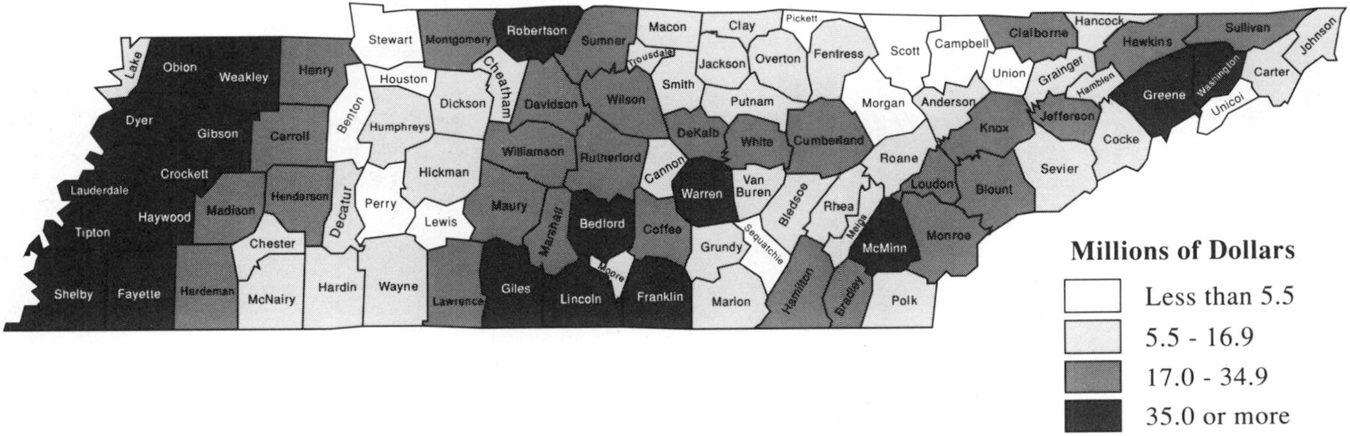

Source: U.S. Department of Commerce, Bureau of Economic Analysis.

TABLE 11.15--CASH RECEIPTS FROM FARM MARKETINGS, COUNTIES, 1987 [In thousands of dollars]

County	Cash receipts	Percentage of total	County	Cash receipts	Percentage of total
Anderson			Cocke		
Marketing total	5,552	100.0	Marketing total	15,074	100.0
Livestock	4,952	89.2	Livestock	8,147	54.0
Crops	600	10.8	Crops	6,927	46.0
Bedford			Coffee		
Marketing total	37,500	100.0	Marketing total	29,508	100.0
Livestock	34,236	91.3	Livestock	22,736	77.1
Crops	3,264	8.7	Crops	6,772	22.9
Benton			Crockett		
Marketing total	5,212	100.0	Marketing total	37,187	100.0
Livestock	2,919	56.0	Livestock	2,998	8.1
Crops	2,293	44.0	Crops	34,189	91.9
Bledsoe			Cumberland		
Marketing total	12,017	100.0	Marketing total	17,213	100.0
Livestock	8,529	71.0	Livestock	10,232	59.4
Crops	3,488	29.0	Crops	6,981	40.6
Blount			Davidson		
Marketing total	21,020	100.0	Marketing total	18,830	100.0
Livestock	13,185	62.7	Livestock	5,772	30.7
Crops	7,835	37.3	Crops	13,058	69.3
Bradley			Decatur		
Marketing total	33,915	100.0	Marketing total	8,391	100.0
Livestock	32,801	96.7	Livestock	7,227	86.1
Crops	1,114	3.3	Crops	1,164	13.9
Campbell			DeKalb		
Marketing total	3,255	100.0	Marketing total	21,628	100.0
Livestock	2,195	67.4	Livestock	5,765	26.7
Crops	1,060	32.6	Crops	15,863	73.3
Cannon			Dickson		
Marketing total	13,382	100.0	Marketing total	13,653	100.0
Livestock	11,562	86.4	Livestock	10,764	78.8
Crops	1,820	13.6	Crops	2,889	21.2
Carroll			Dyer		
Marketing total	19,660	100.0	Marketing total	38,082	100.0
Livestock	9,670	49.2	Livestock	6,922	18.2
Crops	9,990	50.8	Crops	31,160	81.8
Carter			Fayette		
Marketing total	6,430	100.0	Marketing total	73,884	100.0
Livestock	4,144	64.4	Livestock	43,841	59.3
Crops	2,286	35.6	Crops	30,043	40.7
Cheatham			Fentress		
Marketing total	5,802	100.0	Marketing total	12,997	100.0
Livestock	2,738	47.2	Livestock	10,440	80.3
Crops	3,064	52.8	Crops	2,557	19.7
Chester			Franklin		
Marketing total	7,707	100.0	Marketing total	45,338	100.0
Livestock	4,868	63.2	Livestock	26,095	57.6
Crops	2,839	36.8	Crops	19,243	42.4
Claiborne			Gibson		
Marketing total	20,229	100.0	Marketing total	54,196	100.0
Livestock	13,326	65.9	Livestock	18,047	33.3
Crops	6,903	34.1	Crops	36,149	66.7
Clay			Giles		
Marketing total	6,064	100.0	Marketing total	37,130	100.0
Livestock	4,059	66.9	Livestock	34,639	93.3
Crops	2,005	33.1	Crops	2,491	6.7

TABLE 11.15--CASH RECEIPTS FROM FARM MARKETINGS, COUNTIES, 1987 [In thousands of dollars] (Continued)

County	Cash receipts	Percentage of total
Grainger		
Marketing total	11,674	100.0
Livestock	7,390	63.3
Crops	4,284	36.7
Greene		
Marketing total	47,032	100.0
Livestock	34,761	73.9
Crops	12,271	26.1
Grundy		
Marketing total	16,361	100.0
Livestock	13,504	82.5
Crops	2,857	17.5
Hamblen		
Marketing total	13,071	100.0
Livestock	10,746	82.2
Crops	2,325	17.8
Hamilton		
Marketing total	17,137	100.0
Livestock	9,939	58.0
Crops	7,198	42.0
Hancock		
Marketing total	6,031	100.0
Livestock	3,014	50.0
Crops	3,017	50.0
Hardeman		
Marketing total	17,419	100.0
Livestock	6,253	35.9
Crops	11,166	64.1
Hardin		
Marketing total	14,856	100.0
Livestock	10,645	71.7
Crops	4,211	28.3
Hawkins		
Marketing total	17,674	100.0
Livestock	10,661	60.3
Crops	7,013	39.7
Haywood		
Marketing total	42,474	100.0
Livestock	2,894	6.8
Crops	39,580	93.2
Henderson		
Marketing total	19,652	100.0
Livestock	14,478	73.7
Crops	5,174	26.3
Henry		
Marketing total	22,033	100.0
Livestock	12,694	57.6
Crops	9,339	42.4
Hickman		
Marketing total	9,661	100.0
Livestock	8,422	87.2
Crops	1,239	12.8
Houston		
Marketing total	3,155	100.0
Livestock	2,465	78.1
Crops	690	21.9
Humphreys		
Marketing total	9,015	100.0
Livestock	7,246	80.4
Crops	1,769	19.6
Jackson		
Marketing total	5,641	100.0
Livestock	3,335	59.1
Crops	2,306	40.9
Jefferson		
Marketing total	20,999	100.0
Livestock	16,884	80.4
Crops	4,115	19.6
Johnson		
Marketing total	8,967	100.0
Livestock	5,907	65.9
Crops	3,060	34.1
Knox		
Marketing total	22,887	100.0
Livestock	11,287	49.3
Crops	11,600	50.7
Lake		
Marketing total	14,506	100.0
Livestock	44	0.3
Crops	14,462	99.7
Lauderdale		
Marketing total	35,163	100.0
Livestock	4,373	12.4
Crops	30,790	87.6
Lawrence		
Marketing total	29,086	100.0
Livestock	23,968	82.4
Crops	5,118	17.6
Lewis		
Marketing total	1,684	100.0
Livestock	1,329	78.9
Crops	355	21.1
Lincoln		
Marketing total	42,584	100.0
Livestock	34,926	82.0
Crops	7,658	18.0
Loudon		
Marketing total	29,791	100.0
Livestock	15,636	52.5
Crops	14,155	47.5
McMinn		
Marketing total	41,932	100.0
Livestock	39,577	94.4
Crops	2,355	5.6
McNairy		
Marketing total	16,280	100.0
Livestock	10,799	66.3
Crops	5,481	33.7
Macon		
Marketing total	13,366	100.0
Livestock	7,951	59.5
Crops	5,415	40.5

TABLE 11.15--CASH RECEIPTS FROM FARM MARKETINGS, COUNTIES, 1987 [In thousands of dollars] (Continued)

County	Cash receipts	Percentage of total	County	Cash receipts	Percentage of total
Madison			Putnam		
Marketing total	26,651	100.0	Marketing total	13,074	100.0
Livestock	4,864	18.3	Livestock	9,465	72.4
Crops	21,787	81.7	Crops	3,609	27.6
Marion			Rhea		
Marketing total	6,502	100.0	Marketing total	10,752	100.0
Livestock	4,269	65.7	Livestock	6,381	59.3
Crops	2,233	34.3	Crops	4,371	40.7
Marshall			Roane		
Marketing total	28,089	100.0	Marketing total	7,568	100.0
Livestock	26,074	92.8	Livestock	6,495	85.8
Crops	2,015	7.2	Crops	1,073	14.2
Maury			Robertson		
Marketing total	28,495	100.0	Marketing total	57,343	100.0
Livestock	22,700	79.7	Livestock	31,756	55.4
Crops	5,795	20.3	Crops	25,587	44.6
Meigs			Rutherford		
Marketing total	5,563	100.0	Marketing total	28,336	100.0
Livestock	4,956	89.1	Livestock	24,150	85.2
Crops	607	10.9	Crops	4,186	14.8
Monroe			Scott		
Marketing total	20,730	100.0	Marketing total	5,014	100.0
Livestock	17,958	86.6	Livestock	4,766	95.1
Crops	2,772	13.4	Crops	248	4.9
Montgomery			Sequatchie		
Marketing total	24,181	100.0	Marketing total	3,129	100.0
Livestock	14,368	59.4	Livestock	2,723	87.0
Crops	9,813	40.6	Crops	406	13.0
Moore			Sevier		
Marketing total	14,791	100.0	Marketing total	9,077	100.0
Livestock	13,965	94.4	Livestock	6,661	73.4
Crops	826	5.6	Crops	2,416	26.6
Morgan			Shelby		
Marketing total	5,441	100.0	Marketing total	36,125	100.0
Livestock	2,907	53.4	Livestock	7,058	19.5
Crops	2,534	46.6	Crops	29,067	80.5
Obion			Smith		
Marketing total	44,826	100.0	Marketing total	15,046	100.0
Livestock	16,828	37.5	Livestock	10,344	68.7
Crops	27,998	62.5	Crops	4,702	31.3
Overton			Stewart		
Marketing total	13,197	100.0	Marketing total	4,875	100.0
Livestock	11,021	83.5	Livestock	2,823	57.9
Crops	2,176	16.5	Crops	2,052	42.1
Perry			Sullivan		
Marketing total	4,711	100.0	Marketing total	18,018	100.0
Livestock	3,789	80.4	Livestock	12,475	69.2
Crops	922	19.6	Crops	5,543	30.8
Pickett			Sumner		
Marketing total	3,487	100.0	Marketing total	34,013	100.0
Livestock	2,161	62.0	Livestock	24,605	72.3
Crops	1,326	38.0	Crops	9,408	27.7
Polk			Tipton		
Marketing total	16,591	100.0	Marketing total	36,979	100.0
Livestock	16,318	98.4	Livestock	3,889	10.5
Crops	273	1.6	Crops	33,090	89.5

TABLE 11.15--CASH RECEIPTS FROM FARM MARKETINGS, COUNTIES, 1987 [In thousands of dollars] (Continued)

County	Cash receipts	Percentage of total	County	Cash receipts	Percentage of total
Trousdale			Wayne		
Marketing total	6,160	100.0	Marketing total	7,832	100.0
Livestock	3,032	49.2	Livestock	6,984	89.2
Crops	3,128	50.8	Crops	848	10.8
Unicoi			Weakley		
Marketing total	1,355	100.0	Marketing total	37,741	100.0
Livestock	256	18.9	Livestock	17,784	47.1
Crops	1,099	81.1	Crops	19,957	52.9
Union			White		
Marketing total	4,251	100.0	Marketing total	19,387	100.0
Livestock	2,310	54.3	Livestock	17,028	87.8
Crops	1,941	45.7	Crops	2,359	12.2
Van Buren			Williamson		
Marketing total	7,926	100.0	Marketing total	32,736	100.0
Livestock	6,838	86.3	Livestock	27,874	85.1
Crops	1,088	13.7	Crops	4,862	14.9
Warren			Wilson		
Marketing total	114,821	100.0	Marketing total	23,399	100.0
Livestock	21,520	18.7	Livestock	20,677	88.4
Crops	93,301	81.3	Crops	2,722	11.6
Washington					
Marketing total	35,271	100.0			
Livestock	24,556	69.6			
Crops	10,715	30.4			

Source: U.S. Department of Commerce, Bureau of Economic Analysis, Regional Economic Information System, direct subscription.

TABLE 11.16--RURAL FARM POPULATION BY 1980 AND 1970 FARM DEFINITIONS, TENNESSEE AND COUNTIES, 1980

County	Farm population, 1980		County	Farm population, 1980	
	Current definition [1]	Previous definition [2]		Current definition [1]	Previous definition [2]
Anderson	717	1,248	Coffee	2,194	3,295
Bedford	2,591	3,468	Crockett	2,174	2,589
Benton	867	1,505	Cumberland	917	2,077
Bledsoe	938	1,268	Davidson	411	618
Blount	1,961	3,363	Decatur	1,105	1,596
Bradley	1,356	1,898	DeKalb	1,459	2,151
Campbell	950	1,590	Dickson	2,253	3,239
Cannon	1,760	2,591	Dyer	1,917	2,661
Carroll	2,280	3,338	Fayette	2,119	2,894
Carter	957	1,971	Fentress	906	1,573
Cheatham	1,169	1,803	Franklin	2,518	3,448
Chester	861	1,539	Gibson	4,133	5,302
Claiborne	3,261	5,362	Giles	3,258	4,733
Clay	1,611	2,197	Grainger	2,277	4,103
Cocke	2,622	4,106	Greene	6,780	9,589

TABLE 11.16--RURAL FARM POPULATION BY 1980 AND 1970 FARM DEFINITIONS, TENNESSEE AND COUNTIES, 1980 (Continued)

	Farm population, 1980			Farm population, 1980	
County	Current definition [1]	Previous definition [2]	County	Current definition [1]	Previous definition [2]
Grundy	939	1,407	Obion	3,117	4,058
Hamblen	1,897	2,520	Overton	1,839	3,169
Hamilton	762	1,104	Perry	664	1,045
Hancock	1,670	2,950	Pickett	576	1,222
Hardeman	1,029	1,531	Polk	475	646
Hardin	1,127	1,692	Putnam	1,878	3,668
Hawkins	3,343	6,077	Rhea	546	911
Haywood	1,506	2,481	Roane	855	1,389
Henderson	2,151	3,097	Robertson	4,849	5,868
Henry	2,636	3,665	Rutherford	3,276	5,005
Hickman	1,531	2,309	Scott	407	657
Houston	408	760	Sequatchie	282	390
Humphreys	985	1,369	Sevier	1,859	3,569
Jackson	1,433	2,230	Shelby	1,042	2,065
Jefferson	2,359	3,549	Smith	3,067	3,867
Johnson	1,740	3,287	Stewart	1,029	1,431
Knox	1,466	3,139	Sullivan	2,118	3,744
Lake	374	452	Sumner	4,063	6,265
Lauderdale	1,907	2,767	Tipton	1,983	2,769
Lawrence	4,129	5,727	Trousdale	1,021	1,232
Lewis	532	812	Unicoi	519	1,064
Lincoln	4,086	5,573	Union	1,011	1,953
Loudon	1,396	2,043	Van Buren	355	537
McMinn	1,449	2,666	Warren	2,995	3,751
McNairy	1,527	2,503	Washington	3,744	5,903
Macon	3,019	4,169	Wayne	1,566	2,567
Madison	1,856	2,785	Weakley	3,370	4,683
Marion	791	1,062	White	2,314	3,135
Marshall	2,451	2,951	Williamson	3,362	4,711
Maury	3,402	4,374	Wilson	3,042	4,698
Meigs	434	823	TENNESSEE	175,673	263,411
Monroe	1,677	3,108			
Montgomery	2,720	3,299			
Moore	818	1,167			
Morgan	577	876			

Note: For total county population see Table 1.7. For county, urban and rural population see Table 1.9.

1. Under the 1980 definition, the farm population includes all persons living in rural areas on places of 1 or more acres from which at least $1,000 worth of agricultural products were sold during 1979.

2. Under the 1970 definition, the farm population includes all persons living in rural areas on a place of 10 or more acres with at least $50 worth of annual sales or on a place of fewer than 10 acres with at least $250 worth of agricultural sales.

Source: U.S. Department of Commerce, Bureau of the Census, 1980 Census of Population, *Rural and Farm Population by Current (1980) and Previous (1970) Farm Definitions, for States and Counties: 1980*, PC 80-S1-19.

TABLE 11.17--RURAL FARM POPULATION AND PERCENTAGE OF TOTAL POPULATION, SOUTHEASTERN STATES, 1950–1980, DECENNIAL CENSUS YEARS

	1980		1980[a]		1970		1960		1950	
State	Number (1,000)	%	Number (1,000)	%	Number (1,000)	%	Number (1,000)	%	Number (1,000)	%
TENNESSEE	176	3.8	263	5.7	317	8.1	587	16.5	1,016	30.9
Alabama	88	2.3	139	3.6	160	4.6	403	12.3	960	31.4
Arkansas	108	4.7	142	6.2	174	9.0	332	18.6	802	42.0
Florida	59	0.1	85	0.9	72	1.1	105	2.1	233	8.4
Georgia	121	2.2	164	3.0	172	3.7	407	10.3	962	27.9
Kentucky	245	6.7	326	8.9	382	11.9	548	18.0	974	33.1
Louisiana	59	1.4	85	2.0	114	3.1	233	7.2	567	21.1
Mississippi	85	3.4	131	5.2	210	9.5	543	24.9	1,097	50.4
North Carolina	188	3.2	269	4.6	375	7.4	808	17.7	1,377	33.9
South Carolina	54	1.7	84	2.7	112	4.3	351	14.7	701	33.1
Virginia	113	2.1	166	3.1	193	4.1	397	10.0	723	22.1
West Virginia	29	1.5	51	2.6	57	3.3	121	6.5	411	20.5

Note: Percentages computed by the Center for Business and Economic Research.

a. This set of population figures for 1980 is based on the previous farm definition which allowed a place that had as little as $50 of agricultural sales per year to qualify as a farm. For the 1980 Census, the annual dollar value of agricultural sales required for a place to be considered a farm was raised to $1,000. This definitional change is reflected in the 1980 farm population figures shown in the first column.

Source: U.S. Department of Commerce, Bureau of the Census, *1980 Census of Population, General Social and Economic Characteristics*, individual states; "Rural Population by Farm-Nonfarm Residence for Counties in the United States: 1970;" and *Characteristics of the Population*, for 1950 and 1960.

TABLE 11.18--SELECTED FARM STATISTICS, SOUTHEASTERN STATES, 1987

State	Farm acreage	Number of farms	Average size of farm (acres)	Average value of land and buildings		Market value of products sold	
				Per farm	Per acre	Total (1,000)	Per farm
TENNESSEE	11,731,386	79,711	147	$146,126	$1,001	$1,617,636	$20,294
Alabama	9,145,753	43,318	211	168,161	800	1,908,303	44,053
Arkansas	14,355,611	48,242	298	225,604	761	3,320,258	68,825
Florida	11,194,090	36,556	306	543,830	1,790	4,351,383	119,033
Georgia	10,744,718	43,552	247	226,217	920	2,814,592	64,626
Kentucky	14,012,700	92,453	152	135,696	896	2,075,571	22,450
Louisiana	8,007,173	27,350	293	268,630	940	1,340,162	49,000
Mississippi	10,746,190	34,074	315	215,209	697	1,862,903	54,672
North Carolina	9,447,705	59,284	159	199,781	1,263	3,541,419	59,737
South Carolina	4,758,631	20,517	232	201,169	871	878,683	42,827
Virginia	8,676,336	44,799	194	232,374	1,198	1,588,770	35,464
West Virginia	3,372,955	17,237	196	130,802	682	270,639	15,701

Source: U.S. Department of Commerce, Bureau of the Census, *1987 Census of Agriculture*, individual states.

TABLE 11.19--NUMBER AND PERCENTAGE OF FARMS, BY ECONOMIC CLASS, SOUTHEASTERN STATES, 1987

		Economic class (based on farm product sales)							
State	Total	$500,000 or more	$250,000–499,999	$100,000–249,999	$40,000–99,999	$20,000–39,999	$10,000–19,999	$5,000–9,999	Less than $5,000
TENNESSEE									
Number	79,711	296	780	2,388	3,815	5,005	9,472	14,398	43,557
Percentage	100.0	0.4	1.0	3.0	4.8	6.3	11.9	18.1	54.6
Alabama									
Number	43,318	540	1,253	2,693	2,657	2,615	4,218	6,534	22,808
Percentage	100.0	1.2	2.9	6.2	6.1	6.0	9.7	15.1	52.7
Arkansas									
Number	48,242	903	2,511	5,686	4,199	3,139	4,964	7,101	19,739
Percentage	100.0	1.9	5.2	11.8	8.7	6.5	10.3	14.7	40.9
Florida									
Number	36,556	1,455	1,139	2,202	3,151	3,044	3,676	4,470	17,419
Percentage	100.0	4.0	3.1	6.0	8.6	8.3	10.1	12.2	47.7
Georgia									
Number	43,552	935	2,025	3,936	3,821	3,227	4,167	5,805	19,636
Percentage	100.0	2.1	4.6	9.0	8.8	7.4	9.6	13.3	45.1
Kentucky									
Number	92,453	249	631	2,667	6,615	9,413	14,457	17,620	40,801
Percentage	100.0	0.3	0.7	2.9	7.2	10.2	15.6	19.1	44.1
Louisiana									
Number	27,350	386	927	2,396	2,636	1,812	2,441	3,448	13,304
Percentage	100.0	1.4	3.4	8.8	9.6	6.6	8.9	12.6	48.6
Mississippi									
Number	34,074	694	1,318	2,405	2,178	2,066	3,307	5,012	17,094
Percentage	100.0	2.0	3.9	7.1	6.4	6.1	9.7	14.7	50.2
North Carolina									
Number	59,284	1,084	2,177	4,857	5,726	5,213	6,664	8,344	25,219
Percentage	100.0	1.8	3.7	8.2	9.7	8.8	11.2	14.1	42.5

TABLE 11.19--NUMBER AND PERCENTAGE OF FARMS, BY ECONOMIC CLASS, SOUTHEASTERN STATES, 1987 (Continued)

State	Total	Economic class (based on farm product sales)							
		$500,000 or more	$250,000–499,999	$100,000–249,999	$40,000–99,999	$20,000–39,999	$10,000–19,999	$5,000–9,999	Less than $5,000
South Carolina									
Number	20,517	313	478	1,114	1,343	1,395	2,039	2,900	10,935
Percentage	100.0	1.5	2.3	5.4	6.5	6.8	9.9	14.1	53.3
Virginia									
Number	44,799	467	966	2,144	2,963	3,567	5,495	7,580	21,617
Percentage	100.0	1.0	2.2	4.8	6.6	8.0	12.3	16.9	48.3
West Virginia									
Number	17,237	72	115	299	553	699	1,512	2,547	11,440
Percentage	100.0	0.4	0.7	1.7	3.2	4.1	8.8	14.8	66.4

Note: Farms include institutional farms, experiment and research farms, and Indian reservations. Percentages computed by Center for Business and Economic Research.

Source: U.S. Department of Commerce, Bureau of the Census, *1987 Census of Agriculture*, individual states.

TABLE 11.20--TYPE OF FARM OWNERSHIP, SOUTHEASTERN STATES, 1987

State	Farm acreage	Number of farms	Family farms		Partnership farms		Corporate farms	
			Number	%	Number	%	Number	%
TENNESSEE	11,731,386	79,711	71,976	90.3	6,947	8.7	496	0.6
Alabama	9,145,753	43,318	39,553	91.3	3,014	7.0	570	1.3
Arkansas	14,355,611	48,242	42,885	88.9	3,626	7.5	1,542	3.2
Florida	11,194,090	36,556	28,943	79.2	3,289	9.0	3,961	10.8
Georgia	10,744,718	43,552	38,806	89.1	3,382	7.8	1,106	2.5
Kentucky	14,012,700	92,453	78,463	84.9	12,717	13.8	817	0.9
Louisiana	8,007,173	27,350	24,322	88.9	1,926	7.0	905	3.3
Mississippi	10,746,190	34,074	30,326	89.0	2,770	8.1	823	2.4
North Carolina	9,447,705	59,284	52,398	88.4	5,238	8.8	1,355	2.3
South Carolina	4,758,631	20,517	18,337	89.4	1,583	7.7	488	2.4
Virginia	8,676,336	44,799	39,344	87.8	4,004	8.9	1,173	2.6
West Virginia	3,372,955	17,237	15,988	92.8	971	5.6	197	1.1

Note: Percentages computed by Center for Business and Economic Research. Percentages will not add to 100 because cooperative, estate, and institutional farms are not shown separately.

Source: U.S. Department of Commerce, Bureau of the Census, *1987 Census of Agriculture*, individual states.

TABLE 11.21--FARM REAL ESTATE: AVERAGE VALUE OF LAND AND BUILDINGS PER ACRE, SOUTHEASTERN STATES AND UNITED STATES, 1980–1988, SELECTED YEARS

State	Average value of land and buildings per acre ($)					Indexes of average value per acre (1977 = 100)				
	1988	1987	1986	1985	1980	1988	1987	1986	1985	1980
TENNESSEE	1,104	1,012	992	982	976	143	131	128	127	136
Alabama	731	731	761	769	780	146	146	152	154	149
Arkansas	645	634	705	849	918	116	114	126	152	163
Florida	1,596	1,464	1,435	1,527	1,381	154	141	138	147	141[a]
Georgia	865	846	822	865	896	115	113	110	116	132
Kentucky	786	791	870	906	976	112	113	124	129	147
Louisiana	708	734	1,005	1,256	1,256	102	106	145	181	169
Mississippi	657	654	752	835	819	129	128	147	163	156
North Carolina	1,062	1,096	1,130	1,242	1,219	121	125	129	142	141
South Carolina	874	794	872	899	900	118	107	117	121	130
Virginia	1,143	1,111	1,146	1,091	1,028	147	143	147	140	139
West Virginia	542	527	537	554	669	140	136	139	143	150
UNITED STATES	564	547[r]	595	679	737	106	103	112	128	145

r revised.

a. Estimated using the average of the percentage changes in the Alabama and Georgia indexes.

Source: U.S. Department of Commerce, Bureau of the Census, *Statistical Abstract of the United States, 1989*, and earlier editions.

TABLE 11.22--TAXES ON FARM REAL ESTATE, SOUTHEASTERN STATES, 1980–1985, SELECTED YEARS

State	Amount levied on farm real estate ($1,000,000)				Taxes per acre ($)				Taxes per $100 of full value ($)			
	1985	1984	1983	1980	1985	1984	1983	1980	1985	1984	1983	1980
TENNESSEE	46.4	46.4	45.5	41.1	3.73	3.73	3.66	3.25	0.38	0.36	0.40	0.34
Alabama	12.4	12.4	12.2	10.1	1.14	1.14	1.14	0.90	0.15	0.14	0.13	0.11
Arkansas	37.0	37.0	33.6	30.6	2.61	2.61	2.37	2.14	0.31	0.28	0.24	0.23
Florida	85.3	83.6	82.9	78.3	6.97	6.83	6.83	6.21	0.46	0.42	0.47	0.46
Georgia	63.7	59.5	57.1	50.5	4.44	4.15	4.07	3.46	0.51	0.46	0.50	0.40
Kentucky	30.0	29.5	30.0	29.4	2.16	2.12	2.16	2.10	0.24	0.21	0.22	0.22
Louisiana	19.8	19.8	19.6	15.9	2.21	2.21	2.21	1.79	0.18	0.16	0.15	0.14
Mississippi	28.1	28.1	22.2	21.4	2.14	2.14	1.71	1.61	0.26	0.23	0.19	0.20
North Carolina	51.6	49.6	47.2	42.1	4.94	4.75	4.57	3.83	0.40	0.34	0.35	0.32
South Carolina	14.1	14.1	13.1	12.2	2.56	2.56	2.46	2.12	0.28	0.28	0.28	0.24
Virginia	41.5	41.5	40.7	34.8	4.57	4.57	4.48	3.83	0.42	0.41	0.43	0.38
West Virginia	3.4	3.4	3.1	2.7	0.94	0.94	0.92	0.78	0.17	0.14	0.11	0.11

Source: U.S. Department of Agriculture, Statistical Reporting Service, *Agricultural Statistics, 1987*, and earlier editions.

TABLE 11.23--FARM DEBT OUTSTANDING (INCLUDING OPERATOR HOUSEHOLDS), SOUTHEASTERN STATES, 1975–1987, SELECTED YEARS
[In millions of dollars]

State	1987		1986[r]		1985[r]		1980		1975	
	Real estate	Nonreal estate	Real estate	Nonreal estate	Real estate	Nonreal estate	Real estate	Nonreal estate	Real estate	Nonreal estate
TENNESSEE	1,280	999	1,372	1,096	1,509	1,244	1,583	1,493	934	801
Alabama	974	748	1,104	830	1,312	935	1,241	1,129	661	523
Arkansas	1,767	1,454	1,901	1,541	2,062	1,718	1,967	1,642	1,130	837
Florida	2,576	1,045	2,737	1,134	2,893	1,204	2,334	1,294	1,346	668
Georgia	1,805	1,544	1,933	1,614	2,225	1,908	2,273	2,253	1,305	885
Kentucky	1,903	1,043	2,028	1,311	2,180	1,476	2,151	1,627	1,106	897
Louisiana	1,123	1,295	1,246	1,339	1,520	1,416	1,565	1,170	737	530
Mississippi	1,662	1,603	1,803	1,723	2,022	1,877	1,841	1,742	975	740
North Carolina	1,702	1,234	1,895	1,323	2,165	1,581	1,885	1,818	907	855
South Carolina	677	483	765	519	918	606	820	707	482	319
Virginia	1,208	787	1,235	821	1,332	902	1,149	852	644	402
West Virginia	211	93	203	98	221	106	235	125	129	72

Note: Data are as of December 31. Real estate farm debt includes that owed to federal land banks, Farmer's Home Administration, life insurance companies, banks, and individuals. Nonreal estate debt includes that owed to banks, Production Credit Association (excluding loans for aquaculture), federal intermediate credit banks, Farmer's Home Administration and Commodity Credit Corporation.

r revised.

Source: U.S. Department of Agriculture, Economic Research Service, *Economic Indicators of the Farm Sector, State Financial Summary, 1987*.

TABLE 11.24--INDEXES OF PRICES RECEIVED AND PAID BY FARMERS, UNITED STATES, 1973–1987

	Prices received			Prices paid									
					Production items								
Year	All farm products	All crops	Livestock and products	Total	Total [1]	Feed	Seed	Fuels and energy	Interest	Taxes	Wage rates	Ratio [2]	Parity ratio (1910–14=100)
1987	127	106	146	162	147	103	148	161	207	136	167	78	52
1986	123	107r	138	159	144r	108	148	162	219r	134	160	77	51
1985	128	120	136	163	151	116	153	201	237r	133	154	79	52
1984	142	139	146	165	155	135	151	201	257	132	151	86	57
1983	135	128	141	161	152	134	141	202	258	129	148	84	56
1982	133	121	145	159	153	122	141	210	249	124	144	84	56
1981	139	134	143	150	148	134	138	213	216	123	137	93	61
1980	134	125	144	138	138	123	118	188	178	115	127r	97	65
1979	132	116	147	123	125	110	110	137	143	107	117	107	71
1978	115	105	124	108	108	98	105	105	117	100	107	106	70
1976	102	102	101	95	97	103	92	93	88	94	93	107	71
1975	101	105	98	89	91	100	94	88	77	87	85	113	76
1974	105	117	94	81	83	104	82	79	65	81	79	130	86
1973	98	91	104	71	73	86	64	57	55	77	69	138	91

Note: Base year is 1977=100 for prices received, prices paid, and ratio unless otherwise specified.

1. Includes items not shown separately.

2. Ratio of index of prices received by farmers for all farm products to index of prices paid for commodities, services, interest, taxes, and wage rates.

r revised.

Source: U.S. Department of Commerce, Bureau of the Census, *Statistical Abstract of the United States, 1989*, and earlier editions.

TABLE 11.25--FARM MARKETINGS, 1983–1987, AND PRINCIPAL COMMODITIES RANKING, SOUTHEASTERN STATES AND UNITED STATES, 1987
[In millions of dollars]

State	Farm marketings								Principal commodities in order of marketing receipts, 1987
	1987								
	Total	Crops	Livestock and products	Rank in United States	1986 r	1985	1984	1983	
TENNESSEE	1,933	826	1,107	28	1,854	2,091	2,105	1,797	Cattle, dairy products, cotton, greenhouse.
Alabama	2,148	588	1,560	25	2,020	2,074	2,192	2,040	Broilers, cattle, eggs, greenhouse.
Arkansas	3,143	1,027	2,116	16	3,005	3,433	3,285	2,875	Broilers, soybeans, cattle, cotton.
Florida	5,227	4,125	1,102	8	4,714	4,704	4,733	4,609	Greenhouse, oranges, tomatoes, cattle.
Georgia	3,087	1,261	1,826	17	3,195	3,277	3,620	3,196	Broilers, peanuts, cattle, eggs.
Kentucky	2,417	913	1,506	23	2,402	2,934	2,703	2,742	Horses, cattle, tobacco, dairy products.
Louisiana	1,420	899	521	32	1,352	1,485	1,627	1,685	Cotton, soybeans, cattle, sugar.
Mississippi	1,979	939	1,040	27	1,796	2,250	2,164	2,073	Cotton, broilers, soybeans, cattle.
North Carolina	3,715	1,634	2,081	11	3,757	3,929	4,194	3,630	Tobacco, broilers, hogs, turkeys.
South Carolina	931	470	461	36	898	1,036	1,164	994	Tobacco, cattle, dairy products, soybeans.
Virginia	1,692	448	1,244	31	1,629	1,684	1,786	1,453	Cattle, dairy products, broilers, tobacco.
West Virginia	221	52	169	47	215	247	225	211	Cattle, dairy products, broilers, apples.
UNITED STATES	138,094	61,876	76,218	(X)	135,102	144,193	142,153	136,260	Cattle, dairy products, hogs, soybeans.

Note: Cattle include calves.

(X) not applicable.

r revised.

Source: U.S. Department of Commerce, Bureau of the Census, *Statistical Abstract of the United States, 1989.*

TABLE 11.26--CASH RECEIPTS, BY COMMODITY, SOUTHEASTERN STATES, 1987 [In thousands of dollars]

State	Total	Livestock: Total livestock	Percentage of total	Meat animals	Dairy products	Poultry and eggs	Other livestock
TENNESSEE	1,932,695	1,106,790	57.3	689,059	273,076	125,411	19,244
Alabama	2,148,055	1,559,653	72.6	552,404	73,206	899,238	34,805
Arkansas	3,143,394	2,116,476	67.3	461,507	102,098	1,467,798	85,073
Florida	5,226,998	1,101,730	21.1	411,433	360,800	223,554	105,943
Georgia	3,086,887	1,826,053	59.2	495,342	162,590	1,126,778	41,343
Kentucky	2,418,611	1,505,707	62.3	649,763	289,476	23,452	543,016
Louisiana	1,419,707	520,531	36.7	199,377	123,840	149,743	47,571
Mississippi	1,979,027	1,040,150	52.6	255,056	110,870	494,248	179,976
North Carolina	3,715,190	2,081,057	56.0	654,418	222,558	1,152,022	52,059
South Carolina	931,155	460,966	49.5	185,041	83,967	185,667	6,291
Virginia	1,692,179	1,244,029	73.5	537,093	269,730	375,297	61,909
West Virginia	220,937	168,959	76.5	72,483	43,904	51,702	870

State	Crops: Total crop	Percentage of total	Food grains	Feed crops	Cotton	Tobacco	Oil crops	Vege-tables	Fruits and nuts	Other crops
TENNESSEE	825,905	42.7	27,546	71,247	178,157	129,258	163,911	43,894	12,959	198,933
Alabama	588,402	27.4	12,148	28,081	109,475	893	183,881	90,160	18,848	144,916
Arkansas	1,026,918	32.7	269,550	68,250	270,392	0	368,767	20,789	5,080	24,090
Florida	4,125,268	78.9	4,675	29,106	11,456	22,800	71,756	1,259,201	1,360,156	1,366,118
Georgia	1,260,834	40.8	33,905	89,018	67,132	117,000	533,921	160,058	92,498	167,302
Kentucky	912,904	37.7	33,987	189,991	0	441,018	161,555	21,698	11,234	53,421
Louisiana	899,176	63.3	107,147	52,664	282,282	n.a.	197,924	59,566	10,260	189,333
Mississippi	938,877	47.4	71,626	34,807	532,112	0	237,743	27,626	9,963	25,000
North Carolina	1,634,133	44.0	39,036	122,005	35,826	730,079	296,544	145,525	64,882	200,236
South Carolina	470,189	50.5	23,977	41,493	32,444	149,140	92,146	48,303	50,983	31,703
Virginia	448,150	26.5	21,798	33,469	456	113,887	123,494	41,512	60,677	52,857
West Virginia	51,978	23.5	380	10,213	0	3,833	0	1,100	30,149	6,303

Note: Percentages were computed by the Center for Business and Economic Research.

Source: U.S. Department of Agriculture, Economic Research Service, *Economic Indicators of the Farm Sector, State Financial Summary, 1987.*

TABLE 11.27--AGRICULTURAL COOPERATIVE MEMBERS, IN-STATE HEADQUARTERS, AND BUSINESS VOLUME, BY TYPE OF COOPERATIVE, SOUTHEASTERN STATES, 1985

	Marketing			Farm supply			Related services		
State	Members	In-state head-quarters	Business volume[1] ($1,000)	Members	In-state head-quarters	Business volume[1] ($1,000)	Members	In-state head-quarters	Business volume[1] ($1,000)
TENNESSEE	59,954	19	274,925	73,705	80	608,886	1,165	2	6,219
Alabama	22,456	22	498,864	48,100	56	409,223	180	2	7,610
Arkansas	27,983	52	826,566	44,845	49	460,579	135	1	59,295
Florida	13,156	56	1,890,056	6,684	7	358,351	13,063	3	44,422
Georgia	59,278	15	747,711	3,159	6	329,871	0	0	5,566
Kentucky	97,078	24	435,902	128,454	42	341,485	4,276	26	8,576
Louisiana	7,775	35	546,052	10,347	32	250,868	1,118	3	11,988
Mississippi	26,313	73	652,796	64,765	65	446,624	1,048	4	28,233
North Carolina	102,128	30	471,068	40,009	2	195,107	61	2	7,449
South Carolina	25,031	15	235,990	15,578	2	53,270	0	0	899
Virginia	32,090	48	571,754	152,902	52	558,201	3,605	1	8,360
West Virginia	5,520	24	64,622	43,538	20	104,696	528	(a)	1,369

1. Gross business volume. Includes sales between cooperatives.

a. The cooperative with which these members are affiliated has been counted in the state in which the cooperative maintains its headquarters.

Source: U.S. Department of Agriculture, Agricultural Cooperative Service, *Farmer Cooperative Statistics, 1985*.

TABLE 11.28--GOVERNMENT PAYMENTS FOR FARM PROGRAMS, SOUTHEASTERN STATES, 1987 [In thousands of dollars]

State	Total	Conservation[1]	Feed grain program	Wheat program	Rice program	Cotton program	Wool act program	Miscellaneous programs[2]
TENNESSEE	156,745	28,339	47,385	16,326	27	38,556	71	26,041
Alabama	125,228	23,949	17,663	10,801	0	45,542	15	27,258
Arkansas	397,644	10,549	25,465	61,550	198,560	70,376	80	31,064
Florida	42,532	6,261	8,602	1,695	295	3,003	34	22,642
Georgia	245,184	21,962	65,701	35,932	0	33,529	40	88,020
Kentucky	178,338	35,644	112,187	16,539	0	1	152	13,815
Louisiana	209,299	6,001	11,022	8,988	72,933	85,800	53	24,502
Mississippi	302,538	26,322	12,418	21,601	36,758	159,413	24	46,002
North Carolina	190,172	9,025	108,375	16,612	0	10,933	78	45,149
South Carolina	114,086	10,967	36,304	15,444	0	14,757	4	36,610
Virginia	87,285	4,933	42,062	8,648	0	119	1,162	30,361
West Virginia	10,584	1,832	4,649	137	0	0	586	3,380

Note: Includes both cash payments and payment-in-kind (PIK).

1. Includes amount paid under agriculture and conservation programs (Agriculture Conservation, Emergency Conservation, and Great Plains Program.)

2. Programs included are Dairy Indemnity, Dairy Termination, Rural Clean Water, Clean Lakes, Conservation Reserve, Animal Waste Management, Forest Incentive, Water Bank, Emergency Feed, Extended Farm Storage, Extended Warehouse Storage, PIK Storage, Disaster Program Crops, Disaster Program Noncrops, Colorado River Salinity, and Milk Diversion.

Source: U.S. Department of Agriculture, Economic Research Service, *Economic Indicators of the Farm Sector, State Financial Summary, 1987*.

TABLE 11.29--AREA OF COMMERCIAL FOREST LAND, BY AREA CONDITION, AND BY OWNERSHIP CLASSES, TENNESSEE, 1980 [In thousands of acres]

Area-condition class[1]	All owner-ships	National forest	Other public	Forest industry	Farmer	Miscel-laneous private
All classes	12,879.0	557.2	602.6	1,222.8	4,548.1	5,948.3
10	5.6	0.0	0.0	5.6	0.0	0.0
20	5.7	5.5	0.0	0.0	0.0	0.2
30	5.9	0.0	0.0	5.9	0.0	0.0
40	96.4	5.5	20.3	34.5	16.2	19.9
50	2,512.0	246.2	88.4	286.7	823.9	1,066.8
60	7,613.9	244.1	392.1	729.3	2,616.7	3,631.7
70	2,639.5	55.9	101.8	160.8	1,091.3	1,229.7

1. Area-condition class definitions:
   10: Areas 100 percent or more stocked with desirable trees and not overstocked.
   20: Areas 100 percent or more stocked with desirable trees and overstocked with all live trees.
   30: Areas 60 to 100 percent stocked with desirable trees and with less than 30 percent of the area controlled by other trees, inhibiting vegetation, slash, or nonstockable conditions.
   40: Areas 60 to 100 percent stocked with desirable trees and with 30 percent or more of the area controlled by other trees, or conditions that ordinarily prevent occupancy by desirable trees.
   50: Areas less than 60 percent stocked with desirable trees, but with 100 percent or more stocking of growing-stock trees.
   60: Areas less than 60 percent stocked with desirable trees, but with 60 to 100 percent stocking of growing-stock trees.
   70: Areas less than 60 percent stocked with desirable trees and with less than 60 percent stocking of growing-stock trees.

Source: U.S. Department of Agriculture, Forest Service, Southern Forest Experiment Station, New Orleans, direct correspondence.

TABLE 11.30--VOLUME OF GROWING STOCK AND SAWTIMBER ON COMMERCIAL FOREST LAND, TENNESSEE, 1980

	Growing stock (million cu. ft.)			Sawtimber (million board ft.)		
Ownership class	All species	Softwood	Hardwood	All species	Softwood	Hardwood
All ownerships	12,805.2	2,405.5	10,399.7	38,897.3	7,684.3	31,213.0
National forest	797.5	281.0	516.5	2,625.4	1,122.4	1,503.0
Other public	686.2	185.1	501.1	2,356.8	786.1	1,570.7
Forest industry	1,193.6	257.8	935.8	3,600.5	814.3	2,786.2
Farm	4,423.4	595.5	3,827.9	13,359.5	1,793.5	11,566.0
Miscellaneous private	5,704.5	1,086.1	4,618.4	16,955.1	3,168.0	13,787.1

Source: U.S. Department of Agriculture, Forest Service, Southern Forest Experiment Station, New Orleans, direct correspondence.

TABLE 11.31--AVERAGE ANNUAL GROWTH AND REMOVAL OF GROWING STOCK ON COMMERCIAL FOREST LAND, BY OWNERSHIP CLASS, AND BY TYPE OF WOOD, TENNESSEE, 1971–1980 [In millions of cubic feet]

	Periodic annual growth			Periodic annual removals		
Ownership class	All species	Softwood	Hardwood	All species	Softwood	Hardwood
All ownerships[1]	511.4	96.8	414.6	213.7	37.6	176.0
National forest	27.4	9.3	18.1	3.3	1.7	1.6
Other public	26.8	7.0	19.8	24.7	7.1	17.6
Forest industry	44.9	11.0	33.9	24.8	5.6	19.2
Farmer	180.3	22.8	157.5	69.9	9.5	60.4
Miscellaneous private	232.0	46.7	185.3	90.9	13.7	77.2

1. Totals may not add due to independent rounding.

Source: U.S. Department of Agriculture, Forest Service, Southern Forest Experiment Station, New Orleans, direct correspondence.

TABLE 11.32--CHANGES IN COMMERCIAL FOREST LAND, TENNESSEE, 1971–1980 [In thousands of acres]

Resource region	Total area	Commercial forest	Net change	Additions from: Total	Additions from: Agri-culture	Additions from: Other[1]	Diversions to: Total	Diversions to: Agri-culture	Diversions to: Other[1]
All regions	27,035.7	12,879.0	59.2	1,120.9	956.4	164.5	1,061.7	541.2	520.5
West	6,080.6	2,129.0	360.5	588.6	537.1	51.5	228.1	153.8	74.3
West Central	3,422.2	2,183.6	- 107.3	17.9	17.6	0.3	125.2	71.3	53.9
Central	6,305.4	2,139.4	- 136.9	110.3	96.8	13.5	247.2	134.4	112.8
Plateau	4,448.7	2,972.6	- 104.4	72.0	41.2	30.8	176.4	78.2	98.2
East	6,778.9	3,454.4	47.3	332.1	263.7	68.4	284.8	103.5	181.3

1. Includes urban, industrial, highway, noncommercial forest, water, rights-of-way, and other land uses.

Source: U.S. Department of Agriculture, Forest Service, Southern Forest Experiment Station, New Orleans, direct correspondence.

TABLE 11.33--AREA OF COMMERCIAL FOREST LAND, BY FOREST TYPE, AND BY RESOURCE REGION, TENNESSEE, 1980 [In thousands of acres]

Forest type	State	Resource region: West	West Central	Central	Plateau	East
All types	12,879.0	2,129.0	2,183.6	2,139.4	2,972.6	3,454.4
White pine	10.8	0.0	0.0	0.0	5.6	5.2
Loblolly-shortleaf	1,058.3	145.7	101.0	0.0	234.8	576.8
Oak-pine	1,007.6	72.1	39.5	19.6	385.3	491.1
Cedar	651.3	73.9	24.2	392.1	23.8	137.3
Oak-hickory	9,312.6	1,207.7	1,940.8	1,684.0	2,276.3	2,203.8
Oak-gum-cypress	679.7	539.3	66.2	38.7	24.5	11.0
Elm-ash-cottonwood	99.2	71.5	11.9	5.0	10.8	0.0
Maple-beech-birch	59.5	18.8	0.0	0.0	11.5	29.2

Source: U.S. Department of Agriculture, Forest Service, Southern Forest Experiment Station, New Orleans, direct correspondence.

TABLE 11.34--TOTAL LAND AREA AND COMMERCIAL FOREST AREA, TENNESSEE AND COUNTIES, 1980 [Area in thousands of acres]

County	Total land area	Commercial forest area	Commercial forest area as a percentage of total land area	Percent change in commercial forest land 1971–1980
TENNESSEE	27,036.2	12,879.0	48	1
Anderson	218.2	134.2	62	-4
Bedford	308.5	75.6	25	-1
Benton	279.0	161.2	58	-4
Bledsoe	258.6	171.0	66	-1
Blount	373.8	126.0	34	(a)
Bradley	216.3	96.6	45	-10
Campbell	299.5	209.1	70	-7
Cannon	173.4	84.0	48	-3
Carroll	381.4	186.3	49	22
Carter	227.2	151.2	67	4
Cheatham	197.1	104.0	53	-4
Chester	182.4	109.8	60	13
Claiborne	291.2	179.4	62	8
Clay	169.0	97.5	58	-2
Cocke	278.4	174.0	63	4
Coffee	278.4	112.0	40	-5
Crockett	172.2	17.4	10	40
Cumberland	434.5	324.5	75	0
Davidson	341.1	98.0	29	-6
Decatur	225.3	145.0	64	-3
DeKalb	202.9	74.0	36	-16
Dickson	311.0	151.2	49	-6
Dyer	345.6	54.5	16	-17
Fayette	450.5	153.6	34	42
Fentress	319.4	254.2	80	3
Franklin	358.4	174.9	49	-6
Gibson	388.5	60.8	16	24
Giles	396.1	121.8	31	-24
Grainger	199.7	100.7	50	6
Greene	396.1	135.2	34	0
Grundy	229.1	189.0	82	2
Hamblen	111.4	30.4	27	21
Hamilton	375.7	203.0	54	13
Hancock	147.2	100.8	68	18
Hardeman	419.8	248.0	59	12
Hardin	386.6	223.6	58	-1
Hawkins	316.2	185.6	59	11
Haywood	332.2	78.0	23	6
Henderson	329.6	170.8	52	(a)
Henry	384.0	172.5	45	39
Hickman	392.3	275.0	70	2
Houston	133.1	81.9	62	-10
Humphreys	357.8	223.2	62	-10
Jackson	209.3	112.2	54	2
Jefferson	206.1	58.5	28	0
Johnson	191.4	130.0	68	5
Knox	337.9	102.0	30	-4
Lake	122.9	20.1	16	26
Lauderdale	325.8	95.0	29	7
Lawrence	405.8	153.9	38	-16

TABLE 11.34--TOTAL LAND AREA AND COMMERCIAL FOREST AREA, TENNESSEE AND COUNTIES, 1980 [Area in thousands of acres] (Continued)

County	Total land area	Commercial forest area	Commercial forest area as a percentage of total land area	Percent change in commercial forest land 1971–1980
Lewis	182.4	131.1	72	-10
Lincoln	371.2	105.0	28	-10
Loudon	159.4	55.2	35	4
McMinn	278.4	129.8	47	-11
McNairy	364.2	205.2	56	4
Macon	194.6	59.4	31	-19
Madison	358.4	147.0	41	30
Marion	329.6	240.8	73	-3
Marshall	241.3	75.6	31	-3
Maury	393.0	110.0	28	-13
Meigs	139.5	85.8	62	6
Monroe	424.9	290.7	68	-2
Montgomery	347.5	103.4	30	-11
Moore	79.4	28.0	35	-9
Morgan	345.0	270.0	78	-7
Obion	359.0	103.4	29	42
Overton	282.9	167.5	59	-4
Perry	270.7	218.3	81	3
Pickett	111.4	64.8	58	-3
Polk	281.0	208.0	74	-9
Putnam	261.1	136.4	52	-3
Rhea	217.6	124.2	57	-8
Roane	248.3	150.0	60	14
Robertson	304.6	51.2	17	-13
Rutherford	403.2	156.0	39	33
Scott	351.4	302.4	86	-2
Sequatchie	174.7	134.4	77	-4
Sevier	397.2	137.7	35	-14
Shelby	492.1	93.6	19	28
Smith	208.0	75.9	36	5
Stewart	314.9	198.4	63	-10
Sullivan	273.9	99.0	36	-9
Sumner	351.4	73.5	21	-25
Tipton	303.4	100.2	33	80
Trousdale	74.2	24.4	33	3
Unicoi	118.4	96.9	82	3
Union	154.2	108.3	70	28
Van Buren	163.2	124.8	76	(a)
Warren	283.5	94.4	33	-17
Washington	209.3	61.2	29	-1
Wayne	474.2	372.0	78	-2
Weakley	368.6	112.8	31	47
White	246.4	114.4	46	-10
Williamson	379.5	126.0	33	-13
Wilson	371.2	120.7	33	1

a. Percentage less than 0.5.

Source: U.S. Department of Agriculture, Forest Service, Southern Forest Experiment Station: New Orleans, direct correspondence.

TABLE 11.35--SELECTED DATA ON THE LUMBER AND WOOD PRODUCTS INDUSTRY, TENNESSEE, 1982 [Dollar amounts in millions]

Sector of industry	Number of establishments		All employees		Production workers		Value added by manu-facture	Value of ship-ments	New capital expen-ditures
	Total	With 20 or more employees	Number (1,000)	Payroll	Number (1,000)	Wages			
Total lumber and wood products industry	836	163	14.1	$155.2	12.1	$119.7	$266.0	$699.7	$19.2
Logging camps and contractors	140	2	0.5	5.1	0.5	4.5	9.0	28.6	0.9
Sawmills and planing mills	385	76	6.8	75.2	6.0	60.3	129.4	325.1	10.6
Millwork, plywood, and structural members	133	32	2.2	24.0	1.8	17.2	43.5	105.8	1.8
Wood containers	66	20	1.4	16.5	1.2	12.7	23.7	64.5	1.4
Wood buildings and mobile homes	30	15	1.7	17.9	1.4	12.3	33.9	101.5	1.7
Miscellaneous wood products	82	18	1.4	16.5	1.2	12.6	26.6	74.3	2.8

Note: Includes industry groups and industries with 500 employees or more.

Source: U.S. Department of Commerce, Bureau of the Census, *1982 Census of Manufactures, Geographic Area Series, Tennessee.*

Tennessee offers great variety in climate and topography. Elevations range from more than 6,600 feet at the eastern boundary to approximately 200 feet at the Mississippi River. There are nearly 60 national and state parks and recreations areas in Tennessee, as shown in Figure 12.2.

The Tennessee Department of Tourist Development publishes a report entitled *The Economic Impact of Travel on Tennessee Counties.* These data are the results of an annual study by the U.S. Travel Data Center. Presented in Tables 12.5-12.7, data for travel-generated employment and revenues are first detailed at the state level and secondly for individual counties.

Acreage which is located in Tennessee and other southeastern states but owned by various federal agencies is shown in Table 12.17. Additional information on selected federally owned Tennessee lands is given in other tables throughout the chapter. The Army Corps of Engineers maintains the Cumberland River areas in Tennessee, while TVA maintains all Tennessee River areas except for National Wildlife Refuge areas (managed by the U.S. Fish and Wildlife Service). The U.S. Department of the Interior, National Park Service, maintains the Great Smoky Mountains National Park as well as a variety of other areas, as listed in Table 12.9. The Cherokee National Forest is managed by the U.S. Department of Agriculture, National Forest Service. In regard to state-owned properties, the Tennessee Department of Conservation has primary responsibility for these parks and recreation areas. Records of visitations and use, collected and maintained by each of these agencies, are presented in several tables throughout this chapter.

The U.S. Department of Commerce, National Oceanic and Atmospheric Administration, through the Environmental Data Service, National Climate Center, publishes data on weather and climate. The monthly data in Table 12.1 are published for seven metropolitan areas in Tennessee in *Climatological Data Annual Summary, Tennessee, 1988.* "Normal" values of temperature and precipitation shown in this table are based on records for the 30 years between 1951 and 1980. Actual minimum and maximum weekday temperatures and normal and actual cooling degree days and heating degree days are reported for more than 70 Tennessee locations in *Electricity Sales Statistics*, issued monthly by the Tennessee Valley Authority.

Summary information about land and water areas of counties is presented in Table 12.8. These data are collected and published by the U.S. Department of Commerce, Bureau of the Census. Latest measurements were made in 1980.

TABLE OF CONTENTS

FIGURE 12.1
Physiographic Map of Tennessee

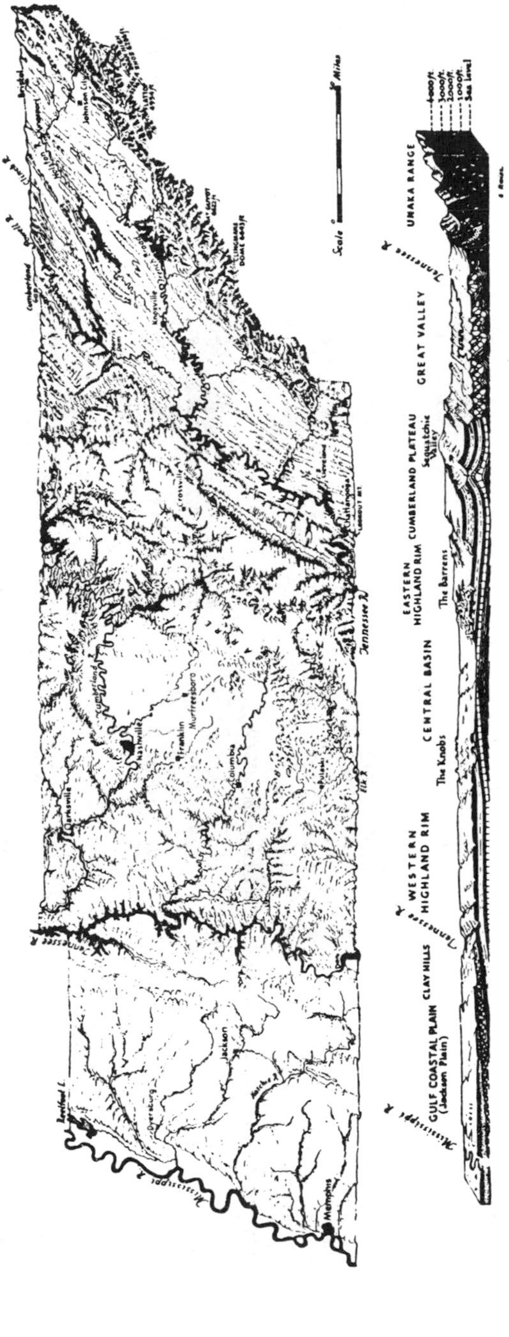

Source: Tennessee Department of Finance and Administration, *Tennessee, Its Resources and Economy*, Volume II.

TABLE 12.1-- CLIMATOLOGICAL DATA, SELECTED METROPOLITAN STATIONS, 1988 AND 30-YEAR NORMALS [Temperatures in degrees Fahrenheit]

Weather station	Jan.	Feb.	Mar.	Apr.	May	June	July	Aug.	Sept.	Oct.	Nov.	Dec.	Annual
BRISTOL - Elevation 1,525 feet, Latitude 36°29′N, Longitude 82°24′W													
1988 average temperature	31.5	37.3	47.8	54.1	62.3	70.5	76.7	77.1	68.1	50.2	47.6	37.6	55.1
Normal average temperature	35.0	37.9	46.3	56.1	64.4	71.5	74.9	74.3	68.8	57.1	46.2	38.2	55.9
1988 precipitation (inches)	2.74	3.20	1.54	2.69	2.48	0.89	3.20	2.78	3.20	1.79	3.44	2.73	30.68
Normal precipitation	3.56	3.43	4.29	3.46	3.61	3.46	4.19	3.23	3.00	2.50	2.98	3.53	41.24
1988 cooling degree days[1]	0	0	0	4	32	214	369	383	120	2	0	0	1,124
CHATTANOOGA - Elevation 676 feet, Latitude 35°02′N, Longitude 85°12′W													
1988 average temperature	35.1	41.0	52.0	60.3	67.0	76.9	79.0	80.5	72.4	55.3	51.7	42.3	59.5
Normal average temperature	38.7	41.9	49.8	60.1	67.8	75.1	78.7	78.1	72.3	60.0	48.9	41.5	59.4
1988 precipitation (inches)	7.10	1.87	1.83	3.30	2.20	0.63	5.85	4.07	6.76	2.10	4.64	3.54	43.89
Normal precipitation	5.20	4.69	6.31	4.57	4.00	3.32	4.55	3.41	4.30	2.92	4.19	5.14	52.60
1988 cooling degree days[1]	0	0	2	27	95	364	442	486	230	17	0	0	1,663
CLARKSVILLE[2] - Elevation 382 feet, Latitude 36°33′N, Longitude 87°22′W													
1988 average temperature	33.1	37.6	48.2	58.1	66.1	75.4	80.4	81.0	71.2	52.5	48.8	39.7	57.7
Normal average temperature	35.7	39.0	47.9	59.0	66.9	74.8	78.7	77.4	71.0	58.9	47.8	39.5	58.1
1988 precipitation (inches)	3.61	3.86	3.24	1.40	2.56	0.46	3.24	3.89	4.00	2.84	7.33	7.01	43.44
Normal precipitation	4.52	4.26	5.92	4.46	4.14	3.74	3.81	3.79	3.31	2.83	4.22	4.64	49.64
1988 cooling degree days[1]	0	0	0	22	93	325	484	501	205	11	0	0	1641
JACKSON[2] - Elevation 433 feet, Latitude 35°36′N, Longitude 88°55′W													
1988 average temperature	35.3	40	51.1	60.9	69.2	77.3	79.6	81.4	73.6	56.3	52.4	42.9	60.0
Normal average temperature	37.8	41.7	50.1	61.2	69.5	77.1	80.4	79.1	72.6	61.1	49.5	41.6	60.2
1988 precipitation (inches)	4.15	4.04	3.23	2.93	2.53	0.56	9.90	1.11	7.22	4.17	6.58	7.54	53.96
Normal precipitation	4.77	4.45	5.24	5.44	4.99	3.81	4.44	2.98	3.52	2.63	4.12	4.60	50.99
1988 cooling degree days[1]	0	0	7	42	151	376	458	516	271	20	0	0	1,841
KNOXVILLE - Elevation 949 feet, Latitude 35°48′N, Longitude 84°00′W													
1988 average temperature	33.9	39.4	50.1	57.2	65.0	74.4	78.7	79.6	71.3	52.7	49.7	40.4	57.7
Normal average temperature	38.2	41.5	49.7	59.6	67.4	74.3	77.6	77.0	71.5	59.5	48.8	41.1	58.9
1988 precipitation (inches)	4.29	2.94	2.42	2.34	2.35	0.51	3.60	3.20	2.68	1.52	4.82	3.99	34.66
Normal precipitation	4.65	4.18	5.49	3.87	3.71	3.95	4.33	3.02	2.99	2.73	3.78	4.59	47.29
1988 cooling degree days[1]	0	0	3	19	74	297	431	458	200	9	0	0	1,491

TABLE 12.1-- CLIMATOLOGICAL DATA, SELECTED METROPOLITAN STATIONS, 1988 AND 30-YEAR NORMALS [Temperatures in degrees Fahrenheit] (Continued)

Weather station	Jan.	Feb.	Mar.	Apr.	May	June	July	Aug.	Sept.	Oct.	Nov.	Dec.	Annual
MEMPHIS - Elevation 265 feet, Latitude 35°03'N, Longitude 90°00'W													
1988 average temperature	36.8	42.2	52.3	62.8	71.8	80.3	81.6	83.7	76.3	59.1	54.6	44.9	62.2
Normal average temperature	39.6	43.6	51.7	62.6	71.0	78.7	82.1	80.6	74.2	62.9	51.3	43.3	61.8
1988 precipitation (inches)	4.25	3.49	4.20	2.85	2.38	2.15	5.21	0.85	4.73	3.62	10.52	5.99	50.24
Normal precipitation	4.61	4.33	5.44	5.77	5.06	3.58	4.03	3.74	3.62	2.37	4.17	4.85	51.57
1988 cooling degree days[1]	0	0	7	52	221	469	518	586	347	24	8	0	2,232
NASHVILLE - Elevation 580 feet, Latitude 36°07'N, Longitude 86°41'W													
1988 average temperature	34.4	38.7	49.3	57.1	67.3	77.3	81.4	81.9	72.8	54.2	51.1	42.4	59.0
Normal average temperature	37.1	40.4	49.0	59.7	68.1	75.8	79.4	78.4	72.3	60.2	48.6	40.9	59.2
1988 precipitation (inches)	3.73	2.02	2.18	2.09	1.86	0.45	3.26	2.39	2.45	1.54	5.49	3.95	31.41
Normal precipitation	4.49	4.03	5.58	4.47	4.56	3.70	3.82	3.40	3.71	2.58	3.52	4.63	48.49
1988 cooling degree days[1]	0	0	5	17	120	380	515	531	246	17	0	0	1,831

Note: Normals are computed over the thirty-year period from 1951 to 1980. They are updated after every tenth year.

1. One cooling degree day is accumulated for each degree that the daily mean temperature exceeds 65°F.

2. Normals computed by the Center for Business and Economic Research.

Source: U.S. Department of Commerce, National Oceanic and Atmospheric Administration, Environmental Data Service, National Climatic Data Center, Asheville, North Carolina, *Climatological Data Annual Summary, Tennessee*, 1988; and *Comparative Climatic Data for the United States*, 1984.

TABLE 12.2-- MAXIMUM RECORDED TEMPERATURE AND COOLING DEGREE DAYS, SELECTED TENNESSEE LOCATIONS, 1987 COOLING YEAR

[Degree day base = 65°F]

Weather station and county	Maximum weekday temperature recorded	Cooling degree days[1] Normal	Cooling degree days[1] Actual[2]	Cooling degree days[1] Actual as a percentage of normal	Weather station and county[3]	Maximum weekday temperature recorded	Actual degree days[2]
Allardt, Fentress	92	905	1,065	118	Ames Plantation, Fayette	100	1,766
Bolivar Water Works, Hardeman	99	1,587	1,800	113	Athens, McMinn	97	1,550
Bristol, Sullivan	97	1,066	1,340	126	Carthage, Smith	98	1,625
Brownsville, Haywood	99	1,873	1,986	106	Centerville Water Plant, Hickman	98	1,522
Chattanooga, Hamilton	100	1,578	1,865	118	Cleveland, Bradley	100	1,652
Clarksville Sewage Plant, Montgomery	100	1,514	1,833	121	Cookeville, Putnam	96	1,303
Columbia, Maury	95	1,497	1,516	101	Crossville, Cumberland	93	987
Covington, Tipton	100	1,733	1,948	112	Dayton, Rhea	97	1,570
Crossville, Cumberland	93	798	987	124	Dresden, Weakley	98	1,734
Dyersburg, Dyer	99	1,840	2,100	114	Elizabethton, Carter	95	1,302
Franklin Sewage Plant, Williamson	98	1,466	1,451	99	Erwin, Unicoi	97	1,128
Greeneville, Greene	96	1,167	1,237	106	Fayetteville, Lincoln	101	1,625
Jackson Exp. Sta., Madison	99	1,625	1,882	116	Huntingdon Water Plant, Carroll	101	1,808
Jackson, Madison	102	1,802	1,925	107	Kingston Springs, Cheatham	98	1,594
Kingsport, Hawkins-Sullivan	97	1,164	1,502	129	LaFayette, Macon	99	1,731
Knoxville, Knox	98	1,449	1,613	111	Lawrenceburg Filtration Plant, Lawrence	95	1,548
Lenoir City, Loudon	98	1,306	1,735	133	Lebanon, Wilson	98	1,693

TABLE 12.2-- MAXIMUM RECORDED TEMPERATURE AND COOLING DEGREE DAYS, SELECTED TENNESSEE LOCATIONS, 1987 COOLING YEAR
[Degree day base = 65°F] (Continued)

Weather station and county	Maximum weekday temperature recorded	Cooling degree days[1]			Weather station and county[3]	Maximum weekday temperature recorded	Actual degree days[2]
		Normal	Actual[2]	Actual as a percentage of normal			
Lewisburg Experimental Sta., Marshall	100	1,383	1,621	117	Morristown Radio, WCRK, Overton	96	1,425
McMinnville, Warren	99	1,375	1,634	119	Moscow, Fayette	96	1,991
Martin, Weakley	101	1,689	1,683	100	Mountain City, Johnson	91	593
Memphis, Shelby	100	2,067	2,384	115	Neapolis Experimental Station, Maury	100	1,607
Milan, Gibson	96	1,580	1,801	114	Norris, Anderson	96	1,230
Monteagle, Grundy-Marion	97	1,087	1,368	126	Pikeville, Bledsoe	97	1,447
Murfreesboro, Rutherford	101	1,573	1,730	110	Portland Sewage Plant, Sumner	98	1,566
Nashville, Davidson	99	1,661	1,907	115	Pulaski Water Plant, Giles	99	1,903
Newbern, Dyer	94	1,653	1,781	108	Rockwood, Roane	95	1,286
Newport, Cocke	98	1,293	1,470	114	Selmer, McNairy	100	1,816
Oak Ridge, Anderson-Roane	97	1,294	1,537	119	Sevierville, Sevier	95	1,440
Paris, Henry	99	1,422	1,644	116	Smithville, DeKalb	97	1,291
Rogersville, Hawkins	94	1,054	1,266	117	Sparta, White	98	1,516
Samburg Wildlife Refuge, Obion	98	1,667	1,686	101	Tazewell Claiborne	96	1,129
Savannah, Hardin	101	1,734	1,975	114	Waverly, Humphreys	97	1,634
Shelbyville, Bedford	99	1,472	1,758	119	Winchester, Franklin	99	1,708
Springfield Exp. Station, Robertson	97	1,380	1,536	111	Woodbury, Cannon	101	1,719

TABLE 12.2-- MAXIMUM RECORDED TEMPERATURE AND COOLING DEGREE DAYS, SELECTED TENNESSEE LOCATIONS, 1987 COOLING YEAR
[Degree day base = 65°F] (Continued)

Weather station and county	Maximum weekday temperature recorded	Cooling degree days[1]			Weather station and county[3]	Maximum weekday temperature recorded	Actual degree days[2]
		Normal	Actual[2]	Actual as a percentage of normal			
Union City, Obion	98	1,426	1,678	118			
Waynesboro, Wayne	95	1,265	1,485	117			

1. A degree day measures the amount by which the mean daily temperature at a location exceeds or falls below a base temperature (usually 65°F). Degree days for a cooling season are the sum of every day's variation from 65°F. TVA's cooling year is from July 1 to June 30.
2. Where temperatures for one or more days are not reported, they are estimated.
3. Data on normal degree days are not available for these stations.

Source: Tennessee Valley Authority, Division of Power Utilization, *Electricity Sales Statistics*, Report No. 638.

TABLE 12.3-- MINIMUM RECORDED TEMPERATURE AND HEATING DEGREE DAYS, SELECTED TENNESSEE LOCATIONS, 1988 HEATING YEAR
[Degree day base = 65°F]

Weather station and county	Minimum weekday temperature recorded	Heating degree days[1] Normal	Heating degree days[1] Actual[2]	Heating degree days[1] Actual as a percentage of normal	Weather station and county[3]	Minimum weekday temperature recorded	Actual degree days[2]
Allardt, Fentress	3[a]	4,491	4,423	98	Ames Plantation, Fayette	-1	3,829
Bolivar Water Works, Hardeman	2[a]	3,608	3,851	107	Athens, McMinn	4	4,040
Bristol, Sullivan	4	4,356	4,503	103	Centerville Water Plant, Hickman	1[a]	4,042
Brownsville, Haywood	3[a]	3,356	3,696	110	Cheatham, Cheatham	5[a]	4,149
Chattanooga, Hamilton	8	3,583	3,488	97	Cookeville, Putnam	-1	4,554
Clarksville Sewage Plant, Montgomery	n.a.	4,014	4,076	102	Crossville, Cumberland	2[a]	4,609
Columbia, Maury	0	3,761	4,302	114	Dayton, Rhea	7[a]	3,728
Covington, Tipton	2[a]	3,707	3,799	102	Dresden, Weakley	3[a]	4,098
Crossville, Cumberland	3[a]	4,896	4,834	99	Elizabethton, Carter	5	4,181
Dickson, Dickson	1	3,759	4,090	109	Erwin, Unicoi	4	4,689
Dover, Stewart	7[a]	4,115	n.a.	n.a.	Fayetteville, Lincoln	-1[a]	4,056
Dyersburg, Dyer	4	3,559	3,397	95	Huntingdon Water Plant, Carroll	4[a]	4,034
Franklin Sewage Plant, Williamson	-1	3,664	4,458	122	Jefferson City, Jefferson	1	4,277
Gatlinburg, Sevier	n.a.	4,263	4,565	107	Kingston Springs, Cheatham	2[a]	4,293
Greeneville, Greene	1	4,063	4,566	112	LaFayette, Macon	6[a]	3,881
Jackson Exp. Sta., Madison	3[a]	3,707	3,800	103	Lawrenceburg Filtration Plant, Lawrence	0	3,966
Jackson, Madison	4[a]	3,540	3,492	99	Lebanon, Wilson	0	4,323

TABLE 12.3-- MINIMUM RECORDED TEMPERATURE AND HEATING DEGREE DAYS, SELECTED TENNESSEE LOCATIONS, 1988 HEATING YEAR
[Degree day base = 65°F] (Continued)

Weather station and county	Minimum weekday temperature recorded	Heating degree days[1] Normal	Heating degree days[1] Actual[2]	Heating degree days[1] Actual as a percentage of normal	Weather station and county[3]	Minimum weekday temperature recorded	Actual degree days[2]
Kingsport, Hawkins-Sullivan	7	3,920	3,937	100	Linden, Perry	1	4,335
Knoxville, Knox	3	3,658	3,952	108	Livingston Radio, WLIV, Hamblen	4[a]	3,809
Lenoir City, Loudon	10[a]	4,023	3,868	96	Morristown Radio, WCRK, Overton	6	4,043
Lewisburg Experimental Sta., Marshall	-1[a]	4,056	4,223	104	Mt. Pleasant, Maury	1[a]	n.a.
McMinnville, Warren	0	3,663	3,631	99	Mountain City, Johnson	0	5,562
Martin, Weakley	1	3,781	4,330	115	Neapolis Experimental Station, Maury	-2	4,153
Memphis, Shelby	6	3,207	3,094	96	Norris, Anderson	5[a]	4,602
Monteagle, Grundy-Marion	5[a]	4,030	4,279	106	Pikeville, Bledsoe	1	3,843
Murfreesboro, Rutherford	-1	3,734	4,201	113	Portland Sewage Plant, Sumner	7[a]	4,064
Nashville, Davidson	5	3,756	3,809	101	Pulaski Water Plant, Giles	1	3,298
Newbern, Dyer	3[a]	3,837	3,997	104	Rockwood, Roane	-4	4,406
Newport, Cocke	n.a.	4,081	4,162	102	Selmer, McNairy	1	3,764
Oak Ridge, Anderson-Roane	8[a]	4,006	3,991	100	Sevierville, Sevier	0	3,946
Paris, Henry	4[a]	4,077	4,259	104	Sparta, White	3[a]	3,731
Rogersville, Hawkins	1	4,220	4,337	103	Tazewell, Claiborne	-3	5,056
Samburg Wildlife Refuge, Obion	1[a]	3,953	4,183	106	Waverly, Humphreys	7[a]	4,246
Savannah, Hardin	5	3,326	3,192	96	Winchester, Franklin	2[a]	3,464

TABLE 12.3-- MINIMUM RECORDED TEMPERATURE AND HEATING DEGREE DAYS, SELECTED TENNESSEE LOCATIONS, 1988 HEATING YEAR
[Degree day base = 65°F] (Continued)

Weather station and county	Minimum weekday temperature recorded	Heating degree days[1] Normal	Heating degree days[1] Actual[2]	Heating degree days[1] Actual as a percentage of normal	Weather station and county[3]	Minimum weekday temperature recorded	Actual degree days[2]
Shelbyville, Bedford	-1	3,610	3,566	99	Woodbury, Cannon	-2[a]	3,824
Springfield Exp. Station, Robertson	6[a]	4,305	4,347	101			
Union City, Obion	-1[a]	4,224	4,274	101			
Waynesboro, Wayne	-5	4,170	4,384	105			

n.a. not available.

a. Indicates Saturday or Sunday temperature was lower.

1. A degree day measures the amount by which the mean daily temperature at a location exceeds or falls below a base temperature (usually 65°F). Degree days for a heating season are the sum of every day's variation from 65°F. TVA's heating year is from July 1 to June 30.

2. Where temperatures for one or more days are not reported, they are estimated.

3. Data on normal degree days are not available for these stations.

Source: Tennessee Valley Authority, Division of Power Utilization, *Electricity Sales Statistics*, Report No. 644.

TABLE 12.4-- MINIMUM TEMPERATURES AND HEATING DEGREE DAYS, TVA REGION,[1] HEATING YEARS 1972–1988

Heating year	Minimum weekday temperatures			Heating degree days[2] (base = 65°F)				
	Dec.	Jan.	Feb.	Dec.	Jan.	Feb.	Total season	Percentage of normal
1988	23	7	16[a]	607	918	708	3,550	99
1987	24	13	19	736	825	569	3,278	92
1986	11	6	15	899	817	520	3,157	88
1985	12	-10	14	463	1,050	727	3,399	95
1984	2[a]	6[a]	10	909	953	614	3,977	111
1983	20	18	21	533	805	616	3,416	96
1982	17[a]	-1[a]	16[a]	813	919	649	3,717	104
1981	16	8	5	730	902	603	3,644	102
1980	17	18	15[a]	715	753	823	3,719	104
1979	22[a]	9	10[a]	664	1,023	794	3,642	102
1978	12	9	11	774	1,105	901	4,129	115
1977	9	-3	13	852	1,180	671	4,197	117
1976	11	7	17	728	899	440	3,292	92
1975	19	15	16	709	669	569	3,514	98
1974	17	26	14	734	538	618	2,943	82
1973	14	13	19	673	852	726	3,635	102
1972	31	15	19	476	686	689	3,099	87
Normal	17	12	17	724	826	651	3,569	100

1. TVA Region is city temperatures weighted by size of heating loads.
2. A degree day measures the amount by which the mean daily temperature at a location exceeds or falls below a base temperature (usually 65°F). Degree days for a heating season are the sum of every day's variation from 65°F. TVA's heating year is from July 1 to June 30.

a. Indicates Saturday or Sunday temperature was lower.

Source: Tennessee Valley Authority, Division of Power Utilization, *Electricity Sales Statistics*, Report No. 644.

TABLE 12.5-- TRAVEL-GENERATED EMPLOYMENT, BY CATEGORY, TENNESSEE, 1986 AND 1987

	1987p		1986r	
	Employment	Percentage of state total	Employment	Percentage of state total
TOTAL	92,320	100.0	87,393	100.0
Public transportation	9,133	9.9	7,470	8.5
Auto transportation	4,247	4.6	3,823	4.4
Lodging	16,602	18.0	15,194	17.4
Food service	45,261	49.0	45,143	51.7
Entertainment/recreation	10,119	11.0	9,503	10.9
General retail trade	5,173	5.6	4,644	5.3
Travel arrangement	1,786	1.9	1,616	1.8

Note: Detail may not add to total due to independent rounding.

p preliminary.

r revised.

Source: U.S. Travel Data Center, *The Economic Impact of Travel on Tennessee Counties, 1987*, a study prepared for the Tennessee Department of Tourist Development.

TABLE 12.6-- ESTIMATES OF TRAVEL ECONOMIC IMPACT, TENNESSEE, 1984–1987

	1987p	1986r	1985	1984
Travel expenditures ($1,000,000)	4,553.1	4,080.8	3,755.7	3,399.6
Travel-generated payroll ($1,000,000)	993.2	885.0	794.6	720.6
Travel-generated employment (1,000)	92.3	87.4	83.4	82.8
Travel-generated state tax revenue ($1,000,000)	222.5	201.0	173.9	164.6
Travel-generated local tax revenue ($1,000,000)	83.2	75.1	65.8	61.3
Out-of-state visitor expenditures ($1,000,000)	3,000.0	2,700.0	2,500.0	2,300.0
Out-of-state travelers (1,000,000)	29.4	27.5	25.2	22.9

Note: Detail may not add to total due to independent rounding.

p preliminary.

r revised.

Source: U.S. Travel Data Center, *The Economic Impact of Travel on Tennessee Counties, 1987*, a study prepared for the Tennessee Department of Tourist Development; and earlier editions.

TABLE 12.7-- TRAVEL EXPENDITURES AND TRAVEL-GENERATED STATE AND LOCAL TAX RECEIPTS AND EMPLOYMENT, TENNESSEE AND COUNTIES, 1986 AND 1987 [Expenditures and receipts in thousands of dollars]

County	1987				1986[r]			
	Total travel expenditures	State tax receipts	Local tax receipts	Travel-generated employment	Total travel expenditures	State tax receipts	Local tax receipts	Travel-generated employment
TENNESSEE	4,553,079	222,491	83,201	92,320	4,080,834	201,006	75,050	87,393
Anderson	31,000	1,787	721	674	28,096	1,610	392	635
Bedford	7,485	437	130	157	9,161	534	159	206
Benton	4,051	157	62	63	3,732	145	58	62
Bledsoe	629	23	10	7	468	13	5	4
Blount	53,330	2,595	1,006	1,040	46,134	2,210	865	935
Bradley	33,841	1,927	687	724	32,694	1,844	656	734
Campbell	23,262	1,367	561	516	25,652	1,499	618	601
Cannon	314	12	4	1	286	11	3	1
Carroll	1,950	91	36	25	2,429	122	46	41
Carter	4,532	163	157	81	4,871	191	162	95
Cheatham	2,117	120	44	43	1,831	102	24	39
Chester	539	21	9	3	431	16	8	2
Claiborne	7,266	435	157	163	5,430	317	116	126
Clay	3,436	179	41	64	3,227	169	38	64
Cocke	18,706	1,098	390	415	18,215	1,058	381	424
Coffee	25,835	1,548	554	585	24,805	1,464	534	589
Crockett	1,662	90	30	31	1,623	88	26	32
Cumberland	23,831	1,417	511	536	12,636	707	267	277
Davidson	1,478,672	73,594	27,594	30,646	1,309,299	66,523	25,051	28,845
Decatur	2,686	104	29	41	2,851	117	31	51
DeKalb	4,371	161	51	64	3,948	144	44	59
Dickson	15,087	909	329	335	13,381	791	289	312
Dyer	10,616	602	261	219	9,968	558	237	214
Fayette	693	27	10	8	556	19	8	7
Fentress	2,007	99	28	38	1,699	82	22	34
Franklin	5,644	283	106	110	5,247	263	82	109
Gibson	5,774	315	118	102	6,604	366	135	131

TABLE 12.7-- TRAVEL EXPENDITURES AND TRAVEL-GENERATED STATE AND LOCAL TAX RECEIPTS AND EMPLOYMENT, TENNESSEE AND COUNTIES, 1986 AND 1987 [Expenditures and receipts in thousands of dollars] (Continued)

County	1987 Total travel expenditures	1987 State tax receipts	1987 Local tax receipts	1987 Travel-generated employment	1986[r] Total travel expenditures	1986[r] State tax receipts	1986[r] Local tax receipts	1986[r] Travel-generated employment
Giles	4,455	249	66	91	4,501	251	67	98
Grainger	1,261	47	20	16	1,154	45	20	15
Greene	11,506	646	186	244	11,463	639	174	257
Grundy	2,347	135	65	50	4,814	284	117	114
Hamblen	17,723	1,022	432	380	18,861	1,086	350	427
Hamilton	226,625	11,892	3,529	4,729	228,161	11,994	3,587	5,032
Hancock	374	4	1	3	352	3	1	3
Hardeman	5,134	248	97	88	6,592	326	132	117
Hardin	2,678	128	35	47	2,456	113	32	44
Hawkins	3,475	136	98	63	3,488	141	96	67
Haywood	1,351	61	17	19	1,280	55	16	20
Henderson	4,292	241	91	84	4,285	237	93	88
Henry	6,546	357	131	135	6,513	354	131	140
Hickman	1,244	56	22	20	1,165	53	21	20
Houston	600	17	8	7	650	20	8	10
Humphreys	8,773	509	184	189	8,578	493	181	196
Jackson	432	10	4	3	351	7	4	2
Jefferson	8,247	439	164	171	7,517	395	149	164
Johnson	1,063	54	14	18	1,165	62	17	23
Knox	307,203	15,827	4,361	6,408	287,327	14,758	4,104	6,303
Lake	3,607	212	75	80	3,587	209	75	83
Lauderdale	1,218	55	18	17	1,142	50	17	17
Lawrence	4,999	282	103	91	4,532	255	95	85
Lewis	4,835	284	91	105	7,212	427	138	170
Lincoln	2,338	124	34	40	2,594	141	39	49
Loudon	8,934	534	139	192	10,110	596	159	231
McMinn	8,584	493	164	180	9,857	565	189	222
McNairy	1,828	89	34	25	1,485	67	27	20

TABLE 12.7-- TRAVEL EXPENDITURES AND TRAVEL-GENERATED STATE AND LOCAL TAX RECEIPTS AND EMPLOYMENT, TENNESSEE AND COUNTIES, 1986 AND 1987 [Expenditures and receipts in thousands of dollars] (Continued)

County	1987				1986[r]			
	Total travel expenditures	State tax receipts	Local tax receipts	Travel-generated employment	Total travel expenditures	State tax receipts	Local tax receipts	Travel-generated employment
Macon	810	34	13	12	739	31	11	12
Madison	60,849	3,538	942	1,354	51,642	2,949	795	1,194
Marion	8,484	492	194	187	8,835	507	201	205
Marshall	5,096	298	109	103	5,022	290	106	106
Maury	11,010	592	206	230	14,399	797	274	324
Meigs	118	1	1	1	111	1	1	1
Monroe	17,660	1,034	334	388	27,458	1,615	578	648
Montgomery	40,971	2,407	873	891	38,655	2,237	827	880
Moore	178	3	2	2	152	3	1	2
Morgan	578	13	4	6	554	12	4	6
Obion	12,249	700	254	257	9,800	545	200	212
Overton	529	17	5	5	515	19	5	6
Perry	609	13	4	4	568	14	3	5
Pickett	304	15	3	5	296	14	3	5
Polk	1,493	82	31	31	1,323	72	27	28
Putnam	24,245	1,401	508	542	16,413	913	337	374
Rhea	4,980	272	98	99	4,603	250	92	93
Roane	14,544	743	288	291	13,598	690	262	285
Robertson	7,566	438	162	147	6,190	350	132	124
Rutherford	37,367	2,104	805	823	36,790	2,050	800	845
Scott	1,405	68	26	24	1,415	68	27	27
Sequatchie	1,921	105	38	41	1,223	63	22	24
Sevier	462,901	28,152	11,943	10,760	415,536	24,887	10,617	10,085
Shelby	1,184,939	43,962	18,096	21,194	1,010,516	37,822	15,556	19,068
Smith	880	35	13	12	851	35	12	13
Stewart	1,065	41	16	15	926	32	14	14
Sullivan	80,360	3,732	1,539	1,529	79,012	3,667	1,541	1,589
Sumner	7,732	403	153	138	8,086	422	162	154

TABLE 12.7-- TRAVEL EXPENDITURES AND TRAVEL-GENERATED STATE AND LOCAL TAX RECEIPTS AND EMPLOYMENT, TENNESSEE AND COUNTIES, 1986 AND 1987 [Expenditures and receipts in thousands of dollars] (Continued)

	1987				1986[r]			
County	Total travel expenditures	State tax receipts	Local tax receipts	Travel-generated employment	Total travel expenditures	State tax receipts	Local tax receipts	Travel-generated employment
Tipton	3,927	221	80	75	3,809	212	79	78
Trousdale	378	18	9	5	347	17	9	5
Unicoi	2,385	126	45	46	2,804	150	55	57
Union	223	6	1	1	993	52	15	21
Van Buren	272	10	3	2	238	9	2	2
Warren	3,090	153	54	53	2,811	137	47	50
Washington	57,203	3,362	1,333	1,270	49,193	2,842	1,138	1,139
Wayne	973	39	12	12	1,092	47	14	18
Weakley	3,330	181	66	60	3,088	165	62	58
White	2,491	123	46	36	2,218	105	39	33
Williamson	50,333	2,859	763	1,125	25,916	1,353	378	580
Wilson	16,623	986	310	358	16,631	973	306	376

Note: Estimates represent expenditures by U.S. residents traveling away from home overnight, or on day trips to places 100 miles or more away from home.

r revised.

Source: U.S. Travel Data Center, *The Economic Impact of Travel on Tennessee Counties, 1987*, a study prepared for the Tennessee Department of Tourist Development.

TABLE 12.8-- LAND AND INLAND WATER AREA, TENNESSEE AND COUNTIES [In square miles]

County	Total area	Land area	Inland water area
TENNESSEE	42,143.56	41,154.74	988.82
Anderson	344.71	338.71	6.00
Bedford	475.35	475.12	0.23
Benton	436.11	392.01	44.10
Bledsoe	407.32	407.32	0.00
Blount	566.77	558.17	8.60
Bradley	331.51	327.41	4.10
Campbell	496.10	479.00	17.10
Cannon	265.65	265.65	0.00
Carroll	599.90	599.60	0.30
Carter	347.69	340.59	7.10
Cheatham	306.85	303.55	3.30
Chester	288.67	288.67	0.00
Claiborne	443.65	432.45	11.20
Clay	259.45	227.04	32.41
Cocke	442.95	432.05	10.90
Coffee	434.44	428.44	6.00
Crockett	266.14	265.94	0.20
Cumberland	684.45	682.32	2.13
Davidson	525.85	500.85	25.00
Decatur	345.06	329.96	15.10
DeKalb	329.35	290.55	38.80
Dickson	491.47	490.57	0.90
Dyer	531.08	519.68	11.40
Fayette	706.03	705.46	0.57
Fentress	498.70	498.00	0.70
Franklin	566.62	542.90	23.72
Gibson	603.14	602.47	0.67
Giles	610.65	610.45	0.20
Grainger	302.63	273.03	29.60
Greene	624.21	618.51	5.70
Grundy	361.21	361.21	0.00
Hamblen	175.84	156.44	19.40
Hamilton	575.63	539.03	36.60
Hancock	223.42	223.42	0.00
Hardeman	671.64	670.34	1.30
Hardin	595.20	578.30	16.90
Hawkins	499.51	485.51	14.00
Haywood	534.16	533.76	0.40
Henderson	525.77	519.99	5.78
Henry	593.09	559.78	33.31
Hickman	612.19	609.59	2.60
Houston	206.95	200.15	6.80
Humphreys	556.64	527.54	29.10
Jackson	321.88	307.86	14.02
Jefferson	313.84	265.44	48.40
Johnson	302.61	297.11	5.50
Knox	525.90	505.90	20.00
Lake	193.61	168.51	25.10
Lauderdale	506.29	474.49	31.80
Lawrence	617.78	617.27	0.51

TABLE 12.8-- LAND AND INLAND WATER AREA, TENNESSEE AND COUNTIES [In square miles] (Continued)

County	Total area	Land area	Inland water area
Lewis	282.55	282.29	0.26
Lincoln	570.78	570.78	0.00
Loudon	247.19	235.09	12.10
McMinn	432.35	428.95	3.40
McNairy	561.59	561.59	0.00
Macon	307.17	307.17	0.00
Madison	558.19	558.19	0.00
Marion	521.13	512.43	8.70
Marshall	376.49	376.49	0.00
Maury	616.40	616.31	0.09
Meigs	216.64	189.24	27.40
Monroe	652.62	648.22	4.40
Montgomery	542.76	538.66	4.10
Moore	130.76	128.69	2.07
Morgan	522.59	522.59	0.00
Obion	555.56	550.31	5.25
Overton	434.46	433.06	1.40
Perry	423.58	411.78	11.80
Pickett	175.18	159.38	15.80
Polk	442.10	437.50	4.60
Putnam	402.67	399.17	3.50
Rhea	336.87	308.97	27.90
Roane	394.92	356.72	38.20
Robertson	475.88	475.88	0.00
Rutherford	623.92	605.52	18.40
Scott	533.36	528.06	5.30
Sequatchie	265.71	265.51	0.20
Sevier	597.87	590.27	7.60
Shelby	785.71	771.61	14.10
Smith	325.62	312.78	12.84
Stewart	493.94	454.32	39.62
Sullivan	429.85	415.25	14.60
Sumner	543.95	529.05	14.90
Tipton	468.95	454.15	14.80
Trousdale	116.39	114.29	2.10
Unicoi	186.44	186.44	0.00
Union	247.15	218.25	28.90
Van Buren	273.62	272.52	1.10
Warren	434.67	430.58	4.09
Washington	329.87	326.27	3.60
Wayne	735.54	733.64	1.90
Weakley	581.93	581.43	0.50
White	376.15	373.00	3.15
Williamson	583.74	583.74	0.00
Wilson	583.09	570.49	12.60

Source: U.S. Department of Commerce, Bureau of the Census, Geography Division, *1980 Area Measurement Report*, October 16, 1981.

TABLE 12.9-- NATIONAL PARKS, ACREAGE, AND RECREATIONAL VISITS, TENNESSEE, 1985–1988
[Visits in thousands]

Name of park	Acreage[1]	Recreational visits 1988	1987	1986	1985
Andrew Johnson National Historic Site	16	76.6	77.1	72.6	68.6
Big South Fork National River[2]	120,000	613.0	n.a.	n.a.	n.a.
Chickamauga and Chattanooga National Military Park[3]	8,095	877.1	1,076.3	1,157.1	1,075.5
Cumberland Gap National Historic Park[4]	20,273	760.8	776.6	788.6	729.7
Fort Donelson National Battlefield	536	285.1	292.1	327.9	300.4
Great Smoky Mountains National Park[5]	241,206	8770.8	10,209.8	9,836.3	9,319.3
Obed Wild and Scenic River	5,101	16.3	6.7	n.a.	n.a.
Shiloh National Military Park	3,753	361.6	336.1	326.0	264.4
Stones River National Battlefield	330	198.2	151.7	210.3	196.3

Note: Data for Appalachian National Scenic Trail are not reported.
n.a. not available.
1. Includes only that part of park located in Tennessee.
2. A part is located in Kentucky.
3. A part is located in Georgia.
4. Parts are located in Kentucky and Virginia.
5. A part is located in North Carolina.
Source: U.S. Department of the Interior, National Park Service, direct correspondence.

TABLE 12.10--SELECTED STATISTICS ON THE GREAT SMOKY MOUNTAINS NATIONAL PARK, NORTH CAROLINA-TENNESSEE, 1960–1988, SELECTED YEARS

Visitor activity	1988[a]	1987	1986	1985
Total number of visitors[1]	8,786,100	10,210,000	9,836,000	9,319,300
Campground campers in tents	200,518	206,530	179,204	197,255
Campground campers in trailers or recreational vehicles	187,092	183,141	177,336	184,692
Campers in organized groups	21,477	19,156	17,343	21,546
Backcountry campers	72,152	76,714	68,375	65,493
Picnickers	622,171	708,717	546,728	494,783
Hikers using park trails	277,389	317,915	276,466	256,911
Horseback riders	72,339	59,546	49,957	63,727
Bicycle riders (Cades Cove Loop)	43,020	48,521	49,664	40,782
		1980	1970	1960
Total number of visitors[1]		8,441,000	6,778,500	4,528,500
Campground campers in tents		198,189	274,300	336,900
Campground campers in trailers or recreational vehicles		207,223	314,400	23,600
Campers in organized groups		26,793	n.a.	n.a.
Backcountry campers		81,500	88,600	19,100
Picnickers		470,161	627,400	558,800
Hikers using park trails		328,951	304,800	203,800
Horseback riders		60,468	43,700	24,000
Bicycle riders (Cades Cove Loop)		16,942	n.a.	n.a.

n.a. not available.

1. Includes categories not shown separately.

a. Starting on January 1, 1988, the method for computing recreational visits was modified; therefore, 1988 figures are not comparable to earlier years.

Source: U.S. Department of the Interior, National Park Service, direct correspondence.

TABLE 12.11--NUMBER OF VISITORS TO THE GREAT SMOKY MOUNTAINS NATIONAL PARK, NORTH CAROLINA-TENNESSEE, MONTHLY, 1970–1988, SELECTED YEARS
[In thousands]

Month	1988[a]	1987[r]	1986	1985	1984	1983	1980	1975	1970
TOTAL	8,786.1	10,209.8	9,836.3	9,319.3	8,508.4	8,435.5	8,441.0	8,541.5	6,778.5
January	169.0	260.1	206.5	174.0	157.6	175.0	207.7	172.8	103.6
February	175.6	227.9	200.2	198.4	231.1	211.1	192.2	191.4	126.1
March	309.0	414.9	456.9	422.0	300.5	288.7	259.7	352.9	228.1
April	504.3	569.6	648.9	598.9	545.7	472.0	553.4	490.7	325.4
May	664.3	868.5	825.4	631.7	638.0	682.6	716.0	770.9	543.9
June	1,245.6	1,316.7	1,283.5	1,215.8	1,140.6	1,059.3	1,105.9	1,222.3	1,017.3
July	1,669.5	1,627.5	1,761.9	1,610.6	1,444.9	1,526.0	1,439.4	1,491.8	1,334.5
August	1,470.6	1,512.7	1,400.4	1,391.1	1,281.5	1,252.0	1,410.2	1,612.3	1,324.6
September	986.9	990.0	920.4	996.0	925.6	880.4	802.5	714.3	600.6
October	969.4	1,576.5	1,285.4	1,340.4	1,133.7	1,266.2	1,075.6	982.8	806.5
November	389.5	586.5	560.4	503.2	430.3	433.8	447.7	356.2	208.3
December	232.4	276.8	286.4	237.2	278.9	188.3	230.7	183.1	159.6

r revised.

a. New method of computing visitation; figures are not comparable to earlier years. In general, the change in computations had a greater impact on the winter months (October through April).

Source: U.S. Department of the Interior, National Park Service, January news releases, and direct correspondence.

TABLE 12.12--NUMBER OF VISITORS TO THE CHEROKEE NATIONAL FOREST, BY TYPE OF ACTIVITY, FISCAL YEAR 1989 [In thousands]

Activity	Visitors	Activity	Visitors
Automobile travel	2,378	Picnicking	1,217
Bicycling	60	Recreation summer homes	32
Boating and sailing	225	Resorts	143
Camping	773	Sports and games	165
Fishing	483	Swimming related activities	714
Hiking and walking	401	Viewing scenery	584
Horseback riding	86	White-water activities	354
Hunting	524	Winter sports	37
Off-road vehicle travel	308	Other	642
		TOTAL	9,126

Note: Cherokee National Forest has 625,350 total acres; within this, there are 29 campgrounds, 29 picnic grounds, 9 swimming beaches, 13 boat launching sites.

Source: U.S. Department of Agriculture, Forest Service, Cleveland, Tennessee, direct correspondence.

TABLE 12.13--STATE PARKS AND RECREATION AREAS: LOCATION, ACREAGE, AND NUMBER OF VISITS, TENNESSEE, FISCAL YEAR 1988

Name of park	County	Size (acres)	Number of visits
Big Cypress Tree	Weakley	330	11,234
Big Hill Pond	McNairy	4,218	86,801
Big Ridge	Union	3,642	211,710
Bledsoe Creek Camping Park	Sumner	164	85,832
Booker T. Washington	Hamilton	353	393,367
Burgess Falls	Putnam-White	155	129,387
Cedars of Lebanon	Wilson	832	548,905
Chickasaw	Chester-Hardeman	1,280	677,405
Cove Lake	Campbell	673	955,734
Cumberland Mountain	Cumberland	1,562	761,543
Cumberland Trail	Campbell	90	24,600
David Crockett Birth Place	Greene	67	398,708
David Crockett State Park	Lawrence	1,071	823,643
Dunbar Cave/Port Royal	Montgomery-Robertson	136	133,747
Edgar Evins	DeKalb	6,279	350,174
Fall Creek Falls	Bledsoe-Van Buren	16,092	937,568
Fort Loudoun	Monroe	407	149,660
Fort Pillow	Lauderdale	1,629	68,919
Frozen Head	Morgan	11,651	133,940
Harrison Bay	Hamilton	1,199	625,010
Henry Horton	Marshall	1,141	910,704
Hiwassee/Ocoee Rivers	Polk	181	300,363
Indian Mountain	Campbell	213	167,507
Long Hunter	Davidson-Rutherford-Wilson	2,315	350,462
Meeman-Shelby Forest	Shelby	12,467	1,055,813
Montgomery Bell	Dickson	3,751	746,537
Mousetail Landing	Perry	1,219	255,517
Natchez Trace	Benton-Carroll-Henderson	11,100	1,193,584
Nathan Bedford Forrest	Benton-Humphreys	2,587	249,020
Norris Dam	Anderson-Campbell	4,038	437,899
Old Stone Fort	Coffee	796	258,464
Panther Creek	Hamblen	1,965	573,383
Paris Landing	Henry	773	1,086,028
Pickett	Pickett	865	311,874
Pickwick Landing	Hardin	1,392	1,634,545
Pinson Mounds	Madison	1,086	84,068
Radnor Lake	Davidson	957	542,505
Red Clay	Bradley	258	382,647
Reelfoot Lake	Lake-Obion	338	1,004,919
Roan Mountain	Carter	1,998	921,882
Rock Island	Warren-White	870	371,721
South Cumberland[1]	Franklin-Grundy-Marion	11,510	778,764
Standing Stone	Overton	1,055	361,028
Sycamore Shoals	Carter	49	134,596
T. O. Fuller	Shelby	384	412,824
Tims Ford	Franklin	413	318,909
Warriors' Path	Sullivan	870	2,420,367

1. The South Cumberland Park is made up of seven smaller parks or areas.

Source: Tennessee Department of Conservation, Division of State Parks, direct correspondence.

FIGURE 12.2
National and State Parks, Tennessee

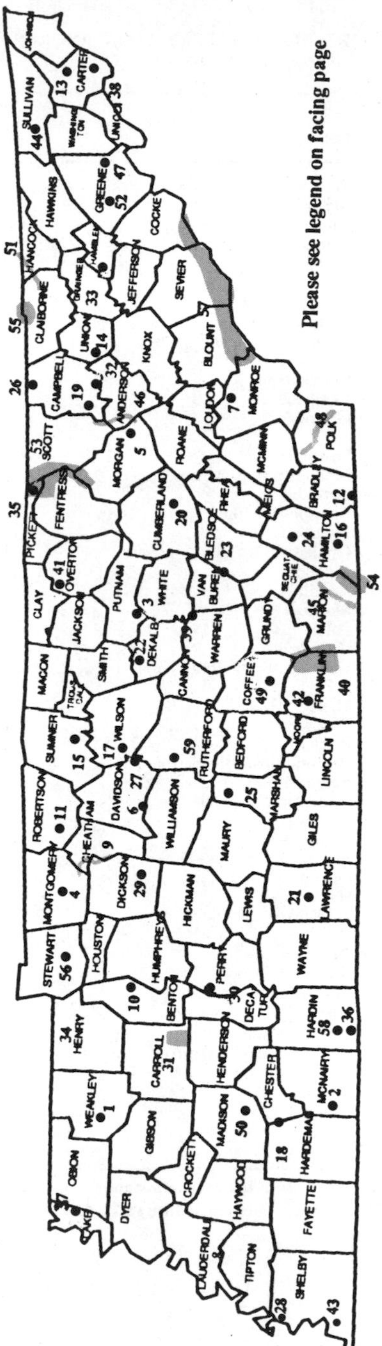

Please see legend on facing page

Legend for Figure 12.2

State Natural Areas

1 Big Cypress Tree
2 Big Hill Pond
3 Burgess Falls
4 Dunbar Cave
5 Frozen Head
6 Radnor Lake

State Historical Areas

7 Fort Loudoun
8 Fort Pillow
9 Harpeth River
10 Nathan Bedford Forrest
11 Port Royal
12 Red Clay
13 Sycamore Shoals

State Parks and Recreation Areas

14 Big Ridge
15 Bledsoe Creek
16 Booker T. Washington
17 Cedars of Lebanon
18 Chickasaw
19 Cove Lake
20 Cumberland Mountain

State Parks and Recreation Areas (Cont.)

21 David Crockett
22 Edgar Evins
23 Fall Creek Falls
24 Harrison Bay
25 Henry Horton
26 Indian Mountain
27 Long Hunter
28 Meeman-Shelby Forest
29 Montgomery Bell
30 Mousetail Landing
31 Natchez Trace
32 Norris Dam
33 Panther Creek
34 Paris Landing
35 Pickett
36 Pickwick Landing
37 Reelfoot Lake
38 Roan Mountain
39 Rock Island
40 South Cumberland[1]
41 Standing Stone
42 Tims Ford
43 T.O. Fuller
44 Warrior's Path

Other State Areas

45 Cumberland State Scenic Trail I
46 Cumberland State Scenic Trail II
47 Davy Crockett Birthplace
48 Hiawassee State Scenic River
49 Old Stone Fort State Archaeological Area
50 Pinson Mounds State Archaeological Area
51 Trail of the Lonesome Pine

National Parks

52 Andrew Johnson
53 Big South Fork
54 Chickamauga
55 Cumberland Gap
56 Fort Donnelson
57 Great Smoky Mountains
58 Shiloh
59 Stones River

Trail or River

Location of largest parks

Note: Does not include national forests.
1. South Cumberland is comprised of seven separate parks and state areas.

Source: Tennessee Department of Tourist Development and Tennessee Department of Conservation, direct correspondence.

TABLE 12.14--HIGHEST AND MEAN ELEVATIONS, SOUTHEASTERN STATES AND UNITED STATES
[Elevations in feet]

State	Highest point: Name	Highest point: Elevation	Approximate mean elevation
TENNESSEE	Clingmans Dome	6,643	900
Alabama	Cheaha Mountain	2,407	500
Arkansas	Magazine Mountain	2,753	650
Florida	Sec. 30, T6N, R20W, Walton County[1]	345	100
Georgia	Brasstown Bald	4,784	600
Kentucky	Black Mountain	4,145	2,000
Louisiana	Driskill Mountain	535	750
Mississippi	Woodall Mountain	806	300
North Carolina	Mount Mitchell	6,684	700
South Carolina	Sassafras Mountain	3,560	350
Virginia	Mount Rogers	5,729	950
West Virginia	Spruce Knob	4,863	1,500
UNITED STATES	Mt. McKinley (Alaska)	20,320	2,500

1. Sec. denotes section; T, township; R, range; N, north; W, west.

Source: U.S. Department of Commerce, Bureau of the Census, *Statistical Abstract of the United States*, 1989.

TABLE 12.15--STATE PARKS AND RECREATION AREAS: ACREAGE, VISITORS AND REVENUE, SOUTHEASTERN STATES AND UNITED STATES, 1984–1987

State	Acreage, 1987 (1,000)	Visitors[1] (1,000)				Revenue, 1987	
		1987	1986	1985	1984	Total ($1,000)	Percentage of operating budget
TENNESSEE	120	24,343	22,255	19,998	19,998	15,662	50.7
Alabama	48	6,099	6,577	6,122	5,441	8,799	57.0
Arkansas	44	7,148	6,490	6,098	6,329	8,799	53.7
Florida	278	14,290	13,659	14,305	14,976	10,459	49.7
Georgia	61	13,310	12,806	11,616	10,888	8,569	48.2
Kentucky	42	24,210	23,492	22,992	23,942	31,858	62.3
Louisiana	38	740	1,100	1,258	1,145	990	23.8
Mississippi	22	4,434	4,691	4,468	4,461	4,246	103.7
North Carolina	125	7,152	6,262	6,554	5,782	1,182	16.4
South Carolina	79	7,803	8,366	9,188	9,487	8,360	61.6
Virginia	54	3,635	3,397	3,497	3,242	1,558	24.8
West Virginia	206	9,129	8,933	8,704	8,656	10,462	53.4
UNITED STATES	13,752	694,432	675,465	661,916	665,524	309,626	36.5

1. Includes overnight visitors.

Source: U.S. Department of Commerce, Bureau of the Census, *Statistical Abstract of the United States*, 1989.

TABLE 12.16--NATIONAL FOREST LAND, SOUTHEASTERN STATES, AS OF SEPTEMBER 30, 1987
[In thousands of acres]

State	Total[1]	National forest system	Other lands within boundaries
TENNESSEE	1,212	626	586
Alabama	1,274	649	625
Arkansas	3,502	2,484	1,019
Florida	1,224	1,100	125
Georgia	1,855	867	988
Kentucky	2,102	665	1,436
Louisiana	1,023	600	422
Mississippi	2,310	1,148	1,162
North Carolina	3,165	1,220	1,946
South Carolina	1,376	606	769
Virginia	3,226	1,638	1,588
West Virginia	1,861	1,003	858

1. Comprises all publicly and privately owned land within authorized boundaries of national forests, purchase units, national grasslands, and land utilization projects.

Source: U.S. Department of Commerce, Bureau of the Census, *Statistical Abstract of the United States*, 1989.

TABLE 12.17--FEDERALLY OWNED LAND, BY AGENCY, SOUTHEASTERN STATES, FISCAL YEAR 1987 [In acres]

	Total federally owned land[1]				
State	Acres	Percentage of total state land area	Forest Service	National Park Service	Fish and Wildlife Service
TENNESSEE	1,875,617.5	7.0	625,574.8	264,258.7	30,860.1
Alabama	1,091,568.6	3.3	645,260.3	6,348.4	12,900.9
Arkansas	3,324,416.1	9.9	2,479,291.2	100,151.6	211,704.5
Florida	4,261,083.0	12.3	1,098,495.8	2,172,245.0	201,521.4
Georgia	2,029,516.7	5.4	877,235.7	37,531.6	464,682.5
Kentucky	1,400,941.5	5.5	673,866.0	62,391.0	2,153.8
Louisiana	1,142,081.3	4.0	597,863.4	6,808.9	355,188.1
Mississippi	1,676,470.8	5.5	1,144,023.4	102,068.5	124,451.7
North Carolina	2,209,548.2	7.0	1,215,683.9	359,092.1	257,492.6
South Carolina	1,161,078.1	6.0	610,394.0	21,021.8	146,154.5
Virginia	2,465,498.2	9.7	1,646,738.0	298,485.2	105,767.8
West Virginia	1,167,711.2	7.6	972,630.3	9,873.1	455.5

State	Military services	Veterans Administration	Corps of Engineers	Tennessee Valley Authority	Department of Energy
TENNESSEE	47,036.7	922.4	272,324.8	560,539.3	73,176.6
Alabama	131,015.5	674.0	69,654.9	221,713.7	0.0
Arkansas	22,017.0	295.1	508,412.3	0.0	58.6
Florida	677,354.7	513.7	19,483.3	0.0	99.2
Georgia	272,052.9	378.4	362,741.9	9,508.7	0.0
Kentucky	160,605.6	264.1	335,251.7	161,394.7	3,423.2
Louisiana	104,374.8	80.6	69,293.8	0.0	1,684.5
Mississippi	17,413.7	290.7	255,277.5	10,764.5	0.0
North Carolina	301,384.3	325.8	44,083.7	21,845.6	0.0
South Carolina	93,530.1	145.7	96,851.5	0.0	192,323.3
Virginia	276,344.1	1,273.5	109,964.3	1,624.5	0.0
West Virginia	49.8	424.2	84,134.7	0.0	131.7

Note: Percentages computed by the Center for Business and Economic Research.

1. Total includes categories not detailed separately.

Source: General Services Administration, Public Buildings Service, direct correspondence.

State-chartered Tennessee banks come under the jurisdiction of the State Department of Financial Institutions, whereas national banks in Tennessee are organized under federal law and are under the jurisdiction of the U.S. Comptroller of the Currency. The Federal Reserve System, including all national banks and those state banks which join voluntarily, was established in 1913 in order to provide some control over bank lending practices across the country. Summary data of U.S. banks are published quarterly in the *Federal Reserve Bulletin.* Some state-lèvel data for Tennessee are available in monthly releases from the Atlanta and St. Louis Federal Reserve District Banks.

The Federal Deposit Insurance Corporation (FDIC) was established in 1933 to insure accounts in its member banks. Nearly all banks belong to the FDIC, and it is a primary source of statistical data on commercial banks. Their semi-annual *Data Book, Operating Banks and Branches* provides deposit information for states, their Metropolitan Statistical Areas, and for counties. The *Annual Report* includes information on bank failures and data on banks receiving FDIC disbursements. A third FDIC publication, *Statistics on Banking*, provides balance sheet and income statement data at the state level. Sheshunoff and Company, Inc. also provides these data at the state level, but its most valuable contribution to banking statistics is the information it provides on individual banks. Performance statistics on banks in Tennessee are taken from *Sheshunoff Banks of Tennessee* and published here by special permission.

For savings and loan institutions, annual statistics of members in the Federal Savings and Loan Insurance Corporation (FSLIC) are reported in *Savings and Home Financing Sourcebook*, published by the Federal Home Loan Bank Board. The name of this supervisory agency was changed to the Office of Thrift Supervision in July 1989. Data on credit unions are available from the Credit Union National Association (CUNA), Inc., established in 1970. The *Credit Union Report*, a statistical supplement formerly included in the *Credit Union National Association Yearbook,* is the source of credit union data for the southeastern states. Additional data on Tennessee credit unions are provided by the Tennessee Department of Financial Institutions in its annual report.

The *Annual Report of the Commissioner of Commerce and Insurance* gives complete data about insurance written in the state of Tennessee by both in-state and out-of-state companies. Because insurance is regulated by the individual states, the federal government does not collect detailed statistics on insurance; however, the American Council of Life Insurance (New York) publishes *Life Insurance Fact Book*, and the Insurance Information Institute publishes *Insurance Facts*. Both are comprehensive statistical booklets on the industry.

TABLE OF CONTENTS

TABLE OF CONTENTS
(Continued)

TABLE 13.1-- NUMBER OF BANKING OFFICES, FDIC-INSURED COMMERCIAL BANKS AND TRUST COMPANIES, BY TYPE OF CHARTER, AND BY INSURANCE STATUS, TENNESSEE, 1940–1987, SELECTED YEARS

			State charter	
Year	Total	National charter	Federal Reserve member	Federal Reserve nonmember
1987	1,370	538	83	749
1986	1,348	546	69	733
1985	1,334	533	66	735
1984	1,317	525	63	729
1983	1,341	478	65	798
1982	1,335	423	72	840
1981	1,407	481	62	864
1980	1,382	479	62	841
1979	1,342	480	60	802
1978	1,301	483	59	759
1977	1,256	474	64	718
1976	1,160	427	66	667
1975	1,114	443	65	606
1974	1,056	427	58	571
1973	974	402	53	519
1972	904	389	55	460
1971	834	371	51	412
1970	791	353	46	392
1969	749	338	44	367
1968	715	324	41	350
1967	698	322	39	337
1966	671	309	36	326
1965	622	281	33	308
1964	585	257	31	297
1963	560	239	31	290
1962	544	224	31	289
1961	526	217	26	283
1960	507	205	25	277
1955	430	153	23	254
1950	387	123	22	242
1945	348	98	21	229
1940	339	89	16	234

Note: Data are as of December 31.

Source: Federal Deposit Insurance Corporation, *Statistics on Banking, 1987*, and earlier editions; and *Annual Report, 1980*, and earlier editions.

TABLE 13.2-- STATEMENT OF CONDITION OF FDIC-INSURED COMMERCIAL BANKS, TENNESSEE, AS OF DECEMBER 31, 1984–1987 [In millions of dollars]

Account	1987	1986	1985	1984
TOTAL ASSETS	41,162	38,921	35,966	32,742
Cash and due from depository institutions	3,992	4,303	4,214	4,030
Securities	9,837	9,235	8,309	7,735
Federal funds sold	1,359	1,494	1,480	1,765
Loans and leases, net	24,065	21,888	19,534	17,303
Real estate	9,544	7,744	6,347	5,473
Commercial and industrial	6,372	6,071	5,422	4,978
Loans to individuals	5,822	5,436	5,005	4,502
Other loans and leases	3,057	3,258	3,357	2,936
Allowance for losses	-361	-285	-238	-209
Unearned income	-368	-335	-360	-376
Other assets	1,909	2,001	2,430	1,910
TOTAL LIABILITIES AND EQUITY CAPITAL	41,162	38,921	35,966	32,742
Total liabilities	38,167	36,158	33,493	30,536
Total deposits	34,054	32,271	29,533	27,422
Federal funds purchased	2,757	2,576	2,209	2,033
Demand notes and other borrowed money	439	352	362	104
Mortgage indebtedness	45	53	57	53
Subordinated notes and debentures	116	40	41	51
Other liabilities	756	866	1,290	873
Total equity capital	2,996	2,763	2,473	2,206
Number of banks	282	283	289	296

Note: Detail may not add to total due to independent rounding.
Source: Federal Deposit Insurance Corporation, *Statistics on Banking, 1987*, and earlier editions.

TABLE 13.3-- INCOME STATEMENT OF COMMERCIAL BANKS, TENNESSEE, 1984–1987
[In thousands of dollars]

Income and expenses	1987	1986	1985	1984
TOTAL OPERATING INCOME	3,821,665	3,715,373	3,694,810	3,603,145
Total interest and fee income	3,315,138	3,193,846	3,233,058	3,203,652
Interest and fees on loans	2,374,026	2,228,265	2,206,791	2,127,980
Income from lease financing receivables	15,269	13,331	12,414	8,972
Interest on balances with banks	70,073	92,027	107,159	133,402
Income on securities	764,411	749,969	778,383	758,938
Income on federal funds sold	91,362	110,252	128,311	174,359
Total non-interest income	506,527	521,527	461,752	399,493
Service charges on deposit accounts	179,680	165,041	154,515	137,416
Other non-interest income	326,847	356,488	307,237	262,075
TOTAL OPERATING EXPENSES	3,377,450	3,306,915	3,313,232	3,272,465
Total interest expense	1,810,475	1,803,938	1,918,480	2,035,176
Interest on deposits	1,600,734	1,623,165	1,727,679	1,811,155
Expense of federal funds purchased	175,624	154,103	163,487	204,976
Interest on other borrowings	27,424	24,683	22,983	13,525
Interest on subordinated notes and debentures	6,694	1,987	4,331	5,521
Total non-interest expense	1,345,008	1,294,207	1,188,751	1,096,972
Salaries and employee benefits	619,207	625,008	600,161	544,741
Expenses of premises and fixed assets	187,676	179,130	181,226	164,522
Other non-interest expense	538,125	490,057	407,364	387,704
Provision for loan and lease losses and allocated transfer risk	221,967	208,770	206,001	140,317
Income before securities gains (losses)	444,215	408,458	381,578	330,680
Securities gains (losses), gross	10,578	30,230	6,287	-5,410
Income before taxes	454,794	438,688	387,865	325,268
Income taxes	-104,573	-87,682	-69,157	-69,192
Income before extraordinary items	350,222	351,011	318,708	256,078
Extraordinary items, net of tax	4,845	9,797	6,544	676
NET INCOME	355,067	360,808	325,252	256,750
Number of full-time equivalent employees	25,117	25,153	25,417	25,194
Number of banks	282	283	289	296

Note: Detail may not add to total due to independent rounding.

Source: Federal Deposit Insurance Corporation, *Statistics on Banking, 1987*, and earlier editions.

FIGURE 13.1
Deposits of Insured Commercial Banks in Tennessee
Annual Percentage Change, 1965–1987

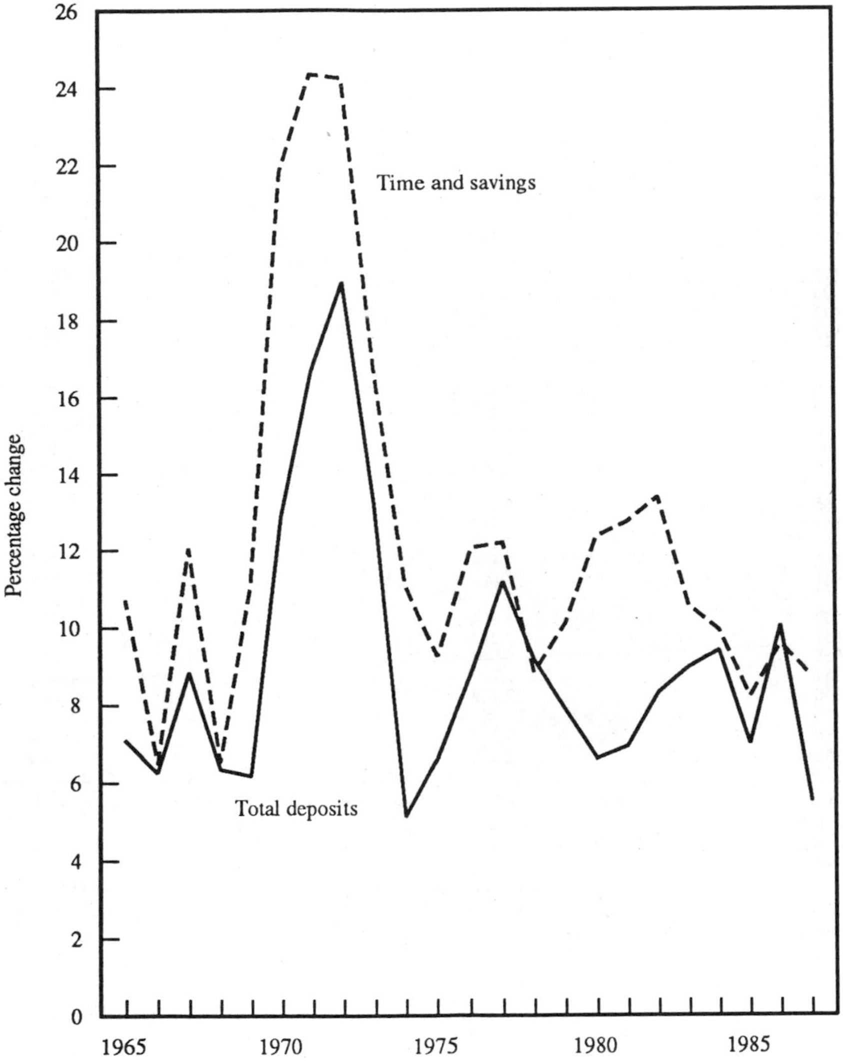

Source: Federal Deposit Insurance Corporation, *Statistics on Banking*, 1987; *Bank Operating Statistics*, 1984, and earlier editions; and U.S. Department of Commerce, Bureau of the Census, *Statistical Abstract of the United States*, 1987.

TABLE 13.4-- DEPOSITS OF INSURED COMMERCIAL BANKS, BY TYPE OF DEPOSIT, TENNESSEE, AS OF DECEMBER 31, 1950–1987, SELECTED YEARS [In millions of dollars]

Year	Total deposits [1]	Time and savings [2]	
		Amount	Percentage
1987	34,054	27,486	80.7
1986	32,271	25,285	78.4
1985	29,334	23,081	78.7
1984	27,422	21,334	77.8
1983	25,070	19,412	77.4
1982	23,012	17,562	76.3
1981	21,251	15,490	72.9
1980	19,875	13,741	69.1
1979	18,645	12,232	65.6
1978	17,288	11,111	64.3
1977	15,840	10,213	64.5
1976	14,249	9,103	63.9
1975	13,098	8,124	62.0
1974	12,288	7,438	60.5
1973	11,691	6,696	57.3
1972	10,329	5,735	55.5
1971	8,682	4,616	53.2
1970	7,442	3,712	49.9
1969	6,593	3,047	46.2
1968	6,209	2,744	44.2
1967	5,839	2,576	44.1
1966	5,365	2,299	42.9
1965	5,050	2,159	42.8
1964	4,717	1,951	41.4
1963	4,183	1,671	39.9
1962	3,806	1,424	37.4
1961	3,617	1,175	32.5
1960	3,314	1,075	32.4
1959	3,212	1,009	31.4
1958	3,044	967	31.8
1957	2,789	838	30.0
1956	2,729	747	27.4
1955	2,632	695	26.4
1950	2,056	459	22.3

1. For 1978 through 1982, deposits in foreign offices were included only in total deposits, as data on the actual breakdown were not available.

2. Beginning in 1986, refers to all interest-bearing deposits, including those held in interest-bearing checking accounts.

Source: Federal Deposit Insurance Corporation, *Statistics on Banking, 1987*, and earlier editions; *Bank Operating Statistics, 1983*, and earlier editions; *Assets and Liabilities, Commercial and Mutual Savings Banks, December 31, 1977*, and earlier editions; and direct correspondence; U.S. Department of Commerce, Bureau of the Census, *Statistical Abstract of the United States, 1987*.

TABLE 13.5-- SELECTED BALANCE SHEET ITEMS OF INSURED SAVINGS INSTITUTIONS, TENNESSEE, AS OF DECEMBER 31, 1950–1987, SELECTED YEARS
[Dollar amounts in millions]

Year	Number of institutions	Total assets	Mortgage loans	Total deposits
1987	63	$11,515	$6,422	$9,240
1986	64	10,624 r	6,197 r	8,942
1985	62	9,819 r	6,207 r	8,570
1984	66 r	9,628 r	5,932 r	8,562
1983	70	7,814	5,276	6,949
1982	81	7,933	5,907	6,826
1981	92	7,684	6,244	6,473
1980	99	7,425	6,097	6,270
1979	98	6,904	5,858	5,728
1978	97	6,417	5,485	5,321
1977	96	5,529	4,699	4,711
1976	76	4,669	3,924	4,036
1975	78	4,031	3,386	3,458
1974	76	3,461	2,963	2,944
1973	72	3,152	2,715	2,696
1972	71	2,817	2,383	2,436
1971	71	2,358	1,969	2,061
1970	70	1,996	1,674	1,727
1969	70	1,808	1,563	1,568
1968	70	1,690	1,443	1,488
1967	68	1,538	1,301	1,362
1966	66	1,375	1,182	1,219
1965	65	1,285	1,103	1,126
1964	65	1,172	1,005	1,031
1963	64	1,080	918	944
1962	63	953	805	840
1961	59	854	718	764
1960	56	744	629	665
1959	52	644	544	570
1958	49	564	471	505
1957	46	492	411	443
1955	44	395	340	349
1950	39	158	132	137

r revised.
Source: Federal Home Loan Bank Board, *Savings and Home Financing Source Book, 1987*, and earlier editions.

TABLE 13.6-- SELECTED DATA ON STATE–CHARTERED CREDIT UNIONS, TENNESSEE, 1979–1987

	1987	1986	1985	1984	1983	1982	1981	1980	1979
Number of credit unions	248	263	280	303	313	337	358	365	361
Average credit union membership	2,588	2,353	2,078	1,820	1,680	1,511	1,411	1,353	1,334
Total number of members	641,979	618,913	581,793	551,497	526,072	509,509	505,207	494,007	481,874
Per member share average	$1,428	$1,507	$1,018	$918	$958	$907	$851	$964	$1,038
Total number of borrowers	264,267	277,716	254,797	244,497	227,232	219,058	229,565	245,573	245,166
Total number of non-borrowers	377,712	341,197	326,996	307,000	298,840	290,451	275,642	248,434	236,708
Total percentage borrowing	41.2	44.9	43.8	44.3	43.2	43.0	45.4	49.7	50.8
Average loan per borrower	$4,977	$4,080	$3,936	$2,861	$3,162	$2,815	$2,632	$2,421	$2,499

Source: Tennessee Department of Financial Institutions, *1987 Fourteenth Annual Report*, and earlier editions.

TABLE 13.7-- STATEMENT OF CONDITION OF STATE–CHARTERED CREDIT UNIONS, TENNESSEE, AS OF DECEMBER 31, 1985, 1986 AND 1987
[In thousands of dollars]

	1987	1986	1985
Cash	48,541	45,807	38,446
Cash and due from banks	46,804	43,229	36,492
Other cash items	1,737	2,578	1,950
Cash short	0	(a)	4
Securities	831,447	813,887	577,936
U.S. government securities	141,800	169,872	122,850
Savings and loan deposits	144,873	126,207	97,169
Other securities	544,774	517,809	357,917
Loans and discounts	1,335,586	1,146,407	1,010,575
Personal and chattel mortgage	1,313,464	1,131,769	1,003,124
Allowance loan losses	-1,835	-1,333	(a)
Loans to other credit unions	23,958	15,970	7,452
Receivables	29,532	16,903	13,584
Accounts receivable	22,392	12,071	9,478
Accrued interest	7,140	4,832	4,106
Fixed assets	24,705	21,755	18,134
Furniture and fixtures	16,922	14,891	12,128
Land and building	17,553	14,759	12,273
Depreciation allowance	-9,770	-7,895	-6,266
Prepaid items and other assets	31,445	42,493	9,002
Prepaid expenses	1,821	1,842	1,796
M.G.C. or NCUA deposit	12,334	7,665	(a)
Other assets	17,290	32,986	7,205
TOTAL ASSETS	2,301,255	2,087,251	1,667,677

	1987	1986	1985
Current liabilities	62,306	50,407	26,376
Accounts payable	18,250	6,473	8,706
Taxes payable	188	180	150
Notes payable	32,870	32,010	9,400
Dividends payable	10,329	11,695	7,963
Bank overdraft	669	27	156
Cash over	0	21	0
Other liabilities	3,283	6,541	2,194
Unearned interest	56	331	381
Miscellaneous liabilities	3,227	6,210	1,812
Members' accounts	2,085,082	1,891,224	1,517,338
Shares	916,815	932,787	592,616
Share drafts	101,621	85,216	63,683
Special accounts	327,118	276,216	396,747
Investment certificates	508,808	411,527	445,634
Christmas club	28,841	22,972	18,659
IRA's	201,879	162,507	(a)
Reserves	107,209	97,749	85,568
Statutory reserve	74,748	66,967	58,522
Special reserves	10,442	10,387	9,238
Reserve for depreciation	445	483	406
Reserve for contingencies	21,573	19,911	17,401
Undivided profits	43,376	41,331	36,202
TOTAL LIABILITIES AND CAPITAL	2,301,255	2,087,251	1,667,677

Note: Detail may not add to total due to independent rounding.

a. Less than $50.

Source: Tennessee Department of Financial Institutions, *1987 Fourteenth Annual Report*, and earlier editions.

TABLE 13.8-- OPERATIONS OF COUNTY MUTUAL FIRE INSURANCE COMPANIES, TENNESSEE, 1930–1987, SELECTED YEARS [In thousands of dollars]

Year	Net risks in force at end of year	New membership fees and assessments	Net losses paid	Net losses paid as a percentage of membership fees and assessments
1987	647,484	3,777	1,928	51.0
1986	669,221	3,678	1,977	53.8
1985	556,097	3,380	1,763	52.2
1984	497,438	3,001	1,916	63.8
1983	497,623	2,965	1,520	51.3
1982	501,184	3,015	1,409	46.7
1981	482,171	2,874	1,785	62.1
1980	500,043	2,492	1,596	64.0
1979	445,629	2,336	1,315	56.3
1978	429,662	2,215	1,048	47.3
1977	398,271	1,906	1,316	69.0
1976	364,401	1,655	926	56.0
1975	353,693	1,408	968	68.8
1974	334,434	1,511	1,135	75.1
1973	334,797	1,876	847	45.1
1972	558,201	1,719	931	54.2
1971	401,022	1,652	972	58.8
1970	378,275	1,418	908	64.0
1960	223,096	853	523	61.3
1950	101,862	416	159	38.2
1940	41,649	171	105	61.4
1930	47,959	266	230	86.5

Note: Percentages computed by the Center for Business and Economic Research.

Source: Tennessee Department of Commerce and Insurance, *Annual Report of the Commissioner of Commerce and Insurance, December 31, 1987,* and earlier editions.

TABLE 13.9-- OPERATIONS OF STOCK, FIRE, AND CASUALTY INSURANCE COMPANIES, TENNESSEE, 1972–1987 [In thousands of dollars]

Year	Premiums earned	Losses incurred	Losses incurred as a percentage of premiums earned
1987	90,233	104,441	115.7
1986	109,779	91,341	83.2
1985	209,816	184,459	87.9
1984	74,247	63,231	85.2
1983	68,803	49,763	72.3
1982	52,524	40,204	76.5
1981	61,825	42,392	68.6
1980	62,436	40,787	65.3
1979	74,858	50,064	66.9
1978	61,231	34,597	56.5
1977	30,461	15,491	50.9
1976	28,808	17,643	61.2
1975	33,532	20,906	62.3
1974	39,921	26,098	65.4
1973	50,415	29,760	59.0
1972	49,688	24,413	49.1

Note: Refers to companies domiciled in Tennessee.

Source: Tennessee Department of Commerce and Insurance, *Annual Report of the Commissioner of Commerce and Insurance, December 31, 1987*, and earlier editions.

TABLE 13.10–NUMBER OF LICENSED INSURANCE COMPANIES, BY TYPE AND BY STATE OF DOMICILE, TENNESSEE, DECEMBER 31, 1984–1987

	Total				Tennessee			
Type of company	1987	1986	1985	1984	1987	1986	1985	1984
Life companies	717	692	660	641	26	24	24	25
Fraternal orders or associations	15	15	15	15	1	1	1	1
Nonprofit hospital and medical associations	4	4	4	4	4	4	4	4
Health maintenance organizations	14	13	9	5	14	13	9	5
Stock fire and casualty companies	553	532	516	492	17	15	15	14
Captive companies	12	11	7	7	12	11	7	7
Mutual fire and casualty companies	80	80	79	82	5	5	5	5
Reciprocal or inter-insurers	15	16	16	16	0	0	0	0
Lloyds, New York	1	1	1	1	0	0	0	0
Title companies	27	27	27	23	3	3	3	3
County mutual fire companies	19	19	19	20	19	19	19	20

Source: Tennessee Department of Commerce and Insurance, *Annual Report of the Commissioner of Commerce and Insurance, December 31, 1987,* and earlier editions.

TABLE 13.11-NUMBER, ASSETS, LIABILITIES, AND SURPLUS OF INSURANCE COMPANIES, BY TYPE, AND BY STATE OF DOMICILE, TENNESSEE, DECEMBER 31, 1987
[In thousands of dollars except number of companies]

Type of company	Number of companies	Admitted assets [1]	Liabilities	Surplus
Life insurance	717	1,017,766,425	957,103,771	60,652,412
Tennessee	26	15,677,906	13,436,036	2,241,869
Out-of-state	691	1,002,088,519	943,667,735	58,410,543
Stock fire and casualty	553	300,872,559	232,028,406	68,854,698
Tennessee	17	229,386	210,203	19,179
Out-of-state	536	300,643,173	231,818,203	68,835,519
Captive companies, Tennessee	12	513,322	387,288	126,031
Mutual fire and casualty	80	76,408,187	49,985,932	26,422,250
Tennessee	5	607,100	365,940	241,160
Out-of-state	75	75,801,087	49,619,992	26,181,090
Reciprocal or inter-insurers, Out-of-state	15	12,023,600	8,129,654	3,893,946
Lloyds, New York	1	9,173	3,959	5,213
County mutual fire companies, Tennessee	19	14,835	187	14,638
Fraternal orders or associations	15	17,226,684	15,474,754	1,751,926
Tennessee	1	37,470	28,478	8,991
Out-of-state	14	17,189,214	15,446,276	1,742,935
Title insurance	27	1,976,464	1,107,796	868,658
Tennessee	3	16,937	6,694	10,243
Out-of-state	24	1,959,527	1,101,102	858,415
Nonprofit hospital and medical associations, Tennessee	4	470,294	238,530	231,763
Health maintenance organizations, Tennessee	14	220,996	195,098	25,899

Note: Detail may not add to total due to independent rounding.

1. Includes capital or guaranty fund for life insurance companies.

Source: Tennessee Department of Commerce and Insurance, *Annual Report of the Commissioner of Commerce and Insurance, December 31, 1987.*

TABLE 13.12--PREMIUMS EARNED AND LOSSES INCURRED BY INSURANCE COMPANIES,[1] BY TYPE, AND BY STATE OF DOMICILE, TENNESSEE, 1987 [In thousands of dollars]

Type of company	Premiums earned	Losses incurred	Losses incurred as a percentage of premiums earned
Stock fire and casualty	109,867,160	71,368,811	65.0
Tennessee	90,233	104,441	115.7
Out-of-state	109,776,927	71,264,370	64.9
Captive companies, Tennessee	63,264	45,494	71.9
Mutual fire and casualty	36,127,235	25,710,380	71.2
Tennessee	240,284	155,285	64.6
Out-of-state	35,886,951	25,555,095	71.2
Reciprocal or inter-insurers, out-of-state	6,975,708	4,633,172	66.4
Lloyds, New York	4,051	2,758	68.1
County mutual fire companies, Tennessee[2]	4,468	1,928	43.2
Fraternal orders or associations[3]	4,299,116	2,972,726	69.1
Tennessee	11,903	7,818	65.7
Out-of-state	4,287,213	2,964,908	69.2
Title insurance	2,920,947	285,281	9.8
Tennessee	12,617	547	4.3
Out-of-state	2,908,330	284,734	9.8

Note: Percentages computed by Center for Business and Economic Research when not given in source.

1. Does not include life insurance companies.

2. Refers to total income and net losses paid.

3. Refers to total income and total paid to policyholders.

Source: Tennessee Department of Commerce and Insurance, *Annual Report of the Commissioner of Commerce and Insurance, December 31, 1987.*

TABLE 13.13--LIFE INSURANCE IN FORCE, BY TYPE, TENNESSEE, 1955–1987 [In millions of dollars]

Year	Total	Ordinary	Group	Industrial	Credit
1987	143,106	76,098	60,398	826	5,784
1986	130,746	67,708	56,618	878	5,542
1985	116,766	60,249	50,353	903	5,261
1984	105,333	53,780	46,180	953	4,420
1983	96,501	47,571	43,739	1,039	4,152
1982	86,316	41,154	40,132	1,105	3,925
1981	77,230	36,064	36,047	1,180	3,939
1980	66,672	32,109	29,011	1,281	4,271
1979	61,051	29,323	25,327	1,383	5,018
1978	54,767	26,438	22,289	1,438	4,602
1977	49,206	23,159	20,791	1,599	3,657
1976	43,512	20,696	18,083	1,597	3,136
1975	39,334	18,679	16,172	1,628	2,855
1974	35,128	16,936	13,808	1,626	2,758
1973	32,348	15,389	12,841	1,625	2,493
1972	29,203	13,663	11,351	1,558	2,631
1971	26,291	12,440	10,140	1,513	2,198
1970	24,077	11,428	9,186	1,533	1,930
1969	21,828	10,611	7,832	1,477	1,908
1968	20,242	9,813	7,221	1,466	1,742
1967	18,265	8,956	6,472	1,436	1,401
1966	16,510	8,070	5,729	1,414	1,297
1965	14,909	7,289	5,020	1,378	1,222
1964	12,762	6,496	3,910	1,332	1,024
1963	11,583	5,838	3,587	1,306	852
1962	10,779	5,329	3,408	1,283	759
1961	9,896	4,890	3,094	1,224	688
1960	9,179	4,527	2,784	1,200	668
1959	8,367	4,145	2,471	1,165	586
1958	7,580	3,716	2,202	1,150	512
1957	7,121	3,387	2,041	1,171	522
1956	6,422	3,064	1,784	1,137	437
1955	5,821	2,762	1,563	1,115	381

Note: Life insurance in force is the sum of the face amounts, plus dividend additions, of life insurance policies outstanding at a given time. Additional amounts payable under accidental death or other special provisions are not included.

Beginning in 1973, credit is limited to life insurance on loans of ten years' duration or less. Ordinary and group include credit life insurance on loans of more than ten years' duration.

Source: American Council of Life Insurance, Washington, D.C., *Life Insurance Fact Book, 1988,* and earlier editions.

TABLE 13.14–LIFE INSURANCE AND ANNUITY BENEFIT PAYMENTS, TENNESSEE, 1950–1987, SELECTED YEARS [In thousands of dollars]

Benefits	1987	1986	1985	1980	1970	1960	1950
TOTAL	1,347,600	1,229,700	1,100,600	612,800	235,100	104,200	42,735
Death payments	381,200	369,600	340,600	230,700	116,300	51,200	22,708
Matured endowments	11,200	12,100	11,900	11,600	12,100	6,700	2,802
Disability payments	8,300	10,100	9,700	11,600	4,400	2,400	1,589
Annuity payments	497,600	371,200	288,400	118,400	20,100	5,500	1,771
Surrender values	241,100	261,600	256,900	118,400	37,600	20,500	6,604
Policy and contract dividends	208,200	205,100	193,100	122,100	44,600	17,900	7,261

Source: American Council of Life Insurance, Washington, D.C., *Life Insurance Fact Book, 1988,* and earlier editions.

TABLE 13.15–OPERATIONS OF NONPROFIT HOSPITAL AND MEDICAL ASSOCIATIONS, TENNESSEE, 1950–1987, SELECTED YEARS [In thousands of dollars]

Year	Premiums earned	Claims incurred	Claims incurred as a percentage of premiums earned
1987	740,230	744,202	100.5
1986	663,053	706,206	106.5
1985	646,410	590,890	91.4
1984	644,872	599,077	92.9
1983	348,428	321,096	92.2
1982	348,890	319,331	91.5
1981	344,671	324,071	94.0
1980	347,495	336,416	96.8
1979	321,424	298,104	92.7
1978	314,692	287,815	91.5
1977	279,190	253,904	90.9
1975	210,596	198,279	94.2
1970	98,245	90,377	92.0
1965	55,028	48,660	88.4
1960	31,525	28,090	89.1
1955	14,674	11,596	79.0
1950	4,349	3,273	75.3

Note: Percentages computed by the Center for Business and Economic Research.

Source: Tennessee Department of Commerce and Insurance, *Annual Report of the Commissioner of Commerce and Insurance, December 31, 1987,* and earlier editions.

TABLE 13.16--NUMBER OF BANKS AND AMOUNT OF DEPOSITS IN INSURED COMMERCIAL BANKS, BY TYPE OF DEPOSIT, METROPOLITAN STATISTICAL AREAS, AS OF JUNE 30, 1987 [Deposits in thousands of dollars]

Metropolitan Statistical Area	Number		Total deposits [1]	Deposits of individuals, partnerships, and corporations			Public funds
	Banks	Banking offices		Transaction [2]	Demand [3]	Non-transaction	
Chattanooga	20	113	2,444,828	756,510	447,192	1,436,421	191,116
Clarksville-Hopkinsville	7	36	802,509	197,160	116,971	510,734	88,055
Jackson	4	21	560,746	161,048	69,309	366,961	25,212
Johnson City-Kingsport-Bristol	20	120	2,242,333	601,345	316,677	1,465,152	134,577
Knoxville	23	149	3,441,688	959,745	582,656	2,246,032	188,790
Memphis	33	195	6,403,222	2,088,250	1,263,232	3,370,920	344,612
Nashville-Davidson	29	229	8,378,867	2,190,997	1,396,623	5,350,651	539,461

1. Includes categories not shown separately.
2. Transaction accounts are deposits/accounts on which the depositor or account holder can make withdrawals by negotiable or transferable instrument, payment orders of withdrawal, telephone transfers, or other similar devices, in order to make payments or transfers to others.
3. Demand deposits are included in transaction accounts.

Source: Federal Deposit Insurance Corporation, *Data Book, Operating Banks and Branches, June 30, 1987.*

TABLE 13.17--SELECTED OPERATING STATISTICS AND ASSET SIZE RANKINGS, BY BANK, CITIES, DECEMBER 31, 1987

City	Name of bank	Rank	Total assets ($1,000)	Total loans to deposits [1]
Adamsville	Bank of Adamsville	228	22,935	56.6
Adamsville	Farmers and Merchants Bank	235	19,605	61.4
Alamo	Bank of Alamo	168	36,644	49.2
Alcoa	American Fidelity Bank	219	24,033	75.3
Alexandria	DeKalb County Bank and Trust Company	132	51,316	68.8
Ardmore	Bank of Ardmore	125	54,935	67.8
Athens	City and County Bank of McMinn County	176	33,518	61.8
Athens	First National Bank and Trust Co. Athens	68	100,025	62.3
Athens	Citizens National Bank of Athens	106	65,986	67.9
Atwood	Citizens Bank and Trust Company	277	7,712	41.3
Barretville	Barretville Bank and Trust Company	31	168,170	57.7
Bartlett	Bank of Bartlett	61	108,360	82.3
Belfast	Bank of Belfast	269	11,575	68.3
Bells	Bank of Crockett	172	34,211	48.1
Bells	Bells Banking Company	236	19,537	74.9
Benton	Benton Banking Company	226	23,274	74.3
Benton	Peoples Bank of Polk County	260	14,271	88.0
Blountville	Tri-City Bank and Trust Company	29	180,865	62.3
Bolivar	Hardeman County Bank	113	60,757	76.7
Bolivar	Bank of Bolivar	189	29,908	56.9
Bradford	Bank of Bradford	227	23,238	38.5
Brentwood	Brentwood National Bank	251	16,071	41.4
Brighton	Brighton Bank	259	14,332	73.6
Brownsville	First State Bank	93	73,462	51.2
Brownsville	Brownsville Bank	81	84,312	84.8
Byrdstown	Peoples Bank and Trust Co. Pickett County	232	21,350	81.0
Byrdstown	Pickett County Bank and Trust Company	204	27,389	41.3
Camden	Bank of Camden	102	68,180	55.3
Carthage	Citizens Bank	44	130,355	65.2
Celina	Clay County Bank	271	10,895	62.9
Centerville	Sovran Bank Hickman County	178	33,255	50.3
Centerville	First National Bank of Centerville	110	63,891	56.3
Chapel Hill	First State Bank	253	15,420	20.8
Chattanooga	Pioneer Bank	17	370,971	51.5
Chattanooga	First American National Bank	27	185,055	81.9
Chattanooga	Volunteer Bank and Trust Company	161	38,345	77.2
Chattanooga	American National Bank and Trust Company	8	1,117,240	78.9
Chattanooga	Sovran Bank Chattanooga	38	141,730	86.1
Clarksville	First National Bank of Clarksville	21	230,199	74.2
Clarksville	Sovran Bank Clarksville	56	116,022	77.1
Clarksville	Northern Bank of Tennessee	24	198,530	88.6
Cleveland	First Citizens Bank	80	85,353	76.4
Cleveland	Merchants Bank	54	117,278	72.3
Cleveland	Cleveland Bank and Trust Company	36	152,533	72.0
Cleveland	Bank of Cleveland	218	24,078	72.4
Clifton	Peoples Bank	229	22,826	66.4
Clinton	Anderson County Bank	203	27,528	48.6
Collierville	First National Bank of Collierville	141	46,563	80.2
Collierville	Citizens Bank	261	14,267	58.9
Columbia	Middle Tennessee Bank	34	155,314	48.8
Columbia	First Bank of Maury County	247	17,341	40.4
Columbia	First Farmers and Merchants National Bank	22	229,845	81.0
Cookeville	Bank of Putnam County	83	83,443	64.7
Cookeville	American Bank and Trust Company	37	151,436	64.9
Cookeville	Citizens Bank	43	131,664	68.3
Copperhill	First National Bank of Polk County	129	52,876	86.2
Cornersville	Farmers Bank	249	16,885	77.2
Covington	First State Bank of Covington	99	69,152	73.7
Covington	Tipton County Bank	39	136,294	51.6

TABLE 13.17--SELECTED OPERATING STATISTICS AND ASSET SIZE RANKINGS, BY BANK, CITIES, DECEMBER 31, 1987 (Continued)

Total capital as a percentage of total assets	Income before extra-ordinary items ($1,000)	Return on average assets	Return on average equity	Yield on average earning assets	Rate on funds [2]	City
9.0	322	1.45	15.75	10.76	4.86	Adamsville
7.8	105	0.58	7.40	9.68	4.75	Adamsville
10.6	346	1.00	9.48	10.13	5.08	Alamo
8.2	174	0.75	10.49	10.76	5.56	Alcoa
7.9	479	0.90	13.48	10.28	5.86	Alexandria
7.1	549	1.05	16.37	10.51	5.33	Ardmore
9.3	304	0.93	11.54	9.63	4.64	Athens
8.2	1,240	1.23	16.16	10.38	5.11	Athens
10.4	1,017	1.62	16.09	10.06	5.06	Athens
9.0	25	0.33	3.56	10.75	6.02	Atwood
15.9	2,696	1.65	10.37	10.41	4.43	Barretville
7.2	780	0.83	12.64	10.47	4.92	Bartlett
8.7	174	1.55	19.73	9.97	5.35	Belfast
8.8	165	0.52	6.51	9.80	5.18	Bells
8.5	193	1.08	12.43	9.77	5.16	Bells
7.9	306	1.35	18.17	11.59	4.71	Benton
9.3	154	1.15	13.89	11.44	6.03	Benton
9.3	905	0.47	5.52	9.60	5.17	Blountville
7.4	328	0.55	9.77	9.99	5.31	Bolivar
6.8	96	0.32	6.23	10.01	5.10	Bolivar
9.5	244	1.07	11.54	8.79	5.05	Bradford
75.4	-204	-1.55	-2.02	0.99	0.19	Brentwood
8.4	173	1.26	17.31	10.40	5.51	Brighton
10.5	651	0.92	9.12	9.84	5.00	Brownsville
10.8	1,129	1.33	13.04	9.89	5.48	Brownsville
7.9	214	1.04	15.49	11.88	6.34	Byrdstown
9.4	294	1.10	12.26	10.49	5.87	Byrdstown
10.7	889	1.33	13.39	10.67	5.09	Camden
15.1	2,689	2.13	15.02	10.84	4.99	Carthage
10.5	-19	-0.17	-1.70	10.31	5.17	Celina
14.4	490	1.52	10.63	10.79	5.22	Centerville
10.5	949	1.56	15.93	11.31	5.27	Centerville
11.1	214	1.43	12.39	9.04	4.59	Chapel Hill
11.4	5,315	1.50	14.38	9.49	4.45	Chattanooga
7.2	1,681	0.96	14.69	10.61	4.97	Chattanooga
8.4	301	0.85	10.89	9.73	5.06	Chattanooga
8.4	9,491	0.87	12.55	9.55	5.00	Chattanooga
7.4	1,144	0.86	12.89	10.10	5.02	Chattanooga
9.5	2,832	1.30	15.37	10.06	5.02	Clarksville
8.7	1,229	1.08	13.74	10.48	5.16	Clarksville
8.4	2,260	1.17	15.24	10.74	5.08	Clarksville
8.2	930	1.15	14.86	10.40	5.28	Cleveland
10.6	1,252	1.08	11.48	9.95	4.90	Cleveland
10.2	1,691	1.14	11.99	10.68	5.20	Cleveland
13.8	-57	-0.42	-2.01	6.06	2.89	Cleveland
4.0	-1,957	-8.27	(b)	9.93	6.25	Clifton
7.1	-427	-2.46	-23.72	6.68	4.75	Clinton
10.3	635	1.45	15.88	11.34	5.29	Collierville
9.0	75	0.54	6.51	10.38	5.27	Collierville
8.7	1,465	0.97	11.67	9.92	5.30	Columbia
3.3	-831	-4.62	(b)	9.13	6.54	Columbia
9.9	2,939	1.31	14.89	10.34	5.09	Columbia
7.9	916	1.16	15.38	9.98	5.20	Cookeville
7.3	1,385	0.98	14.54	10.05	5.43	Cookeville
3.9	-4,467	-3.19	(b)	10.54	5.99	Cookeville
8.9	126	0.25	3.09	11.01	6.32	Copperhill
10.0	231	1.38	17.15	11.04	5.08	Cornersville
9.0	853	1.24	16.34	10.92	5.51	Covington
8.9	1,553	1.22	15.60	9.95	5.28	Covington

TABLE 13.17--SELECTED OPERATING STATISTICS AND ASSET SIZE RANKINGS, BY BANK, CITIES, DECEMBER 31, 1987 (Continued)

City	Name of bank	Rank	Total assets ($1,000)	Total loans to deposits [1]
Covington	Union Savings Bank	162	38,292	61.5
Crossville	First National Bank of Crossville	58	111,110	48.8
Crossville	Cumberland County Bank	135	50,379	49.2
Cumberland City	Cumberland City Bank	241	18,740	64.9
Dayton	Rhea County National Bank	195	29,054	69.6
Decatur	Meigs County Bank	171	34,419	75.4
Decaturville	Decatur County Bank	175	33,574	37.8
Decherd	First National Bank of Franklin County	121	57,062	47.7
Dickson	Bank of Dickson	100	68,938	47.7
Dover	Farmers and Merchants Bank	257	14,665	80.1
Dover	Peoples Bank	152	42,836	77.3
Dresden	Weakley County Bank	201	27,713	66.6
Ducktown	Ducktown Banking Company	143	45,932	68.7
Dukedom	Dukedom Bank	233	20,918	47.4
Dunlap	Sequatchie County Bank	202	27,528	64.9
Dunlap	Citizens Bank Dunlap/Pikeville	224	23,631	88.0
Dyer	Bank of Dyer	262	14,012	39.4
Dyer	Farmers and Merchants Bank	215	24,489	79.0
Dyersburg	First Citizens National Bank	25	193,526	65.2
East Ridge	Bank of East Ridge	248	17,305	67.1
Elizabethton	Carter County Bank	71	96,110	47.6
Elizabethton	Citizens Bank	62	107,261	97.0
Erin	Erin Bank and Trust Company	196	28,877	44.7
Erwin	Erwin National Bank	167	36,734	73.3
Etowah	Southern United Bank McMinn County	221	23,675	38.6
Fayetteville	Lincoln County Bank	126	53,755	82.3
Fayetteville	Union National Bank of Fayetteville	57	113,410	66.9
Fayetteville	Peoples Bank of Elk Valley	210	26,139	69.9
Finger	Home Banking Company	270	11,262	44.7
Frankewing	Bank of Frankewing	242	18,712	77.0
Franklin	First Citizens Bank	264	13,381	97.4
Franklin	Sovran Bank Williamson County	18	345,409	88.7
Friendship	Bank of Friendship	245	17,454	33.1
Gainesboro	Jackson County Bank	160	40,254	48.8
Gainesboro	Citizens Bank	237	19,436	61.2
Gallatin	First and Peoples National Bank Gallatin	101	68,348	58.9
Gates	Gates Banking and Trust Company	243	18,677	45.1
Gatlinburg	First National Bank of Gatlinburg	66	103,305	79.5
Gatlinburg	Tennessee State Bank	85	82,171	87.9
Germantown	Community Bank of Germantown	32	155,353	82.1
Gleason	Bank of Gleason	180	32,395	58.7
Goodlettsville	Bank of Goodlettsville	47	120,579	65.9
Greeneville	Andrew Johnson Bank	188	30,068	71.8
Greeneville	Greene County Bank	26	187,734	62.1
Greeneville	Sovran Bank Greeneville	60	110,125	74.5
Greenfield	Greenfield Banking Company	194	29,111	45.7
Halls	Lauderdale County Bank	273	10,569	67.5
Halls	Bank of Halls	185	30,264	40.8
Harriman	Bank of Roane County	53	117,722	60.8
Harrogate	Commercial Bank Claiborne County	108	64,824	57.0
Hartsville	Bank of Hartsville	212	25,882	67.2
Hartsville	Citizens Bank	217	24,146	75.7
Henderson	First State Bank	87	78,331	32.1
Henderson	Chester County Bank	239	19,257	80.1
Hohenwald	First Citizens Bank Hohenwald	158	41,601	44.1
Hohenwald	Lewis County Bank	246	17,417	87.3
Hornbeak	Reelfoot Bank	147	44,824	67.7
Humboldt	Merchants State Bank	64	104,296	51.2
Huntingdon	Bank of Huntingdon	77	87,546	43.6

TABLE 13.17--SELECTED OPERATING STATISTICS AND ASSET SIZE RANKINGS, BY BANK, CITIES, DECEMBER 31, 1987 (Continued)

Total capital as a percentage of total assets	Income before extra-ordinary items ($1,000)	Return on average assets	Return on average equity	Yield on average earning assets	Rate on funds [2]	City
8.1	476	1.17	16.10	9.82	4.99	Covington
7.9	1,254	1.17	16.48	9.52	5.30	Crossville
5.9	212	0.41	7.80	8.94	5.17	Crossville
9.9	300	1.67	17.34	11.04	5.23	Cumberland City
7.1	314	1.16	16.56	11.48	5.65	Dayton
8.2	381	1.12	14.69	11.72	5.69	Decatur
10.4	348	1.06	10.64	9.97	4.94	Decaturville
9.6	752	1.34	13.93	11.23	4.95	Decherd
9.2	826	1.29	14.97	10.37	5.27	Dickson
7.9	110	0.79	10.74	10.53	5.95	Dover
8.0	489	1.15	12.43	11.76	5.33	Dover
6.1	235	0.85	10.60	9.42	5.40	Dresden
7.6	0	0.00	0.00	10.59	6.13	Ducktown
7.2	151	0.73	12.40	10.22	6.05	Dukedom
15.3	467	1.70	12.10	10.03	4.89	Dunlap
6.8	349	1.56	22.14	12.28	5.96	Dunlap
8.3	122	0.92	11.22	9.80	5.17	Dyer
9.8	306	1.28	14.96	10.53	5.05	Dyer
6.9	1,003	0.53	8.50	10.22	5.42	Dyersburg
12.1	140	0.95	9.15	9.96	4.82	East Ridge
6.9	835	0.89	13.12	10.45	5.50	Elizabethton
8.3	1,133	1.05	11.04	11.32	5.73	Elizabethton
14.7	523	1.92	13.72	10.63	4.48	Erin
8.0	228	0.62	8.30	9.76	5.12	Erwin
7.4	294	1.27	18.75	9.46	5.14	Etowah
9.1	958	1.85	20.37	12.15	4.84	Fayetteville
9.0	750	0.71	8.04	10.97	5.21	Fayetteville
8.1	74	0.29	4.08	10.97	4.94	Fayetteville
7.9	93	0.85	11.36	9.83	5.33	Finger
11.2	262	1.53	14.62	11.32	5.46	Frankewing
28.0	-185	-2.08	-5.65	3.62	1.85	Franklin
8.9	3,576	1.04	13.69	10.54	5.08	Franklin
10.1	144	0.86	9.11	9.80	5.36	Friendship
9.9	495	1.28	14.58	10.23	5.20	Gainesboro
11.2	240	1.30	12.59	10.92	5.31	Gainesboro
8.4	737	1.10	14.59	10.12	5.20	Gallatin
8.1	256	1.45	18.35	9.55	5.25	Gates
7.7	680	0.70	13.15	9.82	5.91	Gatlinburg
6.8	1,031	1.37	21.69	10.95	5.74	Gatlinburg
6.6	1,342	0.94	16.54	11.11	5.19	Germantown
11.2	284	0.88	8.25	9.59	5.26	Gleason
8.3	1,153	0.97	12.76	10.34	5.28	Goodlettsville
8.3	318	1.12	14.79	10.41	5.27	Greeneville
11.2	3,401	1.83	17.54	10.21	5.03	Greeneville
10.2	1,919	1.78	19.07	10.45	4.65	Greeneville
10.1	383	1.34	14.39	9.47	5.24	Greenfield
11.5	61	0.63	5.42	10.69	5.07	Halls
9.5	332	1.13	12.20	9.38	5.18	Halls
8.0	1,149	0.99	13.96	10.36	5.31	Harriman
7.0	261	0.40	6.15	9.79	5.92	Harrogate
10.5	341	1.37	14.26	10.67	5.06	Hartsville
9.8	310	1.35	14.87	10.55	4.79	Hartsville
11.7	914	1.21	11.02	8.79	4.77	Henderson
11.0	182	0.96	9.50	11.02	5.03	Henderson
9.1	514	1.30	15.98	9.89	5.14	Hohenwald
9.8	269	1.61	18.45	10.43	5.61	Hohenwald
8.6	222	0.57	6.95	9.52	4.97	Hornbeak
9.4	1,467	1.51	18.75	10.37	5.29	Humboldt
8.0	831	0.97	12.46	9.34	5.00	Huntingdon

TABLE 13.17--SELECTED OPERATING STATISTICS AND ASSET SIZE RANKINGS, BY BANK, CITIES, DECEMBER 31, 1987 (Continued)

City	Name of bank	Rank	Total assets ($1,000)	Total loans to deposits [1]
Huntland	Bank of Huntland	265	13,311	63.2
Jacksboro	First State Bank	174	33,597	33.8
Jackson	First American National Bank	15	415,757	75.4
Jackson	Jackson National Bank	20	231,794	79.2
Jamestown	Fentress County Bank	197	28,279	55.7
Jamestown	Union Bank	136	48,555	56.2
Jasper	Marion Trust and Banking Company	148	44,594	65.0
Jefferson City	First American National Bank	109	64,463	37.3
Jefferson City	First Peoples Bank	142	46,050	66.4
Jellico	Union Bank	186	30,235	25.7
Johnson City	Hamilton Bank of Upper East Tennessee	23	225,260	67.5
Johnson City	Sovran Bank Tri-Cities	97	71,497	80.1
Kenton	First State Bank	156	42,195	64.0
Kingsport	Bank of Tennessee	74	91,316	69.0
Kingsport	First American National Bank	11	574,073	90.4
Kingsport	Executive Park National Bank	205	27,162	60.6
Kingston Springs	Cheatham State Bank	173	33,813	75.9
Knoxville	NBC Knoxville Bank	211	26,098	71.6
Knoxville	First American Bank	7	1,184,582	78.4
Knoxville	Third National Bank in Knoxville	16	394,224	87.7
Knoxville	Bank of East Tennessee	65	103,842	87.2
Knoxville	Valley Fidelity Bank and Trust Company	14	435,749	68.6
Lafayette	Macon Bank and Trust Company	92	73,787	52.6
Lafayette	Citizens Bank	76	89,510	65.6
LaFollette	Peoples National Bank LaFollette	98	71,233	42.8
LaFollette	First National Bank of LaFollette	115	59,561	43.7
Lake City	Third National Bank in Anderson County	46	123,239	67.3
Lawrenceburg	Community Bank and Trust Company	231	21,526	32.1
Lawrenceburg	First National Bank of Lawrenceburg	63	105,555	37.5
Lebanon	Peoples Bank	105	66,914	69.5
Lebanon	Lebanon Bank	41	136,196	61.1
Lebanon	Wilson Bank and Trust Company	199	27,986	67.8
Lenoir City	First National Bank of Loudon County	52	117,731	73.0
Lenoir City	Bank of Loudon County	94	73,247	79.7
Lewisburg	Sovran Bank Marshall County	107	65,320	81.2
Lewisburg	Peoples and Union Bank	104	67,451	55.8
Lexington	Henderson County Bank	278	7,012	62.8
Lexington	Central State Bank	78	87,027	46.7
Lexington	First National Bank of Lexington	154	42,318	79.9
Liberty	Liberty State Bank	206	26,763	62.3
Linden	First State Bank	182	31,469	52.9
Livingston	Union Bank and Trust Company	164	38,245	75.9
Livingston	First National Bank Cumberlands	153	42,723	71.2
Lobelville	Bank of Perry County	240	18,758	75.8
Loudon	First Heritage National Bank	140	47,104	85.0
Lynchburg	Farmers Bank	150	42,872	25.1
Madison	First Cumberland Bank	276	9,099	11.4
Madisonville	Bank of Madisonville	86	81,189	62.5
Manchester	First National Bank of Manchester	133	51,160	48.1
Manchester	Peoples Bank and Trust Company	177	33,424	57.5
Manchester	Coffee County Bank	250	16,072	61.2
Martin	City State Bank	146	45,272	62.8
Martin	Martin Bank	151	42,865	44.7
Maryville	Citizens Bank of Blount County	67	102,171	61.3
Mason	Bank of Mason	279	5,286	38.1
Maury City	Planters Bank	275	9,310	57.2
Maynardville	First State Bank	216	24,179	52.1
McKenzie	McKenzie Banking Company	157	42,109	50.8
McLemoresville	Carroll Bank and Trust Company	137	47,693	66.5

TABLE 13.17--SELECTED OPERATING STATISTICS AND ASSET SIZE RANKINGS, BY BANK, CITIES, DECEMBER 31, 1987 (Continued)

Total capital as a percentage of total assets	Income before extra-ordinary items ($1,000)	Return on average assets	Return on average equity	Yield on average earning assets	Rate on funds[2]	City
6.9	182	1.45	26.52	10.51	4.99	Huntland
9.0	429	1.28	15.00	9.21	4.83	Jacksboro
7.2	4,027	0.97	15.56	9.72	5.32	Jackson
8.4	2,190	0.95	12.89	10.11	5.05	Jackson
9.2	410	1.45	16.73	10.80	5.14	Jamestown
15.4	807	1.71	11.66	10.90	5.02	Jamestown
8.7	776	1.73	21.29	11.55	4.92	Jasper
7.3	610	1.01	14.88	8.67	5.32	Jefferson City
7.8	266	0.58	8.21	10.35	5.27	Jefferson City
12.8	459	1.55	12.48	10.30	4.62	Jellico
8.3	2,217	0.95	13.04	10.21	4.60	Johnson City
8.3	632	0.89	11.79	9.90	4.93	Johnson City
8.0	116	0.35	4.34	9.49	5.33	Kenton
9.1	1,071	1.15	15.56	10.14	5.54	Kingsport
6.6	4,720	0.85	13.01	9.85	5.10	Kingsport
11.4	67	0.27	2.30	9.46	6.05	Kingsport
7.6	353	1.12	17.84	10.98	5.63	Kingston Springs
10.3	-400	-3.18	-24.98	11.98	5.65	Knoxville
7.5	12,371	1.08	16.41	9.21	4.85	Knoxville
8.3	3,594	0.98	13.51	10.26	4.64	Knoxville
13.2	62	0.07	0.55	10.74	5.02	Knoxville
9.7	7,321	1.72	19.47	9.85	4.75	Knoxville
8.8	647	0.92	11.01	10.06	5.24	Lafayette
8.7	896	1.03	12.26	10.01	5.21	Lafayette
10.8	1,110	1.62	15.68	10.13	4.68	LaFollette
10.3	779	1.34	13.38	9.83	4.86	LaFollette
8.2	876	0.72	9.95	10.13	4.94	Lake City
11.7	28	0.13	1.70	9.01	5.24	Lawrenceburg
9.6	1,476	1.41	16.37	9.86	4.98	Lawrenceburg
9.1	604	0.90	11.56	11.52	5.32	Lebanon
8.9	2,075	1.58	19.88	11.06	5.17	Lebanon
20.5	82	0.51	1.64	5.71	2.89	Lebanon
9.8	1,701	1.47	16.71	10.45	5.42	Lenoir City
9.8	578	0.80	9.80	10.61	5.46	Lenoir City
9.7	668	1.03	11.81	9.89	4.76	Lewisburg
10.6	1,063	1.60	16.86	9.77	4.64	Lewisburg
31.5	50	0.95	2.52	9.12	3.64	Lexington
11.2	1,293	1.52	13.84	10.88	4.82	Lexington
8.4	10	0.02	0.29	9.05	4.99	Lexington
6.9	176	0.70	11.95	9.81	5.70	Liberty
9.5	246	0.77	9.06	9.71	4.90	Linden
9.1	-3,743	-8.35	-67.66	10.05	4.26	Livingston
9.2	452	1.11	12.29	9.43	5.10	Livingston
9.8	251	1.37	15.00	10.17	5.23	Lobelville
7.7	410	0.88	12.17	10.39	5.69	Loudon
12.4	502	1.21	10.09	9.79	5.34	Lynchburg
53.6	-121	-1.78	-2.58	0.25	0.07	Madison
8.8	1,213	1.54	18.58	10.88	5.54	Madisonville
9.6	628	1.27	13.89	10.05	5.09	Manchester
8.7	324	1.00	12.41	9.95	4.84	Manchester
13.7	263	1.66	12.63	9.80	4.68	Manchester
10.0	679	1.52	16.30	10.30	5.30	Martin
9.8	683	1.63	19.42	8.98	5.24	Martin
7.8	1,084	1.16	16.85	9.59	5.19	Maryville
10.7	27	0.55	4.51	9.65	5.03	Mason
11.2	108	1.20	10.37	10.84	4.25	Maury City
7.8	192	0.79	11.13	11.59	5.67	Maynardville
10.5	271	0.64	5.74	10.18	5.15	McKenzie
7.7	459	1.02	14.12	10.04	5.13	McLemoresville

TABLE 13.17--SELECTED OPERATING STATISTICS AND ASSET SIZE RANKINGS, BY BANK, CITIES, DECEMBER 31, 1987 (Continued)

City	Name of bank	Rank	Total assets ($1,000)	Total loans to deposits [1]
McMinnville	City Bank and Trust Company	35	152,998	56.4
McMinnville	First American Bank	193	29,340	80.6
McMinnville	First National Bank of McMinnville	49	119,345	49.2
Medina	Medina Banking Company	238	19,259	43.3
Memphis	First Tennessee Bank	1	5,613,366	85.6
Memphis	Tri State Bank of Memphis	123	55,620	56.1
Memphis	First American Bank	10	642,654	51.2
Memphis	National Bank of Commerce	6	1,317,740	74.0
Memphis	Sovran Bank	19	276,554	83.8
Memphis	United American Bank	33	155,329	72.5
Memphis	Union Planters National Bank	5	2,279,862	98.9
Memphis	Boatmen's Bank of Tennessee	12	516,009	87.1
Middleton	Bank of Middleton	230	21,976	60.7
Milan	Milan Banking Company	111	61,325	29.7
Millington	Tennessee Bank and Trust Company	244	17,681	69.0
Morristown	United Southern Bank	183	31,211	67.3
Morristown	Hamilton Bank of Morristown	50	118,273	77.8
Moscow	Moscow Savings Bank	254	14,988	57.9
Mount Juliet	First Southern Bank	119	58,617	87.6
Mountain City	Johnson County Bank	223	23,638	62.4
Mountain City	Farmers State Bank	128	53,637	51.3
Munford	Munford Union Bank	192	29,374	62.4
Murfreesboro	Mid-South Bank and Trust Company	13	455,468	76.0
Murfreesboro	First Southern Bank Rutherford County	198	28,248	89.3
Murfreesboro	First City Bank	79	86,184	72.9
Nashville	Sovran Bank Central South	3	2,812,954	86.0
Nashville	Nashville Bank of Commerce	138	47,290	89.8
Nashville	Third National Bank in Nashville	4	2,667,834	89.1
Nashville	Dominion Bank of Middle Tennessee	9	921,592	95.4
Nashville	First Union National Bank Tennessee	267	12,912	66.7
Nashville	First American National Bank	2	3,269,986	86.2
Nashville	First American Trust Company	280	4,207	(a)
Nashville	Citizens Savings Bank and Trust Company	179	32,417	73.9
New Tazewell	Citizens Bank	114	60,384	37.4
Newbern	Security State Bank	149	44,101	32.7
Newport	National Bank of Newport	116	59,049	47.3
Newport	Merchants and Planters Bank	48	119,523	42.5
Niota	Bank of Niota	256	14,682	57.7
Oak Ridge	Sovran Bank Eastern	28	181,310	82.3
Oakland	Oakland Deposit Bank	255	14,796	80.8
Obion	Commercial Bank	222	23,646	43.5
Oneida	First Trust and Savings Bank	134	50,696	63.8
Oneida	First National Bank of Oneida	89	75,852	73.9
Paris	Security Bank and Trust Company	122	56,151	89.0
Paris	Commercial Bank and Trust Company	45	126,023	56.5
Parsons	Farmers Bank	207	26,668	53.4
Parsons	Citizens State Bank	234	19,619	60.9
Pikeville	First National Bank of Pikeville	181	31,504	56.9
Portland	Volunteer State Bank	95	73,076	63.9
Portland	Farmers Bank	96	72,014	67.4
Pulaski	First National Bank of Pulaski	42	132,981	68.9
Pulaski	Union Bank	75	91,138	46.2
Ripley	Farmers Union Bank	127	53,752	77.1
Ripley	Bank of Ripley	91	74,530	55.4
Rockwood	First National Bank and Trust Company	51	118,231	55.0
Rogersville	Citizens Union Bank	30	169,920	57.7
Rutledge	Citizens Bank & Trust Co. Grainger County	117	58,882	53.0
Sardis	Peoples Bank	258	14,453	24.5
Savannah	Citizens Bank	144	45,893	45.9

TABLE 13.17-SELECTED OPERATING STATISTICS AND ASSET SIZE RANKINGS, BY BANK, CITIES, DECEMBER 31, 1987 (Continued)

Total capital as a percentage of total assets	Income before extra-ordinary items ($1,000)	Return on average assets	Return on average equity	Yield on average earning assets	Rate on funds [2]	City
9.2	1,881	1.24	15.20	10.57	5.51	McMinnville
6.1	319	1.89	24.52	16.14	8.60	McMinnville
13.5	2,332	2.03	16.08	10.60	4.86	McMinnville
10.1	214	1.17	11.27	10.24	4.95	Medina
8.5	27,986	0.49	8.68	9.96	5.27	Memphis
10.1	678	1.26	13.97	9.75	4.22	Memphis
6.7	5,382	0.89	13.01	9.41	5.07	Memphis
8.2	17,606	1.32	19.45	9.92	4.91	Memphis
7.8	2,950	1.14	17.00	9.78	4.91	Memphis
8.2	1,738	1.14	15.24	9.81	4.05	Memphis
8.7	5,925	0.27	3.46	9.05	4.87	Memphis
7.5	5,128	1.05	16.37	9.93	4.80	Memphis
8.5	170	0.79	10.41	9.77	5.09	Middleton
7.9	530	0.89	11.90	9.11	5.26	Milan
11.4	132	0.74	7.36	11.90	5.30	Millington
6.9	304	1.03	16.19	9.24	4.79	Morristown
8.6	1,296	1.09	15.46	9.60	4.88	Morristown
10.5	119	0.85	8.19	11.10	5.29	Moscow
8.5	799	1.52	19.41	11.35	4.93	Mount Juliet
9.0	175	0.77	8.80	11.17	5.79	Mountain City
11.4	808	1.59	15.28	11.78	5.45	Mountain City
10.1	441	1.54	16.55	11.22	5.33	Munford
7.2	4,542	1.05	16.73	10.75	5.22	Murfreesboro
8.0	210	0.80	10.91	9.80	4.60	Murfreesboro
9.3	301	0.43	6.14	10.11	5.90	Murfreesboro
7.6	29,660	1.14	17.37	10.05	5.19	Nashville
7.9	233	0.77	16.95	16.28	5.58	Nashville
8.3	25,676	0.97	14.29	9.70	5.06	Nashville
6.8	4,770	0.57	8.95	9.94	5.05	Nashville
68.3	-83	-0.87	-5.11	9.80	6.00	Nashville
6.5	17,975	0.60	10.09	9.31	5.29	Nashville
66.8	634	15.39	23.92	9.62	0.00	Nashville
4.8	-658	-1.77	-45.50	9.09	4.12	Nashville
9.5	570	0.95	10.55	9.19	4.92	New Tazewell
7.4	415	0.99	13.66	9.08	5.69	Newbern
8.7	580	0.97	12.43	10.43	5.03	Newport
7.2	1,685	1.45	21.46	10.66	5.49	Newport
8.8	108	0.75	9.03	9.90	4.62	Niota
8.5	1,844	1.04	12.65	9.86	4.52	Oak Ridge
8.2	129	0.92	12.49	11.42	5.54	Oakland
8.9	180	0.90	8.68	10.48	5.46	Obion
8.7	283	0.57	6.82	10.34	5.39	Oneida
9.3	724	0.98	11.44	9.77	5.63	Oneida
8.0	669	1.27	19.28	10.41	5.84	Paris
8.3	1,800	1.46	18.54	9.93	5.14	Paris
7.9	157	0.61	8.29	9.25	4.95	Parsons
7.1	97	0.53	8.47	10.59	4.98	Parsons
9.3	402	1.35	15.71	10.64	5.68	Pikeville
7.8	815	1.16	16.18	10.92	4.92	Portland
10.8	1,268	1.79	18.35	10.38	4.84	Portland
10.8	1,886	1.44	14.61	11.11	5.23	Pulaski
9.8	1,204	1.34	14.83	10.28	5.12	Pulaski
10.2	601	1.18	12.39	9.39	4.91	Ripley
10.9	756	1.04	9.94	10.60	5.27	Ripley
6.5	959	0.85	14.51	11.10	5.60	Rockwood
11.4	2,782	1.67	15.81	10.44	4.84	Rogersville
11.1	1,204	2.13	21.26	11.22	4.60	Rutledge
8.5	106	0.77	9.19	8.13	4.93	Sardis
8.4	613	1.33	18.21	10.09	5.07	Savannah

TABLE 13.17--SELECTED OPERATING STATISTICS AND ASSET SIZE RANKINGS, BY BANK, CITIES, DECEMBER 31, 1987 (Continued)

City	Name of bank	Rank	Total assets ($1,000)	Total loans to deposits [1]
Savannah	Hardin County Bank	118	58,821	70.1
Scotts Hill	Farmers State Bank	187	30,209	75.8
Selmer	Selmer Bank and Trust Company	120	58,105	53.7
Selmer	First National Bank	191	29,526	77.8
Sevierville	Sevier County Bank	69	98,984	51.3
Sevierville	Citizens National Bank	112	60,950	79.4
Sevierville	Third National Bank in Sevier County	59	110,586	71.9
Sharon	Bank of Sharon	159	40,529	53.7
Shelbyville	Bedford County Bank	131	51,999	62.6
Shelbyville	Peoples National Bank Shelbyville	70	97,638	65.0
Shelbyville	First National Bank of Shelbyville	40	136,216	68.6
Smithville	Citizens Bank	124	55,072	49.3
Sneedville	Citizens Bank	252	15,480	78.1
Somerville	Somerville Bank and Trust Company	103	67,746	81.1
Somerville	First State Bank of Fayette County	209	26,509	56.7
South Pittsburg	Citizens State Bank	220	24,022	82.2
South Pittsburg	First Bank of Marion County	73	93,321	78.7
Sparta	First National Bank of Sparta	55	116,911	49.5
Spencer	Citizens Bank	274	10,182	72.6
Spring City	First Bank of Rhea County	170	35,177	71.5
Springfield	First National Bank of Springfield	88	78,175	55.5
Sweetwater	Sweetwater Valley Bank	82	83,797	70.8
Tazewell	Claiborne County Bank	90	75,067	52.5
Tiptonville	First State Bank and Trust Company	208	26,522	51.0
Toone	Merchants and Planters Bank	184	30,344	68.3
Trenton	Bank of Trenton and Trust Company	213	25,527	64.0
Trenton	Citizens State Bank	225	23,431	81.9
Trenton	Bank of Commerce	214	25,404	49.8
Trezevant	Farmers and Merchants Bank	268	12,577	65.4
Troy	Bank of Troy	190	29,751	75.1
Tullahoma	American City Bank Tullahoma	155	42,276	81.2
Tullahoma	Traders National Bank of Tullahoma	169	36,418	72.8
Tullahoma	First National Bank of Tullahoma	139	47,264	69.6
Union City	First Volunteer Bank	266	13,116	74.5
Union City	Sovran Bank	72	93,919	76.7
Vanleer	Peoples Bank	130	52,219	67.8
Wartburg	Citizens Bank and Trust Company	145	45,432	49.2
Waynesboro	Wayne County Bank	166	37,584	83.6
Waynesboro	Bank of Waynesboro	163	38,248	63.4
White Bluff	Farmers and Merchants Bank	263	13,582	49.1
Whiteville	Whiteville Bank	200	27,761	64.1
Winchester	Franklin County Bank	165	37,724	64.8
Woodbury	Bank of Commerce	84	83,046	35.3
Woodland Mills	Farmers Bank	272	10,689	43.2

TABLE 13.17--SELECTED OPERATING STATISTICS AND ASSET SIZE RANKINGS, BY BANK, CITIES, DECEMBER 31, 1987 (Continued)

Total capital as a percentage of total assets	Income before extra-ordinary items ($1,000)	Return on average assets	Return on average equity	Yield on average earning assets	Rate on funds[2]	City
8.0	491	0.84	11.06	10.20	5.35	Savannah
8.9	-99	-0.35	-4.03	10.47	4.81	Scotts Hill
11.1	746	1.31	12.21	10.50	5.03	Selmer
10.4	365	1.25	13.16	10.29	4.97	Selmer
8.7	1,041	1.12	13.61	9.87	5.11	Sevierville
7.8	608	1.06	14.90	10.24	5.08	Sevierville
9.1	1,302	1.22	15.00	9.80	4.73	Sevierville
11.4	630	1.61	14.03	10.27	5.40	Sharon
9.0	621	1.24	15.54	10.21	5.61	Shelbyville
9.2	1,376	1.48	18.64	10.18	5.09	Shelbyville
7.9	1,336	1.01	14.17	10.63	5.51	Shelbyville
8.7	834	1.57	19.66	10.19	5.67	Smithville
10.2	386	2.56	31.09	9.95	4.31	Sneedville
14.4	1,119	1.72	12.89	10.69	5.04	Somerville
8.6	165	0.70	8.09	9.19	5.45	Somerville
9.0	291	1.25	16.07	10.85	5.60	South Pittsburg
8.4	1,233	1.34	16.53	10.51	5.31	South Pittsburg
11.9	1,390	1.36	12.60	9.99	4.94	Sparta
10.9	48	0.45	4.37	10.59	4.54	Spencer
8.3	593	1.79	24.04	11.21	5.38	Spring City
9.8	502	0.65	7.08	10.05	5.15	Springfield
9.4	1,220	1.48	16.30	10.12	4.66	Sweetwater
10.8	858	1.19	11.67	10.80	5.50	Tazewell
11.9	289	1.12	9.92	9.89	4.67	Tiptonville
7.7	308	1.10	15.17	10.90	5.33	Toone
8.3	-782	-2.98	-43.54	9.06	4.99	Trenton
9.6	216	1.01	10.85	9.85	4.63	Trenton
9.7	267	1.06	11.64	9.60	4.85	Trenton
7.6	61	0.51	7.19	10.78	5.58	Trezevant
7.0	-558	-1.85	-26.76	9.96	5.77	Troy
7.3	351	0.89	12.90	9.76	5.35	Tullahoma
7.4	504	1.45	26.55	9.81	4.46	Tullahoma
7.0	222	0.47	7.27	9.70	5.11	Tullahoma
10.0	134	0.88	12.74	10.38	5.41	Union City
10.7	1,368	1.49	15.39	9.89	4.96	Union City
7.7	704	1.47	17.42	11.95	6.06	Vanleer
6.8	287	0.64	9.25	9.98	5.82	Wartburg
12.3	265	0.73	6.41	11.78	5.32	Waynesboro
13.1	540	1.40	11.62	10.81	4.83	Waynesboro
9.9	173	1.37	16.93	11.11	5.31	White Bluff
8.3	167	0.61	8.74	9.55	5.70	Whiteville
8.8	378	1.02	13.04	9.35	4.96	Winchester
7.8	910	1.13	16.79	10.00	5.68	Woodbury
11.3	52	0.49	4.77	8.82	5.35	Woodland Mills

Note: 1987 averages are calculated using each quarter during the year plus year-end 1986. Certain adjustments are made for banks chartered during the year to reflect the number of quarters available. For more information on income statement items, see the original source.

a. Number is too large to be relevant or is otherwise not meaningful.

b. Less than 0.005.

1. Total loans to deposits less public funds.

2. Rate on funds = Total interest expense - Interest on mortgage indebtedness and obligations under capitalized leases/average earning assets.

Source: Sheshunoff and Company, Inc., *Sheshunoff Banks of Tennessee, 1988*. Used by special permission.

TABLE 13.18--NUMBER OF BANKS AND AMOUNT OF DEPOSITS IN INSURED COMMERCIAL BANKS, BY TYPE OF DEPOSIT, TENNESSEE AND COUNTIES, AS OF JUNE 30, 1987
[Deposits in thousands of dollars]

County	Number: Banks [1]	Number: Banking offices	Total deposits [2]	Deposits of individuals, partnerships, and corporations: Transaction [3]	Deposits of individuals, partnerships, and corporations: Demand [4]	Deposits of individuals, partnerships, and corporations: Non-transaction	Public funds
TENNESSEE	282	1,351	32,348,251	8,690,575	5,048,352	20,521,453	2,037,749
Anderson	5	18	356,543	88,844	46,615	253,571	9,950
Bedford	3	10	222,935	48,242	26,797	160,335	13,195
Benton	2	4	122,750	16,258	5,936	101,894	4,444
Bledsoe	2	2	32,271	6,886	3,601	23,298	1,870
Blount	5	23	461,836	112,535	51,443	320,545	26,060
Bradley	5	22	348,864	81,475	48,280	244,036	21,376
Campbell	5	11	198,888	34,306	23,194	150,596	12,621
Cannon	2	4	83,466	11,989	8,329	68,911	2,520
Carroll	5	13	173,657	39,481	20,866	124,886	8,576
Carter	2	13	170,216	38,734	19,998	114,134	16,140
Cheatham	3	7	80,872	22,665	12,268	55,276	2,669
Chester	2	5	82,669	13,657	13,599	62,458	6,001
Claiborne	3	10	155,265	31,043	17,465	111,545	11,825
Clay	2	2	13,228	2,661	1,932	10,223	344
Cocke	2	10	134,620	24,589	16,211	100,746	7,911
Coffee	6	13	189,757	47,586	32,766	128,545	12,385
Crockett	6	9	107,562	27,262	10,517	73,192	6,731
Cumberland	3	10	165,592	46,208	12,792	110,972	7,873
Davidson	12	114	6,044,062	1,578,530	1,052,922	3,770,419	416,218
Decatur	3	5	68,902	18,894	8,642	47,017	2,634
DeKalb	4	8	131,634	27,620	10,178	87,616	15,564
Dickson	4	12	197,347	44,651	23,604	140,024	11,078
Dyer	3	12	277,670	63,257	25,957	188,391	25,510
Fayette	4	6	100,657	21,410	11,694	6,992	8,949
Fentress	2	4	64,412	11,622	8,294	48,847	3,711
Franklin	4	10	158,182	39,556	19,893	111,186	6,993
Gibson	13	21	383,516	89,647	40,476	268,705	24,012
Giles	4	12	260,663	47,709	31,390	193,520	18,167
Grainger	1	3	49,853	12,745	8,899	35,056	2,041
Greene	4	19	314,363	81,112	34,782	208,345	23,020
Grundy	2	6	46,384	9,730	5,506	32,096	4,341
Hamblen	4	13	268,685	85,353	44,956	166,689	15,407
Hamilton	8	81	2,007,295	656,736	386,878	1,147,067	146,977
Hancock	1	1	13,643	3,066	3,066	8,892	1,624
Hardeman	5	10	155,254	33,449	14,830	106,149	14,028
Hardin	3	11	122,970	34,105	17,885	82,926	4,464
Hawkins	3	12	183,871	43,148	24,792	123,802	16,508
Haywood	3	7	139,380	29,670	12,771	92,547	16,812
Henderson	5	10	154,220	34,649	19,129	107,815	10,867
Henry	3	12	204,148	42,724	16,792	145,140	15,778
Hickman	2	3	80,452	17,356	8,358	58,578	4,069
Houston	1	1	22,942	5,337	3,531	16,106	1,466
Humphreys	2	5	83,736	23,079	9,790	58,020	2,431
Jackson	2	6	50,847	9,581	4,816	39,614	1,529
Jefferson	4	12	170,844	35,367	22,188	129,655	5,393

TABLE 13.18--NUMBER OF BANKS AND AMOUNT OF DEPOSITS IN INSURED COMMERCIAL BANKS, BY TYPE OF DEPOSIT, TENNESSEE AND COUNTIES, AS OF JUNE 30, 1987
[Deposits in thousands of dollars] (Continued)

County	Number		Total deposits [2]	Deposits of individuals, partnerships, and corporations			Public funds
	Banks [1]	Banking offices		Transaction [3]	Demand [4]	Non-transaction	
Johnson	2	4	65,410	12,865	6,912	47,553	4,730
Knox	6	65	1,960,319	604,329	390,832	1,210,865	108,617
Lake	2	5	33,545	9,427	4,122	20,308	3,764
Lauderdale	6	9	167,629	33,858	16,910	114,595	18,550
Lawrence	5	14	234,005	50,980	24,435	175,937	6,815
Lewis	2	3	50,332	8,146	4,160	37,464	4,373
Lincoln	4	12	170,839	49,304	30,319	113,327	7,387
Loudon	4	18	234,642	38,528	23,986	167,251	27,743
McMinn	5	13	211,780	51,919	31,560	142,243	13,303
McNairy	5	11	123,128	41,629	16,890	76,442	4,735
Macon	2	8	138,732	29,457	16,222	104,363	4,580
Madison	4	21	560,746	161,048	69,309	366,961	25,212
Marion	3	9	117,699	22,668	12,664	81,333	12,659
Marshall	5	9	154,861	38,810	20,217	106,604	8,933
Maury	4	19	408,943	91,345	42,580	274,932	40,770
Meigs	1	3	32,111	6,918	3,759	22,741	2,243
Monroe	3	14	160,076	37,079	19,813	114,894	6,352
Montgomery	4	21	484,763	113,429	67,459	303,417	63,878
Moore	1	1	36,504	5,030	4,586	29,587	1,636
Morgan	1	3	41,740	9,916	5,387	30,844	850
Obion	8	17	265,368	70,767	33,244	179,869	13,270
Overton	2	4	74,018	18,394	7,586	53,132	2,056
Perry	2	3	45,476	11,903	5,583	29,058	4,313
Pickett	2	2	43,250	5,040	3,487	34,183	3,721
Polk	4	10	124,551	20,768	14,510	93,314	9,342
Putnam	4	17	430,383	79,519	44,893	306,555	40,750
Rhea	3	6	100,637	26,253	11,977	68,853	5,389
Roane	3	12	197,456	46,445	19,822	138,018	11,197
Robertson	4	10	148,746	41,750	18,894	101,479	5,261
Rutherford	7	24	547,054	151,305	90,019	350,433	41,353
Scott	3	7	112,969	15,685	11,437	89,146	7,564
Sequatchie	2	3	38,777	7,499	3,734	26,727	4,351
Sevier	6	23	395,362	96,665	56,776	264,309	31,361
Shelby	15	150	5,801,584	1,918,640	1,166,086	3,000,877	285,410
Smith	2	4	126,294	24,053	10,977	97,283	4,758
Stewart	3	7	66,939	11,993	5,788	50,796	3,719
Sullivan	7	36	720,863	206,836	99,144	420,612	65,266
Sumner	6	26	428,565	121,565	67,469	293,844	11,857
Tipton	6	12	174,077	48,293	21,612	112,793	11,597
Trousdale	2	3	42,334	10,189	5,447	29,929	2,180
Unicoi	2	3	54,005	10,770	6,014	34,228	8,692
Union	2	5	46,931	9,260	5,903	32,031	5,368
Van Buren	1	1	9,509	1,892	1,187	6,624	980
Warren	4	16	258,424	49,487	27,181	199,152	8,547
Washington	5	25	438,183	139,575	79,425	281,526	12,951
Wayne	3	7	86,991	16,704	9,247	62,833	6,331
Weakley	8	12	234,752	61,629	22,563	162,531	9,712

TABLE 13.18--NUMBER OF BANKS AND AMOUNT OF DEPOSITS IN INSURED COMMERCIAL BANKS, BY TYPE OF DEPOSIT, TENNESSEE AND COUNTIES, AS OF JUNE 30, 1987
[Deposits in thousands of dollars] (Continued)

County	Number		Total deposits[2]	Deposits of individuals, partnerships, and corporations			Public funds
	Banks[1]	Banking offices		Transaction[3]	Demand[4]	Non-transaction	
White	3	5	157,805	25,956	10,150	121,104	10,216
Williamson	6	20	598,771	153,636	83,824	404,532	30,744
Wilson	6	17	333,450	76,895	47,623	234,644	20,281

1. Where banks are located in more than one county, they are counted in each one.
2. Includes categories not shown separately.
3. Transaction accounts are deposits/accounts on which the depositor or account holder can make withdrawals by negotiable or transferable instrument, payment orders of withdrawal, telephone transfers, or other similar devices, in order to make payments or transfers to others.
4. Demand deposits are included in transaction accounts.

Source: Federal Deposit Insurance Corporation, *Data Book, Operating Banks and Branches, June 30, 1987.*

TABLE 13.19--SELECTED BALANCE SHEET STATISTICS OF INSURED COMMERCIAL BANKS, SOUTHEASTERN STATES AND UNITED STATES, AS OF DECEMBER 31, 1987
[In millions of dollars]

State	Assets				Deposits	
		Gross loans				
	Total	Total	Commercial and industrial	Real estate	Total	Interest-bearing
TENNESSEE	41,162	24,795	6,372	9,544	34,054	27,486
Alabama	30,808	18,439	4,967	6,947	24,570	19,509
Arkansas	17,761	9,700	2,365	4,295	15,745	13,163
Florida	110,981	69,548	13,829	34,788	91,683	72,763
Georgia	53,670	33,824	9,733	11,932	41,390	30,454
Kentucky	34,902	20,287	5,603	7,303	27,990	22,774
Louisiana	35,550	19,608	5,997	7,756	30,683	24,379
Mississippi	18,262	10,077	2,150	3,958	15,830	13,033
North Carolina	62,597	37,208	10,963	14,609	43,913	34,768
South Carolina	17,930	11,325	2,943	4,334	13,660	10,388
Virginia	56,171	38,101	9,402	13,893	45,073	36,821
West Virginia	15,246	8,136	1,462	3,810	13,150	11,285
UNITED STATES	3,000,914	1,844,481	589,675	599,904	2,334,900	1,857,104

Note: Totals include items not shown separately.

Source: Federal Deposit Insurance Corporation, *Statistics on Banking, 1987.*

TABLE 13.20-NUMBER AND ASSETS OF INSURED COMMERCIAL BANKS, BY ASSET SIZE, SOUTHEASTERN STATES, AS OF DECEMBER 31, 1987
[Assets in millions of dollars]

State	All banks	Less than $25 million	$25 to $49.9 million	$50 to $99.9 million	$100 to $299.9 million	$300 to $499.9 million	$500 to $999.9 million	$1.0 billion or more
TENNESSEE								
Banks	282	68	79	67	50	6	4	8
Assets	41,162	1,122	2,783	4,685	7,238	2,418	2,654	20,263
Alabama								
Banks	225	71	73	48	24	3	2	4
Assets	30,808	1,177	2,601	3,346	4,013	1,228	1,300	17,144
Arkansas								
Banks	257	77	74	64	35	5	2	0
Assets	17,761	1,261	2,688	4,446	5,789	2,094	1,483	0
Florida								
Banks	409	117	91	80	70	20	13	18
Assets	110,981	1,470	3,171	5,335	11,541	7,711	8,949	72,805
Georgia								
Banks	358	114	117	74	41	3	3	6
Assets	53,670	1,765	4,254	5,117	6,358	1,056	1,862	33,260
Kentucky								
Banks	330	76	91	100	51	7	1	4
Assets	34,902	1,234	3,369	6,840	7,856	2,496	738	12,368
Louisiana								
Banks	269	46	85	83	34	9	6	6
Assets	35,550	783	3,079	5,705	5,314	3,564	3,507	13,600
Mississippi								
Banks	128	26	35	39	20	3	1	4
Assets	18,262	440	1,343	2,745	3,101	1,129	905	8,599
North Carolina								
Banks	68	15	17	9	14	3	2	8
Assets	62,597	211	628	672	2,210	976	1,869	56,030

TABLE 13.20-NUMBER AND ASSETS OF INSURED COMMERCIAL BANKS, BY ASSET SIZE, SOUTHEASTERN STATES, AS OF DECEMBER 31, 1987
[Assets in millions of dollars] (Continued)

State	All banks	Less than $25 million	$25 to $49.9 million	$50 to $99.9 million	$100 to $299.9 million	$300 to $499.9 million	$500 to $999.9 million	$1.0 billion or more
South Carolina								
Banks	74	24	16	20	7	2	1	4
Assets	17,930	314	592	1,369	1,537	701	809	12,607
Virginia								
Banks	173	35	43	50	30	3	4	8
Assets	56,171	654	1,597	3,371	4,877	1,107	2,636	41,930
West Virginia								
Banks	207	46	60	60	36	3	2	0
Assets	15,246	725	2,175	4,023	5,751	1,156	1,417	0

Note: Detail may not add to total due to independent rounding.

Source: Federal Deposit Insurance Corporation, *Statistics on Banking, 1987*.

TABLE 13.21--SELECTED BALANCE SHEET AND INCOME STATEMENT ITEMS OF INSURED COMMERCIAL BANKS, SOUTHEASTERN STATES, DECEMBER 31, 1987 [Percentages unless otherwise noted]

State	Number of banks	Total assets ($1,000,000)	Total non-current loans to total loans[1]	Equity capital to total assets	Income before extra-ordinary items ($1,000)	Net income to average assets	Net income to average equity	Net interest income to average earning assets
TENNESSEE	282	41,162	1.30	8.33	350,222	1.11	12.93	4.98
Alabama	225	30,808	1.17	9.73	316,292	1.11	11.27	4.95
Arkansas	257	17,761	2.43	8.99	158,436	1.01	11.12	4.67
Florida	409	110,981	1.33	8.89	790,522	0.34	5.46	5.08
Georgia	358	53,670	1.04	9.34	548,517	1.19	12.35	5.54
Kentucky	330	34,902	1.64	9.00	308,623	1.07	11.55	4.68
Louisiana	269	35,550	6.16	7.80	-20,388	-0.52	-7.29	4.51
Mississippi	128	18,262	1.81	8.93	154,209	0.96	10.48	4.77
North Carolina	68	62,597	0.80	10.19	578,876	0.56	7.22	5.09
South Carolina	74	17,930	1.01	11.02	162,529	0.95	9.15	5.33
Virginia	173	56,171	0.78	9.04	516,991	1.22	13.79	5.29
West Virginia	207	15,246	1.85	9.29	158,229	1.04	11.14	4.93

Note: Ratios correspond to adjusted mean values.

1. Includes lease receivables.

Source: Federal Deposit Insurance Corporation, *Statistics on Banking, 1987.*

TABLE 13.22-NUMBER OF FAILED BANKS, BY TYPE OF LIQUIDATION, SOUTHEASTERN STATES AND UNITED STATES, 1985–1988

State	1988				1987				1986				1985			
	Total	Purchase and assumptions	Payoffs	Insured deposit transfers	Total	Purchase and assumptions	Payoffs	Insured deposit transfers	Total	Purchase and assumptions	Payoffs	Insured deposit transfers	Total	Purchase and assumptions	Payoffs	Insured deposit transfers
TENNESSEE	0	0	0	0	0	0	0	0	2	1	0	1	5	4	0	1
Alabama	0	0	0	0	2	2	0	0	1	1	0	0	1	1	0	0
Arkansas	0	0	0	0	0	0	0	0	0	0	0	0	1	1	0	0
Florida	3	2	0	1	3	2	0	1	3	2	1	0	2	2	0	0
Kentucky	0	0	0	0	1	1	0	0	2	1	0	1	0	0	0	0
Louisiana	11	10	0	1	14[a]	14[a]	0	0	8	8	0	0	0	0	0	0
Mississippi	0	0	0	0	1	1	0	0	0	0	0	0	0	0	0	0
UNITED STATES	200	164	6	30	184	133	11	40	138	98	21	19	116	87	22	7

Note: The U.S. figures include Puerto Rico.

a. Includes one failure handled as a bridge bank.

Source: Federal Deposit Insurance Corporation, *1988 Annual Report*, and earlier editions.

TABLE 13.23--INTERSTATE BANKING LEGISLATION, SOUTHEASTERN STATES, AS OF FEBRUARY 1, 1989

State	Effective date	Area	Number of partner states
TENNESSEE	Currently	Reciprocal, 13 states (AL,AR,FL,GA,IN,KY,LA,MO,MS,NC, SC,VA,WV).	13
Alabama	Currently	Reciprocal, 12 states and D.C.(AR,FL,GA,KY,LA,MD, MS,NC,SC,TN,VA,WV).	13
Arkansas	Currently	Reciprocal, 16 states and D.C.(AL,FL,GA,KS,LA,MD, MS,MO,NE,NC,OK,SC,TN,TX,VA,WV). Reciprocity hinges on commitments to community reinvestment.	17
Florida	Currently	Reciprocal, 11 states and D.C.(AL,AR,GA,LA,MD,MS,NC, SC,TN,VA,WV). Under a 1972 law, NCNB and Northern Trust Corporation are grandfathered and can make further acquisitions.	12
Georgia	Currently	Reciprocal, 10 states and D.C.(AL,FL,KY,LA,MD,MS,NC, SC,TN,VA).	11
Kentucky	Currently	National, reciprocal.	31[a]
Louisiana	Currently	National, reciprocal.	29[a]
Mississippi	Currently	Reciprocal, 4 states (AL,AR,LA,TN).	4
	July 1, 1990	Reciprocal, 13 states (AL,AR,FL,GA,KY,LA,MO,NC,SC,TN, TX,VA,WV).	13
North Carolina	Currently	Reciprocal, 12 states and D.C.(AL,AR,FL,GA,KY,LA,MD, MS,SC,TN,VA,WV).	13
South Carolina	Currently	Reciprocal, 12 states and D.C.(AL,AR,FL,GA,KY,LA,MD, MS,NC,TN,VA,WV).	13
Virginia	Currently	Reciprocal, 12 states and D.C.(AL,AR,FL,GA,KY,LA,MD, MS,NC,SC,TN,WV).	13
West Virginia	Currently	National, reciprocal.	29[a]

a. Does not count the two states where nationwide entry by acquisition of failing banks is possible.
Source: Federal Reserve Bank of Atlanta, *Economic Review*, May/June 1989.

TABLE 13.24--CREDIT UNION MEMBERSHIP AND LOANS OUTSTANDING, SOUTHEASTERN STATES, 1970–1988, SELECTED YEARS
[Loans in thousands of dollars]

	1988		1987		1980		1970	
State	Members	Loans	Members	Loans	Members	Loans	Members	Loans
TENNESSEE	1,166,895	2,591,556	1,125,035	2,340,534	829,780	989,561	423,876	275,520
Alabama	1,017,867	2,080,069	974,441	1,866,245	665,008	721,265	361,802	223,125
Arkansas	176,854	305,394	167,836	262,483	139,890	115,439	86,562	43,712
Florida	2,453,011	5,415,680	2,373,607	4,829,587	1,773,488	1,923,023	722,362	460,612
Georgia	1,151,646	2,259,472	1,091,907	3,308,954	880,791	949,478	398,750	240,974
Kentucky	509,055	939,623	512,478	836,790	373,077	330,570	177,654	89,533
Louisiana	708,610	1,358,465	678,391	1,235,509	589,682	600,302	325,126	166,906
Mississippi	319,309	538,143	312,839	472,639	286,343	246,770	146,189	70,108
North Carolina	1,107,688	3,144,261	1,041,839	2,581,752	752,589	875,689	309,633	154,520
South Carolina	685,998	1,466,486	625,857	1,265,718	443,583	438,129	196,556	105,699
Virginia	2,574,546	5,777,825	1,720,127	5,166,621	1,690,349	1,844,777	370,752	200,659
West Virginia	247,376	463,050	240,342	401,487	182,606	197,883	92,351	56,128

Note: Refers to both state and federally chartered credit unions. All data is stated as preliminary when released.

Source: Credit Union National Association, Inc., direct correspondence; *Credit Union Report, 1988*, and earlier editions; and *Credit Union National Association Yearbook, 1970.*

TABLE 13.25--SELECTED FINANCIAL DATA FOR FSLIC-INSURED THRIFT INSTITUTIONS, SOUTHEASTERN STATES AND UNITED STATES, AS OF DECEMBER 31, 1987 [In millions of dollars]

State	Number of institutions	Total assets	Mortgage loans	Mortgage-backed securities	Cash and investments	Total deposits	FHLB advances and other borrowed money	Regu-latory capital	Net deposit gain [1]
TENNESSEE	63	11,515	6,422	1,606	1,754	9,240	1,301	816	265
Alabama	36	8,969	4,638	1,700	1,375	6,886	1,545	373	177
Arkansas	37	6,796	3,817	1,053	773	5,653	1,331	-272	-633
Florida	148	80,129	40,863	13,051	12,568	60,467	15,117	3,315	2,918
Georgia	69	18,222	10,319	3,510	1,713	13,736	3,315	908	383
Kentucky	67	7,493	4,413	909	1,422	6,340	658	424	53
Louisiana	96	15,619	9,391	943	1,825	12,857	1,716	874	141
Mississippi	42	5,109	2,313	774	781	4,220	544	258	65
North Carolina	137	20,197	13,216	2,076	2,316	16,794	1,859	1,276	422
South Carolina	49	10,874	6,724	977	1,024	8,618	1,521	557	257
Virginia	66	25,617	15,204	3,506	3,119	19,368	4,401	1,440	1,038
West Virginia	18	2,010	1,227	137	312	1,763	136	87	-100
UNITED STATES [2]	3,147	1,250,855	679,249	201,828	169,717	932,616	249,896	46,573	46,573

Note: Data are preliminary.

1. New deposits received less deposits withdrawn plus interest credited.

2. Includes Guam and other territories.

Source: Federal Home Loan Bank Board, *Savings and Home Financing Source Book, 1987.*

TABLE 13.26--SELECTED OPERATING STATISTICS FOR INSURED SAVINGS ASSOCIATIONS, SOUTHEASTERN STATES AND UNITED STATES, 1986 AND 1987

State	1987 Return on assets[1]	1987 Cost of funds[2]	1987 Cost of deposits[3]	1987 Mortgage portfolio yield[4]	1986 Return on assets[1]	1986 Cost of funds[2]	1986 Cost of deposits[3]	1986 Mortgage portfolio yield[4]
TENNESSEE	0.44	6.63	6.54	7.67	0.70	7.55	7.43	9.26
Alabama	-0.10	7.19	6.92	7.27	0.39	7.79	7.79	8.08
Arkansas	-4.72	7.96	8.30	7.00	-4.47	7.98	7.92	10.27
Florida	-0.17	7.07	6.95	7.59	-0.05	7.85	7.71	8.98
Georgia	0.33	6.61	6.77	7.04	0.66	7.67	7.63	8.54
Kentucky	0.01	6.67	6.87	7.80	0.58	8.10	8.22	9.30
Louisiana	-2.04	6.91	6.80	8.07	-1.00	7.96	7.98	8.97
Mississippi	-0.21	6.64	6.56	7.15	0.52	7.25	7.18	8.72
North Carolina	0.55	6.58	6.57	8.32	0.96	7.49	7.50	9.19
South Carolina	0.44	6.56	6.44	8.47	0.61	7.70	7.56	9.69
Virginia	0.15	6.82	6.88	7.74	0.66	7.86	7.75	9.17
West Virginia	-0.79	6.64	6.67	8.61	-0.42	7.84	7.68	10.19
UNITED STATES	-0.64	7.20	6.92	9.70	0.02	8.06	7.84	10.65

1. Net income after taxes divided by average assets.
2. Interest and dividends paid on deposits, FHL Bank advances, and other borrowings divided by average deposits and borrowings balance.
3. Interest and dividends paid on deposits divided by average deposit balance.
4. Interest and discounts earned on mortgage loans divided by average mortgage balance (net of loans in process).

Source: Federal Home Loan Bank Board, *Savings and Home Financing Source Book, 1987.*

TABLE 13.27--NUMBER OF LIFE INSURANCE COMPANIES, SOUTHEASTERN STATES, 1950–1987, SELECTED YEARS

State	1987	1986	1985	1984	1980	1975	1970	1960	1950
TENNESSEE	24	25	24	24	24	22	21	26	11
Alabama	31	31	32	34	34	39	54	42	14
Arkansas	25	25	23	23	23	29	29	35	8
Florida	44	44	41	44	38	38	28	26	17
Georgia	30	30	31	32	27	26	30	30	17
Kentucky	16	16	15	15	14	14	19	11	8
Louisiana	114	115	114	108	99	93	103	127	77
Mississippi	30	28	28	32	25	16	16	19	9
North Carolina	23	24	25	24	21	21	22	26	13
South Carolina	21	22	24	23	29	30	35	54	27
Virginia	17	16	15	12	15	16	16	20	13
West Virginia	2	2	2	2	2	3	4	4	2

Note: Data as of midyear.

Source: American Council of Life Insurance, Washington, D.C., *Life Insurance Fact Book, 1988*, and earlier editions.

TABLE 13.28--LIFE INSURANCE IN FORCE, BY TYPE, SOUTHEASTERN STATES AND UNITED STATES, 1987 [In thousands of policies and millions of dollars]

State	Total		Ordinary		Group	
	Number	Amount	Number	Amount	Certificates	Amount
TENNESSEE	9,988	143,106	3,057	76,098	3,110	60,398
Alabama	12,704	123,408	3,064	67,965	2,393	48,027
Arkansas	2,766	47,459	1,007	27,995	934	17,815
Florida	17,921	322,388	6,653	194,057	5,325	113,713
Georgia	12,646	208,084	4,595	117,735	3,509	81,026
Kentucky	6,069	85,755	2,299	49,057	1,593	32,545
Louisiana	9,065	129,417	2,557	81,115	2,133	42,044
Mississippi	4,188	59,624	1,176	35,135	1,159	21,014
North Carolina	13,498	186,110	4,953	109,404	2,965	68,432
South Carolina	7,757	95,712	2,831	55,094	1,867	35,890
Virginia	13,284	203,094	3,849	104,887	5,035	88,421
West Virginia	3,090	40,196	1,020	19,803	949	17,881
UNITED STATES	394,883	7,452,498	145,174	4,139,071	136,006	3,043,782

State	Industrial		Credit[1]		Average amount of life insurance in force per household ($)
	Number	Amount	Number	Amount	
TENNESSEE	1,858	826	1,963	5,784	78,600
Alabama	5,531	2,245	1,716	5,171	83,200
Arkansas	271	143	554	1,506	53,000
Florida	2,255	1,466	3,688	13,152	67,300
Georgia	2,217	1,340	2,325	7,983	92,200
Kentucky	1,078	623	1,099	3,530	62,800
Louisiana	2,956	1,885	1,419	4,373	82,600
Mississippi	710	434	1,143	3,041	65,600
North Carolina	1,973	1,018	3,607	7,256	77,900
South Carolina	1,542	926	1,517	3,802	79,800
Virginia	1,531	895	2,869	8,891	93,500
West Virginia	360	240	761	2,272	56,900
UNITED STATES	40,783	26,668	72,920	242,977	82,800

1. Includes group credit certificates. "Credit" is limited to life insurance on loans of 10 years' duration or less. "Ordinary" and "Group" include credit insurance on loans of more than 10 years.

Source: American Council of Life Insurance, Washington, D.C., *Life Insurance Fact Book, 1988.*

TABLE 13.29-DIRECT WRITTEN PREMIUMS, SELECTED INSURANCE LINES, SOUTHEASTERN STATES AND UNITED STATES, 1987 [In thousands of dollars]

State	Total [1]	Automobile		Homeowners	Commercial multi-peril	Workers' compensation	Medical malpractice	Fire
		Liability	Physical damage					
TENNESSEE	3,207,038	743,988	635,971	314,328	281,079	410,304	88,838	90,620
Alabama	2,596,553	535,143	521,281	287,901	219,021	340,709	66,541	74,852
Arkansas	1,506,961	363,679	264,306	161,940	123,138	203,366	21,672	57,320
Florida	10,114,380	3,107,096	1,590,670	819,414	1,008,363	1,118,325	191,114	149,274
Georgia	5,024,804	1,407,104	881,807	409,408	387,218	696,960	155,785	109,263
Kentucky	2,158,147	533,209	400,048	191,764	171,763	250,777	63,567	55,095
Louisiana	3,263,098	894,335	444,496	355,517	211,078	438,586	55,841	104,837
Mississippi	1,529,852	326,138	291,793	210,914	90,466	187,149	20,734	82,083
North Carolina	3,791,336	1,068,956	743,572	362,400	296,583	384,813	83,558	92,964
South Carolina	2,208,953	689,188	416,030	210,515	161,375	298,231	9,142	66,917
Virginia	4,166,127	1,247,431	712,237	312,485	365,990	515,682	91,907	79,113
West Virginia	913,996	279,096	218,890	101,035	71,217	2,169[a]	37,619	32,330
UNITED STATES	199,478,139	51,207,423	32,944,974	16,901,952	18,987,341	25,447,780[a]	4,711,610	3,864,080

Note: Direct written premiums are the amounts actually paid by policy holders. These do not reflect the additional exchanges of premiums among insurance companies which contract, through a process known as reinsurance, to absorb specified portions of each other's losses.

1. Total includes categories not shown separately.

a. Does not include state fund premiums.

Source: Insurance Information Institute, *Insurance Facts, 1988–89 Property/Casualty Fact Book.* Data used by special permission.

Official returns from the national elections are collected by the clerk of the U.S. House of Representatives, and state election statistics are collected by the office of the Tennessee Secretary of State. National data are published biennially in *Statistics of Presidential and Congressional Elections*. These data are also included in the *U.S. Statistical Abstract* and the *Tennessee Blue Book*. The Bureau of the Census publishes information about the population of voting age in each decennial Census of Population. Estimates of these populations between decennial censuses are provided in *Current Population Reports*, Series P-25 and P-20. Table 14.13 includes voter registration and participation, in addition to voting age by race and sex, and Table 14.14 details projected voting age populations for November 1, 1988.

The organization of governments below the state level is covered in the Bureau of the Census publication *Governmental Organization*, from the *Census of Governments*. In addition to the 94 county governments (Nashville-Davidson metropolitan government is classified as municipal), data from the 1987 Census cover 334 municipal governments, 14 school districts, and 462 special districts, including airport authorities, housing authorities, and sanitation districts. Information on the number of state and local elected officials is taken from this Census and included for the first time in the *1990 Abstract*. The *Census of Governments*, like the economic censuses, is conducted every five years. The latest Census is published for 1987.

In addition to government units, Tennessee has a number of regional planning areas. Local officials and citizens who wish to receive planning assistance or discuss regional planning coordination will find the names and locations of each of these regional planning agencies in Table 14.2.

In the first judicial restructuring act of this century, Public Chapter 931 established 31 districts in which judges and chancellors serve the same geographical area. The plan allots one judge or chancellor per 42,333 persons per district. Figure 14.2 outlines the geographic boundaries of Tennessee's Judicial Districts.

More information on the organization of Tennessee state government, as well as all state-elected officials and major appointments, will be found in the *Tennessee Blue Book*, which may be ordered from the Office of the Secretary of State.

TABLE OF CONTENTS

TABLE 14.1-- NUMBER OF COUNTY AND MUNICIPAL GOVERNMENTS, BY POPULATION SIZE, TENNESSEE, 1972–1987, CENSUS YEARS

Population size	Number of county governments				Distribution of 1986 county population (1,000)	Percentage of total Tennessee county population
	1987	1982	1977	1972		
Total	94	94	94	94	4,305	100.0
500,000 or more	1	1	(a)	(a)	810	18.8
250,000 to 499,999[a]	2	2	3	3	614	14.3
100,000 to 249,999	2	1	1	1	249	5.8
50,000 to 99,999	14	13	9	8	985	22.9
25,000 to 49,999	27	28	30	25	943	21.9
10,000 to 24,999	34	34	33	38	604	14.0
Less than 10,000	14	15	18	19	101	2.3

Population size	Number of municipalities				Distribution of 1986 municipal population (1,000)	Percentage of total Tennessee municipal population
	1987	1982	1977	1972		
Total	334	335	326	316	2,840	100.0
300,000 or more	2	2	2	2	1,126	39.6
200,000 to 299,999	0	0	0	0	0	0.0
100,000 to 199,999	2	2	2	2	335	11.8
50,000 to 99,999	2	1	1	0	114	4.0
25,000 to 49,999	8	8	7	6	258	9.1
10,000 to 24,999	25	24	22	20	387	13.6
5,000 to 9,999	34	33	32	28	245	8.6
2,500 to 4,999	46	45	44	41	166	5.8
1,000 to 2,499	88	87	70	68	141	5.0
Less than 1,000	127	133	146	149	68	2.4

Note: The Metropolitan Government of Nashville and Davidson County is classified as a municipality in the Census of Governments. Percentages computed by the Center for Business and Economic Research.

a. Data for 1972 and 1977 are for populations of 250,000 or greater.

Source: U.S. Department of Commerce, Bureau of the Census, *1987 Census of Governments, Volume I, Governmental Organization*, and earlier editions.

FIGURE 14.1
Tennessee Development Districts

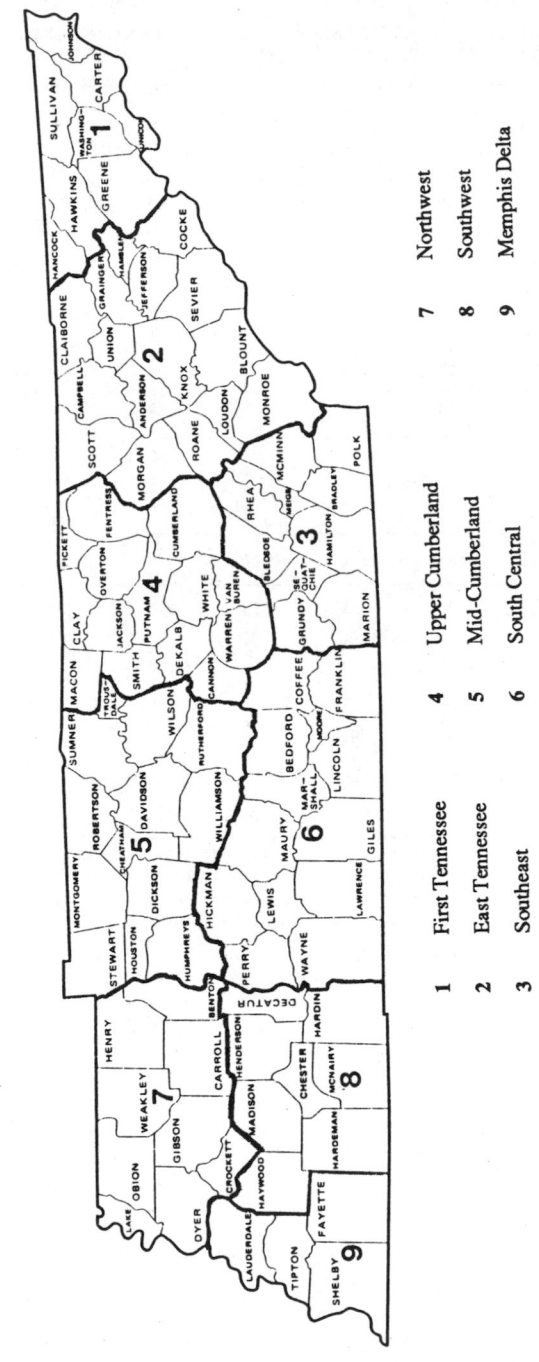

1	First Tennessee	4	Upper Cumberland	7	Northwest
2	East Tennessee	5	Mid-Cumberland	8	Southwest
3	Southeast	6	South Central	9	Memphis Delta

Source: Tennessee State Planning Office.

TABLE 14.2-- TENNESSEE DEVELOPMENT DISTRICTS

East Tennessee Development District
5616 Kingston Pike
P. O. Box 19806
Knoxville, Tennessee 37939-2806

First Tennessee-Virginia Development District
Suite 800
207 North Boone Street
Johnson City, Tennessee 37601

Memphis Delta Development District
157 Poplar Avenue, B-150
Memphis, Tennessee 38103

Greater Nashville Regional Council
Seventh Floor, Stahlman Building
Box 233, 211 Union Street
Nashville, Tennessee 37201

Northwest Tennessee Development District
124 Weldon Street
P. O. Box 63
Martin, Tennessee 38237

South Central Tennessee Development District
P. O. Box 1346
Columbia, Tennessee 38402-1346

Southeast Tennessee Development District
216 W. 8th Street, Suite 300
Chattanooga, Tennessee 37402

Southwest Tennessee Development District
416 East Lafayette Street
Jackson, Tennessee 38301

Upper Cumberland Development District
1225 Burgess Falls Road
Cookeville, Tennessee 38501

Source: Tennessee State Planning Office, direct correspondence.

FIGURE 14.2
Judicial Districts for Tennessee

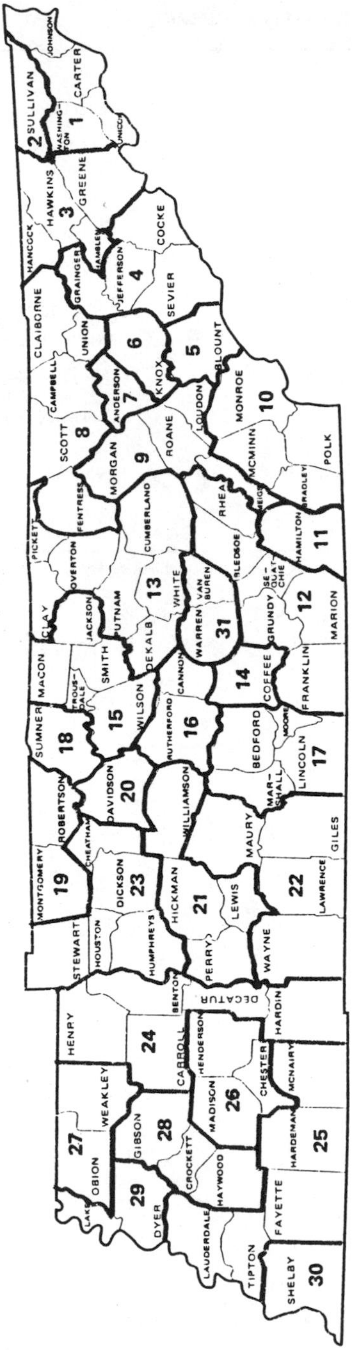

Note: For detail see Public Chapter 931, 93rd General Assembly.
Source: State of Tennessee, Comptroller of the Treasury, *Local Government Newsletter*, September, 1984; and direct correspondence.

TABLE 14.3-- GUBERNATORIAL ELECTION RETURNS, PRIMARY AND GENERAL, TENNESSEE, 1970–1986, ELECTION YEARS

Primary			
Democratic		Republican	
Name	Popular vote	Name	Popular vote
1986			
Jane Eskind	225,551	Winfield Dunn	222,458
Richard H. Fulton	190,016	Hubert Patty	7,660
Ned McWherter	314,449	Charles G. Vick	5,954
Others[1]	10,425	Write-ins	69
1982			
Tom Henry	19,453	Lamar Alexander	259,497
Lutner M. Kindall	7,792	Write-ins	9
John G. Love	10,600		
Boyce McCall	2,577		
Tommy McKnight	10,761		
Virginia Nyabongo	5,885		
Anna Belle Clement O'Brien	254,500		
James W. Thomas	6,052		
Randy Tyree	318,205		
Write-ins	5		
1978			
Jake Butcher	320,329	Lamar Alexander	230,922
Bob Clement	228,577	John H. Harper	2,527
Richard Fulton	122,101	Hubert D. Patty	1,132
Others[2]	51,888	Harold Sterling	34,037
		Write-ins	2
1974			
Ray Blanton	148,062	Lamar Alexander	120,773
Jake Butcher	132,173	Dortch Oldham	35,683
Hudley Crockett	86,852	Melvin Waldron	1,674
Franklin Haney	84,155	Nat Winston	90,980
Stanley Snodgrass	40,211	Write-ins	2
Tom Wiseman	89,061		
Others[3]	70,806		
1970[a]			
Mary Anderson	29,175	Winfield Dunn	81,475
Ralph W. Emerson	12,608	Maxey Jarman	70,420
John J. Hooker, Jr.	261,580	William Jenkins	50,910
James A. Newton, Jr.	3,490	Hubert D. Patty	1,647
Stanley Snodgrass	193,199	Claude Robertson	40,547
Robert L. Taylor	90,009		
Write-ins	48		

TABLE 14.3-- GUBERNATORIAL ELECTION RETURNS, PRIMARY AND GENERAL, TENNESSEE, 1970–1986, ELECTION YEARS (Continued)

General					
Democratic		Republican		Independent	
Name	Popular vote	Name	Popular vote	Name	Popular vote
1986					
Ned McWherter	656,602	Winfield Dunn	553,449	Write-ins	288
1982					
Randy Tyree	500,937	Lamar Alexander	737,963	Write-ins	27
1978					
Jake Butcher	523,495	Lamar Alexander	661,959	Jessie D. McDonald	1,988
				Claude E. Montgomery	921
				William B. Thompson	1,230
				Write-ins	102
1974					
Ray Blanton	576,833	Lamar Alexander	455,467	Jack Comer	2,431
				Hubert D. Patty	845
				James E. Reesor	1,986
				Alfred W. Taylor	2,338
				Arnold J. Zandi	784
				Write-ins	30
1970[a]					
John J. Hooker, Jr.	509,521	Winfield Dunn	575,777	Write-ins	4

1. Joseph L. Crichton, 6,582 votes; Bill Jacox, 3,817 votes; and write-ins, 26 votes.

2. William Jackson, 1,365 votes; Willie Jacox, 2,010 votes; Ben Miller, 1,317 votes; Roger Murray, 40,871 votes; and Shelley Stiles, 6,325 votes.

3. Ross Bass, 36,091 votes; Washington Butler, 14,801 votes; Johnnie David Elkins, 1,694 votes; David Pack, 13,625 votes; James Powers, 13,464 votes; Charles G. Vick, 1,121 votes; and Write-ins, 10 votes.

a. American Party candidate, Douglas L. Heinsohn, received 1,000 votes in the Primary and 22,945 votes in the general election.

Source: Office of the Secretary of State (Nashville), Certificate of Election Returns for the August 7, 1986, Primary Election, and the November 4, 1986, General Election, State of Tennessee; and corresponding dates for earlier years.

TABLE 14.4-- COMPOSITION OF THE STATE LEGISLATURE, BY POLITICAL AFFILIATION, TENNESSEE, 1940–1988, ELECTION YEARS

	Senate		House	
Year	Democrat	Repub-lican	Democrat	Repub-lican
1988	22	11	59	40
1986	23	10	61	38
1984	23	10	62	37
1982[a]	22	11	60	38
1980[b,c]	20	12	57	39
1978[d]	20	12	60	38
1976[d]	23	9	66	32
1974[a,e]	20	12	63	35
1972[e]	19	13	51	48
1970[e]	19	13	55	44
1968[a]	20	13	49	49
1966[a]	25	8	59	39
1964	25	8	75	24
1962	27	6	78	21
1960	27	6	80	19
1958	28	5	82	17
1956	27	6	78	21
1954	28	5	80	19
1952	28	5	81	18
1950	28	5	80	19
1948	29	4	80	19
1946	28	5	84	15
1944	28	5	75	24
1942	30	3	78	21
1940	29	4	84	15

a. One Independent candidate was also elected to the House of Representatives.
b. Two Independent candidates were also elected to the House of Representatives.
c. One Independent candidate was also elected to the Senate.
d. One Independent candidate was also elected to the House and Senate.
e. One American party candidate was also elected to the Senate.
Source: Office of the Secretary of State, direct correspondence; and *Tennessee Blue Book*, 1942–1982.

TABLE 14.5-- ELECTION RETURNS FOR UNITED STATES SENATOR, PRIMARY AND GENERAL ELECTIONS, TENNESSEE, 1972–1988, ELECTION YEARS

	Democratic popular vote			Republican popular vote	
Candidate	Primary	General election	Candidate	Primary	General election
			1988[a]		
Jim Sasser	332,560	1,020,061	Bill Andersen	115,341	541,033
Write-ins	14		Alice Algood	34,413	
			Hubert Patty	8,358	
			Write-ins	11	
			1984[b]		
Albert Gore	345,527	1,000,607	Victor Ashe	145,744	557,016
Write-ins	113		Jack McNeil	17,970	
			Hubert Patty	4,777	
			Write-ins	49	
			1982		
Jim Sasser	511,059	780,113	Robin Beard	205,271	479,642
Charles G. Vick	63,488		William B. Thompson, Jr.	19,277	
			1978		
Jane Eskind	196,156	466,228	Howard H. Baker	205,680	642,644
Jim Boyd	48,458		James D. Boles	8,899	
Walter Bradley	22,130		Harvey Howard	21,154	
Bill Bruce	170,795		Hubert D. Patty	3,941	
James Foster	10,671		Dayton Seiler	3,381	
Douglas Heinsohn	17,787		Francis Tapp	2,994	
J. D. Lee	89,939				
Virginia Nyabongo	7,682				
Charles G. Vick	4,414				
Write-ins	134				
			1976		
Jim Sasser	244,930	751,180	William Brock	173,743	673,231
David Bolin	44,056		Write-ins	1,266	
Edward Brown	4,695				
William T. Hardison	4,461				
John J. Hooker, Jr.	171,716				
Lester Kefauver	29,864				
Harry Sadler	54,125				
			1972[c]		
Ray Blanton	290,717	440,599	Howard H. Baker	242,373	716,539
Herman Frey	18,736		Hubert D. Patty	7,581	
Raymond P. Gibbs	14,897				
Don Palmer	40,600				
Ron Stinnett	15,767				

a. Independent candidate, Muhaymin, received 6,042 votes; there were 45 write-in votes.

b. Independent candidate, McAteer, received 87,234 votes, Muhaymin received 3,179.

c. The totals for the Democratic primary do not include McMinn and McNairy Counties; the totals for the Republican primary do not include Benton and Sequatchie Counties.

Source: Office of the Secretary of State, Certificate of Election Returns for August 4, 1988, Primary Election, and November 8, 1988, General Election, State of Tennessee; and corresponding sources for earlier elections.

TABLE 14.6-- RETURNS FROM THE GENERAL ELECTION FOR THE UNITED STATES HOUSE OF REPRESENTATIVES, TOP TWO CANDIDATES, CONGRESSIONAL DISTRICTS AND COUNTIES, NOVEMBER 4, 1986, AND NOVEMBER 8, 1988

County and district	1988 Democratic candidate	1988 Republican candidate	1986 Democratic candidate	1986 Republican candidate
FIRST DISTRICT	**Smith**	**Quillen**	**Russell**	**Quillen**
Total	29,469	119,526	36,278	80,289
Carter	1,835	11,125	3,422	7,169
Cocke	895	5,620	1,168	4,048
Greene	3,115	11,917	3,825	7,708
Hawkins	3,285	9,681	3,559	5,769
Jefferson	1,721	7,118	1,614	5,411
Johnson	549	3,802	702	2,412
Sevier	2,151	11,635	1,811	7,554
Sullivan	10,924	34,459	12,099	23,631
Unicoi	835	4,057	1,076	2,859
Washington	4,159	20,112	7,002	13,728
SECOND DISTRICT	**Taylor**	**Duncan**	**Bowen**	**Duncan**
Total	77,540	99,631	30,088	96,396
Blount	12,647	15,748	4,870	15,732
Knox	48,801	63,092	15,974	60,368
Loudon	4,385	5,471	1,992	5,705
McMinn	5,224	7,711	2,749	7,704
Monroe	4,450	5,583	2,654	5,017
Polk	2,033	2,026	1,849	1,870
THIRD DISTRICT	**Lloyd**	**Coker**	**Lloyd**	**Golden**
Total	108,264	80,372	75,034	64,084
Anderson	15,233	8,477	12,063	6,521
Bradley	11,388	11,270	7,120	9,897
Grundy	2,987	763	2,353	720
Hamilton	60,946	48,978	39,437	37,272
Marion	6,004	2,876	4,536	2,523
Meigs	1,404	1,148	1,143	1,137
Roane	10,302	6,860	8,382	6,014
FOURTH DISTRICT	**Cooper**	(a)	**Cooper**	(a)
Total	94,129		86,997	
Bedford	6,678		6,182	
Bledsoe	1,946		1,855	
Campbell	5,186		4,674	
Claiborne	4,036		3,587	
Coffee	8,916		7,950	
Cumberland	6,177		5,408	
Fentress	2,693		2,075	
Franklin	7,325		6,581	
Giles	4,847		4,379	
Grainger	1,891		1,741	
Hamblen	7,864		7,093	
Hancock	800		729	
Lawrence	6,551		6,341	
Lincoln	4,826		3,998	
Moore	954		931	
Morgan	2,703		3,076	
Rhea	3,633		3,528	
Scott	2,297		2,210	
Sequatchie	1,649		1,471	
Union	1,769		1,553	
Van Buren	1,018		1,080	

TABLE 14.6-- RETURNS FROM THE GENERAL ELECTION FOR THE UNITED STATES HOUSE OF REPRESENTATIVES, TOP TWO CANDIDATES, CONGRESSIONAL DISTRICTS AND COUNTIES, NOVEMBER 4, 1986, AND NOVEMBER 8, 1988 (Continued)

County and district	1988 Democratic candidate	1988 Republican candidate	1986 Democratic candidate	1986 Republican candidate
Warren	6,267		6,383	
White	4,103		4,172	
FIFTH DISTRICT	**Clement**	(b)	**Boner**	**Holcomb**
Total	155,068		85,126	58,701
Davidson	146,806		78,658	56,407
Robertson	8,262		6,468	2,294
SIXTH DISTRICT	**Gordon**	**Embry**	**Gordon**	**Vail**
Total	123,652	38,033	102,180	30,823
Cannon	2,570	443	2,416	427
Clay	1,463	479	1,407	448
DeKalb	3,208	697	3,066	650
Jackson	2,428	323	2,500	333
Lewis	2,014	437	2,237	424
Macon	2,569	820	2,230	777
Marshall	4,043	1,073	4,094	905
Maury	8,991	3,905	9,091	2,764
Overton	3,187	581	3,104	595
Pickett	884	523	828	556
Putnam	10,709	2,537	8,759	2,334
Rutherford	24,512	6,102	16,596	4,557
Smith	3,245	555	3,467	518
Sumner	19,880	6,639	16,736	4,781
Trousdale	1,538	213	1,284	124
Williamson	18,231	8,271	12,056	7,330
Wilson	14,180	4,435	12,309	3,300
SEVENTH DISTRICT	**Bloodworth**	**Sundquist**	**Hiler**	**Sundquist**
Total	35,237	142,025	35,966	93,902
Cheatham	1,689	3,357	2,108	2,594
Chester	1,029	2,778	1,132	2,069
Decatur	1,156	2,174	1,456	1,900
Dickson	2,689	5,272	3,468	4,405
Fayette	2,033	3,843	2,127	2,885
Hardeman	1,605	3,532	1,862	2,799
Hardin	1,401	4,299	1,772	3,422
Henderson	1,001	5,072	1,555	4,325
Hickman	1,389	2,149	2,026	1,991
Houston	887	977	1,085	759
Humphreys	1,604	2,383	1,933	2,294
McNairy	1,775	4,829	2,339	4,256
Montgomery	4,262	13,667	4,227	9,802
Perry	687	904	972	768
Shelby	11,210	83,757	6,765	47,319
Wayne	820	3,032	1,139	2,314
EIGHTH DISTRICT	**Tanner**	**Bryant**	**Jones**	**Campbell**
Total	94,571	56,893	101,699	24,792
Benton	3,518	1,105	4,505	600
Carroll	5,486	3,645	6,916	1,917
Crockett	2,407	1,504	2,829	591
Dyer	6,308	3,713	6,056	1,744
Gibson	10,439	4,780	11,327	1,997
Haywood	3,569	1,755	3,818	882

TABLE 14.6-- RETURNS FROM THE GENERAL ELECTION FOR THE UNITED STATES HOUSE OF REPRESENTATIVES, TOP TWO CANDIDATES, CONGRESSIONAL DISTRICTS AND COUNTIES, NOVEMBER 4, 1986, AND NOVEMBER 8, 1988 (Continued)

	1988		1986	
County and district	Democratic candidate	Republican candidate	Democratic candidate	Republican candidate
Henry	6,286	2,475	7,544	1,236
Lake	1,321	265	1,212	167
Lauderdale	4,944	1,594	4,345	969
Madison	12,858	15,151	18,288	5,623
Obion	8,460	1,561	5,820	1,480
Shelby	14,829	11,208	13,061	4,042
Stewart	1,896	651	2,205	435
Tipton	5,430	4,406	5,751	1,294
Weakley	6,820	3,080	8,022	1,815
NINTH DISTRICT	**Ford**	(c)	**Ford**	(d)
Total	126,280		83,006	
Shelby	126,280		83,006	

a. Jim Cooper ran unopposed. There were 22 write-in votes in 1988; 8 in 1986.

b. Bob Clement ran unopposed. There were 72 write-in votes.

c. There was no Republican candidate. Independent candidate, Isaac Richmond, received 28,522 votes.

d. There was no Republican candidate. Independent candidate, Isaac Richmond, received 16,221 votes, and there were 289 write-in votes cast.

Source: State of Tennessee, Office of the Secretary of State (Nashville), Certificate of Election Returns for the November 4, 1986, and the November 8, 1988, General Elections, State of Tennessee.

FIGURE 14.3
United States Congressional Districts in Tennessee

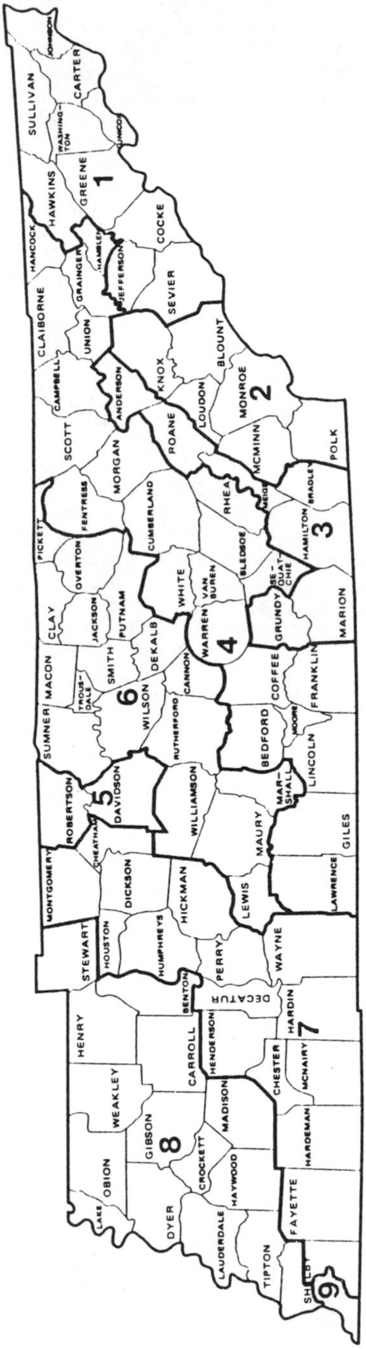

Source: State of Tennessee, Office of Legislative Services of the Tennessee General Assembly.

TABLE 14.7-- RETURNS FROM THE GENERAL ELECTION FOR THE UNITED STATES SENATE, TOP TWO CANDIDATES, TENNESSEE AND COUNTIES, NOVEMBER 6, 1984, AND NOVEMBER 8, 1988

	1988		1984	
County	Democratic candidate	Republican candidate	Democratic candidate	Republican candidate
	Sasser	**Andersen**	**Gore**	**Ashe**
TENNESSEE	1,020,061	541,033	1,000,607	557,016
Anderson	14,997	8,459	15,971	9,348
Bedford	6,275	2,182	7,075	1,702
Benton	4,042	998	4,573	1,214
Bledsoe	1,824	1,353	1,749	1,554
Blount	15,039	13,016	13,431	13,068
Bradley	11,834	10,578	9,444	12,086
Campbell	5,852	2,919	5,827	3,887
Cannon	2,445	728	2,825	627
Carroll	6,188	2,759	6,520	3,504
Carter	8,484	6,751	6,906	8,002
Cheatham	4,890	1,870	5,071	1,708
Chester	2,659	1,612	2,643	1,605
Claiborne	4,568	2,273	3,662	3,145
Clay	1,522	673	1,795	778
Cocke	3,523	3,119	3,113	4,848
Coffee	8,955	4,069	9,522	3,416
Crockett	2,866	1,093	2,772	1,360
Cumberland	6,074	4,872	5,793	4,594
Davidson	126,569	55,900	132,696	43,309
Decatur	2,885	1,086	2,786	1,243
DeKalb	3,279	1,019	3,922	909
Dickson	7,312	2,621	8,668	2,369
Dyer	6,992	3,015	6,166	3,702
Fayette	4,727	2,109	4,577	2,364
Fentress	2,871	1,295	2,791	1,725
Franklin	7,549	2,721	8,534	2,419
Gibson	11,403	3,350	11,729	4,579
Giles	5,060	1,787	5,240	1,805
Grainger	2,126	1,727	2,010	2,424
Greene	8,895	6,982	7,056	8,016
Grundy	2,957	672	2,993	746
Hamblen	8,280	6,125	7,452	6,628
Hamilton	60,154	49,296	54,623	48,548
Hancock	987	760	783	1,068
Hardeman	4,828	1,624	4,494	1,854
Hardin	4,234	2,196	4,504	2,685
Hawkins	8,184	5,589	6,413	6,540
Haywood	4,150	1,462	4,005	1,506
Henderson	4,309	2,915	4,423	2,843
Henry	7,104	2,044	7,426	2,563
Hickman	3,564	1,079	3,983	1,161
Houston	1,840	436	2,077	402
Humphreys	4,067	1,000	4,780	980
Jackson	2,485	506	3,971	496
Jefferson	5,060	4,251	4,733	5,148
Johnson	2,459	2,118	1,563	2,900
Knox	66,540	45,081	65,091	47,269
Lake	1,187	268	1,312	454

TABLE 14.7-- RETURNS FROM THE GENERAL ELECTION FOR THE UNITED STATES SENATE, TOP TWO CANDIDATES, TENNESSEE AND COUNTIES, NOVEMBER 6, 1984, AND NOVEMBER 8, 1988 (Continued)

County	1988 Democratic candidate	1988 Republican candidate	1984 Democratic candidate	1984 Republican candidate
	Sasser	**Andersen**	**Gore**	**Ashe**
Lauderdale	5,164	1,555	4,893	1,894
Lawrence	6,778	3,612	7,359	4,126
Lewis	2,007	643	2,424	665
Lincoln	5,327	1,765	5,606	1,505
Loudon	5,886	4,087	5,190	4,631
McMinn	7,262	5,875	7,478	7,169
McNairy	5,205	2,419	5,121	2,961
Macon	2,721	1,370	3,770	1,296
Madison	18,824	9,130	18,791	8,637
Marion	6,079	2,646	5,399	3,016
Marshall	4,073	1,416	4,717	1,378
Maury	9,431	4,457	10,990	4,042
Meigs	1,412	991	1,270	1,133
Monroe	5,337	4,713	5,408	5,159
Montgomery	13,959	6,617	14,946	6,013
Moore	1,039	370	1,294	324
Morgan	2,983	1,297	3,001	1,747
Obion	7,105	1,836	5,903	3,853
Overton	3,304	834	4,089	864
Perry	1,602	391	1,783	408
Pickett	818	703	1,087	784
Polk	2,738	1,528	2,678	2,091
Putnam	10,719	4,304	12,183	3,638
Rhea	3,951	3,434	3,674	3,730
Roane	10,583	6,152	9,914	6,897
Robertson	8,374	2,645	8,403	2,201
Rutherford	21,070	10,687	21,737	6,852
Scott	2,385	1,379	2,499	1,923
Sequatchie	1,786	876	1,616	1,215
Sevier	6,657	7,642	5,652	8,235
Shelby	204,815	88,768	187,944	102,831
Smith	3,455	914	5,107	633
Stewart	2,454	707	2,591	666
Sullivan	29,928	19,046	25,537	20,289
Sumner	19,851	9,903	21,292	6,954
Tipton	6,853	3,104	6,072	3,391
Trousdale	1,643	337	1,706	215
Unicoi	2,933	2,241	2,460	2,616
Union	1,993	1,321	1,946	1,758
Van Buren	1,195	289	1,167	311
Warren	6,417	2,293	7,272	1,949
Washington	17,527	10,512	14,915	11,859
Wayne	2,329	1,932	2,154	2,223
Weakley	7,239	2,559	7,277	3,444
White	3,967	1,305	4,751	1,245
Williamson	14,764	13,294	14,286	8,442
Wilson	14,025	6,776	15,762	4,702

Source: State of Tennessee, Office of the Secretary of State (Nashville), Certificate of Election Returns for the November 6, 1984, and the November 8, 1988, General Elections, State of Tennessee.

TABLE 14.8-- POPULAR VOTE FOR UNITED STATES PRESIDENT, TOP THREE CANDIDATES, TENNESSEE AND COUNTIES, 1984 AND 1988

	1988			1984		
County	Michael Dukakis	George Bush	Ron Paul	Walter Mondale	Ronald Reagan	David Bergland
TENNESSEE	679,794	947,233	2,041	711,714	990,212	3,072
Anderson	9,589	15,056	35	10,415	16,783	62
Bedford	4,046	4,856	9	4,499	4,699	25
Benton	2,826	2,167	1	3,398	2,481	5
Bledsoe	1,274	1,858	5	1,316	1,950	3
Blount	9,602	20,027	38	9,188	20,525	48
Bradley	6,122	15,829	16	6,085	16,322	40
Campbell	4,188	5,197	5	4,692	5,685	9
Cannon	1,726	1,604	4	1,846	1,669	7
Carroll	4,151	5,635	3	4,568	6,017	19
Carter	4,634	12,036	18	4,642	13,153	33
Cheatham	3,067	4,132	15	3,007	4,109	22
Chester	1,757	2,781	2	1,854	2,793	2
Claiborne	2,977	4,071	6	2,870	4,474	9
Clay	1,183	1,291	0	1,281	1,338	8
Cocke	2,115	5,430	9	2,068	6,665	16
Coffee	5,686	7,837	29	5,691	7,695	26
Crockett	1,742	2,214	0	1,937	2,479	6
Cumberland	3,964	7,557	22	3,605	7,083	20
Davidson	89,270	98,599	299	89,498	98,155	355
Decatur	1,880	2,286	7	2,031	2,390	3
DeKalb	2,452	2,098	6	2,645	2,337	8
Dickson	5,129	5,343	13	5,809	5,846	21
Dyer	3,690	6,508	5	3,991	6,610	14
Fayette	3,292	3,573	11	3,634	3,733	11
Fentress	1,856	3,103	2	1,755	2,922	4
Franklin	5,442	5,381	16	5,846	5,705	21
Gibson	7,542	8,415	16	8,334	9,484	56
Giles	3,918	3,518	10	3,812	3,875	16
Grainger	1,423	2,734	5	1,565	3,212	10
Greene	5,077	11,947	44	4,763	13,215	27
Grundy	2,415	1,429	0	2,596	1,396	5
Hamblen	5,061	10,418	27	4,922	11,144	41
Hamilton	40,990	68,111	157	41,449	69,626	128
Hancock	737	1,303	8	619	1,491	10
Hardeman	3,526	3,547	13	3,797	3,712	23
Hardin	2,808	4,252	5	3,051	4,632	21
Hawkins	5,212	9,356	24	4,802	9,863	31
Haywood	2,923	2,687	3	3,308	2,839	6
Henderson	2,296	5,418	21	2,426	5,362	9
Henry	5,138	4,784	3	5,407	5,376	11
Hickman	2,643	2,246	14	2,941	2,370	8
Houston	1,467	882	4	1,716	882	2
Humphreys	3,037	2,132	1	3,668	2,249	5
Jackson	1,962	1,168	5	2,894	1,544	15
Jefferson	3,168	6,832	13	3,185	7,721	20
Johnson	1,329	3,715	3	999	3,853	3
Knox	41,829	73,092	190	43,448	76,965	228
Lake	935	806	1	1,191	878	11

TABLE 14.8-- POPULAR VOTE FOR UNITED STATES PRESIDENT, TOP THREE CANDIDATES, TENNESSEE AND COUNTIES, 1984 AND 1988 (Continued)

	1988			1984		
County	Michael Dukakis	George Bush	Ron Paul	Walter Mondale	Ronald Reagan	David Bergland
Lauderdale	3,296	3,308	4	3,506	3,566	7
Lawrence	4,903	6,273	0	5,458	6,034	13
Lewis	1,419	1,324	8	1,556	1,733	4
Lincoln	3,672	4,288	21	4,103	3,982	10
Loudon	3,480	7,122	14	3,227	7,113	14
McMinn	4,568	8,462	19	5,141	9,604	16
McNairy	3,510	4,625	10	3,825	4,776	7
Macon	1,538	2,962	5	1,747	3,330	3
Madison	11,001	16,952	3	12,006	17,819	21
Marion	4,175	4,407	6	3,942	4,337	20
Marshall	2,795	2,975	2	2,935	3,416	9
Maury	6,280	8,397	11	6,950	9,008	27
Meigs	1,048	1,507	2	1,012	1,575	3
Monroe	4,000	6,355	9	4,223	6,665	17
Montgomery	9,145	12,599	24	9,939	13,228	66
Moore	731	786	3	808	863	2
Morgan	1,941	2,576	2	2,121	2,903	15
Obion	4,785	6,037	8	4,769	6,384	18
Overton	2,511	1,873	1	2,749	2,054	12
Perry	1,208	854	3	1,316	948	2
Pickett	634	1,118	0	706	1,246	2
Polk	2,073	2,297	3	2,112	2,785	13
Putnam	6,606	9,547	24	7,443	8,999	25
Rhea	2,595	5,144	6	2,804	5,692	16
Roane	6,535	10,881	6	6,623	11,882	43
Robertson	5,884	5,714	12	5,756	5,445	20
Rutherford	12,245	20,397	34	11,618	19,503	60
Scott	1,611	2,562	3	1,810	3,107	13
Sequatchie	1,196	1,659	2	1,238	1,785	9
Sevier	3,643	11,920	13	3,384	12,517	28
Shelby	149,759	157,457	375	165,947	169,717	564
Smith	2,522	2,138	2	3,258	2,393	7
Stewart	1,979	1,302	2	2,174	1,285	6
Sullivan	17,396	32,996	33	16,925	36,516	212
Sumner	11,702	19,523	41	11,535	18,442	59
Tipton	3,824	6,052	6	3,895	5,945	11
Trousdale	1,193	969	1	1,142	781	2
Unicoi	1,794	3,664	5	1,696	4,249	24
Union	1,431	2,110	3	1,495	2,447	5
Van Buren	796	780	0	810	718	0
Warren	4,646	4,529	5	4,813	4,811	16
Washington	10,087	19,615	63	9,452	21,762	50
Wayne	1,516	3,405	3	1,534	3,332	1
Weakley	4,239	5,701	15	4,752	6,480	24
White	2,562	2,646	10	3,033	2,895	8
Williamson	7,864	20,847	52	6,929	17,975	28
Wilson	8,360	13,317	24	8,433	12,858	57

Source: State of Tennessee, Office of the Secretary of State (Nashville), Certificate of Election Returns for the November 8, 1988, General Election, State of Tennessee, and corresponding source for 1984 election year.

TABLE 14.9-- REGISTERED VOTERS AS A PERCENTAGE OF VOTING AGE POPULATION, 1980, AND NUMBER OF REGISTERED VOTERS AND VOTES, TENNESSEE AND COUNTIES, 1988

County	Population age 18 and over in 1980[a]	Registered voters in 1980 as a percentage of voting age population	Registered voters as of 12/1/88[b]	Total voters in 1988[c]
TENNESSEE	3,292,560	65.3	2,590,923	1,636,250
Anderson	48,762	66.9	35,277	24,788
Bedford	19,966	69.1	14,873	8,939
Benton	10,919	82.6	9,220	5,009
Bledsoe	6,632	88.8	6,079	3,147
Blount	56,796	60.6	44,839	29,776
Bradley	47,161	62.8	36,029	22,031
Campbell	24,207	66.0	18,568	9,416
Cannon	7,411	75.9	5,923	3,348
Carroll	20,540	76.4	16,485	9,830
Carter	36,622	72.7	25,133	16,778
Cheatham	14,626	58.3	10,926	7,250
Chester	9,395	68.1	7,172	4,555
Claiborne	17,185	72.5	14,682	7,082
Clay	5,530	77.9	5,111	2,493
Cocke	20,327	76.1	14,523	7,579
Coffee	27,226	68.8	19,984	13,615
Crockett	10,633	89.7	7,963	3,970
Cumberland	20,089	82.2	17,692	11,594
Davidson	358,134	60.4	289,690	188,946
Decatur	7,938	86.2	7,147	4,191
DeKalb	9,801	76.1	8,773	4,581
Dickson	20,998	61.8	18,105	10,536
Dyer	24,502	65.6	18,722	10,243
Fayette	16,522	65.1	12,092	6,921
Fentress	10,156	69.3	9,303	4,992
Franklin	22,861	61.4	17,166	10,886
Gibson	35,801	60.8	24,108	16,038
Giles	17,799	57.7	13,454	7,478
Grainger	11,740	68.0	7,523	4,174
Greene	39,314	59.8	29,241	17,132
Grundy	9,221	75.5	6,807	3,857
Hamblen	34,722	67.6	25,132	15,565
Hamilton	208,839	61.9	163,027	109,709
Hancock	4,866	(d)	4,512	2,082
Hardeman	16,274	61.3	12,391	7,138
Hardin	15,834	72.5	11,932	7,089
Hawkins	30,859	61.1	23,180	14,646
Haywood	13,558	66.0	9,783	5,640
Henderson	15,230	79.4	13,071	7,819
Henry	21,215	65.0	15,175	9,975
Hickman	10,927	63.3	9,461	4,918
Houston	4,886	81.2	3,909	2,367
Humphreys	11,148	72.8	8,334	5,188
Jackson	6,806	88.8	6,258	3,144
Jefferson	22,792	67.8	15,487	10,069
Johnson	9,709	84.8	7,502	5,079
Knox	239,058	65.2	171,905	115,521
Lake	5,229	89.7	3,421	1,750
Lauderdale	17,057	68.0	12,428	6,639
Lawrence	23,856	68.8	17,715	11,183
Lewis	6,555	72.2	5,424	2,761
Lincoln	19,165	61.5	13,099	8,017

TABLE 14.9-- REGISTERED VOTERS AS A PERCENTAGE OF VOTING AGE POPULATION, 1980, AND NUMBER OF REGISTERED VOTERS AND VOTES, TENNESSEE AND COUNTIES, 1988 (Continued)

County	Population age 18 and over in 1980 [a]	Registered voters in 1980 as a percentage of voting age population	Registered voters as of 12/1/88 [b]	Total voters in 1988 [c]
Loudon	20,858	68.9	17,387	10,679
McMinn	29,720	69.5	20,875	13,078
McNairy	16,178	67.5	12,363	8,191
Macon	11,232	69.6	9,506	4,531
Madison	53,336	64.5	42,380	28,039
Marion	16,956	84.0	18,130	8,618
Marshall	14,285	61.5	9,445	5,791
Maury	36,583	59.8	24,200	14,788
Meigs	5,098	76.9	5,232	2,568
Monroe	19,924	81.6	18,552	10,393
Montgomery	59,494	43.4	32,634	21,856
Moore	3,151	71.6	2,709	1,530
Morgan	11,433	69.0	8,363	4,546
Obion	23,429	66.9	16,789	10,858
Overton	12,465	72.1	8,660	4,397
Perry	4,414	76.1	3,778	2,076
Pickett	3,130	(d)	3,709	1,756
Polk	9,353	88.9	8,325	4,391
Putnam	35,949	55.6	24,484	16,285
Rhea	16,872	78.3	11,722	7,776
Roane	34,420	71.0	35,977	17,497
Robertson	25,923	58.8	18,140	11,672
Rutherford	60,167	61.7	50,718	32,801
Scott	12,683	71.1	10,244	4,193
Sequatchie	5,877	83.9	5,216	2,869
Sevier	29,718	68.5	25,209	15,631
Shelby	546,442	68.5	473,538	308,988
Smith	10,833	80.6	9,563	4,686
Stewart	6,349	87.5	5,403	3,296
Sullivan	104,385	57.0	76,946	50,977
Sumner	58,586	56.3	46,250	31,389
Tipton	22,067	61.3	15,860	9,918
Trousdale	4,483	77.6	3,561	2,173
Unicoi	12,000	71.8	9,167	5,486
Union	8,128	75.4	7,994	3,564
Van Buren	3,261	78.6	3,300	1,580
Warren	23,182	58.1	15,443	9,218
Washington	65,451	58.6	43,931	29,887
Wayne	9,698	75.4	8,300	4,951
Weakley	25,039	57.8	16,816	9,989
White	14,103	58.0	10,496	5,249
Williamson	39,657	64.1	41,153	28,823
Wilson	38,849	60.0	32,699	21,793

Note: Percentages were computed by the Center for Business and Economic Research.

a. Computed by Center for Business and Economic Research using *1980 Census of Population, General Population Characteristics, Tennessee.*

b. Data by direct correspondence, Office of the Secretary of State.

c. Total who voted for President in Tennessee General Election, November 8, 1988.

d. Percentage is greater than 100.

Source: Office of the Secretary of State, Certificate of Election Returns for the November 8, 1988, General Election, State of Tennessee; and direct correspondence.

FIGURE 14.4
Legislative Districts of Tennessee

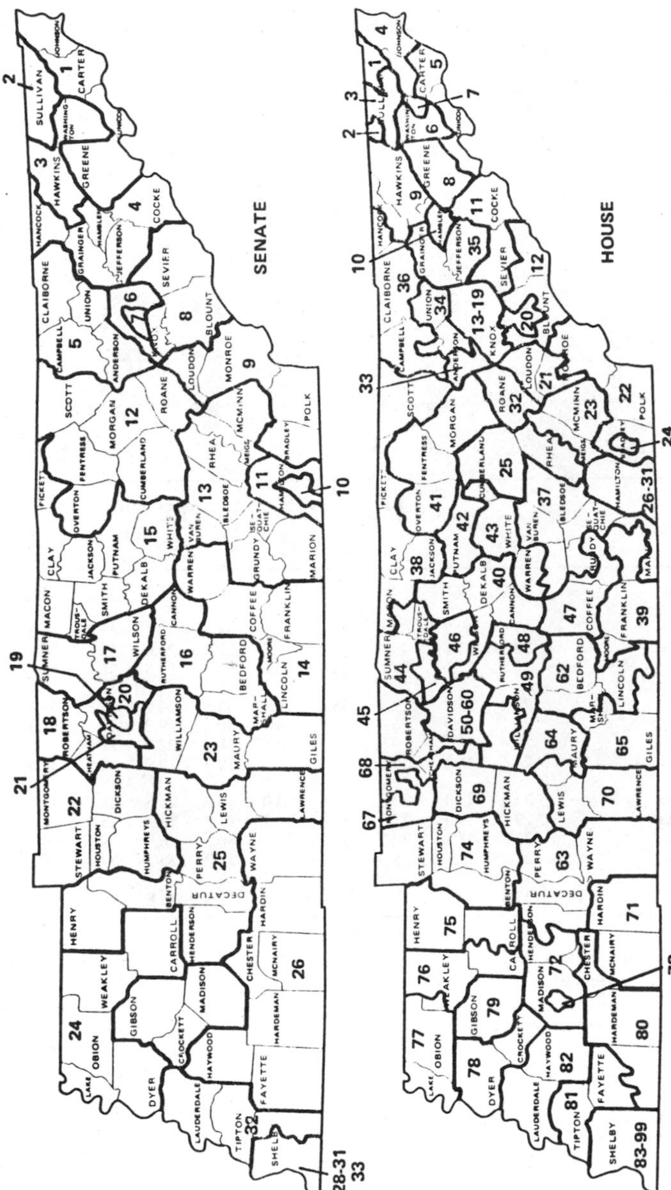

Source: State of Tennessee, Office of Legislative Services of the Tennessee General Assembly.

TABLE 14.10--ESTIMATES OF THE PERCENTAGE OF THE VOTING AGE POPULATION VOTING FOR PRESIDENTIAL ELECTORS, 1960–1988, AND VOTING FOR U.S. REPRESENTATIVES, 1960–1986, SOUTHEASTERN STATES AND UNITED STATES, SELECTED ELECTION YEARS

State	Percentage voting for presidential electors[1]							
	1988	1984	1980	1976	1972	1968	1964	1960
TENNESSEE	44.7	49.1	48.7	48.7	43.5	53.7	51.7	49.8
Alabama	45.8	49.9	48.7	46.3	43.3	52.7	35.9	30.8
Arkansas	47.0	51.8	51.5	51.1	48.1	53.3	50.6	40.8
Florida	44.7	48.2	48.7	49.2	48.6	53.0	51.2	48.6
Georgia	38.8	42.0	41.3	42.0	37.3	43.4	43.3	29.2
Kentucky	48.2	50.8	49.9	48.0	48.0	51.2	53.3	57.6
Louisiana	51.3	54.5	53.0	48.7	44.0	54.8	47.3	44.6
Mississippi	51.1	52.2	51.8	48.0	44.2	53.2	33.9	25.3
North Carolina	43.4	47.4	43.4	43.0	42.8	54.3	52.3	52.9
South Carolina	38.9	40.7	40.4[r]	40.3	38.2	46.7	39.4	30.4
Virginia	48.2	50.7	47.5	47.0	44.7	50.1	41.1	32.8
West Virginia	46.7	51.8[r]	52.7	57.2	62.5	71.1	75.5	78.0
UNITED STATES	50.2	53.1	52.6	53.5	55.2	60.7	61.8	63.1

	Percentage voting for U.S. representatives[1]										
	1986	1984[r]	1982[r]	1980	1978	1976	1974	1972	1968	1964	1960
TENNESSEE	31.0	37.7	34.5	39.3	33.4	41.2	31.2	39.9	43.6	46.8	30.5
Alabama	37.9	39.7	34.0	36.8	24.1	38.5	23.1	41.8	45.7	32.2	23.7
Arkansas[2]	38.5	27.1	45.6	12.4	18.6	22.4	29.6	13.8	26.1	11.7	36.0
Florida[2]	23.5	28.1	27.1	40.9	23.6	32.5	17.7	36.4	42.9	39.1	39.3
Georgia	24.0	35.9	22.4	35.0	16.1	35.8	24.6	28.3	33.1	31.7	22.9
Kentucky	23.1	44.0	26.4	40.7	18.9	40.6	29.3	44.4	41.9	48.6	46.8
Louisiana[3]	12.4	20.5	16.9	26.3	4.7	38.7	22.0	28.4	31.4	31.7	28.7
Mississippi	28.6	48.2	36.2	45.8	31.0	39.7	19.9	40.2	36.5	29.9	21.9
North Carolina	33.2	47.0	29.9	40.6	25.0	40.2	26.5	38.1	47.9	47.9	50.4
South Carolina	29.2	39.0	28.5	37.5	27.3	39.3	27.5	35.8	44.0	32.9	25.8
Virginia	23.8	43.4	32.7	39.5	27.8	40.5	26.9	39.0	46.7	36.6	27.2
West Virginia	28.0	49.5	38.5	49.0	32.5	51.3	33.3	59.1	67.1	73.4	76.3
UNITED STATES	33.4	47.7	38.0	47.4	34.5	48.9	35.8	50.7	55.2	57.8	58.7

r revised.

1. Votes cast as a percentage of the population of voting age.

2. State law does not require tabulation of votes for unopposed candidates.

3. Since 1978, Louisiana has had an open primary for Congressional elections. The general election is used for runoff purposes in the event that no candidate receives a majority of the votes in the primary.

Source: U.S. Department of Commerce, Bureau of the Census, *Statistical Abstract of the United States, 1989*, and earlier editions.

TABLE 14.11--POPULAR VOTE FOR PRESIDENTIAL ELECTORS, BY MAJOR POLITICAL PARTY, SOUTHEASTERN STATES, 1972–1988, ELECTION YEARS
[In thousands of votes]

	1988			1984			1980			1976			1972		
State	Total[1]	Demo-cratic	Repub-lican	Total[1]	Demo-cratic	Repub-lican	Total[1]	Demo-cratic	Repub-lican	Total[1]	Demo-cratic	Repub-lican	Total[1]	Demo-cratic	Repub-lican
TENNESSEE	1,617	678	939	1,712	712	990	1,618	783	788	1,476	826	634	1,201	357	813
Alabama	1,357	547	810	1,442	552	873	1,342	637	654	1,183	659	504	1,006	257	729
Arkansas	809	345	464	884	339	535	838	398	403	768	499	268	651	200	449
Florida	4,171	1,632	2,539	4,180	1,449	2,730	3,687	1,419	2,047	3,151	1,636	1,470	2,583	718	1,858
Georgia	1,786	716	1,070	1,776	707	1,069	1,597	891	654	1,467	979	484	1,175	290	881
Kentucky	1,311	579	731	1,369	540	822	1,295	616	635	1,167	616	532	1,067	371	676
Louisiana	1,596	716	881	1,707	652	1,037	1,549	708	793	1,278	661	587	1,051	298	687
Mississippi	913	361	552	941	352	582	893	429	441	769	381	367	646	127	505
North Carolina	2,122	890	1,232	2,175	824	1,346	1,856	876	915	1,679	927	742	1,519	439	1,055
South Carolina	967	368	600	969	344	616	894	430	442	803	451	346	674	187	477
Virginia	2,166	861	1,305	2,147	796	1,337	1,866	752	990	1,697	814	837	1,457	439	988
West Virginia	647	339	308	736	328	405	738	367	334	751	436	315	762	277	485

1. Includes candidates other than official Democratic and Republican nominees.

Source: U.S. Department of Commerce, Bureau of the Census, Statistical Abstract of the United States, 1989, and earlier editions; original source for data is Elections Research Center, *America Votes*, biennial, used by special permission; and *Congressional Quarterly, Inc.*, Washington, D.C., *Congressional Quarterly Weekly Report*, Vol. 46, No. 46, Nov. 12, 1988, used by special permission.

TABLE 14.12--POPULATION OF VOTING AGE, SOUTHEASTERN STATES AND UNITED STATES, NOVEMBER 1, 1964–1988, SELECTED ELECTION YEARS
[In thousands of voters]

State	1988[a]	1986[a]	1984	1982	1980	1978	1976	1972	1968	1964
TENNESSEE	3,661	3,563	3,490	3,375	3,293	3,179	3,033	2,763	2,325	2,212
Alabama	3,010	2,949	2,893	2,812	2,732	2,669	2,554	2,325	1,993	1,919
Arkansas	1,761	1,729	1,705	1,650	1,615	1,575	1,502	1,354	1,143	1,108
Florida	9,614	9,111	8,631	8,169	7,387	6,862	6,408	5,313	4,124	3,623
Georgia	4,665	4,402	4,228	4,040	3,817	3,667	3,494	3,153	2,851	2,634
Kentucky	2,746	2,728	2,696	2,620	2,578	2,528	2,434	2,223	2,063	1,964
Louisiana	3,175	3,186	3,124	3,055	2,875	2,760	2,623	2,389	2,002	1,894
Mississippi	1,867	1,833	1,804	1,745	1,706	1,672	1,603	1,462	1,229	1,207
North Carolina	4,913	4,748	4,600	4,417	4,224	4,088	3,907	3,548	2,921	2,723
South Carolina	2,534	2,467	2,389	2,291	2,180	2,104	1,993	1,762	1,427	1,333
Virginia	4,544	4,377	4,241	4,078	3,872	3,794	3,613	3,257	2,717	2,539
West Virginia	1,398	1,435	1,432	1,408	1,390	1,363	1,314	1,219	1,061	1,049
UNITED STATES	182,628	178,335	174,447	169,342	162,791	158,369	152,308	140,777	120,285	114,085

Note: Data include Armed Forces stationed in each state. Data through 1970 are for population 21 years old and over, except in Georgia and Kentucky, where it is 18 years. Beginning in 1972, data are for population 18 years old and over.

a. Projected for November 1.

Source: U.S. Department of Commerce, Bureau of the Census, *Current Population Reports*, Series P-25, No. 1019, and earlier editions.

TABLE 14.13--REPORTED VOTING AND REGISTRATION, BY RACE AND BY SEX, SOUTHEASTERN STATES AND UNITED STATES, NOVEMBER 1988 [Percentages]

State	All persons 18 years and over	Reported registered	Reported voted
Tennessee	100.0	65.3	51.4
Male	47.2	65.2	50.9
Female	52.8	65.4	51.9
White	84.3	64.4	50.7
Black	14.7	74.0	57.9
Alabama	100.0	73.3	56.9
Male	46.6	69.7	54.3
Female	53.4	76.4	59.2
White	77.0	75.0	58.4
Black	22.3	68.4	52.4
Arkansas	100.0	67.4	55.8
Male	49.2	66.5	54.6
Female	50.7	68.3	57.0
White	87.0	67.9	57.3
Black	11.6	68.0	49.6
Florida	100.0	63.0	54.5
Male	47.3	61.5	53.5
Female	52.7	64.3	55.5
White	85.5	64.3	57.1
Black	13.4	57.7	40.8
Hispanic origin	11.2	37.7	34.1
Georgia	100.0	61.4	49.6
Male	46.8	59.5	49.1
Female	53.2	63.0	50.1
White	68.6	63.9	53.2
Black	30.6	56.8	42.4
Kentucky	100.0	62.2	49.7
Male	45.8	62.2	50.6
Female	54.2	62.2	49.0
White	94.3	63.4	50.9
Black	5.1	45.8	32.3
Louisiana	100.0	75.1	65.2
Male	47.5	73.6	63.3
Female	52.4	76.5	67.0
White	71.3	75.1	67.5
Black	26.8	77.1	61.5
Mississippi	100.0	78.2	62.7
Male	47.0	76.1	60.9
Female	53.0	80.0	64.2
White	67.0	80.5	64.2
Black	32.5	74.2	60.3
North Carolina	100.0	63.6	52.9
Male	48.4	63.1	53.0
Female	51.6	64.0	52.8
White	77.7	65.6	55.2
Black	21.0	58.2	46.6
South Carolina	100.0	60.4	49.2
Male	46.0	59.4	48.7
Female	54.0	61.1	49.5
White	73.6	61.8	52.3
Black	26.1	56.7	40.7

TABLE 14.13--REPORTED VOTING AND REGISTRATION, BY RACE AND BY SEX, SOUTHEASTERN STATES AND UNITED STATES, NOVEMBER 1988 [Percentages] (Continued)

State	All persons 18 years and over	Reported registered	Reported voted
Virginia	100.0	66.9	58.0
Male	47.3	65.4	58.0
Female	52.7	68.2	58.1
White	80.4	68.5	61.1
Black	18.1	63.8	47.7
West Virginia	100.0	64.8	52.7
Male	46.9	64.8	52.7
Female	53.1	65.3	54.4
White	96.5	65.1	53.1
United States	100.0	66.6	57.4
Male	47.5	65.2	56.4
Female	52.5	67.8	58.3
White	85.8	67.9	59.1
Black	11.1	64.5	51.5
Hispanic origin	7.2	35.5	28.8

Note: Data are percentages of total voting age population by race and by sex. Data from household surveys have the limitation of generally overestimating voter turnout. For example, data from the November 1988, CPS indicate that 102.2 million persons reported voting in the 1988 elections, some 10.6 million more than actually voted, according to ballot counts.

Source: U.S. Department of Commerce, Bureau of the Census, *Current Population Reports*, Series P-20, No. 440.

TABLE 14.14--PROJECTIONS OF THE POPULATION, BY VOTING AGE, SOUTHEASTERN STATES, NOVEMBER 1, 1988 [In thousands]

State	Total, 18 and over	Age			
		18–24	25–44	45–64	65 and over
TENNESSEE					
Number	3,661	532	1,569	944	616
Percentage of total	100.0	14.5	42.8	25.8	16.8
Alabama					
Number	3,010	451	1,277	766	516
Percentage of total	100.0	15.0	42.4	25.5	17.1
Arkansas					
Number	1,761	249	704	454	354
Percentage of total	100.0	14.1	40.0	25.8	20.1
Florida					
Number	9,614	1,179	3,569	2,583	2,283
Percentage of total	100.0	12.3	37.1	26.9	23.7
Georgia					
Number	4,665	746	2,117	1,152	649
Percentage of total	100.0	16.0	45.4	24.7	13.9
Kentucky					
Number	2,746	416	1,178	691	462
Percentage of total	100.0	15.1	42.9	25.1	16.8
Louisiana					
Number	3,175	507	1,433	765	470
Percentage of total	100.0	16.0	45.1	24.1	14.8
Mississippi					
Number	1,867	302	779	462	324
Percentage of total	100.0	16.2	41.7	24.8	17.3
North Carolina					
Number	4,913	757	2,112	1,259	784
Percentage of total	100.0	15.4	43.0	25.6	16.0
South Carolina					
Number	2,534	409	1,122	623	380
Percentage of total	100.0	16.1	44.3	24.6	15.0
Virginia					
Number	4,544	706	2,049	1,141	648
Percentage of total	100.0	15.5	45.1	25.1	14.3
West Virginia					
Number	1,398	194	581	359	265
Percentage of total	100.0	13.9	41.5	25.7	18.9

Note: Detail may not add to total due to independent rounding.

Source: U.S. Department of Commerce, Bureau of the Census, *Current Population Reports*, Series P-25, No. 1019, January 1988.

TABLE 14.15--NUMBER OF LOCAL GOVERNMENT UNITS, BY TYPE, SOUTHEASTERN STATES, 1987

State	Total	County	Municipal	School district	Special district
TENNESSEE	904	94	334	14	462
Alabama	1,053	67	436	129	421
Arkansas	1,396	75	483	333	505
Florida	965	66	390	95	414
Georgia	1,286	158	532	186	410
Kentucky	1,303	119	437	178	569
Louisiana	452	61	301	66	24
Mississippi	853	82	293	171	307
North Carolina	916	100	495	0	321
South Carolina	707	46	269	92	300
Virginia	430	95	229	0	106
West Virginia	630	55	230	55	290

Source: U.S. Department of Commerce, Bureau of the Census, *1987 Census of Governments, Volume I, Government Organization.*

TABLE 14.16--NUMBER OF STATE AND LOCAL ELECTED OFFICIALS, SOUTHEASTERN STATES, 1987

State	Elected officials: Total	Elected officials: State	Elected officials: Local	Number of local governments	Elected officials per local government
TENNESSEE	6,841	322	6,519	904	7.6
Alabama	4,315	423	3,892	1,053	4.1
Arkansas	8,331	310	8,021	1,396	6.0
Florida	5,368	817	4,551	965	5.6
Georgia	6,556	447	6,109	1,286	5.1
Kentucky	7,481	560	6,921	1,303	5.7
Louisiana	4,985	582	4,403	452	11.0
Mississippi	4,950	294	4,656	853	5.8
North Carolina	5,554	549	5,005	916	6.0
South Carolina	3,692	195	3,497	707	5.2
Virginia	3,118	143	2,975	430	7.3
West Virginia	2,838	205	2,633	630	4.5
United States	503,862	18,171	485,691	83,186	6.1

Source: United States Department of Commerce, Bureau of the Census, *1987 Census of Governments, Preliminary Report*, GC87-2(P).

Because governments have traditionally been required to maintain records in order to answer to constituents or serve the needs of higher levels of government, revenues and expenditures are among the best documented fields. One principal source of data concerning state and local government finances is the Bureau of the Census, which publishes the annual reports, *State Government Finances, City Government Finances*, and *County Government Finances*, in addition to the multiple volume, *Census of Governments*, which is issued quinquennially. The geographic distribution of federal funds is reported in an annual report, *Federal Expenditures by State*. Another report that provides data at the county level is *Consolidated Federal Funds Report*, Volume I.

For those who need a variety of statistics on state finance, including relative tax burdens, *Facts and Figures on Government Finance* is a convenient compendium of state-level governmental data published biennially by the Tax Foundation, Inc. Data relating to federal tax collections by source are available in the *Statistics of Income Bulletin* and the *Annual Report of the Commissioner of Internal Revenue*, Department of the Treasury.

A comprehensive collection of data on Tennessee local and county government finances is published by the the Tennessee Association of Business (formerly the Tennessee Manufacturers and Taxpayers Association) in a report titled *Annual Survey of State and Local Government in Tennessee*. Much of the data used to report sales and use tax collections, property taxes, valuations and tax rates in the *Annual Survey* are provided by the Tennessee State Board of Equalization and the Office of the Comptroller of the Treasury, State of Tennessee. The State Board of Equalization publishes the annual *Tax Aggregate Report*, and the Comptroller's Office provides fiscal year data in a report titled *County and Municipal Finances*. These original source reports have been used to prepare most of the tabular data for this edition of the *Abstract*. The Tennessee Budget, available from the Department of Finance and Administration, is another source of Tennessee financial information.

Tennessee Rankings, Chapter 20 of the *Abstract*, provides interesting comparative statistics on per capita measures of state tax collections in Figure 20.1 and its corresponding table. However, data users should exercise caution when making comparisons among governments in *Rankings* and throughout the *Abstract*. Programs may be administered by different levels of governments in different states, and sources of funding and program content may vary greatly. Rigorous use of the data may require that the user make specific inquiries of the governments concerned.

TABLE OF CONTENTS

Table Number / Page Number

TABLE OF CONTENTS
(Continued)

TABLE 15.1-- STATE GOVERNMENT REVENUE AND EXPENDITURE, TENNESSEE, 1950–1987, SELECTED YEARS [In thousands of dollars]

	Revenue[1]		
Year	Total	Tax [2]	Expenditure [3]
1987	7,382,678	3,603,331	6,641,241
1986	6,812,908	3,271,963	6,080,204
1985	6,142,245	2,998,373	5,439,026
1984	5,334,595	2,511,631	4,829,728
1983	4,783,433	2,246,288	4,578,341
1982	4,521,319	2,146,242	4,298,381
1981	4,271,237	1,958,427	4,230,952
1980	4,028,047	1,886,992	3,873,736
1979	3,614,601	1,843,906	3,361,000
1978	3,275,928	1,703,951	3,091,556
1977	2,933,213	1,529,531	2,854,020
1976	2,643,189	1,273,215	2,807,698
1975	2,234,018	1,152,054	2,417,217
1974	2,036,318	1,092,405	1,910,117
1973	1,882,304	1,002,356	1,675,600
1972	1,636,377	887,450	1,522,748
1971	1,422,737	735,440	1,457,612
1970	1,272,728	686,936	1,271,209
1969	1,127,971	645,758	1,113,043
1968	1,034,971	577,320	993,351
1967	962,743	514,422	956,603
1966	858,856	480,949	841,020
1965	751,947	432,844	702,747
1964	706,179	408,244	658,856
1963	618,321	352,098	591,100
1962	557,035	329,078	559,975
1961	535,316	311,352	522,299
1960	517,311	304,590	494,351
1955	314,935	204,761	320,469
1950	238,860	149,782	247,803

1. Revenue is all money received from external sources, net of refunds and correcting transactions, other than from issue of debt, liquidation of investments, and agency and private trust transactions. State university student fees are included in revenue.

2. Tax revenue is all money received from taxes imposed, including interest, penalties, and money shared or redistributed to local governments, but excluding protested amounts, refunds, and local government revenues collected by the state as agent.

3. Expenditure is all money paid out, net of recoveries and correcting transactions, other than for retirement of debt, investment in securities, extension of credit, or agency transactions. Expenditure includes only external transactions. All state university general spending is included in expenditure.

Source: U.S. Department of Commerce, Bureau of the Census, *State Government Finances in 1987*, and earlier editions.

TABLE 15.2-- PER CAPITA GENERAL REVENUE AND EXPENDITURES OF THE STATE GOVERNMENT, BY TYPE, TENNESSEE, 1960–1987, SELECTED YEARS [In dollars]

Revenue, by source	1987	1986	1985	1980	1975	1970	1960
Total general revenue	1299.34	1225.54	1123.75	778.01	486.46	301.24	133.39
Taxes, total[1]	742.19	681.23	629.65	411.02	275.08	175.05	85.39
General sales	410.78	388.49	365.05	213.95	113.90	61.45	29.41
Motor fuel sales	100.77	76.89	60.58	49.40	41.33	33.29	21.38
Motor vehicle licenses[2]	26.85	26.38	25.36	20.28	18.31	14.81	7.10
Individual income	14.03	14.04	12.98	6.71	4.40	3.09	1.46
Corporation net income[2]	61.51	55.93	54.43	43.18	30.26	15.20	6.00
Total aid received from other governments[2]	387.94	385.78	346.09	270.38	155.88	95.21	41.62
Federal	381.52	377.30	338.44	263.09	151.73	91.29	39.34
Local	6.42	8.48	7.65	7.29	4.15	3.92	2.28
Charges and miscellaneous	169.21	158.52	148.02	96.61	55.49	30.97	6.39

Expenditures, by function	1987	1986	1985	1980	1975	1970	1960
Total general expenditures	1269.15	1180.70	1055.30	771.81	522.39	308.64	128.85
Education	484.78	464.17	420.62	308.45	225.53	133.65	41.82
Highways	166.08	166.47	147.13	132.76	96.05	67.96	45.67
Public welfare	244.14	210.60	179.09	124.24	69.23	39.09	16.54
Health and hospitals[2]	112.94	100.58	93.24	62.96	45.55	21.33	8.47
Correction	45.59	39.28	32.69	21.43	9.48	5.35	1.34
Natural resources[2]	19.88	18.78	18.37	15.66	16.11	9.17	3.30
Employment security administration[2]	9.67	10.29	10.25	9.20	5.49	2.86	n.a.
General control[2,3]	14.50	12.78	11.51	9.25	5.22	2.29	1.78
Financial administration[2]	14.83	12.43	11.23	8.23	7.93	3.92	n.a.
Miscellaneous[4]	156.74	145.32	131.17	79.63	41.80	23.02	9.93

Note: Detail may not add to total due to independent rounding.

n.a. not available.

1. Includes amounts for categories not shown separately.
2. Calculated by the Center for Business and Economic Research when not given in the source. Per capita amounts are based on population estimates as of July 1, for intercensal years and are computed on the basis of amounts rounded to the nearest thousand.
3. Consists of judicial and legal, legislative, and other governmental administration expenditures.
4. Calculated by the Center for Business and Economic Research as the residual of total general expenditures and the sum of all other per capita expenditure classifications.

Source: U.S. Department of Commerce, Bureau of the Census, *State Government Finances in 1987*, and earlier editions.

FIGURE 15.1
General Revenues and Expenditures of Tennessee Government, by Source and Percentage Distribution, 1987

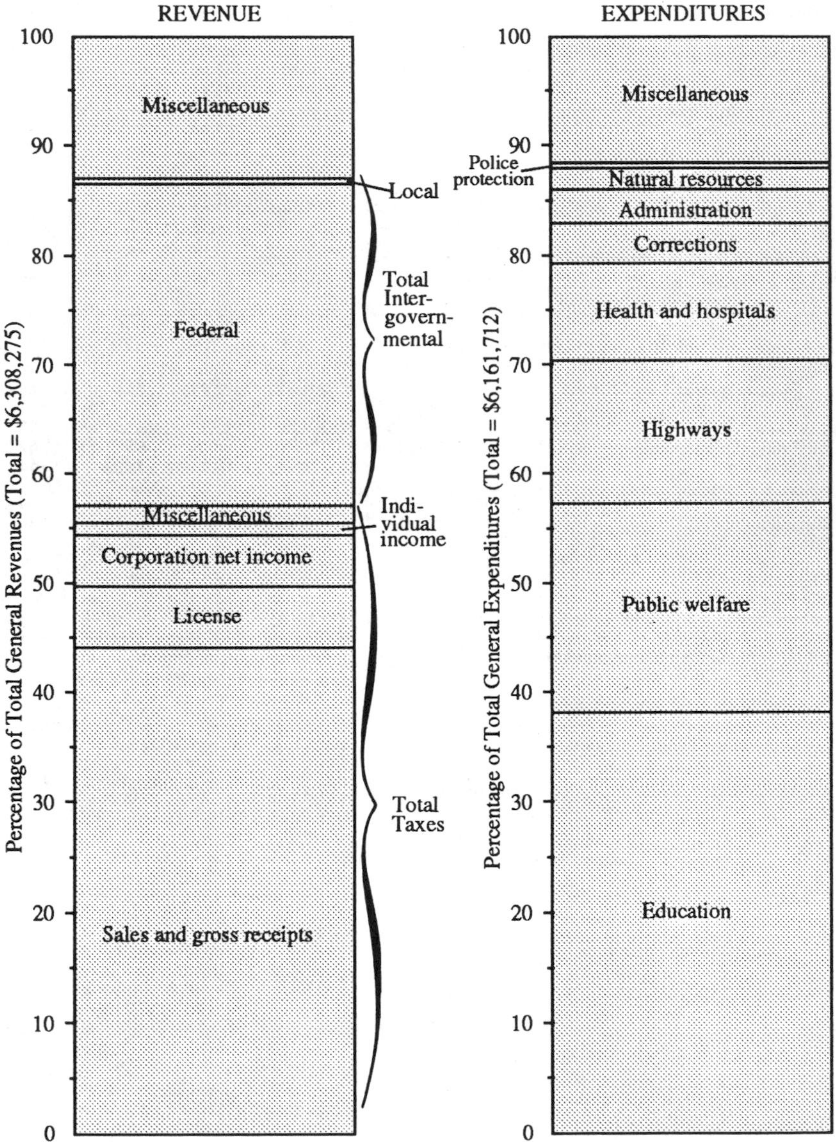

Note: See Tables 15.3 and 15.6 for data.
Source: U.S. Department of Commerce, Bureau of the Census, *State Government Finances in 1987*.

TABLE 15.3-- GENERAL REVENUE OF THE STATE GOVERNMENT, BY SOURCE, TENNESSEE, 1970–1987, SELECTED YEARS [Amounts in thousands of dollars]

	1987		1986		1985		1980		1970	
Source of revenue	Amount	%	Amount	%	Amount	%	Amount	%	Amount	%
Total general revenue[1]	6,308,275	100.0	5,886,272	100.0	5,351,295	100.0	3,571,842	100.0	1,182,101	100.0
Taxes, total	3,603,331	57.1	3,271,963	55.6	2,998,373	56.0	1,886,992	52.8	686,936	58.1
Sales and gross receipts	2,785,525	44.2	2,517,290	42.8	2,292,690	42.8	1,415,967	39.6	473,806	40.1
General	1,994,313	31.6	1,865,934	31.7	1,738,375	32.5	982,251	27.5	241,151	20.4
Selective[2]	791,212	12.5	651,356	11.1	554,315	10.4	433,716	12.1	232,655	19.7
License	351,296	5.6	332,259	5.6	303,268	5.7	181,522	5.1	116,417	9.8
Motor vehicle and operator	144,816	2.3	136,655	2.3	140,692	2.6	102,651	2.9	62,631	5.3
Other[3]	206,480	3.3	195,604	3.3	162,576	3.0	78,871	2.2	53,786	4.6
Individual income	68,123	1.1	67,432	1.1	61,825	1.2	30,800	0.9	12,113	1.0
Corporation net income	298,644	4.7	268,618	4.6	259,198	4.8	198,222	5.5	59,633	5.0
Miscellaneous[4]	99,743	1.6	86,364	1.5	81,392	1.5	60,481	1.7	24,967	2.1
Intergovernmental revenue	1,883,423	29.9	1,852,921	31.5	1,648,068	30.8	1,241,306	34.8	373,623	31.6
Federal	1,852,262	29.4	1,812,191	30.8	1,611,640	30.1	1,207,833	33.8	358,231	30.3
Local	31,161	0.5	40,730	0.7	36,428	0.7	33,473	0.9	15,392	1.3
Charges and miscellaneous	821,521	13.0	761,388	12.9	704,854	13.2	443,544	12.4	121,542	10.3

Note: For each source item, the percentage relates to total general revenue, not to category totals. Percentages were computed by the Center for Business and Economic Research.

1. General revenue is all state revenue except insurance trust revenue.

2. Includes motor fuels, alcoholic beverages, tobacco products, insurance, public utilities, amusements, and parimutuels.

3. Includes corporations in general, public utilities, alcoholic beverage, amusements, occupations and businesses not elsewhere classified, and hunting and fishing.

4. Includes property (back taxes only), death and gift, document and stock transfer, and severance.

Source: U.S. Department of Commerce, Bureau of the Census, *State Government Finances in 1987*, and earlier editions.

TABLE 15.4-- INTERGOVERNMENTAL REVENUE FROM LOCAL GOVERNMENTS TO THE STATE GOVERNMENT, BY FUNCTION, TENNESSEE, 1955–1987 [In thousands of dollars]

Year	Total	Education	Highways	Public welfare	Health and hospitals	Other
1987	31,161	5,966	10,758	895	10,678	2,864
1986	40,730	5,391	18,426	911	12,872	3,130
1985	36,428	6,500	13,074	1,349	11,955	3,550
1984	31,713	4,498	11,820	1,250	12,042	2,103
1983	29,484	4,686	10,366	1,264	11,022	2,146
1982	34,101	3,560	16,005	766	10,847	2,923
1981	32,332	6,239	7,363	5,265	11,976	1,489
1980	33,473	6,224	10,436	5,539	9,784	1,490
1979	25,103	4,353	6,376	4,816	8,096	1,462
1978	23,004	4,095	6,676	3,183	7,804	1,246
1977	16,325	3,309	3,900	1,417	6,640	1,059
1976	14,816	2,296	4,167	508	6,472	1,373
1975	17,384	2,670	5,943	547	7,310	914
1974	24,068	2,806	9,453	477	10,232	1,100
1973	29,859	1,955	5,216	9,333	12,416	939
1972	22,635	1,147	4,460	7,067	9,286	675
1971	20,117	1,329	3,774	6,888	7,706	420
1970	15,392	1,570	2,099	5,885	5,380	458
1969	12,086	1,159	981	5,103	4,397	446
1968	15,784	1,010	5,854	4,608	3,814	498
1967	21,702	1,703	11,387	4,008	3,166	1,438
1966	9,780	1,109	1,338	3,290	3,121	922
1965	7,362	313	459	2,668	3,580	342
1964	7,307	638	265	2,383	3,558	463
1963	6,168	149	125	2,256	3,232	406
1962	6,401	235	0	2,412	3,267	487
1961	8,609	230	2,276	2,401	3,118	584
1960	8,129	312	1,756	2,564	2,902	595
1959	6,376	0	122	2,277	3,184	793
1958	5,686	0	146	2,154	2,633	753
1957	5,203	0	314	2,168	2,347	374
1956	5,232	0	593	2,439	1,640	560
1955	4,687	0	125	2,207	1,535	820

Source: U.S. Department of Commerce, Bureau of the Census, *State Government Finances in 1987*, and earlier editions.

TABLE 15.5-- INTERGOVERNMENTAL REVENUE FROM THE FEDERAL GOVERNMENT TO THE STATE GOVERNMENT, BY FUNCTION, TENNESSEE, 1950–1987, SELECTED YEARS [In thousands of dollars]

Year	Total	Education	Highways	Public welfare	Health and hospitals	Employment security adminis-tration	Natural resources	General revenue sharing	Other
1987	1,852,262	323,953	277,766	835,821	82,331	45,318	24,203	(X)	262,870[a]
1986	1,812,191	328,882	341,393	729,678	83,435	48,097	20,692	(X)	260,014[a]
1985	1,611,640	311,171	282,280	599,975	90,955	48,093	24,302	(X)	254,864[a]
1984	1,462,876	285,676	263,483	553,208	71,534	46,498	24,036	(X)	218,441
1983	1,287,327	274,438	182,782	495,982	59,761	51,181	20,040	(X)	203,143
1982	1,230,529	263,578	194,847	463,593	52,056	47,697	20,632	(X)	188,126
1981	1,322,402	292,940	256,755	454,090	49,511	46,664	20,155	22,053	180,234
1980	1,207,833	266,546	230,308	404,750	43,929	43,441	21,430	43,163	154,266
1979	1,004,156	221,430	170,027	342,945	38,261	40,139	18,835	41,721	130,798
1978	909,753	196,660	155,146	307,416	37,645	39,413	17,192	41,172	115,109
1977	817,356	177,321	155,885	280,990	30,819	33,691	19,179	40,736	78,735
1976	769,930	178,392	165,940	245,829	25,718	27,830	16,181	39,306	70,734
1975	635,458	159,406	125,903	193,007	19,904	23,157	15,056	39,508	59,517
1974	523,553	129,768	80,444	174,467	16,347	18,182	13,814	37,877	52,654
1973	524,875	132,135	87,020	188,681	13,467	16,199	11,907	41,249	34,217
1972	452,402	116,498	110,163	161,729	13,868	15,126	9,887	(X)	25,131
1971	434,029	117,981	114,243	145,128	14,936	13,041	10,971	(X)	17,729
1970	358,231	98,709	101,691	111,351	13,592	11,436	8,146	(X)	13,306
1965	209,587	20,733	110,379	54,463	6,893	6,195	4,734	(X)	6,190
1960	140,319	11,398	66,825	43,115	6,811	4,401	3,703	(X)	4,066
1955	63,737[b]	4,956	11,801	35,497	3,353	3,286	2,556	(X)	1,601
1950	58,495	12,251	8,488	28,162	0	3,063	0	(X)	6,531

(X) not applicable.

a. Includes housing and community development.

b. Total includes defense revenue.

Source: U.S. Department of Commerce, Bureau of the Census, *State Government Finances in 1987*, and earlier editions.

TABLE 15.6-- GENERAL EXPENDITURES OF THE STATE GOVERNMENT, BY FUNCTION, TENNESSEE, 1960–1987, SELECTED YEARS [Amounts in thousands of dollars]

	1987		1986		1985	
Function	Amount	%	Amount	%	Amount	%
Total general expenditure	6,161,712	100.0	5,670,889	100.0	5,025,340	100.0
Education	2,353,584	38.2	2,229,420	39.3	2,002,990	39.9
Highways	806,296	13.1	799,577	14.1	700,620	13.9
Public welfare	1,185,317	19.2	1,011,510	17.8	852,837	17.0
Health and hospitals	548,334	8.9	483,079	8.5	443,982	8.8
Police protection	46,943	0.8	41,819	0.7	35,299	0.7
Correction	221,333	3.6	188,669	3.3	155,683	3.1
Natural resources	96,516	1.6	90,210	1.6	87,499	1.7
Employment security administration	46,950	0.8	49,415	0.9	48,823	1.0
General control[1]	70,395	1.1	61,391	1.1	54,828	1.1
Financial administration	72,016	1.2	59,687	1.1	53,466	1.1
Miscellaneous[2]	714,028	11.6	656,112	11.6	589,313	11.7

	1980		1970		1960	
Function	Amount	%	Amount	%	Amount	%
Total general expenditure	3,543,378	100.0	1,211,150	100.0	459,618	100.0
Education	1,416,092	40.0	524,467	43.3	149,184	32.5
Highways	609,508	17.2	266,680	22.0	162,913	35.4
Public welfare	570,382	16.1	153,411	12.7	58,994	12.8
Health and hospitals	289,093	8.2	83,699	6.9	30,214	6.6
Police protection	23,629	0.7	8,301	0.7	3,919	0.9
Correction	98,408	2.8	20,999	1.7	4,763	1.0
Natural resources	71,906	2.0	35,982	3.0	11,786	2.6
Employment security administration	42,241	1.2	11,213	0.9	4,223	0.9
General control[1]	42,482	1.2	8,992	0.7	6,366	1.4
Financial administration	37,805	1.1	15,384	1.3	(a)	(a)
Miscellaneous[2]	341,832	9.6	82,022	6.8	27,256	5.9

Note: Percentages computed by the Center for Business and Economic Research.

1. General control includes judicial and legal, legislative, and other governmental administration expenditures.

2. Calculated by the Center for Business and Economic Research as the residual of total general expenditure and the sum of all other general expenditure classifications. Includes protective inspection and regulation, governmental administration of general public buildings, airports, libraries, veterans' services, housing and community development, parks and recreation, and interest on general debt.

a. Included in general control.

Source: U.S. Department of Commerce, Bureau of the Census, *State Government Finances in 1987*, and earlier editions.

TABLE 15.7-- FEDERAL INTERNAL REVENUE COLLECTIONS, BY SOURCE, TENNESSEE, 1950–1986, SELECTED FISCAL YEARS [In thousands of dollars]

Year	Total internal revenue collections	Corporation income tax [1]	Individual income and employment taxes	Estate tax	Gift tax	Excise taxes			
						Alcohol	Tobacco	Manufac-turers'	All other [2]
1986	12,332,044	1,353,819	10,372,346	78,714	3,994	131,563	1,570	200,469	189,569
1985	10,415,894	932,042	8,986,352	60,556	3,316	151,615	699	109,447	171,867
1984	8,735,857	897,731	7,431,231	56,480	2,883	132,157	695	87,805	126,876
1983	8,105,423	814,255	6,926,651	75,214	432	135,119	21,099	49,074	83,579
1982	7,324,593	689,183	6,384,576	91,435	713	134,170	593	36,829	-12,907[a]
1981	6,463,109	826,216	5,347,281	79,695	1,294	119,297	595	38,197	50,534
1980	6,419,433	751,552	5,395,421	82,281	2,140	96,197	3,222	28,501	60,119
1979	5,669,707	755,715	4,691,426	59,679	1,947	83,516	617	40,853	35,954
1978	5,034,752	765,897	3,992,077	132,221	1,782	79,720	633	35,106	27,316
1977	9,912,327	1,276,123	7,876,730	63,411	22,767	90,786	546	24,025	557,940
1976[b]	1,026,156	156,565	805,884	15,717	1,552	26,097	149	6,468	13,722
1975	3,511,943	509,719	2,814,829	49,920	3,211	90,177	508	20,206	23,372
1974	3,212,037	461,615	2,569,150	59,003	5,354	79,660	470	17,959	18,826
1973	2,811,214	420,016	2,225,562	51,211	11,762	66,247	379	26,256	9,782
1972	2,349,423	361,813	1,864,023	50,006	4,866	38,105	262	15,600	14,747
1971	2,023,831	308,691	1,625,638	30,752	3,034	27,029	211	15,147	13,331
1970	1,996,748	329,379	1,585,723	31,461	2,734	22,950	162	13,528	10,811
1965	1,055,239	199,128	770,756	21,615	3,404	15,329	1,537	23,914	19,558
1960	757,815	158,406	551,955	10,312	2,047	7,663	2,010	14,723	10,698
1955	505,123	107,944	360,412	6,821	870	6,087	2,148	8,153	12,686
1950	316,036	87,097	80,641[c]	4,435	245	3,777	4,025	3,956	n.a.

1. Includes tax on unrelated business income of exempt organizations.

2. Includes retailer's and special fuel taxes, miscellaneous excise tax, and unclassified excise tax.

a. Negative figures result from the classification of amounts previously reported as unclassified.

b. July 1–September 30, 1976. The Budget and Impoundment Control Act, effective in calendar year 1976, changed the fiscal year for the U.S. government. These figures represent transitional figures.

c. Individual income taxes only.

Source: U.S. Department of the Treasury, Internal Revenue Service, Commissioner of Internal Revenue, *Annual Report, 1986*, and earlier editions.

TABLE 15.8-- OPERATING REVENUE, BY SOURCE, COUNTY GOVERNMENTS, FISCAL YEAR 1987
[In thousands of dollars]

County	Total [1]	Federal government	State government	Local sources: Total [1]	Local sources: Property taxes	Local sources: Local sales taxes
TENNESSEE	3,037,795	192,396	900,971	1,944,436	878,190	546,640
Anderson	35,987	3,035	11,102	21,849	12,738	3,046
Bedford	17,201	1,025	8,062	8,115	3,929	2,223
Benton	9,709	671	5,040	4,001	1,048	1,328
Bledsoe	6,022	644	3,424	1,954	1,100	378
Blount	44,481	2,025	13,937	28,521	11,493	10,767
Bradley	38,353	1,680	11,301	25,370	11,112	8,526
Campbell	22,752	2,705	10,579	9,467	4,380	2,860
Cannon	6,420	444	3,398	2,580	1,401	423
Carroll	10,824	271	3,396	7,156	3,435	1,946
Carter	24,943	2,520	10,016	12,409	5,994	3,426
Cheatham	15,870	901	6,913	8,058	3,821	1,336
Chester	7,252	613	3,858	2,782	1,264	691
Claiborne	15,578	2,303	7,351	5,923	2,788	1,403
Clay	5,900	1,011	3,055	1,836	970	187
Cocke	16,519	2,121	7,025	7,373	3,604	2,241
Coffee	20,158	1,101	6,001	13,056	5,295	5,502
Crockett	7,969	618	3,438	3,912	1,978	696
Cumberland	21,255	1,737	8,267	11,250	3,943	3,766
Davidson [2]	543,224	43,740	101,080	398,404	183,298	88,537
Decatur	6,545	539	3,814	2,193	1,075	636
DeKalb	8,235	1,283	4,128	2,825	1,519	707
Dickson	21,491	1,142	9,073	11,275	3,658	3,797
Dyer	19,709	1,300	6,564	11,846	3,333	4,319
Fayette	16,235	3,064	7,152	6,019	3,248	1,167
Fentress	8,282	1,359	4,636	2,286	920	665
Franklin	17,330	1,917	8,828	6,585	2,085	2,414
Gibson	12,756	79	2,373	10,303	4,351	4,239
Giles	17,791	1,088	7,021	9,682	3,671	1,565
Grainger	9,102	885	4,660	3,557	2,099	506
Greene	27,298	1,970	10,555	14,773	6,169	3,625
Grundy	8,969	1,259	4,678	3,031	1,654	553
Hamblen	33,517	2,333	11,958	19,228	8,381	6,374
Hamilton	146,960	6,825	32,234	107,901	62,963	24,884
Hancock	5,318	1,181	3,113	1,023	457	172
Hardeman	14,804	1,660	7,972	5,172	2,175	1,625
Hardin	14,836	1,677	6,644	6,514	3,015	1,404
Hawkins	27,093	2,416	10,797	13,881	8,154	2,446
Haywood	14,472	2,261	6,441	5,770	2,781	972
Henderson	11,288	897	5,912	4,480	1,515	1,802
Henry	16,842	921	6,357	9,563	4,171	2,964
Hickman	10,608	796	5,145	4,667	2,367	519
Houston	4,845	394	2,686	1,765	824	416
Humphreys	12,361	762	5,626	5,973	3,371	1,486
Jackson	6,383	1,217	2,857	2,309	1,068	361
Jefferson	19,081	1,768	8,046	9,268	3,963	2,174
Johnson	9,286	1,035	4,291	3,961	2,331	509
Knox	163,680	6,543	38,879	118,257	57,384	41,406
Lake	5,594	665	2,563	2,366	874	395
Lauderdale	14,759	1,795	7,415	5,548	1,994	1,501
Lawrence	22,386	1,497	9,347	11,542	5,642	3,095

TABLE 15.8-- OPERATING REVENUE, BY SOURCE, COUNTY GOVERNMENTS, FISCAL YEAR 1987
[In thousands of dollars] (Continued)

County	Total [1]	Federal government	State government	Local sources: Total [1]	Local sources: Property taxes	Local sources: Local sales taxes
Lewis	5,672	484	3,306	1,882	743	545
Lincoln	13,875	949	6,862	6,065	2,900	1,679
Loudon	16,740	909	6,542	9,290	6,069	1,480
McMinn	22,763	1,212	8,544	13,006	8,578	2,301
McNairy	14,113	1,988	6,601	5,526	2,141	1,525
Macon	8,386	514	4,558	3,314	1,698	1,101
Madison	36,976	1,702	10,976	24,299	10,175	9,027
Marion	14,910	1,297	6,925	6,687	2,893	2,310
Marshall	14,347	704	5,660	7,982	3,768	2,128
Maury	38,157	2,239	13,098	22,820	7,937	6,947
Meigs	5,817	804	2,890	2,121	907	288
Monroe	17,418	2,128	7,034	8,257	2,957	2,583
Montgomery	56,512	4,083	20,397	32,034	12,049	9,889
Moore	3,946	192	2,126	1,628	1,105	110
Morgan	11,785	1,153	5,312	5,321	3,508	520
Obion	20,044	1,031	7,095	11,917	5,324	3,418
Overton	11,155	1,206	5,479	4,470	1,898	854
Perry	5,165	278	2,799	2,089	1,137	275
Pickett	3,461	382	1,824	1,254	572	154
Polk	10,446	1,049	4,883	4,512	2,693	770
Putnam	29,886	1,501	11,204	17,181	6,112	7,079
Rhea	15,024	1,344	6,504	7,177	3,830	1,952
Roane	23,250	1,619	9,665	11,966	4,844	3,141
Robertson	24,622	1,414	10,106	13,101	6,886	3,232
Rutherford	65,688	2,248	19,718	43,722	14,450	14,375
Scott	12,040	1,928	5,542	4,570	2,595	1,238
Sequatchie	6,958	560	3,593	2,803	1,089	665
Sevier	35,009	1,872	11,194	21,941	6,242	11,806
Shelby	478,743	13,128	70,160	395,454	156,738	130,658
Smith	9,600	522	4,131	4,947	2,182	1,084
Stewart	6,598	548	4,076	1,975	691	524
Sullivan	100,817	3,584	23,283	73,950	40,944	21,239
Sumner	62,987	2,611	23,424	36,951	16,029	9,311
Tipton	20,717	1,569	8,581	10,566	5,633	2,279
Trousdale	4,626	215	2,390	2,021	1,313	392
Unicoi	10,832	1,422	4,541	4,869	2,311	1,008
Union	6,918	784	3,978	2,156	1,293	314
Van Buren	3,677	498	2,233	946	456	98
Warren	23,484	1,169	8,671	13,643	3,045	3,100
Washington	42,583	2,515	11,616	28,452	11,543	12,568
Wayne	10,318	834	4,865	4,622	1,921	596
Weakley	17,598	1,122	7,580	8,896	3,697	2,483
White	12,089	874	5,865	5,350	2,751	1,532
Williamson	48,846	1,240	13,773	33,835	19,395	6,192
Wilson	34,924	1,278	12,359	21,289	12,345	3,890

Note: Detail may not add to total due to independent rounding.

1. Includes items not shown separately.

2. Data are for Metropolitan Nashville-Davidson County.

Source: State of Tennessee, Report of the Comptroller of the Treasury, Division of Local Finance, *County and Municipal Finances for Fiscal Year Ended June 30, 1987*.

TABLE 15.9-- PER CAPITA MAJOR OPERATING REVENUE SOURCES, TENNESSEE AND COUNTIES, YEAR ENDING JUNE 30, 1987

County	Per capita major revenue sources[1]				Percentage of total operating revenue by source		
	Property tax	Local sales tax	Federal government	State government	Federal	State	Local
Anderson	$182	$43	$43	$158	8	31	61
Bedford	134	76	35	275	6	47	47
Benton	70	89	45	338	7	52	41
Bledsoe	110	38	64	342	11	57	32
Blount	137	129	24	167	5	31	64
Bradley	152	117	23	155	4	29	66
Campbell	125	82	77	302	12	46	42
Cannon	129	39	41	312	7	53	40
Carroll	122	69	10	121	3	31	66
Carter	116	66	49	194	10	40	50
Cheatham	148	52	35	267	6	44	51
Chester	97	53	47	297	8	53	38
Claiborne	106	53	87	278	15	47	38
Clay	123	24	128	387	17	52	31
Cocke	123	76	72	240	13	43	45
Coffee	127	132	26	144	5	30	65
Crockett	140	49	44	244	8	43	49
Cumberland	121	115	53	253	8	39	53
Davidson-Nashville	362	175	86	199	8	19	73
Decatur	97	57	49	344	8	58	34
DeKalb	105	49	89	287	16	50	34
Dickson	108	112	34	268	5	42	52
Dyer	97	125	38	190	7	33	60
Fayette	123	44	117	272	19	44	37
Fentress	59	42	87	295	16	56	28
Franklin	61	71	56	259	11	51	38
Gibson	90	87	2	49	1	19	81
Giles	147	63	44	281	6	39	54
Grainger	121	29	51	269	10	51	39
Greene	109	64	35	187	7	39	54
Grundy	113	38	86	320	14	52	34
Hamblen	163	124	45	233	7	36	57
Hamilton	217	86	24	111	5	22	73
Hancock	66	25	171	451	22	59	19
Hardeman	90	67	68	328	11	54	35
Hardin	135	63	75	297	11	45	44
Hawkins	181	54	54	239	9	40	51
Haywood	132	46	107	305	16	45	40
Henderson	67	79	40	260	8	52	40
Henry	142	101	31	216	5	38	57
Hickman	144	32	49	314	8	49	44
Houston	116	59	55	378	8	55	36
Humphreys	211	93	48	352	6	46	48
Jackson	114	38	129	304	19	45	36
Jefferson	119	65	53	242	9	42	49
Johnson	165	36	73	304	11	46	43
Knox	174	126	20	118	4	24	72
Lake	114	51	86	333	12	46	42
Lauderdale	79	60	72	295	12	50	38
Lawrence	161	88	43	267	7	42	52
Lewis	71	52	46	315	9	58	33
Lincoln	107	62	35	252	7	49	44

TABLE 15.9-- PER CAPITA MAJOR OPERATING REVENUE SOURCES, TENNESSEE AND COUNTIES, YEAR ENDING JUNE 30, 1987 (Continued)

County	Per capita major revenue sources[1]				Percentage of total operating revenue by source		
	Property tax	Local sales tax	Federal government	State government	Federal	State	Local
Loudon	196	48	29	212	5	39	55
McMinn	196	53	28	196	5	38	57
McNairy	90	64	83	276	14	47	39
Macon	105	68	32	283	6	54	40
Madison	130	116	22	141	5	30	66
Marion	114	91	51	273	9	46	45
Marshall	178	100	33	267	5	39	56
Maury	144	126	41	238	6	34	60
Meigs	111	35	98	352	14	50	36
Monroe	95	83	69	227	12	40	47
Montgomery	128	105	43	217	7	36	57
Moore	230	23	40	443	5	54	41
Morgan	198	29	65	300	10	45	45
Obion	161	103	31	214	5	35	59
Overton	106	48	67	306	11	49	40
Perry	178	43	43	437	5	54	40
Pickett	124	33	83	397	11	53	36
Polk	194	55	75	351	10	47	43
Putnam	118	137	29	217	5	37	57
Rhea	153	78	54	260	9	43	48
Roane	98	63	33	195	7	42	51
Robertson	164	77	34	241	6	41	53
Rutherford	135	134	21	184	3	30	67
Scott	125	60	93	266	16	46	38
Sequatchie	122	75	63	404	8	52	40
Sevier	128	242	38	230	5	32	63
Shelby	193	161	16	86	3	15	83
Smith	147	73	35	279	5	43	52
Stewart	74	56	58	434	8	62	30
Sullivan	278	144	24	158	4	23	73
Sumner	160	93	26	234	4	37	59
Tipton	151	61	42	231	8	41	51
Trousdale	215	64	35	392	5	52	44
Unicoi	138	60	85	272	13	42	45
Union	104	25	63	321	11	58	31
Van Buren	95	20	104	465	14	61	26
Warren	89	91	34	254	5	37	58
Washington	126	138	28	127	6	27	67
Wayne	135	42	59	343	8	47	45
Weakley	113	76	34	233	6	43	51
White	136	75	43	289	7	49	44
Williamson	258	82	17	183	3	28	69
Wilson	185	58	19	186	4	35	61
TENNESSEE	181	113	40	186	6	30	64

Note: Figures computed by the Center for Business and Economic Research. Sum of percentages may not equal 100 due to independent rounding.

1. Population figures used are provisional estimates as of July 1, 1987.

Source: State of Tennessee, Report of the Comptroller of the Treasury, Division of Local Finance, *County and Municipal Finances For Fiscal Year Ended June 30, 1987*; U.S. Department of Commerce, Bureau of the Census, *Current Population Reports, Local Population Estimates*, Series P-26, No. 86-S-SC.

TABLE 15.10--OPERATING EXPENDITURES, BY FUNCTION, COUNTY GOVERNMENTS, FISCAL YEAR 1987 [In thousands of dollars]

County	Total [1]	General purpose	Schools	Highways and streets	Debt service	
					Principal	Interest
Anderson	31,545	6,750	19,227	2,529	2,466	573
Bedford	18,933	2,821	11,913	2,395	1,045	759
Benton	9,941	1,874	5,715	1,647	555	150
Bledsoe	6,328	925	3,612	1,324	278	189
Blount	36,914	7,146	22,640	2,596	2,928	1,604
Bradley	35,399	7,045	19,338	2,596	4,548	1,872
Campbell	23,009	3,210	16,325	1,725	943	806
Cannon	6,143	992	3,710	1,044	270	127
Carroll	6,778	3,413	1,416	1,747	170	32
Carter	23,223	4,163	15,897	1,677	987	499
Cheatham	16,295	2,627	9,959	1,780	1,006	923
Chester	6,975	1,412	4,024	1,083	235	221
Claiborne	15,704	2,429	11,076	1,379	365	455
Clay	5,705	827	3,672	992	146	68
Cocke	15,456	2,299	9,806	1,801	1,074	476
Coffee	14,490	3,563	8,422	1,314	633	558
Crockett	7,568	1,618	3,722	1,490	345	393
Cumberland	19,009	4,438	12,075	1,278	687	531
Davidson [2]	608,907	278,433	231,334	30,751	24,953	43,436
Decatur	6,139	1,067	3,940	966	105	61
DeKalb	8,283	1,824	5,003	1,083	268	105
Dickson	20,334	4,586	12,682	2,103	680	283
Dyer	15,062	3,566	8,589	1,847	645	415
Fayette	16,179	2,463	10,008	2,939	323	446
Fentress	9,196	1,499	5,471	1,711	355	160
Franklin	17,736	2,595	11,636	1,367	1,600	538
Gibson	6,210	2,884	1	2,470	502	353
Giles	16,861	2,202	10,663	2,319	1,133	544
Grainger	8,807	1,247	5,760	1,150	318	332
Greene	23,867	4,264	15,047	3,016	925	615
Grundy	8,974	1,569	5,667	1,092	438	208
Hamblen	29,762	3,862	22,381	1,182	1,967	370
Hamilton	117,404	49,218	53,410	5,172	5,520	4,084
Hancock	5,355	1,115	3,150	992	78	20
Hardeman	13,921	2,215	9,675	1,655	113	263
Hardin	14,964	2,302	9,593	1,369	757	943
Hawkins	25,801	5,247	15,551	2,673	1,372	958
Haywood	13,022	1,937	8,998	1,772	140	175
Henderson	11,233	1,658	6,854	1,251	1,085	385
Henry	21,178	2,324	7,849	2,293	8,023	689
Hickman	10,503	1,392	6,005	1,727	870	509
Houston	4,571	689	2,736	892	164	90
Humphreys	11,118	1,669	6,740	1,502	675	532
Jackson	7,105	1,672	3,103	1,165	918	247
Jefferson	18,048	2,104	12,281	1,639	927	1,097
Johnson	8,720	1,514	5,449	1,175	297	285
Knox	139,912	60,363	59,610	6,432	9,986	3,521
Lake	5,491	967	2,788	757	736	243
Lauderdale	14,322	1,668	9,574	1,902	772	406
Lawrence	20,357	3,105	12,801	2,440	904	1,107

TABLE 15.10--OPERATING EXPENDITURES, BY FUNCTION, COUNTY GOVERNMENTS, FISCAL YEAR 1987 [In thousands of dollars] (Continued)

County	Total [1]	General purpose	Schools	Highways and streets	Debt service	
					Principal	Interest
Lewis	5,482	930	3,213	1,075	143	121
Lincoln	13,110	1,813	8,268	1,839	696	494
Loudon	15,652	3,149	8,729	1,169	1,465	1,140
McMinn	20,510	2,906	12,513	2,463	1,720	908
McNairy	13,770	1,366	8,650	2,356	737	661
Macon	7,821	1,337	5,163	994	252	75
Madison	29,950	9,090	15,288	2,768	1,673	1,131
Marion	14,055	2,271	9,656	1,220	483	425
Marshall	13,140	2,394	8,283	1,468	488	507
Maury	34,141	6,264	21,233	2,486	2,751	1,407
Meigs	5,426	1,043	3,260	979	46	98
Monroe	14,749	2,474	9,814	1,821	423	217
Montgomery	58,823	8,663	35,099	3,868	8,405	2,788
Moore	3,833	595	2,226	927	66	19
Morgan	11,569	1,792	6,930	1,037	725	1,085
Obion	17,725	2,111	9,718	3,067	2,226	603
Overton	14,533	1,697	6,615	1,555	4,169	497
Perry	4,730	949	2,438	975	151	217
Pickett	3,411	698	1,709	875	61	68
Polk	12,385	1,814	5,750	1,382	2,781	658
Putnam	26,952	5,546	16,648	1,482	2,506	770
Rhea	14,187	2,292	8,911	1,106	1,162	716
Roane	23,674	6,168	14,214	1,847	923	522
Robertson	23,833	3,871	15,270	2,077	1,313	1,302
Rutherford	70,532	10,378	33,338	3,277	2,893	3,993
Scott	11,104	2,287	6,697	1,334	442	344
Sequatchie	6,875	1,110	4,342	1,132	118	173
Sevier	29,428	5,231	18,475	2,127	2,384	1,211
Shelby	245,509	131,125	70,980	7,633	13,128	22,643
Smith	8,953	1,759	5,185	1,219	446	344
Stewart	6,420	950	4,046	1,080	208	136
Sullivan	78,615	15,917	50,420	5,983	3,980	2,315
Sumner	58,150	7,685	40,490	3,210	4,305	2,460
Tipton	19,797	2,495	11,594	3,610	821	1,277
Trousdale	4,287	887	2,222	885	97	196
Unicoi	10,784	1,671	6,423	1,170	1,021	499
Union	7,058	1,230	4,265	1,113	289	161
Van Buren	3,470	769	1,769	896	30	6
Warren	22,207	4,297	12,864	1,122	3,049	875
Washington	32,346	6,133	19,717	2,950	2,144	1,402
Wayne	13,251	1,843	5,733	1,282	3,948	445
Weakley	16,324	1,721	10,929	2,307	912	455
White	12,059	1,977	7,277	1,468	782	555
Williamson	41,473	6,413	25,389	4,149	2,702	2,820
Wilson	36,407	5,049	19,136	8,093	1,908	2,221

1. Includes detail not shown separately.

2. Data are for Metropolitan Nashville-Davidson County.

Source: State of Tennessee, Report of the Comptroller of the Treasury, Division of Local Finance, *County and Municipal Finances for Fiscal Year Ended June 30, 1987.*

TABLE 15.11--STATE SALES AND USE TAX COMPARISON, COUNTIES, FISCAL YEAR 1988

County	Total collections	Percentage of state total	Percent change 1987–1988	Per capita collections [1]
Anderson	$32,777,331	1.54	14.94	$464
Bedford	9,313,642	0.44	8.89	316
Benton	3,950,649	0.19	3.67	265
Bledsoe	1,072,653	0.05	2.30	108
Blount	37,278,974	1.75	7.85	441
Bradley	26,989,988	1.26	6.88	363
Campbell	8,069,904	0.38	1.48	231
Cannon	1,527,175	0.07	6.07	140
Carroll	6,102,387	0.29	3.24	217
Carter	10,943,337	0.51	9.39	213
Cheatham	3,553,199	0.17	-1.80	133
Chester	2,441,210	0.11	2.42	189
Claiborne	4,320,622	0.20	12.08	161
Clay	1,251,128	0.06	11.76	158
Cocke	7,299,133	0.34	6.09	248
Coffee	20,451,333	0.96	6.07	485
Crockett	2,399,566	0.11	5.90	171
Cumberland	10,650,163	0.50	6.87	319
Davidson	361,810,348	16.95	5.07	713
Decatur	2,814,219	0.13	7.64	258
DeKalb	3,412,639	0.16	6.65	237
Dickson	11,987,954	0.56	6.90	345
Dyer	14,091,479	0.66	11.44	403
Fayette	3,328,168	0.16	4.63	126
Fentress	2,588,464	0.12	5.48	165
Franklin	7,757,103	0.36	2.09	225
Gibson	13,519,064	0.63	3.73	280
Giles	6,864,607	0.32	8.21	273
Grainger	1,548,929	0.07	6.94	89
Greene	16,272,090	0.76	6.00	289
Grundy	1,483,706	0.07	-0.14	103
Hamblen	22,186,188	1.04	13.93	429
Hamilton	147,715,634	6.92	8.23	506
Hancock	521,025	0.02	5.01	77
Hardeman	5,124,686	0.24	3.67	210
Hardin	7,049,158	0.33	9.05	315
Hawkins	8,151,334	0.38	7.17	180
Haywood	4,896,473	0.23	6.03	232
Henderson	5,532,167	0.26	5.72	243
Henry	9,630,614	0.45	6.84	328
Hickman	2,779,260	0.13	8.24	166
Houston	968,764	0.05	3.64	135
Humphreys	4,505,177	0.21	-2.18	280
Jackson	1,023,818	0.05	2.99	109
Jefferson	6,587,788	0.31	9.42	197
Johnson	2,351,414	0.11	6.31	168
Knox	187,973,598	8.80	7.97	568
Lake	975,368	0.05	2.02	130
Lauderdale	5,238,720	0.25	9.37	209
Lawrence	9,684,320	0.45	11.24	275
Lewis	1,818,993	0.09	9.95	172
Lincoln	7,377,814	0.35	5.25	267

TABLE 15.11--STATE SALES AND USE TAX COMPARISON, COUNTIES, FISCAL YEAR 1988 (Continued)

County	Total collections	Percentage of state total	Percent change 1987–1988	Per capita collections [1]
Loudon	7,732,747	0.36	5.19	248
McMinn	14,849,312	0.70	7.72	341
McNairy	4,380,157	0.21	1.42	183
Macon	3,382,440	0.16	7.44	209
Madison	39,376,572	1.84	4.70	504
Marion	7,212,613	0.34	11.37	282
Marshall	6,781,832	0.32	7.51	318
Maury	22,123,048	1.04	9.51	400
Meigs	1,587,183	0.07	11.82	189
Monroe	7,731,276	0.36	6.26	249
Montgomery	30,982,989	1.45	8.65	319
Moore	875,168	0.04	82.74	179
Morgan	1,768,241	0.08	10.37	100
Obion	10,247,100	0.48	4.85	313
Overton	3,178,011	0.15	7.19	178
Perry	905,321	0.04	2.82	139
Pickett	706,344	0.03	10.43	157
Polk	2,033,332	0.10	-3.50	146
Putnam	21,600,658	1.01	9.31	413
Rhea	5,600,670	0.26	-0.14	221
Roane	19,980,949	0.94	29.01	403
Robertson	10,108,706	0.47	7.71	236
Rutherford	46,313,533	2.17	6.11	415
Scott	3,502,739	0.16	7.63	170
Sequatchie	1,894,958	0.09	2.51	211
Sevier	33,774,096	1.58	13.04	678
Shelby	394,123,972	18.46	5.53	481
Smith	3,417,349	0.16	-2.50	231
Stewart	1,435,129	0.07	-0.52	153
Sullivan	64,118,568	3.00	5.87	435
Sumner	27,300,214	1.28	7.18	267
Tipton	6,833,540	0.32	7.40	179
Trousdale	1,041,620	0.05	5.99	168
Unicoi	3,233,904	0.15	9.46	194
Union	1,380,610	0.06	2.06	109
Van Buren	377,110	0.02	5.34	80
Warren	10,168,408	0.48	6.31	297
Washington	37,514,831	1.76	6.26	409
Wayne	2,193,693	0.10	-2.83	154
Weakley	7,503,768	0.35	7.26	230
White	5,195,167	0.24	5.92	253
Williamson	29,719,155	1.39	3.88	382
Wilson	18,562,118	0.87	9.25	271

Note: Percent change was computed by the Center for Business and Economic Research.

1. Per capita figures were computed by the Center for Business and Economic Research using provisional estimates of the population of counties as of July, 1988.

Source: Tennessee Association of Business, *The 1988 Annual Survey of State and Local Government in Tennessee*; and earlier editions.

TABLE 15.12--ESTIMATED CURRENT PROPERTY VALUE, ASSESSED VALUE, BY CLASSIFICATION, AND PROPERTY TAXES LEVIED, COUNTIES, 1987
[In thousands of dollars]

County	County taxes levied	Estimated current property value	Assessed value				
				Real property			
			Total	Residential and farm	Industrial and commercial	Personal property [1]	Public utilities [2]
Anderson	12,738	1,415,454	392,740	235,562	106,974	22,711	26,715
Bedford	3,929	633,193	182,141	122,239	35,092	5,286	19,524
Benton	1,048	263,680	64,340	49,181	7,892	2,472	4,795
Bledsoe	1,100	193,351	53,960	39,806	4,844	1,326	7,551
Blount	11,493	2,269,150	657,853	400,504	170,107	45,787	41,320
Bradley	11,112	1,759,047	515,051	272,388	156,539	56,145	29,646
Campbell	4,380	588,212	162,972	96,889	34,422	12,549	16,520
Cannon	1,401	183,985	51,560	38,313	7,605	734	4,908
Carroll	3,435	430,757	109,254	72,336	18,436	9,007	9,475
Carter	5,994	785,010	222,322	151,898	52,398	7,925	9,960
			33,197				
Cheatham	3,821	536,289	89,517	69,619	7,773	4,807	7,318
Chester	1,264	205,944	57,645	41,995	7,287	1,970	6,392
Claiborne	2,788	504,824	115,901	80,214	19,326	3,486	11,480
Clay	970	119,914	32,031	22,605	4,299	2,228	2,896
Cocke	3,604	437,542	128,190	76,049	32,254	7,960	11,926
Coffee	5,295	884,982	261,153	153,352	77,344	13,384	17,011
Crockett	1,978	313,427	87,473	62,651	9,314	6,356	9,153
Cumberland	3,943	797,787	139,844	92,303	22,192	12,789	12,302
Davidson-Nashville	183,298	20,709,547	5,532,142	2,034,117	2,758,600	463,113	276,313
Decatur	1,075	210,063	48,254	34,814	6,077	2,599	4,755
DeKalb	1,519	319,236	73,677	52,777	12,084	3,847	4,969
Dickson	3,658	781,241	131,033	86,084	29,006	5,935	10,008
Dyer	3,333	828,738	122,230	70,923	28,478	12,371	10,458
Fayette	3,248	569,338	134,548	91,328	18,120	6,799	18,301
Fentress	920	260,319	69,618	49,953	9,666	2,500	6,247
Franklin	2,085	689,745	160,047	120,802	19,964	5,669	13,613
Gibson	4,351	890,913	234,652	149,827	45,990	17,958	20,877

TABLE 15.12--ESTIMATED CURRENT PROPERTY VALUE, ASSESSED VALUE, BY CLASSIFICATION, AND PROPERTY TAXES LEVIED, COUNTIES, 1987
[In thousands of dollars] (Continued)

County	County taxes levied	Estimated current property value	Assessed value: Total	Real property: Residential and farm	Real property: Industrial and commercial	Personal property[1]	Public utilities[2]
Giles	3,671	568,891	133,627	77,990	25,962	14,520	11,429
Grainger	2,099	269,310	72,355	56,696	6,982	704	7,910
Greene	6,169	1,209,349	313,800	195,851	77,004	23,830	17,107
Grundy	1,654	191,030	47,921	33,788	4,496	968	8,561
Hamblen	8,381	1,233,498	362,125	172,895	116,256	48,315	24,628
Hamilton	62,963	8,385,761	2,115,707	865,937	861,686	250,255	137,829
Hancock	457	114,688	23,348	17,541	2,646	67	3,054
Hardeman	2,175	422,786	103,590	70,033	14,121	8,375	11,061
Hardin	3,015	592,352	165,701	85,905	21,309	42,494	15,929
Hawkins	8,154	1,033,999	214,516	103,816	62,161	29,882	18,658
Haywood	2,781	480,456	142,441	81,945	24,009	14,688	21,799
Henderson	1,515	347,374	91,241	62,868	13,692	6,510	8,170
Henry	4,171	595,630	168,978	106,060	34,012	13,870	15,014
Hickman	2,367	353,346	91,786	64,421	9,125	3,190	14,341
Houston	824	118,278	22,723	16,506	2,409	1,793	2,015
Humphreys	3,371	424,774	121,116	58,452	27,066	23,825	11,774
Jackson	1,068	155,807	40,387	28,323	3,779	2,838	5,441
Jefferson	3,963	710,919	163,775	108,932	31,222	8,496	14,028
Johnson	2,331	271,803	51,007	32,240	8,346	6,225	4,106
Knox	57,384	8,548,934	2,520,351	1,263,400	942,129	163,309	151,513
Lake	874	127,083	35,178	25,551	5,142	940	3,546
Lauderdale	1,994	386,959	100,618	66,890	16,537	7,017	10,175
Lawrence	5,642	674,690	182,800	117,826	35,219	17,012	12,743
Lewis	743	142,879	25,624	16,639	3,872	566	4,545
Lincoln	2,900	584,712	161,422	118,691	26,565	8,307	7,859
Loudon	6,069	794,445	229,401	126,943	62,594	26,332	13,529

TABLE 15.12--ESTIMATED CURRENT PROPERTY VALUE, ASSESSED VALUE, BY CLASSIFICATION, AND PROPERTY TAXES LEVIED, COUNTIES, 1987
[In thousands of dollars] (Continued)

			Assessed value				
				Real property			
County	County taxes levied	Estimated current property value	Total	Residential and farm	Industrial and commercial	Personal property [1]	Public utilities [2]
McMinn	8,578	1,125,675	330,232	141,109	86,417	83,442	19,203
McNairy	2,141	397,263	114,449	73,992	16,997	6,158	17,296
Macon	1,698	294,628	86,708	56,973	10,825	3,398	15,512
Madison	10,175	1,892,531	501,440	255,387	165,396	50,119	30,538
Marion	2,893	515,808	137,053	77,397	25,409	17,899	15,216
Marshall	3,768	561,719	105,879	54,011	22,142	22,156	7,556
Maury	7,937	1,556,951	348,397	188,110	84,188	50,136	24,533
Meigs	907	187,124	28,150	19,542	2,567	3,072	2,969
Monroe	2,957	528,698	120,537	72,237	26,288	7,778	14,234
Montgomery	12,049	1,639,756	345,667	181,074	102,567	37,232	24,794
Moore	1,105	164,684	45,320	20,965	16,086	6,217	2,052
Morgan	3,508	245,395	70,475	46,394	4,554	2,316	16,379
Obion	5,324	750,548	183,739	120,087	32,284	13,501	17,868
Overton	1,898	255,778	71,177	49,319	11,811	1,809	8,043
Perry	1,137	169,847	30,334	20,737	3,831	352	5,410
Pickett	572	78,195	21,883	16,231	2,705	677	2,129
Polk	2,693	256,233	71,007	38,947	8,895	9,186	12,721
Putnam	6,112	1,074,509	319,274	181,417	88,910	22,045	26,674
Rhea	3,830	451,065	120,656	71,924	24,404	7,998	15,687
Roane	4,844	931,532	261,489	177,336	45,841	15,600	22,703
Robertson	6,886	969,759	196,074	137,506	32,874	9,599	16,095
Rutherford	14,450	2,863,377	815,759	418,765	288,457	59,423	48,914
Scott	2,595	303,635	76,078	38,052	12,744	9,646	15,195
Sequatchie	1,089	209,927	59,437	37,317	8,290	5,863	4,458
Sevier	6,242	1,716,504	303,641	164,162	122,937	7,883	8,646
Shelby	156,738	21,563,122	4,508,919	2,191,574	1,531,419	536,468	249,457
Smith	2,182	312,306	73,468	44,221	14,104	6,806	7,112

TABLE 15.12--ESTIMATED CURRENT PROPERTY VALUE, ASSESSED VALUE, BY CLASSIFICATION, AND PROPERTY TAXES LEVIED, COUNTIES, 1987
[In thousands of dollars] (Continued)

County	County taxes levied	Estimated current property value	Assessed value: Total	Real property: Residential and farm	Real property: Industrial and commercial	Personal property[1]	Public utilities[2]
Stewart	691	180,009	43,816	33,499	3,925	1,426	4,946
Sullivan	40,944	4,278,419	1,210,441	535,299	336,968	261,941	76,232
Sumner	16,029	2,523,984	714,274	492,063	158,186	25,653	38,316
Tipton	5,633	731,472	150,170	109,661	20,634	6,307	13,568
Trousdale	1,313	109,904	30,560	18,868	5,101	1,236	5,355
Unicoi	2,311	299,480	63,664	41,117	10,724	6,461	5,358
Union	1,293	204,317	51,669	38,808	6,571	2,411	3,852
Van Buren	456	116,527	27,642	23,752	1,394	144	2,068
Warren	3,045	650,932	180,675	115,530	40,554	11,378	13,213
Washington	11,543	2,131,852	582,209	308,795	195,922	41,050	36,430
Wayne	1,921	268,157	74,544	50,480	6,632	2,878	14,511
Weakley	3,697	618,262	133,363	83,937	25,406	13,591	10,429
White	2,751	373,335	100,769	63,846	20,269	8,174	8,320
Williamson	19,395	3,494,364	473,353	301,598	92,479	35,386	39,768
Wilson	12,345	1,782,944	406,846	301,421	67,799	11,673	25,943

1. Includes industrial and commercial, residential, farm, and intangible personal property.

2. Includes utilities assessed by the Public Service Commission as well as those locally assessed.

Source: Tennessee State Board of Equalization, *1987 Tax Aggregate Report*; and State of Tennessee, Report of the Comptroller of the Treasury, Division of Local Finance, *County and Municipal Finances for Fiscal Year Ended June 30, 1987*.

FIGURE 15.2
Equalized Property Tax Rate, Tennessee Counties, 1987
(Tennessee Mean Rate = $2.45)

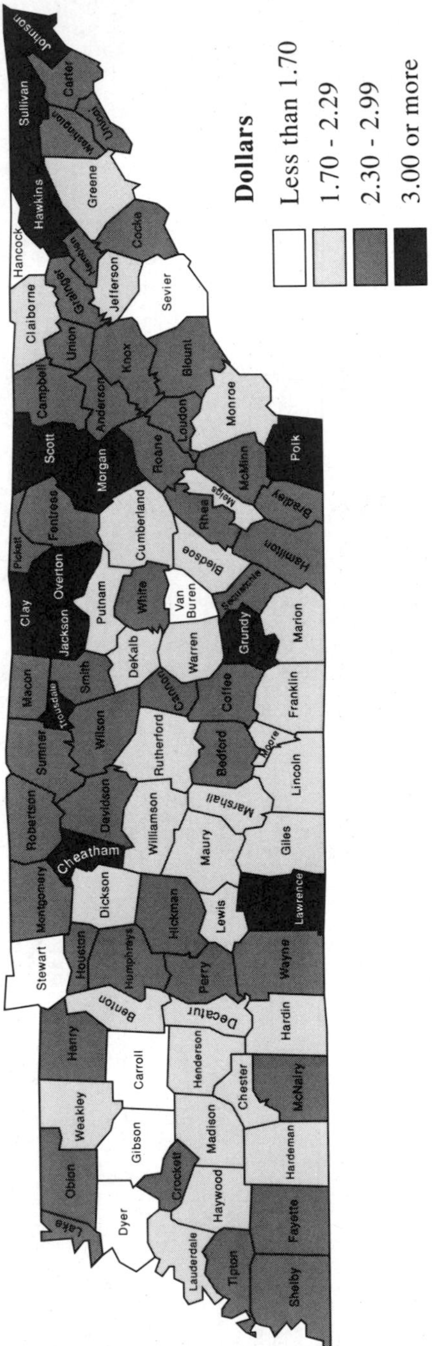

Source: State of Tennessee, State Board of Equalization, *1987 Tax Aggregate Report of Tennessee*.

TABLE 15.13--ACTUAL AND EFFECTIVE PROPERTY TAX RATES, APPRAISAL RATIO, AND YEAR OF LATEST APPRAISAL, COUNTIES, 1987

County	Actual tax rate[1]	Appraisal ratio (%)[2]	Year of appraisal	Equalized tax rate[3]	Effective tax rate by class of property[4]				Weighted average effective rate[5]
					Commercial and industrial real (40 %)	Residential and farm real (25 %)	Commercial and industrial personal (30%)	Public utilities (55 %)	
Anderson	$2.99	94.62	1981	$2.83	$1.13	$0.71	$0.90	$1.56	$0.83
Bedford	2.90	100.00	1987	2.90	1.16	0.72	0.87	1.59	0.83
Benton	2.25	88.72	1983	2.00	0.80	0.50	0.67	1.10	0.55
Bledsoe	2.32	98.73	1984	2.29	0.92	0.57	0.70	1.26	0.65
Blount	2.43	100.00	1987	2.43	0.97	0.61	0.73	1.34	0.70
Bradley	2.70	98.90	1986	2.67	1.06	0.66	0.81	1.46	0.79
Campbell	2.99	94.99	1983	2.84	1.14	0.71	0.90	1.56	0.83
Cannon	2.65	100.00	1987	2.65	1.06	0.66	0.79	1.46	0.74
Carroll	1.55	89.00	1979	1.38	0.55	0.34	0.46	0.76	0.39
Carter	2.85	100.00	1987	2.85	1.14	0.71	0.85	1.57	0.81
Cheatham	5.33	60.00	1979	3.20	1.28	0.80	1.60	1.76	0.89
Chester	2.24	99.57	1981	2.23	0.89	0.56	0.67	1.23	0.63
Claiborne	2.54	80.22	1981	2.04	0.82	0.51	0.76	1.12	0.58
Clay	3.56	94.67	1984	3.37	1.35	0.84	1.07	1.85	0.95
Cocke	2.95	100.00	1984	2.95	1.18	0.74	0.88	1.62	0.86
Coffee	2.43	100.00	1987	2.43	0.97	0.61	0.73	1.34	0.72
Crockett	2.35	100.00	1981	2.35	0.94	0.59	0.70	1.29	0.66
Cumberland	2.93	59.54	1975	1.74	0.70	0.44	0.88	0.96	0.51
Davidson	2.89	81.38	1984	2.35	0.94	0.59	0.87	1.29	0.77
Decatur	2.32	81.14	1981	1.88	0.75	0.47	0.70	1.04	0.53
DeKalb	2.10	81.82	1983	1.72	0.69	0.43	0.63	0.95	0.48
Dickson	3.06	57.36	1978	1.76	0.70	0.44	0.92	0.97	0.51
Dyer	2.80	47.72	1975	1.34	0.53	0.33	0.84	0.73	0.41
Fayette	2.85	81.94	1983	2.34	0.93	0.58	0.85	1.28	0.67
Fentress	2.45	94.69	1985	2.32	0.93	0.58	0.73	1.28	0.66
Franklin	2.30	83.53	1983	1.92	0.77	0.48	0.69	1.06	0.53
Gibson	0.92	90.92	1983	0.84	0.33	0.21	0.28	0.46	0.24
Giles	2.90	78.82	1983	2.29	0.91	0.57	0.87	1.26	0.68

TABLE 15.13--ACTUAL AND EFFECTIVE PROPERTY TAX RATES, APPRAISAL RATIO, AND YEAR OF LATEST APPRAISAL, COUNTIES, 1987 (Continued)

County	Actual tax rate[1]	Appraisal ratio (%)[2]	Year of appraisal	Equalized tax rate[3]	Effective tax rate by class of property[4]: Commercial and industrial real (40 %)	Residential and farm real (25 %)	Commercial and industrial personal (30%)	Public utilities (55 %)	Weighted average effective rate[5]
Grainger	2.91	97.78	1984	2.85	1.14	0.71	0.87	1.56	0.78
Greene	2.35	89.56	1982	2.10	0.84	0.53	0.70	1.16	0.61
Grundy	3.62	86.67	1979	3.14	1.25	0.78	1.09	1.73	0.91
Hamblen	2.77	96.40	1986	2.67	1.07	0.67	0.83	1.47	0.81
Hamilton	3.26	78.13	1980	2.55	1.02	0.64	0.98	1.40	0.82
Hancock	1.92	72.03	1983	1.38	0.55	0.35	0.58	0.76	0.39
Hardeman	2.29	85.88	1979	1.97	0.79	0.49	0.69	1.08	0.56
Hardin	2.09	94.86	1986	1.98	0.79	0.50	0.63	1.09	0.58
Hawkins	4.71	65.10	1977	3.07	1.23	0.77	1.41	1.69	0.98
Haywood	2.17	100.00	1987	2.17	0.87	0.54	0.65	1.19	0.64
Henderson	2.33	92.78	1983	2.16	0.86	0.54	0.70	1.19	0.61
Henry	2.94	98.33	1985	2.89	1.16	0.72	0.88	1.59	0.83
Hickman	2.55	90.48	1986	2.31	0.92	0.58	0.76	1.27	0.66
Houston	3.68	67.52	1978	2.48	0.99	0.62	1.10	1.37	0.71
Humphreys	2.84	94.40	1984	2.68	1.07	0.67	0.85	1.47	0.81
Jackson	3.67	90.67	1984	3.33	1.33	0.83	1.10	1.83	0.95
Jefferson	2.73	80.00	1980	2.18	0.87	0.55	0.82	1.20	0.63
Johnson	5.20	62.92	1978	3.27	1.31	0.82	1.56	1.80	0.98
Knox	2.76	96.39	1983	2.66	1.06	0.67	0.83	1.46	0.81
Lake	2.65	100.00	1982	2.65	1.06	0.66	0.79	1.46	0.73
Lauderdale	2.07	90.89	1986	1.88	0.75	0.47	0.62	1.03	0.54
Lawrence	3.21	94.67	1982	3.04	1.22	0.76	0.96	1.67	0.87
Lewis	3.60	60.12	1979	2.16	0.87	0.54	1.08	1.19	0.65
Lincoln	2.06	100.00	1987	2.06	0.82	0.51	0.62	1.13	0.57
Loudon	2.80	98.00	1983	2.74	1.10	0.69	0.84	1.51	0.81
McMinn	2.64	97.12	1982	2.56	1.03	0.64	0.79	1.41	0.77
McNairy	2.40	99.21	1985	2.38	0.95	0.60	0.72	1.31	0.69

TABLE 15.13--ACTUAL AND EFFECTIVE PROPERTY TAX RATES, APPRAISAL RATIO, AND YEAR OF LATEST APPRAISAL, COUNTIES, 1987 (Continued)

County	Actual tax rate[1]	Appraisal ratio (%)[2]	Year of appraisal	Equalized tax rate[3]	Effective tax rate by class of property[4]				Weighted average effective rate[5]
					Commercial and industrial real (40 %)	Residential and farm real (25 %)	Commercial and industrial personal (30%)	Public utilities (55 %)	
Macon	2.58	100.00	1986	2.58	1.03	0.64	0.77	1.42	0.76
Madison	2.47	86.96	1981	2.15	0.86	0.54	0.74	1.18	0.65
Marion	2.15	89.30	1982	1.92	0.77	0.48	0.64	1.06	0.57
Marshall	3.86	58.72	1978	2.27	0.91	0.57	1.16	1.25	0.73
Maury	2.35	73.01	1985	1.72	0.69	0.43	0.70	0.94	0.53
Meigs	4.30	50.94	1974	2.19	0.88	0.55	1.29	1.20	0.65
Monroe	3.00	76.26	1978	2.29	0.92	0.57	0.90	1.26	0.68
Montgomery	3.68	67.86	1965	2.50	1.00	0.62	1.10	1.37	0.78
Moore	2.43	88.84	1984	2.16	0.86	0.54	0.73	1.19	0.67
Morgan	5.65	100.00	1987	5.65	2.26	1.41	1.69	3.11	1.62
Obion	3.18	84.55	1980	2.69	1.08	0.67	0.95	1.48	0.78
Overton	3.51	96.96	1981	3.40	1.36	0.85	1.05	1.87	0.98
Perry	3.91	60.83	1978	2.38	0.95	0.59	1.17	1.31	0.70
Pickett	2.50	100.00	1987	2.50	1.00	0.63	0.75	1.37	0.70
Polk	3.95	93.33	1982	3.69	1.47	0.92	1.18	2.03	1.09
Putnam	1.85	100.00	1987	1.85	0.74	0.46	0.55	1.02	0.55
Rhea	3.18	91.43	1984	2.91	1.16	0.73	0.95	1.60	0.85
Roane	2.71	99.39	1986	2.69	1.08	0.67	0.81	1.48	0.76
Robertson	3.78	70.88	1980	2.68	1.07	0.67	1.13	1.47	0.76
Rutherford	2.20	93.63	1986	2.06	0.82	0.51	0.66	1.13	0.63
Scott	3.90	81.51	1979	3.18	1.27	0.79	1.17	1.75	0.98
Sequatchie	2.33	98.55	1984	2.30	0.92	0.57	0.70	1.26	0.66
Sevier	2.20	58.00	1977	1.28	0.51	0.32	0.66	0.70	0.39
Shelby	3.78	66.60	1980	2.52	1.01	0.63	1.13	1.38	0.79
Smith	2.93	80.00	1984	2.34	0.94	0.59	0.88	1.29	0.69
Stewart	1.59	87.33	1983	1.39	0.56	0.35	0.48	0.76	0.39
Sullivan	3.96	92.05	1983	3.65	1.46	0.91	1.19	2.00	1.12
Sumner	2.55	100.00	1987	2.55	1.02	0.64	0.76	1.40	0.72

TABLE 15.13--ACTUAL AND EFFECTIVE PROPERTY TAX RATES, APPRAISAL RATIO, AND YEAR OF LATEST APPRAISAL, COUNTIES, 1987 (Continued)

County	Actual tax rate[1]	Appraisal ratio (%)[2]	Year of appraisal	Equalized tax rate[3]	Effective tax rate by class of property[4]: Commercial and industrial real (40 %)	Residential and farm real (25 %)	Commercial and industrial personal (30%)	Public utilities (55 %)	Weighted average effective rate[5]
Tipton	3.70	72.81	1980	2.69	1.08	0.67	1.11	1.48	0.76
Trousdale	4.14	92.77	1982	3.84	1.54	0.96	1.24	2.11	1.15
Unicoi	3.94	73.52	1979	2.90	1.16	0.72	1.18	1.59	0.84
Union	2.52	91.37	1983	2.30	0.92	0.58	0.76	1.27	0.64
Van Buren	1.86	88.76	1981	1.65	0.66	0.41	0.56	0.91	0.44
Warren	1.98	96.00	1981	1.90	0.76	0.48	0.59	1.05	0.55
Washington	2.58	90.11	1983	2.32	0.93	0.58	0.77	1.28	0.70
Wayne	2.72	94.87	1981	2.58	1.03	0.65	0.82	1.42	0.76
Weakley	2.96	73.33	1978	2.17	0.87	0.54	0.89	1.19	0.64
White	2.99	93.20	1982	2.79	1.11	0.70	0.90	1.53	0.81
Williamson	4.81	45.09	1977	2.17	0.87	0.54	1.44	1.19	0.65
Wilson	2.83	81.67	1986	2.31	1.06	0.67	0.98	1.46	0.74

1. Does not include special school district rates or differing county rates charged in municipalities by some counties.
2. Based on sales ratio studies and certified by the Tennessee State Board of Equalization.
3. Computed by the Center for Business and Economic Research. Equalized rate = actual rate x appraisal ratio.
4. Effective tax rate is the percentage that tax liability is of the market value. Effective rate = equalized rate x assessment ratio.
5. Weighted average effective rate is the ratio of the total assessed value to the total estimated current property value multiplied by the appropriate tax rate.

Source: State of Tennessee, State Board of Equalization, *1987 Tax Aggregate Report of Tennessee.*

TABLE 15.14--FEDERAL GOVERNMENT DIRECT EXPENDITURES OR OBLIGATIONS, COUNTIES, FISCAL YEAR 1988 [In thousands of dollars]

County	Total	Grant awards	Total salaries and wages	Total direct payments for individuals	Total procurement contract awards	Other federal expenditures or obligations
Anderson	1,649,226	22,017	75,593	132,402	1,419,001	213
Bedford	62,431	7,956	3,388	46,115	3,422	1,550
Benton	46,749	11,143	1,551	32,864	138	1,052
Bledsoe	20,580	4,065	531	13,265	2,143	576
Blount	176,496	15,722	11,053	147,489	1,357	873
Bradley	123,297	13,053	10,598	96,214	2,815	617
Campbell	96,157	16,183	3,760	72,638	3,377	199
Cannon	24,624	3,806	941	17,219	2,038	621
Carroll	136,888	9,000	3,621	58,202	61,485	4,581
Carter	97,951	15,000	4,686	76,217	1,684	364
Cheatham	32,310	3,133	2,331	25,785	724	338
Chester	27,153	4,738	1,926	18,584	75	1,831
Claiborne	58,901	12,068	2,377	42,752	1,347	358
Clay	20,124	6,236	1,593	11,472	530	293
Cocke	64,080	15,721	2,506	45,212	344	297
Coffee	369,796	9,610	14,921	71,163	272,635	1,467
Crockett	39,743	5,160	1,854	24,192	1,858	6,680
Cumberland	74,717	8,207	3,386	62,077	528	519
Davidson	1,260,616	192,336	259,008	776,947	13,875	18,450
Decatur	25,444	3,590	1,465	18,651	1,009	729
DeKalb	33,717	6,439	1,758	24,750	392	379
Dickson	62,748	6,294	3,098	52,544	416	397
Dyer	106,780	15,674	4,863	60,268	20,649	5,325
Fayette	53,220	13,496	2,099	30,814	455	6,356
Fentress	36,880	8,067	1,439	25,816	1,008	551
Franklin	75,567	7,528	5,812	58,882	2,020	1,325
Gibson	172,214	19,270	8,389	91,996	42,544	10,016
Giles	64,519	10,826	3,091	48,328	418	1,855
Grainger	34,144	6,363	1,507	24,860	1,220	193
Greene	117,595	16,795	5,842	80,302	12,860	1,796
Grundy	30,553	4,164	1,283	23,674	1,198	233
Hamblen	102,018	17,328	5,611	73,132	5,541	407
Hamilton	1,124,833	83,701	411,119	505,283	121,337	3,393

TABLE 15.14--FEDERAL GOVERNMENT DIRECT EXPENDITURES OR OBLIGATIONS, COUNTIES, FISCAL YEAR 1988 [In thousands of dollars] (Continued)

County	Total	Grant awards	Total salaries and wages	Total direct payments for individuals	Total procurement contract awards	Other federal expenditures or obligations
Hancock	16,112	4,793	416	10,751	37	115
Hardeman	78,580	12,894	2,521	39,410	20,620	3,134
Hardin	51,701	7,668	4,399	36,760	743	2,131
Hawkins	195,358	15,903	13,704	63,422	101,775	553
Haywood	51,174	11,047	1,867	30,072	858	7,329
Henderson	49,736	7,652	2,088	35,822	365	3,809
Henry	107,347	6,689	5,264	61,431	548	33,414
Hickman	32,103	3,418	2,277	25,624	266	518
Houston	17,342	2,543	662	13,887	82	167
Humphreys	58,270	8,512	19,164	28,519	1,450	624
Jackson	18,996	4,192	847	13,554	172	232
Jefferson	67,766	8,892	4,585	52,909	380	999
Johnson	33,098	5,782	1,349	25,540	131	296
Knox	1,045,919	119,976	284,002	545,861	91,945	4,135
Lake	21,053	3,542	853	13,862	452	2,344
Lauderdale	62,942	14,337	2,264	39,754	1,337	5,249
Lawrence	76,255	9,108	4,018	60,087	385	2,657
Lewis	17,555	1,618	871	14,822	52	191
Lincoln	62,923	9,255	2,476	47,713	1,420	2,057
Loudon	82,976	6,054	5,437	53,208	17,784	493
McMinn	84,231	9,781	5,033	67,267	1,230	920
McNairy	60,743	12,211	2,908	42,564	234	2,826
Macon	30,295	6,723	1,430	21,308	121	713
Madison	184,673	27,189	19,412	130,402	2,606	5,064
Marion	72,157	14,235	3,132	41,909	12,404	477
Marshall	45,452	4,554	2,591	35,342	2,048	916
Maury	109,531	12,330	8,444	86,639	990	1,128
Meigs	16,109	2,714	969	11,976	60	391
Monroe	59,971	9,504	3,112	45,876	855	623
Montgomery	168,500	19,507	7,780	136,801	808	3,604
Moore	6,290	1,530	171	4,472	15	101
Morgan	41,612	5,890	1,157	24,038	10,234	294
Obion	96,275	12,584	4,353	53,353	17,283	8,703
Overton	40,940	10,197	1,771	27,505	475	992

TABLE 15.14--FEDERAL GOVERNMENT DIRECT EXPENDITURES OR OBLIGATIONS, COUNTIES, FISCAL YEAR 1988 [In thousands of dollars] (Continued)

County	Total	Grant awards	Total salaries and wages	Total direct payments for individuals	Total procurement contract awards	Other federal expenditures or obligations
Perry	15,824	2,104	562	12,548	56	554
Pickett	10,513	2,061	304	7,299	706	144
Polk	35,067	4,407	3,535	26,410	227	488
Putnam	117,899	19,206	8,856	86,392	2,713	731
Rhea	168,737	7,303	110,286	43,056	7,542	551
Roane	129,348	13,161	22,792	89,690	3,142	563
Robertson	70,049	9,156	2,935	53,306	712	3,940
Rutherford	202,623	20,431	50,289	123,737	5,935	2,232
Scott	53,598	11,426	2,006	33,384	6,610	172
Sequatchie	25,887	2,229	738	11,661	11,110	150
Sevier	87,467	8,395	8,413	68,510	1,708	441
Shelby	2,453,879	354,714	678,860	1,278,769	123,694	17,841
Smith	47,886	10,952	9,495	24,725	1,786	929
Stewart	71,287	3,689	44,223	20,170	2,981	224
Sullivan	657,008	35,977	20,352	245,325	354,489	864
Sumner	160,509	13,252	20,128	119,797	5,839	1,493
Tipton	74,716	12,672	3,657	52,365	1,562	4,461
Trousdale	12,933	1,258	2,493	9,015	41	125
Unicoi	102,668	4,600	2,314	32,932	62,707	115
Union	20,063	3,749	809	15,275	138	92
Van Buren	8,705	1,910	266	4,950	1,428	152
Warren	76,003	11,309	6,161	55,235	1,833	1,465
Washington	256,964	28,106	48,964	164,342	13,613	1,939
Wayne	28,562	5,221	1,434	20,928	226	753
Weakley	90,028	9,107	7,113	53,054	12,347	8,408
White	44,191	6,900	1,926	34,614	179	571
Williamson	106,312	10,040	7,395	74,894	12,666	1,317
Wilson	94,691	9,554	5,128	78,972	488	549

Note: Detail may not add to total because of independent rounding. Undistributed federal obligations of $641,485,000 are not shown.

Source: U.S. Department of Commerce, Bureau of the Census, *Consolidated Federal Funds Report, Volume I: County Areas, Fiscal Year 1988.*

TABLE 15.15--OPERATING REVENUE, BY SOURCE, MUNICIPALITIES, FISCAL YEAR 1987
[In thousands of dollars]

Municipality	Total	Property tax	Local sales tax	Other local sources [1]	Federal government	State government
Adams	79	15	10	15	2	37
Adamsville	586	105	108	251	10	111
Alamo	1,322	153	85	185	143	575
Alcoa	12,540	3,081	2,259	4,051	470	2,678
Alexandria	134	39	15	24	2	55
Algood	535	116	62	194	15	147
Allardt	55	0	7	6	1	39
Altamont	64	0	17	4	2	41
Ardmore	224	13	56	101	3	53
Arlington	511	147	80	161	7	115
Ashland City	678	188	191	139	10	150
Athens	9,784	1,740	1,413	1,525	539	3,215
Atoka	144	2	34	64	1	43
Atwood	120	0	23	28	2	69
Auburntown	37	0	4	20	1	13
Baileyton	69	0	24	21	4	20
Baneberry	9	0	0	9	0	0
Bartlett	7,049	2,534	1,044	2,112	29	1,332
Baxter	275	63	24	84	17	86
Beersheba Springs	256	0	4	8	2	242
Bell Buckle	64	8	4	13	1	39
Belle Meade	2,550	998	0	693	4	854
Bells	1,098	124	46	278	61	446
Benton	194	31	62	30	3	68
Berry Hill	1,009	0	477	426	12	95
Bethel Springs	103	5	11	35	1	51
Big Sandy	120	18	30	28	4	40
Blaine	115	0	32	8	2	73
Bluff City	267	42	68	31	10	117
Bolivar	1,721	380	427	403	53	457
Braden	29	0	2	9	0	17
Bradford	214	39	25	70	2	79
Brentwood	6,085	2,132	963	1,964	15	1,011
Brighton	146	12	34	35	2	62
Bristol	23,175	5,425	2,404	2,607	776	6,415
Brownsville	2,615	561	410	803	85	755
Bruceton	339	85	43	109	6	96
Bulls Gap	167	33	15	7	0	113
Burlison	32	0	5	4	0	22
Byrdstown	152	44	38	4	6	59
Calhoun	73	14	7	15	1	36
Camden	1,259	116	425	356	14	348
Carthage	852	226	48	256	131	190
Caryville	353	0	79	138	7	128
Cedar Hill	40	4	4	6	1	27
Celina	312	102	43	57	10	100
Centertown	19	0	0	1	1	16
Centerville	883	164	268	169	17	265
Chapel Hill	114	24	13	21	3	53
Charleston	202	14	27	80	4	76

TABLE 15.15--OPERATING REVENUE, BY SOURCE, MUNICIPALITIES, FISCAL YEAR 1987
[In thousands of dollars] (Continued)

Municipality	Total	Property tax	Local sales tax	Other local sources[1]	Federal government	State government
Charlotte	142	10	42	39	3	49
Chattanooga	188,740	42,360	19,965	56,722	12,782	39,023
Church Hill	587	66	124	131	12	250
Clarksburg	38	0	9	6	0	23
Clarksville	20,647	3,073	2,111	4,735	7,172	3,557
Cleveland	19,831	2,687	2,817	3,432	705	6,832
Clifton	165	36	0	63	4	62
Clinton	7,999	1,178	1,373	3,517	227	1,704
Coalmont	77	0	8	12	1	56
Collegedale	1,131	455	140	229	21	285
Collierville	4,331	1,041	975	1,637	54	623
Collinwood	233	94	0	69	6	65
Columbia	8,543	1,452	2,808	2,411	103	1,770
Cookeville	7,500	1,171	2,283	2,790	148	1,106
Copperhill	263	18	118	92	3	31
Cornersville	106	33	7	15	1	50
Cottage Grove	29	1	1	14	0	13
Covington	4,870	830	850	1,484	173	1,533
Cowan	296	70	23	91	5	107
Crab Orchard	155	0	37	50	4	64
Cross Plains	138	0	38	42	4	55
Crossville	3,576	522	1,399	834	68	753
Cumberland City	105	9	9	58	2	27
Cumberland Gap	235	4	9	178	1	43
Dandridge	339	92	95	50	3	99
Dayton	3,013	181	677	706	200	975
Decatur	292	56	69	84	6	77
Decaturville	209	76	38	27	6	60
Decherd	861	195	235	183	109	139
Dickson	3,628	790	878	1,489	64	407
Dover	287	75	62	59	8	83
Dowelltown	23	0	1	0	0	22
Doyle	40	0	4	13	8	15
Dresden	976	251	153	329	15	229
Ducktown	151	20	67	17	3	45
Dunlap	736	161	110	204	29	233
Dyer	556	135	130	120	10	161
Dyersburg	15,370	1,787	3,008	4,551	443	5,181
Eagleville	106	15	42	16	1	32
East Ridge	4,048	877	1,022	817	17	1,315
Eastview	76	0	10	32	2	33
Elizabethton	11,464	1,841	1,319	2,251	677	3,926
Elkton	132	3	7	84	5	33
Englewood	362	112	35	101	2	111
Enville	78	1	1	60	0	16
Erin	389	55	138	80	15	101
Erwin	1,437	490	322	257	37	332
Estill Springs	553	66	24	74	306	84
Ethridge	81	0	14	30	2	34
Etowah	2,369	394	208	434	99	878

TABLE 15.15--OPERATING REVENUE, BY SOURCE, MUNICIPALITIES, FISCAL YEAR 1987
[In thousands of dollars] (Continued)

Municipality	Total	Property tax	Local sales tax	Other local sources[1]	Federal government	State government
Fairview	742	130	197	175	12	229
Farragut	1,254	0	450	378	11	414
Fayetteville	n.a.	n.a.	n.a.	n.a.	n.a.	n.a.
Finger	35	0	5	15	0	14
Forest Hills	582	0	152	120	6	305
Franklin	6,546	2,226	0	1,281	33	3,006
Friendship	133	21	9	48	1	54
Friendsville	89	0	10	20	1	58
Gadsden	73	0	6	26	0	41
Gallatin	7,346	1,643	1,817	2,699	52	1,135
Gallaway	255	0	24	123	47	61
Garland	42	0	11	13	0	18
Gates	82	22	0	14	2	44
Gatlinburg	10,213	550	1,369	7,370	20	903
Germantown	11,768	5,139	1,379	3,199	19	2,029
Gibson	78	15	10	25	1	27
Gilt Edge	44	0	5	14	0	25
Gleason	313	68	47	92	17	90
Goodlettsville	4,452	226	2,554	963	57	652
Gordonsville	182	77	16	32	4	54
Grand Junction	147	32	35	46	3	30
Graysville	153	21	11	38	3	81
Greenback	95	0	12	40	1	41
Greenbrier	370	99	44	37	7	183
Greeneville	14,076	3,594	1,461	1,763	903	4,500
Greenfield	479	83	96	157	10	134
Gruetli-Laager	253	0	41	87	5	120
Guys	104	0	9	95	0	0
Halls	578	110	0	229	48	190
Harriman	7,586	1,501	890	1,548	334	3,313
Hartsville	1,117	145	169	390	232	181
Henderson	890	188	98	240	13	351
Hendersonville	n.a.	n.a.	n.a.	0	n.a.	n.a.
Henning	131	16	0	71	3	40
Henry	114	10	5	78	1	19
Hickory Valley	34	1	14	3	1	15
Hohenwald	1,076	194	182	403	42	254
Hollow Rock	138	11	11	32	2	82
Hornbeak	62	6	0	10	1	45
Hornsby	65	7	6	27	1	24
Humboldt	8,980	1,296	1,234	1,257	473	3,820
Huntingdon	1,424	253	399	460	13	299
Huntland	216	61	26	69	3	57
Huntsville	130	7	0	31	3	89
Jacksboro	274	0	39	44	84	104
Jackson	38,735	8,966	2,947	9,658	2,554	10,153
Jamestown	555	103	108	120	65	159
Jasper	676	136	171	193	9	166
Jefferson City	1,437	308	433	244	46	405
Jellico	1,563	79	128	907	283	167
Johnson City	35,941	8,334	5,237	6,791	1,750	9,793

TABLE 15.15--OPERATING REVENUE, BY SOURCE, MUNICIPALITIES, FISCAL YEAR 1987
[In thousands of dollars] (Continued)

Municipality	Total	Property tax	Local sales tax	Other local sources[1]	Federal government	State government
Jonesborough	985	272	237	218	26	232
Kenton	311	79	60	71	3	98
Kimball	262	17	54	113	5	73
Kingsport	38,386	9,545	6,467	4,652	1,693	8,381
Kingston	985	252	222	183	15	315
Kingston Springs	192	63	24	36	3	65
Knoxville	138,568	35,135	16,221	29,509	9,111	39,484
Lafayette	1,685	203	431	339	454	259
LaFollette	2,610	453	875	663	84	536
LaGrange	36	9	2	13	1	12
Lake City	1,742	78	256	1,238	26	142
Lakeland	367	0	220	89	4	55
Lakesite	77	17	3	14	1	42
Lakewood	428	0	0	192	2	235
LaVergne	1,319	0	498	398	17	406
Lawrenceburg	4,433	724	1,139	1,344	174	1,053
Lebanon	4,350	620	1,320	1,443	61	894
Lenoir City	5,891	1,190	639	1,471	336	2,254
Lewisburg	3,546	1,446	377	875	268	580
Lexington	4,244	507	564	1,568	178	1,330
Liberty	53	4	9	11	0	29
Linden	323	82	93	66	10	71
Livingston	1,137	450	183	220	32	252
Lobelville	180	60	21	15	2	80
Lookout Mountain	1,560	913	25	112	1	510
Loretto	304	31	96	70	7	100
Loudon	1,727	646	148	641	40	252
Luttrell	78	0	11	6	2	59
Lynchburg	166	39	32	47	3	45
Lynnville	50	10	3	11	1	25
McEwen	391	57	61	65	124	84
McKenzie	1,909	185	339	592	332	460
McLemoresville	70	11	6	32	1	19
McMinnville	3,755	1,267	269	1,227	72	921
Madisonville	1,025	131	426	249	26	194
Manchester	6,080	1,082	798	1,014	279	1,974
Martin	2,757	284	680	1,135	87	571
Maryville	16,940	4,285	3,704	3,129	591	5,120
Mason	157	7	35	83	3	31
Maury City	180	31	27	56	6	61
Maynardville	180	0	68	50	6	57
Medina	139	54	23	13	2	48
Medon	18	0	0	4	0	13
Memphis	631,387	108,505	55,762	126,370	63,779	167,927
Michie	96	0	11	47	2	36
Middleton	285	24	109	100	6	48
Milan	2,733	354	630	1,174	42	533
Milledgeville	230	0	7	19	179	23
Millersville	224	11	31	59	2	120
Millington	3,627	413	1,095	790	90	1,239
Minor Hill	236	0	6	187	12	31

TABLE 15.15--OPERATING REVENUE, BY SOURCE, MUNICIPALITIES, FISCAL YEAR 1987
[In thousands of dollars] (Continued)

Municipality	Total	Property tax	Local sales tax	Other local sources[1]	Federal government	State government
Mitchellville	25	6	1	4	0	13
Monterey	509	116	110	105	19	160
Morrison	63	2	0	25	1	36
Morristown	10,452	3,322	2,644	2,106	735	1,571
Moscow	190	25	43	85	6	32
Mosheim	181	0	26	59	3	94
Mount Carmel	454	0	123	92	5	235
Mount Juliet	849	0	423	199	6	221
Mount Pleasant	1,290	153	158	566	198	216
Mountain City	692	170	175	174	23	151
Munford	422	53	77	122	2	169
Murfreesboro	26,686	5,844	6,063	5,450	550	6,979
Nashville[2]	543,224	183,298	88,537	126,569	43,740	101,080
New Hope	60	8	2	9	1	42
New Johnsonville	464	73	80	190	11	111
New Market	187	0	40	61	5	82
New Tazewell	931	0	260	98	466	108
Newbern	744	143	104	305	16	175
Newport	4,868	992	1,243	941	348	1,343
Niota	155	42	19	38	3	53
Normandy	11	1	0	0	0	8
Norris	480	182	23	172	4	101
Oak Hill	603	0	0	135	14	455
Oak Ridge	25,640	3,384	3,537	6,833	979	7,776
Oakdale	482	13	4	16	426	24
Oakland	118	9	21	53	2	33
Obion	279	58	38	90	6	87
Oliver Springs	771	229	149	146	21	225
Oneida	1,245	270	0	246	15	715
Orlinda	33	0	3	3	1	27
Orme	14	0	0	1	1	12
Palmer	91	0	7	21	2	61
Paris	3,831	541	1,195	1,324	73	699
Parker's Crossroads	91	0	35	41	1	14
Parrottsville	11	0	0	3	0	8
Parsons	692	127	19	371	6	167
Pegram	114	0	16	31	0	66
Petersburg	113	21	28	41	2	22
Philadelphia	45	0	5	10	1	30
Pigeon Forge	6,231	208	1,900	3,009	24	1,090
Pikeville	445	57	62	182	10	133
Piperton	65	0	6	13	1	45
Pittman Center	112	38	21	21	1	31
Pleasant Hill	53	0	9	9	1	33
Portland	1,529	339	356	511	47	276
Powell's Crossroads	97	0	10	31	1	55
Pulaski	2,554	427	417	1,153	57	476
Puryear	107	14	10	43	1	41
Ramer	158	0	13	93	24	28
Red Bank	2,373	646	461	436	20	813

TABLE 15.15--OPERATING REVENUE, BY SOURCE, MUNICIPALITIES, FISCAL YEAR 1987
[In thousands of dollars] (Continued)

Municipality	Total	Property tax	Local sales tax	Other local sources [1]	Federal government	State government
Red Boiling Springs	263	59	56	67	8	72
Ridgely	413	95	27	166	11	114
Ridgeside	107	62	1	8	0	36
Ridgetop	179	46	26	30	2	75
Ripley	1,938	678	0	766	40	454
Rives	49	14	2	4	1	27
Rockford	94	0	44	10	3	37
Rockwood	1,689	367	346	490	38	447
Rogersville	3,146	804	547	391	445	959
Rossville	118	24	15	51	3	24
Rutherford	328	77	41	119	5	85
Rutledge	341	0	53	46	1	240
St. Joseph	369	7	33	266	8	54
Saltillo	195	0	6	6	158	26
Samburg	95	0	19	46	3	28
Sardis	49	5	8	16	0	20
Saulsbury	26	0	9	6	0	10
Savannah	1,687	321	309	511	43	503
Scotts Hill	129	15	42	21	3	48
Selmer	1,143	213	323	327	15	266
Sevierville	3,209	294	1,278	1,002	50	585
Sharon	392	88	44	176	6	79
Shelbyville	5,237	1,475	575	1,151	1,138	898
Signal Mountain	2,487	1,292	150	469	16	562
Silerton	7	0	1	0	0	6
Smithville	906	181	182	279	19	245
Smyrna	4,881	594	1,171	2,362	58	696
Sneedville	196	0	61	50	5	80
Soddy-Daisy	1,494	336	311	306	22	518
Somerville	777	74	290	236	25	153
South Carthage	335	50	18	196	6	65
South Fulton	550	137	81	133	11	188
South Pittsburg	1,263	158	272	547	28	258
Sparta	1,741	602	337	422	43	336
Spencer	114	0	13	32	2	66
Spring City	542	173	108	107	5	150
Spring Hill	1,076	27	33	877	4	135
Springfield	4,268	952	608	1,540	481	687
Stanton	67	13	5	12	1	36
Stantonville	96	0	1	6	73	17
Surgoinsville	175	0	16	64	1	94
Sweetwater	4,630	828	834	840	453	1,667
Tazewell	396	0	113	136	18	131
Tellico Plains	204	26	43	67	6	60
Tennessee Ridge	185	38	45	15	6	80
Tiptonville	740	92	44	375	19	211
Toone	50	2	5	17	1	26
Townsend	139	0	45	43	25	25
Trenton	1,934	343	406	848	28	308
Trezevant	162	23	23	56	4	57

TABLE 15.15--OPERATING REVENUE, BY SOURCE, MUNICIPALITIES, FISCAL YEAR 1987
[In thousands of dollars] (Continued)

Municipality	Total	Property tax	Local sales tax	Other local sources[1]	Federal government	State government
Trimble	118	28	12	28	3	45
Troy	262	64	65	60	6	68
Tullahoma	15,014	3,204	2,439	3,929	768	4,673
Tusculum	206	0	12	60	3	131
Union City	9,500	1,324	1,806	1,374	826	3,131
Vanleer	46	2	5	13	0	25
Viola	175	0	0	4	162	9
Vonore	105	0	16	47	11	32
Walden	242	112	6	39	2	84
Wartburg	216	0	92	64	14	45
Wartrace	198	32	0	79	47	41
Watauga	87	4	46	9	4	23
Waverly	1,375	296	404	330	65	280
Waynesboro	512	197	0	161	20	134
Westmoreland	465	76	97	104	81	107
White House	801	295	203	160	6	137
Whiteville	251	45	31	85	4	85
Whitwell	266	14	0	98	6	149
Williston	34	0	6	3	1	24
Winchester	2,093	697	322	618	37	418
Woodbury	519	158	86	116	14	146
Woodland Mills	68	0	5	30	1	31
Yorkville	29	0	4	6	0	19

Note: Detail may not add to total due to independent rounding.

n.a. not available.

1. Refers to in-lieu property tax payments by utilities, business tax, local beer tax, and other county and municipal sources.

2. It should be noted that the data for Nashville are Davidson County figures, which include both the General Services District and the Urban Services District of the Unified City and County Government. These data are presented also in Table 15.8.

Source: State of Tennessee, Report of the Comptroller of the Treasury, Division of Local Finance, *County and Municipal Finances for Fiscal Year Ended June 30, 1987.*

TABLE 15.16--OPERATING EXPENDITURES, BY FUNCTION, MUNICIPALITIES, FISCAL YEAR 1987
[In thousands of dollars]

Municipality	Total [1]	General purpose	Schools	Highways and streets	Debt service Principal	Debt service Interest
Adams	59	48	0	11	0	0
Adamsville	793	408	0	34	310	41
Alamo	1,449	1,258	52	104	10	25
Alcoa	11,521	5,355	4,659	399	616	492
Alexandria	114	88	0	13	8	5
Algood	558	278	0	91	140	49
Allardt	35	26	0	9	0	0
Altamont	53	40	0	12	0	1
Ardmore	275	222	0	53	0	0
Arlington	466	350	0	59	15	42
Ashland City	457	278	0	179	0	0
Athens	9,560	3,077	4,885	815	545	238
Atoka	203	177	0	26	0	0
Atwood	79	74	0	5	0	0
Auburntown	24	17	0	5	1	1
Baileyton	46	43	0	3	0	0
Baneberry	5	5	0	0	0	0
Bartlett	11,621	5,887	0	832	4,616	286
Baxter	212	187	0	15	8	2
Beersheba Springs	42	33	0	9	0	0
Bell Buckle	44	40	0	4	0	0
Belle Meade	3,732	1,179	0	130	2,090	293
Bells	1,136	246	661	58	51	120
Benton	206	152	0	54	0	0
Berry Hill	900	880	0	20	0	0
Bethel Springs	155	132	0	17	4	2
Big Sandy	99	85	0	14	0	0
Blaine	116	54	0	62	0	0
Bluff City	343	255	0	88	0	0
Bolivar	1,722	1,378	0	344	0	0
Braden	28	25	1	2	0	0
Bradford	193	157	0	28	7	1
Brentwood	5,264	3,605	0	682	389	588
Brighton	132	104	0	28	0	0
Bristol	29,427	8,176	14,951	1,487	1,713	3,100
Brownsville	2,611	1,466	0	1,032	63	50
Bruceton	366	271	0	95	0	0
Bulls Gap	140	106	0	23	10	1
Burlison	30	13	0	17	0	0
Byrdstown	152	82	0	47	15	8
Calhoun	68	53	0	15	0	0
Camden	1,044	722	0	291	30	1
Carthage	940	772	9	156	0	3
Caryville	515	255	0	208	44	8
Cedar Hill	33	19	0	14	0	0
Celina	298	172	0	94	25	7
Centertown	33	13	0	20	0	0
Centerville	793	712	0	35	29	17
Chapel Hill	105	102	0	3	0	0
Charleston	175	150	0	25	0	0

TABLE 15.16--OPERATING EXPENDITURES, BY FUNCTION, MUNICIPALITIES, FISCAL YEAR 1987
[In thousands of dollars] (Continued)

Municipality	Total [1]	General purpose	Schools	Highways and streets	Debt service	
					Principal	Interest
Charlotte	144	78	0	66	0	0
Chattanooga	172,412	95,269	67,454	5,657	2,852	1,180
Church Hill	603	471	0	132	0	0
Clarksburg	24	16	0	8	0	0
Clarksville	17,762	10,828	0	2,647	3,383	904
Cleveland	20,466	7,057	11,237	1,239	390	284
Clifton	176	96	0	65	8	7
Clinton	8,268	1,928	2,751	816	2,773	0
Coalmont	57	51	0	6	0	0
Collegedale	1,219	591	0	444	121	63
Collierville	7,998	3,219	0	796	3,640	343
Collinwood	233	139	0	46	39	9
Columbia	8,055	6,358	0	1,494	0	203
Cookeville	12,900	4,595	0	737	6,766	802
Copperhill	296	199	0	97	0	0
Cornersville	90	79	0	6	3	2
Cottage Grove	13	10	0	3	0	0
Covington	4,909	1,771	2,236	857	14	31
Cowan	274	175	0	88	5	6
Crab Orchard	166	81	0	85	0	0
Cross Plains	154	111	0	43	0	0
Crossville	3,097	2,234	0	773	66	24
Cumberland City	89	63	0	26	0	0
Cumberland Gap	159	120	0	39	0	0
Dandridge	244	176	0	68	0	0
Dayton	3,139	1,227	1,491	410	9	2
Decatur	254	146	0	108	0	0
Decaturville	181	122	0	43	7	7
Decherd	752	513	0	213	13	13
Dickson	3,197	2,340	0	844	11	2
Dover	285	215	0	70	0	0
Dowelltown	31	16	0	15	0	0
Doyle	19	7	0	12	0	0
Dresden	819	496	0	199	107	17
Ducktown	82	43	0	39	0	0
Dunlap	681	491	0	156	23	11
Dyer	452	328	0	124	0	0
Dyersburg	14,406	5,001	7,938	1,191	234	42
Eagleville	91	91	0	0	0	0
East Ridge	3,411	2,382	0	730	255	44
Eastview	91	52	0	6	27	6
Elizabethton	11,224	3,654	6,233	729	466	142
Elkton	116	81	0	35	0	0
Englewood	345	239	0	106	0	0
Enville	86	73	0	13	0	0
Erin	379	287	0	46	39	7
Erwin	1,474	966	0	349	70	89
Estill Springs	528	444	0	68	13	3
Ethridge	88	87	0	1	0	0
Etowah	2,542	1,165	1,020	74	217	66

TABLE 15.16--OPERATING EXPENDITURES, BY FUNCTION, MUNICIPALITIES, FISCAL YEAR 1987
[In thousands of dollars] (Continued)

Municipality	Total [1]	General purpose	Schools	Highways and streets	Debt service Principal	Debt service Interest
Fairview	709	478	0	231	0	0
Farragut	1,007	758	0	249	0	0
Fayetteville	n.a.	n.a.	n.a.	n.a.	n.a.	n.a.
Finger	32	22	0	10	0	0
Forest Hills	381	131	0	250	0	0
Franklin	6,980	6,348	0	359	112	161
Friendship	132	115	0	17	0	0
Friendsville	95	53	0	34	8	0
Gadsden	64	41	0	23	0	0
Gallatin	8,599	4,782	0	878	2,567	372
Gallaway	226	183	0	43	0	0
Garland	40	24	0	16	0	0
Gates	76	63	0	13	0	0
Gatlinburg	11,770	7,071	199	875	3,037	588
Germantown	8,881	6,439	0	952	785	705
Gibson	60	48	0	12	0	0
Gilt Edge	51	39	0	12	0	0
Gleason	344	274	0	70	0	0
Goodlettsville	4,216	3,527	0	689	0	0
Gordonsville	178	104	0	71	0	3
Grand Junction	119	106	0	13	0	0
Graysville	159	139	0	20	0	0
Greenback	71	65	0	0	6	0
Greenbrier	341	241	0	68	32	0
Greeneville	13,817	3,786	7,995	1,242	513	281
Greenfield	415	345	0	53	15	2
Gruetli-Laager	215	160	0	55	0	0
Guys	11	11	0	0	0	0
Halls	667	523	0	131	3	10
Harriman	7,045	1,635	4,951	189	154	116
Hartsville	1,418	1,084	0	334	0	0
Henderson	1,178	798	0	332	27	21
Hendersonville	n.a.	n.a.	n.a.	n.a.	n.a.	n.a.
Henning	115	87	0	28	0	0
Henry	70	51	0	19	0	0
Hickory Valley	22	18	0	4	0	0
Hohenwald	1,003	610	0	368	17	8
Hollow Rock	134	104	0	30	0	0
Hornbeak	69	55	0	14	0	0
Hornsby	47	43	0	4	0	0
Humboldt	9,335	2,358	6,206	386	200	185
Huntingdon	1,482	1,098	0	267	78	39
Huntland	180	114	0	33	28	5
Huntsville	120	94	0	17	6	3
Jacksboro	296	247	0	49	0	0
Jackson	39,759	19,047	16,795	2,253	440	1,224
Jamestown	508	371	0	131	1	5
Jasper	644	580	0	64	0	0
Jefferson City	1,467	1,020	0	370	56	21
Jellico	1,529	1,231	0	210	65	23

TABLE 15.16--OPERATING EXPENDITURES, BY FUNCTION, MUNICIPALITIES, FISCAL YEAR 1987
[In thousands of dollars] (Continued)

Municipality	Total [1]	General purpose	Schools	Highways and streets	Debt service	
					Principal	Interest
Johnson City	38,594	18,679	15,825	2,913	525	652
Jonesborough	1,016	617	0	264	50	85
Kenton	325	267	0	58	0	0
Kimball	307	278	0	29	0	0
Kingsport	37,367	16,877	18,687	460	650	693
Kingston	973	789	0	170	0	14
Kingston Springs	212	126	0	86	0	0
Knoxville	146,313	57,710	71,006	4,692	4,879	8,026
Lafayette	1,334	1,111	0	223	0	0
LaFollette	2,591	1,797	0	550	119	125
LaGrange	36	29	0	7	0	0
Lake City	1,615	1,471	0	128	14	2
Lakeland	132	108	0	24	0	0
Lakesite	87	49	0	38	0	0
Lakewood	342	275	0	67	0	0
LaVergne	893	739	0	154	0	0
Lawrenceburg	4,535	3,671	0	811	43	10
Lebanon	3,075	2,778	0	244	48	5
Lenoir City	6,052	1,257	4,016	415	310	54
Lewisburg	3,171	2,475	0	504	127	65
Lexington	4,134	989	1,397	775	72	109
Liberty	87	32	0	55	0	0
Linden	235	210	0	22	1	2
Livingston	1,222	841	0	217	126	38
Lobelville	157	118	0	39	0	0
Lookout Mountain	1,338	785	97	229	125	102
Loretto	268	243	0	25	0	0
Loudon	1,829	1,066	0	522	62	179
Luttrell	68	60	0	8	0	0
Lynchburg	178	114	0	64	0	0
Lynnville	42	37	0	5	0	0
McEwen	387	311	0	4	27	45
McKenzie	2,155	1,610	0	396	85	64
McLemoresville	75	29	0	22	16	8
McMinnville	3,655	3,075	0	379	120	81
Madisonville	946	727	0	178	31	10
Manchester	5,817	1,957	3,118	350	320	72
Martin	3,424	3,045	0	379	0	0
Maryville	17,253	5,901	8,510	1,850	475	517
Mason	153	104	0	49	0	0
Maury City	140	105	0	35	0	0
Maynardville	210	164	0	46	0	0
Medina	116	98	0	15	0	3
Medon	16	13	0	3	0	0
Memphis	679,598	385,208	233,126	12,482	26,661	22,121
Michie	76	60	0	10	4	2
Middleton	239	208	0	24	2	5
Milan	2,603	1,710	0	543	220	130
Milledgeville	211	206	0	5	0	0
Millersville	193	186	0	7	0	0

TABLE 15.16--OPERATING EXPENDITURES, BY FUNCTION, MUNICIPALITIES, FISCAL YEAR 1987
[In thousands of dollars] (Continued)

Municipality	Total [1]	General purpose	Schools	Highways and streets	Debt service: Principal	Debt service: Interest
Millington	2,928	2,104	0	785	30	9
Minor Hill	211	209	0	2	0	0
Mitchellville	41	37	0	3	0	1
Monterey	739	360	0	379	0	0
Morrison	94	67	0	27	0	0
Morristown	10,207	7,711	0	978	1,200	318
Moscow	161	99	0	62	0	0
Mosheim	162	88	0	74	0	0
Mount Carmel	441	364	0	65	9	3
Mount Juliet	760	374	0	367	6	13
Mount Pleasant	1,146	789	0	301	22	34
Mountain City	678	579	0	99	0	0
Munford	382	293	0	89	0	0
Murfreesboro	32,830	12,153	9,548	1,501	7,904	1,724
Nashville[2]	608,907	278,433	231,334	30,751	24,953	43,436
New Hope	73	44	0	26	0	3
New Johnsonville	447	335	0	112	0	0
New Market	115	85	0	30	0	0
New Tazewell	932	758	0	168	3	3
Newbern	783	527	0	212	15	29
Newport	4,676	2,226	1,565	656	178	51
Niota	166	138	0	28	0	0
Normandy	9	5	0	4	0	0
Norris	484	427	0	27	26	4
Oak Hill	489	237	0	252	0	0
Oak Ridge	25,999	7,704	15,833	760	1,435	267
Oakdale	470	461	0	9	0	0
Oakland	104	90	7	7	0	0
Obion	232	194	0	38	0	0
Oliver Springs	1,116	750	0	344	6	16
Oneida	1,843	850	0	768	208	17
Orlinda	28	21	0	7	0	0
Orme	8	6	0	2	0	0
Palmer	111	81	0	30	0	0
Paris	3,846	2,876	0	738	178	54
Parker's Crossroads	73	60	0	13	0	0
Parrottsville	5	3	0	2	0	0
Parsons	470	298	0	77	61	34
Pegram	128	112	0	16	0	0
Petersburg	98	73	0	20	4	1
Philadelphia	41	29	0	12	0	0
Pigeon Forge	4,561	3,772	0	789	0	0
Pikeville	449	331	0	64	23	31
Piperton	38	36	0	2	0	0
Pittman Center	71	64	0	7	0	0
Pleasant Hill	40	27	0	13	0	0
Portland	1,960	1,494	0	466	0	0
Powell's Crossroads	77	58	0	19	0	0
Pulaski	2,584	1,932	0	594	54	4
Puryear	89	68	0	21	0	0

TABLE 15.16--OPERATING EXPENDITURES, BY FUNCTION, MUNICIPALITIES, FISCAL YEAR 1987
[In thousands of dollars] (Continued)

Municipality	Total [1]	General purpose	Schools	Highways and streets	Debt service Principal	Debt service Interest
Ramer	127	71	0	51	2	3
Red Bank	2,303	2,047	0	251	0	5
Red Boiling Springs	263	210	0	53	0	0
Ridgely	381	293	0	88	0	0
Ridgeside	111	57	0	54	0	0
Ridgetop	143	102	0	13	13	15
Ripley	1,850	1,175	0	549	125	1
Rives	34	19	0	15	0	0
Rockford	75	44	0	31	0	0
Rockwood	1,737	1,262	0	353	86	36
Rogersville	3,467	1,703	1,184	291	119	170
Rossville	131	123	4	4	0	0
Rutherford	367	324	2	31	8	2
Rutledge	352	311	0	41	0	0
St. Joseph	213	203	0	10	0	0
Saltillo	184	169	0	9	5	1
Samburg	75	53	0	22	0	0
Sardis	37	35	0	2	0	0
Saulsbury	11	9	0	2	0	0
Savannah	1,564	1,232	0	249	49	34
Scotts Hill	103	96	0	7	0	0
Selmer	1,084	832	0	252	0	0
Sevierville	3,369	2,252	0	736	364	17
Sharon	365	308	0	48	8	1
Shelbyville	4,877	4,582	0	295	0	0
Signal Mountain	2,017	1,272	0	571	96	78
Silerton	3	2	0	1	0	0
Smithville	761	596	0	108	20	37
Smyrna	2,353	1,826	0	474	31	22
Sneedville	215	137	0	65	9	4
Soddy-Daisy	1,406	1,072	0	203	78	53
Somerville	717	528	0	189	0	0
South Carthage	421	370	0	51	0	0
South Fulton	530	358	0	127	35	10
South Pittsburg	1,282	900	0	198	80	104
Sparta	1,965	1,523	0	333	40	69
Spencer	101	72	0	13	8	8
Spring City	482	369	0	102	11	0
Spring Hill	667	457	0	204	0	6
Springfield	4,795	3,221	0	768	656	150
Stanton	68	40	0	28	0	0
Stantonville	110	100	0	5	1	4
Surgoinsville	167	141	0	26	0	0
Sweetwater	4,445	1,185	2,708	369	147	36
Tazewell	430	255	0	109	65	1
Tellico Plains	200	146	0	54	0	0
Tennessee Ridge	218	117	0	90	9	2
Tiptonville	687	511	0	137	30	9
Toone	25	21	0	4	0	0
Townsend	124	115	0	4	5	0

TABLE 15.16--OPERATING EXPENDITURES, BY FUNCTION, MUNICIPALITIES, FISCAL YEAR 1987
[In thousands of dollars] (Continued)

Municipality	Total [1]	General purpose	Schools	Highways and streets	Debt service	
					Principal	Interest
Trenton	1,843	1,420	0	323	85	15
Trezevant	158	89	0	36	28	5
Trimble	108	98	0	10	0	0
Troy	178	143	0	35	0	0
Tullahoma	15,272	4,173	9,103	621	715	660
Tusculum	118	56	0	62	0	0
Union City	10,065	3,626	5,750	689	0	0
Vanleer	30	27	0	3	0	0
Viola	171	169	0	1	0	1
Vonore	99	87	0	12	0	0
Walden	215	144	0	71	0	0
Wartburg	197	124	0	73	0	0
Wartrace	162	105	0	57	0	0
Watauga	93	88	0	5	0	0
Waverly	1,318	567	0	443	167	141
Waynesboro	463	401	0	62	0	0
Westmoreland	496	463	0	27	0	6
White House	718	530	0	55	40	93
Whiteville	226	120	0	106	0	0
Whitwell	235	227	0	8	0	0
Williston	16	13	2	1	0	0
Winchester	2,005	1,242	0	330	394	39
Woodbury	481	348	0	133	0	0
Woodland Mills	135	67	0	68	0	0
Yorkville	27	22	0	5	0	0

n.a. not available.

1. Includes detail not shown separately.

2. It should be noted that the data for Nashville are Davidson County figures, which include both General Services District and the Urban Services District of the Unified City and County Government. These data are presented also in Table 15.10.

Source: State of Tennessee, Report of the Comptroller of the Treasury, Division of Local Finance, *County and Municipal Finances for Fiscal Year Ended June 30, 1987.*

TABLE 15.17--ESTIMATED CURRENT PROPERTY VALUE, ASSESSED VALUE, BY CLASSIFICATION, AND PROPERTY TAXES LEVIED, MUNICIPALITIES, 1987

[In thousands of dollars]

			Assessed value					
				Real property				
Municipality	City property taxes levied	Estimated current property value	Total	Residential and farm	Industrial and commercial	Personal property [1]	Public utilities [2]	County
Adams	15	9,084	1,945	1,202	62	10	671	Robertson
Adamsville	105	41,542	13,366	4,453	4,816	2,529	1,568	McNairy
Alamo	153	34,759	10,412	5,812	2,915	596	1,090	Crockett
Alcoa	3,081	417,321	142,222	27,525	69,405	33,441	11,851	Blount
Alexandria	39	14,549	3,882	1,883	803	205	990	DeKalb
Algood	116	38,435	11,791	6,268	3,805	667	1,051	Putnam
Allardt	0	10,711	2,645	2,376	170	23	76	Fentress
Altamont	0	4,388	1,056	836	76	2	140	Grundy
Ardmore	13	20,383	4,944	2,435	1,945	423	142	Giles
Arlington	147	43,042	9,817	3,667	2,138	2,689	1,323	Shelby
Ashland City	188	64,938	13,579	5,059	3,703	3,604	1,213	Cheatham
Athens	1,740	325,028	100,777	33,558	40,356	21,618	5,245	McMinn
Atoka	2	8,592	1,735	1,299	241	76	118	Tipton
Atwood	0	8,909	2,188	1,628	199	118	243	Carroll
Auburntown	0	2,860	830	582	115	0	133	Cannon
Baileyton	0	642	316	0	0	0	316	Greene
Baneberry	0	10,325	2,131	1,958	166	0	7	Jefferson
Bartlett	2,534	673,533	123,840	96,432	16,150	4,236	7,022	Shelby
Baxter	63	17,810	5,267	3,205	1,188	275	598	Putnam
Beersheba Springs	0	630	298	2	0	0	296	Grundy
Bell Buckle	8	4,751	1,308	1,018	130	7	153	Bedford
Belle Meade	998	298,490	61,412	59,933	360	162	956	Davidson
Bells	124	33,612	10,596	3,801	3,957	2,063	775	Crockett
Benton	31	13,092	4,008	1,910	900	109	1,089	Polk
Berry Hill	0	90,580	27,261	3,098	19,480	4,451	232	Davidson
Bethel Springs	5	9,058	2,620	1,841	213	10	556	McNairy
Big Sandy	18	6,651	1,757	1,108	300	47	301	Benton

TABLE 15.17--ESTIMATED CURRENT PROPERTY VALUE, ASSESSED VALUE, BY CLASSIFICATION, AND PROPERTY TAXES LEVIED, MUNICIPALITIES, 1987
[In thousands of dollars] (Continued)

			Assessed value					
				Real property				
Municipality	City property taxes levied	Estimated current property value	Total	Residential and farm	Industrial and commercial	Personal property [1]	Public utilities [2]	County
Blaine	0	16,517	4,166	3,803	321	27	16	Grainger
Bluff City	42	22,161	6,254	3,402	1,371	408	1,073	Sullivan
Bolivar	380	89,250	23,931	10,739	7,233	4,450	1,508	Hardeman
Braden	0	3,962	910	658	67	7	178	Fayette
Bradford	39	16,436	4,302	2,938	913	21	430	Gibson
Brentwood	2,132	1,126,593	160,242	89,094	37,647	11,890	21,611	Williamson
Brighton	12	12,311	2,460	1,925	305	51	180	Tipton
Bristol	5,425	628,017	183,922	79,972	66,779	18,719	18,451	Sullivan
Brownsville	561	195,475	60,392	24,984	21,482	10,698	3,227	Haywood
Bruceton	85	26,047	7,217	3,356	2,123	758	979	Carroll
Bulls Gap	33	11,227	2,253	1,287	291	30	644	Hawkins
Burlison	0	218	87	0	0	0	87	Tipton
Byrdstown	44	15,690	5,003	2,087	1,976	455	484	Pickett
Calhoun	14	9,731	2,761	1,615	583	169	394	McMinn
Camden	116	67,269	18,150	9,712	5,758	1,230	1,449	Benton
Carthage	226	53,325	13,809	5,847	5,788	937	1,236	Smith
Caryville	0	28,134	8,341	3,945	3,982	96	318	Campbell
Cedar Hill	4	3,871	807	523	97	5	182	Robertson
Celina	102	25,476	7,517	3,439	2,819	763	495	Clay
Centertown	0	4,619	1,450	811	28	0	611	Warren
Centerville	164	69,949	20,031	8,992	6,618	2,168	2,253	Hickman
Chapel Hill	24	14,654	2,615	1,607	453	82	473	Marshall
Charleston	14	12,004	3,789	1,871	512	51	1,355	Bradley
Charlotte	10	15,388	2,693	1,621	551	152	368	Dickson
Chattanooga	42,360	4,701,714	1,314,518	272,462	722,734	224,196	95,126	Hamilton
Church Hill	66	73,599	14,486	8,404	4,294	412	1,377	Hawkins

TABLE 15.17--ESTIMATED CURRENT PROPERTY VALUE, ASSESSED VALUE, BY CLASSIFICATION, AND PROPERTY TAXES LEVIED, MUNICIPALITIES, 1987
[In thousands of dollars] (Continued)

			Assessed value					
				Real property				
Municipality	City property taxes levied	Estimated current property value	Total	Residential and farm	Industrial and commercial	Personal property [1]	Public utilities [2]	County
Clarksburg	0	3,552	874	672	109	2	92	Carroll
Clarksville	3,073	1,186,503	248,771	130,292	84,385	22,827	11,266	Montgomery
Cleveland	2,687	807,612	254,739	88,358	113,890	39,472	13,020	Bradley
Clifton	36	8,425	2,343	1,517	310	156	360	Wayne
Clinton	1,178	195,404	56,992	27,797	23,084	3,384	2,727	Anderson
Coalmont	0	1,633	777	0	0	0	777	Grundy
Collegedale	455	119,273	30,552	10,983	11,356	7,124	1,090	Hamilton
Collierville	1,041	356,122	71,117	42,727	14,193	11,408	2,789	Shelby
Collinwood	94	20,424	6,282	2,659	2,210	478	934	Wayne
Columbia	1,452	757,328	174,342	82,409	65,196	18,144	8,593	Maury
Cookeville	1,171	549,699	175,866	67,970	76,088	18,585	13,222	Putnam
Copperhill	18	9,558	3,323	787	1,066	114	1,356	Polk
Cornersville	33	11,871	2,048	1,328	349	39	332	Marshall
Cottage Grove	1	1,255	417	206	37	1	174	Henry
Covington	830	141,723	34,386	12,509	14,602	4,493	2,782	Tipton
Cowan	70	19,646	4,654	3,293	664	215	482	Franklin
Crab Orchard	0	6,759	1,262	724	150	261	127	Cumberland
Cross Plains	0	10,349	2,074	1,505	377	43	148	Robertson
Crossville	522	171,323	38,360	9,015	15,662	10,143	3,540	Cumberland
Cumberland City	9	5,083	1,428	791	142	11	484	Stewart
Cumberland Gap	4	7,026	1,940	539	1,308	0	93	Claiborne
Dandridge	92	38,253	9,846	4,271	3,861	769	945	Jefferson
Dayton	181	132,229	39,772	12,490	17,997	6,470	2,815	Rhea
Decatur	56	26,721	4,721	1,881	1,381	304	1,155	Meigs
Decaturville	76	15,628	3,931	2,027	1,295	219	390	Decatur
Decherd	195	44,896	11,938	5,209	4,947	1,011	771	Franklin
Dickson	790	223,621	43,862	14,935	22,192	3,725	3,011	Dickson

TABLE 15.17--ESTIMATED CURRENT PROPERTY VALUE, ASSESSED VALUE, BY CLASSIFICATION, AND PROPERTY TAXES LEVIED, MUNICIPALITIES, 1987
[In thousands of dollars] (Continued)

Municipality	City property taxes levied	Estimated current property value	Assessed value: Total	Real property: Residential and farm	Real property: Industrial and commercial	Personal property [1]	Public utilities [2]	County
Dover	75	32,494	8,869	4,365	2,396	996	1,113	Stewart
Dowelltown	0	4,665	1,102	718	254	80	51	DeKalb
Doyle	0	2,961	859	515	90	0	254	White
Dresden	251	63,038	16,193	4,247	7,916	3,006	1,025	Weakley
Ducktown	20	7,486	2,314	785	1,199	190	140	Polk
Dunlap	161	65,720	20,053	9,662	7,164	1,424	1,803	Sequatchie
Dyer	135	39,622	10,683	6,171	2,683	1,036	793	Gibson
Dyersburg	1,787	310,154	58,559	21,003	24,181	10,807	2,568	Dyer
Eagleville	15	11,090	3,114	1,877	740	75	421	Rutherford
East Ridge	877	524,901	128,095	60,723	58,399	5,962	3,012	Hamilton
Eastview	0	586	319	0	0	0	319	McNairy
Elizabethton	1,841	249,581	78,327	35,024	34,973	4,381	3,950	Carter
Elkton	3	8,043	1,928	1,075	693	17	143	Giles
Englewood	112	19,517	5,366	3,695	1,008	183	479	McMinn
Enville	1	1,639	466	344	48	1	73	Chester/McNairy
Erin	55	23,898	5,602	1,855	2,006	1,121	620	Houston
Erwin	490	108,072	24,660	12,137	6,333	3,792	2,397	Unicoi
Estill Springs	66	26,695	6,392	4,500	850	132	910	Franklin
Ethridge	0	5,907	1,608	1,125	238	37	208	Lawrence
Etowah	394	61,087	18,287	10,177	5,796	737	1,577	McMinn
Fairview	130	87,293	11,487	7,916	2,066	692	813	Williamson
Farragut	0	9,937	5,037	0	0	0	5,037	Knox
Fayetteville	n.a.	172,371	54,071	21,899	21,752	7,373	3,047	Lincoln
Finger	0	181	79	0	0	0	79	McNairy
Forest Hills	0	339,144	69,502	68,390	594	3	516	Davidson
Franklin	2,226	718,283	112,873	42,462	46,513	18,651	5,247	Williamson
Friendship	21	6,422	2,032	1,061	324	122	525	Crockett

TABLE 15.17--ESTIMATED CURRENT PROPERTY VALUE, ASSESSED VALUE, BY CLASSIFICATION, AND PROPERTY TAXES LEVIED, MUNICIPALITIES, 1987
[In thousands of dollars] (Continued)

Municipality	City property taxes levied	Estimated current property value	Assessed value: Total	Real property: Residential and farm	Real property: Industrial and commercial	Personal property[1]	Public utilities[2]	County
Friendsville	0	1,070	580	0	0	0	580	Blount
Gadsden	0	541	226	0	0	0	226	Crockett
Gallatin	1,643	453,604	139,623	65,265	58,414	11,237	4,707	Sumner
Gallaway	0	9,061	2,591	534	511	1,151	395	Fayette
Garland	0	196	78	0	0	0	78	Tipton
Gates	22	7,017	1,845	1,158	517	41	130	Lauderdale
Gatlinburg	550	499,967	96,188	34,154	59,295	1,023	1,716	Sevier
Germantown	5,139	1,451,588	258,568	217,480	27,522	7,208	6,358	Shelby
Gibson	15	4,829	1,358	824	90	6	439	Gibson
Gilt Edge	0	158	63	0	0	0	63	Tipton
Gleason	68	17,335	3,798	2,256	687	574	282	Weakley
Goodlettsville	226	407,596	133,014	45,667	72,125	10,852	4,369	Davidson/Sumner
Gordonsville	77	38,979	9,686	2,997	3,596	2,704	390	Smith
Grand Junction	32	10,236	2,895	974	839	625	456	Hardeman
Graysville	21	10,938	2,635	2,254	186	7	188	Rhea
Greenback	0	1,003	460	0	0	0	460	Loudon
Greenbrier	99	49,564	10,071	7,007	1,732	170	1,163	Robertson
Greeneville	3,594	428,179	125,802	42,254	59,797	17,808	5,943	Greene
Greenfield	83	31,338	6,804	4,201	1,255	797	551	Weakley
Gruetli-Laager	0	14,058	3,470	2,604	274	0	592	Grundy
Guys	0	431	170	0	0	0	170	McNairy
Halls	110	34,185	9,672	4,386	2,245	1,807	1,234	Lauderdale
Harriman	1,501	126,735	39,474	16,454	13,987	5,057	3,976	Roane
Hartsville	145	43,240	12,958	5,309	4,965	1,220	1,464	Trousdale
Henderson	188	59,154	18,006	9,994	4,895	563	2,554	Chester
Hendersonville	n.a.	976,156	275,918	189,210	70,946	8,454	7,307	Sumner

TABLE 15.17--ESTIMATED CURRENT PROPERTY VALUE, ASSESSED VALUE, BY CLASSIFICATION, AND PROPERTY TAXES LEVIED, MUNICIPALITIES, 1987
[In thousands of dollars] (Continued)

Municipality	City property taxes levied	Estimated current property value	Assessed value: Total	Real property: Residential and farm	Real property: Industrial and commercial	Personal property[1]	Public utilities[2]	County
Henning	16	5,605	1,567	900	321	15	331	Lauderdale
Henry	10	6,262	1,967	519	567	705	175	Henry
Hickory Valley	1	2,065	505	341	128	22	14	Hardeman
Hohenwald	194	53,065	9,704	5,359	2,963	409	974	Lewis
Hollow Rock	11	8,893	2,206	1,615	349	22	219	Carroll
Hornbeak	6	5,523	1,476	841	156	43	436	Obion
Hornsby	7	4,962	1,293	587	184	474	48	Hardeman
Humboldt	1,296	165,653	47,309	20,394	15,719	7,419	3,776	Gibson
Huntingdon	253	90,684	25,786	9,812	9,676	4,793	1,506	Carroll
Huntland	61	17,217	4,271	2,534	1,156	289	292	Franklin
Huntsville	7	9,342	2,582	989	976	108	509	Scott
Jacksboro	0	11,495	3,330	1,820	1,246	25	239	Campbell
Jackson	8,966	1,217,988	341,434	132,225	151,808	40,156	17,245	Madison
Jamestown	103	37,150	12,096	3,545	6,493	746	1,311	Fentress
Jasper	136	91,258	26,128	7,835	5,670	11,224	1,399	Marion
Jefferson City	308	87,882	23,678	8,303	11,871	1,064	2,439	Jefferson
Jellico	79	35,061	10,602	4,632	3,909	753	1,308	Campbell
Johnson City	8,334	1,171,182	344,915	129,394	160,726	30,602	24,192	Carter/Washington
Jonesborough	272	62,367	17,292	8,949	6,429	537	1,376	Washington
Kenton	79	21,248	5,524	3,147	1,280	729	368	Gibson/Obion
Kimball	17	29,528	8,567	3,400	3,896	485	786	Marion
Kingsport	9,545	1,716,200	523,372	116,624	209,679	173,366	23,702	Hawkins/Sullivan
Kingston	252	87,086	25,097	16,405	6,051	637	2,005	Roane
Kingston Springs	63	29,525	4,903	3,679	955	95	174	Cheatham
Knoxville	35,135	4,138,313	1,314,247	453,304	651,375	108,753	100,816	Knox
Lafayette	203	79,924	25,556	10,696	8,451	2,868	3,541	Macon
LaFollette	453	131,881	40,960	14,937	18,882	3,513	3,628	Campbell

TABLE 15.17--ESTIMATED CURRENT PROPERTY VALUE, ASSESSED VALUE, BY CLASSIFICATION, AND PROPERTY TAXES LEVIED, MUNICIPALITIES, 1987
[In thousands of dollars] (Continued)

Municipality	City property taxes levied	Estimated current property value	Assessed value: Total	Real property: Residential and farm	Real property: Industrial and commercial	Personal property[1]	Public utilities[2]	County
LaGrange	9	4,758	1,064	786	77	4	197	Fayette
Lake City	78	29,477	9,017	3,678	4,083	321	936	Anderson
Lakeland	0	52,535	10,524	6,015	3,566	671	271	Shelby
Lakesite	17	17,185	3,491	3,134	284	22	50	Hamilton
Lakewood	0	38,977	8,569	6,911	1,196	249	212	Davidson
LaVergne	0	266,396	80,751	22,640	33,017	22,161	2,933	Rutherford
Lawrenceburg	724	258,025	76,368	30,003	28,008	15,336	3,022	Lawrence
Lebanon	620	363,526	97,974	35,588	46,864	9,743	5,778	Wilson
Lenoir City	1,190	126,052	40,157	13,480	18,341	5,795	2,541	Loudon
Lewisburg	1,446	267,972	58,935	15,130	20,225	21,624	1,957	Marshall
Lexington	507	114,847	32,992	14,512	10,320	6,009	2,150	Henderson
Liberty	4	4,891	1,158	782	166	60	151	DeKalb
Linden	82	22,932	4,810	1,603	2,403	180	624	Perry
Livingston	450	65,898	20,637	8,641	8,417	1,199	2,381	Overton
Lobelville	60	19,615	4,356	1,531	956	66	1,804	Perry
Lookout Mountain	913	113,038	22,752	21,257	670	77	748	Hamilton
Loretto	31	27,808	7,802	4,836	1,981	65	920	Lawrence
Loudon	646	220,419	72,796	13,100	38,516	19,324	1,857	Loudon
Luttrell	0	498	197	0	0	0	197	Union
Lynchburg	39	13,064	3,718	1,753	1,229	155	581	Moore
Lynnville	10	4,690	1,054	765	114	3	172	Giles
McEwen	57	19,490	5,453	3,352	989	302	810	Humphreys
McKenzie	185	73,189	19,774	10,240	6,202	2,079	1,252	Carroll/Henry/Weakley
McLemoresville	11	3,418	829	637	133	0	58	Carroll
McMinnville	1,267	227,158	71,227	26,643	32,915	5,627	6,042	Warren
Madisonville	131	60,783	15,298	6,151	6,034	996	2,117	Monroe
Manchester	1,082	174,634	56,093	23,071	26,810	2,539	3,674	Coffee

TABLE 15.17--ESTIMATED CURRENT PROPERTY VALUE, ASSESSED VALUE, BY CLASSIFICATION, AND PROPERTY TAXES LEVIED, MUNICIPALITIES, 1987
[In thousands of dollars] (Continued)

Municipality	City property taxes levied	Estimated current property value	Assessed value: Total	Real property: Residential and farm	Real property: Industrial and commercial	Personal property[1]	Public utilities[2]	County
Martin	284	126,845	30,306	12,526	11,152	4,501	2,126	Weakley
Maryville	4,285	501,843	151,963	80,136	58,859	6,774	6,194	Blount
Mason	7	6,018	1,399	678	430	66	225	Tipton
Maury City	31	9,615	2,867	1,772	520	117	457	Crockett
Maynardville	0	2,564	1,282	0	0	0	1,282	Union
Medina	54	8,742	2,360	1,497	457	32	374	Gibson
Medon	0	145	69	0	0	0	69	Madison
Memphis	108,505	14,277,209	3,319,872	1,388,472	1,286,230	434,670	210,501	Shelby
Michie	0	476	260	0	0	0	260	McNairy
Middleton	24	12,934	3,625	1,355	947	675	649	Hardeman
Milan	354	137,461	37,775	19,244	11,917	4,744	1,869	Gibson
Milledgeville	0	704	382	0	0	0	382	Chester/Hardin/McNairy
Millersville	11	22,574	6,248	4,570	1,407	186	85	Sumner
Millington	413	146,417	32,582	12,530	13,709	3,196	3,146	Shelby
Minor Hill	0	382	166	0	0	0	166	Giles
Mitchellville	6	2,211	640	425	47	18	150	Sumner
Monterey	116	34,893	10,542	5,441	2,598	1,351	1,151	Putnam
Morrison	2	20,557	5,923	1,424	304	4,068	127	Warren
Morristown	3,322	593,609	193,815	57,802	87,446	35,463	13,105	Hamblen
Moscow	25	8,726	2,232	1,116	560	144	412	Fayette
Mosheim	0	4,597	1,463	522	374	26	542	Greene
Mount Carmel	0	36,427	6,686	4,848	1,010	330	498	Hawkins
Mount Juliet	0	116,352	27,869	18,286	6,439	370	2,774	Wilson
Mount Pleasant	153	79,627	16,909	10,783	4,113	1,234	778	Maury
Mountain City	170	48,046	10,423	4,105	4,085	795	1,439	Johnson
Munford	53	33,530	7,188	4,661	1,524	197	805	Tipton

TABLE 15.17--ESTIMATED CURRENT PROPERTY VALUE, ASSESSED VALUE, BY CLASSIFICATION, AND PROPERTY TAXES LEVIED, MUNICIPALITIES, 1987
[In thousands of dollars] (Continued)

			Assessed value					
				Real property				
Municipality	City property taxes levied	Estimated current property value	Total	Residential and farm	Industrial and commercial	Personal property [1]	Public utilities [2]	County
Murfreesboro	5,844	1,235,261	374,591	143,287	190,913	24,247	16,144	Rutherford
Nashville	183,298	14,627,097	4,036,188	1,221,131	2,206,123	386,014	222,920	Davidson
New Hope	8	11,319	2,779	2,222	36	4	517	Marion
New Johnsonville	73	31,130	8,675	5,270	1,845	427	1,133	Humphreys
New Market	0	18,111	4,561	2,670	362	70	1,460	Jefferson
New Tazewell	0	3,408	1,433	0	0	0	1,433	Claiborne
Newbern	143	34,961	5,881	3,335	1,496	656	394	Dyer
Newport	992	124,495	40,513	15,004	19,382	2,971	3,155	Cocke
Niota	42	14,111	4,287	1,963	1,676	253	395	McMinn
Normandy	1	1,905	533	398	38	0	98	Bedford
Norris	182	27,993	7,465	5,443	939	135	947	Anderson
Oak Hill	0	270,308	55,417	54,477	382	42	516	Davidson
Oak Ridge	3,384	750,168	214,979	110,965	74,926	15,029	14,059	Anderson/Roane
Oakdale	13	4,025	1,390	465	23	2	901	Morgan
Oakland	9	10,389	2,801	827	429	1,433	112	Fayette
Obion	58	18,485	4,686	2,618	814	792	461	Obion
Oliver Springs	229	58,163	16,200	9,959	4,179	469	1,592	Anderson/Morgan/Roane
Oneida	270	76,760	20,698	7,269	8,302	2,954	2,173	Scott
Orlinda	0	217	74	2	0	29	43	Robertson
Orme	0	45	22	0	0	0	22	Marion
Palmer	0	120	56	0	0	0	56	Grundy
Paris	541	199,246	61,596	25,086	25,248	7,766	3,497	Henry
Parker's Crossroads	0	296	151	0	0	0	151	Henderson
Parrottsville	0	22	11	0	0	0	11	Cocke
Parsons	127	42,291	11,014	4,853	3,775	1,195	1,192	Decatur
Pegram	0	721	198	0	0	0	198	Cheatham
Petersburg	21	6,414	1,851	1,232	373	64	183	Lincoln/Marshall

TABLE 15.17--ESTIMATED CURRENT PROPERTY VALUE, ASSESSED VALUE, BY CLASSIFICATION, AND PROPERTY TAXES LEVIED, MUNICIPALITIES, 1987
[In thousands of dollars] (Continued)

			Assessed value					
				Real property				
Municipality	City property taxes levied	Estimated current property value	Total	Residential and farm	Industrial and commercial	Personal property [1]	Public utilities [2]	County
Philadelphia	0	560	226	0	0	0	226	Loudon
Pigeon Forge	208	200,153	41,328	8,759	31,977	77	515	Sevier
Pikeville	57	33,275	11,292	3,695	4,158	880	2,559	Bledsoe
Piperton	0	24,943	6,277	3,200	1,133	1,259	684	Fayette
Pittman Center	38	17,712	2,900	2,063	730	7	99	Sevier
Pleasant Hill	0	5,473	1,035	578	163	8	286	Cumberland
Portland	339	105,787	33,826	13,804	13,008	3,302	3,712	Sumner
Powell's Crossroads	0	454	223	0	0	0	223	Marion
Pulaski	427	150,528	38,154	16,069	17,780	2,414	1,891	Giles
Puryear	14	8,191	2,286	1,689	222	11	365	Henry
Ramer	0	533	230	0	0	0	230	McNairy
Red Bank	646	270,716	67,079	31,524	26,369	3,391	5,795	Hamilton
Red Boiling Springs	59	15,151	4,676	2,441	1,476	202	556	Macon
Ridgely	95	15,731	4,578	2,968	1,137	77	396	Lake
Ridgeside	62	15,500	3,063	2,981	5	9	68	Hamilton
Ridgetop	46	24,067	4,521	3,866	404	33	219	Davidson/Robertson
Ripley	678	89,676	25,957	11,130	11,261	1,576	1,990	Lauderdale
Rives	14	3,074	722	555	31	4	133	Obion
Rockford	0	219	97	0	0	0	97	Blount
Rockwood	367	82,527	25,095	11,759	7,587	2,245	3,504	Roane
Rogersville	804	97,430	22,350	7,102	8,210	4,416	2,621	Hawkins
Rossville	24	7,539	1,994	735	615	452	192	Fayette
Rutherford	77	20,719	5,587	3,373	982	492	740	Gibson
Rutledge	0	16,996	5,562	2,236	1,823	234	1,270	Grainger
St. Joseph	7	11,520	3,131	2,150	560	66	354	Lawrence
Saltillo	0	3,666	954	760	94	14	85	Hardin
Samburg	0	147	68	0	0	0	68	Obion

TABLE 15.17--ESTIMATED CURRENT PROPERTY VALUE, ASSESSED VALUE, BY CLASSIFICATION, AND PROPERTY TAXES LEVIED, MUNICIPALITIES, 1987
[In thousands of dollars] (Continued)

Municipality	City property taxes levied	Estimated current property value	Assessed value: Total	Real property: Residential and farm	Real property: Industrial and commercial	Personal property [1]	Public utilities [2]	County
Sardis	5	4,328	1,191	796	118	25	252	Henderson
Saulsbury	0	1,625	409	231	99	9	70	Hardeman
Savannah	321	127,987	37,529	18,786	12,946	2,434	3,363	Hardin
Scotts Hill	15	10,320	2,841	1,608	571	89	572	Decatur/Henderson
Selmer	213	79,638	25,393	10,066	9,558	2,748	3,021	McNairy
Sevierville	294	171,709	33,557	11,899	18,109	974	2,575	Sevier
Sharon	88	17,057	3,944	1,937	647	936	425	Weakley
Shelbyville	1,475	270,937	85,478	38,915	32,477	4,736	9,350	Bedford
Signal Mountain	1,292	247,529	52,383	42,535	7,144	567	2,138	Hamilton
Silerton	0	674	147	142	2	0	3	Chester/Hardeman
Smithville	181	85,610	22,175	9,650	8,225	3,342	958	DeKalb
Smyrna	594	350,196	106,913	38,984	50,613	8,988	8,328	Rutherford
Sneedville	0	2,098	831	0	0	0	831	Hancock
Soddy Daisy	336	135,425	31,108	18,998	6,723	1,342	4,046	Hamilton
Somerville	74	47,371	13,104	4,849	4,869	1,129	2,257	Fayette
South Carthage	50	21,802	5,915	2,292	2,074	301	1,247	Smith
South Fulton	137	41,558	10,068	6,685	3,121	0	263	Obion
South Pittsburg	158	66,696	19,758	6,746	8,845	2,342	1,824	Marion
Sparta	602	106,923	32,436	11,414	14,149	4,549	2,323	White
Spencer	0	1,105	517	0	0	33	484	Van Buren
Spring City	173	38,702	10,624	6,147	2,398	272	1,807	Rhea
Spring Hill	27	30,250	6,044	4,270	934	304	536	Maury/Williamson
Springfield	952	236,852	54,996	21,770	24,044	6,424	2,757	Robertson
Stanton	13	5,464	1,675	899	432	51	293	Haywood
Stantonville	0	67	36	0	0	0	36	McNairy
Surgoinsville	0	18,581	3,542	2,346	415	411	370	Hawkins

TABLE 15.17--ESTIMATED CURRENT PROPERTY VALUE, ASSESSED VALUE, BY CLASSIFICATION, AND PROPERTY TAXES LEVIED, MUNICIPALITIES, 1987
[In thousands of dollars] (Continued)

			Assessed value					
				Real property				
Municipality	City property taxes levied	Estimated current property value	Total	Residential and farm	Industrial and commercial	Personal property [1]	Public utilities [2]	County
Sweetwater	828	102,659	25,845	9,972	10,543	2,921	2,409	Monroe
Tazewell	0	3,493	1,528	0	0	0	1,528	Claiborne
Tellico Plains	26	13,580	3,529	1,361	1,258	141	768	Monroe
Tennessee Ridge	38	17,029	3,145	2,586	147	19	392	Houston
Tiptonville	92	26,185	8,221	4,149	2,721	186	1,165	Lake
Toone	2	2,663	632	475	92	36	29	Hardeman
Townsend	0	805	443	0	0	0	443	Blount
Trenton	343	86,493	25,259	10,442	10,174	2,426	2,217	Gibson
Trezevant	23	10,731	2,682	1,881	417	115	268	Carroll
Trimble	28	7,900	1,128	750	158	75	145	Dyer/Obion
Troy	64	16,820	4,415	2,292	877	579	667	Obion
Tullahoma	3,204	381,380	116,080	57,901	45,382	8,148	4,649	Coffee/Franklin
Tusculum	0	21,600	4,957	4,665	220	2	71	Greene
Union City	1,324	216,076	57,694	25,926	22,914	5,205	3,649	Obion
Vanleer	2	5,222	892	591	120	0	173	Dickson
Viola	0	136	67	0	0	0	67	Warren
Vonore	0	7,481	1,705	988	333	28	356	Monroe
Walden	112	54,971	11,264	9,928	417	629	290	Hamilton
Wartburg	0	11,698	3,965	1,354	1,967	96	549	Morgan
Wartrace	32	7,831	2,443	1,403	350	6	684	Bedford
Watauga	4	5,148	1,420	1,072	103	165	80	Carter
Waverly	296	80,637	23,614	12,120	7,741	912	2,841	Humphreys
Waynesboro	197	38,159	11,273	5,244	2,724	1,775	1,529	Wayne
Westmoreland	76	29,049	8,883	4,654	2,882	444	904	Sumner
White House	295	78,085	16,606	9,954	4,326	815	1,511	Robertson/Sumner
Whiteville	45	14,375	3,744	2,081	876	374	413	Hardeman
Whitwell	14	23,296	6,395	3,414	1,901	327	754	Marion

TABLE 15.17--ESTIMATED CURRENT PROPERTY VALUE, ASSESSED VALUE, BY CLASSIFICATION, AND PROPERTY TAXES LEVIED, MUNICIPALITIES, 1987
[In thousands of dollars] (Continued)

			Assessed value					
				Real property				
Municipality	City property taxes levied	Estimated current property value	Total	Residential and farm	Industrial and commercial	Personal property[1]	Public utilities[2]	County
Williston	0	4,396	965	831	47	3	84	Fayette
Winchester	697	116,809	29,767	16,009	9,134	2,251	2,373	Franklin
Woodbury	158	46,150	14,644	6,395	6,738	635	877	Cannon
Woodland Mills	0	88	41	0	0	0	41	Obion
Yorkville	0	603	301	0	0	0	301	Gibson

Note: Data for Special School districts are not shown.

1. Includes industrial and commercial, residential, farm, and intangible personal property.

2. Includes utilities assessed by the Public Service Commission as well as those locally assessed.

Source: Tennessee State Board of Equalization, *1987 Tax Aggregate Report*; and State of Tennessee, Report of the Comptroller of the Treasury, Division of Local Finance, *County and Municipal Finances for Fiscal Year Ended June 30, 1987*.

TABLE 15.18--ACTUAL AND EFFECTIVE PROPERTY TAX RATES AND APPRAISAL RATIO, MUNICIPALITIES, 1987

Municipality	Actual tax rates: City tax rate	Actual tax rates: County tax rate in city	Actual tax rates: Total tax rate for city [1]	Appraisal ratio (%)	Equalized tax rate [2]	Effective tax rate by class of property: Commercial and industrial real (40 %)	Residential and farm real (25 %)	Commercial and industrial personal (30 %)	Public utilities (55 %)	Weighted average effective rate	County
Adams	0.75	3.78	4.53	70.88	3.21	1.28	0.80	1.36	1.77	0.97	Robertson
Adamsville	0.82	2.40	3.22	99.21	3.19	1.28	0.80	0.97	1.76	1.04	McNairy
Alamo	1.15	2.35	3.50	100.00	3.50	1.40	0.87	1.05	1.92	1.05	Crockett
Alcoa	1.76	2.43	4.19	100.00	4.19	1.68	1.05	1.26	2.30	1.43	Blount
Alexandria	1.20	2.10	3.30	81.82	2.70	1.08	0.68	0.99	1.49	0.88	DeKalb
Algood	1.08	1.85	2.93	100.00	2.93	1.17	0.73	0.88	1.61	0.90	Putnam
Allardt	0.00	2.45	2.45	94.69	2.32	0.93	0.58	0.73	1.28	0.61	Fentress
Altamont	0.00	3.62	3.62	86.67	3.14	1.25	0.78	1.09	1.73	0.87	Grundy
Ardmore	0.26	2.90	3.16	78.82	2.49	1.00	0.62	0.95	1.37	0.77	Giles
Arlington	1.45	3.78	5.23	66.60	3.48	1.39	0.87	1.57	1.92	1.19	Shelby
Ashland City	1.25	5.33	6.58	60.00	3.95	1.58	0.99	1.97	2.17	1.38	Cheatham
Athens	1.85	2.64	4.49	97.12	4.36	1.74	1.09	1.35	2.40	1.39	McMinn
Atoka	0.15	3.70	3.85	72.81	2.80	1.12	0.70	1.15	1.54	0.78	Tipton
Atwood	0.00	1.55	1.55	89.00	1.38	0.55	0.34	0.46	0.76	0.38	Carroll
Auburntown	0.00	2.65	2.65	100.00	2.65	1.06	0.66	0.79	1.46	0.77	Cannon
Baileyton	0.00	2.35	2.35	89.56	2.10	0.84	0.53	0.70	1.16	1.16	Greene
Baneberry	0.00	2.73	2.73	80.00	2.18	0.87	0.55	0.82	1.20	0.56	Jefferson
Bartlett	2.27	3.78	6.05	66.60	4.03	1.61	1.01	1.81	2.22	1.11	Shelby
Baxter	1.50	1.85	3.35	100.00	3.35	1.34	0.84	1.00	1.84	0.99	Putnam
Beersheba Springs	0.00	3.62	3.62	86.67	3.14	1.25	0.78	1.09	1.73	1.71	Grundy
Bell Buckle	0.51	2.90	3.41	100.00	3.41	1.36	0.85	1.02	1.88	0.94	Bedford
Belle Meade	1.60	2.89	4.49	81.38	3.65	1.46	0.91	1.35	2.01	0.92	Davidson
Bells	1.45	2.35	3.80	100.00	3.80	1.52	0.95	1.14	2.09	1.20	Crockett
Benton	0.80	3.95	4.75	93.33	4.43	1.77	1.11	1.42	2.44	1.45	Polk
Berry Hill	0.00	2.89	2.89	81.38	2.35	0.94	0.59	0.87	1.29	0.87	Davidson
Bethel Springs	0.24	2.40	2.64	99.21	2.62	1.05	0.65	0.79	1.44	0.76	McNairy
Big Sandy	1.05	2.25	3.30	88.72	2.93	1.17	0.73	0.99	1.61	0.87	Benton
Blaine	0.00	2.91	2.91	97.78	2.85	1.14	0.71	0.87	1.56	0.73	Grainger

TABLE 15.18--ACTUAL AND EFFECTIVE PROPERTY TAX RATES AND APPRAISAL RATIO, MUNICIPALITIES, 1987 (Continued)

Municipality	Actual tax rates: City tax rate	Actual tax rates: County tax rate in city	Actual tax rates: Total tax rate for city[1]	Appraisal ratio (%)	Equalized tax rate[2]	Effective tax rate by class of property: Commercial and industrial real (40 %)	Residential and farm real (25 %)	Commercial and industrial personal (30 %)	Public utilities (55 %)	Weighted average effective rate	County
Bluff City	1.10	3.96	5.06	92.05	4.66	1.86	1.16	1.52	2.56	1.43	Sullivan
Bolivar	1.05	2.29	3.34	85.88	2.87	1.15	0.72	1.00	1.58	0.90	Hardeman
Braden	0.00	2.85	2.85	81.94	2.34	0.93	0.58	0.85	1.28	0.65	Fayette
Bradford	0.94	0.92	1.86	90.92	1.69	0.68	0.42	0.56	0.93	0.49	Gibson
Brentwood	1.52	4.29	5.81	45.09	2.62	1.05	0.65	1.74	1.44	0.83	Williamson
Brighton	0.50	3.70	4.20	72.81	3.06	1.22	0.76	1.26	1.68	0.84	Tipton
Bristol	2.99	3.51	6.50	92.05	5.98	2.56	1.60	2.08	3.52	2.04	Sullivan
Brownsville	1.10	2.17	3.27	100.00	3.27	1.31	0.82	0.98	1.80	1.01	Haywood
Bruceton	1.43	1.55	2.98	89.00	2.65	1.06	0.66	0.89	1.46	0.83	Carroll
Bulls Gap	1.50	4.71	6.21	65.10	4.04	1.62	1.01	1.86	2.22	1.25	Hawkins
Burlison	0.00	3.70	3.70	72.81	2.69	1.08	0.67	1.11	1.48	1.48	Tipton
Byrdstown	0.85	2.50	3.35	100.00	2.44	1.34	0.84	1.00	1.84	1.07	Pickett
Calhoun	0.60	2.64	3.24	97.12	3.15	1.26	0.79	0.97	2.73	0.92	McMinn
Camden	0.64	2.25	2.89	88.72	2.56	1.03	0.64	0.87	1.41	0.78	Benton
Carthage	1.95	2.93	4.88	80.00	3.90	1.56	0.98	1.46	2.15	1.26	Smith
Caryville	0.00	2.99	2.99	94.99	2.84	1.14	0.71	0.90	1.56	0.89	Campbell
Cedar Hill	0.51	3.78	4.29	70.88	3.04	1.22	0.76	1.29	1.67	0.89	Robertson
Celina	1.44	3.56	5.00	94.67	4.73	1.89	1.18	1.50	2.60	1.48	Clay
Centertown	0.00	1.98	1.98	96.00	1.90	0.76	0.48	0.59	1.05	0.62	Warren
Centerville	0.80	2.55	3.35	90.48	3.03	1.21	0.76	1.00	1.67	0.96	Hickman
Chapel Hill	1.00	3.86	4.86	58.72	2.85	1.14	0.71	1.46	1.57	0.87	Marshall
Charleston	0.50	2.70	3.20	98.09	3.14	1.26	0.78	0.96	1.73	1.01	Bradley
Charlotte	0.40	3.06	3.46	57.36	1.98	0.79	0.50	1.04	1.09	0.61	Dickson
Chattanooga	3.51	3.26	6.77	78.13	5.29	2.12	1.32	2.03	2.91	1.89	Hamilton
Church Hill	0.55	4.71	5.26	65.10	3.42	1.37	0.86	1.58	1.88	1.04	Hawkins
Clarksburg	0.00	1.55	1.55	89.00	1.38	0.55	0.34	0.46	0.76	0.38	Carroll
Clarksville	1.60	3.68	5.28	67.86	3.58	1.43	0.90	1.58	1.97	1.11	Montgomery
Cleveland	1.08	2.70	3.78	98.09	3.71	1.48	0.93	1.13	2.04	1.19	Bradley
Clifton	1.85	2.72	4.57	94.87	4.34	1.73	1.08	1.37	2.38	1.27	Wayne

TABLE 15.18--ACTUAL AND EFFECTIVE PROPERTY TAX RATES AND APPRAISAL RATIO, MUNICIPALITIES, 1987 (Continued)

	Actual tax rates					Effective tax rate by class of property					
Municipality	City tax rate	County tax rate in city	Total tax rate for city [1]	Appraisal ratio (%)	Equalized tax rate [2]	Commercial and industrial real (40 %)	Residential and farm real (25 %)	Commercial and industrial personal (30 %)	Public utilities (55 %)	Weighted average effective rate	County
Clinton	0.84	2.98	3.82	94.62	3.61	1.45	0.90	1.15	1.99	1.11	Anderson
Coalmont	0.00	3.62	3.62	86.67	3.14	1.25	0.78	1.09	1.73	1.72	Grundy
Collegedale	1.65	3.26	4.91	78.13	3.84	1.53	0.96	1.47	2.11	1.26	Hamilton
Collierville	2.27	3.78	6.05	66.60	4.03	1.61	1.01	1.81	2.22	1.21	Shelby
Collinwood	1.70	2.72	4.42	94.87	4.19	1.68	1.05	1.33	2.31	1.36	Wayne
Columbia	0.91	2.35	3.26	73.01	2.38	0.95	0.60	0.98	1.31	0.75	Maury
Cookeville	0.75	1.85	2.60	100.00	2.60	1.04	0.65	0.78	1.43	0.83	Putnam
Copperhill	1.25	3.95	5.20	93.33	4.85	1.94	1.21	1.56	2.67	1.81	Polk
Cornersville	1.75	3.86	5.61	58.72	3.29	1.32	0.82	1.68	1.81	0.97	Marshall
Cottage Grove	0.30	2.94	3.24	98.33	3.19	1.27	0.80	0.97	1.75	1.08	Henry
Covington	2.00	3.70	5.70	72.81	4.15	1.66	1.04	1.71	2.28	1.38	Tipton
Cowan	1.75	2.23	3.98	83.53	3.32	1.33	0.83	1.19	1.83	0.94	Franklin
Crab Orchard	0.00	2.93	2.93	59.54	1.74	0.70	0.44	0.88	0.96	0.55	Cumberland
Cross Plains	0.00	3.78	3.78	70.88	2.68	1.07	0.67	1.13	1.47	0.76	Robertson
Crossville	1.55	2.93	4.48	59.54	2.67	1.07	0.67	1.34	1.47	1.00	Cumberland
Cumberland City	1.00	1.59	2.59	87.33	2.26	0.90	0.57	0.78	1.24	0.73	Stewart
Cumberland Gap	0.22	2.54	2.76	80.22	2.21	0.89	0.55	0.83	1.22	0.76	Claiborne
Dandridge	1.00	2.73	3.73	80.00	2.98	1.19	0.75	1.12	1.64	0.96	Jefferson
Dayton	0.50	3.18	3.68	91.43	3.36	1.35	0.84	1.10	1.85	1.11	Rhea
Decatur	1.25	4.30	5.55	50.94	2.83	1.13	0.71	1.66	1.55	0.98	Meigs
Decaturville	1.80	2.32	4.12	81.14	3.34	1.34	0.84	1.24	1.84	1.04	Decatur
Decherd	1.50	2.23	3.73	83.53	3.12	1.25	0.78	1.12	1.71	0.99	Franklin
Dickson	1.90	3.06	4.96	57.36	2.85	1.14	0.71	1.49	1.56	0.97	Dickson
Dover	0.85	1.59	2.44	87.33	2.13	0.85	0.53	0.73	1.17	0.67	Stewart
Dowelltown	0.00	2.10	2.10	81.82	1.72	0.69	0.43	0.63	0.95	0.50	DeKalb
Doyle	0.00	2.99	2.99	93.20	2.79	1.11	0.70	0.90	1.53	0.87	White
Dresden	1.75	2.96	4.71	73.33	3.45	1.38	0.86	1.41	1.90	1.21	Weakley
Ducktown	0.90	3.95	4.85	93.33	4.53	1.81	1.13	1.45	2.49	1.50	Polk

TABLE 15.18--ACTUAL AND EFFECTIVE PROPERTY TAX RATES AND APPRAISAL RATIO, MUNICIPALITIES, 1987 (Continued)

	Actual tax rates					Effective tax rate by class of property					
Municipality	City tax rate	County tax rate in city	Total tax rate for city[1]	Appraisal ratio (%)	Equalized tax rate[2]	Commercial and industrial real (40 %)	Residential and farm real (25 %)	Commercial and industrial personal (30 %)	Public utilities (55 %)	Weighted average effective rate	County
Dunlap	0.89	2.33	3.22	98.55	3.17	1.27	0.79	0.97	1.75	0.98	Sequatchie
Dyer	1.32	0.92	2.24	90.92	2.04	0.81	0.51	0.67	1.12	0.60	Gibson
Dyersburg	2.50	2.80	5.30	47.72	2.53	1.16	0.72	1.59	1.59	1.00	Dyer
Eagleville	0.65	2.20	2.85	93.63	2.67	1.07	0.67	0.85	1.45	0.80	Rutherford
East Ridge	0.70	3.26	3.96	78.13	3.09	1.24	0.77	1.19	1.70	0.97	Hamilton
Eastview	0.00	2.40	2.40	99.21	2.38	0.95	0.60	0.72	1.31	1.31	McNairy
Elizabethton	2.48	2.85	5.33	100.00	5.33	2.13	1.33	1.60	2.93	1.67	Carter
Elkton	0.18	2.90	3.08	78.82	2.43	0.97	0.61	0.92	1.34	0.74	Giles
Englewood	2.18	2.64	4.82	97.12	4.68	1.87	1.17	1.45	2.57	1.33	McMinn
Enville	0.00	2.24	2.24	99.57	2.23	0.89	0.56	0.67	1.23	0.64	Chester/McNairy
Erin	1.00	3.68	4.68	67.52	3.16	1.26	0.79	1.40	1.74	1.10	Houston
Erwin	1.85	3.94	5.79	73.52	4.26	1.70	1.06	1.74	2.34	1.32	Unicoi
Estill Springs	1.04	2.23	3.27	83.53	2.73	1.09	0.68	0.98	1.50	0.78	Franklin
Ethridge	0.00	3.21	3.21	94.67	3.04	1.22	0.76	0.96	1.67	0.87	Lawrence
Etowah	2.00	2.64	4.64	97.12	4.51	1.86	1.16	1.39	2.55	1.39	McMinn
Fairview	1.35	4.29	5.64	45.09	2.54	1.02	0.64	1.69	1.40	0.74	Williamson
Farragut	0.00	2.76	2.76	96.39	2.66	1.06	0.67	0.83	1.46	1.40	Knox
Fayetteville	1.75	2.06	3.81	100.00	3.81	1.52	0.95	1.14	2.10	1.20	Lincoln
Finger	0.00	2.40	2.40	99.21	2.38	0.95	0.60	0.72	1.31	1.04	McNairy
Forest Hills	0.00	2.89	2.89	81.38	2.35	0.94	0.59	0.87	1.29	0.59	Davidson
Franklin	2.15	4.09	6.24	45.09	2.81	1.13	0.70	1.87	1.55	0.98	Williamson
Friendship	1.05	2.35	3.40	100.00	3.40	1.36	0.85	1.02	1.87	1.08	Crockett
Friendsville	0.00	2.43	2.43	100.00	2.43	0.97	0.61	0.73	1.34	1.32	Blount
Gadsden	0.00	2.35	2.35	100.00	2.35	0.94	0.59	0.70	1.29	0.98	Crockett
Gallatin	1.22	2.55	3.77	100.00	3.77	1.51	0.94	1.13	2.07	1.16	Sumner
Gallaway	0.00	2.85	2.85	81.94	2.34	0.93	0.58	0.85	1.28	0.81	Fayette
Garland	0.00	3.70	3.70	72.81	2.69	1.08	0.67	1.11	1.48	1.48	Tipton
Gates	1.45	2.07	3.52	90.89	3.20	1.28	0.80	1.06	1.76	0.93	Lauderdale

TABLE 15.18--ACTUAL AND EFFECTIVE PROPERTY TAX RATES AND APPRAISAL RATIO, MUNICIPALITIES, 1987 (Continued)

	Actual tax rates					Effective tax rate by class of property					
Municipality	City tax rate	County tax rate in city	Total tax rate for city[1]	Appraisal ratio (%)	Equalized tax rate[2]	Commercial and industrial real (40 %)	Residential and farm real (25 %)	Commercial and industrial personal (30 %)	Public utilities (55 %)	Weighted average effective rate	County
Gatlinburg	0.58	2.20	2.78	58.00	1.61	0.64	0.40	0.83	0.89	0.53	Sevier
Germantown	2.16	3.78	5.94	66.60	3.96	1.58	0.99	1.78	2.18	1.06	Shelby
Gibson	1.07	0.92	1.99	90.92	1.81	0.72	0.45	0.60	1.00	0.56	Gibson
Gilt Edge	0.00	3.70	3.70	72.81	2.69	1.08	0.67	1.11	1.48	1.48	Tipton
Gleason	2.10	2.96	5.06	73.33	3.71	1.48	0.93	1.52	2.04	1.11	Weakley
Goodlettsville	0.22	2.89	3.11	81.38	2.53	1.24	0.78	0.93	1.71	1.06	Davidson
Gordonsville	0.91	2.93	3.84	80.00	3.07	1.23	0.77	1.15	1.69	0.95	Smith
Grand Junction	1.00	2.29	3.29	85.88	2.83	1.13	0.71	0.99	1.55	0.93	Hardeman
Graysville	0.74	3.18	3.92	91.43	3.58	1.43	0.90	1.18	1.97	0.94	Rhea
Greenback	0.00	2.80	2.80	98.00	2.74	1.10	0.69	0.84	1.51	1.28	Loudon
Greenbrier	1.10	3.78	4.88	70.88	3.46	1.38	0.86	1.46	1.90	0.99	Robertson
Greeneville	2.90	1.95	4.85	89.56	4.34	1.74	1.09	1.45	2.39	1.42	Greene
Greenfield	1.25	2.96	4.21	73.33	3.09	1.23	0.77	1.26	1.70	0.91	Weakley
Gruetli-Laager	0.00	3.62	3.62	86.67	3.14	1.25	0.78	1.09	1.73	0.89	Grundy
Guys	0.00	2.40	2.40	99.21	2.38	0.95	0.60	0.72	1.31	0.95	McNairy
Halls	1.16	2.07	3.23	90.89	2.94	1.17	0.73	0.97	1.61	0.91	Lauderdale
Harriman	2.87	2.55	5.42	99.39	5.39	2.15	1.35	1.63	2.96	1.69	Roane
Hartsville	1.10	4.14	5.24	92.77	4.86	1.94	1.22	1.57	2.67	1.57	Trousdale
Henderson	1.07	2.24	3.31	99.57	3.30	1.32	0.82	0.99	1.81	1.01	Chester
Hendersonville	0.67	2.55	3.22	100.00	3.22	1.29	0.80	0.97	1.77	0.91	Sumner
Henning	1.30	2.07	3.37	90.89	3.06	1.23	0.77	1.01	1.68	0.94	Lauderdale
Henry	0.57	2.94	3.51	98.33	3.45	1.38	0.86	1.05	1.90	1.10	Henry
Hickory Valley	0.25	2.29	2.54	85.88	2.18	0.87	0.55	0.76	1.20	0.62	Hardeman
Hohenwald	2.00	3.60	5.60	60.12	3.37	1.33	0.83	1.68	1.83	1.02	Lewis
Hollow Rock	0.60	1.55	2.15	89.00	1.91	0.77	0.48	0.64	1.05	0.53	Carroll
Hornbeak	0.40	3.18	3.58	84.55	3.03	1.21	0.76	1.07	1.66	0.96	Obion
Hornsby	0.50	2.29	2.79	85.88	2.40	0.96	0.60	0.84	1.32	0.73	Hardeman
Humboldt	2.65	0.92	3.57	90.92	3.25	1.30	0.81	1.07	1.79	1.02	Gibson
Huntingdon	1.35	1.55	2.90	89.00	2.58	1.03	0.65	0.87	1.42	0.82	Carroll

TABLE 15.18--ACTUAL AND EFFECTIVE PROPERTY TAX RATES AND APPRAISAL RATIO, MUNICIPALITIES, 1987 (Continued)

Municipality	Actual tax rates: City tax rate	Actual tax rates: County tax rate in city	Actual tax rates: Total tax rate for city[1]	Appraisal ratio (%)	Equalized tax rate[2]	Effective tax rate by class of property: Commercial and industrial real (40 %)	Residential and farm real (25 %)	Commercial and industrial personal (30 %)	Public utilities (55 %)	Weighted average effective rate	County
Huntland	1.40	2.23	3.63	83.53	3.03	1.21	0.76	1.09	1.67	0.90	Franklin
Huntsville	0.30	3.90	4.20	81.51	3.42	1.37	0.86	1.26	1.88	1.16	Scott
Jacksboro	0.00	2.99	2.99	94.99	2.84	1.14	0.71	0.90	1.56	0.87	Campbell
Jackson	2.75	2.47	5.22	86.96	4.54	1.82	1.13	1.57	2.50	1.46	Madison
Jamestown	0.95	2.45	3.40	94.69	3.22	1.29	0.80	1.02	1.77	1.11	Fentress
Jasper	0.54	2.15	2.69	89.30	2.40	0.96	0.60	0.81	1.32	0.77	Marion
Jefferson City	1.32	2.73	4.05	80.00	3.24	1.30	0.81	1.21	1.78	1.09	Jefferson
Jellico	0.74	2.99	3.73	94.99	3.54	1.42	0.89	1.12	1.95	1.13	Campbell
Johnson City	2.43	2.58	5.01	90.11	4.51	1.81	1.13	1.50	2.48	1.47	Washington
Jonesborough	1.54	2.58	4.12	90.11	3.71	1.49	0.93	1.24	2.04	1.14	Washington
Kenton	1.40	0.92	2.32	90.92	2.11	0.84	0.53	0.70	1.16	0.59	Gibson/Obion
Kimball	0.25	2.15	2.40	89.30	2.14	0.86	0.54	0.72	1.18	0.70	Marion
Kingsport	2.00	3.51	5.51	92.05	5.07	2.03	1.27	1.65	2.79	1.69	Sullivan
Kingston	1.25	2.71	3.96	99.39	3.94	1.57	0.98	1.19	2.16	1.14	Roane
Kingston Springs	1.45	5.33	6.78	60.00	4.07	1.63	1.02	2.03	2.24	1.13	Cheatham
Knoxville	3.40	2.76	6.16	96.39	5.94	2.38	1.48	1.85	3.27	1.96	Knox
Lafayette	1.00	2.58	3.58	100.00	3.58	1.43	0.89	1.07	1.97	1.14	Macon
LaFollette	1.12	2.99	4.11	94.99	3.90	1.56	0.98	1.23	2.15	1.28	Campbell
LaGrange	0.90	2.85	3.75	81.94	3.07	1.23	0.77	1.12	1.69	0.84	Fayette
Lake City	1.10	2.99	4.09	94.62	3.87	1.55	0.97	1.23	2.13	1.25	Anderson
Lakeland	0.00	3.78	3.78	66.60	2.52	1.01	0.63	1.13	1.38	0.76	Shelby
Lakesite	0.50	3.26	3.76	78.13	2.94	1.18	0.73	1.13	1.62	0.76	Hamilton
Lakewood	0.00	2.89	2.89	81.38	2.35	0.94	0.59	0.87	1.29	0.64	Davidson
LaVergne	0.00	2.20	2.20	93.63	2.06	0.82	0.51	0.66	1.13	0.67	Rutherford
Lawrenceburg	1.17	3.21	4.38	94.67	4.15	1.66	1.04	1.31	2.28	1.30	Lawrence
Lebanon	0.65	2.83	3.48	81.67	2.84	1.14	0.71	1.04	1.56	0.94	Wilson
Lenoir City	1.03	2.55	3.58	98.00	3.51	1.40	0.88	1.07	1.93	1.14	Loudon
Lewisburg	2.70	3.86	6.56	58.72	3.85	1.54	0.96	1.97	2.12	1.44	Marshall

TABLE 15.18--ACTUAL AND EFFECTIVE PROPERTY TAX RATES AND APPRAISAL RATIO, MUNICIPALITIES, 1987 (Continued)

	Actual tax rates					Effective tax rate by class of property					
Municipality	City tax rate	County tax rate in city	Total tax rate for city[1]	Appraisal ratio (%)	Equalized tax rate[2]	Commercial and industrial real (40 %)	Residential and farm real (25 %)	Commercial and industrial personal (30 %)	Public utilities (55 %)	Weighted average effective rate	County
Lexington	1.25	2.33	3.58	92.78	3.32	1.33	0.83	1.07	1.83	1.03	Henderson
Liberty	0.25	2.10	2.35	81.82	1.92	0.77	0.48	0.70	1.06	0.56	DeKalb
Linden	1.30	3.91	5.21	60.83	4.26	1.27	0.79	1.56	1.74	1.09	Perry
Livingston	2.20	3.51	5.71	96.96	3.47	2.21	1.38	1.71	3.05	1.79	Overton
Lobelville	1.50	3.91	5.41	60.83	5.25	1.32	0.82	1.62	1.81	1.20	Perry
Lookout Mountain	3.90	3.26	7.16	78.13	5.59	2.24	1.40	2.15	3.08	1.44	Hamilton
Loretto	0.40	3.21	3.61	94.67	3.42	1.37	0.85	1.08	1.88	1.01	Lawrence
Loudon	0.89	2.80	3.69	98.00	3.62	1.45	0.90	1.11	1.99	1.22	Loudon
Luttrell	0.00	2.52	2.52	91.37	2.30	0.92	0.58	0.76	1.27	1.00	Union
Lynchburg	1.15	2.43	3.58	88.84	3.18	1.27	0.80	1.07	1.75	1.02	Moore
Lynnville	1.00	2.90	3.90	78.82	3.07	1.23	0.77	1.17	1.69	0.88	Giles
McEwen	1.06	2.84	3.90	94.40	3.68	1.47	0.92	1.17	2.02	1.09	Humphreys
McKenzie	1.00	1.55	2.55	89.00	2.27	0.91	0.57	0.76	1.25	0.68	Carroll
McLemoresville	1.25	1.55	2.80	89.00	2.49	1.00	0.62	0.84	1.37	0.68	Carroll
McMinnville	1.88	1.98	3.86	96.00	3.71	1.48	0.93	1.16	2.04	1.21	Warren
Madisonville	0.85	3.00	3.85	76.26	2.94	1.17	0.73	1.15	1.61	0.97	Monroe
Manchester	2.15	2.38	4.53	100.00	4.53	1.81	1.13	1.36	2.49	1.46	Coffee
Martin	1.00	2.96	3.96	73.33	2.90	1.16	0.73	1.19	1.60	0.95	Weakley
Maryville	2.01	2.43	4.44	100.00	4.44	1.78	1.11	1.33	2.44	1.34	Blount
Mason	0.75	3.70	4.45	72.81	3.24	1.30	0.81	1.33	1.78	1.03	Tipton
Maury City	1.00	2.35	3.35	100.00	3.35	1.34	0.84	1.00	1.84	1.00	Crockett
Maynardville	0.00	2.52	2.52	91.37	2.30	0.92	0.58	0.76	1.27	1.26	Union
Medina	2.00	0.92	2.92	90.92	2.65	1.06	0.66	0.88	1.46	0.79	Gibson
Medon	0.00	2.47	2.47	89.96	2.22	0.86	0.54	0.74	1.18	1.17	Madison
Memphis	3.31	3.78	7.09	66.60	4.72	2.05	1.28	2.13	2.82	1.65	Shelby
Michie	0.00	2.40	2.40	99.21	2.38	0.95	0.60	0.72	1.31	1.31	McNairy
Middleton	0.65	2.29	2.94	85.88	2.52	1.01	0.63	0.88	1.39	0.82	Hardeman
Milan	0.96	0.92	1.88	90.92	1.71	0.68	0.43	0.56	0.94	0.52	Gibson

TABLE 15.18--ACTUAL AND EFFECTIVE PROPERTY TAX RATES AND APPRAISAL RATIO, MUNICIPALITIES, 1987 (Continued)

	Actual tax rates					Effective tax rate by class of property					
Municipality	City tax rate	County tax rate in city	Total tax rate for city [1]	Appraisal ratio (%)	Equalized tax rate [2]	Commercial and industrial real (40 %)	Residential and farm real (25 %)	Commercial and industrial personal (30 %)	Public utilities (55 %)	Weighted average effective rate	County
Milledgeville	0.00	2.24	2.24	99.57	2.23	0.89	0.56	0.67	1.23	1.22	Chester/Hardin/McNairy
Millersville	0.29	2.55	2.84	100.00	2.84	1.14	0.71	0.85	1.56	0.79	Sumner
Millington	1.50	3.78	5.28	66.60	3.52	1.41	0.88	1.58	1.93	1.17	Shelby
Minor Hill	0.00	2.90	2.90	78.82	2.29	0.91	0.57	0.87	1.26	1.26	Giles
Mitchellville	0.97	2.55	3.52	100.00	3.52	1.41	0.88	1.06	1.94	1.02	Sumner
Monterey	1.00	1.85	2.85	100.00	2.85	1.14	0.71	0.85	1.57	0.86	Putnam
Morrison	0.13	1.98	2.11	96.00	2.03	0.81	0.51	0.63	1.11	0.61	Warren
Morristown	1.41	2.40	3.81	96.40	3.67	1.52	0.95	1.14	2.10	1.24	Hamblen
Moscow	1.05	2.85	3.90	81.94	3.20	1.28	0.80	1.17	1.76	1.00	Fayette
Mosheim	0.00	2.35	2.35	89.56	2.10	0.84	0.53	0.70	1.16	0.75	Greene
Mount Carmel	0.00	4.71	4.71	65.10	3.07	1.23	0.77	1.41	1.69	0.86	Hawkins
Mount Juliet	0.00	2.83	2.83	81.67	2.31	0.93	0.58	0.85	1.28	0.68	Wilson
Mount Pleasant	1.08	2.35	3.43	73.01	2.50	1.00	0.63	1.03	1.38	0.73	Maury
Mountain City	1.97	5.20	7.17	62.92	4.51	1.85	1.16	2.15	2.55	1.56	Johnson
Munford	0.85	3.70	4.55	72.81	3.31	1.33	0.83	1.36	1.82	0.98	Tipton
Murfreesboro	1.75	2.20	3.95	93.63	3.70	1.48	0.92	1.18	2.03	1.20	Rutherford
Nashville	1.03	2.89	3.92	81.38	3.19	1.28	0.80	1.18	1.75	1.08	Davidson
New Hope	0.30	2.15	2.45	89.30	2.19	0.88	0.55	0.73	1.20	0.60	Marion
New Johnsonville	1.00	2.84	3.84	94.40	3.62	1.45	0.91	1.15	1.99	1.07	Humphreys
New Market	0.00	2.73	2.73	80.00	2.18	0.87	0.55	0.82	1.20	0.69	Jefferson
New Tazewell	0.00	2.54	2.54	80.22	2.04	0.82	0.51	0.76	1.12	1.07	Claiborne
Newbern	2.50	2.80	5.30	47.72	2.53	1.16	0.72	1.59	1.59	0.89	Dyer
Newport	2.22	2.95	5.17	100.00	5.17	2.07	1.29	1.55	2.84	1.68	Cocke
Niota	1.05	2.64	3.69	97.12	3.58	1.43	0.90	1.11	1.97	1.12	McMinn
Normandy	0.27	2.90	3.17	100.00	3.17	1.27	0.79	0.95	1.74	0.89	Bedford
Norris	2.55	2.99	5.54	94.62	5.24	2.08	1.30	1.66	2.86	1.48	Anderson
Oak Hill	0.00	2.89	2.89	81.38	2.35	0.94	0.59	0.87	1.29	0.59	Davidson
Oak Ridge	1.67	2.64	4.31	94.62	4.08	1.62	1.01	1.29	2.22	1.24	Anderson
Oakdale	1.25	5.65	6.90	100.00	6.90	2.76	1.72	2.07	3.79	2.38	Morgan

TABLE 15.18--ACTUAL AND EFFECTIVE PROPERTY TAX RATES AND APPRAISAL RATIO, MUNICIPALITIES, 1987 (Continued)

Municipality	Actual tax rates: City tax rate	Actual tax rates: County tax rate in city	Actual tax rates: Total tax rate for city[1]	Appraisal ratio (%)	Equalized tax rate[2]	Effective tax rate by class of property: Commercial and industrial real (40 %)	Effective tax rate by class of property: Residential and farm real (25 %)	Effective tax rate by class of property: Commercial and industrial personal (30 %)	Effective tax rate by class of property: Public utilities (55 %)	Weighted average effective rate	County
Oakland	0.43	2.85	3.28	81.94	2.69	1.08	0.67	0.98	1.48	0.88	Fayette
Obion	1.25	3.18	4.43	84.55	3.75	1.50	0.94	1.33	2.06	1.12	Obion
Oliver Springs	1.31	2.99	4.30	94.62	4.07	1.63	1.02	1.29	2.24	1.17	Anderson/Morgan/Roane
Oneida	1.25	3.90	5.15	81.51	4.20	1.68	1.05	1.54	2.31	1.39	Scott
Orlinda	0.00	3.78	3.78	70.88	2.68	1.07	0.67	1.13	1.47	1.28	Robertson
Orme	0.00	2.15	2.15	89.30	1.92	0.77	0.48	0.64	1.06	1.05	Marion
Palmer	0.00	3.62	3.62	86.67	3.14	1.25	0.78	1.09	1.73	1.69	Grundy
Paris	0.70	2.94	3.64	98.33	3.58	1.43	0.89	1.09	1.97	1.13	Henry
Parker's Crossroads	0.00	2.33	2.33	92.78	2.16	0.86	0.54	0.70	1.19	1.19	Henderson
Parrottsville	0.00	2.95	2.95	100.00	2.95	1.18	0.74	0.88	1.62	1.55	Cocke
Parsons	1.25	2.32	3.57	81.14	2.90	1.16	0.72	1.07	1.59	0.93	Decatur
Pegram	0.00	5.33	5.33	60.00	3.20	1.28	0.80	1.60	1.76	1.46	Cheatham
Petersburg	1.18	2.06	3.24	100.00	3.24	1.30	0.81	0.97	1.78	0.91	Lincoln/Marshall
Philadelphia	0.00	2.80	2.80	98.00	2.74	1.10	0.69	0.84	1.51	1.13	Loudon
Pigeon Forge	0.55	2.20	2.75	58.00	1.60	0.64	0.40	0.82	0.88	0.57	Sevier
Pikeville	0.70	2.32	3.02	98.73	2.98	1.19	0.75	0.91	1.64	1.02	Bledsoe
Piperton	0.00	2.85	2.85	81.94	2.34	0.93	0.58	0.85	1.28	0.72	Fayette
Pittman Center	1.00	2.20	3.20	58.00	1.86	0.74	0.46	0.96	1.02	0.52	Sevier
Pleasant Hill	0.00	2.93	2.93	59.54	1.74	0.70	0.44	0.88	0.96	0.55	Cumberland
Portland	1.15	2.55	3.70	100.00	3.70	1.48	0.92	1.11	2.03	1.18	Sumner
Powell's Crossroads	0.00	2.15	2.15	89.30	1.92	0.77	0.48	0.64	1.06	1.05	Marion
Pulaski	1.20	2.90	4.10	78.82	3.23	1.29	0.81	1.23	1.78	1.04	Giles
Puryear	0.67	2.94	3.61	98.33	3.55	1.42	0.89	1.08	1.95	1.01	Henry
Ramer	0.00	2.40	2.40	99.21	2.38	0.95	0.60	0.72	1.31	1.04	McNairy
Red Bank	0.95	3.26	4.21	78.13	3.29	1.32	0.82	1.26	1.81	1.04	Hamilton
Red Boiling Springs	1.43	2.58	4.01	100.00	4.01	1.60	1.00	1.20	2.21	1.24	Macon
Ridgely	2.00	2.65	4.65	100.00	4.65	1.86	1.16	1.39	2.56	1.35	Lake
Ridgeside	3.50	3.26	6.76	78.13	5.28	2.11	1.32	2.03	2.90	1.34	Hamilton

TABLE 15.18--ACTUAL AND EFFECTIVE PROPERTY TAX RATES AND APPRAISAL RATIO, MUNICIPALITIES, 1987 (Continued)

Municipality	Actual tax rates: City tax rate	County tax rate in city	Total tax rate for city[1]	Appraisal ratio (%)	Equalized tax rate[2]	Effective tax rate by class of property: Commercial and industrial real (40 %)	Residential and farm real (25 %)	Commercial and industrial personal (30 %)	Public utilities (55 %)	Weighted average effective rate	County
Ridgetop	1.00	2.89	3.89	81.38	3.17	1.27	0.79	1.17	1.74	0.95	Davidson/Robertson
Ripley	2.00	2.07	4.07	90.89	3.70	1.48	0.92	1.22	2.03	1.18	Lauderdale
Rives	2.00	3.18	5.18	84.55	4.38	1.75	1.09	1.55	2.41	1.22	Obion
Rockford	0.00	2.43	2.43	100.00	2.43	0.97	0.61	0.73	1.34	1.08	Blount
Rockwood	1.40	2.71	4.11	99.39	4.08	1.63	1.02	1.23	2.25	1.25	Roane
Rogersville	2.25	4.71	6.96	65.10	4.53	1.81	1.13	2.09	2.49	1.60	Hawkins
Rossville	1.03	2.85	3.88	81.94	3.18	1.27	0.79	1.16	1.75	1.03	Fayette
Rutherford	1.42	0.92	2.34	90.92	2.13	0.85	0.53	0.70	1.17	0.63	Gibson
Rutledge	0.00	2.91	2.91	97.78	2.85	1.14	0.71	0.87	1.56	0.95	Grainger
St. Joseph	0.22	3.21	3.43	94.67	3.25	1.30	0.81	1.03	1.79	0.93	Lawrence
Saltillo	0.00	2.09	2.09	94.86	1.98	0.79	0.50	0.63	1.09	0.54	Hardin
Samburg	0.00	3.18	3.18	84.55	2.69	1.08	0.67	0.95	1.48	1.47	Obion
Sardis	0.37	2.33	2.70	92.78	2.51	1.00	0.63	0.81	1.38	0.74	Henderson
Saulsbury	0.00	2.29	2.29	85.88	1.97	0.79	0.49	0.69	1.08	0.58	Hardeman
Savannah	0.90	2.09	2.99	94.86	2.84	1.13	0.71	0.90	1.56	0.88	Hardin
Scotts Hill	0.52	2.32	2.84	81.14	2.30	0.92	0.58	0.85	1.27	0.64	Decatur/Henderson
Selmer	0.90	2.40	3.30	99.21	3.27	1.31	0.82	0.99	1.80	1.05	McNairy
Sevierville	1.08	2.20	3.28	58.00	1.90	0.76	0.48	0.98	1.05	0.64	Sevier
Sharon	2.39	2.96	5.35	73.33	3.92	1.57	0.98	1.60	2.16	1.24	Weakley
Shelbyville	1.95	2.90	4.85	100.00	4.85	1.94	1.21	1.45	2.67	1.53	Bedford
Signal Mountain	2.50	3.26	5.76	78.13	4.50	1.80	1.13	1.73	2.48	1.22	Hamilton
Silerton	0.00	2.24	2.24	99.57	2.23	0.89	0.56	0.67	1.23	1.23	Chester/Hardeman
Smithville	0.85	2.10	2.95	81.82	2.41	0.97	0.60	0.88	1.33	0.76	DeKalb
Smyrna	0.62	2.20	2.82	93.63	2.64	1.06	0.66	0.85	1.45	0.86	Rutherford
Sneedville	0.00	1.92	1.92	72.03	1.38	0.55	0.35	0.58	0.76	0.76	Hancock
Soddy-Daisy	1.00	3.26	4.26	78.13	3.33	1.33	0.83	1.28	1.83	0.98	Hamilton
Somerville	0.58	2.85	3.43	81.94	2.81	1.12	0.70	1.03	1.55	0.95	Fayette
South Carthage	1.10	2.93	4.03	80.00	3.22	1.29	0.81	1.21	1.77	1.09	Smith

TABLE 15.18--ACTUAL AND EFFECTIVE PROPERTY TAX RATES AND APPRAISAL RATIO, MUNICIPALITIES, 1987 (Continued)

Municipality	Actual tax rates: City tax rate	Actual tax rates: County tax rate in city	Actual tax rates: Total tax rate for city[1]	Appraisal ratio (%)	Equalized tax rate[2]	Effective tax rate by class of property: Commercial and industrial real (40 %)	Effective tax rate by class of property: Residential and farm real (25 %)	Effective tax rate by class of property: Commercial and industrial personal (30 %)	Effective tax rate by class of property: Public utilities (55 %)	Weighted average effective rate	County
South Fulton	1.30	3.18	4.48	84.55	3.79	1.52	0.95	1.34	2.08	1.09	Obion
South Pittsburg	0.86	2.15	3.01	89.30	2.69	1.08	0.67	0.90	1.48	0.89	Marion
Sparta	1.89	2.99	4.88	93.20	4.55	1.82	1.14	1.46	2.50	1.48	White
Spencer	0.00	1.86	1.86	88.76	1.65	0.66	0.41	0.56	0.91	0.87	Van Buren
Spring City	1.60	3.18	4.78	91.43	4.37	1.75	1.09	1.43	2.40	1.31	Rhea
Spring Hill	0.61	2.35	2.96	73.01	2.16	0.86	0.54	0.89	1.19	0.62	Maury/Williamson
Springfield	1.85	3.78	5.63	70.88	3.99	1.60	1.00	1.69	2.19	1.31	Robertson
Stanton	0.81	2.17	2.98	100.00	2.98	1.19	0.74	0.89	1.64	0.91	Haywood
Stantonville	0.00	2.40	2.40	99.21	2.38	0.95	0.60	0.72	1.31	1.30	McNairy
Surgoinsville	0.00	4.71	4.71	65.10	3.07	1.23	0.77	1.41	1.69	0.90	Hawkins
Sweetwater	1.60	3.00	4.60	76.26	3.51	1.40	0.88	1.38	1.93	1.16	Monroe
Tazewell	0.00	2.54	2.54	80.22	2.04	0.82	0.51	0.76	1.12	1.11	Claiborne
Tellico Plains	1.25	3.00	4.25	76.26	3.24	1.30	0.81	1.27	1.78	1.10	Monroe
Tennessee Ridge	1.25	3.68	4.93	67.52	3.33	1.33	0.83	1.48	1.83	0.91	Houston
Tiptonville	1.35	2.65	4.00	100.00	4.00	1.60	1.00	1.20	2.20	1.26	Lake
Toone	0.30	2.29	2.59	85.88	2.22	0.89	0.56	0.78	1.22	0.61	Hardeman
Townsend	0.00	2.43	2.43	100.00	2.43	0.97	0.61	0.73	1.34	1.34	Blount
Trenton	1.36	0.92	2.28	90.92	2.07	0.83	0.52	0.68	1.14	0.67	Gibson
Trezevant	0.90	1.55	2.45	89.00	2.18	0.87	0.55	0.73	1.20	0.61	Carroll
Trimble	2.80	2.80	5.60	47.72	2.67	1.07	0.67	1.68	1.47	0.79	Dyer/Obion
Troy	1.70	3.18	4.88	84.55	4.13	1.65	1.03	1.46	2.27	1.28	Obion
Tullahoma	1.87	2.15	4.02	100.00	4.02	1.61	1.00	1.21	2.21	1.23	Coffee
Tusculum	0.00	2.35	2.35	89.56	2.10	0.84	0.53	0.70	1.16	0.54	Greene
Union City	2.36	2.28	4.64	84.55	3.92	1.57	0.98	1.39	2.16	1.24	Obion
Vanleer	0.25	3.06	3.31	57.36	1.90	0.76	0.47	0.99	1.04	0.57	Dickson
Viola	0.00	1.98	1.98	96.00	1.90	0.76	0.48	0.59	1.05	0.98	Warren
Vonore	0.00	3.00	3.00	76.26	2.29	0.92	0.57	0.90	1.26	0.68	Monroe
Walden	1.00	3.26	4.26	78.13	3.33	1.33	0.83	1.28	1.83	0.87	Hamilton
Wartburg	0.00	5.65	5.65	100.00	5.65	2.26	1.41	1.69	3.11	1.92	Morgan

TABLE 15.18--ACTUAL AND EFFECTIVE PROPERTY TAX RATES AND APPRAISAL RATIO, MUNICIPALITIES, 1987 (Continued)

	Actual tax rates					Effective tax rate by class of property					
Municipality	City tax rate	County tax rate in city	Total tax rate for city[1]	Appraisal ratio (%)	Equalized tax rate[2]	Commercial and industrial real (40 %)	Residential and farm real (25 %)	Commercial and industrial personal (30 %)	Public utilities (55 %)	Weighted average effective rate	County
Wartrace	1.28	2.90	4.18	100.00	4.18	1.67	1.04	1.25	2.30	1.30	Bedford
Watauga	0.30	2.85	3.15	100.00	3.15	1.26	0.79	0.94	1.73	0.87	Carter
Waverly	1.34	2.84	4.18	94.40	3.95	1.58	0.99	1.25	2.17	1.22	Humphreys
Waynesboro	1.70	2.72	4.42	94.87	4.19	1.68	1.05	1.33	2.31	1.31	Wayne
Westmoreland	0.95	2.55	3.50	100.00	3.50	1.40	0.87	1.05	1.92	1.07	Sumner
White House	2.00	3.78	5.78	70.88	4.10	1.64	1.02	1.73	2.25	1.24	Robertson/Sumner
Whiteville	1.30	2.29	3.59	85.88	3.08	1.23	0.77	1.08	1.70	0.94	Hardeman
Whitwell	0.25	2.15	2.40	89.30	2.14	0.86	0.54	0.72	1.18	0.66	Marion
Williston	0.00	2.85	2.85	81.94	2.34	0.93	0.58	0.85	1.28	0.63	Fayette
Winchester	2.15	2.23	4.38	83.53	3.66	1.46	0.91	1.31	2.01	1.12	Franklin
Woodbury	1.07	2.65	3.72	100.00	3.72	1.49	0.93	1.12	2.05	1.18	Cannon
Woodland Mills	0.00	3.18	3.18	84.55	2.69	1.08	0.67	0.95	1.48	1.47	Obion
Yorkville	0.00	0.92	0.92	90.92	0.84	0.33	0.21	0.28	0.46	0.46	Gibson

1. Excludes Special School District rate.

2. Equal to total tax rate multiplied by the appraisal ratio; computed by the Center for Business and Economic Research; see Table 15.13 for additional footnotes.

Source: State of Tennessee, State Board of Equalization, *1987 Tax Aggregate Report of Tennessee*.

TABLE 15.19--GENERAL REVENUE OF STATE GOVERNMENTS, BY SOURCE, SOUTHEASTERN STATES AND UNITED STATES, 1987 [In thousands of dollars]

State	Total	Intergovernmental revenue		Taxes	Current charges	Miscel-laneous
		Federal	Local			
TENNESSEE	6,308,275	1,852,262	31,161	3,603,331	546,009	275,512
Alabama	5,953,977	1,481,298	33,419	3,222,201	748,691	468,368
Arkansas	3,252,525	908,755	4,222	1,889,066	245,074	205,408
Florida	14,435,691	2,799,133	102,972	9,846,189	780,590	906,807
Georgia	8,631,416	2,287,425	54,945	5,323,689	610,374	354,983
Kentucky	5,859,962	1,411,147	13,473	3,520,409	525,784	389,149
Louisiana	7,718,612	2,450,735	25,312	3,448,641	719,659	1,074,265
Mississippi	3,617,723	1,149,563	16,288	1,943,388	323,634	184,850
North Carolina	9,764,630	2,029,557	164,580	6,235,163	865,387	469,943
South Carolina	5,271,248	1,197,157	35,350	3,158,453	542,801	337,487
Virginia	9,224,246	1,948,921	136,609	5,526,557	1,051,013	561,146
West Virginia	3,239,733	914,581	13,146	1,830,168	228,705	253,133
UNITED STATES	419,486,709	95,462,932	6,917,727	246,933,216	31,900,381	38,272,453

Source: U.S. Department of Commerce, Bureau of the Census, *State Government Finances in 1987*.

TABLE 15.20--PER CAPITA GENERAL REVENUE OF STATE GOVERNMENTS, BY SOURCE, SOUTHEASTERN STATES AND UNITED STATES, 1987 [In dollars]

State	Total	Intergovernmental revenue		Taxes	Current charges [1]	Miscel-laneous [1]
		Federal	Local			
TENNESSEE	1,299.34	381.52	6.42	742.19	112.46	56.75
Alabama	1,458.24	362.80	8.18	789.17	183.37	114.71
Arkansas	1,362.03	380.55	1.77	791.07	102.63	86.02
Florida	1,200.67	232.81	8.56	818.95	64.92	75.42
Georgia	1,387.24	367.64	8.83	855.62	98.10	57.05
Kentucky	1,572.30	378.63	3.61	944.57	141.07	104.41
Louisiana	1,730.24	549.37	5.67	773.06	161.32	240.81
Mississippi	1,378.18	437.93	6.20	740.34	123.29	70.42
North Carolina	1,522.63	316.48	25.66	972.27	134.94	73.28
South Carolina	1,539.05	349.53	10.32	922.18	158.48	98.54
Virginia	1,562.37	330.10	23.14	936.07	178.02	95.05
West Virginia[1]	1,707.82	482.12	6.93	964.77	120.56	133.44
UNITED STATES	1,727.86	393.21	28.50	1,017.11	131.06	157.24

Note: Population estimates are as of July 1.

1. Computed by Center for Business and Economic Research. Per capita amounts are computed on the basis of figures rounded to nearest thousand.

Source: U.S. Department of Commerce, Bureau of the Census, *State Government Finances in 1987*.

TABLE 15.21--STATE TAX REVENUE, BY SOURCE, SOUTHEASTERN STATES, FISCAL YEAR 1987 [In thousands of dollars]

State	Total	General sales and gross receipts	Selective sales and gross receipts [1]	Total license	Individual income	Corporation net income	Property	Severance	Death and gift	Other taxes [2]
TENNESSEE	3,603,331	1,994,313	791,212	351,296	68,123	298,644	0	1,581	31,757	66,405
Alabama	3,222,201	883,762	856,983	279,291	887,807	161,832	68,640	53,342	16,351	14,193
Arkansas	1,889,066	715,636	366,354	124,624	535,317	115,620	5,669	15,130	6,010	4,706
Florida	9,846,189	5,478,278	2,110,152	662,708	0	596,434	221,959	81,268	151,653	543,737
Georgia	5,323,689	1,739,304	747,786	169,623	2,149,111	449,176	17,801	0	30,289	20,599
Kentucky	3,520,409	892,042	671,133	254,499	920,968	267,378	251,246	211,203	49,334	2,606
Louisiana	3,448,641	1,189,690	765,274	369,550	438,643	191,189	4,552	449,576	40,167	0
Mississippi	1,943,388	1,015,402	285,645	164,131	315,449	102,865	285	49,190	10,421	0
North Carolina	6,235,163	1,456,024	1,074,066	415,486	2,565,878	566,480	78,316	1,436	77,477	0
South Carolina	3,158,453	1,175,411	564,561	167,592	1,008,938	190,474	8,465	0	26,981	16,031
Virginia	5,526,557	1,102,670	1,156,962	329,803	2,445,816	320,598	23,510	1,714	32,800	112,684
West Virginia	1,830,168	790,406	343,621	111,390	482,205	89,890	1,944	0	6,761	3,951

Note: Total does not include unemployment insurance tax collections.

1. Includes collections of motor fuels, alcoholic beverages, tobacco products, insurance, public utilities, parimutuels, and amusements.

2. Includes document and stock transfer taxes.

Source: U.S. Department of Commerce, Bureau of the Census, *State Government Finances in 1987*.

TABLE 15.22--GROSS ASSESSED VALUE OF LOCALLY ASSESSED TAXABLE REAL PROPERTY, ESTIMATED DISTRIBUTION BY USE CATEGORY, SOUTHEASTERN STATES AND UNITED STATES, 1986 [In millions of dollars]

State	Total	Residential (nonfarm)			Acreage	Vacant platted lots	Commercial and industrial		
		Total	Single-family	Multi-family			Total	Commercial	Industrial
TENNESSEE[1]	24,345	12,284	11,562	722	2,961	935	8,104	6,825	1,280
Alabama[2]	8,874	5,084	4,603	481	1,535	324	1,915	1,635	280
Arkansas	8,871	5,014	4,699	315	1,752	348	1,745	1,329	416
Florida	344,042	227,631	203,481	24,150	16,035	29,217	70,151	59,775	10,377
Georgia[3]	50,768	31,481	28,086	3,395	6,209	1,837	11,189	9,210	1,979
Kentucky[1]	54,240	32,616	30,098	2,519	9,575	842	10,900	8,586	2,314
Louisiana[4]	8,852	5,424	4,858	567	805	377	2,242	2,001	241
Mississippi	4,807	2,824	2,544	280	866	189	920	764	156
North Carolina[3,5]	121,397	75,767	69,902	5,865	16,645	4,050	24,327	18,137	6,190
South Carolina[1,2]	3,174	1,819	1,607	212	241	213	881	519	362
Virginia[3]	166,460	110,689	100,852	9,837	15,475	7,186	32,536	27,088	5,448
West Virginia[2]	8,697	5,369	5,025	344	562	294	1,802	1,169	632
UNITED STATES	4,104,549	2,511,599	2,180,289	331,310	309,308	189,224	997,462	710,546	286,916

Note: These data are estimates subject to sampling variation. Valuation date was January 1, 1986, unless otherwise stated.

1. Estimates for "Single-family" residential may include all or some parcels in "Multi-family" use.

2. Alabama valuation date was October 1, 1985; South Carolina, December 31, 1985; and West Virginia, July 1, 1985.

3. Estimates for "Vacant platted lots" may include "Acreage" parcels, and vice versa.

4. Louisiana manufacturing plant value was inconsistently allocated between realty and personalty components in reported data. As a result, the total realty value amount shown may be overstated or understated to the extent influenced by inconsistent reporting.

5. North Carolina assessed values reported as gross are actually net values for those counties which did not report the amounts of their partial exemptions.

Source: U.S. Department of Commerce, Bureau of the Census, *1987 Census of Governments, Volume 2, Taxable Property Values.*

TABLE 15.23--GENERAL EXPENDITURES OF STATE GOVERNMENTS, BY FUNCTION, SOUTHEASTERN STATES AND UNITED STATES, 1987
[In thousands of dollars]

State	Total[1]	Education	Highways	Public welfare	Health and hospitals	Natural resources	General control	Financial adminis-tration	Interest on general debt
TENNESSEE	6,161,712	2,353,584	806,296	1,185,317	548,334	96,516	70,395	72,016	159,812
Alabama	5,769,291	2,746,552	555,098	635,826	623,724	120,652	94,001	108,549	255,699
Arkansas	3,219,547	1,346,723	468,403	540,055	230,143	98,985	30,009	61,729	98,630
Florida	14,570,274	5,744,313	1,466,365	1,905,156	1,374,271	516,356	345,209	185,681	568,347
Georgia	8,423,176	3,645,183	926,762	1,430,849	714,716	232,182	73,812	111,897	163,149
Kentucky	5,844,453	2,318,365	850,602	985,769	308,722	174,827	136,214	115,317	281,489
Louisiana	7,204,836	2,590,472	711,646	1,046,149	725,022	262,039	106,402	58,419	606,585
Mississippi	3,555,483	1,497,570	386,804	544,760	278,955	102,142	33,547	27,881	106,868
North Carolina	9,379,549	4,473,137	923,098	1,205,315	818,391	197,319	175,611	99,931	176,028
South Carolina	5,107,330	2,355,267	395,287	610,690	588,156	120,180	54,304	81,580	147,228
Virginia	9,039,910	3,677,587	1,316,372	1,059,112	985,781	142,242	142,065	173,362	321,227
West Virginia	3,238,828	1,286,900	462,632	510,870	161,534	86,420	44,710	61,423	139,060
UNITED STATES	403,937,262	149,900,675	38,272,844	78,453,819	32,130,934	7,815,820	6,191,157	6,458,626	18,583,419

1. Includes items not shown separately.

Source: U.S. Department of Commerce, Bureau of the Census, *State Government Finances in 1987*.

TABLE 15.24--PER CAPITA GENERAL EXPENDITURES OF STATE GOVERNMENTS, BY FUNCTION, SOUTHEASTERN STATES AND UNITED STATES, 1987
[In dollars]

State	Total[1]	Education	Highways	Public welfare	Health and hospitals	General control[2]	Financial adminis-tration[2]	Interest on general debt
TENNESSEE	1,269.15	484.78	166.08	244.14	112.94	14.50	14.83	32.92
Alabama	1,413.00	672.68	135.95	155.73	152.77	23.02	26.59	62.63
Arkansas	1,348.22	563.95	196.15	226.15	96.37	12.57	25.85	41.30
Florida	1,211.87	477.78	121.96	158.46	114.31	28.71	15.44	47.27
Georgia	1,353.77	585.85	148.95	229.97	114.87	11.86	17.98	26.22
Kentucky	1,568.14	622.05	228.23	264.49	82.84	36.55	30.94	75.53
Louisiana	1,615.07	580.69	159.53	234.51	162.53	23.85	13.10	135.98
Mississippi	1,354.47	570.50	147.35	207.53	106.27	12.78	10.62	40.71
North Carolina	1,462.58	697.51	143.94	187.95	127.61	27.38	15.58	27.45
South Carolina	1,491.19	687.67	115.41	178.30	171.73	15.86	23.82	42.99
Virginia	1,531.15	622.90	222.96	179.39	166.97	24.06	29.36	54.41
West Virginia	1,687.77	670.61	241.08	266.22	84.18	23.57	32.38	72.46
UNITED STATES	1,663.81	617.44	157.65	323.15	132.35	25.44	26.54	76.54

Note: Population estimates are as of July 1.

1. Includes items not shown separately.

2. Computed by Center for Business and Economic Research. Per capita amounts are computed on the basis of figures rounded to nearest thousand.

Source: U.S. Department of Commerce, Bureau of the Census, *State Government Finances in 1987*.

TABLE 15.25--DISTRIBUTION OF FEDERAL FUNDS AND RANK BY STATE, SOUTHEASTERN STATES, 1988

State	Per capita federal funds ($)		Federal funds received ($1,000,000)					
	Amount	Rank	Total	Grants to state and local govern-ments	Salaries and wages	Direct payments to individuals	Procure-ment	Other
TENNESSEE	3,193	32	15,705	2,225	2,356	7,855	2,927	342
Alabama	3,478	20	14,354	1,721	2,665	7,182	2,428	357
Arkansas	3,090	37	7,485	1,011	822	4,406	835	411
Florida	3,474	21	42,997	3,419	5,662	26,800	6,590	526
Georgia	2,882	42	18,451	2,964	4,175	8,866	1,944	502
Kentucky	2,872	43	10,686	1,766	1,861	6,142	629	288
Louisiana	2,869	44	12,682	2,135	1,585	6,479	2,036	448
Mississippi	3,767	12	9,895	1,324	1,208	4,465	2,586	311
North Carolina	2,719	47	17,743	2,299	3,691	9,504	1,690	560
South Carolina	3,130	34	10,934	1,354	2,322	5,139	1,932	187
Virginia	5,954	1	35,698	1,961	9,841	10,597	12,288	1,011
West Virginia	3,111	35	5,861	1,056	530	3,838	372	65

Note: Detail may not add to total due to independent rounding.

Source: U.S. Department of Commerce, Bureau of the Census, *Federal Expenditures by State for Fiscal Year 1988*.

TABLE 15.26--FEDERAL GRANTS TO STATE AND LOCAL GOVERNMENTS, PER CAPITA, BY PROGRAM, SOUTHEASTERN STATES AND UNITED STATES, 1988
[In dollars]

State	Total	Dept. of Agriculture child nutrition programs	Dept. of Education compensatory education for disadvantaged	EPA construction of wastewater treatment works	Medical assistance (Medicaid)	Social services block grant	Family support payments (A.F.D.C.)
TENNESSEE	452.41	17.27	15.75	7.28	148.35	12.34	22.06
Alabama	417.11	25.45	18.11	4.87	86.94	10.48	14.81
Arkansas	417.44	21.22	19.94	6.21	133.02	11.22	17.84
Florida	276.20	15.31	14.47	5.18	71.88	9.93	17.81
Georgia	463.07	21.03	15.59	6.56	117.96	10.46	33.46
Kentucky	474.67	22.45	18.11	6.75	138.17	11.26	32.52
Louisiana	483.07	31.76	21.27	5.97	156.65	10.12	31.31
Mississippi	504.17	40.71	26.51	10.30	138.58	10.36	26.14
North Carolina	352.27	19.50	13.74	5.36	105.69	10.10	23.11
South Carolina	387.60	21.33	16.48	11.83	104.91	10.41	25.87
Virginia	327.03	10.93	12.25	7.21	70.01	12.47	20.90
West Virginia	560.62	22.25	18.27	32.00	127.03	11.56	51.16
UNITED STATES	459.56	16.36	16.10	10.07	121.58	10.39	43.16

TABLE 15.26- FEDERAL GRANTS TO STATE AND LOCAL GOVERNMENTS, PER CAPITA, BY PROGRAM, SOUTHEASTERN STATES AND UNITED STATES, 1988
[In dollars] (Continued)

	Department of Housing and Urban Development		Department of Labor		Department of Transportation		
State	Community development	Housing assistance	Job Training Partner-ship Act	State employment services	Highway trust fund	Urban Mass Transpor-tation Adminis-tration	Other
TENNESSEE	8.91	22.65	13.06	6.82	65.01	4.38	108.53
Alabama	12.72	23.62	16.34	8.28	78.49	4.60	112.39
Arkansas	9.91	21.12	12.87	9.09	48.65	2.01	104.34
Florida	9.99	15.67	8.37	5.39	50.01	6.42	45.78
Georgia	10.94	21.07	8.80	6.86	82.47	7.89	119.98
Kentucky	12.50	25.64	15.08	7.52	61.09	6.85	116.73
Louisiana	14.05	24.14	12.62	9.24	72.02	4.98	88.94
Mississippi	10.29	25.54	13.90	8.47	57.65	1.95	133.76
North Carolina	9.86	20.81	11.57	7.04	42.08	3.94	79.47
South Carolina	10.67	19.85	11.67	8.22	57.00	2.70	86.67
Virginia	8.81	24.04	8.42	6.84	61.79	3.88	79.47
West Virginia	10.05	29.15	14.58	10.00	104.05	3.37	127.15
UNITED STATES	12.23	26.23	11.89	9.73	72.89	12.98	95.93

Note: Detail may not add to total due to independent rounding.

Source: U.S. Department of Commerce, Bureau of the Census, *Federal Expenditures by State for Fiscal Year 1988*.

TABLE 15.27--FEDERAL INDIVIDUAL INCOME TAX, SOUTHEASTERN STATES AND UNITED STATES, 1986 [Money amounts in thousands of dollars, except as indicated]

State	Number of returns	Adjusted gross income	Salaries and wages	Tax liability Total	Tax liability Average ($)
TENNESSEE	1,967,923	41,071,250	34,740,998	6,072,049	3,748
Alabama	1,537,065	32,055,361	26,967,941	4,421,503	3,530
Arkansas	882,648	16,573,801	13,506,122	2,205,280	3,086
Florida	5,300,996	123,771,406	86,085,972	20,901,193	4,705
Georgia	2,547,529	58,644,369	50,354,128	8,596,520	4,032
Kentucky	1,382,471	27,961,310	22,904,413	3,932,907	3,459
Louisiana	1,606,074	32,810,721	27,518,645	4,776,941	3,759
Mississippi	917,726	16,395,149	13,942,359	2,100,578	2,972
North Carolina	2,710,326	57,576,908	47,803,806	7,932,772	3,503
South Carolina	1,346,996	27,774,612	23,231,645	3,650,940	3,293
Virginia	2,583,679	65,737,990	54,426,286	9,851,527	4,422
West Virginia	663,519	13,552,665	11,058,758	1,845,691	3,356
United States	103,633,570	2,472,559,803	2,012,988,154	380,561,579	4,362

Source: U.S. Department of the Treasury, Internal Revenue Service, *Statistics of Income Bulletin, Fall 1988.*

TABLE 15.28--FEDERAL INTERNAL REVENUE COLLECTIONS, SOUTHEASTERN STATES AND UNITED STATES, 1949–1986, SELECTED FISCAL YEARS [In millions of dollars]

	1986[a]		1985		1979	
State	Total	Income and employment taxes	Total	Income and employment taxes	Total	Income and employment taxes
TENNESSEE	12,332.0	11,726.2	10,415.9	8,986.4	5,669.7	5,447.1
Alabama	7,271.7	6,941.7	6,683.0	5,741.1	4,130.5	3,948.6
Arkansas	3,284.8	3,115.1	3,728.0	2,956.7	2,018.9	1,939.4
Florida	28,546.2	27,152.4	26,254.4	23,367.4	13,328.6	12,482.9
Georgia	18,225.4	16,850.9	15,590.6	11,963.8	7,314.7	6,735.2
Kentucky	6,517.3	5,020.6	7,560.6	5,099.8	5,272.0	3,928.0
Louisiana	8,068.1	7,755.1	8,424.9	7,542.9	5,486.7	5,334.5
Mississippi	3,049.1	2,887.6	2,801.5	2,455.6	1,755.6	1,702.8
North Carolina	17,017.2	13,590.9	16,292.5	10,528.7	8,936.4	7,427.8
South Carolina	5,678.3	5,470.5	5,058.9	4,405.5	3,030.6	2,959.5
Virginia	15,758.6	14,379.9	14,165.1	11,514.2	7,626.9	6,761.7
West Virginia	2,040.2	1,958.1	2,374.4	2,127.2	1,770.7	1,708.7
UNITED STATES	782,251.8	741,384.8	742,871.5	621,874.1	453,859.1	432,697.8

	1969		1959		1949	
State	Total	Income and employment taxes	Total	Income and employment taxes	Total	Income and employment taxes
TENNESSEE	1,868.1	1,788.4	644.7	605.4	333.2	295.7
Alabama	1,332.6	1,222.5	534.7	512.6	259.5	236.2
Arkansas	651.8	609.5	197.5	188.6	115.9	105.6
Florida	3,625.6	3,381.7	1,147.3	1,039.3	342.6	286.6
Georgia	2,614.8	2,428.8	888.9	778.7	403.5	322.9
Kentucky	2,541.0	1,314.1	1,541.0	547.3	812.3	282.1
Louisiana	1,639.9	1,542.3	689.2	610.7	357.4	291.8
Mississippi	619.6	574.0	193.1	176.7	100.7	91.6
North Carolina	4,065.6	2,801.4	1,983.7	875.0	1,166.7	423.7
South Carolina	963.1	931.4	287.6	272.6	205.0	191.5
Virginia	2,829.1	2,250.5	1,231.5	843.3	770.3	393.4
West Virginia	630.1	595.6	308.0	287.4	242.7	219.8
UNITED STATES	187,919.3	168,846.7	78,652.1	66,642.2	40,351.4	31,983.3

Note: Collections in various states do not necessarily indicate the actual Federal tax burden on the residents of each state.

a. Data for 1986 are not strictly comparable to prior years because amounts in 1986 are classified according to state of taxpayer's residence; previously, amounts were classified according to state where tax payments were made.

Source: Tax Foundation, Inc., *Facts and Figures on Government Finance, 1988–1989.*

TABLE 15.29--FEDERAL TAX BURDEN, SOUTHEASTERN STATES AND UNITED STATES, FISCAL YEARS 1980 AND 1987

State	Amount ($1,000,000) 1987	Amount ($1,000,000) 1980	Percentage of total burden 1987	Percentage of total burden 1980	Per capita ($) 1987[a]	Per capita ($) 1980
TENNESSEE	13,141	8,115	1.60	1.62	2,725	1,768
Alabama	10,227	6,512	1.25	1.30	2,515	1,674
Arkansas	5,558	3,457	0.68	0.69	2,355	1,512
Florida	39,348	19,186	4.81	3.83	3,269	1,970
Georgia	17,869	9,468	2.18	1.89	2,893	1,733
Kentucky	9,241	6,412	1.13	1.28	2,466	1,751
Louisiana	12,418	7,715	1.52	1.54	2,770	1,835
Mississippi	5,375	3,457	0.66	0.69	2,031	1,371
North Carolina	17,476	10,069	2.13	2.01	2,732	1,714
South Carolina	8,259	5,010	1.01	1.00	2,406	1,606
Virginia	20,065	11,572	2.45	2.31	3,435	2,164
West Virginia	4,542	3,457	0.55	0.69	2,356	1,773
UNITED STATES	818,856	500,950[b]	100.00	100.00	3,365	2,212

Note: The burden by state is estimated on the basis of a special formula designed by the Tax Foundation, Inc. Data on federal tax collections by state do not accurately reflect the distribution of the burden.

a. Based on estimates of resident population as of July 1, 1987.

b. Total receipts minus refunds and miscellaneous receipts.

Source: Tax Foundation, Inc., *Facts and Figures on Government Finance, 1988–1989*; and earlier editions.

Many of the tables in Chapter 16 are from the Tennessee Department of Education's *Annual Statistical Report*, which provides detailed data for each county and school district as well as data for special education and vocational-technical education. In the absence of a current *Report*, data have been provided by the Tennessee Department of Education from departmental records. Public library data are available from the Tennessee State Library and Archives. The Tennessee Higher Education Commission publishes data on public and private institutions of higher education in its annual *Statistical Abstract of Tennessee Higher Education*. While some information on private institutions of higher education is given in this report, additional information can be obtained from the Tennessee Council of Private Colleges.

The Tennessee Education Association (TEA) publishes a series of research bulletins annually which provide details on economic status, taxing effort and ability, revenue sources, salaries, and employment in education for county and local areas as well as data aggregated for the state. The Research Bulletins may be ordered from the TEA in Nashville. The National Education Association (NEA) publication, *Estimates of School Statistics*, is a detailed comparison of the 50 states and is the source for many of the southeastern comparisons. NEA also publishes a variety of reports on special topics at the state and national level.

The Bureau of the Census, in its decennial censuses, provides data on the educational attainment of the population. The first data were percentages of the illiterate population and number of children attending school. Beginning in 1950, data became available concerning school attendance and number of years of school completed, by sex and race. Table 16.15 contains information on the educational level of the population by race for each of the southeastern states and the U.S. Additional data from this Census include school enrollments in public, private, and church-related schools. These are presented in Table 16.3. *Current Population Reports* from the Bureau of the Census provide occasional intercensal reports on educational attainment. However, these data are usually reported at the national or regional level and are not included in this *Abstract*.

The U.S. Department of Education, National Center for Education Statistics, collects data on institutions of higher education. Data such as enrollments, degrees conferred, current revenues and current expenditures were formerly published in an annual *Digest of Education Statistics*. These data are currently provided through direct correspondence with the National Center for Education Statistics.

TABLE OF CONTENTS

TABLE OF CONTENTS
(Continued)

Table Number Page Number

TABLE 16.1-- NET ENROLLMENT, AVERAGE DAILY MEMBERSHIP, AND AVERAGE DAILY ATTENDANCE IN PUBLIC SCHOOLS, TENNESSEE, 1950–1988, SELECTED SCHOLASTIC YEARS

	Net enrollment [1]						
Year	Total	Kinder-garten	Elementary (grades 1–8)	Secondary (grades 9–12)	Special education [2]	Average daily membership	Average daily attendance
1988	860,101	66,429	524,432	250,110	19,130	816,678	766,651
1987	855,157	66,060	518,069	251,440	19,588	813,576	766,521
1986	846,823	62,079	517,685	247,284	19,775	808,303	762,225
1985	849,047	63,571	524,175	243,224	18,077	811,232	769,862
1984	854,318	61,568	533,431	242,289	17,030	816,666	774,346
1983	860,708	61,083	539,171	245,465	14,989	821,719	778,321
1982	874,589	57,576	547,925	253,075	16,013	831,854	785,336
1981	889,847	58,647	553,514	260,744	16,942	846,922	797,237
1980	898,997	58,815	561,173	263,785	15,224	857,373	806,696
1979	911,347	59,069	570,384	268,076	13,818	865,509	808,512
1978	918,552	59,642	579,383	265,995	13,532	873,317	819,028
1977	925,184	62,905	581,974	263,407	16,898	877,030	821,698
1976	918,684	59,482	584,922	261,327	12,953	876,322	826,335
1975	913,103	53,245	587,208	256,853	15,797	871,681	823,394
1970	916,862	(X)	645,315	256,661	14,886	880,172	836,010
1965	893,908	(X)	647,175	235,833	10,900	859,198	821,192
1960	810,300	(X)	628,562	181,738	(a)	775,516	735,660
1955	740,933	(X)	590,408	150,525	(a)	n.a.	663,738
1950	659,785	(X)	539,445	120,340	(a)	n.a.	583,126

n.a. not available.

1. Represents the total number of original entries in public schools; pupils enrolled who change school districts during the school year are counted more than once.

2. Applies only to that portion of students receiving special education who are in the comprehensive development classrooms; the remainder of special education students are included in the regular graded classifications. Prior to 1962, all types of special education were included in the regular graded classifications. Prior to 1976, includes ungraded or unclassified enrollment.

a. Included in regular graded classifications.

Source: Tennessee Department of Education, direct correspondence; and *Annual Statistical Report, 1950–1983.*

TABLE 16.2-- NUMBER OF PUPILS IN PROGRAMS OTHER THAN KINDERGARTEN THROUGH TWELFTH GRADES RUN BY LOCAL BOARDS OF EDUCATION, TENNESSEE, SCHOLASTIC YEARS 1972–1988

Year	Total	Headstart	Summer school	Adult education	Other
1988	104,616	404	26,882	29,855	47,475
1987	97,778	448	20,617	24,549	52,164
1986	93,459	1,031	17,946	25,972	48,510
1985	84,730	802	15,485	23,956	44,487
1984	84,363	682	16,629	25,553	41,499
1983	54,664	894	16,737	25,729	11,304
1982	n.a.	n.a.	n.a.	n.a.	n.a.
1981	82,541	1,845	17,605	26,999	36,092
1980	86,870	2,017	24,501	26,277	34,075
1979	77,372	1,842	20,449	21,964	33,117
1978	96,959	6,497	20,812	64,229	5,421
1977	116,492	1,693	27,427	73,358	14,014
1976	100,261	1,945	23,772	56,719	17,825
1975	92,150	6,837	21,683	55,785	7,845
1974	84,850	2,985	24,529	48,125	9,211
1973	102,291	6,052	27,872	56,143	12,224
1972	101,322	7,421	36,113	41,426	16,362

n.a. not available.

Source: Tennessee Department of Education, direct correspondence; and *Annual Statistical Report, 1972–1984*.

TABLE 16.3-- SCHOOL ENROLLMENT, BY TYPE OF SCHOOL, URBAN AND RURAL AREAS, TENNESSEE, 1980

	Total	Urban	Rural
Persons 3 years old and over enrolled in school	1,217,290	765,575	451,715
Nursery school	40,814	30,321	10,493
Public	14,958	10,362	4,596
Church-related	16,603	13,136	3,467
Other private	9,253	6,823	2,430
Percentage private	63.4	65.8	56.2
Kindergarten	67,181	39,660	27,521
Public	57,981	32,214	25,767
Church-related	6,844	5,683	1,161
Other private	2,356	1,763	593
Percentage private	13.7	18.8	6.4
Elementary	599,393	343,198	256,195
Public	553,366	305,621	247,745
Church-related	36,423	30,351	6,072
Other private	9,604	7,226	2,378
Percentage private	7.7	10.9	3.3
High School	293,400	174,817	118,583
Public	269,427	155,049	114,378
Church-related	16,421	14,057	2,364
Other private	7,552	5,711	1,841
Percentage private	8.2	11.3	3.5
College	216,502	177,579	38,923
Public	172,171	139,547	32,624
Private	44,331	38,032	6,299
Percentage private	20.5	21.4	16.2

Note: Percentages were computed by the Center for Business and Economic Research.

Source: U.S. Department of Commerce, Bureau of the Census, *1980 Census of Population, General Social and Economic Characteristics, Tennessee.*

TABLE 16.4-- TOTAL AND AVERAGE ANNUAL EXPENDITURES IN PUBLIC SCHOOL SYSTEMS, TENNESSEE, 1930–1988, SELECTED FISCAL YEARS

Year	Total expenditures ($1,000)	Current expenditures ($1,000)		Number of pupils in ADA[2]	Average expenditures per pupil in ADA[2] ($)		
						Current	
		Total[1]	Operating		Total	Total[1]	Operating
1988	2,489,574	2,370,392	2,130,743	766,651	3,247.34	3,091.88	2,779.29
1987	2,312,393	2,198,866	1,963,035	766,521	3,016.74	2,868.63	2,560.97
1986	2,140,542	2,035,219	1,762,328	762,225	2,808.28	2,670.10	2,312.08
1985	1,958,473	1,855,909	1,625,030	769,862	2,543.93	2,410.70	2,110.81
1984	1,747,960	1,657,646	1,451,590	774,346	2,257.34	2,140.70	1,874.60
1983	1,658,544	1,602,577	1,399,623	778,321	2,130.92	2,059.01	1,798.26
1982	1,530,144	1,522,227	1,319,432	785,336	1,948.39	1,938.31	1,680.09
1981	1,539,979	1,462,835	1,275,764	797,237	1,931.65	1,834.89	1,600.23
1980	1,391,576	1,322,072	1,176,179	806,696	1,725.03	1,638.87	1,458.02
1979	1,247,582	1,194,166	1,056,241	808,512	1,543.06	1,476.99	1,307.50
1978	1,133,315	1,094,249	960,126	819,028	1,383.73	1,336.03	1,172.27
1977	1,018,612	993,196	875,767	821,698	1,239.64	1,208.71	1,065.80
1976	959,114	877,524	783,168	826,335	1,160.68	1,061.95	947.76
1975	878,926	789,868	727,404	823,394	1,067.44	959.28	883.42
1974	735,743	671,882	611,881	817,902	899.55	821.47	748.11
1973	660,292	616,726	555,301	832,087	793.54	741.18	667.36
1972	642,122	578,766	516,091	846,190	758.84	683.97	609.90
1971	598,667	519,937	472,882	849,882	704.41	611.78	556.41
1970	509,164	472,440	427,920	836,010	609.04	565.11	511.86
1969	470,809	421,460	376,960	835,076	563.79	504.70	451.41
1968	430,620	382,884	342,084	830,568	518.46	460.99	411.87
1967	395,855	337,531	312,581	828,091	478.03	407.60	377.47
1965	275,555	249,733	231,633	821,192	335.55	304.11	282.07
1960	205,446	n.a.	159,885	735,660	279.27	n.a.	217.34
1955	130,794	n.a.	103,965	663,738	196.06	n.a.	156.64
1950	109,680	n.a.	78,715	583,126	188.09	n.a.	134.99
1945	36,574	n.a.	34,773	498,305	73.40	n.a.	69.78
1940	29,035	n.a.	23,371	536,717	54.10	n.a.	43.54
1935	20,257	n.a.	17,189	521,079	38.88	n.a.	32.99
1930	23,837	n.a.	20,614	481,962	49.46	n.a.	42.77

Note: Averages computed by the Center for Business and Economic Research when not available in the source.
n.a. not available.

1. Beginning in 1965 the Department of Education calculated a second series of current expenditures including administration of State Department of Education, retirement of teachers, and value of commodities distributed by the U.S. Department of Agriculture.
2. Average daily attendance in regular classes and special education classes.

Source: Tennessee Department of Education, direct correspondence; and *Annual Statistical Report, 1930–1988.*

TABLE 16.5-- NUMBER OF TEACHERS EMPLOYED IN PUBLIC SCHOOL SYSTEMS, BY LEVEL OF TRAINING, TENNESSEE, SCHOLASTIC YEARS, 1950–1988, SELECTED YEARS

Year	Total	Ph.D. degree	Ed.S. degree	Master's degree [1]	Bachelor's degree	3 years college	2 years college	1 year college or less
1988	49,920	538	1,002	22,920	23,375	38	13	34
1987	48,965	508	949	21,926	25,428	27	16	111
1986	48,645	470	926	21,653	25,430	39	20	107
1985	47,487	439	874	20,911	25,118	55	22	68
1984	47,022	401	846	20,283	25,318	65	34	75
1983	46,691	378	799	19,780	25,545	69	40	80
1982	47,494	365	751	19,465	26,661	118	57	77
1981	49,021	340	709	19,329	28,311	165	81	86
1980	49,133	289	619	18,560	29,298	217	112	38
1979	48,479	253	534	17,613	29,599	288	117	75
1978	48,302	217	466	16,897	30,142	364	155	61
1977	47,569	186	386	15,918	30,289	472	216	102
1976	46,483	144	267	14,626	30,450	603	295	98
1975	45,942	97	186	13,361	31,008	795	405	90
1974	44,161	77	116	11,969	30,296	1,064	534	105
1973	43,124	67	93	11,007	29,771	1,285	728	173
1972	41,942	62	(X)	10,030	29,219	1,552	975	104
1971	41,531	36	(X)	9,084	29,115	1,957	1,163	176
1970	40,458	29	(X)	8,502	28,385	2,023	1,331	188
1969	39,164	28	(X)	7,860	27,278	2,253	1,485	260
1968	38,016	29	(X)	7,612	26,204	2,230	1,698	243
1967	36,111	33	(X)	7,341	24,624	2,185	1,708	220
1966	35,123	28	(X)	7,015	23,363	2,666	1,877	174
1965	34,231	27	(X)	6,954	22,632	2,387	2,028	203
1964	33,393	27	(X)	6,636	21,744	2,501	2,239	246
1963	32,402	26	(X)	6,306	20,744	2,567	2,483	276
1962	31,635	21	(X)	6,036	19,903	2,590	2,724	361
1961	30,907	25	(X)	5,808	19,028	2,642	2,967	437
1960	29,936	34	(X)	5,358	18,076	2,685	3,162	621
1959	29,092	29	(X)	5,034	17,265	2,607	3,412	745
1958	28,252	23	(X)	4,788	16,172	2,724	3,593	952
1957	27,899	17	(X)	4,551	15,412	2,764	3,933	1,222
1956	27,088	20	(X)	4,112	14,689	2,775	4,265	1,227
1955	26,363	16	(X)	3,726	14,019	2,730	4,582	1,290
1950	23,067	5	(X)	1,787	9,886	2,394	5,795	3,200

(X) not applicable.

1. Includes master's degree plus 45 hours.

Source: Tennessee Department of Education, direct correspondence; and *Annual Statistical Report, 1950–1983*.

TABLE 16.6-- NUMBER OF TEACHERS EMPLOYED IN PUBLIC SCHOOL SYSTEMS, BY SEX, TENNESSEE, 1930–1988, SELECTED SCHOLASTIC YEARS

Year	Total	Male	Female
1988	49,920	12,252	37,668
1987	48,965	12,318	36,647
1986	48,645	12,320	36,325
1985	47,487	12,463	35,024
1984	47,022	12,370	34,652
1983	46,691	12,406	34,285
1982	47,494	12,647	34,847
1981	49,021	13,242	35,779
1980	49,133	13,277	35,856
1979	48,479	13,179	35,300
1978	48,302	13,304	34,998
1977	47,569	13,196	34,373
1976	46,483	12,679	33,804
1975	45,942	12,269	33,673
1974	44,161	11,898	32,263
1973	43,124	11,815	31,309
1972	41,942	11,157	30,785
1971	41,531	10,890	30,641
1970	40,458	10,452	30,006
1969	39,164	9,885	29,279
1968	38,016	9,414	28,602
1967	36,111	8,843	27,268
1966	35,123	8,763	26,360
1965	34,231	8,591	25,640
1964	33,393	8,307	25,086
1963	32,402	7,967	24,435
1962	31,635	7,751	23,884
1961	30,907	7,415	23,492
1960	29,936	7,118	22,818
1959	29,092	6,725	22,367
1958	28,252	6,353	21,899
1957	27,899	6,121	21,778
1956	27,088	5,947	21,141
1955	26,363	5,719	20,644
1954	25,251	5,410	19,841
1953	24,532	5,349	19,183
1952	24,106	5,234	18,872
1951	23,897	5,252	18,645
1950	23,067	4,734	18,333
1945	20,562	2,916	17,646
1940	20,664	5,353	15,311
1935	19,592	4,869	14,723
1930	19,058	4,050	15,008

Source: Tennessee Department of Education, direct correspondence; and *Annual Statistical Report, 1930–1983.*

TABLE 16.7-- AVERAGE ANNUAL SALARIES IN PUBLIC SCHOOL SYSTEMS, TENNESSEE, 1956–1988, SCHOLASTIC YEARS

Year	Average, all salaries
1988	$24,535.86
1987	23,323.46
1986	21,874.02
1985	20,812.05
1984	18,243.65
1983	17,697.58
1982	16,581.52
1981	15,395.82
1980	14,072.70
1979	13,158.45
1978	12,272.02
1977	11,338.44
1976	10,326.93
1975	9,949.37
1974	9,028.70
1973	8,470.07
1972	8,153.89
1971	7,694.73
1970	7,187.29
1969	6,621.43
1968	6,145.71
1967	5,755.06
1966	5,216.57
1965	4,941.49
1964	4,769.39
1963	4,329.10
1962	4,151.47
1961	4,136.85
1960	3,818.85
1959	3,538.32
1958	3,427.45
1957	3,174.33
1956	3,051.50

Note: After 1980, refers to instructional personnel, which includes teachers, principals, supervisors, guidance counselors, attendance teachers, librarians and psychological personnel.

Source: Tennessee Department of Education, direct correspondence; and *Annual Statistical Report, 1955–1983*.

TABLE 16.8-- SELECTED PUBLIC LIBRARY STATISTICS, METROPOLITAN AND CITY LIBRARIES AND REGIONAL LIBRARY CENTERS, FISCAL YEAR 1987

Location and name of library or regional library center	Number of libraries and branches	Total per-sonnel	Total book-stock	Total circu-lation	Total expendi-tures
Metropolitan and city libraries					
Chattanooga, Chattanooga-Hamilton County Bicentennial Library	4	98	388,280	805,470	$2,517,641
Kingsport, Kingsport Public Library	2	15	106,579	173,889	447,500
Knoxville, Knox County Public Library	17	88	639,197	1,518,865	3,318,583
Memphis, Memphis Public Library and Information Center	22	333	1,605,965	2,310,470	10,045,049
Nashville, Public Library of Nashville and Davidson County	18	220	608,346	1,945,454	4,893,622
Oak Ridge, Oak Ridge Public Library	1	24	105,395	229,118	526,106
Regional centers[1]					
Athens, Fort Loudoun Regional Library System	26	67	401,473	1,023,778	1,212,265
Clarksville, Warioto Regional Library System	11	37	271,836	723,562	880,478
Clinton, Clinch-Powell Regional Library System	20	34	177,409	402,885	505,080
Columbia, Blue Grass Regional Library System	19	64	330,045	828,339	1,149,139
Cookeville, Upper Cumberland Regional Library System	16	23	272,722	478,999	614,376
Halls, Forked Deer Regional Library System	12	30	235,325	386,004	509,550
Jackson, Shiloh Regional Library System	12	31	330,663	544,959	824,086
Johnson City, Watauga Regional Library System	16	67	449,121	1,081,023	1,441,886
Martin, Reelfoot Regional Library System	13	32	308,408	598,918	749,097
Morristown, Nolichucky Regional Library System	20	48	292,788	580,538	770,020
Murfreesboro, Highland Rim Regional Library System	16	54	502,801	1,145,448	1,125,312
Sparta, Caney Fork Regional Library System	15	34	212,855	473,781	499,377

1. Statistics include local libraries in each region.

Source: Tennessee State Library and Archives, *Tennessee Public Library Statistics, July 1, 1986–June 30, 1987.*

FIGURE 16.1
Public Higher Educational Institutions in Tennessee

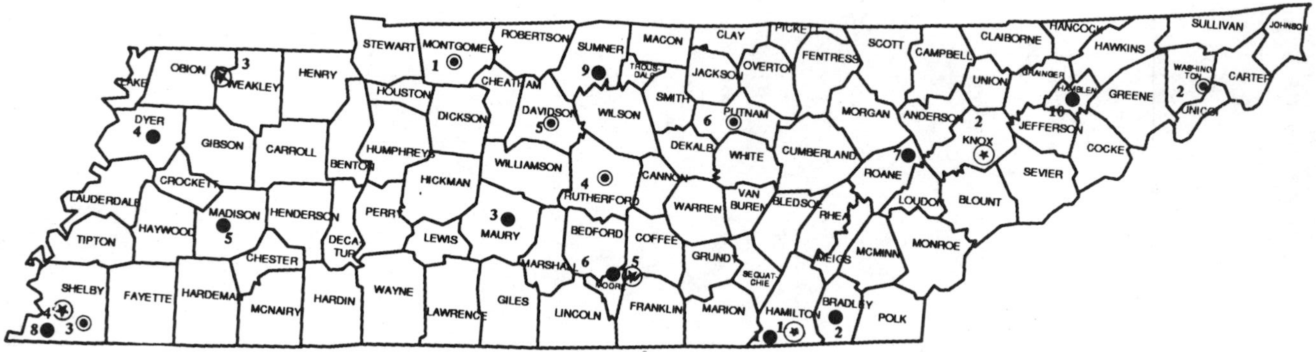

● Board of Regents Community Colleges

1 Chattanooga State Technical
2 Cleveland State
3 Columbia State
4 Dyersburg State
5 Jackson State
6 Motlow State
7 Roane State
8 Shelby State
9 Volunteer State
10 Walters State

◉ Board of Regents Universities

1 Austin Peay State
2 East Tennessee State
3 Memphis State
4 Middle Tennessee State
5 Tennessee State
6 Tennessee Technological

⊛ University of Tennessee System

1 U.T. Chattanooga
2 U.T. Knoxville
3 U.T. Martin
4 U.T. Center for Health Sciences
5 U.T. Space Institute

Source: Tennessee Higher Education Commission, *Statistical Abstract of Tennessee Higher Education.*

TABLE 16.9-- FALL ENROLLMENT IN STATE INSTITUTIONS OF HIGHER EDUCATION, TENNESSEE, 1986, 1987 AND 1988

Institution	1988 Headcount enrollment	1988 Full-time equated enrollment[1]	1987 Headcount enrollment	1987 Full-time equated enrollment[1]	1986 Headcount enrollment	1986 Full-time equated enrollment[1]
Board of Regents' Universities	64,840	52,570	62,700	50,402	60,715	48,788
Austin Peay State	5,168	3,983	5,111	4,160	4,943	4,015
East Tennessee State	10,754	8,728	9,976	8,213	9,736	7,984
Memphis State	20,270	15,285	20,473	15,144	20,046	14,838
Middle Tennessee State	13,165	11,388	11,975	10,398	11,408	9,915
Tennessee State	7,353	5,815	7,012	5,426	6,734	5,134
Tennessee Technological	7,901	7,371	7,935	7,061	7,625	6,902
East Tennessee State-Medical	229	(X)	218	(X)	223	(X)
The University of Tennessee System	38,936	30,794	39,889	31,909	39,955	31,707
U.T. Chattanooga	7,526	5,769	7,355	5,557	7,484	5,727
U.T. Knoxville	24,568	20,569	25,525	21,695	25,463	21,298
U.T. Martin	4,653	4,283	4,785	4,473	4,923	4,531
U.T. Center for Health Sciences, Memphis	1,772	(X)	1,763	(X)	1,706	(X)
U.T. Space Institute	417	173	461	184	379	151
Community Colleges	33,605	20,828	33,237	20,364	31,462	18,934
Chattanooga State	6,391	3,710	5,829	3,416	4,821	2,942
Cleveland State	2,977	1,798	2,978	1,707	2,735	1,586
Columbia State	2,667	1,606	2,866	1,563	3,040	1,560
Dyersburg State	1,742	976	1,664	962	1,651	1,001
Jackson State	2,774	1,663	2,835	1,704	2,445	1,473
Motlow State	2,392	1,438	2,336	1,392	2,331	1,316
Roane State	3,853	2,663	4,194	2,909	3,597	2,518
Shelby State	3,822	2,588	3,399	2,282	3,730	2,484
Volunteer State	3,474	2,110	3,415	2,034	3,366	1,853
Walters State	3,513	2,276	3,721	2,395	3,746	2,201
State Technical Institutes	17,672	9,415	16,845	9,154	17,409	9,329
Nashville	5,358	2,335	5,176	2,452	5,255	2,439
Memphis	7,398	3,950	7,638	4,198	7,657	4,192
Pellissippi	3,261	2,038	2,221	1,333	2,658	1,495
Tri-Cities	1,655	1,092	1,810	1,171	1,839	1,203

(X) not applicable.

1. Full-time equated enrollment is the total number of degree credits taken by undergraduate students divided by 15; for graduate/professional, divided by 12. Enrollments in medical schools are not included.

Source: Tennessee Higher Education Commission, *Statistical Abstract of Tennessee Higher Education, 1988–89.*

FIGURE 16.2
State Technical Institutes and Area Vocational–Technical Schools

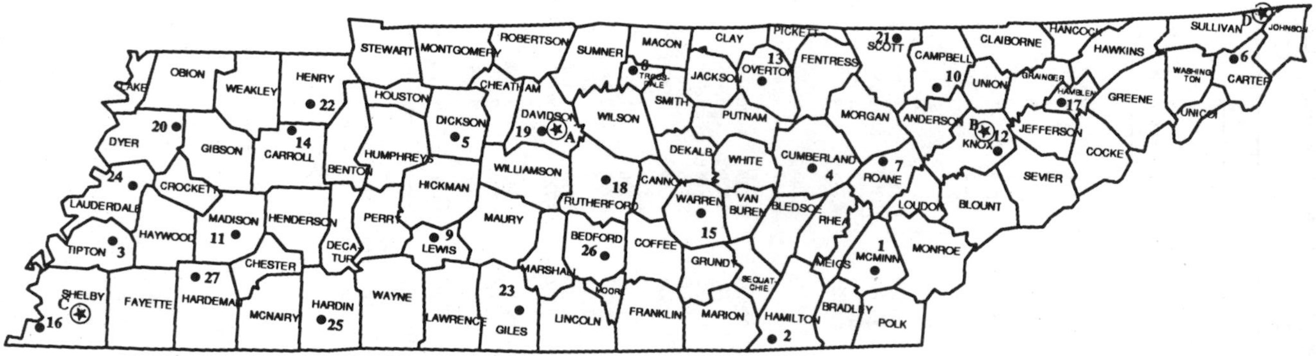

State Technical Institutes

A	Nashville State Technical Institute
B	State Technical Institute at Knoxville
C	State Technical Institute at Memphis
D	Tri-Cities State Technical Institute

• Vocational-Technical Schools

1	Athens	8	Hartsville	15	McMinnville	22	Paris
2	Chattanooga	9	Hohenwald	16	Memphis	23	Pulaski
3	Covington	10	Jacksboro	17	Morristown	24	Ripley
4	Crossville	11	Jackson	18	Murfreesboro	25	Savannah
5	Dickson	12	Knoxville	19	Nashville	26	Shelbyville
6	Elizabethton	13	Livingston	20	Newbern	27	Whiteville
7	Harriman	14	McKenzie	21	Oneida		

Source: Tennessee Higher Education Commission, *Statistical Abstract of Tennessee Higher Education.*

TABLE 16.10--VOCATIONAL-TECHNICAL EDUCATION ENROLLMENTS, BY INSTRUCTIONAL CATEGORY AND BY GRADE LEVEL, TENNESSEE, FISCAL YEAR 1988

Instructional category	Grade level 6	7	8	9	10	11	12	Adult supplementary
TOTAL	2,584	5,147	8,060	48,402	45,509	47,364	56,335	25,223
Agriculture	39	21	54	6,014	4,407	3,576	4,051	496
Marketing and distributive education	4	4	3	150	588	3,971	6,651	413
Office occupations	68	39	72	6,770	9,773	10,471	12,936	10,959
Technical	0	0	0	21	34	117	201	280
Health occupations	1	0	2	493	1,178	1,071	962	1,021
Consumer and homemaking	459	1,335	2,481	14,426	8,238	7,913	11,382	1,921
Occupational home economics	21	20	55	772	1,682	1,984	2,139	3,202
Industrial arts	1,721	3,652	5,135	9,720	3,097	2,336	2,579	0
Trades and industry	91	12	131	7,265	12,747	12,842	12,207	6,931
Special programs	180	64	127	2,771	3,765	3,083	3,227	0

Source: Tennessee Department of Education, direct correspondence.

TABLE 16.11–NUMBER OF DEGREES CONFERRED BY STATE INSTITUTIONS OF HIGHER EDUCATION, BY TYPE OF DEGREE, TENNESSEE, SCHOLASTIC YEAR 1988

Institution and location	Bachelor's degrees	Master's degrees	Ed.S. or education specialist degrees	Professional degrees	Doctoral degrees
U.T. Chattanooga	817	230	0	0	0
U.T. Knoxville	3,368	1,110	11	217	217
U.T. Martin	701	68	0	0	0
U.T. Center for Health Sciences, Memphis	148	42	0	289	8
Austin Peay State University, Clarksville	511	83	1	0	0
East Tennessee State University, Johnson City	1,202	331	10	49	11
Memphis State University, Memphis	1,791	714	5	146	58
Middle Tennessee State University, Murfreesboro	1,439	282	21	0	13
Tennessee State University, Nashville	511	196	1	0	16
Tennessee Technological University, Cookeville	999	206	32	0	5

Note: Excludes duplicates for double majors.

Source: Tennessee Higher Education Commission, *Statistical Abstract of Tennessee Higher Education, 1988–89.*

TABLE 16.12–ACCREDITED PRIVATE INSTITUTIONS OF HIGHER EDUCATION, TENNESSEE, 1988

Institution	Location	Controlling body
Aquinas Junior College[1]	Nashville	Roman Catholic
Belmont College	Nashville	Southern Baptist
Bethel College	McKenzie	Cumberland Presbyterian
Bryan (Wm. Jennings) College	Dayton	Independent
Carson-Newman College	Jefferson City	Southern Baptist
Christian Brothers College	Memphis	Roman Catholic
Cumberland College	Lebanon	Independent
David Lipscomb College	Nashville	Church of Christ
Fisk University	Nashville	Independent
Freed-Hardeman College	Henderson	Church of Christ
Hiwassee College[1]	Madisonville	United Methodist
John A. Gupton College[2]	Nashville	Independent
Johnson Bible College	Knoxville	Christian
King College	Bristol	Presbyterian
Lambuth College	Jackson	United Methodist
Lane College	Jackson	United Methodist
Lee College	Cleveland	Church of God
LeMoyne-Owen College	Memphis	United Church of Christ
Lincoln Memorial University	Harrogate	Independent
Martin College[1]	Pulaski	United Methodist
Maryville College	Maryville	Presbyterian
Meharry Medical College	Nashville	Independent
Memphis Academy of Arts	Memphis	Independent
Milligan College	Milligan College	Christian
Morristown College[1]	Morristown	United Methodist
Rhodes College[3]	Memphis	Presbyterian
Southern College of Optometry[2]	Memphis	Independent
Southern College[4]	Collegedale	Seventh Day Adventist
Tennessee Wesleyan	Athens	United Methodist
Tomlinson College	Cleveland	Church of God
Trevecca Nazarene College	Nashville	Church of the Nazarene
Tusculum College	Greeneville	Presbyterian
Union University	Jackson	Southern Baptist
University of the South	Sewanee	Episcopal
Vanderbilt University	Nashville	Independent

Note: Associations accredited by the Southern Association of Colleges and Schools.

1. Junior college.

2. Private professional schools.

3. Formerly Southwestern at Memphis.

4. Formerly Southern Missionary College.

Source: Tennessee Council of Private Colleges, direct correspondence.

TABLE 16.13--FALL ENROLLMENT IN PRIVATE INSTITUTIONS OF HIGHER EDUCATION, TENNESSEE, 1985–1988

	Headcount				Full-time equivalent[1]			
Institution	1988	1987	1986	1985	1988	1987	1986	1985
TOTAL	43,219	39,721	38,380	37,752	39,276	35,655	35,133	34,685
Aquinas	443	330	293	310	284	232	222	236
Belmont	2,580	2,677	2,364	2,257	2,104	2,112	1,943	1,891
Bethel	596	633	495	469	486	487	415	420
Bryan	517	452	442	508	460	406	431	498
Carson-Newman	1,974	1,883	1,681	1,590	1,870	1,810	1,632	1,553
Christian Brothers	1,798	1,740	1,642	1,543	1,542	1,280	1,369	1,287
Cumberland[2]	645	693	570	640	415	437	410	383
David Lipscomb	2,330	2,330	2,245	2,262	2,208	2,306	2,224	2,136
Fisk	774	650	538	506	786	691	541	531
Freed-Hardeman	1,169	1,193	1,083	1,050	1,154	1,157	1,098	1,047
Hiwassee	584	594	661	591	503	505	590	546
John A. Gupton	55	48	50	49	56	48	52	51
Johnson Bible	430	380	392	397	419	391	402	390
King	589	597	555	588	632	531[a]	507	498
Knoxville	1,310	633	436	370	1,199	608	407	335
Lambuth	767	671	638	688	687	600	549	595
Lane	541	501	531	632	514	463	508	609
Lee	1,535	1,324	1,214	1,204	1,483	1,275	1,172	1,219
LeMoyne-Owen	1,130	n.a.	885	951	1,020	n.a.	830	831
Lincoln Memorial	1,582	1,410	1,348	1,314	1,315	1,157	1,155	1,147
Martin	330	295	271	256	319	255	243	234
Maryville	787	647	676	654	648	503	533	523
Meharry Medical	683	742	725	778	683	742	725	778
Memphis College of Arts	254	247	278	262	225	222	240	228
Milligan	658	586	607	603	636	618	617	618
Morristown	(b)	183	178	148	(b)	n.a.	n.a.	171
Rhodes	1,346	1,308	1,226	1,063	1,293	1,272	1,215	1,053
Southern	1,443	1,366	1,327	1,468	1,208	1,111	1,075	1,168
Southern College of Optometry	382	373	386	397	407	608	585	587
Tennessee Wesleyan	600	572	546	503	510	473	478	445
Tomlinson	248	188	227	224	255	190	240	238
Trevecca Nazarene	1,977	1,727	1,404	1,058	1,378	1,288	1,120	918
Tusculum	953	884	801	660	1,252	870	788	590
Union	2,017	1,761	1,546	1,511	1,636	1,479	1,247	1,250
University of the South	1,171	1,142	1,151	1,179	1,160	1,127	1,141	1,162
Vanderbilt	9,021	8,961	8,968	9,069	8,529	8,401	8,429	8,519

n.a. not available.

1. Represents the total number of degree credits taken by undergraduates divided by 15; for graduates the total is divided by 12.

2. Prior to 1986, Cumberland University's headcount included non-degree students.

a. The FTE number for 1987 was obtained directly from King College and differs from that given in source.

b. Morristown College merged with Knoxville College in 1988.

Source: Tennessee Higher Education Commission, *Statistical Abstract of Tennessee Higher Education, 1988–89.*

FIGURE 16.3
Expenditures per Pupil in Average Daily Attendance in Tennessee County School Districts, Scholastic Year 1988
(Tennessee average = $3,092)

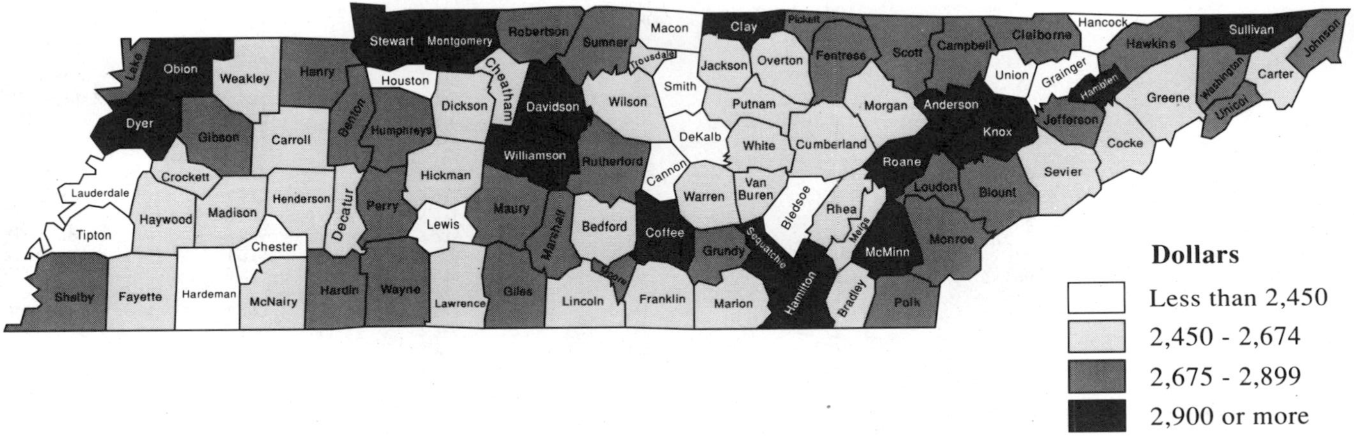

Note: For city school district per capita expenditures, see Table 16.14.
*Per pupil expenditures in Carroll and Gibson Counties are not comparable with other county school systems. They include special school systems.
Source: Tennessee Department of Education, direct correspondence.

TABLE 16.14--SELECTED PUBLIC SCHOOL STATISTICS, COUNTY AND CITY SCHOOL DISTRICTS, SCHOLASTIC YEAR 1988

County and local district	Net enrollment[1]	Average daily attendance	Number of teachers employed	Number of public schools	Total current expenditures ($1,000)	Expenditure per pupil in ADA[2] ($)
TENNESSEE	860,101	766,651	49,920	1,626	2,370,392	3,092
Anderson	6,868	6,155	476	18	22,064	3,585
Clinton	1,180	1,093	76	3	3,175	2,905
Oak Ridge	4,570	4,095	308	9	18,970	4,633
Bedford	5,554	5,184	301	10	12,978	2,504
Benton	2,628	2,386	156	7	6,802	2,851
Bledsoe	1,703	1,527	91	6	3,737	2,447
Blount	9,890	8,899	524	18	25,190	2,831
Alcoa	1,335	1,263	95	3	5,411	4,284
Maryville	3,506	3,235	240	5	10,671	3,299
Bradley	9,587	8,471	506	18	22,165	2,617
Cleveland	4,547	3,951	282	8	12,979	3,285
Campbell	7,329	6,332	413	18	18,046	2,850
Cannon	1,849	1,717	112	7	4,111	2,394
Carroll	0	0	18	3	1,418	0
Hollow Rock-Bruceton[3]	834	749	48	2	1,831	2,444
Huntingdon[3]	1,449	1,370	83	4	3,137	2,290
McKenzie[3]	1,384	1,290	83	3	3,114	2,414
South Carroll[3]	377	358	24	1	849	2,371
West Carroll[3]	1,171	1,072	64	6	2,694	2,513
Carter	6,778	6,117	423	17	15,589	2,548
Elizabethton	2,519	2,250	161	5	8,175	3,633
Cheatham	5,141	4,581	273	10	11,698	2,554
Chester	2,263	2,077	120	6	4,489	2,161
Claiborne	5,164	4,599	332	12	12,796	2,782
Clay	1,379	1,288	90	4	4,122	3,200
Cocke	4,813	4,257	247	12	10,932	2,568
Newport	793	736	45	1	1,881	2,556
Coffee	3,542	3,151	219	10	9,391	2,980
Manchester	1,185	1,034	76	3	3,799	3,674
Tullahoma	3,146	2,847	210	7	10,864	3,816

TABLE 16.14--SELECTED PUBLIC SCHOOL STATISTICS, COUNTY AND CITY SCHOOL DISTRICTS, SCHOLASTIC YEAR 1988 (Continued)

County and local district	Net enrollment [1]	Average daily attendance	Number of teachers employed	Number of public schools	Total current expenditures ($1,000)	Expenditure per pupil in ADA [2] ($)
Crockett	1,731	1,562	102	6	4,165	2,666
Alamo	452	430	22	1	888	2,066
Bells	340	310	19	1	716	2,309
Cumberland	5,999	5,360	319	10	13,853	2,585
Davidson-Nashville (Metro)	69,697	61,150	4,433	120	261,747	4,280
Decatur	1,934	1,807	112	5	4,537	2,511
DeKalb	2,623	2,378	145	5	5,750	2,418
Dickson	6,860	6,197	368	14	15,700	2,533
Dyer	3,404	3,023	196	8	10,101	3,341
Dyersburg	3,495	3,127	203	4	9,595	3,068
Fayette	4,905	4,457	256	9	11,410	2,560
Fentress	2,474	2,284	153	10	6,293	2,755
Franklin	6,173	5,720	349	17	14,100	2,465
Gibson	0	0	0	0	0	0
Humboldt	2,461	2,264	155	6	6,259	2,764
Milan	2,163	1,980	128	4	5,375	2,715
Trenton [3]	1,473	1,370	89	3	3,795	2,770
Bradford [3]	703	653	33	1	1,574	2,411
Gibson [3]	1,993	1,860	115	7	5,122	2,754
Giles	4,766	4,318	268	7	11,786	2,729
Grainger	3,143	2,880	171	7	6,734	2,338
Greene	7,049	6,405	404	18	16,892	2,637
Greeneville	2,789	2,601	208	7	10,319	3,967
Grundy	2,758	2,409	170	9	6,716	2,788
Hamblen	9,315	8,426	558	20	25,555	3,033
Hamilton	22,874	19,957	1,324	39	65,486	3,281
Chattanooga	24,288	21,330	1,609	53	82,849	3,884
Hancock	1,410	1,346	85	6	3,281	2,438
Hardeman	5,122	4,675	284	10	11,223	2,401
Hardin	4,553	3,912	248	12	10,547	2,696

TABLE 16.14--SELECTED PUBLIC SCHOOL STATISTICS, COUNTY AND CITY SCHOOL DISTRICTS, SCHOLASTIC YEAR 1988 (Continued)

County and local district	Net enrollment[1]	Average daily attendance	Number of teachers employed	Number of public schools	Total current expenditures ($1,000)	Expenditure per pupil in ADA[2] ($)
Hawkins	7,178	6,460	433	17	17,814	2,758
Rogersville	530	487	32	1	1,347	2,766
Haywood	4,407	4,042	244	6	10,479	2,592
Henderson	3,347	3,067	193	11	7,618	2,484
Lexington	831	779	40	1	1,778	2,283
Henry	3,557	3,207	206	7	9,027	2,815
Paris[3]	1,364	1,292	87	3	3,745	2,898
Hickman	2,877	2,575	164	5	6,710	2,606
Houston	1,433	1,280	79	3	3,096	2,418
Humphreys	3,100	2,859	171	6	7,890	2,760
Jackson	1,531	1,352	91	4	3,431	2,537
Jefferson	5,732	5,197	333	10	14,424	2,776
Johnson	2,694	2,264	158	10	6,541	2,889
Knox	54,725	46,759	3,295	93	151,995	3,251
Lake	1,248	1,106	77	3	3,073	2,778
Lauderdale	5,119	4,690	276	6	11,483	2,448
Lawrence	6,453	5,858	370	14	15,508	2,647
Lewis	1,844	1,659	98	3	3,518	2,121
Lincoln	4,339	3,876	236	9	10,055	2,594
Fayetteville	929	879	57	2	2,406	2,737
Loudon	3,865	3,518	233	11	9,981	2,837
Lenoir City	1,892	1,658	95	3	4,481	2,702
McMinn	5,920	5,283	337	10	15,322	2,900
Athens	1,893	1,704	120	5	5,916	3,472
Etowah	488	438	25	1	1,257	2,869
McNairy	4,420	4,003	210	9	9,940	2,483
Macon	2,841	2,584	147	7	5,751	2,226
Madison	7,702	7,057	420	15	18,378	2,604
Jackson	6,557	5,754	410	13	18,418	3,201

TABLE 16.14--SELECTED PUBLIC SCHOOL STATISTICS, COUNTY AND CITY SCHOOL DISTRICTS, SCHOLASTIC YEAR 1988 (Continued)

County and local district	Net enrollment [1]	Average daily attendance	Number of teachers employed	Number of public schools	Total current expenditures ($1,000)	Expenditure per pupil in ADA [2] ($)
Marion	5,280	4,551	281	11	11,521	2,532
Richard City[3]	189	176	14	1	417	2,368
Marshall	3,883	3,537	221	7	9,913	2,803
Maury	9,694	9,010	548	16	24,961	2,770
Meigs	1,624	1,444	88	6	3,694	2,558
Monroe	4,779	4,262	258	13	12,217	2,867
Sweetwater	1,287	1,132	64	3	2,832	2,502
Montgomery-Clarksville	16,716	14,162	881	19	41,970	2,964
Moore	980	890	58	2	2,543	2,858
Morgan	3,476	3,234	160	8	8,002	2,474
Obion	4,338	3,949	256	9	11,498	2,912
Union City	2,182	2,034	134	5	6,349	3,122
Overton	3,155	2,868	186	9	7,221	2,518
Perry	1,095	999	68	4	2,719	2,722
Pickett	793	741	53	2	1,994	2,691
Polk	2,721	2,373	157	6	6,629	2,794
Putnam	8,652	7,846	483	14	19,967	2,545
Rhea	4,324	3,750	240	7	9,927	2,647
Dayton	653	592	34	1	1,350	2,281
Roane	6,304	5,694	362	15	16,818	2,954
Harriman	1,996	1,789	125	7	5,579	3,118
Robertson	7,969	7,222	449	15	19,411	2,688
Rutherford	17,302	15,523	862	23	43,035	2,772
Murfreesboro	3,957	3,671	250	7	11,933	3,251
Scott	3,052	2,834	175	7	7,669	2,706
Oneida[3]	1,271	1,165	68	2	2,741	2,352
Sequatchie	1,843	1,674	125	6	5,131	3,065
Sevier	9,086	8,034	476	19	21,219	2,641
Shelby	35,616	31,430	1,701	36	86,505	2,752
Memphis	112,670	99,519	6,710	165	345,489	3,472

TABLE 16.14--SELECTED PUBLIC SCHOOL STATISTICS, COUNTY AND CITY SCHOOL DISTRICTS, SCHOLASTIC YEAR 1988 (Continued)

County and local district	Net enrollment[1]	Average daily attendance	Number of teachers employed	Number of public schools	Total current expenditures ($1,000)	Expenditure per pupil in ADA[2] ($)
Smith	2,678	2,492	148	10	5,725	2,297
Stewart	1,631	1,468	78	3	4,406	3,001
Sullivan	16,615	14,906	1,063	34	54,323	3,644
Bristol	3,694	3,255	267	8	14,329	4,402
Kingsport	5,223	4,665	373	11	20,362	4,365
Sumner	19,862	17,874	1,078	33	49,360	2,762
Tipton	6,717	5,951	316	6	13,512	2,271
Covington	1,088	997	58	1	2,630	2,638
Trousdale	1,133	1,057	66	2	2,642	2,500
Unicoi	2,947	2,649	177	9	7,349	2,774
Union	2,387	2,155	125	5	4,941	2,293
Van Buren	856	755	49	3	1,906	2,525
Warren	6,561	5,787	355	12	14,445	2,496
Washington	9,064	8,304	512	15	22,285	2,684
Johnson City	5,730	5,093	340	11	18,462	3,625
Wayne	2,711	2,433	173	10	6,617	2,720
Weakley	5,265	4,868	321	13	12,990	2,668
White	3,652	3,358	224	9	8,622	2,568
Williamson	11,118	10,129	592	18	30,035	2,965
Franklin[3]	3,259	2,952	211	5	9,496	3,217
Wilson	10,381	9,204	510	16	22,567	2,452
Lebanon[3]	2,395	2,232	138	4	5,305	2,377

1. Net enrollment consists of ungraded or unclassified, special education, and grades K-12.

2. Average daily attendance.

3. Special school district.

Source: Tennessee Department of Education, direct correspondence.

TABLE 16.15--MEDIAN YEARS OF SCHOOL COMPLETED BY PERSONS 25 YEARS OLD AND OLDER, BY RACE, SOUTHEASTERN STATES AND UNITED STATES, 1940–1980, DECENNIAL CENSUS YEARS

	Total					White					Nonwhite[1]				
State	1980	1970	1960	1950	1940	1980	1970	1960	1950	1940	1980	1970	1960	1950	1940
TENNESSEE	12.2	10.6	8.8	8.4	8.1	12.5	11.1	9.0	8.6	8.3	11.6	8.8	7.5	6.5	5.8
Alabama	12.2	10.8	9.1	7.9	7.1	12.5	11.6	10.2	8.8	8.2	11.5	8.1	6.5	5.4	4.5
Arkansas	12.4	10.5	8.9	8.3	7.9	12.5	11.1	9.5	8.7	8.4	10.8	8.0	6.5	5.6	5.2
Florida	12.2	11.3	10.9	9.6	8.6	12.2	11.8	11.6	10.9	9.3	12.1	7.6	7.0	5.8	5.2
Georgia	12.4	10.8	9.0	7.8	7.1	12.6	11.5	10.3	8.8	8.1	11.5	8.0	6.1	4.9	4.2
Kentucky	12.3	9.9	8.7	8.4	8.2	12.4	10.0	8.7	8.5	8.3	12.1	9.3	8.2	7.3	6.3
Louisiana	12.2	10.8	8.8	7.6	6.6	12.4	12.0	10.5	8.8	8.1	10.7	7.9	6.0	4.6	3.9
Mississippi	12.4	10.7	8.9	8.1	7.2	12.7	12.1	11.0	9.9	8.9	10.4	7.5	6.0	5.1	4.7
North Carolina	12.4	10.6	8.9	7.9	7.3	12.6	11.1	9.8	8.6	7.7	11.8	8.6	7.0	5.9	5.1
South Carolina	12.1	10.5	8.7	7.6	6.7	12.3	11.4	10.3	9.0	8.5	10.4	7.7	5.9	4.8	3.9
Virginia	12.4	11.7	9.9	8.5	7.5	12.5	12.1	10.8	9.3	7.9	11.0	8.7	7.2	6.1	5.1
West Virginia	12.2	10.6	8.8	8.5	8.3	12.2	10.6	8.8	8.6	8.3	12.1	9.6	8.4	7.6	6.5
UNITED STATES	12.5	12.1	10.6	9.3	8.6	12.5	12.1	10.9	9.7	8.7	12.0	9.8	8.2	6.9	5.8

1. In the 1980 Census, the category entitled "Black" most closely approximates the Nonwhite category.

Source: U.S. Department of Commerce, Bureau of the Census, *1980 Census of Population, General Social and Economic Characteristics, United States Summary*; and individual states; and earlier editions.

TABLE 16.16–ESTIMATED PUBLIC SCHOOL FALL ENROLLMENT, AVERAGE DAILY MEMBERSHIP AND ATTENDANCE, DAILY ATTENDANCE AS A PERCENTAGE OF FALL ENROLLMENT, AND NUMBER OF PUBLIC HIGH SCHOOL GRADUATES, SOUTHEASTERN STATES AND UNITED STATES, SCHOLASTIC YEAR 1989

State	Fall enrollment			Average daily membership	Average daily attendance		Number of public high school graduates
	Total	Elementary	Secondary		Number	Percentage of fall enrollment	
TENNESSEE	829,898	591,577	238,321	818,840	767,400	92.5	48,350
Alabama	730,032	408,151	321,881	723,577	686,285	94.0	43,415
Arkansas	436,387	242,259	194,128	429,559	411,535	94.3	28,317
Florida	1,724,939	949,062	775,877	1,769,113	1,644,744	95.4	91,255
Georgia[1]	1,111,365	779,067	332,298	1,079,135	1,034,890	93.1	62,285
Kentucky	637,627	433,482	204,145	606,125	574,000	90.0	40,742
Louisiana	782,900	578,300	204,600	750,900	707,500	90.4	37,900
Mississippi[1]	503,326	316,149	187,177	511,092	490,085	97.4	27,896
North Carolina	1,081,138	759,529	321,609	1,069,800	1,009,615	93.4	69,893
South Carolina	615,500	438,600	176,900	594,600	575,000	93.4	36,800
Virginia	982,081	628,445	353,636	974,028	917,147	93.4	65,700
West Virginia	335,912	197,270	138,642	n.a.	311,592	92.8	22,591
UNITED STATES	40,292,308	25,506,170	14,786,138	n.a.	37,240,835	92.4	2,445,411

Note: With some exceptions, enrollment data are based on organizational level; i.e., kindergarten and grades 1–6 as elementary; and junior and senior high school, grades 7–12, as secondary.

n.a. not available.

1. NEA Research estimates based on regression equations. Used where state did not submit data.

Source: National Education Association, *Estimates of School Statistics, 1988–89*. Used by special permission.

TABLE 16.17–ESTIMATED TOTAL CURRENT EXPENDITURES AND AVERAGE EXPENDITURE PER PUPIL IN PUBLIC SCHOOLS, SOUTHEASTERN STATES AND UNITED STATES, SCHOLASTIC YEARS 1988 AND 1989

	Total current expenditures[1] (1,000)		Average expenditure per pupil in ADA	
State	1989	1988	1989	1988
TENNESSEE	$2,536,319	$2,370,392	$3,305	$3,092
Alabama	2,000,532	1,899,500	2,915	2,754
Arkansas	1,110,278	1,071,671	2,698	2,618
Florida	7,380,475	6,661,680	4,487	4,353
Georgia[2]	4,287,594	3,842,715	4,143	3,715
Kentucky	2,098,120	1,993,960	3,655	3,444
Louisiana[2]	2,371,220	2,237,500	3,352	3,148
Mississippi[2]	1,394,632	1,302,241	2,846	2,716
North Carolina	3,908,800	3,687,400	3,872	3,639
South Carolina	1,992,511	1,891,470	3,465	3,340
Virginia	4,350,504	4,056,036	4,744	4,436
West Virginia	1,208,800	1,179,300	3,879	3,693
UNITED STATES	167,931,394	157,655,582	4,509	4,257

Note: Data for 1988 are revised, and data for 1989 are preliminary and subject to future revision.

1. Refers to expenditures for public elementary and secondary day schools. Excludes current expenditures for other programs, capital outlay, and interest on school debt.

2. NEA Research estimates based on regression equations. Used where state did not submit data.

Source: National Education Association, *Estimates of School Statistics, 1988–89*. Used by special permission.

TABLE 16.18--ESTIMATED AVERAGE ANNUAL SALARIES OF TOTAL INSTRUCTIONAL STAFF AND OF CLASSROOM TEACHERS, SOUTHEASTERN STATES AND UNITED STATES, SCHOLASTIC YEARS 1988 AND 1989 [In dollars except percentages]

State	1989					1988[r]			
	Average salary of instructional staff	Average salary of classroom teachers				Average salary of instructional staff	Average salary of classroom teachers		
		All teachers	Percentage increase 1988-89	Elementary school	Secondary school		All teachers	Elementary school	Secondary school
TENNESSEE[1]	26,512	25,619	7.7	25,560	25,715	24,536	23,785	23,726	23,880
Alabama	26,150	25,190	8.0	25,190	25,190	24,210	23,320	23,320	23,320
Arkansas	22,503	21,692	6.6	20,959	22,408	21,097	20,340	19,650	21,006
Florida	28,697	26,648	5.8	27,025	25,834	27,052[a]	25,198	25,622	24,548
Georgia[2]	29,752	28,038	7.1	27,743	28,512	27,606	26,190	25,964	26,554
Kentucky	26,020	24,920	2.8	24,310	26,206	25,327	24,253	23,655	25,505
Louisiana	23,100	22,470	5.9	22,090	23,240	21,802	21,209	20,847	21,936
Mississippi[2]	22,664	22,036	7.2	21,691	22,499	21,175	20,562	20,189	21,037
North Carolina	26,761	25,650	3.0	25,529	25,827	25,900	24,900	24,821	25,011
South Carolina	26,200	25,060	2.7	24,474	26,116	25,505	24,403	23,832	25,431
Virginia	29,503	29,056	6.9	28,205	30,207	27,705	27,193	26,395	28,268
West Virginia	22,889	21,904	0.8	21,460	22,500	22,711	21,736	21,302	22,335
UNITED STATES	30,853	29,567	5.6	28,909	30,293	29,177	28,008	27,420	28,829

r revised.

1. Includes career ladder supplement.

2. NEA Research estimates based on regression equation. Used where state did not submit data.

a. See footnote 2.

Source: National Education Association, *Estimates of School Statistics, 1988–89*. Used by special permission.

TABLE 16.19--STATE AND LOCAL GOVERNMENT FULL-TIME EQUIVALENT EMPLOYMENT AND PAYROLL IN EDUCATION, SOUTHEASTERN STATES, OCTOBER 1987

	Number of employees				October payroll ($1,000)			
State	Total	Elementary and secondary schools	Institutions of higher education	Other education[1]	Total	Elementary and secondary schools	Institutions of higher education	Other education[1]
TENNESSEE	110,765	82,681	26,188	1,896	189,219	135,771	49,878	3,570
Alabama	103,068	72,976	25,689	4,403	174,609	111,402	54,522	8,685
Arkansas	58,974	45,290	11,869	1,815	88,933	63,686	22,254	2,993
Florida	249,384	198,454	48,529	2,401	499,097	394,678	100,297	4,121
Georgia	157,767	125,838	28,711	3,218	274,085	204,699	63,268	6,117
Kentucky	94,855	71,729	18,922	4,204	155,665	114,421	33,113	8,130
Louisiana	116,492	88,396	24,274	3,822	183,065	131,737	44,488	6,840
Mississippi	74,279	54,834	18,078	1,367	104,608	71,706	30,570	2,332
North Carolina	175,363	125,249	46,826	3,288	335,649	229,422	99,322	6,905
South Carolina	94,676	68,823	22,904	2,949	161,427	112,192	43,849	5,386
Virginia	160,688	121,871	36,163	2,654	312,261	224,622	82,281	5,358
West Virginia	55,116	43,479	10,118	1,519	95,286	73,107	19,708	2,471

Note: Detail may not add to total due to independent rounding.

1. State government only.

Source: U.S. Department of Commerce, Bureau of the Census, *Public Employment in 1987*.

TABLE 16.20–ESTIMATED PUBLIC SCHOOL REVENUE AND PERCENTAGE DISTRIBUTIONS, BY SOURCE, SOUTHEASTERN STATES AND UNITED STATES, SCHOLASTIC YEAR 1989

State	Total receipts[1] ($1,000)	Total revenue receipts ($1,000)	Percentage of revenue receipts by source		
			Federal	State	Local and other
TENNESSEE	2,839,748	2,646,049	9.6	49.7	40.7
Alabama	2,240,300	2,130,300	11.7	71.4	16.9
Arkansas	1,382,064	1,358,420	9.3	60.8	29.8
Florida	9,139,469	8,511,866	6.3	53.8	40.0
Georgia[2]	4,530,513	4,521,453	7.1	59.7	33.2
Kentucky	2,424,620	2,219,590	9.9	69.9	20.1
Louisiana[2]	2,693,520	2,482,910	12.1	55.1	32.8
Mississippi[2]	1,598,617	1,488,402	15.0	54.4	30.5
North Carolina[2]	4,241,390	4,215,490	6.9	63.6	29.6
South Carolina	2,450,900	2,291,900	8.0	54.5	37.5
Virginia	4,680,558	4,591,083	4.7	34.6	60.7
West Virginia	1,326,216	1,323,816	8.6	63.4	28.0
UNITED STATES	192,975,635	185,121,978	6.3	50.2	43.5

Note: Data are preliminary estimates.

1. Includes non-revenue receipts.

2. NEA Research estimates based on regression equations. Used where state did not submit data.

Source: National Education Association, *Estimates of School Statistics, 1988–89*. Used by special permission.

TABLE 16.21--SELECTED STATISTICS FOR INSTITUTIONS OF HIGHER EDUCATION, SOUTHEASTERN STATES AND UNITED STATES, 1986–1988, ACADEMIC YEARS

State	Number of institutions, 1987–88			Fall enrollment, 1987p			Degrees conferred, 1986–87p		
	Total	Public	Private	Total	Public	Private	Bachelor's	Master's and first-profes-sional	Doctor's
TENNESSEE	87	24	63	202,006	154,104	47,902	17,328	5,344	576
Alabama	93	59	34	183,348	162,278	21,070	15,981	4,743	279
Arkansas	38	20	18	79,273	68,313	10,960	7,036	2,202	112
Florida	94	38	56	489,964	405,292	84,672	31,430	11,149	1,109
Georgia	95	49	46	224,066	174,355	49,711	19,103	7,642	654
Kentucky	60	22	38	153,351	122,019	31,332	11,708	4,405	281
Louisiana	34	20	14	173,229	148,492	24,737	16,221	5,364	301
Mississippi	47	29	18	105,510	93,284	12,226	9,173	2,498	272
North Carolina	127	75	52	321,251	258,930	62,321	24,919	7,298	788
South Carolina	64	33	31	140,841	113,352	27,489	12,559	4,007	266
Virginia	79	39	40	319,026	275,583	43,443	24,010	7,232	693
West Virginia	29	16	13	77,256	67,959	9,297	7,518	2,080	110
UNITED STATES	3,587	1,591	1,996	12,768,307	9,975,064	2,793,243	991,339	362,307	34,120

p preliminary.
Source: U.S. Department of Education, National Center for Education Statistics, direct correspondence.

TABLE 16.22--CURRENT FUNDS REVENUES OF INSTITUTIONS OF HIGHER EDUCATION, BY SOURCE, SOUTHEASTERN STATES, FISCAL YEAR 1986
[In thousands of dollars]

State	All institutions					Publicly controlled institutions	Privately controlled institutions
	Total	Student tuition and fees	Revenue from governmental appropriations				
			Federal	State	Local		
TENNESSEE	1,877,193	342,651	16,195	498,842	387	1,138,091	739,102
Alabama	1,641,730	230,650	12,216	627,784	5,509	1,445,286	196,445
Arkansas	643,441	91,045	11,200	256,238	0	562,620	80,821
Florida	2,652,329	625,046	7,237	1,079,951	4,236	1,869,120	783,209
Georgia	2,047,512	359,423	10,769	645,499	12,415	1,294,853	752,659
Kentucky	1,188,616	214,760	16,015	450,831	3,231	973,553	215,063
Louisiana	1,475,458	273,557	13,120	532,749	1,773	1,102,462	372,996
Mississippi	849,753	129,832	21,475	330,527	19,837	777,216	72,537
North Carolina	2,747,945	389,959	22,289	992,447	39,577	1,899,142	848,803
South Carolina	1,189,513	217,443	11,367	471,241	10,982	981,908	207,605
Virginia	2,329,990	492,878	76,771	741,665	1,601	1,911,614	418,375
West Virginia	478,126	88,358	7,491	212,551	0	401,635	76,491

Note: Total includes items not shown separately. Detail may not add to total due to independent rounding.

Source: U.S. Department of Education, National Center for Education Statistics, direct correspondence.

TABLE 16.23-CURRENT FUNDS EXPENDITURES OF PUBLIC AND PRIVATE INSTITUTIONS OF HIGHER EDUCATION, SOUTHEASTERN STATES, FISCAL YEARS 1985 AND 1986 [In thousands of dollars]

	1986				1985		
State	All institutions	Percentage change 1985–1986	Public	Private	All institutions	Public	Private
TENNESSEE	1,819,524	11.0	1,115,025	704,500	1,639,121	989,248	649,872
Alabama	1,569,104	10.2	1,368,367	200,738	1,424,251	1,229,522	194,729
Arkansas	632,008	8.9	552,265	79,743	580,251	504,532	75,718
Florida	2,594,198	8.1	1,841,210	752,988	2,398,730	1,701,865	696,865
Georgia	1,998,237	10.4	1,283,345	714,892	1,809,285	1,166,932	642,353
Kentucky	1,137,605	6.5	929,204	208,401	1,067,963	871,944	196,019
Louisiana	1,445,413	5.7	1,085,697	359,715	1,367,252	1,036,901	330,351
Mississippi	819,274	6.9	748,783	70,491	766,451	697,040	69,410
North Carolina	2,697,651	9.4	1,841,191	856,461	2,466,095	1,669,337	796,757
South Carolina	1,183,595	10.3	975,985	207,610	1,073,048	875,434	197,614
Virginia	2,259,218	9.1	1,860,619	398,599	2,070,441	1,712,808	357,633
West Virginia	470,400	5.9	392,757	77,643	444,265	367,984	76,281

Note: Detail may not add to total due to independent rounding.

Source: U.S. Department of Education, National Center for Education Statistics, direct correspondence.

Users of health statistics data should be aware that funding cuts in the proposed fiscal year 1991 federal statistical budget threaten statistical programs for the National Center for Health Statistics (NCHS). This agency compiles and publishes details of birth, death, marriage and divorce for the United States and for state-by-state comparisons in its annual report, *Vital Statistics of the United States*. A *Monthly Vital Statistics Report* is also issued. NCHS also collects data on hospitals and health care. Other national data sources providing comparative data for states include the U.S. Health Care Financing Administration, which publishes *Health Care Financing Review*; the American Medical Association; the American Dental Association; the American Hospital Association, publisher of *Hospital Statistics* (copyright); and the Health Insurance Association of America, which publishes the *Source Book of Health Insurance*. These sources of national health and vital statistics data are noted in order to provide *Abstract* users with complete source information. The *Statistical Abstract of the United States* is an intermediary source for much of the state and national data used in this chapter.

In Tennessee, the Department of Health and Environment, Center for Health Statistics, provides state and county data on births, deaths, marriage, and divorce, as well as details of morbidity, health care, and medical personnel and facilities. Publications include the *Annual Bulletin of Vital Statistics*; the *Annual Report of Hospitals, Nursing Homes, and Homes for the Aged in Tennessee; Teenage Childbearing; Induced Abortions Reported in Tennessee;* and *Vital Signs*. The State Licensing Board for the Healing Arts and the State Board of Dentistry, also in the Department of Health and Environment, publish annual directories of doctors of medicine, osteopathy and dentistry. These reports provide a good picture of health care resources and vital statistics in Tennessee and its local and county areas.

In cases where the publication of reports significantly lags data collection, the Tennessee Department of Health and Environment has graciously provided the needed data from department files. Hence, many tables in this chapter carry a source citation, "unpublished data."

In most cases, the tables of this chapter contain "resident data." These include all births or deaths of residents of the specific area, regardless of the place of occurrence. "Recorded data," data by place of occurrence, are for a specific area, regardless of the place of residence of the individual. Recorded data are used for marriage and divorce information.

TABLE OF CONTENTS

TABLE OF CONTENTS
(Continued)

FIGURE 17.1
Live Birth and Death Rates per 1,000 Population, Tennessee, 1940–1987

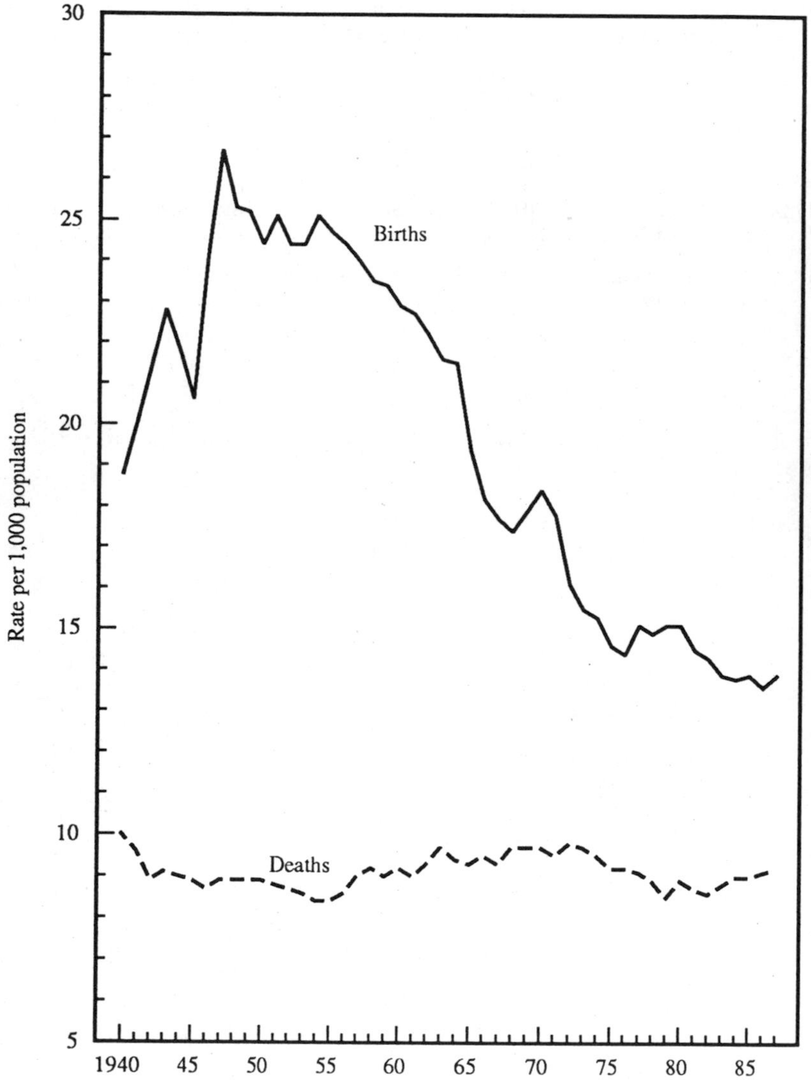

Source: Tennessee Department of Health and Environment, *Annual Bulletin of Vital Statistics*, and direct correspondence.

TABLE 17.1--NUMBER OF LIVE BIRTHS, NUMBER OF DEATHS, AND BIRTH AND DEATH RATES, BY RACE, TENNESSEE, 1935–1987, SELECTED YEARS

Year	Number of live births			Total live birth rate	Number of deaths			Total death rate
	Total	White	Nonwhite		Total	White	Nonwhite	
1987	67,942	51,410	16,528	13.9	44,884	37,307	7,572	9.2
1986	66,246	50,445	15,798	13.6	44,237	36,674	7,561	9.1
1985	66,730	50,989	15,735	13.9	43,176	35,729	7,444	9.0
1984	64,937	49,951	14,979	13.8	42,221	35,031	7,183	9.0
1983	65,465	50,469	14,989	13.9	41,604	34,438	7,161	8.8
1982	67,078	51,748	15,327	14.3	40,260	33,238	7,021	8.6
1981	67,050	51,429	15,614	14.5	40,480	33,533	6,941	8.7
1980	69,102	52,967	16,129	15.1	40,713	33,416	7,291	8.9
1979	68,326	52,303	16,021	15.1	38,712	31,837	6,875	8.5
1978	66,466	51,183	15,275	14.9	38,654	31,964	6,690	8.9
1977	66,632	52,110	14,521	15.1	39,080	32,110	6,970	9.1
1976	62,514	48,750	13,760	14.4	38,938	32,086	6,847	9.2
1975	62,265	48,453	13,808	14.6	38,522	31,504	7,013	9.2
1974	64,154	50,201	13,952	15.3	39,376	32,214	7,158	9.5
1973	64,303	50,113	14,187	15.5	39,724	32,319	7,394	9.7
1972	65,802	51,609	14,191	16.1	39,345	32,039	7,306	9.8
1971	71,202	56,075	15,125	17.8	37,783	30,671	7,112	9.5
1970	72,273	56,777	15,493	18.4	38,079	30,878	7,200	9.7
1969	69,921	55,133	14,788	17.9	37,832	30,441	7,391	9.7
1968	67,029	52,779	14,249	17.4	37,373	29,827	7,545	9.7
1967	67,740	52,991	14,749	17.7	35,736	28,843	6,893	9.3
1966	68,871	53,769	15,102	18.2	36,108	28,873	7,235	9.5
1965	72,990	56,380	16,610	19.4	35,049	28,116	6,933	9.3
1964	80,100	62,526	17,572	21.5	34,815	27,597	7,218	9.4
1963	79,715	62,145	17,570	21.6	35,633	28,223	7,410	9.7
1962	80,893	62,945	17,948	22.2	34,025	26,852	7,173	9.3
1961	82,067	63,830	18,236	22.7	32,625	25,744	6,880	9.0
1960	81,892	63,551	18,341	22.9	32,892	25,849	7,043	9.2
1959	82,956	64,555	18,401	23.4	31,813	24,990	6,823	9.0
1958	82,679	64,963	17,716	23.5	32,305	25,256	7,049	9.2
1957	83,923	65,469	18,454	24.0	31,329	24,328	7,001	9.0
1956	84,527	66,026	18,499	24.4	29,698	23,232	6,465	8.6
1955	84,713	66,661	18,048	24.7	28,886	22,463	6,422	8.4
1954	85,401	67,492	17,907	25.1	28,517	22,222	6,295	8.4
1953	82,585	65,402	17,183	24.4	29,106	22,362	6,744	8.6
1952	81,750	65,334	16,406	24.4	29,124	22,380	6,744	8.7
1951	83,521	67,007	16,501	25.1	29,281	22,425	6,856	8.8
1950	80,559	64,541	16,016	24.4	29,197	22,395	6,802	8.9
1949	82,307	67,047	15,258	25.2	29,012	22,248	6,764	8.9
1948	81,490	67,006	14,480	25.3	28,597	21,990	6,607	8.9
1947	85,284	71,845	13,437	26.7	28,456	21,891	6,563	8.9
1946	75,839	64,234	11,588	24.1	27,356	20,920	6,432	8.7
1945	64,101	53,473	10,622	20.6	27,680	21,052	6,624	8.9
1944	67,100	56,357	10,731	21.8	27,652	21,036	6,610	9.0
1943	69,205	58,391	10,808	22.8	27,782	20,752	7,030	9.1
1942	64,557	54,319	10,224	21.5	26,787	19,896	6,886	8.9
1941	59,415	50,127	9,284	20.1	28,373	20,959	7,406	9.6
1940	54,958	46,445	8,510	18.8	29,231	21,488	7,733	10.0
1935	52,827	44,511	8,302	19.0	29,425	21,632	7,785	10.6

Note: All data are by place of residence. Rates are per 1,000 population. For years where total does not equal the sum of the components, the total includes births and deaths with race unknown.

Source: Tennessee Department of Health and Environment, Center for Health Statistics, *Annual Bulletin of Vital Statistics*, 1986, and earlier editions; and unpublished data.

TABLE 17.2--NUMBER OF DEATHS, BY SELECTED MAJOR CAUSE, TENNESSEE, 1960–1987

Year	All causes [1]	Diseases of heart	Athero-sclerosis	Malignant neoplasms	Pneumonia and influenza	Conditions origi-nating in perinatal period
1987	44,884	15,779	347	10,004	1,361	405
1986	44,237	15,722	411	9,549	1,471	338
1985	43,176	15,740	429	9,220	1,437	367
1984	42,221	15,361	475	9,127	1,133	366
1983	41,604	15,206	495	8,768	1,117	395
1982	40,260	14,843	552	8,660	973	376
1981	40,480	14,894	620	8,355	1,174	445
1980	40,713	14,872	570	8,304	1,037	454
1979	38,712	14,115	642	7,792	908	464
1978	38,654	14,176	615	7,492	1,159	460
1977	39,080	14,497	582	7,507	1,070	481
1976	38,938	14,580	570	7,198	1,240	522
1975	38,522	14,303	622	6,869	1,101	526
1974	39,376	14,738	669	6,718	1,024	619
1973	39,724	15,011	641	6,501	1,197	726
1972	39,345	14,946	617	6,266	1,264	754
1971	37,783	14,528	558	6,070	1,193	847
1970	38,079	14,312	538	5,984	1,351	889
1969	37,832	14,345	634	5,737	1,402	881
1968	37,373	14,182	633	5,713	1,377	859
1967	35,736	13,173	709	5,465	1,247	913
1966	36,108	13,518	761	5,202	1,435	965
1965	35,049	12,763	744	5,108	1,356	1,094
1964	34,815	12,558	690	4,888	1,523	1,209
1963	35,633	12,561	668	5,134	1,880	1,192
1962	34,025	11,996	756	4,650	1,443	1,269
1961	32,625	11,119	701	4,634	1,326	1,256
1960	32,892	11,284	666	4,381	1,449	1,293

TABLE 17.2--NUMBER OF DEATHS, BY SELECTED MAJOR CAUSE, TENNESSEE, 1960–1987 (Continued)

Congenital anomalies	Diabetes Mellitus	Accidents (including motor vehicle)	Motor vehicle accidents	Suicide	Homicide and legal inter-vention	Year
230	701	2,334	1,298	623	495	1987
247	672	2,435	1,289	642	517	1986
244	597	2,185	1,135	598	431	1985
267	627	2,144	1,154	658	414	1984
275	646	2,173	1,076	604	440	1983
271	557	2,093	1,091	589	482	1982
262	609	2,205	1,132	577	510	1981
317	514	2,453	1,178	566	551	1980
280	552	2,350	1,268	607	474	1979
278	525	2,460	1,294	548	456	1978
281	565	2,440	1,245	588	477	1977
228	548	2,262	1,160	559	492	1976
298	612	2,310	1,142	567	568	1975
304	629	2,510	1,290	544	569	1974
325	610	2,698	1,442	490	550	1973
384	651	2,602	1,401	469	549	1972
339	675	2,467	1,337	490	486	1971
381	619	2,582	1,406	497	441	1970
339	607	2,531	1,358	461	423	1969
376	571	2,502	1,252	413	412	1968
372	498	2,466	1,286	404	379	1967
391	492	2,468	1,250	385	333	1966
387	461	2,247	1,143	379	316	1965
447	448	2,162	1,061	395	307	1964
422	428	2,100	977	359	266	1963
405	455	1,967	901	401	264	1962
420	419	1,825	795	346	263	1961
434	420	1,969	859	333	268	1960

Note: Data are by place of residence at time of death. Cause titles are shown according to the Ninth Revision International Classification of Disease, 1975, adopted for use January 1, 1979. Where necessary, regrouping of causes for 1960–1978 has been done to make numbers for these years correspond as nearly as possible with those for 1979–1987.

1. Includes categories not detailed separately.

Source: Tennessee Department of Health and Environment, Center for Health Statistics, *Annual Bulletin of Vital Statistics, 1986*; and unpublished data.

TABLE 17.3--DEATH RATES PER 100,000 POPULATION, BY MAJOR CAUSE, TENNESSEE, 1960–1987

Year	Diseases of the heart	Malig- nant neo- plasms	Cerebro- vascular disease	Accidents and adverse effects	Chronic obstructive pulmonary disease and allied conditions	Pneu- monia and in- fluenza	Sui- cide	Homi- cide and legal inter- vention	Dia- betes melli- tus
1987	321.7	204.0	77.3	47.6	32.8	27.8	12.7	10.1	14.3
1986	323.8	196.7	74.8	50.1	34.6	30.3	13.2	10.6	13.8
1985	327.3	191.7	74.9	45.4	33.0	29.9	12.4	9.0	12.4
1984	325.7	193.5	82.7	45.5	30.9	24.0	14.0	8.8	13.3
1983	321.8	185.5	87.6	46.0	27.3	23.6	12.8	9.3	13.7
1982	317.1	185.0	84.7	44.7	27.0	20.8	12.6	10.3	11.9
1981	321.3	180.2	88.2	47.6	27.9	25.3	12.4	11.0	13.1
1980	323.9	180.9	93.9	53.4	26.9	22.6	12.3	12.0	11.2
1979	311.4	171.9	92.9	51.8	23.2	20.0	13.4	10.5	12.2
1978	317.7	167.9	96.0	55.1	25.7	26.0	12.3	10.2	11.8
1977	329.3	170.5	103.6	55.4	23.7	24.3	13.4	10.8	12.8
1976	336.8	166.3	112.3	52.3	23.0	28.6	12.9	11.4	12.7
1975	335.7	161.2	115.0	54.2	21.9	25.8	13.3	13.3	14.4
1974	350.8	159.9	123.9	59.7	22.4	24.4	12.9	13.5	15.0
1973	362.7	157.1	129.0	65.2	21.8	28.9	11.8	13.3	14.7
1972	365.6	153.3	127.6	63.7	20.5	30.9	11.5	13.4	15.9
1971	362.3	151.4	124.6	61.5	17.0	29.8	12.2	12.1	16.8
1970	364.5	152.4	128.8	65.8	18.3	34.4	12.7	11.2	15.8
1969	368.1	147.2	130.8	64.9	17.9	36.0	11.8	10.9	15.6
1968	367.3	148.0	133.3	64.8	16.8	35.7	10.7	10.7	14.8
1967	344.3	142.9	131.2	64.5	16.5	32.6	10.6	9.9	13.0
1966	356.7	137.3	132.6	65.1	16.5	37.9	10.2	8.8	13.0
1965	340.0	136.1	131.4	59.9	17.2	36.1	10.1	8.4	12.3
1964	337.7	131.4	131.2	58.1	13.5	41.0	10.6	8.3	12.0
1963	341.1	139.4	136.0	57.0	14.4	51.0	9.7	7.2	11.6
1962	328.9	127.5	135.0	53.9	13.1	39.6	11.0	7.2	12.5
1961	307.9	128.3	130.2	50.5	11.4	36.7	9.6	7.3	11.6
1960	315.5	122.5	130.9	55.1	11.3	40.5	9.3	7.5	11.7

Note: Cause titles are shown according to the Ninth Revision International Classification of Disease, 1975, adopted for use on January 1, 1979. Where necessary, regrouping of causes for 1960–1978 has been done to make numbers for these years correspond as closely as possible with those for 1979–1987. Rates are based on number of deaths by place of residence at time of death.

Source: Tennessee Department of Health and Environment, Center for Health Statistics, *Annual Bulletin of Vital Statistics*, 1986; and unpublished data.

TABLE 17.4-- NUMBER OF INFANT AND NEONATAL DEATHS AND RATES PER 1,000 LIVE BIRTHS, BY RACE, RESIDENT DATA, TENNESSEE, 1960–1987, SELECTED YEARS

	Infant deaths[1]						Neonatal deaths[2]					
	Total		White		All other races		Total		White		All other races	
Year	Number	Rate	Number	Rate	Number	Rate	Number	Rate	Number	Rate	Number	Rate
1987	792	11.7	473	9.2	319	19.3	515	7.6	302	5.9	213	12.9
1986	726	11.0	437	8.7	289	18.3	456	6.9	281	5.6	175	11.1
1985	757	11.3	451	8.8	306	19.4	501	7.5	277	5.4	224	14.2
1984	768	11.8	491	9.8	277	18.5	516	7.9	319	6.4	197	13.2
1983	833	12.7	537	10.6	296	19.7	545	8.3	352	7.0	193	12.9
1982	804	12.0	519	10.0	285	18.6	532	7.9	339	6.6	193	12.6
1981	846[a]	12.6	522	10.1	321	20.6	593[a]	8.8	356	6.9	235	15.1
1980	929	13.4	625	11.8	304	18.8	626	9.1	424	8.0	202	12.5
1979	925	13.5	600	11.5	325	20.3	620	9.1	397	7.6	223	13.9
1978	981	14.8	664	13.0	317	20.8	691	10.4	461	9.0	230	15.1
1977	1,022	15.3	691	13.3	331	22.8	719	10.8	487	9.3	232	16.0
1976	1,007	16.1	674	13.8	333	24.2	724	11.6	491	10.1	233	16.9
1975	1,004	16.1	672	13.9	332	24.0	729	11.7	485	10.0	244	17.7
1974	1,110	17.3	756	15.1	354	25.4	828	12.9	570	11.4	258	18.5
1973	1,303[a]	20.3	898	17.9	404	28.5	956[a]	14.9	670	13.4	285	20.1
1972	1,384	21.0	925	17.9	459	32.3	1,021	15.5	687	13.3	334	23.5
1971	1,469	20.6	1,054	18.8	415	27.4	1,092	15.3	791	14.1	301	19.9
1970	1,540	21.3	1,061	18.7	479	30.9	1,173	16.2	839	14.8	334	21.6
1969	1,529	21.9	1,031	18.7	498	33.7	1,126	16.1	770	14.0	356	24.1
1968	1,549[a]	23.1	1,039	19.7	509	35.7	1,117	16.7	787	14.9	330	23.2
1967	1,649	24.3	1,107	20.9	542	36.7	1,176	17.4	825	15.6	351	23.8
1966	1,790	26.0	1,186	22.1	604	40.0	1,243	18.0	854	15.9	389	25.8
1965	2,024	27.7	1,327	23.5	697	42.0	1,409	19.3	970	17.2	439	26.4
1964	2,255	28.2	1,547	24.7	708	40.3	1,569	19.6	1,098	17.6	471	26.8
1960	2,399	29.3	1,610	25.3	789	43.0	1,651	20.2	1,180	18.6	471	25.7

1. A death of a live-born infant under one year of age.
2. A death of a live-born infant under 28 days of age.
a. Includes deaths with race not stated.
Source: Tennessee Department of Health and Environment, Center for Health Statistics, *Annual Bulletin of Vital Statistics*, 1986; and unpublished data.

TABLE 17.5--NUMBER OF INFANT DEATHS AND RATES PER 1,000 LIVE BIRTHS, BY CAUSE AND BY RACE, RESIDENT DATA, TENNESSEE, 1987

	Total		White		Nonwhite	
Cause of death	Number	Rate	Number	Rate	Number	Rate
Total[1]	792	11.7	473	9.2	319	19.3
Congenital anomalies	147	2.2	97	1.9	50	3.0
Sudden infant death syndrome	120	1.8	66	1.3	54	3.3
Respiratory distress syndrome	80	1.2	68	1.3	12	0.7
Immaturity	65	1.0	35	0.7	30	1.8
Accidents and adverse effects	30	0.4	19	0.4	11	0.7
Infections specific to the perinatal period	22	0.3	13	0.3	9	0.5
Intrauterine hypoxia and birth asphyxia	19	0.3	9	0.2	10	0.6
Maternal complications of pregnancy	14	0.2	7	0.1	7	0.4
Neonatal hemorrhage	13	0.2	1	0.0	12	0.7
Complications of placenta, cord and membranes	10	0.1	10	0.2	0	0.0

1. Total includes subcategories not listed separately.

Source: Tennessee Department of Health and Environment, Center for Health Statistics, unpublished data.

TABLE 17.6--ILLEGITIMATE BIRTHS AS A PERCENTAGE OF LIVE BIRTHS, BY RACE, TENNESSEE, 1950--1987

Year	Total	White	Nonwhite
1987	26.3	13.8	65.3
1986	25.3	13.0	64.6
1985	24.3	12.2	63.3
1984	22.9	11.2	62.0
1983	22.0	10.5	60.9
1982	20.9	9.7	58.7
1981	20.4	9.2	57.0
1980	19.8	8.8	56.2
1979	19.1	8.1	55.1
1978	18.2	7.4	54.1
1977	16.6	6.7	52.2
1976	16.5	6.1	53.3
1975	15.8	5.9	50.6
1974	14.9	5.4	49.3
1973	14.9	5.3	49.0
1972	14.4	5.2	47.9
1971	12.9	4.5	43.9
1970	12.5	4.6	41.5
1969	11.8	4.5	39.3
1968	11.8	4.4	39.1
1967	11.8	4.1	39.6
1966	11.3	4.0	37.2
1965	11.2	3.8	36.4
1964	9.9	3.2	33.9
1963	9.7	3.1	32.8
1962	9.5	3.1	32.1
1961	9.3	3.0	31.3
1960	8.7	2.7	29.4
1959	8.4	2.8	27.8
1958	8.0	2.7	27.3
1957	7.8	2.6	26.2
1956	7.6	2.5	25.7
1955	7.3	2.4	25.5
1954	7.0	2.4	24.6
1953	6.7	2.2	24.0
1952	6.0	2.2	21.1
1951	6.1	2.7	19.7
1950	5.8	2.1	20.6

Source: Tennessee Department of Health and Environment, Center for Health Statistics. ***Annual Bulletin of Vital Statistics***, 1986; and unpublished data.

FIGURE 17.2
Age-Specific Fertility Rates per 1,000 Female Population Aged 15-44 Years, Resident Data, Tennessee, 1970 and 1985

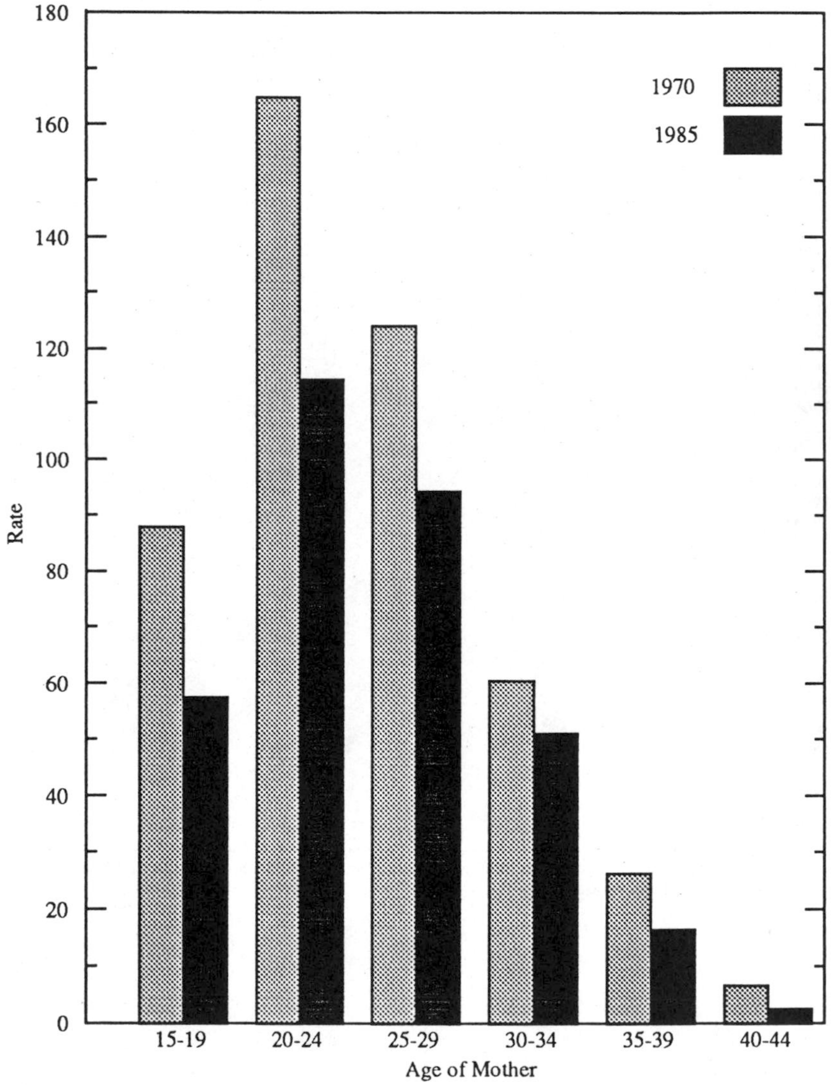

Note: Fertility rates refer to the number of live births per 1,000 female population.
Source: Tennessee Department of Health and Environment, Center for Health Statistics, unpublished data.

TABLE 17.7--TEENAGE PREGNANCIES, LIVE BIRTHS, AND PERCENTAGE OF LIVE BIRTHS THAT WERE ILLEGITIMATE, BY AGE GROUP AND BY RACE OF MOTHER, TENNESSEE, 1974-1987

Females 10-14 years of age

	Teenage pregnancies, all races[1]		Live births						
			All races		White		Other races		Percentage illeg-itimate, all races
Year	Number	Rate	Number	Rate	Number	Rate	Number	Rate	
1987	521	3.1	279	1.7	100	0.8	179	4.9	92.8
1986	580	3.4	293	1.7	99	0.7	194	5.3	91.8
1985	555	3.2	294	1.7	99	0.7	195	5.3	89.5
1984	497	2.9	252	1.5	80	0.6	172	5.0	90.9
1983	506	2.9	272	1.6	104	0.8	168	4.8	91.5
1982	494	2.8	292	1.6	113	0.8	179	5.1	85.3
1981	495	2.8	299	1.7	105	0.7	194	5.4	87.0
1980	527	2.9	291	1.6	118	0.8	173	4.7	85.2
1979	574	3.4	334	2.0	148	1.1	186	5.9	80.2
1978	565	3.2	359	2.0	159	1.1	200	6.0	81.3
1977	595	3.3	380	2.1	168	1.2	212	6.2	81.8
1976	616	3.4	384	2.1	150	1.0	234	6.7	77.1
1975	596	3.1	425	2.2	164	1.1	261	6.8	80.0
1974	606	3.1	455	2.4	175	1.1	280	7.1	75.2

Females 15-19 years of age

	Teenage pregnancies, all races[1]		Live births						
			All races		White		Other races		Percentage illeg-itimate, all races
Year	Number	Rate	Number	Rate	Number	Rate	Number	Rate	
1987	16,313	87.3	11,145	59.6	7,309	49.3	3,836	99.1	55.9
1986	16,110	84.9	10,972	57.8	7,326	48.7	3,646	93.0	52.2
1985	16,052	83.3	11,120	57.7	7,521	49.2	3,599	90.6	51.4
1984	15,927	80.1	11,016	55.9	7,562	47.8	3,454	89.1	48.7
1983	16,685	82.7	11,557	57.7	7,907	49.3	3,650	91.5	47.4
1982	17,511	85.5	12,221	59.7	8,434	51.4	3,787	93.1	44.7
1981	18,012	86.7	12,716	61.2	8,713	52.5	4,003	95.5	43.9
1980	19,276	91.5	13,468	63.9	9,206	54.9	4,262	98.8	42.5
1979	19,816	100.4	13,841	70.2	9,386	58.6	4,455	119.7	41.1
1978	18,759	94.5	13,830	69.7	9,376	58.3	4,453	118.1	40.3
1977	18,706	94.0	14,176	71.2	9,809	60.9	4,347	114.0	37.9
1976	18,964	95.8	14,243	71.9	9,660	60.5	4,583	120.0	37.0
1975	18,371	91.7	14,950	74.6	10,252	64.4	4,698	113.9	33.8
1974	18,538	93.6	15,943	80.5	10,858	68.8	5,085	126.0	32.1

Note: Rate is per 1,000 female population in specified race and age group.

1. Live births plus fetal deaths plus abortions.

Source: Tennessee Department of Health and Environment, Center for Health Statistics, *Teenage Childbearing, Resident Data, Tennessee, 1950–1982*, April 1984; and unpublished data.

TABLE 17.8-- NUMBER AND PERCENTAGE DISTRIBUTION OF WOMEN RECEIVING ABORTIONS, BY SELECTED CHARACTERISTICS, TENNESSEE, 1980–1987, SELECTED YEARS

	1987		1986		1985		1984		1983		1980	
Characteristics	Number	%	Number	%	Number	%	Number	%	Number	%	Number	%
Total	21,621	100.0	21,938	100.0	21,069	100.0	21,124	100.0	20,726	100.0	23,274	100.0
Age												
9 years or less	6,232	28.8	6,210	28.3	6,056	28.7	6,000	28.4	6,373	30.7	7,400	31.8
20--24 years	7,097	32.8	7,342	33.5	7,208	34.2	7,201	34.1	6,982	33.7	8,101	34.8
25 years and over	8,286	38.3	8,373	38.2	7,794	37.0	7,900	37.4	7,367	35.5	7,741	33.3
Race												
White	14,754	68.2	15,039	68.6	14,721	69.9	14,926	70.7	15,445	74.5	17,199	73.9
All other races	6,826	31.6	6,878	31.4	6,305	29.9	6,159	29.2	5,278	25.5	5,950	25.6
Marital status												
Married[1]	4,817	22.3	4,850	22.1	4,835	22.9	4,785	22.7	4,708	22.7	5,982	25.7
Unmarried	16,496	76.3	16,936	77.2	16,146	76.6	16,200	76.7	15,971	77.1	17,131	73.6
Number of living children												
None	11,846	54.8	12,198	55.6	12,117	57.5	12,173	57.6	12,469	60.2	13,619	58.5
One	5,277	24.4	5,235	23.1	4,788	22.7	4,684	22.2	4,440	21.4	4,841	20.8
Two	3,089	14.3	3,079	14.0	2,884	13.7	2,895	13.7	2,617	12.6	3,034	13.0
Three	961	4.4	976	4.4	861	4.1	908	4.3	785	3.8	1,072	4.6
Four	287	1.3	283	1.3	270	1.3	257	1.2	260	1.3	337	1.4
Five or more	140	0.6	152	0.7	133	0.6	163	0.8	151	0.7	225	1.0
Number of previous abortions												
None	14,799	68.4	15,138	69.0	14,522	68.9	14,492	68.6	14,793	71.4	17,190	73.9
One	4,904	22.7	4,887	22.3	4,788	22.7	4,787	22.7	4,574	22.1	4,718	20.3
Two	1,287	6.0	1,295	5.9	1,229	5.8	1,294	6.1	1,025	4.9	890	3.8
Three	398	1.8	401	1.8	340	1.6	373	1.8	254	1.2	164	0.7
Four	121	0.6	125	0.6	110	0.5	78	0.4	57	0.3	45	0.2
Five or more	79	0.4	64	0.3	60	0.3	52	0.2	19	0.1	10	(a)

Note: Percentages do not add to 100 as total includes observations with "characteristics not stated."

1. Married includes separated.

a. Percentage less than 0.05.

Source: Tennessee Department of Health and Environment, Center for Health Statistics, *Induced Abortions Reported in Tennessee*, 1987.

TABLE 17.9-- REPORTED CASES OF SELECTED COMMUNICABLE DISEASES, TENNESSEE, 1960–1987, SELECTED YEARS

Year	Encephalitis (all types)	Hepatitis (all types)	Measles	Meningococcal infections	Pertussis (whooping cough)	Salmonellosis[1]	Primary and secondary syphilis	Gonorrhea
1987	14	636	0	35	23	507	721	19,886
1986	13	793 r	55	45	18	474	624	26,891
1985	8	818 r	0	44	27	486	631	29,658
1984	22	901 r	2	52	7	450	543	30,748
1983	23	1,004 r	0	58	8	521	588	30,949
1982	33	1,012 r	6	79	26	455	656	32,663
1981	89	1,029	2	71	16	598	686	31,817
1980	35	1,023	170	61	37	546	926	29,932
1979	38	1,149	69	54	31	508	686	31,059
1978	34	1,249	952	58	60	513	387	31,201
1977	55	1,582	769	47	56	588	253	35,195
1976	78	1,663	187	64	33	363	289	35,362
1975	181	1,631	165	62	78	525	416	33,124
1974	98	1,976	54	51	80	485	450	30,188
1973	42	1,886	164	40	55	686	453	26,688
1972	41	1,548	195	35	128	527	509	26,891
1971	59	1,531	1,028	85	192	429	355	20,783
1970	64	1,344	608	75	161	880	179	16,366
1969	53	1,097	21	75	110	277	289	14,432
1968	48	1,058	64	72	180	313	310	12,456
1967	84	860	2,058	78	479	436	298	12,163
1966	58	1,015	12,955	100	313	229	305	11,105
1965	28	805	8,994	75	286	191	497	9,905
1964	47	910	25,309	71	578	220	480	9,369
1963	26	1,459	7,880	79	865	148	396	8,210
1960	36	2,100	19,202	66	1,111	97	448	9,881

r revised.

1. Excluding typhoid fever.

Source: Tennessee Department of Health and Environment, Center for Health Statistics, unpublished data.

TABLE 17.10--SELECTED DATA ON SHORT-TERM NON-FEDERAL HOSPITALS, BY TYPE OF OWNERSHIP, TENNESSEE, 1980–1985

Year and type of ownership	Number of hospitals	Staffed beds: Number	Staffed beds: Per 1,000 popu-lation	Average daily census	Average length of stay (days)	Percent-age occupancy	Full-time equivalent employees per 100 staffed beds
1985							
Total	151	24,000	5.0	15,015	6.4	62.5	285.1
State/local government	33	4,676	1.0	2,885	5.8	61.9	313.7
Nonprofit	59	13,273	2.8	9,077	6.8	68.0	321.9
Profit	59	6,051	1.3	3,054	6.0	50.9	182.3
1984							
Total	153	24,571	5.2	16,065	6.6	67.4	248.0
State/local government	35	5,046	1.1	2,961	5.8	66.4	214.2
Nonprofit	57	13,381	2.8	9,837	7.0	73.3	281.2
Profit	61	6,144	1.3	3,367	6.1	55.0	203.3
1983							
Total	152	25,127	5.4	17,189	6.7	71.7	261.8
State/local government	38	6,114	1.3	4,268	6.0	71.4	225.2
Nonprofit	53	12,966	2.8	9,294	7.2	76.3	306.6
Profit	61	6,047	1.3	3,626	6.5	62.5	202.6
1982							
Total	154	24,993	5.4	17,518	6.8	73.3	260.7
State/local government	41	6,062	1.3	4,197	6.0	70.7	238.3
Nonprofit	52	13,070	2.8	9,831	7.4	78.9	298.3
Profit	61	5,861	1.3	3,490	6.6	63.3	200.2
1981							
Total	152	24,614	5.3	18,040	6.8	74.6	251.4
State/local government	50	6,399	1.4	4,470	5.9	71.9	240.1
Nonprofit	45	13,006	2.8	10,247	7.4	79.1	281.2
Profit	57	5,209	1.1	3,323	6.5	66.4	191.1
1980							
Total	152	24,114	5.3	17,315	6.8	74.8	257.3
State/local government	57	7,083	1.5	5,036	6.1	72.3	223.7
Nonprofit	40	12,105	2.6	8,993	7.5	78.8	300.2
Profit	55	4,926	1.1	3,286	6.6	68.9	200.3

Note: Computed variables such as average length of stay were based on only those facilities which reported sufficient data necessary for the calculations. In addition, not every hospital reported every variable.

Source: Tennessee Department of Health and Environment, Center for Health Statistics, *Vital Signs*, Vol. 3, No. 1, April 1986; and unpublished data.

TABLE 17.11--NUMBER OF HOSPITALS, BY OWNERSHIP AND BY TYPE, TENNESSEE, 1983–1985

Year and type of hospital	Total	Government Ownership: Federal	Government Ownership: State and local	Private Ownership: Nonprofit	Private Ownership: Proprietary
1985 Total	173	6	39	64	64
Short-term	156	5	33	59	59
General	149	5	33	54	57
Specialty	7	0	0	5	2
Long-term	17	1	6	5	5
Psychiatric	15	1	5	4	5
Geriatric	2	0	1	1	0
1984 Total	172	6	41	61	64
Short-term	157	5	35	57	60
General	150	5	35	53	57
Specialty	7	0	0	4	3
Long-term	15	1	6	4	4
Psychiatric	13	1	5	3	4
Geriatric	2	0	1	1	0
1983 Total	171	5	44	57	65
Short-term	155	4	38	53	60
General	149	4	38	49	58
Specialty	6	0	0	4	2
Long-term	16	1	6	4	5
Psychiatric	14	1	5	3	5
Geriatric	2	0	1	1	0

Note: Includes only those facilities which reported to the Department of Health and Environment.

Source: Tennessee Department of Health and Environment, Center for Health Statistics, *Annual Report of Hospitals, Nursing Homes, and Homes for the Aged, 1980*; and unpublished data.

TABLE 17.12--AVERAGE EXPENSES PER PATIENT DAY FOR SHORT-TERM HOSPITALS REPORTING, BY SIZE OF HOSPITAL, TENNESSEE, 1963–1985 [In dollars]

Year	All hospitals	Size of hospital (in number of beds) Under 25	25–49	50–99	100–249	250–499	500 and over
1985	497.36	425.67	655.51	428.90	458.22	502.26	548.54
1984	419.03	356.33	520.10	350.22	399.84	428.33	448.51
1983	370.19	305.44	421.25	296.94	341.44	377.75	406.19
1982	327.06	283.65	348.13	268.37	304.02	331.35	362.95
1981	284.63	226.31	311.94	242.26	270.25	283.55	307.97
1980	234.03	170.57	276.08	193.28	216.31	248.38	247.33
1979	210.98	145.53	242.61	177.56	189.65	211.79	244.87
1978	181.24	123.33	147.38	145.66	168.09	182.38	211.20
1977	159.38	116.34	131.33	127.98	144.09	159.34	188.12
1976	140.27	102.30	111.36	119.28	131.37	146.30	155.14
1975	121.99	97.84	93.55	103.45	118.33	124.31	133.65
1974	88.38	70.07	76.79	81.90	104.50	99.48	102.84
1973	79.48	61.11	69.74	76.43	91.16	90.57	108.15
1972	74.08	60.03	71.06	70.06	83.01	86.02	90.04
1971	61.43	64.22	56.11	57.52	65.53	74.57	76.38
1970	55.54	50.47	49.53	52.11	61.13	70.41	79.88
1969	49.11	49.61	45.47	46.36	49.42	60.98	65.68
1968	43.45	46.86	40.27	39.70	46.73	51.69	55.40
1967	37.36	41.79	32.64	34.52	41.01	48.53	47.40
1966	33.18	31.18	31.35	31.62	35.77	42.27	40.05
1965	29.23	22.68	27.14	30.33	31.38	38.86	34.01
1964	27.30	23.54	25.08	27.54	29.23	36.87	30.52
1963	25.36	22.52	22.73	26.56	27.77	32.67	29.26

Note: Federal hospitals are not included. Data include only those hospitals reporting total cost, total annual depreciation, and total inpatient days, the three items necessary for computation.

Source: Tennessee Department of Health and Environment, Center for Health Statistics, *Annual Report of Hospitals, Nursing Homes, and Homes for the Aged in Tennessee, 1980*, and earlier editions; and unpublished data.

TABLE 17.13--NUMBER OF PERSONNEL AND TRAINEES IN REPORTING HOSPITALS, BY TYPE OF HOSPITAL AND BY TYPE OF PERSONNEL, TENNESSEE, 1985

Type of personnel and trainees	Total		Short-term[1]		Long-term			
					Psychiatric		Geriatric	
	FTE Employees	Per 100 beds	FTE Employees	Per 100 beds	FTE Employees	Per 100 beds	FTE Employees	Per 100 beds
Total personnel	81,501.3	271.4	75,013.5	287.3	5,837.2	181.3	650.6	92.9
Professional nurse (R.N.)	15,648.6	52.1	15,015.2	57.5	592.4	18.4	41.0	5.9
Licensed practical nurse (L.P.N.)	6,629.9	22.1	6,225.7	23.8	339.7	10.6	64.5	9.2
Nurse technician	2,608.1	8.7	1,629.5	6.2	930.6	28.9	48.0	6.9
Nurse aide	3,823.0	12.7	3,277.4	12.6	323.6	10.1	222.0	31.7
Orderly	922.9	3.1	920.4	3.5	0.0	0.0	2.5	0.4
Other ward unit personnel	3,136.2	10.4	2,993.6	11.5	129.1	4.0	13.5	1.9
Medical lab director	146.0	0.5	144.0	0.6	2.0	0.1	0.0	0.0
Medical lab supervisor	425.8	1.4	420.8	1.6	4.0	0.1	1.0	0.1
Medical lab technologist	1,736.4	5.8	1,713.6	6.6	20.8	0.6	2.0	0.3
Medical lab technician	1,939.2	6.5	1,917.6	7.3	20.6	0.6	1.0	0.1
Radiologic technologist	1,455.0	4.8	1,440.0	5.5	13.5	0.4	1.5	0.2
Radiologic technician	248.6	0.8	244.6	0.9	4.0	0.1	0.0	0.0
Other radiologic personnel	1,071.8	3.6	1,069.8	4.1	2.0	0.1	0.0	0.0
Physical therapist	308.6	1.0	304.1	1.2	3.0	0.1	1.5	0.2
Physical therapy assistant and aide	450.6	1.5	435.4	1.7	10.7	0.3	4.5	0.6
Occupational therapist	101.4	0.3	88.1	0.3	13.3	0.4	0.0	0.0
Occupational therapy assistant and aide	67.5	0.2	46.5	0.2	20.0	0.6	1.0	0.1
Inhalation therapist	1,155.9	3.8	1,143.9	4.4	11.0	0.3	1.0	0.1
Recreational therapist	156.6	0.5	56.2	0.2	100.4	3.1	0.0	0.0
Registered pharmacist	850.3	2.8	813.3	3.1	33.0	1.0	4.0	0.6
Pharmacy technician	860.9	2.9	828.7	3.2	28.7	0.9	3.5	0.5
Medical social worker	385.5	1.3	273.0	1.0	108.5	3.4	4.0	0.6
Other social worker	226.0	0.8	147.0	0.6	78.0	2.4	1.0	0.1
Registered records administrator	132.8	0.4	122.8	0.5	9.0	0.3	1.0	0.1
Accredited records technician	281.9	0.9	273.4	1.0	8.0	0.2	0.5	0.1
Chief executive officer and assistant	484.0	1.6	410.0	1.6	70.0	2.2	4.0	0.6
Administrative staff	1,867.1	6.2	1,421.3	5.4	433.8	13.5	12.0	1.7
Registered dietician	296.5	1.0	273.9	1.0	20.6	0.6	2.0	0.3
Dietary employee	1,388.1	4.6	1,245.1	4.8	85.5	2.7	57.5	8.2

TABLE 17.13--NUMBER OF PERSONNEL AND TRAINEES IN REPORTING HOSPITALS, BY TYPE OF HOSPITAL AND BY TYPE OF PERSONNEL, TENNESSEE, 1985 (Continued)

					Long-term			
	Total		Short-term[1]		Psychiatric		Geriatric	
Type of personnel and trainees	FTE Employees	Per 100 beds	FTE Employees	Per 100 beds	FTE Employees	Per 100 beds	FTE Employees	Per 100 beds
Housekeeping	4,763.7	15.9	4,378.3	16.8	335.9	10.4	49.5	7.1
Maintenance and grounds	2,167.8	7.2	1,844.8	7.1	301.5	9.4	21.5	3.1
Laundry	752.0	2.5	676.0	2.6	67.0	2.1	9.0	1.3
Other health	4,313.2	14.4	3,717.6	14.2	584.1	18.1	11.5	1.6
Resident and intern	1,090.0	3.6	1,053.8	4.0	36.2	1.1	0.0	0.0
Extern	63.4	0.2	63.4	0.2	0.0	0.0	0.0	0.0
Radiologist	116.9	0.4	113.4	0.4	3.5	0.1	0.0	0.0
Pathologist	96.5	0.3	95.5	0.4	1.0	0.0	0.0	0.0
Dentist	38.6	0.1	31.5	0.1	7.0	0.2	0.1	0.0
Dental intern and assistant	11.0	0.0	10.0	0.0	1.0	0.0	0.0	0.0
Podiatrist	4.5	0.0	3.0	0.0	0.5	0.0	1.0	0.1
Other physician	937.5	3.1	811.6	3.1	124.9	3.9	1.0	0.1
Other non-health	18,340.6	61.1	17,319.3	66.3	958.8	29.8	62.5	8.9
Total in training	3,431.3	11.4	3,424.3	13.1	7.0	0.2	0.0	0.0
Professional student nurse	2,617.5	8.7	2,613.5	10.0	4.0	0.1	0.0	0.0
Practical student nurse	295.0	1.0	295.0	1.1	0.0	0.0	0.0	0.0
Paramedical training program	195.5	0.7	195.5	0.7	0.0	0.0	0.0	0.0
Other	323.3	1.1	320.3	1.2	3.0	0.1	0.0	0.0

Note: Number of personnel includes full-time plus the full-time equivalent (FTE) of part-time personnel.

1. Includes both general and specialty hospitals.

Source: Tennessee Department of Health and Environment, Center for Health Statistics, unpublished data.

TABLE 17.14--NUMBER OF NURSING HOMES AND SELECTED UTILIZATION DATA, TENNESSEE, 1970–1987

Year	Nursing homes	Beds	Admissions	Patient days[1]	Percentage occupancy
1987	284	31,993	25,625	10,685,768	94.4
1986	278	30,200	23,638	10,103,795	93.7
1985	268	29,128	21,834	9,702,449	94.7
1984	261	27,756	21,539	9,503,802	95.5
1983	258	27,169	20,155	9,116,368	94.2
1982	251	26,208	18,664	8,696,774	92.9
1981	242	24,984	17,961	8,210,423	93.4
1980	235	22,990	15,989	7,484,862	95.4
1979	218	20,557	14,715	6,778,172	94.7
1978	209	18,369	13,326	6,196,139	96.0
1977	205	17,320	12,636	5,618,718	94.1
1976	200	15,700	12,090	5,226,232	95.1
1975	199	14,410	12,510	4,766,637	94.6
1974	203	13,109	11,375	4,243,999	94.0
1973	198	11,924	12,681	3,934,953	92.0
1972	200	11,977	14,023	3,693,078	88.1
1971	207	11,792	14,348	3,445,248	82.1
1970	208	11,475	14,281	3,186,815	80.4

1. 1970–1978 data are inpatient days. After 1978 data are patient days of care.

Source: Tennessee Department of Health and Environment, Center for Health Statistics, *Annual Report of Hospitals, Nursing Homes, and Homes for the Aged in Tennessee, 1980*, and earlier editions; and unpublished data.

FIGURE 17.3
Birth Rates per 1,000 Population by County of Residence, Tennessee, 1987
(Tennessee average birth rate = 13.9)

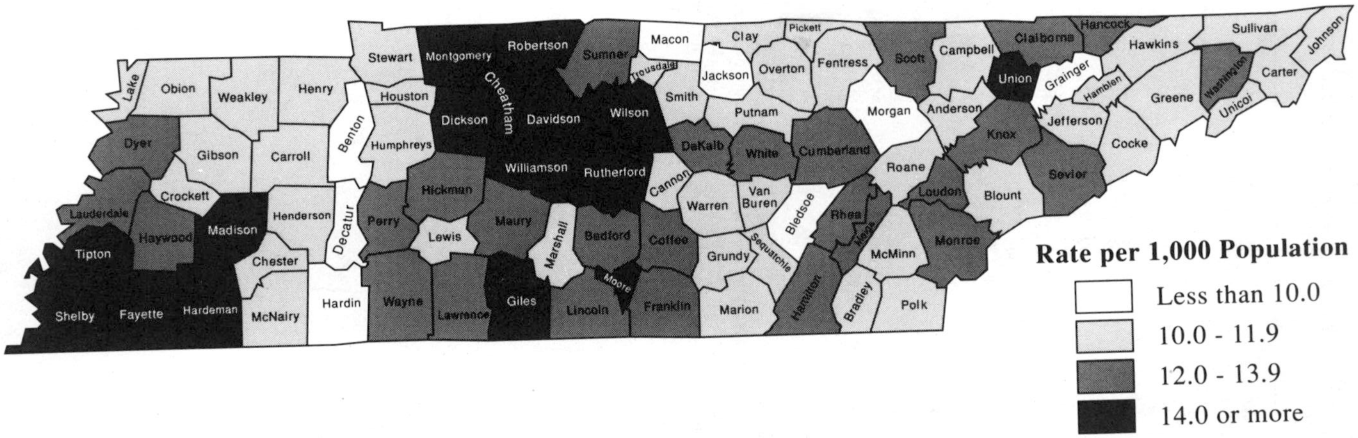

Source: Tennessee Department of Health and Environment, Center for Health Statistics, direct correspondence.

TABLE 17.15--LIVE BIRTHS AND DEATHS, BY RACE, TENNESSEE AND COUNTY OF RESIDENCE, 1987

	Live births						Deaths					
	Total[1]		White		Nonwhite		Total[2]		White		Nonwhite	
County	Number	Rate	Number	Rate	Number	Rate	Number	Rate	Number	Rate	Number	Rate
TENNESSEE	67,942	13.9	51,410	12.7	16,528	19.4	44,884	9.2	37,307	9.2	7,572	8.9
Anderson	789	11.2	723	10.9	66	17.0	667	9.5	641	9.7	26	6.7
Bedford	372	12.7	315	12.2	57	17.1	315	10.8	282	10.9	33	9.9
Benton	134	8.6	125	8.2	9	22.6	188	12.0	181	11.9	7	17.5
Bledsoe	94	9.2	94	9.5	0	0.0	91	8.9	87	8.8	4	12.9
Blount	958	11.6	915	11.5	43	13.6	753	9.1	716	9.0	37	11.7
Bradley	882	11.8	833	11.7	49	14.1	593	8.0	563	7.9	30	8.6
Campbell	460	11.9	458	12.0	2	6.6	382	9.9	382	10.0	0	0.0
Cannon	116	10.8	114	10.9	2	9.3	109	10.2	105	10.0	4	18.7
Carroll	340	11.6	298	11.6	42	12.0	383	13.1	357	13.9	26	7.4
Carter	567	10.8	555	10.7	12	20.1	500	9.5	494	9.5	6	10.1
Cheatham	359	14.1	356	14.3	3	4.7	185	7.3	178	7.2	7	11.1
Chester	150	11.0	119	9.8	31	20.9	115	8.4	100	8.2	15	10.1
Claiborne	333	12.6	331	12.7	2	5.0	256	9.7	255	9.8	1	2.5
Clay	79	10.0	78	10.1	1	7.9	71	9.0	70	9.0	1	7.9
Cocke	334	11.2	328	11.3	6	8.4	317	10.6	308	10.6	9	12.6
Coffee	556	13.7	524	13.5	32	18.0	376	9.2	359	9.2	17	9.6
Crockett	170	11.2	135	11.1	35	11.4	166	10.9	143	11.8	23	7.5
Cumberland	396	12.6	396	12.6	0	(a)	305	9.7	305	9.7	0	(a)
Davidson	8,157	16.4	5,710	15.3	2,446	19.6	4,514	9.1	3,451	9.3	1,061	8.5
Decatur	89	7.9	88	8.2	1	1.9	142	12.6	138	12.8	4	7.7
DeKalb	180	12.5	173	12.3	6	18.6	149	10.3	146	10.4	3	9.3
Dickson	499	15.0	473	15.1	26	13.7	322	9.7	300	9.6	22	11.6
Dyer	443	12.1	353	11.1	90	19.9	382	10.5	325	10.2	57	12.6
Fayette	391	14.3	171	12.2	220	16.4	248	9.0	121	8.7	127	9.4
Fentress	184	11.8	183	11.7	1	(a)	168	10.7	168	10.7	0	(a)
Franklin	416	12.3	387	12.4	29	11.2	337	10.0	311	10.0	26	10.1
Gibson	580	11.6	412	10.3	168	16.3	632	12.6	521	13.1	111	10.8
Giles	368	14.2	306	13.7	62	16.8	286	11.0	250	11.2	36	9.8

TABLE 17.15--LIVE BIRTHS AND DEATHS, BY RACE, TENNESSEE AND COUNTY OF RESIDENCE, 1987 (Continued)

	Live births						Deaths					
	Total[1]		White		Nonwhite		Total[2]		White		Nonwhite	
County	Number	Rate	Number	Rate	Number	Rate	Number	Rate	Number	Rate	Number	Rate
Grainger	174	9.8	172	9.8	2	14.5	160	9.0	160	9.1	0	0.0
Greene	610	10.7	587	10.7	23	12.6	575	10.1	561	10.2	14	7.7
Grundy	166	11.0	166	11.0	0	(a)	128	8.5	127	8.4	1	(a)
Hamblen	597	11.2	564	11.2	33	11.8	485	9.1	456	9.1	29	10.4
Hamilton	4,048	13.3	2,911	12.2	1,137	17.3	2,709	8.9	2,092	8.7	617	9.4
Hancock	84	12.0	84	12.0	0	(a)	91	13.0	91	13.0	0	(a)
Hardeman	357	14.1	174	11.3	183	18.6	247	9.8	167	10.8	80	8.1
Hardin	234	9.9	220	9.7	14	13.3	233	9.8	220	9.7	13	12.4
Hawkins	511	10.8	504	10.9	7	7.2	403	8.5	393	8.5	10	10.3
Haywood	278	12.9	112	10.9	166	14.6	237	11.0	128	12.5	109	9.6
Henderson	264	11.5	229	11.0	35	17.1	243	10.6	224	10.7	19	9.3
Henry	342	11.3	299	11.2	43	12.6	393	13.0	344	12.8	49	14.4
Hickman	204	12.7	194	12.7	10	11.1	179	11.1	168	11.0	11	12.2
Houston	82	11.4	79	11.5	3	9.0	76	10.5	68	9.9	8	24.0
Humphreys	189	11.2	178	11.0	11	14.8	183	10.8	172	10.7	11	14.8
Jackson	95	9.8	95	9.8	0	(a)	145	15.0	145	15.0	0	(a)
Jefferson	332	10.0	322	10.0	10	9.3	283	8.5	280	8.7	3	2.8
Johnson	159	11.0	159	11.1	0	0.0	146	10.1	146	10.2	0	0.0
Knox	4,409	13.2	3,832	12.8	577	16.5	3,024	9.0	2,725	9.1	299	8.5
Lake	79	10.6	60	10.1	19	12.6	93	12.5	77	13.0	16	10.6
Lauderdale	350	13.0	207	11.4	143	16.1	266	9.9	177	9.8	89	10.0
Lawrence	493	13.7	488	13.8	5	7.9	344	9.5	342	9.7	2	3.2
Lewis	120	10.7	120	10.9	0	0.0	91	8.1	88	8.0	3	13.8
Lincoln	347	12.7	302	12.4	45	15.6	290	10.6	261	10.7	29	10.0
Loudon	376	12.6	370	12.6	6	12.0	331	11.1	326	11.1	5	10.0
McMinn	494	11.2	462	11.1	32	12.8	423	9.6	399	9.6	24	9.6
McNairy	251	10.4	216	9.6	35	20.1	258	10.6	244	10.8	14	8.0
Macon	161	9.5	159	9.4	2	(a)	187	11.0	186	11.0	1	(a)
Madison	1,143	14.4	667	12.2	476	19.0	854	10.7	580	10.6	274	11.0
Marion	295	11.5	281	11.4	14	12.4	229	8.9	212	8.6	17	15.0

TABLE 17.15--LIVE BIRTHS AND DEATHS, BY RACE, TENNESSEE AND COUNTY OF RESIDENCE, 1987 (Continued)

	Live births						Deaths					
	Total[1]		White		Nonwhite		Total[2]		White		Nonwhite	
County	Number	Rate	Number	Rate	Number	Rate	Number	Rate	Number	Rate	Number	Rate
Marshall	235	11.4	208	11.3	27	12.5	232	11.3	203	11.0	29	13.4
Maury	742	13.6	594	13.2	148	15.7	550	10.1	441	9.8	109	11.6
Meigs	99	12.0	97	11.9	2	16.9	74	8.9	72	8.8	2	16.9
Monroe	390	12.7	371	12.5	19	19.6	296	9.6	285	9.6	11	11.3
Montgomery	1,692	17.8	1,255	16.6	437	22.0	594	6.2	463	6.1	131	6.6
Moore	74	14.9	73	15.2	1	6.1	28	5.7	27	5.6	1	6.1
Morgan	176	9.9	176	9.9	0	0.0	191	10.7	191	10.8	0	0.0
Obion	345	10.1	304	10.0	41	11.1	350	10.3	318	10.5	32	8.6
Overton	195	10.6	195	10.7	0	(a)	213	11.6	213	11.7	0	(a)
Perry	77	12.1	77	12.4	0	0.0	81	12.7	80	12.9	1	6.0
Pickett	55	11.8	55	11.8	0	(a)	47	10.1	47	10.1	0	(a)
Polk	156	10.9	156	10.9	0	(a)	146	10.2	146	10.2	0	(a)
Putnam	566	11.0	552	11.0	14	10.1	417	8.1	410	8.2	7	5.1
Rhea	333	12.3	320	12.1	13	16.2	228	8.4	220	8.3	8	10.0
Roane	520	10.0	502	10.0	18	10.2	468	9.0	452	9.0	16	9.0
Robertson	587	14.4	501	14.2	86	15.4	354	8.7	291	8.2	62	11.1
Rutherford	1,689	17.8	1,462	17.3	227	22.4	690	7.3	581	6.9	109	10.7
Scott	284	13.4	283	13.4	1	(a)	178	8.4	178	8.4	0	(a)
Sequatchie	99	10.7	99	10.7	0	(a)	65	7.0	65	7.0	0	(a)
Sevier	582	12.5	576	12.4	6	17.4	386	8.3	385	8.3	1	2.9
Shelby	14,672	17.6	6,371	14.2	8,301	21.6	7,154	8.6	3,911	8.7	3,241	8.5
Smith	181	11.4	176	11.6	5	8.4	159	10.0	155	10.2	4	6.7
Stewart	94	10.4	92	10.4	2	12.9	99	11.0	99	11.2	0	0.0
Sullivan	1,643	11.1	1,602	11.0	41	12.2	1,384	9.3	1,358	9.4	26	7.7
Sumner	1,385	13.9	1,275	13.6	110	17.7	690	6.9	633	6.8	57	9.2
Tipton	636	17.8	412	15.9	224	23.2	335	9.4	243	9.4	92	9.5
Trousdale	71	10.8	61	10.7	10	11.0	73	11.1	59	10.4	14	15.3
Unicoi	175	10.6	173	10.5	1	(a)	168	10.2	168	10.2	0	(a)
Union	185	14.5	185	14.5	0	(a)	120	9.4	120	9.4	0	(a)
Van Buren	56	10.8	55	10.6	1	(a)	46	8.9	46	8.9	0	(a)

TABLE 17.15--LIVE BIRTHS AND DEATHS, BY RACE, TENNESSEE AND COUNTY OF RESIDENCE, 1987 (Continued)

	Live births						Deaths					
	Total[1]		White		Nonwhite		Total[2]		White		Nonwhite	
County	Number	Rate	Number	Rate	Number	Rate	Number	Rate	Number	Rate	Number	Rate
Warren	396	11.3	371	11.0	25	18.9	348	9.9	332	9.8	16	12.1
Washington	1,129	12.1	1,058	11.8	71	18.8	863	9.2	824	9.2	39	10.3
Wayne	177	12.2	173	12.1	4	24.0	144	9.9	143	10.0	1	6.0
Weakley	344	10.2	314	10.0	30	13.2	349	10.4	328	10.5	21	9.2
White	260	12.7	255	12.8	5	9.8	186	9.1	185	9.3	1	2.0
Williamson	1,064	15.3	966	15.2	98	16.7	414	6.0	373	5.9	41	7.0
Wilson	938	14.5	849	14.4	88	15.2	506	7.8	446	7.6	60	10.4

Note: Data are by place of residence. Rates are per 1,000 population.

1. Includes births with race unknown.

2. Includes deaths with race unknown.

a. Rate not calculated when population is less than 100.

Source: Tennessee Department of Health and Environment, Center for Health Statistics, unpublished data.

TABLE 17.16--NUMBER OF MARRIAGES AND DIVORCES, TENNESSEE AND COUNTY OF OCCURRENCE, 1987

County	Marriages	Divorces	County	Marriages	Divorces
Anderson	806	388	Lewis	108	80
Bedford	293	209	Lincoln	527	204
Benton	195	114	Loudon	429	188
Bledsoe	111	26	McMinn	577	318
Blount	898	550	McNairy	329	158
Bradley	886	529	Macon	213	96
Campbell	1,359	250	Madison	876	454
Cannon	182	59	Marion	366	172
Carroll	319	172	Marshall	261	153
Carter	538	314	Maury	552	346
Cheatham	185	173	Meigs	126	47
Chester	201	417	Monroe	420	197
Claiborne	495	105	Montgomery	1,400	821
Clay	215	48	Moore	64	29
Cocke	404	181	Morgan	205	104
Coffee	506	264	Obion	392	199
Crockett	158	52	Overton	204	98
Cumberland	446	247	Perry	69	32
Davidson	5,732	3,155	Pickett	98	23
Decatur	136	48	Polk	211	44
DeKalb	207	103	Putnam	570	330
Dickson	444	218	Rhea	311	151
Dyer	479	335	Roane	493	310
Fayette	266	140	Robertson	2,154	232
Fentress	268	125	Rutherford	1,127	681
Franklin	411	197	Scott	224	100
Gibson	550	330	Sequatchie	147	67
Giles	360	149	Sevier	4,036	310
Grainger	178	78	Shelby	8,321	3,896
Greene	663	394	Smith	153	98
Grundy	162	84	Stewart	117	49
Hamblen	690	374	Sullivan	1,474	728
Hamilton	2,934	2,030	Sumner	974	690
Hancock	75	33	Tipton	525	436
Hardeman	291	94	Trousdale	292	44
Hardin	365	188	Unicoi	203	98
Hawkins	493	261	Union	205	56
Haywood	195	114	Van Buren	54	23
Henderson	281	139	Warren	357	236
Henry	305	186	Washington	965	537
Hickman	168	87	Wayne	147	83
Houston	94	33	Weakley	362	206
Humphreys	190	108	White	245	76
Jackson	134	41	Williamson	608	418
Jefferson	342	183	Wilson	668	321
Johnson	193	94	TENNESSEE	61,358	30,324
Knox	3,518	2,500			
Lake	103	55			
Lauderdale	335	219			
Lawrence	440	192			

Source: Tennessee Department of Health and Environment, Center for Health Statistics, unpublished data.

TABLE 17.17--ILLEGITIMATE LIVE BIRTHS, BY RACE, TENNESSEE AND COUNTY OF RESIDENCE OF MOTHER, 1987

County	Total		White		Nonwhite	
	Number	Percentage of live births	Number	Percentage of live births	Number	Percentage of live births
TENNESSEE	17,892	26.3	7,101	13.8	10,791	65.3
Anderson	164	20.8	123	17.0	41	62.1
Bedford	80	21.5	43	13.7	37	64.9
Benton	29	21.6	22	17.6	7	(a)
Bledsoe	15	16.0	15	16.0	0	(a)
Blount	164	17.1	142	15.5	22	51.2
Bradley	150	17.0	118	14.2	32	65.3
Campbell	113	24.6	112	24.5	1	(a)
Cannon	11	9.5	10	8.8	1	(a)
Carroll	61	17.9	36	12.1	25	59.5
Carter	93	16.4	89	16.0	4	33.3
Cheatham	49	13.6	48	13.5	1	(a)
Chester	37	24.7	18	15.1	19	61.3
Claiborne	52	15.6	51	15.4	1	(a)
Clay	12	15.2	12	15.4	0	(a)
Cocke	74	22.2	69	21.0	5	(a)
Coffee	101	18.2	91	17.4	10	31.2
Crockett	41	24.1	18	13.3	23	65.7
Cumberland	70	17.7	70	17.7	0	(a)
Davidson	2,318	28.4	811	14.2	1,507	61.6
Decatur	7	7.9	6	6.8	1	(a)
DeKalb	31	17.2	29	16.8	2	(a)
Dickson	97	19.4	79	16.7	18	69.2
Dyer	132	29.8	68	19.3	64	71.1
Fayette	171	43.7	22	12.9	149	67.7
Fentress	36	19.6	36	19.7	0	(a)
Franklin	65	15.6	48	12.4	17	58.6
Gibson	167	28.8	48	11.7	119	70.8
Giles	76	20.7	35	11.4	41	66.1
Grainger	20	11.5	18	10.5	2	(a)
Greene	127	20.8	116	19.8	11	47.8
Grundy	39	23.5	39	23.5	0	(a)
Hamblen	114	19.1	94	16.7	20	60.6
Hamilton	1,207	29.8	408	14.0	799	70.3
Hancock	15	17.9	15	17.9	0	(a)
Hardeman	141	39.5	15	8.6	126	68.9
Hardin	41	17.5	34	15.5	7	50.0
Hawkins	59	11.5	58	11.5	1	(a)
Haywood	125	45.0	14	12.5	111	66.9
Henderson	46	17.4	28	12.2	18	51.4
Henry	77	22.5	49	16.4	28	65.1
Hickman	29	14.2	24	12.4	5	50.0
Houston	15	18.3	14	17.7	1	(a)
Humphreys	35	18.5	27	15.2	8	72.7
Jackson	16	16.8	16	16.8	0	(a)
Jefferson	57	17.2	51	15.8	6	60.0
Johnson	41	25.8	41	25.8	0	(a)
Knox	878	19.9	513	13.4	365	63.3
Lake	25	31.6	10	16.7	15	78.9

TABLE 17.17--ILLEGITIMATE LIVE BIRTHS, BY RACE, TENNESSEE AND COUNTY OF RESIDENCE OF MOTHER, 1987 (Continued)

County	Total		White		Nonwhite	
	Number	Percentage of live births	Number	Percentage of live births	Number	Percentage of live births
Lauderdale	124	35.4	31	15.0	93	65.0
Lawrence	54	11.0	52	10.7	2	(a)
Lewis	19	15.8	19	15.8	0	(a)
Lincoln	66	19.0	35	11.6	31	68.9
Loudon	58	15.4	53	14.3	5	(a)
McMinn	91	18.4	70	15.2	21	65.6
McNairy	51	20.3	27	12.5	24	68.6
Macon	23	14.3	23	14.5	0	(a)
Madison	389	34.0	77	11.5	312	65.5
Marion	63	21.4	54	19.2	9	64.3
Marshall	57	24.3	41	19.7	16	59.3
Maury	199	26.8	93	15.7	106	71.6
Meigs	21	21.2	19	19.6	2	(a)
Monroe	60	15.4	48	12.9	12	63.2
Montgomery	279	16.5	127	10.1	152	34.8
Moore	3	4.1	3	4.1	0	(a)
Morgan	32	18.2	32	18.2	0	(a)
Obion	63	18.3	38	12.5	25	61.0
Overton	34	17.4	34	17.4	0	(a)
Perry	8	10.4	8	10.4	0	(a)
Pickett	7	12.7	7	12.7	0	(a)
Polk	25	16.0	25	16.0	0	(a)
Putnam	98	17.3	92	16.7	6	42.9
Rhea	74	22.2	66	20.6	8	61.5
Roane	95	18.3	82	16.3	13	72.2
Robertson	117	19.9	51	10.2	66	76.7
Rutherford	331	19.6	196	13.4	135	59.5
Scott	46	16.2	46	16.3	0	(a)
Sequatchie	11	11.1	11	11.1	0	(a)
Sevier	86	14.8	84	14.6	2	(a)
Shelby	6,313	43.0	657	10.3	5,656	68.1
Smith	15	8.3	13	7.4	2	(a)
Stewart	7	7.4	6	6.5	1	(a)
Sullivan	264	16.1	248	15.5	16	39.0
Sumner	219	15.8	151	11.8	68	61.8
Tipton	209	32.9	67	16.3	142	63.4
Trousdale	17	23.9	11	18.0	6	60.0
Unicoi	31	17.7	30	17.3	1	(a)
Union	26	14.1	26	14.1	0	(a)
Van Buren	7	12.5	6	10.9	1	(a)
Warren	68	17.2	53	14.3	15	60.0
Washington	201	17.8	167	15.8	34	47.9
Wayne	20	11.3	17	9.8	3	(a)
Weakley	38	11.0	23	7.3	15	50.0
White	45	17.3	42	16.5	3	(a)
Williamson	157	14.8	94	9.7	63	64.3
Wilson	148	15.8	93	11.0	55	62.5

a. Percentage not calculated when number of births is less than 10.

Source: Tennessee Department of Health and Environment, Center for Health Statistics, unpublished data.

TABLE 17.18--SELECTED STATISTICS ON MEDICAL RESOURCES, TENNESSEE AND COUNTIES, 1986 AND 1988

County	No. of hospitals (1986)	No. of staffed beds (1986)	No. of medical doctors (1988)	No. of dentists (1988)	No. of osteopaths (1988)
TENNESSEE	168	27,567	8,892	2,731	101
Anderson	3	307	132	44	0
Bedford	1	79	20	10	0
Benton	1	93	10	5	0
Bledsoe	1	32	3	3	1
Blount	2	358	103	42	1
Bradley	2	281	89	35	4
Campbell	2	117	22	9	0
Cannon	1	65	9	3	0
Carroll	2	126	14	10	1
Carter	1	100	37	17	0
Cheatham	0	0	3	2	0
Chester	0	0	3	2	0
Claiborne	1	67	16	4	0
Clay	1	36	4	1	1
Cocke	1	63	14	8	0
Coffee	3	227	43	25	15
Crockett	0	0	6	2	0
Cumberland	1	184	41	11	0
Davidson	17	4,986[a]	2,039	375	5
Decatur	1	40	4	1	0
DeKalb	2	69	11	4	0
Dickson	1	132	27	13	0
Dyer	1	125	47	13	0
Fayette	1	38	11	1	1
Fentress	1	72	8	3	0
Franklin	2	122	30	14	1
Gibson	4	281	32	20	5
Giles	1	95	18	10	0
Grainger	0	0	4	2	1
Greene	2	277	65	20	0
Grundy	0	0	1	2	3
Hamblen	2	283	63	28	4
Hamilton	11	2,036	734	175	8
Hancock	1	31	4	1	0
Hardeman	2	409	20	6	3
Hardin	1	83	14	8	1
Hawkins	1	55	17	10	1
Haywood	1	62	8	6	1
Henderson	1	42	9	6	0
Henry	1	140	24	12	2
Hickman	1	28	5	4	0
Houston	1	40	4	2	0
Humphreys	1	52	11	5	0
Jackson	1	41	5	3	0
Jefferson	1	81	14	11	0
Johnson	1	66	9	2	2
Knox	8	2,749	885	220	9
Lake	0	0	1	2	0
Lauderdale	1	70	11	6	0
Lawrence	2	126	21	12	0

TABLE 17.18--SELECTED STATISTICS ON MEDICAL RESOURCES, TENNESSEE AND COUNTIES, 1986 AND 1988 (Continued)

County	No. of hospitals (1986)	No. of staffed beds (1986)	No. of medical doctors (1988)	No. of dentists (1988)	No. of osteopaths (1988)
Lewis	1	49	6	3	0
Lincoln	1	91	32	11	0
Loudon	1	50	19	7	0
McMinn	2	181	41	21	1
McNairy	1	86	14	7	0
Macon	1	43	4	3	0
Madison	3	805	193	46	2
Marion	2	114	21	7	1
Marshall	1	119	19	5	0
Maury	1	235	72	24	0
Meigs	0	0	3	1	0
Monroe	1	59	18	8	0
Montgomery	2	421	92	27	3
Moore	0	0	0	1	0
Morgan	0	0	3	2	0
Obion	1	121	35	15	0
Overton	1	106	12	4	0
Perry	1	53	4	2	2
Pickett	0	0	2	2	0
Polk	1	(a)	14	4	0
Putnam	2	182	61	20	2
Rhea	1	57	10	6	1
Roane	2	151	40	21	0
Robertson	1	121	26	13	0
Rutherford	3	221[a]	119	48	0
Scott	1	99	11	4	0
Sequatchie	1	49	4	2	3
Sevier	1	45	25	14	1
Shelby	16	6,333	2,275	591	9
Smith	2	95	7	3	1
Stewart	0	0	3	1	0
Sullivan	4	1,033	360	93	0
Sumner	3	263	88	39	1
Tipton	1	99	18	10	1
Trousdale	1	34	3	3	0
Unicoi	1	48	7	6	0
Union	0	0	0	2	0
Van Buren	0	0	1	1	0
Warren	2	152	31	11	0
Washington	5	633[a]	309	54	0
Wayne	1	70	4	3	1
Weakley	1	100	25	11	1
White	1	54	13	6	0
Williamson	1	145	61	39	1
Wilson	2	284	61	20	0

Note: Number of hospitals and beds are reported as of December 31, 1986; Health care professionals are as of August 15, 1988. Totals may include health professionals with county unstated.

a. Includes hospitals that did not report data.

Source: Tennessee Department of Health and Environment, Center for Health Statistics, unpublished data.

TABLE 17.19--LIVE BIRTHS AND DEATHS, BY RESIDENCE, CITIES WITH 1980 POPULATION OF 10,000 OR MORE, 1987

City	Live births Number	Live births Rate[1]	Deaths Number	Deaths Rate[1]
Athens	172	13.4	133	10.3
Bartlett	265	14.0	75	4.0
Bristol	249	10.1	285	11.5
Chattanooga	2,377	13.1	1,798	9.9
Clarksville	1,336	21.3	401	6.4
Cleveland	387	13.0	352	11.9
Columbia	413	14.3	305	10.6
Cookeville	214	9.2	157	6.8
Dyersburg	241	14.4	209	12.5
East Ridge	146	6.6	224	10.1
Elizabethton	149	11.4	159	12.2
Franklin	336	21.6	167	10.7
Gallatin	323	16.2	190	9.5
Germantown	298	12.9	125	5.4
Greeneville	172	11.6	206	13.9
Hendersonville	413	13.2	180	5.8
Humboldt	160	15.2	130	12.4
Jackson	790	15.0	668	12.7
Johnson City	544	11.5	498	10.6
Kingsport	414	12.5	464	14.0
Knoxville	2,354	12.8	2,010	10.9
Lawrenceburg	145	13.5	157	14.6
Lebanon	234	14.4	233	14.3
McMinnville	158	12.5	161	12.7
Maryville	265	14.0	247	13.1
Memphis	11,967	17.1	6,588	9.4
Millington	407	19.4	79	3.8
Morristown	314	13.4	279	11.9
Murfreesboro	624	16.9	361	9.8
Nashville	8,157	16.4	4,514	9.1
Oak Ridge	275	9.5	273	9.4
Paris	123	10.8	179	15.7
Red Bank	39	2.8	89	6.4
Shelbyville	171	11.9	176	12.3
Springfield	183	15.1	142	11.8
Tullahoma	226	13.4	152	9.0
Union City	133	11.9	111	9.9

1. Rates are per 1,000 population and are based on population estimates from the Census Bureau.

Source: Tennessee Department of Health and Environment, Center for Health Statistics, unpublished data.

TABLE 17.20--NUMBER OF DEATHS AND RATE PER 1,000 POPULATION, SOUTHEASTERN STATES AND UNITED STATES, 1950–1986, SELECTED YEARS [Number in thousands]

	1986		1985		1984		1983		1982	
State	Number	Rate	Number	Rate	Number	Rate	Number	Rate	Number	Rate
TENNESSEE	44	9.2	43	9.1	42	9.0	42	8.9	40	8.7
Alabama	38	9.3	38	9.3	37	9.2	36	9.0	35	8.9
Arkansas	24	10.1	24	10.2	24	10.1	23	10.0	22	9.7
Florida	124	10.6	121	10.7	115	10.4	113	10.5	109	10.4
Georgia	49	8.1	49	8.1	47	8.0	46	8.0	44	7.8
Kentucky	35	9.3	35	9.4	34	9.0	34	9.2	33	8.9
Louisiana	36	8.1	37	8.3	36	8.0	36	8.2	36	8.2
Mississippi	24	9.3	25	9.4	24	9.2	24	9.3	23	9.1
North Carolina	55	8.6	53	8.5	51	8.3	50	8.3	49	8.1
South Carolina	28	8.3	27	8.1	26	8.0	26	8.0	25	7.8
Virginia	47	8.0	45	7.9	44	7.9	44	7.9	42	7.6
West Virginia	20	10.4	19	10.0	19	9.8	19	9.9	19	9.7
UNITED STATES	2,105	8.7	2,086	8.7	2,039	8.6	2,019	8.6	1,975	8.5

	1980		1970		1960		1950	
State	Number	Rate	Number	Rate	Number	Rate	Number	Rate
TENNESSEE	41	8.9	38	9.7	33	9.2	29	8.9
Alabama	36	9.1	34	9.8	30	9.3	27	8.8
Arkansas	23	9.9	21	10.7	18	10.0	15	8.1
Florida	105	10.7	75	11.0	48	9.7	27	9.6
Georgia	44	8.1	42	9.1	35	9.0	30	8.8
Kentucky	34	9.2	33	10.3	30	9.9	28	9.5
Louisiana	36	8.5	33	9.2	30	9.1	24	8.8
Mississippi	24	9.4	23	10.5	22	10.0	21	9.5
North Carolina	48	8.2	45	8.8	38	8.4	31	7.7
South Carolina	25	8.1	23	8.8	21	8.7	18	8.5
Virginia	43	8.0	39	8.4	34	8.7	30	9.0
West Virginia	19	9.9	20	11.5	18	9.7	17	8.7
UNITED STATES	1,990	8.8	1,921	9.5	1,712	9.5	1,452	9.6

Note: Data by place of residence. Rates are based on total population residing in area. Beginning in 1970, data exclude nonresidents of the U.S.

Source: U.S. Department of Commerce, Bureau of the Census, *Statistical Abstract of the United States, 1989*, and earlier editions.

TABLE 17.21--NUMBER OF LIVE BIRTHS AND RATE PER 1,000 POPULATION, SOUTHEASTERN STATES AND UNITED STATES, 1950–1986, SELECTED YEARS [Number in thousands]

	1986		1985		1984		1983		1982	
State	Number	Rate	Number	Rate	Number	Rate	Number	Rate	Number	Rate
TENNESSEE	66	13.8	67	14.0	65	13.8	65	14.0	67	14.4
Alabama	59	14.7	60	14.9	59	14.8	59	14.9	60	15.3
Arkansas	34	14.5	35	14.9	35	14.9	35	15.1	35	15.3
Florida	168	14.3	164	14.4	155	14.1	149	13.9	145	13.8
Georgia	98	16.1	96	16.1	92	15.8	90	15.7	90	16.0
Kentucky	52	13.9	53	14.2	53	14.3	55	14.7	57	15.4
Louisiana	78	17.3	81	18.2	81	18.3	83	18.6	85	19.3
Mississippi	42	16.0	43	16.6	44	16.9	44	17.0	46	17.9
North Carolina	90	14.3	89	14.3	86	14.0	84	13.8	86	14.3
South Carolina	52	15.3	52	15.6	51	15.3	51	15.6	52	16.0
Virginia	87	15.0	86	15.1	83	14.7	81	14.5	81	14.8
West Virginia	23	12.1	24	12.5	25	12.6	26	13.2	27	13.9
UNITED STATES[1]	3,757	15.6	3,761	15.8	3,669	15.5	3,639	15.5	3,681	15.9

	1980		1970		1960		1950	
State	Number	Rate	Number	Rate	Number	Rate	Number	Rate
TENNESSEE	69	15.1	72	18.4	82	23.0	84	25.6
Alabama	64	16.3	67	19.4	81	24.7	86	28.1
Arkansas	37	16.3	35	18.5	41	22.7	52	27.1
Florida	132	13.5	115	16.9	116	23.3	66	23.9
Georgia	92	16.9	97	21.1	100	25.3	97	28.0
Kentucky	60	16.3	60	18.7	72	23.8	79	26.9
Louisiana	82	19.5	74	20.4	90	27.7	80	29.7
Mississippi	48	19.0	49	22.1	59	27.2	66	30.4
North Carolina	84	14.4	98	19.3	110	24.1	111	27.3
South Carolina	52	16.6	52	20.1	60	25.1	64	30.2
Virginia	78	14.7	86	18.6	96	24.1	84	25.4
West Virginia	29	15.1	31	17.8	39	21.2	53	26.6
UNITED STATES[1]	3,612	15.9	3,731	18.4	4,258	23.7	3,632	24.1

Note: Data are by place of residence. Rates are based on total population residing in area. Beginning in 1970, births to nonresidents of the U.S. are excluded.

1. Beginning in 1960, includes Alaska and Hawaii.

Source: U.S. Department of Commerce, Bureau of the Census, *Statistical Abstract of the United States, 1989*, and earlier editions.

TABLE 17.22--NUMBER OF MARRIAGES, AND RATE PER 1,000 POPULATION, SOUTHEASTERN STATES AND UNITED STATES, 1950–1987, SELECTED YEARS [Number in thousands]

	1987[p]		1986[p]		1985[r]		1984		1983	
State	Number	Rate	Number	Rate	Number	Rate	Number	Rate	Number	Rate
TENNESSEE	57.5	11.8	58.9	12.3	55.0	11.5	55.2	11.7	56.5	12.1
Alabama	44.0	10.8	46.5	11.5	46.1	11.5	47.5	11.9	47.5	12.0
Arkansas	32.2	13.5	31.2	13.1	31.7	13.4	31.4	13.4	30.1	12.9
Florida	138.2	11.5	129.0	11.1	125.5	11.0	124.1	11.3	119.0	11.1
Georgia	65.3	10.5	72.0	11.8	72.3	12.1	75.8	13.0	73.4	12.8
Kentucky	47.6	12.8	47.1	12.6	46.0	12.3	44.0	11.8	37.4[a]	10.1[a]
Louisiana	36.8	8.2	36.7	8.1	39.4	8.8	41.3	9.3	43.2	9.7
Mississippi	23.9	9.1	24.1	9.2	24.8	9.5	26.2	10.1	26.9	10.4
North Carolina	50.5	7.9	50.2	7.9	50.5	8.1	52.1	8.5	52.1	8.6
South Carolina	53.5	15.6	54.1	16.0	52.8	15.8	55.9	16.9	53.7	16.5
Virginia	67.1	11.4	66.8	11.5	66.5	11.7	66.0	11.7	61.9	11.1
West Virginia	13.5	7.1	13.8	7.2	14.6	7.5	15.5	7.9	15.9	8.1
UNITED STATES	2,421.0	9.9	2,400.0	10.0	2,412.6	10.1	2,487.0	10.5	2,445.6	10.5

	1980		1970		1960		1950	
State	Number	Rate	Number	Rate	Number	Rate	Number	Rate
TENNESSEE	59.2	12.9	45.4	11.6	30.7	8.6	21.7	6.6
Alabama	49.0	12.6	47.0	13.6	31.9	9.8	22.8	7.5
Arkansas	26.5	11.6	23.3	12.1	18.3	10.3	51.6	27.0
Florida	108.3	11.1	69.2	10.2	39.3	7.9	27.6	10.0
Georgia	70.6	12.9	63.9	13.9	49.4	12.5	44.1	12.8
Kentucky	32.7[a]	8.9[a]	36.3	11.3	26.5	8.7	33.0	11.2
Louisiana	43.5	10.3	35.4	9.7	23.5	7.2	26.9	10.0
Mississippi	27.9	11.1	26.3	11.9	21.2	9.7	56.7	26.0
North Carolina	46.7	7.9	48.3	9.5	31.7	6.9	29.8	7.3
South Carolina	53.9	17.3	57.9	22.3	39.0	16.4	46.2	21.8
Virginia	60.2	11.3	52.0	11.2	37.5	9.5	36.7	11.1
West Virginia	17.4	8.9	15.9	9.1	13.6	7.3	17.2	8.6
UNITED STATES	2,390.3	10.6	2,158.8	10.6	1,523.4	8.5	1,667.2	11.1

Note: Data are by place of occurrence. Rates are based on total population residing in area.

p preliminary.

r revised.

a. Incomplete.

Source: U.S. Department of Commerce, Bureau of the Census, *Statistical Abstract of the United States, 1989*, and earlier editions.

TABLE 17.23--NUMBER OF DIVORCES, AND RATE PER 1,000 POPULATION, SOUTHEASTERN STATES AND UNITED STATES, 1950–1987, SELECTED YEARS [Number in thousands]

	1987[p]		1986[r]		1985[r]		1984		1983	
State	Number	Rate	Number	Rate	Number	Rate	Number	Rate	Number	Rate
TENNESSEE	31.0	6.4	29.2	6.1	29.9	6.3	30.7	6.5	29.4	6.3
Alabama	24.7	6.0	25.3	6.2	25.0	6.2	25.5	6.4	25.2	6.4
Arkansas	16.2	6.8	16.6	7.0	16.5	7.0	15.6	6.6	15.7[a]	6.7[a]
Florida	79.7	6.6	77.6	6.6	77.5	6.8	75.3	6.9	71.2	6.6
Georgia	33.5	5.4	32.6	5.3	33.4	5.6	34.1	5.8	33.3	5.8
Kentucky	19.9	5.3	19.3	5.2	18.3	4.9	17.4	4.7	17.0[a]	4.6[a]
Louisiana	n.a.	n.a.	n.a.	n.a.	17.6[a]	n.a.	n.a.	n.a.	16.2[a]	3.6[a]
Mississippi	12.4	4.7	14.2	5.4	13.0	5.0	12.5	4.8	13.4	5.2
North Carolina	31.6	4.9	31.7	5.0	30.2	4.8	29.1	4.7	30.1	5.0
South Carolina	14.0	4.1	13.5	4.0	13.5	4.0	13.8	4.2	13.6	4.2
Virginia	25.6	4.3	25.0	4.3	24.1	4.2	24.8	4.4	25.5	4.6
West Virginia	9.1	4.8	9.8	5.1	9.9	5.1	9.5	4.9	10.1	5.2
UNITED STATES[1]	1,157.0	4.8	1,159.0	4.8	1,190.0	5.0	1,155.0	4.9	1,158.0	4.9

	1980		1970		1960		1950	
State	Number	Rate	Number	Rate	Number	Rate	Number	Rate
TENNESSEE	30.2	6.6	16.6	4.2	9.0	2.5	7.8	2.4
Alabama	26.7	6.9	15.1	4.4	17.3	5.3	8.7	2.9
Arkansas	15.9[a]	6.9[a]	9.3[a]	4.8[a]	5.4[a]	(b)	8.8	4.6
Florida	71.6	7.3	37.2	5.5	19.6	3.9	18.0	6.5
Georgia	34.7	6.4	18.6	4.1	8.9	2.3	9.5	2.8
Kentucky	16.7[a]	4.6[a]	10.7	3.3	7.5[a]	(b)	8.1	2.8
Louisiana	18.1[a]	4.3[a]	5.1[a]	(b)	4.1[a]	(b)	5.4	2.0
Mississippi	13.8	5.5	8.2	3.7	5.2	2.4	6.1	2.8
North Carolina	28.1	4.8	13.7	2.7	6.0	1.3	6.4	1.6
South Carolina	13.6	4.4	5.8	2.3	3.0	1.3	2.3	1.1
Virginia	23.6	4.4	11.9	2.6	7.4	1.9	5.9	1.8
West Virginia	10.3	5.3	5.6	3.2	3.6	1.9	4.2	2.1
UNITED STATES[1]	1,189.0	5.2	708.0	3.5	393.0	2.2	385.0	2.6

Note: Data are by place of occurrence and include reported annulments. Rates are based on total population residing in area.

n.a. not available.

p preliminary.

r revised.

1. Estimated.

a. Incomplete.

b. Does not meet publication standards because reporting was less than 90 percent complete.

Source: U.S. Department of Commerce, Bureau of the Census, *Statistical Abstract of the United States, 1989*, and earlier editions.

TABLE 17.24--NUMBER OF PHYSICIANS, 1980–1986, SELECTED YEARS, SOUTHEASTERN STATES AND UNITED STATES

	1986		1985			
State	Number	Rate	Number	Rate	1983	1980
TENNESSEE	8,673	181	8,492	179	7,851	7,169
Alabama	5,903	147	5,769	144	5,336	4,856
Arkansas	3,342	141	3,274	140	3,059	2,772
Florida	23,083	199	22,295	198	19,899	17,479
Georgia	9,863	164	9,614	163	8,732	7,728
Kentucky	5,754	156	5,640	153	5,364	4,820
Louisiana	7,999	179	7,936	178	7,392	6,501
Mississippi	3,176	122	3,081	119	2,933	2,664
North Carolina	10,755	173	10,489	171	9,708	8,874
South Carolina	5,052	153	4,912	149	4,490	4,129
Virginia	11,331	202	11,075	200	10,110	9,154
West Virginia	3,117	163	3,122	161	2,940	2,610
UNITED STATES	491,503	205	483,905	204	455,192	413,692

Note: "Physicians" refers to all active, non-federal physicians. Rates are per 100,000 civilian population and are based on U.S. Bureau of the Census estimates as of July 1.

Source: Copyright 1987, American Medical Association, as printed in U.S. Department of Commerce, Bureau of the Census, *Statistical Abstract of the United States, 1989*, 109th edition, page 98; and earlier editions.

TABLE 17.25--NUMBER OF DENTISTS, 1979–1987, SELECTED YEARS, SOUTHEASTERN STATES AND UNITED STATES

	1987			
State	Number	Rate	1982	1979
TENNESSEE	2,491	51.3	2,226	2,034
Alabama	1,615	39.5	1,489	1,314
Arkansas	911	38.1	838	714
Florida	5,960	49.6	4,878	4,323
Georgia	2,864	46.0	2,388	2,167
Kentucky	1,944	52.2	1,741	1,490
Louisiana	1,953	43.9	1,808	1,586
Mississippi	962	36.7	872	763
North Carolina	2,674	41.7	2,451	2,175
South Carolina	1,412	41.2	1,242	1,130
Virginia	3,264	55.2	2,876	2,599
West Virginia	784	41.3	797	703
UNITED STATES	n.a.	n.a.	126,985	117,223

Note: "Dentists" refers to all professionally active dentists. Active occupation categories include the following: clinical practitioners, dental school faculty or staff, armed forces dentists, government-employed dentists, health/dental organization staff members, interns/ residents, and other students. Rates are per 100,000 civilian population and are based on U.S. Bureau of the Census estimates as of July 1.

Source: American Dental Association, *Distribution of Dentists in the United States by Region and State*, 1979, 1982 and 1987.

Information on payments to individuals for reasons of public assistance, unemployment, or retirement benefits is the subject of this chapter. These payments are considered transfer payments–income payments which are not a compensation for current work effort. Program payments are frequently from a combination of federal, state, and local sources, and total payments distributed to local areas are reported in two sources. The Tennessee Department of Human Services provides data on levels of funding for various programs in its *Annual Report.* Comparisons of assistance funds to Tennessee counties for Aid to Families with Dependent Children and food stamps, previously found in the *Annual Report*, were provided from departmental records in Tables 18.3 and 18.4.

The second and most comprehensive source of local information on transfer payments is compiled by the Bureau of Economic Analysis (BEA), U.S. Department of Commerce. Estimates of transfer payments to residents of metropolitan statistical areas and counties are available for dissemination to members of BEA's Regional Economics Information System. Usually published in total, transfer payments are detailed by type for each county in Tennessee in Table 2.18, in the chapter on income. The effects of changes in the level of transfer payments may be more easily estimated by consideration of two additional measures, per capita transfer payments and transfers as a percentage of total personal income. These data are provided for each Tennessee county in Table 2.19. Revisions for earlier years could not be published here due to lack of space; however, these revised data are available upon request from the Center for Business and Economic Research.

Though transfer payments to residents in local areas are often substantial, they do not necessarily cover local needs. The 1980 decennial Census of Population reported on the incidence of poverty in counties and municipalities. These data are presented in Chapter 2, Table 2.17, of the *Abstract.*

For state- and United States-level information on public assistance or social insurance programs, a number of federal publications are available to the public. The Social Security Administration in its monthly *Social Security Bulletin* gives information on Supplemental Security Income, Aid to Families with Dependent Children, and Social Security payments. Year-end data are published in the *Annual Statistical Supplement.*

Table 18.8 provides data on the Food and Nutrition Service Programs for Tennessee and other southeastern states. These data are published in *Agricultural Statistics* by the U.S. Department of Agriculture, Statistical Reporting Service.

TABLE OF CONTENTS

TABLE 18.1--EXPENDITURES FOR HUMAN SERVICES PROGRAMS, TENNESSEE, FISCAL YEARS 1988 AND 1989

Program	Amount 1988–89	Amount 1987–88	Percentage change
Total expenditures	$476,979,078	$434,940,662	9.7
Rehabilitation services			
Case services	24,188,933	21,716,335	11.4
Workshops for the blind	487,700	485,288	0.5
Facility operation	7,670,284	7,142,870	7.4
Hearing impaired contracts	500,009	343,357	45.6
Family assistance			
Aid to dependent children grants	141,176,352	124,709,508	13.2
Child support			
Contracted services	6,595,010	5,314,180	24.1
Family and incentive payments	9,508,445	7,717,901	23.2
Refugee assistance grants	63,000	127,081	-50.4
Social services			
Vendor day care	3,431,358	3,320,649	3.3
Board and care (includes foster care)	28,426,865	21,086,783	34.8
Work incentive program			
Day care	78,772	242,432	-67.5
Other	78,651	132,770	-40.8
Social services contracts	42,100,531	36,895,877	14.1
Refugee resettlement contracts	484,617	511,375	-5.2
Low income energy assistance contracts	14,714,493	20,995,114	-29.9
Weatherization assistance contracts	7,186,543	11,966,863	-39.9
Administration			
General	67,080,921	64,221,853	4.5
Direct services	33,562,633	30,216,728	11.1
Purchased services	2,811,258	2,739,353	2.6
Family assistance	58,160,840	51,372,284	13.2
Disability determination	15,881,654	14,167,997	12.1
Child support	2,056,936	1,683,877	22.2
Rehabilitation services	10,733,273	7,830,187	37.1

Note: The following amounts in Certified Public Expenditures were not included in the figures above:

	1988–1989	1987–1988
Child support	$1,439,518	$1,237,109
Social services contracts	6,711,576	5,630,336

Source: Tennessee Department of Human Services, direct correspondence.

FIGURE 18.1
Unemployment Insurance Benefit Payments as a Percentage of Contributions

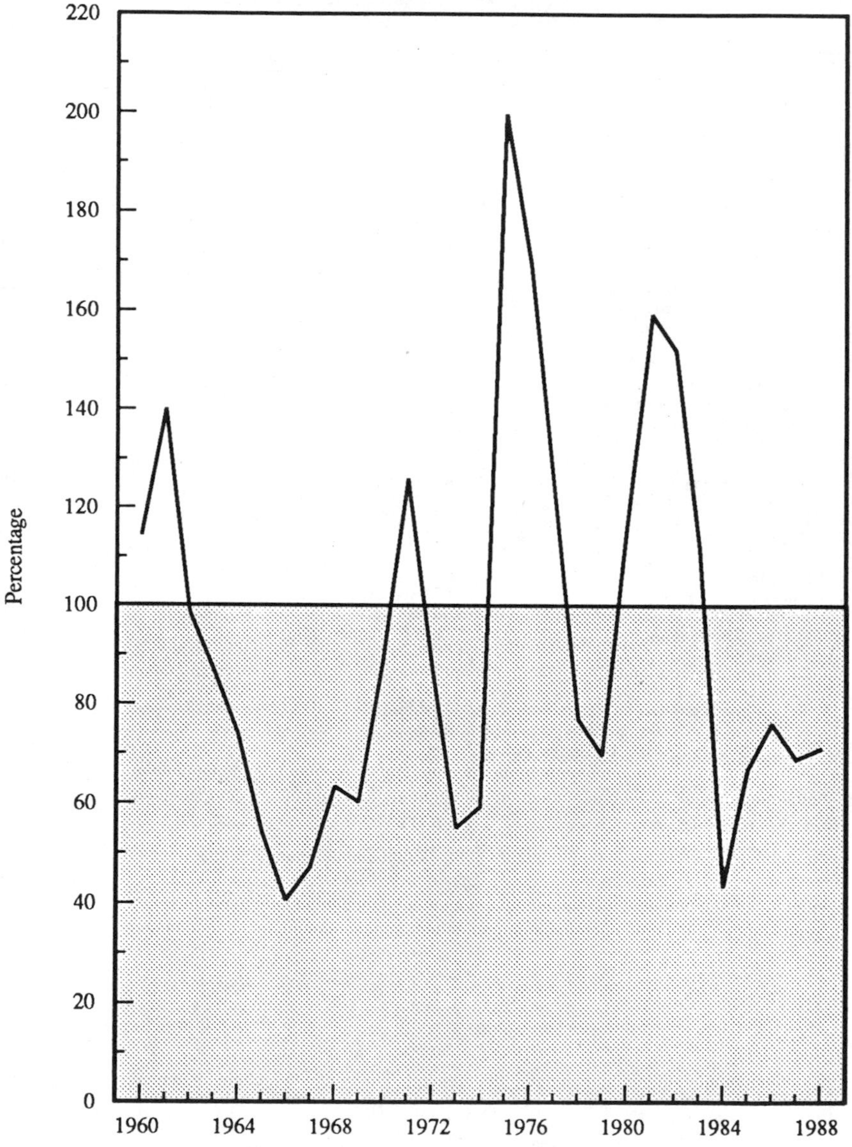

Source: Tennessee Department of Employment Security, "Statement of Revenues, Expenditures, and Changes in Fund Balance, 1988," and earlier editions; U.S. Department of Commerce, Bureau of the Census, State Government Finances in 1984, and earlier editions; and Tennessee Department of Employment Security, 30th Annual Report, 1966.

TABLE 18.2--CONTRIBUTIONS, BENEFIT PAYMENTS, AND FUND ASSETS UNDER UNEMPLOYMENT INSURANCE PROGRAM, TENNESSEE, 1955–1988, SELECTED YEARS
[In thousands of dollars]

				Assets[2]		
Year	Contributions	Benefit payments	Payments as a percentage of contributions[1]	Total	Trust fund account in United States Treasury[1]	Other[1]
1988	258,031	183,399	71.1	567,185	569,816	-2,631
1987	243,069	167,358	68.9	492,553	495,636	-3,083
1986	233,053	177,255	76.1	416,842	421,401	-4,559
1985	272,008	182,067	66.9	361,044	365,438	-4,394
1984	344,617	149,488	43.4	271,103	271,957	-854
1983	276,646	309,237	111.8	37,771	40,847	-3,076
1982	181,031	275,098	152.0	69,571	76,461	-6,890
1981	143,308	228,197	159.2	156,905	159,876	-2,971
1980	157,304	182,349	115.9	249,065	249,115	-50
1979	161,735	112,949	69.8	254,841	254,406	435
1978	130,972	100,838	77.0	192,145	190,950	1,195
1977	93,209	115,617	124.0	156,446	155,950	497
1976	79,996	135,503	169.4	180,676	179,273	1,402
1975	80,367	160,492	199.7	247,423	245,783	1,640
1974	80,939	48,002	59.3	316,101	315,705	396
1973	69,117	38,101	55.1	267,079	266,710	369
1972	52,346	45,721	87.3	224,145	223,993	152
1971	45,807	57,714	126.0	207,006	206,662	344
1970	45,766	40,490	88.5	208,013	207,383	630
1969	45,056	27,148	60.3	193,481	193,539	-58
1968	48,439	30,753	63.5	167,465	166,999	466
1967	50,524	23,853	47.2	149,884	149,745	139
1966	46,604	18,922	40.6	123,060	122,855	205
1965	42,663	23,112	54.2	94,316	94,014	302
1964	39,295	29,123	74.1	76,897	74,711	2,186
1963	35,936	31,187	86.8	65,001	64,356	645
1962	33,079	32,610	98.6	62,136	61,629	507
1960	30,120	34,508	114.6	72,886	72,127	759
1955	21,528	29,009	134.8	92,855	91,879	976

Note: Prior to 1984, the data were obtained from State Government Finances. Beginning in 1984, the source becomes the Tennessee Department of Employment Security. As a result, the data may not be directly comparable.

1. Computed by the Center for Business and Economic Research when not given in the source.

2. At end of fiscal year.

Source: Tennessee Department of Employment Security, "Statement of Revenues, Expenditures, and Changes in Fund Balance, 1988," and earlier editions; U.S. Department of Commerce, Bureau of the Census, *State Government Finances in 1984*, and earlier editions; and Tennessee Department of Employment Security, *30th Annual Report, 1966*.

TABLE 18.3--AID TO FAMILIES WITH DEPENDENT CHILDREN, CASES AND GRANT PAYMENTS, TENNESSEE AND COUNTIES, FISCAL YEARS 1987 AND 1988

County	1988 Families	1988 Children	1988 Grant payments ($)	1987 Families	1987 Children	1987 Grant payments ($)
TENNESSEE	66,845	123,834	124,935,953	63,816	117,744	114,417,230
Anderson	894	1,556	1,564,527	810	1,410	1,381,166
Bedford	209	382	381,306	224	410	397,471
Benton	136	229	245,935	130	210	221,201
Bledsoe	122	200	211,249	118	201	200,720
Blount	713	1,122	1,232,929	723	1,155	1,216,736
Bradley	449	777	844,645	409	698	735,096
Campbell	914	1,596	1,606,545	843	1,463	1,442,204
Cannon	70	125	128,474	68	122	115,563
Carroll	291	533	564,811	271	483	484,717
Carter	535	878	947,371	506	833	869,906
Cheatham	169	309	316,320	138	258	244,909
Chester	124	204	226,351	121	205	211,608
Claiborne	435	746	761,530	408	697	688,130
Clay	72	122	124,979	83	137	137,517
Cocke	646	1,049	1,115,157	649	1,058	1,069,700
Coffee	384	664	727,575	334	567	607,794
Crockett	172	306	326,416	184	331	329,978
Cumberland	288	509	527,585	295	498	516,176
Davidson	7,356	13,886	13,984,348	6,926	13,044	12,603,511
Decatur	56	92	99,833	67	113	115,271
DeKalb	174	306	329,705	163	285	293,822
Dickson	327	559	607,178	332	565	580,013
Dyer	564	945	1,019,243	536	883	914,297
Fayette	636	1,324	1,199,400	626	1,272	1,137,409
Fentress	299	503	521,547	278	472	471,530
Franklin	311	517	533,174	308	499	503,969
Gibson	615	1,115	1,128,846	602	1,092	1,063,631
Giles	324	565	587,896	305	536	529,200
Grainger	200	324	337,511	194	325	326,532
Greene	578	921	1,001,585	496	776	819,348
Grundy	259	462	471,460	259	461	452,051
Hamblen	736	1,247	1,301,258	664	1,112	1,133,202
Hamilton	4,072	7,515	7,503,312	4,073	7,406	7,186,626
Hancock	205	357	353,567	199	354	337,401
Hardeman	696	1,270	1,237,893	668	1,211	1,152,365
Hardin	300	516	541,133	289	483	493,574
Hawkins	492	867	919,810	451	802	802,011
Haywood	630	1,101	1,142,441	631	1,121	1,083,294
Henderson	198	322	338,350	187	315	313,769
Henry	255	450	477,222	240	430	430,755
Hickman	140	245	249,216	136	231	226,965
Houston	80	129	146,504	78	131	133,850
Humphreys	122	223	231,167	120	219	213,436
Jackson	74	122	130,409	70	116	117,661
Jefferson	349	544	586,396	344	527	558,407
Johnson	260	450	479,121	245	416	427,390
Knox	4,293	7,495	7,752,103	4,020	7,054	7,063,203
Lake	167	289	306,177	184	305	308,734

TABLE 18.3--AID TO FAMILIES WITH DEPENDENT CHILDREN, CASES AND GRANT PAYMENTS, TENNESSEE AND COUNTIES, FISCAL YEARS 1987 AND 1988 (Continued)

	1988			1987		
County	Families	Children	Grant payments ($)	Families	Children	Grant payments ($)
Lauderdale	522	1,004	967,836	532	1,021	961,638
Lawrence	248	417	453,172	239	406	414,225
Lewis	109	187	195,648	102	171	173,546
Lincoln	204	347	358,932	196	331	326,320
Loudon	286	471	494,279	273	436	454,218
McMinn	435	717	771,123	409	663	695,708
McNairy	294	483	506,373	278	464	463,119
Macon	122	201	214,884	106	168	176,431
Madison	1,485	2,754	2,752,999	1,337	2,507	2,379,468
Marion	424	693	759,215	392	636	668,170
Marshall	201	351	362,618	185	310	317,932
Maury	671	1,155	1,178,446	621	1,042	1,035,583
Meigs	89	155	164,761	90	157	161,216
Monroe	308	521	561,029	309	526	522,606
Montgomery	730	1,302	1,372,144	669	1,206	1,223,410
Moore	19	28	29,291	18	24	24,999
Morgan	251	440	447,245	260	451	445,024
Obion	337	582	614,896	315	547	543,807
Overton	176	276	306,138	159	241	270,131
Perry	40	65	68,133	40	69	68,858
Pickett	38	63	63,258	39	59	61,143
Polk	92	145	162,783	85	142	150,073
Putnam	294	507	531,523	275	474	488,710
Rhea	437	741	777,137	417	698	727,088
Roane	539	873	930,155	517	855	872,845
Robertson	375	648	706,617	373	656	668,738
Rutherford	634	1,156	1,196,977	583	1,040	1,045,261
Scott	472	860	858,221	452	808	794,770
Sequatchie	123	207	219,093	127	204	212,413
Sevier	371	590	625,648	364	580	595,353
Shelby	19,874	40,720	39,200,605	19,160	39,038	36,198,293
Smith	115	202	212,199	112	194	196,843
Stewart	56	83	92,615	53	83	87,526
Sullivan	1,102	1,808	2,028,489	1,013	1,655	1,776,998
Sumner	402	722	802,034	393	685	715,714
Tipton	806	1,612	1,497,448	732	1,468	1,315,510
Trousdale	36	65	69,400	42	68	72,336
Unicoi	146	211	244,344	135	204	226,912
Union	209	368	378,853	196	347	342,704
Van Buren	47	75	79,381	45	72	75,202
Warren	287	498	550,423	253	429	457,110
Washington	928	1,591	1,694,656	849	1,455	1,473,084
Wayne	97	173	166,252	87	149	146,251
Weakley	202	348	372,842	183	305	309,086
White	111	198	201,363	119	212	209,866
Williamson	354	635	666,843	338	596	593,771
Wilson	356	618	656,122	339	600	613,402

Note: Number of families and children are monthly averages.

Source: Tennessee Department of Human Services, direct correspondence.

TABLE 18.4--VALUE OF FOOD STAMP COUPONS AND NUMBER OF HOUSEHOLDS PARTICIPATING, TENNESSEE AND COUNTIES, FISCAL YEARS 1987 AND 1988 [Value in thousands]

County	1988 Number of house-holds [1]	1988 Value of coupons	1987 Number of house-holds [1]	1987 Value of coupons
TENNESSEE	184,285	$288,180	185,511	$278,154
Anderson	2,704	4,314	2,651	4,048
Bedford	697	956	759	1,035
Benton	630	870	634	836
Bledsoe	497	751	492	717
Blount	2,429	3,341	2,565	3,511
Bradley	1,797	2,444	1,893	2,575
Campbell	2,771	4,556	2,810	4,509
Cannon	314	426	336	424
Carroll	1,250	1,441	1,224	1,378
Carter	2,029	2,971	2,079	2,909
Cheatham	410	736	344	575
Chester	635	757	666	791
Claiborne	1,551	2,452	1,551	2,403
Clay	386	444	388	455
Cocke	2,036	2,955	2,152	3,067
Coffee	1,280	1,968	1,197	1,751
Crockett	560	692	598	756
Cumberland	1,179	1,756	1,248	1,838
Davidson	15,272	26,666	14,740	23,536
Decatur	499	476	545	543
DeKalb	569	839	578	852
Dickson	875	1,419	842	1,322
Dyer	1,831	2,192	1,937	2,215
Fayette	1,456	2,399	1,408	2,232
Fentress	1,146	1,821	1,176	1,887
Franklin	1,001	1,430	989	1,369
Gibson	2,083	2,679	2,103	2,674
Giles	1,055	1,498	1,043	1,383
Grainger	785	1,135	770	1,082
Greene	2,174	3,137	2,126	2,952
Grundy	891	1,509	940	1,538
Hamblen	1,896	2,908	1,892	2,842
Hamilton	10,587	16,308	11,027	16,115
Hancock	676	1,135	714	1,172
Hardeman	1,733	2,594	1,706	2,462
Hardin	1,476	1,914	1,506	1,915
Hawkins	1,980	3,069	2,047	3,139
Haywood	1,805	2,420	1,825	2,473
Henderson	1,039	1,254	1,044	1,214
Henry	1,220	1,573	1,207	1,507
Hickman	544	730	518	679
Houston	285	431	300	404
Humphreys	434	567	480	590
Jackson	408	573	424	569
Jefferson	1,272	1,798	1,274	1,783
Johnson	1,074	1,552	1,084	1,480
Knox	10,515	16,007	10,544	15,488
Lake	610	798	658	872

TABLE 18.4--VALUE OF FOOD STAMP COUPONS AND NUMBER OF HOUSEHOLDS PARTICIPATING, TENNESSEE AND COUNTIES, FISCAL YEARS 1987 AND 1988 [Value in thousands] (Continued)

County	1988 Number of households [1]	1988 Value of coupons	1987 Number of households [1]	1987 Value of coupons
Lauderdale	1,467	1,964	1,527	1,989
Lawrence	1,305	1,794	1,379	1,807
Lewis	478	629	500	650
Lincoln	783	1,000	766	917
Loudon	1,014	1,435	1,112	1,545
McMinn	1,463	2,217	1,486	2,182
McNairy	1,289	1,567	1,332	1,546
Macon	472	663	479	640
Madison	3,674	5,295	3,663	4,930
Marion	1,241	1,996	1,230	1,880
Marshall	619	847	643	862
Maury	2,024	2,866	1,938	2,580
Meigs	310	501	286	463
Monroe	1,327	1,972	1,369	1,938
Montgomery	2,231	3,538	2,152	3,286
Moore	91	108	94	115
Morgan	970	1,506	1,061	1,680
Obion	1,270	1,607	1,272	1,575
Overton	762	1,025	791	1,046
Perry	258	302	270	317
Pickett	205	273	194	241
Polk	488	664	507	677
Putnam	1,137	1,544	1,200	1,589
Rhea	1,312	2,043	1,306	1,977
Roane	1,867	2,626	1,872	2,609
Robertson	944	1,261	952	1,273
Rutherford	1,650	2,566	1,595	2,347
Scott	1,704	2,687	1,720	2,693
Sequatchie	505	772	506	745
Sevier	1,525	2,186	1,610	2,271
Shelby	40,859	74,399	41,208	71,628
Smith	378	553	388	531
Stewart	273	397	269	358
Sullivan	4,876	7,245	4,712	6,833
Sumner	1,513	2,208	1,412	1,986
Tipton	1,990	3,173	1,954	3,005
Trousdale	168	254	170	241
Unicoi	769	973	807	1,014
Union	576	993	596	958
Van Buren	182	270	198	300
Warren	1,037	1,599	1,022	1,482
Washington	2,939	4,516	2,960	4,382
Wayne	619	809	659	849
Weakley	928	1,052	904	987
White	527	688	586	775
Williamson	891	1,356	859	1,212
Wilson	1,029	1,580	961	1,377

1. Monthly average number of participating households.

Source: Tennessee Department of Human Services, Research and Statistics Division, direct correspondence.

TABLE 18.5--MEDICARE AND MEDICAID BENEFITS, SOUTHEASTERN STATES, 1987

	Medicare[1]		Medicaid[2]	
State	Benefits paid ($1,000,000)	Persons enrolled (1,000)	Benefits paid ($1,000,000)	Recipients[3] (1,000)
TENNESSEE	1,357	654	811	443
Alabama	1,215	553	366	289
Arkansas	785	377	410	212
Florida	5,720	2,135	1,178	640
Georgia	1,526	685	901	506
Kentucky	946	510	606	411
Louisiana	1,253	504	824	464
Mississippi	757	353	363	342
North Carolina	1,448	821	825	386
South Carolina	798	406	422	267
Virginia	1,230	670	662	318
West Virginia	686	297	244	215

Note: Preliminary data.

1. Payments are for calendar year and represent total disbursements from federal hospital and supplementary medical insurance trust funds. Estimates of distribution by state based on interim reimbursements. Enrollment is as of July 1.

2. For fiscal year ending September 30.

3. Persons receiving Medicaid at any time during year.

Source: U.S. Department of Commerce, Bureau of the Census, *Statistical Abstract of the United States, 1989.*

TABLE 18.6--PUBLIC HEALTH PROGRAM EXPENDITURES, BY SOURCE, SOUTHEASTERN STATES, 1984 [In thousands of dollars]

State	Total	Federal grant and contract funds	State funds	Local funds	Fees, reimbursements, and other sources[1]
TENNESSEE	130,112	58,878	52,171	6,186	12,876
Alabama	67,477	44,379	21,282	0	1,817
Arkansas	56,111	25,500	30,007	0	604
Florida	247,022	69,221	98,208	32,823	46,770
Georgia	176,872	72,174	71,157	23,287	10,254
Kentucky	221,537	52,748	103,526	15,647	49,616
Louisiana	113,882	63,089	33,762	8,060	8,971
Mississippi	88,108	46,251	16,601	6,604	18,653
North Carolina	202,980	63,204	55,217	0	84,559
South Carolina	136,095	55,232	57,898	2,209	20,755
Virginia	160,702	43,962	66,397	32,314	18,029
West Virginia	153,229	48,767	90,734	4,766	8,962

Note: Data exclude those funds expended for public health purposes by other state agencies such as separate mental health authorities, environmental agencies, and hospital authorities. Details may not add to total due to rounding.

1. Includes funds from unknown sources.

Source: Health Insurance Association of America, *Source Book of Health Insurance Data*, 1986–87, used by special permission.

TABLE 18.7--AID TO FAMILIES WITH DEPENDENT CHILDREN, NUMBER OF RECIPIENTS AND AMOUNT OF PAYMENTS, SOUTHEASTERN STATES AND UNITED STATES, 1986

State	Recipients (1,000)	Amount of payments: Total ($1,000,000)	Amount of payments: Monthly average per family ($)
TENNESSEE	177	104	143
Alabama	139	68	114
Arkansas	66	49	178
Florida	286	267	227
Georgia	246	232	228
Kentucky	161	140	193
Louisiana	256	164	168
Mississippi	170	76	116
North Carolina	173	184	228
South Carolina	130	104	186
Virginia	151	178	255
West Virginia	115	109	247
UNITED STATES	10,875	15,961	n.a.

Note: Recipients are as of December.

n.a. not available.

Source: U.S. Department of Commerce, Bureau of the Census, *Statistical Abstract of the United States*, 1989.

TABLE 18.8--CASH PAYMENTS MADE UNDER FOOD AND NUTRITION SERVICE PROGRAMS, SOUTHEASTERN STATES, FISCAL YEAR 1986
[In thousands of dollars]

State	Total[1]	Child Care Food	Summer Feeding	Special Milk	National School Lunch	Breakfast	Special Supplemental Food (WIC)[2]	Commodity Distribution[2]	Food Stamp Program[2]
TENNESSEE	440,223	6,184	1,291	34	61,787	12,311	27,674	30,233	277,928
Alabama	441,433	9,385	3,068	39	70,756	11,457	25,705	21,870	278,062
Arkansas	205,392	3,583	106	29	35,541	5,403	15,220	12,543	120,704
Florida	646,725	16,267	5,770	121	119,330	20,114	41,994	45,812	361,940
Georgia	482,369	12,221	3,074	57	90,711	14,881	42,999	32,748	269,645
Kentucky	471,098	4,620	1,052	106	55,801	12,837	27,348	24,430	320,492
Louisiana	599,609	13,746	2,057	84	86,119	13,487	39,867	38,603	389,822
Mississippi	410,606	12,901	3,496	14	62,736	13,065	35,573	16,736	263,351
North Carolina	427,573	9,422	2,201	103	83,911	19,254	37,232	33,523	225,885
South Carolina	309,226	5,114	3,197	32	57,804	8,316	27,706	19,628	178,730
Virginia	311,199	6,458	1,445	139	53,241	6,117	24,928	25,417	180,805
West Virginia	223,808	2,324	492	29	26,507	8,050	10,721	9,130	156,376

Note: Data are preliminary.

1. Total includes items not shown separately.

2. The amounts shown for WIC, Commodity Distribution, and Food Stamp programs are the values of the food benefits provided.

Source: U.S. Department of Agriculture, Statistical Reporting Service, *Agricultural Statistics*, 1987.

TABLE 18.9-- SOCIAL SECURITY BENEFICIARIES AND BENEFIT PAYMENTS, SOUTHEASTERN STATES AND UNITED STATES, 1987

	Number of beneficiaries (1,000)				Benefit payments ($1,000,000)				Average monthly payments ($)		
State	Total [1]	Retired workers [2]	Survivors	Disabled workers [2]	Total [1]	Retired workers [2]	Survivors [3]	Disabled workers [2]	Retired workers [4]	Disabled workers	Widows and widowers
TENNESSEE	787	519	163	105	3,832	2,482	862	488	471	477	414
Alabama	680	430	155	95	3,257	2,010	801	446	466	484	406
Arkansas	454	301	90	63	2,125	1,373	461	291	454	479	400
Florida	2,439	1,866	369	205	13,088	9,768	2,244	1,076	512	517	483
Georgia	832	533	176	123	4,046	2,548	919	579	468	477	411
Kentucky	624	389	137	98	2,996	1,811	732	453	466	499	415
Louisiana	622	372	155	94	3,002	1,750	826	426	477	506	425
Mississippi	439	268	98	73	1,949	1,174	462	313	436	462	375
North Carolina	1,003	682	195	126	4,920	3,296	1,014	610	472	472	403
South Carolina	506	330	103	73	2,472	1,593	528	351	473	476	403
Virginia	787	537	157	93	3,972	2,630	879	463	480	492	433
West Virginia	362	220	85	57	1,878	1,105	492	281	506	538	446
UNITED STATES	37,283	26,455	6,954	3,874	200,995	139,582	41,490	19,923	515	511	471

Note: A person eligible to receive more than one type of benefit is generally classified or counted only once as a retired worker beneficiary.

1. Includes special benefits for persons aged 72 and over not insured under regular or transitional provisions of Social Security Act.
2. Includes benefits payable to dependents.
3. Includes lump-sum payments to survivors of deceased workers.
4. Excludes persons with special benefits.

Source: U.S. Department of Commerce, Bureau of the Census, *Statistical Abstract of the United States*, 1989.

TABLE 18.10--SUPPLEMENTAL SECURITY INCOME FOR THE AGED, BLIND, AND DISABLED, SOUTHEASTERN STATES, 1987

	State-administered supplementation		Federally-administered supplementation[1]							
					Aged		Blind		Disabled	
	Total recipients	Total payments ($1,000)	Total recipients	Total payments ($1,000)	Recipients	Average monthly payment ($)	Recipients	Average monthly payment ($)	Recipients	Average monthly payment ($)
TENNESSEE	0	0	131,915	308,219	45,792	125.36	2,018	245.01	84,105	244.90
Alabama	15,837	11,159	130,955	293,379	55,782	133.49	1,738	231.92	73,435	242.37
Arkansas	0	0	73,855	153,775	31,324	120.15	1,310	223.44	41,221	224.32
Florida	10,539	11,681	195,969	506,709	78,449	187.80	3,108	245.05	114,412	251.35
Georgia	0	0	155,296	350,274	56,048	128.54	2,778	231.69	96,470	233.99
Kentucky	6,840	10,081	103,478	259,254	31,388	134.41	2,076	255.60	70,014	254.88
Louisiana	0	0	129,099	313,836	45,319	140.86	2,281	240.50	81,499	248.97
Mississippi	0	0	112,807	255,648	46,961	132.54	1,727	228.37	64,119	240.05
North Carolina	14,048	49,471	141,523	322,431	51,467	132.09	2,668	232.86	87,388	235.90
South Carolina	2,983	4,908	87,989	196,702	31,756	127.31	1,836	241.87	54,397	230.92
Virginia	5,336	13,288	88,949	204,556	30,333	132.27	1,494	238.43	57,122	237.02
West Virginia	0	0	44,118	117,633	9,859	134.74	692	246.51	33,567	266.20

Note: Number of recipients and average monthly payments are for the month of December.

1. Includes federal SSI payments and federally administered state supplementation.

Source: U.S. Department of Health and Human Services, Social Security Administration, *Social Security Bulletin, Annual Statistical Supplement*, 1988.

TABLE 18.11--INSURANCE SUMMARY FOR COVERED EMPLOYMENT, SOUTHEASTERN STATES, 1987

State	Average weekly insured unemployment		Average weekly unemployment benefits	Beneficiaries, first payments	Benefits paid
	Number (1,000)	%[1]	($)	(1,000)	($1,000,000)
TENNESSEE	40	2.2	98	148	167
Alabama	37	2.7	101	149	166
Arkansas	27	3.4	123	88	131
Florida	52	1.1	128	159	269
Georgia	41	1.6	120	199	236
Kentucky	29	2.4	108	101	141
Louisiana	61	4.2	142	150	382
Mississippi	26	3.2	100	75	100
North Carolina	42	1.6	124	185	202
South Carolina	22	1.8	104	82	88
Virginia	21	0.9	133	118	128
West Virginia	20	3.6	145	59	126

1. Insured unemployment as a percentage of average covered employment in preceding year.

Source: U.S. Department of Commerce, Bureau of the Census, *Statistical Abstract of the United States*, 1989.

Law enforcement statistics are generally either records of police agencies or prison data. Records of prosecutions and court actions do not lend themselves to statistical presentation because of the complexity of reporting litigation. The U.S. Department of Justice, Federal Bureau of Investigation, reports the most common local crimes in its *Crime in the United States, Uniform Crime Reports.* It is important to remember that crime statistics included here represent only those crimes reported to police and represent fewer than the number actually committed; that reporting procedures vary from place to place or over time; that differences exist among governmental units in the scope of responsibilities and administration; and finally, that many factors influence the frequency of crimes and the level of enforcement needed. Therefore, data users are advised to exercise caution in making comparisons in the area of law enforcement statistics.

The *Sourcebook of Criminal Justice Statistics*, published by the U.S. Department of Justice, Bureau of Justice Statistics, provides prisoner detail and governmental expenditures data for criminal justice. However, more current data and place-specific details are provided in annual reports of state government departments. The most current data on Tennessee state and local expenditures for law enforcement can be found in Chapter 15, Government Finance. Prisoner and prison statistics are published by the Department of Corrections in its annual report. When published reports are not available in time to be included in the *Abstract*, the Department of Corrections has graciously provided these data from their files. Information on the number of deaths from homicide is supplied by another department of state government. These data, detailed by race and sex, are collected and published by the Tennessee Department of Health and Environment.

Traffic accidents and deaths are reported in the Tennessee Department of Safety's *Tennessee Motor Vehicle Traffic Accident Facts.* Note that a change in reporting laws and procedures occurred in 1971; therefore, data reported prior to this date are not comparable to data reported later. However, two years of comparable data have been given here in order to provide an easier transition for the data user.

Information on the number of lawyers licensed in Tennessee and in each of the other southeastern states is published here by special permission of the American Bar Foundation. A map featuring judicial districts in Tennessee might also be of interest to data users interested in law enforcement. This information is included in Chapter 14.

TABLE OF CONTENTS

FIGURE 19.1
Crime Rates per 100,000 Population by Type of Crime, Tennessee, 1977–1987

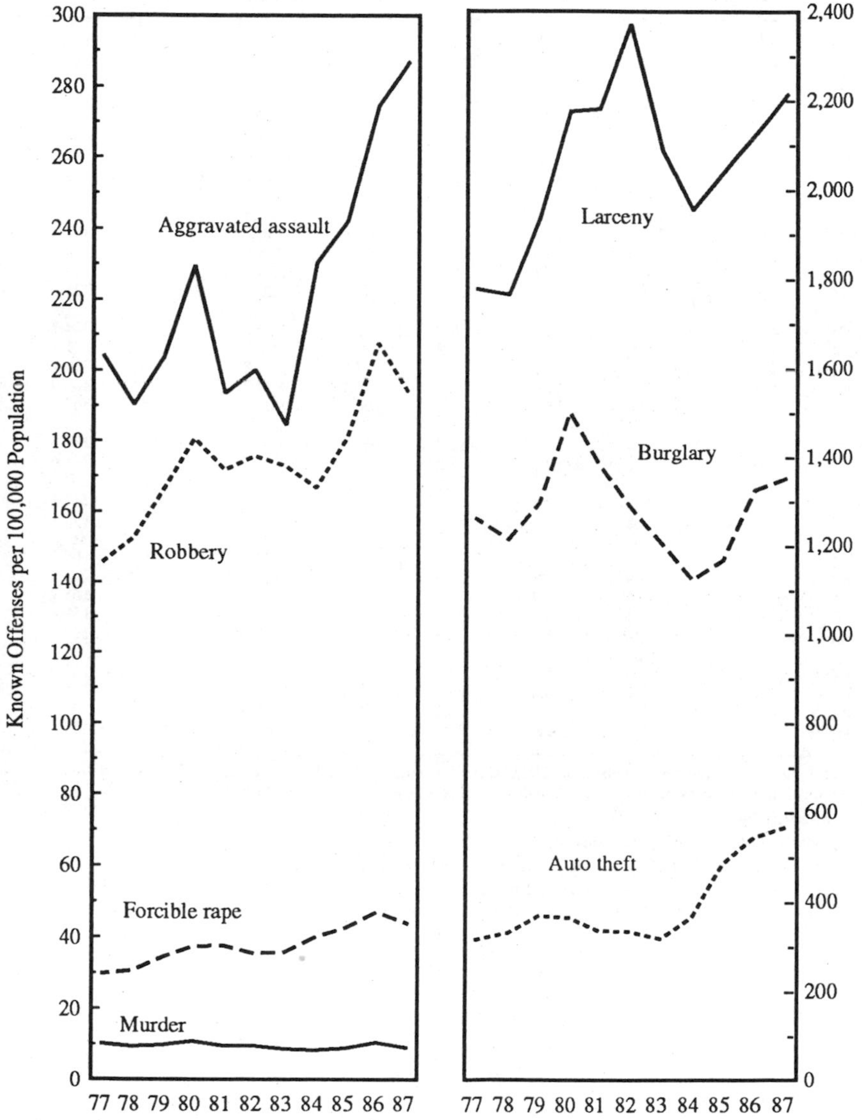

Note: Rates are known offenses based on Bureau of the Census population estimates as of July 1 except in decennial census years, when it is April 1.
Source: U.S. Department of Justice F.B.I., *Crime in the United States, Uniform Crime Reports*, 1987.

TABLE 19.1-- CRIME RATES PER 100,000 POPULATION, BY TYPE OF CRIME, TENNESSEE, 1957–1987

Year	Total offenses	Murder[1]	Forcible rape	Robbery	Aggra- vated assault	Burglary	Larceny $50 and over[2]	Auto theft
1987	4,665.6	9.1	43.9	193.8	286.6	1,351.8	2,213.4	566.9
1986	4,534.2	10.4	47.0	207.7	274.5	1,325.2	2,125.8	543.6
1985	4,166.7	9.0	42.6	180.9	242.0	1,166.8	2,040.3	485.2
1984	3,889.6	8.4	40.0	166.8	230.3	1,123.6	1,954.1	366.4
1983	4,011.7	8.8	35.9	172.8	184.6	1,205.9	2,087.2	316.5
1982	4,413.6	9.7	35.5	175.7	200.2	1,288.6	2,371.9	332.0
1981	4,311.4	9.7	37.6	171.7	193.5	1,384.2	2,180.6	334.1
1980	4,497.9	10.8	37.4	180.6	229.4	1,501.5	2,175.2	363.1
1979	4,013.4	9.8	34.5	166.1	203.6	1,294.7	1,937.2	367.4
1978	3,690.4	9.4	30.6	152.4	190.2	1,213.6	1,766.1	328.1
1977	3,739.7	10.1	29.7	145.8	203.9	1,259.7	1,776.5	314.0
1976	4,258.4	11.0	25.4	147.5	209.4	1,320.5	2,218.6	325.9
1975	4,270.5	11.4	26.1	166.8	192.6	1,379.3	2,129.5	364.7
1974	3,659.1	13.4	25.7	157.2	190.4	1,350.1	1,575.6	346.7
1973	3,060.1	13.2	26.9	130.5	187.5	1,009.8	1,362.2	330.1
1972	2,101.5	11.3	19.9	101.1	186.7	894.3	587.4	300.9
1971	2,060.3	12.4	18.1	86.5	196.8	901.4	541.7	303.5
1970	1,888.3	8.8	15.5	82.0	168.6	806.7	517.4	289.3
1969	1,665.5	9.6	12.7	75.2	134.3	715.0	437.2	281.6
1968	1,598.0	8.7	11.6	71.2	129.0	719.7	390.3	267.4
1967	1,531.3	8.9	12.5	56.5	130.5	711.8	368.0	243.1
1966	1,275.6	7.8	10.8	34.4	105.2	602.5	321.7	193.1
1965	1,082.9	8.0	11.1	28.6	91.1	523.0	254.5	166.7
1964	1,103.8	5.9	8.8	30.2	73.6	561.4	248.0	175.8
1963	1,014.0	6.5	6.7	28.4	60.7	515.9	230.2	165.7
1962	919.2	6.1	6.6	34.8	56.1	461.6	195.9	158.1
1961	875.5	8.0	6.7	30.4	63.0	462.0	166.1	139.2
1960	847.2	8.5	5.2	27.8	50.4	469.4	153.5	132.2
1959	821.5	7.0	6.6	26.9	56.2	437.8	151.4	135.7
1958	791.7	8.4	7.4	26.2	59.2	416.5	142.1	131.9
1957	745.0	9.2	n.a.	27.1	70.5	360.5	139.2	138.6

Note: Rates represent offenses known per 100,000 population, based on the Bureau of the Census provisional population estimate as of July 1, except in decennial census years, when it is April 1.

n.a. not available.

1. Murder includes nonnegligent manslaughter.

2. Beginning in 1973, includes all larceny–theft not using force or fraud.

Source: U.S. Department of Justice, Federal Bureau of Investigation, *Crime in the United States, Uniform Crime Reports, 1987*, and earlier editions (prior to 1961 titled *Uniform Crime Reports for the United States*).

TABLE 19.2-- NUMBER OF CRIMINAL OFFENSES, BY TYPE OF CRIME, TENNESSEE, 1957–1987

Year	Total offenses	Murder[1]	Forcible rape	Robbery	Aggra-vated assault	Burglary	Larceny $50 and over[2]	Auto theft
1987	226,516	444	2,133	9,409	13,914	65,632	107,459	27,525
1986	217,780	501	2,256	9,978	13,184	63,649	102,103	26,109
1985	198,419	429	2,027	8,614	11,522	55,563	97,159	23,105
1984	183,472	394	1,887	7,867	10,862	53,002	92,176	17,284
1983	187,946	410	1,682	8,094	8,650	56,498	97,785	14,827
1982	205,278	452	1,651	8,173	9,310	59,934	110,316	15,442
1981	198,756	448	1,735	7,916	8,920	63,811	100,526	15,400
1980	204,456	489	1,700	8,208	10,427	68,251	98,876	16,505
1979	175,786	430	1,511	7,277	8,917	56,710	84,850	16,091
1978	160,792	411	1,335	6,639	8,286	52,876	76,948	14,297
1977	160,768	434	1,276	6,266	8,767	54,154	76,371	13,500
1976	179,448	462	1,072	6,215	8,825	55,647	93,493	13,734
1975	178,850	477	1,095	6,987	8,068	57,766	89,184	15,273
1974	151,085	555	1,062	6,490	7,862	55,745	65,055	14,316
1973	126,259	544	1,108	5,383	7,736	41,663	56,206	13,619
1972	84,713	455	802	4,076	7,525	36,049	23,678	12,128
1971	82,207	496	721	3,452	7,851	35,964	21,612	12,111
1970	74,101	346	607	3,218	6,616	31,656	20,305	11,353
1969	66,371	382	505	2,996	5,352	28,492	17,421	11,223
1968	63,535	345	460	2,830	5,131	28,616	15,520	10,633
1967	59,605	347	486	2,199	5,079	27,703	14,323	9,468
1966	49,529	304	421	1,337	4,083	23,394	12,492	7,498
1965	41,635	307	425	1,100	3,501	20,107	9,787	6,408
1964	41,920	225	336	1,148	2,796	21,321	9,418	6,676
1963	37,458	239	247	1,048	2,243	19,056	8,503	6,122
1962	33,404	220	241	1,266	2,040	16,772	7,119	5,746
1961	31,648	290	242	1,100	2,278	16,702	6,005	5,031
1960	30,220	304	187	993	1,799	16,744	5,477	4,716
1959	29,014	247	232	950	1,984	15,461	5,347	4,793
1958	27,468	293	258	908	2,054	14,448	4,930	4,577
1957	25,651	316	n.a.	932	2,427	12,411	4,794	4,771

n.a. not available.

1. Murder includes nonnegligent manslaughter.

2. Beginning in 1973, includes all larceny–theft not using force or fraud.

Source: U.S. Department of Justice, Federal Bureau of Investigation, *Crime in the United States, Uniform Crime Reports, 1987*, and earlier editions.

TABLE 19.3--POPULATION AND PER CAPITA EXPENDITURES OF ADULT AND JUVENILE CORRECTIONAL INSTITUTIONS AND REHABILITATIVE SERVICE CENTERS, TENNESSEE, FISCAL YEAR 1988

Institution	Population [1]	Average daily count	Designated capacity	Average daily cost per resident
Adult				
Brushy Mountain State Penitentiary	404	382	408	$66.94
Middle Tennessee Reception Center	583	571	600	46.21
Mark H. Luttrell Reception Center (formerly West Tennessee Reception Center)	419	399	411	52.87
Fort Pillow Prison and Farm	609	546	632	51.54
Turney Center Industrial Prison	783	771	782	45.19
Tennessee State Penitentiary	978	918	1,068	65.39
Tennessee Prison For Women	379	363	374	46.46
DeBerry Correctional Institute	268	260	285	72.90
Southeastern Tennessee State Regional Correctional Facility	836	796	806	41.56
Morgan County Regional Correctional Facility	844	808	815	37.06
Lake County Regional Correctional Facility	733	717	725	37.26
Rehabilitative Services				
Nashville Community Service Center	273	270	350	41.20
Chattanooga Community Service Center	95	95	120	46.11
Knoxville Community Service Center	148	124	150	48.75
Wayne County Work Camp	120	112	120	63.91
Carter County Work Camp	181	125	180	53.32
Juvenile				
John S. Wilder Youth Development Center	144	169	188	66.20
Tennessee Youth Center	47	69	75	107.41
Spencer Youth Center	225	246	219	80.21
James M. Taft Youth Center	181	192	203	85.24

Note: Adult population does not include 2,089 felons in local jails awaiting transfer to TDOC institutions and 2,011 locally sentenced felons. In addition to the data detailed above, there are twelve group homes with a total population of 66.

1. As of June 30, 1988.

Source: Tennessee Department of Correction, direct correspondence.

TABLE 19.4-- SENTENCED PRISONERS RECEIVED FROM COURT DURING YEAR AND PRESENT AT END OF YEAR IN STATE PRISONS, TENNESSEE AND UNITED STATES, 1940–1986, SELECTED YEARS

Year	Received from court: Tennessee	Received from court: United States	Tennessee as % of U.S.	Present at end of year: Tennessee	Present at end of year: United States	Tennessee as % of U.S.
1986	3,011	219,382	1.37	7,591	522,245	1.45
1985	n.a.	n.a.	n.a.	7,127	480,568	1.48
1984	3,991	180,418	2.21	7,302	443,838	1.65
1983	3,632	187,408	1.94	8,201	419,346	1.96
1982	3,238	177,109	1.83	7,869	395,516	1.99
1981	3,814	160,272	2.38	7,897	353,167	2.24
1980	2,947	142,122	2.07	7,022	315,974	2.22
1979	2,809	131,047	2.14	6,629	301,470	2.20
1978	2,415	126,121	1.91	5,835	293,546	1.99
1977	2,608	128,050	2.04	5,480	278,141	1.97
1976	2,482	121,997	2.03	4,817	262,833	1.83
1975	2,353	122,715	1.92	4,371	233,900	1.87
1974	1,895	103,754	1.83	3,771	218,205	1.73
1973	1,861	127,686	1.46	3,454	204,349	1.69
1972	1,797	119,316	1.51	3,329	196,183	1.70
1971	1,741	n.a.	n.a.	3,454	198,061	1.74
1970	1,611	67,304	2.39	3,268	176,391	1.85
1969	1,474	63,688	2.31	3,148	176,384	1.78
1968	1,379	60,938	2.26	2,999	167,211	1.79
1967	1,313	66,403	1.98	2,980	175,317	1.70
1966	1,214	66,349	1.83	2,968	180,409	1.65
1965	1,403	74,724	1.88	3,213	189,855	1.69
1964	1,300	75,096	1.73	3,187	192,627	1.65
1963	1,275	74,944	1.70	3,246	194,155	1.67
1962	1,221	75,568	1.62	3,167	194,886	1.63
1961	1,288	79,996	1.61	3,144	196,453	1.60
1960	1,294	74,852	1.73	3,134	189,735	1.65
1959	1,283	73,394	1.75	2,914	185,613	1.57
1958	1,073	74,922	1.43	2,712	184,094	1.47
1957	956	67,252	1.42	2,657	174,994	1.52
1956	931	64,534	1.44	2,713	169,431	1.60
1955	984	63,128	1.56	2,723	165,692	1.64
1950	1,026	55,236	1.86	2,780	148,989	1.87
1945	624	39,041	1.60	2,232	115,011	1.94
1940	1,278	57,995	2.20	3,233	154,446	2.09

Note: Percentages computed by the Center for Business and Economic Research. The United States numbers include federal institutions.

n.a. not available.

Source: U.S. Department of Justice, Bureau of Justice Statistics, *Source Book of Criminal Justice Statistics, 1987*, and earlier editions; and *National Prisoner Statistics, Prisoners in State and Federal Institutions on December 31, 1980*, and earlier editions.

TABLE 19.5-- MOTOR VEHICLE TRAFFIC ACCIDENTS AND DEATHS ON TENNESSEE HIGHWAYS, 1955–1986

Year	Accidents: Total	Accidents: Fatal	Accidents: Non-fatal	Property damage only	Number of deaths	Number of injuries
1986	167,584	1,102	45,990	120,492	1,230	67,741
1985	164,317	997	42,760	120,560	1,101	62,092
1984	156,957	1,006	39,868	116,083	1,111	57,380
1983	149,706	927	37,521	111,258	1,046	54,229
1982	135,491	961	34,134	100,396	1,074	49,266
1981	137,098	978	34,884	101,236	1,119	50,338
1980	137,829	1,014	34,989	101,826	1,161	50,712
1979	149,942	1,070	35,944	112,928	1,268	51,955
1978	144,572	1,109	35,091	108,372	1,252	51,199
1977	133,723	1,072	32,828	99,823	1,218	47,940
1976	126,947	1,009	31,191	94,747	1,146	45,789
1975	121,046	1,002	29,535	90,509	1,162	43,194
1974	111,981	1,081	26,354	84,546	1,274	38,439
1973	140,020	1,256	31,322	108,328	1,444	42,800
(1972)	(23,578)	(1,205)	(7,840)	(14,533)	(1,414)	(12,100)
1972[a]	133,626	1,205	30,487	101,934	1,431	38,315
(1971)	(21,750)	(1,146)	(7,324)	(13,280)	(1,373)	(11,513)
1971[a]	107,154	1,158	26,690	79,306	1,373	36,754
1970	15,661	1,153	5,826	8,682	1,390	9,655
1969	16,877	1,126	6,161	9,590	1,371	9,551
1968	17,925	1,045	6,249	10,631	1,201	9,809
1967	18,720	1,043	6,509	11,160	1,258	10,639
1966	63,802	1,064	n.a.	n.a.	1,272	27,475
1965	49,595	925	17,259	31,411	1,077	27,787
1964	48,688	904	17,853	29,931	1,060	26,047
1963	49,255	779	17,305	31,171	941	25,405
1962	44,810	688	16,366	27,756	811	24,238
1961	50,508	628	16,153	33,727	742	23,725
1960	68,209	663	14,916	52,630	787	22,079
1959	51,344	674	11,706	38,964	771	17,706
1958	43,208	606	9,789	32,813	719	15,360
1957	39,414	600	8,886	29,928	699	13,741
1956	35,468	670	7,732	27,066	765	12,029
1955	29,758	708	6,558	22,492	906	10,135

n.a. not available.

a. Data prior to 1971 are not comparable to data reported after this date due to changes in reporting laws and procedures. Comparable data based on earlier reporting procedures are given in parentheses for 1971 and 1972.

Source: Tennessee Department of Safety, Planning and Research Section, *Tennessee Motor Vehicle Traffic Accident Facts, 1986*, and earlier editions.

TABLE 19.6-- TRAFFIC FATALITIES AND INJURIES, BY AGE, AND BY SEX, TENNESSEE, 1986

	Fatalities				Injuries			
Age	Total	Male	Female	Percentage pedestrian[1]	Total	Male	Female	Percentage pedestrian[1]
Total[1]	1,230	890	340	10.7	67,741[a]	35,251	32,463	2.4
0–4	19	13	6	21.1	1,608	906	702	7.6
5–9	17	12	5	58.8	2,091	1,129	962	12.6
10–14	39	27	12	25.6	2,548	1,304	1,244	6.9
15–19	193	140	53	3.1	12,067	6,546	5,521	1.4
20–24	224	184	40	4.9	11,295	6,416	4,879	1.4
25–34	291	223	68	6.9	14,391	7,632	6,759	1.6
35–44	135	98	37	11.9	8,167	3,959	4,208	1.5
45–54	83	50	33	15.7	4,574	2,147	2,427	2.3
55–64	75	52	23	16.0	3,424	1,597	1,827	2.1
65–74	69	42	27	14.5	2,382[a]	1,041	1,314	2.4
75 and over	73	42	31	24.7	1,298	593	705	4.3
Age not stated	12	7	5	16.7	3,896	1,981	1,915	2.3

1. Computed by the Center for Business and Economic Research.

a. There were 27 injuries in the 65–74 age group not classified according to sex.

Source: Tennessee Department of Safety, Planning and Research Section, *Tennessee Motor Vehicle Traffic Accident Facts, 1986.*

TABLE 19.7-- NUMBER OF DEATHS FROM HOMICIDE AND LEGAL INTERVENTION, BY RACE AND BY SEX, RESIDENT DATA, TENNESSEE, 1980–1987

			White				All other races			
	All races		Male		Female		Male		Female	
Year	Number	Rate	Number	Rate	Number	Rate	Number	Rate	Number	Rate
1987	495	10.1	181	9.1	49	2.4	204	49.9	61	13.7
1986	517	10.6	192	9.8	56	2.7	223	55.3	46	10.5
1985	431	9.0	174	8.9	59	2.9	157	39.5	41	9.5
1984	414	8.8	181	9.4	55	2.7	157	44.6	21	5.2
1983	440	9.3	168	8.7	54	2.6	179	51.3	39	9.8
1982	482	10.3	194	10.2	57	2.8	189	53.9	42	10.5
1981	510	11.0	223	11.8	60	3.0	181	51.4	46	11.5
1980	551	12.0	234	12.6	66	3.3	207	58.5	44	11.0

Note: Rate is per 100,000 population.

Source: Tennessee Department of Health and Environment, Center for Health Statistics, *Vital Signs*, Vol. 4, No. 1, February, 1988, and unpublished data.

TABLE 19.8-- NUMBER OF CRIMES AND CRIME RATES PER 100,000 POPULATION, BY TYPE OF CRIME, METROPOLITAN STATISTICAL AREAS, 1987

Metropolitan Statistical Area	Total offenses	Murder[1]	Forcible rape	Robbery	Aggravated assault	Burglary	Larceny-theft	Auto theft
Chattanooga								
Number	21,698	32	176	638	1,769	5,792	10,885	2,406
Rate	5,039.6	7.4	40.9	148.2	410.9	1,345.3	2,528.2	558.8
Clarksville-Hopkinsville								
Number	5,610	9	52	104	521	1,579	3,033	312
Rate	3,610.1	5.8	33.5	66.9	335.3	1,016.1	1,951.8	200.8
Jackson								
Number	5,497	4	47	169	504	1,291	3,206	276
Rate	6,971.8	5.1	59.6	214.3	639.2	1,637.4	4,066.2	350.0
Johnson City-Kingsport-Bristol								
Number	13,232	21	66	153	606	3,479	8,157	750
Rate	2,948.4	4.7	14.7	34.1	135.0	775.2	1,817.6	167.1
Knoxville								
Number	22,430	40	147	591	1,359	7,829	10,103	2,361
Rate	3,922.8	7.0	25.7	103.4	237.7	1,369.2	1,766.9	412.9
Memphis								
Number	77,202	169	987	4,998	3,849	22,807	29,497	14,895
Rate	7,967.0	17.4	101.9	515.8	397.2	2,353.6	3,044.0	1,537.1
Nashville-Davidson								
Number	57,792	115	601	2,609	3,478	15,486	30,772	4,731
Rate	6,186.7	12.3	64.3	279.3	372.3	1,657.8	3,294.2	506.5

Note: Where reporting area is less than 100%, data are estimated to include that portion not reporting. See Figure 0.1 for area of each Metropolitan Statistical Area.

1. Includes nonnegligent manslaughter.

Source: U.S. Department of Justice, Federal Bureau of Investigation, *Crime in the United States, Uniform Crime Reports, 1987.*

TABLE 19.9--NUMBER OF OFFENSES KNOWN TO POLICE, BY TYPE OF CRIME, CITIES AND TOWNS WITH POPULATION OF 10,000 OR MORE, 1987

City	Murder[1]	Forcible rape	Robbery	Aggra-vated assault	Burglary	Larceny $50 and over[2]	Auto theft
Athens	0	3	6	20	82	292	44
Bartlett	0	2	14	38	217	423	55
Brentwood	0	0	2	17	83	149	17
Bristol	2	1	12	36	204	720	42
Brownsville	0	3	6	47	108	233	23
Chattanooga	26	121	552	1,394	3,445	7,255	1,796
Clarksville	3	31	58	258	791	1,523	190
Cleveland	2	8	14	87	412	683	127
Collierville	0	4	3	31	66	294	25
Columbia	1	4	12	64	301	845	69
Cookeville	0	3	6	36	254	412	69
Dyersburg	0	4	12	88	181	666	35
East Ridge	1	5	20	43	233	786	120
Franklin	1	9	35	119	311	523	64
Gallatin	2	4	16	105	178	603	54
Germantown	0	1	6	5	95	436	21
Greeneville	0	0	5	0	164	409	54
Hendersonville	0	10	9	124	240	526	33
Jackson	3	38	157	467	1,043	2,874	244
Johnson City	3	12	27	50	538	1,557	135
Kingsport	5	4	28	115	328	1,776	96
Knoxville	20	86	439	831	4,008	4,854	1,490
Lawrenceburg	0	2	4	20	109	190	34
McMinnville	3	5	2	43	107	194	27
Maryville	0	0	6	1	153	308	66
Memphis	143	831	4,696	3,163	18,451	22,971	13,569
Millington	2	2	23	96	115	271	56
Morristown	0	12	8	39	325	555	114
Murfreesboro	2	12	42	197	472	1,582	170
Nashville	99	509	2,350	2,295	11,358	22,602	3,788
Oak Ridge	1	7	22	93	268	830	49
Red Bank	0	6	6	16	126	276	28
Shelbyville	3	6	2	15	199	246	37
Smyrna	0	3	11	28	213	292	38
Springfield	1	2	19	79	115	314	17
Tullahoma	1	1	11	9	194	363	63
Union City	1	12	6	38	150	526	22

1. Murder includes nonnegligent manslaughter.

2. Includes all larceny–theft not using force or fraud.

Source: U.S. Department of Justice, Federal Bureau of Investigation, *Crime in the United States, Uniform Crime Reports, 1987.*

TABLE 19.10–NUMBER OF TOTAL OFFENSES AND MURDERS KNOWN TO POLICE, SELECTED CITIES, 1975–1987, SELECTED YEARS

Year	Chatta-nooga	Clarksville	Jackson	Johnson City	Kingsport	Knoxville	Memphis	Nashville[1]	Oak Ridge
1987									
Total	14,589	2,854	4,826	2,322	2,352	11,728	63,824	43,001	1,270
Murder	26	3	3	3	5	20	143	99	1
1986									
Total	13,283	2,825	4,462	2,496	2,117	11,872	64,856	38,240	1,278
Murder	25	6	6	3	0	29	161	93	0
1985									
Total	13,461	2,630	4,310	2,308	2,160	10,838	59,965	31,863	1,163
Murder	26	4	5	2	3	16	122	81	0
1984									
Total	13,212	2,623	4,088	2,128	2,026	9,796	52,792	31,125	1,259
Murder	22	4	10	0	1	20	113	72	1
1983									
Total	13,051	2,546	3,828	2,319	1,923	9,994	55,222	31,213	1,543
Murder	22	3	9	1	2	19	127	81	0
1982									
Total	16,280	2,546	4,831	2,436	1,996	11,863	55,931	35,206	1,510
Murder	34	5	7	3	2	19	122	67	3
1981									
Total	13,555	2,548	4,998	2,504	2,053	12,527	53,325	33,604	1,467
Murder	29	5	9	4	2	25	133	79	1
1980									
Total	16,019	2,585	4,660	2,563	2,385	12,423	50,921	34,886	1,731
Murder	26	5	2	2	1	21	152	87	4
1975									
Total	12,538	n.a.	3,246	1,898	1,329	11,151	54,302	32,828	1,071
Murder	30	n.a.	10	2	4	24	120	93	2

Note: Murder includes nonnegligent manslaughter.

n.a. not available.

1. 1975 is not comparable with later years.

Source: U.S. Department of Justice, Federal Bureau of Investigation, *Crime in the United States, Uniform Crime Reports, 1987*, and earlier editions.

TABLE 19.11--NUMBER OF FULL-TIME POLICE AND CIVILIAN LAW ENFORCEMENT PERSONNEL, SELECTED CITIES, 1970–1987, SELECTED YEARS

	Total					Police officers					Civilians [1]				
City	1987	1986	1985	1980	1970	1987	1986	1985	1980	1970	1987	1986	1985	1980	1970
Chattanooga	510	483	481	482	282	356	351	364	387	256	154	132	117	95	26
Clarksville	121	114	n.a.	n.a.	n.a.	99	93	n.a.	n.a.	n.a.	22	21	n.a.	n.a.	n.a.
Jackson	169	172	167	153	85	127	131	130	124	76	42	41	37	29	9
Johnson City	131	122	120	127	74	103	98	96	105	65	28	24	24	22	9
Kingsport	90	86	89	87	76	74	71	71	72	56	16	15	18	15	20
Knoxville	357	379	389	431	334	301	272	288	325	260	56	107	101	106	74
Memphis	1,658	1,572	1,563	1,661	1,272	1,231	1,139	1,154	1,210	1,089	427	433	409	451	183
Nashville	1,306	1,254	1,238	1,157	716	1,019	970	984	1,006	593	287	284	254	151	123
Oak Ridge	50	49	54	51	47	43	41	44	42	44	7	8	10	9	3

Note: Data for 1970 are as of December 31; data for later years are as of October 31.

n.a. not available.

1. Employees of police departments who are not sworn personnel.

Source: U.S. Department of Justice, Federal Bureau of Investigation, *Crime in the United States, Uniform Crime Reports, 1987*, and earlier editions.

TABLE 19.12-NUMBER OF ADULT COMMITMENTS TO CORRECTIONAL INSTITUTIONS, TENNESSEE AND COUNTY OF COMMITMENT, FISCAL YEARS 1986–1988

County	Commitments 1988	1987	1986	County	Commitments 1988	1987	1986
Anderson	32	38	32	Lewis	1	3	5
Bedford	19	10	23	Lincoln	12	4	15
Benton	6	14	13	Loudon	17	16	14
Bledsoe	6	2	3	McMinn	13	14	18
Blount	61	50	45	McNairy	5	3	9
Bradley	26	37	25	Macon	4	3	8
Campbell	3	5	3	Madison	70	66	99
Cannon	13	5	4	Marion	3	7	12
Carroll	13	14	13	Marshall	21	11	12
Carter	14	7	5	Maury	24	22	24
Cheatham	9	4	26	Meigs	4	5	3
Chester	6	6	14	Monroe	19	29	4
Claiborne	6	5	9	Montgomery	42	25	22
Clay	3	0	0	Moore	2	1	0
Cocke	21	14	18	Morgan	5	5	2
Coffee	47	24	43	Obion	25	24	11
Crockett	5	5	26	Overton	0	4	2
Cumberland	7	19	19	Perry	0	1	2
Davidson	338	423	629	Pickett	0	1	0
Decatur	8	5	6	Polk	5	11	1
DeKalb	8	8	10	Putnam	5	11	16
Dickson	22	39	38	Rhea	7	4	4
Dyer	41	50	39	Roane	12	17	12
Fayette	12	23	19	Robertson	12	21	16
Fentress	6	2	3	Rutherford	57	62	87
Franklin	18	17	7	Scott	6	6	7
Gibson	23	32	56	Sequatchie	2	5	9
Giles	7	8	15	Sevier	25	24	21
Grainger	5	7	7	Shelby	808	1,021	1,094
Greene	18	29	66	Smith	6	4	8
Grundy	7	6	7	Stewart	1	3	4
Hamblen	26	33	84	Sullivan	48	109	101
Hamilton	177	314	320	Sumner	58	51	68
Hancock	0	2	6	Tipton	13	24	15
Hardeman	16	15	16	Trousdale	4	3	1
Hardin	16	15	24	Unicoi	6	5	2
Hawkins	17	14	17	Union	2	1	4
Haywood	20	6	23	Van Buren	0	5	5
Henderson	16	13	11	Warren	10	26	34
Henry	17	9	18	Washington	24	22	29
Hickman	6	7	4	Wayne	0	3	3
Houston	1	1	4	Weakley	10	12	24
Humphreys	8	15	9	White	8	8	6
Jackson	1	0	3	Williamson	54	69	51
Jefferson	10	13	10	Wilson	23	36	17
Johnson	0	3	3	TENNESSEE	5,751	6,417	6,953
Knox	100	178	250				
Lake	8	5	9				
Lauderdale	1	8	10				
Lawrence	17	19	25				

Note: Does not include felons in local jails.

Source: Tennessee Department of Correction, direct correspondence.

TABLE 19.13--COMMITMENTS TO JUVENILE CORRECTIONAL INSTITUTIONS, PROBATION REGIONS, FISCAL YEARS 1984–1988

Probation region	1988	1987	1986	1985	1984
TOTAL	1,363	1,519	1,777	2,038	3,344
First Tennessee	138	130	138	125	278
East Tennessee	178	219	349	253	420
Southeast	228	255	127	285	419
Upper Cumberland	153	157	393	165	457
Mid-Cumberland	204	199	178	294	429
South Central	120	142	118	148	413
Southwest Tennessee	117	135	114	109	282
Northwest Tennessee	81	88	49	83	314
Delta	144	194	311	576	332

Source: Tennessee Department of Correction, direct correspondence.

TABLE 19.14--CRIME RATES PER 100,000 POPULATION, BY TYPE OF CRIME, SOUTHEASTERN STATES, 1987

State	Total offenses	Murder[1]	Forcible rape	Robbery	Aggravated assault	Burglary	Larceny-theft	Auto theft
TENNESSEE	4,665.6	9.1	43.9	193.8	286.6	1,351.8	2,213.4	566.9
Alabama	4,451.4	9.3	27.8	112.2	409.9	1,198.3	2,431.1	262.8
Arkansas	4,245.2	7.6	32.6	79.1	292.6	1,078.0	2,548.7	206.5
Florida	8,503.2	11.4	50.2	356.6	606.3	2,256.9	4,545.2	676.7
Georgia	5,792.0	11.8	43.1	209.2	312.4	1,552.1	3,171.0	492.4
Kentucky	3,270.0	7.5	21.0	90.2	219.1	847.1	1,892.5	192.7
Louisiana	5,873.3	11.1	35.9	179.0	467.0	1,444.5	3,323.2	412.5
Mississippi	3,438.6	10.2	29.2	57.0	173.3	1,201.4	1,807.0	160.5
North Carolina	4,649.9	8.1	29.1	93.9	352.9	1,356.1	2,586.0	223.8
South Carolina	5,161.9	9.3	43.7	101.1	510.8	1,358.0	2,858.2	280.8
Virginia	3,959.5	7.4	26.0	105.8	155.8	806.9	2,603.2	254.4
West Virginia	2,190.7	4.8	22.6	31.2	78.7	603.6	1,288.1	161.7

Note: Rates represent offenses known per 100,000 population, based on the Bureau of the Census provisional population estimate as of July 1.

1. Murder includes nonnegligent manslaughter.

Source: U.S. Department of Justice, Federal Bureau of Investigation, *Crime in the United States, Uniform Crime Reports, 1987.*

TABLE 19.15–PRISON POPULATION IN STATE INSTITUTIONS, SOUTHEASTERN STATES, AS OF DECEMBER 31, 1950–1987, SELECTED YEARS

State	1987	1986	1985	1984	1983	1980	1975	1970	1960	1950
TENNESSEE[1, 2]	7,624	7,591 r	7,127	7,302	8,201	7,022	4,561	3,268	3,134	2,780
Alabama	12,827	11,710	11,015	10,482	9,856	6,543	4,420	3,790	5,369	4,454
Arkansas[1]	5,443	4,701	4,611	4,454	4,244	2,911	2,162	n.a.	2,016	1,541
Florida[2]	32,445	32,237 r	28,600	27,106	26,334	20,735	15,315	9,187	7,084	3,973
Georgia[2]	18,575	17,363	16,014	15,731	15,358	12,178	10,102	5,113	6,985	4,545
Kentucky[1]	5,471	5,288 r	5,801	5,502	4,752	3,588	3,393	2,849	3,603	3,259
Louisiana	15,375	14,300 r	13,890	13,919	12,812	8,889	4,835	4,196	3,749	2,674
Mississippi	6,831	6,747	6,392	6,115	5,586	3,902	2,422	1,730	1,975	2,158
North Carolina	17,249	17,698 r	17,344	16,371	15,395	15,513	11,449	5,969	5,977	5,004
South Carolina	12,664	11,676	10,510	10,011	9,576	7,862	5,600	2,726	2,080	1,513
Virginia[3]	13,321	12,930	12,073	10,667	10,093	8,920	5,497	4,648	5,775	4,439
West Virginia	1,461	1,482	1,725	1,599	1,624	1,257	1,176	938	2,407	2,904

r revised.

n.a. not available.

1. Excludes state prisoners held in local jails because of overcrowding.

2. Numbers are custodial, not jurisdictional counts.

3. Year-end 1983 data are for January 1, 1984; 1984 data are for December 28, 1984; and 1985 data are for January 3, 1986.

Source: U.S. Department of Commerce, Bureau of the Census, *Statistical Abstract of the United States, 1989*, and earlier editions; and U.S. Department of Justice, Bureau of Justice Statistics, *National Prisoner Statistics, Prisoners in State and Federal Institutions on December 31, 1982*, and earlier editions.

TABLE 19.16--DEATHS FROM MOTOR VEHICLE ACCIDENTS, SOUTHEASTERN STATES AND UNITED STATES, 1970–1986, SELECTED YEARS

State	1986	1985	1980	1975	1972 [a]	1970
TENNESSEE	1,372	1,219	1,280	1,280	1,526	1,525
Alabama	1,180	1,005	1,054	1,087	1,356	1,297
Arkansas	624	580	607	577	750	595
Florida	2,925	2,968	2,967	2,067	2,570	2,181
Georgia	1,604	1,462	1,558	1,420	1,940	1,825
Kentucky	829	749	865	885	1,114	1,081
Louisiana	987	1,011	1,261	993	1,136	1,194
Mississippi	785	691	796	629	976	947
North Carolina	1,727	1,553	1,588	1,560	2,026	1,801
South Carolina	1,077	943	895	837	1,148	1,070
Virginia	1,141	1,021	1,111	1,069	1,256	1,251
West Virginia	470	461	583	499	578	561
UNITED STATES	48,140	46,159	53,476	46,032	56,528	54,845

a. Represents peak year for deaths from motor vehicle accidents.
Source: U.S. Department of Commerce, Bureau of the Census, *Statistical Abstract of the United States, 1989.*

TABLE 19.17--LAWYERS LICENSED IN THE UNITED STATES, SOUTHEASTERN STATES, 1970, 1980 AND 1985

State	1985			1980	1970
	Total	Private practice	Population ratio per lawyer [1]		
TENNESSEE	8,782	6,206	537	7,802	4,770
Alabama	6,679	4,747	597	5,466	3,291
Arkansas	3,741	2,586	628	3,188	1,969
Florida	30,444	21,709	361	23,521	10,917
Georgia	13,652	10,097	428	11,087	5,517
Kentucky	7,017	4,941	531	6,200	3,625
Louisiana	10,569	8,272	422	8,752	5,089
Mississippi	4,270	3,198	608	3,850	2,517
North Carolina	9,265	6,520	665	7,459	4,367
South Carolina	5,021	3,755	657	4,195	2,236
Virginia	13,390	9,031	421	10,895	6,401
West Virginia	2,835	2,033	689	2,566	1,719

Note: Data are weighted to account for non-reporters and duplicate listings.

1. Based on Bureau of the Census estimated resident population, including Armed Forces stationed in area as of July 1, 1984.

Source: U.S. Department of Commerce, Bureau of the Census, *Statistical Abstract of the United States, 1988*; and American Bar Foundation, Chicago, IL., *The Lawyer Statistical Report: A Statistical Profile of the U.S. Legal Profession in the 1980's* (copyright), by special permission.

TABLE 19.18--SELECTED DATA ON FULL-TIME STATE POLICE AND HIGHWAY PATROL EMPLOYEES, SOUTHEASTERN STATES, 1987

State	Total	Police officers	Civilians	Miles of primary highway per police officer[1]	State motor vehicle registrations per police officer[2]
TENNESSEE	1,325	744	581	9.6	5,412.0
Alabama	1,248	717	531	10.6	4,946.4
Arkansas	613	452	161	12.7	3,196.9
Florida	2,025	1,537	488	6.0	6,950.9
Georgia	1,564	775	789	14.6	6,485.4
Kentucky	1,617	955	662	4.8	2,848.4
Louisiana	998	713	285	5.4	4,055.0
Mississippi	842	504	338	12.7	3,493.8
North Carolina	1,523	1,207	316	4.4	4,035.0
South Carolina	1,068	893	175	7.2	2,649.7
Virginia	2,012	1,502	510	4.3	3,081.2
West Virginia	837	528	309	5.5	2,261.4

Note: Data as of October 31.

1. Miles of primary highway taken from U.S. Department of Transportation publication, *Highway Statistics, 1987*. Includes federal-aid primary system and interstate system.

2. State motor vehicle registration data, which include automobile, bus, and truck registrations, taken from U.S. Department of Transportation publication, *Highway Statistics, 1987*.

Source: U.S. Department of Justice, Federal Bureau of Investigation, *Crime in the United States, Uniform Crime Reports, 1987*.

TABLE 19.19--STATE AND LOCAL GOVERNMENT DIRECT EXPENDITURES FOR CRIMINAL JUSTICE SYSTEM, BY TYPE OF ACTIVITY, SOUTHEASTERN STATES, FISCAL YEAR 1985 [In thousands of dollars]

State	Total	Police protection	Judicial and legal services			Corrections	Others
			Courts only	Prosecution and legal services	Public defense		
TENNESSEE	540,076	262,700	73,547	24,498	6,296	172,680	355
Alabama	456,022	207,062	62,627	22,600	5,444	155,412	2,877
Arkansas	204,362	100,830	20,970	10,937	1,188	66,406	4,031
Florida	1,993,356	961,012	232,913	106,533	45,003	615,679	32,216
Georgia	785,390	364,406	107,162	31,360	3,648	277,930	884
Kentucky	390,705	178,479	62,670	26,160	4,643	117,149	1,604
Louisiana	688,229	336,464	92,682	35,230	2,014	220,054	1,785
Mississippi	214,688	112,622	26,242	9,248	1,007	65,382	187
North Carolina	808,685	369,398	119,318	39,168	13,613	259,173	8,015
South Carolina	391,134	178,325	40,283	13,675	3,411	152,100	3,340
Virginia	855,312	397,296	94,236	30,740	9,484	317,037	6,519
West Virginia	159,092	80,129	29,302	9,322	5,087	33,642	1,610

Source: U.S. Department of Justice, Bureau of Justice Statistics, *Source Book of Criminal Justice Statistics, 1987.*

Tennessee Rankings presents comparative socioeconomic data for Tennessee and other southeastern states in key interest areas. This section is a particularly useful feature for speech writers, planners and others who need readily accessible comparative information on Tennessee. Unlike other chapters, *Tennessee Rankings* changes substantially from one edition to the next in accordance with current interests and the availability of new data. The content of this edition reflects interests in funding for the arts, radioactive waste disposal, financing state government, residential electricity costs, part-time employment, funding for research and development and foreign trade.

The first seven tables are from primary data areas: population, income and employment. The ranking of states and cities according to these topics provides a current assessment of growth and general well-being. Population rankings are published by the U.S. Department of Commerce, Bureau of the Census. Income items include measures of per capita disposable personal income for states as well as per capita personal income for states and metropolitan areas. These are estimated and published by the Bureau of Economic Analysis (BEA), also in the U.S. Department of Commerce.

Employment data are collected and published by the U.S. Department of Labor, Bureau of Labor Statistics. Rankings include percentage change in total nonagricultural jobs and manufacturing jobs and an analysis of part-time employment, by reason for part-time status.

Heightened interest in foreign trade and foreign ownership of business in Tennessee and the U.S. determined the inclusion of data on foreign direct investment for the 1989 edition of the *Abstract*. These benchmark survey results, developed and published by the BEA, are updated for this *Abstract* in Tables 20.15 and 20.16. Information on the value of exports and imports for each of the southeastern states is reported in Table 20.14.

The Council of State Governments publishes useful data in *The Book of States*. Data on the volume and activity of low-level radioactive waste disposal in southeastern states were selected from this source, while comparisons of typical residential electric bills were taken from a report issued by the U.S. Energy Information Administration.

Finally, state legislative arts appropriations and many other helpful and interesting statistics complete *Tennessee Rankings*. These data were gathered by the U.S. Department of Commerce, Bureau of the Census, and published in the *Statistical Abstract of the United States*.

TABLE OF CONTENTS

TABLE 20.1-- POPULATION ESTIMATES, BY AGE, AND MEDIAN AGE, SOUTHEASTERN STATES AND UNITED STATES, JULY 1, 1988
[In thousands except median age]

State	Total	Under 5 years	5 to 14 years	15 to 24 years	25 to 34 years	35 to 44 years	45 to 54 years	55 to 64 years	65 to 74 years	75 to 84 years	85 years and over	Median age	
												Years	Rank
TENNESSEE	4,895	332	693	764	853	705	503	434	359	194	58	32.7	13
Alabama	4,102	296	618	657	706	557	399	355	303	163	47	31.7	36
Arkansas	2,395	173	362	370	376	317	234	213	200	116	34	32.7	13
Florida	12,335	848	1,470	1,667	1,929	1,618	1,231	1,370	1,297	715	189	36.4	1
Georgia	6,342	496	967	1,045	1,123	932	632	509	385	196	56	30.8	42
Kentucky	3,727	253	551	600	653	523	365	319	270	148	45	31.9	30
Louisiana	4,408	372	720	708	808	593	391	336	289	145	44	29.9	47
Mississippi	2,620	206	439	440	433	330	240	211	186	104	31	30.0	46
North Carolina	6,489	449	887	1,046	1,154	930	660	589	473	235	66	32.3	21
South Carolina	3,470	259	521	576	626	490	332	287	240	109	29	30.9	41
Virginia	6,015	430	782	967	1,111	934	632	521	393	189	58	32.4	17
West Virginia	1,876	113	274	293	311	266	181	171	158	85	25	33.3	8
UNITED STATES	245,807	18,456	34,655	37,398	43,675	35,264	24,163	21,830	17,897	9,521	2,948	32.3	(X)

Note: Population includes Armed Forces residing in each state.

(X) not applicable.

Source: U.S. Department of Commerce, Bureau of the Census, *Current Population Reports*, Series P-25, No. 1044.

TABLE 20.2-- POPULATION ESTIMATES AND PERCENTAGE CHANGE, METROPOLITAN STATISTICAL AREAS, SOUTHEASTERN STATES, 1980–1988

MSA	Population 1988	Population 1980	Percent change 1980–1988	Rank in United States	Rank in Southeast
Albany, GA	116,300	112,394	3.5	243	78
Alexandria, LA	137,800	135,282	1.9	204	67
Anderson, SC	143,100	133,235	7.4	198	65
Anniston, AL	123,300	119,761	3.0	229	75
Asheville, NC	173,100	160,934	7.6	169	55
Athens, GA	144,700	130,015	11.3	196	63
Atlanta, GA	2,736,600	2,138,143	28.0	13	2
Augusta, GA-SC	396,400	345,923	14.6	89	26
Baton Rouge, LA	536,500	494,151	8.6	68	19
Biloxi-Gulfport, MS	205,000	182,161	12.5	154	50
Birmingham, AL	923,400	883,993	4.5	46	12
Bradenton, FL	186,900	148,445	25.9	161	52
Burlington, NC	105,800	99,319	6.5	252	81
Charleston, SC	510,800	430,346	18.7	73	21
Charleston, WV	260,800	269,595	-3.3	126	38
Charlotte-Gastonia-Rock Hill, NC-SC	1,112,000	971,447	14.5	35	6
Charlottesville, VA	123,800	113,568	9.0	227	74
CHATTANOOGA, TN-GA	438,100	426,540	2.7	81	25
CLARKSVILLE-HOPKINSVILLE, TN-KY	158,900	150,220	5.8	180	58
Columbia, SC	456,500	409,955	11.4	78	23
Columbus, GA-AL	246,900	239,196	3.2	132	41
Danville, VA	108,100	111,789	-3.3	250	80
Daytona Beach, FL	348,400	258,762	34.6	105	32
Decatur, AL	132,700	120,401	10.2	209	69
Dothan, AL	131,100	122,453	7.1	214	70
Fayetteville, NC	255,700	247,160	3.5	130	40
Fayetteville-Springdale, AR	110,600	100,494	10.1	249	79
Florence, AL	135,500	135,065	0.3	208	68
Florence, SC	118,000	110,163	7.1	238	76
Fort Myers-Cape Coral, FL	309,100	205,266	50.6	115	35
Fort Pierce, FL	231,800	151,196	53.3	141	44
Fort Smith, AR-OK	180,700	162,813	11.0	167	54
Fort Walton Beach, FL	150,600	109,920	37.0	186	60
Gadsden, AL	102,900	103,057	-0.2	256	82
Gainesville, FL	207,600	171,392	21.1	153	49
Greensboro--Winston-Salem--High Point, NC	924,700	851,444	8.6	45	11
Greenville-Spartanburg, SC	621,400	570,211	9.0	62	17
Hickory, NC	222,100	202,711	9.6	144	46
Houma-Thibodaux, LA	183,100	176,876	3.5	163	53
Huntington-Ashland, WV-KY-OH	322,300	336,410	-4.2	111	34
Huntsville, AL	236,700	196,966	20.2	139	43
Jackson, MS	396,200	362,038	9.4	90	27
JACKSON, TN	78,200	74,546	4.9	276	85
Jacksonville, FL	898,100	722,252	24.3	47	13
Jacksonville, NC	126,500	112,784	12.2	220	72
JOHNSON CITY-KINGSPORT-BRISTOL, TN-VA	442,300	433,638	2.0	80	24
KNOXVILLE, TN	599,600	565,970	5.9	65	18
Lafayette, LA	209,600	190,231	10.2	152	48
Lake Charles, LA	172,400	167,223	3.1	170	56
Lakeland-Winter Haven, FL	395,800	321,652	23.1	91	28

TABLE 20.2-- POPULATION ESTIMATES AND PERCENTAGE CHANGE, METROPOLITAN STATISTICAL AREAS, SOUTHEASTERN STATES, 1980–1988 (Continued)

MSA	Population 1988	Population 1980	Percent change 1980–1988	Rank in United States	Rank in Southeast
Lexington-Fayette, KY	347,900	317,548	9.6	106	33
Little Rock-North Little Rock, AR	513,100	474,464	8.1	72	20
Louisville, KY-IN	967,000	956,436	1.1	42	10
Lynchburg, VA	145,500	141,289	3.0	194	61
Macon-Warner Robbins, GA	286,700	263,591	8.8	118	37
Melbourne-Titusville-Palm Bay, FL	388,300	272,959	42.3	94	29
MEMPHIS, TN-AR-MS	979,300	913,472	7.2	39	7
Miami-Fort Lauderdale, FL[1]	3,000,500	2,643,766	13.5	11	1
Mobile, AL	485,600	443,536	9.5	76	22
Monroe, LA	144,000	139,241	3.4	197	64
Montgomery, AL	300,800	272,687	10.3	116	36
Naples, FL	138,500	85,971	61.1	202	66
NASHVILLE, TN	971,800	850,505	14.3	40	8
New Orleans, LA	1,306,900	1,256,668	4.0	31	5
Norfolk-Virginia Beach-Newport News, VA	1,380,200	1,160,311	19.0	28	4
Ocala, FL	189,800	122,488	55.0	159	51
Orlando, FL	971,200	699,906	38.8	41	9
Owensboro, KY	87,800	85,949	2.2	268	84
Panama City, FL	125,500	97,740	28.4	222	73
Parkersburg-Marietta, WV-OH	154,400	157,889	-2.2	183	59
Pascagoula, MS	128,100	118,015	8.5	218	71
Pensacola, FL	349,900	289,782	20.7	103	31
Pine Bluff, AR	90,800	90,718	0.1	267	83
Raleigh-Durham, NC	683,500	560,775	21.9	55	16
Richmond-Petersburg, VA	844,300	761,311	10.9	49	14
Roanoke, VA	221,600	220,393	0.5	145	47
Sarasota, FL	260,600	202,251	28.8	127	39
Savannah, GA	244,400	220,553	10.8	133	42
Shreveport, LA	359,100	333,158	7.8	99	30
Tallahassee, FL	228,600	190,329	20.1	142	45
Tampa-St. Petersburg-Clearwater, FL	1,995,100	1,613,600	23.6	21	3
Tuscaloosa, AL	145,400	137,541	5.7	195	62
West Palm Beach-Boca Raton-Delray Beach, FL	818,500	576,754	41.9	51	15
Wheeling, WV-OH	171,500	185,566	-7.6	172	57
Wilmington, NC	117,300	103,471	13.4	240	77

Note: Population counts for 1980 include MSA boundaries as defined by the Office of Management and Budget, June, 1989.

1. Consolidated Metropolitan Statistical Area consisting of two Primary Metropolitan Statistical Areas: Miami-Hialeah, Fla., and Fort Lauderdale-Hollywood-Pompano Beach, Fla.

Source: U.S. Department of Commerce, Bureau of the Census, *News*, September 8, 1989.

TABLE 20.3-- POPULATION ESTIMATES AND PERCENTAGE CHANGE, CITIES WITH 1988 POPULATION OF 100,000 OR MORE, SOUTHEASTERN STATES, 1980–1988

City	Population 1988	Population 1980	Percent change 1980–1988	Rank in United States	Rank in Southeast
Alexandria, VA	108,400	103,217	5.0	163	40
Atlanta, GA	420,220	425,022	-1.1	31	5
Baton Rouge, LA	235,270	220,394	6.7	65	14
Birmingham, AL	277,280	284,413	-2.5	58	12
Charlotte, NC	367,860	315,474	16.6	42	7
CHATTANOOGA, TN	162,670	169,520	-4.0	99	26
Chesapeake, VA	147,800	114,486	29.1	115	32
Columbus, GA	177,680	169,441	4.9	93	24
Durham, NC	115,430	101,149	14.1	150	39
Fort Lauderdale, FL	145,610	153,279	-5.0	117	34
Greensboro, NC	181,970	155,642	16.9	87	22
Hampton, VA	130,800	122,617	6.7	132	35
Hialeah, FL	162,080	145,254	11.6	100	27
Hollywood, FL	120,140	121,323	-1.0	144	37
Huntsville, AL	159,450	142,513	11.9	104	29
Jackson, MS	201,250	202,895	-0.8	77	19
Jacksonville, FL	635,430	540,920	17.5	16	2
KNOXVILLE, TN	172,080	175,045	-1.7	94	25
Lexington-Fayette, KY	225,700	204,165	10.5	67	15
Little Rock, AR	180,090	159,159	13.2	89	23
Louisville, KY	281,880	298,694	-5.6	55	10
Macon, GA	117,940	116,896	0.9	147	38
MEMPHIS, TN	645,190	646,170	-0.2	15	1
Miami, FL	371,100	346,681	7.0	39	6
Mobile, AL	208,820	200,452	4.2	76	18
Montgomery, AL	193,510	177,857	8.8	78	20
NASHVILLE-DAVIDSON, TN	481,400	455,651	5.7	26	4
New Orleans, LA	531,700	557,927	-4.7	21	3
Newport News, VA	160,100	144,903	10.5	103	28
Norfolk, VA	286,500	266,979	7.3	53	9
Orlando, FL	155,950	128,291	21.6	108	30
Portsmouth, VA	107,500	104,577	2.8	167	41
Raleigh, NC	186,720	150,255	24.3	84	21
Richmond, VA	213,300	219,214	-2.7	73	17
Savannah, GA	145,980	141,658	3.1	116	33
Shreveport, LA	218,010	206,989	5.3	71	16
St. Petersburg, FL	235,450	238,647	-1.3	64	13
Tallahassee, FL	125,640	81,548	54.1	136	36
Tampa, FL	281,790	271,578	3.8	56	11
Virginia Beach, VA	365,300	262,199	39.3	43	8
Winston-Salem, NC	148,690	131,885	12.7	112	31

Source: U.S. Department of Commerce, Bureau of the Census, *News*, November 22, 1989.

TABLE 20.4-- PER CAPITA DISPOSABLE PERSONAL INCOME, SOUTHEASTERN STATES AND UNITED STATES, 1983–1988 [In dollars]

State	1988 Amount	1988 Percentage of U.S. average	1988 Rank	1987	1986	1985	1984	1983
TENNESSEE	12,212	87	35	11,353	10,579	9,798	9,356	8,491
Alabama	11,040	78	43	10,258	9,717	9,099	8,731	8,009
Arkansas	10,670	76	47	9,924	9,586	9,169	8,579	7,917
Florida	14,338	102	16	13,374	12,548	11,925	11,244	10,494
Georgia	12,886	91	28	12,079	11,390	10,545	9,925	8,983
Kentucky	11,081	79	42	10,321	9,715	9,276	9,056	8,266
Louisiana	10,890	77	44	10,191	9,993	9,836	9,551	9,066
Mississippi	9,612	68	50	8,876	8,437	8,012	7,701	7,157
North Carolina	12,259	87	34	11,355	10,657	9,891	9,517	8,610
South Carolina	11,102	79	41	10,321	9,732	9,219	8,798	8,008
Virginia	15,050	107	10	13,980	13,163	12,280	11,561	10,590
West Virginia	10,306	73	49	9,624	9,198	8,803	8,360	7,851
UNITED STATES	14,107	100	(X)	13,128	12,474	11,863	11,257	10,350

(X) not applicable.

Source: U.S. Department of Commerce, Bureau of Economic Analysis, *Survey of Current Business*, August 1989, Volume 69, Number 8.

TABLE 20.5-- PER CAPITA PERSONAL INCOME, METROPOLITAN AREAS, SOUTHEASTERN STATES, 1986–1987

Metropolitan area	Dollars 1987	Dollars 1986	Dollars Percent change 1986–1987	Percentage of U.S. 1987	Percentage of U.S. 1986	Rank 1987	Rank 1986
Albany, GA	11,626	11,077	5.0	75.1	75.8	291	293
Alexandria, LA	11,151	10,894	2.4	72.0	74.6	304	297
Anderson, SC	11,876	11,059	7.4	76.7	75.7	287	295
Anniston, AL	11,108	10,560	5.2	71.7	72.3	305	302
Asheville, NC	13,395	12,554	6.7	86.5	85.9	208	215
Athens, GA	12,966	12,294	5.5	83.7	84.2	233	233
Atlanta, GA	17,293	16,341	5.8	111.7	111.9	46	44
Augusta, GA-SC	12,977	12,468	4.1	83.8	85.3	230	220
Baton Rouge, LA	12,734	12,375	2.9	82.2	84.7	247	227
Biloxi-Gulfport, MS	10,926	10,459	4.5	70.6	71.6	307	308
Birmingham, AL	13,722	12,994	5.6	88.6	88.9	183	184
Bradenton, FL	16,180	15,198	6.5	104.5	104.0	67	71
Burlington, NC	14,615	13,642	7.1	94.4	93.4	134	151
Charleston, SC	11,741	11,210	4.7	75.8	76.7	289	288
Charleston, WV	13,432	12,965	3.6	86.7	88.7	205	188
Charlotte-Gastonia-Rock Hill. NC-SC	15,267	14,164	7.8	98.6	97.0	107	125
Charlottesville, VA	15,522	14,475	7.2	100.2	99.1	90	104
CHATTANOOGA, TN-GA	13,429	12,420	8.1	86.7	85.0	206	224
CLARKSVILLE-HOPKINSVILLE, TN-KY	11,087	10,341	7.2	71.6	70.8	306	309
Columbia, SC	13,714	12,935	6.0	88.6	88.5	185	190
Columbus, GA-AL	12,261	11,312	8.4	79.2	77.4	270	284
Danville, VA	12,510	11,629	7.6	80.8	79.6	256	271
Daytona Beach, FL	13,895	13,134	5.8	89.7	89.9	172	177
Decatur, AL	12,272	11,526	6.5	79.3	78.9	268	277
Dothan, AL	12,119	11,350	6.8	78.3	77.7	278	281
Fayetteville, NC	11,494	10,878	5.7	74.2	74.5	296	298
Fayetteville-Springdale, AR	12,150	11,634	4.4	78.5	79.6	275	270
Florence, AL	11,160	10,507	6.2	72.1	71.9	302	305
Florence, SC	11,279	10,540	7.0	72.8	72.1	299	303
Fort Lauderdale-Hollywood-Pompano Beach, FL	19,238	17,971	7.1	124.2	123.0	22	23

TABLE 20.5-- PER CAPITA PERSONAL INCOME, METROPOLITAN AREAS, SOUTHEASTERN STATES, 1986–1987 (Continued)

Metropolitan area	Dollars 1987	Dollars 1986	Dollars Percent change 1986–1987	Percentage of U.S. 1987	Percentage of U.S. 1986	Rank 1987	Rank 1986
Fort Myers-Cape Coral, FL	15,908	14,992	6.1	102.7	102.6	80	80
Fort Pierce, FL	16,291	15,142	7.6	105.2	103.6	65	73
Fort Smith, AR-OK	11,626	11,139	4.4	75.1	76.2	291	290
Fort Walton Beach, FL	12,485	11,739	6.4	80.6	80.4	257	265
Gadsden, AL	11,251	10,510	7.1	72.7	71.9	300	304
Gainesville, FL	12,187	11,465	6.3	78.7	78.5	271	278
Greensboro--Winston-Salem--High Point, NC	15,396	14,395	7.0	99.4	98.5	101	109
Greenville-Spartanburg, SC	13,488	12,584	7.2	87.1	86.1	199	214
Hickory, NC	13,333	12,336	8.1	86.1	84.4	214	228
Houma-Thibodaux, LA	10,582	10,489	0.9	68.3	71.8	311	307
Huntington-Ashland, WV-KY-OH	11,195	10,575	5.9	72.3	72.4	301	301
Huntsville, AL	15,082	14,190	6.3	97.4	97.1	116	124
Jackson, MS	12,591	11,961	5.3	81.3	81.9	251	251
JACKSON, TN	12,145	11,268	7.8	78.4	77.1	276	287
Jacksonville, FL	14,611	13,865	5.4	94.4	94.9	136	136
Jacksonville, NC	10,668	10,100	5.6	68.9	69.1	310	311
JOHNSON CITY-KINGSPORT-BRISTOL, TN-VA	11,547	10,898	6.0	74.6	74.6	294	296
KNOXVILLE, TN	13,144	12,234	7.4	84.9	83.7	223	237
Lafayette, LA	12,363	12,440	-0.6	79.8	85.2	264	222
Lake Charles, LA	11,819	11,339	4.2	76.3	77.6	288	283
Lakeland-Winter Haven, FL	12,479	11,679	6.8	80.6	79.9	259	268
Lexington-Fayette, KY	14,953	13,986	6.9	96.6	95.7	123	132
Little Rock-North Little Rock, AR	13,966	13,474	3.7	90.2	92.2	168	161
Louisville, KY-IN	14,599	13,656	6.9	94.3	93.5	137	149
Lynchburg, VA	12,868	11,976	7.4	83.1	82.0	242	249
Macon-Warner Robins, GA	13,291	12,431	6.9	85.8	85.1	216	223
Melbourne-Titusville-Palm Bay, FL	14,650	13,887	5.5	94.6	95.1	131	134
MEMPHIS, TN-AR-MS	14,271	13,285	7.4	92.2	90.9	154	173
Miami-Hialeah, FL	15,689	14,592	7.5	101.3	99.9	86	93
Mobile, AL	11,566	11,087	4.3	74.7	75.9	293	292

TABLE 20.5-- PER CAPITA PERSONAL INCOME, METROPOLITAN AREAS, SOUTHEASTERN STATES, 1986–1987 (Continued)

Metropolitan area	Dollars 1987	Dollars 1986	Dollars Percent change 1986–1987	Percentage of U.S. 1987	Percentage of U.S. 1986	Rank 1987	Rank 1986
Monroe, LA	11,442	11,203	2.1	73.9	76.7	298	289
Montgomery, AL	13,106	12,416	5.6	84.6	85.0	225	225
Naples, FL	19,906	18,398	8.2	128.6	125.9	19	20
NASHVILLE, TN	15,253	14,322	6.5	98.5	98.0	110	116
New Orleans, LA	13,130	12,845	2.2	84.8	87.9	224	196
Norfolk-Virginia Beach-Newport News, VA	14,462	13,748	5.2	93.4	94.1	143	144
Ocala, FL	11,543	10,871	6.2	74.5	74.4	295	299
Orlando, FL	15,421	14,480	6.5	99.6	99.1	98	103
Owensboro, KY	12,775	12,149	5.2	82.5	83.2	244	241
Panama City, FL	12,271	11,745	4.5	79.2	80.4	269	264
Parkersburg-Marietta, WV-OH	12,390	11,776	5.2	80.0	80.6	263	263
Pascagoula, MS	10,231	9,957	2.8	66.1	68.2	312	312
Pensacola, FL	12,174	11,601	4.9	78.6	79.4	273	272
Pine Bluff, AR	10,878	10,578	2.8	70.3	72.4	308	300
Raleigh-Durham, NC	16,613	15,614	6.4	107.3	106.9	59	62
Richmond-Petersburg, VA	17,446	16,178	7.8	112.7	110.7	44	46
Roanoke, VA	15,672	14,625	7.2	101.2	100.1	89	92
Sarasota, FL	20,594	19,238	7.0	133.0	131.7	13	13
Savannah, GA	14,067	13,335	5.5	90.8	91.3	163	169
Shreveport, LA	12,574	12,263	2.5	81.2	83.9	253	236
Tallahassee, FL	12,632	11,678	8.2	81.6	79.9	250	269
Tampa-St. Petersburg-Clearwater, FL	15,435	14,541	6.1	99.7	99.5	95	98
Tuscaloosa, AL	12,076	11,432	5.6	78.0	78.3	280	279
West Palm Beach-Boca Raton-Delray Beach, FL	21,246	19,990	6.3	137.2	136.8	10	11
Wheeling, WV-OH	11,920	11,346	5.1	77.0	77.7	286	282
Wilmington, NC	13,484	12,874	4.7	87.1	88.1	200	193

Note: Rank is out of 318 metropolitan areas. Includes Metropolitan Statistical Areas and Primary Metropolitan Statistical Areas.

Source: U.S. Department of Commerce, Bureau of Economic Analysis, *News*, May 4, 1989.

TABLE 20.6-- NONAGRICULTURAL AND MANUFACTURING JOBS, SOUTHEASTERN STATES AND UNITED STATES, 1985–1988 [In thousands of persons]

State	Nonagricultural jobs						Manufacturing jobs					
					1987–1988						1987–1988	
	1988	1987	1986	1985	Percent change	Rank	1988	1987	1986	1985	Percent change	Rank
TENNESSEE	2,065.8	2,011.6	1,929.8	1,867.8	2.69	30	508.2	497.4	490.5	492.4	2.17	28
Alabama	1,549.7	1,507.7	1,463.3	1,427.1	2.79	27	379.0	368.8	358.6	358.1	2.77	23
Arkansas	859.9	836.6	813.8	797.1	2.79	28	228.4	219.6	211.8	209.6	4.01	15
Florida	5,080.2	4,848.1	4,599.4	4,410.0	4.79	2	540.8	531.0	517.2	514.4	1.85	30
Georgia	2,879.1	2,782.0	2,672.4	2,569.8	3.49	14	574.0	571.2	564.6	557.1	0.49	38
Kentucky	1,370.3	1,328.2	1,274.1	1,250.3	3.17	18	274.2	262.5	253.8	255.3	4.46	11
Louisiana	1,501.5	1,483.6	1,518.5	1,591.2	1.21	46	170.1	164.5	166.0	178.0	3.40	19
Mississippi	894.8	864.4	848.2	838.9	3.52	13	238.5	228.6	223.7	221.6	4.33	12
North Carolina	2,967.7	2,862.6	2,744.1	2,651.2	3.67	12	866.9	856.0	832.8	828.6	1.27	33
South Carolina	1,447.8	1,392.2	1,338.0	1,296.2	3.99	8	383.5	374.0	365.2	365.4	2.54	26
Virginia	2,780.6	2,680.4	2,557.7	2,454.7	3.74	10	427.3	428.9	424.7	423.4	-0.37	43
West Virginia	610.9	599.0	597.5	597.2	1.99	36	87.0	86.2	86.8	89.5	0.93	37
UNITED STATES	106,039.0	102,310.0	99,525.0	97,519.0	3.64	(X)	19,539.0	19,065.0	18,965.0	19,260.0	2.49	(X)

(X) not applicable.

Source: U.S. Department of Labor, Bureau of Labor Statistics, *Employment and Earnings*, May 1989.

TABLE 20.7-- CIVILIAN EMPLOYED PERSONS BY FULL OR PART-TIME STATUS, AND BY REASON FOR PART-TIME STATUS, SOUTHEASTERN STATES AND UNITED STATES, 1988 ANNUAL AVERAGES (Numbers in thousands)

			Part-time						
			Total		Economic reasons			Voluntary reasons	
						Percentage of total			
State	Total employment	Full-time	Number	Percentage of total	Number	%	Rank	Number	Percentage of total
TENNESSEE	2,214	1,833	382	17.25	114	5.15	20	268	12.10
Alabama	1,751	1,438	312	17.82	97	5.54	16	215	12.28
Arkansas	1,037	839	199	19.19	67	6.46	10	132	12.73
Florida	5,800	4,834	965	16.64	243	4.19	34	722	12.45
Georgia	3,007	2,527	480	15.96	123	4.09	36	357	11.87
Kentucky	1,575	1,256	319	20.25	85	5.40	17	234	14.86
Louisiana	1,712	1,376	335	19.57	122	7.13	5	213	12.44
Mississippi	1,048	874	175	16.70	69	6.58	9	106	10.11
North Carolina	3,222	2,712	510	15.83	126	3.91	38	384	11.92
South Carolina	1,604	1,343	260	16.21	70	4.36	31	190	11.85
Virginia	2,973	2,475	497	16.72	109	3.67	41	388	13.05
West Virginia	669	539	130	19.43	48	7.17	4	82	12.26

Note: Persons employed on a part-time basis for economic reasons are those working fewer than 35 hours per week whose employers are experiencing slack work, material shortages, or repairs to plant and equipment or persons who are unable to find a full-time job.

Source: U.S. Department of Labor, Bureau of Labor Statistics, *Geographic Profile of Employment and Unemployment, 1988.*

TABLE 20.8-- TYPICAL MONTHLY ELECTRIC BILLS FOR RESIDENTIAL SERVICE, BY CONSUMPTION LEVEL, SOUTHEASTERN STATES AND UNITED STATES, 1988

State	250 kWh		500 kWh		750 kWh		1,000 kWh		2,500 kWh	
	Amount	Rank	Amount	Rank	Amount	Rank	Amount	Rank	Amount	Rank
TENNESSEE	$16.54	45	$29.78	46	$43.01	46	$56.24	44	$138.52	34
Alabama	20.58	28	35.19	35	49.79	32	62.19	36	136.10	36
Arkansas	25.57	6	44.39	11	61.60	11	80.06	12	151.25	26
Florida	23.65	14	41.53	18	59.41	18	78.68	16	194.35	8
Georgia	21.08	27	35.51	34	49.49	33	62.47	34	139.81	31
Kentucky	16.29	46	29.19	47	39.81	47	51.29	47	115.71	46
Louisiana	18.06	40	33.72	39	49.07	35	63.76	31	149.28	27
Mississippi	22.21	23	39.79	22	50.19	31	63.41	32	130.27	40
North Carolina	23.22	16	39.92	21	56.69	21	73.52	20	164.65	17
South Carolina	22.67	19	39.33	25	54.30	24	69.88	24	162.20	21
Virginia	22.22	22	38.39	28	54.55	23	68.03	27	144.04	28
West Virginia	17.93	42	33.57	40	47.11	40	60.58	40	139.73	33
UNITED STATES	22.26	(X)	41.21	(X)	57.39	(X)	74.15	(X)	171.13	(X)

(X) not applicable.

Source: Energy Information Administration, *Typical Electric Bills, Based on January 1, 1988 Rates.*

TABLE 20.9-- LOW-LEVEL RADIOACTIVE WASTE DISTRIBUTION,[1] SOUTHEASTERN STATES, 1984

	Volume		Activity	
State	Amount (M3)	Percentage of U.S.	Curies	Rank in U.S.
TENNESSEE	6,787	9.0	3,005	15
Alabama	4,282	5.7	6,241	11
Arkansas	947	1.3	1,375	18
Florida	2,506	3.3	71,299	3
Georgia	2,471	3.3	2,453	16
Kentucky	47	0.1	4	34
Louisiana	14	(a)	0	40
Mississippi	432	0.6	9	33
North Carolina	2,825	3.7	5,527	12
South Carolina	7,211	9.6	7,898	10
Virginia	2,781	3.7	2,250	17
West Virginia	6	(a)	0	40

Note: There were 11 states with activity level of 0. These states all share a ranking of 40.

1. As reported by disposal site operators.

a. Less than 0.05.

Source: The Council of State Governments, *The Book of the States, 1986–87.*

TABLE 20.10–STATE LEGISLATIVE ARTS APPROPRIATIONS, SOUTHEASTERN STATES, 1980–1988, SELECTED FISCAL YEARS [In thousands of dollars]

State	1988			1987			1986	1985	1980
		Per capita[1]			Per capita[1]				
	Total	Amount ($)	Rank	Total	Amount ($)	Rank			
TENNESSEE	1,523	0.31	42	1,383	0.29	40	3,616[a]	719	517
Alabama	1,319	0.32	40	921	0.23	43	1,045	1,000	525
Arkansas	1,016	0.43	31	970	0.41	30	836	796	846
Florida	17,340	1.44	6	12,710	1.12	8	9,761	9,045	2,378
Georgia	3,001	0.48	27	2,688	0.45	29	2,201	1,720	1,102
Kentucky	2,032	0.55	23	1,983	0.53	21	1,564	1,536	857
Louisiana	978	0.22	47	713	0.16	48	1,205	1,133	857
Mississippi	421	0.16	50	412	0.16	48	466	436	307
North Carolina	4,485	0.70	19	4,051	0.65	19	3,936	2,921	1,379
South Carolina	2,801	0.82	16	2,772	0.83	14	2,556	1,858	941
Virginia	2,980	0.50	25	2,980	0.52	23	1,948	1,748	1,230
West Virginia	1,811	0.95	11	2,242	1.16	7	2,117	1,849	1,563

1. Based on estimated resident population as of July 1, 1987.

a. Includes $2.5 million one-time gift.

Source: U.S. Department of Commerce, Bureau of the Census, *Statistical Abstract of the United States, 1989.*

TABLE 20.11--STATE GOVERNMENT PER CAPITA GENERAL EXPENDITURES, BY TYPE OF EXPENDITURE, SOUTHEASTERN STATES, 1987

		Per capita general expenditures ($)											
	Total general expendi-tures	Total[1]		Education		Public welfare		Hospitals		Highways		Police	
State	($1,000)	Amount	Rank	Amount	Rank	Amount	Rank	Amount	Rank	Amount	Rank	Amount	Rank
TENNESSEE	6,161,712	1,269	47	485	44	244	27	61	28	166	29	10	45
Alabama	5,769,291	1,413	38	673	14	156	47	102	8	136	42	12	40
Arkansas	3,219,547	1,348	44	564	38	226	33	56	34	196	20	11	43
Florida	14,570,274	1,212	49	478	46	158	46	33	46	122	45	17	19
Georgia	8,423,176	1,354	43	586	28	230	31	66	27	149	36	14	32
Kentucky	5,844,453	1,568	29	622	21	264	23	42	42	228	12	20	12
Louisiana	7,204,836	1,615	27	581	30	235	28	124	3	160	32	23	8
Mississippi	3,555,483	1,354	42	571	34	208	39	67	26	147	37	12	41
North Carolina	9,379,549	1,463	35	698	12	188	42	78	19	144	38	16	23
South Carolina	5,107,330	1,491	32	688	13	178	44	96	12	115	46	17	22
Virginia	9,039,910	1,531	31	623	20	179	43	114	4	223	13	15	26
West Virginia	3,238,828	1,688	23	671	15	266	22	31	47	241	8	14	34

1. Includes categories not shown separately.

Source: U.S. Department of Commerce, Bureau of the Census, *State Government Finances in 1987*.

TABLE 20.12-STATE GOVERNMENT PER CAPITA TAX COLLECTIONS, BY TYPE OF TAX, SOUTHEASTERN STATES, 1988

		Per capita tax collections ($)											
	Total state tax	Total[1]		General sales		Personal income		Motor fuel		Motor vehicle license		Death and gift	
State	($1,000)	Amount	Rank	Amount	Rank	Amount	Rank	Amount	Rank	Amount	Rank	Amount	Rank
TENNESSEE	3,855,027	784	47	436	8	16	43	102	4	29	35	7	30
Alabama	3,374,056	818	44	225	42	225	35	67	37	26	40	4	40
Arkansas	2,020,721	834	42	321	24	246	33	90	20	28	38	2	45
Florida	11,460,299	926	33	554	4	(X)	(X)	62	41	31	34	14	13
Georgia	5,782,747	903	36	290	36	374	17	64	40	12	50	8	27
Kentucky	3,663,591	985	24	256	39	271	29	87	26	21	46	13	14
Louisiana	3,774,225	854	40	294	35	130	40	83	28	17	48	9	25
Mississippi	2,126,254	809	45	383	15	134	39	87	25	28	39	6	33
North Carolina	6,922,990	1,061	21	249	40	427	12	91	15	33	27	10	23
South Carolina	3,438,186	984	25	358	19	327	22	88	24	20	47	10	21
Virginia	6,136,607	1,023	22	198	45	460	10	99	6	39	19	7	28
West Virginia	1,743,871	926	34	285	37	209	36	89	21	36	23	3	41

Note: Rank is among 50 states and is based on unrounded figures.

(X) not applicable.

1. Includes categories not shown separately.

Source: U.S. Department of Commerce, Bureau of the Census, *State Government Tax Collections in 1988.*

FIGURE 20.1
State Tax Collections Per Capita by Selected Categories
Southeastern States, 1988

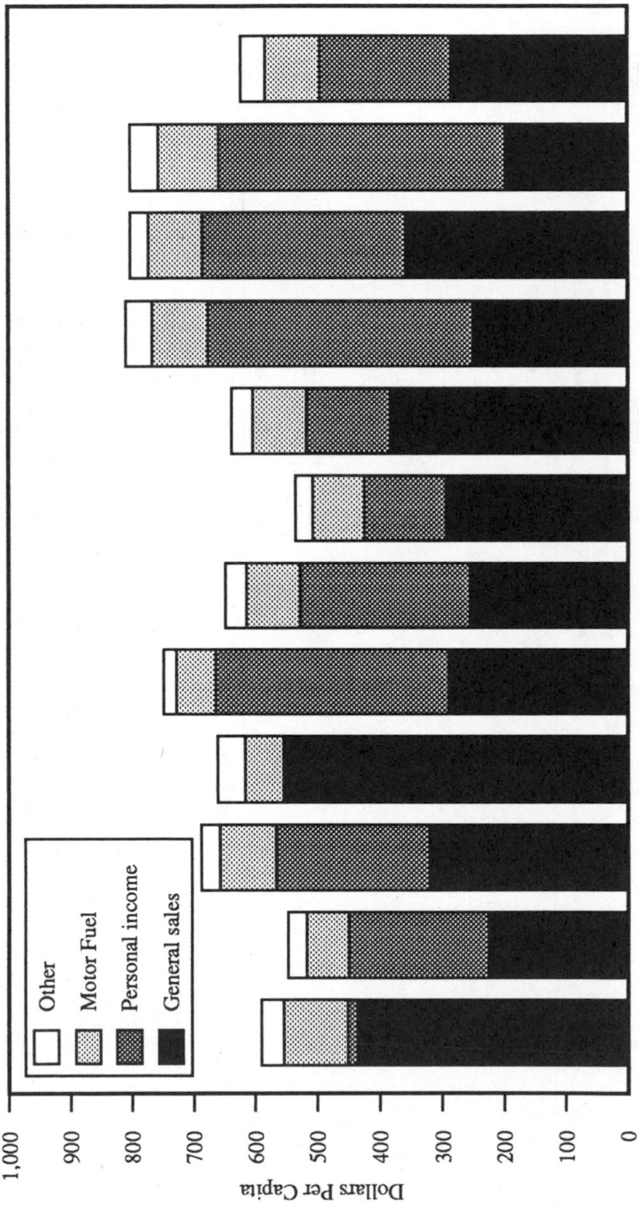

Source: U.S. Department of Commerce, Bureau of the Census, *State Government Tax Collections in 1988*.

TABLE 20.13–RESEARCH AND DEVELOPMENT EXPENDITURES, BY PERFORMING SECTOR, SOUTHEASTERN STATES, 1985 [In millions of dollars]

State	Total		Industry			Federal government	Universities and colleges	Other nonprofit
	Amount	Rank	Amount	Rank	Largest R&D-performing industry			
TENNESSEE	734	27	538	24	Aircraft and missiles	86	98	11
Alabama	973	23	387	28	Aircraft and missiles	462	104	20
Arkansas	68	43–51	15	40–51	Other industries	22	30	1
Florida	2,404	13	1,832	13	Aircraft and missiles	362	203	6
Georgia	831	24–26	515	25	Aircraft and missiles	86	226	4
Kentucky	306	38	221	35–39	Machinery, computer (SIC 357)	31	54	0
Louisiana	348	37	187	35–39	Chemicals, industrial (SIC 281-2,286)	34	126	2
Mississippi	245	39–42	62	40–51	Electrical equipment, other (SIC 361-5,369)	122	53	7
North Carolina	1,193	22	797	21–22	Machinery, computer (SIC 357)	137	245	14
South Carolina	476	31	389	27	Machinery	20	66	1
Virginia	1,947	16	800	20	Machinery, computer (SIC 357)	868	168	112
West Virginia	153–301 [a]	39–42	94–242 [a]	35–39	Chemicals, industrial (SIC 281-2,286)	30	29	0

Note: Because data for industrial R&D performance were suppressed for some states, total and industrial sector rankings must be grouped for these states to avoid disclosure.

a. For the industry sector, reported data fall within the range specified but have been withheld by the Census Bureau to avoid disclosing individual company operations. Range for state total is R&D performance of Federal Government, universities and colleges, and other nonprofit institutions, plus the low and high ends of the industry R&D performance range.

Source: National Science Foundation, *Geographic Patterns: R&D in the United States, Special Report*, NSF 89–317.

TABLE 20.14--VALUE OF EXPORTS AND GENERAL IMPORTS, SOUTHEASTERN STATES, 1987
[Dollar amounts in millions]

	Exports			Imports		
State	Value	Percentage of total	Rank	Value	Percentage of total	Rank
TENNESSEE	$1,902	0.8	22	$2,519	0.6	21
Alabama	1,850	0.7	23	1,032	0.2	34
Arkansas	519	0.2	40	1,002	0.2	35
Florida	7,624	3.0	7	9,212	2.2	10
Georgia	3,009	1.2	18	4,623	1.1	15
Kentucky	1,833	0.7	24	2,445	0.6	23
Louisiana	9,775	3.9	6	1,661	0.4	29
Mississippi	973	0.4	33	3,055	0.7	18
North Carolina	4,466	1.8	14	4,705	1.1	13
South Carolina	1,729	0.7	26	2,486	0.6	22
Virginia	5,642	2.2	11	4,634	1.1	14
West Virginia	1,020	0.4	32	90	(a)	47

Note: Exports on f.a.s. value basis; general imports on c.i.f. value basis.

a. Less than 0.05 percent.

Source: U.S. Department of Commerce, Bureau of the Census, *Statistical Abstract of the United States, 1989.*

TABLE 20.15--GROSS BOOK VALUE OF PROPERTY, PLANT AND EQUIPMENT OF U.S. AFFILIATES OF FOREIGN COMPANIES, BY INDUSTRY OF AFFILIATE, SOUTHEASTERN STATES, 1987 [In millions of dollars]

State	All industries		Manufacturing		Petroleum	Wholesale trade	Retail trade	Finance, except banking	Insurance	Real estate	Services	Other industries
	Value	Rank	Value	Rank								
TENNESSEE	5,553	16	3,253	15	166	1,179	208	49	74	352	63	211
Alabama	3,883	25	2,268	18	317	981	35	2	23	67	39	153
Arkansas	1,256	44	548	36	99	195	(D)	1	21	133	23	(D)
Florida	9,484	11	2,568	17	248	492	797	206	59	4,001	432	681
Georgia	8,879	12	4,348	10	214	463	475	100	204	2,145	281	648
Kentucky	4,377	21	2,254	19	469	296	70	1	3	133	46	1,105
Louisiana	14,289	5	4,578	8	7,127	361	359	(D)	16	590	605	(D)
Mississippi	2,387	36	800	31	1,093	245	31	2	15	72	41	87
North Carolina	9,515	10	5,337	6	(D)	766	593	39	83	643	46	(D)
South Carolina	6,012	15	3,941	12	67	1,126	320	6	5	286	155	106
Virginia	6,632	14	3,599	13	366	386	357	111	14	1,231	70	499
West Virginia	4,987	18	3,327	14	357	(D)	19	1	1	22	13	(D)

(D) Withheld to avoid disclosing data of individual operations.

Source: U.S. Department of Commerce, Bureau of Economic Analysis, *Foreign Direct Investment in the United States, 1987 Benchmark Survey, Preliminary Results.*

TABLE 20.16-GROSS BOOK VALUE OF PROPERTY, PLANT AND EQUIPMENT OF U.S. AFFILIATES OF FOREIGN COMPANIES, BY INDUSTRY OF AFFILIATE, TENNESSEE, 1977–1987 [In millions of dollars]

Year	All industries[1]	Petroleum	Manufacturing: Total	Manufacturing: Food and kindred products	Manufacturing: Chemicals and allied products	Manufacturing: Primary and fabricated metals	Manufacturing: Machinery	Manufacturing: Other manufacturing	Wholesale trade	Retail trade	Finance, except banking	Insurance	Real estate
1987	5,553	166	3,253	100	1,591	321	562	679	1,179	208	49	74	352
1986	5,182	165	2,854	101	1,487	384	492	389	1,087	243	37	25	352
1985	4,609	101	2,863	91	1,604	437	330	400	867	161	n.a.	9	329
1984	4,465	85	2,890	82	1,779	436	270	323	785	116	n.a.	9	296
1983	4,730	73	3,523	80	1,725	799	233	685	730	86	n.a.	8	169
1982	4,514	72	3,488	48	1,747	709	307	678	540	83	7	7	187
1981	3,747	77	3,142	41	1,677	698	213	513	177	70	n.a.	4	142
1980	2,208	36	1,798	23	553	668	137	417	129	46	5	4	104
1979	1,897	42	1,624	8	517	650	85	364	120	n.a.	4	4	66
1978	1,576	85	1,362	8	489	501	n.a.	n.a.	53	9	3	1	53
1977	1,335	32	1,159	6	453	386	n.a.	n.a.	80	3	0	0	44

n.a. not available.

1. Includes other categories not shown separately.

Source: U.S. Department of Commerce, Bureau of Economic Analysis, *Foreign Direct Investment in the United States, 1987 Benchmark Survey, Preliminary Results*, and earlier editions.

TABLE 20.17--TENNESSEE: SIGNIFICANT RANKINGS AMONG 50 STATES

Item	Rank	Tennessee	U.S.
Total population, 1988	16th	4,895,000	245,807,000
Land area, 1980 (square miles)	34th	41,155	3,539,289
Population per square mile, 1988	19th	119.5	69.5
Percent change in population, 1980–1988	22nd	7.1%	8.5%
Median age, 1980 (years)	15th	30.1	30.0
Population 65 years old and over, 1987, percent	24th	12.4% of population	12.3% of population
Non-white population, 1980	20th	16.5% of population	16.9% of population
Spanish population, 1980	43rd	0.7% of population	6.4% of population
Metropolitan population, 1987, percent	25th	67.0% of population	76.9% of population
Persons living in different state in 1975 (5 yrs. +) 1980	27th	10.6% of population	9.7% of population
Birth rate[1], 1986	46th	13.8	15.6
Infant mortality rate[2], 1986	15th	11.0	10.4
Marriage rate[1], 1987 (preliminary)	8th	11.8	9.9
Divorce rate[1], 1986 (preliminary)	8th	6.4	4.8
Legal abortions per 1,000 live births, 1985	27th	315	425
Physicians per 100,000 population, 1986	23rd	181	205
Hospital beds per 100,000 population, 1986	7th	644	532
Total housing units, 1980	17th	1,747,422	88,411,263
Year-round housing units, 1980, percent			
Built between 1970 and 1980	19th	31.1%	25.9%
Prior to 1940	37th	16.7%	26.1%
With 5 or more units in structure	31st	11.5%	17.5%
With air conditioning	7th	74.0%	55.0%
Homeownership rate, 1980	23rd	68.6%	64.4%
Median value of specified owner-occupied units, 1980	44th	$35,600	$47,200
Median gross rent of specified renter-occupied units, 1980	43rd	$203	$243
Violent crime rate[3], 1987	19th	534	609
Federal and state prisoners per 100,000 population, 1987	29th	156	228
Public elementary and secondary schools, 1988			
Expenditures per capita	47th	$542	$705
Current expenditures per pupil	41st	$3,189	$4,209
Public school teachers' salaries, 1988	37th	$23,785	$28,044
Percent high school graduates (25 years old +), 1980	44th	56.2%	66.5%
Enrollment, higher education, 1986	20th	197,000	12,501,000
Percent change in nonagricultural employment, 1980–1987	17th	15.0%	13.2%
Unemployment rate, 1987	19th	6.6%	6.2%
Manufacturing employment, 1987			
Number	15th	495,000	19,065,000
Percent of total employed	9th	24.6%	18.6%

TABLE 20.17--TENNESSEE: SIGNIFICANT RANKINGS AMONG 50 STATES (Continued)

Item	Rank	Tennessee	U.S.
Average annual pay, 1987	33rd	$18,501	$20,855
Median household money income, 1979	44th	$14,142	$16,841
Percent of population receiving food stamps, 1987	7th	10.0%	7.5%
Percent below poverty level, 1979			
Persons	10th	16.5%	12.4%
Children under 18 years	9th	20.6%	16.0%
State and local governments, 1986			
Direct general expenditures per capita	47th	$1,920	$2,504
Tax revenues per capita	47th	$1,077	$1,547
Debt outstanding per capita	38th	$2,041	$2,733
Federal grants per capita, 1987	29th	$416	$427
Percent of population casting votes for U.S. President, 1988	45th	44.7%	50.2%
Automobile registration per 1,000 population, 1987	4th	679	571
Means of transportation to work, 1980			
Percent of workers commuting in carpools	10th	23.2%	19.7%
Percent using car, truck, or van	3rd	91.3%	84.1%
Vehicle traffic fatalities per 100,000 population, 1986	8th	28.6	20.0
Energy consumption per capita, 1986	14th	345 mil. Btu	308 mil. Btu
Temperature, average annual	14th	58.5 °F.	53.2 °F.
Precipitation, average annual	5th	51.7 in.	28.8 in.
Acreage per farm, 1988	46th	136 acres	463 acres
Average value of farm land and buildings per acre, 1988	15th	$1,104	$564
Farm debt/asset ratio, 1987	40th	11.2	18.9
Percent change in housing starts, 1986--1987	29th	-8.0%	-10.2%
Manufacturing value added, 1986	16th	$23.6 bil.	$1,035.8 bil.
Retail sales per capita, 1987	34th	$5,902	$6,348

1. Per 1,000 resident population.

2. Deaths of infants under 1 year old per 1,000 live births. Excludes fetal deaths.

3. Per 100,000 resident population.

Source: U.S. Department of Commerce, Bureau of the Census, *Statistical Abstract of the United States, 1989*.

INDEX

I

R

S

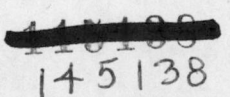